RANDOM HOUSE
ATLAS
OF THE
WORLD

THIRD COMPACT EDITION

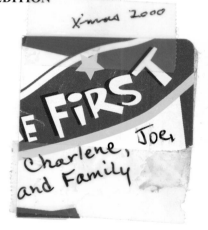

Xmas 2000

Charlene, Joe, and Family

Random House Atlas of the World, Third Compact Edition

Copyright © 2000 by Times Books Group Ltd. and Bartholomew Ltd.

This book is available for special purchases in bulk by organizations and institutions, not for resale, at special discounts. Please direct your inquiries to the Random House Special Sales Department, toll-free 888-591-1200 or fax 212-572-4961.

Please address inquiries about electronic licensing of reference products, for use on a network or in software or on CD-ROM, to the Subsidiary Rights Department, Random House Reference & Information Publishing, fax 212-940-7370.

This edition was originally published in Great Britain by Times Books, London in 2000. First published as The Times Atlas of the World, Compact Edition, in 1994.

Library of Congress Cataloging-in-Publication data is available.

Visit the Random House Information and Publishing Web site at www.randomwords.com

Typeset and printed in the UK

Third Edition

0 9 8 7 6 5 4 3 2 1

February 2001

ISBN 0-375-71952-0
SAP Network: 10059688

New York Toronto London Sydney Auckland

RANDOM HOUSE
ATLAS
OF THE
WORLD
THIRD COMPACT EDITION

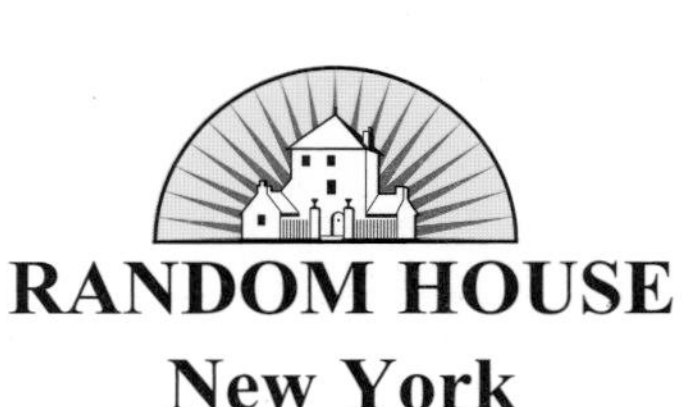

RANDOM HOUSE
New York

CONTENTS

THE WORLD TODAY

Pages	Title	Scal
8-31	STATES AND TERRITORIES OF THE WORLD	
32	CITIES	
33	CONTINENTS, OCEANS AND SEAS	
34-35	ISLANDS, MOUNTAINS, LAKES AND RIVERS	
36-37	CLIMATE	
38-39	LAND COVER	
40-41	POPULATION	
42-43	TRAVEL	

ATLAS OF THE WORLD

44	INTRODUCTION TO THE ATLAS	
45	MAP SYMBOLS	
46-47	**WORLD** COUNTRIES	1:120 000 00(
48-49	**OCEANIA**	1:50 000 00(
50-51	**AUSTRALIA**	1:20 000 00(
52-53	**AUSTRALIA** SOUTHEAST	1:7 500 00(
54	**NEW ZEALAND**	1:7 500 00(
55	**ANTARCTICA**	1:45 000 00(

CONTENTS

Pages	Title	Scale
6-57	**ASIA**	1:55 000 000
8-59	**SOUTHEAST ASIA**	1:25 000 000
0-61	**MALAYSIA AND INDONESIA** WEST	1:12 000 000
2-63	**CONTINENTAL SOUTHEAST ASIA**	1:12 000 000
4	**PHILIPPINES**	1:12 000 000
5	**NORTH KOREA AND SOUTH KOREA**	1:6 500 000
6-67	**JAPAN**	1:7 500 000
8-69	**CHINA AND MONGOLIA**	1:25 000 000
0-71	**CHINA** CENTRAL	1:12 000 000
2-73	**SOUTH ASIA**	1:15 000 000
4-75	**PAKISTAN, INDIA** NORTH AND **BANGLADESH**	1:12 000 000
6-77	**CENTRAL ASIA**	1:15 000 000
8-79	**ARABIAN PENINSULA**	1:12 000 000
0-81	**EAST MEDITERRANEAN**	1:12 000 000
2-83	**RUSSIAN FEDERATION**	1:30 000 000
4-85	**EUROPE**	1:25 000 000
6-87	**EUROPEAN RUSSIAN FEDERATION**	1:15 000 000
8-89	**NORTHEAST EUROPE**	1:6 000 000
0-91	**UKRAINE AND MOLDOVA**	1:6 000 000

CONTENTS

Pages	Title	Scale
	EUROPE (continued)	
92-93	SCANDINAVIA AND ICELAND	1:7 500 000
94-95	BRITISH ISLES	1:6 000 000
96	SCOTLAND	1:3 000 000
97	IRELAND	1:3 000 000
98-99	ENGLAND AND WALES	1:3 000 000
100-101	NORTHWEST EUROPE	1:3 000 000
102-103	CENTRAL EUROPE	1:6 000 000
104-105	FRANCE AND SWITZERLAND	1:6 000 000
106-107	SPAIN AND PORTUGAL	1:6 000 000
108-109	ITALY AND THE BALKANS	1:6 000 000
110-111	GREECE, ROMANIA AND BULGARIA	1:6 000 000
112-113	**AFRICA**	1:45 000 000
114-115	NORTHWEST AFRICA	1:20 000 000
116-117	NORTHEAST AFRICA	1:20 000 000
118-119	CENTRAL AFRICA	1:15 000 000
120-121	SOUTHERN AFRICA	1:15 000 000
122-123	REPUBLIC OF SOUTH AFRICA	1:7 500 000
124-125	**NORTH AMERICA**	1:40 000 000
126-127	CANADA	1:25 000 000
128-129	CANADA WEST	1:12 000 000

CONTENTS

Pages	Title	Scale

NORTH AMERICA (continued)

Pages	Title	Scale
130-131	CANADA EAST	1:12 000 000
132-133	UNITED STATES OF AMERICA	1:20 000 000
134-135	USA WEST	1:8 000 000
136-137	USA NORTH CENTRAL	1:8 000 000
138-139	USA SOUTH CENTRAL	1:8 000 000
140-141	USA NORTHEAST	1:8 000 000
142-143	USA SOUTHEAST	1:8 000 000
144-145	MEXICO	1:12 000 000
146-147	CENTRAL AMERICA AND THE CARIBBEAN	1:15 000 000

SOUTH AMERICA

Pages	Title	Scale
148-149	SOUTH AMERICA	1:35 000 000
150-151	SOUTH AMERICA NORTH	1:20 000 000
152-153	SOUTH AMERICA SOUTH	1:20 000 000
154-155	BRAZIL SOUTHEAST	1:7 500 000

OCEANS

Pages	Title	Scale
156-157	PACIFIC OCEAN	1:90 000 000
158	ATLANTIC OCEAN	1:90 000 000
159	INDIAN OCEAN	1:90 000 000
160	ARCTIC OCEAN	1:45 000 000

INDEX

161-240	INDEX

STATES AND TERRITORIES OF THE WORLD

All independent countries and major territories are included in this list of the states and territories of the world; the list is arranged in alphabetical order by the conventional name form. For independent states, the full country name is given below the conventional name, if this is different; for territories, the status is given. The capital city name is given in the conventional form with the local name or alternate name in brackets.

The statistics used for the area and population are the latest available and include estimates. The information on languages and religions is based on the latest information on 'de facto' speakers of the language or 'de facto' adherents of the religion. The information available on languages and religions varies greatly from country to country, some countries include questions in censuses others do not, in which case best estimates are used. The order of the languages and religions reflect their relative importance within the country; generally, languages or religions are included when more than one per cent of the population are estimated to be speakers or adherents.

Membership of the following international organizations is shown by the abbreviations below, territories are not shown as having separate memberships of these organizations.

APEC	Asia-Pacific Economic Cooperation
ASEAN	Association of Southeast Asian Nations
CARICOM	Caribbean Community
CIS	Commonwealth of Independent States
Comm.	The Commonwealth
EU	European Union
OECD	Organization for Economic Co-operation and Development
OPEC	Organization of Petroleum Exporting Countries
SADC	Southern African Development Community
UN	United Nations

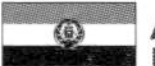

 AFGHANISTAN
Islamic Emirate of Afghanistan

Area Sq Km	652 225	Religions	Sunni Muslim, Shi'a
Area Sq Miles	251 825		Muslim
Population	21 354 000	Currency	Afghani
Capital	Kābul	Organizations	UN
Languages	Dari, Pushtu, Uzbek, Turkmen	Map page	76-77

 ALBANIA
Republic of Albania

Area Sq Km	28 748	Religions	Sunni Muslim,
Area Sq Miles	11 100		Albanian Orthodox,
Population	3 119 000		Roman Catholic *
Capital	Tirana (Tiranë)	Currency	Lek
Languages	Albanian, Greek	Organizations	UN
		Map page	109

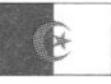

 ALGERIA
Democratic and Popular Republic of Algeria

Area Sq Km	2 381 741	Religions	Sunni Muslim
Area Sq Miles	919 595	Currency	Dinar
Population	30 081 000	Organizations	OPEC, UN
Capital	Algiers (Alger)	Map page	114-115
Languages	Arabic, French, Berber		

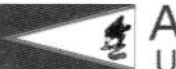

 American Samoa
United States Unincorporated Territory

Area Sq Km	197	Religions	Protestant, Roman
Area Sq Miles	76		Catholic
Population	63 000	Currency	US dollar
Capital	Fagatogo	Map page	49
Languages	Samoan, English		

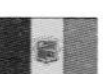

 ANDORRA
Principality of Andorra

Area Sq Km	465	Religions	Roman Catholic
Area Sq Miles	180	Currency	French franc,
Population	72 000		Spanish peseta
Capital	Andorra la Vella	Organizations	UN
Languages	Spanish, Catalan, French	Map page	104

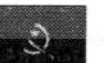

 ANGOLA
Republic of Angola

Area Sq Km	1 246 700	Religions	Roman Catholic,
Area Sq Miles	481 354		Protestant, traditional
Population	12 092 000		beliefs
Capital	Luanda	Currency	Kwanza
Languages	Portuguese, Bantu, local languages	Organizations	SADC, UN
		Map page	120

Anguilla
United Kingdom Overseas Territory

Area Sq Km	155	Religions	Protestant, Roman
Area Sq Miles	60		Catholic
Population	8 000	Currency	E. Carib. dollar
Capital	The Valley	Map page	147
Languages	English		

ANTIGUA AND BARBUDA

Area Sq Km	442	Religions	Protestant, Roman
Area Sq Miles	171		Catholic
Population	67 000	Currency	E. Carib. dollar
Capital	St John's	Organizations	CARICOM,
Languages	English, creole		Comm.,UN
		Map page	147

ARGENTINA
Argentine Republic

Area Sq Km	2 766 889	Religions	Roman Catholic,
Area Sq Miles	1 068 302		Protestant
Population	36 123 000	Currency	Peso
Capital	Buenos Aires	Organizations	UN
Languages	Spanish, Italian,	Map page	152-153
	Amerindian		
	languages		

ARMENIA
Republic of Armenia

Area Sq Km	29 800	Religions	Armenian Orthodox
Area Sq Miles	11 506	Currency	Dram
Population	3 536 000	Organizations	CIS, UN
Capital	Yerevan (Erevan)	Map page	81
Languages	Armenian, Azeri		

Aruba
Self-governing Netherlands Territory

Area Sq Km	193	Religions	Roman Catholic,
Area Sq Miles	75		Protestant
Population	94 000	Currency	Florin
Capital	Oranjestad	Map page	147
Languages	Papiamento, Dutch,		
	English		

Ascension
Dependency of St Helena

Area Sq Km	88	Religions	Protestant, Roman
Area Sq Miles	34		Catholic
Population	1 100	Currency	Pound sterling
Capital	Georgetown	Map page	113
Languages	English		

AUSTRALIA
Commonwealth of Australia

Area Sq Km	7 682 395	Religions	Protestant, Roman
Area Sq Miles	2 966 189		Catholic, Orthodox
Population	18 520 000	Currency	Dollar
Capital	Canberra	Organizations	APEC, Comm.,
Languages	English, Italian,		OECD, UN
	Greek	Map page	50-51

Australian Capital Territory (Federal Territory)

Area Sq Km	2 400	Population	299 243
Area Sq Miles	927	Capital	Canberra

Jervis Bay Territory

Area Sq Km	73
Area Sq Miles	28

New South Wales (State)

Area Sq Km	801 600	Population	6 038 696
Area Sq Miles	309 499	Capital	Sydney

Northern Territory

Area Sq Km	1 346 200	Population	195 101
Area Sq Miles	519 771	Capital	Darwin

Queensland (State)

Area Sq Km	1 727 200	Population	3 368 850
Area Sq Miles	666 876	Capital	Brisbane

South Australia (State)

Area Sq Km	984 000	Population	1 427 936
Area Sq Miles	379 925	Capital	Adelaide

Tasmania (State)

Area Sq Km	67 800	Population	459 659
Area Sq Miles	26 178	Capital	Hobart

Victoria (State)

Area Sq Km	227 600	Population	4 373 520
Area Sq Miles	87 877	Capital	Melbourne

Western Australia (State)

Area Sq Km	2 525 500	Population	1 726 095
Area Sq Miles	975 101	Capital	Perth

AUSTRIA
Republic of Austria

Area Sq Km	83 855	Religions	Roman Catholic,
Area Sq Miles	32 377		Protestant
Population	8 140 000	Currency	Schilling, Euro
Capital	Vienna (Wien)	Organizations	EU, OECD, UN
Languages	German, Croatian,	Map page	102-103
	Turkish		

AZERBAIJAN
Azerbaijani Republic

Area Sq Km	86 600	Religions	Shi'a Muslim, Sunni
Area Sq Miles	33 436		Muslim, Russian and
Population	7 669 000		Armenian Orthodox
Capital	Baku (Bakı)	Currency	Manat
Languages	Azeri, Armenian,	Organizations	CIS, UN
	Russian, Lezgian	Map page	81

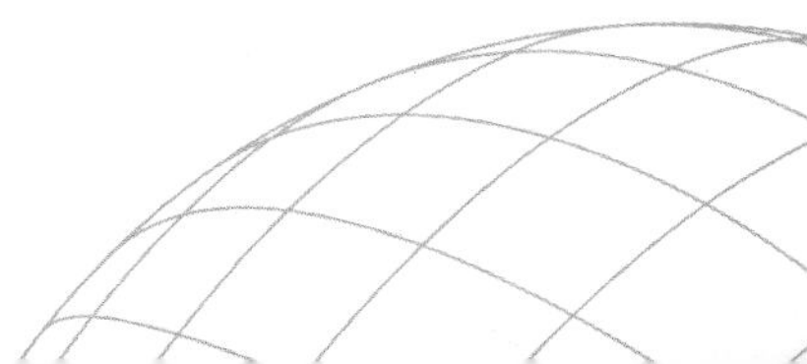

Azores (Arquipélago dos Açores)
Autonomous Region of Portugal

Area Sq Km	2 300	Religions	Roman Catholic,
Area Sq Miles	888		Protestant
Population	243 600	Currency	Portuguese escudo
Capital	Ponta Delgada	Map page	112
Languages	Portuguese		

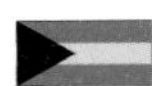

THE BAHAMAS
Commonwealth of the Bahamas

Area Sq Km	13 939	Religions	Protestant, Roman
Area Sq Miles	5 382		Catholic
Population	296 000	Currency	Dollar
Capital	Nassau	Organizations	CARICOM, Comm.,
Languages	English, creole		UN
		Map page	146-147

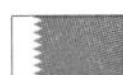

BAHRAIN
State of Bahrain

Area Sq Km	691	Religions	Shi'a Muslim, Sunni
Area Sq Miles	267		Muslim, Christian
Population	595 000	Currency	Dinar
Capital	Manama	Organizations	UN
	(Al Manāmah)	Map page	79
Languages	Arabic, English		

BANGLADESH
People's Republic of Bangladesh

Area Sq Km	143 998	Religions	Sunni Muslim, Hindu
Area Sq Miles	55 598	Currency	Taka
Population	124 774 000	Organizations	Comm.,UN
Capital	Dhaka (Dacca)	Map page	75
Languages	Bengali, English		

BARBADOS

Area Sq Km	430	Religions	Protestant, Roman
Area Sq Miles	166		Catholic
Population	268 000	Currency	Dollar
Capital	Bridgetown	Organizations	CARICOM,
Languages	English, creole		Comm.,UN
		Map page	147

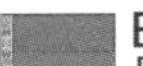

BELARUS
Republic of Belarus

Area Sq Km	207 600	Religions	Belorussian Orthodox,
Area Sq Miles	80 155		Roman Catholic
Population	10 315 000	Currency	Rouble
Capital	Minsk	Organizations	CIS, UN
Languages	Belorussian, Russian	Map page	88-89

BELGIUM
Kingdom of Belgium

Area Sq Km	30 520	Religions	Roman Catholic,
Area Sq Miles	11 784		Protestant
Population	10 141 000	Currency	Franc, Euro
Capital	Brussels (Bruxelles)	Organizations	EU, OECD, UN
Languages	Dutch (Flemish),	Map page	100
	French (Walloon),		
	German		

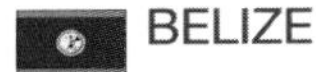

BELIZE

Area Sq Km	22 965	Religions	Roman Catholic,
Area Sq Miles	8 867		Protestant
Population	230 000	Currency	Dollar
Capital	Belmopan	Organizations	CARICOM, Comm.,
Languages	English, Spanish,		UN
	Mayan, creole	Map page	147

BENIN
Republic of Benin

Area Sq Km	112 620	Religions	Traditional beliefs,
Area Sq Miles	43 483		Roman Catholic, Sunni
Population	5 781 000		Muslim
Capital	Porto-Novo	Currency	CFA franc
Languages	French, Fon,	Organizations	UN
	Yoruba, Adja,	Map page	114
	local languages		

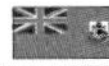

Bermuda
United Kingdom Overseas Territory

Area Sq Km	54	Religions	Protestant, Roman
Area Sq Miles	21		Catholic
Population	64 000	Currency	Dollar
Capital	Hamilton	Map page	125
Languages	English		

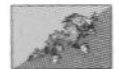

BHUTAN
Kingdom of Bhutan

Area Sq Km	46 620	Religions	Buddhist, Hindu
Area Sq Miles	18 000	Currency	Ngultrum
Population	2 004 000	Organizations	UN
Capital	Thimphu	Map page	75
Languages	Dzongkha,		
	Nepali, Assamese		

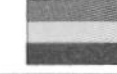

BOLIVIA
Republic of Bolivia

Area Sq Km	1 098 581	Religions	Roman Catholic,
Area Sq Miles	424 164		Protestant, Baha'i
Population	7 957 000	Currency	Boliviano
Capital	La Paz/Sucre	Organizations	UN
Languages	Spanish, Quechua,	Map page	152
	Aymara		

Bonaire
part of Netherlands Antilles

Area Sq Km	288	Religions	Roman Catholic,
Area Sq Miles	111		Protestant
Population	14 218	Currency	NA guilder
Capital	Kralendijk	Map page	147
Languages	Dutch, Papiamento		

Bonin Islands (Ogasawara-shotō)
part of Japan

Area Sq Km	104	Map page	69
Area Sq Miles	40		
Population	2 300		
Capital	Omura		

BOSNIA-HERZEGOVINA
Republic of Bosnia and Herzegovina

Area Sq Km	51 130	Religions	Sunni Muslim, Serbian
Area Sq Miles	19 741		Orthodox, Roman
Population	3 675 000		Catholic, Protestant
Capital	Sarajevo	Currency	Marka
Languages	Bosnian, Serbian,	Organizations	UN
	Croatian	Map page	109

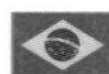

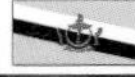

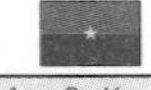

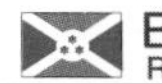

BURUNDI
Republic of Burundi

Area Sq Km	27 835	Religions	Roman Catholic,
Area Sq Miles	10 747		traditional beliefs,
Population	6 457 000		Protestant
Capital	Bujumbura	Currency	Franc
Languages	Kirundi (Hutu,	Organizations	UN
	Tutsi), French	Map page	119

BOTSWANA
Republic of Botswana

Area Sq Km	581 370	Religions	Traditional beliefs,
Area Sq Miles	224 468		Protestant, Roman
Population	1 570 000		Catholic
Capital	Gaborone	Currency	Pula
Languages	English,Setswana,	Organizations	Comm., SADC, UN
	Shona, local	Map page	120
	languages		

CAMBODIA
Kingdom of Cambodia

Area Sq Km	181 000	Religions	Buddhist, Roman
Area Sq Miles	69 884		Catholic, Sunni Muslim
Population	10 716 000	Currency	Riel
Capital	Phnom Pénh (Phnom	Organizations	ASEAN, UN
	Penh)	Map page	63
Languages	Khmer, Vietnamese		

BRAZIL
Federative Republic of Brazil

Area Sq Km	8 547 379	Religions	Roman Catholic,
Area Sq Miles	3 300 161		Protestant
Population	165 851 000	Currency	Real
Capital	Brasília	Organizations	UN
Languages	Portuguese	Map page	150-151

CAMEROON
Republic of Cameroon

Area Sq Km	475 442	Religions	Roman Catholic,
Area Sq Miles	183 569		traditional beliefs,
Population	14 305 000		Sunni Muslim,
Capital	Yaoundé		Protestant
Languages	French, English,	Currency	CFA franc
	Fang, Bamileke, local	Organizations	Comm., UN
	languages	Map page	118

BRUNEI
State of Brunei Darussalam

Area Sq Km	5 765	Religions	Sunni Muslim, Buddhist,
Area Sq Miles	2 226		Christian
Population	315 000	Currency	Dollar
Capital	Bandar Seri Begawan	Organizations	APEC, ASEAN,
Languages	Malay, English,		Comm., UN
	Chinese	Map page	61

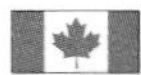

CANADA
Federation

Area Sq Km	9 970 610	Religions	Roman Catholic,
Area Sq Miles	3 849 674		Protestant, Eastern
Population	30 563 000		Orthodox, Jewish
Capital	Ottawa	Currency	Dollar
Languages	English, French,	Organizations	APEC, Comm.,
	Inuktitut		OECD, UN
		Map page	126-127

BULGARIA
Republic of Bulgaria

Area Sq Km	110 994	Religions	Bulgarian Orthodox,
Area Sq Miles	42 855		Sunni Muslim
Population	8 336 000	Currency	Lev
Capital	Sofia (Sofiya)	Organizations	UN
Languages	Bulgarian, Turkish,	Map page	110
	Romany,		
	Macedonian		

Alberta (Province)

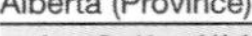

Area Sq Km	661 190	Population	2 914 900
Area Sq Miles	255 287	Capital	Edmonton

British Columbia (Province)

Area Sq Km	947 800	Population	4 009 900
Area Sq Miles	365 948	Capital	Victoria

Manitoba (Province)

Area Sq Km	649 950	Population	1 138 000
Area Sq Miles	250 947	Capital	Winnipeg

BURKINA
Democratic Republic of Burkina Faso

Area Sq Km	274 200	Religions	Sunni Muslim,
Area Sq Miles	105 869		traditional beliefs,
Population	11 305 000		Roman Catholic
Capital	Ouagadougou	Currency	CFA franc
Languages	French, Moore	Organizations	UN
	(Mossi), Fulani, local	Map page	114
	languages		

New Brunswick (Province)

Area Sq Km	73 440	Population	753 000
Area Sq Miles	28 355	Capital	Fredericton

Newfoundland (Province)

Area Sq Km	405 720	Population	544 400
Area Sq Miles	156 649	Capital	St John's

Northwest Territories (Territory)

Area Sq Km	1 432 320	Population	45 500
Area Sq Miles	553 022	Capital	Yellowknife

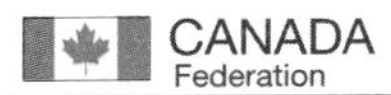

CANADA
Federation

Nova Scotia (Province)
Area Sq Km 55 490	Population 934 000
Area Sq Miles 21 425	Capital Halifax

Nunavut (Territory)
Area Sq Km 1 994 000	Population 22 000
Area Sq Miles 769 888	Capital Iqaluit

Ontario (Province)
Area Sq Km 1 068 580	Population 11 411 500
Area Sq Miles 412 581	Capital Toronto

Prince Edward Island (Province)
Area Sq Km 5 660	Population 136 400
Area Sq Miles 2 185	Capital Charlottetown

Québec (Province)
Area Sq Km 1 540 680	Population 7 333 300
Area Sq Miles 594 860	Capital Québec

Saskatchewan (Province)
Area Sq Km 652 330	Population 1 024 400
Area Sq Miles 251 866	Capital Regina

Yukon Territory (Territory)
Area Sq Km 483 450	Population 31 700
Area Sq Miles 186 661	Capital Whitehorse

Canary Islands (Islas Canarias)
Autonomous Community of Spain
Area Sq Km 7 447	Religions Roman Catholic
Area Sq Miles 2 875	Currency Peseta
Population 1 606 522	Map page 114
Capital Santa Cruz de Tenerife	
Languages Spanish	

CAPE VERDE
Republic of Cape Verde
Area Sq Km 4 033	Religions Roman Catholic,
Area Sq Miles 1 557	Protestant
Population 408 000	Currency Escudo
Capital Praia	Organizations UN
Languages Portuguese, creole	Map page 46

Cayman Islands
United Kingdom Overseas Territory
Area Sq Km 259	Religions Protestant, Roman
Area Sq Miles 100	Catholic
Population 36 000	Currency Dollar
Capital George Town	Map page 146
Languages English	

CENTRAL AFRICAN REPUBLIC
Area Sq Km 622 436	Religions Protestant, Roman
Area Sq Miles 240 324	Catholic, traditional
Population 3 485 000	beliefs, Sunni Muslim
Capital Bangui	Currency CFA franc
Languages French, Sango,	Organizations UN
Banda, Baya, local	Map page 118
languages	

Ceuta
Spanish Territory
Area Sq Km 19	Religions Roman Catholic,
Area Sq Miles 7	Muslim
Population 68 796	Currency Peseta
Capital Ceuta	Map page 106
Languages Spanish, Arabic	

CHAD
Republic of Chad
Area Sq Km 1 284 000	Religions Sunni Muslim, Roman
Area Sq Miles 495 755	Catholic, Protestant,
Population 7 270 000	traditional beliefs
Capital Ndjamena	Currency CFA franc
Languages Arabic, French, Sara,	Organizations UN
local languages	Map page 115

Chatham Islands
part of New Zealand
Area Sq Km 963	Religions Protestant
Area Sq Miles 372	Currency Dollar
Population 732	Map page 49
Capital Waitangi	
Languages English	

CHILE
Republic of Chile
Area Sq Km 756 945	Religions Roman Catholic,
Area Sq Miles 292 258	Protestant
Population 14 824 000	Currency Peso
Capital Santiago	Organizations APEC, UN
Languages Spanish, Amerindian	Map page 152-153
languages	

CHINA
People's Republic of China
Area Sq Km 9 584 492	Religions Confucian, Taoist,
Area Sq Miles 3 700 593	Buddhist, Christian,
Population 1 262 817 000	Sunni Muslim
Capital Beijing (Peking)	Currency Yuan
Languages Mandarin, Wu,	Organizations APEC, UN
Cantonese, Hsiang,	Map page 68-69
regional languages	

Anhui (Province)
Area Sq Km 139 000	Population 60 130 000
Area Sq Miles 53 668	Capital Hefei

Bejing (Municipality)
Area Sq Km 16 800	Population 12 510 000
Area Sq Miles 6 487	Capital Beijing (Peking)

Chongqing (Municipality)
Area Sq Km 23 000	Population 14 600 000
Area Sq Miles 8 880	Capital Chongqing

Fujian (Province)
Area Sq Km 121 400	Population 32 370 000
Area Sq Miles 46 873	Capital Fuzhou

Gansu (Province)

Area Sq Km 453 700	Population 24 380 000
Area Sq Miles 175 175	Capital Lanzhou

Guangdong (Province)

Area Sq Km 178 000	Population 68 680 000
Area Sq Miles 68 726	Capital Guangzhou

Guangxi Zhuangzu Zizhiqu (Autonomous Region)

Area Sq Km 236 000	Population 45 430 000
Area Sq Miles 91 120	Capital Nanning

Guizhou (Province)

Area Sq Km 176 000	Population 35 080 000
Area Sq Miles 67 954	Capital Guiyang

Hainan (Province)

Area Sq Km 34 000	Population 7 240 000
Area Sq Miles 13 127	Capital Haikou

Hebei (Province)

Area Sq Km 187 700	Population 64 370 000
Area Sq Miles 72 471	Capital Shijiazhuang

Heilongjiang (Province)

Area Sq Km 454 600	Population 37 010 000
Area Sq Miles 175 522	Capital Harbin

Henan (Province)

Area Sq Km 167 000	Population 91 000 000
Area Sq Miles 64 479	Capital Zhengzhou

Hong Kong (Special Administrative Region)

Area Sq Km 1 075	Population 6 706 965
Area Sq Miles 415	Capital Hong Kong
	Currency Hong Kong dollar
	Organizations ASEAN

Hubei (Province)

Area Sq Km 185 900	Population 57 720 000
Area Sq Miles 71 776	Capital Wuhan

Hunan (Province)

Area Sq Km 210 000	Population 63 920 000
Area Sq Miles 81 081	Capital Changsha

Jiangsu (Province)

Area Sq Km 102 600	Population 70 660 000
Area Sq Miles 39 614	Capital Nanjing

Jiangxi (Province)

Area Sq Km 166 900	Population 40 630 000
Area Sq Miles 64 440	Capital Nanchang

Jilin (Province)

Area Sq Km 187 000	Population 25 920 000
Area Sq Miles 72 201	Capital Changchun

Liaoning (Province)

Area Sq Km 147 400	Population 40 920 000
Area Sq Miles 56 911	Capital Shenyang

Macau (Special Administrative Region)

Area Sq Km 17	Population 459 000
Area Sq Miles 7	Capital Macau
	Currency Pataca

Nei Mongol Zizhiqu (Inner Mongolia) (Autonomous Region)

Area Sq Km 1 183 000	Population 22 840 000
Area Sq Miles 456 759	Capital Huhhot

Ningxia Huizu Zizhiqu (Autonomous Region)

Area Sq Km 66 400	Population 5 130 000
Area Sq Miles 25 637	Capital Yinchuan

Qinghai (Province)

Area Sq Km 721 000	Population 4 810 000
Area Sq Miles 278 380	Capital Xining

Shaanxi (Province)

Area Sq Km 205 600	Population 35 140 000
Area Sq Miles 79 383	Capital Xi'an

Shandong (Province)

Area Sq Km 153 300	Population 87 050 000
Area Sq Miles 59 189	Capital Jinan

Shanghai (Municipality)

Area Sq Km 6 300	Population 14 150 000
Area Sq Miles 2 432	Capital Shanghai

Shanxi (Province)

Area Sq Km 156 300	Population 30 770 000
Area Sq Miles 60 348	Capital Taiyuan

Sichuan (Province)

Area Sq Km 569 000	Population 98 650 000
Area Sq Miles 219 692	Capital Chengdu

Tianjin (Municipality)

Area Sq Km 11 300	Population 9 420 000
Area Sq Miles 4 363	Capital Tianjin

Xinjiang Uygur Zizhiqu (Sinkiang) (Autonomous Region)

Area Sq Km 1 600 000	Population 16 610 000
Area Sq Miles 617 763	Capital Ürümqi

Xizang Zizhiqu (Tibet) (Autonomous Region)

Area Sq Km 1 228 400	Population 2 400 000
Area Sq Miles 474 288	Capital Lhasa

Yunnan (Province)

Area Sq Km 394 000	Population 39 900 000
Area Sq Miles 152 124	Capital Kunming

Zhejiang (Province)

Area Sq Km 101 800	Population 43 190 000
Area Sq Miles 39 305	Capital Hangzhou

14

Christmas Island

Australian External Territory

Area Sq Km	135	Religions	Buddhist, Sunni
Area Sq Miles	52		Muslim, Protestant,
Population	2 195		Roman Catholic
Capital	The Settlement	Currency	Australian dollar
Languages	English	Map page	58

Cook Islands

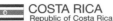

Self-governing New Zealand Territory

Area Sq Km	293	Religions	Protestant, Roman
Area Sq Miles	113		Catholic
Population	19 000	Currency	Dollar
Capital	Avarua	Map page	49
Languages	English, Maori		

Cocos Islands (Keeling Islands)
Australian External Territory

Area Sq Km	14	Religions	Sunni Muslim,
Area Sq Miles	5		Christian
Population	637	Currency	Australian dollar
Capital	West Island	Map page	58
Languages	English		

COSTA RICA

Republic of Costa Rica

Area Sq Km	51 100	Religions	Roman Catholic,
Area Sq Miles	19 730		Protestant
Population	3 841 000	Currency	Colón
Capital	San José	Organizations	UN
Languages	Spanish	Map page	146

COLOMBIA

Republic of Colombia

Area Sq Km	1 141 748	Religions	Roman Catholic,
Area Sq Miles	440 831		Protestant
Population	40 803 000	Currency	Peso
Capital	Bogotá	Organizations	APEC, UN
Languages	Spanish, Amerindian	Map page	150
	languages		

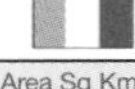

CÔTE D'IVOIRE

Republic of Côte d'Ivoire

Area Sq Km	322 463	Religions	Sunni Muslim, Roman
Area Sq Miles	124 504		Catholic, traditonal
Population	14 292 000		beliefs, Protestant
Capital	Yamoussoukro	Currency	CFA franc
Languages	French, creole, Akan,	Organizations	UN
	local languages	Map page	114

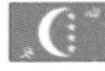

COMOROS

Federal Islamic Republic of the Comoros

Area Sq Km	1 862	Religions	Sunni Muslim, Roman
Area Sq Miles	719		Catholic
Population	658 000	Currency	Franc
Capital	Moroni	Organizations	UN
Languages	Comorian, French,	Map page	121
	Arabic		

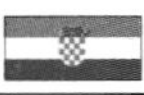

CROATIA

Republic of Croatia

Area Sq Km	56 538	Religions	Roman Catholic,
Area Sq Miles	21 829		Serbian Orthodox,
Population	4 481 000		Sunni Muslim
Capital	Zagreb	Currency	Kuna
Languages	Croatian, Serbian	Organizations	UN
		Map page	109

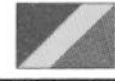

CONGO

Republic of Congo

Area Sq Km	342 000	Religions	Roman Catholic,
Area Sq Miles	132 047		Protestant, traditional
Population	2 785 000		beliefs, Sunni Muslim
Capital	Brazzaville	Currency	CFA franc
Languages	French, Kongo,	Organizations	UN
	Monokutuba, local	Map page	118
	languages		

CUBA

Republic of Cuba

Area Sq Km	110 860	Religions	Roman Catholic,
Area Sq Miles	42 803		Protestant
Population	11 116 000	Currency	Peso
Capital	Havana (La Habana)	Organizations	UN
Languages	Spanish	Map page	146

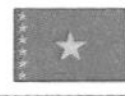

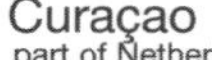

Curaçao
part of Netherlands Antilles

Area Sq Km	444	Religions	Roman Catholic,
Area Sq Miles	171		Protestant
Population	115 448	Currency	NA guilder
Capital	Willemstad	Map page	147
Languages	Dutch, Papiamento		

CONGO, DEMOCRATIC REPUBLIC OF

Area Sq Km	2 345 410	Religions	Christian, Sunni
Area Sq Miles	905 568		Muslim
Population	49 139 000	Currency	Franc
Capital	Kinshasa	Organizations	SADC, UN
Languages	French, Lingala,	Map page	118-119
	Swahili, Kongo, local		
	languages		

CYPRUS

Republic of Cyprus

Area Sq Km	9 251	Religions	Greek Orthodox, Sunni
Area Sq Miles	3 572		Muslim
Population	771 000	Currency	Pound
Capital	Nicosia (Lefkosia)	Organizations	Comm., UN
Languages	Greek, Turkish,	Map page	80
	English		

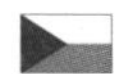

CZECH REPUBLIC

Area Sq Km	78 864	Religions	Roman Catholic,
Area Sq Miles	30 450		Protestant
Population	10 282 000	Currency	Koruna
Capital	Prague (Praha)	Organizations	UN
Languages	Czech, Moravian,	Map page	102-103
	Slovak		

 DENMARK
Kingdom of Denmark

Area Sq Km	43 075	Religions	Protestant
Area Sq Miles	16 631	Currency	Krone
Population	5 270 000	Organizations	EU, OECD, UN
Capital	Copenhagen	Map page	93
	(København)		
Languages	Danish		

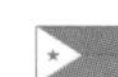

 DJIBOUTI
Republic of Djibouti

Area Sq Km	23 200	Religions	Sunni Muslim,
Area Sq Miles	8 958		Christian
Population	623 000	Currency	Franc
Capital	Djibouti	Organizations	UN
Languages	Somali, Afar, French,	Map page	117
	Arabic		

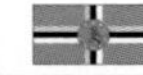

 DOMINICA
Commonwealth of Dominica

Area Sq Km	750	Religions	Roman Catholic,
Area Sq Miles	290		Protestant
Population	71 000	Currency	E. Carib. dollar
Capital	Roseau	Organizations	CARICOM, Comm.,
Languages	English, creole		UN
		Map page	147

■■ DOMINICAN REPUBLIC

Area Sq Km	48 442	Religions	Roman Catholic,
Area Sq Miles	18 704		Protestant
Population	8 232 000	Currency	Peso
Capital	Santo Domingo	Organizations	UN
Languages	Spanish, creole	Map page	147

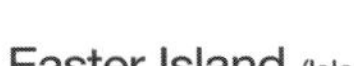

Easter Island (Isla de Pascua)
part of Chile

Area Sq Km	171	Religions	Roman Catholic
Area Sq Miles	66	Currency	Peso
Population	2 764	Map page	157
Capital	Hanga Roa		
Languages	Spanish		

East Timor
under UN Transitional Administration

Area Sq Km	14 874	Religions	Roman Catholic
Area Sq Miles	5 743	Currency	Rupiah
Population	857 000	Map page	59
Capital	Dili		
Languages	Portuguese, Tetun,		
	English		

 ECUADOR
Republic of Ecuador

Area Sq Km	272 045	Religions	Roman Catholic
Area Sq Miles	105 037	Currency	Sucre
Population	12 175 000	Organizations	APEC, UN
Capital	Quito	Map page	150
Languages	Spanish, Quechua,		
	Amerindian languages		

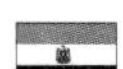

■■ EGYPT
Arab Republic of Egypt

Area Sq Km	1 000 250	Religions	Sunni Muslim, Coptic
Area Sq Miles	386 199		Christian
Population	65 978 000	Currency	Pound
Capital	Cairo (El Qâhira)	Organizations	UN
Languages	Arabic	Map page	116

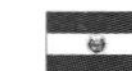

 EL SALVADOR
Republic of El Salvador

Area Sq Km	21 041	Religions	Roman Catholic,
Area Sq Miles	8 124		Protestant
Population	6 032 000	Currency	Colón
Capital	San Salvador	Organizations	UN
Languages	Spanish	Map page	146

 EQUATORIAL GUINEA
Republic of Equatorial Guinea

Area Sq Km	28 051	Religions	Roman Catholic,
Area Sq Miles	10 831		traditional beliefs
Population	431 000	Currency	CFA franc
Capital	Malabo	Organizations	UN
Languages	Spanish, French, Fang	Map page	118

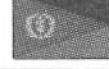

 ERITREA
State of Eritrea

Area Sq Km	117 400	Religions	Sunni Muslim, Coptic
Area Sq Miles	45 328		Christian
Population	3 577 000	Currency	Nakfa
Capital	Asmara	Organizations	UN
Languages	Tigrinya, Tigre	Map page	116

■■ ESTONIA
Republic of Estonia

Area Sq Km	45 200	Religions	Protestant, Estonian
Area Sq Miles	17 452		and Russian Orthodox
Population	1 429 000	Currency	Kroon
Capital	Tallinn	Organizations	UN
Languages	Estonian, Russian	Map page	88

 ETHIOPIA
Federal Democratic Republic of Ethiopia

Area Sq Km	1 133 880	Religions	Ethiopian Orthodox,
Area Sq Miles	437 794		Sunni Muslim,
Population	59 649 000		traditional beliefs
Capital	Addis Ababa	Currency	Birr
	(Ādīs Ābeba)	Organizations	UN
Languages	Oromo, Amharic,	Map page	117
	Tigrinya, local		
	languages		

16

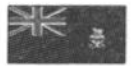

 ## Falkland Islands
United Kingdom Overseas Territory

Area Sq Km	12 170	Religions	Protestant, Roman
Area Sq Miles	4 699		Catholic
Population	2 000	Currency	Pound
Capital	Stanley	Map page	153
Languages	English		

 ## GABON
Gabonese Republic

Area Sq Km	267 667	Religions	Roman Catholic,
Area Sq Miles	103 347		Protestant, traditonal
Population	1 167 000		beliefs
Capital	Libreville	Currency	CFA franc
Languages	French, Fang, local	Map page	118
	languages		

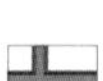

 ## Faroe Islands
Self-governing Danish Territory

Area Sq Km	1 399	Religions	Protestant
Area Sq Miles	540	Currency	Danish krone
Population	43 000	Map page	94
Capital	Tórshavn		
	(Thorshavn)		
Languages	Faroese, Danish		

Galapagos Islands (Islas Galápagos)
part of Ecuador

Area Sq Km	8 010	Religions	Roman Catholic
Area Sq Miles.	3 093	Currency	Sucre
Population	10 207	Map page	125
Capital	Puerto Baquerizo		
	Moreno		
Languages	Spanish		

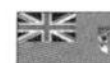

 ## FIJI
Sovereign Democratic Republic of Fiji

Area Sq Km	18 330	Religions	Christian, Hindu, Sunni
Area Sq Miles	7 077		Muslim
Population	796 000	Currency	Dollar
Capital	Suva	Organizations	UN, Comm.
Languages	English, Fijian,	Map page	49
	Hindi		

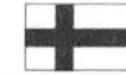

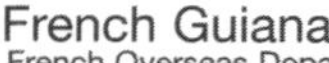

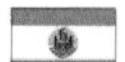

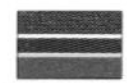

 ## THE GAMBIA
Republic of The Gambia

Area Sq Km	11 295	Religions	Sunni Muslim,
Area Sq Miles	4 361		Protestant
Population	1 229 000	Currency	Dalasi
Capital	Banjul	Organizations	Comm., UN
Languages	English, Malinke,	Map page	114
	Fulani, Wolof		

 ## FINLAND
Republic of Finland

Area Sq Km	338 145	Religions	Protestant, Greek
Area Sq Miles	130 559		Orthodox
Population	5 154 000	Currency	Markka, Euro
Capital	Helsinki (Helsingfors)	Organizations	EU, OECD, UN
Languages	Finnish, Swedish	Map page	92-93

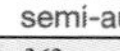

Gaza
semi-autonomous region

Area Sq Km	363	Religions	Sunni Muslim, Shi'a
Area Sq Miles	140		Muslim
Population	1 036 000	Currency	Israeli shekel
Capital	Gaza	Map page	80
Languages	Arabic		

 ## FRANCE
French Republic

Area Sq Km	543 965	Religions	Roman Catholic,
Area Sq Miles	210 026		Protestant, Sunni
Population	58 683 000		Muslim
Capital	Paris	Currency	Franc, Euro
Languages	French, Arabic	Organizations	EU, OECD, UN
		Map page	104-105

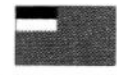

 ## GEORGIA
Republic of Georgia

Area Sq Km	69 700	Religions	Georgian Orthodox,
Area Sq Miles	26 911		Russian Orthodox,
Population	5 059 000		Sunni Muslim
Capital	T'bilisi	Currency	Lari
Languages	Georgian, Russian,	Organizations	CIS, UN
	Armenian, Azeri,	Map page	81
	Ossetian, Abkhaz		

French Guiana
French Overseas Department

Area Sq Km	90 000	Religions	Roman Catholic
Area Sq Miles	34 749	Currency	French franc
Population	167 000	Map page	151
Capital	Cayenne		
Languages	French, creole		

 ## GERMANY
Federal Republic of Germany

Area Sq Km	357 028	Religions	Protestant, Roman
Area Sq Miles	137 849		Catholic
Population	82 133 000	Currency	Mark, Euro
Capital	Berlin	Organizations	EU, OECD, UN
Languages	German, Turkish	Map page	102

 ## French Polynesia
French Overseas Territory

Area Sq Km	3 265	Religions	Protestant, Roman
Area Sq Miles	1 261		Catholic
Population	227 000	Currency	Pacific franc
Capital	Papeete	Map page	49
Languages	French, Tahitian,		
	Polynesian languages		

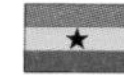

 ## GHANA
Republic of Ghana

Area Sq Km	238 537	Religions	Christian, Sunni
Area Sq Miles	92 100		Muslim, traditional
Population	19 162 000		beliefs
Capital	Accra	Currency	Cedi
Languages	English, Hausa,	Organizations	Comm., UN
	Akan, local languages	Map page	114

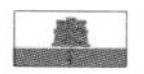

Gibraltar
United Kingdom Overseas Territory

Area Sq Km	7	Religions	Roman Catholic,
Area Sq Miles	3		Protestant, Sunni
Population	25 000		Muslim
Capital	Gibraltar	Currency	Pound
Languages	English, Spanish	Map page	106

Guernsey
United Kingdom Crown Dependency

Area Sq Km	78	Religions	Protestant, Roman
Area Sq Miles	30		Catholic
Population	64 555	Currency	Pound
Capital	St Peter Port	Map page	95
Languages	English, French		

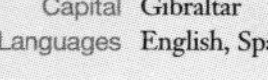

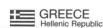

GREECE
Hellenic Republic

Area Sq Km	131 957	Religions	Greek Orthodox, Sunni
Area Sq Miles	50 949		Muslim
Population	10 600 000	Currency	Drachma
Capital	Athens (Athina)	Organizations	EU, OECD, UN
Languages	Greek	Map page	111

GUINEA
Republic of Guinea

Area Sq Km	245 857	Religions	Sunni Muslim,
Area Sq Miles	94 926		traditional beliefs,
Population	7 337 000		Christian
Capital	Conakry	Currency	Franc
Languages	French, Fulani,	Organizations	UN
	Malinke, local	Map page	114
	languages		

Greenland
Self-governing Danish Territory

Area Sq Km	2 175 600	Religions	Protestant
Area Sq Miles	840 004	Currency	Danish krone
Population	56 000	Map page	127
Capital	Nuuk (Godthåb)		
Languages	Greenlandic, Danish		

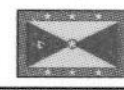

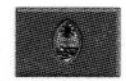

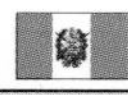

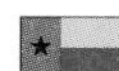

GUINEA-BISSAU
Republic of Guinea-Bissau

Area Sq Km	36 125	Religions	Traditional beliefs,
Area Sq Miles	13 948		Sunni Muslim,
Population	1 161 000		Christian
Capital	Bissau	Currency	CFA franc
Languages	Portuguese, crioulo,	Organizations	UN
	local languages	Map page	114

GRENADA

Area Sq Km	378	Religions	Roman Catholic,
Area Sq Miles	146		Protestant
Population	93 000	Currency	E. Carib. dollar
Capital	St George's	Organizations	CARICOM, Comm.,
Languages	English, creole		UN
		Map page	147

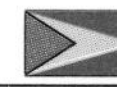

GUYANA
Co-operative Republic of Guyana

Area Sq Km	214 969	Religions	Protestant, Hindu,
Area Sq Miles	83 000		Roman Catholic, Sunni
Population	850 000		Muslim
Capital	Georgetown	Currency	Dollar
Languages	English, creole,	Organizations	CARICOM, Comm.,
	Amerindian		UN
	languages	Map page	150

Guadeloupe
French Overseas Department

Area Sq Km	1 780	Religions	Roman Catholic
Area Sq Miles	687	Currency	French franc
Population	443 000	Map page	147
Capital	Basse-Terre		
Languages	French, creole		

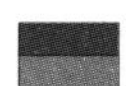

HAITI
Republic of Haiti

Area Sq Km	27 750	Religions	Roman Catholic,
Area Sq Miles	10 714		Protestant, Voodoo
Population	7 952 000	Currency	Gourde
Capital	Port-au-Prince	Organizations	UN
Languages	French, creole	Map page	147

Guam
United States Unincorporated Territory

Area Sq Km	541	Religions	Roman Catholic
Area Sq Miles	209	Currency	US dollar
Population	161 000	Map page	59
Capital	Hagåtña		
Languages	Chamorro, English,		
	Tagalog		

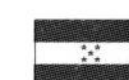

HONDURAS
Republic of Honduras

Area Sq Km	112 088	Religions	Roman Catholic,
Area Sq Miles	43 277		Protestant
Population	6 147 000	Currency	Lempira
Capital	Tegucigalpa	Organizations	UN
Languages	Spanish, Amerindian	Map page	147
	languages		

GUATEMALA
Republic of Guatemala

Area Sq Km	108 890	Religions	Roman Catholic,
Area Sq Miles	42 043		Protestant
Population	10 801 000	Currency	Quetzal
Capital	Guatemala	Organizations	UN
	(Guatemala City)	Map page	146
Languages	Spanish, Mayan		
	languages		

HUNGARY
Republic of Hungary

Area Sq Km	93 030	Religions	Roman Catholic,
Area Sq Miles	35 919		Protestant
Population	10 116 000	Currency	Forint
Capital	Budapest	Organizations	OECD, UN
Languages	Hungarian	Map page	103

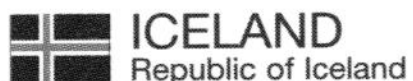

ICELAND
Republic of Iceland

Area Sq Km	102 820	Religions	Protestant
Area Sq Miles	39 699	Currency	Króna
Population	276 000	Organizations	OECD, UN
Capital	Reykjavík	Map page	92
Languages	Icelandic		

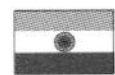

 ## INDIA
Republic of India

Area Sq Km	3 065 027	Religions	Hindu, Sunni Muslim,
Area Sq Miles	1 183 414		Shi'a Muslim, Sikh,
Population	982 223 000		Christian
Capital	New Delhi	Currency	Rupee
Languages	Hindi, English, many	Organizations	Comm., UN
	regional languages	Map page	72-73

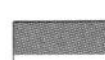

 ## INDONESIA
Republic of Indonesia

Area Sq Km	1 919 445	Religions	Sunni Muslim,
Area Sq Miles	741 102		Protestant, Roman
Population	206 338 000		Catholic, Hindu,
Capital	Jakarta		Buddhist
Languages	Indonesian, local	Currency	Rupiah
	languages	Organizations	APEC, ASEAN,
			OPEC, UN
		Map page	58-59

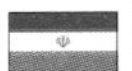

 ## IRAN
Islamic Republic of Iran

Area Sq Km	1 648 000	Religions	Shi'a Muslim, Sunni
Area Sq Miles	636 296		Muslim
Population	65 758 000	Currency	Rial
Capital	Tehrān	Organizations	OPEC, UN
Languages	Farsi, Azeri, Kurdish,	Map page	81
	regional languages		

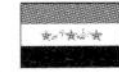

 ## IRAQ
Republic of Iraq

Area Sq Km	438 317	Religions	Shi'a Muslim, Sunni
Area Sq Miles	169 235		Muslim, Christian
Population	21 800 000	Currency	Dinar
Capital	Baghdād	Organizations	OPEC, UN
Languages	Arabic, Kurdish,	Map page	81
	Turkmen		

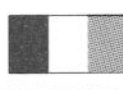

 ## IRELAND, REPUBLIC OF

Area Sq Km	70 282	Religions	Roman Catholic,
Area Sq Miles	27 136		Protestant,
Population	3 681 000	Currency	Punt, Euro
Capital	Dublin	Organizations	EU, OECD, UN
	(Baile Átha Cliath)	Map page	97
Languages	English, Irish		

Isle of Man
United Kingdom Crown Dependency

Area Sq Km	572	Religions	Protestant, Roman
Area Sq Miles	221		Catholic
Population	77 000	Currency	Pound
Capital	Douglas	Map page	98
Languages	English		

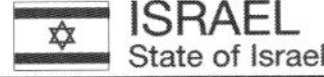

 ## ISRAEL
State of Israel

Area Sq Km	20 770	Religions	Jewish, Sunni Muslim,
Area Sq Miles	8 019		Christian, Druze
Population	5 984 000	Currency	Shekel
Capital	Jerusalem	Organizations	UN
	(Yerushalayim)	Map page	80
	(El Quds)		
Languages	Hebrew, Arabic		

 ## ITALY
Italian Republic

Area Sq Km	301 245	Religions	Roman Catholic
Area Sq Miles	116 311	Currency	Lira, Euro
Population	57 369 000	Organizations	EU, OECD, UN
Capital	Rome (Roma)	Map page	108-109
Languages	Italian		

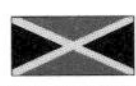

 ## JAMAICA

Area Sq Km	10 991	Religions	Protestant, Roman
Area Sq Miles	4 244		Catholic
Population	2 538 000	Currency	Dollar
Capital	Kingston	Organizations	CARICOM, Comm.,
Languages	English, creole		UN
		Map page	146

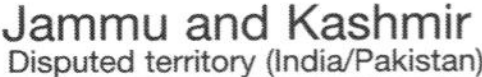

Jammu and Kashmir
Disputed territory (India/Pakistan)

Area Sq Km	222 236	Map page	74-75
Area Sq Miles	85 806		
Population	13 000 000		
Capital	Srinagar		

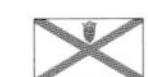

 ## JAPAN

Area Sq Km	377 727	Religions	Shintoist, Buddhist,
Area Sq Miles	145 841		Christian
Population	126 281 000	Currency	Yen
Capital	Tōkyō	Organizations	APEC, OECD, UN
Languages	Japanese	Map page	66-67

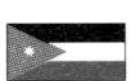

 ## Jersey
United Kingdom Crown Dependency

Area Sq Km	116	Religions	Protestant, Roman
Area Sq Miles	45		Catholic
Population	89 136	Currency	Pound
Capital	St Helier	Map page	95
Languages	English, French		

 ## JORDAN
Hashemite Kingdom of Jordan

Area Sq Km	89 206	Religions	Sunni Muslim,
Area Sq Miles	34 443		Christian
Population	6 304 000	Currency	Dinar
Capital	'Ammān	Organizations	UN
Languages	Arabic	Map page	80

Juan Fernández Islands
part of Chile

Area Sq Km	179	Religions	Roman Catholic
Area Sq Miles	69	Map page	157
Population	516		
Capital	San Juan Bautista		
Languages	Spanish		

LATVIA
Republic of Latvia

Area Sq Km	63 700	Religions	Protestant, Roman
Area Sq Miles	24 595		Catholic, Russian
Population	2 424 000		Orthodox
Capital	Riga	Currency	Lat
Languages	Latvian, Russian	Organizations	UN
		Map page	88

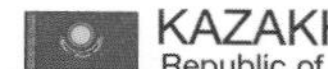

 ## KAZAKHSTAN
Republic of Kazakhstan

Area Sq Km	2 717 300	Religions	Sunni Muslim, Russian
Area Sq Miles	1 049 155		Orthodox, Protestant
Population	16 319 000	Currency	Tenge
Capital	Astana (Akmola)	Organizations	CIS, UN
Languages	Kazakh, Russian,	Map page	76-77
	Ukrainian, German,		
	Uzbek, Tatar		

LEBANON
Republic of Lebanon

Area Sq Km	10 452	Religions	Shi'a Muslim, Sunni
Area Sq Miles	4 036		Muslim, Christian
Population	3 191 000	Currency	Pound
Capital	Beirut (Beyrouth)	Organizations	UN
Languages	Arabic, Armenian,	Map page	80
	French		

 ## KENYA
Republic of Kenya

Area Sq Km	582 646	Religions	Christian, traditional
Area Sq Miles	224 961		beliefs
Population	29 008 000	Currency	Shilling
Capital	Nairobi	Organizations	Comm., UN
Languages	Swahili, English, local	Map page	119
	languages		

LESOTHO
Kingdom of Lesotho

Area Sq Km	30 355	Religions	Christian, traditional
Area Sq Miles	11 720		beliefs
Population	2 062 000	Currency	Loti
Capital	Maseru	Organizations	Comm., SADC, UN
Languages	Sesotho, English,	Map page	123
	Zulu		

 ## KIRIBATI
Republic of Kiribati

Area Sq Km	717	Religions	Roman Catholic,
Area Sq Miles	277		Protestant
Population	81 000	Currency	Australian dollar
Capital	Bairiki	Organizations	Comm., UN
Languages	Gilbertese, English	Map page	49

LIBERIA
Republic of Liberia

Area Sq Km	111 369	Religions	Traditional beliefs,
Area Sq Miles	43 000		Christian, Sunni
Population	2 666 000		Muslim
Capital	Monrovia	Currency	Dollar
Languages	English, creole, local	Organizations	UN
	languages	Map page	114

 ## KUWAIT
State of Kuwait

Area Sq Km	17 818	Religions	Sunni Muslim, Shi'a
Area Sq Miles	6 880		Muslim, Christian,
Population	1 811 000		Hindu
Capital	Kuwait (Al Kuwayt)	Currency	Dinar
Languages	Arabic	Organizations	OPEC, UN
		Map page	78

LIBYA
Socialist People's Libyan Arab Jamahiriya

Area Sq Km	1 759 540	Religions	Sunni Muslim
Area Sq Miles	679 362	Currency	Dinar
Population	5 339 000	Organizations	OPEC, UN
Capital	Tripoli (Ṭarābulus)	Map page	115
Languages	Arabic, Berber		

 ## KYRGYZSTAN
Kyrgyz Republic

Area Sq Km	198 500	Religions	Sunni Muslim, Russian
Area Sq Miles	76 641		Orthodox
Population	4 643 000	Currency	Som
Capital	Bishkek (Frunze)	Organizations	CIS, UN
Languages	Kyrgyz, Russian,	Map page	77
	Uzbek		

LIECHTENSTEIN
Principality of Liechtenstein

Area Sq Km	160	Religions	Roman Catholic,
Area Sq Miles	62		Protestant
Population	32 000	Currency	Swiss franc
Capital	Vaduz	Organizations	UN
Languages	German	Map page	105

 ## LAOS
Lao People's Democratic Republic

Area Sq Km	236 800	Religions	Buddhist, traditional
Area Sq Miles	91 429		beliefs
Population	5 163 000	Currency	Kip
Capital	Vientiane	Organizations	ASEAN, UN
	(Viangchan)	Map page	62-63
Languages	Lao, local languages		

 ## LITHUANIA
Republic of Lithuania

Area Sq Km	65 200	Religions	Roman Catholic,
Area Sq Miles	25 174		Protestant, Russian
Population	3 694 000		Orthodox
Capital	Vilnius	Currency	Litas
Languages	Lithuanian, Russian,	Organizations	UN
	Polish	Map page	88

Lord Howe Islands
part of Australia

Area Sq Km	17	Population	371
Area Sq Miles	6	Map page	51

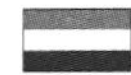

LUXEMBOURG
Grand Duchy of Luxembourg

Area Sq Km	2 586	Religions	Roman Catholic
Area Sq Miles	998	Currency	Franc, Euro
Population	422 000	Organizations	EU, OECD, UN
Capital	Luxembourg	Map page	100
Languages	Letzeburgish, German, French		

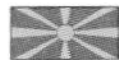

MACEDONIA (F.Y.R.O.M.)
Republic of Macedonia

Area Sq Km	25 713	Religions	Macedonian Orthodox,
Area Sq Miles	9 928		Sunni Muslim
Population	1 999 000	Currency	Denar
Capital	Skopje	Organizations	UN
Languages	Macedonian, Albanian, Turkish	Map page	111

MADAGASCAR
Republic of Madagascar

Area Sq Km	587 041	Religions	Traditional beliefs,
Area Sq Miles	226 658		Christian, Sunni
Population	15 057 000		Muslim
Capital	Antananarivo	Currency	Franc
Languages	Malagasy, French	Organizations	UN
		Map page	121

Madeira
Autonomous Region of Portugal

Area Sq Km	779	Religions	Roman Catholic,
Area Sq Miles	301		Protestant
Population	259 000	Currency	Portuguese escudo
Capital	Funchal	Map page	114
Languages	Portuguese		

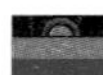

MALAWI
Republic of Malawi

Area Sq Km	118 484	Religions	Christian, traditional
Area Sq Miles	45 747		beliefs, Sunni Muslim
Population	10 346 000	Currency	Kwacha
Capital	Lilongwe	Organizations	Comm.,SADC, UN
Languages	Chichewa, English, local languages	Map page	121

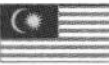

MALAYSIA
Federation of Malaysia

Area Sq Km	332 965	Religions	Sunni Muslim, Buddhist,
Area Sq Miles	128 559		Hindu, Christian,
Population	21 410 000		traditional beliefs
Capital	Kuala Lumpur	Currency	Ringgit
Languages	Malay, English, Chinese, Tamil, local languages	Organizations	APEC, ASEAN, Comm., UN
		Map page	60-61

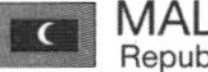

MALDIVES
Republic of the Maldives

Area Sq Km	298	Religions	Sunni Muslim
Area Sq Miles	115	Currency	Rufiyaa
Population	271 000	Organizations	Comm., UN
Capital	Male	Map page	56
Languages	Divehi (Maldivian)		

MALI
Republic of Mali

Area Sq Km	1 240 140	Religions	Sunni Muslim,
Area Sq Miles	478 821		traditional beliefs,
Population	10 694 000		Christian
Capital	Bamako	Currency	CFA franc
Languages	French, Bambara, local languages	Organizations	UN
		Map page	114

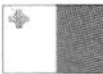

MALTA
Republic of Malta

Area Sq Km	316	Religions	Roman Catholic
Area Sq Miles	122	Currency	Lira
Population	384 000	Organizations	Comm.,UN
Capital	Valletta	Map page	84
Languages	Maltese, English		

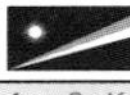

MARSHALL ISLANDS
Republic of Marshall Islands

Area Sq Km	181	Religions	Protestant, Roman
Area Sq Miles	70		Catholic
Population	60 000	Currency	US dollar
Capital	Dalap-Uliga-Darrit	Organizations	UN
Languages	English, Marshallese	Map page	48

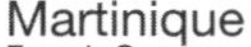

Martinique
French Overseas Department

Area Sq Km	1 079	Religions	Roman Catholic,
Area Sq Miles	417		traditional beliefs
Population	389 000	Currency	French franc
Capital	Fort-de-France	Map page	147
Languages	French, creole		

MAURITANIA
Islamic Arab and African Republic of Mauritania

Area Sq Km	1 030 700	Religions	Sunni Muslim
Area Sq Miles	397 955	Currency	Ouguiya
Population	2 529 000	Organizations	UN
Capital	Nouakchott	Map page	114
Languages	Arabic, French, local languages		

MAURITIUS
Republic of Mauritius

Area Sq Km	2 040	Religions	Hindu, Roman
Area Sq Miles	788		Catholic, Sunni Muslim
Population	1 141 000	Currency	Rupee
Capital	Port Louis	Organizations	Comm., SADC, UN
Languages	English, creole, Hindi, Bhojpurī, French	Map page	113

Mayotte
French Territorial Collectivity

Area Sq Km	373	Religions	Sunni Muslim,
Area Sq Miles	144		Christian
Population	144 944	Currency	French franc
Capital	Dzaoudzi	Map page	121
Languages	French, Mahorian		

Melilla
Spanish Territory

Area Sq Km	13	Religions	Roman Catholic,
Area Sq Miles	5		Muslim
Population	59 576	Currency	Peseta
Capital	Melilla	Map page	114
Languages	Spanish, Arabic		

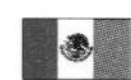

MEXICO
United Mexican States

Area Sq Km	1 972 545	Religions	Roman Catholic,
Area Sq Miles	761 604		Protestant
Population	95 831 000	Currency	Peso
Capital	México (Mexico	Organizations	APEC, OECD, UN
	City)	Map page	144-145
Languages	Spanish, Amerindian		
	languages		

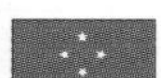

MICRONESIA, FEDERATED STATES OF

Area Sq Km	701	Religions	Roman Catholic,
Area Sq Miles	271		Protestant
Population	114 000	Currency	US dollar
Capital	Palikir	Organizations	UN
Languages	English, Chuukese,	Map page	48
	Pohnpeian, local		
	languages		

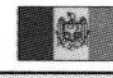

MOLDOVA
Republic of Moldova

Area Sq Km	33 700	Religions	Romanian Orthodox,
Area Sq Miles	13 012		Russian Orthodox
Population	4 378 000	Currency	Leu
Capital	Chişinău (Kishinev)	Organizations	CIS, UN
Languages	Romanian,	Map page	90
	Ukrainian, Gagauz,		
	Russian		

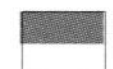

MONACO
Principality of Monaco

Area Sq Km	2	Religions	Roman Catholic
Area Sq Miles	1	Currency	French franc
Population	33 000	Organizations	UN
Capital	Monaco-Ville	Map page	105
Languages	French, Monegasque,		
	Italian		

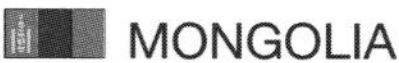

MONGOLIA

Area Sq Km	1 565 000	Religions	Buddhist, Sunni Muslim
Area Sq Miles	604 250	Currency	Tugrik
Population	2 579 000	Organizations	UN
Capital	Ulaanbaatar	Map page	68-69
	(Ulan Bator)		
Languages	Khalka (Mongolian),		
	Kazakh, local languages		

Montserrat
United Kingdom Overseas Territory

Area Sq Km	100	Religions	Protestant, Roman
Area Sq Miles	39		Catholic
Population	11 000	Currency	E. Carib. dollar
Capital	Plymouth	Organizations	CARICOM
Languages	English	Map page	147

MOROCCO
Kingdom of Morocco

Area Sq Km	446 550	Religions	Sunni Muslim
Area Sq Miles	172 414	Currency	Dirham
Population	27 377 000	Organizations	UN
Capital	Rabat	Map page	114
Languages	Arabic, Berber,		
	French		

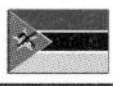

MOZAMBIQUE
Republic of Mozambique

Area Sq Km	799 380	Religions	Traditional beliefs,
Area Sq Miles	308 642		Roman Catholic, Sunni
Population	18 880 000		Muslim
Capital	Maputo	Currency	Metical
Languages	Portuguese, Makua,	Organizations	Comm., SADC, UN
	Tsonga, local	Map page	121
	languages		

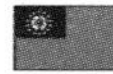

MYANMAR
Union of Myanmar

Area Sq Km	676 577	Religions	Buddhist, Christian,
Area Sq Miles	261 228		Sunni Muslim
Population	44 497 000	Currency	Kyat
Capital	Yangôn (Rangoon)	Organizations	ASEAN, UN
Languages	Burmese, Shan,	Map page	62-63
	Karen, local languages		

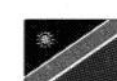

NAMIBIA
Republic of Namibia

Area Sq Km	824 292	Religions	Protestant, Roman
Area Sq Miles	318 261		Catholic
Population	1 660 000	Currency	Dollar
Capital	Windhoek	Organizations	Comm., SADC, UN
Languages	English, Afrikaans,	Map page	121
	German, Ovambo,		
	local languages		

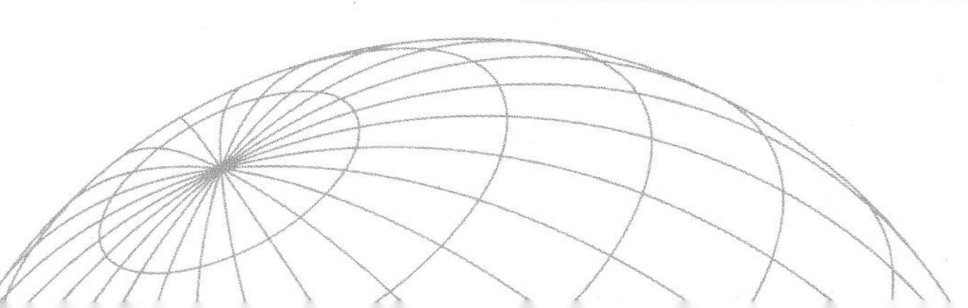

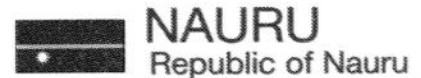

NAURU
Republic of Nauru

Area Sq Km	21	Religions	Protestant, Roman
Area Sq Miles	8		Catholic
Population	11 000	Currency	Australian dollar
Capital	Yaren	Organizations	Comm., UN
Languages	Nauruan, English	Map page	48

NEPAL

Kingdom of Nepal

Area Sq Km	147 181	Religions	Hindu, Buddhist, Sunni
Area Sq Miles	56 827		Muslim
Population	22 847 000	Currency	Rupee
Capital	Kathmandu	Organizations	UN
Languages	Nepali, Maithili, Bhojpuri, English, local languages	Map page	75

NETHERLANDS
Kingdom of the Netherlands

Area Sq Km	41 526	Religions	Roman Catholic,
Area Sq Miles	16 033		Protestant, Sunni
Population	15 678 000		Muslim
Capital	Amsterdam/The Hague ('s-Gravenhage)	Currency	Guilder, Euro
		Organizations	EU, OECD, UN
		Map page	100
Languages	Dutch, Frisian		

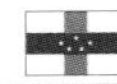

Netherlands Antilles
Self-governing Netherlands Territory

Area Sq Km	800	Religions	Roman Catholic,
Area Sq Miles	309		Protestant
Population	213 000	Currency	NA guilder
Capital	Willemstad	Map page	147
Languages	Dutch, Papiamento, English		

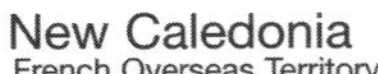

New Caledonia
French Overseas Territory

Area Sq Km	19 058	Religions	Roman Catholic,
Area Sq Miles	7 358		Protestant, Sunni
Population	206 000		Muslim
Capital	Nouméa	Currency	Pacific franc
Languages	French, local languages	Map page	48

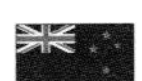

 ## NEW ZEALAND

Area Sq Km	270 534	Religions	Protestant, Roman
Area Sq Miles	104 454		Catholic
Population	3 796 000	Currency	Dollar
Capital	Wellington	Organizations	APEC, Comm., OECD, UN
Languages	English, Maori		
		Map page	54

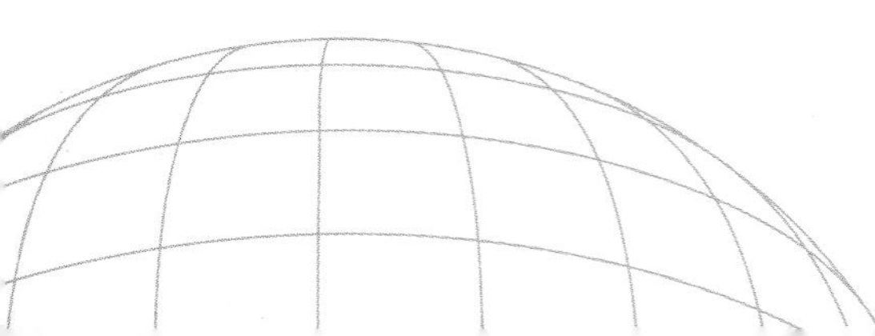

NICARAGUA
Republic of Nicaragua

Area Sq Km	130 000	Religions	Roman Catholic,
Area Sq Miles	50 193		Protestant
Population	4 807 000	Currency	Córdoba
Capital	Managua	Organizations	UN
Languages	Spanish, Amerindian languages	Map page	146

NIGER

Republic of Niger

Area Sq Km	1 267 000	Religions	Sunni Muslim,
Area Sq Miles	489 191		traditional beliefs
Population	10 078 000	Currency	CFA franc
Capital	Niamey	Organizations	UN
Languages	French, Hausa, Fulani, local languages	Map page	115

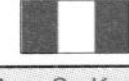

NIGERIA
Federal Republic of Nigeria

Area Sq Km	923 768	Religions	Sunni Muslim,
Area Sq Miles	356 669		Christian, traditional
Population	106 409 000		beliefs
Capital	Abuja	Currency	Naira
Languages	English, Hausa, Yoruba, Ibo, Fulani, local languages	Organizations	Comm., OPEC, UN
		Map page	115

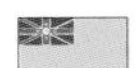

 ### Niue
Self-governing New Zealand Overseas Territory

Area Sq Km	258	Religions	Christian
Area Sq Miles	100	Currency	NZ dollar
Population	2 000	Map page	48
Capital	Alofi		
Languages	English, Polynesian		

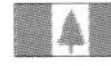

 ### Norfolk Island
Australian External Territory

Area Sq Km	35	Religions	Protestant, Roman
Area Sq Miles	14		Catholic
Population	2 000	Currency	Australian dollar
Capital	Kingston	Map page	48
Languages	English		

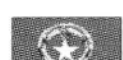

Northern Mariana Islands
United States Commonwealth

Area Sq Km	477	Religions	Roman Catholic
Area Sq Miles	184	Currency	US dollar
Population	70 000	Map page	59
Capital	Saipan		
Languages	English, Chamorro, local languages		

NORTH KOREA
People's Democratic Republic of North Korea

Area Sq Km	120 538	Religions	Traditional beliefs,
Area Sq Miles	46 540		Chondoist, Buddhist
Population	23 348 000	Currency	Won
Capital	P'yŏngyang	Organizations	UN
Languages	Korean	Map page	65

NORWAY
Kingdom of Norway

Area Sq Km	323 878	Religions	Protestant, Roman
Area Sq Miles	125 050		Catholic
Population	4 419 000	Currency	Krone
Capital	Oslo	Organizations	OECD, UN
Languages	Norwegian	Map page	92-93

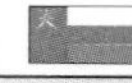

OMAN
Sultanate of Oman

Area Sq Km	309 500	Religions	Ibadhi Muslim, Sunni
Area Sq Miles	119 499		Muslim
Population	2 382 000	Currency	Rial
Capital	Muscat (Masqat)	Organizations	UN
Languages	Arabic, Baluchi,	Map page	79
	Indian languages		

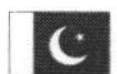

PAKISTAN
Islamic Republic of Pakistan

Area Sq Km	803 940	Religions	Sunni Muslim, Shi'a
Area Sq Miles	310 403		Muslim, Christian,
Population	148 166 000		Hindu
Capital	Islamabad	Currency	Rupee
Languages	Urdu, Punjabi,	Organizations	Comm., UN
	Sindhi, Pushtu,	Map page	74
	English		

PALAU
Republic of Palau

Area Sq Km	497	Religions	Roman Catholic,
Area Sq Miles	192		Protestant, traditional
Population	19 000		beliefs
Capital	Koror	Currency	US dollar
Languages	Palauan, English	Organizations	UN
		Map page	59

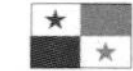

PANAMA
Republic of Panama

Area Sq Km	77 082	Religions	Roman Catholic,
Area Sq Miles	29 762		Protestant, Sunni
Population	2 767 000		Muslim
Capital	Panamá	Currency	Balboa
	(Panama City)	Organizations	UN
Languages	Spanish, English,	Map page	146
	Amerindian languages		

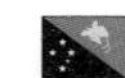

PAPUA NEW GUINEA
Independent State of Papua New Guinea

Area Sq Km	462 840	Religions	Protestant, Roman
Area Sq Miles	178 704		Catholic, traditional
Population	4 600 000		beliefs
Capital	Port Moresby	Currency	Kina
Languages	English, Tok Pisin	Organizations	Comm., UN
	(creole), local	Map page	59
	languages		

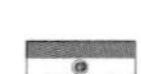

PARAGUAY
Republic of Paraguay

Area Sq Km	406 752	Religions	Roman Catholic,
Area Sq Miles	157 048		Protestant
Population	5 222 000	Currency	Guaraní
Capital	Asunción	Organizations	UN
Languages	Spanish, Guaraní	Map page	152

PERU
Republic of Peru

Area Sq Km	1 285 216	Religions	Roman Catholic,
Area Sq Miles	496 225		Protestant
Population	24 797 000	Currency	Sol
Capital	Lima	Organizations	APEC, UN
Languages	Spanish, Quechua,	Map page	150
	Aymara		

PHILIPPINES
Republic of the Philippines

Area Sq Km	300 000	Religions	Roman Catholic,
Area Sq Miles	115 831		Protestant, Sunni
Population	72 944 000		Muslim, Aglipayan
Capital	Manila	Currency	Peso
Languages	English, Pilipino,	Organizations	APEC, ASEAN, UN
	Cebuano, local	Map page	64
	languages		

Pitcairn Islands
United Kingdom Overseas Territory

Area Sq Km	45	Religions	Protestant
Area Sq Miles	17	Currency	NZ dollar
Population	46	Map page	49
Capital	Adamstown		
Languages	English		

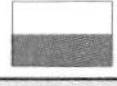

POLAND
Polish Republic

Area Sq Km	312 683	Religions	Roman Catholic, Polish
Area Sq Miles	120 728		Orthodox
Population	38 718 000	Currency	Złoty
Capital	Warsaw (Warszawa)	Organizations	OECD, UN
Languages	Polish, German	Map page	103

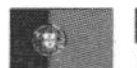

PORTUGAL
Portuguese Republic

Area Sq Km	88 940	Religions	Roman Catholic,
Area Sq Miles	34 340		Protestant
Population	9 869 000	Currency	Escudo, Euro
Capital	Lisbon (Lisboa)	Organizations	EU, OECD, UN
Languages	Portuguese	Map page	106

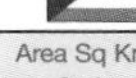

Puerto Rico
United States Commonwealth

Area Sq Km	9 104	Religions	Roman Catholic,
Area Sq Miles	3 515		Protestant
Population	3 810 000	Currency	US dollar
Capital	San Juan	Map page	147
Languages	Spanish, English		

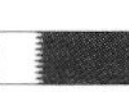

QATAR
State of Qatar

Area Sq Km	11 437	Religions	Sunni Muslim
Area Sq Miles	4 416	Currency	Riyal
Population	579 000	Organizations	OPEC, UN
Capital	Doha (Ad Dawḥah)	Map page	79
Languages	Arabic		

24

Réunion
French Overseas Department

Area Sq Km	2 551	Religions	Roman Catholic
Area Sq Miles	985	Currency	French franc
Population	682 000	Map page	113
Capital	St-Denis		
Languages	French, creole		

St Eustatius
part of Netherlands Antilles

Area Sq Km	21	Religions	Protestant, Roman
Area Sq Miles	8		Catholic
Population	1 900	Currency	NA guilder
Capital	Oranjestad	Map page	147
Languages	Dutch, English		

Rodrigues Island
part of Mauritius

Area Sq Km	104	Religions	Christian
Area Sq Miles	40	Currency	Rupee
Population	35 221	Map page	159
Capital	Port Mathurin		
Languages	English, creole		

St Helena
United Kingdom Overseas Territory

Area Sq Km	121	Religions	Protestant, Roman
Area Sq Miles	47		Catholic,
Population	5 644	Currency	Pound sterling
Capital	Jamestown	Map page	113
Languages	English		

ROMANIA

Area Sq Km	237 500	Religions	Romanian Orthodox,
Area Sq Miles	91 699		Protestant, Roman
Population	22 474 000		Catholic
Capital	Bucharest (Bucureşti)	Currency	Leu
Languages	Romanian, Hungarian	Organizations	UN
		Map page	110

ST KITTS AND NEVIS
Federation of St Kitts and Nevis

Area Sq Km	261	Religions	Protestant, Roman
Area Sq Miles	101		Catholic
Population	39 000	Currency	E. Carib. dollar
Capital	Basseterre	Organizations	CARICOM, Comm.,
Languages	English, creole		UN
		Map page	147

RUSSIAN FEDERATION

Area Sq Km	17 075 400	Religions	Russian Orthodox,
Area Sq Miles	6 592 849		Sunni Muslim,
Population	147 434 000		Protestant
Capital	Moscow (Moskva)	Currency	Rouble
Languages	Russian, Tatar,	Organizations	APEC, CIS, UN
	Ukrainian, local	Map page	82-83
	languages		

ST LUCIA

Area Sq Km	616	Religions	Roman Catholic,
Area Sq Miles	238		Protestant
Population	150 000	Currency	E. Carib. dollar
Capital	Castries	Organizations	CARICOM, Comm.,
Languages	English, creole		UN
		Map page	147

RWANDA
Republic of Rwanda

Area Sq Km	26 338	Religions	Roman Catholic,
Area Sq Miles	10 169		traditional beliefs,
Population	6 604 000		Protestant
Capital	Kigali	Currency	Franc
Languages	Kinyarwanda,	Organizations	UN
	French, English	Map page	119

St Maarten
part of Netherlands Antilles

Area Sq Km	34	Religions	Protestant, Roman
Area Sq Miles	13		Catholic
Population	38 567	Currency	NA guilder
Capital	Philipsburg	Map page	147
Languages	Dutch, English		

Saba
part of Netherlands Antilles

Area Sq Km	13	Religions	Roman Catholic,
Area Sq Miles	5		Protestant
Population	1 200	Currency	NA guilder
Capital	Bottom	Map page	147
Languages	Dutch, English		

Saint Martin
Dependency of Guadeloupe

Area Sq Km	54	Religions	Roman Catholic
Area Sq Miles	21	Currency	French franc
Population	28 518	Map page	147
Capital	Marigot		
Languages	French, creole		

St Barthélémy
Dependency of Guadeloupe

Area Sq Km	21	Languages	French, creole
Area Sq Miles	8	Religions	Roman Catholic
Population	5 038	Currency	French franc
Capital	Gustavia	Map page	147

St Pierre and Miquelon
French Territorial Collectivity

Area Sq Km	242	Religions	Roman Catholic
Area Sq Miles	93	Currency	French franc
Population	7 000	Map page	131
Capital	St-Pierre		
Languages	French		

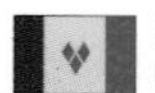

ST VINCENT AND THE GRENADINES

Area Sq Km	389	Religions	Protestant, Roman
Area Sq Miles	150		Catholic
Population	112 000	Currency	E. Carib. dollar
Capital	Kingstown	Organizations	CARICOM, Comm.,
Languages	English, creole		UN
		Map page	147

SAMOA
Independent State of Samoa

Area Sq Km	2 831	Religions	Protestant, Roman
Area Sq Miles	1 093		Catholic
Population	174 000	Currency	Tala
Capital	Apia	Organizations	Comm., UN
Languages	Samoan, English	Map page	49

SAN MARINO
Republic of San Marino

Area Sq Km	61	Religions	Roman Catholic
Area Sq Miles	24	Currency	Italian lira
Population	26 000	Organizations	UN
Capital	San Marino	Map page	108
Languages	Italian		

SÃO TOMÉ AND PRÍNCIPE
Democratic Republic of São Tomé and Príncipe

Area Sq Km	964	Religions	Roman Catholic,
Area Sq Miles	372		Protestant
Population	141 000	Currency	Dobra
Capital	São Tomé	Organizations	UN
Languages	Portuguese, creole	Map page	113

SAUDI ARABIA
Kingdom of Saudi Arabia

Area Sq Km	2 200 000	Religions	Sunni Muslim, Shi'a
Area Sq Miles	849 425		Muslim
Population	20 181 000	Currency	Riyal
Capital	Riyadh (Ar Riyāḍ)	Organizations	OPEC, UN
Languages	Arabic	Map page	78-79

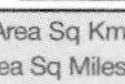

SENEGAL
Republic of Senegal

Area Sq Km	196 720	Religions	Sunni Muslim, Roman
Area Sq Miles	75 954		Catholic, traditional
Population	9 003 000		beliefs
Capital	Dakar	Currency	CFA franc
Languages	French, Wolof, Fulani,	Organizations	UN
	local languages	Map page	114

SEYCHELLES
Republic of the Seychelles

Area Sq Km	455	Religions	Roman Catholic,
Area Sq Miles	176		Protestant
Population	76 000	Currency	Rupee
Capital	Victoria	Organizations	Comm., SADC, UN
Languages	English, French,	Map page	113
	creole		

SIERRA LEONE
Republic of Sierra Leone

Area Sq Km	71 740	Religions	Sunni Muslim,
Area Sq Miles	27 699		traditional beliefs
Population	4 568 000	Currency	Leone
Capital	Freetown	Organizations	Comm., UN
Languages	English, creole,	Map page	114
	Mende, Temne, local		
	languages		

SINGAPORE
Republic of Singapore

Area Sq Km	639	Religions	Buddhist, Taoist, Sunni
Area Sq Miles	247		Muslim, Christian,
Population	3 476 000		Hindu
Capital	Singapore	Currency	Dollar
Languages	Chinese, English,	Organizations	APEC, ASEAN,
	Malay, Tamil		Comm., UN
		Map page	60

SLOVAKIA
Slovak Republic

Area Sq Km	49 035	Religions	Roman Catholic,
Area Sq Miles	18 933		Protestant, Orthodox
Population	5 377 000	Currency	Koruna
Capital	Bratislava	Organizations	UN
Languages	Slovak, Hungarian,	Map page	103
	Czech		

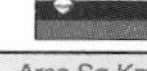

SLOVENIA
Republic of Slovenia

Area Sq Km	20 251	Religions	Roman Catholic,
Area Sq Miles	7 819		Protestant
Population	1 993 000	Currency	Tólar
Capital	Ljubljana	Organizations	UN
Languages	Slovene, Croatian,	Map page	108-109
	Serbian		

SOLOMON ISLANDS

Area Sq Km	28 370	Religions	Protestant, Roman
Area Sq Miles	10 954		Catholic
Population	417 000	Currency	Dollar
Capital	Honiara	Organizations	Comm., UN
Languages	English, creole, local	Map page	48
	languages		

SOMALIA
Somali Democratic Republic

Area Sq Km	637 657	Religions	Sunni Muslim
Area Sq Miles	246 201	Currency	Shilling
Population	9 237 000	Organizations	UN
Capital	Muqdisho	Map page	117
	(Mogadishu)		
Languages	Somali, Arabic		

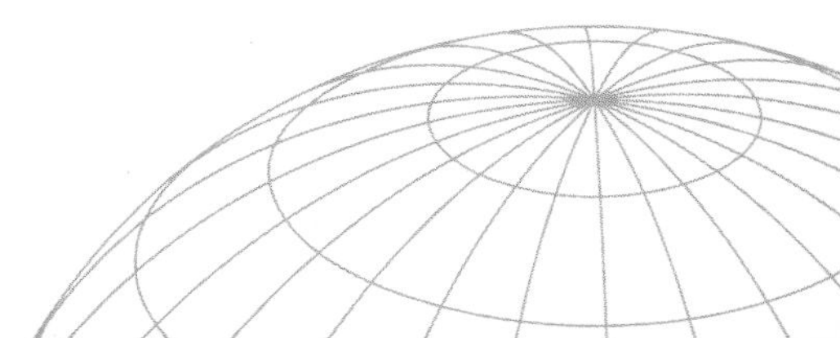

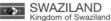

SOUTH AFRICA, REPUBLIC OF

Area Sq Km	1 219 090	Religions	Protestant, Roman
Area Sq Miles	470 693		Catholic, Sunni
Population	39 357 000		Muslim, Hindu
Capital	Pretoria/Cape Town	Currency	Rand
Languages	Afrikaans, English,	Organizations	Comm., SADC, UN
	nine official local	Map page	122-123
	languages		

SOUTH KOREA
Republic of South Korea

Area Sq Km	99 274	Religions	Buddhist, Protestant,
Area Sq Miles	38 330		Roman Catholic
Population	46 109 000	Currency	Won
Capital	Seoul (Sŏul)	Organizations	APEC, UN
Languages	Korean	Map page	65

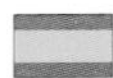

SPAIN
Kingdom of Spain

Area Sq Km	504 782	Religions	Roman Catholic
Area Sq Miles	194 897	Currency	Peseta, Euro
Population	39 628 000	Organizations	EU, OECD, UN
Capital	Madrid	Map page	106-107
Languages	Castilian, Catalan,		
	Galician, Basque		

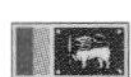

SRI LANKA
Democratic Socialist Republic of Sri Lanka

Area Sq Km	65 610	Religions	Buddhist, Hindu,
Area Sq Miles	25 332		Sunni Muslim, Roman
Population	18 455 000		Catholic
Capital	Sri Jayewardenepura	Currency	Rupee
	Kotte	Organizations	Comm., UN
Languages	Sinhalese, Tamil,	Map page	73
	English		

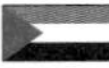

SUDAN
Republic of the Sudan

Area Sq Km	2 505 813	Religions	Sunni Muslim,
Area Sq Miles	967 500		traditional beliefs,
Population	28 292 000		Christian
Capital	Khartoum	Currency	Dinar
Languages	Arabic, Dinka,	Organizations	UN
	Nubian, Beja, Nuer,	Map page	116-117
	local languages		

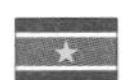

SURINAME
Republic of Suriname

Area Sq Km	163 820	Religions	Hindu, Roman Catholic,
Area Sq Miles	63 251		Protestant,
Population	414 000		Sunni Muslim
Capital	Paramaribo	Currency	Guilder
Languages	Dutch,	Organizations	CARICOM, UN
	Surinamese,	Map page	151
	English, Hindi		

Svalbard
part of Norway

Area Sq Km	61 229	Religions	Protestant
Area Sq Miles	23 641	Currency	Krone
Population	2 591	Map page	82
Capital	Longyearbyen		
Languages	Norwegian		

SWAZILAND
Kingdom of Swaziland

Area Sq Km	17 364	Religions	Christian, traditional
Area Sq Miles	6 704		beliefs
Population	952 000	Currency	Lilangeni
Capital	Mbabane	Organizations	Comm., SADC, UN
Languages	Swazi, English	Map page	123

SWEDEN
Kingdom of Sweden

Area Sq Km	449 964	Religions	Protestant,
Area Sq Miles	173 732		Roman Catholic
Population	8 875 000	Currency	Krona
Capital	Stockholm	Organizations	EU, OECD, UN
Languages	Swedish	Map page	92-93

SWITZERLAND
Swiss Confederation

Area Sq Km	41 293	Religions	Roman Catholic,
Area Sq Miles	15 943		Protestant,
Population	7 299 000	Currency	Franc
Capital	Bern (Berne)	Organizations	OECD
Languages	German, French,	Map page	105
	Italian, Romansch		

SYRIA
Syrian Arab Republic

Area Sq Km	185 180	Religions	Sunni Muslim, Shi'a
Area Sq Miles	71 498		Muslim, Christian
Population	15 333 000	Currency	Pound
Capital	Damascus (Dimashq)	Organizations	UN
Languages	Arabic, Kurdish,	Map page	80
	Armenian		

TAIWAN
Republic of China

Area Sq Km	36 179	Religions	Buddhist, Taoist,
Area Sq Miles	13 969		Confucian, Christian
Population	21 908 135	Currency	Dollar
Capital	T'aipei	Organizations	APEC
Languages	Mandarin, Min,	Map page	71
	Hakka, local		
	languages		

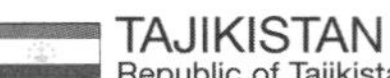

TAJIKISTAN
Republic of Tajikistan

Area Sq Km	143 100	Religions	Sunni Muslim
Area Sq Miles	55 251	Currency	Rouble
Population	6 015 000	Organizations	CIS, UN
Capital	Dushanbe	Map page	77
Languages	Tajik, Uzbek, Russian		

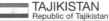

TANZANIA
United Republic of Tanzania

Area Sq Km	945 087	Religions	Shi'a Muslim, Sunni
Area Sq Miles	364 900		Muslim, traditional
Population	32 102 000		beliefs, Christian
Capital	Dodoma	Currency	Shilling
Languages	Swahili, English,	Organizations	Comm., SADC, UN
	Nyamwezi, local	Map page	119
	languages		

THAILAND
Kingdom of Thailand

Area Sq Km	513 115	Religions	Buddhist, Sunni
Area Sq Miles	198 115		Muslim
Population	60 300 000	Currency	Baht
Capital	Bangkok (Krung	Organizations	APEC, ASEAN, UN
	Thep)	Map page	62-63
Languages	Thai, Lao, Chinese,		
	Malay, Mon-Khmer		
	languages		

TOGO
Republic of Togo

Area Sq Km	56 785	Religions	Traditional beliefs,
Area Sq Miles	21 925		Christian, Sunni
Population	4 397 000		Muslim
Capital	Lomé	Currency	CFA franc
Languages	French, Ewe, Kabre,	Organizations	UN
	local languages	Map page	114

Tokelau
New Zealand Overseas Territory

Area Sq Km	10	Religions	Christian
Area Sq Miles	4	Currency	NZ dollar
Population	1 000	Map page	49
Capital	none		
Languages	English, Tokelauan		

TONGA
Kingdom of Tonga

Area Sq Km	748	Religions	Protestant, Roman
Area Sq Miles	289		Catholic
Population	98 000	Currency	Pa'anga
Capital	Nuku'alofa	Organizations	Comm., UN
Languages	Tongan, English	Map page	49

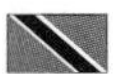

TRINIDAD AND TOBAGO
Republic of Trinidad and Tobago

Area Sq Km	5 130	Religions	Roman Catholic,
Area Sq Miles	1 981		Hindu, Protestant,
Population	1 283 000		Sunni Muslim
Capital	Port of Spain	Currency	Dollar
Languages	English, creole,	Organizations	CARICOM, Comm.,
	Hindi		UN
		Map page	147

Tristan da Cunha
Dependency of St Helena

Area Sq Km	98	Religions	Protestant, Roman
Area Sq Miles	38		Catholic
Population	300	Currency	Pound sterling
Capital	Settlement of	Map page	113
	Edinburgh		
Languages	English		

TUNISIA
Republic of Tunisia

Area Sq Km	164 150	Religions	Sunni Muslim
Area Sq Miles	63 379	Currency	Dinar
Population	9 335 000	Organizations	UN
Capital	Tunis	Map page	115
Languages	Arabic, French		

TURKEY
Republic of Turkey

Area Sq Km	779 452	Religions	Sunni Muslim, Shi'a
Area Sq Miles	300 948		Muslim
Population	64 479 000	Currency	Lira
Capital	Ankara	Organizations	OECD, UN
Languages	Turkish, Kurdish	Map page	80

TURKMENISTAN
Republic of Turkmenistan

Area Sq Km	488 100	Religions	Sunni Muslim, Russian
Area Sq Miles	188 456		Orthodox
Population	4 309 000	Currency	Manat
Capital	Ashgabat (Ashkhabad)	Organizations	CIS, UN
Languages	Turkmen, Uzbek,	Map page	76
	Russian		

Turks and Caicos Islands
United Kingdom Overseas Territory

Area Sq Km	430	Religions	Protestant
Area Sq Miles	166	Currency	US dollar
Population	16 000	Map page	147
Capital	Grand Turk		
	(Cockburn Town)		
Languages	English		

TUVALU
Monarchy

Area Sq Km	25	Religions	Protestant
Area Sq Miles	10	Currency	Dollar
Population	11 000	Organizations	Comm.
Capital	Vaiaku	Map page	49
Languages	Tuvaluan, English		

UGANDA
Republic of Uganda

Area Sq Km	241 038	Religions	Roman Catholic,
Area Sq Miles	93 065		Protestant, Sunni
Population	20 554 000		Muslim, traditional
Capital	Kampala		beliefs
Languages	English, Swahili,	Currency	Shilling
	Luganda, local	Organizations	Comm., UN
	languages	Map page	119

UKRAINE
Republic of Ukraine

Area Sq Km	603 700	Religions	Ukrainian Orthodox,
Area Sq Miles	233 090		Ukrainian Catholic,
Population	50 861 000		Roman Catholic
Capital	Kiev (Kyiv)	Currency	Hryvnia
Languages	Ukrainian, Russian	Organizations	CIS, UN
		Map page	90-91

UNITED ARAB EMIRATES
Federation of Emirates

Area Sq Km	83 600	Religions	Sunni Muslim, Shi'a
Area Sq Miles	32 278		Muslim
Population	2 377 453	Currency	Dirham
Capital	Abu Dhabi	Organizations	OPEC, UN
	(Abū Ẓabī)	Map page	79
Languages	Arabic, English		

Abu Dhabi (Abū Ẓabī) (Emirate)

Area Sq Km	73 060	Population	928 360
Area Sq Miles	28 209	Capital	Abu Dhabi (Abū Ẓabī)

Ajman (Emirate)

Area Sq Km	260	Population	118 812
Area Sq Miles	100	Capital	Ajman

Dubai (Emirate)

Area Sq Km	3 900	Population	674 101
Area Sq Miles	1 506	Capital	Dubai

Fujairah (Emirate)

Area Sq Km	1 300	Population	76 254
Area Sq Miles	502	Capital	Fujairah

Ras al Khaimah (Emirate)

Area Sq Km	1 700	Population	144 430
Area Sq Miles	656	Capital	Ras al Khaimah

Sharjah (Emirate)

Area Sq Km	2 600	Population	400 339
Area Sq Miles	1 004	Capital	Sharjah

Umm al Qaiwain (Emirate)

Area Sq Km	780	Population	35 157
Area Sq Miles	301	Capital	Umm al Qaiwain

UNITED KINGDOM
of Great Britain and Northern Ireland

Area Sq Km	244 082	Religions	Protestant, Roman
Area Sq Miles	94 241		Catholic, Muslim
Population	58 649 000	Currency	Pound
Capital	London	Organizations	Comm., EU, OECD,
Languages	English, Welsh,		UN
	Gaelic	Map page	94-95

England (Constituent country)

Area Sq Km	130 423	Population	49 284 200
Area Sq Miles	50 357	Capital	London

Northern Ireland (Province)

Area Sq Km	14 121	Population	1 675 000
Area Sq Miles	5 452	Capital	Belfast

Scotland (Constituent country)

Area Sq Km	78 772	Population	5 122 500
Area Sq Miles	30 414	Capital	Edinburgh

Wales (Principality)

Area Sq Km	20 766	Population	2 926 900
Area Sq Miles	8 018	Capital	Cardiff

UNITED STATES OF AMERICA

Area Sq Km	9 809 378	Religions	Protestant, Roman
Area Sq Miles	3 787 422		Catholic, Sunni Muslim,
Population	274 028 000		Jewish
Capital	Washington D.C.	Currency	Dollar
Languages	English, Spanish	Organizations	APEC, OECD, UN
		Map page	132-133

Alabama (State)

Area Sq Km	135 775	Population	4 351 999
Area Sq Miles	52 423	Capital	Montgomery

Alaska (State)

Area Sq Km	1 700 130	Population	614 010
Area Sq Miles	656 424	Capital	Juneau

Arizona (State)

Area Sq Km	295 274	Population	4 668 631
Area Sq Miles	114 006	Capital	Phoenix

Arkansas (State)

Area Sq Km	137 741	Population	2 538 303
Area Sq Miles	53 182	Capital	Little Rock

California (State)

Area Sq Km	423 999	Population	32 666 550
Area Sq Miles	163 707	Capital	Sacramento

Colorado (State)

Area Sq Km	269 618	Population	3 970 971
Area Sq Miles	104 100	Capital	Denver

Connecticut (State)

Area Sq Km	14 359	Population	3 274 069
Area Sq Miles	5 544	Capital	Hartford

Delaware (State)	
Area Sq Km 6 446	Population 743 603
Area Sq Miles 2 489	Capital Dover

Maryland (State)	
Area Sq Km 32 134	Population 5 134 808
Area Sq Miles 12 407	Capital Annapolis

District of Columbia (District)	
Area Sq Km 176	Population 523 124
Area Sq Miles 68	Capital Washington

Massachusetts (State)	
Area Sq Km 27 337	Population 6 147 132
Area Sq Miles 10 555	Capital Boston

Florida (State)	
Area Sq Km 170 312	Population 14 915 980
Area Sq Miles 65 758	Capital Tallahassee

Michigan (State)	
Area Sq Km 250 737	Population 9 817 242
Area Sq Miles 96 810	Capital Lansing

Georgia (State)	
Area Sq Km 153 951	Population 7 642 207
Area Sq Miles 59 441	Capital Atlanta

Minnesota (State)	
Area Sq Km 225 181	Population 4 725 419
Area Sq Miles 86 943	Capital St Paul

Hawaii (State)	
Area Sq Km 28 314	Population 1 193 001
Area Sq Miles 10 932	Capital Honolulu

Mississippi (State)	
Area Sq Km 125 443	Population 2 752 092
Area Sq Miles 48 434	Capital Jackson

Idaho (State)	
Area Sq Km 216 456	Population 1 228 684
Area Sq Miles 83 574	Capital Boise

Missouri (State)	
Area Sq Km 180 545	Population 5 438 559
Area Sq Miles 69 709	Capital Jefferson City

Illinois (State)	
Area Sq Km 150 007	Population 13 045 326
Area Sq Miles 57 918	Capital Springfield

Montana (State)	
Area Sq Km 380 847	Population 880 453
Area Sq Miles 147 046	Capital Helena

Indiana (State)	
Area Sq Km 94 327	Population 5 899 195
Area Sq Miles 36 420	Capital Indianapolis

Nebraska (State)	
Area Sq Km 200 356	Population 1 662 719
Area Sq Miles 77 358	Capital Lincoln

Iowa (State)	
Area Sq Km 145 754	Population 2 862 447
Area Sq Miles 56 276	Capital Des Moines

Nevada (State)	
Area Sq Km 286 367	Population 1 746 898
Area Sq Miles 110 567	Capital Carson City

Kansas (State)	
Area Sq Km 213 109	Population 2 629 067
Area Sq Miles 82 282	Capital Topeka

New Hampshire (State)	
Area Sq Km 24 219	Population 1 185 048
Area Sq Miles 9 351	Capital Concord

Kentucky (State)	
Area Sq Km 104 664	Population 3 936 499
Area Sq Miles 40 411	Capital Frankfort

New Jersey (State)	
Area Sq Km 22 590	Population 8 115 011
Area Sq Miles 8 722	Capital Trenton

Louisiana (State)	
Area Sq Km 134 273	Population 4 368 967
Area Sq Miles 51 843	Capital Baton Rouge

New Mexico (State)	
Area Sq Km 314 937	Population 1 736 931
Area Sq Miles 121 598	Capital Santa Fe

Maine (State)	
Area Sq Km 91 652	Population 1 244 250
Area Sq Miles 35 387	Capital Augusta

New York (State)	
Area Sq Km 141 090	Population 18 175 301
Area Sq Miles 54 475	Capital Albany

☰ UNITED STATES OF AMERICA

North Carolina (State)

Area Sq Km 139 396	Population 7 546 493
Area Sq Miles 53 821	Capital Raleigh

North Dakota (State)

Area Sq Km 183 123	Population 638 244
Area Sq Miles 70 704	Capital Bismarck

Ohio (State)

Area Sq Km 116 104	Population 11 209 493
Area Sq Miles 44 828	Capital Columbus

Oklahoma (State)

Area Sq Km 181 048	Population 3 346 713
Area Sq Miles 69 903	Capital Oklahoma City

Oregon (State)

Area Sq Km 254 819	Population 3 281 974
Area Sq Miles 98 386	Capital Salem

Pennsylvania (State)

Area Sq Km 119 290	Population 12 001 451
Area Sq Miles 46 058	Capital Harrisburg

Rhode Island (State)

Area Sq Km 4 002	Population 988 480
Area Sq Miles 1 545	Capital Providence

South Carolina (State)

Area Sq Km 82 898	Population 3 835 962
Area Sq Miles 32 007	Capital Columbia

South Dakota (State)

Area Sq Km 199 742	Population 738 171
Area Sq Miles 77 121	Capital Pierre

Tennessee (State)

Area Sq Km 109 158	Population 5 430 621
Area Sq Miles 42 146	Capital Nashville

Texas (State)

Area Sq Km 695 673	Population 19 759 614
Area Sq Miles 268 601	Capital Austin

Utah (State)

Area Sq Km 219 900	Population 2 099 758
Area Sq Miles 84 904	Capital Salt Lake City

Vermont (State)

Area Sq Km 24 903	Population 590 883
Area Sq Miles 9 615	Capital Montpelier

Virginia (State)

Area Sq Km 110 771	Population 6 791 345
Area Sq Miles 42 769	Capital Richmond

Washington (State)

Area Sq Km 184 674	Population 5 689 263
Area Sq Miles 71 303	Capital Olympia

West Virginia (State)

Area Sq Km 62 758	Population 1 811 156
Area Sq Miles 24 231	Capital Charleston

Wisconsin (State)

Area Sq Km 169 652	Population 5 223 500
Area Sq Miles 65 503	Capital Madison

Wyoming (State)

Area Sq Km 253 347	Population 480 907
Area Sq Miles 97 818	Capital Cheyenne

☰ URUGUAY
Oriental Republic of Uruguay

Area Sq Km 176 215	Religions Roman Catholic,
Area Sq Miles 68 037	Protestant, Jewish
Population 3 289 000	Currency Peso
Capital Montevideo	Organizations UN
Languages Spanish	Map page 153

☰ UZBEKISTAN
Republic of Uzbekistan

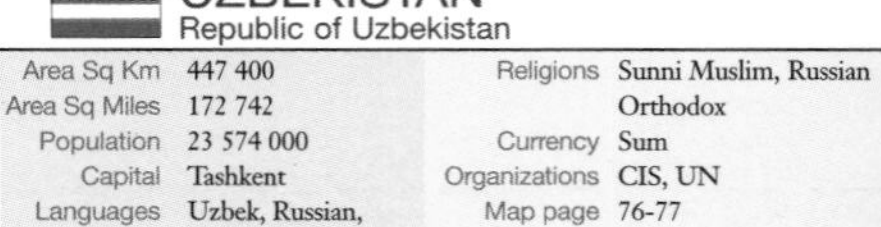

Area Sq Km 447 400	Religions Sunni Muslim, Russian
Area Sq Miles 172 742	Orthodox
Population 23 574 000	Currency Sum
Capital Tashkent	Organizations CIS, UN
Languages Uzbek, Russian,	Map page 76-77
Tajik, Kazakh	

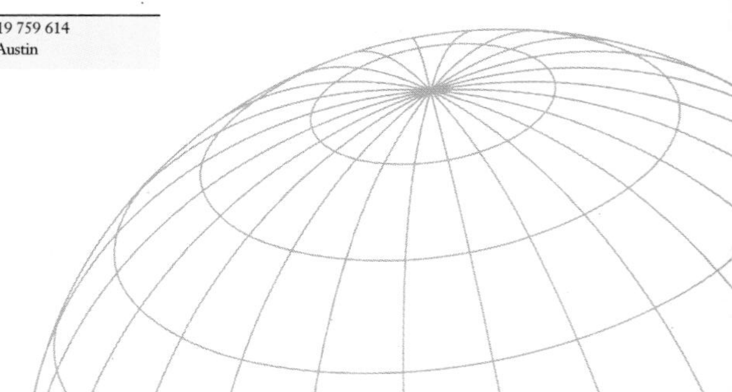

VANUATU
Republic of Vanuatu

Area Sq Km	12 190	Religions	Protestant, Roman
Area Sq Miles	4 707		Catholic, traditional
Population	182 000		beliefs
Capital	Port Vila	Currency	Vatu
Languages	English, Bislama	Organizations	Comm., UN
	(creole),French	Map page	48

VATICAN CITY
Vatican City State

Area Sq Km	0.5	Religions	Roman Catholic
Area Sq Miles	0.2	Currency	Italian lira
Population	480	Map page	108
Capital	Vatican City		
Languages	Italian		

VENEZUELA
Republic of Venezuela

Area Sq Km	912 050	Religions	Roman Catholic,
Area Sq Miles	352 144		Protestant
Population	23 242 000	Currency	Bolívar
Capital	Caracas	Organizations	OPEC, UN
Languages	Spanish, Amerindian	Map page	150
	languages		

VIETNAM
Socialist Republic of Vietnam

Area Sq Km	329 565	Religions	Buddhist, Taoist,
Area Sq Miles	127 246		Roman Catholic,
Population	77 562 000		Cao Dai, Hoa Hoa
Capital	Ha Nôi (Hanoi)	Currency	Dong
Languages	Vietnamese, Thai,	Organizations	APEC, ASEAN, UN
	Khmer, Chinese,	Map page	62-63
	local languages		

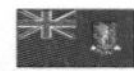

Virgin Islands (U.K.)
United Kingdom Overseas Territory

Area Sq Km	153	Religions	Protestant, Roman
Area Sq Miles	59		Catholic
Population	20 000	Currency	US dollar
Capital	Road Town	Map page	147
Languages	English		

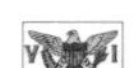

Virgin Islands (U.S.)
United States Unincorporated Territory

Area Sq Km	352	Religions	Protestant,
Area Sq Miles	136		Roman Catholic
Population	94 000	Currency	US dollar
Capital	Charlotte Amalie	Map page	147
Languages	English, Spanish		

Wallis and Futuna Islands
French Overseas Territory

Area Sq Km	274	Religions	Roman Catholic
Area Sq Miles	106	Currency	Pacific franc
Population	14 000	Map page	49
Capital	Matā'utu		
Languages	French, Wallisian,		
	Futunian		

West Bank
Territory occupied by Israel

Area Sq Km	5 860	Religions	Sunni Muslim, Jewish,
Area Sq Miles	2 263		Shi'a Muslim, Christian
Capital	none	Map page	80
Languages	Arabic, Hebrew		

Western Sahara
Disputed territory (Morocco)

Area Sq Km	266 000	Religions	Sunni Muslim
Area Sq Miles	102 703	Currency	Moroccan dirham
Population	275 000	Map page	114
Capital	Laâyoune		
Languages	Arabic		

YEMEN
Republic of Yemen

Area Sq Km	527 968	Religions	Sunni Muslim, Shi'a
Area Sq Miles	203 850		Muslim
Population	16 887 000	Currency	Rial
Capital	Şan'a'	Organizations	UN
Languages	Arabic	Map page	78-79

YUGOSLAVIA
Federal Republic of Yugoslavia

Area Sq Km	102 173	Religions	Serbian Orthodox,
Area Sq Miles	39 449		Montenegrin Orthodox,
Population	10 635 000		Sunni Muslim
Capital	Belgrade (Beograd)	Currency	Dinar
Languages	Serbian, Albanian,	Organizations	UN
	Hungarian	Map page	109

ZAMBIA
Republic of Zambia

Area Sq Km	752 614	Religions	Christian, traditional
Area Sq Miles	290 586		beliefs
Population	8 781 000	Currency	Kwacha
Capital	Lusaka	Organizations	Comm., SADC, UN
Languages	English, Bemba,	Map page	120-121
	Nyanja, Tonga, local		
	languages		

ZIMBABWE
Republic of Zimbabwe

Area Sq Km	390 759	Religions	Christian, traditional
Area Sq Miles	150 873		beliefs
Population	11 377 000	Currency	Dollar
Capital	Harare	Organizations	Comm., SADC, UN
Languages	English, Shona,	Map page	121
	Ndebele		

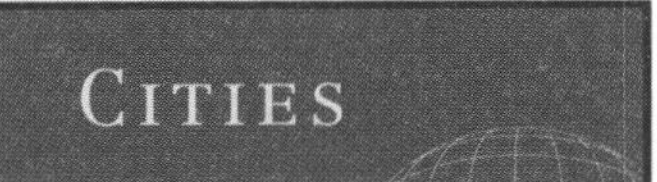

CITIES

THE WORLD'S LARGEST CITIES

Figures are for the urban agglomeration, defined as the population contained within the contours of a contiguous territory inhabited at urban levels without regard to administrative boundaries. They incorporate the population within a city plus the surburban fringe lying outside of, but adjacent to, the city boundaries.

City	Population	Region
Tōkyō Japan	28 025 000	Asia
México Mexico	18 131 000	North America
Mumbai India	18 042 000	Asia
São Paulo Brazil	17 711 000	South America
New York USA	16 626 000	North America
Shanghai China	14 173 000	Asia
Lagos Nigeria	13 488 000	Africa
Los Angeles USA	13 129 000	North America
Calcutta India	12 900 000	Asia
Buenos Aires Argentina	12 431 000	South America
Seoul South Korea	12 215 000	Asia
Beijing China	12 033 000	Asia
Karachi Pakistan	11 774 000	Asia
Delhi India	11 680 000	Asia
Dhaka Bangladesh	10 979 000	Asia
Manila Philippines	10 818 000	Asia
Cairo Egypt	10 772 000	Africa
Ōsaka Japan	10 609 000	Asia
Rio de Janeiro Brazil	10 556 000	South America
Tianjin China	10 239 000	Asia
Jakarta Indonesia	9 815 000	Asia
Paris France	9 638 000	Europe
İstanbul Turkey	9 413 000	Asia
Moscow Russian Federation	9 299 000	Europe
London United Kingdom	7 640 000	Europe
Lima Peru	7 443 000	South America
Tehrān Iran	7 380 000	Asia
Bangkok Thailand	7 221 000	Asia
Chicago USA	6 945 000	North America
Bogotá Colombia	6 834 000	South America
Hyderabad India	6 833 000	Asia
Chennai India	6 639 000	Asia
Essen Germany	6 559 000	Europe
Hangzhou China	6 389 000	Asia
Hong Kong China	6 097 000	Asia
Lahore Pakistan	6 030 000	Asia
Shenyang China	5 681 000	Asia
Changchun China	5 566 000	Asia
Bangalore India	5 544 000	Asia
Harbin China	5 475 000	Asia
Chengdu China	5 293 000	Asia
Santiago Chile	5 261 000	South America
Guangzhou China	5 162 000	Asia
St Petersburg Russian Federation	5 132 000	Europe
Kinshasa Dem. Rep. Congo	5 068 000	Africa
Baghdād Iraq	4 796 000	Asia
Jinan China	4 789 000	Asia
Wuhan China	4 750 000	Asia
Toronto Canada	4 657 000	North America
Yangôn Myanmar	4 458 000	Asia
Algiers Algeria	4 447 000	Africa
Philadelphia USA	4 398 000	North America
Qingdao China	4 376 000	Asia
Milan Italy	4 251 000	Europe
Pusan South Korea	4 239 000	Asia
Belo Horizonte Brazil	4 160 000	South America
Ahmadabad India	4 154 000	Asia
Madrid Spain	4 072 000	Europe
San Francisco USA	4 051 000	North America
Alexandria Egypt	3 995 000	Africa
Washington D.C. USA	3 927 000	North America
Dallas USA	3 912 000	North America
Guadalajara Mexico	3 908 000	North America
Chongqing China	3 896 000	Asia
Medellín Colombia	3 831 000	South America
Detroit USA	3 785 000	North America
Handan China	3 763 000	Asia
Frankfurt Germany	3 700 000	Europe
Porto Alegre Brazil	3 699 000	South America
Ha Nôi Vietnam	3 678 000	Asia
Sydney Australia	3 665 000	Oceania
Santo Domingo Dominican Republic	3 601 000	North America
Singapore Singapore	3 587 000	Asia
Casablanca Morocco	3 535 000	Africa
Katowice Poland	3 488 000	Europe
Pune India	3 485 000	Asia
Bandung Indonesia	3 420 000	Asia
Monterrey Mexico	3 416 000	North America
Montréal Canada	3 401 000	North America
Nagoya Japan	3 377 000	Asia
Nanjing China	3 375 000	Asia
Houston USA	3 365 000	North America
Abidjan Côte d'Ivoire	3 359 000	Africa
Xi'an China	3 352 000	Asia
Berlin Germany	3 337 000	Europe
Riyadh Saudi Arabia	3 328 000	Asia
Recife Brazil	3 307 000	South America
Düsseldorf Germany	3 251 000	Europe
Ankara Turkey	3 190 000	Asia
Melbourne Australia	3 188 000	Oceania
Salvador Brazil	3 180 000	South America
Dalian China	3 153 000	Asia
Caracas Venezuela	3 153 000	South America
Addis Ababa Ethiopia	3 112 000	Africa
Athens Greece	3 103 000	Europe
Cape Town South Africa	3 092 000	Africa
Cologne Germany	3 067 000	Europe
Maputo Mozambique	3 017 000	Africa
Naples Italy	3 012 000	Europe
Fortaleza Brazil	3 007 000	South America
San Diego USA	2 983 000	North America
Boston USA	2 915 000	North America
Chittagong Bangladesh	2 906 000	Asia
Kita-Kyūshū Japan	2 898 000	Asia
Kiev Ukraine	2 897 000	Europe
T'aipei Taiwan	2 880 000	Asia
Inch'ôn South Korea	2 837 000	Asia
Barcelona Spain	2 819 000	Europe
Khartoum Sudan	2 748 000	Africa
P'yôngyang North Korea	2 726 000	Asia
Kābul Afghanistan	2 716 000	Asia
Guatemala Guatemala	2 697 000	North America
Atlanta USA	2 689 000	North America
Stuttgart Germany	2 688 000	Europe
Rome Italy	2 688 000	Europe
Hamburg Germany	2 680 000	Europe
Luanda Angola	2 665 000	Africa
Eşfahān Iran	2 644 000	Asia
Phoenix USA	2 607 000	North America
Lucknow India	2 565 000	Asia
Taegu South Korea	2 559 000	Asia
Curitiba Brazil	2 519 000	South America
Surabaya Indonesia	2 507 000	Asia
Tashkent Uzbekistan	2 495 000	Asia
Kanpur India	2 447 000	Asia
Johannesburg South Africa	2 412 000	Africa
İzmir Turkey	2 399 000	Asia
Mashhad Iran	2 378 000	Asia
Arbīl Iraq	2 368 000	Asia
Minneapolis USA	2 363 000	North America
Surat India	2 341 000	Asia
Damascus Syria	2 335 000	Asia
Nairobi Kenya	2 320 000	Africa
Munich Germany	2 306 000	Europe
Havana Cuba	2 302 000	North America
Taiyuan China	2 280 000	Asia
Zhengzhou China	2 275 000	Asia
Birmingham United Kingdom	2 271 000	Europe
Warsaw Poland	2 269 000	Europe
Manchester United Kingdom	2 252 000	Europe
Guiyang China	2 230 000	Asia
Faisalabad Pakistan	2 228 000	Asia
Miami USA	2 210 000	North America
Aleppo Syria	2 173 000	Asia
Tel Aviv-Yafo Israel	2 170 000	Asia
Jaipur India	2 143 000	Asia
Bucharest Romania	2 130 000	Europe
Guayaquil Ecuador	2 127 000	South America
Peshawar Pakistan	2 094 000	Asia
Seattle USA	2 084 000	North America
Cali Colombia	2 082 000	South America
Dakar Senegal	2 077 000	Africa
Vienna Austria	2 072 000	Europe
St Louis USA	2 071 000	North America
Nagpur India	2 060 000	Asia
Beirut Lebanon	2 058 000	Asia
Dar es Salaam Tanzania	2 051 000	Africa
Tampa USA	2 051 000	North America
Gujranwala Pakistan	2 048 000	Asia
Tripoli Libya	2 041 000	Africa
Baltimore USA	2 040 000	North America
Lanzhou China	2 021 000	Asia
Budapest Hungary	2 017 000	Europe
Accra Ghana	2 010 000	Africa

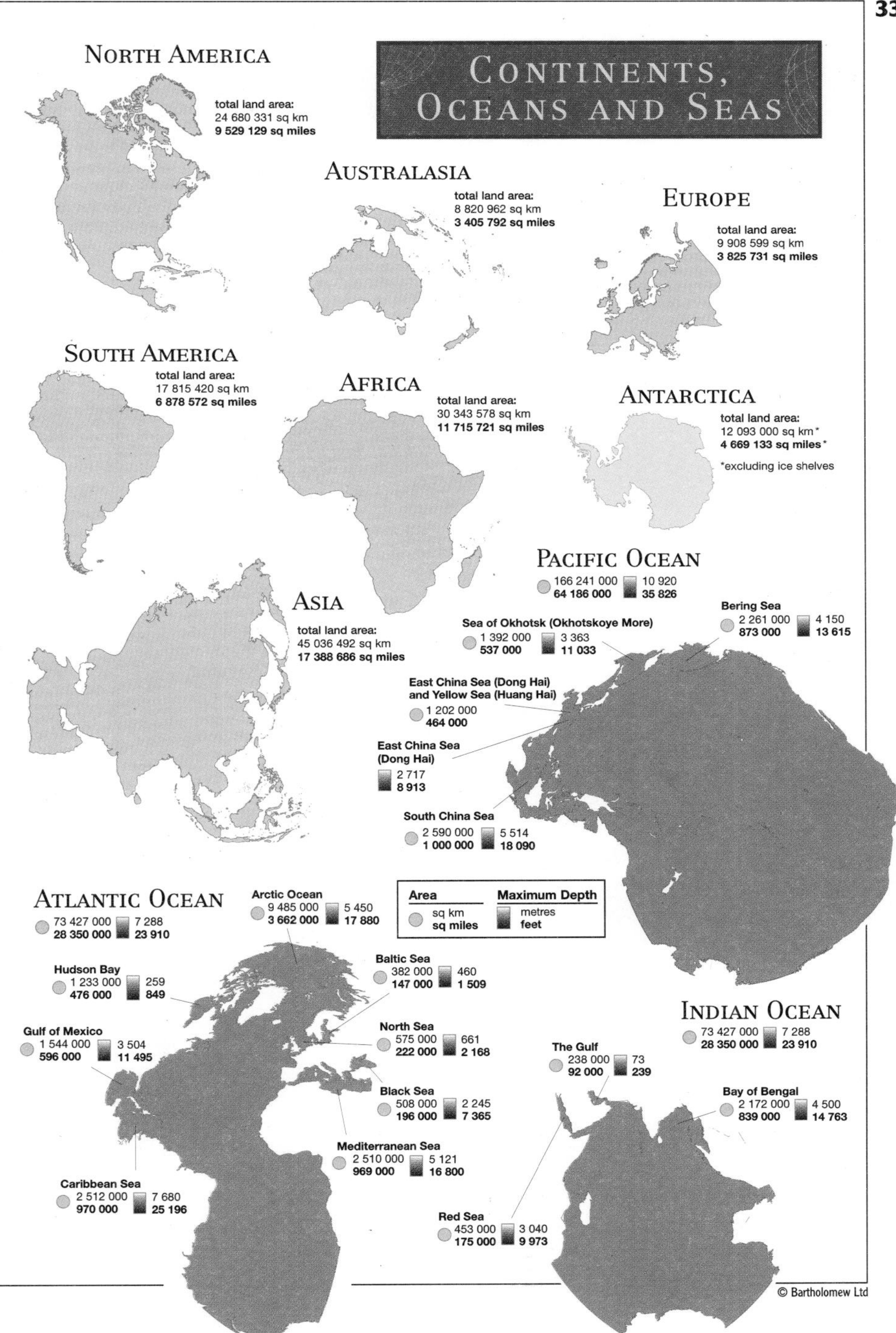

NORTH AMERICA

total land area:
24 680 331 sq km
9 529 129 sq miles

CONTINENTS, OCEANS AND SEAS

AUSTRALASIA

total land area:
8 820 962 sq km
3 405 792 sq miles

EUROPE

total land area:
9 908 599 sq km
3 825 731 sq miles

SOUTH AMERICA

total land area:
17 815 420 sq km
6 878 572 sq miles

AFRICA

total land area:
30 343 578 sq km
11 715 721 sq miles

ANTARCTICA

total land area:
12 093 000 sq km*
4 669 133 sq miles*

*excluding ice shelves

ASIA

total land area:
45 036 492 sq km
17 388 686 sq miles

PACIFIC OCEAN

166 241 000 / 10 920
64 186 000 / **35 826**

Bering Sea
2 261 000 / 4 150
873 000 / **13 615**

Sea of Okhotsk (Okhotskoye More)
1 392 000 / 3 363
537 000 / **11 033**

**East China Sea (Dong Hai)
and Yellow Sea (Huang Hai)**
1 202 000
464 000

**East China Sea
(Dong Hai)**
2 717
8 913

South China Sea
2 590 000 / 5 514
1 000 000 / **18 090**

ATLANTIC OCEAN

73 427 000 / 7 288
28 350 000 / **23 910**

Arctic Ocean
9 485 000 / 5 450
3 662 000 / **17 880**

Area	Maximum Depth
sq km	metres
sq miles	feet

Hudson Bay
1 233 000 / 259
476 000 / **849**

Baltic Sea
382 000 / 460
147 000 / **1 509**

Gulf of Mexico
1 544 000 / 3 504
596 000 / **11 495**

North Sea
575 000 / 661
222 000 / **2 168**

The Gulf
238 000 / 73
92 000 / **239**

INDIAN OCEAN

73 427 000 / 7 288
28 350 000 / **23 910**

Bay of Bengal
2 172 000 / 4 500
839 000 / **14 763**

Black Sea
508 000 / 2 245
196 000 / **7 365**

Mediterranean Sea
2 510 000 / 5 121
969 000 / **16 800**

Caribbean Sea
2 512 000 / 7 680
970 000 / **25 196**

Red Sea
453 000 / 3 040
175 000 / **9 973**

© Bartholomew Ltd

ISLANDS, MOUNTAINS, LAKES AND RIVERS

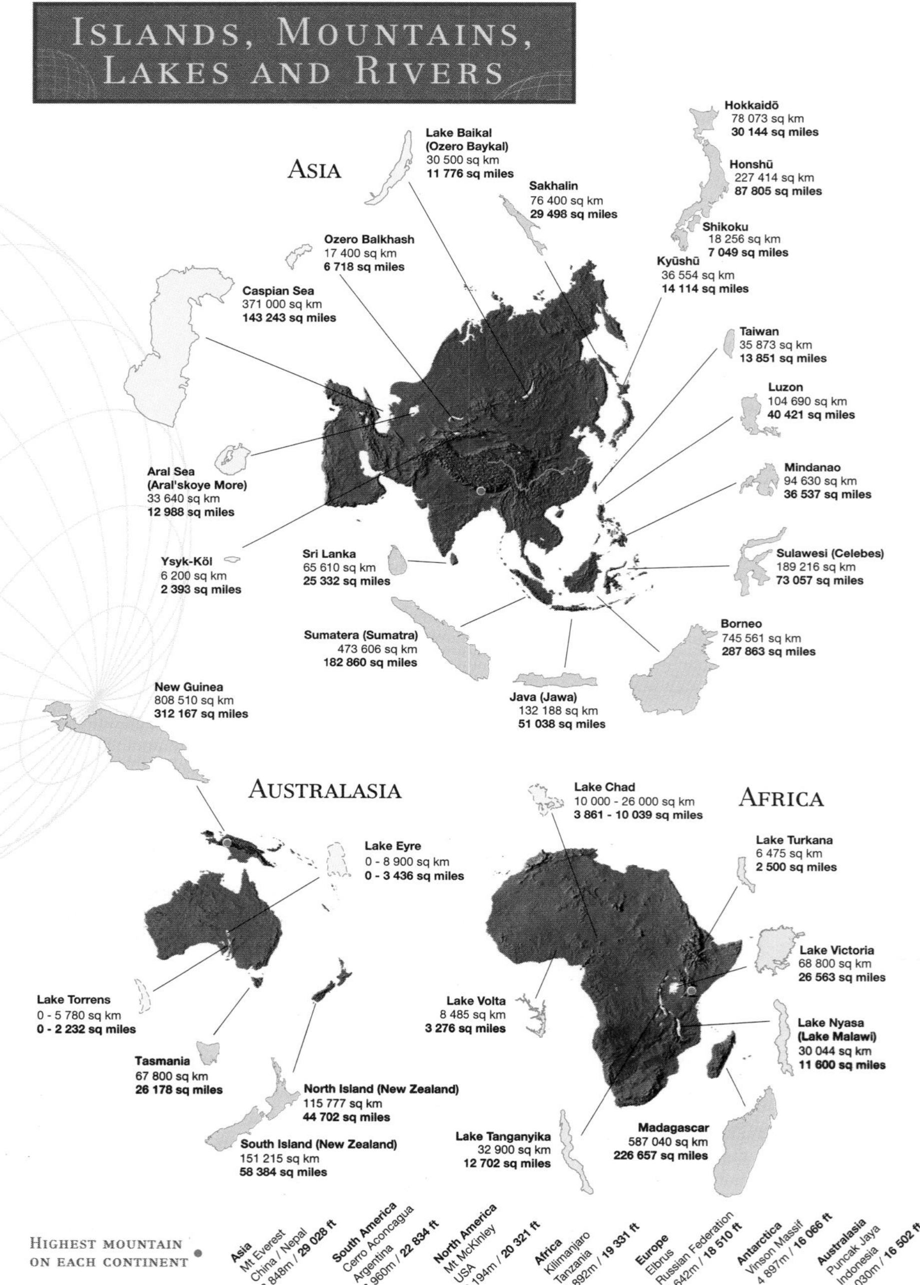

ASIA

Lake Baikal
(Ozero Baykal)
30 500 sq km
11 776 sq miles

Hokkaidō
78 073 sq km
30 144 sq miles

Honshū
227 414 sq km
87 805 sq miles

Sakhalin
76 400 sq km
29 498 sq miles

Shikoku
18 256 sq km
7 049 sq miles

Kyūshū
36 554 sq km
14 114 sq miles

Ozero Balkhash
17 400 sq km
6 718 sq miles

Caspian Sea
371 000 sq km
143 243 sq miles

Taiwan
35 873 sq km
13 851 sq miles

Luzon
104 690 sq km
40 421 sq miles

Aral Sea
(Aral'skoye More)
33 640 sq km
12 988 sq miles

Mindanao
94 630 sq km
36 537 sq miles

Ysyk-Köl
6 200 sq km
2 393 sq miles

Sri Lanka
65 610 sq km
25 332 sq miles

Sulawesi (Celebes)
189 216 sq km
73 057 sq miles

Borneo
745 561 sq km
287 863 sq miles

New Guinea
808 510 sq km
312 167 sq miles

Sumatera (Sumatra)
473 606 sq km
182 860 sq miles

Java (Jawa)
132 188 sq km
51 038 sq miles

AUSTRALASIA

Lake Chad
10 000 - 26 000 sq km
3 861 - 10 039 sq miles

AFRICA

Lake Eyre
0 - 8 900 sq km
0 - 3 436 sq miles

Lake Turkana
6 475 sq km
2 500 sq miles

Lake Victoria
68 800 sq km
26 563 sq miles

Lake Torrens
0 - 5 780 sq km
0 - 2 232 sq miles

Lake Volta
8 485 sq km
3 276 sq miles

Lake Nyasa
(Lake Malawi)
30 044 sq km
11 600 sq miles

Tasmania
67 800 sq km
26 178 sq miles

North Island (New Zealand)
115 777 sq km
44 702 sq miles

South Island (New Zealand)
151 215 sq km
58 384 sq miles

Lake Tanganyika
32 900 sq km
12 702 sq miles

Madagascar
587 040 sq km
226 657 sq miles

HIGHEST MOUNTAIN
ON EACH CONTINENT •

Asia
Mt Everest
China / Nepal
8 848m / 29 028 ft

South America
Cerro Aconcagua
Argentina
6 960m / 22 834 ft

North America
Mt McKinley
USA
6 194m / 20 321 ft

Africa
Kilimanjaro
Tanzania
5 892m / 19 331 ft

Europe
Elbrus
Russian Federation
5 642m / 18 510 ft

Antarctica
Vinson Massif
4 897m / 16 066 ft

Australasia
Puncak Jaya
Indonesia
5 030m / 16 502 ft

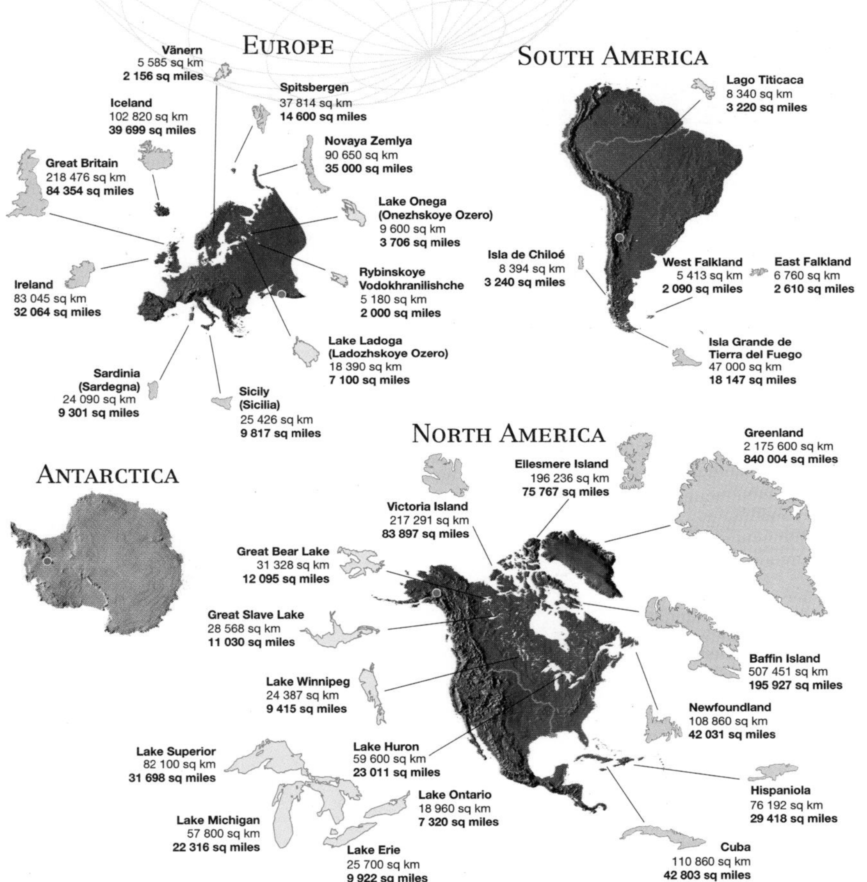

EUROPE

Vänern
5 585 sq km
2 156 sq miles

Iceland
102 820 sq km
39 699 sq miles

Spitsbergen
37 814 sq km
14 600 sq miles

Novaya Zemlya
90 650 sq km
35 000 sq miles

Great Britain
218 476 sq km
84 354 sq miles

**Lake Onega
(Onezhskoye Ozero)**
9 600 sq km
3 706 sq miles

**Rybinskoye
Vodokhranilishche**
5 180 sq km
2 000 sq miles

Ireland
83 045 sq km
32 064 sq miles

**Lake Ladoga
(Ladozhskoye Ozero)**
18 390 sq km
7 100 sq miles

**Sardinia
(Sardegna)**
24 090 sq km
9 301 sq miles

**Sicily
(Sicilia)**
25 426 sq km
9 817 sq miles

SOUTH AMERICA

Lago Titicaca
8 340 sq km
3 220 sq miles

Isla de Chiloé
8 394 sq km
3 240 sq miles

West Falkland
5 413 sq km
2 090 sq miles

East Falkland
6 760 sq km
2 610 sq miles

**Isla Grande de
Tierra del Fuego**
47 000 sq km
18 147 sq miles

NORTH AMERICA

Greenland
2 175 600 sq km
840 004 sq miles

Ellesmere Island
196 236 sq km
75 767 sq miles

Victoria Island
217 291 sq km
83 897 sq miles

Great Bear Lake
31 328 sq km
12 095 sq miles

Great Slave Lake
28 568 sq km
11 030 sq miles

Lake Winnipeg
24 387 sq km
9 415 sq miles

Baffin Island
507 451 sq km
195 927 sq miles

Newfoundland
108 860 sq km
42 031 sq miles

Lake Superior
82 100 sq km
31 698 sq miles

Lake Huron
59 600 sq km
23 011 sq miles

Lake Ontario
18 960 sq km
7 320 sq miles

Hispaniola
76 192 sq km
29 418 sq miles

Lake Michigan
57 800 sq km
22 316 sq miles

Lake Erie
25 700 sq km
9 922 sq miles

Cuba
110 860 sq km
42 803 sq miles

ANTARCTICA

HIGHEST MOUNTAINS IN THE WORLD

Mt Everest China/Nepal	Asia	8 848m / 29 028ft	
K2 China/Jammu and Kashmir	Asia	8 611m / 28 251ft	
Kangchenjunga India/Nepal	Asia	8 586m / 28 169ft	
Lhotse China/Nepal	Asia	8 516m / 27 939ft	
Makalu China/Nepal	Asia	8 463m / 27 765ft	
Cho Oyu China/Nepal	Asia	8 201m / 26 906ft	
Dhaulagiri Nepal	Asia	8 167m / 26 794ft	
Manaslu Nepal	Asia	8 163m / 26 781ft	
Nanga Parbat Jammu and Kashmir	Asia	8 126m / 26 660ft	
Annapurna I Nepal	Asia	8 091m / 26 545ft	
Gasherbrum I China/Jammu and Kashmir	Asia	8 068m / 26 469ft	
Broad Peak China/Jammu and Kashmir	Asia	8 047m / 26 401ft	
Gasherbrum II China/Jammu and Kashmir	Asia	8 035m / 26 361ft	
Xixabangma Feng China	Asia	8 012m / 26 286ft	
Annapurna II Nepal	Asia	7 937m / 26 040ft	
Nuptse Nepal	Asia	7 885m / 25 869ft	
Himalchul Nepal	Asia	7 864m / 25 800ft	
Masherbrum Jammu and Kashmir	Asia	7 821m / 25 659ft	
Nanda Devi India	Asia	7 816m / 25 643ft	
Rakaposhi Jammu and Kashmir	Asia	7 788m / 25 551ft	
Namjagbarwa Feng China	Asia	7 756m / 25 446ft	
Kamet China	Asia	7 756m / 25 446ft	

LONGEST RIVERS IN THE WORLD

Nile	Africa	6 695 km / 4 160 mls
Amazon (Amazonas)	South America	6 516 km / 4 049 mls
Yangtze (Chang Jiang)	Asia	6 380 km / 3 964 mls
Mississippi-Missouri	North America	5 969 km / 3 709 mls
Ob'-Irtysh	Asia	5 568 km / 3 459 mls
Yenisey-Angara-Selenga	Asia	5 550 km / 3 448 mls
Huang He (Yellow River)	Asia	5 464 km / 3 395 mls
Congo	Africa	4 667 km / 2 900 mls
Río de la Plata-Paraná	South America	4 500 km / 2 796 mls
Irtysh	Asia	4 440 km / 2 759 mls
Mekong	Asia	4 425 km / 2 749 mls
Heilong Jiang (Amur)-Argun'	Asia	4 416 km / 2 744 mls
Lena-Kirenga	Asia	4 400 km / 2 734 mls
Mackenzie-Peace-Finlay	North America	4 241 km / 2 635 mls
Niger	Africa	4 184 km / 2 599 mls
Yenisey	Asia	4 090 km / 2 541 mls
Missouri	North America	4 086 km / 2 539 mls
Mississippi	North America	3 765 km / 2 339 mls
Murray-Darling	Australasia	3 750 km / 2 330 mls
Ob'	Asia	3 701 km / 2 300 mls
Volga	Europe	3 688 km / 2 291 mls
Purus	South America	3 218 km / 2 000 mls

CLIMATE

MAJOR CLIMATIC REGIONS AND SUB-TYPES

Köppen classification system

Winkel Tripel Projection
scale: 1:150 000 000

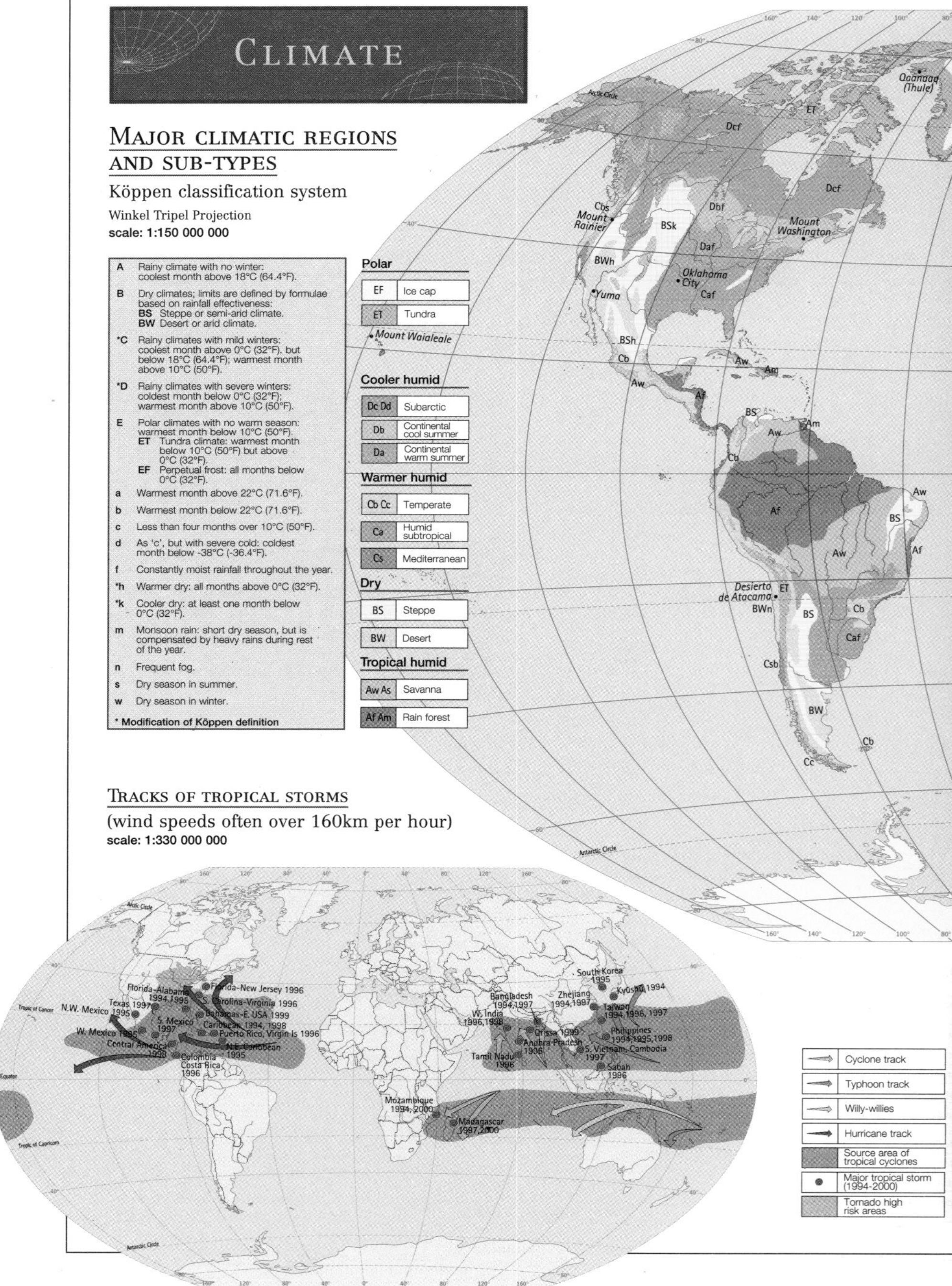

A Rainy climate with no winter: coolest month above 18°C (64.4°F).

B Dry climates; limits are defined by formulae based on rainfall effectiveness:
BS Steppe or semi-arid climate.
BW Desert or arid climate.

*C Rainy climates with mild winters: coolest month above 0°C (32°F), but below 18°C (64.4°F); warmest month above 10°C (50°F).

*D Rainy climates with severe winters: coldest month below 0°C (32°F); warmest month above 10°C (50°F).

E Polar climates with no warm season: warmest month below 10°C (50°F).
ET Tundra climate: warmest month below 10°C (50°F) but above 0°C (32°F).
EF Perpetual frost: all months below 0°C (32°F).

a Warmest month above 22°C (71.6°F).

b Warmest month below 22°C (71.6°F).

c Less than four months over 10°C (50°F).

d As 'c', but with severe cold: coldest month below -38°C (-36.4°F).

f Constantly moist rainfall throughout the year.

*h Warmer dry: all months above 0°C (32°F).

*k Cooler dry: at least one month below 0°C (32°F).

m Monsoon rain: short dry season, but is compensated by heavy rains during rest of the year.

n Frequent fog.

s Dry season in summer.

w Dry season in winter.

* Modification of Köppen definition

Polar

EF	Ice cap
ET	Tundra

Cooler humid

Dc Dd	Subarctic
Db	Continental cool summer
Da	Continental warm summer

Warmer humid

Cb Cc	Temperate
Ca	Humid subtropical
Cs	Mediterranean

Dry

BS	Steppe
BW	Desert

Tropical humid

Aw As	Savanna
Af Am	Rain forest

TRACKS OF TROPICAL STORMS

(wind speeds often over 160km per hour)
scale: 1:330 000 000

→	Cyclone track
→	Typhoon track
→	Willy-willies
→	Hurricane track
▬	Source area of tropical cyclones
•	Major tropical storm (1994-2000)
▬	Tornado high risk areas

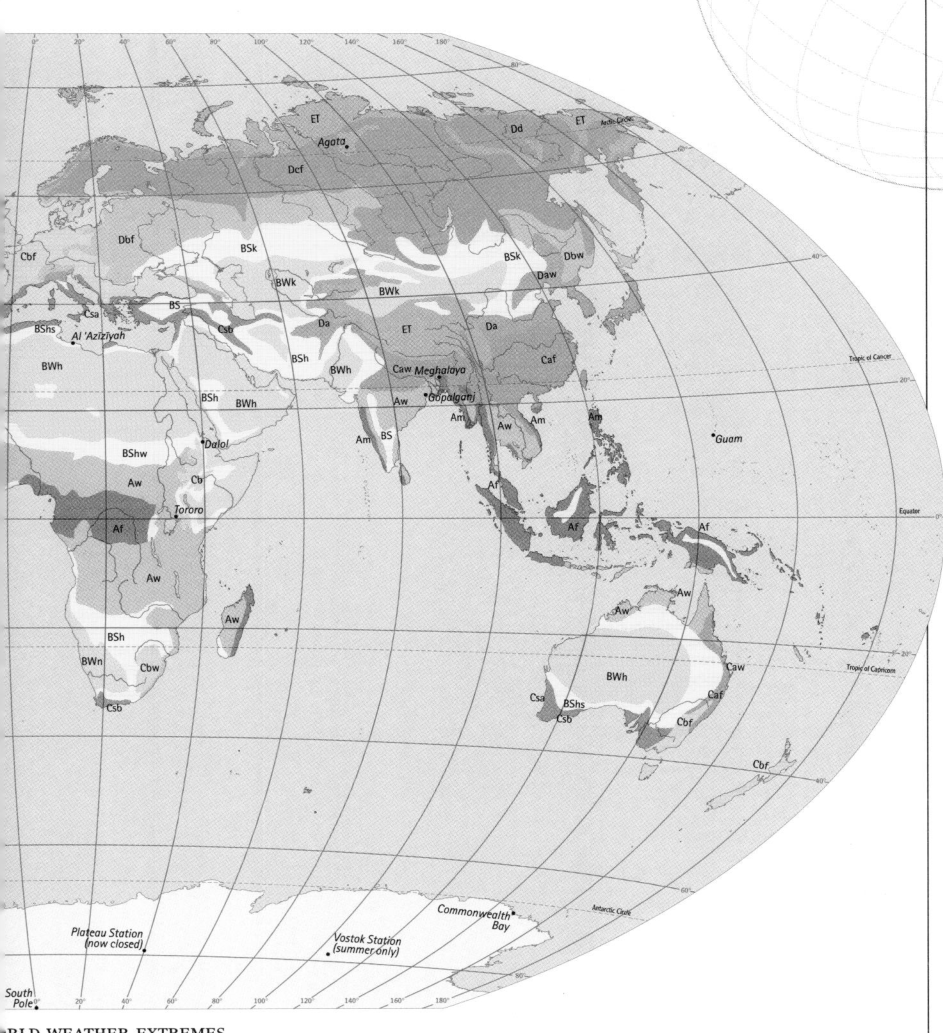

RLD WEATHER EXTREMES

			Highest surface wind speed		
est shade temperature	57.8°C/136°F Al 'Azīzīyah, Libya (13th September 1922)		High altitude		372 km per hour/231 miles per hour Mount Washington, New Hampshire, USA, (12th April 1934)
est place — Annual mean	34.4°C/93.9°F Dalol, Ethiopia		Low altitude		333 km per hour/207 miles per hour Qaanaaq (Thule), Greenland (8th March 1972)
st place — Annual mean	0.1 mm/0.004 inches Desierto de Atacama, Chile		Tornado		512 km per hour/318 miles per hour Oklahoma City, Oklahoma, USA (3rd May 1999)
t sunshine — Annual mean	90% Yuma, Arizona, USA (over 4 000 hours)		Greatest snowfall		31 102 mm/1 224.5 inches Mount Rainier, Washington, USA (19th February 1971 — 18th February 1972)
t sunshine	Nil for 182 days each year, South Pole				
est screen temperature	-89.2°C/-128.6°F Vostok Station, Antarctica (21st July 1983)		Heaviest hailstones		1 kg/2.21 lb Gopalganj, Bangladesh (14th April 1986)
lest place — Annual mean	-56.6°C/-69.9°F Plateau Station, Antarctica		Thunder-days Average		251 days per year Tororo, Uganda
test place — Annual mean	11 873 mm/467.4 inches Meghalaya, India		Highest barometric pressure		1 083.8 mb Agata, Siberia, Rus. Fed. (31st December 1968)
t rainy days	Up to 350 per year Mount Waialeale, Hawaii, USA		Lowest barometric pressure		870 mb 483 km/300 miles west of Guam, Pacific Ocean (12th October 1979)
diest place	322 km per hour/200 miles per hour in gales, Commonwealth Bay, Antarctica				

LAND COVER

WORLD LAND COVER

Goode Interrupted Homolosine Projection
scale: 1: 125 000 000
DISCover map courtesy of IGBP, JRC and USGS

1. Evergreen needleleaf forest

2. Evergreen broadleaf forest

3. Deciduous needleleaf forest

4. Deciduous broadleaf forest

5. Mixed forest

6. Closed shrublands

7. Open shrublands

8. Woody savannas

9. Savannas

10. Grasslands

11. Permanent wetlands

12. Croplands

13. Urban and built-up

14. Cropland/Natural vegetation mosaic

15. Snow and Ice

16. Barren or sparsely vegetated

17. Water bodies

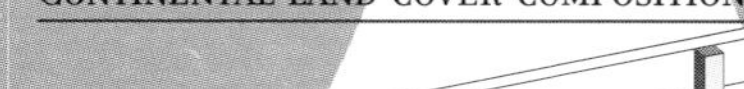

CONTINENTAL LAND COVER COMPOSITION

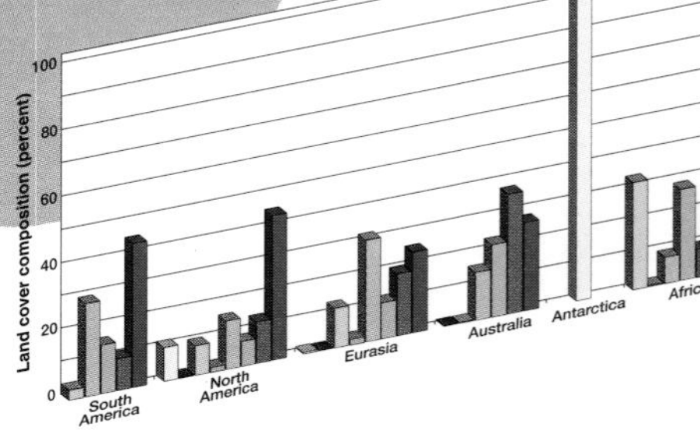

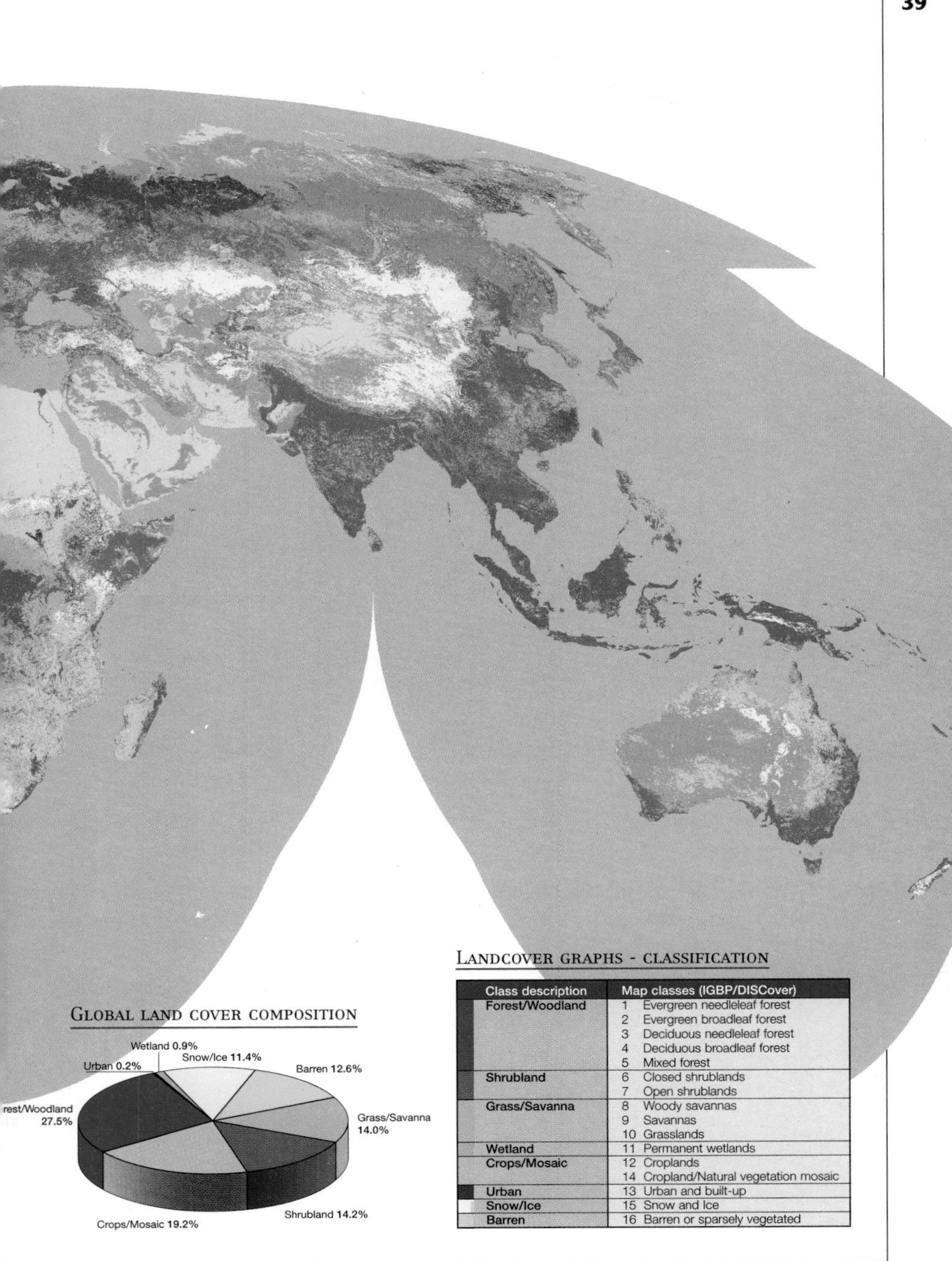

LANDCOVER GRAPHS - CLASSIFICATION

Class description	Map classes (IGBP/DISCover)	
Forest/Woodland	1	Evergreen needleleaf forest
	2	Evergreen broadleaf forest
	3	Deciduous needleleaf forest
	4	Deciduous broadleaf forest
	5	Mixed forest
Shrubland	6	Closed shrublands
	7	Open shrublands
Grass/Savanna	8	Woody savannas
	9	Savannas
	10	Grasslands
Wetland	11	Permanent wetlands
Crops/Mosaic	12	Croplands
	14	Cropland/Natural vegetation mosaic
Urban	13	Urban and built-up
Snow/Ice	15	Snow and ice
Barren	16	Barren or sparsely vegetated

GLOBAL LAND COVER COMPOSITION

Wetland 0.9%
Urban 0.2%
Snow/Ice 11.4%
Barren 12.6%
rest/Woodland 27.5%
Grass/Savanna 14.0%
Crops/Mosaic 19.2%
Shrubland 14.2%

© Bartholomew Ltd

POPULATION

WORLD POPULATION DISTRIBUTION AND THE WORLD'S MAJOR CITIES

Winkel Tripel Projection
scale : 1:145 000 000

POPULATION DENSITY

per sq mile
| 500 | 100 | 25 | 5 | 0 |

Inhabitants | Uninhabited

| 200 | 40 | 10 | 2 | 0 |
per sq km

URBAN AGGLOMERATIONS WITH OVER 5 MILLION INHABITANTS

- 5 million - 10 million
- 10 million - 20 million
- over 20 million

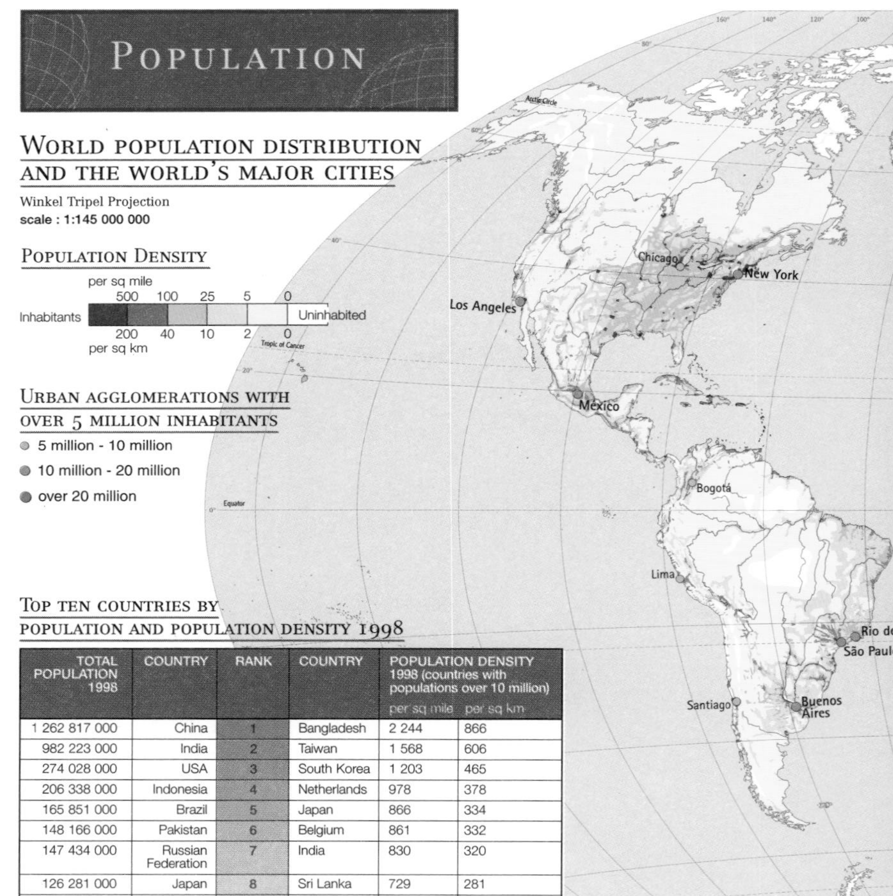

TOP TEN COUNTRIES BY POPULATION AND POPULATION DENSITY 1998

TOTAL POPULATION 1998	COUNTRY	RANK	COUNTRY	POPULATION DENSITY 1998 (countries with populations over 10 million)	
				per sq mile	per sq km
1 262 817 000	China	1	Bangladesh	2 244	866
982 223 000	India	2	Taiwan	1 568	606
274 028 000	USA	3	South Korea	1 203	465
206 338 000	Indonesia	4	Netherlands	978	378
165 851 000	Brazil	5	Japan	866	334
148 166 000	Pakistan	6	Belgium	861	332
147 434 000	Russian Federation	7	India	830	320
126 281 000	Japan	8	Sri Lanka	729	281
124 774 000	Bangladesh	9	Philippines	630	243
106 409 000	Nigeria	10	UK	622	240

KEY POPULATION STATISTICS FOR MAJOR REGIONS

	Population 1998 (millions)	Growth (per cent)	Infant mortality rate	Total fertility rate (years)	Life expectancy
World	5 901	1.33	57	2.7	65
More developed regions	1 182	0.28	9	1.6	75
Less developed regions	4 719	1.59	63	3.0	63
Africa	749	2.37	87	5.1	51
Asia	3 585	1.38	57	2.6	66
Europe	729	0.03	12	1.4	73
Latin America and the Caribbean	504	1.57	36	2.7	69
North America	305	0.85	7	1.9	77
Oceania	30	1.30	24	2.4	74

Except for population (1998), the data are annual averages projected for the period 1995-2000. Regional and continental areas follow United Nations definitions.

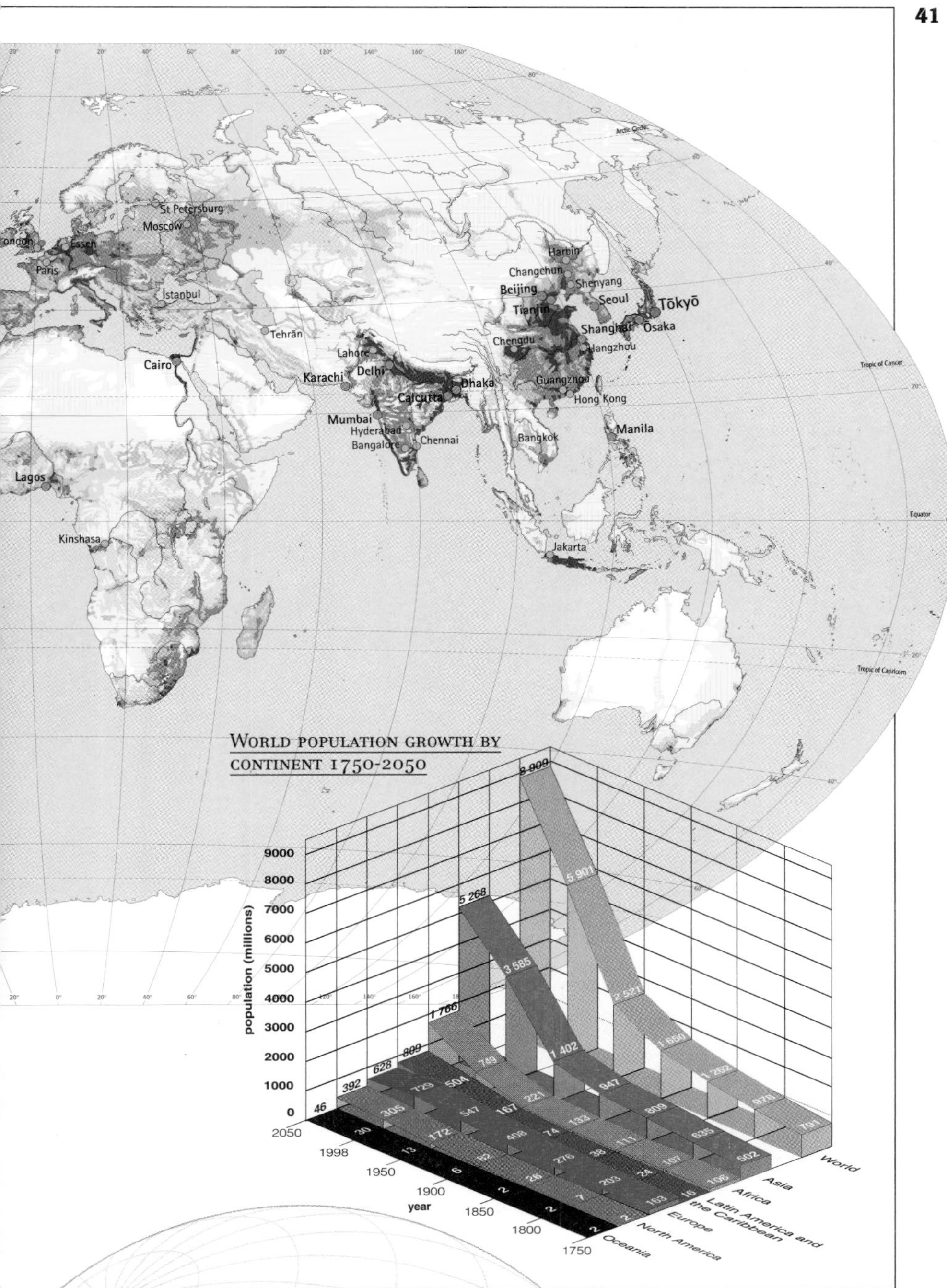

WORLD POPULATION GROWTH BY CONTINENT 1750-2050

© Bartholomew Ltd

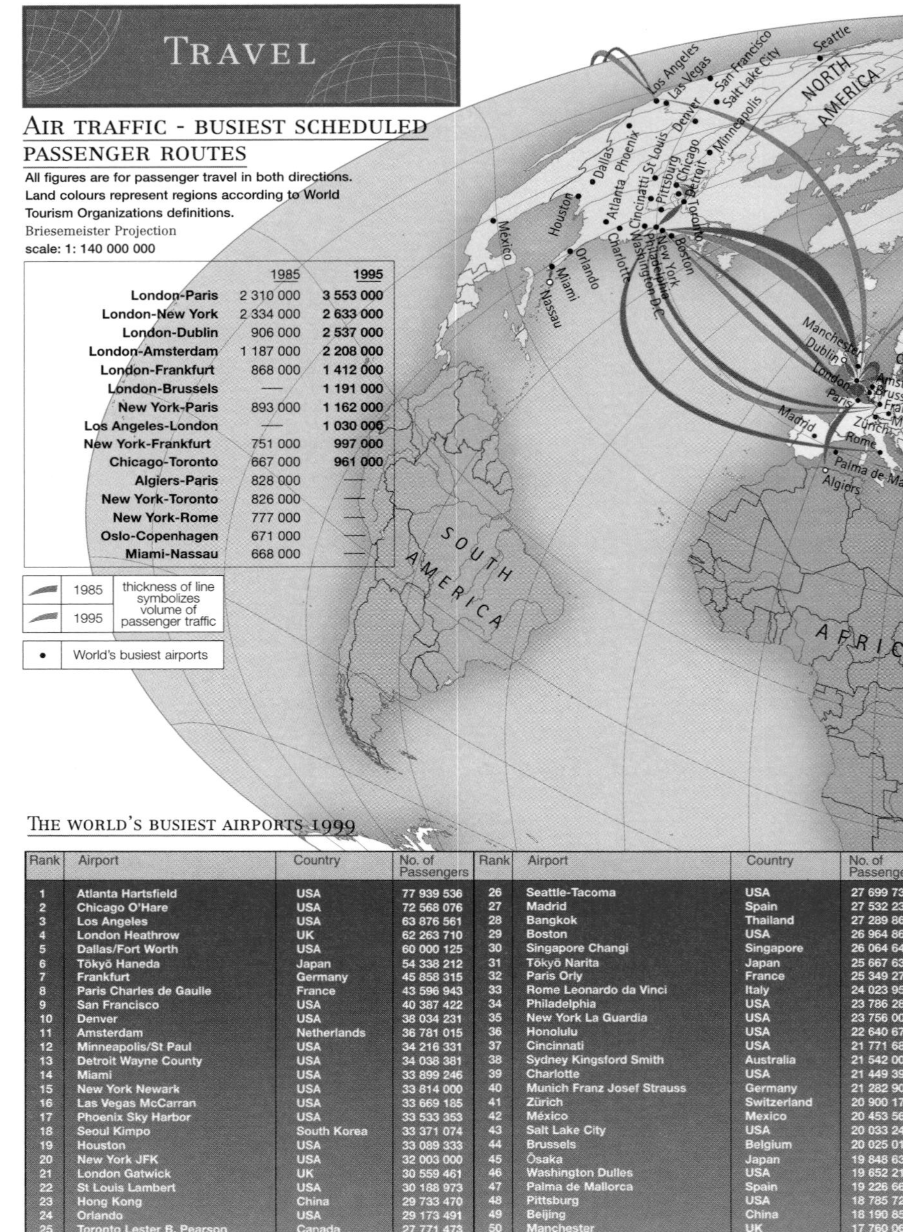

TRAVEL

AIR TRAFFIC - BUSIEST SCHEDULED PASSENGER ROUTES

All figures are for passenger travel in both directions.
Land colours represent regions according to World
Tourism Organizations definitions.
Briesemeister Projection
scale: 1: 140 000 000

	1985	1995
London-Paris	2 310 000	3 553 000
London-New York	2 334 000	2 633 000
London-Dublin	906 000	2 537 000
London-Amsterdam	1 187 000	2 208 000
London-Frankfurt	868 000	1 412 000
London-Brussels	—	1 191 000
New York-Paris	893 000	1 162 000
Los Angeles-London	—	1 030 000
New York-Frankfurt	751 000	997 000
Chicago-Toronto	667 000	961 000
Algiers-Paris	828 000	—
New York-Toronto	826 000	—
New York-Rome	777 000	—
Oslo-Copenhagen	671 000	—
Miami-Nassau	668 000	—

1985	thickness of line symbolizes volume of passenger traffic
1995	

• World's busiest airports

THE WORLD'S BUSIEST AIRPORTS 1999

Rank	Airport	Country	No. of Passengers	Rank	Airport	Country	No. of Passengers
1	Atlanta Hartsfield	USA	77 939 536	26	Seattle-Tacoma	USA	27 699 733
2	Chicago O'Hare	USA	72 568 076	27	Madrid	Spain	27 532 237
3	Los Angeles	USA	63 876 561	28	Bangkok	Thailand	27 289 863
4	London Heathrow	UK	62 263 710	29	Boston	USA	26 964 864
5	Dallas/Fort Worth	USA	60 000 125	30	Singapore Changi	Singapore	26 064 645
6	Tōkyō Haneda	Japan	54 338 212	31	Tōkyō Narita	Japan	25 667 634
7	Frankfurt	Germany	45 858 315	32	Paris Orly	France	25 349 270
8	Paris Charles de Gaulle	France	43 596 943	33	Rome Leonardo da Vinci	Italy	24 023 952
9	San Francisco	USA	40 387 422	34	Philadelphia	USA	23 786 285
10	Denver	USA	38 034 231	35	New York La Guardia	USA	23 756 000
11	Amsterdam	Netherlands	36 781 015	36	Honolulu	USA	22 640 676
12	Minneapolis/St Paul	USA	34 216 331	37	Cincinnati	USA	21 771 689
13	Detroit Wayne County	USA	34 038 381	38	Sydney Kingsford Smith	Australia	21 542 000
14	Miami	USA	33 899 246	39	Charlotte	USA	21 449 392
15	New York Newark	USA	33 814 000	40	Munich Franz Josef Strauss	Germany	21 282 906
16	Las Vegas McCarran	USA	33 669 185	41	Zürich	Switzerland	20 900 179
17	Phoenix Sky Harbor	USA	33 533 353	42	México	Mexico	20 453 568
18	Seoul Kimpo	South Korea	33 371 074	43	Salt Lake City	USA	20 033 241
19	Houston	USA	33 089 333	44	Brussels	Belgium	20 025 014
20	New York JFK	USA	32 003 000	45	Ōsaka	Japan	19 848 635
21	London Gatwick	UK	30 559 461	46	Washington Dulles	USA	19 652 213
22	St Louis Lambert	USA	30 188 973	47	Palma de Mallorca	Spain	19 226 669
23	Hong Kong	China	29 733 470	48	Pittsburg	USA	18 785 728
24	Orlando	USA	29 173 491	49	Beijing	China	18 190 852
25	Toronto Lester B. Pearson	Canada	27 771 473	50	Manchester	UK	17 760 065

For airport locations see map

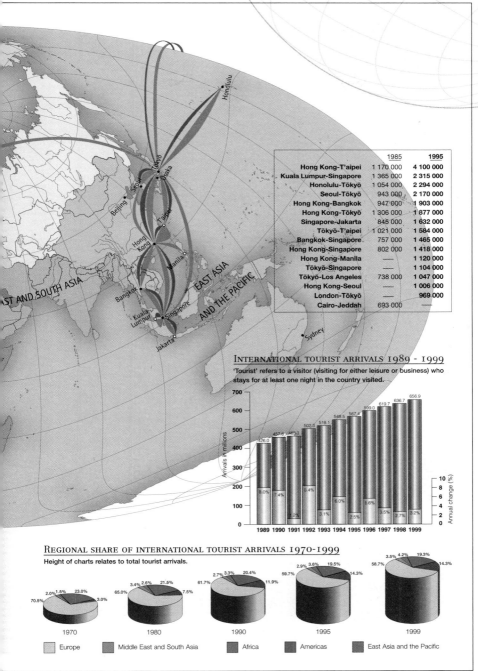

	1985	1995
Hong Kong-T'aipei	1 170 000	4 100 000
Kuala Lumpur-Singapore	1 365 000	2 315 000
Honolulu-Tōkyō	1 054 000	2 294 000
Seoul-Tōkyō	943 000	2 170 000
Hong Kong-Bangkok	947 000	1 903 000
Hong Kong-Tōkyō	1 306 000	1 877 000
Singapore-Jakarta	845 000	1 632 000
Tōkyō-T'aipei	1 021 000	1 584 000
Bangkok-Singapore	757 000	1 465 000
Hong Kong-Singapore	802 000	1 418 000
Hong Kong-Manila	—	1 120 000
Tōkyō-Singapore	—	1 104 000
Tōkyō-Los Angeles	738 000	1 047 000
Hong Kong-Seoul	—	1 006 000
London-Tōkyō	—	969 000
Cairo-Jeddah	693 000	—

INTERNATIONAL TOURIST ARRIVALS 1989 - 1999

'Tourist' refers to a visitor (visiting for either leisure or business) who stays for at least one night in the country visited.

Arrivals in millions:
- 1989: 426.0 — 8.0%
- 1990: 452.6 — 7.4%
- 1991: 463.0 — 1.2%
- 1992: 502.5 — 9.4%
- 1993: 518.1 — 3.1%
- 1994: 549.5 — 6.0%
- 1995: 567.4 — 2.5%
- 1996: 599.0 — 5.6%
- 1997: 619.7 — 3.5%
- 1998: 636.7 — 2.7%
- 1999: 656.9 — 3.2%

Annual change (%)

REGIONAL SHARE OF INTERNATIONAL TOURIST ARRIVALS 1970-1999

Height of charts relates to total tourist arrivals.

1970: 70.5% | 2.0% | 1.5% | 23.0% | 3.0%

1980: 65.0% | 3.4% | 2.6% | 21.5% | 7.5%

1990: 61.7% | 2.7% | 3.3% | 20.4% | 11.9%

1995: 59.7% | 2.9% | 3.6% | 19.5% | 14.3%

1999: 58.7% | 3.5% | 4.2% | 19.3% | 14.3%

- Europe
- Middle East and South Asia
- Africa
- Americas
- East Asia and the Pacific

© Bartholomew Ltd

INTRODUCTION TO THE ATLAS

PLACE NAMES

The spelling of place names on maps has always been a matter of great complexity, because of the variety of the world's languages and the systems used to write them down. There is no standard way of spelling names or of converting them from one alphabet, or symbol set, to another. Instead, conventional ways of spelling have evolved in each of the world's major languages, and the results often differ significantly from the name as it is spelled in the original language. Familiar examples of English conventional names include Munich (München), Florence (Firenze) and Moscow (from the transliterated form, Moskva).

In this atlas, local name forms are used where these are in the Roman alphabet, though for major cities, and main physical features, conventional English names are given first. The local forms are those which are officially recognized by the government of the country concerned, usually as represented by its official mapping agency. This is a basic principle laid down by the United Kingdom government's Permanent Committee on Geographical Names (PCGN) and the equivalent United States Board on Geographic Names, (BGN). Prominent English-language and historic names are not neglected, however. These, and significant superseded names and alternate spellings, are included in brackets on the maps where space permits, and are cross-referenced in the index.

Country names are shown in conventional English form and include any recent changes promulgated by national governments and adopted by the United Nations. The names of continents, oceans, seas and under-water features in international waters also appear in English throughout the atlas, as do those of other international features where such an English form exists and is in common use. International features are defined as features crossing one or more international boundary.

BOUNDARIES

The status of nations, their names and their boundaries, are shown in this atlas as they are at the time of going to press, as far as can be ascertained. Where an international boundary symbol appears in the sea or ocean it does not necessarily infer a legal maritime boundary, but shows which off-shore islands belong to which country. The extent of island nations is shown by a short boundary symbol at the extreme limits of the area of sea or ocean within which all land is part of that nation.

Where international boundaries are the subject of dispute it may be that no portrayal of them will meet with the approval of any of the countries involved, but it is not seen as the function of this atlas to try to adjudicate between the rights and wrongs of political issues. Although reference mapping at atlas scales is not the ideal medium for indicating the claims of many

separatist and irredentist movements, every reasonable attempt is made to show where an active territorial dispute exists, and where there is an important difference between 'de facto' (existing in fact, on the ground) and 'de jure' (according to law) boundaries. This is done by the use of a different symbol where international boundaries are disputed, or where the alignment is unconfirmed, to that used for settled international boundaries. Cease-fire lines are also shown by a separate symbol. For clarity, disputed boundaries and areas are annotated where this is considered necessary. The atlas aims to take a strictly neutral viewpoint of all such cases, based on advice from expert consultants.

PROJECTIONS

Map projections have been selected specifically for the area and scale of each map, or suite of maps. As the only way to show the Earth with absolute accuracy is on a globe, all map projections are compromises. Some projections seek to maintain correct area relationships (equal area projections), true distances and bearings from a point (equidistant projections) or correct angles and shapes (conformal projections); others attempt to achieve a balance between these properties. The choice of projections used in this atlas has been made on an individual continental and regional basis. Projections used, and their individual parameters, have been defined to minimize distortion and to reduce scale errors as much as possible. The projection used is indicated at the bottom left of each map page.

SCALE

In order to directly compare like with like throughout the world it would be necessary to maintain a single scale throughout the atlas. However, the desirability of mapping the more densely populated areas of the world at larger scales, and other geographical considerations, such as the need to fit a homogeneous physical region within a uniform rectangular page format, mean that a range of scales have been used. Scales for continental maps range between 1:25 000 000 and 1:55 000 000, depending on the size of the continental land mass being covered. Scales for regional maps are typically in the range 1:15 000 000 to 1:25 000 000. Mapping for most countries is at scales between 1:6 000 000 and 1:12 000 000, although for the more densely populated areas of Europe the scale increases to 1:3 000 000.

ABBREVIATIONS

Arch.	Archipelago		
B.	Bay		
	Bahía, Baía	Portuguese	bay
	Bahia	Spanish	bay
	Baie	French	bay
C.	Cape		
	Cabo	Portuguese, Spanish	cape, headland
	Cap	French	cape, headland
Co	Cerro	Spanish	hill, peak, summit
E.	East, Eastern		
Est.	Estrecho	Spanish	strait
G.	Gebel	Arabic	hill, mountain
Gt	Great		
I.	Island, Isle		
	Ilha	Portuguese	island
	Islas	Spanish	island
Is	Islands, Isles		
	Islas	Spanish	islands
Khr.	Khrebet	Russian	mountain range
L.	Lake		
	Loch	(Scotland)	lake
	Lough	(Ireland)	lake
	Lac	French	lake
	Lago	Portuguese, Spanish	lake
M.	Mys	Russian	cape, point
Mt	Mount		
	Mont	French	hill, mountain
Mt.	Mountain		

Mte	Monte	Portuguese, Spanish	hill, mountain
Mts	Mountains		
	Monts	French	hills, mountains
N.	North, Northern		
O.	Ostrov	Russian	island
Pt	Point		
Pta	Punta	Italian, Spanish	cape, point
R.	River		
	Rio	Portuguese	river
	Río	Spanish	river
	Rivière	French	river
Ra.	Range		
S.	South, Southern		
	Salar, Salina, Salinas	Spanish	salt pan, salt pans
Sa	Serra	Portuguese	mountain range
	Sierra	Spanish	mountain range
Sd	Sound		
S.E.	Southeast, Southeastern		
St	Saint		
	Sankt	German	saint
	Sint	Dutch	saint
Sta	Santa	Italian, Portuguese, Spanish	saint
Ste	Sainte	French	saint
Str.	Strait		
W.	West, Western		
	Wadi, Wādi, Wâdi	Arabic	watercourse

TRANSPORT

═══	Motorway
────	Main road
- - -	Track
────	Main railway
┴┴┴┴	Canal
⊕	Main airport

BOUNDARIES

▬▬▬	International boundary
·■·	Disputed international boundary or alignment unconfirmed
✒	Undefined international boundary in the sea. All land within this boundary is part of state or territory named.
▬▬▬	Administrative boundary Shown for selected countries only.
●●●●	Ceasefire line or other boundary described on the map

MAP SYMBOLS

LAND AND WATER FEATURES

⬭	Lake	────	River
⬭	Impermanent lake	- - - -	Impermanent river
⬭	Salt lake or lagoon	⬭	Ice cap / Glacier
⬭	Impermanent salt lake	‿123	Pass Height in metres
⬭	Dry salt lake or salt pan	∴	Site of special interest
		⌄	Oasis
		⌂⌂⌂⌂	Wall

RELIEF

Contour intervals used in layer-colouring, for land height and sea depth

METRES FEET		Ocean pages METRES FEET	
5000	16404	0	0
3000	9843	200	656
2000	6562	2000	6562
1000	3281	3000	9843
500	1640	4000	13124
200	656	5000	16404
0	0	6000	19686
LAND B.S.L.		7000	22967
200	656	9000	29529
4000	13124	123	Ocean deep in metres.
6000	19686		

1234 Summit
△ Height in metres

STYLES OF LETTERING

Cities and towns are explained separately

		Physical features	
Country	FRANCE	Island	*Gran Canaria*
Overseas Territory/Dependency	Guadeloupe	Lake	*Lake Erie*
Disputed Territory	AKSAI CHIN	Mountain	*Mt Blanc*
Administrative name Shown for selected countries only.	SCOTLAND	River	*Thames*
Area name	PATAGONIA	Region	*LAPPLAND*

CITIES AND TOWNS

Population	National Capital	Administrative Capital Shown for selected countries only	Other City or Town
over 1 million	BEIJING □	Sydney ○	New York ○
500 000 to 1 million	BANGUI □	Edmonton ○	Jeddah ○
100 000 to 500 000	WELLINGTON □	Edinburgh ○	Apucarana ○
50 000 to 100 000	PORT OF SPAIN □	Bismarck ○	Invercargill ○
under 50 000	MALABO □	Charlottetown ○	Ceres ○

⬭ Built-up area
Scale 1:3 000 000 only

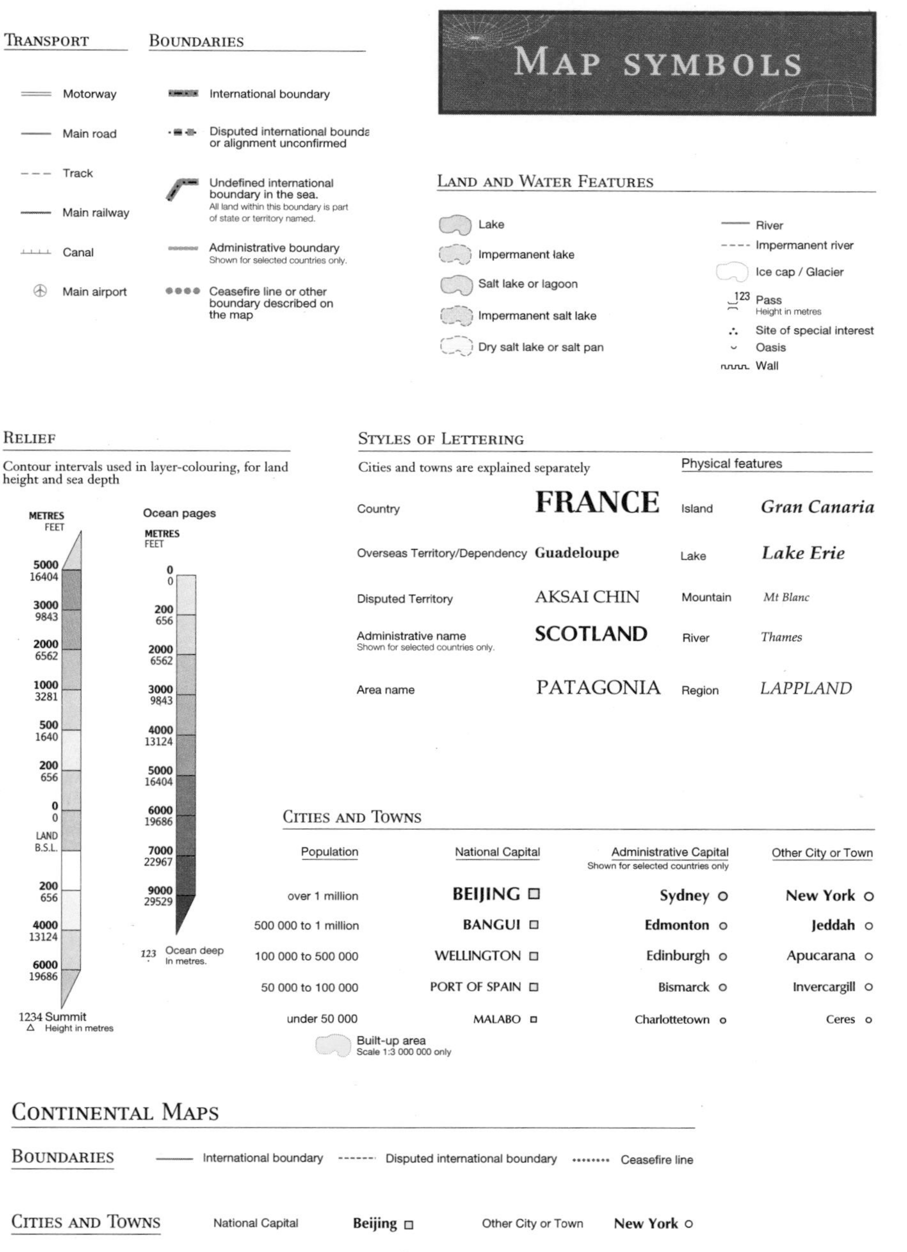

CONTINENTAL MAPS

BOUNDARIES

──── International boundary   ------ Disputed international boundary   ········ Ceasefire line

CITIES AND TOWNS

National Capital   **Beijing □**   Other City or Town   **New York ○**

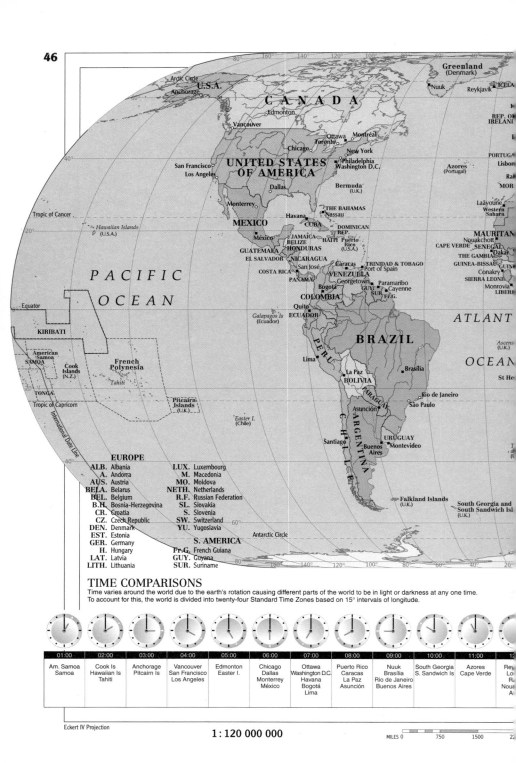

Greenland
(Denmark)

Nuuk   Reykjavik   ICELA

Arctic Circle
U.S.A.
Anchorage

C A N A D A

Edmonton

Vancouver

Ottawa   Montréal
Toronto
Chicago
New York
Philadelphia
Washington D.C.

San Francisco   UNITED STATES
Los Angeles   OF AMERICA

Dallas

Monterrey

Bermuda
(U.K.)

THE BAHAMAS
Nassau
Havana
MEXICO   CUBA
DOMINICAN
México   JAMAICA   REP.
BELIZE   HAITI   Puerto
GUATEMALA   HONDURAS   Rico
EL SALVADOR   NICARAGUA   (U.S.A.)
San José   Caracas   TRINIDAD & TOBAGO
COSTA RICA   VENEZUELA   Port of Spain
PANAMA   Georgetown   Paramaribo
Bogotá   GUY.   Cayenne
COLOMBIA   SUR.   F.G.

Quito
Galápagos Is   ECUADOR
(Ecuador)

PERU

B R A Z I L

Lima

La Paz   Brasília
BOLIVIA

Rio de Janeiro
São Paulo
PARAGUAY
Asunción

Santiago   URUGUAY
Buenos   Montevideo
Aires

ARGENTINA

C H I L E

Falkland Islands
(U.K.)   South Georgia and
South Sandwich Isl
(U.K.)

Tropic of Cancer
Hawaiian Islands
(U.S.A.)

P A C I F I C

O C E A N

Equator

KIRIBATI

American
Samoa
SAMOA   Cook   French
Islands   Polynesia
(N.Z.)
Tahiti

TONGA
Tropic of Capricorn

Pitcairn
Islands
(U.K.)

Easter I.
(Chile)

International Date Line

REP. OF
IRELAND

PORTUG
Lisbon
Azores   Ra
(Portugal)   MOR

Laâyoune
Western
Sahara

MAURITAN
Nouakchott
CAPE VERDE   SENEGAL
THE GAMBIA   Dakar
GUINEA-BISSAU   GUIN
Conakry
SIERRA LEONE
Monrovia
LIBER

A T L A N T

Ascens
(U.K.)

O C E A N

St He

EUROPE

ALB. Albania	LUX. Luxembourg
A. Andorra	M. Macedonia
AUS. Austria	MO. Moldova
BELA. Belarus	NETH. Netherlands
BEL. Belgium	R.F. Russian Federation
B.H. Bosnia-Herzegovina	SL. Slovakia
CR. Croatia	S. Slovenia
CZ. Czech Republic	SW. Switzerland
DEN. Denmark	YU. Yugoslavia
EST. Estonia	
GER. Germany	**S. AMERICA**
H. Hungary	Fr.G. French Guiana
LAT. Latvia	GUY. Guyana
LITH. Lithuania	SUR. Suriname

Antarctic Circle

TIME COMPARISONS

Time varies around the world due to the earth's rotation causing different parts of the world to be in light or darkness at any one time.
To account for this, the world is divided into twenty-four Standard Time Zones based on 15° intervals of longitude.

01:00	02:00	03:00	04:00	05:00	06:00	07:00	08:00	09:00	10:00	11:00	1
Am. Samoa	Cook Is	Anchorage	Vancouver	Edmonton	Chicago	Ottawa	Puerto Rico	Nuuk	South Georgia	Azores	Rey
Samoa	Hawaiian Is	Pitcairn Is	San Francisco	Easter I.	Dallas	Washington D.C.	Caracas	Brasília	S. Sandwich Is	Cape Verde	Lo
	Tahiti		Los Angeles		Monterrey	Havana	La Paz	Rio de Janeiro			R
					México	Bogotá	Asunción	Buenos Aires			Nou
						Lima					A

Eckert IV Projection

1 : 120 000 000

MILES 0   750   1500   2

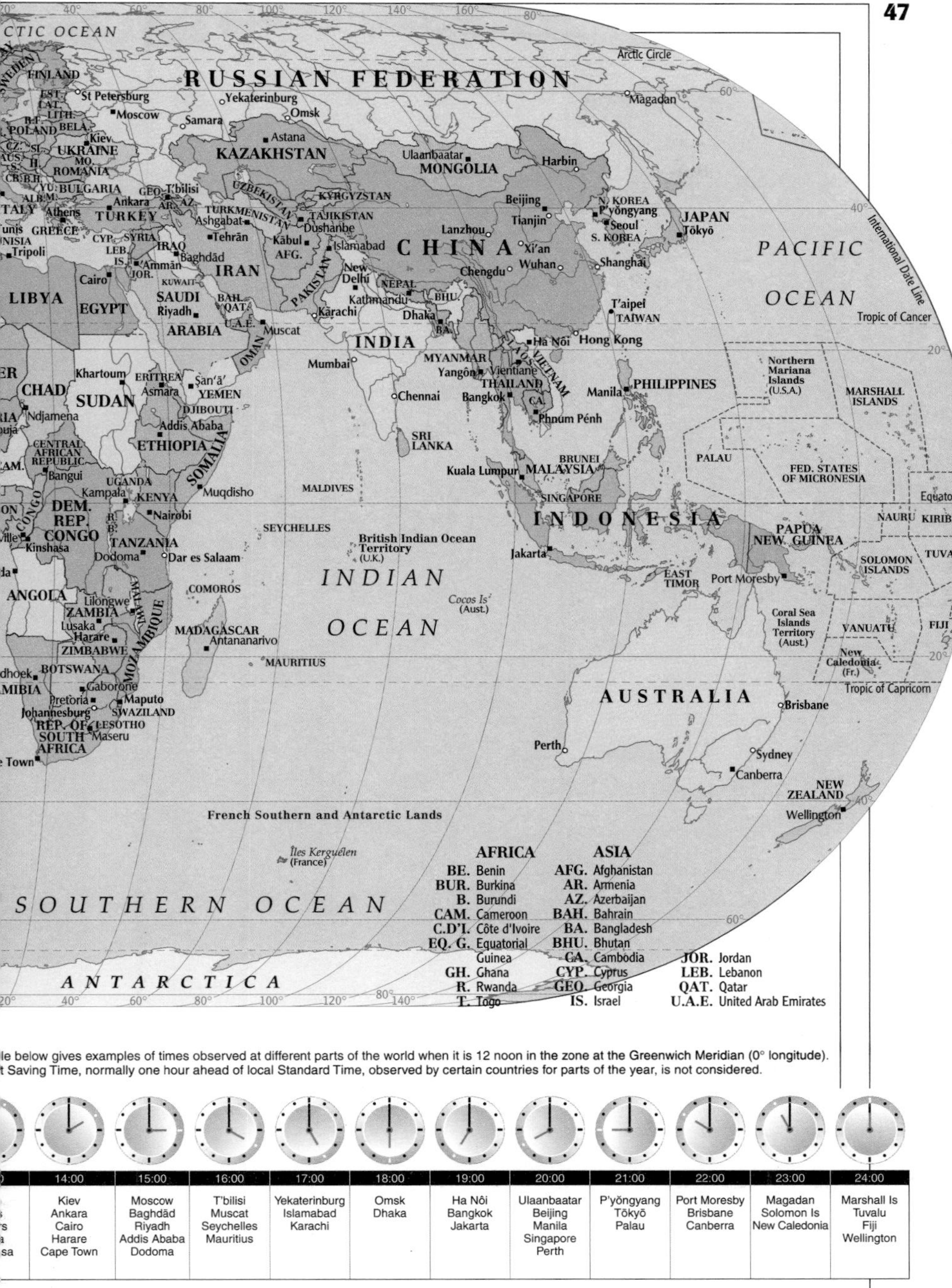

The below gives examples of times observed at different parts of the world when it is 12 noon in the zone at the Greenwich Meridian (0° longitude).
t Saving Time, normally one hour ahead of local Standard Time, observed by certain countries for parts of the year, is not considered.

14:00	15:00	16:00	17:00	18:00	19:00	20:00	21:00	22:00	23:00	24:00
Kiev	Moscow	T'bilisi	Yekaterinburg	Omsk	Ha Nôi	Ulaanbaatar	P'yŏngyang	Port Moresby	Magadan	Marshall Is
Ankara	Baghdād	Muscat	Islamabad	Dhaka	Bangkok	Beijing	Tōkyō	Brisbane	Solomon Is	Tuvalu
Cairo	Riyadh	Seychelles	Karachi		Jakarta	Manila	Palau	Canberra	New Caledonia	Fiji
Harare	Addis Ababa	Mauritius				Singapore				Wellington
Cape Town	Dodoma					Perth				

AFRICA
BE. Benin
BUR. Burkina
B. Burundi
CAM. Cameroon
C.D'I. Côte d'Ivoire
EQ. G. Equatorial Guinea
GH. Ghana
R. Rwanda
T. Togo

ASIA
AFG. Afghanistan
AR. Armenia
AZ. Azerbaijan
BAH. Bahrain
BA. Bangladesh
BHU. Bhutan
CA. Cambodia
CYP. Cyprus
GEO. Georgia
IS. Israel
JOR. Jordan
LEB. Lebanon
QAT. Qatar
U.A.E. United Arab Emirates

1500   3000   4500 KILOMETRES

© Bartholomew Ltd

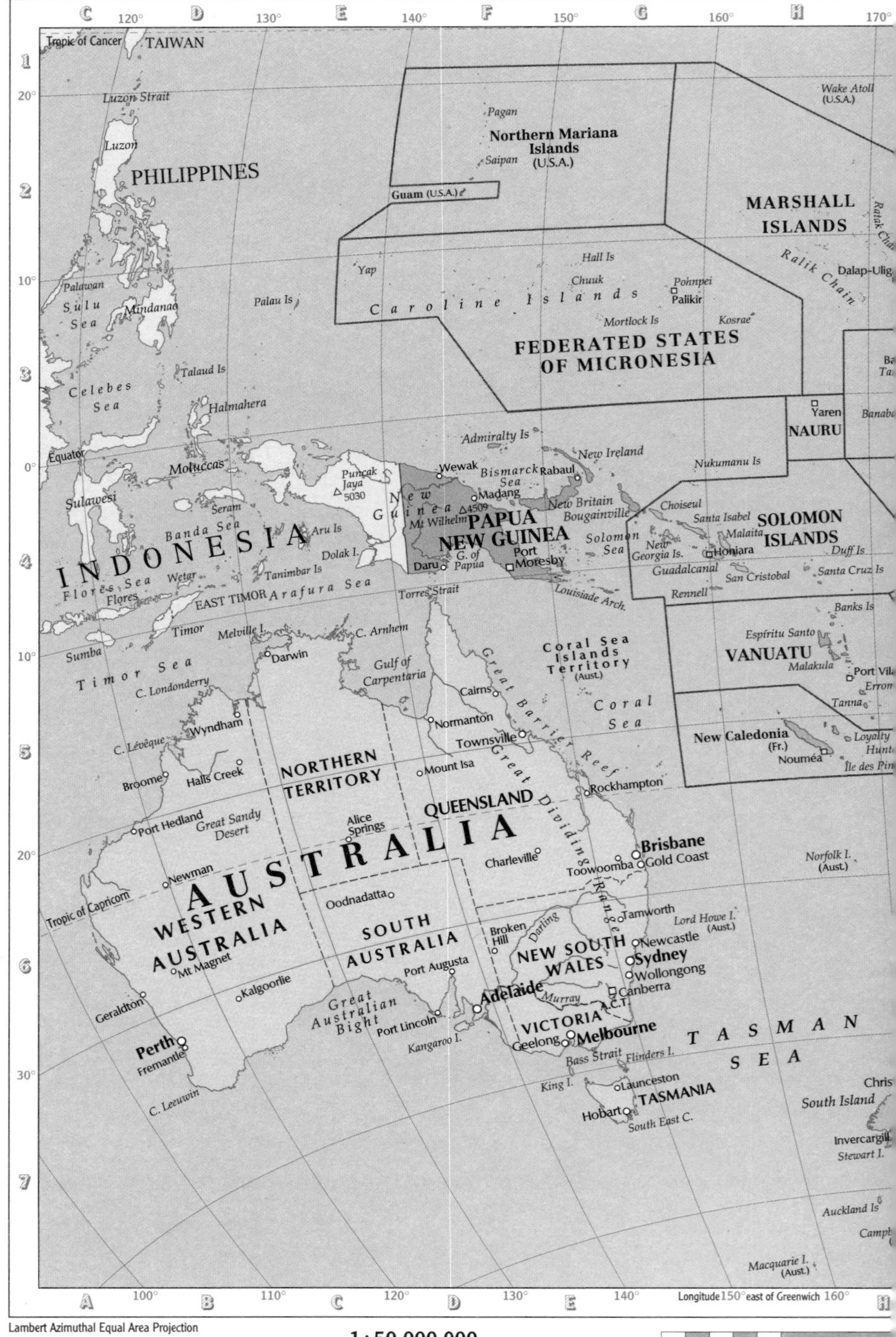

Tropic of Cancer · TAIWAN

120° · 130° · 140° · 150° · 160° · 170°

20° · Luzon Strait

Pagan

Northern Mariana
Islands
Saipan (U.S.A.)

Wake Atoll
(U.S.A.)

Luzon

PHILIPPINES

Guam (U.S.A.)

MARSHALL
ISLANDS

Ralik Chain

10° · Palawan

Yap

Hall Is

Chuuk

Pohnpei
Palikir

Dalap-Ulig

Sulu
Sea · Mindanao

Palau Is

C a r o l i n e   I s l a n d s

Mortlock Is

Kosrae

FEDERATED STATES
OF MICRONESIA

Ba
Ta

3° · Celebes
Sea

Talaud Is

Halmahera

Admiralty Is

New Ireland

Nukumanu Is

Yaren

NAURU

Banaba

0° · Equator

Moluccas

Puncak
Jaya
5030

Wewak

Bismarck
Sea

Rabaul

New w
u i n e a 4509
Mt Wilhelm

Madang

PAPUA
NEW GUINEA

New Britain

Bougainville

Choiseul

Santa Isabel

SOLOMON
ISLANDS

Sulawesi

Seram

Banda Sea

INDONESIA

Aru Is

G
u i n e a

Dolak I.

G. of
Papua

Port
Moresby

Solomon
Sea

New
Georgia Is.

Honiara

Malaita

Duff Is

4° · Flores Sea

Wetar

Tanimbar Is

Daru

Guadalcanal

San Cristobal

Santa Cruz Is

Flores

EAST TIMOR Arafura Sea

Torres Strait

Louisiade Arch.

Rennell

Banks Is

Timor

Melville I.

C. Arnhem

Espíritu Santo

10° · Sumba

Timor Sea

Darwin

Gulf of
Carpentaria

Coral Sea
Islands
Territory
(Aust.)

VANUATU

Malakula

Port Vil

Erron

C. Londonderry

Cairns

Coral
Sea

Tanna

C. Lévêque

Wyndham

Normanton

Townsville

Great Barrier Reef

New Caledonia
(Fr.)

Nouméa

Loyalty
Hunt
Île des Pin

Broome

Halls Creek

NORTHERN
TERRITORY

Mount Isa

Rockhampton

Norfolk I.
(Aust.)

Port Hedland

Great Sandy
Desert

Alice
Springs

QUEENSLAND

Great Dividing Range

20° · Newman

AUSTRALIA

Charleville

Toowoomba

Brisbane
Gold Coast

Tropic of Capricorn

WESTERN
AUSTRALIA

Mt Magnet

Oodnadatta

SOUTH
AUSTRALIA

Broken
Hill

Tamworth

Lord Howe I.
(Aust.)

Geraldton

Kalgoorlie

Great
Australian
Bight

Port Augusta

NEW SOUTH
WALES

Newcastle

Sydney
Wollongong

Perth

Port Lincoln

Adelaide

Murray

Canberra
A.C.T.

T A S M A N

Fremantle

Kangaroo I.

VICTORIA

Geelong

Melbourne

S E A

30° · C. Leeuwin

Bass Strait

King I.

Flinders I.

Launceston

TASMANIA

South Island

Chris

Hobart

South East C.

Invercargill

Stewart I.

Auckland Is

Camp

Macquarie I.
(Aust.)

100° · 110° · 120° · 130° · 140° · Longitude 150° east of Greenwich 160°

Lambert Azimuthal Equal Area Projection

1 : 50 000 000

MILES 0 · 500

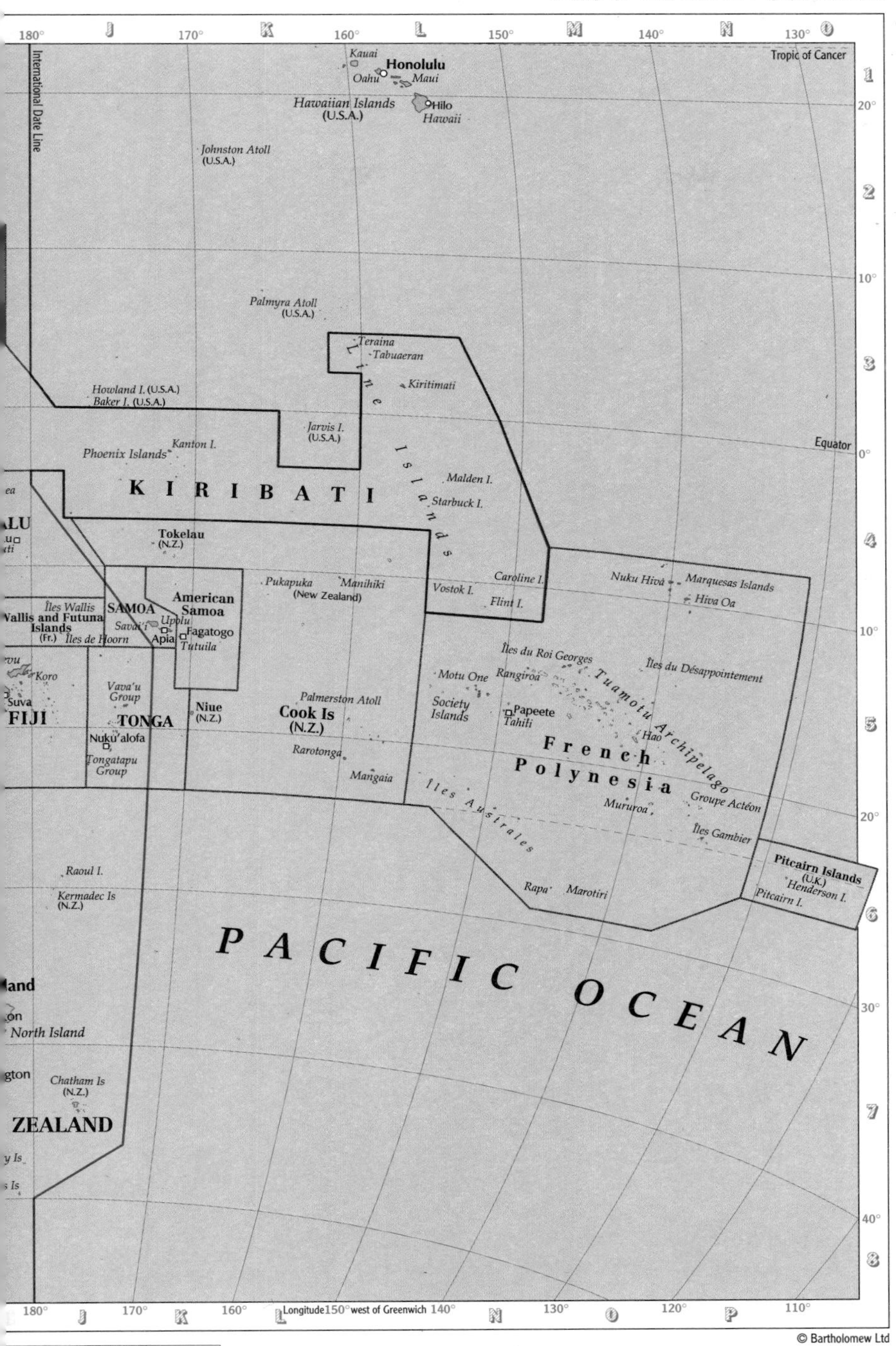

© Bartholomew Ltd

International Date Line
Tropic of Cancer
Equator
Kauai
Honolulu
Oahu
Maui
Hawaiian Islands
(U.S.A.)
Hilo
Hawaii
Johnston Atoll
(U.S.A.)
Palmyra Atoll
(U.S.A.)
Teraina
Tabuaeran
Kiritimati
Line Islands
Howland I. (U.S.A.)
Baker I. (U.S.A.)
Jarvis I.
(U.S.A.)
Kanton I.
Phoenix Islands
KIRIBATI
Malden I.
Starbuck I.
Tokelau
(N.Z.)
Pukapuka
Manihiki
(New Zealand)
Vostok I.
Caroline I.
Flint I.
Nuku Hiva
Marquesas Islands
Hiva Oa
Îles Wallis
Wallis and Futuna
Islands
(Fr.)
Îles de Hoorn
SAMOA
Savai'i
Upolu
Apia
American
Samoa
Fagatogo
Tutuila
Îles du Roi Georges
Îles du Désappointement
Motu One
Rangiroa
Tuamotu Archipelago
Koro
Suva
FIJI
Vava'u
Group
TONGA
Nuku'alofa
Tongatapu
Group
Niue
(N.Z.)
Palmerston Atoll
Cook Is
(N.Z.)
Rarotonga
Mangaia
Society
Islands
Papeete
Tahiti
Hao
French
Polynesia
Îles Australes
Mururoa
Groupe Actéon
Îles Gambier
Pitcairn Islands
(U.K.)
Henderson I.
Pitcairn I.
Rapa
Marotiri
Raoul I.
Kermadec Is
(N.Z.)
PACIFIC OCEAN
North Island
Chatham Is
(N.Z.)
ZEALAND
Longitude 150° west of Greenwich
180° 170° 160° 150° 140° 130° 120° 110°
20° 10° 0° 10° 20° 30° 40°
J K L M N O P
1 2 3 4 5 6 7 8
500 1000 1500 KILOMETRES

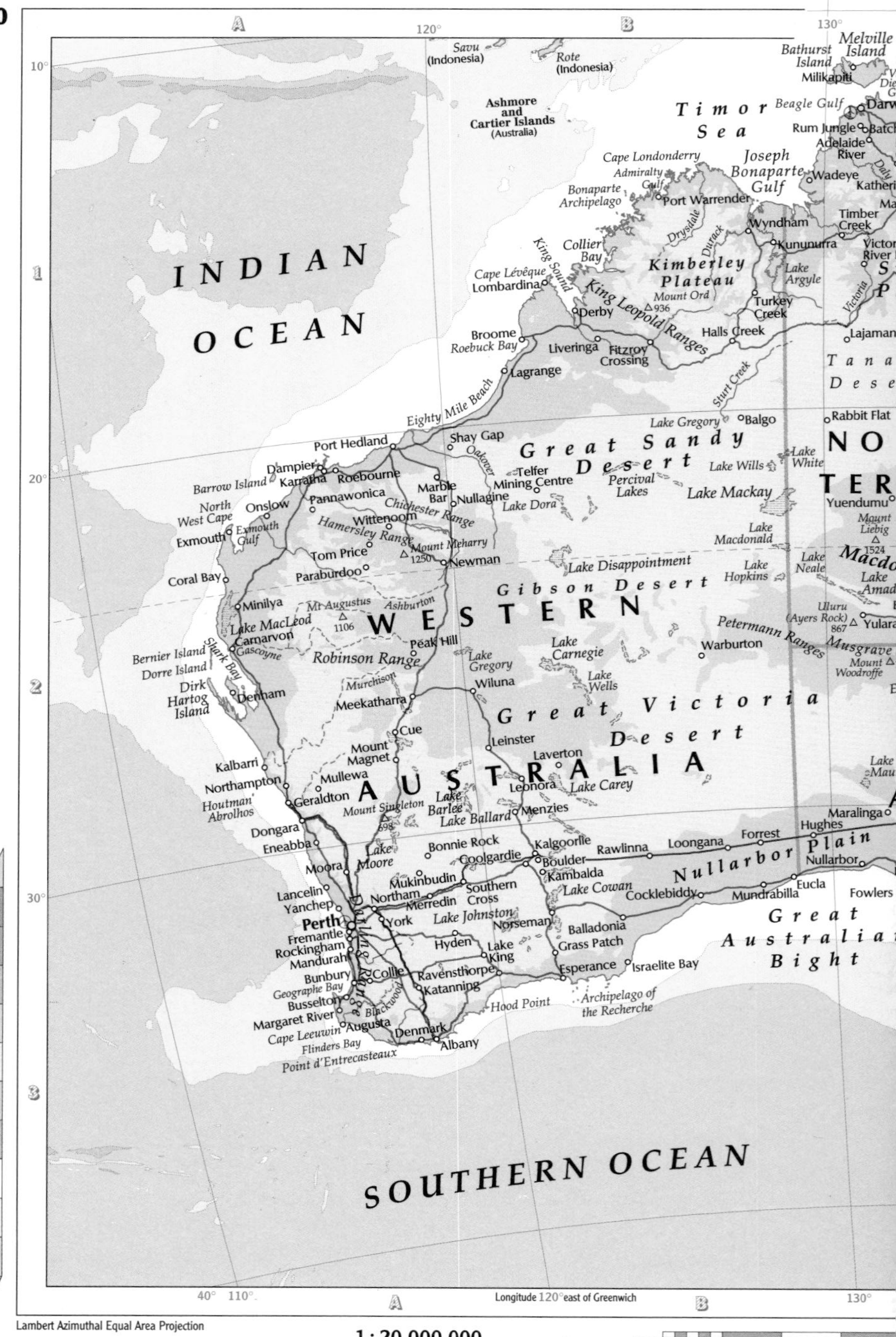

Lambert Azimuthal Equal Area Projection

1 : 20 000 000

MILES 0   100   200   300

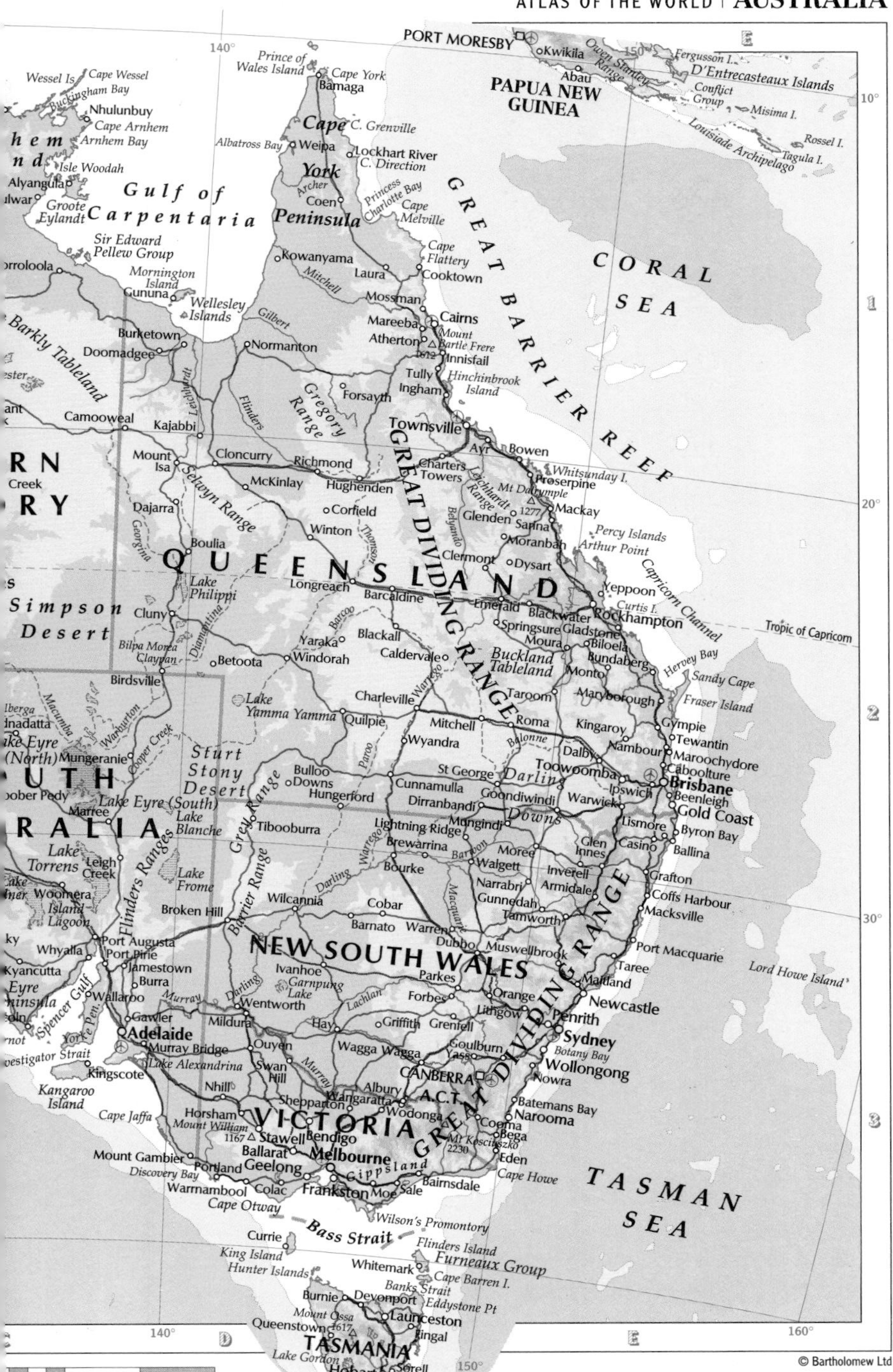

Wessel Is ‹Cape Wessel
Buckingham Bay
Nhulunbuy
h e m ‹Cape Arnhem
Arnhem Bay
n d‹Isle Woodah
Alyangula›
ulwar› Groote
Eylandt
Sir Edward
Pellew Group
orroloola›
Mornington
Island
Gununa
Wellesley
Burketown‹ Islands
Doomadgee‹
ester›
Camooweal

Gulf of
Carpentaria

PORT MORESBY
Prince of
Wales Island
Cape York
Bamaga
Cape
C. Grenville
Weipa
Lockhart River
York C. Direction
Archer
Coen‹ Princess
Charlotte Bay
Cape
Melville
Peninsula
Kowanyama
Mitchell
Laura
Cooktown
Mossman
Mareeba‹ Cairns
Atherton Mount
Bartle Frere
Innisfail
Tully‹ Hinchinbrook
Ingham‹ Island
Forsayth

PAPUA NEW
GUINEA

Kwikila
Abau
Conflict
Group
Misima I.

Fergusson I.
D'Entrecasteaux Islands

Rossel I.
Louisiade Archipelago Tagula I.

C O R A L
S E A

Albatross Bay
Normanton

G R E A T   B A R R I E R   R E E F

Kajabbi
Cloncurry
Mount Richmond
Isa McKinlay
Dajarra
Corfield
Boulia
Winton
Clermont

Charters
Towers
Hughenden
Mt Dalrymple
1277
Glenden Saina
Moranbah
Dysart

Townsville
Ayr Bowen
Proserpine Whitsunday I.
Mackay
Percy Islands
Arthur Point

Yeppoon
Rockhampton
Curtis I.
Capricorn Channel

Tropic of Capricorn

S i m p s o n
D e s e r t

Cluny
Bilpa Morea
Claypan
Birdsville

Lake
Philippi
Yaraka
Blackall
Windorah
Caldervale
Betoota
Longreach
Barcaldine
Emerald
Blackwater
Springsure
Moura
Buckland
Tableland
Biloela
Gladstone
Bundaberg
Monto
Hervey Bay
Sandy Cape

Iberga
inadatta
ke Eyre
(North)
Mungeranie
Sturt
Stony
Desert
Charleville
Yamma Yamma
Quilpie
Taroom
Maryborough
Fraser Island

Gympie
Tewantin

sober Pedy
Marree‹
Lake Eyre (South)
Lake
Blanche
Tibooburra
Mitchell
Wyandra
Roma
Kingaroy
Nambour
Maroochydore
Caloundra

UTH
RALIA
Lake
Torrens Leigh
Creek
Lake
Frome
Bulloo
Downs
Hungerford
Cunnamulla
St George
Dirranbandi
Goondiwindi
Balonne
Dalby
Toowoomba
Warwick
Ipswich
Brisbane
Beenleigh
Gold Coast
Byron Bay
Ballina

Lightning Ridge
Mungindi
Lismore
Casino

ky
Whyalla
Port Augusta
Port Pirie
Wilcannia
Brewarrina
Bourke
Moree
Walgett
Narrabri
Inverell
Gunnedah
Tamworth
Grafton
Coffs Harbour
Macksville

Woomera
Broken Hill
Cobar
Warren
Dubbo
Muswellbrook
Port Macquarie
Lord Howe Island

Kyancutta
Eyre
ninsula
Jamestown
Burra
Ivanhoe
Garnpung
Lake
Parkes
Orange
Maitland
Taree

NEW SOUTH WALES

Gawler
Wallaroo
Mildura
Wentworth
Hay
Griffith
Grenfell
Lithgow
Penrith
Newcastle

Adelaide
Murray Bridge
Ouyen
Wagga Wagga
CANBERRA
A.C.T.
Goulburn
Sydney
Botany Bay
Wollongong
Nowra

Kingscote
Lake Alexandrina
Swan
Hill
Albury
Wangaratta
Wodonga
Cooma
Batemans Bay
Narooma

Kangaroo
Island
Cape Jaffa
Nhill
Horsham
Mount William
1167
Stawell
VICTORIA
Shepparton
Bendigo
Mt Kosciuszko
2230
Bega
Eden

Mount Gambier
Portland
Ballarat
Melbourne
Geelong
Frankston Moe
Sale
Bairnsdale
Cape Howe

T A S M A N
S E A

Warrnambool
Colac
Cape Otway
Wilson's Promontory

Bass Strait
Flinders Island
Furneaux Group

Currie
King Island
Hunter Islands
Whitemark
Cape Barren I.

Burnie
Devonport
Eddystone Pt

Mount Ossa
1617
Launceston
Queenstown
Fingal

TASMANIA
Lake Gordon
Sorell
Hobart
Kingston
Port Arthur

© Bartholomew Ltd

200   400   600 KILOMETRES

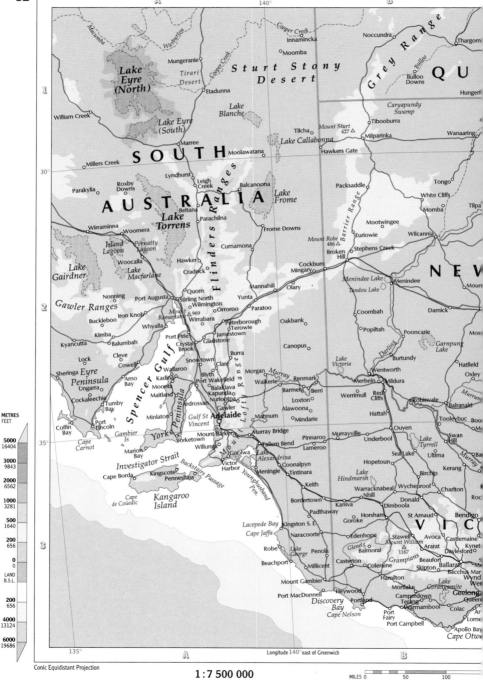

Conic Equidistant Projection

1:7 500 000

MILES 0   50   100

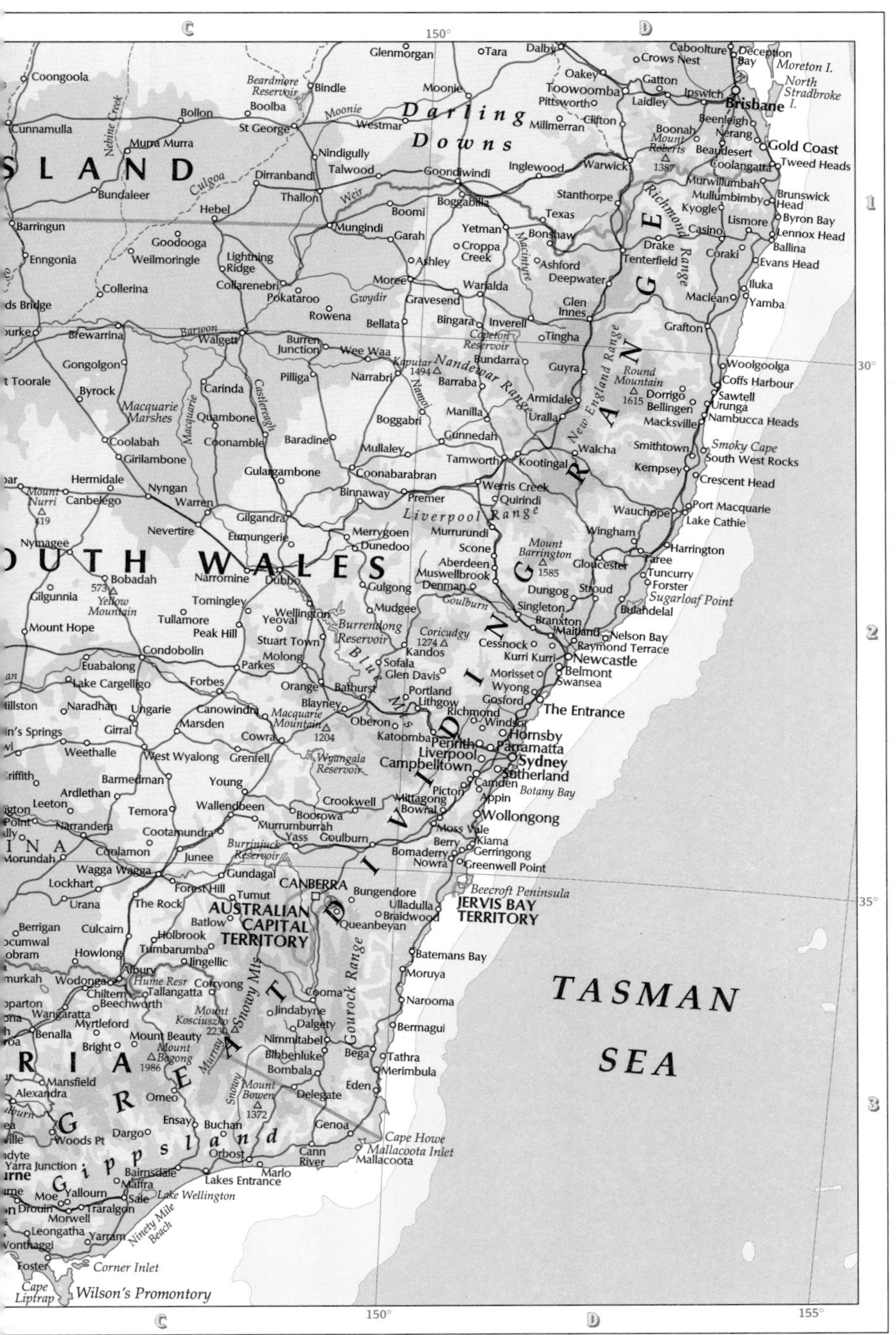

Coongoola
Cunnamulla
Murra Murra
Nebine Creek
Bollon
St George
Boolba
Beardmore Reservoir
Bindle
Moonie
Westmar
Darling
Downs
Glenmorgan
Tara
Dalby
Oakey
Toowoomba
Pittsworth
Clifton
Millmerran
Crows Nest
Gatton
Laidley
Ipswich
Caboolture
Deception Bay
Moreton I.
North Stradbroke I.
Beenleigh
Nerang
Brisbane
Boonah
Mount Roberts
Beaudesert
Murwillumbamby
Coolangatta
Gold Coast
Tweed Heads

SLAND
Bundaleer
Culgoa
Dirranbandi
Thallon
Hebel
Talwood
Nindigully
Goondiwindi
Inglewood
Warwick
1387
Stanthorpe
Kyogle
Mullumbimby
Casino
Lismore
Brunswick Head
Byron Bay
Lennox Head
Ballina

Barringun
Goodooga
Weilmoringle
Mungindi
Boomi
Garah
Yetman
Bonshaw
Ashford
Texas
Drake
Tenterfield
Coraki
Evans Head

Ennonia
Collerina
Lightning Ridge
Collarenebri
Croppa Creek
Deepwater
Iluka
Maclean
Yamba

ds Bridge
Pokataroo
Rowena
Gwydir
Moree
Warialda
Gravesend
Bellata
Bingara
Inverell
Glen Innes
Grafton

ourke
Brewarrina
Barwon
Walgett
Burren Junction
Wee Waa
Coghton Reservoir
Tingha
Guyra
Round Mountain
Dorrigo
Woolgoolga
Coffs Harbour
Sawtell

t Toorale
Gongolgon
Byrock
Carinda
Pilliga
Narrabri
Kaputar
1494
Barraba
Armidale
1615
Bellingen
Urunga
Nambucca Heads

Macquarie Marshes
Quambone
Boggabri
Manilla
Uralla
Macksville

Coolabah
Girilambone
Coonamble
Baradine
Mullaley
Gunnedah
Walcha
Smithtown
Smoky Cape
South West Rocks
Crescent Head

Hermidale
Nyngan
Gulargambone
Coonabarabran
Tamworth
Kempsey
Port Macquarie
Lake Cathie

ar
Mount Nurri
419
Canbelego
Warren
Nevertire
Gilgandra
Binnaway
Premer
Werris Creek
Quirindi
Wauchope
Wingham
Harrington

Nymagee
Bobadah
573
Yellow Mountain
Narromine
Dubbo
Tominglev
Merrygoen
Dunedoo
Scone
Aberdeen
Muswellbrook
Mount Barrington
1585
Gloucester
Taree
Tuncurry
Forster

Gilgunnia
Mount Hope
Tullamore
Peak Hill
Wellington
Yeoval
Mudgee
Denman
Dungog
Stroud
Sugarloaf Point

Euabalong
Condobolin
Stuart Town
Molong
Parkes
Burrendong Reservoir
Coricudgy
1274
Singleton
Branxton
Maitland
Cessnock
Kandos
Kurri Kurri
Newcastle
Nelson Bay
Raymond Terrace
Belmont

Lake Cargelligo
Naradhan
Forbes
Orange
Sofala
Glen Davis
Portland
Morisset
Wyong
Swansea

n
Ungarie
Marsden
Canowindra
Blayney
Bathurst
Lithgow
Gosford
The Entrance

in's Springs
Girral
Cowra
Macquarie Mountains
1204
Oberon
Katoomba
Penrith
Windsor
Hornsby
Parramatta

Weethalle
West Wyalong
Grenfell
Wyangala Reservoir
Liverpool
Sydney

riffith
Barmedman
Young
Crookwell
Wrightville
Bowral
Camden
Appin
Campbelltown
Sutherland
Botany Bay

ton Point
Leeton
Temora
Wallendbeen
Boorowa
Picton
Wollongong

ally
Narrandera
Cootamundra
Murrumburrah
Yass
Goulburn
Moss Vale
Kiama

INA
Morundah
Coolamon
Junee
Burrinjuck Reservoir
Bomaderry
Berry
Cerringong
Nowra
Greenwell Point

Lockhart
Wagga Wagga
Gundagai
CANBERRA
Bungendore
Beecroft Peninsula

Urana
Forest Hill
The Rock
Tumut
Batlow
Ulladulla
Braidwood
Queanbeyan
JERVIS BAY
TERRITORY

Berrigan
ocumwal
obram
Culcairn
Howlong
Tumbarumba
Jingellic
AUSTRALIAN
CAPITAL
TERRITORY
Batemans Bay

murkah
Wodonga
Chiltern
Tallangatta
Cooyong
Mount Kosciuszko
2230
Cooma
Moruya

parton
Wangaratta
Beechworth
Jindabyne
Narooma

ha
Benalla
Myrtleford
Dalgety
Bermagui

Bright
Mount Beauty
Nimmitabel
Bega
Tathra
Merimbula

RIA
Mansfield
Alexandra
Omeo
Mount Bogong
1986
Mount Bowen
1372
Bibbenluke
Bombala
Delegate
Eden

GRE
Ensay
Buchan
Genoa
Cape Howe
Mallacoota Inlet

un
ville
Woods Pt
Dargo
Orbost
Cann River
Mallacoota

adyte
Yarra Junction
urne
Moe
Yallourn
Bairnsdale
Maffra
Sale
Marlo
Lakes Entrance

Drouin
Morwell
Leongatha
Traralgon
Lake Wellington
Ninety Mile Beach

onthaggi
Yarram

Foster
Corner Inlet
Cape Liptrap
Wilson's Promontory
Gippsland

TASMAN

SEA

SOUTH WALES

NEW ENGLAND RANGE

Liverpool Range

GREAT DIVIDING RANGE

Gourock Range

100   200 KILOMETRES

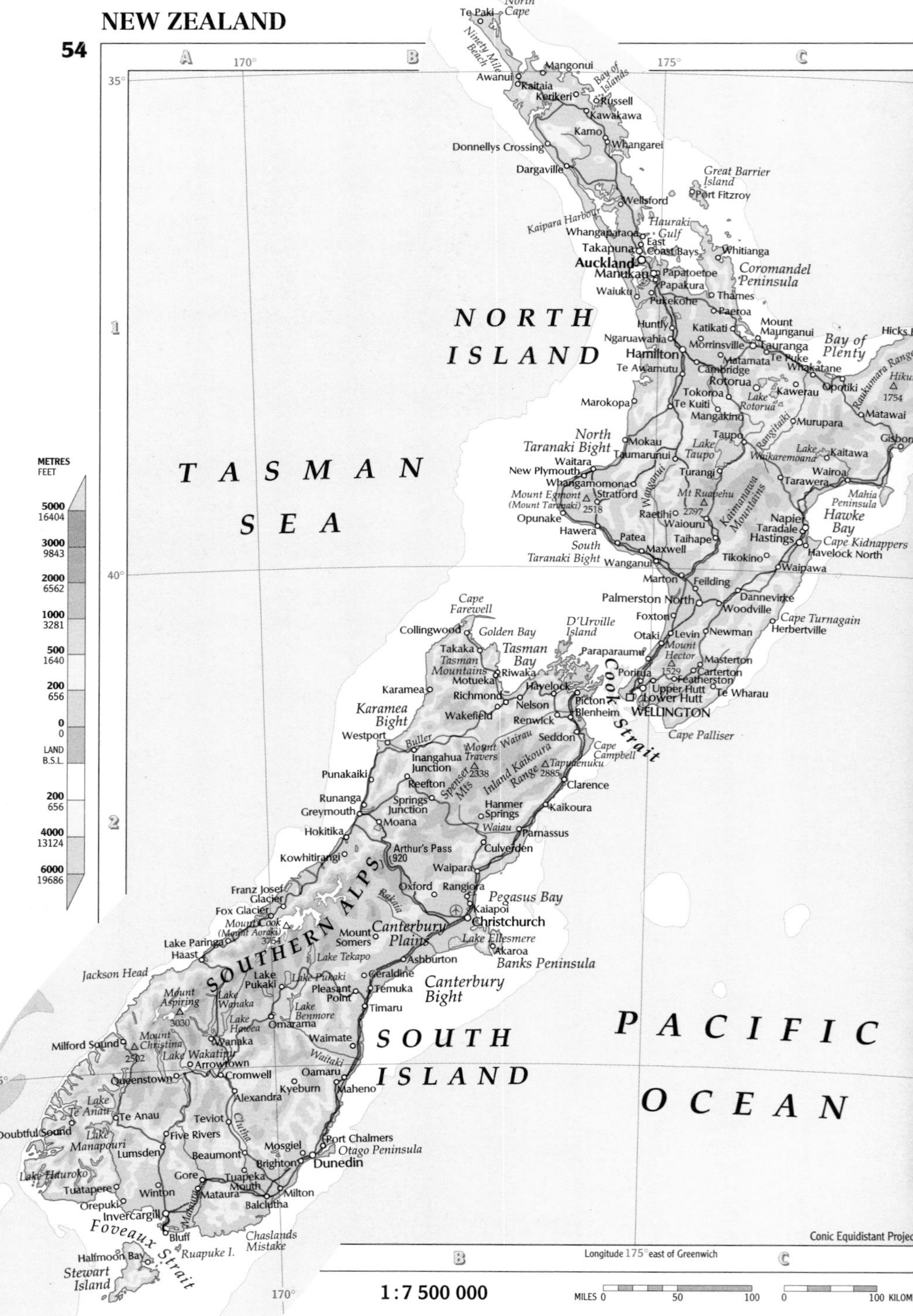

NEW ZEALAND

54

North Cape
Te Paki
North
Ninety Mile Beach
Awanui
Mangonui
Kaitaia
Kerikeri
Bay of Islands
Russell
Kawakawa
Kamo
Donnellys Crossing
Whangarei
Dargaville
Great Barrier Island
Port Fitzroy
Wellsford
Kaipara Harbour
Hauraki Gulf
Whangaparaoa
East Coast Bays
Whitianga
Takapuna
Coromandel Peninsula
Auckland
Manukau
Papatoetoe
Papakura
Thames
Waiuku
Pukekohe
Paeroa

NORTH ISLAND

Huntly
Katikati
Mount Maunganui
Hicks B
Ngaruawahia
Morrinsville
Tauranga
Bay of Plenty
Hamilton
Matamata
Te Puke
Whakatane
Te Awamutu
Cambridge
Rotorua
Kawerau
Opotiki
Hikur
1754
Tokoroa
Lake Kaweau
Te Kuiti
Lake Rotorua
Marokopa
Mangakino
Murupara
Matawai
Mokau
Taupo
Gisborn
North Taranaki Bight
Taumarunui
Lake Taupo
Lake Waikaremoana
Kaitaia
New Plymouth
Waitara
Turangi
Wairoa
Whangamomona
Stratford
Mt Ruapehu
Tarawera
Mahia Peninsula
Mount Egmont (Mount Taranaki) 2518
2797
Opunake
Raetihi
Waiouru
Napier
Hawke Bay
Hawera
Patea
Taihape
Taradale
Hastings
South Taranaki Bight
Maxwell
Wanganui
Tikokino
Havelock North
Cape Kidnappers
Marton
Feilding
Waipawa
Palmerston North
Woodville
Dannevirke
Foxton
Cape Turnagain
Cape Farewell
D'Urville Island
Otaki
Levin
Newman
Herbertville
Collingwood
Golden Bay
Paraparaumu
Mount Hector 1529
Masterton
Takaka
Tasman Bay
Porirua
Carterton
Tasman Mountains
Riwaka
Motueka
WELLINGTON
Upper Hutt
Featherston
Karamea
Hayelock
Lower Hutt
Te Wharau
Karamea Bight
Richmond
Nelson
Picton
Wakefield
Blenheim
Westport
Renwick
Seddon
Cape Palliser
Buller
Mount Travers 2338
Cape Campbell
Inangahua Junction
Tapuaenuku 2885
Punakaiki
Reefton
Inland Kaikoura Range
Clarence
Runanga
Springs Junction
Hanmer Springs
Kaikoura
Greymouth
Moana
Waiau
Parnassus
Hokitika
Arthur's Pass (920)
Culverden
Kowhitirangi
Waipara
Franz Josef Glacier
Oxford
Rangiora
Pegasus Bay
Fox Glacier
Kaiapoi
Christchurch
Mount Cook (Mount Aoraki) 3754
Mount Somers
Canterbury Plains
Akaroa
Lake Paringa
Lake Tekapo
Ashburton
Banks Peninsula
Haast
Lake Pukaki
Geraldine
Canterbury Bight
Jackson Head
Pleasant Point
Temuka
Mount Aspiring 3030
Lake Wanaka
Lake Benmore
Timaru
Lake Hawea
Milford Sound
Mount Christina 2502
Wanaka
Omarama
Waimate
Lake Wakatipu
Waitaki

SOUTH ISLAND

Arrowtown
Cromwell
Oamaru
Queenstown
Kyeburn
Maheno
Lake Te Anau
Alexandra
Doubtful Sound
Teviot
Lake Manapouri
Five Rivers
Mosgiel
Port Chalmers
Te Anau
Lumsden
Beaumont
Brighton
Otago Peninsula
Lake Hauroko
Gore
Tuapeka Mouth
Dunedin
Tuatapere
Winton
Mataura
Milton
Orepuki
Balclutha
Invercargill
Chaslands Mistake
Foveaux Strait
Bluff
Ruapuke I.
Halfmoon Bay
Stewart Island

TASMAN SEA

PACIFIC OCEAN

Cook Strait

Longitude 175° east of Greenwich

1 : 7 500 000

MILES 0   50   100   0   100 KILOMI

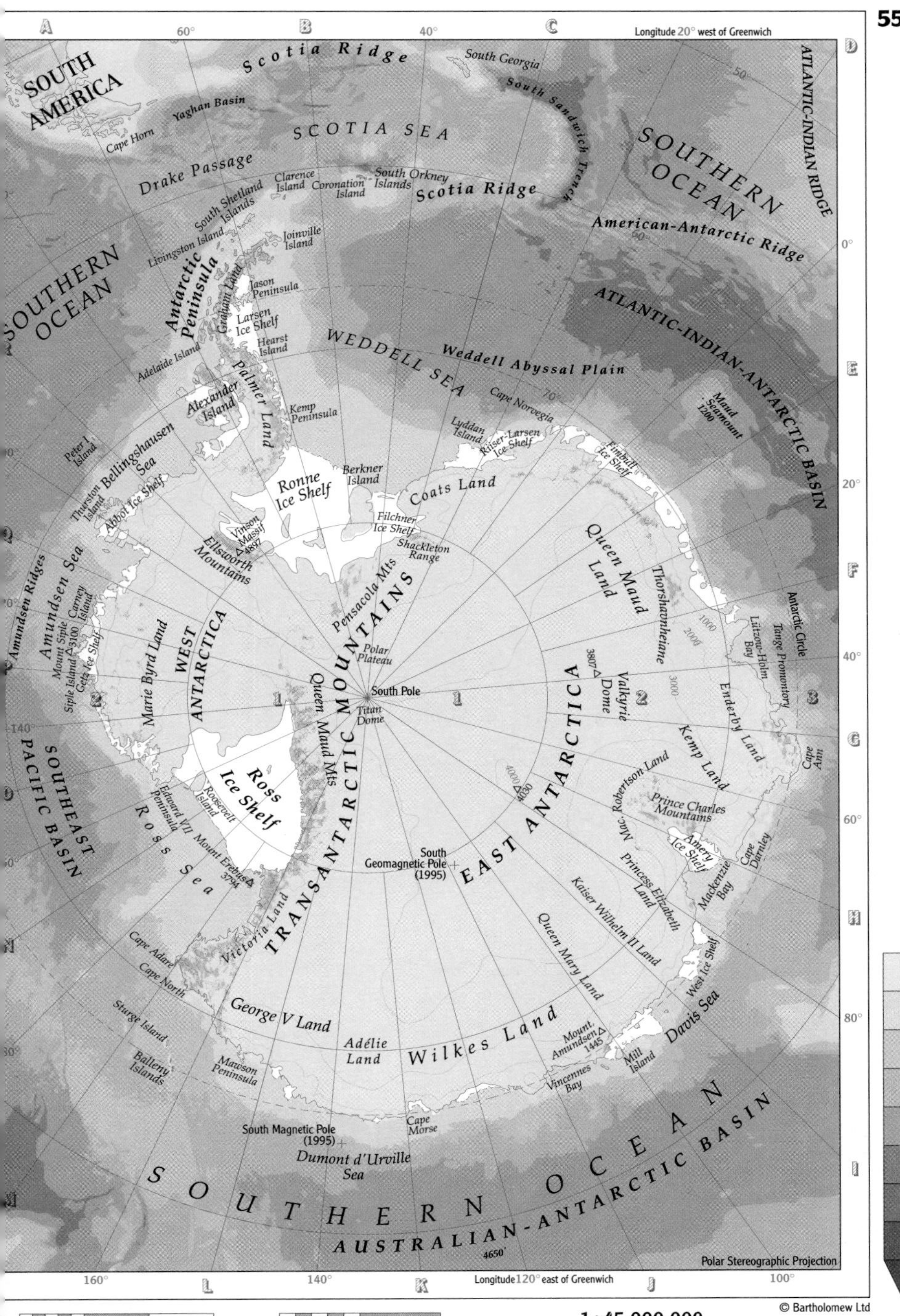

SOUTH AMERICA

Scotia Ridge

South Georgia

South Sandwich Islands

Longitude 20° west of Greenwich

Cape Horn

Yaghan Basin

SCOTIA SEA

Drake Passage

ATLANTIC-INDIAN RIDGE

SOUTHERN OCEAN

Clarence Island
Coronation Island
South Orkney Islands
South Shetland Islands
Livingston Island

Scotia Ridge

American-Antarctic Ridge

Joinville Island

SOUTHERN OCEAN

Antarctic Peninsula
Graham Land
Jason Peninsula

Larsen Ice Shelf

Hearst Island

WEDDELL SEA

Weddell Abyssal Plain

ATLANTIC-INDIAN-ANTARCTIC BASIN

Adelaide Island

Alexander Island

Palmer Land

Kemp Peninsula

Cape Norvegia

Lyddan Island
Riiser-Larsen Ice Shelf
Fimbull Ice Shelf

Maud Seamount
1200

Peter I Island

Thurston Island
Bellingshausen Sea

Abbot Ice Shelf

Berkner Island

Ronne Ice Shelf

Coats Land

Filchner Ice Shelf
Shackleton Range

Queen Maud Land

Thorshammerne

Antarctic Circle

Tange Promontory

Lützow-Holm Bay

Erskine Land

Amundsen Ridges

Amundsen Sea

Carney Island
Siple Island
3100
Mount Siple

Getz Ice Shelf

Vinson Massif 4897
Ellsworth Mountains

Pensacola Mts

Polar Plateau

Valkyrie Dome
3807

1000

2000

3000

WEST ANTARCTICA

TRANSANTARCTIC MOUNTAINS

South Pole

Titan Dome

EAST ANTARCTICA

Kemp Land

Cape Ann

Marie Byrd Land

Queen Maud Mts

Mac-Robertson Land

Prince Charles Mountains

Amery Ice Shelf

Cape Darnley

SOUTHEAST PACIFIC BASIN

Ross Ice Shelf

Roosevelt Island

Ross Sea

Edward VII Peninsula

Mount Erebus 3794

South Geomagnetic Pole (1995)

4009

450

Princess Elizabeth Land

Kaiser Wilhelm II Land

Mackenzie Bay

West Ice Shelf

Davis Sea

Cape Adare
Cape North

Victoria Land

George V Land

Queen Mary Land

Mount Amundsen 1445

Mill Island

Sturge Island

Balleny Islands

Mawson Peninsula

Adélie Land

Wilkes Land

Vincennes Bay

South Magnetic Pole (1995)

Cape Morse

Dumont d'Urville Sea

SOUTHERN OCEAN

AUSTRALIAN-ANTARCTIC BASIN

4650

Polar Stereographic Projection

Longitude 120° east of Greenwich

METRES	FEET
0	0
200	656
2000	6562
3000	9843
4000	13124
5000	16404
6000	19686
7000	22967
9000	29529

ES 0   250   500   750   0   500   1000 KILOMETRES

1 : 45 000 000

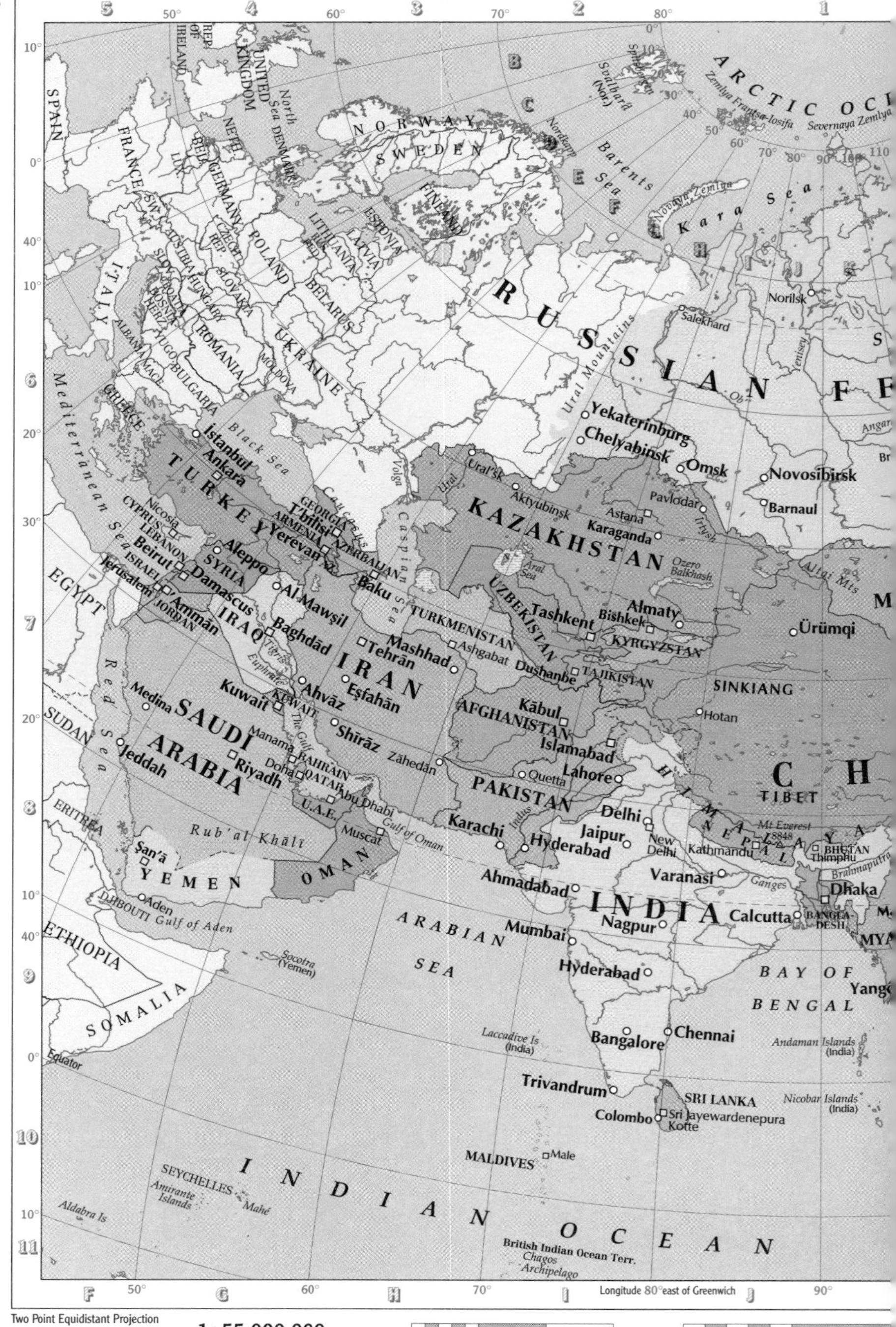

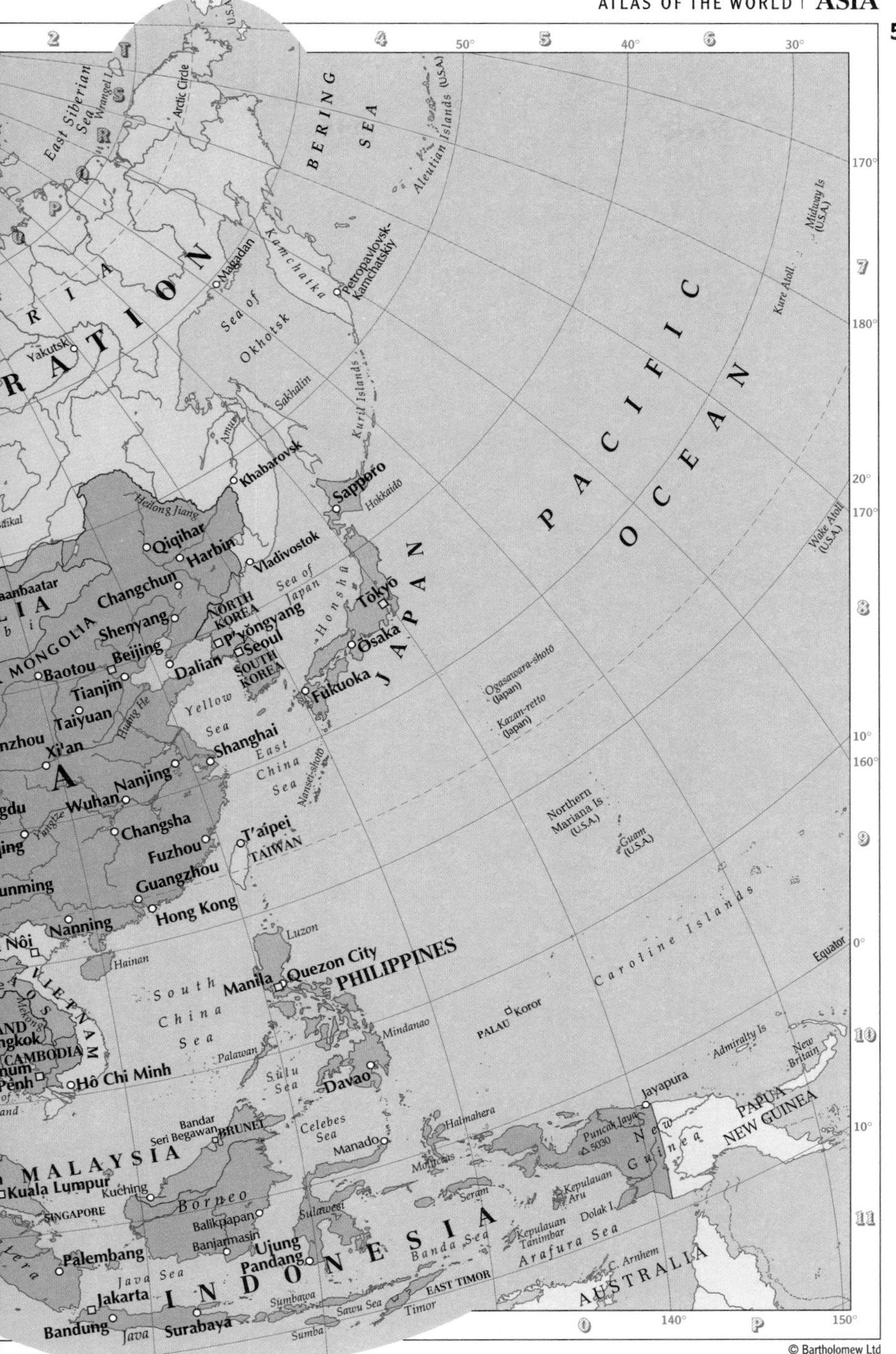

East Siberian Sea
Wrangel I
Arctic Circle
U.S.A.

BERING SEA

Aleutian Islands (U.S.A.)

Midway Is (U.S.A.)

170°
180°
170°
160°

RATION

ERIA

P

RIA

Yakutsk

Magadan

Kamchatka

Petropavlovsk-Kamchatskiy

Sea of Okhotsk

Sakhalin

Kuril Islands

Kure Atoll

Wake Atoll (U.S.A.)

PACIFIC OCEAN

Hedong Jiang

Qiqihar

Harbin

Khabarovsk

Sapporo

Hokkaidō

Vladivostok

Sea of Japan

Changchun

NORTH KOREA

P'yŏngyang

Tokyo

JAPAN

Honshū

aanbaatar

MONGOLIA

Shenyang

Seoul

SOUTH KOREA

Ōsaka

Ogasawara-shotō (Japan)

Baotou

Beijing

Dalian

Fukuoka

Kazan-rettō (Japan)

Tianjin

Huang He

Yellow Sea

Taiyuan

A

Xi'an

Shanghai

East China Sea

Nanjing

Northern Mariana Is (U.S.A.)

Wuhan

Changsha

T'aipei

Guam (U.S.A.)

Fuzhou

TAIWAN

Guangzhou

Hong Kong

Luzon

Caroline Islands

Nanning

Quezon City

PHILIPPINES

Equator 0°

Hainan

South China Sea

Manila

Koror

VIETNAM

Mindanao

PALAU

New Britain

Bangkok

CAMBODIA

Hô Chi Minh

Sulu Sea

Davao

Admiralty Is

Penh

Palawan

Jayapura

PAPUA NEW GUINEA

10°

MALAYSIA

Bandar Seri Begawan

BRUNEI

Celebes Sea

Manado

Halmahera

Puncak Jaya

New Guinea

Kuala Lumpur

Kuching

Borneo

Sulawesi

Seram

Kepulauan Aru

SINGAPORE

Balikpapan

Kepulauan Tanimbar

Dolak I.

Palembang

Banjarmasin

Ujung

Banda Sea

C. Arnhem

Java Sea

Pandang

EAST TIMOR

Arafura Sea

INDONESIA

AUSTRALIA

Jakarta

Sumbawa

Sawu Sea

Timor

Bandung

Java

Surabaya

Sumba

140°
150°

© Bartholomew Ltd

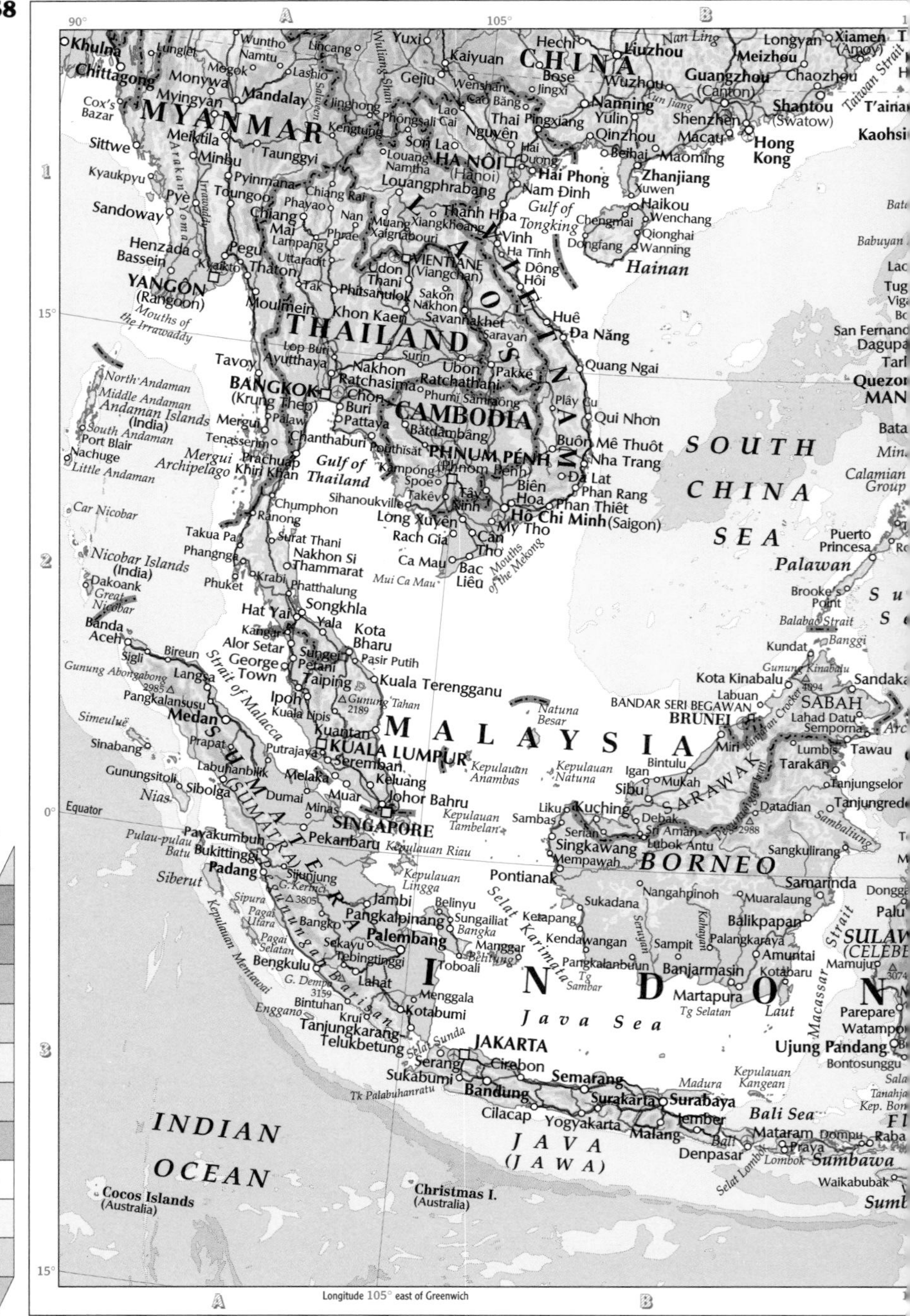

Albers Equal Area Conic Projection

1 : 25 000 000

MILES 0   250

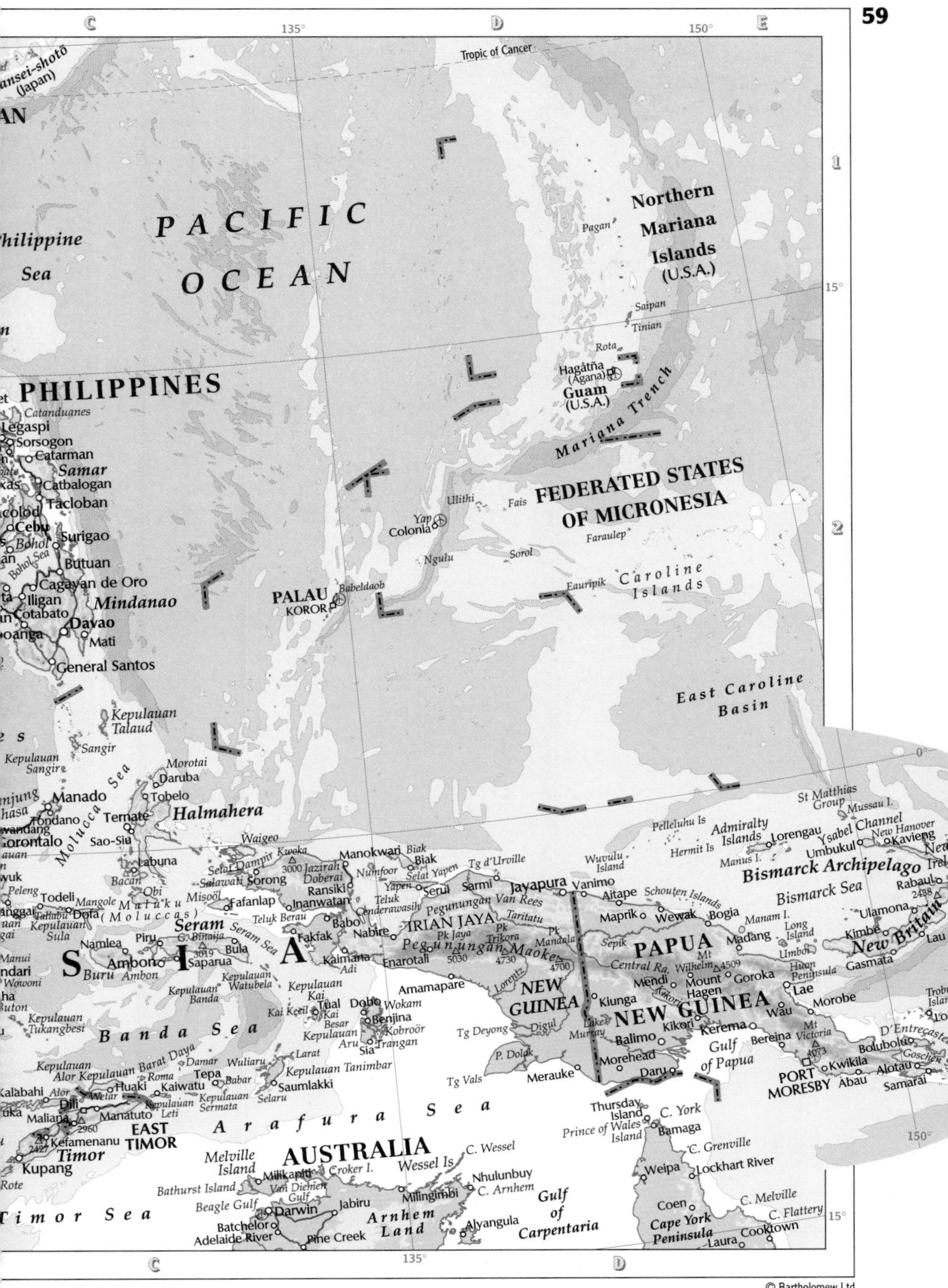

135° · D · 150° · E

Tropic of Cancer

ansei-shotō
(Japan)

PACIFIC

AN

Philippine
Sea

OCEAN

Northern
Mariana
Islands
(U.S.A.)

Pagan

15°

Saipan
Tinian

n

PHILIPPINES

Rota

Hagåtña
(Agana)
Guam
(U.S.A.)

Mariana Trench

FEDERATED STATES
OF MICRONESIA

et
Catanduanes
Legaspi
Sorsogon
Catarman
as
Samar
Catbalogan
colod
Tacloban
Cebu
Surigao
Bohol
Butuan
an
Bohol Sea
Cagayan de Oro
Iligan
Cotabato
Mindanao
oanga
Davao
Mati
General Santos

Yap
Colonia

Ulithi

Fais

Faraulep

Ngulu

Sorol

Eauripik

*Caroline
Islands*

East Caroline
Basin

PALAU
KOROR
Babeldaob

*Kepulauan
Talaud*

0°

*Kepulauan
Sangire*

Sangir

Morotai
Daruba

Tobelo

St Matthias
Group

Mussau I.

hasa
Pidono
Manado
nwandang
Gorontalo
Sao-Siu
Ternate

Halmahera

Waigeo

Admiralty
Hermit Is Islands

Pelleluhu Is

Isabel Channel
Lorengau
Manus I.
Umbukul
Kavieng
New Hanover

Bismarck Archipelago Ireland

Peleng
Todeli
Labuna
Bacan
Obi
Mangole
Matu'ku
Misool
Kwoka
Doberai
Ransiki
Nimfoor

Selat Dampir Sorong

3000 Jazirah

Manokwari Biak

Selat Yapen
Yapen

Sermu Sarmi

Tg d'Urville

Wuvulu
Island

Vanimo

Schouten Islands

Aitape

Wewak
Maprik

Manam I.

Bismarck Sea

Bogia

Ulamona
2438

Rabaul

New

nggai
Kepulauan
Luan
Tatabu Dola
(Moluccas)

Seram

Salawati
Inanwatan

Teluk Berau
Fakfak

Teluk
Onderawasih
Pegunungan Van Rees

Babo
Nabire

IRIAN JAYA
Pk Jaya

Jayapura

Pegunungan

Taritatu

Madang

Mt

New Britain

Kimbe

Umboi

Lau

Manui
ndari
Wowoni
buton

Piru
Ambon

Namlea
Saparua

Buru

S

Bula

I

Ambon

Kaimana

Adi

Enarotali

Pk Trikora
Mandala
Maoke
4700
5030

Sepik

Central Ra.
Mendi

Mt
Wilhelm 4509
Mount
Hagen

Huon
Peninsula

Goroka

Gasmata

Trobriand
Islands

PAPUA

Morobe

Wau

D'Entrecasteaux
Is

rosula

Goschen Strait

Kepulauan
Watubela
Kepulauan
Banda

Banda Sea

Kepulauan
Kai Kecil
Kai

Dobo
Besar

Kepulauan

Amamapare

**NEW
GUINEA**

Lorentz

NEW GUINEA

Kiunga

Kikori
Kerema

Bereina
Victoria

PORT
MORESBY

Kwikila
Abau

Alotau
Samarai

Kepulauan
Barat Daya
Alor Kepulauan

Damar Wuliaru
Roma

Benjina
Kobroör

Wokam
Aru

Tg Deyong

Digul

Murray

Balimo

Morehead

Gulf
of Papua

Daru

Arafura Sea

Kepulauan
Serdata
Kefamenanu
TIMOR

Alor
Weri
Huaki
Leti

Tepa
Kaiwatu

Damar
Babar

Larat

Kepulauan Tanimbar
Saumlakki

P. Dolak
Tg Vals

Merauke

Thursday
Island
Prince of Wales
Island

C. York
Bamaga

EAST

AUSTRALIA

C. Wessel

C. Grenville

Maliana
Dili
Manatuto

Kalabahi
tika

2960

Kupang

Rote

**Timor
Sea**

Melville
Island

Bathurst Island

Beagle Gulf

Batchelor
Adelaide River

Milikapiti

Van Diemen
Gulf

Darwin

Jabiru

Pine Creek

Croker I.

Wessel Is

Nhulunbuy

C. Arnhem

Milingimbi

Alyangula

*Arnhem
Land*

Gulf
of
Carpentaria

Welpa
Lockhart River

Coen

C. Melville

Cape York
Peninsula

Laura

C. Flattery

Cooktown

15°

135° · C · D

© Bartholomew Ltd

250 · 500 · 750 KILOMETRES

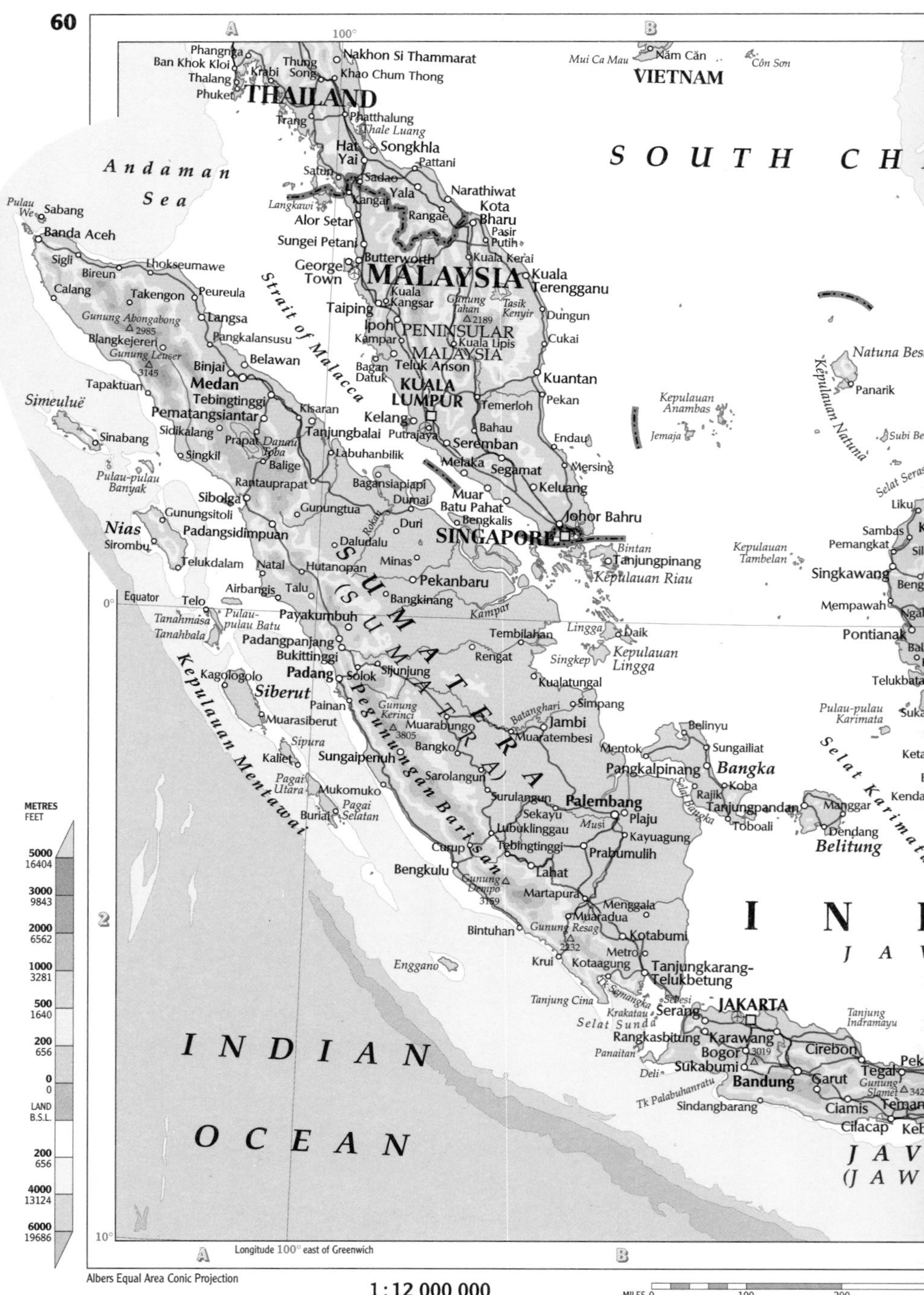

100°

A

B

Phangnga
Ban Khok Kloi
Thalang
Phuket

Thung
Krabi Song

Nakhon Si Thammarat
Khao Chum Thong

Mui Ca Mau
Nam Căn
Côn Son

VIETNAM

Trang
Phatthalung
Thale Luang

Andaman
Sea

Hat
Yai
Songkhla

Satun
Pattani

S O U T H   C H I

Pulau
We
Sabang

Langkawi
Yala
Narathiwat

Banda Aceh

Langsa
Kangar

Rangae
Kota
Bharu

Sigli
Bireun
Lhokseumawe
Sungei Petani

Pasir
Putih

Kuala Kerai

Calang
Takengon
Peureula

George
Town
Butterworth

Kuala
Terengganu

Gunung Abongabong
△2985
Langsa
Taiping

Kuala
Kangsar

MALAYSIA

Blangkejeren
Pangkalansusu
Ipoh

Gunung
Tahan
△2189

Tasik
Kenyir

Dungun

Gunung Leuser
△3145
Binjai
Belawan
Bagan
Datuk

PENINSULAR
MALAYSIA
Kampar

Kuala Lipis

Cukai

Simeuluë

Medan
Tebingtinggi
Kisaran

Teluk Anson

Kuantan

Pematangsiantar

KUALA
LUMPUR

Temerloh
Pekan

Kepulauan
Anambas

Sinabang
Sidikalang
Prapat
Danau
Toba

Tanjungbalai

Kelang

Putrajaya
Bahau

Endau

Jemaja

Singkil
Balige
Labuhanbilik
Seremban

Mersing

Pulau-pulau
Banyak
Sibolga
Rantauprapat
Bagansiapiapi

Melaka
Segamat

Keluang

Nias
Sirombu
Gunungsitoli
Gunungtua

Dumai
Duri

Muar
Batu Pahat
Bengkalis

Johor Bahru

Padangsidimpuan
Daludalu

SINGAPORE

Bintan
Tanjungpinang

Kepulauan
Tambelan

Telukdalam
Natal
Hutanopan
Minas

Pekanbaru

Kepulauan Riau

Airbangis
Talu
Bangkinang

0°
Equator
Telo
Tanahmasa
Tanahbala
Pulau-
pulau Batu
Payakumbuh

Kampar
Lingga
Daik

Kepulauan Mentawai
Padangpanjang
Bukittinggi
Padang
Solok
Sijunjung

Tembilahan

Rengat

Singkep

Kepulauan
Lingga

Painan
Gunung
Kerinci
△3805

Kualatungal

Simpang

Pulau-pulau
Karimata

Sipura
Muarasiberut

Muarabungo
Muaratembesi

Jambi

Belinyu

Kaliet
Sungaipenuh

Bangko

Mentok
Sungailiat

Pagai
Utara
Mukomuko

Sarolangun

Pangkalpinang
Bangka

Pagai
Selatan
Burai

Surulangun
Palembang

Rajik
Koba

Tanjungpandan
Manggar

Sekayu
Lubuklinggau
Plaju

Toboali

Dendang
Belitung

Curup
Tebingtinggi
Prabumulih

Musi
Kayuagung

Bengkulu
Lahat

Martapura

Gunung
Dempo
△3159

Menggala

Muaradua

I N

J A W

Bintuhan
Gunung Resag

Kotabumi

Gunung
△3332

Krui
Kotaagung
Metro

JAKARTA

Enggano
Tanjung Cina
Serang

Tanjungkarang-
Telukbetung

Tanjung
Indramayu

I N D I A N

Krakatau
Panaitan
Selat Sunda

Rangkasbitung
Karawang

Cirebon

Deli

Sukabumi
Bogor
△3019

Tk Palabuhanratu
Bandung

Garut

Tegal

O C E A N

Sindangbarang

Ciamis

Cilacap

J A V
(J A W

Albers Equal Area Conic Projection

1 : 12 000 000

MILES 0
100
200

METRES
FEET

5000
16404

3000
9843

2000
6562

1000
3281

500
1640

200
656

0
0

LAND
B.S.L.

200
656

4000
13124

6000
19686

Strait of Malacca

S U M A T E R A

Selat Serasa

Kepulauan Natuna

Natuna Besa

Panarik

Subi Bes

Liku
Sambas
Pemangkat

K
Silu

Singkawang

Bengk

Mempawah

Ngal

Pontianak

Bala
K

Telukbata

Suka

Keta

Bi

Selat Karimat a

Kenda

2

10°

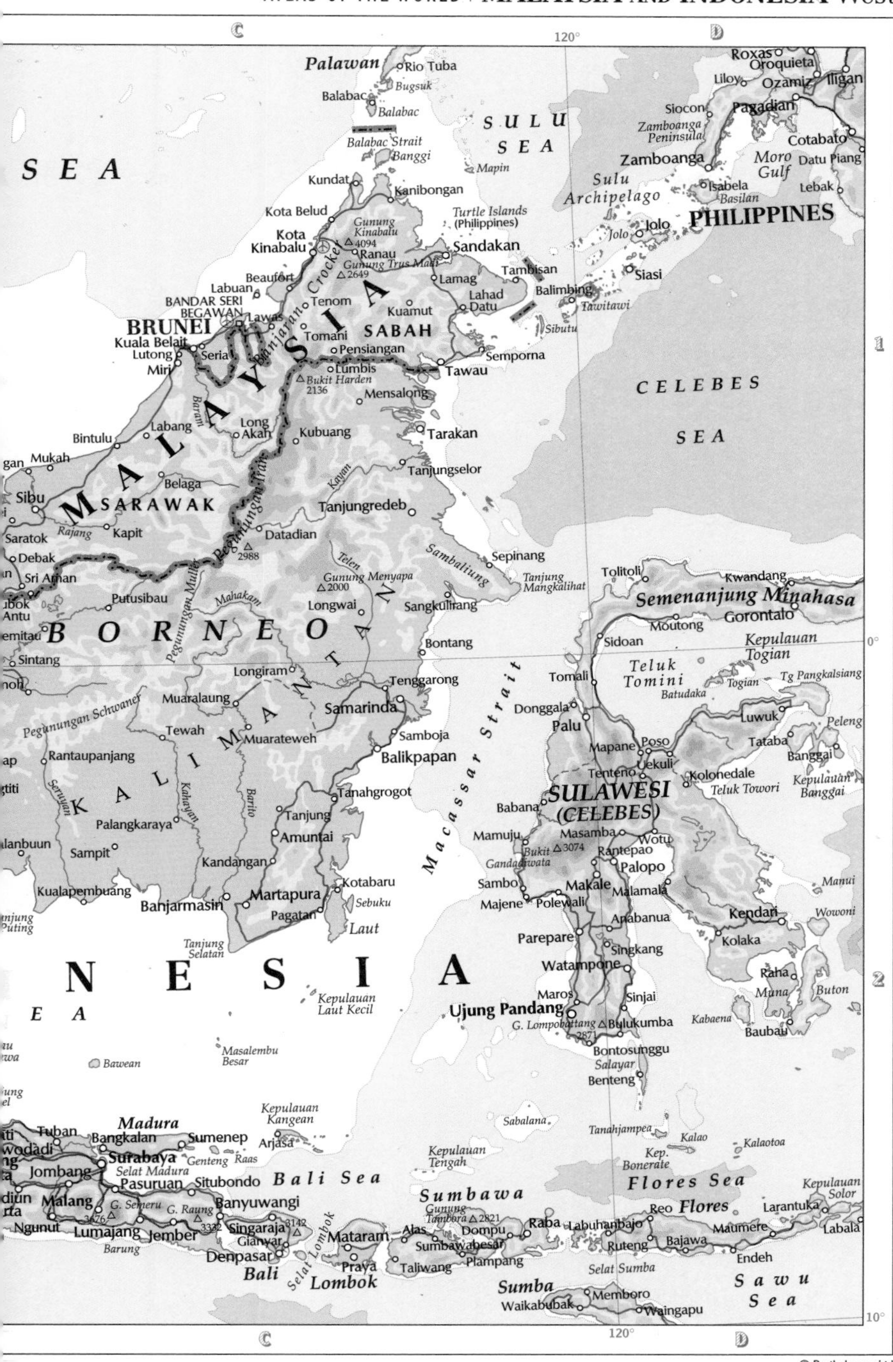

120°

Palawan
Rio Tuba
Balabac Bugsuk
Balabac
Balabac Strait
Banggi
Kundat
Kanibongan
Kota Belud
Gunung
Kota Kinabalu
Kinabalu △4094
Ranau
Gunung Trus Madi
Beaufort △2649
Labuan
Lamag
BANDAR SERI
BEGAWAN
BRUNEI Tenom
Kuala Belait Kuamut
Lutong Seria Tomani
Miri Lumbis
△ Bukit Harden
2136 Mensalong
Labang Long
Bintulu Akah Kubuang
Mukah Belaga
Sibu **SARAWAK**
Saratok Rajang Kapit
Debak Datadian
Sri Aman △2988
Putusibau Longwai
Antu
Sintang Longiram
Muaralaung
Tewah Muarateweh
Rantaupanjang
Palangkaraya Tanjung
Amuntai
Sampit Kandangan
Kualapembuang Kotabaru
Banjarmasin Martapura Sebuku
Pagatan
Tanjung
Selatan *Laut*

S U L U
S E A
Mapin
Turtle Islands
(Philippines)
Sandakan
Tambisan
Lahad
Datu
Balimbing
Semporna
Tawau

Siocon
Zamboanga
Peninsula
Zamboanga
Sulu
Archipelago
Jolo Jolo
Isabela
Basilan
Siasi
Tawitawi
Sibutu

Roxas
Oroquieta
Liloy Ozamiz Iligan
Pagadian
Cotabato
Moro Datu Piang
Gulf Lebak

PHILIPPINES

C E L E B E S

S E A

Tarakan
Tanjungselor
Tanjungredeb
Sepinang
Tolitoli Kwandang
Semenanjung Minahasa
Gorontalo
Moutong
Bontang Sidoan *Kepulauan*
Togian
Tomali *Teluk* Togian Tg Pangkalsiang
Tomini Togian Batudaka
Donggala Palu Luwuk
Mapane Poso Tataba Peleng
Uekuli Banggai
Tentena Kolonedale *Kepulauan*
Babana Teluk Towori Banggai
SULAWESI
(CELEBES)
Mamuju Masamba
Bukit △3074 Wotu Manui
Gandadiwata Rantepao
Sambo Palopo Wowoni
Majene Polewali Malamala
Apabanua Kendari
Parepare Kolaka
Singkang
Watampone
Maros Sinjai Raha Buton
Mana
Ujung Pandang Kabaena Baubau
G. Lompobattang △Bulukumba
2871
Bontosunggu
Salayar
Benteng

Mahakam
Kutai

Barito

Macassar Strait

I N D O N E S I A
Kepulauan
Laut Kecil
Tanjung
Puting

Bintulu

Barun

Bangkalan Sumenep Arjasa
Tuban
Madura Raas
Surabaya Genteng
Jombang Selat Madura
Pasuruan Situbondo *Bali Sea*
Malang Banyuwangi
G. Semeru G. Raung
Ngunut Lumajang Jember Singaraja
Gianyar
Denpasar Mataram
Bali Praya
Lombok

Kepulauan
Kangean
Kepulauan
Tengah

Sabalana
Tanahjampea Kalao Kalaotoa
Kep.
Bonerate
Kepulauan
Flores Sea Solor
Sumbawa Larantuka Labala
Gunung
Tambora △2821
Alas Raba Labuhanbajo *Flores* Maumere
Sumbawabesar Ruteng Bajawa
Plampang Endeh
Sumba Selat Sumba *S a w u*
Waikabubak Memboro *S e a*
Waingapu

120°

Masalembu
Besar
Bawean

200   400 KILOMETRES

© Bartholomew Ltd

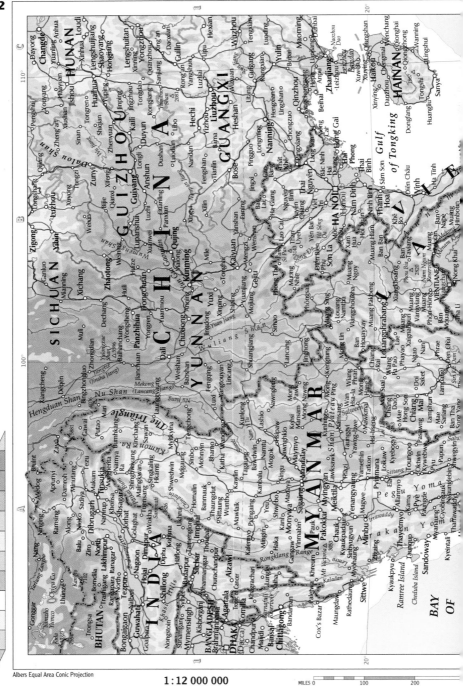

Albers Equal Area Conic Projection

1:12 000 000

METRES
FEET

5000	16404
3000	9843
2000	6562
1000	3281
500	1640
200	656
0	0
LAND B.S.L.	
200	656
4000	13124
6000	19686

MILES 0   100   200

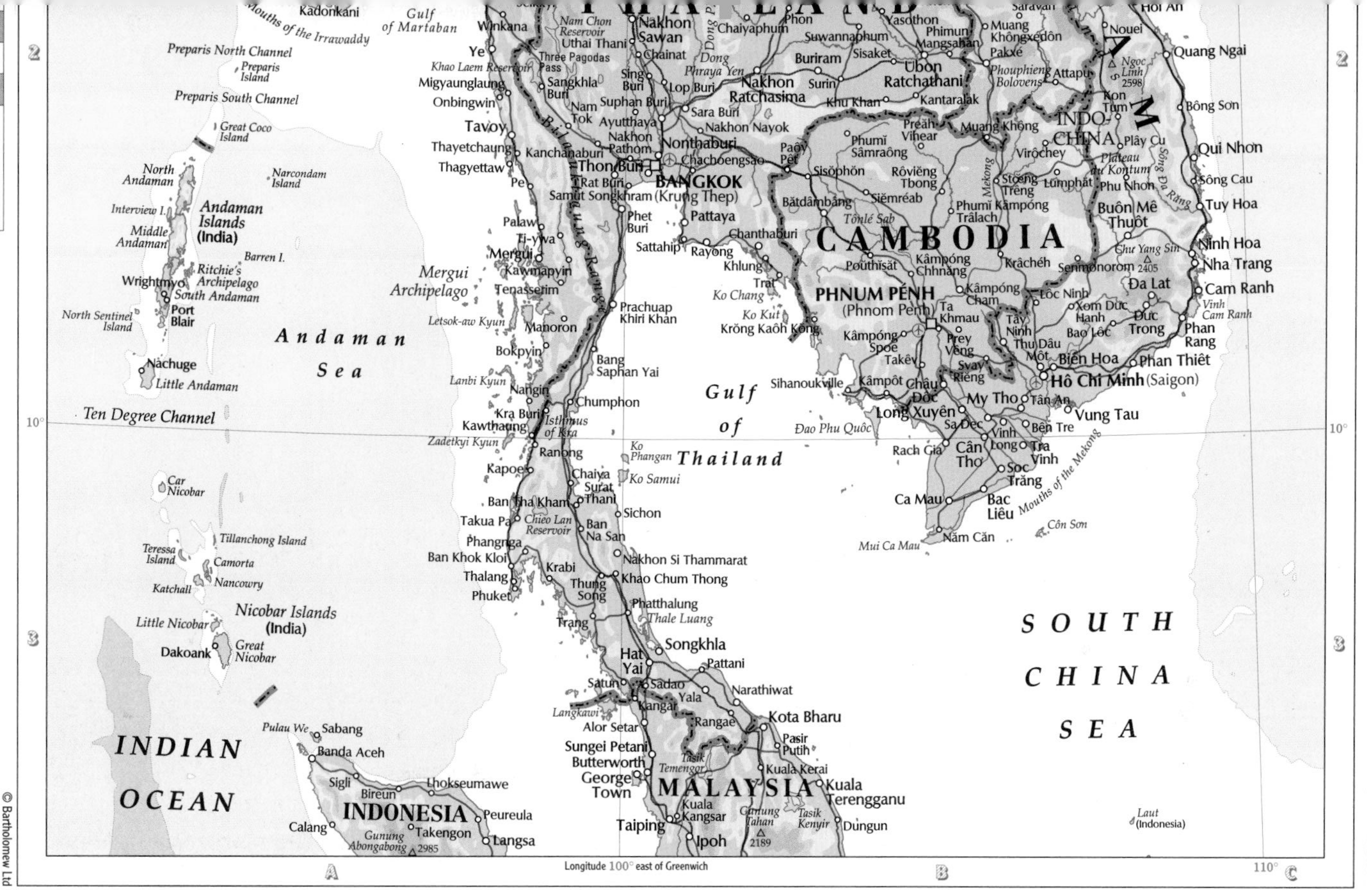
CAMBODIA
PHNUM PÉNH
(Phnom Penh)
BANGKOK
(Krung Thep)
MALAYSIA
INDONESIA
S O U T H
C H I N A
S E A
Gulf of Thailand
Andaman Sea
INDIAN OCEAN
Gulf of Martaban
Mouths of the Irrawaddy
Mouths of the Mekong
Preparis North Channel
Preparis Island
Preparis South Channel
Great Coco Island
North Andaman
Narcondam Island
Interview I.
Middle Andaman
Andaman Islands (India)
Barren I.
Ritchie's Archipelago
South Andaman
Wrightmyo
Port Blair
North Sentinel Island
Nachuge
Little Andaman
Ten Degree Channel
Car Nicobar
Tillanchong Island
Teressa Island
Camorta
Nancowry
Katchall
Nicobar Islands (India)
Little Nicobar
Great Nicobar
Dakoank
Mergui Archipelago
Letsok-aw Kyun
Lanbi Kyun
Zadetkyi Kyun
Kadonkani
Winkana
Ye
Khao Laem Reservoir
Migyaunglaung
Onbingwin
Tavoy
Thayetchaung
Thagyettaw
Pe
Palaw
Ti-ywa
Mergui
Kawmapyin
Tenasserim
Manoron
Bokpyin
Nangin
Kra Buri
Kawthaung
Isthmus of Kra
Ranong
Kapoe
Ban Tha Kham
Takua Pa
Chieo Lan Reservoir
Phangnga
Ban Khok Kloi
Thalang
Phuket
Krabi
Trang
Satun
Langkawi
Alor Setar
Sungei Petani
Butterworth
George Town
Taiping
Kuala Kangsar
Ipoh
Tasik Temengor
Gunung Tahan 2189
Tasik Kenyir
Dungun
Kuala Terengganu
Kuala Kerai
Pasir Putih
Kota Bharu
Rangae
Narathiwat
Yala
Kangar
Sadao
Hat Yai
Pattani
Songkhla
Thale Luang
Phatthalung
Thung Song
Khao Chum Thong
Nakhon Si Thammarat
Ban Na San
Sichon
Surat Thani
Chaiya
Ko Samui
Ko Phangan
Chumphon
Bang Saphan Yai
Prachuap Khiri Khan
Bilauktaung Range
Nam Chon Reservoir
Uthai Thani
Three Pagodas Pass
Sangkhla Buri
Nam Tok
Kanchanaburi
Nakhon Pathom
Thon Buri
Rat Buri
Samut Songkhram
Phet Buri
Sattahip
Rayong
Pattaya
Chanthaburi
Khlung
Trat
Ko Chang
Ko Kut
Krŏng Kaôh Kŏng
Nakhon Sawan
Chainat
Sing Buri
Suphan Buri
Ayutthaya
Lop Buri
Sara Buri
Nonthaburi
Chachoengsao
Nakhon Nayok
Dong Phraya Yen
Chaiyaphum
Nakhon Ratchasima
Buriram
Surin
Sisaket
Suwannaphum
Yasothon
Ubon Ratchathani
Kantaralak
Khu Khan
Paôy Pêt
Sisŏphŏn
Bătdâmbâng
Tônlé Sab
Siĕmréab
Phumĭ Sâmraông
Preăh Vihear
Rôviĕng Tbong
Phumĭ Kâmpóng Trâlach
Pouthĭsăt
Kâmpóng Chhnăng
Kâmpóng Cham
Krâchéh
Sênmônoŭrôm
Ta Khmau
Prey Vêng
Svay Riĕng
Takêv
Kâmpóng Spoe
Kâmpôt
Sihanoukville
Đao Phu Quôc
Châu Đôc
Long Xuyên
Rach Gia
Sa Đec
Cân Thơ
My Tho
Vinh Long
Tra Vinh
Bên Tre
Soc Trăng
Bac Liêu
Ca Mau
Năm Căn
Mui Ca Mau
Côn Sơn
Tân An
Vung Tau
Hô Chi Minh (Saigon)
Biên Hoa
Thu Dâu Môt
Tây Ninh
Lôc Ninh
Bao Lôc
Xom Dưc Hanh
Đưc Trong
Đa Lat
Phan Thiêt
Phan Rang
Vinh Cam Ranh
Cam Ranh
Nha Trang
Ninh Hoa
Chu Yang Sin 2405
Buôn Mê Thuôt
Tuy Hoa
Sông Cau
Qui Nhơn
Sông Đa Rang
Phu Nhơn
Plateau du Kontum
Plây Cu
Kon Tum
Ngoc Linh 2598
Bông Sơn
Quang Ngai
Hoi An
Nouei
Attapu
Phouphieng Bolovens
Pakxé
Muang Khôngxédôn
Muang Khŏng
Mangsahan
Phimun
INDO-CHINA
Virôchey
Stœng Trêng
Lumphăt
Mekong
Saravan
Laut (Indonesia)
Pulau We
Sabang
Banda Aceh
Sigli
Bireun
Lhokseumawe
Peureula
Langsa
Takengon
Gunung Abongabong 2985
Calang
Longitude 100° east of Greenwich
10°
110°
A
B
C
2
3
200
400 KILOMETRES

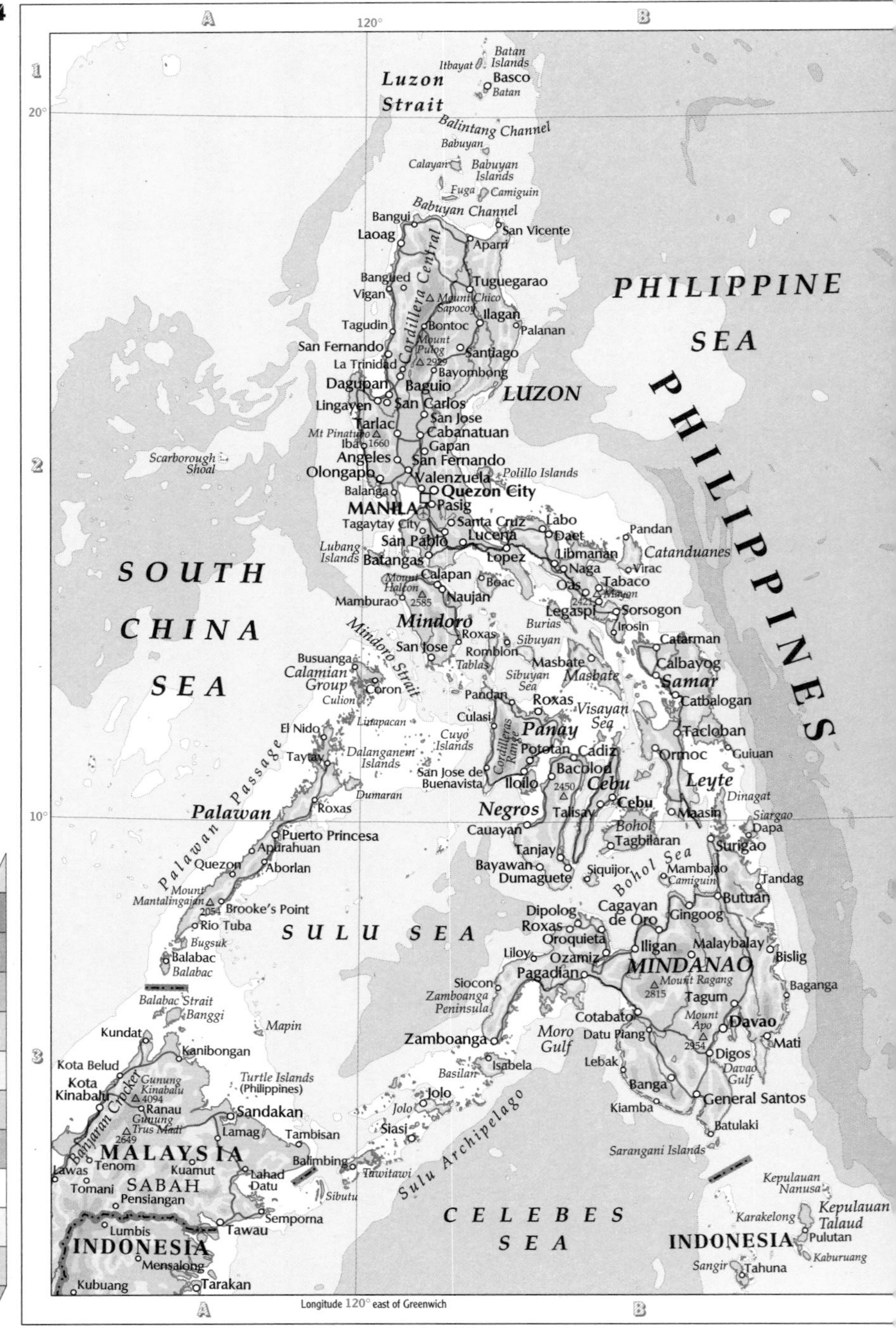

Longitude 120° east of Greenwich

Albers Equal Area Conic Projection

1 : 12 000 000

METRES
FEET

5000
16404

3000
9843

2000
6562

1000
3281

500
1640

200
656

0
0

LAND
B.S.L.

200
656

4000
13124

6000
19686

KILOMETRES 0   200

MILES 0   100   200

SEA

OF

JAPAN

Korea Bay

YELLOW

SEA

(HUANG HAI)

Cheju-haehyŏp

Cheju-do
(S. Korea)

JAPAN

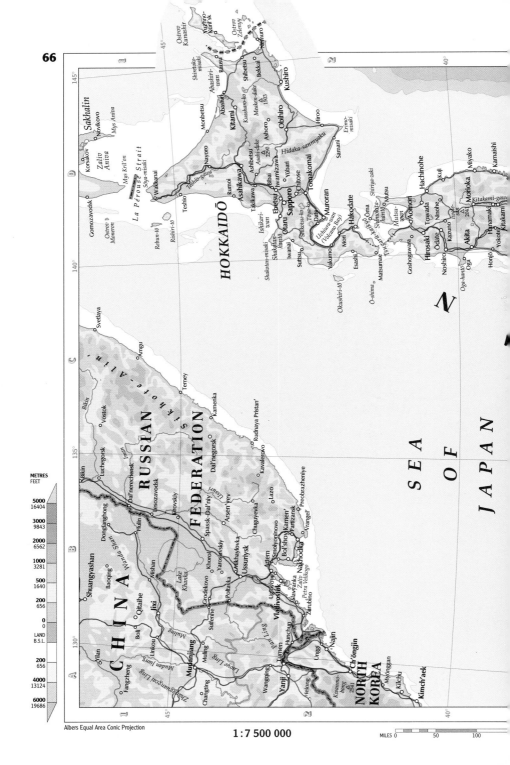

METRES
FEET

5000	16404
3000	9843
2000	6562
1000	3281
500	1640
200	656
0	0
LAND	B.S.L.
200	656
4000	13124
6000	19686

Albers Equal Area Conic Projection

1 : 7 500 000

MILES 0   50   100

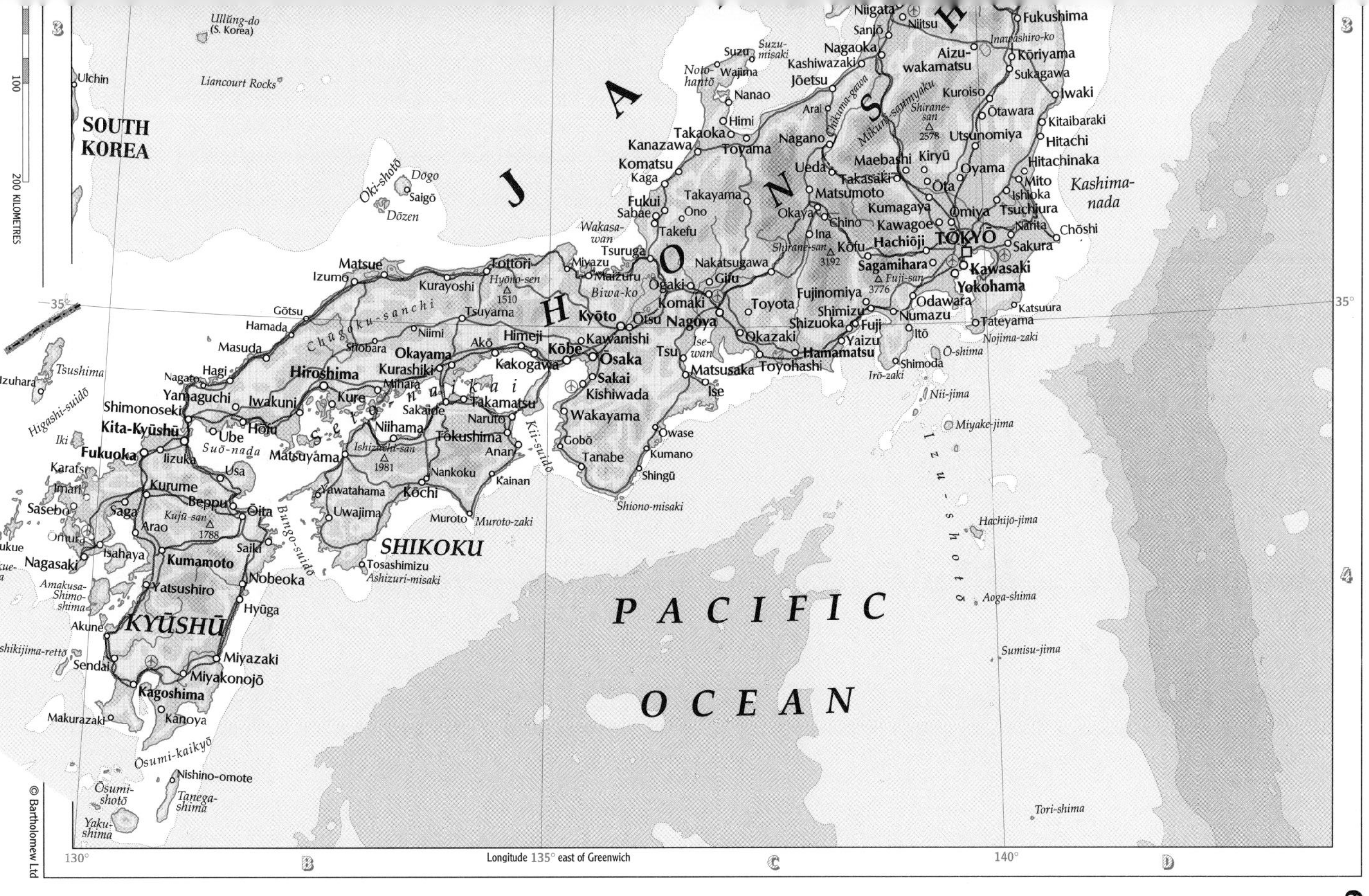

PACIFIC

OCEAN

SHIKOKU

KYŪSHŪ

SOUTH
KOREA

Izu-shotō

TOKYO
Yokohama
Kawasaki

Kyōto
Ōsaka
Kōbe

Hiroshima

Fukuoka
Kita-Kyūshū

Nagasaki

Kagoshima

Kumamoto

Tori-shima

Sumisu-jima

Aoga-shima

Hachijō-jima

Miyake-jima

Longitude 135° east of Greenwich

© Bartholomew Ltd

100   200 KILOMETRES

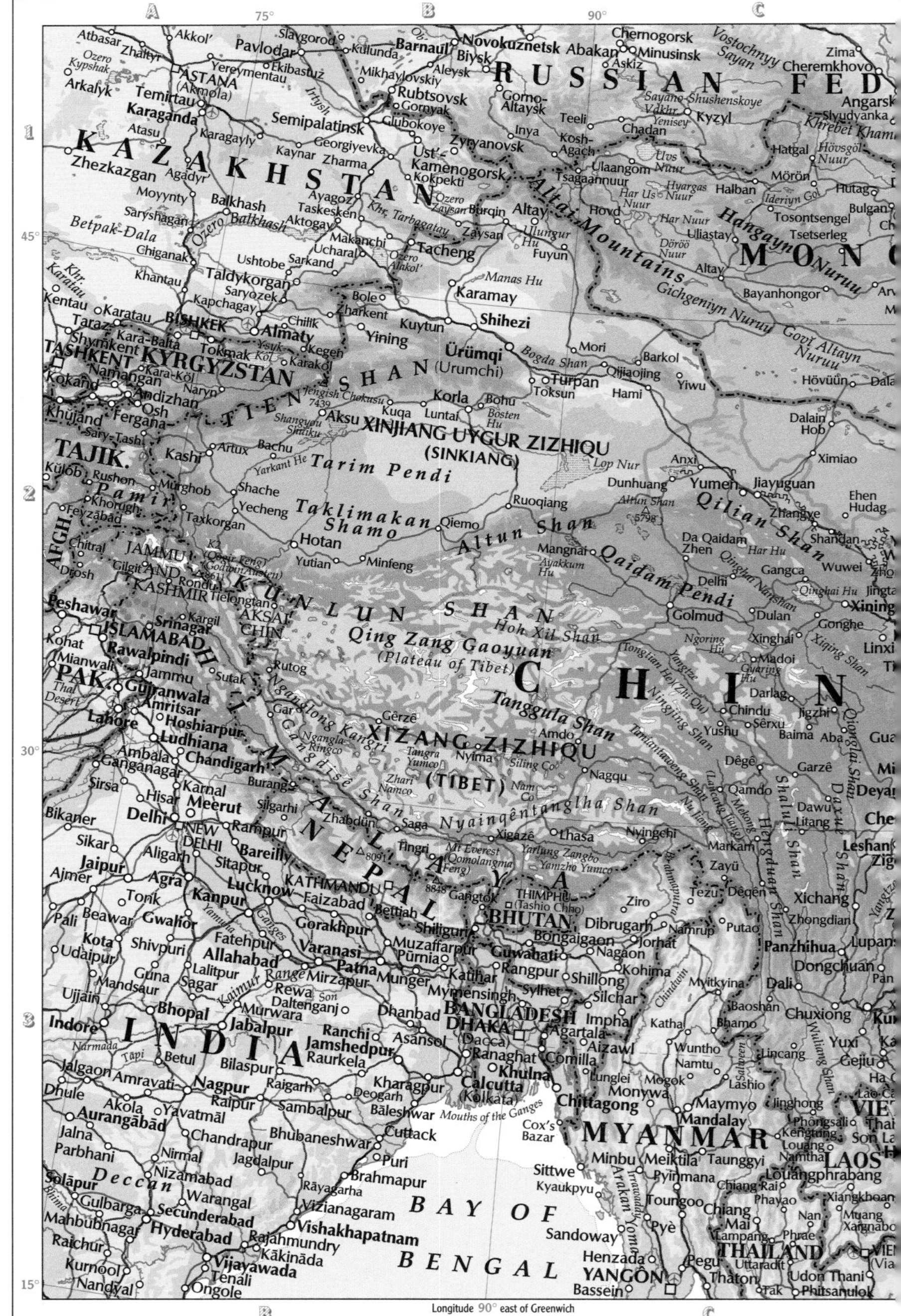

METRES
FEET

5000
16404

3000
9843

2000
6562

1000
3281

500
1640

200
656

0
0
LAND
B.S.L.

200
656

4000
13124

6000
19686

Longitude 90° east of Greenwich

Albers Equal Area Conic Projection

1 : 25 000 000

MILES 0   250

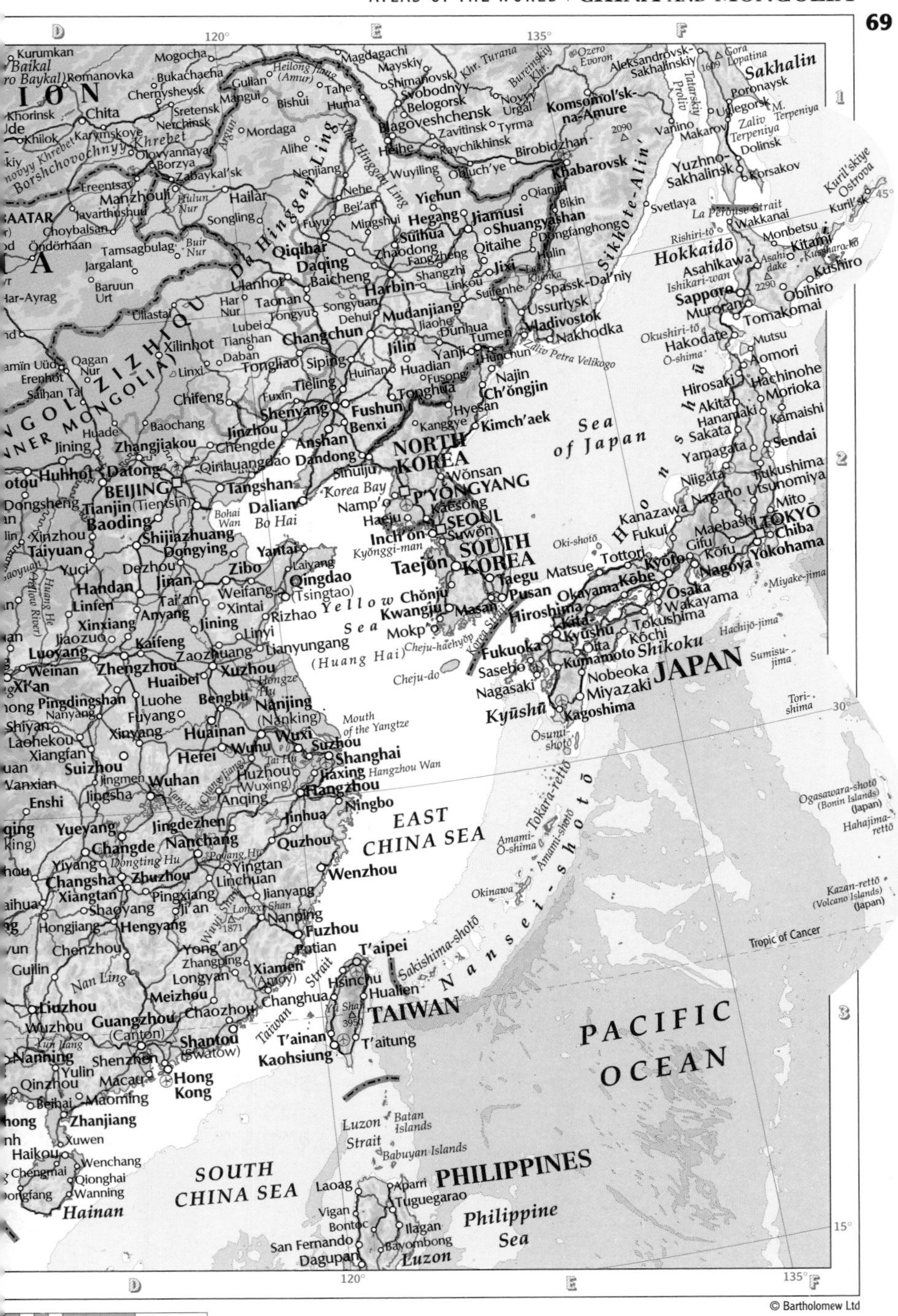
D
E
F
120°
135°
45°
30°
15°
1
2
3
Sakhalin
Poronaysk
Uglegorsk
Zaliv Terpeniya
Dolinsk
Yuzhno-Sakhalinsk
Korsakov
Kuril'skiye Ostrova
Kuril'sk
La Pérouse Strait
Wakkanai
Monbetsu
Kitami
Kushiro
Obihiro
Rishiri-tō
Hokkaidō
Asahikawa
Asahi-dake
2290
Ishikari-wan
Sapporo
Muroran
Tomakomai
Okushiri-tō
Hakodate
Ō-shima
Mutsu
Aomori
Hirosaki
Hachinohe
Morioka
Akita
Hanamaki
Kamaishi
Sakata
Sendai
Yamagata
Niigata
Fukushima
Utsunomiya
Mito
Nagano
Maebashi
TŌKYŌ
Chiba
Kanazawa
Fukui
Gifu
Kōfu
Yokohama
Nagoya
Kyōto
Ōsaka
Kōbe
Wakayama
Miyake-jima
Tottori
Matsue
Okayama
Hiroshima
Tokushima
Kōchi
Shikoku
Hachijō-jima
Fukuoka
Kitakyūshū
Ōita
Kumamoto
Nobeoka
Miyazaki
Kagoshima
Sasebo
Nagasaki
Kyūshū
JAPAN
Sumisu-jima
Tori-shima
Ōsumi-shotō
Honshū
Oki-shotō
Sea of Japan
Tatarskiy Proliv
Vanino
Makarov
Komsomol'sk-na-Amure
Khabarovsk
Birobidzhan
Sikhote-Alin'
Svetlaya
Aleksandrovsk-Sakhalinskiy
Ozero Evoron
Bureinskiy Khr.
Khr. Turana
Magdagachi
Mayskiy
Shimanovsk
Svobodnyy
Belogorsk
Novyy Urgal
Blagoveshchensk
Zavitinsk
Tyrma
Heihe
Raychikhinsk
Obluch'ye
Wuyiling
Yichun
Hegang
Jiamusi
Shuangyashan
Qitaihe
Bikin
Dongfanghong
Jixi
Hulin
Spassk-Dal'niy
Ussuriysk
Vladivostok
Nakhodka
Zaliv Petra Velikogo
Suifenhe
Linkou
Mudanjiang
Harbin
Shangzhi
Suihua
Zhaodong
Fangzheng
Daqing
Qiqihar
Baicheng
Ulanhot
Taonan
Songyuan
Dehui
Changchun
Jilin
Dunhua
Tumen
Yanji
Hunchun
Huadian
Huinan
Siping
Tongliao
Tieling
Fushun
Shenyang
Benxi
Anshan
Jinzhou
Chifeng
Dandong
Tonghua
Hyesan
Kanggye
Najin
Ch'ŏngjin
Kimch'aek
NORTH KOREA
Sinuiju
Wŏnsan
P'YŎNGYANG
Korea Bay
Namp'o
Haeju
Kaesŏng
SEOUL
Inch'ŏn
Suwŏn
Kyŏnggi-man
SOUTH KOREA
Taejŏn
Taegu
Pusan
Masan
Chŏnju
Kwangju
Mokp'o
Korea Strait
Cheju-haehyŏp
Cheju-do
Yellow Sea
(Huang Hai)
Bohai Wan
Bo Hai
Dalian
Yantai
Laiyang
Qingdao
(Tsingtao)
Weifang
Xintai
Rizhao
Linyi
Lianyungang
Zibo
Jinan
Dezhou
Dongying
Tai'an
Jining
Shijiazhuang
Tianjin (Tientsin)
BEIJING
Tangshan
Qinhuangdao
Chengde
Zhangjiakou
Datong
Hohhot
Baotou
Dongsheng
Baoding
Taiyuan
Xinzhou
Yuci
Handan
Linfen
Anyang
Xinxiang
Jiaozuo
Kaifeng
Luoyang
Zhengzhou
Weinan
Xi'an
Zaozhuang
Xuzhou
Huaibei
Pingdingshan
Nanyang
Luohe
Bengbu
Hongze Hu
Fuyang
Xinyang
Huainan
Nanjing
(Nanking)
Mouth of the Yangtze
Wuxi
Suzhou
Shanghai
Tai Hu
Jiaxing
Hangzhou Wan
Huzhou
(Wuxing)
Hangzhou
Wuhu
Hefei
Anqing
Ningbo
Jinhua
Shiyan
Laohekou
Xiangfan
Suizhou
Jingmen
Wuhan
Jingsha
Enshi
Yangtze (Chang Jiang)
Yueyang
Jingdezhen
Changde
Nanchang
Poyang Hu
Yiyang
Dongting Hu
Changsha
Zhuzhou
Xiangtan
Yingtan
Linchuan
Quzhou
EAST CHINA SEA
Wenzhou
Shaoyang
Hengyang
Pingxiang
Ji'an
Jianyang
Longxi Shan
1871
Wuyi Shan
Nanping
Fuzhou
Hongjiang
Chenzhou
Yong'an
Zhangping
Putian
Xiamen
(Amoy)
Longyan
Guilin
Nan Ling
Meizhou
Taiwan Strait
Chaozhou
Changhua
Liuzhou
Wuzhou
Guangzhou
(Canton)
Xun Jiang
Shantou
(Swatow)
Nanning
Shenzhen
Hong Kong
Yulin
Macau
Qinzhou
Beihai
Maoming
Zhanjiang
Xuwen
Haikou
Wenchang
Chengmai
Qionghai
Wanning
Hainan
T'aipei
Hsinchu
Hualien
TAIWAN
Yü Shan
3950
T'ainan
T'aitung
Kaohsiung
Sakishima-shotō
Nansei-shotō
Okinawa
Amami-Ō-shima
Amami-shotō
Tokara-rettō
Ogasawara-shotō
(Bonin Islands)
(Japan)
Hahajima-rettō
Kazan-rettō
(Volcano Islands)
(Japan)
Tropic of Cancer
PACIFIC OCEAN
Luzon Strait
Batan Islands
Babuyan Islands
SOUTH CHINA SEA
PHILIPPINES
Laoag
Aparri
Tuguegarao
Vigan
Bontoc
Ilagan
Bayombong
San Fernando
Dagupan
Luzon
Philippine Sea
Kurumkan
Baikal
Romanovka
Mogocha
Bukachacha
Chernyshevsk
Sretensk
Nerchinsk
Chita
Khorinsk
Khilok
Karymskoye
Olovyannaya
Borzya
Zabaykal'sk
Borshchovochnyy Khrebet
Gulian
Mangui
Heilong Jiang (Amur)
Bishui
Tahe
Huma
Mordaga
Alihe
Argun
Nenjiang
Nehe
Bei'an
Mingshui
Fuyu
Da Hinggan Ling
Xiao Hinggan Ling
Manzhouli
Hulun Nur
Hailar
Ereentsav
Choybalsan
Öndörhaan
Tamsagbulag
Buir Nur
Jargalant
Baruun Urt
Songling
Uliastai
Har Nur
Lubei
Tianshan
Daban
Xilinhot
Linxi
Qagan Nur
Erenhot
Saihan Tal
Baochang
Huade
Jining
NEI MONGOL ZIZHIQU
INNER MONGOLIA
Huang He (Yellow River)
2090

250 500 750 KILOMETRES

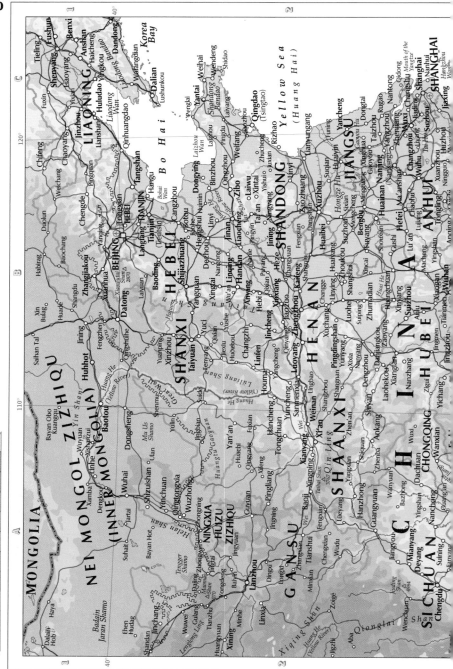

METRES
FEET

5000	16404
3000	9843
2000	6562
1000	3281
500	1640
200	656
0	0
LAND B.S.L.	
200	656
4000	13124
6000	19686

Albers Equal Area Conic Projection

1 : 12 000 000

MILES 0   100   200

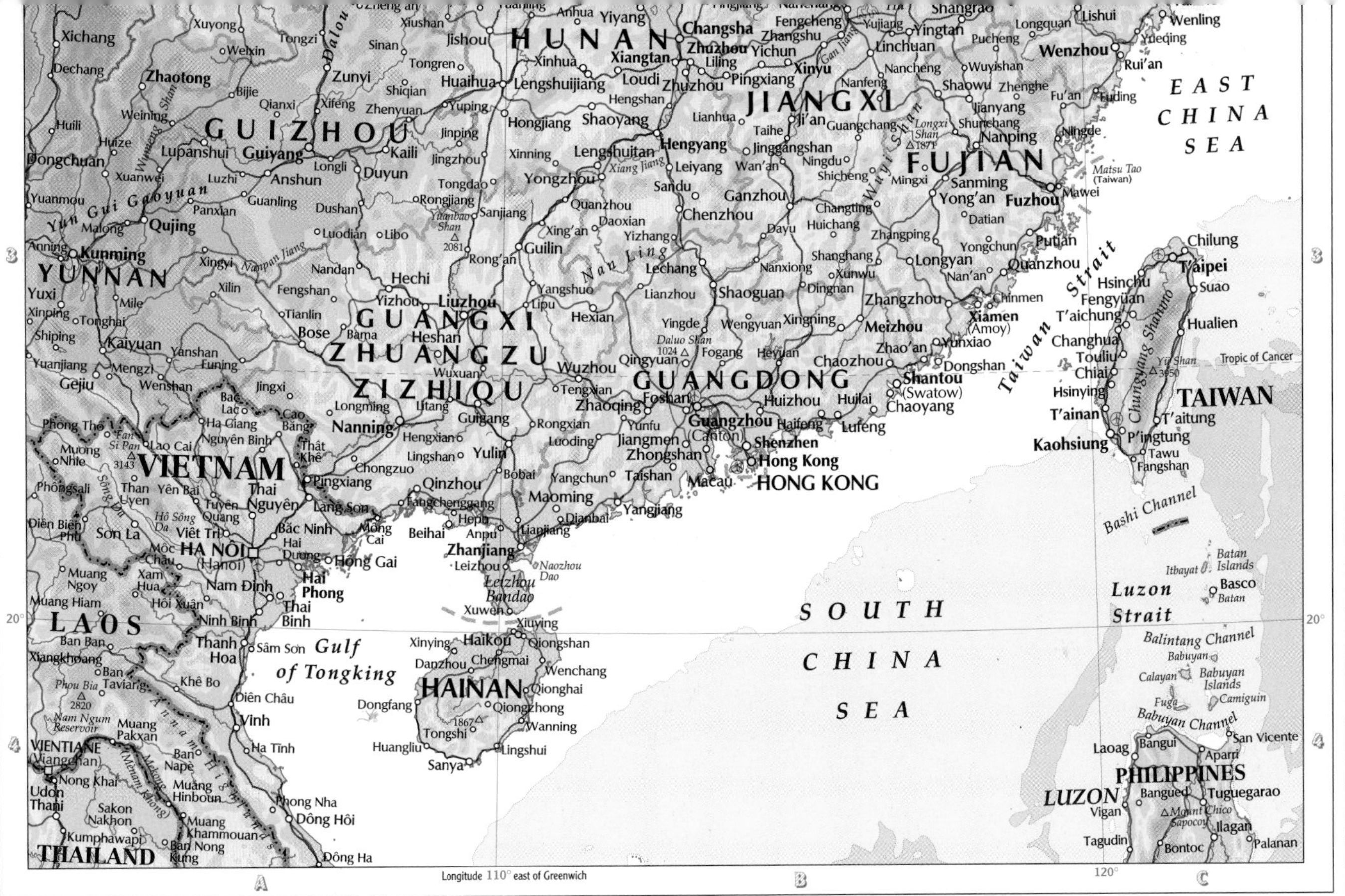
EAST CHINA SEA
SOUTH CHINA SEA
Gulf of Tongking
Luzon Strait
Taiwan Strait
Bashi Channel
Balintang Channel
Babuyan Channel
Tropic of Cancer
HUNAN
JIANGXI
FUJIAN
GUANGDONG
GUANGXI ZHUANGZU ZIZHIQU
GUIZHOU
YUNNAN
HAINAN
TAIWAN
HONG KONG
VIETNAM
LAOS
THAILAND
PHILIPPINES
LUZON
Changsha
Zhuzhou
Xiangtan
Hengyang
Guangzhou (Canton)
Shenzhen
Hong Kong
Macau
Shantou (Swatow)
Xiamen (Amoy)
Fuzhou
Wenzhou
Taipei
Kaohsiung
Nanning
Guiyang
Kunming
Zhanjiang
Haikou
HA NOI (Hanoi)
Hai Phong
Longitude 110° east of Greenwich
20°
120°
A
B
C
200
400 KILOMETRES

METRES
FEET

5000
16404

3000
9843

2000
6562

1000
3281

500
1640

200
656

0
0

LAND
B.S.L.

200
656

4000
13124

6000
19686

Albers Equal Area Conic Projection

1 : 15 000 000

MILES 0   100   200

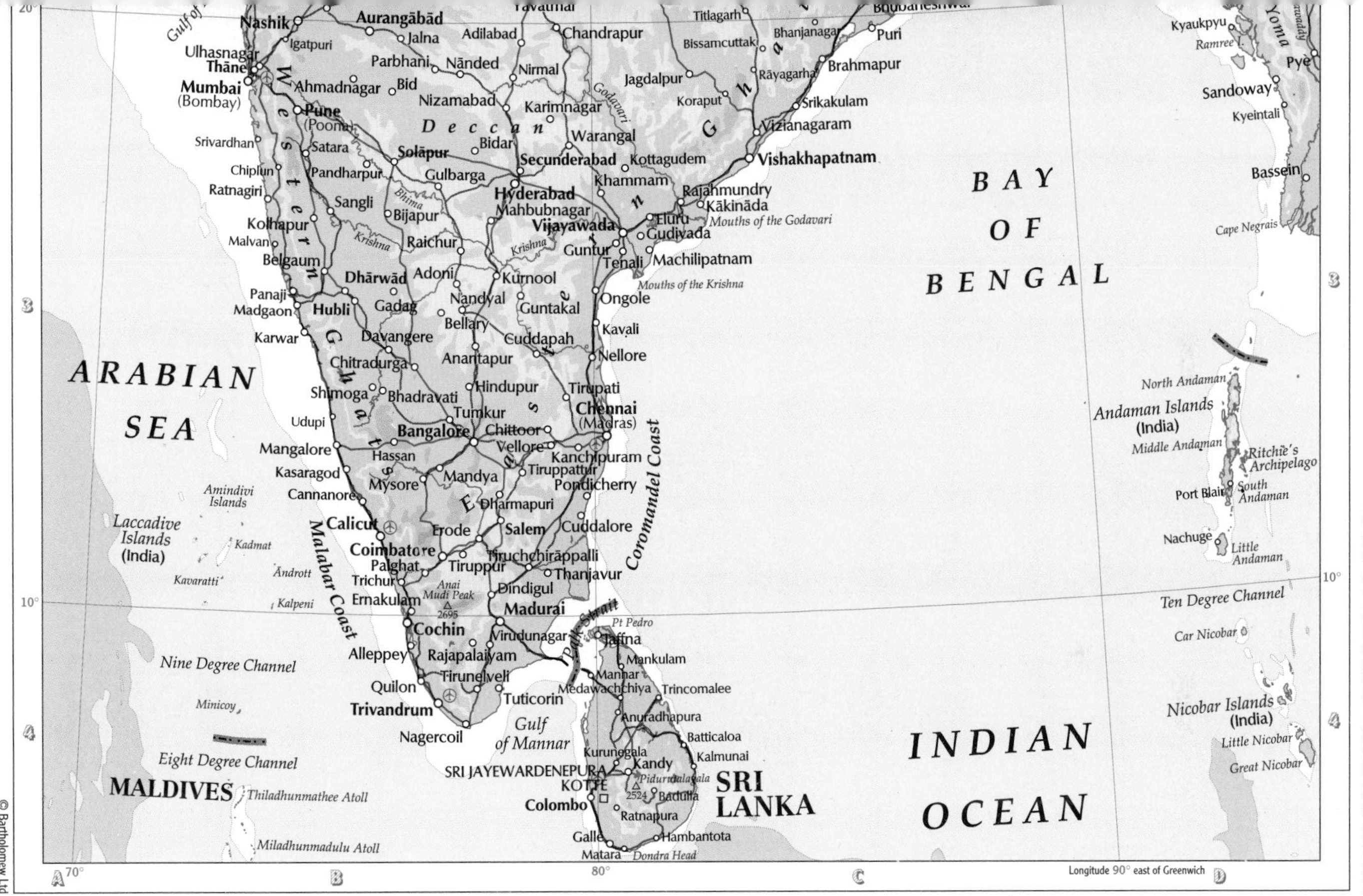
BAY OF BENGAL
ARABIAN SEA
INDIAN OCEAN
SRI LANKA
MALDIVES
Andaman Islands (India)
Nicobar Islands (India)
Laccadive Islands (India)
Deccan
Western Ghats
Eastern Ghats
Malabar Coast
Coromandel Coast
Gulf of Mannar
Ten Degree Channel
Nine Degree Channel
Eight Degree Channel
Mouths of the Godavari
Mouths of the Krishna
North Andaman
Middle Andaman
South Andaman
Little Andaman
Ritchie's Archipelago
Car Nicobar
Little Nicobar
Great Nicobar
Port Blair
Nachuge
Cape Negrais
Bassein
Sandoway
Kyeintali
Kyaukpyu
Ramree
Pye
Mumbai (Bombay)
Thane
Ulhasnagar
Nashik
Igatpuri
Pune (Poona)
Ahmadnagar
Aurangabad
Jalna
Parbhani
Nanded
Bid
Nizamabad
Adilabad
Nirmal
Chandrapur
Karimnagar
Warangal
Secunderabad
Hyderabad
Mahbubnagar
Kottagudem
Khammam
Vijayawada
Guntur
Tenali
Eluru
Gudivada
Machilipatnam
Rajahmundry
Kakinada
Vishakhapatnam
Vizianagaram
Srikakulam
Brahmapur
Puri
Bhanjanagar
Rayagarha
Bissamcuttak
Titlagarh
Jagdalpur
Koraput
Solapur
Gulbarga
Bidar
Satara
Pandharpur
Sangli
Bijapur
Raichur
Kolhapur
Belgaum
Dharwad
Hubli
Gadag
Adoni
Kurnool
Nandyal
Guntakal
Bellary
Anantapur
Cuddapah
Ongole
Kavali
Nellore
Tirupati
Chennai (Madras)
Kanchipuram
Vellore
Chittoor
Hindupur
Tumkur
Bangalore
Davangere
Chitradurga
Shimoga
Bhadravati
Hassan
Mandya
Mysore
Dharmapuri
Tiruppattur
Pondicherry
Cuddalore
Salem
Erode
Tiruchchirappalli
Thanjavur
Tiruppur
Dindigul
Madurai
Virudunagar
Rajapalaiyam
Tirunelveli
Tuticorin
Nagercoil
Trivandrum
Quilon
Alleppey
Cochin
Ernakulam
Trichur
Palghat
Coimbatore
Calicut
Cannanore
Kasaragod
Mangalore
Udupi
Karwar
Panaji
Madgaon
Malvan
Ratnagiri
Chiplun
Srivardhan
Anai Mudi Peak 2695
Palk Strait
Jaffna
Pt Pedro
Mannar
Mankulam
Trincomalee
Anuradhapura
Medawachchiya
Kurunegala
Kandy
Batticaloa
Kalmunai
Badulla
Ratnapura
Pidurutalagala 2524
SRI JAYEWARDENEPURA KOTTE
Colombo
Galle
Matara
Hambantota
Dondra Head
Amindivi Islands
Kadmat
Andrott
Kalpeni
Kavaratti
Minicoy
Thiladhunmathee Atoll
Miladhunmadulu Atoll
Longitude 90° east of Greenwich
10°
80°
70°
20°
© Bartholomew Ltd
250
500 KILOMETRES

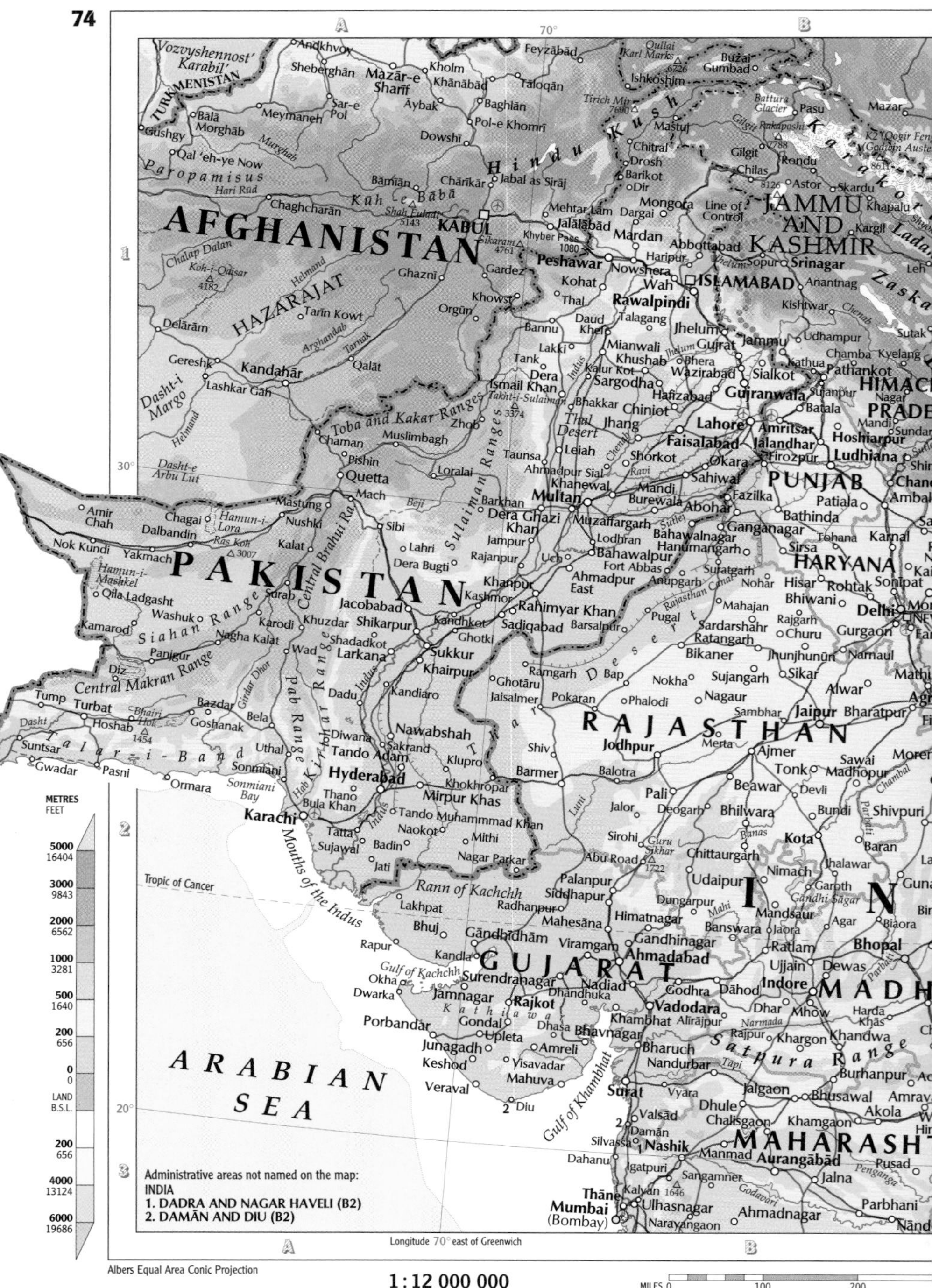

70°

A

B

Vozvyshennost' Karabil'
TURKMENISTAN
Andkhvoy
Sheberghán
Mazār-e Sharīf
Kholm
Khānābād
Talōqan
Feyzābād
Qullai Karl Marksa 6226
Ishkoshim
Buzai Gumbad

Bālā Morghāb
Gushgy
Qal 'eh-ye Now
Meymaneh
Sar-e Pol
Āybak
Baghlān
Pol-e Khomrī
Dowshī
Maştūj
Chitrāl
Tirich Mir 7690
Gilgit Rakaposhi 7788
K2 (Qogir Feng) Godwin Austen 8611
Pasu
Mazar

Murghab
Paropamisus
Hari Rūd
Bāmiān
Chārīkār
Jabal as Sirāj
Drosh
Barikot
Dir
Chilas
Rondu
Astor
Skardu

Chaghcharān
Kūh e Bābā
Shah Fulādi 5143
KABUL
Mehtar Lām
Dargai
Mongola
Jalālābād
Line of Control
JAMMU
Khapalu
AND

AFGHANISTAN
HAZARAJAT
Helmand
Ghaznī
Gardēz
Sīkaram 4761
Khyber Pass
Mardan
Abbottābād
KASHMIR
Kargil
Ladā
Leh

Delārām
Tarīn Kowt
Khowst
Orgūn
Thal
Kohat
Haripur
Nowshera
Peshāwar
Wah
Rawalpindi
ISLAMABAD
Srīnagar
Anantnag
Zaska

Gereshk
Kandahār
Qalāt
Bannu
Lakki
Tank
Khōst
Talagang
Jhelum
Gujrāt
Jammu
Udhampur
Kishtwar
Chenab
Sutak

Dasht-i Margo
Lashkar Gāh
Khanewal
Muslimbagh
Zhōb
Takht-i-Sulaimān 3374
Ismail Khan
Dera
Mianwali
Khushab
Sargodha
Hafizabad
Wazirabad
Sialkot
Gujranwala
Batala
HIMAC
PRADE
Nagar
Mandi
Sundar

Chaman
Pishīn
Taunsa
Leiah
Jhang
Chiniot
Lahore
Amritsar
Faisalabad
Jalandhar
Ludhiana
Hoshiarpur
Shin

Dasht-e Arbu Lut
Quetta
Loralai
Barkhan
Khanewal
Mandi
Sahiwal
Shorkot
Firozpur
PUNJAB
Chan
Ambal

30°
Amir Chah
Nok Kundi
Chagai
Dalbandin
Hamun-i-Lora
Nushki
Kalat
Mach
Beji
Sibi
Lahri
Dera Ghazi Khan
Muzaffargarh
Multan
Lodhran
Bahawalnagar
Burewala
Abohar
Ganganagar
Fazilka
Bathinda
Tohana
Patiala
Sirsa
Karnal
HARYANA

Yakmach
Hamun-i-Mashkel
Qila Ladgasht
Washuk
Kamarod
Siahan Range
Nagha Kalat
Karodi
Khuzdar
Shadadkot
Jacobabad
Kandhkot
Ghotki
Jampur
Rajanpur
Uch
Ahmadpur East
Fort Abbas
Sadiqabad
Rahimyar Khan
Barsalpur
Anupgarh
Suratgarh
Pugal
Nohar
Mahajan
Sardarshahr
Bikaner
Ratangarh
Hisar
Rohtak
Bhiwani
Rajgarh
Churu
Jhunjhunū
Delhi
Gurgaon
Namaul
LINE

Diz
Central Makran Range
Panjgur
Ras Koh
Wad
Larkana
Sukkur
Khairpur
Dadu
Kandiaro
Ghotāru
Jaisalmer
Pokaran
Phalodi
Nagaur
Sujangarh
Sikar
Alwar
Nokha
Bap
Mathi
Agi

Tump
Turbat
Hoshab
Suntsar
Gwadar
Bhairi 1454
Bazdar
Goshanak
Bela
Diwana
Sakrand
Nawabshah
Shiv
Barmer
Jodhpur
Merta
Balotra
Pali
Jaisalmer
Ramgarh
Jaipur
Bharatpur
Sambhar
Ajmer
Sawai Madhopur
Chambal
Fi

Pasni
Ormara
Sonmiani
Sonmiani Bay
Uthal
Thano Bula Khan
Hyderabad
Mirpur Khas
Tando Adam
Klupro
Khokhropar
Tando Muhammmad Khan
Jalor
Deogarh
Bhilwara
Beawar
Devli
Bundi
Tonk
Kota
Morer
Shivpuri

METRES FEET
Karachi
Tatta
Badin
Mithi
Naokot
Nagar Parkar
Siroh
Abu Road
Chittaurgarh
Udaipur
Nimach
Jhalawar
Baran
La

5000 16404
Mouths of the Indus
Sujawal
Jati
Rann of Kachchh
Palanpur
Siddhapur
Radhanpur
Dungarpur
Mahi
Mandsaur
Agar
Biaora
Guna
Garoth

3000 9843
Tropic of Cancer
Lakhpat
Bhuj
Gandhidham
Mahesāna
Himatnagar
Banswara
Jaora
Gandhi Sagar
Bhopal

2000 6562
Rapur
Kandla
Viramgam
Gandhinagar
Ahmadabad
Ratlam
Dewas

1000 3281
Gulf of Kachchh
Okha
Dwarka
Surendranagar
Nadiad
Dhandhuka
Godhra
Dāhod
Ujjain
Indore
MADH

500 1640
Jamnagar
Rajkot
Vadodara
Dhar
Mhow
Harda
Khāś

200 656
Porbandar
Gondal
Upleta
Dhasa
Bhavnagar
Khambhat
Aliräjpur
Rajpur
Khargon
Khandwa

0 0
LAND B.S.L.
Junagadh
Keshod
Amreli
Bharuch
Nandurbar
Sāt
pura
Range
Burhanpur
Ch

ARABIAN SEA
Veraval
Mahuva
Visavadar
Diu
Gulf of Khambhat
Vyara
Jalgaon
Bhusawal
Amrav
Akola

200 656
20°
Surat
Valsād
Dhule
Chalisgaon
Khamgaon
Hir

4000 13124
Silvassa
Daman
Dahanu
Nashik
Manmad
Aurangabad
Jalna
Pusad

6000 19686
Administrative areas not named on the map:
INDIA
1. DADRA AND NAGAR HAVELI (B2)
2. DAMĀN AND DIU (B2)
Gatpuri
Sangamner
Mumbai (Bombay)
Thāne
Kalyan 1646
Ulhasnagar
Godavari
Ahmadnagar
Narayangaon
Parbhani
Nānde
MAHARASHT

Longitude 70° east of Greenwich

A

B

Albers Equal Area Conic Projection

1 : 12 000 000

MILES 0   100   200

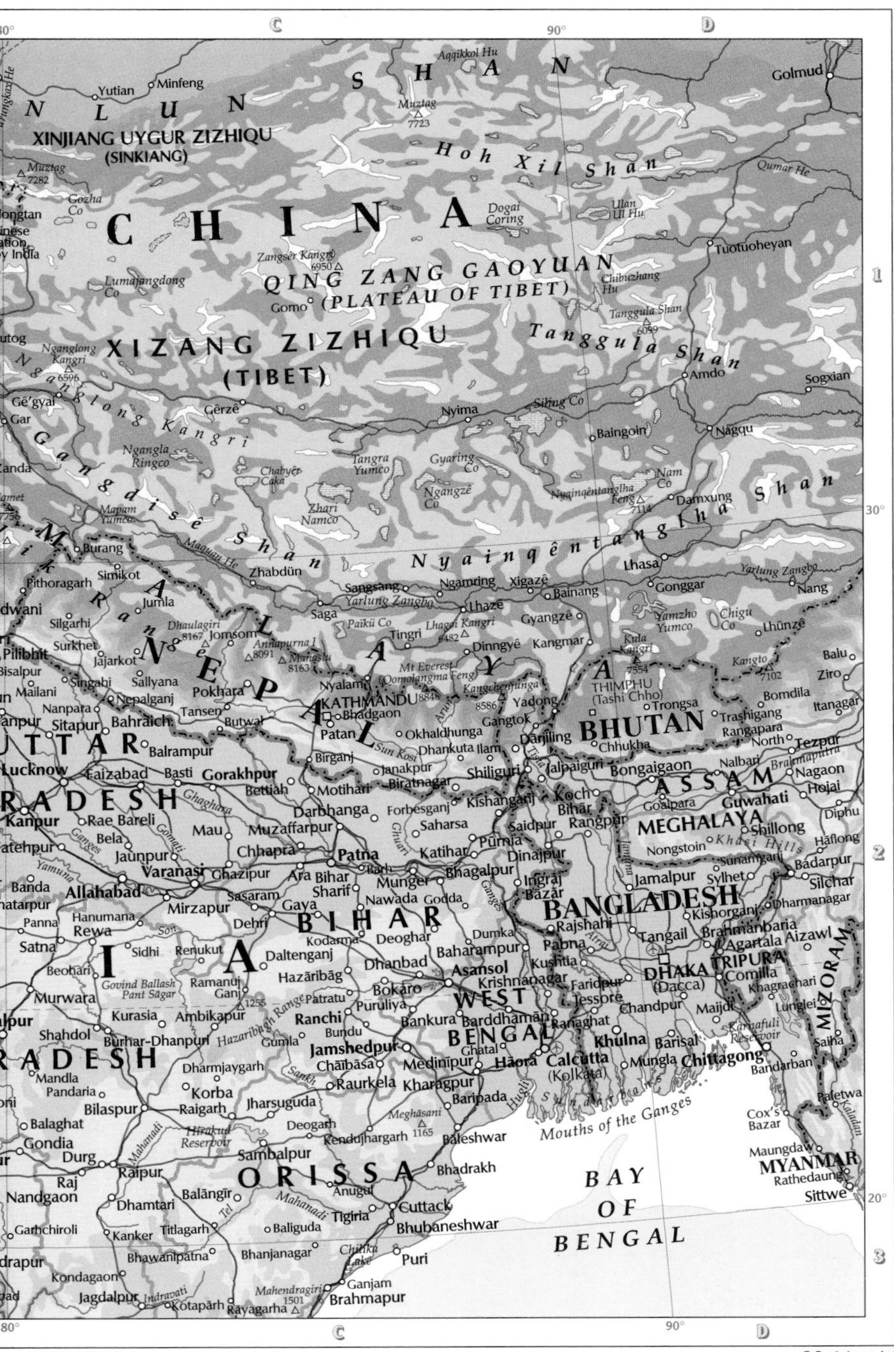

30°   ℂ   90°   𝔻

Aqqikkol Hu

N L U N Yutian Minfeng **S H A N** Golmud

XINJIANG UYGUR ZIZHIQU Muztag 7723

(SINKIANG) *H o h X i l S h a n* Qumar He

Muztag 7282

Gozha Co Dogai Coring Ulan UI Hu

longtan **C H I N A**

inese ation y India Lumajangdong Co Zangser Kangri 6950△ **QING ZANG GAOYUAN** Chibzhang Hu Tuotuoheyan

Gomo **(PLATEAU OF TIBET)** Tanggula Shan 6099

utog Nganglong Kangri **XIZANG ZIZHIQU** *T a n g g u l a* Amdo Sogxian

6596 **(TIBET)** *S h a n*

Ge'gyai Gerze Nyima Siling Co Nagqu

Gar *K a n g r i* Baingoin

zanda Ngangla Ringco Tangra Yumco Gyaring Co Nam Co *S h a n*

amet 7523 Mapam Yumco Chabyêr Caka Ngangzê Co Nyainqêntanglha Feng 7114 Damxung 30°

Burang Zhari Namco *N y a i n q ê n t a n g l h a*

Pithoragarh Simikot Zhabdün Sangsang Ngamring Xigazê Lhasa Yarlung Zangbo Nang

dwani Jumla Saga Yarlung Zangbo Lhazê Bainang Gonggar

Silgarhi Surkhet Dhaulagiri 8167 Jomsom Paikü Co Lhagoi Kangri 6482△ Tingri Dinngyê Gyangzê Kangmar Kula Kangri Yamzho Yumco Chigu Co Lhünzê

Pilibhit Jajarkot **N E P A L** Annapurna 8091 △ Manaslu 8163 Mt Everest Qomolangma Feng 8848 Kangchenjunga 8586 7554 Kangto 7102 Balu

Bisalpur Singahi Sallyana Pokhara Nyalam THIMPHU (Tashi Chho) Yadong Trongsa Bomdila Ziro

Mailani Nepalganj Tansen **KATHMANDU** Trashigang Itanagar

n Nanpara Butwal Bhadgaon Gangtok **BHUTAN** Rangapara Tezpur

anpur Sitapur Bahraich Patan Okhaldhunga Darjiling North Brahmaputra

U T T A R Balrampur Birganj Sun Kosi Dhankuta Ilam Chhukha Nalbari Nagaon

Lucknow Faizabad Basti **Gorakhpur** Janakpur Biratnagar Jalpaiguri Bongaigaon **A S S A M** Hojai

R A D E S H Bettiah Motihari Ghaghara Shiliguri Koch Bihar Goalpara Guwahati Diphu

Kanpur Rae Bareli Darbhanga Forbesganj Kishanganj Rangpur **MEGHALAYA** Shillong Haflong

atehpur Bela Jaunpur Mau Muzaffarpur Saharsa Saidpur Purnia Dinajpur Nongstoin *Khasi Hills* Badarpur

Ganges Chhapra **Patna** Katihar Sunamganj Silchar

Yamuna **Varanasi** Ghazipur Ara Bihar Bhagalpur Jamalpur Sylhet

Banda **Allahabad** Mirzapur Sasaram Sharif Munger Ingraj Bazar Dharmanagar

hatarpur Panna Rewa Dehri **B I H A R** Gaya Nawada Godda Rajshahi **B A N G L A D E S H** Kishorganj Brahmanbaria Aizawl

Satna Sidhi Son Kodarma Deoghar Dumka Pabna Tangail Agartala **MIZORAM**

Beohari Renukut Daltenganj Dhanbad Kushtia **DHAKA** (Dacca) Comilla **TRIPURA**

Murwara Govind Ballash Pant Sagar Ramanuj Ganj Hazaribag Asansol Krishnagar Faridpur Chandpur Khagrachari

alpur Kurasia Ambikapur 1255 Patratu Bokaro Puruliya **WEST** Jessore Maijdi Lunglei Saiha

Shahdol Burhar-Dhanpuri *Hazaribagh Range* **Ranchi** Bankura Barddhaman **BENGAL** Ranaghat Khulna Barisal **Chittagong** Karnaphuli

R A D E S H Gumla **Jamshedpur** Ghatal **Haora** **Calcutta** Mungla Bandarban

Mandla Dharmjaygarh Chaibasa Medinipur (Kolkata)

Pandaria Korba Raurkela Kharagpur

oni Bilaspur Raigarh Jharsuguda Baripada Paletwa

Balaghat Deogarh Meghasani 1165△ Cox's Bazar

Gondia Hirakud Reservoir Kendujhargarh Baleshwar *Mouths of the Ganges*

ir Durg Mahanadi Sambalpur Bhadrakh Maungdaw

Raj Raipur Balangir Anugul **B A Y** **MYANMAR** Rathedaung

Nandgaon Dhamtari Tel Tigiria Cuttack **O F** Sittwe 20°

athchiroli Kanker Titlagarh Baliguda Bhubaneshwar **BENGAL**

drapur Bhawanipatna Bhanjanagar Chilka Lake Puri

ad Jagdalpur Indravati Mahendragiri 1501△ Ganjam **Brahmapur**

Kondagaon Kotaparh Rayagarha△

80°   ℂ   90°   𝔻

© Bartholomew Ltd

200   400 KILOMETRES

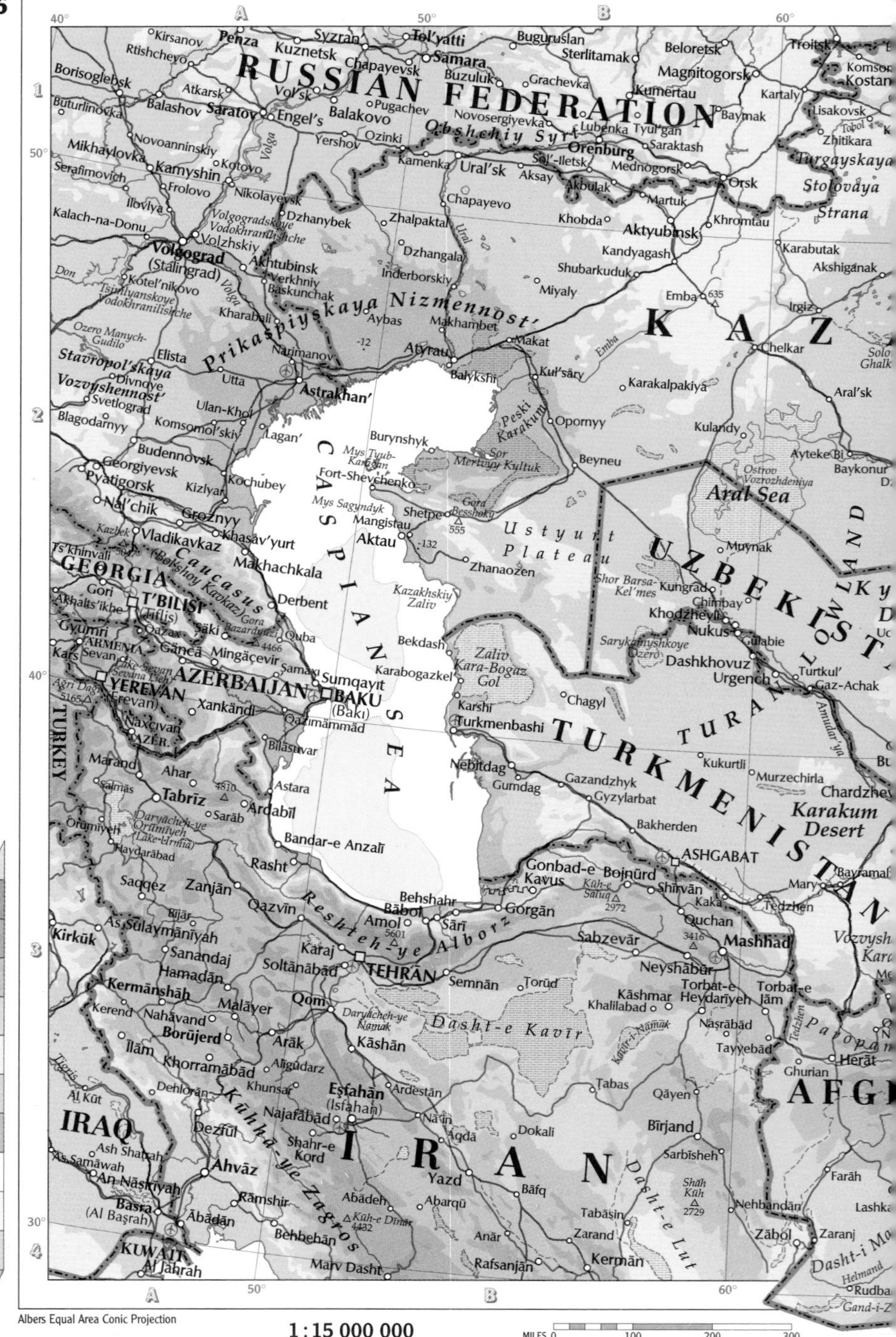

METRES
FEET

5000
16404

3000
9843

2000
6562

1000
3281

500
1640

200
656

0
0

LAND
B.S.L.

200
656

4000
13124

6000
19686

Albers Equal Area Conic Projection

1 : 15 000 000

MILES 0   100   200   300

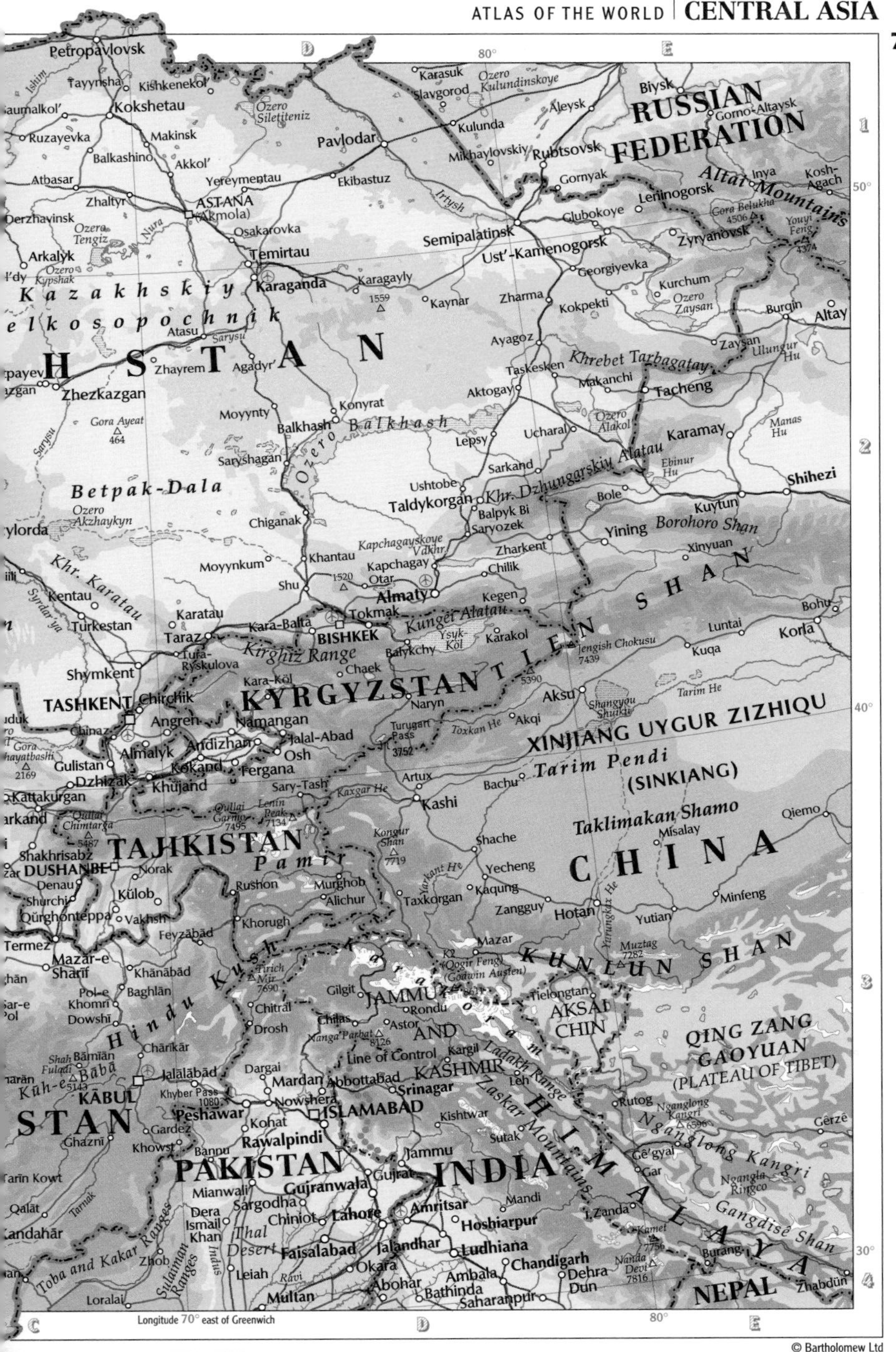

Petropavlovsk
Tayyrisha
Kishkenekol
Islim
Karasuk
80°
Slavgorod
Ozero
Kulundinskoye
Biysk
RUSSIAN
Gorno-Altaysk
saumalkol'
Kokshetau
Ozero
Siletiteniz
Ajeysk
FEDERATION
Ruzayevka
Makinsk
Pavlodar
Kulunda
Rubtsovsk
Mikhaylovskiy
Altai Mountains
Kosh-Agach
inya
Balkashino
Akkol'
Ekibastuz
Gornyak
Leninogorsk
Gora Belukha
4506
Youyi
Feng
4374
50°
Atbasar
Yereymentau
Irtysh
Zhaltyr
ASTANA
(Akmola)
Osakarovka
Glubokoye
Zyryanovsk
Derzhavinsk
Ozero
Tengiz
Nura
Temirtau
Semipalatinsk
Ust'-Kamenogorsk
Georgiyevka
Kurchum
l'dy
Kypshak
Arkalyk
Karaganda
Karagayly
1559
Kaynar
Zharma
Kokpekti
Ozero
Zaysan
Burqin
Altay
K a z a k h s k i y
payev
e l k o s o p o c h n i k
Atasu
Sarysu
Ayagoz
Zaysan
Ulungur
Hu
zgan
H
S
T
A
N
Zhayrem
Agadyr'
Taskesken
Khrebet Tarbagatay
Makanchi
Tacheng
Ulungur
Hu
Zhezkazgan
Moyynty
Konyrat
Aktogay
Ozero
Alakol
Karamay
Manas
Hu
Gora Ayeat
464
Balkhash
B a l k h a s h
Lepsy
Ucharal
Ehinur
Hu
Shihezi
Betpak-Dala
Ozero
Akzhaykyn
Saryshagan
Ozero
Balkhash
Sarkand
Ushtobe
Kuytun
ylorda
Chiganak
Taldykorgan
Khr. Dzhungarskiy Alatau
Bole
Yining
Borohoro Shan
Xinyuan
Shu
Khantau
Moyynkum
Kapchagayskoye
Vdkhr.
Balpyk Bi
Saryozek
Zharkent
Khr. Karatau
Kapchagay
Otar.
1520
Chilik
Kegen
T
I
E
N
Bohu
illn
Kentau
Syrdar'ya
Almaty
S
H
A
N
Turkestan
Karatau
Kara-Balta
Tokmak
Kunger Alatau
Ysyk-
Köl
Karakol
Luntai
Korla
Taraz
BISHKEK
Jengish Chokusu
7439
Kuqa
Shymkent
Tura-
Ryskulova
Kirghiz Range
Balykchy
5390
Aksu
Tarim He
TASHKENT
Chitchik
Chaek
Kara-köl
Naryn
Shanyou
Shukhi
uduk
Angren
Namangan
Turugart
Pass
Akqi
XINJIANG UYGUR ZIZHIQU
40°
Gora
hayatbashi
Almalyk
Andizhan
Jalal-Abad
Osh
3752
Toxkan He
Artux
Bachu
Tarim Pendi
Dzhizak
Kokand
Fergana
Sary-Tash
Raxgar He
Kashi
(SINKIANG)
Kattakurgan
Khujand
Lenin Peak
7134
Qiemo
arkand
Qullai
Garmo
7495
Kongur
Shan
7719
Shache
Taklimakan Shamo
Misalay
Shakhrisabz
TAJIKISTAN
P a m i r
Yecheng
C
H
I
N
A
zar
DUSHANBE
Norak
Rushon
Murghob
Kaqung
Denau
Shurchi
Kulob
Alichur
Taxkorgan
Zangguy
Hotan
Minfeng
Qurghonteppa
Vakhsh
Khorugh
Yutian
Termez
Mazar-e
Sharif
Khanabad
Zirich
Mt
7690
Mazar
Muztag
7282
K U N L U N
S H A N
han
Pol-e
Khomri
Baghlan
Gilgit
Qogir Feng)
(Godwin Austen)
Tilongtan
Rutog
Dowshi
Charikar
Chitral
Drosh
Chilas
Astor
JAMMU
Nanga Parbat
8126
Rondu
AKSAI
CHIN
QING ZANG
GAOYUAN
(PLATEAU OF TIBET)
Gerze
Kuh-e-Baba
Jalalabad
Dargai
Mardan
AND
Ladakh Range
Leh
Ngangla
Kangri
Gar
 Get'yal
Ge'gyal
KABUL
Khyber Pass
1080
Nowshera
Abbottabad
Srinagar
Kargil
Line of Control
KASHMIR
Karan
Khowst
Peshawar
Kohat
Kishtwar
S
T
A
N
Ghazni
Gardez
Banpu
Rawalpindi
Jammu
Sutak
Zanskar
Gerze
Ngangong Kangri
6596
arin Kowt
Khowst
ISLAMABAD
Mandi
PAKISTAN
INDIA
H
Qalat
Mianwali
Sargodha
Gujranwala
Gujrat
Amritsar
Zanda
Ngangla
6536
Gangdise Shan
andahar
Dera
Ismail
Khan
Chiniot
Lahore
Hoshiarpur
Ludhiana
Chandigarh
M
Burang
Kamet
7816
30°
Toba and Kakar Ranges
Thal
Desert
Faisalabad
Jalandhar
A
Dehra
Dun
Nanda
Devi
7816
Zhabdun
Loralai
Zhob
Leiah
Okara
Ambala
Saharanpur
L
A
Y
A
NEPAL
Multan
Abohar
Bathinda
Longitude 70° east of Greenwich
80°

© Bartholomew Ltd

250   500 KILOMETRES

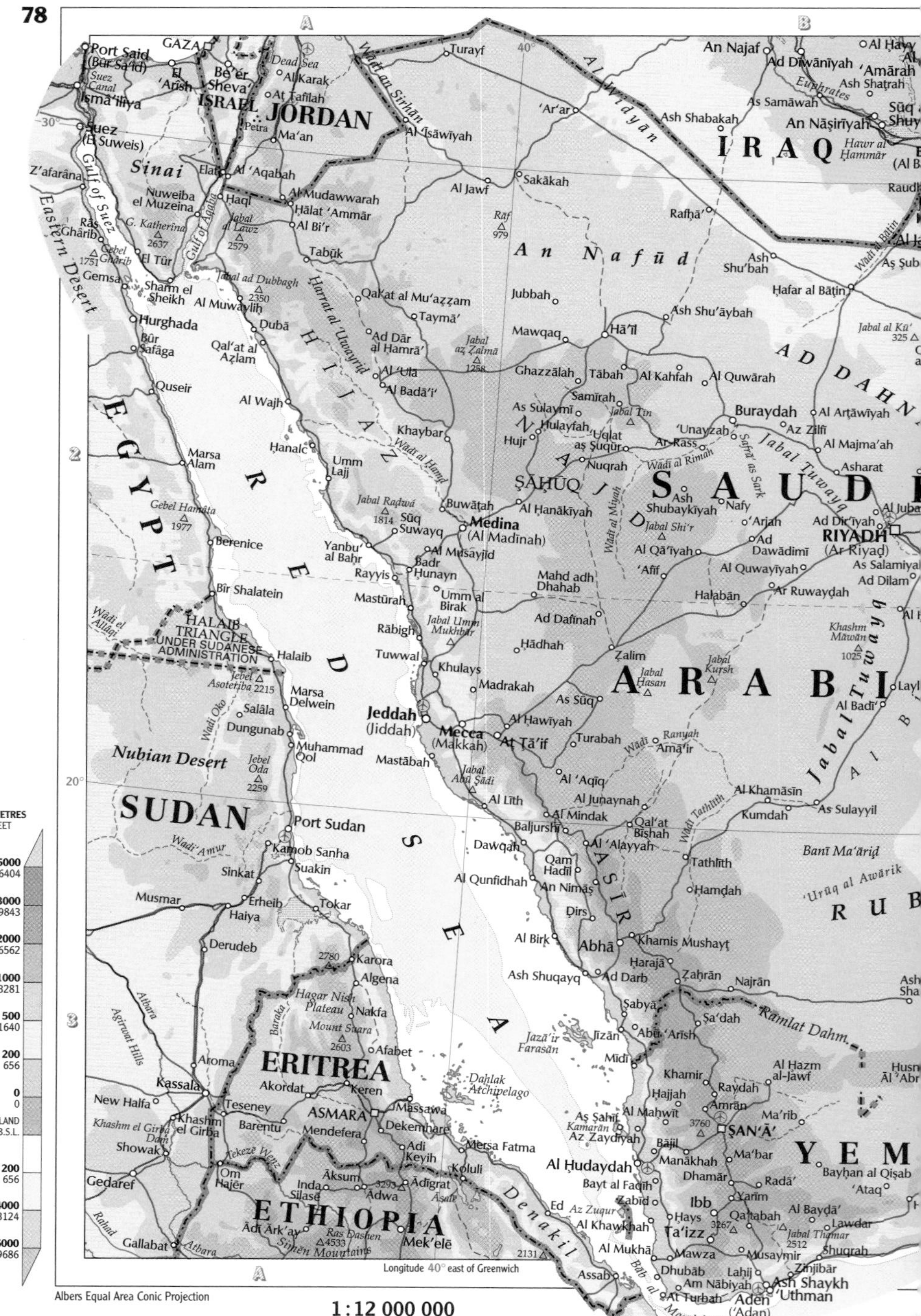
A
B
Port Said
(Bûr Sa'îd)
Suez Canal
Isma'iliya
Suez
(El Suweis)
GAZA
El 'Arîsh
Be'ér Sheva'
ISRAEL
JORDAN
Petra
Dead Sea
Al Karak
At Tafilah
Ma'an
Sinai
Elat
Al 'Aqabah
Z'afarâna
Gulf of Suez
Eastern Desert
Nuweiba el Muzeina
Gulf of Aqaba
Haql
Al Mudawwarah
Hâlat 'Ammâr
Al Bi'r
Jabal al Lawz
2579
G. Katherina
2637
Râs Ghârib
Gebel Ghârib
1751
El Tûr
Gemsa
Sharm el Sheikh
Tabūk
Jabal ad Dubbagh
2350
Al Muwaylih
Hurghada
Bûr Safâga
Dubā
Qal'at al Azlam
Quseir
Al Wajh
EGYPT
Marsa Alam
Gebel Hamâta
1977
Berenice
Bîr Shalatein
Wâdi el Allâqi
HALAIB TRIANGLE
UNDER SUDANESE ADMINISTRATION
Halaib
Jebel Asoteriba 2215
Marsa Delwein
Salâla
Dungunab
Wadi Oko
Muhammad Qol
Nubian Desert
Jebel Oda
2259
SUDAN
Port Sudan
Wadi Amur
Kamob Sanha
Suakin
Sinkat
Musmar
Erheib
Tokar
Haiya
Derudeb
Atbara
Agirwat Hills
Aroma
Kassala
New Halfa
Khashm el Girba Dam
Khashm el Girba
Showak
Gedaref
Rahad
Gallabat
Atbara
Turayf
Wadi as Sirhan
Al 'Isawiyah
'Ar'ar
Al Widyan
An Najaf
Ad Dīwānīyah
Al Hayy
'Amārah
Euphrates
Ash Shatrah
As Samāwah
Sūq ash Shuyūkh
Ash Shabakah
An Nāşirīyah
IRAQ
Hawr al Hammār
Al Jawf
Sakākah
Rafhā'
Raf
979
An Nafūd
Ash Shu'bah
Wadi al Batin
Hafar al Bātin
Aş Şubayhīyah
Qal'at al Mu'azzam
Taymā'
Jubbah
Ash Shu'āybah
Harrat al 'Uwayrid
HIJAZ
Ad Dār al Hamrā'
Jabal az Zalmā
1258
Mawqaq
Hā'il
Jabal al Kū'
325
AD DAHNĀ
Al 'Ulā
Al Badā'i'
Ghazzālah
Tābah
Al Kahfah
Al Quwārah
Samīrah
As Sulaymī
Jabal Tin
Buraydah
Al Artāwīyah
Az Zilfī
Khaybar
Hulayfah
Hujr
'Uqlat aş Şuqūr
'Unayzah
Ar Rass
Al Majma'ah
Jabal Tuwayq
Hanalc
Wādī al Hamd
Umm Lajj
Nuqrah
Wādī al Rimah
Safrā' as Sark
Asharat
NAJD
ŞAHŪQ
SAUDI
RED SEA
Jabal Radwā
1814
Sūq Suwayq
Buwātah
Medina
(Al Madīnah)
Al Hanākīyah
Ash Shubaykīyah
Nafy
Wādī al Miyah
Jabal Shi'r
'Arjah
Ad Dir'īyah
Al Jubayl
RIYADH
(Ar Riyad)
Yanbu' al Bahr
Al Musayjīd
Badr Hunayn
Al Qā'īyah
Ad Dawādimī
'Afīf
Al Quwayīyah
As Salamiyah
Ad Dilam
Rayyis
Umm al Birak
Mahd adh Dhahab
Halabān
Ar Ruwaydah
Mastūrah
Jabal Umm Mukhbar
Ad Dafīnah
Rābigh
Hādhah
Khashm Māwān
1025
Tuwwal
Zalim
Jabal Kursh
Khulays
Madrakah
Jabal Hasan
ARABIA
Laylā
Jeddah
(Jiddah)
As Sūq
Al Badī'
Mecca
(Makkah)
Al Hawīyah
At Tā'if
Turabah
Ranyah
Wādī
Āmā'ir
Mastābah
Jabal Abū Sādi
Al 'Aqīq
Al Līth
Al Junaynah
Al Khamāsīn
Kumdah
As Sulayyil
Al Mindak
Baljurshī
Qal'at Bīshah
Wādī Tathlīth
Dawqah
Al 'Alayyah
Banī Ma'ārid
Qam Hadīl
Tathlīth
'Urūq al Awārik
Al Qunfidhah
An Nimāş
'ASIR
Hamdah
Dirs
RUB
Al Birk
Abhā
Khamis Mushayt
Harajā
Ash Shuqayq
Ad Darb
Zahrān
Najrān
Ash Sharawrah
Şabyā
Şa'dah
Ramlat Dahm
Jazā'ir Farasān
Jīzān
Abū 'Arīsh
Karora
2780
Algena
Hagar Nish Plateau
Nakfa
Baraka
Mount Soara
2603
Afabet
Mīdī
Al Hazm al-Jawf
Husn Āl 'Abr
ERITREA
Akordat
Keren
Dahlak Archipelago
Khamir
Raydah
Hajjah
Amrān
Teseney
Barentu
ASMARA
Massawa
Al Mahwīt
Aş Şalīf
Kamarān
Az Zaydīyah
3760
ŞAN'Ā'
Ma'rib
Tekeze Wenz
Mendefera
Dekemhare
Adi Keyih
Mersa Fatma
Bājil
Manākhah
Ma'bar
YEMEN
Bayhan al Qişab
Om Hajër
Āksum
3293
Ādīgrat
Koluli
Al Hudaydah
Dhamār
Radā'
'Ataq
Inda Silasē
Ādwa
Āsalē
Bayt al Faqīh
Zabīd
Yarīm
Ibb
Qa'tabah
Al Baydā'
Lawdar
ETHIOPIA
Denakil
Ed
Az Zuqur
Al Khawkhah
Hays
3267
Jabal Thamar
2512
Ādī Ārk'ay
Ras Dashen
4533
Simēn Mountains
Mek'elē
2131
Al Mukhā
Ta'izz
Mawza
Musaymir
Shuqrah
Dhubāb
Lahij
Zinjibār
Assab
Bāb al Mandab
Am Nābiyah
At Turbah
Aden
('Adan)
Ash Shaykh 'Uthman
Longitude 40° east of Greenwich
30°
40°
2
3
20°
METRES
FEET
5000
16404
3000
9843
2000
6562
1000
3281
500
1640
200
656
0
0
LAND B.S.L.
200
656
4000
13124
6000
19686

Albers Equal Area Conic Projection

1:12 000 000

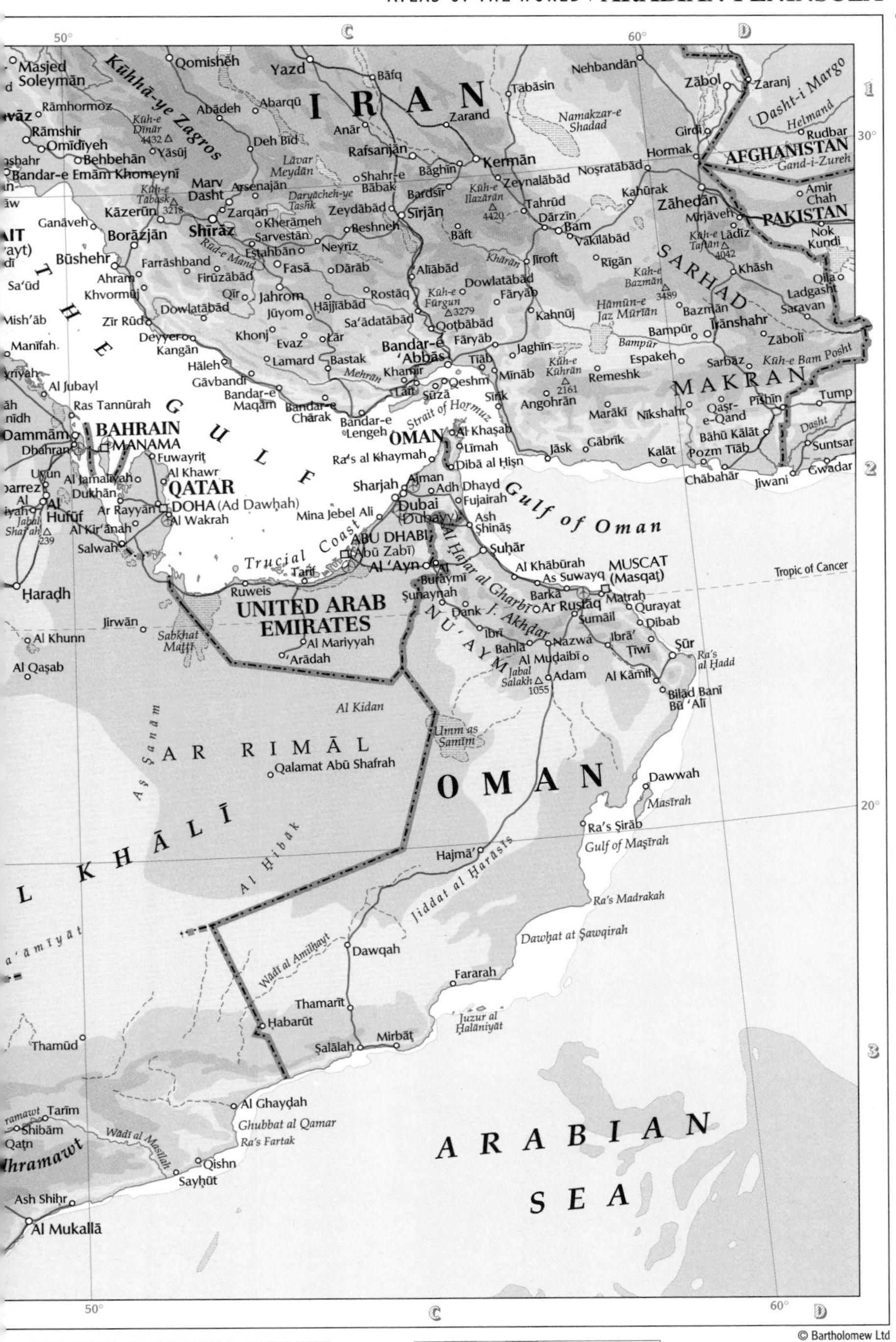

MILES 0   100   200   300   0   200   400 KILOMETRES

© Bartholomew Ltd

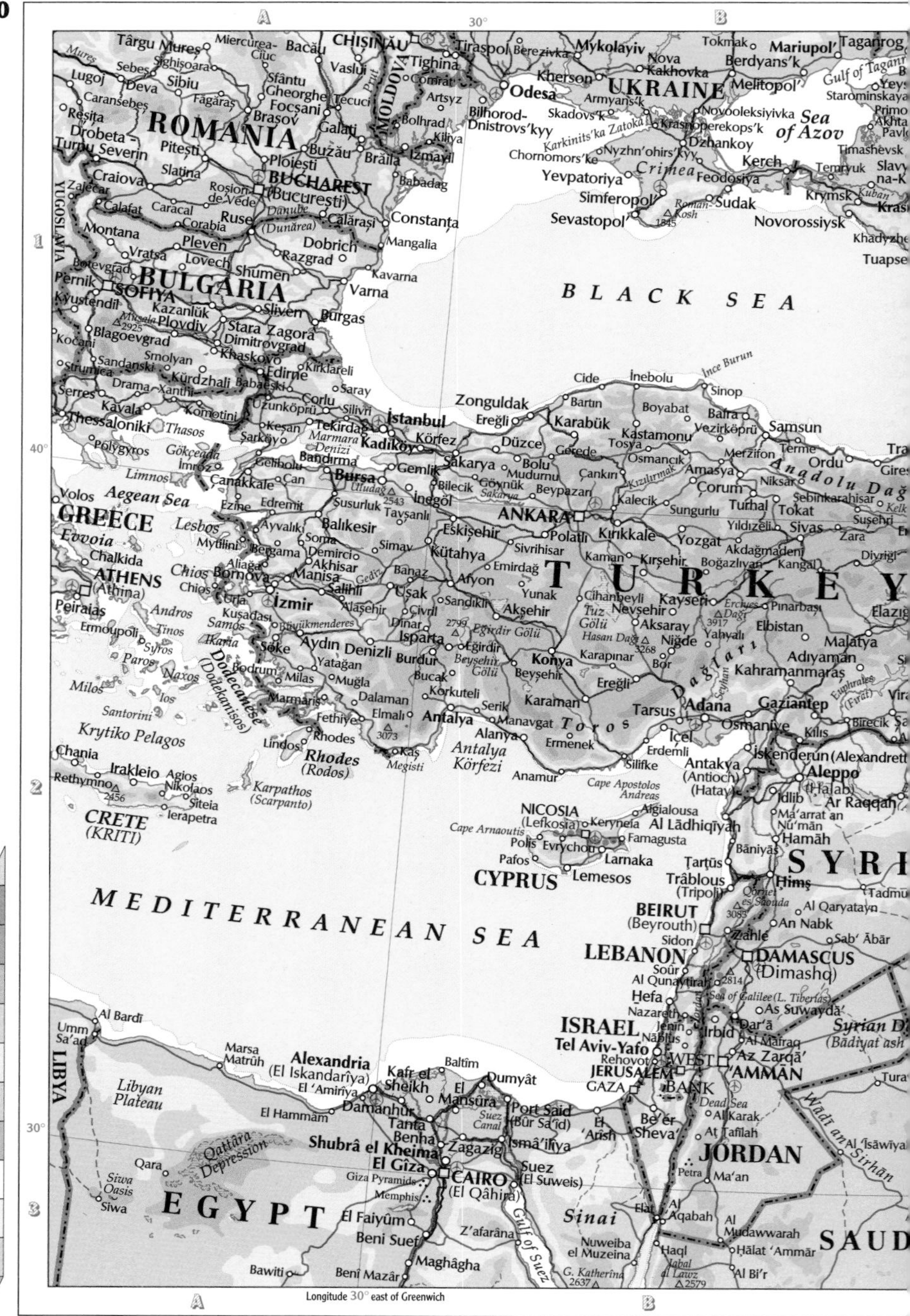

A 30° B

Târgu Mureş Miercurea- Bacău CHIŞINĂU Tiraspol Berezivka Mykolayiv Tokmak Mariupol' Taganrog
Mureş Sebeş Ghisoara Ciuc Vaslui Tighina Nova Berdyans'k B
Lugoj Deva Sibiu Sfântu Comrat Kherson Kakhovka Melitopol' Gulf of Taganrog Yeya
Caransebeş Făgăraş Gheorghe Tecuci Artsyz Odesa Armyans'k UKRAINE Staromins'ka
Reşiţa Drobeta Braşov Focşani Bilhorod- Skadovs'k Novooleksiyivka Sea Primo
Drobeta ROMANIA Galaţi Bolhrad Dnistrovs'kyy Krasnoperekops'k of Azov Akhta
Turnu Severin Piteşti Buzău Brăila Izmayil Kiliya Karkinits'ka Zatoka Dzhankoy Pavlo
Slatina Ploieşti Babadag Chornomors'ke Nyzhn'ohirs'kyy Kerch Temryuk Slavy
Craiova Rosiori BUCHAREST Yevpatoriya Crimea Feodosiya na-K
Zalecar de-Vede (Bucureşti) Simferopol' Roman Krymsk Kuban Krasr
Calafat Caracal Ruse Dunărea Călăraşi Constanţa Sevastopol' Kosh Sudak Novorossiysk
Montana Corabia (Dunărea) Dobrich Mangalia Khadyzhe
Vratsa Lovech Pleven Razgrad Kavarna Tuapse
Borovgrad Shumen BULGARIA SOFIYA Varna BLACK SEA
Pernik Kyustendil Kazanlŭk Sliven Bŭrgas
Blagoevgrad Plovdiv Stara Zagora
Kočani Sandanski Smolyan Dimitrovgrad Khaskovo Ince Burun
Strumica Drama Xanthi Kŭrdzhali Babaeski Edirne Kırklareli Cide İnebolu Sinop
Serres Kavala Komotini Üzünköprü Silivri İstanbul Ereğli Bartın Boyabat Bafra Samsun
Thessaloniki Thasos Tekirdağ Kadıköy Körfez Karabük Kastamonu Vezirköprü Terme
Limnos Gelibolu Marmara Düzce Tosya Merzifon Ordu Giresun
Volos Aegean Sea İmroz Bandırma Gemlik Sakarya Bolu Gerede Osmancık Amasya Çorum Niksar Sebinkarahisar
GREECE Lesbos Edremit Bursa Uludağ Bilecik Mudurnu Beypazarı Çankırı Kalecik Sungurlu Tokat Sivas
Evvoia Mytilini Ayvalık Balıkesir Taysanlı İnegöl Eskişehir Polatlı Kırıkkale Yıldızeli Zara
Chalkida Chios Bergama Demirci Simav Kütahya Sivrihisar ANKARA Kaman Kırşehir Akdağmadeni Divriği
ATHENS Aliağa Akhisar Banaz Afyon Emirdağ Yunak Boğazlıyan Kangal
Peiraias (Athína) Manisa Gediz Uşak Sandıklı Cihanbeyli Kayseri Erciyes Pınarbaşı Elazığ
Andros İzmir Alaşehir Civril Akşehir Tuz Nevşehir Elbistan
Ermoupoli Kuşadası Söke Büyükmenderes Dinar Eğirdir Gölü Gölü Aksaray Niğde Yahyalı Malatya
Tinos Samos Aydın Denizli Burdur Isparta Beyşehir Konya Karapınar Bor Adıyaman
Paros Naxos Bodrum Milas Muğla Bucak Beyşehir Ereğli Kahramanmaraş
Milos İos Marmaris Dalaman Korkuteli Karaman Toros Tarsus Adana Gaziantep Euphrates Vira
Santorini Fethiye Elmalı Antalya Manavgat İçel Osmaniye Birecik
Krytiko Pelagos Kaş Alanya Ermenek Silifke Antakya İskenderun (Alexandretta) Aleppo
Chania Irakleio Agios Rhodes Antalya Anamur Cape Apostolos Antakya (Halab)
Rethymno Nikolaos Karpathos (Rodos) Körfezi Andreas (Hatay) İdlib Ar Raqqah
Siteia Ierapetra (Scarpanto) Aigialousa Ma'arrat an Nu'mān
CRETE Megisti NICOSIA Keryneia Al Lādhiqīyah Hamāh
(KRITI) Cape Arnaoutis (Lefkosia) Famagusta Bāniyās SYRI
Polis Evrychou Tartūs Hamāh
Pafos CYPRUS Lemesos Larnaca Trâblous Hims
MEDITERRANEAN SEA (Tripoli) Tadmu
BEIRUT Al Qaryatayn
(Beyrouth) An Nabk
Sidon Zahlé Sab' Ābar
LEBANON DAMASCUS
Soûr Al Qunaytirah (Dimashq)
Hefa Sea of Galilee (L. Tiberias) Syrian D
Al Bardi Nazareth As Suwaydā' (Bādiyat ash
ISRAEL Jenin Dar'ā
Umm Tel Aviv-Yafo Nāblus Irbid Al Mafraq Tura
Sa'ad Rehovot WEST 'Az Zarqā'
Marsa Alexandria Baltīm JERUSALEM BANK AMMAN
Matrûh (El Iskandarīya) Kafr el Dumyât GAZA Dead Sea
LIBYA Libyan El 'Amirīya Sheikh El Mansûra Be'er Al Karak
Plateau El Hammam Damanhûr Tanta Port Said 'Arîsh Sheva' At Tafîlah JORDAN
Qattâra Shubrâ el Kheima Zagazig Ismâ'îlîya Wādī an al Sirhan
Qara Depression El Gîza Suez Ma'an Petra
Siwa Giza Pyramids CAIRO (El Suweis) Hal
Oasis Memphis (El Qâhira) Al Aqabah Mudawwarah
Siwa EGYPT El Faiyûm Sinai Al Hālat 'Ammār SAUD
Beni Suef Nuweiba Haql Jabal
Bawiti Z'afarâna el Muzeina al Lawz Al Bi'r
Beni Mazâr Maghâgha G. Katherina A 2579

METRES
FEET

5000 16404
3000 9843
2000 6562
1000 3281
500 1640
200 656
0 0
LAND B.S.L.
200 656
4000 13124
6000 19686

Longitude 30° east of Greenwich

Albers Equal Area Conic Projection

1 : 12 000 000

MILES 0   100   200   30

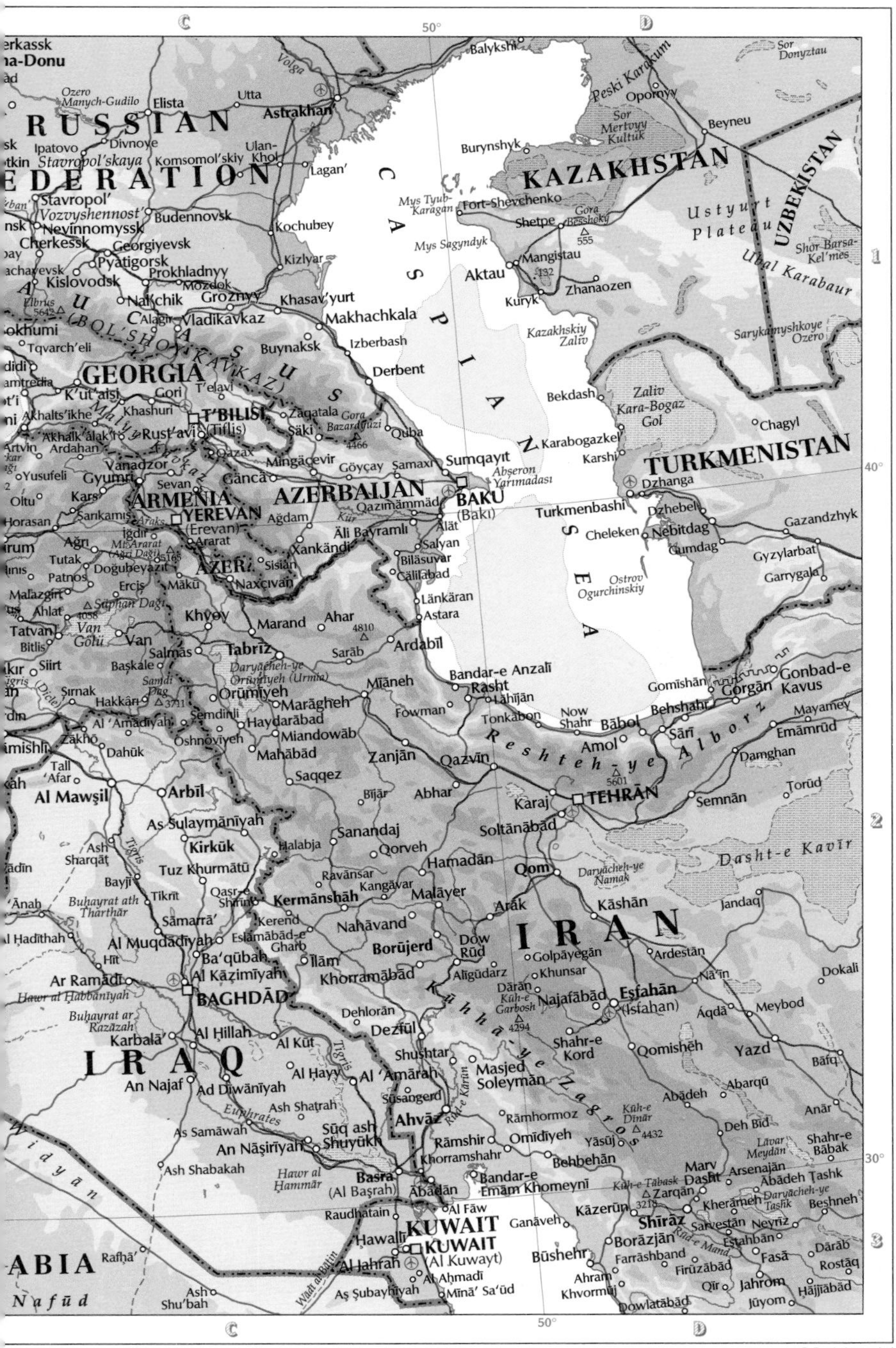
RUSSIAN FEDERATION
KAZAKHSTAN
UZBEKISTAN
TURKMENISTAN
GEORGIA
ARMENIA
AZERBAIJAN
IRAN
IRAQ
KUWAIT
CASPIAN SEA
Astrakhan'
Elista
Stavropol'
Groznyy
Makhachkala
Derbent
Aktau
Fort-Shevchenko
Beyneu
Turkmenbashi
T'BILISI (Tiflis)
YEREVAN (Erevan)
BAKU (Bakı)
Gyumri
Gäncä
Sumqayıt
Tabrīz
Ardabīl
Rasht
Bandar-e Anzalī
Orūmīyeh
Zanjān
Qazvīn
Karaj
TEHRĀN
Qom
Hamadān
Kermānshāh
Arāk
Kāshān
Eşfahān (Isfahan)
Yazd
Shīrāz
Būshehr
Ahvāz
Dezfūl
Khorramābād
Borūjerd
Al Mawşil
Arbīl
Kirkūk
As Sulaymānīyah
BAGHDĀD
Karbalā'
An Najaf
Basra (Al Başrah)
Ābādān
KUWAIT (Al Kuwayt)
Dasht-e Kavīr
Reshteh-ye Alborz
Kūhhā-ye Zāgros
Ustyurt Plateau
Zaliv Kara-Bogaz Gol
5601
5642
5165
4466
4432
4294
50°
40°
30°
C
D
1
2
3
200
400 KILOMETRES
© Bartholomew Ltd

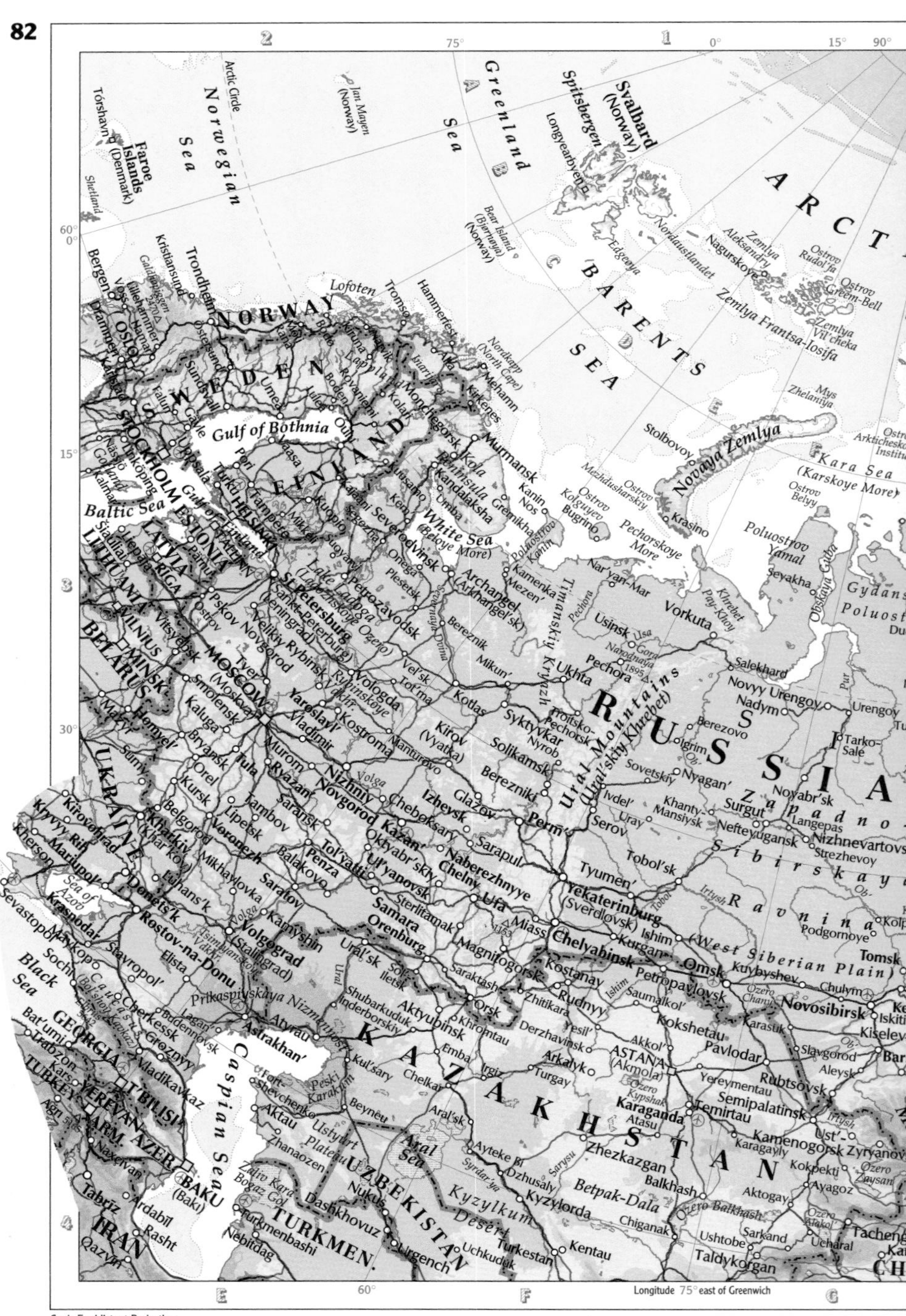

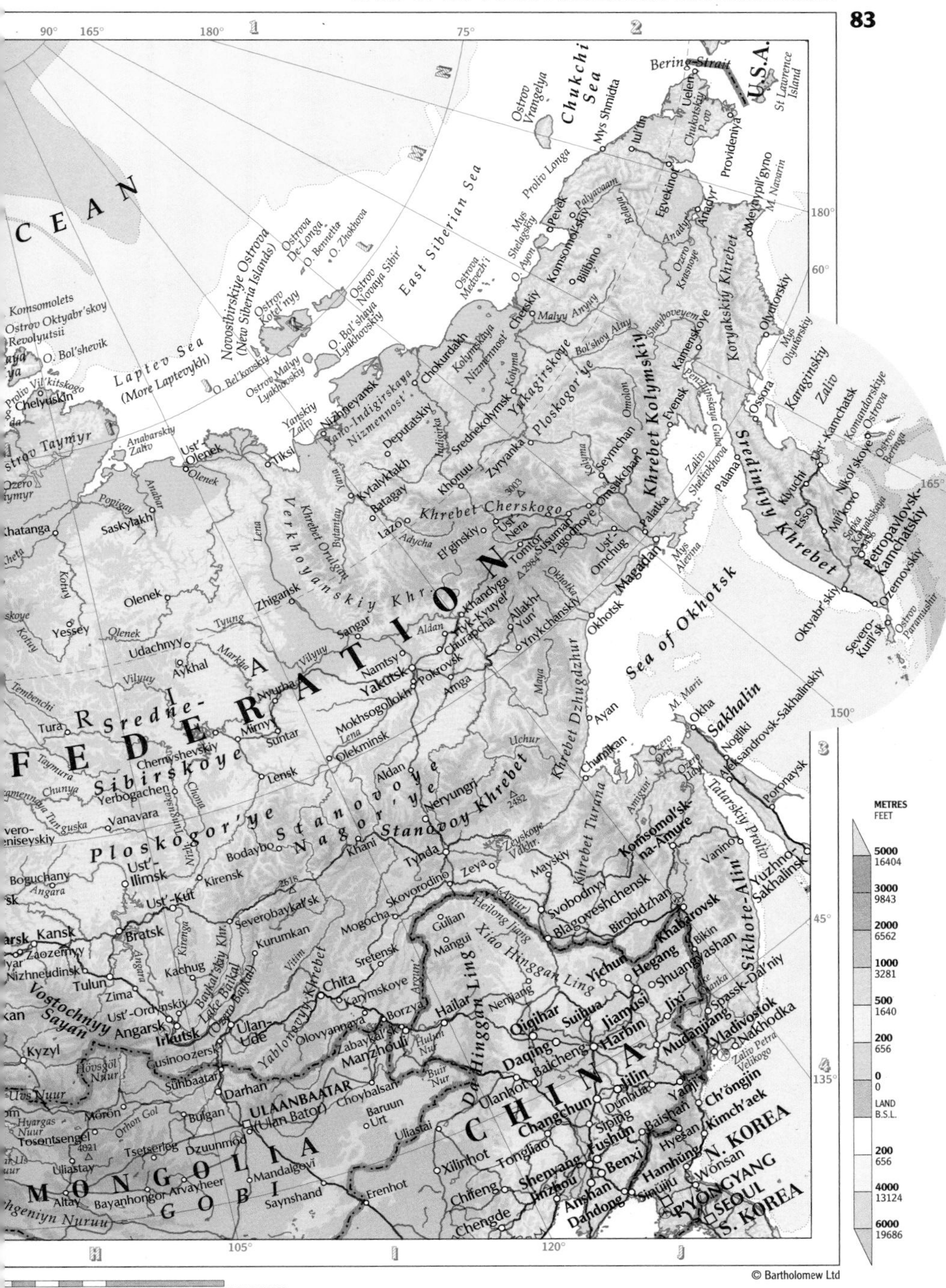
RUSSIAN FEDERATION
CHINA
MONGOLIA
N. KOREA
S. KOREA
U.S.A.
Chukchi Sea
East Siberian Sea
Laptev Sea
(More Laptevykh)
Sea of Okhotsk
Bering Strait
Verkhoyanskiy Khr.
Khrebet Cherskogo
Khrebet Kolymskiy
Sredne-Sibirskoye Ploskogor'ye
Stanovoye Nagor'ye
Stanovoy Khrebet
Sikhote-Alin'
Sakhalin
GOBI
Yakutsk
Magadan
Petropavlovsk-Kamchatskiy
Khabarovsk
Vladivostok
Irkutsk
Ulan-Ude
Chita
Harbin
ULAANBAATAR
(Ulan Bator)
P'YONGYANG
SEOUL
Lake Baikal
METRES
FEET
5000
16404
3000
9843
2000
6562
1000
3281
500
1640
200
656
0
0
LAND
B.S.L.
200
656
4000
13124
6000
19686
500
1000 KILOMETRES

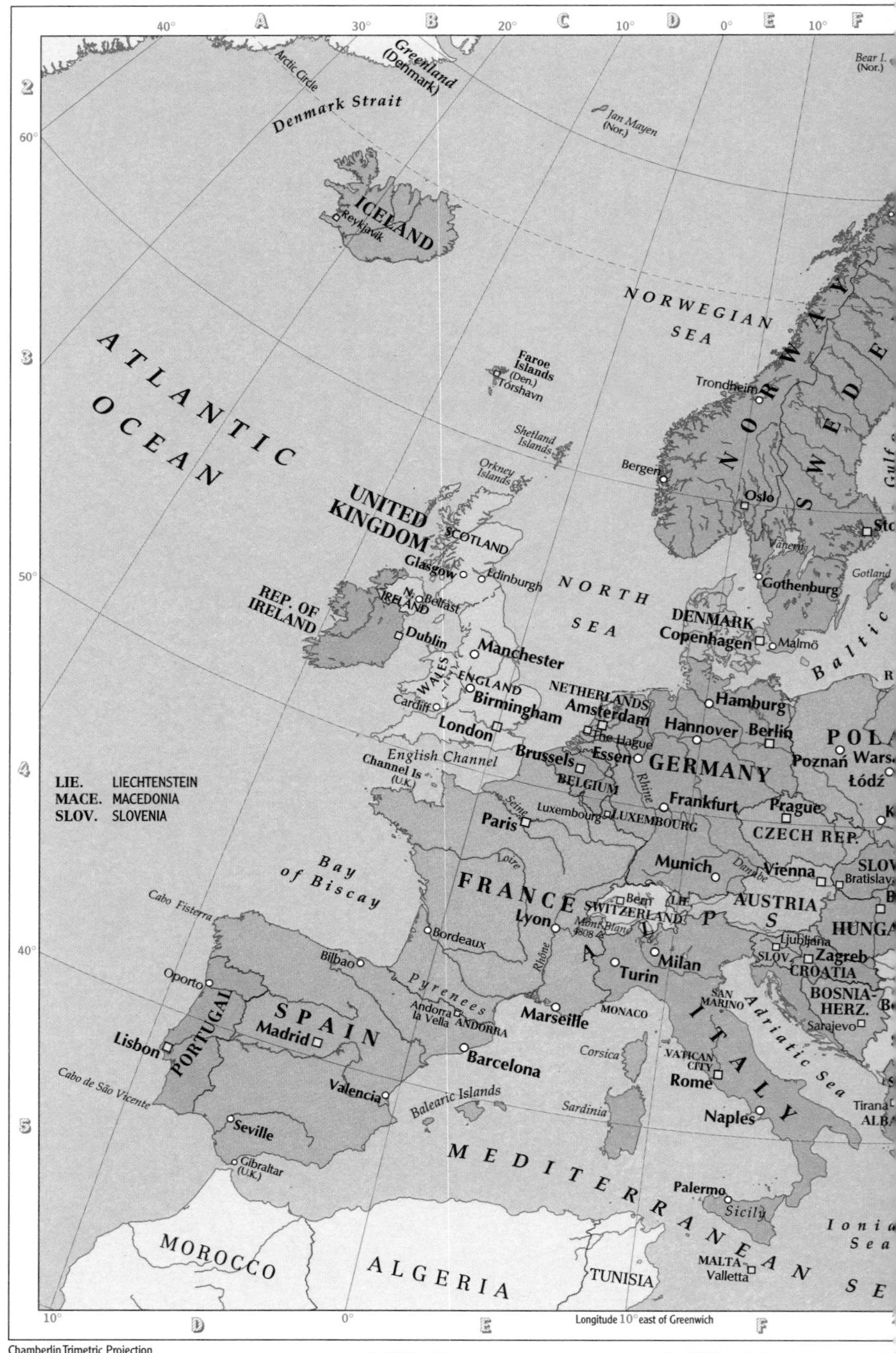

40° **A** 30° **B** 20° **C** 10° **D** 0° **E** 10° **F**

Bear I.
(Nor.)

Arctic Circle

Greenland
(Denmark)

Denmark Strait

Jan Mayen
(Nor.)

60°

ICELAND
Reykjavík

N O R W E G I A N
S E A

ATLANTIC

Faroe
Islands
(Den.)
Tórshavn

Trondheim

Bergen

Oslo

Shetland
Islands

OCEAN

Orkney
Islands

UNITED
KINGDOM
SCOTLAND

Glasgow
Edinburgh

N O R T H
S E A

Gothenburg

Gotland

50°

REP. OF
IRELAND

N.
Belfast
IRELAND

Dublin

Manchester

DENMARK
Copenhagen
Malmö

St

WALES
ENGLAND
Cardiff
Birmingham

London

NETHERLANDS
Amsterdam

Hamburg

Hannover
Berlin

POL

English Channel
Channel Is
(U.K.)

The Hague
Brussels
Essen

GERMANY

Poznań
Warsz

Łódź

BELGIUM

Luxembourg
LUXEMBOURG

Frankfurt

Prague

LIE. LIECHTENSTEIN
MACE. MACEDONIA
SLOV. SLOVENIA

Paris

CZECH REP.

Munich
Vienna

SLOV
Bratislava

Bay
of Biscay

F R A N C E
SWITZERLAND
Bern (LIE.)
Lyon
Mont Blanc
4808

AUSTRIA

HUNGA

Ljubljana
SLOV.
Zagreb
CROATIA

Cabo Fisterra

Milan

Turin

SAN
MARINO

BOSNIA-
HERZ.

Sarajevo

40°

Bilbao

Bordeaux

Pyrenees

Oporto

Andorra
la Vella ANDORRA

Marseille

MONACO

Corsica

VATICAN
CITY
Rome

Tirana
ALB

SPAIN

Madrid

Barcelona

Lisbon
PORTUGAL

Valencia

Balearic Islands

Sardinia

Naples

Cabo de São Vicente

Seville

M E D I T E R R
Palermo

Sicily

I o n i a
S e a

Gibraltar
(U.K.)

MOROCCO

ALGERIA

TUNISIA

MALTA
Valletta

A N

S E

10° **D** 0° **E** Longitude 10° east of Greenwich **F**

Chamberlin Trimetric Projection

1 : 25 000 000

MILES 0   250

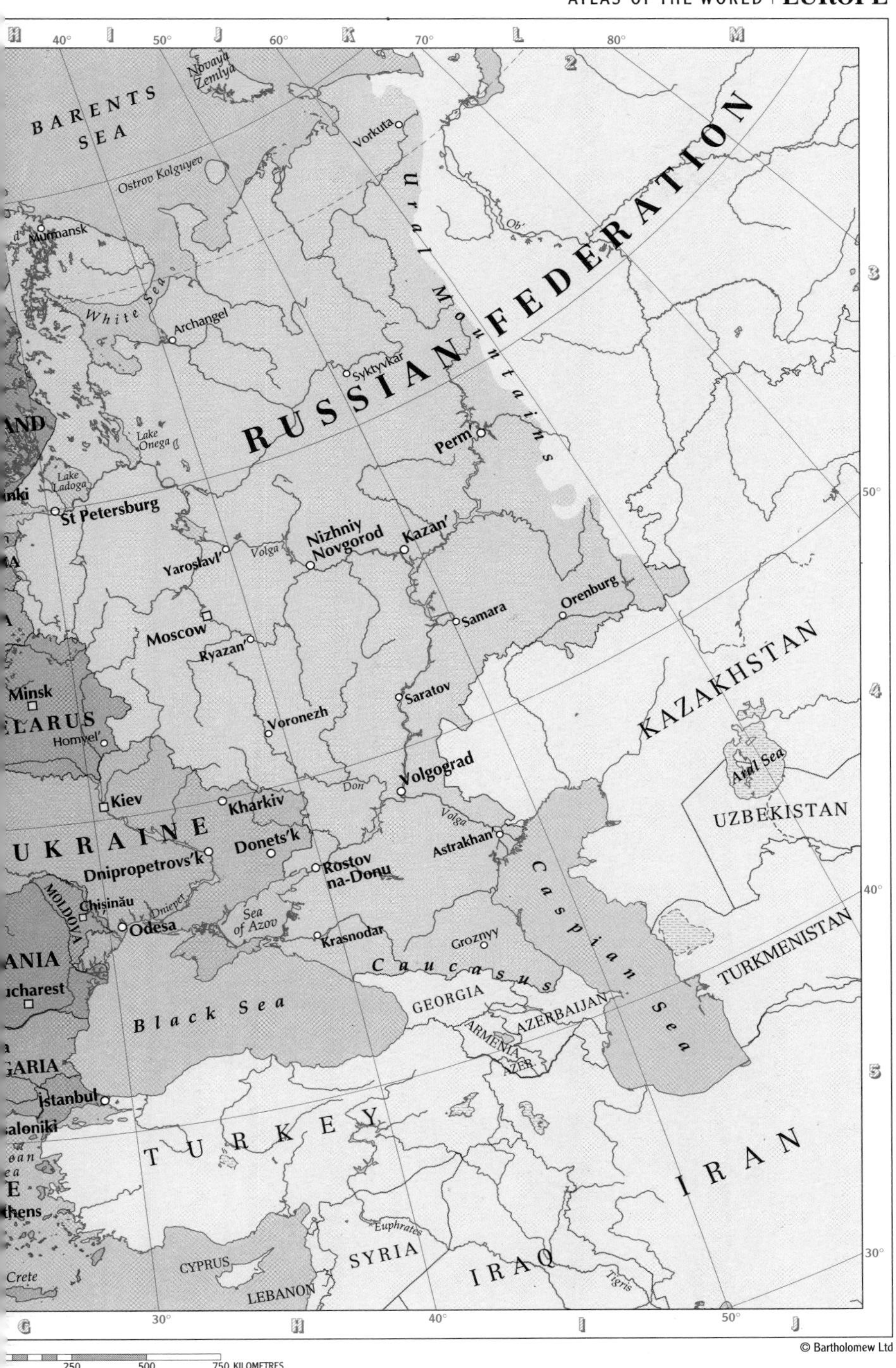

BARENTS SEA

Novaya Zemlya

Ostrov Kolguyev

Vorkuta

Murmansk

White Sea

Archangel

RUSSIAN FEDERATION

Syktyvkar

Ob'

Ural Mountains

FINLAND

Lake Onega

Lake Ladoga

St Petersburg

Perm'

Helsinki

Yaroslavl'

Nizhniy Novgorod

Kazan'

Volga

Orenburg

Moscow

Ryazan'

Samara

Minsk

BELARUS

Homyel'

Voronezh

Saratov

KAZAKHSTAN

Kiev

Kharkiv

Volgograd

Don

Aral Sea

UKRAINE

Dnipropetrovs'k

Donets'k

Volga

UZBEKISTAN

Chişinău

Dnieper

Rostov na-Donu

Astrakhan'

MOLDOVA

Odesa

Sea of Azov

Krasnodar

Caspian Sea

TURKMENISTAN

ROMANIA

Bucharest

Black Sea

Caucasus

Groznyy

GEORGIA

AZERBAIJAN

BULGARIA

Istanbul

ARMENIA

AZER.

IRAN

Thessaloniki

T U R K E Y

Aegean Sea

GREECE

Athens

Euphrates

Crete

CYPRUS

SYRIA

IRAQ

Tigris

LEBANON

250   500   750 KILOMETRES

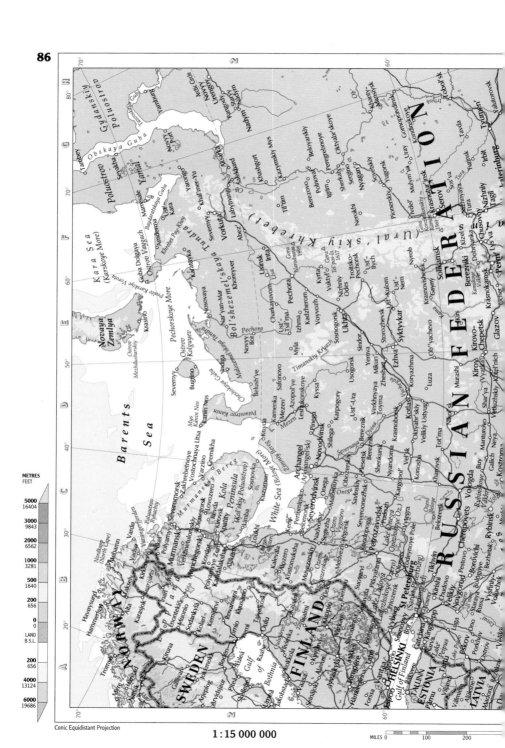

METRES
FEET

5000 16404
3000 9843
2000 6562
1000 3281
500 1640
200 656
0 0
LAND B.S.L.
200 656
4000 13124
6000 19686

Conic Equidistant Projection

1 : 15 000 000

MILES 0   100   200

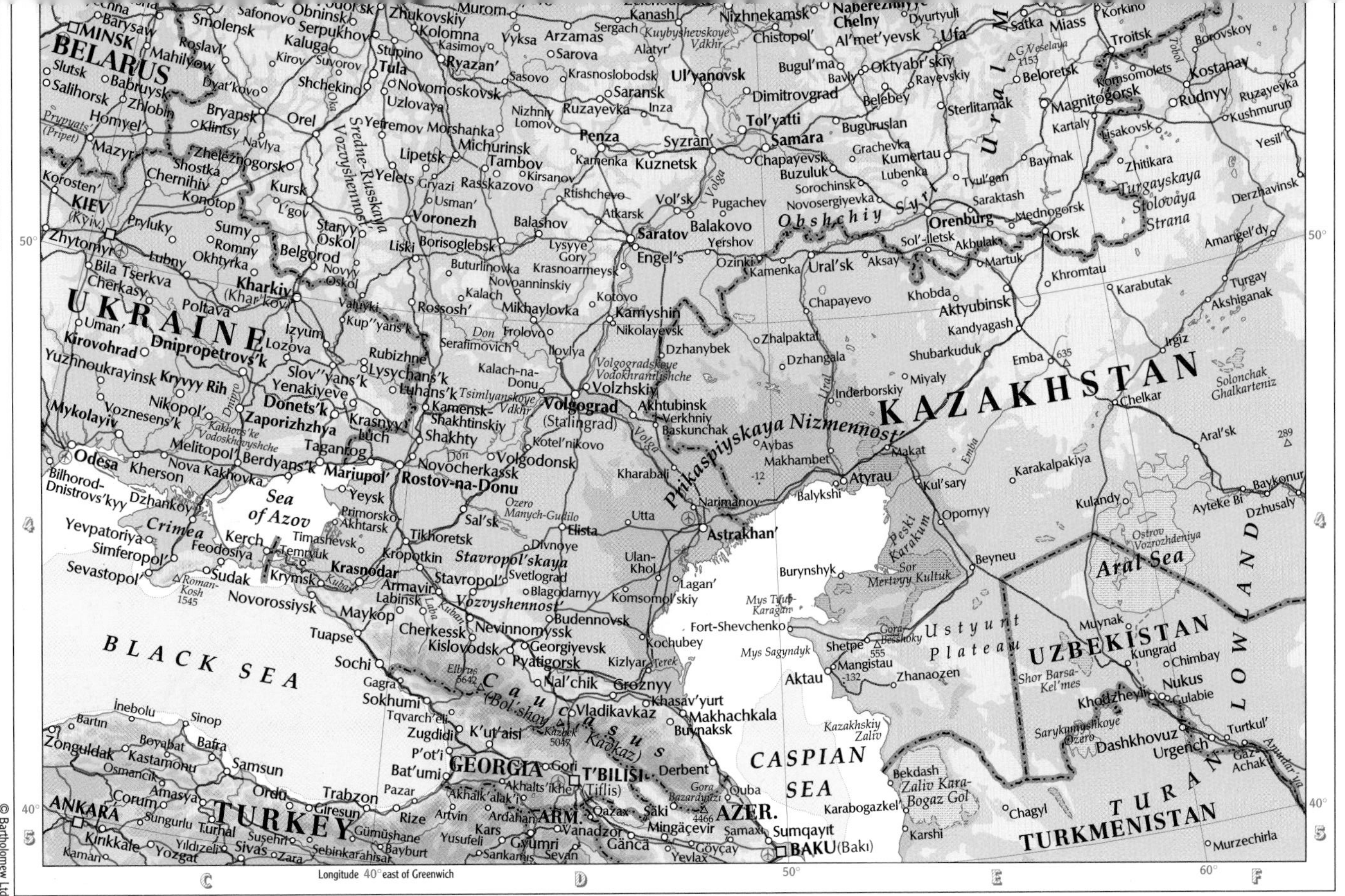
BELARUS
MINSK
UKRAINE
KIEV (Kyiv)
KAZAKHSTAN
UZBEKISTAN
TURKMENISTAN
GEORGIA
T'BILISI (Tiflis)
ARM.
AZER.
BAKU (Bakı)
TURKEY
ANKARA
BLACK SEA
CASPIAN SEA
Sea of Azov
Aral Sea
Crimea
Prikaspiyskaya Nizmennost'
Obshchiy Syrt
Ural M
Ustyurt Plateau
TURAN LOWLAND
Caucasus (Bol'shoy Kavkaz)
Sredne-Russkaya Vozvyshennost'
Stavropol'skaya Vozvyshennost'
Turgayskaya Stolovaya Strana
Volgograd (Stalingrad)
Saratov
Samara
Astrakhan'
Rostov-na-Donu
Orenburg
Voronezh
Kharkiv (Khar'kov)
Longitude 40° east of Greenwich
250
500 KILOMETRES

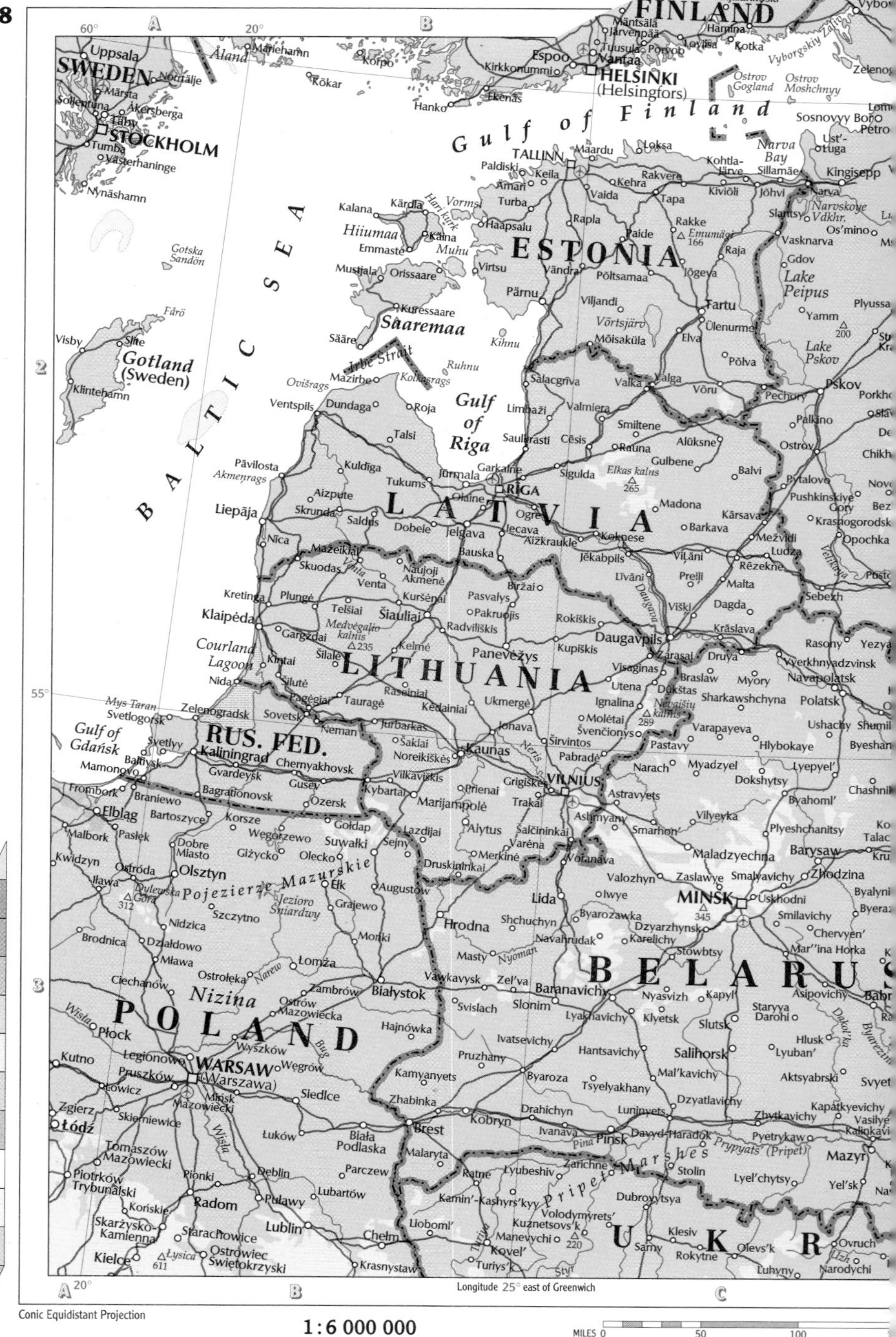

METRES
FEET

5000
16404

3000
9843

2000
6562

1000
3281

500
1640

200
656

0
0

LAND
B.S.L.

200
656

4000
13124

6000
19686

Conic Equidistant Projection

1:6 000 000

Longitude 25° east of Greenwich

MILES 0   50   100

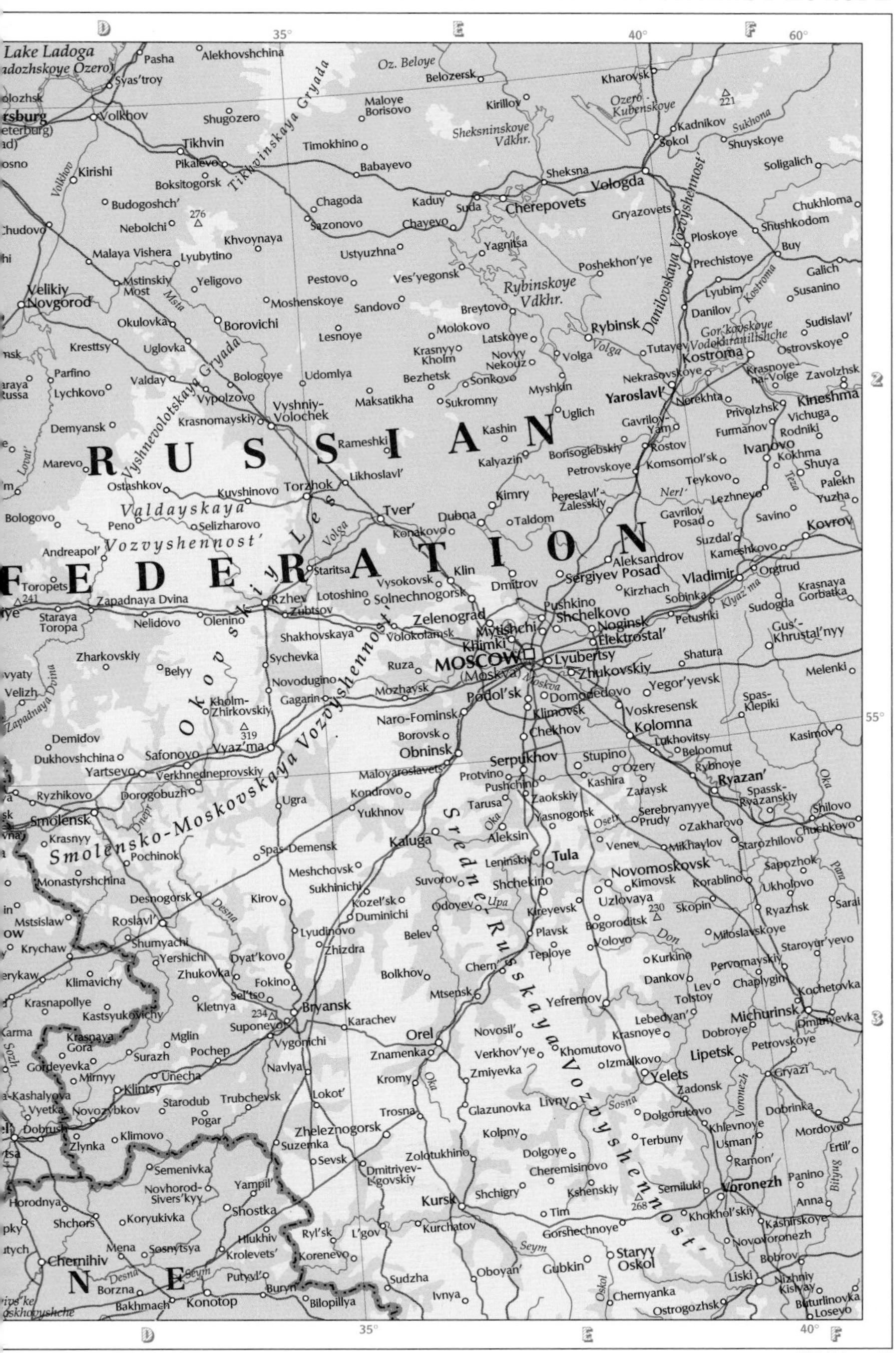
D
35°
E
40°
F
60°
Lake Ladoga
Pasha
Alekhovshchina
Syas'troy
Oz. Beloye
Belozersk
Kharovsk
221
Maloye Borisovo
Kirillov
Ozero Kubenskoye
Volkhov
Shugozero
Tikhvinskaya Gryada
Sheksninskoye Vdkhr.
Kadnikov
Sukhona
Sokol
Shuyskoye
Tikhvin
Timokhino
Pikalevo
Babayevo
Soligalich
Kirishi
Volkhov
Boksitogorsk
Sheksna
Vologda
Budogoshch'
Chagoda
Kaduy
Suda
Cherepovets
Gryazovets
Chukhloma
276
Nebolchi
Sazonovo
Chayevo
Shushkodom
Khvoynaya
Ploskoye
Malaya Vishera
Lyubytino
Ustyuzhna
Yagnitsa
Buy
Poshekhon'ye
Prechistoye
Danilovskaya Vozvyshennost'
Mstinskiy Most
Yeligovo
Pestovo
Ves'yegonsk
Rybinskoye Vdkhr.
Galich
Velikiy Novgorod
Msta
Moshenskoye
Sandovo
Breytovo
Lyubim
Kostroma
Susanino
Danilov
Okulovka
Borovichi
Molokovo
Rybinsk
Sudislavl'
Lesnoye
Latskoye
Gor'kovskoye Vodokhranilishche
Kresttsy
Uglovka
Krasnyy Kholm
Novyy Nekouz
Volga
Tutayev
Ostrovskoye
Kostroma
Parfino
Bezhetsk
Sonkovo
Krasnoye-na-Volge
Zavolzhsk
Valday
Bologoye
Udomlya
Nekrasovskoye
2
Lychkovo
Vypolzovo
Vyshniy-Volochek
Maksatikha
Sukromny
Myshkin
Yaroslavl'
Nerekhta
Kineshma
Demyansk
Krasnomayskiy
Uglich
Gavrilov-Yam
Privolzhsk
Vichuga
Furmanov
Rodniki
Rameshki
Kashin
Rostov
Marevo
Vyshnevolotskaya Gryada
Kalyazin
Borisoglebskiy
Ivanovo
Kokhma
Lovat'
Likhoslavl'
Petrovskoye
Komsomol'sk
Shuya
Ostashkov
Kuvshinovo
Torzhok
Teykovo
Teza
Palekh
Kimry
Pereslavl'-Zalesskiy
Nerl'
Lezhnevo
Yuzha
Valdayskaya
Tver'
Dubna
Taldom
Gavrilov Posad
Savino
Bologovo
Peno
Selizharovo
Volga
Konakovo
Suzdal'
Kovrov
Vozvyshennost'
Andreapol'
Kameshkovo
Aleksandrov
Staritsa
Klin
Sergiyev Posad
Vladimir
Orgtrud
Toropets
Vysokovsk
Dmitrov
Kirzhach
Krasnaya Gorbatka
241
Zapadnaya Dvina
Rzhev
Lotoshino
Solnechnogorsk
Pushkino
Sobinka
Klyaz'ma
Sudogda
Staraya Toropa
Nelidovo
Olenino
Zubtsov
Zelenograd
Shchelkovo
Noginsk
Petushki
Gus'-Khrustal'nyy
Shakhovskaya
Volokolamsk
Mytishchi
Elektrostal'
Khimki
Zharkovskiy
Sychevka
MOSCOW
(Moskva)
Lyubertsy
Shatura
Melenki
Belyy
Ruza
Zhukovskiy
Velizh
Zapadnaya Dvina
Novodugino
Mozhaysk
Moskva
Yegor'yevsk
Domodedovo
Podol'sk
Spas-Klepiki
Kholm-Zhirkovskiy
Gagarin
Okop skiy Les
Voskresensk
Naro-Fominsk
Klimovsk
55°
Kolomna
Demidov
319
Borovsk
Chekhov
Kasimov
Lukhovitsy
Dukhovshchina
Safonovo
Vyaz'ma
Obninsk
Beloomut
Serpukhov
Stupino
Yartsevo
Verkhnedneprovskiy
Maloyaroslavets
Ozery
Rybnoye
Oka
Protvino
Kashira
Ryazan'
Pushchino
Zaraysk
Ryzhikovo
Dorogobuzh
Kondrovo
Zaokskiy
Spassk-Ryazanskiy
Ugra
Tarusa
Serebryanyye Prudy
Shilovo
Smolensk
Yukhnov
Yasnogorsk
Osetr
Zakharovo
Dnepr
Smolensko-Moskovskaya Vozvyshennost'
Chuchkovo
Krasnyy
Kaluga
Aleksin
Venev
Mikhaylov
Starozhilovo
Pochinok
Spas-Demensk
Tula
Sredne-Russkaya Vozvyshennost'
Leninskiy
Novomoskovsk
Sapozhok
Para
Meshchovsk
Kimovsk
Monastyrshchina
Sukhinichi
Suvorov
Shchekino
Korablino
Ukholovo
Desnogorsk
Kirov
Kozel'sk
Uzlovaya
230
Skopin
Ryazhsk
Sarai
Mstsislaw
Duminichi
Odoyev
Upa
Kireyevsk
Roslavl'
Desna
Lyudinovo
Bogoroditsk
Don
Miloslavskoye
Belev
Plavsk
Volovo
Krychaw
Shumyachi
Zhizdra
Teploye
Staroyur'yevo
Yershichi
Dyat'kovo
Kurkino
Klimavichy
Zhukovka
Bolkhov
Chern'
Pervomayskiy
Fokino
Dankov
Chaplygin
Mtsensk
Lev Tolstoy
Kochetovka
Krasnapollye
Sel'tso
Kletnya
Bryansk
Yefremov
Michurinsk
3
Kastsyukovichy
234
Suponevo
Karachev
Lebedyan'
Dmitriyevka
Krasnaya Gora
Mglin
Vygonichi
Orel
Novosil'
Dobroye
Sozh
Pochep
Khomutovo
Krasnoye
Petrovskoye
Surazh
Znamenka
Verkhov'ye
Izmalkovo
Lipetsk
Gordeyevka
Navlya
Zmiyevka
Mirnyy
Unecha
Kromy
Oka
Yelets
Gryazi
Klintsy
Zadonsk
Kashalyova
Starodub
Trubchevsk
Lokot'
Livny
Sosna
Voronezh
Vyetka
Novozybkov
Trosna
Glazunovka
Dolgorukovo
Dobrinka
Pogar
Dobrush
Kolpny
Khlevnoye
Mordovo
Klimovo
Zheleznogorsk
Terbuny
Zlynka
Suzemka
Usman'
Ertil'
Dolgoye
Sevsk
Zolotukhino
Semenivka
Cheremisinovo
Ramon'
Dmitriyev-L'govskiy
Bityug
Panino
Novhorod-Sivers'kyy
Yampil'
Voronezh
Semiluki
Kursk
Shchigry
Kshenskiy
Anna
Horodnya
Shostka
268
Tim
Khokhol'skiy
Shchors
Koryukivka
Ryl'sk
L'gov
Kurchatov
Kashirskoye
Hlukhiv
Gorshechnoye
Novovoronezh
Mena
Sosnytsya
Seym
Krolevets'
Korenevo
Staryy Oskol
Bobrov
Chernihiv
Gubkin
Desna
Seym
Putyvl'
Sudzha
Oboyan'
Liski
Nizhniy Kislyay
Borzna
Buryn'
Oskol
Chernyanka
Ivnya
Bilopillya
Buturlinovka
Bakhmach
Konotop
Ostrogozhsk
Losevo
D
35°
E
40°
F
RUSSIAN FEDERATION
UKRAINE

100 200 KILOMETRES

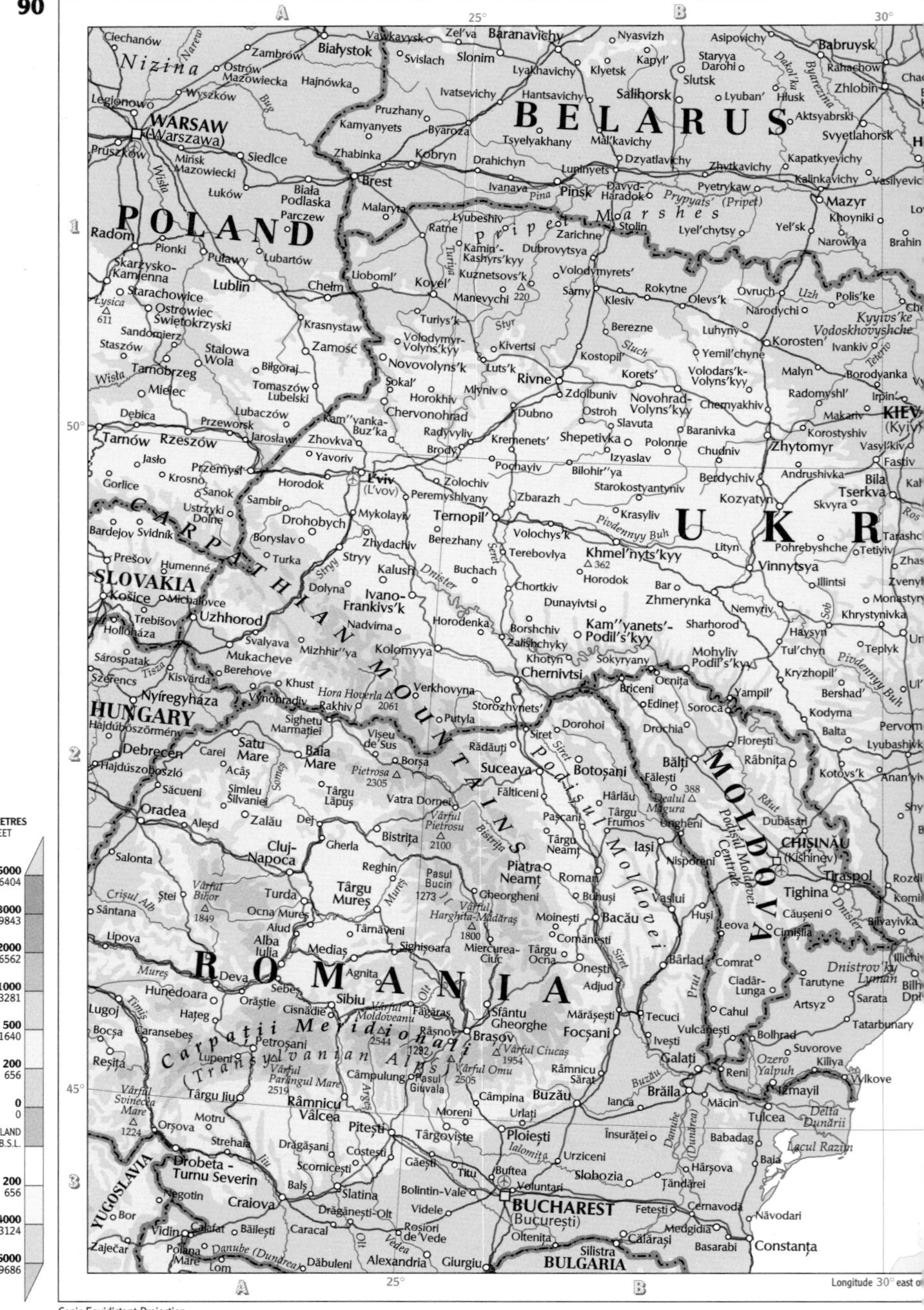

A map of Eastern Europe showing parts of Poland, Belarus, Ukraine, Slovakia, Hungary, Romania, Moldova, and Bulgaria.

METRES / FEET scale:
5000 / 16404
3000 / 9843
2000 / 6562
1000 / 3281
500 / 1640
200 / 656
0 / 0
LAND B.S.L.
200 / 656
4000 / 13124
6000 / 19686

Conic Equidistant Projection

1 : 6 000 000

MILES 0   50   100

Longitude 30° east of

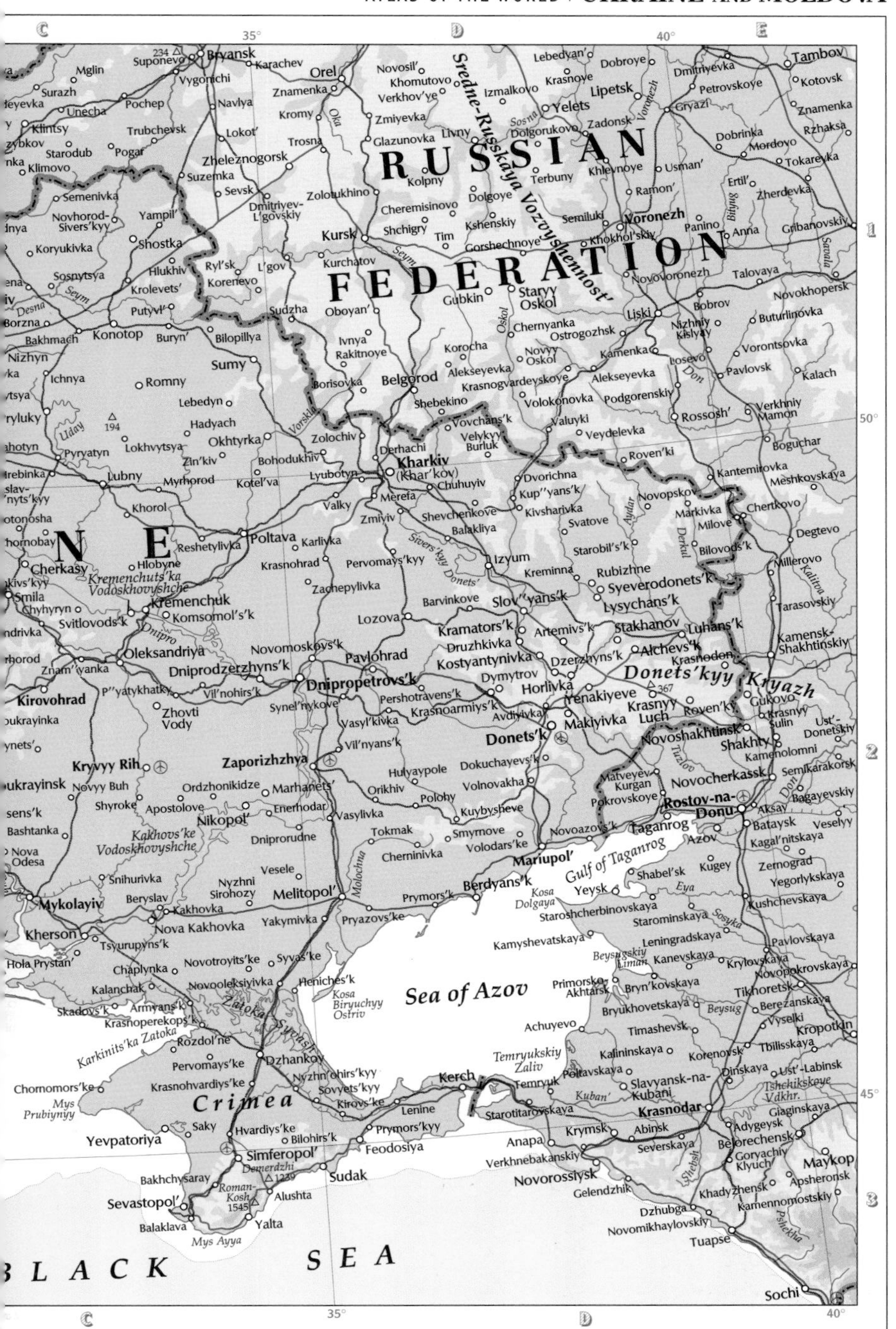
C
35°
D
40°
E
RUSSIAN FEDERATION
Sredne-Russkaya Vozvyshennost'
Bryansk
Suponevo
Karachev
Mglin
Surazh
Vygonichi
Unecha
Pochep
Navlya
Klintsy
Trubchevsk
Lokot'
Starodub
Pogar
Klimovo
Zheleznogorsk
Suzemka
Sevsk
Orel
Znamenka
Kromy
Trosna
Oka
Novosil'
Khomutovo
Verkhov'ye
Zmiyevka
Glazunovka
Livny
Izmalkovo
Lebedyan'
Krasnoye
Dobroye
Lipetsk
Yelets
Dolgorukovo
Zadonsk
Sosna
Voronezh
Dmitriyevka
Petrovskoye
Gryazi
Tambov
Kotovsk
Znamenka
Rzhaksa
Dobrinka
Mordovo
Tokarevka
Usman'
Khlevnoye
Terbuny
Kolpny
Dolgoye
Ramon'
Ertil'
Zherdevka
Bityug
Zolotukhino
Dmitriyev-L'govskiy
Cheremisinovo
Shchigry
Tim
Kshenskiy
Semiluki
Voronezh
Khokhol'skiy
Panino
Anna
Gribanovskiy
Savala
Kursk
Seym
Gorshechnoye
Kurchatov
Novovoronezh
Talovaya
Novokhopersk
Semenivka
Novhorod-Sivers'kyy
Yampil'
Shostka
Koryukivka
Hlukhiv
Ryl'sk
L'gov
Korenevo
Sosnytsya
Krolevets'
Putyvl'
Desna
Borzna
Bakhmach
Konotop
Buryn'
Bilopillya
Sudzha
Oboyan'
Gubkin
Staryy Oskol
Oskol
Chernyanka
Ostrogozhsk
Liski
Bobrov
Nizhniy Kislyay
Buturlinovka
Vorontsovka
Pavlovsk
Kalach
Losevo
Don
Kamenka
Alekseyevka
Korocha
Novyy Oskol
Ivnya
Rakitnoye
Belgorod
Borisovka
Shebekino
Krasnogvardeyskoye
Volokonovka
Podgorenskiy
Rossosh'
Verkhniy Mamon
50°
Nizhyn
Ichnya
Romny
Sumy
Lebedyn
Hadyach
Okhtyrka
Vorskla
Zolochiv
Pryluky
Uday
194
Lokhvytsya
Pyryatyn
Zin'kiv
Bohodukhiv
Derhachi
Vovchans'k
Velykyy Burluk
Valuyki
Veydelevka
Roven'ki
Boguchar
Lubny
Myrhorod
Kotel'va
Lyubotyn
Kharkiv (Khar'kov)
Chuhuyiv
Merefa
Valky
Dvorichna
Kup''yans'k
Kivsharivka
Kantemirovka
Meshkovskaya
Novopskov
Markivka
Chertkovo
Milove
Khorol
Zmiyiv
Shevchenkove
Balakliya
Svatove
Aydar
Derkul
Bilovods'k
Degtevo
Zolotonosha
Chornobay
UKRAINE
Reshetylivka
Poltava
Karlivka
Hlobyne
Cherkasy
Kremenchuts'ka Vodoskhovyshche
Smila
Krasnohrad
Pervomays'kyy
Sivers'kyy Donets'
Izyum
Starobil's'k
Millerovo
Kalitva
Kremenchuk
Komsomol's'k
Chyhyryn
Svitlovods'k
Zachepylivka
Kreminna
Rubizhne
Syeverodonets'k
Lysychans'k
Tarasovskiy
Barvinkove
Slov''yans'k
Lozova
Kramators'k
Artemivs'k
Stakhanov
Luhans'k
Kamensk-Shakhtinskiy
Dnipro
Oleksandriya
Novomoskovs'k
Druzhkivka
Kostyantynivka
Alchevs'k
Krasnodon
Znam''yanka
Dniprodzerzhyns'k
Pavlohrad
Dzerzhyns'k
Dymytrov
Horlivka
Donets'kyy Kryazh
367
Kirovohrad
P''yatykhatky
Vil'nohirs'k
Dnipropetrovs'k
Pershotravens'k
Synel'nykove
Krasnoarmiys'k
Yenakiyeve
Krasnyy Luch
Roven'ky
Gukovo
Krasnyy Sulin
Zhovti Vody
Vasyl'kivka
Avdiyivka
Makiyivka
Donets'k
Novoshakhtinsk
Shakhty
Ust'-Donetskiy
Kamenolomni
Vil'nyans'k
Kryvyy Rih
Zaporizhzhya
Dokuchayevs'k
Tuzlov
Semikarakorsk
Novyy Buh
Ordzhonikidze
Marhanets'
Hulyaypole
Volnovakha
Matveyev Kurgan
Pokrovskoye
Novocherkassk
Shyroke
Apostolove
Orikhiv
Polohy
Kuybysheve
Rostov-na-Donu
Aksay
Bagayevskiy
Bashtanka
Nikopol'
Enerhodar
Vasylivka
Tokmak
Smyrnove
Novoazovs'k
Taganrog
Azov
Bataysk
Veselyy
Kakhovs'ke Vodoskhovyshche
Dniprorudne
Cherninivka
Volodars'ke
Mariupol'
Gulf of Taganrog
Kagal'nitskaya
Nova Odesa
Molochna
Vesele
Kugey
Zernograd
Shabel'sk
Yegorlykskaya
Snihurivka
Nyzhni Sirohozy
Melitopol'
Berdyans'k
Prymors'k
Kosa Dolgaya
Yeysk
Eya
Mykolayiv
Beryslav
Kakhovka
Kushchevskaya
Nova Kakhovka
Yakymivka
Pryazovs'ke
Starosherbinovskaya
Starominskaya
Sosyka
Kherson
Tsyurupyns'k
Kamyshevatskaya
Leningradskaya
Pavlovskaya
Hola Prystan'
Novotroyits'ke
Syvas'ke
Beysugskiy Liman
Kanevskaya
Krylovskaya
Chaplynka
Novooleksiyivka
Heniches'k
Sea of Azov
Primorsko-Akhtarsk
Bryn'kovskaya
Novopokrovskaya
Kalanchak
Kosa Biryuchyy Ostriv
Tikhoretsk
Skadovs'k
Armyans'k
Zatoka Syvash
Bryukhovetskaya
Beysug
Berezanskaya
Krasnoperekops'k
Achuyevo
Vyselki
Kropotkin
Karkinits'ka Zatoka
Rozdol'ne
Timashevsk
Tbilisskaya
Dzhankoy
Temryukskiy Zaliv
Kalininskaya
Korenovsk
Pervomays'ke
Nyzhn'ohirs'kyy
Dinskaya
Ust'-Labinsk
Chornomors'ke
Krasnohvardiys'ke
Sovyets'kyy
Kerch
Temryuk
Poltavskaya
Slavyansk-na-Kubani
Tshchikskoye Vdkhr.
45°
Mys Prubiynyy
Crimea
Kirovs'ke
Lenine
Kuban'
Krasnodar
Giaginskaya
Starotitarovskaya
Adygeysk
Saky
Hvardiys'ke
Bilohirs'k
Prymors'kyy
Krymsk
Abinsk
Belorechensk
Yevpatoriya
Feodosiya
Anapa
Severskaya
Simferopol'
Verkhnebakanskiy
Goryachiy Klyuch
Maykop
Demerdzhi
1239
Shebsh
Bakhchysaray
Sudak
Novorossiysk
Apsheronsk
Roman-Kosh
1545
Alushta
Gelendzhik
Khadyzhensk
Kamennomostskiy
Sevastopol'
Dzhubga
Balaklava
Yalta
Novomikhaylovskiy
Pshekha
Mys Ayya
Tuapse
BLACK SEA
Sochi
1
2
3
100
200 KILOMETRES
© Bartholomew Ltd

METRES
FEET

METRES	FEET
6000	19686
4000	13124
200	656
LAND B.S.L.	
0	0
200	656
500	1640
1000	3281
2000	6562
3000	9843
5000	16404

ICELAND
AT THE SAME SCALE

NORWEGIAN SEA

Conic Equidistant Projection

1:7 500 000

MILES 0 50 100

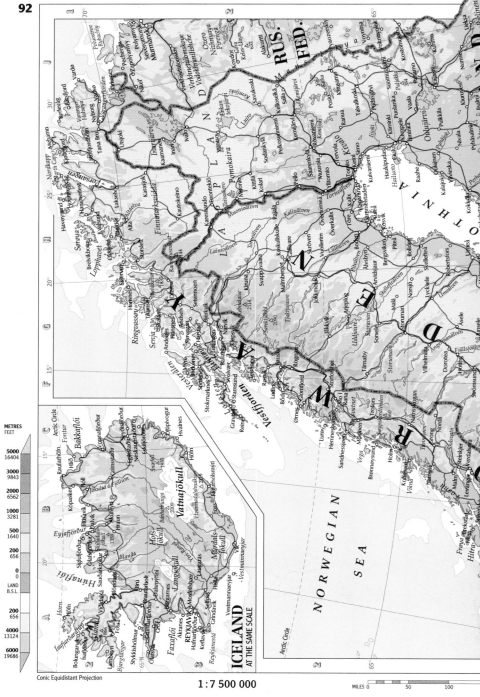

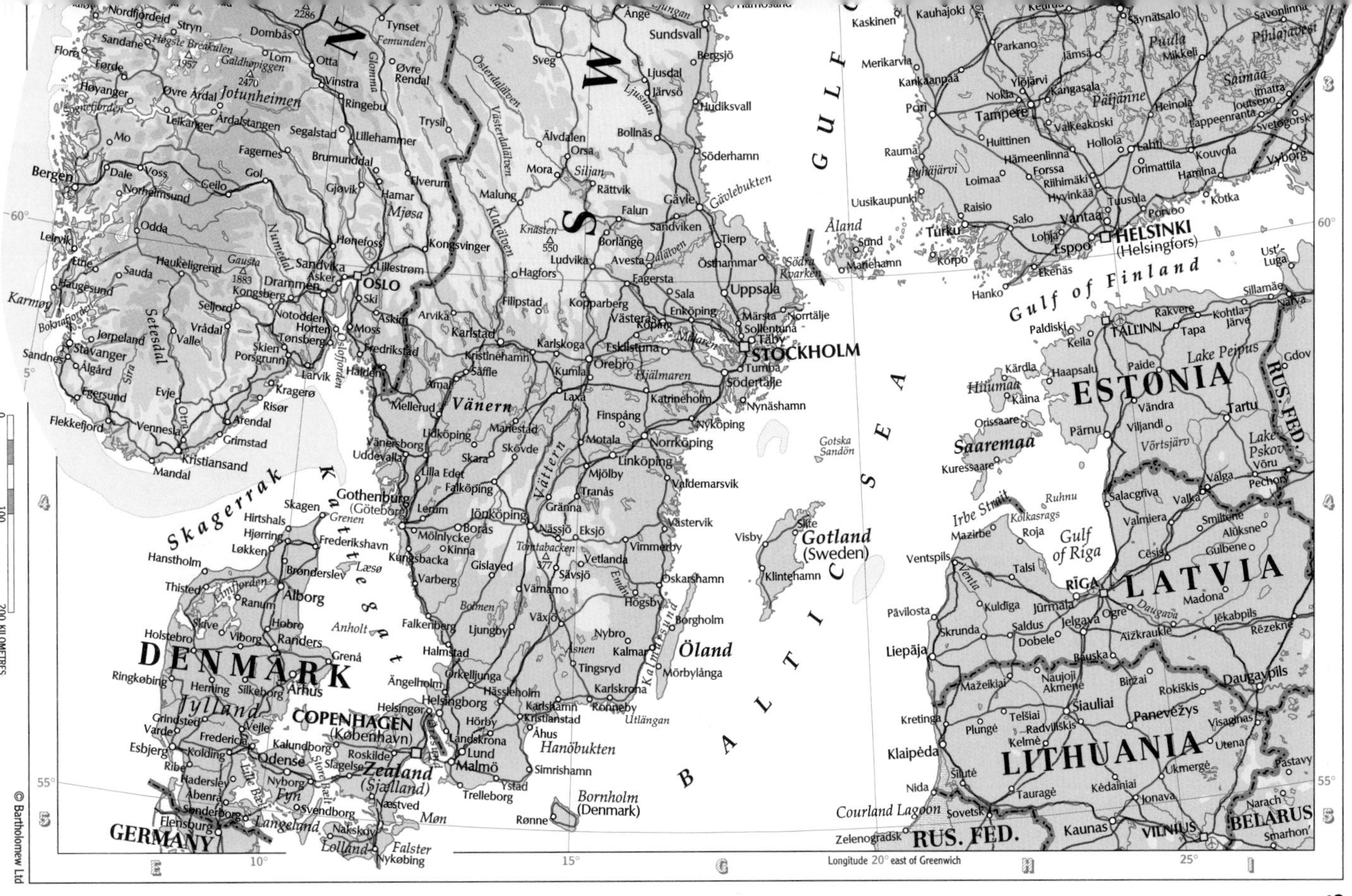

© Bartholomew Ltd

0   100   200 KILOMETRES

ESTONIA
LATVIA
LITHUANIA
BELARUS
RUS. FED.
DENMARK
GERMANY
HELSINKI
(Helsingfors)
TALLINN
RĪGA
VILNIUS
STOCKHOLM
OSLO
COPENHAGEN
(København)
Gulf of Finland
Gulf of Riga
BALTIC SEA
GULF
Kattegat
Skagerrak
Gotland
(Sweden)
Öland
Bornholm
(Denmark)
Saaremaa
Hiiumaa
Åland
Zealand
(Sjælland)
Jylland
Fyn
Lolland
Falster
Vänern
Vättern
Lake Peipus
Jotunheimen
Setesdal
Courland Lagoon
Longitude 20° east of Greenwich
60°
55°
25°
15°
5°

METRES
FEET

5000	16404
3000	9843
2000	6562
1000	3281
500	1640
200	656
0	0
LAND	B.S.L.
200	656
4000	13124
6000	19686

NORTH SEA

Shetland Islands

Herma Ness
Yell Unst
Fetlar
Isbister
Lerwick
Mainland
Foula ⊙
Sumburgh Head
Fair Isle

Orkney Islands
Westray
Rousay
Sanday
Mainland
Stromness
Kirkwall
Hoy
John o'Groats
Pentland Firth
Thurso
Wick
Tongue
Helmsdale

Peterhead
Fraserburgh
Banff
Huntly
Inverie
Aberdeen
Elgin
Grampian
Grantown-on-Spey
Mountains
Ballater
Inverness
Moray Firth
SCOTLAND
Montrose
Arbroath
Forfar
Dundee
Perth
Crieff

Cape
Wrath
Durness
Ben Hope
927
Loch
Shin
Scourie
Ullapool
An Teallach
1062
Dingwall
Ben
Nevis
1344
Comrie

The Minch

Butt of
Lewis
Stornoway
Isle of
Lewis
Harris
799
Little Minch
Kyle of
Lochalsh
Mallaig
Portree
Skye
Fort William
Spean Bridge
Fort Augustus
Kinloch
Rum

Outer Hebrides

St Kilda
North Uist
Benbecula
South Uist
Barra
Coll
Tiree
Mull

Faroe Islands
(Denmark)
Streymoy
Norðoyar
Vestmanna
Klaksvík
882
Borðoy
Miðvágur
Eysturoy
Vágar
Tórshavn
Sandur
Sandoy
Vágur
Suðuroy

ATLANTIC
OCEAN

Rockall

Conic Equidistant Projection

1:6 000 000

MILES 0   50   100

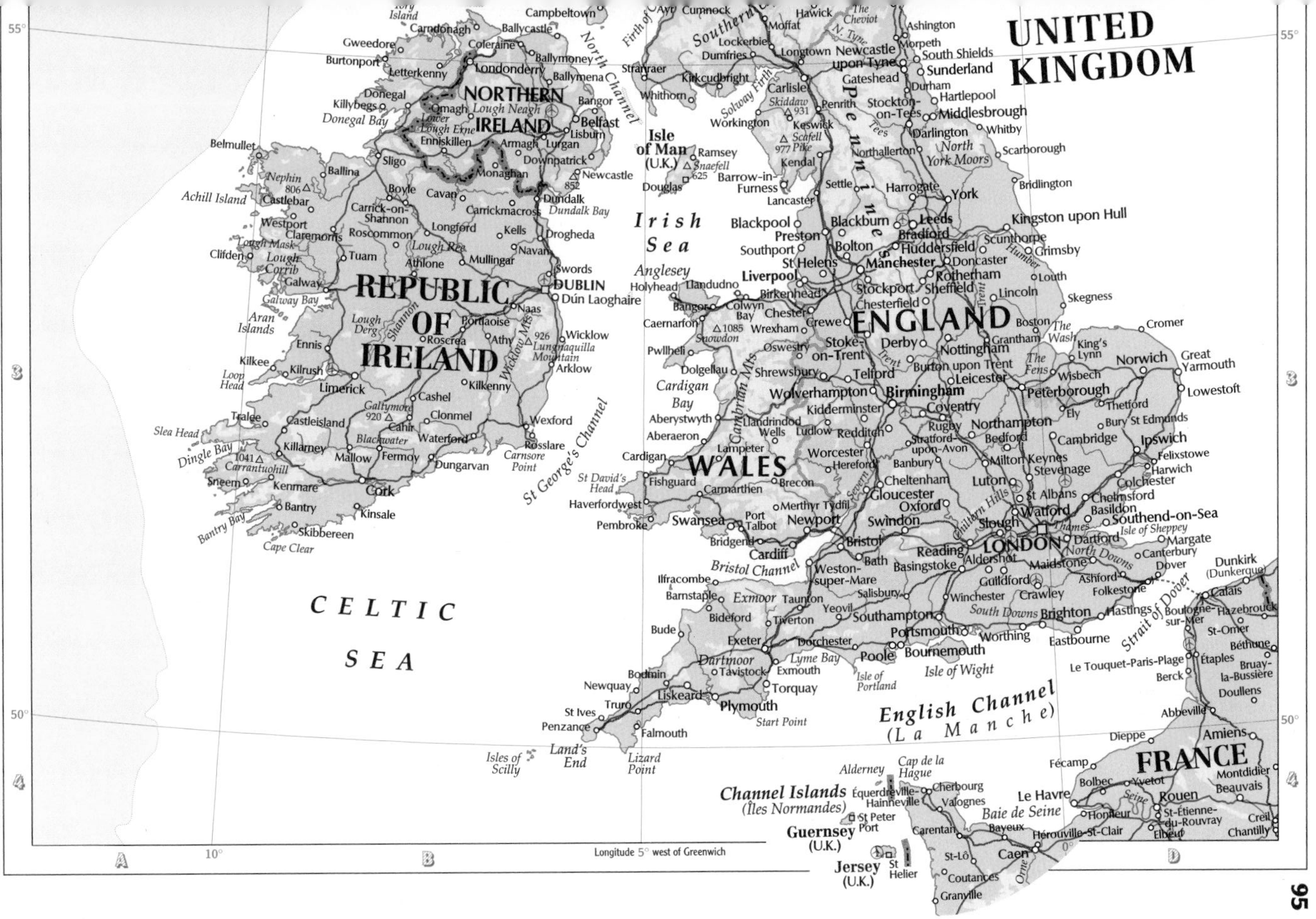

© Bartholomew Ltd

100   200 KILOMETRES

UNITED KINGDOM
ENGLAND
WALES
NORTHERN IRELAND
REPUBLIC OF IRELAND
FRANCE
LONDON
DUBLIN
Irish Sea
CELTIC SEA
English Channel
(La Manche)
North Channel
St George's Channel
Bristol Channel
Strait of Dover
Cardigan Bay
Solway Firth
Pennines
Cambrian Mts
Isle of Man (U.K.)
Anglesey
Channel Islands (Îles Normandes)
Guernsey (U.K.)
Jersey (U.K.)
Isle of Wight
Isles of Scilly
Land's End
Lizard Point
Birmingham
Manchester
Liverpool
Leeds
Sheffield
Bristol
Cardiff
Swansea
Newcastle upon Tyne
Belfast
Londonderry
Cork
Limerick
Galway
Waterford
Wexford
Plymouth
Southampton
Portsmouth
Norwich
Cambridge
Oxford
Nottingham
Leicester
Coventry
York
Kingston upon Hull
Le Havre
Caen
Rouen
Calais
Dunkirk (Dunkerque)
Cherbourg
Amiens
Longitude 5° west of Greenwich
55°
50°

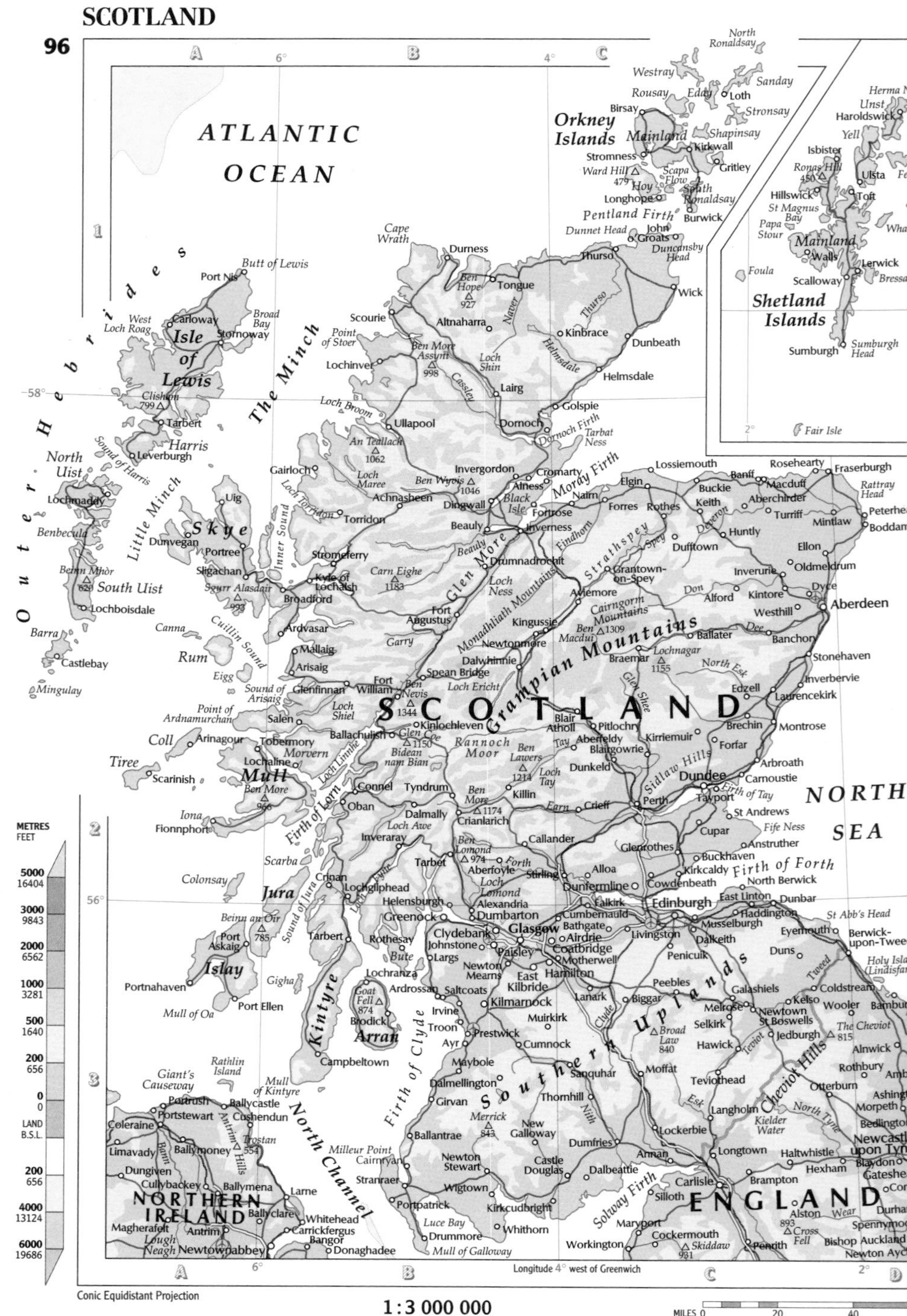

SCOTLAND

ATLANTIC
OCEAN

NORTH
SEA

SCOTLAND

NORTHERN
IRELAND

ENGLAND

Orkney Islands

North Ronaldsay, Westray, Rousay, Eddy, Loth, Sanday, Birsay, Stronsay, Mainland, Shapinsay, Kirkwall, Stromness, Scapa Flow, Gritley, Ward Hill, 479, Hoy, South Ronaldsay, Longhope, Burwick, John o'Groats, Pentland Firth, Dunnet Head, Duncansby Head

Shetland Islands

Herma N, Unst, Haroldswick, Yell, Isbister, Ronas Hill, 450, Uista, Toft, Hillswick, St Magnus Bay, Papa Stour, Wha, Foula, Mainland, Walls, Lerwick, Scalloway, Bressa, Sumburgh, Sumburgh Head, Fair Isle

Outer Hebrides

Butt of Lewis, Port Nis, West Loch Roag, Broad Bay, Carloway, Stornoway, Isle of Lewis, Clishom 799, Tarbert, Harris, Leverburgh, Sound of Harris, North Uist, Lochmaddy, Benbecula, Beinn Mhòr, South Uist, Lochboisdale, Barra, Castlebay, Mingulay

Cape Wrath, Durness, Thurso, Wick, Ben Hope 927, Tongue, Scourie, Altnaharra, Point of Stoer, Ben More Assynt 998, Lochinver, Loch Shin, Lairg, Kinbrace, Dunbeath, Helmsdale, An Teallach 1062, Ullapool, Loch Broom, Dornoch, Golspie, Tarbat Ness, Clishom, Gairloch, Loch Maree, Ben Wyvis 1046, Achnasheen, Dingwall, Invergordon, Cromarty, Alness, Moray Firth, Elgin, Lossiemouth, Rosehearty, Fraserburgh, Banff, Macduff, Rattray Head, Peterhead, Boddam, Uig, Torridon, Beauly, Nairn, Forres, Rothes, Keith, Aberchirder, Turriff, Mintlaw, Skye, Inverness, Dufftown, Huntly, Ellon, Oldmeldrum, Dunvegan, Portree, Stromferry, Carn Eighe 1183, Drumnadrochit, Glen More, Grantown-on-Spey, Strathspey, Inverurie, Dyce, Aberdeen, Sligachan, Kyle of Lochalsh, Loch Ness, Aviemore, Cairngorm Mountains, Alford, Kintore, Westhill, Sgurr Alasdair 993, Broadford, Fort Augustus, Kingussie, Cairngorm 1309, Don, Banchory, Stonehaven, Canna, Ardvasar, Mallaig, Newtonmore, Macdui 1309, Ballater, Lochnagar 1155, North Esk, Cuillin Sound, Garry, Dalwhinnie, Braemar, Dee, Inverbervie, Rum, Arisaig, Spean Bridge, Loch Ericht, Grampian Mountains, Edzell, Laurencekirk, Eigg, Sound of Arisaig, Fort William, Ben Nevis 1344, Glen Spean, Rannoch Moor, Blair Atholl, Pitlochry, Brechin, Montrose, Point of Ardnamurchan, Salen, Glenfinnan, Loch Shiel, Bidean nam Bian 1150, Ben Lawers 1214, Tay, Aberfeldy, Blairgowrie, Kirriemuir, Forfar, Arbroath, Coll, Arinagour, Tobermory, Morvern, Ballachulish, Kinlochleven, Loch Linnhe, Black Mount, Loch Tay, Dunkeld, Camoustie, Tiree, Scarinish, Lochaline, Ben More 966, Connel, Tyndrum, Ben More 1174, Killin, Earn, Crieff, Perth, Dundee, Firth of Tay, Tayport, Iona, Fionnphort, Oban, Dalmally, Crianlarich, Sidlaw Hills, St Andrews, NORTH SEA, Loch Awe, Inveraray, Callander, Cupar, Fife Ness, Anstruther, Scarba, Ben Lomond 974, Aberfoyle, Stirling, Glenrothes, Buckhaven, Crinan, Forth, Alloa, Cowdenbeath, Kirkcaldy, Firth of Forth, North Berwick, Colonsay, Lochgilphead, Helensburgh, Loch Lomond, Dunfermline, Falkirk, Edinburgh, East Linton, Dunbar, Beinn an Oir 785, Greenock, Dumbarton, Cumbernauld, Bathgate, Musselburgh, Haddington, St Abb's Head, Port Askaig, Clydebank, Glasgow, Airdrie, Coatbridge, Livingston, Dalkeith, Eyemouth, Berwick-upon-Tweed, Islay, Gigha, Johnstone, Paisley, Motherwell, Penicuik, Duns, Holy Island, Portnahaven, Mull of Oa, Port Ellen, Lochranza, Newton Mearns, East Kilbride, Hamilton, Peebles, Galashiels, Coldstream, Goat Fell 874, Ardrossan, Saltcoats, Kilbride, Lanark, Biggar, Melrose, Kelso, Wooler, Bamburgh, Arran, Brodick, Irvine, Kilmarnock, Muirkirk, Selkirk, St Boswells, Jedburgh, The Cheviot 815, Alnwick, Kintyre, Troon, Prestwick, Cumnock, Hawick, Broad Law 840, Campbeltown, Ayr, Maybole, Sanquhar, Moffat, Teviothead, Cheviot Hills, Otterburn, Rothbury, Amb, Rathlin Island, Mull of Kintyre, Dalmellington, Girvan, Thornhill, Nith, Langholm, Kielder Water, Morpeth, Bedlington, Giant's Causeway, Merrick 843, New Galloway, Dumfries, Lockerbie, Esk, North Tyne, Newcastle upon Tyne, Blaydon, Gateshead, Portrush, Portstewart, Coshendun, Ballantrae, Milleur Point, Cairnryan, Newton Stewart, Castle Douglas, Dalbeattie, Annan, Longtown, Haltwhistle, Hexham, Coleraine, Ballycastle, Trostan 554, Wigtown, Kirkcudbright, Solway Firth, Carlisle, Brampton, Alston, Wear, Durham, Limavady, Ballymoney, Stranraer, Luce Bay, Whithorn, Silloth, Maryport, Cockermouth, Penrith, Cross Fell 893, Bishop Auckland, Dungiven, Cullybackey, Ballymena, Larne, Portpatrick, Drummore, Mull of Galloway, Workington, Skiddaw 931, Newton Aycliffe, Magherafelt, Antrim, Ballyclare, Whitehead, Carrickfergus, Bangor, Donaghadee, Lough Neagh, Newtownabbey

Atlantic, Mull, Loch Linnhe, Firth of Lorn, Sound of Jura, Jura, Kintyre, North Channel, Firth of Clyde, Bute, The Minch, Little Minch, Inner Sound, Sound of Sleat, Cuillin Sound, Sound of Mull

METRES / FEET

METRES	FEET
5000	16404
3000	9843
2000	6562
1000	3281
500	1640
200	656
0	0
LAND B.S.L.	
200	656
4000	13124
6000	19686

Longitude 4° west of Greenwich

Conic Equidistant Projection

1 : 3 000 000

MILES 0   20   40

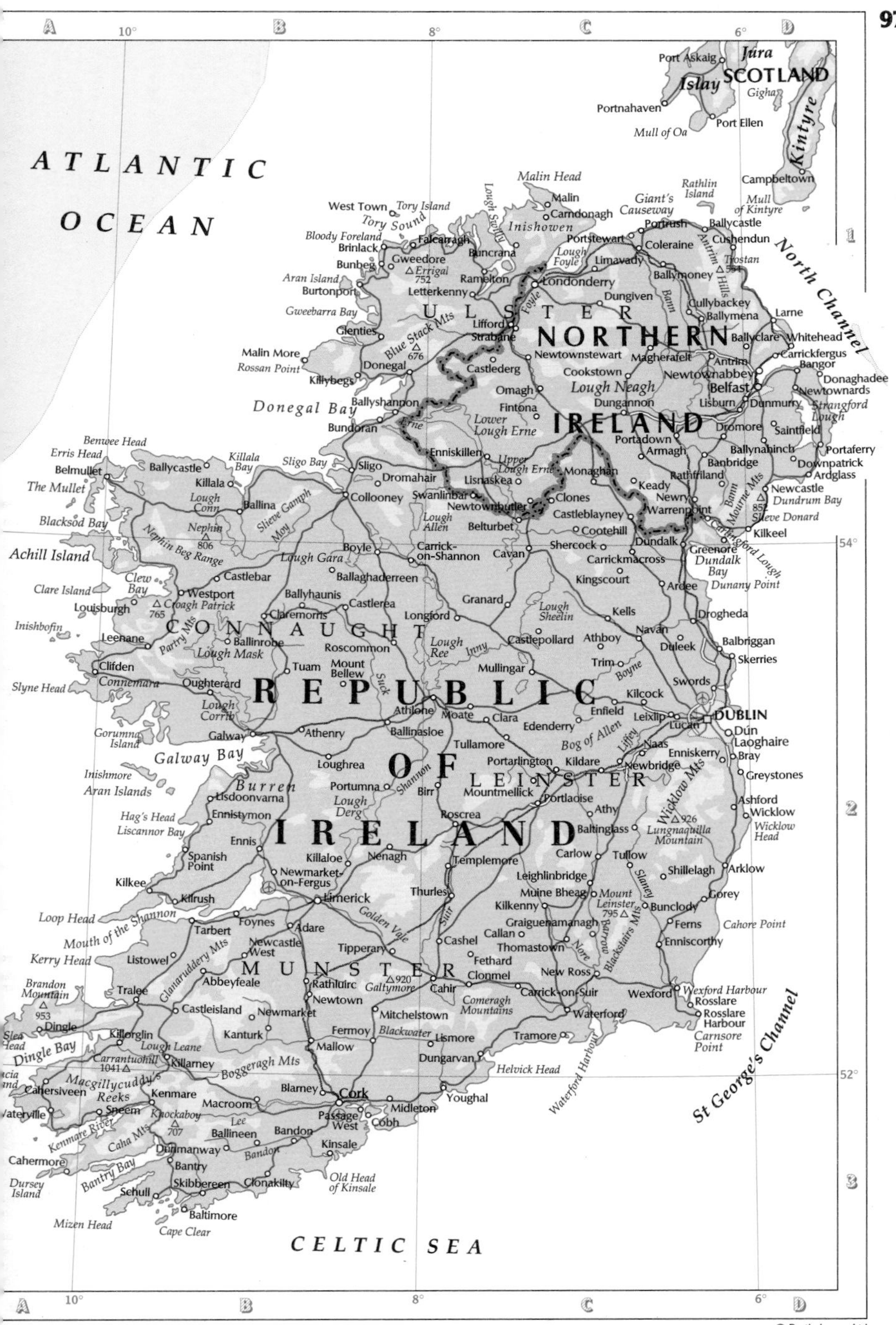

ATLANTIC

OCEAN

Port Askaig *Jura*
Islay SCOTLAND
Portnahaven *Gigha*
Mull of Oa Port Ellen

Malin Head
West Town *Tory Island* Malin *Rathlin* Campbeltown
Tory Sound Carndonagh *Island*
Inishowen *Giant's* Mull
Bloody Foreland Falcarragh Portstewart *Causeway* Portrush of Kintyre
Brinlack Buncrana Coleraine Ballycastle
Bunbeg Gweedore Portstewart Cushendun *Tristan*
Aran Island △Errigal Rathmelton Limavady Ballymoney
Burtonport 752 Londonderry
Letterkenny Dungiven Cullybackey
Gweebarra Bay Lifford Ballymena Larne
Glenties Strabane Whitehead
Malin More *Blue Stack Mts* Newtownstewart Magherafelt Ballyclare Carrickfergus
Rossan Point 676△ Antrim Bangor
Killybegs Donegal Castlederg Cookstown Newtownabbey Donaghadee
Omagh *Lough Neagh* Belfast Newtownards
Donegal Bay Ballyshannon Fintona Dungannon Lisburn Dunmurry Strangford
Bundoran *Erne* Lower Portadown Dromore *Lough*
Lough Erne Armagh Saintfield
Benvee Head Enniskillen Upper Ballynahinch Portaferry
Erris Head *Lough Erne* Monaghan Banbridge Downpatrick
Belmullet Ballycastle Killala Sligo Bay Sligo Dromahair Lisnaskea Keady Rathfriland Ardglass
The Mullet Bay Killala Clones Newry Newcastle
Collooney Swanlinbar Newtownbutler Castleblayney Warrenpoint Dundrum Bay
Blacksod Bay Ballina Belturbet Cootehill Kilkeel
Nephin Lough Allen Carrick- Shercock Dundalk Greenore
Achill Island 806△ Boyle on-Shannon Cavan Carrickmacross Dundalk
Clare Island Clew Castlebar Ballaghaderreen Kingscourt Bay
Westport Ballyhaunis Granard Ardee Dunany Point
Louisburgh Croagh Patrick Claremorris Castlerea Longford Lough Kells Drogheda
Inishbofin 765△ Sheelin
Leenane Ballinrobe Roscommon Castlepollard Athboy Navan Balbriggan
Clifden Lough Mask Tuam Mount Lough Mullingar Trim Duleek Skerries
Slyne Head Connemara Oughterard Bellew Ree Swords
Lough Athlone Moate Clara Kilcock DUBLIN
Gorumna Corrib Athenry Ballinasloe Edenderry Enfield Leixlip Dún
Island Galway Tullamore Naas Lucan Laoghaire
Galway Bay Loughrea *Bog of Allen* Newbridge Bray
Inishmore Portumna Birr Portarlington Kildare Enniskerry Greystones
Aran Islands Burren Lisdoonvarna Mountmellick Portlaoise Athy Ashford
Hag's Head Lough Roscrea Baltinglass Wicklow
Liscannor Bay Ennistymon Derg Lungnaquilla Head
Ennis Killaloe Nenagh Templemore Carlow Tullow Mountain
Spanish Newmarket- Thurles Kilkenny Shillelagh Arklow
Point on-Fergus Limerick Muine Bheag Gorey
Kilkee Kilrush Golden Vale Kilkenny Mount Bunclody
Loop Head Foynes Adare Thurles Graiguenamanagh Leinster Ferns Cahore Point
Mouth of the Shannon Tarbert Tipperary Callan 795△ Enniscorthy
Kerry Head Listowel Newcastle Cashel Thomastown
West Fethard
Abbeyfeale Clonmel New Ross Wexford Wexford Harbour
Brandon MUNSTER Rathluirc Galtymore Cahir Carrick-on-Suir Rosslare
Mountain Tralee Newtown Comeragh Waterford Rosslare
953△ Dingle Castleisland Newmarket Mitchelstown Mountains Carnsore
Killorglin Fermoy Blackwater Lismore Tramore Point
Dingle Bay Lough Leane Kanturk Mallow Dungarvan
Carrantuohill Boggeragh Mts Helvick Head
Caherciveen Macgillycuddy's 1041△ Killarney Blarney
Reeks Kenmare Macroom Cork Youghal
Waterville Sneem Knockalough Lee Midleton
Cahermore Ballineen Bandon Passage
Dunmanway West Cobh
Bantry Bandon Kinsale
Dursey Schull Skibbereen Clonakilty Old Head
Island Baltimore of Kinsale
Mizen Head Cape Clear

CELTIC SEA

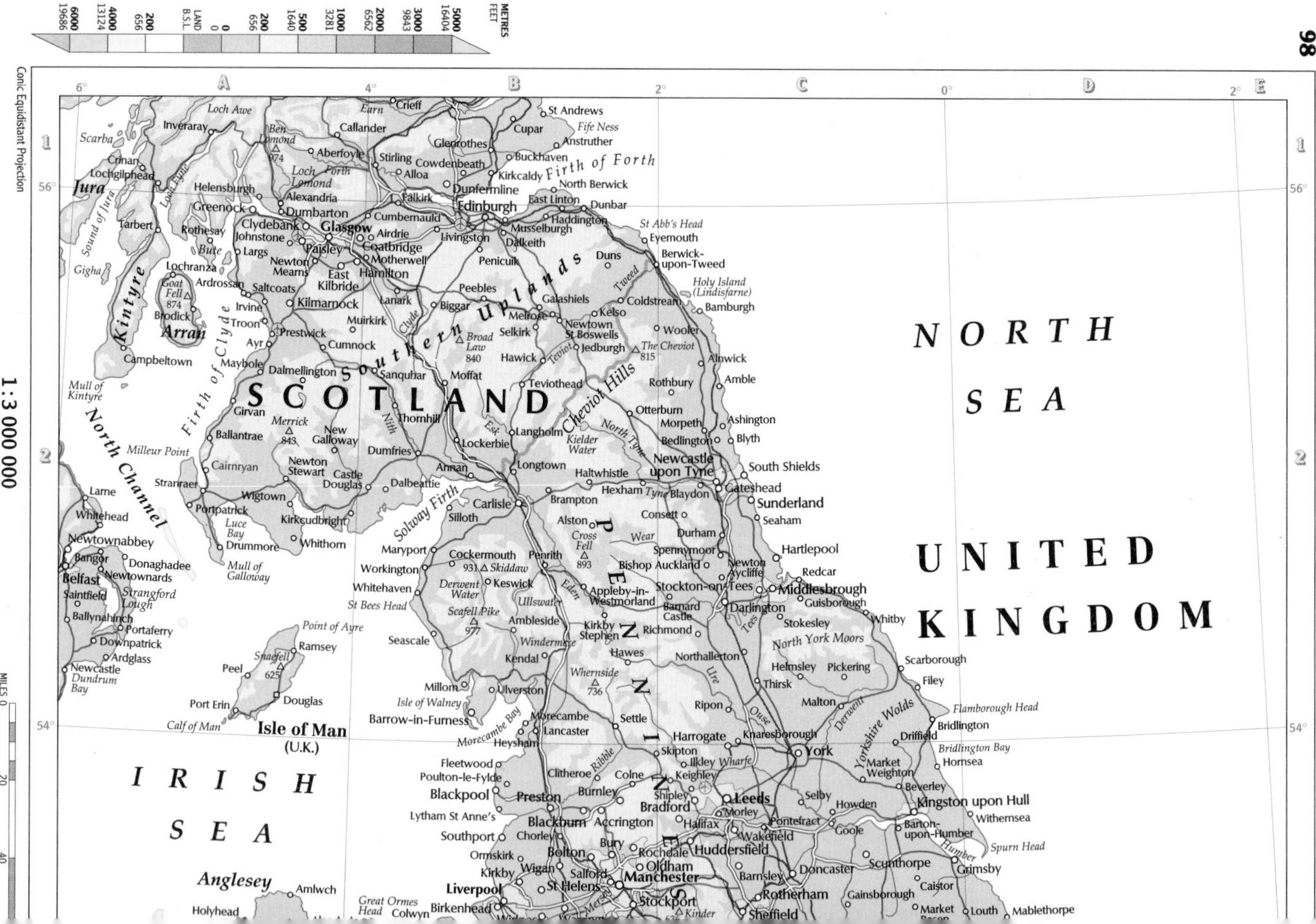

1:3 000 000

MILES 0   20   40

METRES
FEET

5000	16404
3000	9843
2000	6562
1000	3281
500	1640
200	656
0	0
LAND	B.S.L.
200	656
4000	13124
6000	19686

NORTH SEA

UNITED KINGDOM

SCOTLAND

PENNINES

IRISH SEA

Anglesey

Isle of Man (U.K.)

North Channel

Firth of Forth

Firth of Clyde

Kintyre

Southern Uplands

Cheviot Hills

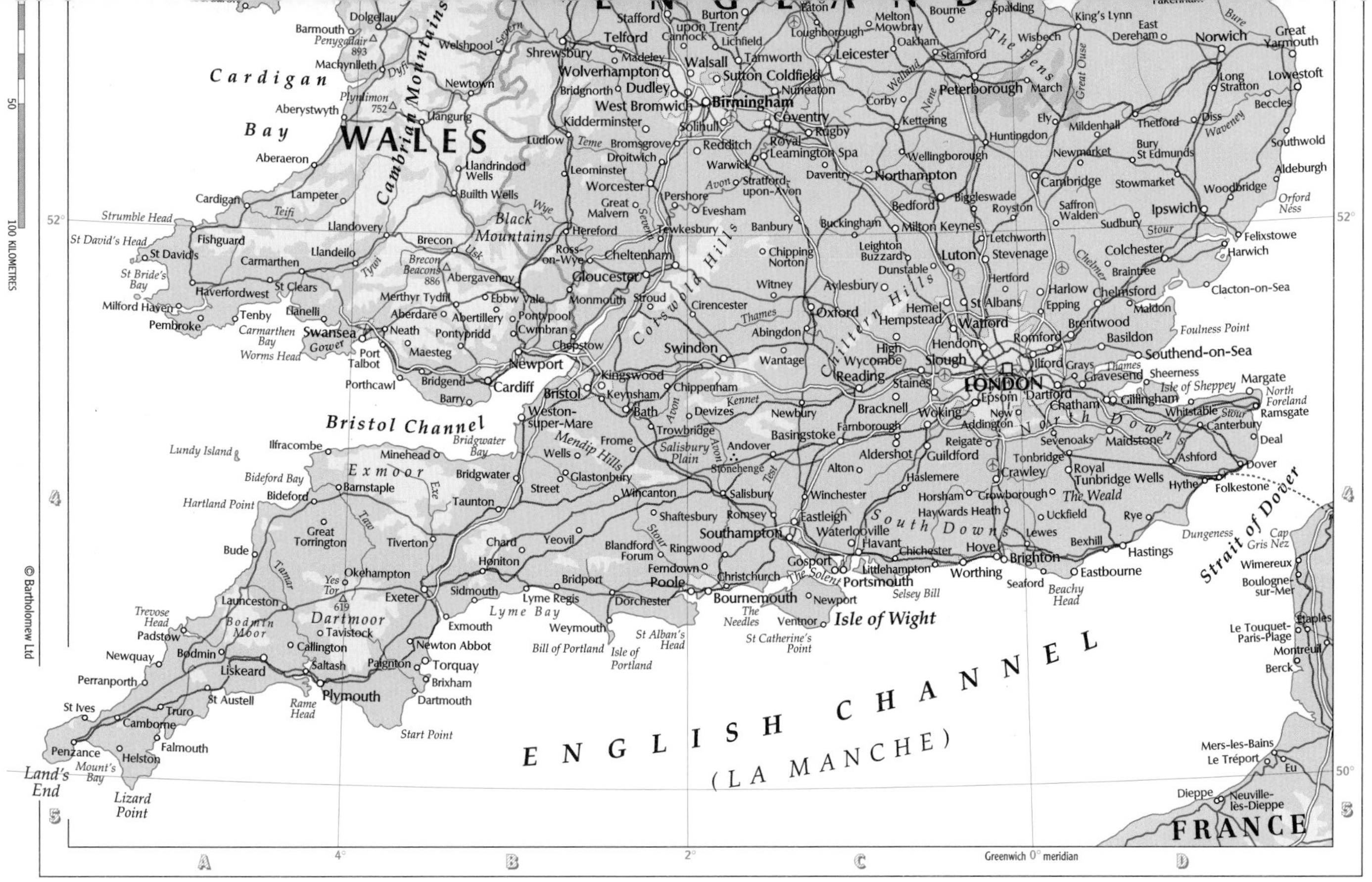

© Bartholomew Ltd

50   100 KILOMETRES

ENGLISH CHANNEL
(LA MANCHE)
FRANCE
WALES
Strait of Dover
Bristol Channel
Cardigan Bay
Isle of Wight
LONDON
Birmingham
Bristol
Cardiff
Swansea
Newport
Plymouth
Southampton
Portsmouth
Brighton
Norwich
Ipswich
Colchester
Cambridge
Oxford
Reading
Swindon
Gloucester
Cheltenham
Worcester
Coventry
Leicester
Northampton
Peterborough
Luton
Bedford
Milton Keynes
Wolverhampton
Telford
Shrewsbury
Hereford
Exeter
Torquay
Bournemouth
Poole
Salisbury
Winchester
Canterbury
Dover
Folkestone
Hastings
Eastbourne
Maidstone
Southend-on-Sea
Chelmsford
Great Yarmouth
Lowestoft
King's Lynn
Carmarthen
Aberystwyth
Pembroke
Penzance
Truro
Land's End
Lizard Point
Dartmoor
Exmoor
Cotswold Hills
Chiltern Hills
Mendip Hills
Black Mountains
Cambrian Mountains
North Downs
South Downs
The Weald
The Fens
Dieppe
Boulogne-sur-Mer
Greenwich 0° meridian
52°

A 4° B 6° C

NORTH

SEA

West Frisian Islands

East Frisian Islands
Spiek
Norderney Langeoog
Juist Norderney
Borkum Norden
Borkum Westerho
Westerho OSTFRIE
Hinte Aurich
Emden
Delfzijl Emden
Appingedam Leer
Groningen (Ostfriesland)
Winschoten Strücklin
Hoogezand- (Saterlan
Sappemeer Pap
Veendam F
Assen Walchu
Stadskanaal Sustrum
Beilen Emmen Haren (Er
Hoogeveen Meppe
Coevorden Meppe
Hardenberg Groß-Hesepe Q
Ommen Unger
Kloosterhaar (Ems)
Vriezenveen Nordhorn
Raalte Almelo Oldenzaal
Nijverdal Borne Rhein
Deventer Hengelo Gronau
Apeldoorn Enschede (Westfalen)
Emsdetten
Eibergen Steinfurt
Zutphen Ahaus Greve
Doesburg Hoog- Winterswijk Havixbeck
Keppel Coesfeld
Arnhem Borken Dülmen
Bocholt
Wesel MÜNSTERLA
Kleve Marl
Goch Dorsten Recklingha
Kevelaer Gelsenkirchen Herne
Dinslaken Bottrop
Venray Duisburg Essen Bochum
Deurne Mülheim an der Ruhr Hagen
Venlo Krefeld Ratingen Hattingen
Viersen Düsseldorf Wuppertal
Mönchengladbach Hilden Lüdenscheid
Roermond Neuss Remscheid
Wegberg Solingen
Maaseik Grevenbroich Leverkusen
Erkelenz Bergisch Gladbach
Heinsberg Köln/Cologne (Köln)
Kerkrade Erft Brühl
Herzogenrath Hennef
Aachen Düren Bonn St. Augustin
Stolberg Kreuzau Königswinter
Eschweiler (Rheinland) Zülpich Meckenheim
Düpeye Rach Bad Neuenahr- Ahrweiler
Ververs Mechernich Spa Ahrweiler
Kallo Blankenheim
Malmédy Dahlem Adenau Neuwied
St.-Vith Hillesheim Mayen Koblenz
Vielsalm Gerolstein Lahnstein
Marche- Prüm Daun Cochem
en-Famenne Kelberg
Houffalize Manderscheid Blankenrath
Clervaux Wittlich Bernkastel-Kues
Wiltz Bitburg
Neuerburg Salmtal
Ettelbruck Kern Morbach Bad Kre
Neufchâteau Echternach Trier Erbeskopf Sobernheim
Redange Mersch Konz
Echternach Reinsfeld Idar-Ober
LUXEMBOURG Konz Nohfelden
Pétange Mettlach St. Wendel
Esch-Alzette Merzig
Thionville Orange Saarlouis Neunkirchen
Hayange Hombu

Texel
Den Helder
Schagen
IJsselmeer
Alkmaar
Haarlem
AMSTERDAM
Leiden
THE HAGUE ('s-Gravenhage)
Hoek van Holland (Hook of Holland)
Rotterdam
Dordrecht
NETHERLANDS
Utrecht
Amersfoort

Westkapelle
Middelburg
Vlissingen
Zeebrugge
Ostend (Oostende)
Bruges (Brugge)
Antwerpen (Anvers)
BRUSSELS (Bruxelles)
Gent (Gand)
BELGIUM
Mechelen
Leuven
Maastricht
Hasselt
Liège
Charleroi Namur
Mons
Lille

FRANCE
Reims
St.-Quentin
Laon

Longitude 6° east of Greenwich

METRES
FEET
5000 16404
3000 9843
2000 6562
1000 3281
500 1640
200 656
0 0
LAND
B.S.L.
200 656
4000 13124
6000 19686

Conic Equidistant Projection

1 : 3 000 000

MILES 0   20   40

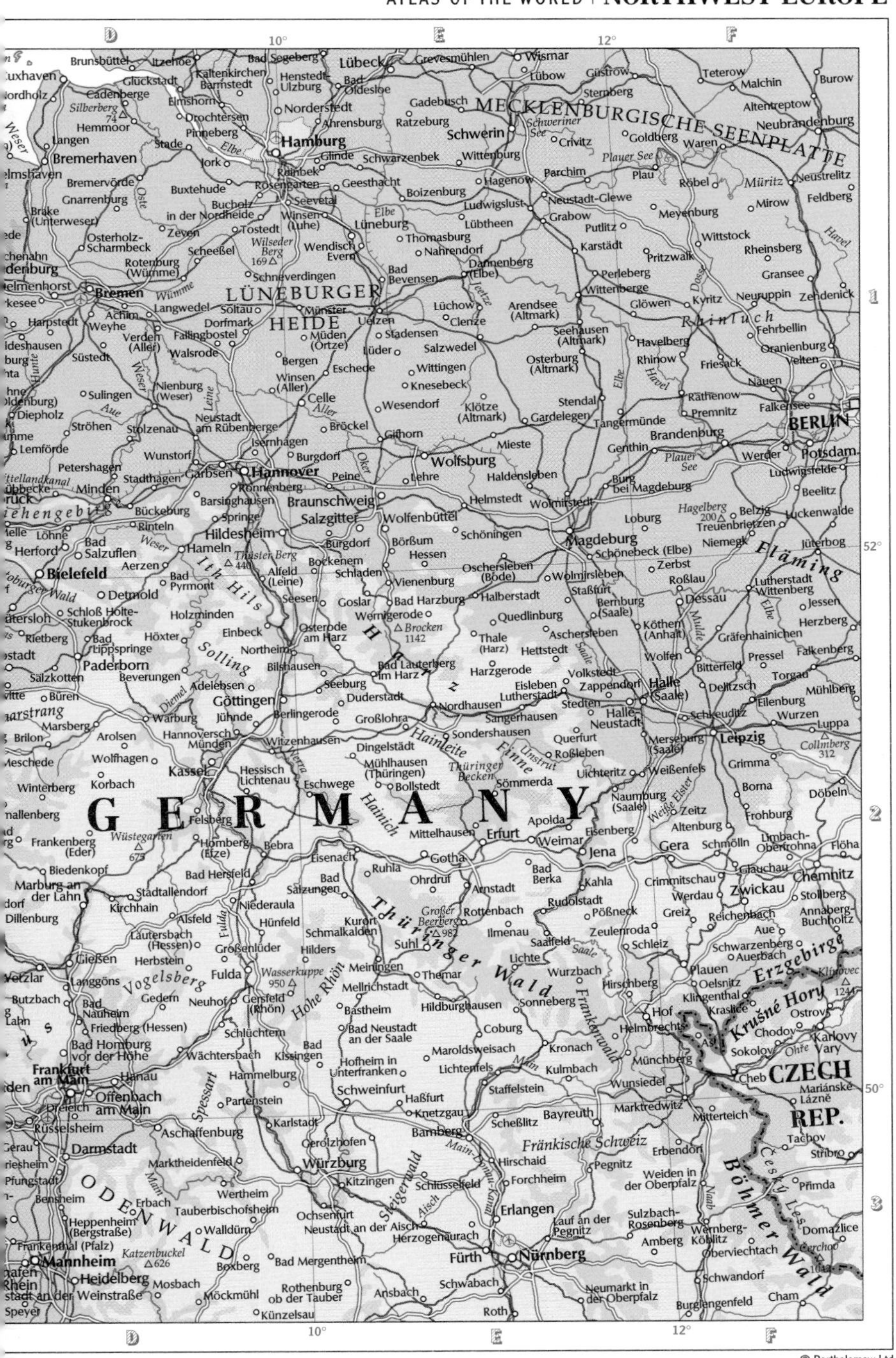
D
E
F
10°
12°
52°
50°
1
2
3
Brunsbüttel
Itzehoe
Bad Segeberg
Lübeck
Grevesmühlen
Wismar
Cuxhaven
Glückstadt
Kaltenkirchen
Henstedt-Ulzburg
Bad Oldesloe
Lübow
Güstrow
Teterow
Malchin
Burow
Barmstedt
Cadenberge
Elmshorn
Norderstedt
Gadebusch
Sternberg
Altentreptow
Silberberg
74
Drochtersen
Ahrensburg
Ratzeburg
MECKLENBURGISCHE SEENPLATTE
Neubrandenburg
Hemmoor
Pinneberg
Schwerin
Schweriner See
Goldberg
Langen
Stade
Hamburg
Crivitz
Waren
Elbe
Glinde
Schwarzenbek
Wittenburg
Plauer See
Bremerhaven
Jork
Reinbek
Neustrelitz
Bremervörde
Rosengarten
Geesthacht
Hagenow
Parchim
Plau
Röbel
Müritz
Buxtehude
Boizenburg
Gnarrenburg
Oste
Seevetal
Ludwigslust
Neustadt-Glewe
Feldberg
Mirow
Brake (Unterweser)
Buchholz in der Nordheide
Winsen (Luhe)
Lüneburg
Lübtheen
Grabow
Meyenburg
Tostedt
Putlitz
Zeven
Osterholz-Scharmbeck
Wilseder Berg
169
Thomasburg
Karstädt
Wittstock
Havel
Scheeßel
Wendisch Evern
Nahrendorf
Pritzwalk
Rheinsberg
Rotenburg (Wümme)
Bad Bevensen
Dannenberg (Elbe)
Perleberg
Gransee
Schneverdingen
Wittenberge
Dosse
Bremen
Wümme
LÜNEBURGER HEIDE
Jeetze
Glöwen
Kyritz
Neuruppin
Zehdenick
Langwedel
Soltau
Münster
Uelzen
Lüchow
Arendsee (Altmark)
Harpstedt
Achim
Dorfmark
Clenze
Rhinluch
Fehrbellin
Weyhe
Verden (Aller)
Fallingbostel
Müden (Örtze)
Stadensen
Seehausen (Altmark)
Havelberg
Oranienburg
Süstedt
Walsrode
Lüder
Salzwedel
Rhinow
Velten
Hunte
Bergen
Eschede
Wittingen
Osterburg (Altmark)
Friesack
Nauen
Winsen (Aller)
Knesebeck
Sulingen
Nienburg (Weser)
Leine
Celle
Rathenow
Aue
Aller
Wesendorf
Klötze (Altmark)
Stendal
Premnitz
Falkensee
Diepholz
Neustadt am Rübenberge
Gardelegen
Tangermünde
BERLIN
Ströhen
Stolzenau
Bröckel
Lemförde
Isernhagen
Gifhorn
Mieste
Genthin
Brandenburg
Wunstorf
Burgdorf
Oker
Wolfsburg
Plauer See
Werder
Potsdam
Petershagen
Garbsen
Hannover
Peine
Lehre
Haldensleben
Ludwigsfelde
Stadthagen
Minden
Ronnenberg
Burg bei Magdeburg
Barsinghausen
Braunschweig
Helmstedt
Wolmirstedt
Beelitz
Bückeburg
Springe
Salzgitter
Wolfenbüttel
Loburg
Hagelberg
200
Belzig
Luckenwalde
Rinteln
Treuenbrietzen
Löhne
Bad Salzuflen
Hildesheim
Schöningen
Magdeburg
Niemegk
Jüterbog
Herford
Hameln
Burgdorf
Börßum
Hessen
Schönebeck (Elbe)
Fläming
Weser
Thüster Berg
440
Bockenem
Oschersleben (Bode)
Zerbst
Bielefeld
Aerzen
Bad Pyrmont
Alfeld (Leine)
Schladen
Wolmirsleben
Roßlau
Ith
Hils
Vienenburg
Staßfurt
Lutherstadt Wittenberg
Teutoburger Wald
Detmold
Seesen
Goslar
Bad Harzburg
Halberstadt
Bernburg (Saale)
Dessau
Jessen
Schloß Holte-Stukenbrock
Holzminden
Wernigerode
Quedlinburg
Elbe
Herzberg
Gütersloh
Brocken
1142
Köthen (Anhalt)
Mulde
Rietberg
Bad Lippspringe
Einbeck
Osterode am Harz
Thale (Harz)
Aschersleben
Gräfenhainichen
Höxter
Northeim
HARZ
Hettstedt
Wolfen
Pressel
Falkenberg
Paderborn
Solling
Bilshausen
Bad Lauterberg im Harz
Harzgerode
Saale
Bitterfeld
Torgau
Salzkotten
Beverungen
Adelebsen
Seeburg
Volkstedt
Eisleben
Zappendorf
Halle (Saale)
Delitzsch
Mühlberg
Büren
Diemel
Göttingen
Duderstadt
Nordhausen
Lutherstadt
Stedten
Eilenburg
Haarstrang
Warburg
Jühnde
Berlingerode
Großlohra
Sangerhausen
Halle-Neustadt
Schkeuditz
Wurzen
Marsberg
Brilon
Arolsen
Hannoversch Münden
Witzenhausen
Sondershausen
Querfurt
Merseburg (Saale)
Leipzig
Luppa
Collmberg
312
Hainleite
Dingelstädt
Finne
Unstrut
Roßleben
Meschede
Wolfhagen
Kassel
Werra
Mühlhausen (Thüringen)
Thüringer Becken
Grimma
Hessisch Lichtenau
Eschwege
Bollstedt
Uichteritz
Weißenfels
Winterberg
Korbach
Sömmerda
Borna
Döbeln
Naumburg (Saale)
GERMANY
Hainich
Weiße Elster
Zeitz
Frohburg
Schmallenberg
Felsberg
Apolda
Altenburg
Limbach-Oberfrohna
Frankenberg (Eder)
Wüstegarten
675
Homberg (Efze)
Bebra
Mittelhausen
Erfurt
Eisenberg
Weimar
Jena
Gera
Schmölln
Flöha
Biedenkopf
Bad Hersfeld
Eisenach
Gotha
Glauchau
Chemnitz
Ruhla
Bad Berka
Marburg an der Lahn
Stadtallendorf
Bad Salzungen
Ohrdruf
Arnstadt
Kahla
Crimmitschau
Zwickau
Werdau
Stollberg
Kirchhain
Niederaula
Rudolstadt
Dillenburg
Alsfeld
Hünfeld
Thüringer Wald
Kurort
Großer Beerberg
982
Rottenbach
Pößneck
Greiz
Reichenbach
Annaberg-Buchholz
Fulda
Schmalkalden
Ilmenau
Zeulenroda
Lautersbach (Hessen)
Saalfeld
Aue
Großenlüder
Hilders
Suhl
Schleiz
Schwarzenberg
Gießen
Herbstein
Lichte
Saale
Auerbach
Erzgebirge
Wetzlar
Vogelsberg
Fulda
Wasserkuppe
950
Meiningen
Themar
Wurzbach
Plauen
Klínovec
Langgöns
Gedern
Mellrichstadt
Frankenwald
Hirschberg
Oelsnitz
1244
Butzbach
Bad Nauheim
Neuhof
Gersfeld (Rhön)
Hohe Rhön
Bastheim
Hildburghausen
Sonneberg
Klingenthal
Kraslice
Krušné Hory
Ostrov
Lahn
Friedberg (Hessen)
Schlüchtern
Bad Neustadt an der Saale
Coburg
Hof
Helmbrechts
Chodov
Karlovy Vary
Bad Homburg vor der Höhe
Wächtersbach
Bad Kissingen
Maroldsweisach
Kronach
Aš
Sokolov
Ohře
Frankfurt am Main
Hofheim in Unterfranken
Lichtenfels
Main
Kulmbach
Münchberg
Cheb
CZECH REP.
Hanau
Hammelburg
Schweinfurt
Staffelstein
Wunsiedel
Mariánské Lázně
Offenbach am Main
Spessart
Partenstein
Haßfurt
Dreieich
Knetzgau
Scheßlitz
Bayreuth
Marktredwitz
Rüsselsheim
Karlstadt
Bamberg
Mitterteich
Aschaffenburg
Fränkische Schweiz
Tachov
Darmstadt
Gerolzhofen
Erbendorf
Stříbro
Griesheim
Marktheidenfeld
Main-Donau-Kanal
Hirschaid
Pegnitz
Český Les
Pfungstadt
Würzburg
Forchheim
Weiden in der Oberpfalz
Böhmer Wald
ODENWALD
Kitzingen
Schlüsselfeld
Steigerwald
Přimda
Bensheim
Erbach
Wertheim
Aisch
Main
Heppenheim (Bergstraße)
Tauberbischofsheim
Ochsenfurt
Erlangen
Sulzbach-Rosenberg
Naab
Walldürn
Neustadt an der Aisch
Herzogenaurach
Lauf an der Pegnitz
Wernberg-Köblitz
Domažlice
Frankenthal (Pfalz)
Katzenbuckel
626
Amberg
Oberviechtach
Čerchov
1042
Mannheim
Boxberg
Bad Mergentheim
Fürth
Nürnberg
Heidelberg
Mosbach
Schwabach
Schwandorf
Rhein
Möckmühl
Rothenburg ob der Tauber
Ansbach
Neumarkt in der Oberpfalz
Cham
Speyer
Künzelsau
Roth
Burglengenfeld

50 100 KILOMETRES

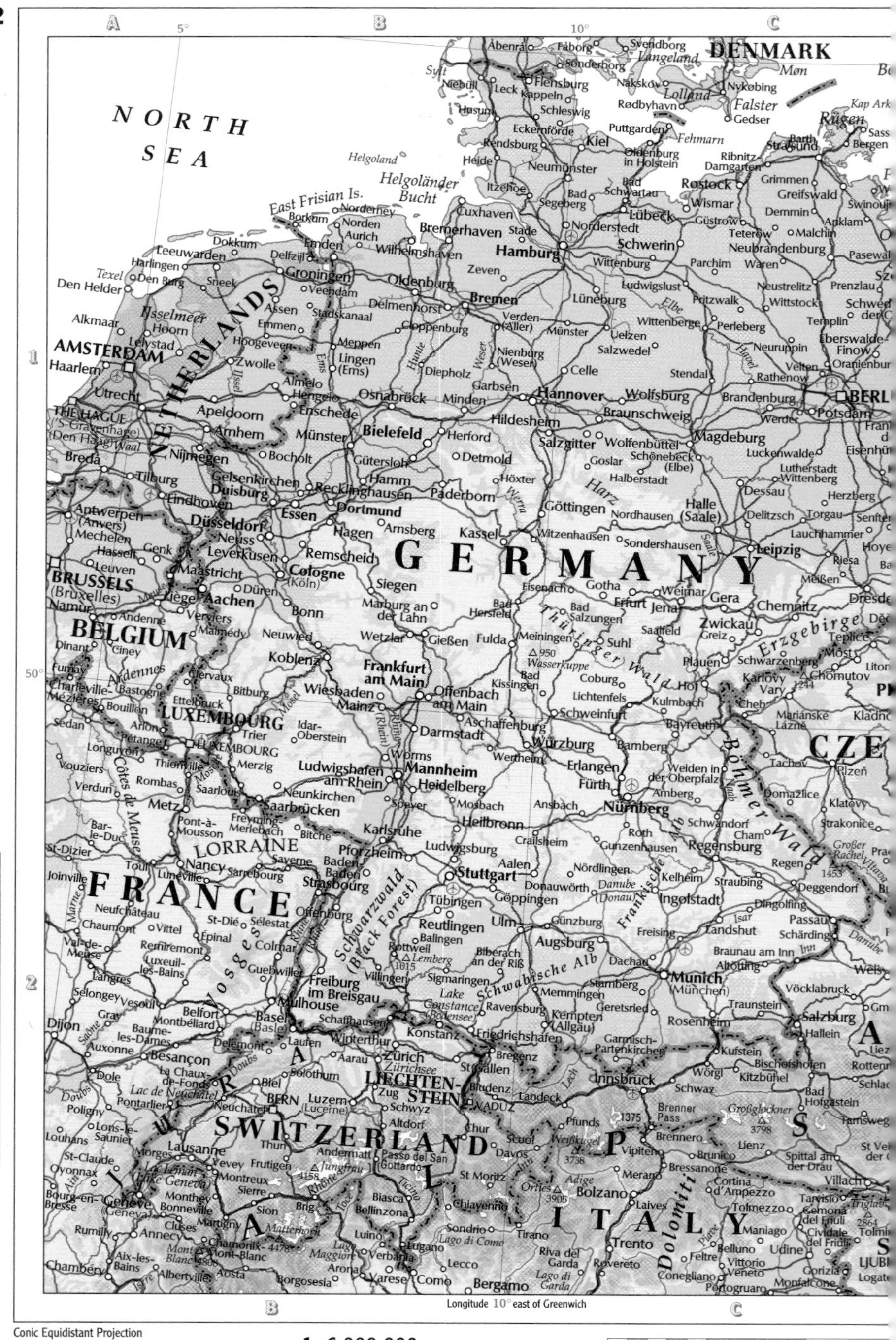

NORTH SEA

DENMARK

NETHERLANDS

AMSTERDAM

BELGIUM

BRUSSELS
(Bruxelles)

GERMANY

Hamburg

Bremen

Hannover

BERL

LUXEMBOURG

Frankfurt
am Main

CZE

LORRAINE

FRANCE

Stuttgart

Nürnberg

Munich
(München)

Salzburg

SWITZERLAND

LIECHTEN-
STEIN

ITALY

Conic Equidistant Projection

1 : 6 000 000

Longitude 10° east of Greenwich

MILES 0   50   100

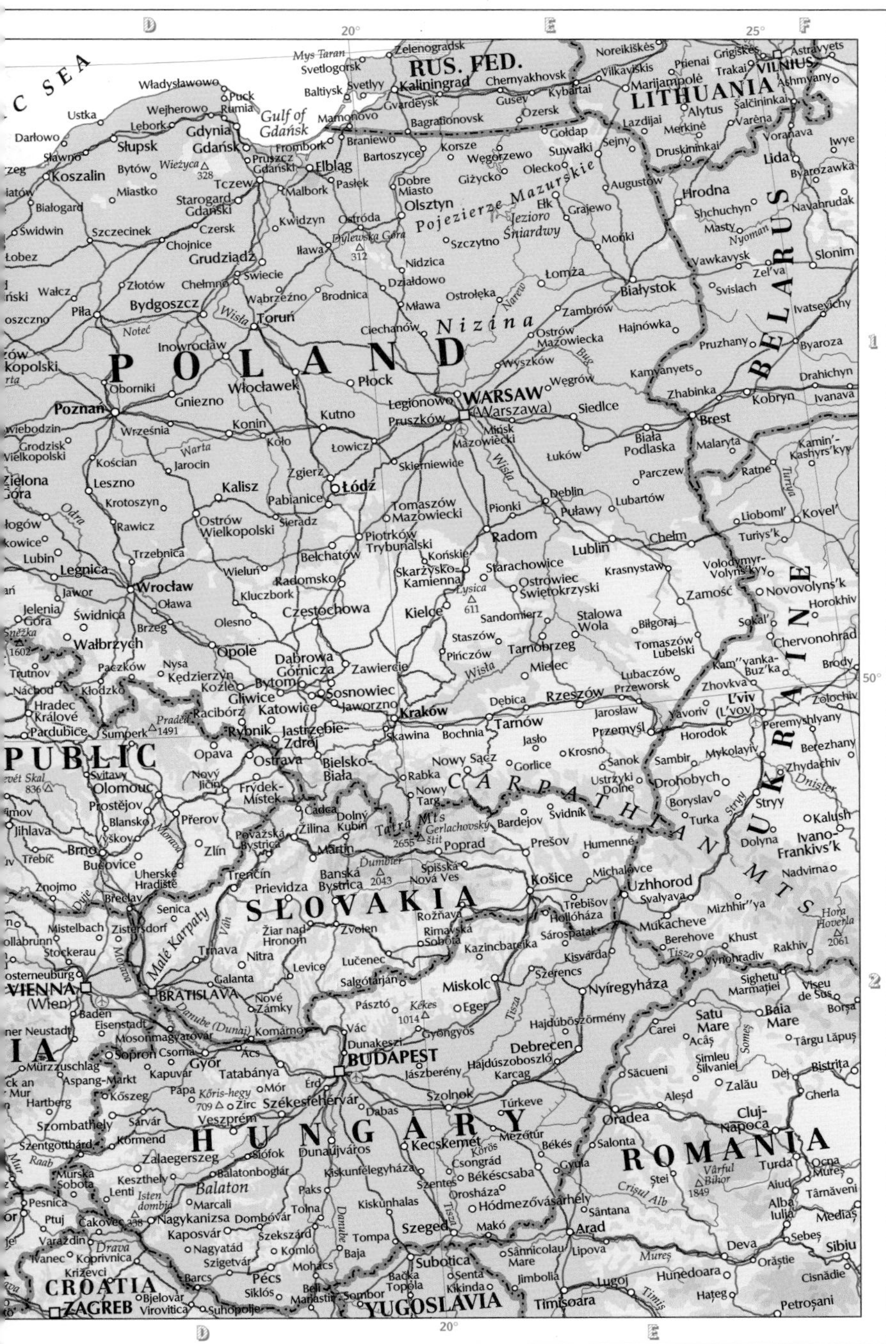
POLAND
SLOVAKIA
HUNGARY
ROMANIA
CROATIA
YUGOSLAVIA
RUS. FED.
LITHUANIA
BELARUS
UKRAINE
C SEA
Gulf of Gdańsk
WARSAW (Warszawa)
BUDAPEST
VIENNA (Wien)
BRATISLAVA
ZAGREB
VILNIUS
Kaliningrad
Gdańsk
Gdynia
Elbląg
Olsztyn
Białystok
Bydgoszcz
Toruń
Poznań
Łódź
Wrocław
Kraków
Katowice
Lublin
Radom
Kielce
Częstochowa
Rzeszów
Przemyśl
Brest
Hrodna
Lida
L'viv (L'vov)
Uzhhorod
Košice
Prešov
Poprad
Žilina
Banská Bystrica
Trenčín
Nitra
Miskolc
Debrecen
Nyíregyháza
Szeged
Kecskemét
Pécs
Győr
Sopron
Székesfehérvár
Oradea
Arad
Timişoara
Cluj-Napoca
Baia Mare
Satu Mare
Subotica
Brno
Olomouc
Ostrava
Opole
Pojezierze Mazurskie
Nizina
CARPATHIAN MTS
Tatra Mts
Gerlachovský štít 2655
Balaton
Danube (Dunaj)
Wisła
Odra
Tisza
Mureş
Dniester
20°
25°
50°
D
E
F
1
2

100 200 KILOMETRES

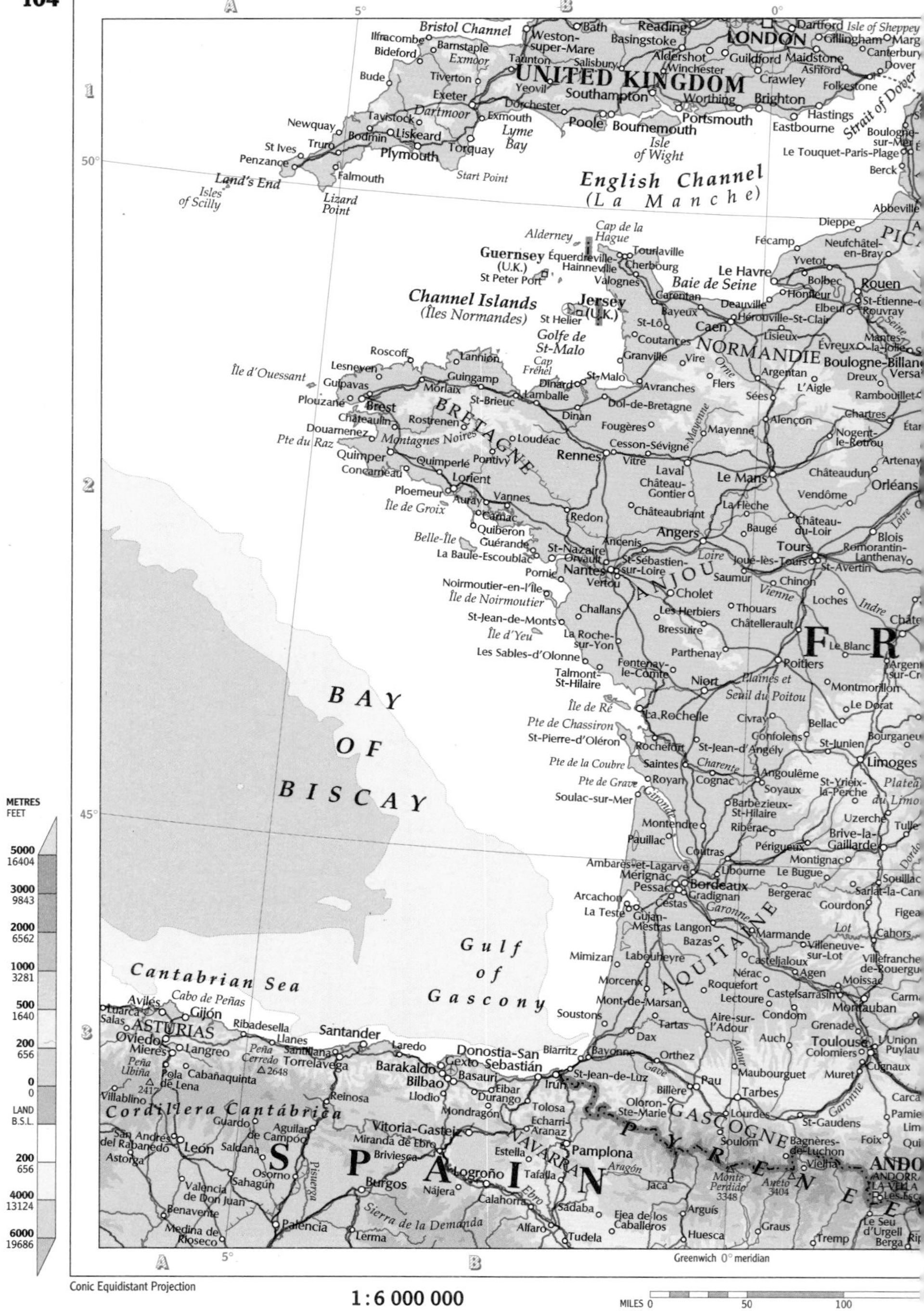

METRES / FEET

METRES	FEET
5000	16404
3000	9843
2000	6562
1000	3281
500	1640
200	656
0	0
LAND	B.S.L.
200	656
4000	13124
6000	19686

Conic Equidistant Projection

1 : 6 000 000

MILES 0   50   100

Greenwich 0° meridian

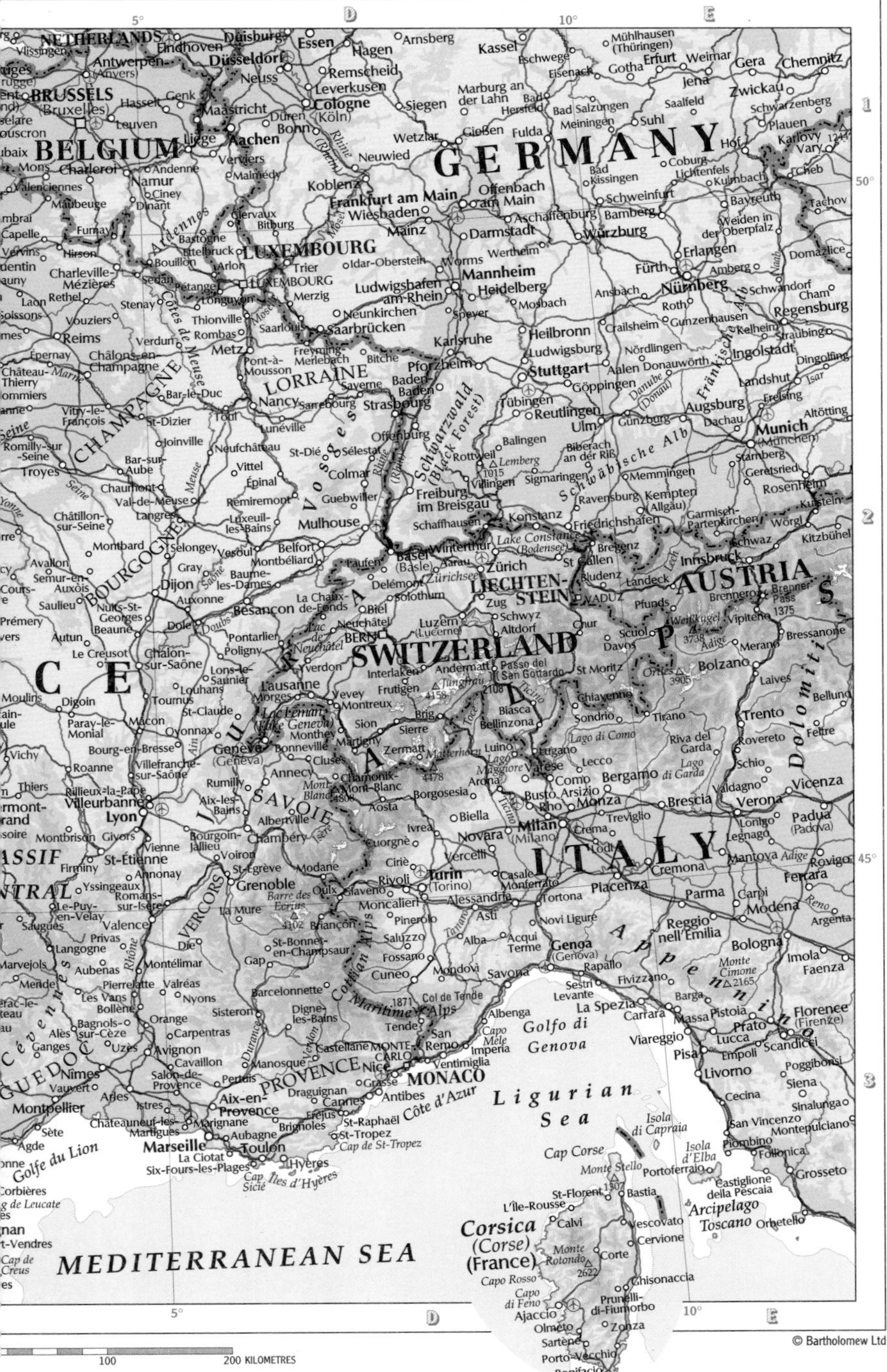
NETHERLANDS
BRUSSELS
(Bruxelles)
BELGIUM
GERMANY
LUXEMBOURG
LORRAINE
CHAMPAGNE
BOURGOGNE
SWITZERLAND
LIECHTENSTEIN
VADUZ
AUSTRIA
ITALY
SAVOIE
PROVENCE
MONACO
Corsica
(Corse)
(France)
MEDITERRANEAN SEA
Ligurian Sea
Golfo di Genova
Golfe du Lion
Côte d'Azur
Lake Constance
(Bodensee)
Lac Léman
(Lake Geneva)
Schwarzwald
(Black Forest)
Schwäbische Alb
Vosges
Appennino
Dolomiti
Cottian Alps
Maritime Alps
Rhine
Rhône
Danube
(Donau)
Düsseldorf
Cologne
(Köln)
Aachen
Frankfurt am Main
Mannheim
Stuttgart
Nürnberg
Munich
(München)
Regensburg
Augsburg
Strasbourg
Basel
(Basle)
Zürich
BERN
Luzern
(Lucerne)
Genève
(Geneva)
Lausanne
Lyon
Dijon
Besançon
Grenoble
Marseille
Toulon
Nice
Aix-en-Provence
Nîmes
Montpellier
Avignon
Turin
(Torino)
Milan
(Milano)
Genoa
(Genova)
Verona
Florence
(Firenze)
Bologna
Trento
Bolzano
Innsbruck
Ajaccio
Bastia
Bonifacio
Isola d'Elba
Arcipelago Toscano
50°
45°
5°
10°
D
E
1
2
3
© Bartholomew Ltd
100
200 KILOMETRES

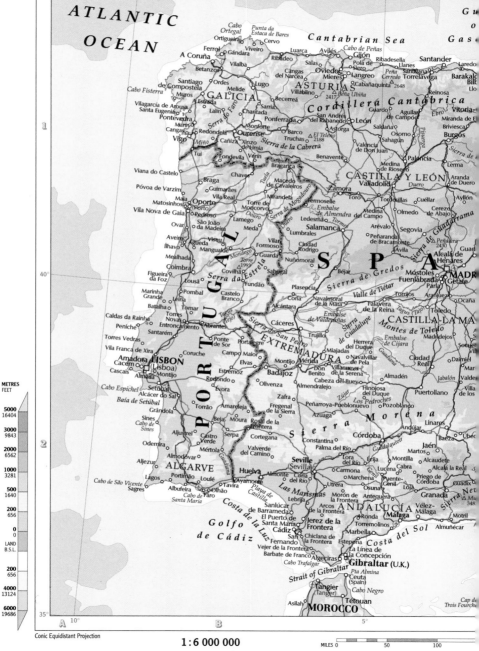

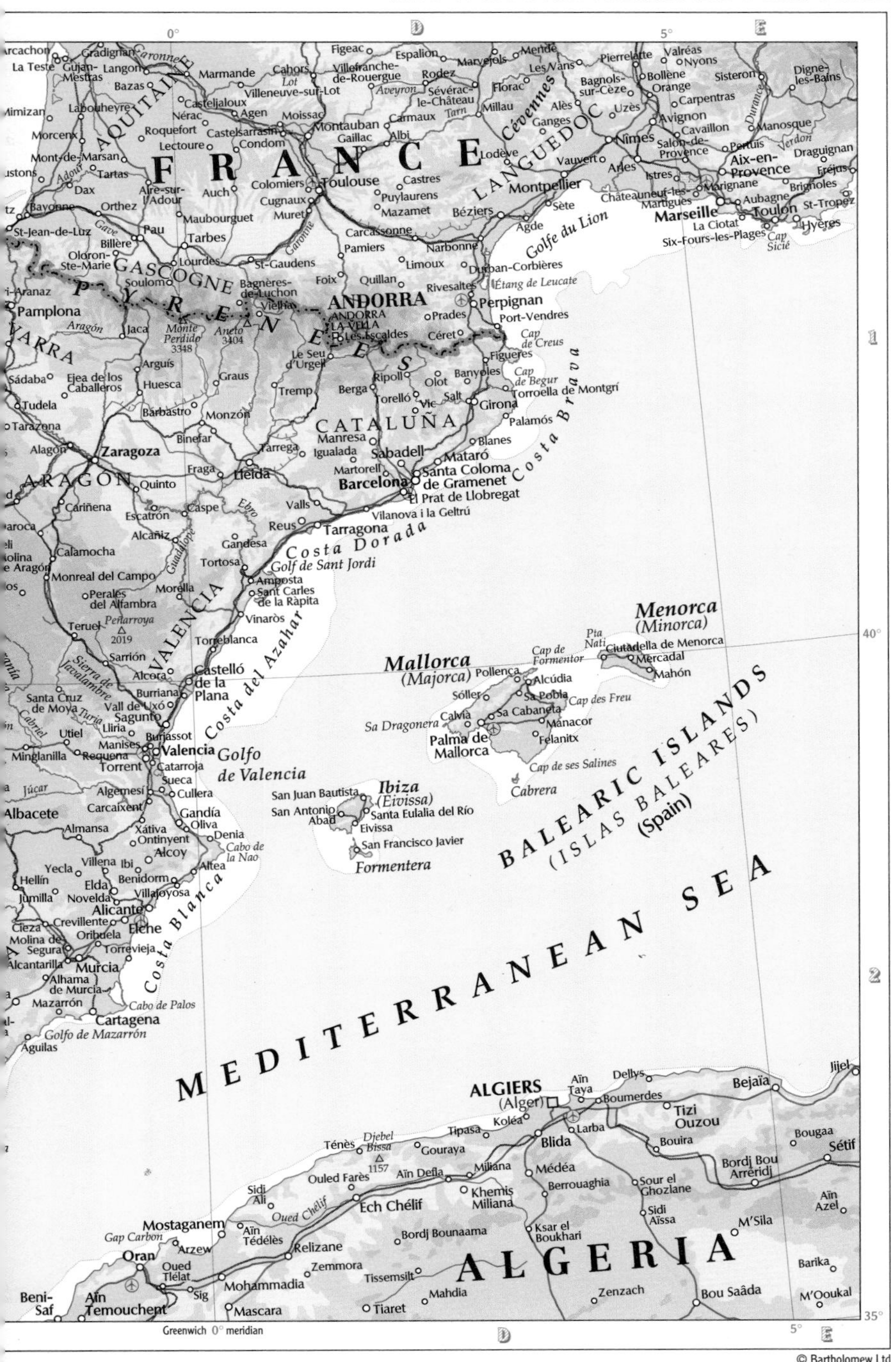

© Bartholomew Ltd

100   200 KILOMETRES

FRANCE
AQUITAINE
GASCOGNE
LANGUEDOC
Cévennes
PYRENEES
ANDORRA
ANDORRA LA VELLA
Les Escaldes
CATALUÑA
ARAGÓN
VALENCIA
Costa Brava
Costa Dorada
Costa del Azahar
Costa Blanca
Golfe du Lion
Golf de Sant Jordi
Golfo de Valencia
Golfo de Mazarrón
Cabo de Palos
Cabo de la Nao
Cap de Creus
Cap de Begur
Étang de Leucate
Cap Sicié
Menorca (Minorca)
Mallorca (Majorca)
Ibiza (Eivissa)
Formentera
Cabrera
Sa Dragonera
Cap de Formentor
Pta Nati
Cap des Freu
Cap de ses Salines
BALEARIC ISLANDS (ISLAS BALEARES) (Spain)
MEDITERRANEAN SEA
ALGERIA
ALGIERS (Alger)
Toulouse
Marseille
Montpellier
Perpignan
Zaragoza
Lleida
Barcelona
Tarragona
Valencia
Castelló de la Plana
Alicante
Murcia
Cartagena
Albacete
Palma de Mallorca
Oran
Mostaganem
Blida
Médéa
Ech Chélif
Relizane
Bejaïa
Sétif
Tizi Ouzou
Pamplona
Tudela
Huesca
Teruel
Monte Perdido 3348
Aneto 3404
Peñarroya 2019
Djebel Bissa 1157
Gap Carbon
Oued Chélif
Sierra de Javalambre
Ebro
Júcar
Turia
Cabriel
Garonne
5°
40°
35°
Greenwich 0° meridian

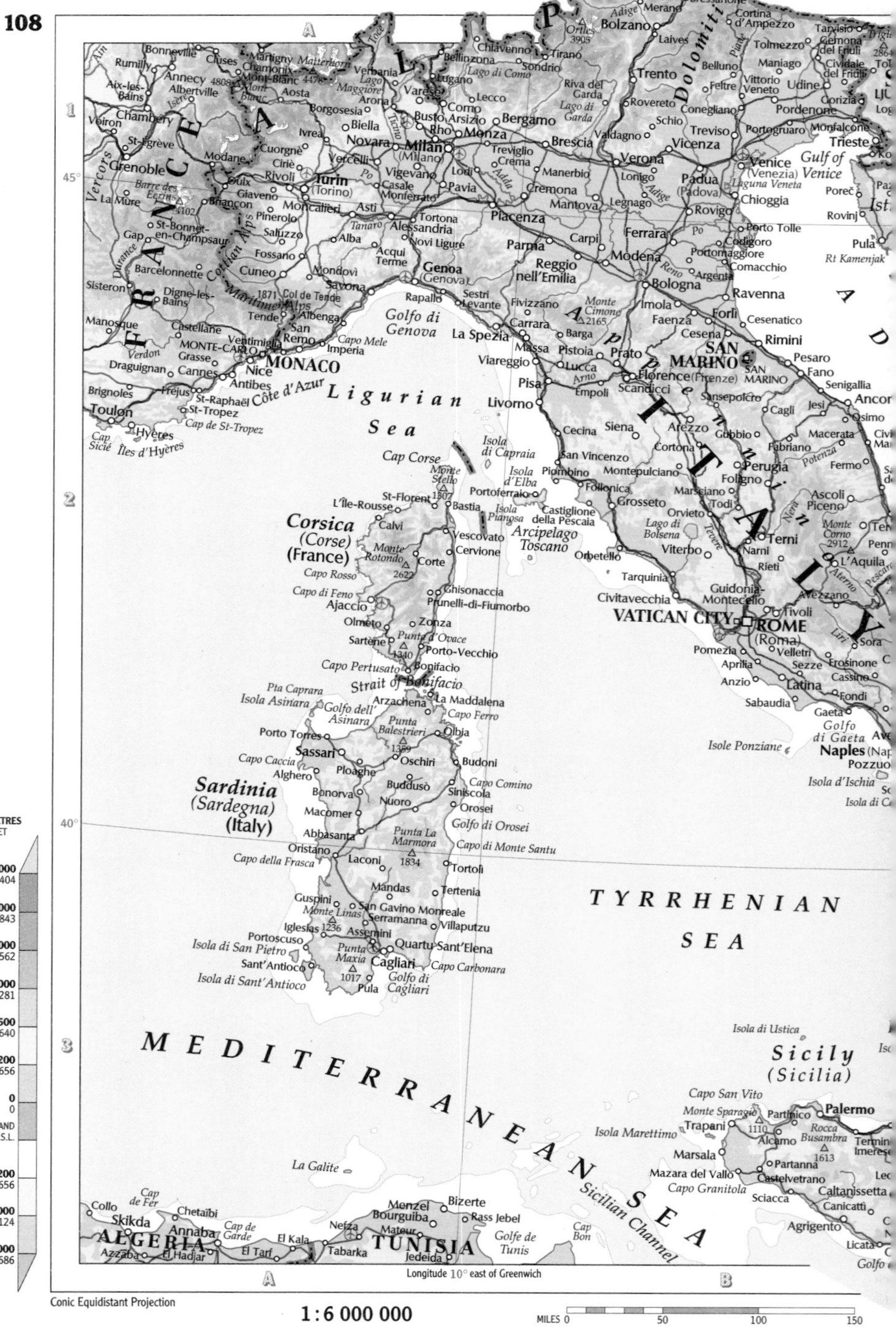

METRES
FEET

5000	16404
3000	9843
2000	6562
1000	3281
500	1640
200	656
0	0
LAND	B.S.L.
200	656
4000	13124
6000	19686

Conic Equidistant Projection

1 : 6 000 000

MILES 0   50   100   150

Longitude 10° east of Greenwich

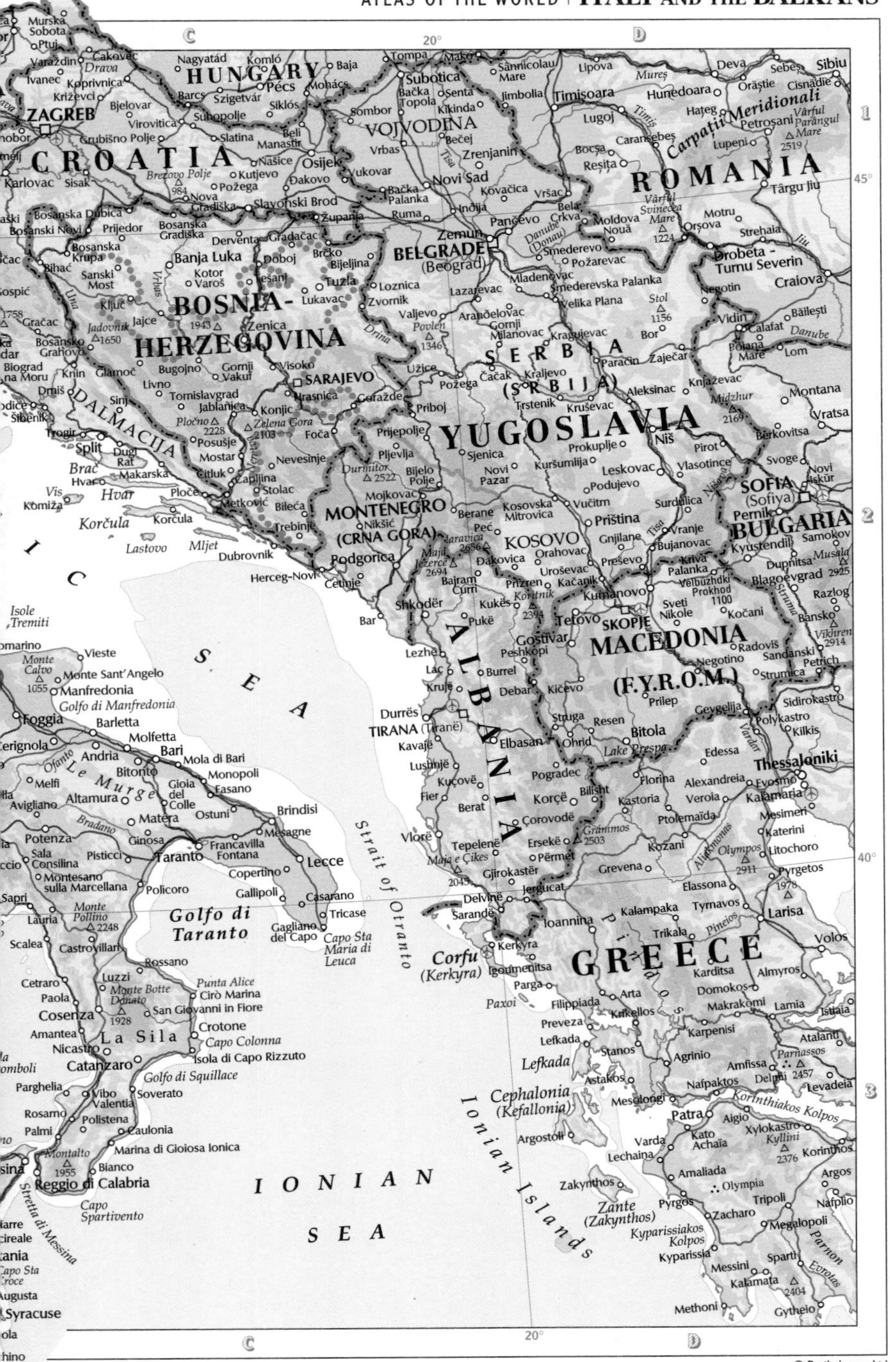
HUNGARY
CROATIA
BOSNIA-HERZEGOVINA
VOJVODINA
ROMANIA
SERBIA (SRBIJA)
YUGOSLAVIA
MONTENEGRO (CRNA GORA)
KOSOVO
ALBANIA
MACEDONIA (F.Y.R.O.M.)
BULGARIA
GREECE
DALMACIJA
ZAGREB
BELGRADE (Beograd)
SARAJEVO
TIRANA (Tiranë)
SKOPJE
SOFIA (Sofiya)
Carpații Meridionali
Danube (Donau)
Drava
Tisa
Drina
Una
Vrbas
Mureș
Timiș
Jiu
Vardar
Struma
Lake Prespa
Osijek
Novi Sad
Subotica
Sombor
Zrenjanin
Pančevo
Zemun
Smederevo
Požarevac
Kragujevac
Kraljevo
Čačak
Niš
Priština
Prizren
Peć
Podgorica
Nikšić
Cetinje
Bar
Herceg-Novi
Dubrovnik
Mostar
Split
Banja Luka
Tuzla
Zenica
Doboj
Bihać
Slavonski Brod
Vukovar
Pécs
Szigetvár
Baja
Mohács
Timișoara
Lugoj
Reșița
Hunedoara
Petroșani
Sibiu
Craiova
Drobeta - Turnu Severin
Vidin
Lom
Montana
Vratsa
Pernik
Kyustendil
Blagoevgrad
Sandanski
Bitola
Prilep
Ohrid
Struga
Tetovo
Kumanovo
Kičevo
Shkodër
Durrës
Elbasan
Vlorë
Berat
Korçë
Gjirokastër
Sarandë
Thessaloniki
Kavala
Veroia
Kozani
Larisa
Volos
Trikala
Ioannina
Arta
Preveza
Lefkada
Agrinio
Mesolongi
Patra
Korinthos
Tripoli
Kalamata
Pyrgos
Corfu (Kerkyra)
Cephalonia (Kefallonia)
Zante (Zakynthos)
Olympos 2911
Musala 2925
Korinthiakos Kolpos
Kyparissiakos Kolpos
Foggia
Manfredonia
Golfo di Manfredonia
Barletta
Molfetta
Bari
Mola di Bari
Monopoli
Brindisi
Lecce
Taranto
Golfo di Taranto
Matera
Altamura
Potenza
Le Murge
Gallipoli
Capo Sta Maria di Leuca
Crotone
Catanzaro
Cosenza
La Sila
Golfo di Squillace
Reggio di Calabria
Capo Spartivento
Stretta di Messina
Syracuse
Isole Tremiti
Vieste
Strait of Otranto
Ionian Islands
IONIAN SEA
Lastovo
Mljet
Korčula
Hvar
Brač
Vis
20°
45°
40°
C
D
1
2
3

0 100 200 KILOMETRES

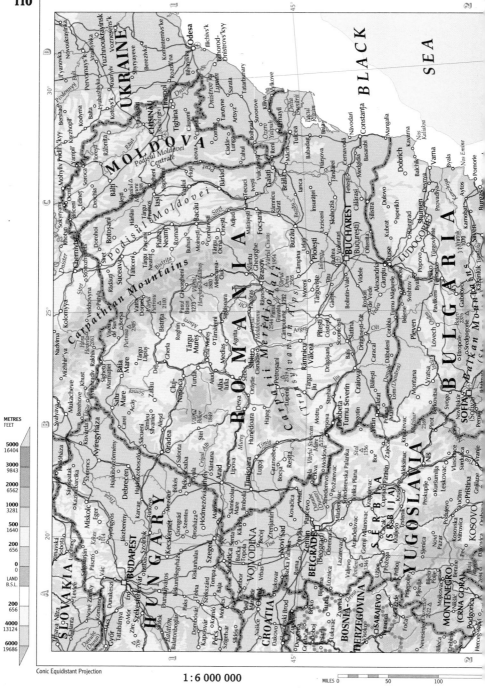

METRES
FEET

5000
16404

3000
9843

2000
6562

1000
3281

500
1640

200
656

0
0

LAND
B.S.L.

200
656

4000
13124

6000
19686

Conic Equidistant Projection

1 : 6 000 000

MILES 0   50   100

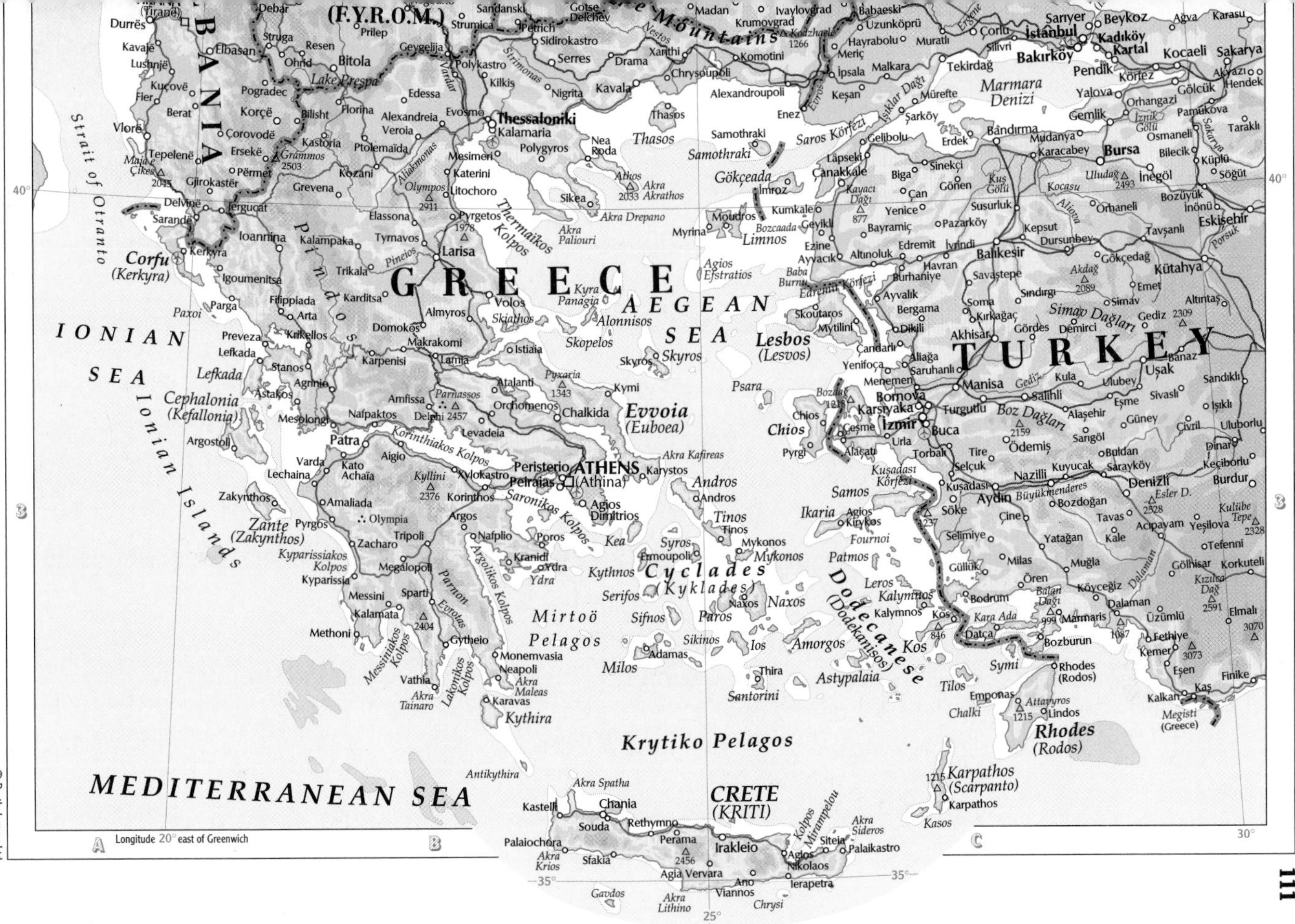
GREECE
TURKEY
(F.Y.R.O.M.)
AEGEAN SEA
IONIAN SEA
MEDITERRANEAN SEA
CRETE
(KRITI)
Krytiko Pelagos
Mirtoö Pelagos
Cyclades
(Kyklades)
Dodecanese
(Dodekanisos)
Ionian Islands
Strait of Otranto
Marmara Denizi
Lesbos
(Lesvos)
Chios
Samos
Rhodes
(Rodos)
Karpathos
(Scarpanto)
Evvoia
(Euboea)
Corfu
(Kerkyra)
Cephalonia
(Kefallonia)
Zante
(Zakynthos)
Kythira
Thasos
Samothraki
Limnos
Skyros
Naxos
Santorini
Milos
ATHENS
(Athina)
Thessaloniki
İzmir
İstanbul
Bursa
Larisa
Patra
Irakleio
Chania
Thermaikos Kolpos
Saronikos Kolpos
Argolikos Kolpos
Pindos
Longitude 20° east of Greenwich
100
200 KILOMETRES

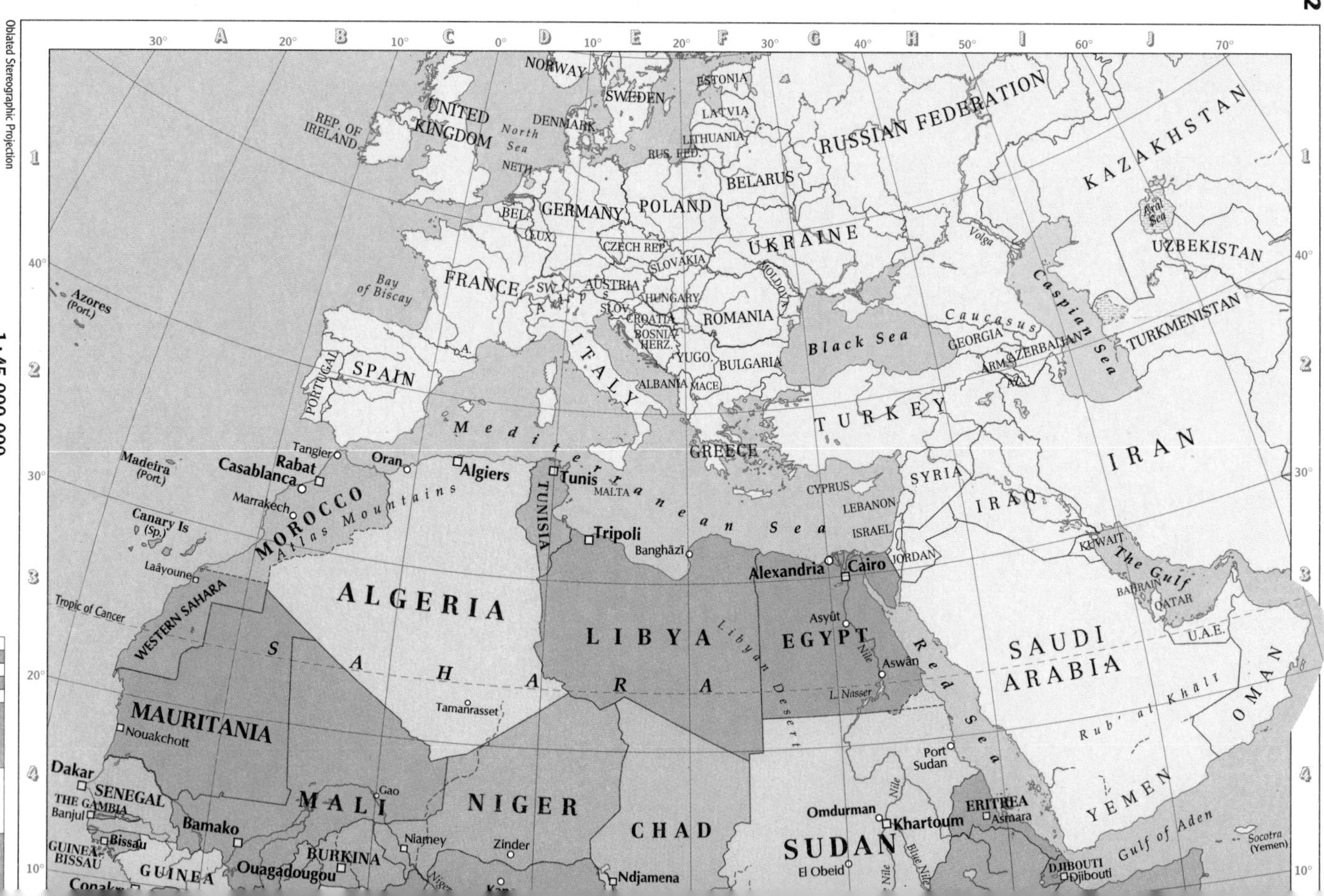

Oblated Stereographic Projection

1 : 45 000 000

MILES 0   250   500   750

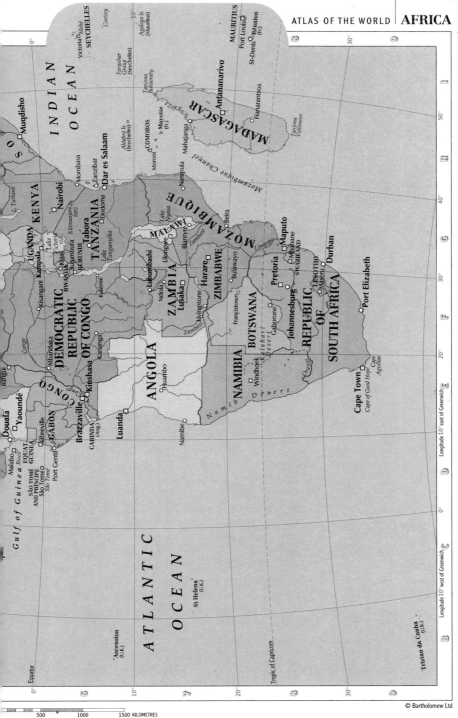

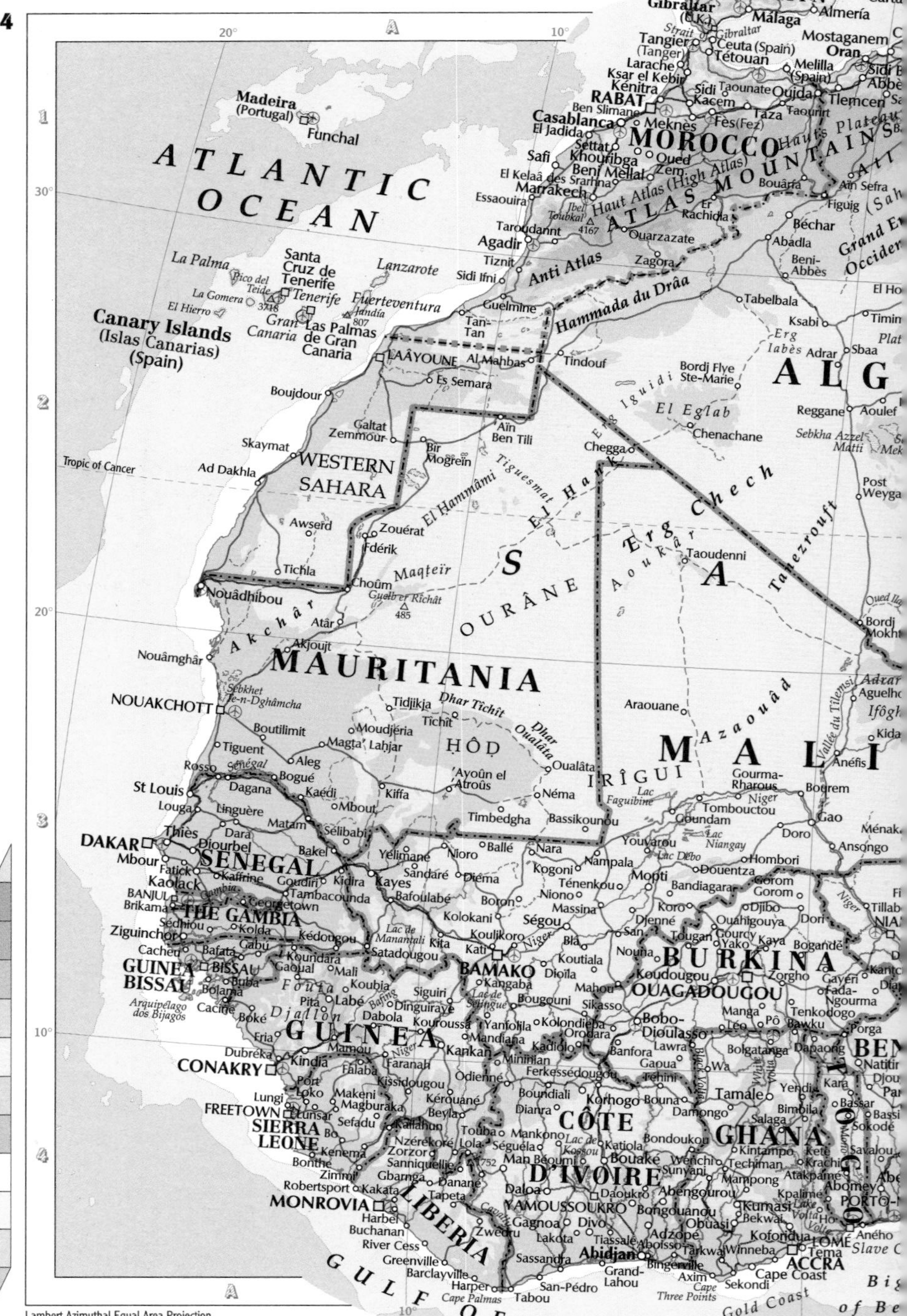

METRES
FEET

5000
16404

3000
9843

2000
6562

1000
3281

500
1640

200
656

0
0

LAND
B.S.L.

200
656

4000
13124

6000
19686

Lambert Azimuthal Equal Area Projection

ATLANTIC OCEAN

Madeira (Portugal)
Funchal

La Palma
Santa Cruz de Tenerife
Pico del Teide
La Gomera
El Hierro
Tenerife
Gran Canaria
Las Palmas de Gran Canaria
Canary Islands (Islas Canarias) (Spain)
Lanzarote
Fuerteventura

Tropic of Cancer

WESTERN SAHARA

Skaymat
Ad Dakhla
Awserd
Tichla
Nouâdhibou
Nouâmghâr

MAURITANIA

NOUAKCHOTT
Akjoujt
Atâr
Fdérik
Zouérat
Choûm
Galtat Zemmour
Bir Mogreïn
Aïn Ben Tili
Tidjikja
Moudjéria
Tichit
Dhar Tichît
HÔD
Boutilimit
Tiguent
Magta' Lahjar
Aleg
Bogué
Rosso
Kaédi
St Louis
Louga
Dagana
Linguère
Matam
Sélibabi
Mbout
Kiffa
Néma
Ayoûn el Atroûs
Oualâta
Timbedgha
Bassikounou

DAKAR
Thiès
Diourbel
Mbour
Fatick
Kaolack
Kaffrine
SENEGAL
Gossas
Bakel
Yélimané
Nioro
Ballé
Nara
THE GAMBIA
BANJUL
Brikama
Georgetown
Kolda
Ziguinchor
Sedhiou
Cacheu
Bafatá
Gabú
Kédougou
Kidira
Tambacounda
Goudiri
Kayes
Diéma
Nampala
Kogoni
Niono
Massina
Ségou
GUINEA BISSAU
BISSAU
Bolama
Buba
Bubaque
Arquipélago dos Bijagós
Boké
Cacine
Koundara
Gaoual
Koubia
Mali
Siguiri
Kita
Koulikoro
Kati
BAMAKO
Kangaba
Dioïla
Koutiala
San
Tougan
Nouna
BURKINA
OUAGADOUGOU
Erla
Pita
Labé
Dabola
Dinguiraye
Kouroussa
Koubia
GUINEA
Fouta Djallon
Mamou
Kindia
CONAKRY
Forécariah
Télimélé
Dubréka
Falaba
Faranah
Kissidougou
Kankan
Mandiana
Kérouané
Kadidô
Mandiana
Touba
Odienné
Boundiali
Korhogo
Bouna
Tamale
Yendi
Lungi
Port Loko
Makéni
Magburaka
Kérouané
Dianra
Ferkessédougou
Salala
FREETOWN
Kambia
Bo
Kenema
Zimmi
Zorzor
Sanniquellie
Man
Séguéla
Bouaké
Katiola
Dabakala
Bondoukou
Sunyani
SIERRA LEONE
Bonthe
Robertsport
Harbel
Buchanan
River Cess
Greenville
Barclayville
Harper
MONROVIA
Zimmi
Gbarnga
Tapeta
Zwedru
Gagnoa
Daloa
Divo
Yamoussoukro
Bongouanou
Adzopé
Obuasi
D'IVOIRE
CÔTE
Abidjan
Aboisso
Grand-Lahou
Sassandra
San-Pédro
Tabou
Cape Palmas
LIBERIA
Danané
Duékoué
Daoukro
Abengourou
Bondoukou
Agnibilékrou
Kumasi
GHANA
Kintampo
Techiman
Mampong
Koforidua
ACCRA
Tema
Cape Coast
Sekondi
Takoradi
Winneba
LOMÉ
Aného

GULF OF GUINEA

SPAIN
Gibraltar
Málaga
Almería
Tangier (Tanger)
Strait of Gibraltar
Ceuta (Spain)
Tétouan
Mostaganem
Oran
Melilla (Spain)
Larache
Ksar el Kebir
Kénitra
Sidi Slimane
RABAT
Ben Slimane
Casablanca
El Jadida
Meknès
Fès (Fez)
Taza
Taourirt
Oujda
Tlemcen
Safi
Settat
Khouribga
Oued Zem
Beni Mellal
El Kelaâ des Srarhna
Marrakech
Haut Atlas (High Atlas)
ATLAS MOUNTAINS
Aïn Sefra
Essaouira
Toubkal 4167
Haut Atlas
Rachidia
Figuig
Béchar
Taroudannt
Ouarzazate
Zagora
Abadla
Beni-Abbès
Agadir
Anti Atlas
Tiznit
Sidi Ifni
Guelmine
Hammada du Drâa
Tabelbala
Ksabi
El Ho
Tan-Tan
Timin
Erg Iabès
Plat
Adrar
Sbaa
LAÂYOUNE
Al Mahbas
El Aaiún
Es Semara
Tindouf
Bordj Flye Ste-Marie
El Eglab
Reggane
Aoulef
Boujdour
Galtat Zemmour
Chenachane
Sebkha Azzel Matti
Mek
Chegga
El Ham
Iguîdi
El Hammâmi
Tiguesmat
Erg Chech
Taoudenni
Post Weyga
Maqteïr
Guelb er Richât 485
Aouker
Azaouâd
SAHARA
S
A
Tahezrouft
MALI
Araouane
Azaouâd
Kidal
Anéfis
Ménaka
Gao
Ansongo
Tillab
Gourma-Rharous
Tombouctou
Hombori
Douentza
Mopti
Bandiagara
Gorom-Gorom
Dori
Koro
Ouahigouya
Gourcy
Kaya
Bogandé
Kongoussi
Zorgho
Kantchari
Gayéri
Fada-N'gourma
Tenkodogo
Pô
Bawku
BEN
Natitingou
Djougou
Parakou
Bassila
Bassar
Sokodé
Bondoukou
Kara
Sinématiali
Tchamba
Atakpamé
Kpalimé
PORTO-N
Volta
Kete
Krachi
Gambaga
Nalerigu
Savelugu
Bimbilla
Yendi
Salaga

Aïoun
Gourma

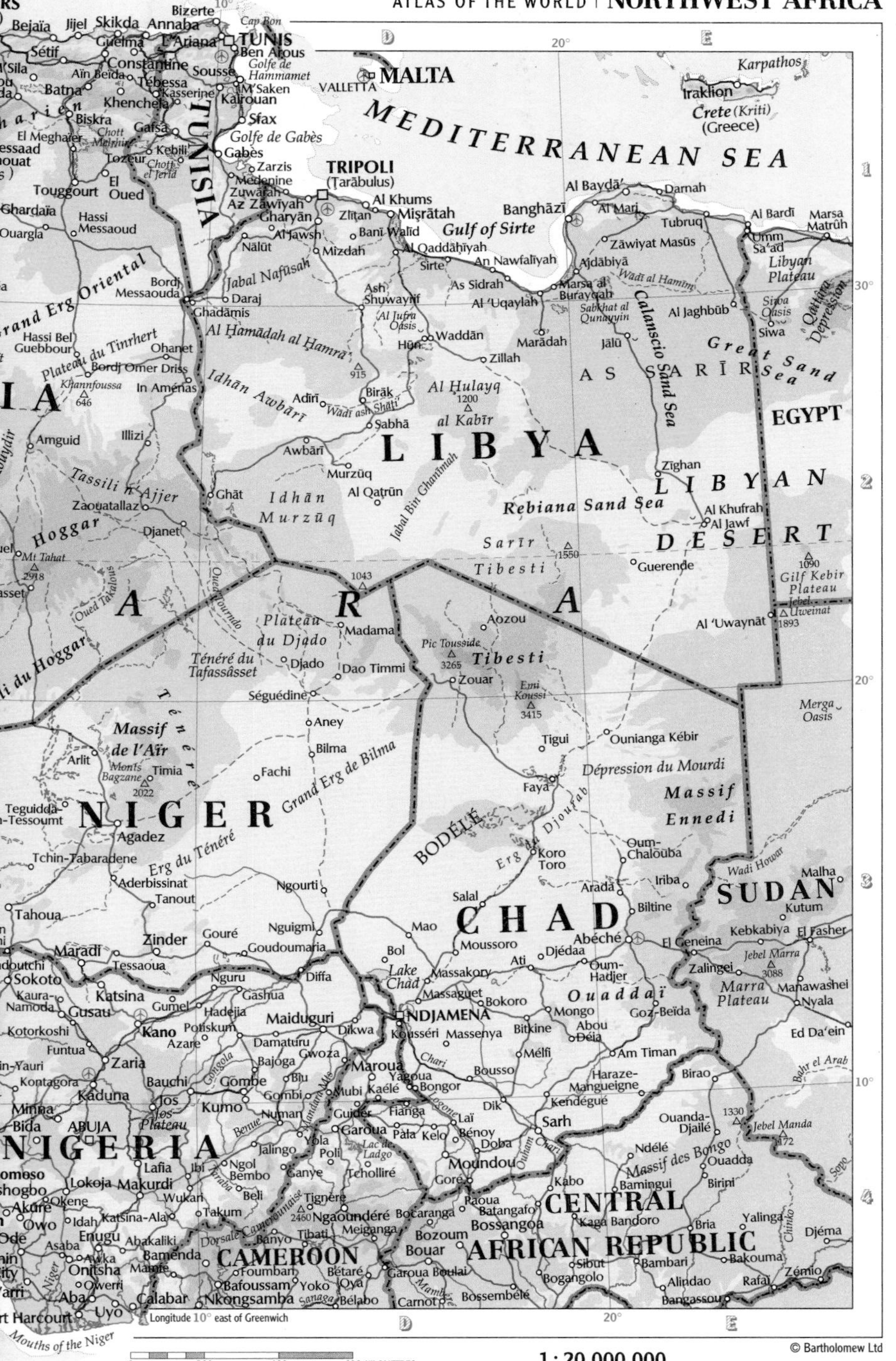

© Bartholomew Ltd

MEDITERRANEAN SEA
MALTA
VALLETTA
Karpathos
Iraklion
Crete (Kriti)
(Greece)
TUNIS
Bizerte
Cap Bon
Ben Arous
Golfe de Hammamet
Sousse
M'Saken
Kairouan
Sfax
Golfe de Gabès
Gabès
Zarzis
Medenine
TUNISIA
Bejaïa
Jijel
Skikda
Annaba
Guelma
L'Ariana
Sétif
Constantine
Aïn Beïda
Tébessa
Kasserine
Batna
Khenchela
Biskra
Gafsa
El Meghaier
Chott Melrhir
Kebili
Tozeur
Chott el Jerid
El Oued
Touggourt
Ghardaïa
Hassi Messaoud
Ouargla
Grand Erg Oriental
Bordj Messaouda
Hassi Bel Guebbour
Plateau du Tinrhert
Ohanet
Bordj Omer Driss
In Aménas
Khanfoussa
646
Amguid
Illizi
Tassili n'Ajjer
Zaouatallaz
Djanet
Hoggar
Mt Tahat
2918
Oued Tafassasset
du Hoggar
TRIPOLI
(Tarābulus)
Zuwārah
Az Zawiyah
Gharyān
Al Khums
Zlītan
Mişrātah
Al Jawsh
Banī Walīd
Nālūt
Mizdah
Jabal Nafūsah
Daraj
Ghadāmis
Al Hamādah al Hamrā'
Idhān Awbārī
Gulf of Sirte
Al Qaddāhiyah
Sirte
An Nawfalīyah
As Sidrah
Ash Shuwayrif
Al Jufra Oasis
Hūn
Waddān
Zillah
915
Adīrī
Birāk
Wadi ash Shāti'
Sabhā
Al Hulayq al Kabīr
1200
Awbārī
Murzūq
Ghāt
Al Qatrūn
Idhān Murzūq
Jabal Bin Ghanīmah
LIBYA
Banghāzī
Al Baydā'
Darnah
Al Marj
Tubruq
Zāwiyat Masūs
Ajdābiyā
Wādī al Hamīm
Marsa al Burayqah
Al 'Uqaylah
Sabkhat al Qunayyin
Marādah
Jālū
Calanscio Sand Sea
AS SARĪR
Al Jaghbūb
Al Bardī
Umm Sa'ad
Marsa Matrūh
Libyan Plateau
Siwa Oasis
Siwa
Qattara Depression
Great Sand Sea
EGYPT
Zighan
LIBYAN DESERT
Al Khufrah
Al Jawf
Rebiana Sand Sea
Sarīr Tibesti
1550
Guerende
1090
Gilf Kebir Plateau
Jebel Uweinat
1893
Al 'Uwaynāt
1043
SAHARA
Plateau du Djado
Madama
Djado
Dao Timmi
Ténéré du Tafassâsset
Séguédine
Oued Tourndo
Aozou
Pic Toussidé
3265
Tibesti
Zouar
Emi Koussi
3415
Aney
Bilma
Grand Erg de Bilma
Fachi
Ténéré
Massif de l'Aïr
Arlit
Monts Bagzane
2022
Timia
Tigui
Ounianga Kébir
Dépression du Mourdi
Faya
Massif Ennedi
Merga Oasis
NIGER
Teguidda-n-Tessoumt
Agadez
Erg du Ténéré
Tchin-Tabaradene
Aderbissinat
Tanout
Tahoua
Ngourti
BODÉLÉ
Djourab
Erg du Djourab
Koro Toro
Oum-Chalouba
Wadi Howar
Malha
Arada
Iriba
SUDAN
Biltine
Kutum
Salal
CHAD
Kebkabiya
El Fasher
Zinder
Gouré
Nguigmi
Goudoumaria
Mao
Moussoro
Abéché
El Geneina
Maradi
Tessaoua
Bol
Djédaa
Lake Chad
Ati
Oum-Hadjer
Jebel Marra
3088
Zalingei
Sokoto
Nguru
Diffa
Massakory
Marra Plateau
Manawashei
Nyala
Kaura-Namoda
Katsina
Gashua
Massaguet
Bokoro
Ouaddaï
Gusau
Gumel
Hadejia
NDJAMENA
Mongo
Goz-Beïda
Kotorkoshi
Kano
Potiskum
Maiduguri
Dikwa
Kousséri
Massenya
Bitkine
Abou Déia
Ed Da'ein
Funtua
Azare
Damaturu
Gwoza
Mélfi
Am Timan
Zaria
Bajoga
Maroua
Chari
Bousso
Bahr el Arab
Kontagora
Bauchi
Gombe
Biu
Yagoua
Bongor
Haraze-Mangueigne
Birao
Kaduna
Jos
Gombi
Mubi
Kaélé
Dik
Kendégué
Minna
Jos Plateau
Kumo
Numan
Guider
Fianga
Logone
Laï
Sarh
Bida
ABUJA
Benue
Garoua
Pala
Kelo
Bénoy
Doba
Ouanda-Djailé
1330
Jebel Manda
1172
NIGERIA
Jalingo
Yola
Poli
Lac de Lagdo
Mandara Mts
Moundou
Ouham
Ndélé
Massif des Bongo
Ouadda
Lafia
Ibi
Ngol Bembo
Ganye
Tcholliré
Goré
Kabo
Bamingui
Biriní
Sopo
Omoso
Oshogbo
Lokoja
Makurdi
Wukari
Beli
Tignère
Raoua
Batangafo
CENTRAL
Okene
Akure
Takum
2460
Ngaoundéré
Bocaranga
Kaga Bandoro
Bria
Yalinga
Djéma
Owo
Idah
Katsina-Ala
Tibati
Meiganga
Bossangoa
Chinko
Ode
Asaba
Enugu
Abakaliki
Dorsale Camerounaise
Banyo
Bozoum
AFRICAN REPUBLIC
Bamenda
CAMEROON
Bouar
Onitsha
Awka
Mamfe
Foumban
Bétaré Oya
Garoua Boulaï
Sibut
Bambari
Bakouma
Zémio
Niger
Owerri
Bafoussam
Yoko
Mambéré
Bogangolo
Alindao
Rafaï
Aba
Calabar
Nkongsamba
Sanaga
Bélabo
Carnot
Bossembélé
Bangassou
Port Harcourt
Uyo
Mouths of the Niger
Longitude 10° east of Greenwich
10°
20°
30°
1
2
3
4

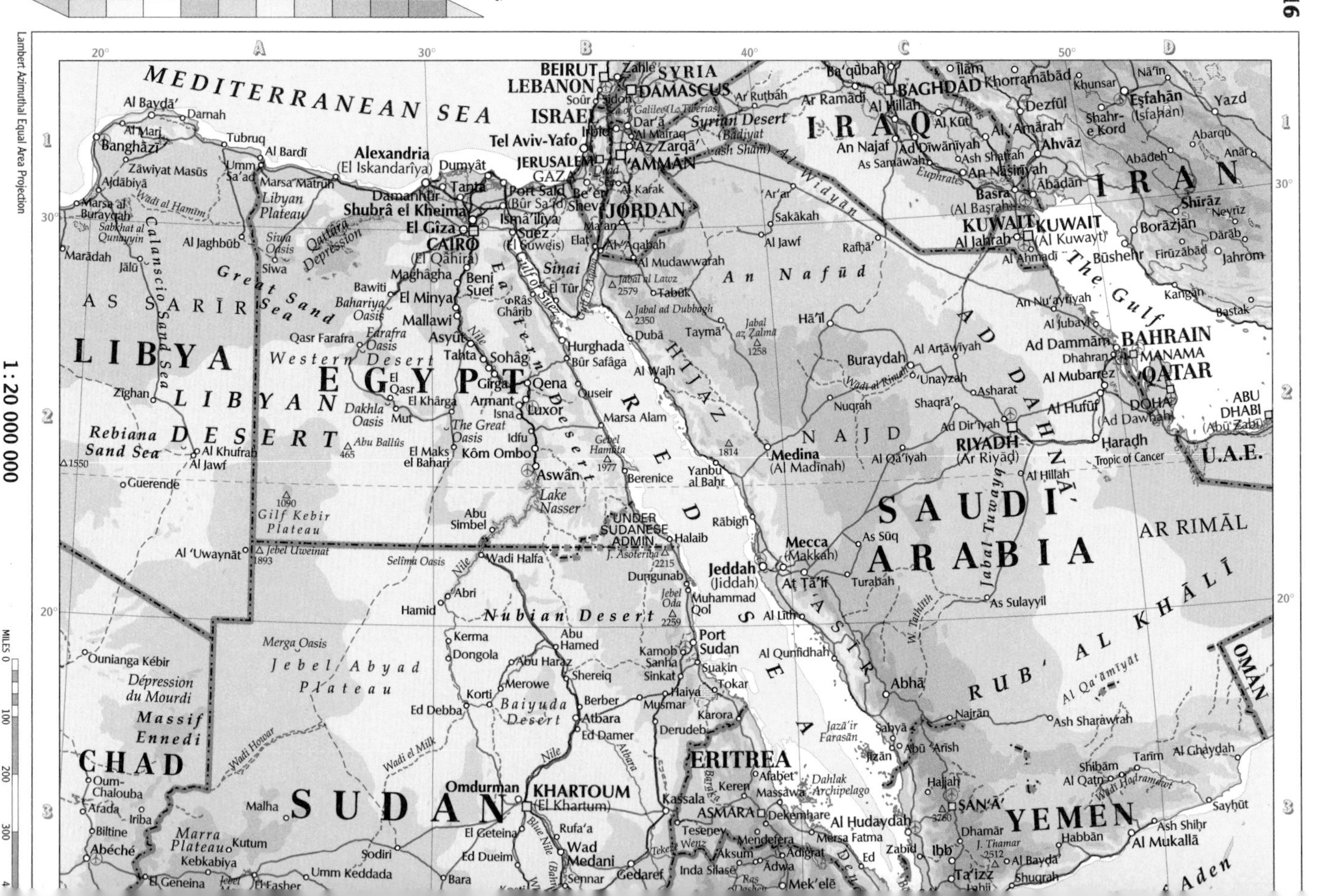

Lambert Azimuthal Equal Area Projection

1 : 20 000 000

MILES 0   100   200   300   4

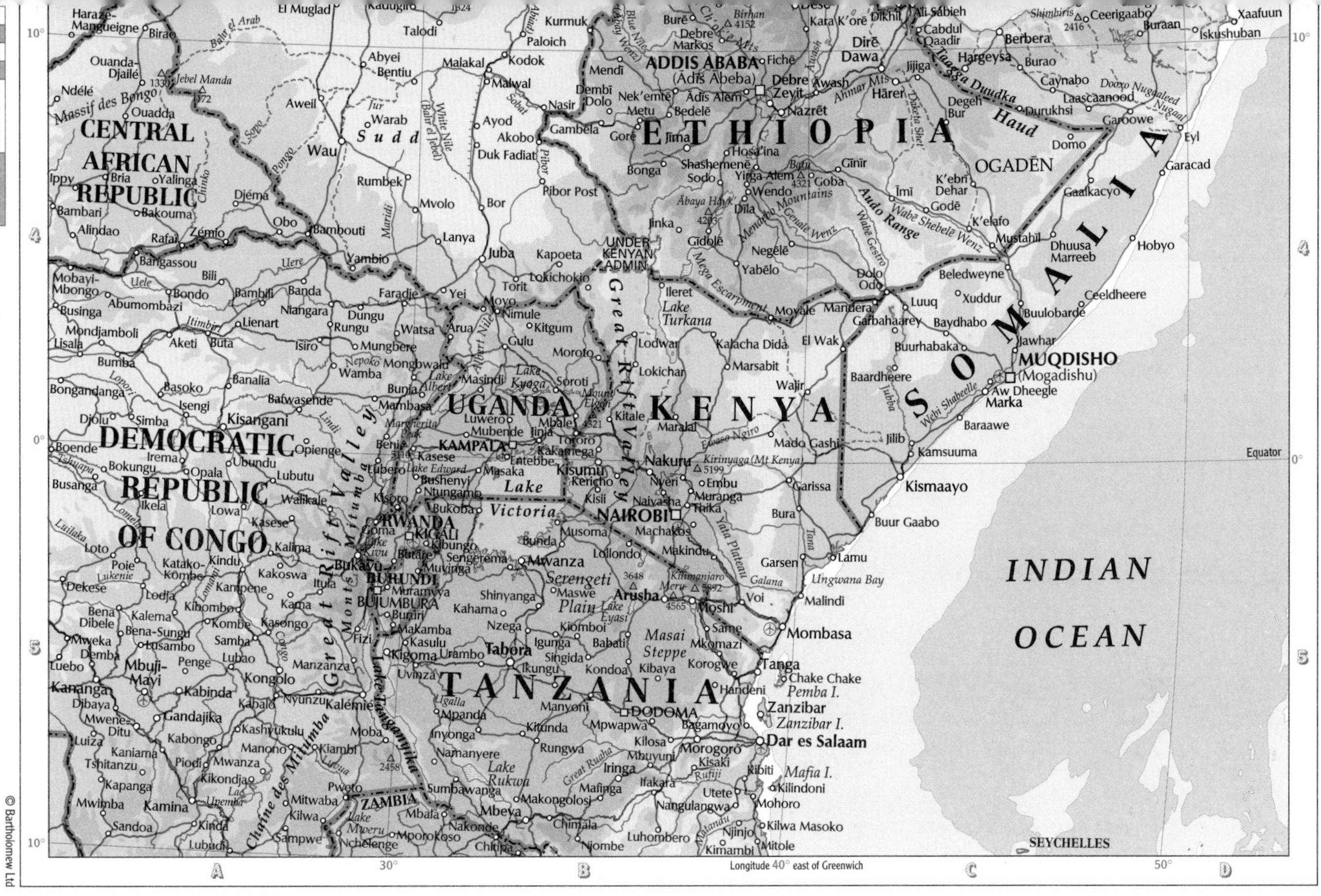
ETHIOPIA
SOMALIA
KENYA
UGANDA
TANZANIA
RWANDA
BURUNDI
DEMOCRATIC REPUBLIC OF CONGO
CENTRAL AFRICAN REPUBLIC
ZAMBIA
INDIAN OCEAN
ADDIS ABABA (Adis Abeba)
MUQDISHO (Mogadishu)
NAIROBI
KAMPALA
KIGALI
BUJUMBURA
DODOMA
Dar es Salaam
Mombasa
Zanzibar
Kismaayo
Juba
OGADĒN
Haud
Great Rift Valley
Lake Turkana
Lake Victoria
Lake Tanganyika
Lake Rukwa
Serengeti Plain
Masai Steppe
Yata Plateau
Mega Escarpment
Sudd
SEYCHELLES
Equator
Longitude 40° east of Greenwich

0 200 400 600 KILOMETRES

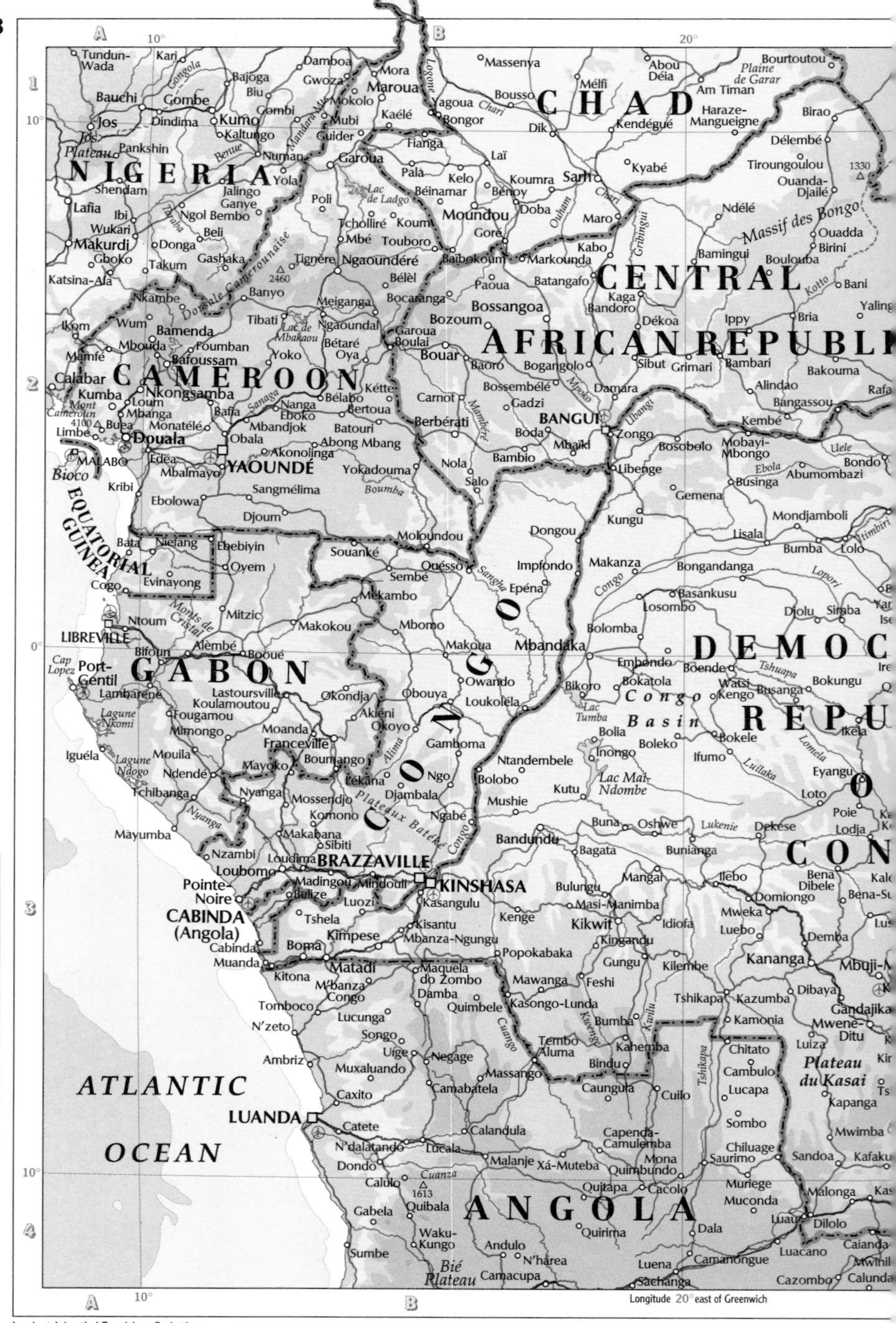

⒈

CHAD

NIGERIA

CENTRAL

AFRICAN REPUBLI

CAMEROON

⒉

BANGUI

YAOUNDÉ

EQUATORIAL GUINEA

LIBREVILLE

GABON

DEMOC

0°

CONGO

REPU

Congo Basin

O

CON

KINSHASA

BRAZZAVILLE

⒊

Pointe-Noire

CABINDA (Angola)

METRES	FEET
5000	16404
3000	9843
2000	6562
1000	3281
500	1640
200	656
0 LAND B.S.L.	0
200	656
4000	13124
6000	19686

ATLANTIC

OCEAN

LUANDA

ANGOLA

⒋

Lambert Azimuthal Equal Area Projection

10° ⒶＡ ⒷＢ

Longitude 20° east of Greenwich

1 : 15 000 000

MILES 0   100   200   3

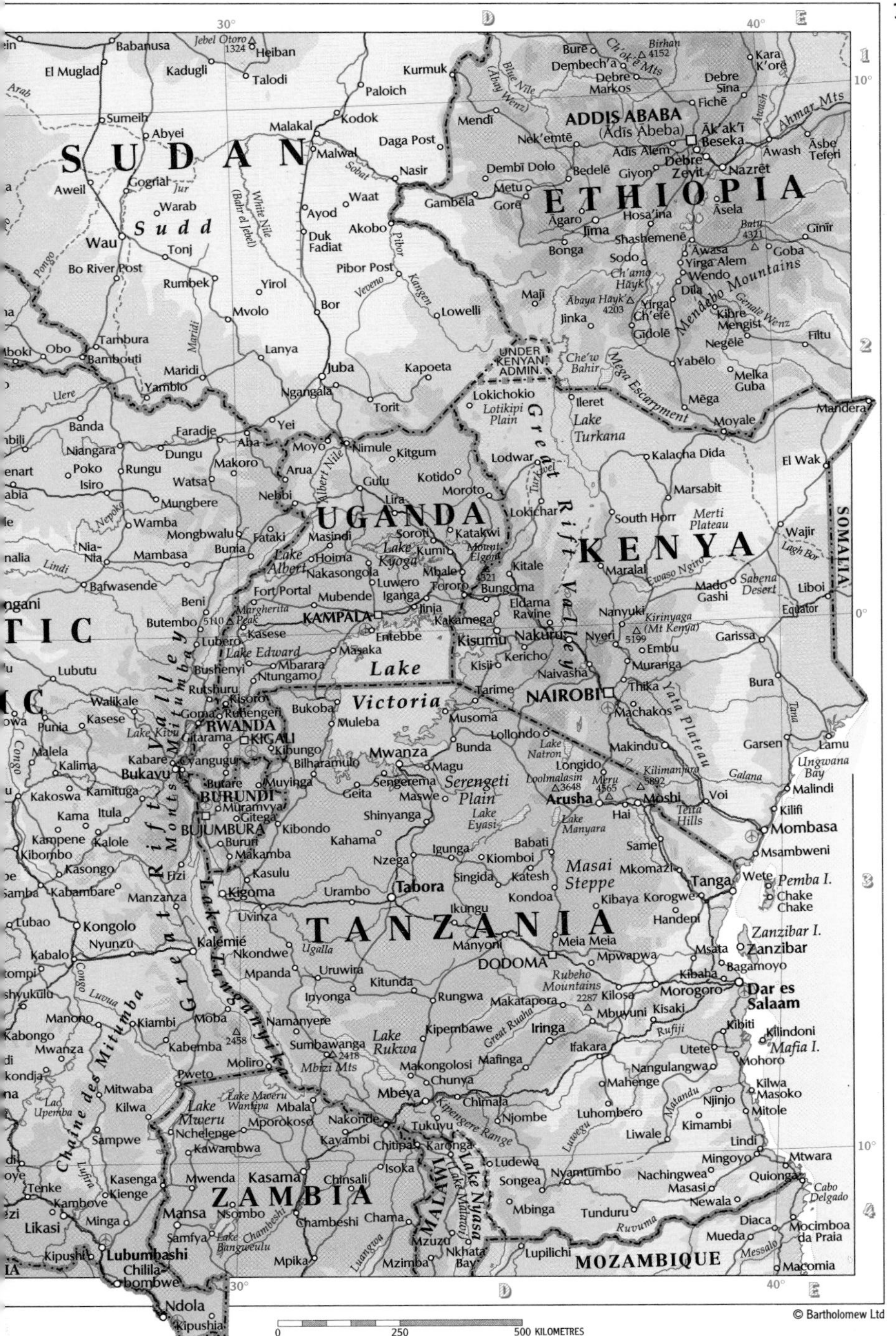
30°
D
40°
E
1
2
3
4
10°
0°
10°
SUDAN
ETHIOPIA
UGANDA
KENYA
SOMALIA
TANZANIA
ZAMBIA
MALAWI
MOZAMBIQUE
RWANDA
BURUNDI
TIC
IC
Babanusa
Jebel Otoro
1324
Heiban
El Muglad
Kadugli
Talodi
Kurmuk
Paloich
Arab
Sumeih
Abyei
Kodok
Malakal
Malwal
Daga Post
Sobat
Nasir
Aweil
Gogrial
Jur
Warab
Sudd
Ayod
Waat
White Nile
(Bahr el Jebel)
Wau
Tonj
Duk Fadiat
Akobo
Pibor
Pongo
Bo River Post
Pibor Post
Veveno
Kangen
Rumbek
Yirol
Mvolo
Bor
Lowelli
Maridi
Tambura
Obo
Bambouti
Lanya
Maridi
Yambio
Juba
Ngangala
Kapoeta
Torit
Uere
Yei
Banda
Faradje
Aba
Niangara
Dungu
Moyo
Nimule
Kitgum
Poko
Rungu
Makoro
Arua
Albert Nile
Isiro
Watsa
Gulu
Kotido
Moroto
Nebbi
Lira
Mungbere
Nepoko
Wamba
Mongbwalu
Fataki
Masindi
Soroti
Katakwi
Nia-Nia
Mambasa
Bunia
Lake Albert
Hoima
Lake Kyoga
Kumi
Mount Elgon
4321
Lindi
Nakasongola
Mbale
Bafwasende
Luwero
Tororo
Beni
Fort Portal
Mubende
Iganga
Margherita Peak
5110
KAMPALA
Jinja
Butembo
Kasese
Entebbe
Lubero
Lake Edward
Masaka
Lake
Lubutu
Mbarara
Bushenyi
Ntungamo
Rutshuru
Kisoro
Ruhengeri
Bukoba
Victoria
Walikale
Goma
Kasese
Punia
Muleba
Lake Kivu
Gitarama
KIGALI
Congo
Malela
Kabare
Cyangugu
Kibungo
Kalima
Bukavu
Bilharamulo
Mwanza
Kakoswa
Kamituga
Butare
Muyinga
Muramvya
Kama
Itula
Gitega
BUJUMBURA
Kibondo
Kampene
Kalole
Bururi
Kibombo
Makamba
Kasongo
Fizi
Kasulu
Kabambare
Manzanza
Kigoma
Uvinza
Lubao
Kongolo
Nyunzu
Kalémié
Kabalo
Nkondwe
Ugalla
Mpanda
Uruwira
Congo
Luvua
Manono
Kiambi
Moba
Kabongo
Mwanza
Kabemba
2458
Moliro
Pweto
Mitwaba
Lac Upemba
Kilwa
Lake Mweru
Lake Mweru Wantipa
Nchelenge
Kawambwa
Sampwe
Lufira
Tenke
Kasenga
Kienge
Kambove
Minga
Likasi
Kipushi
Lubumbashi
Chililabombwe
Ndola
Kipushia
Mwenda
Kasama
Mansa
Nsombo
Samfya
Lake Bangweulu
Chambeshi
Mbala
Mporokoso
Chinsali
Chambeshi
Chama
Isoka
Mpika
Luangwa
Mzuzu
Mzimba
Nkhata Bay
Lake Nyasa
(Lake Malawi)
Chitipa
Karonga
Tukuyu
Kyela
Kayambi
Nakonde
Mbeya
Chunya
Makongolosi
Mbizi Mts
2418
Sumbawanga
Lake Rukwa
Namanyere
Kipembawe
Inyonga
Kitunda
Rungwa
Mafinga
Chimala
Njombe
Kipengere Range
Ludewa
Songea
Mbinga
Lupilichi
Chaine des Mitumba
Monts Mitumba
Great Rift Valley
Lake Tanganyika
Mendi
Blue Nile
(Abay Wenz)
Bure
Dembech'a
Debre Markos
Ch'ok'e Mts
Birhan
4152
Kara K'orē
Debre Sina
Fichē
Awash
Ahmar Mts
ADDIS ABABA
(Ādīs Ābeba)
Āk'ak'ī Beseka
Nek'emtē
Adis Alem
Debre Zeyit
Nazrēt
Āwash
Āsbe Teferi
Dembī Dolo
Bedelē
Giyon
Metu
Gorē
Gambēla
Āgaro
Jīma
Hosa'ina
Āsela
Batu
4321
Gīnīr
Bonga
Shashemenē
Āwasa
Goba
Sodo
Yirga Alem
Wendo
Ch'amo Hāyk'
Dila
Mendebo Mountains
Genale Wenz
Maji
Ābaya Hāyk'
4203
Yirga Ch'efē
Kibre Mengist
Jinka
Gidolē
Filtu
Negēlē
UNDER KENYAN ADMIN.
Che'w Bahir
Mega Escarpment
Yabēlo
Melka Guba
Mēga
Lokichokio
Lotikipi Plain
Ileret
Lake Turkana
Moyale
Mandera
Kalacha Dida
Lodwar
Turkwel
Marsabit
El Wak
Lokichar
South Horr
Merti Plateau
Wajir
Lagh Bor
Great Rift Valley
Kitale
Maralal
Ewaso Ngiro
Mado Gashi
Sabena Desert
Liboi
Bungoma
Eldama Ravine
Nanyuki
Kirinyaga
(Mt Kenya)
5199
Equator
Kakamega
Kisumu
Nakuru
Nyeri
Garissa
Kericho
Embu
Kisii
Muranga
Naivasha
Bura
Tarime
Thika
NAIROBI
Yata Plateau
Machakos
Tana
Musoma
Lollondo
Lake Natron
Bunda
Makindu
Garsen
Lamu
Ungwana Bay
Magu
Longido
Kilimanjaro
5892
Galana
Sengerema
Serengeti Plain
Loolmalasin
3648
Meru
4565
Malindi
Geita
Maswe
Arusha
Moshi
Voi
Kilifi
Shinyanga
Lake Eyasi
Hai
Taita Hills
Lake Manyara
Mombasa
Kahama
Babati
Same
Msambweni
Igunga
Kiomboi
Masai Steppe
Mkomazi
Nzega
Singida
Katesh
Tanga
Wete
Pemba I.
Tabora
Urambo
Kondoa
Kibaya
Korogwe
Chake Chake
Ikungu
Handeni
Manyoni
Meia Meia
Zanzibar I.
Msata
Zanzibar
DODOMA
Mpwapwa
Bagamoyo
Rubeho Mountains
2287
Kilosa
Kibaha
Morogoro
Dar es Salaam
Makatapora
Mbuyuni
Kisaki
Great Ruaha
Iringa
Rufiji
Kibiti
Kilindoni
Mafia I.
Ifakara
Utete
Mohoro
Nangulangwa
Mahenge
Kilwa Masoko
Matandu
Njinjo
Luhombero
Mitole
Luwegu
Kimambi
Liwale
Lindi
Mingoyo
Mtwara
Nyamtumbo
Nachingwea
Quionga
Masasi
Cabo Delgado
Newala
Tunduru
Ruvuma
Diaca
Mocimboa da Praia
Mueda
Messalo
Macomia

0 250 500 KILOMETRES

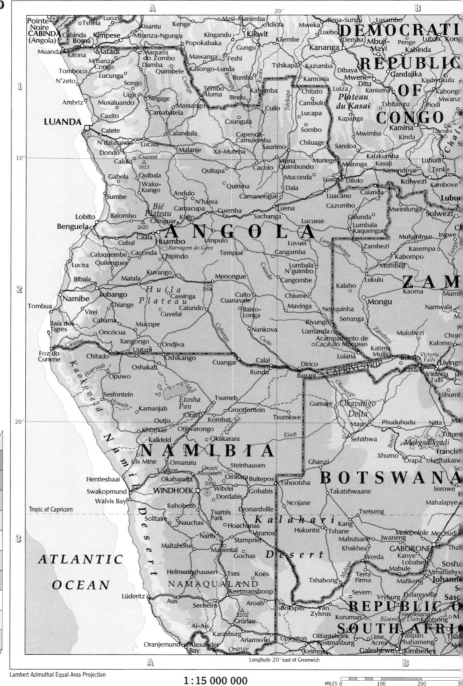

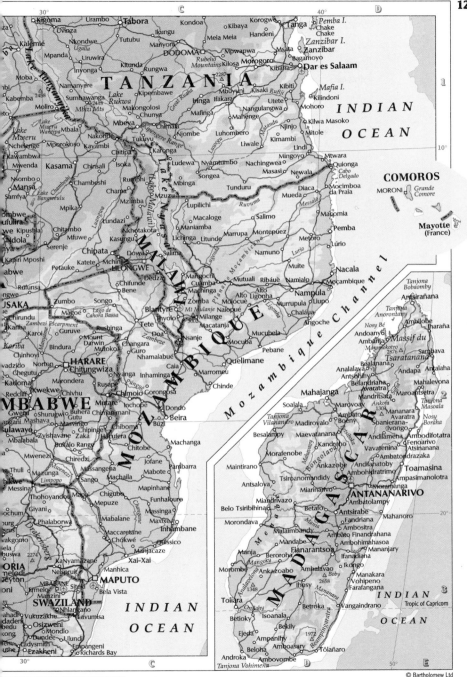

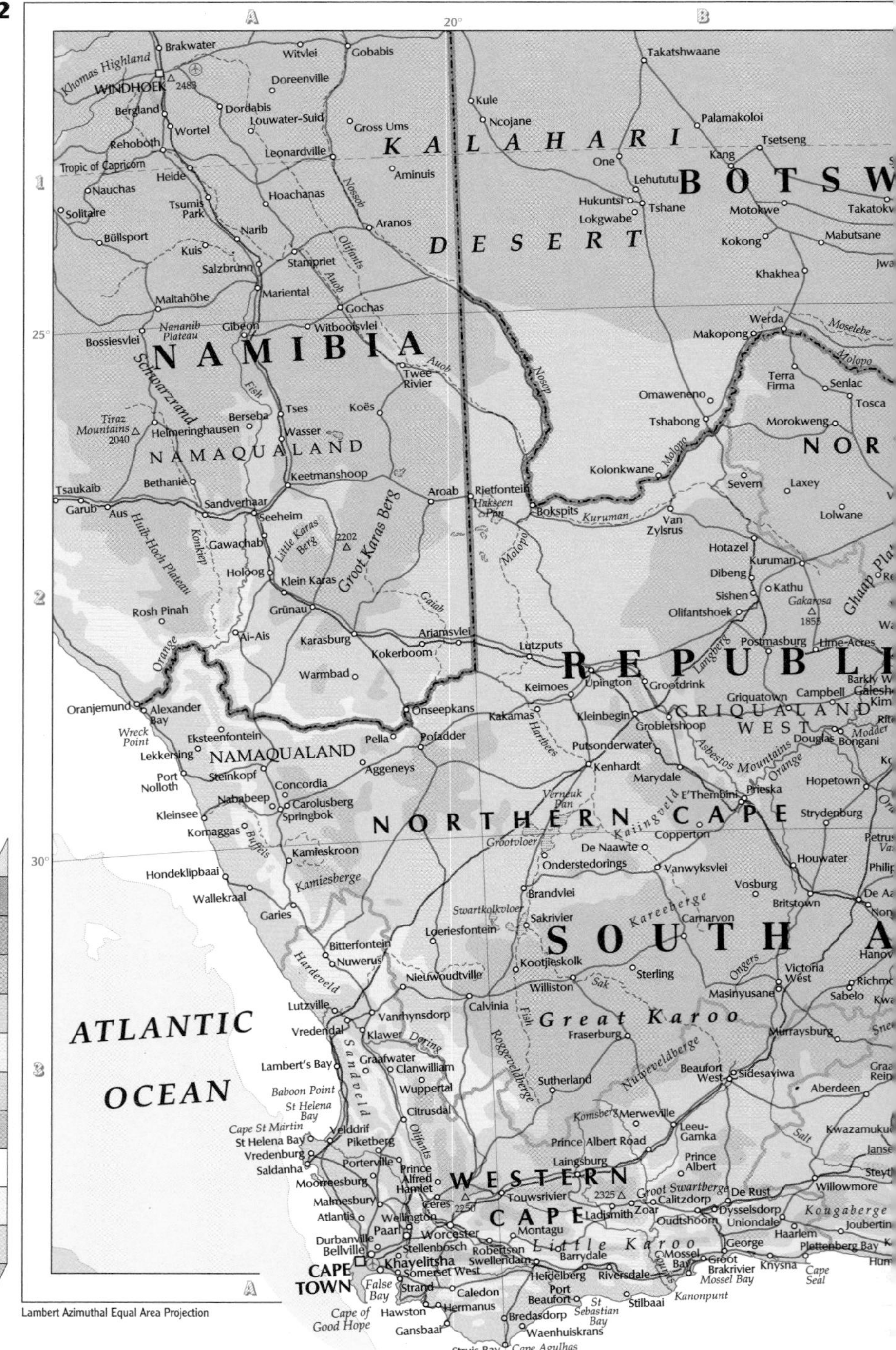

METRES
FEET

5000
16404

3000
9843

2000
6562

1000
3281

500
1640

200
656

0
0

LAND
B.S.L.

200
656

4000
13124

6000
19686

Lambert Azimuthal Equal Area Projection

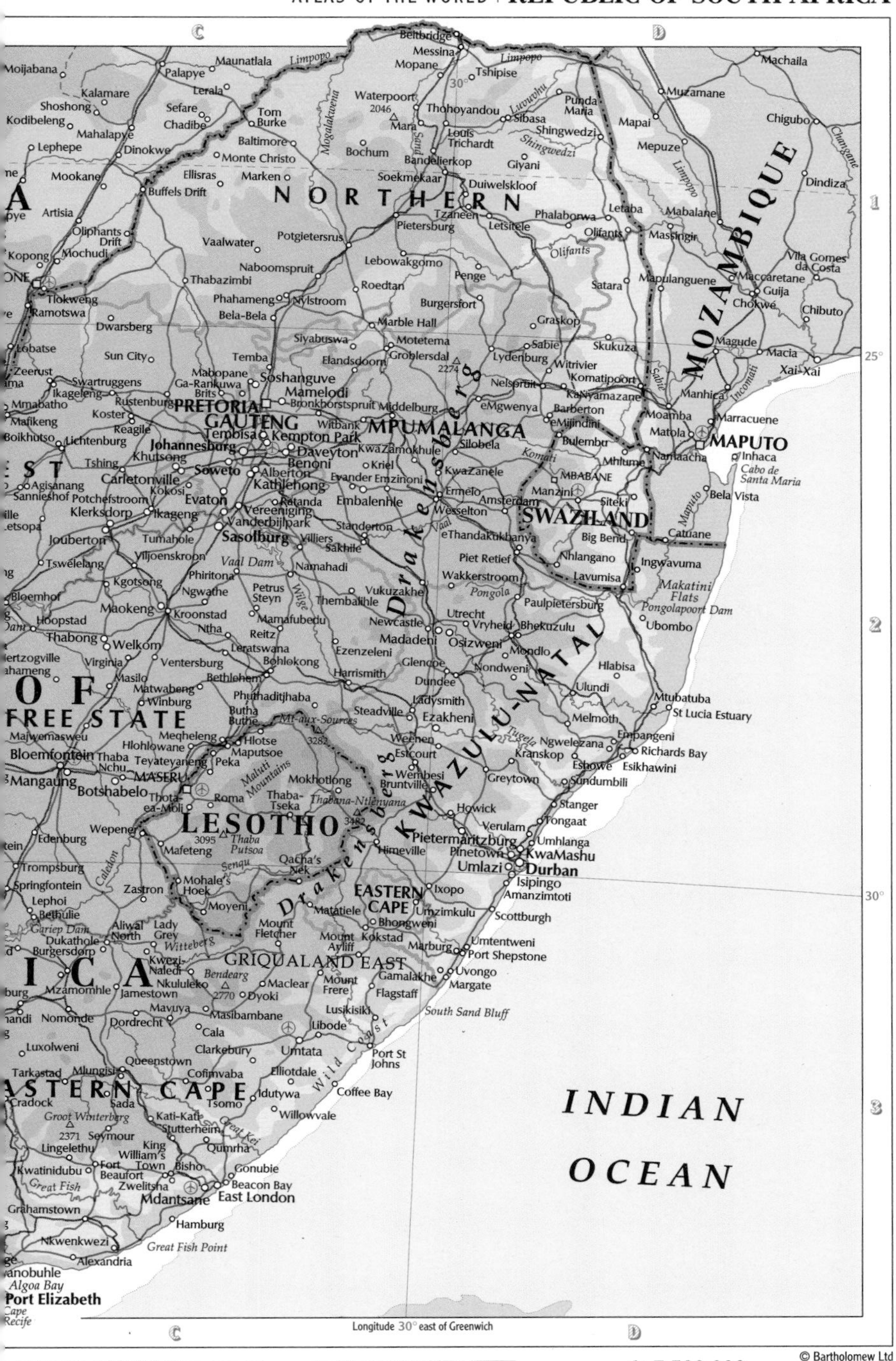

INDIAN

OCEAN

Longitude 30° east of Greenwich

© Bartholomew Ltd

ES 0   50   100   150   0   100   200 KILOMETRES   **1 : 7 500 000**

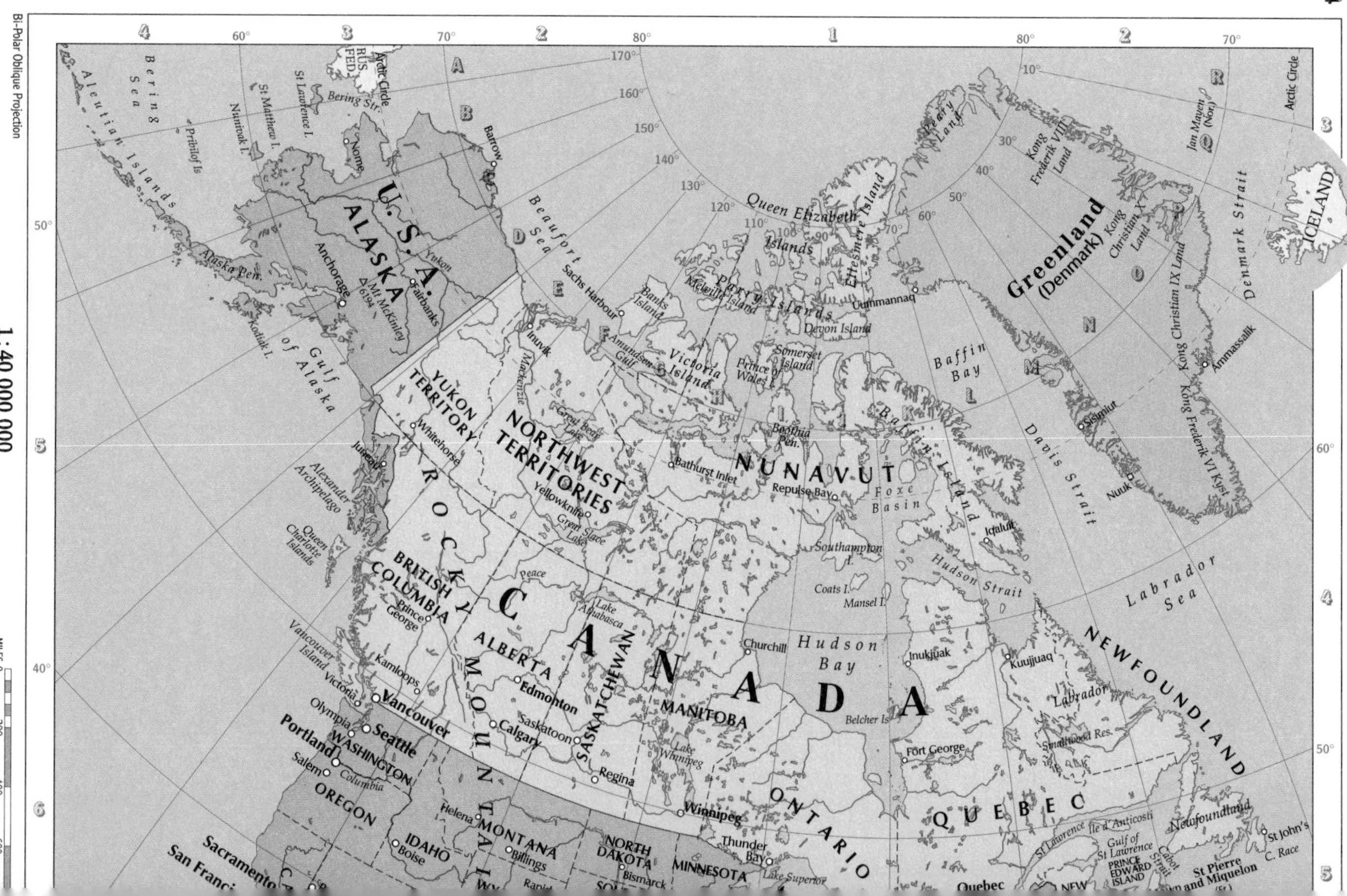

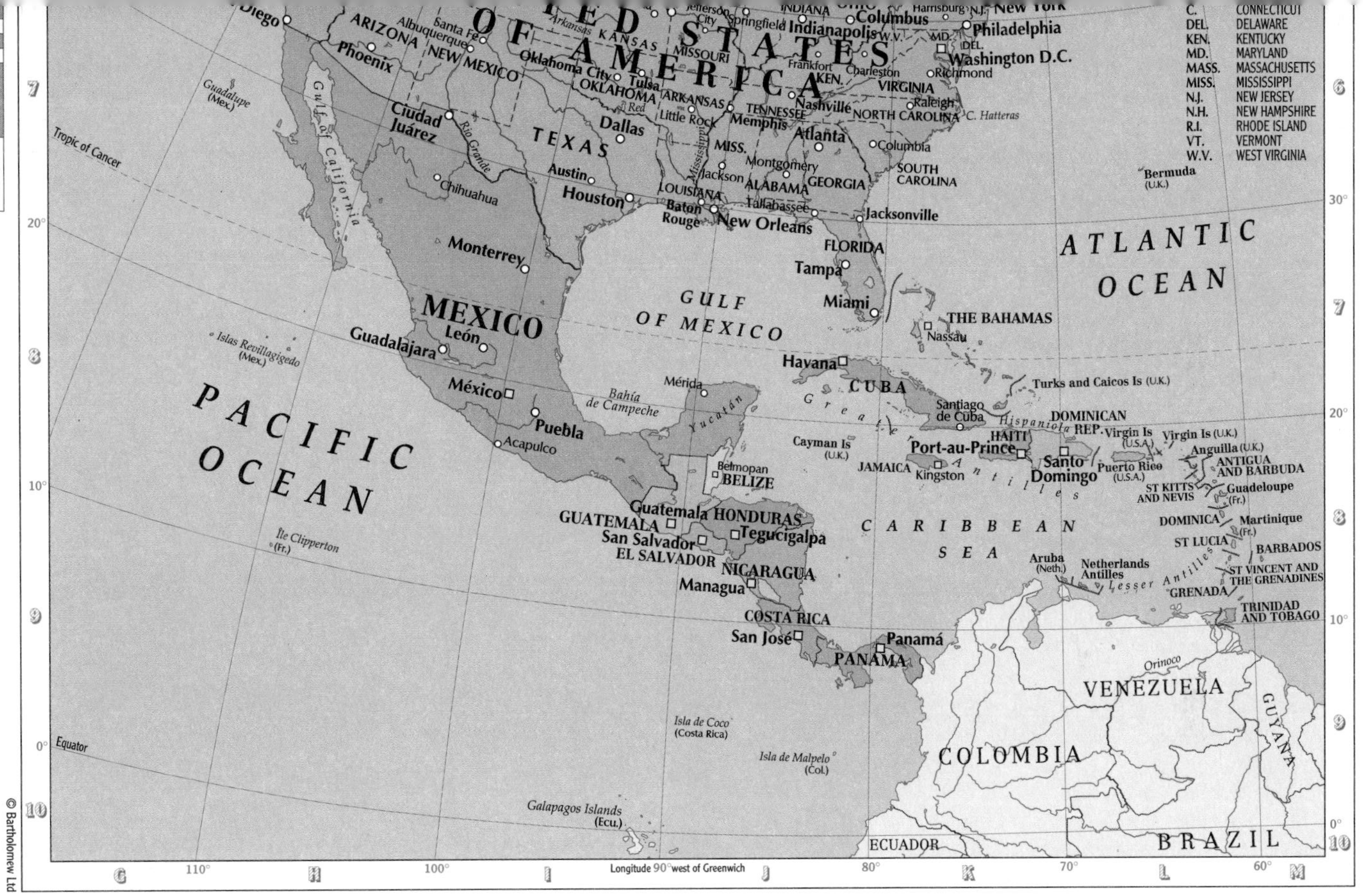

© Bartholomew Ltd

400   800   1200 KILOMETRES

UNITED STATES OF AMERICA
C. DEL. KEN. MD. MASS. MISS. N.J. N.H. R.I. VT. W.V.
CONNECTICUT DELAWARE KENTUCKY MARYLAND MASSACHUSETTS MISSISSIPPI NEW JERSEY NEW HAMPSHIRE RHODE ISLAND VERMONT WEST VIRGINIA
ATLANTIC OCEAN
PACIFIC OCEAN
GULF OF MEXICO
CARIBBEAN SEA
MEXICO
CUBA
THE BAHAMAS
HAITI
DOMINICAN REP.
JAMAICA
BELIZE
GUATEMALA
HONDURAS
EL SALVADOR
NICARAGUA
COSTA RICA
PANAMA
COLOMBIA
VENEZUELA
GUYANA
BRAZIL
ECUADOR
ARIZONA
NEW MEXICO
KANSAS
MISSOURI
OKLAHOMA
ARKANSAS
TEXAS
LOUISIANA
MISS.
ALABAMA
GEORGIA
TENNESSEE
KEN.
VIRGINIA
NORTH CAROLINA
SOUTH CAROLINA
FLORIDA
Diego
Phoenix
Albuquerque
Santa Fe
Oklahoma City
Tulsa
Dallas
Austin
Houston
Little Rock
Memphis
Jackson
Baton Rouge
New Orleans
Montgomery
Tallahassee
Atlanta
Nashville
Frankfort
Charleston
Columbia
Jacksonville
Tampa
Miami
Springfield
Indianapolis
Columbus
Harrisburg
New York
Philadelphia
Washington D.C.
Richmond
Raleigh
C. Hatteras
Bermuda (U.K.)
Ciudad Juárez
Chihuahua
Monterrey
León
Guadalajara
México
Puebla
Acapulco
Mérida
Havana
Nassau
Santiago de Cuba
Port-au-Prince
Santo Domingo
Kingston
Belmopan
Guatemala
San Salvador
Tegucigalpa
Managua
San José
Panamá
Turks and Caicos Is (U.K.)
Cayman Is (U.K.)
Virgin Is (U.S.A.)
Virgin Is (U.K.)
Puerto Rico (U.S.A.)
Anguilla (U.K.)
ANTIGUA AND BARBUDA
ST KITTS AND NEVIS
Guadeloupe (Fr.)
DOMINICA
Martinique (Fr.)
ST LUCIA
BARBADOS
ST VINCENT AND THE GRENADINES
GRENADA
TRINIDAD AND TOBAGO
Aruba (Neth.)
Netherlands Antilles
Hispaniola
Greater Antilles
Lesser Antilles
Orinoco
Rio Grande
Red
Arkansas
Mississippi
Gulf of California
Bahía de Campeche
Yucatán
Guadalupe (Mex.)
Islas Revillagigedo (Mex.)
Île Clipperton (Fr.)
Isla de Coco (Costa Rica)
Isla de Malpelo (Col.)
Galapagos Islands (Ecu.)
Tropic of Cancer
Equator
Longitude 90° west of Greenwich

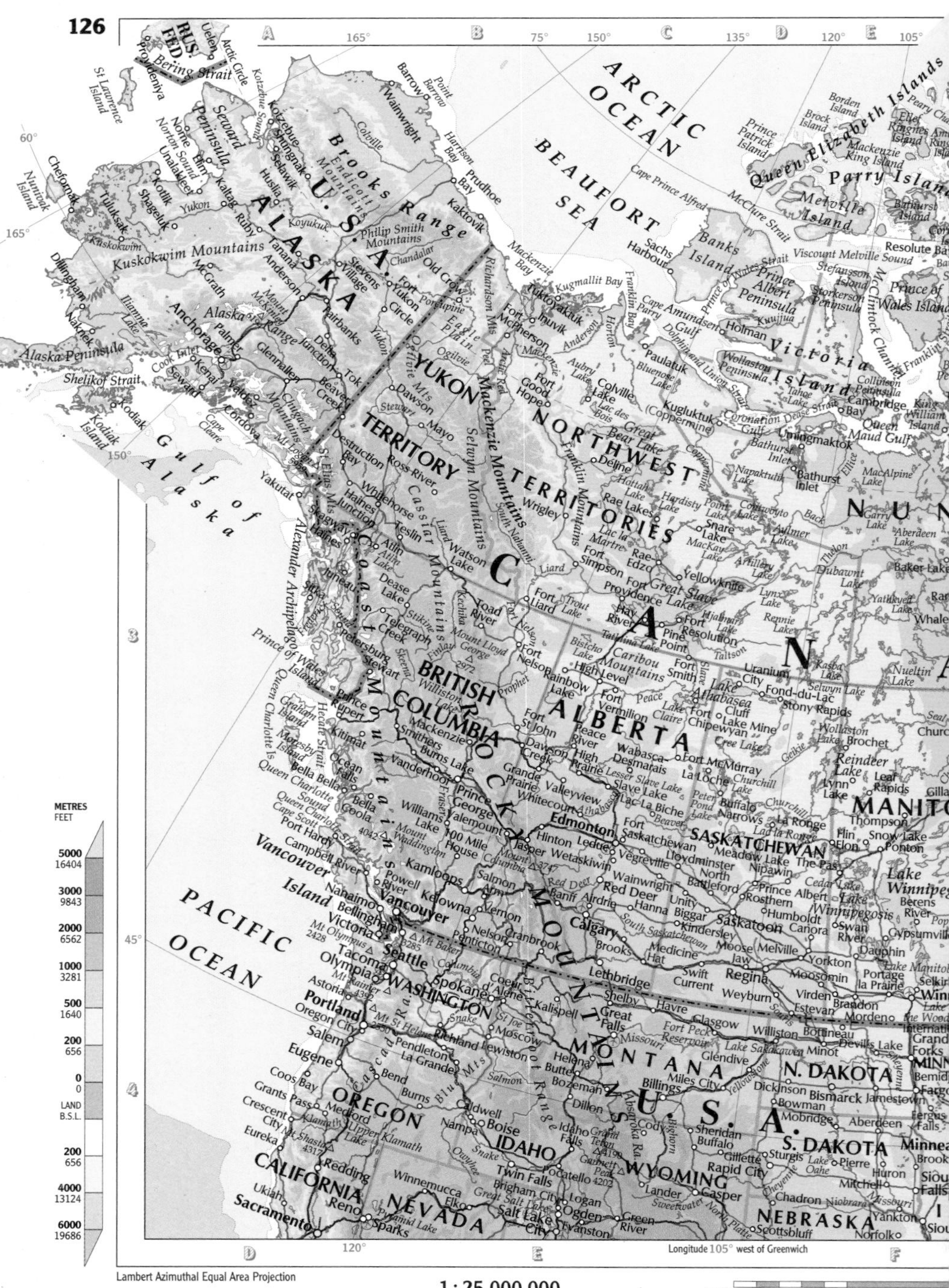

Lambert Azimuthal Equal Area Projection

1 : 25 000 000

MILES 0   250

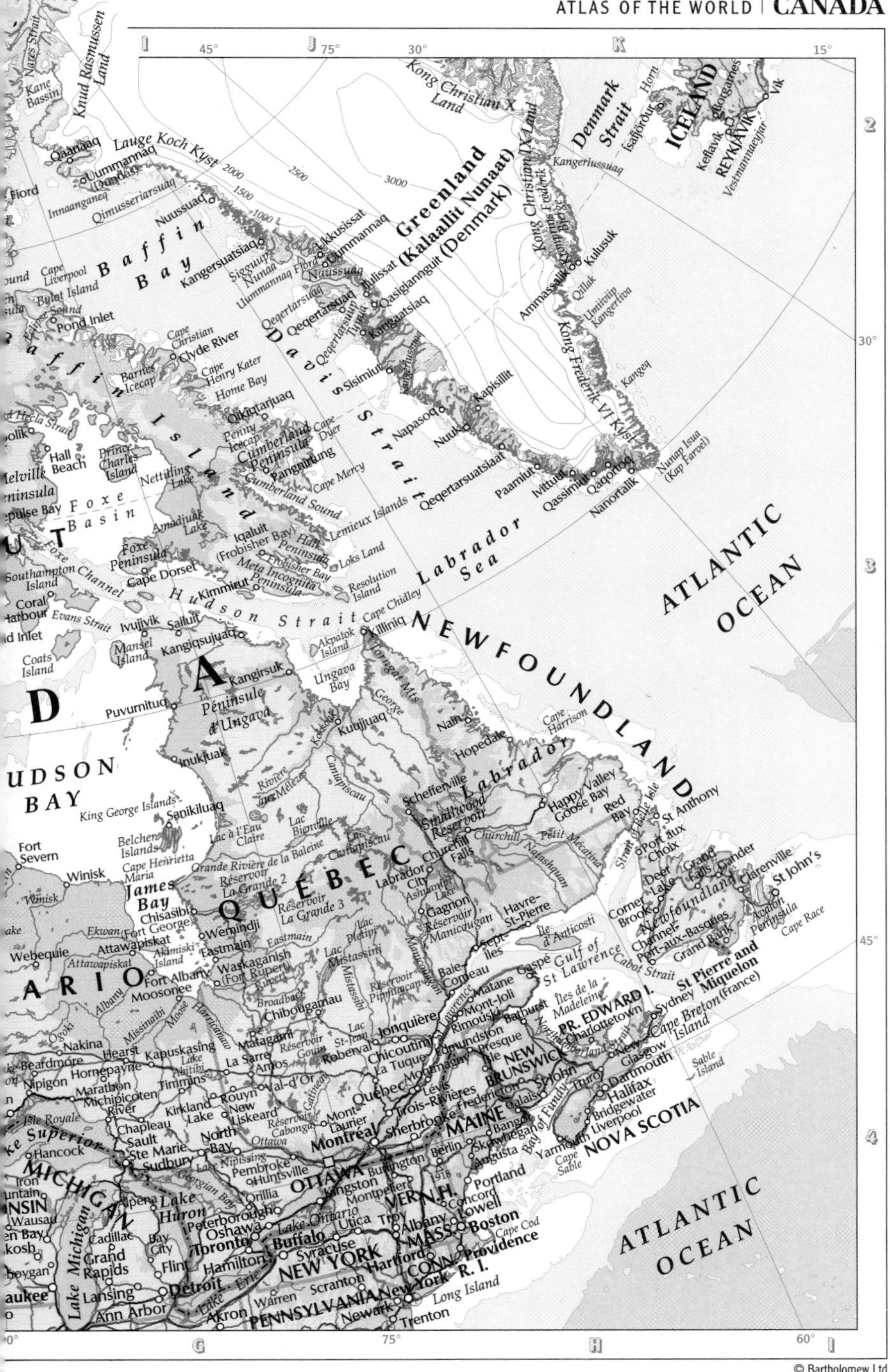
Greenland
(Kalaallit Nunaat)
(Denmark)
ICELAND
REYKJAVIK
Denmark Strait
Baffin Bay
Baffin Island
Davis Strait
Labrador Sea
ATLANTIC OCEAN
NEWFOUNDLAND
Labrador
QUÉBEC
HUDSON BAY
James Bay
Hudson Strait
Foxe Basin
NOVA SCOTIA
NEW BRUNSWICK
PR. EDWARD I.
St Pierre and Miquelon (France)
Gulf of St Lawrence
MAINE
NEW YORK
PENNSYLVANIA
MICHIGAN
OTTAWA
Montréal
Québec
Toronto
Boston
New York
Halifax
St John's
Nuuk
250 500 750 KILOMETRES

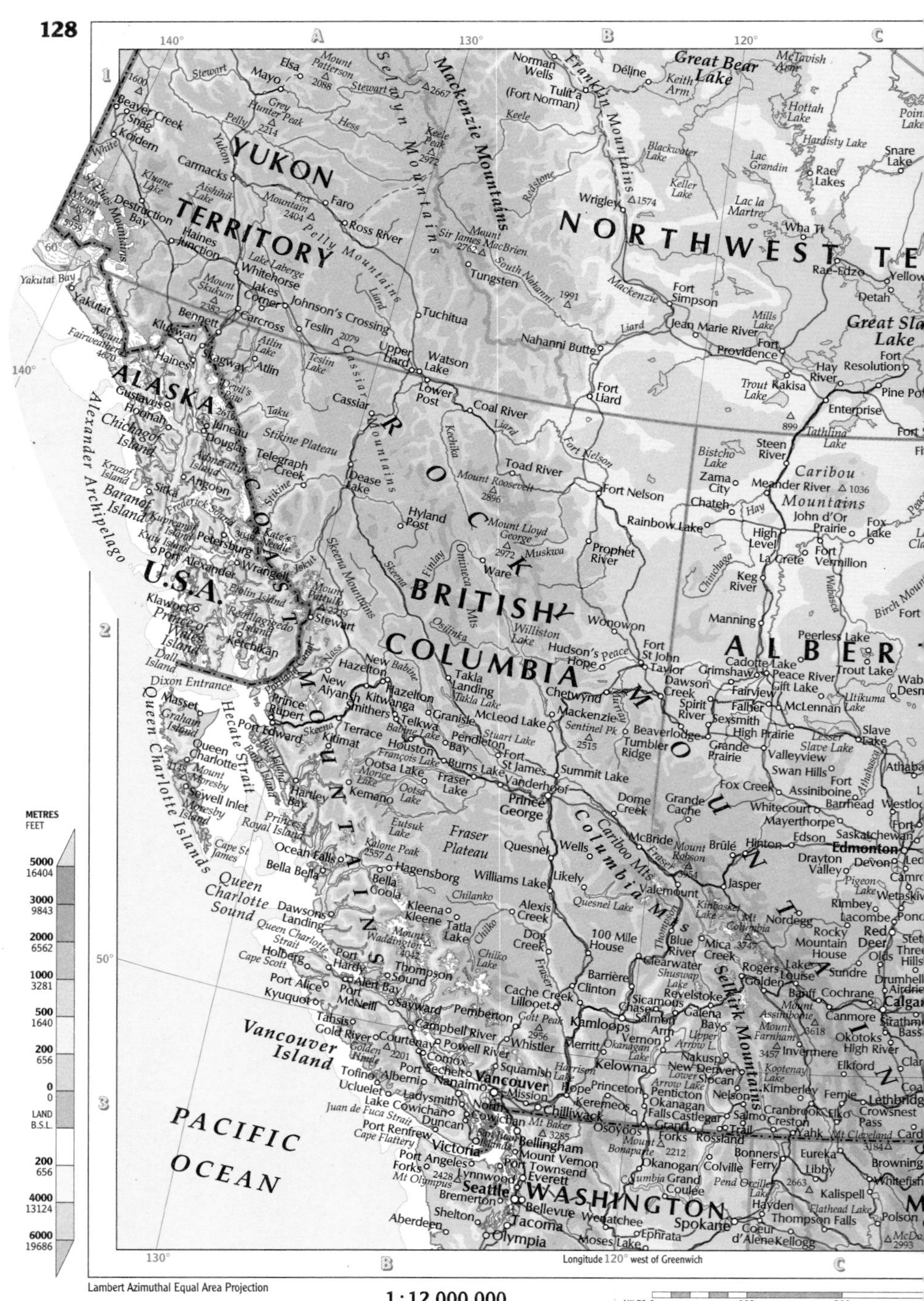

Lambert Azimuthal Equal Area Projection

1 : 12 000 000

MILES 0   100   200

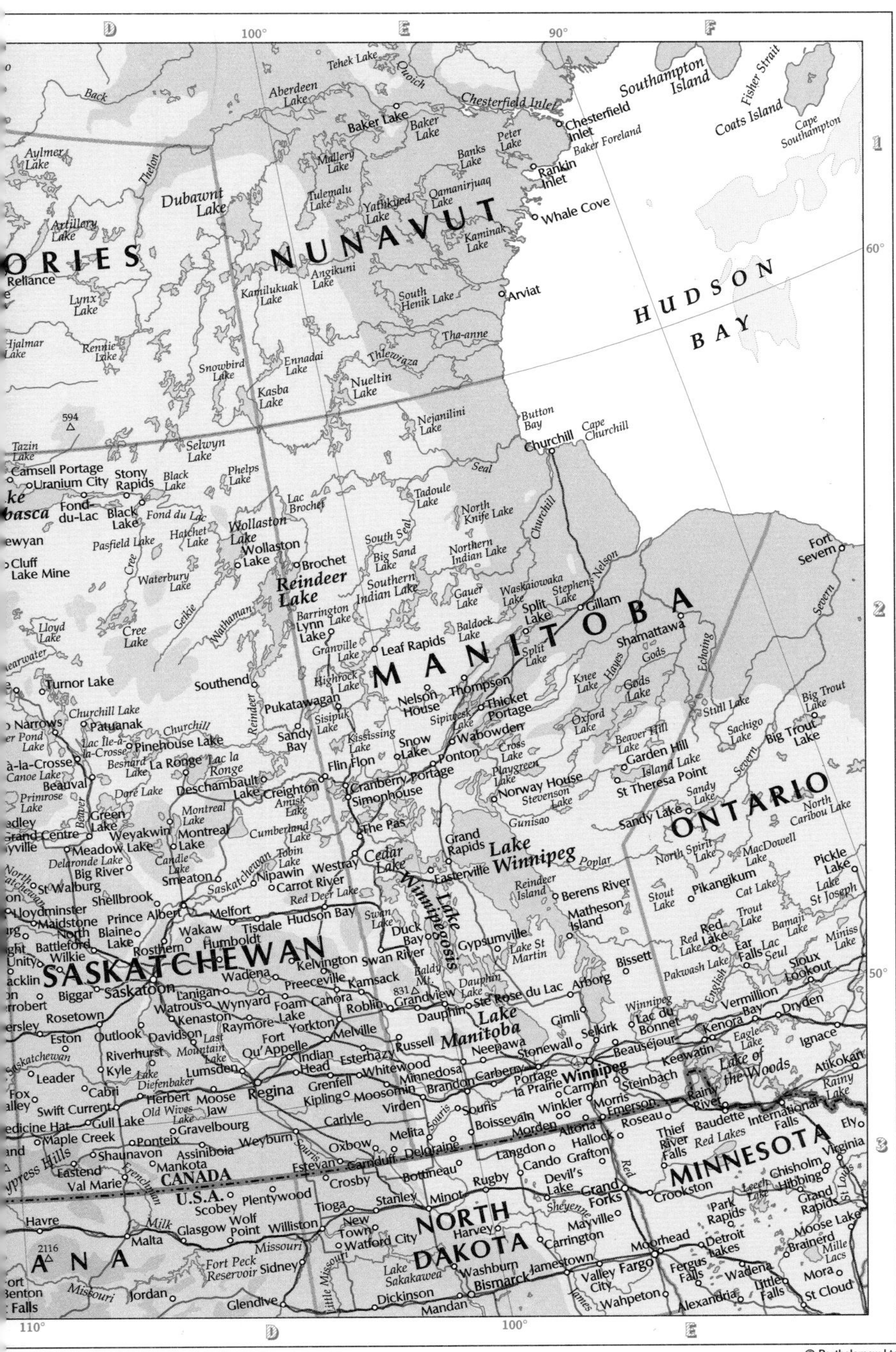

© Bartholomew Ltd

200   400 KILOMETRES

100°
90°
F
1
3
60°
50°
110°
100°
NUNAVUT
MANITOBA
SASKATCHEWAN
ONTARIO
MINNESOTA
NORTH DAKOTA
HUDSON BAY
CANADA
U.S.A.
Southampton Island
Fisher Strait
Coats Island
Cape Southampton
Chesterfield Inlet
Chesterfield Inlet
Baker Foreland
Rankin Inlet
Whale Cove
Arviat
Tehek Lake
Quoich
Back
Aberdeen Lake
Baker Lake
Baker Lake
Peter Lake
Banks Lake
Aylmer Lake
Thelon
Mallery Lake
Dubawnt Lake
Tulemalu Lake
Yathkyed Lake
Qamanirjuaq Lake
Kaminak Lake
Artillery Lake
Reliance
Angikuni Lake
Kamilukuak Lake
Lynx Lake
South Henik Lake
Tha-anne
Hjalmar Lake
Rennie Lake
Thlewiaza
Snowbird Lake
Ennadai Lake
Nueltin Lake
Kasba Lake
594
Nejanilini Lake
Button Bay
Cape Churchill
Churchill
Tazin Lake
Selwyn Lake
Camsell Portage
Uranium City
Stony Rapids
Black Lake
Phelps Lake
Seal
Fond-du-Lac
Black Lake
Fond du Lac
Lac Brochet
Tadoule Lake
Hatchet Lake
Wollaston Lake
Wollaston Lake
North Knife Lake
Churchill
Pasfield Lake
South Seal
Cree
Brochet
Big Sand Lake
Northern Indian Lake
Cluff Lake Mine
Waterbury Lake
Reindeer Lake
Southern Indian Lake
Gauer Lake
Waskaiowaka Lake
Stephens Lake
Nelson
Fort Severn
Severn
Barrington Lake
Lynn Lake
Split Lake
Gillam
Lloyd Lake
Cree Lake
Geikie
Wathaman
Baldock Lake
Shamattawa
Granville Lake
Leaf Rapids
Split Lake
Echoing
Gods
Knee Lake
Hayes
Gods Lake
Turnor Lake
Southend
Highrock Lake
Nelson House
Thompson
Churchill Lake
Reindeer
Pukatawagan
Sipiwesk Lake
Thicket Portage
Oxford Lake
Still Lake
Big Trout Lake
Patuanak
Churchill
Sisipuk Lake
Wabowden
Beaver Hill Lake
Sachigo Lake
Big Trout Lake
Lac Île-à-la-Crosse
Pinehouse Lake
Sandy Bay
Kississing Lake
Snow Lake
Cross Lake
Garden Hill
Île-à-la-Crosse
Canoe Lake
Besnard Lake
La Ronge
Lac la Ronge
Flin Flon
Ponton
Playgreen Lake
Island Lake
Beauval
Deschambault Lake
Creighton
Cranberry Portage
St Theresa Point
Primrose Lake
Doré Lake
Amisk Lake
Simonhouse
Norway House
Stevenson Lake
Sandy Lake
Severn
North Caribou Lake
Green Lake
Montreal Lake
The Pas
Sandy Lake
Bonnyville
Grand Centre
Weyakwin
Montreal Lake
Cumberland Lake
Gunisao
Meadow Lake
Delaronde Lake
Candle Lake
Tobin Lake
Cedar Lake
Grand Rapids
Lake Winnipeg
Poplar
North Spirit Lake
MacDowell Lake
Pickle Lake
Big River
Smeaton
Nipawin
Saskatchewan
Westray
Easterville
St Walburg
Carrot River
Reindeer Island
Berens River
Pikangikum
Cat Lake
Lake St Joseph
Red Deer Lake
Lake Winnipegosis
Stout Lake
Lloydminster
Shellbrook
Melfort
Hudson Bay
Matheson Island
Trout Lake
Maidstone
Prince Albert
Swan Lake
Bamaji Lake
North Battleford
Blaine Lake
Wakaw
Tisdale
Duck Bay
Gypsumville
Red Lake
Red Lake
Miniss Lake
Battleford
Rosthern
Humboldt
Lake St Martin
Ear Falls
Lac Seul
Wilkie
Unity
Kelvington
Swan River
Bissett
Pakwash Lake
Sioux Lookout
Kindersley
Saskatoon
Wadena
Preeceville
Kamsack
Baldy Mt.
831
Dauphin Lake
English
Biggar
Lanigan
Wynyard
Foam Lake
Canora
Grandview
Ste Rose du Lac
Arborg
Winnipeg
Vermillion Bay
Dryden
Rosetown
Watrous
Kenaston
Raymore
Yorkton
Roblin
Dauphin
Lake Manitoba
Gimli
Lac du Bonnet
Kenora
Eston
Outlook
Davidson
Last Mountain Lake
Fort Qu'Appelle
Melville
Russell
Neepawa
Selkirk
Beauséjour
Eagle Lake
Ignace
Saskatchewan
Riverhurst
Indian Head
Esterhazy
Stonewall
Keewatin
Lake of the Woods
Atikokan
Leader
Kyle
Lake Diefenbaker
Lumsden
Whitewood
Minnedosa
Carberry
Portage la Prairie
Winnipeg
Steinbach
Rainy Lake
Cabri
Herbert
Moose Jaw
Regina
Grenfell
Kipling
Moosomin
Brandon
Carman
Rainy River
Swift Current
Gull Lake
Old Wives Lake
Morris
Emerson
International Falls
Ely
Carlyle
Virden
Souris
Boissevain
Winkler
Roseau
Baudette
Medicine Hat
Maple Creek
Gravelbourg
Melita
Souris
Morden
Altona
Hallock
Thief River Falls
Red Lakes
Ponteix
Assiniboia
Weyburn
Oxbow
Deloraine
Langdon
Grafton
Virginia
Cypress Hills
Shaunavon
Mankota
Estevan
Carnduff
Cando
Devil's Lake
Red
St Louis
Eastend
Bottineau
Rugby
Chisholm
Hibbing
Val Marie
Frenchman
Crosby
Grand Forks
Crookston
Leech Lake
Grand Rapids
Scobey
Plentywood
Tioga
Stanley
Minot
Sheyenne
Park Rapids
Havre
Milk
Wolf Point
Williston
New Town
Harvey
Mayville
Moose Lake
Glasgow
Watford City
Carrington
Moorhead
Detroit Lakes
Brainerd
2116
Malta
Missouri
Mille Lacs
Fort Peck Reservoir
Sidney
Little Missouri
Lake Sakakawea
Washburn
Jamestown
Fargo
Fergus Falls
Wadena
Mora
Fort Benton
Missouri
Jordan
Glendive
Bismarck
Valley City
Little Falls
St Cloud
Great Falls
Dickinson
Mandan
James
Wahpeton
Alexandria

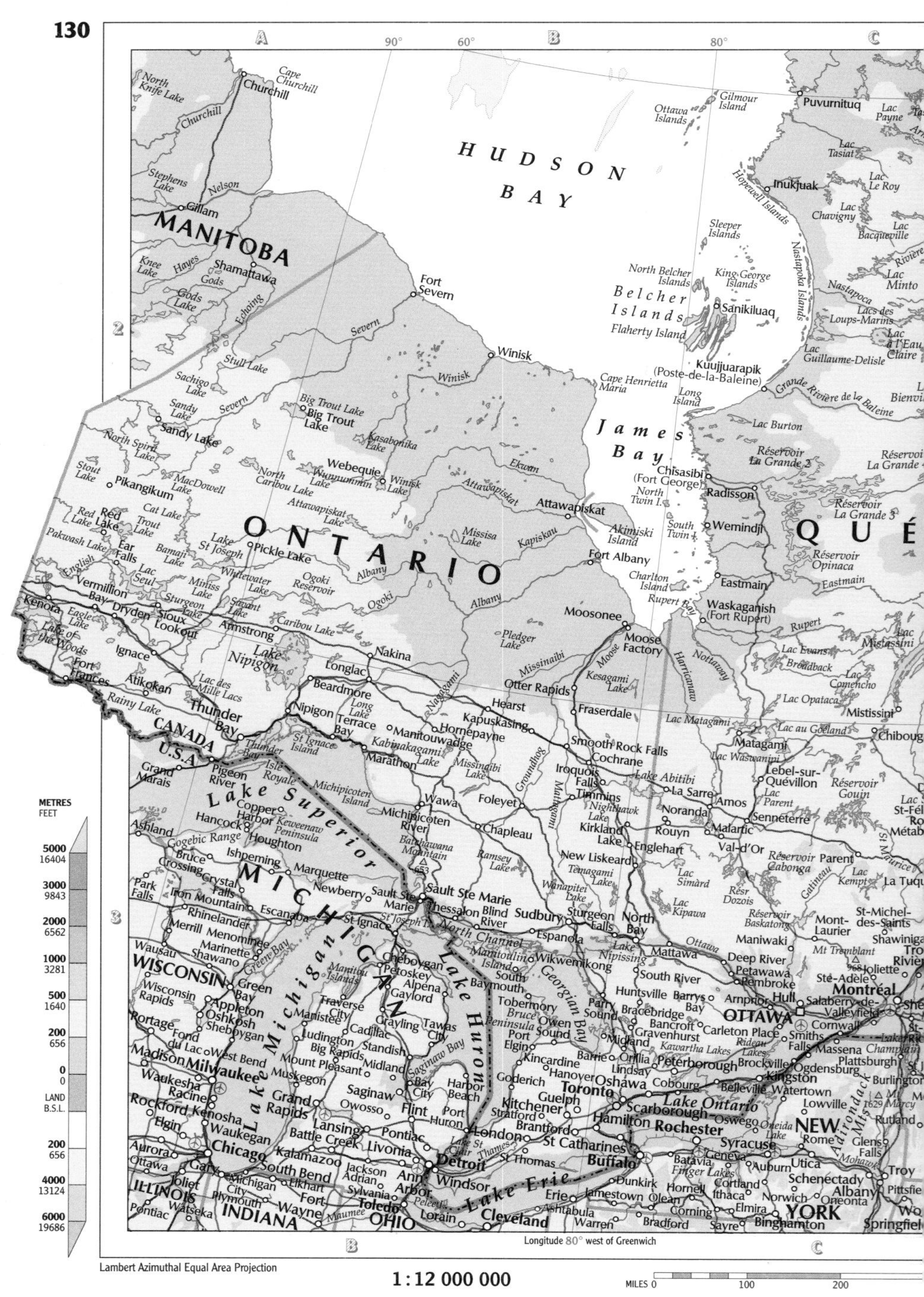

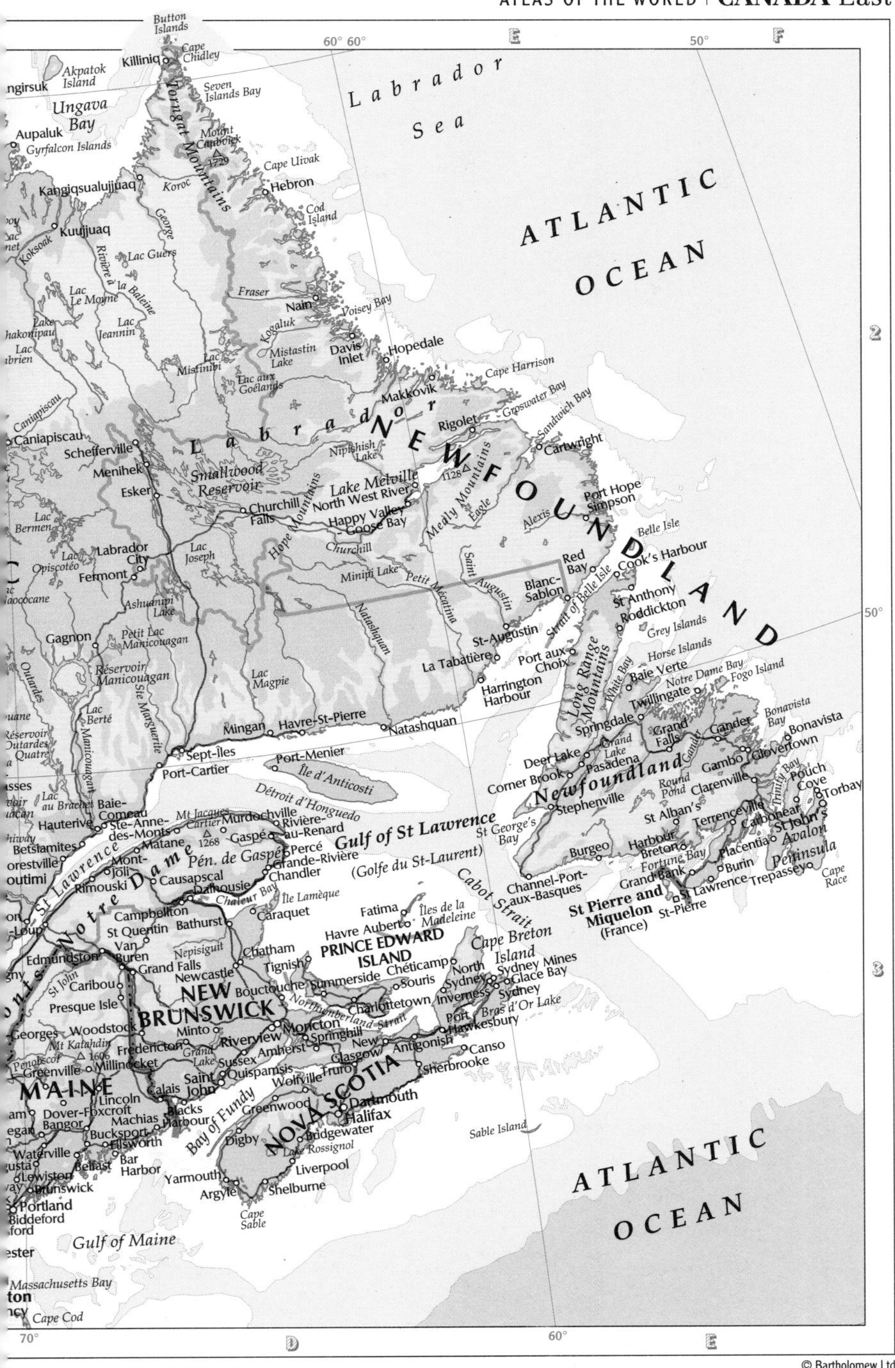

ATLANTIC OCEAN

Labrador Sea

ATLANTIC OCEAN

Gulf of Maine

Massachusetts Bay

Cape Cod

© Bartholomew Ltd

200   400 KILOMETRES

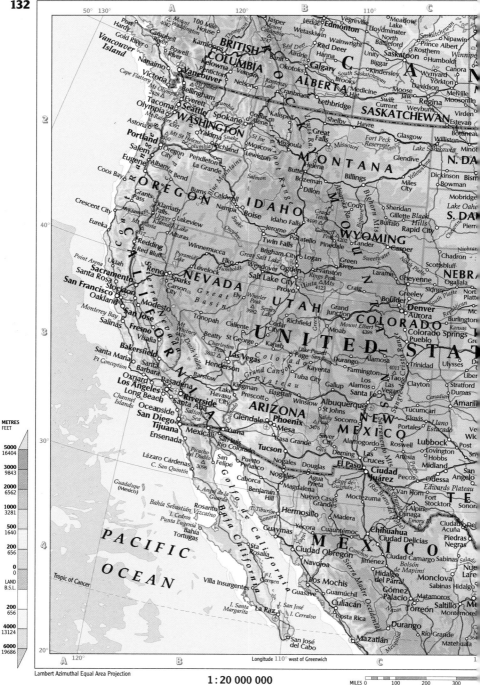

Lambert Azimuthal Equal Area Projection

1 : 20 000 000

METRES
FEET

5000
16404

3000
9843

2000
6562

1000
3281

500
1640

200
656

0
0

LAND
B.S.L.

200
656

4000
13124

6000
19686

MILES 0   100   200   300

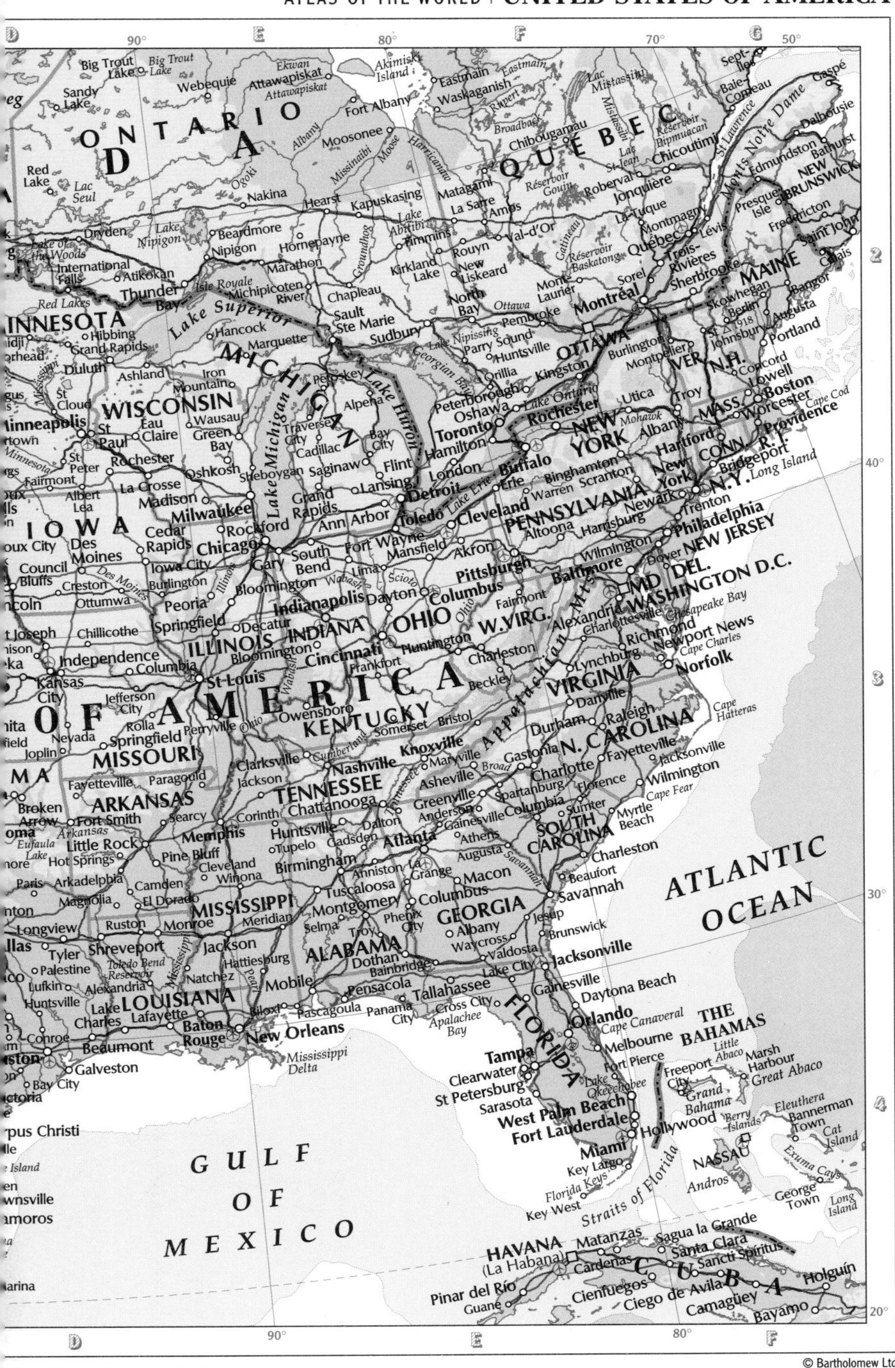
ONTARIO
QUÉBEC
NEW BRUNSWICK
MAINE
VER.
N.H.
MASS.
CONN.
R.I.
NEW YORK
N.Y.
PENNSYLVANIA
NEW JERSEY
DEL.
MD
WASHINGTON D.C.
W.VIRG.
VIRGINIA
N. CAROLINA
SOUTH CAROLINA
GEORGIA
FLORIDA
ALABAMA
MISSISSIPPI
LOUISIANA
ARKANSAS
TENNESSEE
KENTUCKY
OHIO
INDIANA
ILLINOIS
MICHIGAN
WISCONSIN
INNESOTA
IOWA
MISSOURI
OF AMERICA
ATLANTIC OCEAN
GULF OF MEXICO
THE BAHAMAS
CUBA
Lake Superior
Lake Michigan
Lake Huron
Lake Erie
Lake Ontario
Appalachian Mts
Straits of Florida
Big Trout Lake
Webequie
Attawapiskat
Fort Albany
Moosonee
Eastmain
Waskaganish
Chibougamau
Chicoutimi
Sept-Îles
Baie-Comeau
Gaspé
Dalhousie
Bathurst
Edmundston
Fredericton
Saint John
Calais
Red Lake
Sandy Lake
Nakina
Hearst
Kapuskasing
Matagami
La Sarre
Amos
Roberval
Jonquière
La Tuque
Dryden
Beardmore
Nipigon
Hornepayne
Timmins
Rouyn
Val-d'Or
Québec
Lévis
Trois-Rivières
Sherbrooke
International Falls
Atikokan
Thunder Bay
Marathon
Michipicoten River
Chapleau
Kirkland Lake
New Liskeard
North Bay
Mont-Laurier
Montréal
Sorel
Sault Ste Marie
Sudbury
Parry Sound
Huntsville
Pembroke
OTTAWA
Kingston
Orillia
Peterborough
Oshawa
Toronto
Hamilton
London
Bangor
Augusta
Portland
Burlington
Montpelier
Concord
Lowell
Boston
Worcester
Providence
Cape Cod
Hibbing
Grand Rapids
Duluth
Ashland
Hancock
Marquette
Iron Mountain
Petoskey
Alpena
Traverse City
Cadillac
Bay City
Saginaw
Flint
Lansing
Detroit
Ann Arbor
Toledo
Cleveland
Erie
Buffalo
Rochester
Utica
Albany
Troy
Hartford
New York
Bridgeport
Long Island
Binghamton
Scranton
Warren
Newark
Trenton
Philadelphia
Harrisburg
Altoona
Pittsburgh
Akron
Mansfield
Fort Wayne
South Bend
Gary
Chicago
Rockford
Milwaukee
Sheboygan
Oshkosh
Green Bay
Wausau
Eau Claire
St Paul
Minneapolis
St Cloud
Rochester
La Crosse
Madison
Albert Lea
Cedar Rapids
Des Moines
Iowa City
Council Bluffs
Creston
Ottumwa
Burlington
Peoria
Bloomington
Springfield
Decatur
Indianapolis
Dayton
Columbus
Lima
Wilmington
Dover
Baltimore
Alexandria
Charlottesville
Richmond
Newport News
Norfolk
Chesapeake Bay
Cape Charles
Cape Hatteras
Fairmont
Huntington
Charleston
Lynchburg
Danville
Durham
Raleigh
Fayetteville
Jacksonville
Wilmington
Cape Fear
Chillicothe
Independence
Kansas City
Columbia
St Louis
Jefferson City
Rolla
Nevada
Springfield
Joplin
Cincinnati
Frankfort
Owensboro
Perryville
Beckley
Bristol
Somerset
Knoxville
Maryville
Clarksville
Nashville
Jackson
Paragould
Fayetteville
Fort Smith
Little Rock
Hot Springs
Searcy
Memphis
Corinth
Chattanooga
Huntsville
Tupelo
Asheville
Greenville
Anderson
Spartanburg
Gastonia
Charlotte
Florence
Columbia
Sumter
Myrtle Beach
Charleston
Beaufort
Savannah
Athens
Gainesville
Augusta
Atlanta
Dalton
Gadsden
Birmingham
Anniston
La Grange
Macon
Columbus
Tuscaloosa
Montgomery
Selma
Troy
Phenix City
Albany
Waycross
Valdosta
Jesup
Brunswick
Jacksonville
Lake City
Gainesville
Daytona Beach
Orlando
Cape Canaveral
Melbourne
Fort Pierce
Tampa
Clearwater
St Petersburg
Sarasota
West Palm Beach
Fort Lauderdale
Hollywood
Miami
Key Largo
Key West
Florida Keys
Lake Okeechobee
Tallahassee
Cross City
Apalachee Bay
Panama City
Pensacola
Mobile
Pascagoula
Biloxi
Dothan
Bainbridge
Hattiesburg
Meridian
Jackson
Natchez
Cleveland
Winona
Pine Bluff
Camden
El Dorado
Magnolia
Arkadelphia
Ruston
Monroe
Shreveport
Alexandria
Lafayette
Lake Charles
Baton Rouge
New Orleans
Mississippi Delta
Beaumont
Galveston
Bay City
Tyler
Palestine
Lufkin
Huntsville
Conroe
Longview
Toledo Bend Reservoir
Freeport
Grand Bahama
Marsh Harbour
Great Abaco
Berry Islands
Eleuthera
Bannerman Town
Cat Island
NASSAU
Andros
Exuma Cays
George Town
Long Island
HAVANA (La Habana)
Matanzas
Cárdenas
Sagua la Grande
Santa Clara
Sancti Spíritus
Cienfuegos
Ciego de Avila
Camagüey
Holguín
Bayamo
Pinar del Río
Guane

200 400 600 KILOMETRES

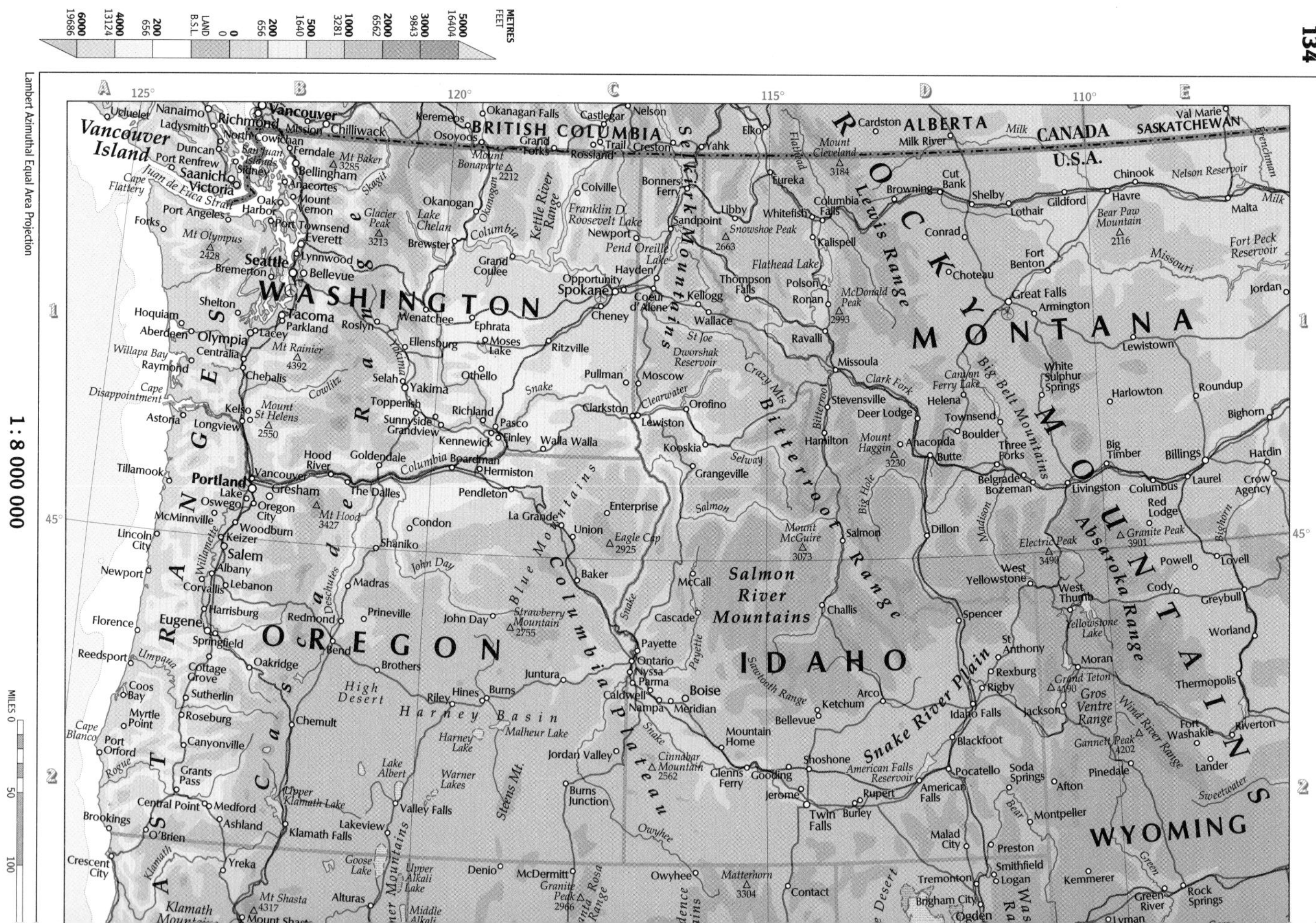

METRES
FEET

5000 16404

3000 9843

2000 6562

1000 3281

500 1640

200 656

0 0

LAND
B.S.L.

200 656

4000 13124

6000 19686

Lambert Azimuthal Equal Area Projection

1 : 8 000 000

MILES 0   50   100

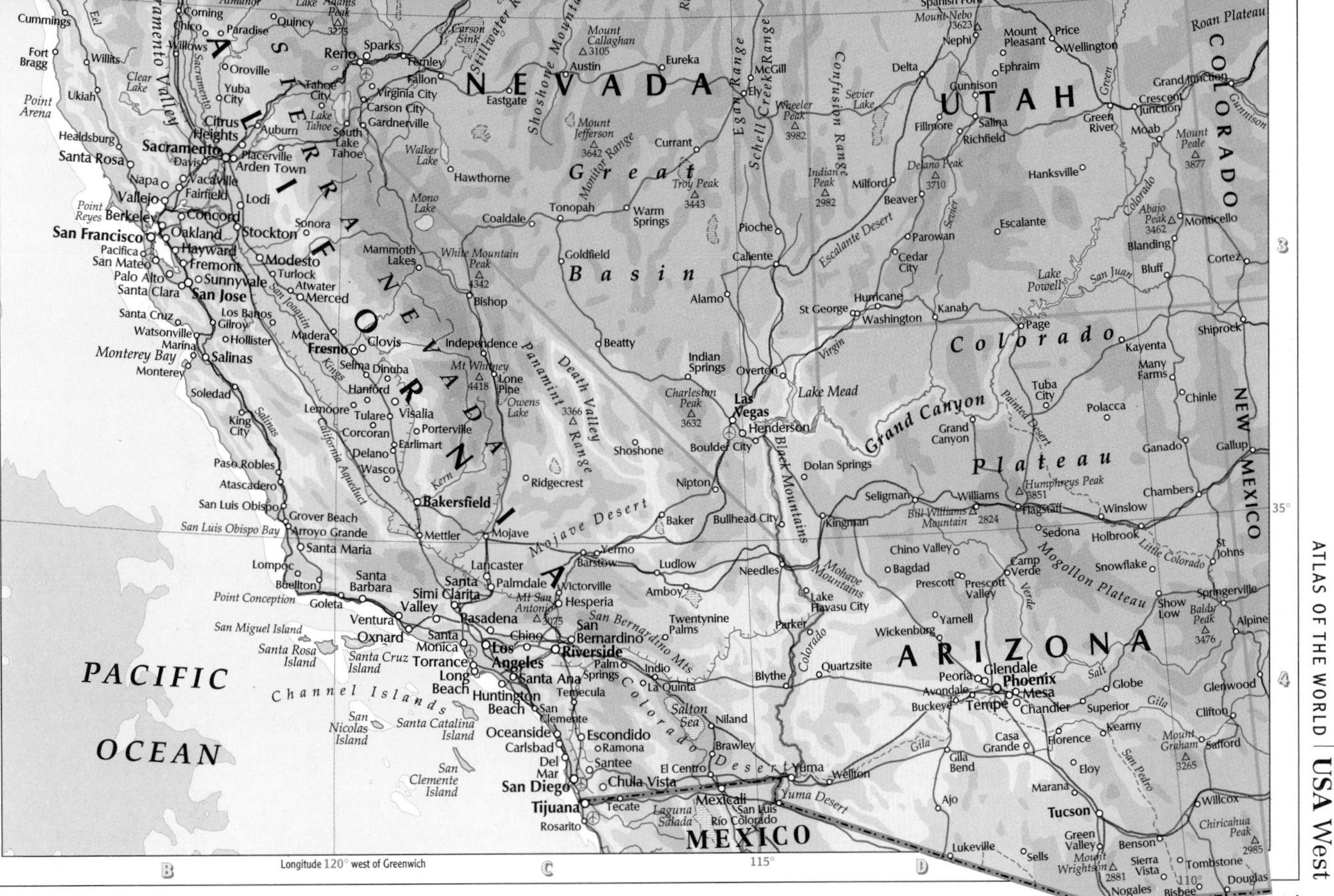

COLORADO

NEW MEXICO

UTAH

ARIZONA

NEVADA

CALIFORNIA

Colorado Plateau

Grand Canyon

Great Basin

Sierra Nevada

Death Valley

Mojave Desert

Sonoran Desert

Colorado Desert

MEXICO

PACIFIC OCEAN

Channel Islands

Sacramento Valley

Confusion Range

Schell Creek Range

Egan Range

Shoshone Mountains

Black Mountains

Panamint Range

San Bernardino Mts

Roan Plateau

Las Vegas

San Francisco

Los Angeles

San Diego

Tijuana

Sacramento

Fresno

Bakersfield

Phoenix

Tucson

Reno

Longitude 120° west of Greenwich

© Bartholomew Ltd

100   200 KILOMETRES

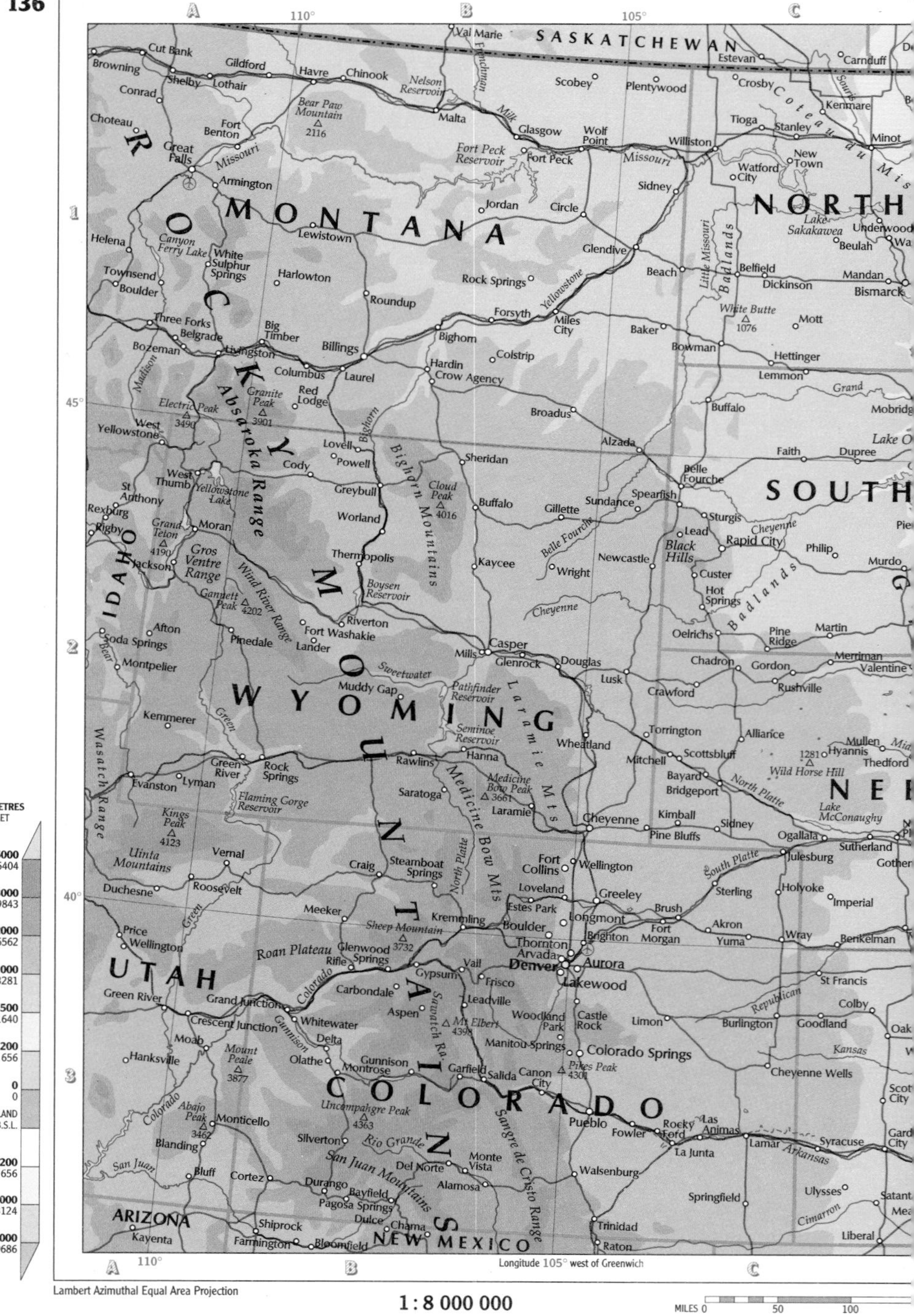

Lambert Azimuthal Equal Area Projection

1 : 8 000 000

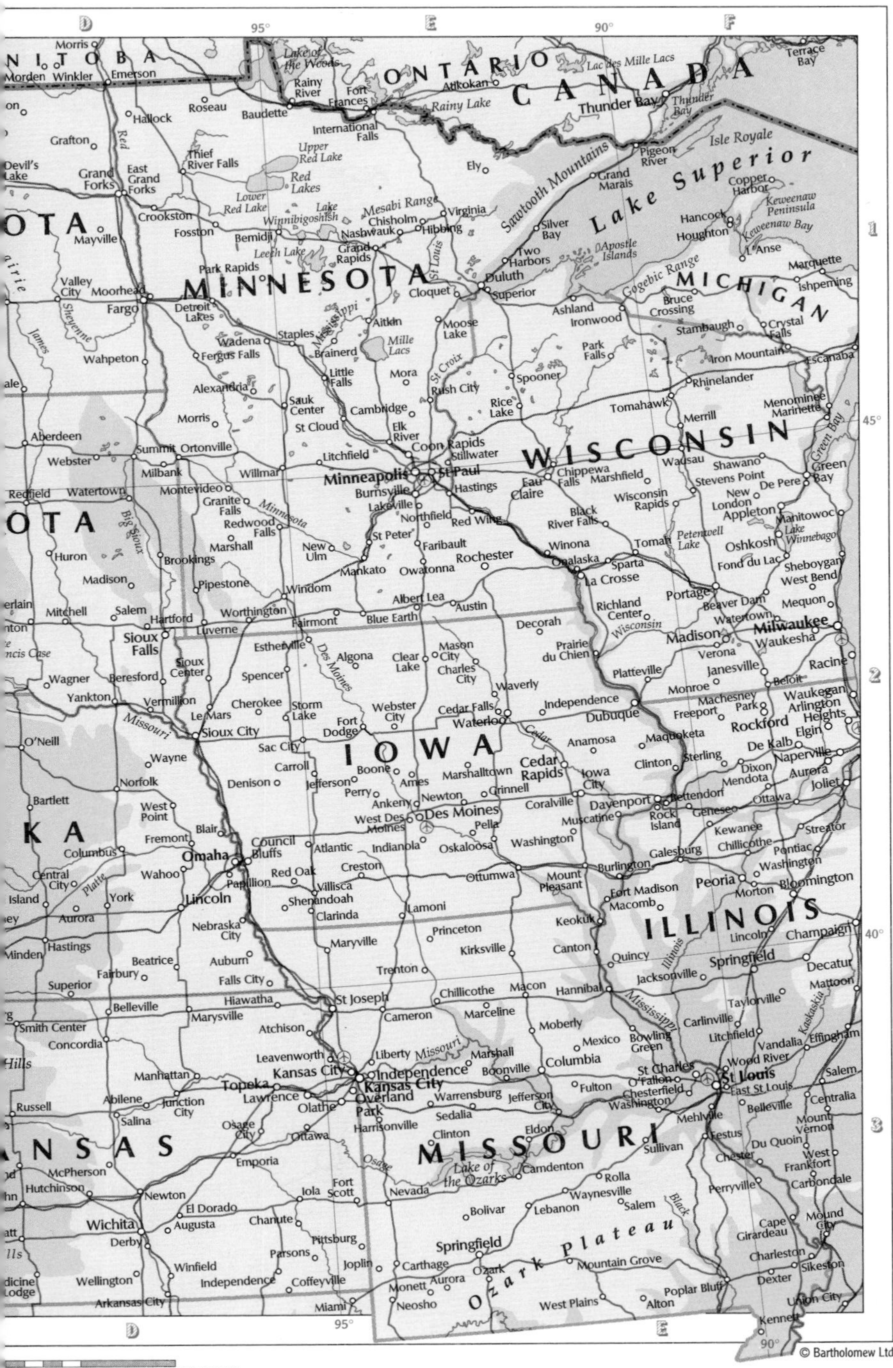

© Bartholomew Ltd

100   200 KILOMETRES

95°
90°
F
ONTARIO
CANADA
MINNESOTA
WISCONSIN
MICHIGAN
IOWA
ILLINOIS
MISSOURI
Lake of the Woods
Morris
Morden
Winkler
Emerson
Rainy River
Fort Frances
Atikokan
Lac des Mille Lacs
Terrace Bay
Rainy Lake
Thunder Bay
Roseau
Baudette
Hallock
International Falls
Upper Red Lake
Red Lakes
Lower Red Lake
Grafton
Thief River Falls
Grand Forks
East Grand Forks
Devil's Lake
Crookston
Fosston
Mayville
Bemidji
Lake Winnibigoshish
Leech Lake
Mesabi Range
Chisholm
Nashwauk
Hibbing
Virginia
Grand Rapids
Ely
Isle Royale
Pigeon River
Grand Marais
Sawtooth Mountains
Lake Superior
Silver Bay
Two Harbors
Apostle Islands
Copper Harbor
Keweenaw Peninsula
Keweenaw Bay
Hancock
Houghton
L'Anse
Marquette
Ishpeming
Gogebic Range
Park Rapids
Valley City
Moorhead
Fargo
Detroit Lakes
Duluth
Superior
Cloquet
St Louis
Ashland
Ironwood
Bruce Crossing
Stambaugh
Crystal Falls
Aitkin
Moose Lake
Mille Lacs
Wadena
Staples
Fergus Falls
Brainerd
Mississippi
Wahpeton
Sheyenne
James
Red
Little Falls
Mora
St Croix
Park Falls
Iron Mountain
Escanaba
Alexandria
Rush City
Spooner
Rhinelander
Sauk Center
Cambridge
Rice Lake
Tomahawk
Menominee
Marinette
Morris
St Cloud
Elk River
Merrill
Aberdeen
Summit
Ortonville
Coon Rapids
Stillwater
Green Bay
Webster
Milbank
Litchfield
Minneapolis
St Paul
Wausau
Shawano
Willmar
Chippewa Falls
Marshfield
Stevens Point
Green Bay
Redfield
Watertown
Montevideo
Burnsville
Hastings
Eau Claire
New London
De Pere
Granite Falls
Lakeville
Wisconsin Rapids
Appleton
Minnesota
Northfield
Black River Falls
Manitowoc
Redwood Falls
Red Wing
Petenwell Lake
Lake Winnebago
Big Sioux
St Peter
Faribault
Winona
Tomah
Oshkosh
Huron
Marshall
New Ulm
Rochester
Onalaska
Sparta
Fond du Lac
Sheboygan
Brookings
Mankato
Owatonna
La Crosse
West Bend
Madison
Pipestone
Windom
Portage
Mequon
Albert Lea
Austin
Richland Center
Beaver Dam
Mitchell
Salem
Hartford
Worthington
Fairmont
Blue Earth
Decorah
Watertown
Milwaukee
Sioux Falls
Luverne
Wisconsin
Madison
Waukesha
Estherville
Mason City
Prairie du Chien
Verona
Racine
Algona
Clear Lake
Charles City
Des Moines
Platteville
Janesville
Sioux Center
Spencer
Beloit
Wagner
Beresford
Waverly
Monroe
Machesney Park
Waukegan
Yankton
Vermillion
Cherokee
Storm Lake
Webster City
Cedar Falls
Independence
Freeport
Arlington Heights
Le Mars
Fort Dodge
Waterloo
Dubuque
Rockford
Elgin
Missouri
Sioux City
Cedar
Anamosa
Maquoketa
O'Neill
Sac City
De Kalb
Wayne
Carroll
Boone
Marshalltown
Cedar Rapids
Clinton
Sterling
Dixon
Naperville
Norfolk
Denison
Jefferson
Ames
Iowa City
Mendota
Aurora
Joliet
Perry
Ankeny
Newton
Grinnell
Bettendorf
Bartlett
Coralville
Davenport
Ottawa
West Point
West Des Moines
Des Moines
Muscatine
Rock Island
Geneseo
Blair
Pella
Kewanee
Streator
Fremont
Council Bluffs
Atlantic
Washington
Chillicothe
Columbus
Omaha
Indianola
Oskaloosa
Galesburg
Pontiac
Red Oak
Creston
Burlington
Washington
Central City
Wahoo
Papillion
Ottumwa
Mount Pleasant
Peoria
Villisca
Morton
Bloomington
Platte
York
Lincoln
Shenandoah
Fort Madison
Island
Aurora
Clarinda
Lamoni
Macomb
Keokuk
Nebraska City
Princeton
Lincoln
Champaign
Hastings
Maryville
Kirksville
Canton
Illinois
Minden
Beatrice
Auburn
Quincy
Springfield
Decatur
Fairbury
Trenton
Superior
Falls City
Jacksonville
Mattoon
Chillicothe
Macon
Hannibal
Hiawatha
St Joseph
Taylorville
Belleville
Marysville
Cameron
Marceline
Mississippi
Kaskaskia
Smith Center
Carlinville
Concordia
Atchison
Moberly
Litchfield
Effingham
Mexico
Bowling Green
Vandalia
Liberty
Missouri
Marshall
Leavenworth
Columbia
Wood River
Hills
Manhattan
Kansas City
Independence
Boonville
St Charles
St Louis
Salem
Topeka
Kansas City
O'Fallon
Abilene
Junction City
Lawrence
Overland Park
Warrensburg
Fulton
Chesterfield
East St Louis
Centralia
Russell
Olathe
Jefferson City
Washington
Belleville
Salina
Osage City
Harrisonville
Sedalia
Mehlville
Mount Vernon
Ottawa
Clinton
Eldon
Festus
Du Quoin
NSAS
Sullivan
Emporia
Osage
Lake of the Ozarks
Camdenton
Chester
West Frankfort
McPherson
Rolla
Hutchinson
Fort Scott
Iola
Nevada
Waynesville
Perryville
Carbondale
Newton
El Dorado
Black
Salem
Augusta
Chanute
Bolivar
Lebanon
Cape Girardeau
Mound City
Wichita
Derby
Pittsburg
Springfield
Ozark Plateau
Charleston
Parsons
Joplin
Carthage
Ozark
Mountain Grove
Sikeston
Winfield
Independence
Coffeyville
Dexter
Wellington
Monett
Aurora
Poplar Bluff
Arkansas City
Miami
Neosho
West Plains
Alton
Union City
Kennett
45°
40°
3

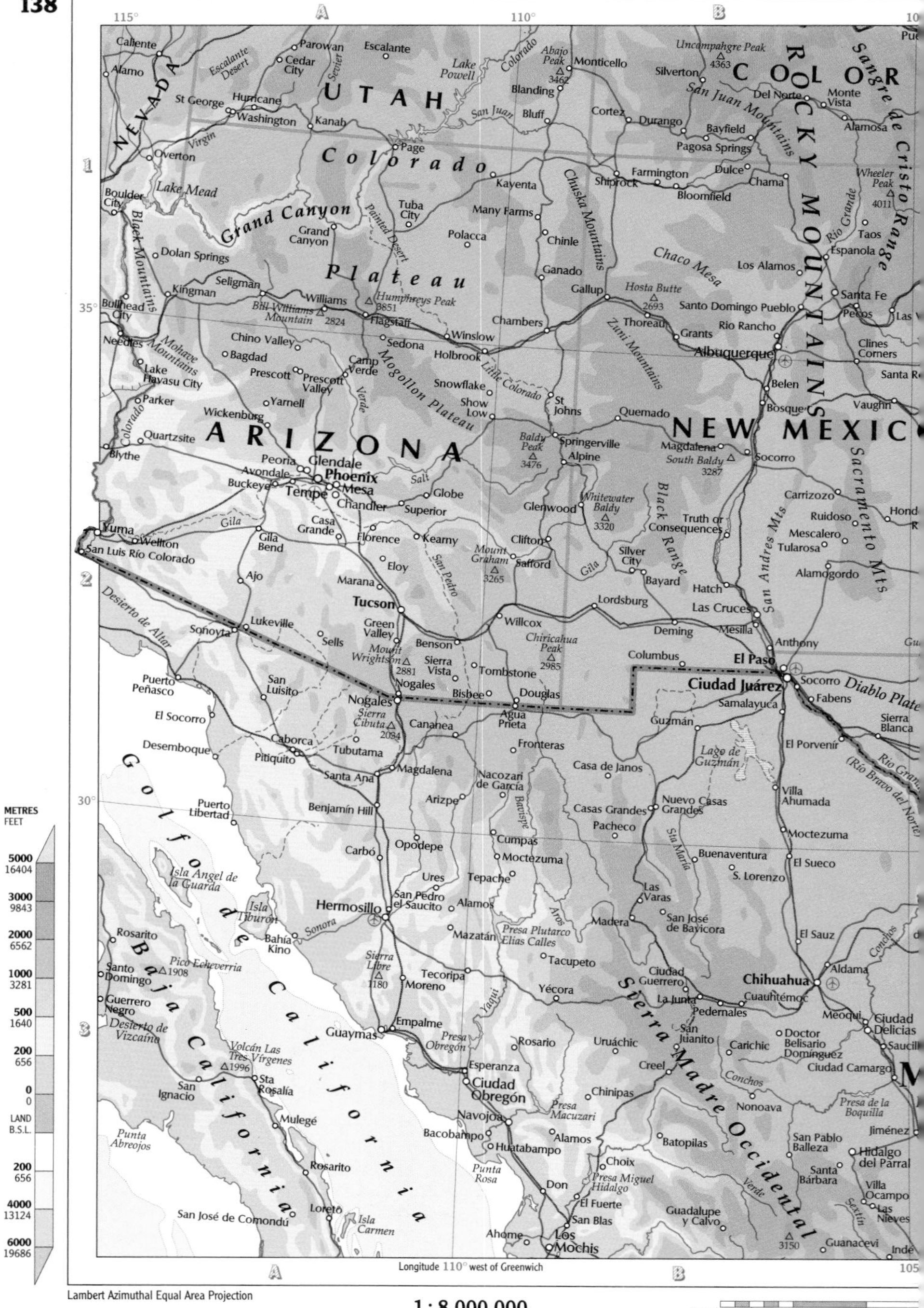

METRES
FEET

5000
16404

3000
9843

2000
6562

1000
3281

500
1640

200
656

0
0

LAND
B.S.L.

200
656

4000
13124

6000
19686

Lambert Azimuthal Equal Area Projection

Longitude 110° west of Greenwich

1 : 8 000 000

MILES 0   50   100

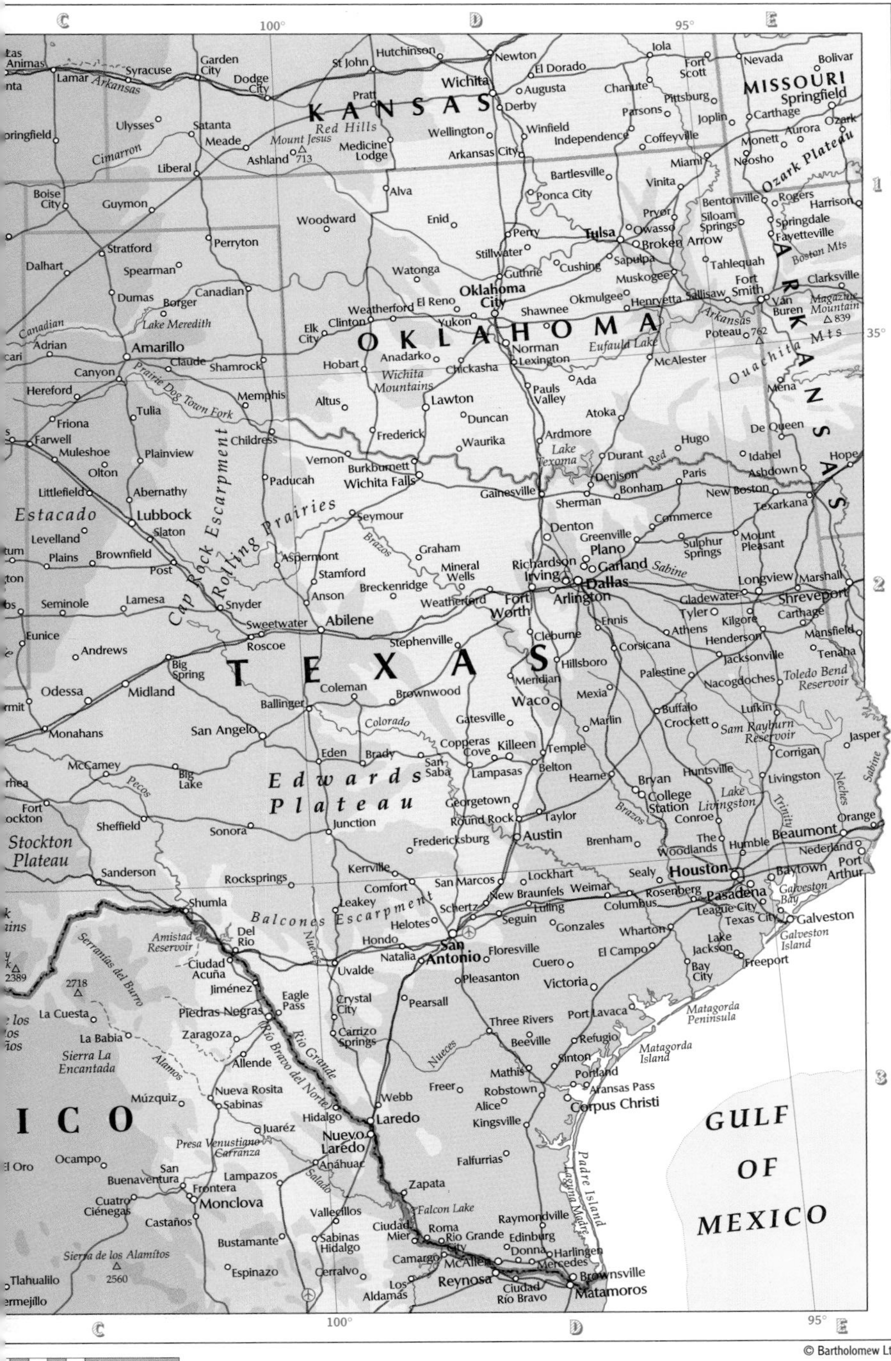
KANSAS
OKLAHOMA
TEXAS
MISSOURI
ARKANSAS
GULF OF MEXICO
Wichita
Oklahoma City
Tulsa
Amarillo
Lubbock
Abilene
Fort Worth
Dallas
Arlington
Waco
Austin
San Antonio
Houston
Corpus Christi
Laredo
Nuevo Laredo
Brownsville
Matamoros
Shreveport
Beaumont
Galveston
Edwards Plateau
Llano Estacado
Red Hills
Ozark Plateau
Ouachita Mts
Balcones Escarpment
Cap Rock Escarpment
Rolling Prairies
Wichita Mountains
Stockton Plateau
Padre Island
Matagorda Island
Rio Grande
Red
Brazos
Colorado
Pecos
Nueces
Sabine
Trinity
Arkansas
Canadian
Cimarron
100°
95°
35°
© Bartholomew Ltd
100
200 KILOMETRES

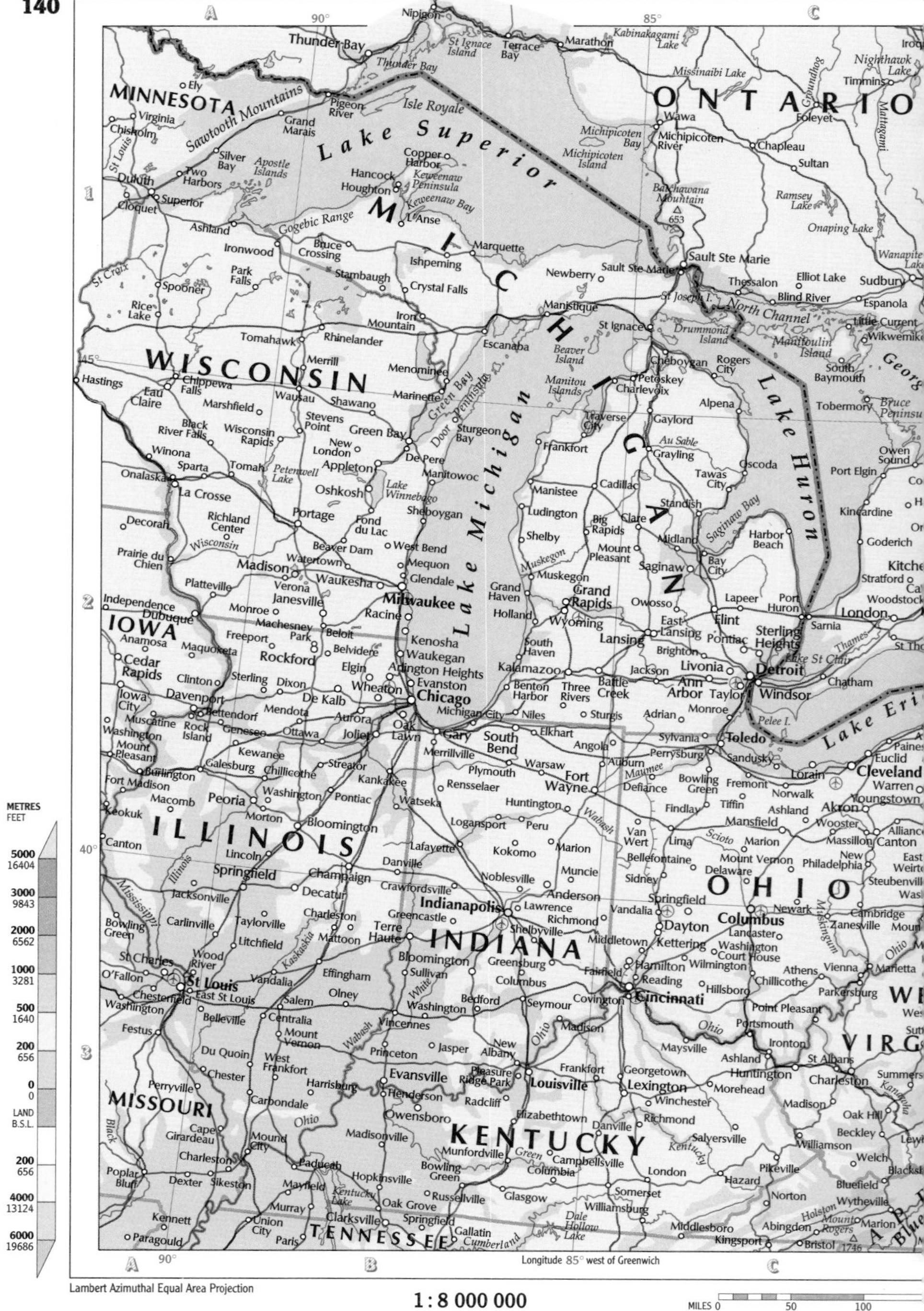

Lambert Azimuthal Equal Area Projection

1 : 8 000 000

MILES 0   50   100

METRES
FEET

5000	16404
3000	9843
2000	6562
1000	3281
500	1640
200	656
0	0
LAND	B.S.L.
200	656
4000	13124
6000	19686

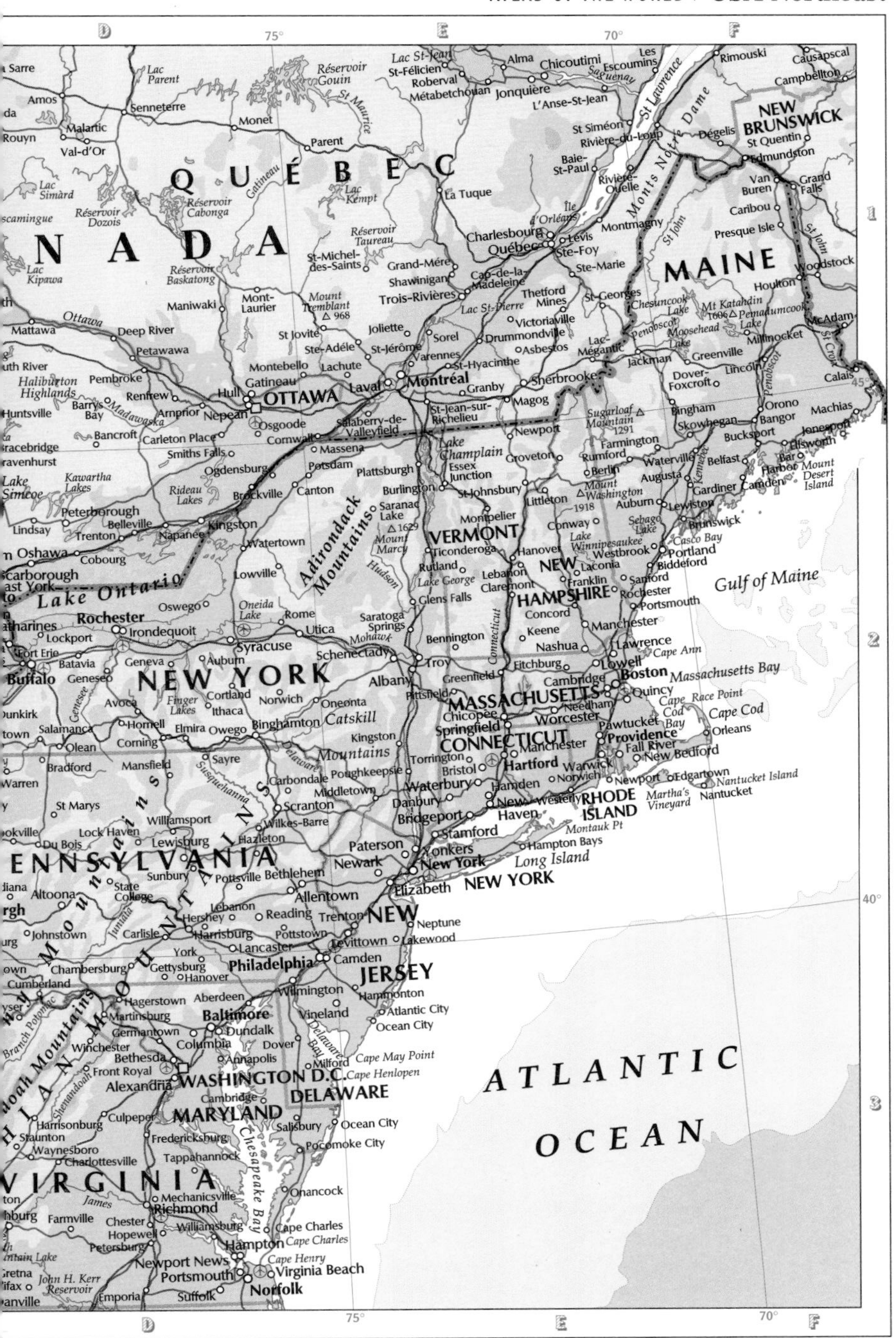
D
75°
E
70°
F
QUÉBEC
CANADA
MAINE
NEW BRUNSWICK
VERMONT
NEW HAMPSHIRE
MASSACHUSETTS
CONNECTICUT
RHODE ISLAND
NEW YORK
PENNSYLVANIA
NEW JERSEY
DELAWARE
MARYLAND
VIRGINIA
WASHINGTON D.C.
OTTAWA
Montréal
Québec
Boston
New York
Philadelphia
Baltimore
Richmond
Norfolk
Hartford
Providence
Rochester
Buffalo
Syracuse
Albany
Gulf of Maine
Massachusetts Bay
Cape Cod
Nantucket Island
Martha's Vineyard
Long Island
Lake Ontario
Lake Champlain
Adirondack Mountains
Catskill Mountains
Appalachian Mountains
Chesapeake Bay
Delaware Bay
Cape May Point
Cape Henlopen
Cape Charles
Cape Henry
Montauk Pt
Cape Ann
St Lawrence
Monts Notre Dame
Mt Katahdin 1606
Mount Washington 1918
Sugarloaf Mountain 1291
Mount Marcy 1629
Mount Tremblant 968
Lac St-Jean
Réservoir Gouin
Réservoir Cabonga
Réservoir Baskatong
Réservoir Taureau
Lake Winnipesaukee
Moosehead Lake
Sebago Lake
Finger Lakes
Oneida Lake
Connecticut
Hudson
Susquehanna
Delaware
Potomac
James
Mount Desert Island
1
2
3
40°
45°
ATLANTIC OCEAN

100 200 KILOMETRES

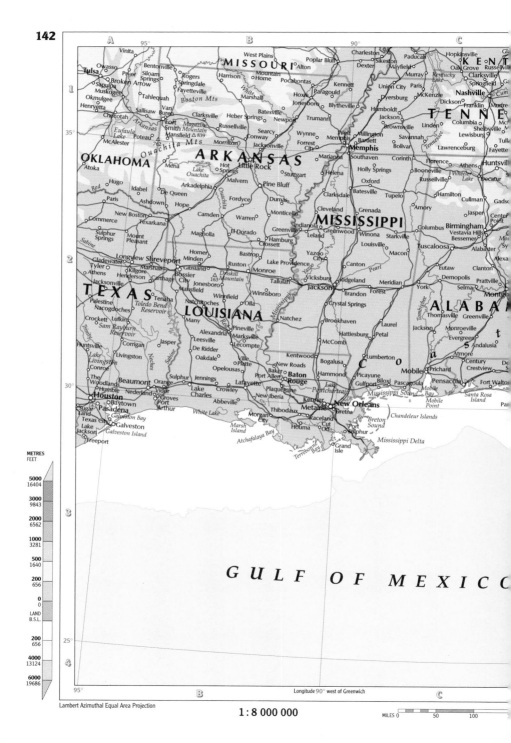

METRES
FEET

5000 16404
3000 9843
2000 6562
1000 3281
500 1640
200 656
0 0
LAND B.S.L.
200 656
4000 13124
6000 19686

Lambert Azimuthal Equal Area Projection

1 : 8 000 000

Longitude 90° west of Greenwich

MILES 0   50   100

GULF OF MEXICO

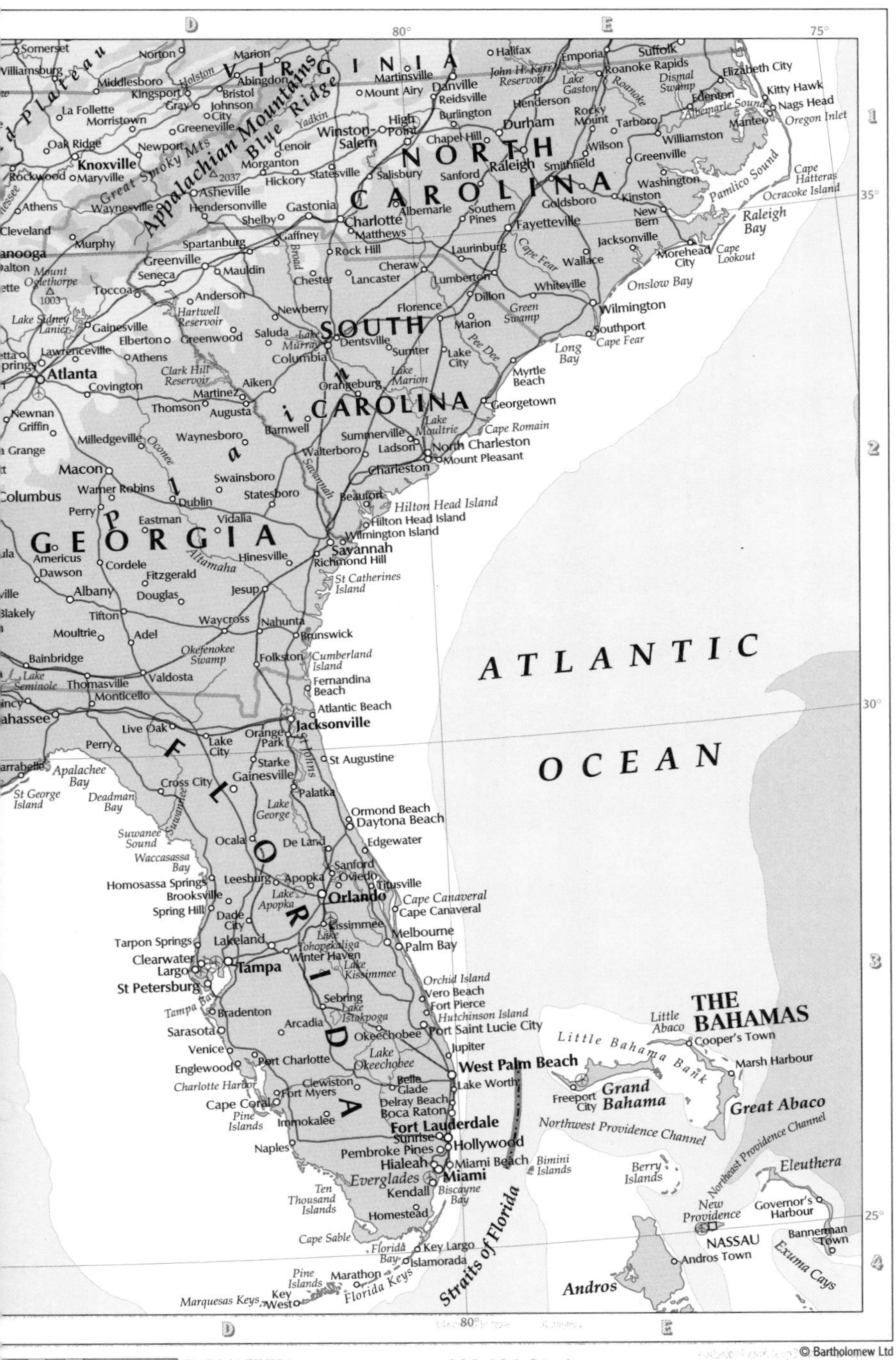
D
E
80°
75°
35°
30°
25°
1
2
3
4
VIRGINIA
NORTH CAROLINA
SOUTH CAROLINA
GEORGIA
FLORIDA
Appalachian Mountains
Blue Ridge
Great Smoky Mts
2037
Appalachian
ATLANTIC
OCEAN
THE BAHAMAS
Somerset
Williamsburg
Norton
Marion
Abingdon
Bristol
Middlesboro
Kingsport
Gray
Johnson City
La Follette
Morristown
Greeneville
Oak Ridge
Knoxville
Newport
Rockwood
Maryville
Athens
Cleveland
Murphy
Waynesville
Asheville
Hendersonville
Lenoir
Morganton
Hickory
Statesville
Salisbury
Winston-Salem
High Point
Martinsville
Mount Airy
Danville
Reidsville
Burlington
Chapel Hill
Durham
Raleigh
Sanford
Smithfield
Henderson
Rocky Mount
Tarboro
Wilson
Greenville
Washington
Kinston
New Bern
Goldsboro
Halifax
John H. Kerr Reservoir
Lake Gaston
Emporia
Roanoke Rapids
Roanoke
Suffolk
Dismal Swamp
Elizabeth City
Edenton
Albemarle Sound
Kitty Hawk
Nags Head
Manteo
Oregon Inlet
Williamston
Pamlico Sound
Cape Hatteras
Ocracoke Island
Raleigh Bay
Morehead City
Cape Lookout
Jacksonville
Onslow Bay
Wallace
Whiteville
Wilmington
Southport
Cape Fear
Long Bay
Holston
Yadkin
Gastonia
Shelby
Charlotte
Matthews
Albemarle
Southern Pines
Fayetteville
Cape Fear
Laurinburg
Gaffney
Spartanburg
Rock Hill
Greenville
Mauldin
Seneca
Chester
Lancaster
Cheraw
Lumberton
Dillon
Broad
Anderson
Toccoa
Mount Oglethorpe
1003
Hartwell Reservoir
Newberry
Florence
Marion
Green Swamp
Lake Sidney Lanier
Gainesville
Elberton
Greenwood
Saluda
Lake Murray
Columbia
Dentsville
Sumter
Lake City
Pee Dee
Myrtle Beach
Lawrenceville
Athens
Atlanta
Covington
Clark Hill Reservoir
Aiken
Martinez
Augusta
Thomson
Orangeburg
Lake Marion
Georgetown
Newnan
Griffin
Milledgeville
Waynesboro
Barnwell
Summerville
Lake Moultrie
Cape Romain
Ladson
North Charleston
Mount Pleasant
Charleston
Walterboro
La Grange
Macon
Oconee
Swainsboro
Savannah
Warner Robins
Columbus
Perry
Dublin
Statesboro
Beaufort
Hilton Head Island
Eastman
Vidalia
Wilmington Island
Americus
Cordele
Dawson
Fitzgerald
Altamaha
Hinesville
Richmond Hill
St Catherines Island
Albany
Douglas
Jesup
Blakely
Tifton
Waycross
Nahunta
Brunswick
Moultrie
Adel
Bainbridge
Okefenokee Swamp
Folkston
Cumberland Island
Lake Seminole
Thomasville
Valdosta
Monticello
Fernandina Beach
Atlantic Beach
Jacksonville
Live Oak
Perry
Lake City
Orange Park
St Johns
St Augustine
Starke
Gainesville
Apalachee Bay
Cross City
St George Island
Deadman Bay
Suwannee
Palatka
Lake George
Ormond Beach
Daytona Beach
Suwanee Sound
Ocala
De Land
Edgewater
Waccasassa Bay
Sanford
Oviedo
Leesburg
Apopka
Titusville
Homosassa Springs
Brooksville
Lake Apopka
Orlando
Cape Canaveral
Spring Hill
Dade City
Kissimmee
Melbourne
Palm Bay
Tarpon Springs
Lakeland
Lake Tohopekaliga
Winter Haven
Clearwater
Largo
Tampa
Lake Kissimmee
St Petersburg
Orchid Island
Vero Beach
Fort Pierce
Tampa Bay
Bradenton
Sebring
Lake Istokpoga
Hutchinson Island
Sarasota
Arcadia
Okeechobee
Port Saint Lucie City
Venice
Port Charlotte
Lake Okeechobee
Jupiter
Englewood
West Palm Beach
Charlotte Harbor
Clewiston
Belle Glade
Lake Worth
Fort Myers
Delray Beach
Cape Coral
Boca Raton
Pine Islands
Immokalee
Fort Lauderdale
Sunrise
Hollywood
Naples
Pembroke Pines
Hialeah
Miami Beach
Miami
Everglades
Kendall
Biscayne Bay
Ten Thousand Islands
Homestead
Cape Sable
Florida Bay
Key Largo
Islamorada
Pine Islands
Marathon
Florida Keys
Marquesas Keys
Key West
Straits of Florida
Little Abaco
Cooper's Town
Little Bahama Bank
Marsh Harbour
Freeport City
Grand Bahama
Great Abaco
Northwest Providence Channel
Northeast Providence Channel
Bimini Islands
Berry Islands
Eleuthera
New Providence
NASSAU
Governor's Harbour
Bannerman Town
Andros Town
Exuma Cays
Andros

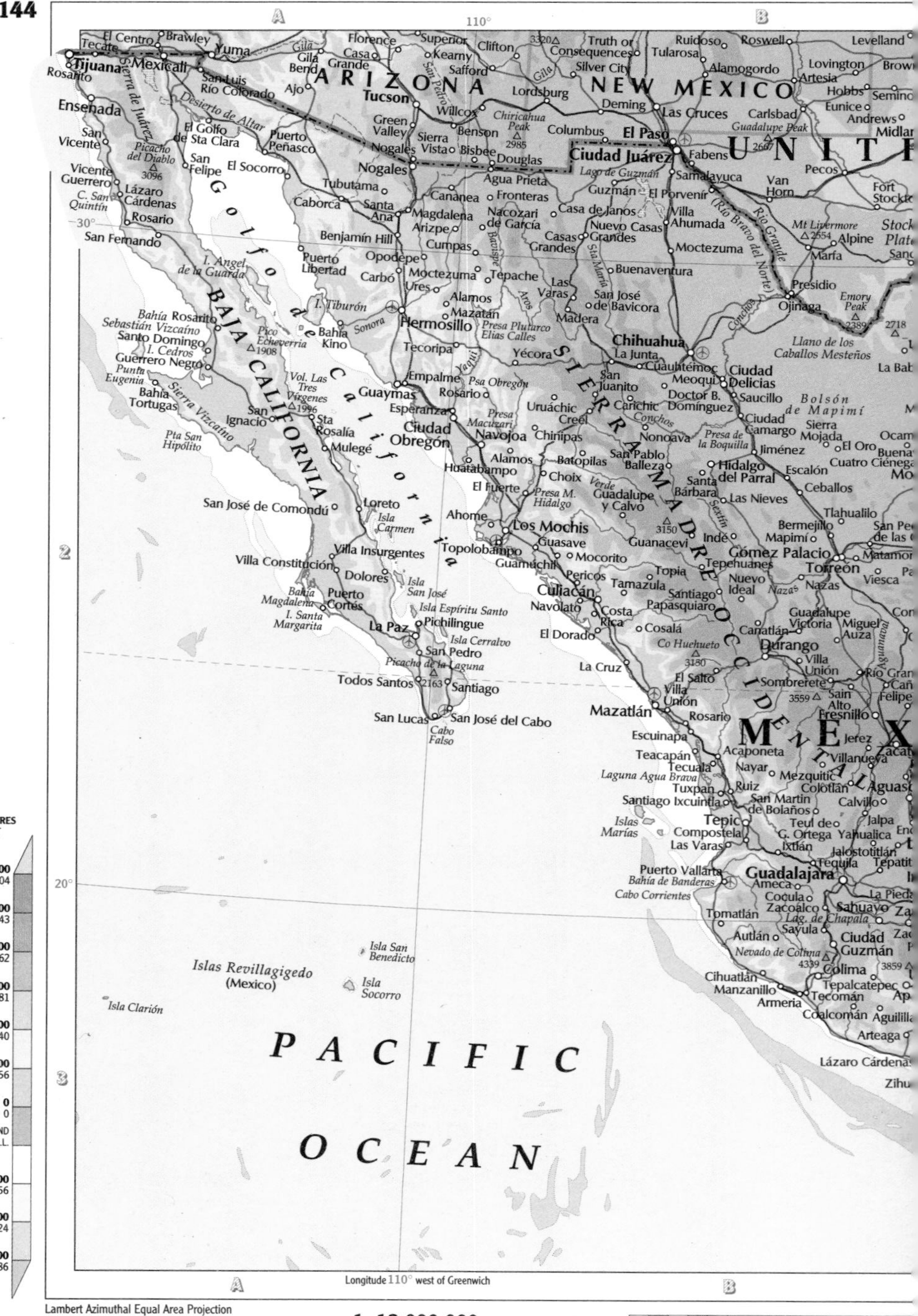

METRES / FEET

5000 / 16404
3000 / 9843
2000 / 6562
1000 / 3281
500 / 1640
200 / 656
0 / 0
LAND B.S.L.
200 / 656
4000 / 13124
6000 / 19686

Lambert Azimuthal Equal Area Projection

1 : 12 000 000

MILES 0   100   200

Longitude 110° west of Greenwich

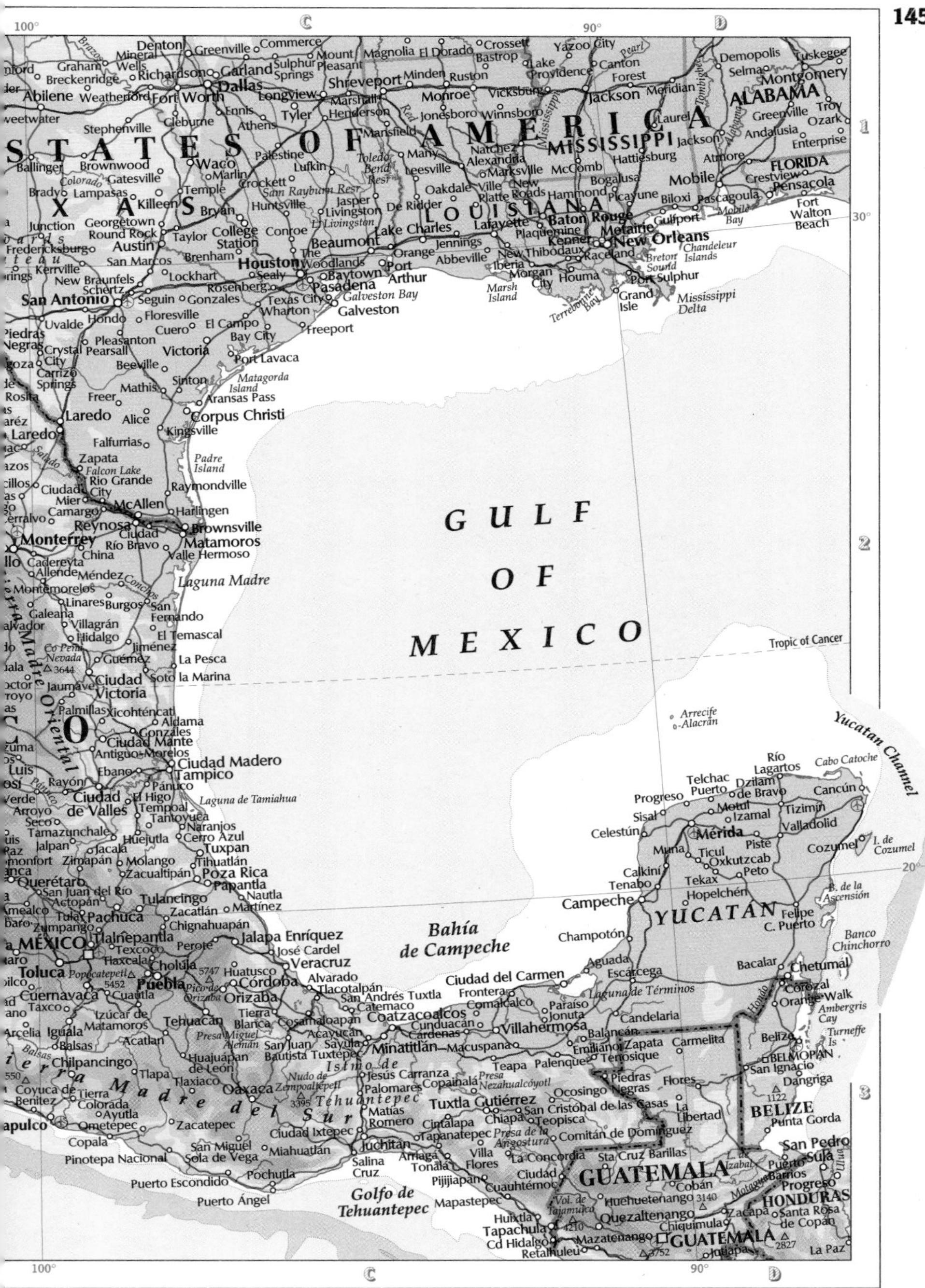

G U L F

O F

M E X I C O

Tropic of Cancer

Laguna Madre

Laguna de Tamiahua

Bahía
de Campeche

YUCATÁN

Golfo de
Tehuantepec

GUATEMALA

BELIZE

HONDURAS

200   400 KILOMETRES

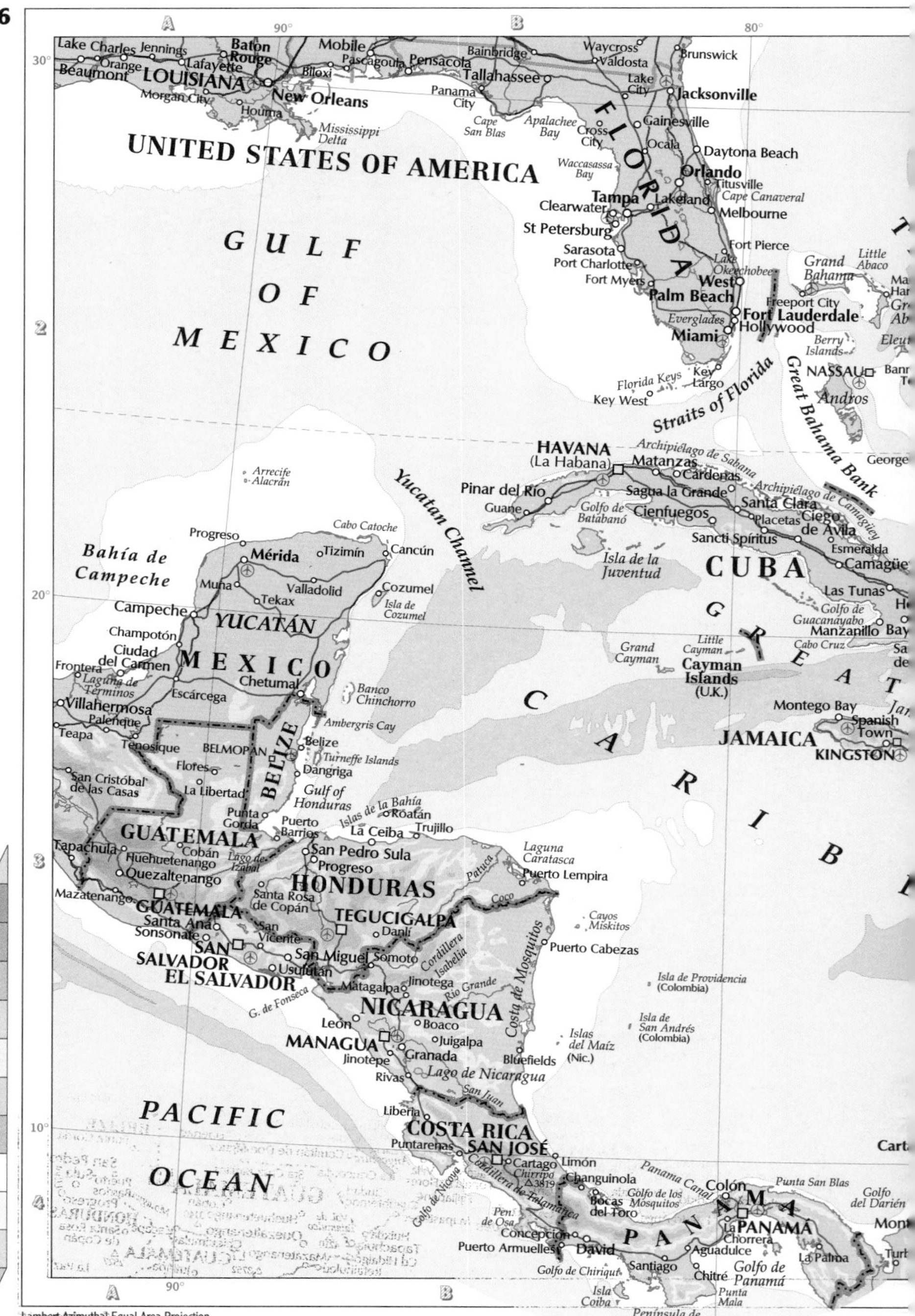
UNITED STATES OF AMERICA
GULF OF MEXICO
LOUISIANA
FLORIDA
New Orleans
Baton Rouge
Mobile
Pensacola
Tallahassee
Jacksonville
Orlando
Tampa
Miami
Fort Lauderdale
Key West
Straits of Florida
HAVANA
(La Habana)
CUBA
Yucatan Channel
YUCATÁN
MEXICO
Mérida
Cancún
Bahía de Campeche
BELIZE
BELMOPAN
GUATEMALA
HONDURAS
TEGUCIGALPA
SAN SALVADOR
EL SALVADOR
NICARAGUA
MANAGUA
COSTA RICA
SAN JOSÉ
PANAMA
PACIFIC OCEAN
CARIBBEAN
Cayman Islands
(U.K.)
JAMAICA
KINGSTON
Great Bahama Bank
NASSAU
Grand Bahama
Andros
Gulf of Honduras
Lago de Nicaragua
Golfo de Panamá
METRES
FEET
5000
16404
3000
9843
2000
6562
1000
3281
500
1640
200
656
0
0
LAND
B.S.L.
200
656
4000
13124
6000
19686
Lambert Azimuthal Equal Area Projection
1:15 000 000

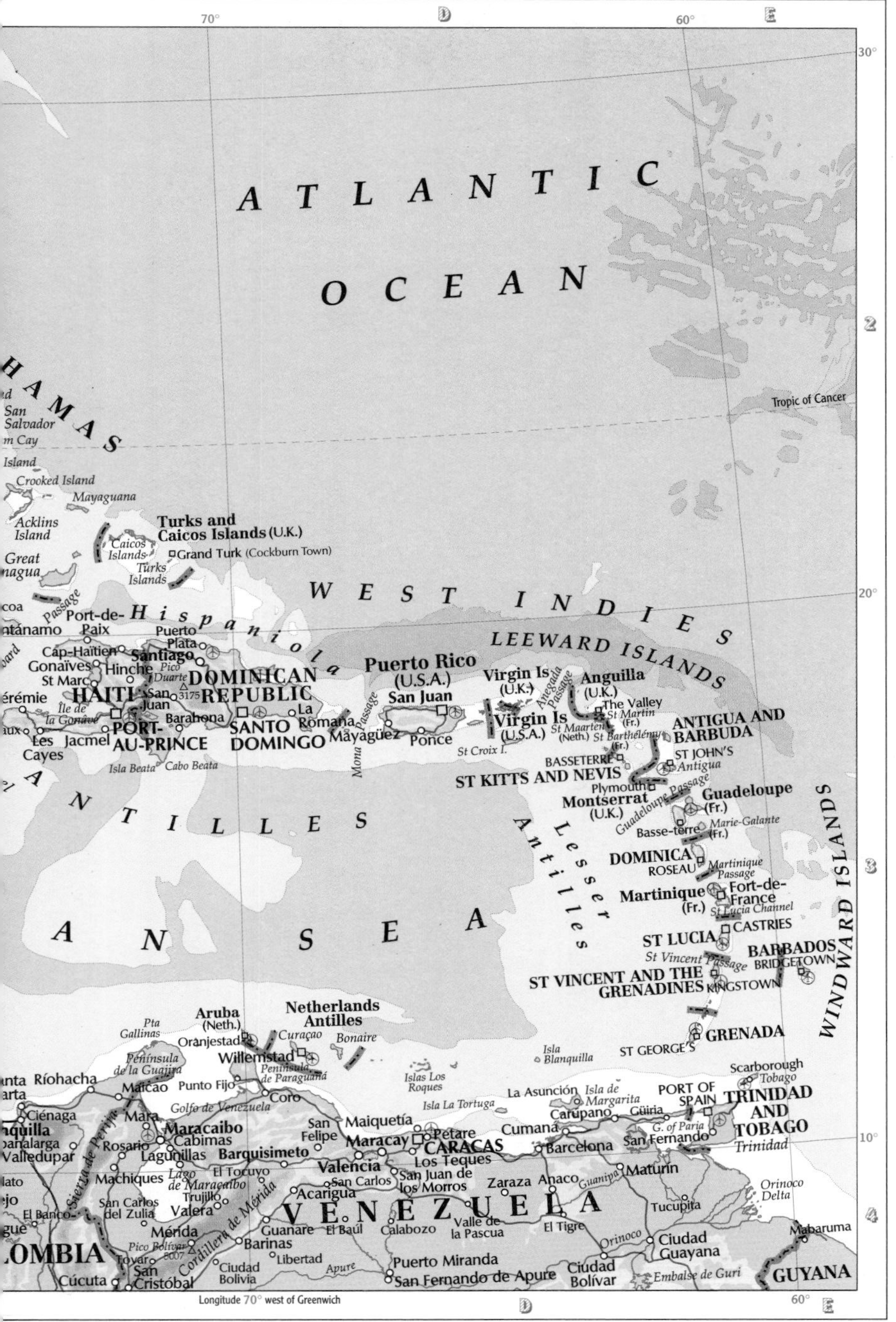

70°　　　　　　　　Ⓓ　　　　　60°　　Ⓔ

30°

A T L A N T I C

O C E A N

Ⓑ

Tropic of Cancer

ad
San
Salvador
m Cay

Island

Crooked Island
Mayaguana

Acklins
Island　　**Turks and**
　　　　　Caicos Islands (U.K.)
Caicos　　□Grand Turk (Cockburn Town)
Islands
Turks
Islands

coa　　　　　　W　E　S　T　　　　I　N　D　I　E　S　　　20°

ntánamo　Port-de-　H *i* s *p* a n *i* o *l* a
Paix　　Puerto　　　　　　　L E E W A R D　　I S L A N D S
Cap-Haïtien　Plata　　**Puerto Rico**
Gonaïves　Santiago○　　　　**(U.S.A.)**　　Virgin Is　Anguilla
St Marc　Hinche *Pico*　　　　　　　　(U.K.)　(U.K.)
érémie　**HAITI** *San* ○3175　**DOMINICAN**　**San Juan**　　The Valley
Île de　　*Juan* *Duarte*　**REPUBLIC**　　Virgin Is　St Martin
la Gonâve　Barahona○　　　　　　　**(U.S.A.)** St Maarten　(Fr.)
aux○　Les　Jacmel　**SANTO**　○La　　　　　(Neth.) St Barthélémy　**ANTIGUA AND**
Cayes　　**PORT-**　**DOMINGO** *Mayagüez*　　　　　　　**BARBUDA**
　　　　AU-PRINCE　　　Ponce　St Croix I.　　　ST JOHN'S
　　Isla Beata *Cabo Beata*　　　　　　　　　BASSETERRE□　□Antigua
N　　　　　　　　　　　　　　**ST KITTS AND NEVIS**
　　　　　　　　　　　　　　　　　Plymouth□　**Guadeloupe**
T　　*I*　　*L*　　*L*　　*E*　　*S*　　　**Montserrat**　　□(Fr.)
　　　　　　　　　　　　　　　　(U.K.)　Basse-terre□　Marie-Galante
A　　　　　　*S*　　　*E*　　*A*　　　　　　　　**DOMINICA**
　　　　　　　　　　　　　　　　　ROSEAU□　Martinique
　　　　　　　　　　　　　　　　　　　　Martinique □Fort-de-
　　　　　　　　　　　　　　　　　　　　(Fr.)　□France
　　　　　　　　　　　　　　　　　　　　　ST LUCIA □CASTRIES

Ⓒ

W
I
N
D
W
A
R
D

I
S
L
A
N
D
S

St Vincent Passage
ST VINCENT AND THE　　**BARBADOS**
GRENADINES KINGSTOWN　BRIDGETOWN

Pta　**Aruba**　**Netherlands**
Gallinas　**(Neth.)**　**Antilles**
　　　Oranjestad□　Curaçao　Bonaire　　　　ST GEORGE'S □　**GRENADA**
Península　Willemstad□
de la Guajíra　　　*Península*　*Isla*
nta Ríohacha　Maicao Punto Fijo○*de Paraguaná*　*Blanquilla*　　　　　　Scarborough
arta　　　　Coro　　　　　　*Islas Los*　　　　　　　　　○ Tobago
○Ciénaga　*Golfo de Venezuela*　*Roques*　La Asunción *Isla de*　**PORT OF**
aquilla　　Maracaibo○　　San　○Maiquetía　*Isla La Tortuga*　*Margarita* Güiria　**SPAIN** **TRINIDAD**
banalarga　○Cabimas　Felipe○　**Maracay**　　Cumaná　Carúpano○　　**AND**
Valledupar○　Rosario○ Lagunillas **Barquisimeto**○　**CARACAS**　　　Barcelona San Fernando○　**TOBAGO**
lato　Machiques○ *El Toruvo*　**Valencia**○ Los Teques　　　　　　　Trinidad
jo　　San Carlos *de Maracaibo*　○San Carlos San Juan de　Zaraza Anaco○*Guanipa* Maturín
El Banco○ *del Zulia* Trujillo○　Acarigua　los Morros　　　　　　Tucupita
gue○　　Valera○　**V E N E Z U E L A**　　　El Tigre○　Orinoco
OMBIA　　*Pico Bolívar* Barinas○ El Baúl　Calabozo Valle de
　　　Mérida○　Guanare○　　　　　la Pascua　　　○Ciudad
　　Tovar Libertad○　Apure　**Puerto Miranda**　　　Guayana
　Cúcuta○ Ciudad　　　　**San Fernando de Apure** Ciudad
　　San Bolivia　　　　　　　　　Bolívar *Embalse de Guri*　**GUYANA**
　　Cristóbal○

Orinoco
Delta

Mabaruma

10°

4

60° Ⓔ

Longitude 70° west of Greenwich　　Ⓓ

© Bartholomew Ltd

ES 0　　100　　200　　300　　　　0　　250　　500 KILOMETRES

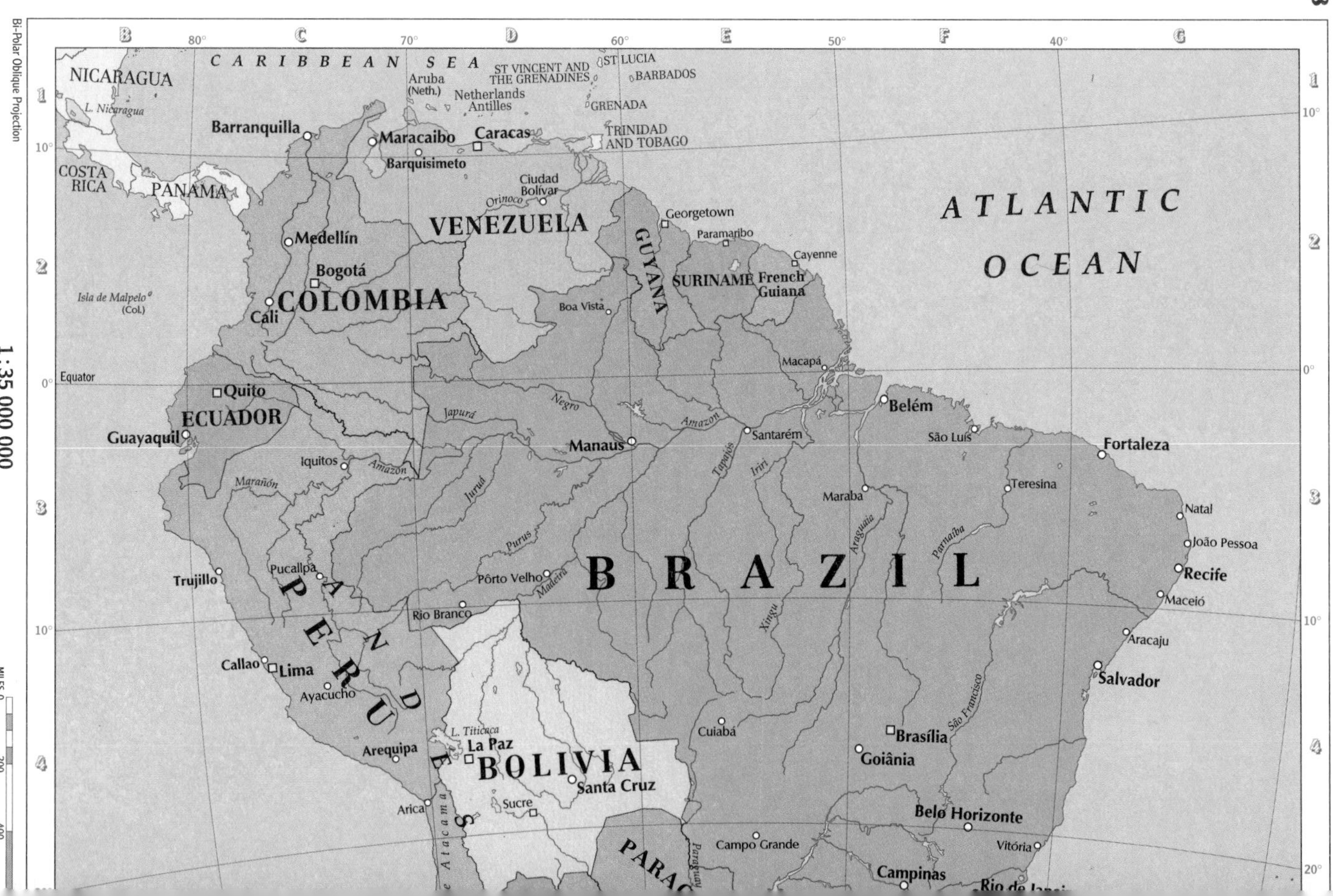
CARIBBEAN SEA
NICARAGUA
L. Nicaragua
COSTA RICA
PANAMA
Aruba (Neth.)
Netherlands Antilles
ST VINCENT AND THE GRENADINES
ST LUCIA
BARBADOS
GRENADA
TRINIDAD AND TOBAGO
ATLANTIC OCEAN
Isla de Malpelo (Col.)
Equator
VENEZUELA
COLOMBIA
ECUADOR
PERU
BOLIVIA
GUYANA
SURINAME
French Guiana
BRAZIL
ANDES
Atacama
Barranquilla
Maracaibo
Caracas
Barquisimeto
Ciudad Bolívar
Orinoco
Medellín
Bogotá
Cali
Georgetown
Paramaribo
Cayenne
Boa Vista
Macapá
Quito
Guayaquil
Belém
São Luís
Fortaleza
Manaus
Santarém
Iquitos
Japurá
Negro
Amazon
Marañón
Juruá
Purus
Madeira
Tapajós
Iriri
Xingu
Araguaia
Parnaíba
São Francisco
Marabá
Teresina
Natal
João Pessoa
Recife
Maceió
Aracaju
Salvador
Trujillo
Pucallpa
Pôrto Velho
Rio Branco
Callao
Lima
Ayacucho
Arequipa
Arica
L. Titicaca
La Paz
Santa Cruz
Sucre
Cuiabá
Brasília
Goiânia
Belo Horizonte
Vitória
Campo Grande
Campinas
Paraguay
80°
70°
60°
50°
40°
10°
0°
10°
20°

1:35 000 000

MILES 0 200 400

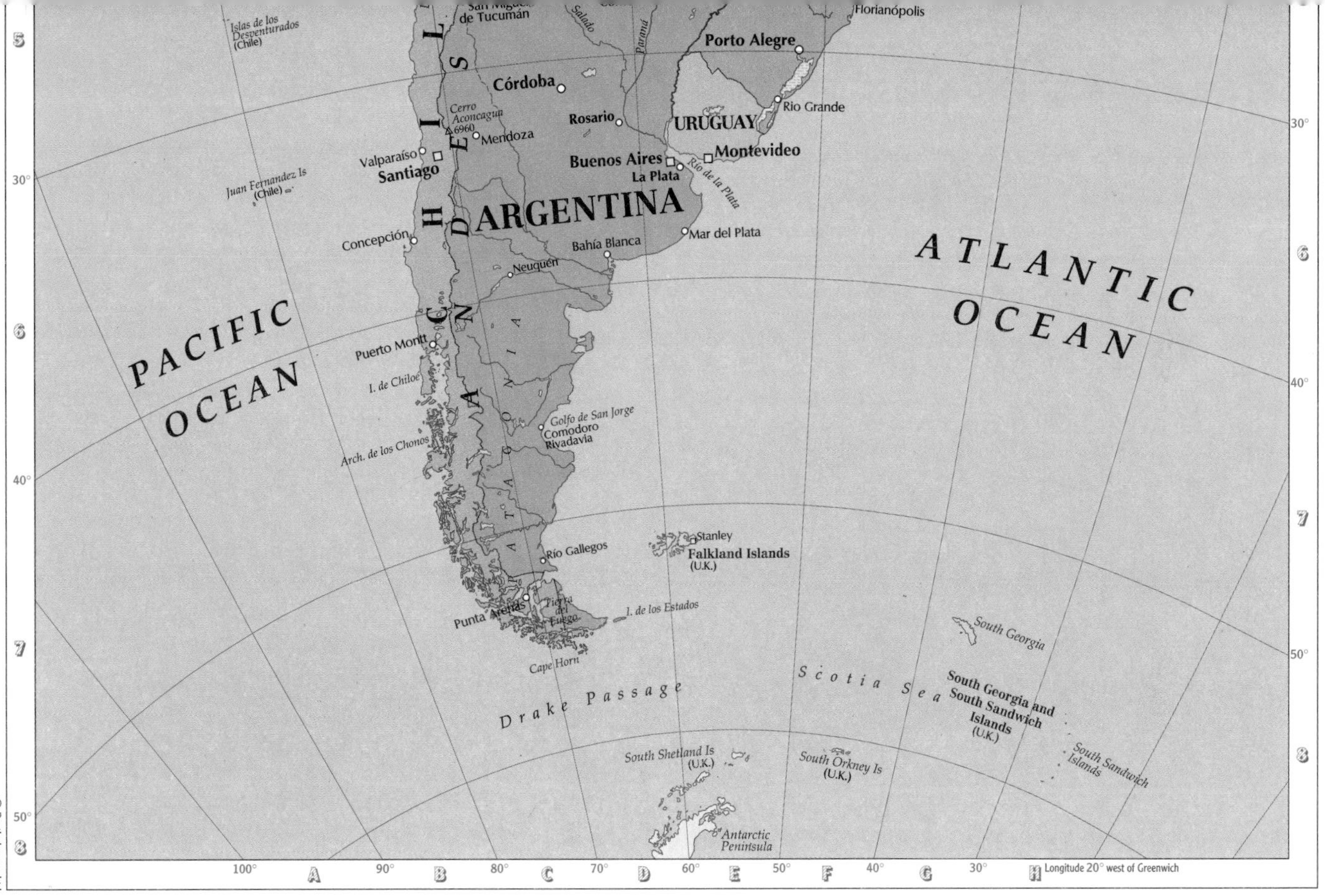

ATLANTIC
OCEAN

PACIFIC
OCEAN

Florianópolis
Porto Alegre
Rio Grande
URUGUAY
Montevideo
Río de la Plata
Mar del Plata
La Plata
Buenos Aires
Rosario
Córdoba
San Miguel
de Tucumán
Cerro
Aconcagua
Mendoza
ARGENTINA
Neuquén
Bahía Blanca
Paraná
Salado
Valparaíso
Santiago
Concepción
Puerto Montt
I. de Chiloé
Arch. de los Chonos
Golfo de San Jorge
Comodoro
Rivadavia
Río Gallegos
Punta Arenas
Cape Horn
I. de los Estados
Drake Passage
Islas de los
Desventurados
(Chile)
Juan Fernández Is
(Chile)
Stanley
Falkland Islands
(U.K.)
Scotia Sea
South Georgia
South Georgia and
South Sandwich
Islands
(U.K.)
South Sandwich
Islands
South Orkney Is
(U.K.)
South Shetland Is
Antarctic
Peninsula

Longitude 20° west of Greenwich

© Bartholomew Ltd

500   1000 KILOMETRES

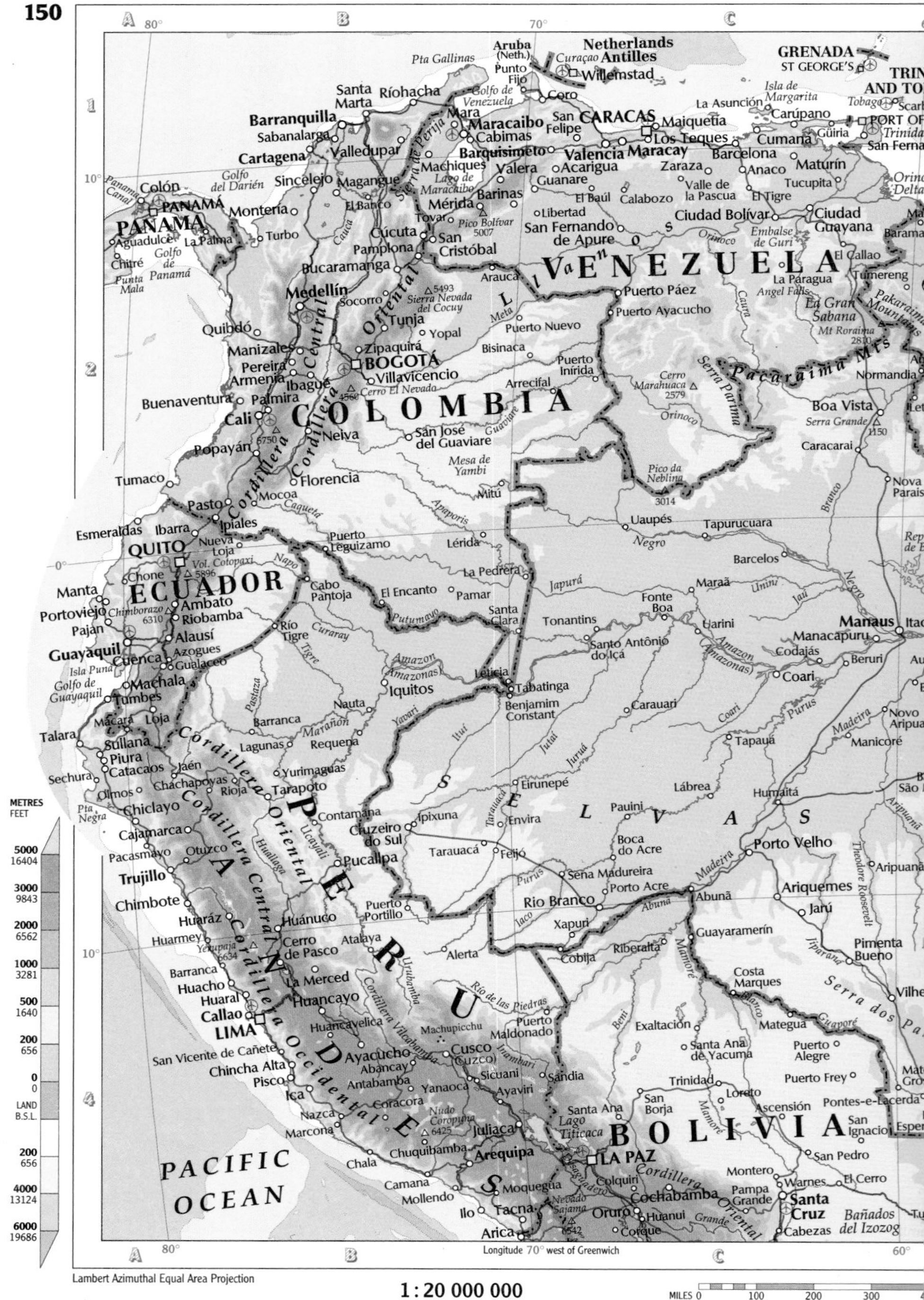

A 80°   B   70°   C

Pta Gallinas
Punto
Filo
Netherlands
Aruba
(Neth.) Curaçao **Antilles**
Willemstad
GRENADA
ST GEORGE'S
TRIN
AND TO

Santa Ríohacha
Marta
Golfo de
Venezuela
Coro
Isla de
Margarita
La Asunción
Tobaga
Scarl

Barranquilla
Sabanalarga
Mara
Maracaibo
Cabimas
Felipe
Majquetia
CARACAS
Carúpano
PORT OF
Trinida
Sabanalarga
Cartagena
Valledupar
Barquisimeto
Valencia Maracay
Los Teques
Cumana
Güiria
San Ferna

Colón
Golfo
del Darién
Sincelejo
Magangue
Machiques
Valera
Acarigua
Guanare
El Baúl
Valle de
la Pascua
El Tigre
Maturín
Orinc
Delta

PANAMÁ
Montería
El Banco
Mérida
Tovar
Barinas
San Fernando
de Apure
Calabozo
Ciudad Bolívar
Ciudad
Guayana
Bara

Aguadulce
La Palma
Turbo
Pamplona
San
Cristóbal
Pico Bolívar
5007
El Libertad
Puerto Páez
Embalse
de Guri
El Callao
Túmereno

PACIFIC
OCEAN
Lambert Azimuthal Equal Area Projection

Longitude 70° west of Greenwich

1 : 20 000 000

MILES 0   100   200   300

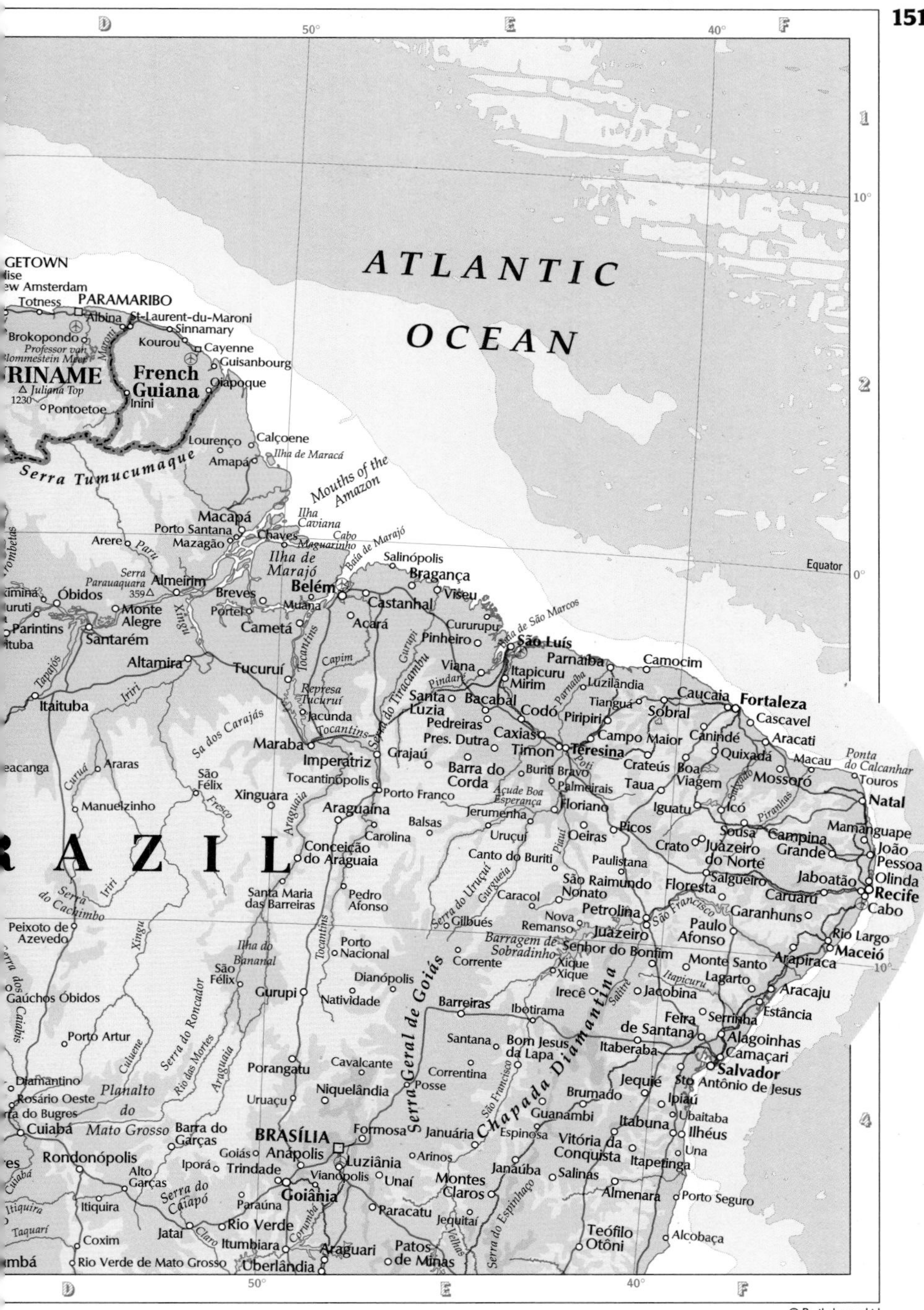
ATLANTIC
OCEAN
Mouths of the Amazon
Equator
PARAMARIBO
French Guiana
Cayenne
Kourou
Sinnamary
St-Laurent-du-Maroni
Albina
Oiapoque
Serra Tumucumaque
Macapá
Ilha de Marajó
Belém
Bragança
Castanhal
São Luís
Baía de São Marcos
Teresina
Fortaleza
Natal
João Pessoa
Olinda
Recife
Jaboatão
Maceió
Aracaju
Salvador
Ilhéus
Porto Seguro
Santarém
Altamira
Marabá
Imperatriz
Araguaína
Tucuruí
Caxias
Timon
Sobral
Mossoró
Campina Grande
Caruaru
Petrolina
Juazeiro
Feira de Santana
Vitória da Conquista
Montes Claros
BRASÍLIA
Goiânia
Anápolis
Uberlândia
Cuiabá
Rondonópolis
Serra Geral de Goiás
Chapada Diamantina
Planalto do Mato Grosso
Barragem de Sobradinho
Ponta do Calcanhar
© Bartholomew Ltd
200
400
600 KILOMETRES

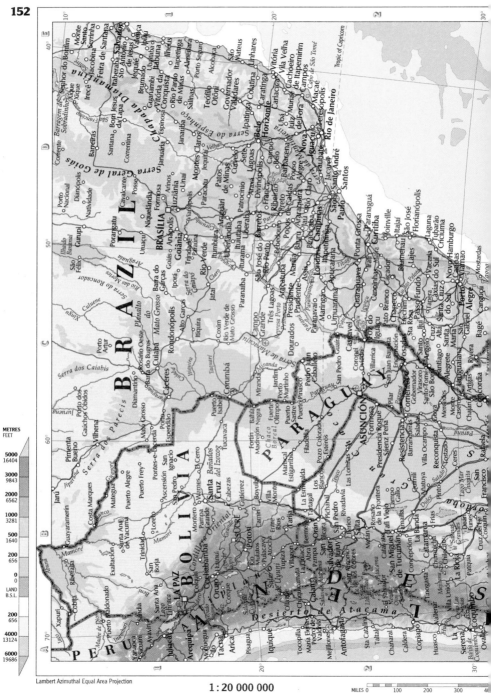

Lambert Azimuthal Equal Area Projection

1 : 20 000 000

METRES
FEET

5000
16404

3000
9843

2000
6562

1000
3281

500
1640

200
656

0
0

LAND
B.S.L.

200
656

4000
13124

6000
19686

MILES 0   100   200   300   40

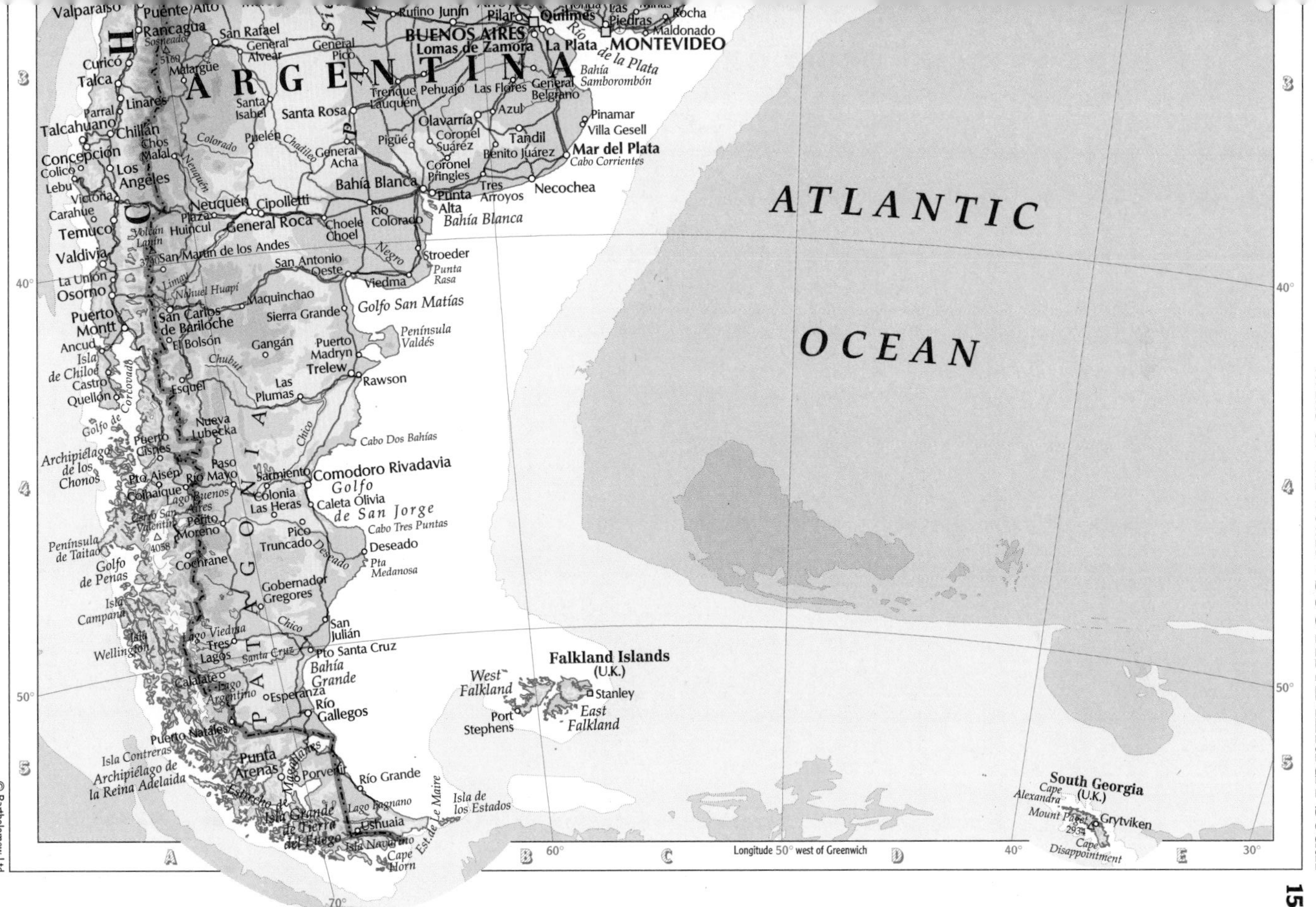

ATLANTIC

OCEAN

South Georgia
Cape (U.K.) *Cape*
Alexandra Mount Paget *Disappointment*

Longitude 50° west of Greenwich

Falkland Islands
(U.K.)
West Stanley
Falkland East
Falkland
Port
Stephens

Isla de
los Estados

Estrecho Le Maire

Cabo San
Diego

ARGENTINA

PATAGONIA

Comodoro Rivadavia

BUENOS AIRES
Lomas de Zamora
La Plata MONTEVIDEO
Mar del Plata

200   400   600 KILOMETRES

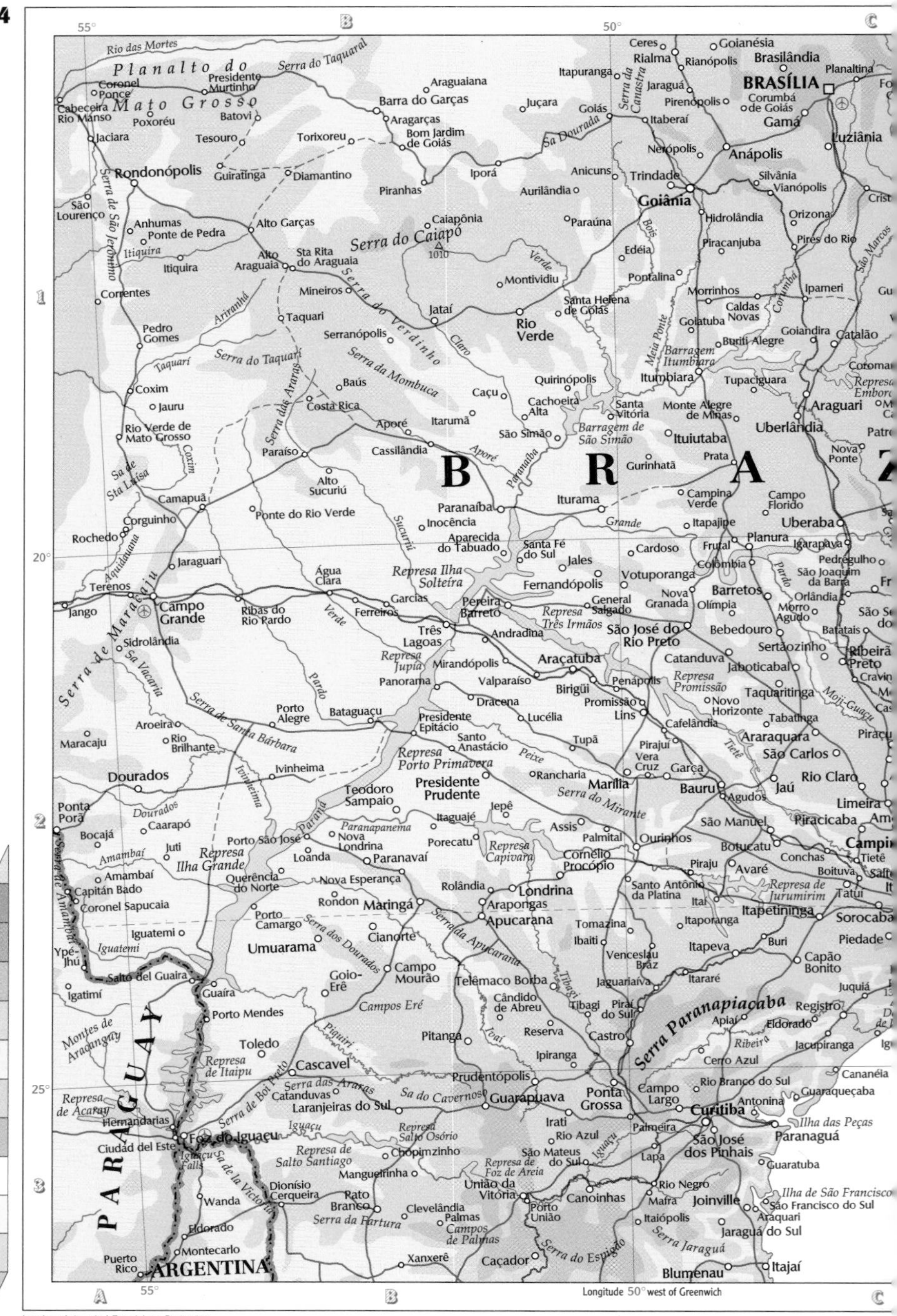

Lambert Azimuthal Equal Area Projection

1 : 7 500 000

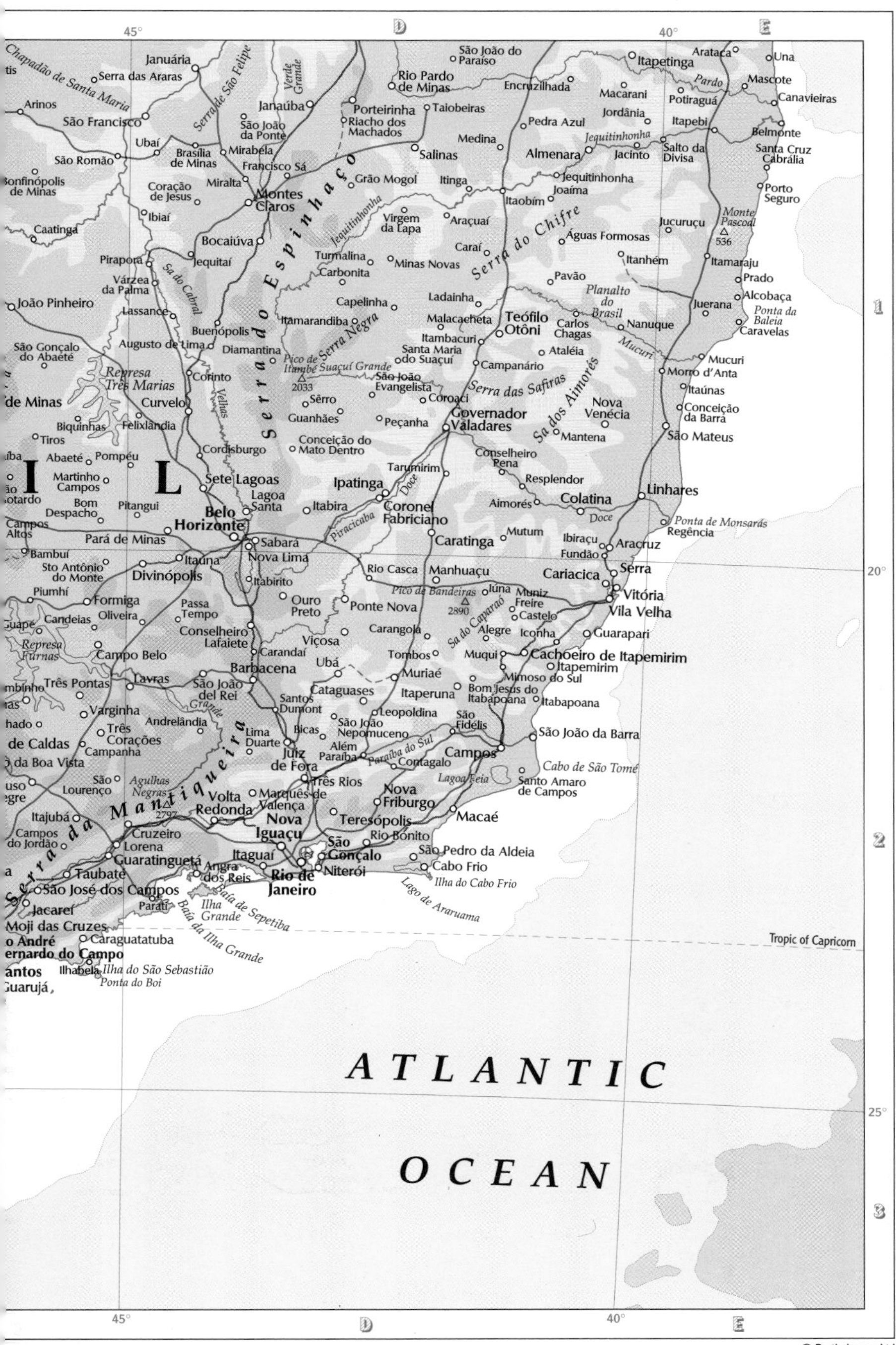

ATLANTIC

OCEAN

Tropic of Capricorn

100   200 KILOMETRES

© Bartholomew Ltd

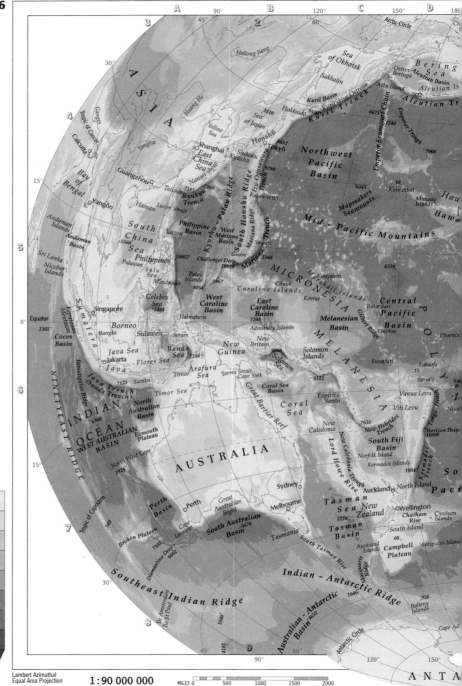

METRES
FEET

0	0
200	656
2000	6562
3000	9843
4000	13124
5000	16404
6000	19686
7000	22967
9000	29529

Lambert Azimuthal
Equal Area Projection

1 : 90 000 000

MILES 0   500   1000   1500   2000

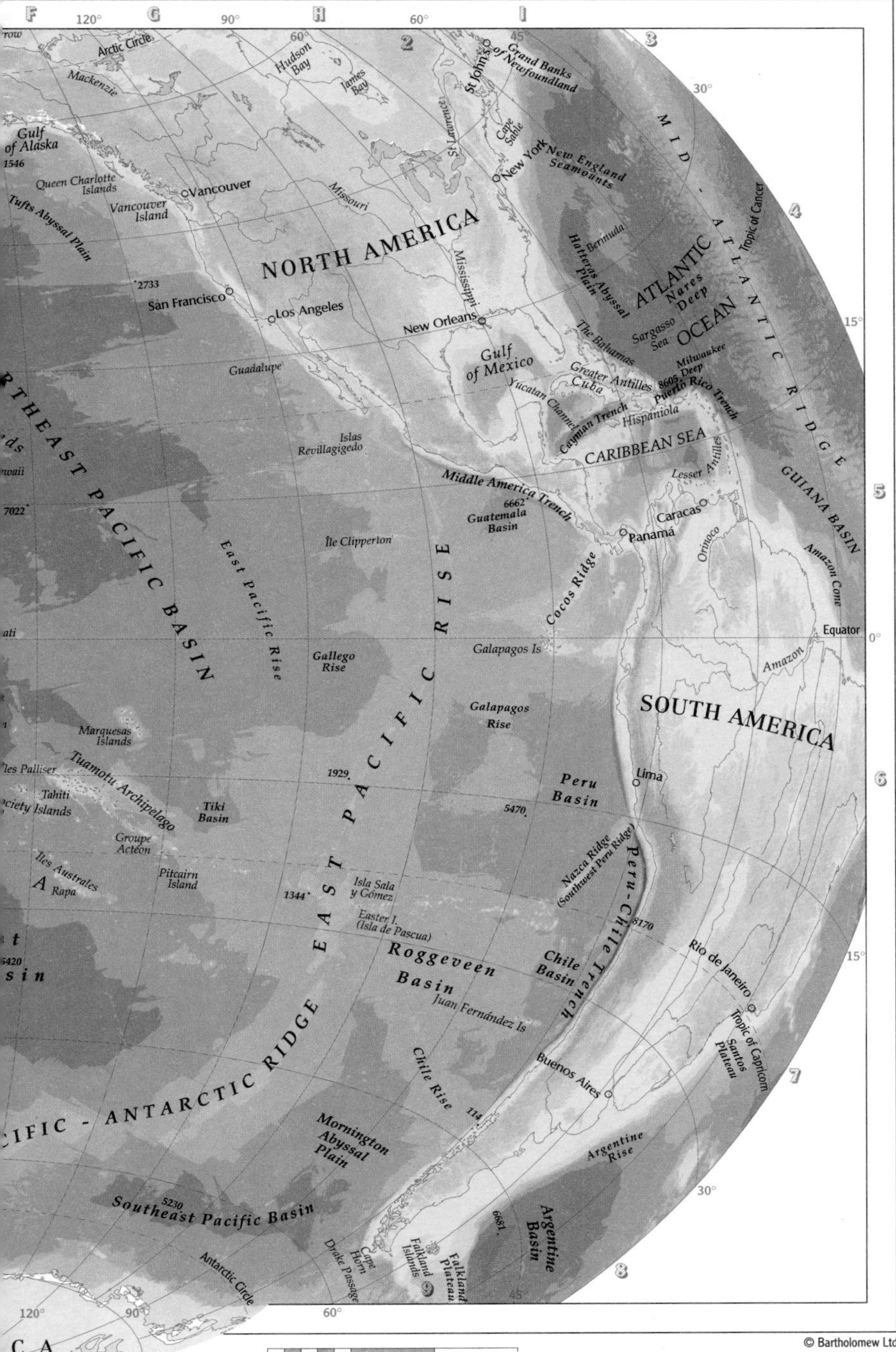

row

Arctic Circle

Mackenzie

Hudson Bay

James Bay

St John's

Grand Banks of Newfoundland

30°

Gulf of Alaska
1546

Queen Charlotte Islands

Vancouver

Vancouver Island

Cape Sable

New York

New England Seamounts

M I D

A T L A N T I C

Tropic of Cancer

4

Tufts Abyssal Plain

Missouri

Bermuda

Hatteras Abyssal Plain

15°

NORTH AMERICA

Mississippi

2733

San Francisco

Los Angeles

ATLANTIC

Nares Deep

OCEAN

R I D G E

New Orleans

Sargasso Sea

The Bahamas

Guadalupe

Gulf of Mexico

Yucatan Channel

Greater Antilles
Cuba

Milwaukee Deep
8605

Puerto Rico Trench

5

EAST PACIFIC BASIN

Islas Revillagigedo

Cayman Trench

Hispaniola

Lesser Antilles

GUIANA BASIN

awaii

Middle America Trench

CARIBBEAN SEA

7022

6662
Guatemala Basin

Cocos Ridge

Caracas

Panamá

Orinoco

Amazon Cone

Île Clipperton

East Pacific Rise

Galapagos Is

Equator 0°

ati

Gallego Rise

Amazon

Marquesas Islands

Galapagos Rise

SOUTH AMERICA

6

Tuamotu Archipelago

1929

Lima

les Palliser

Tahiti

Tiki Basin

5470

Peru Basin

ciety Islands

Groupe Actéon

Nazca Ridge (Southwest Peru Ridge)

Îles Australes

Pitcairn Island

Isla Sala y Gómez

A   Rapa

1344

Easter I. (Isla de Pascua)

8170

Río de Janeiro

15°

t

5420

Roggeveen Basin

Chile Basin

Peru-Chile Trench

s i n

Juan Fernández Is

Tropic of Capricorn

Chile Rise

Buenos Aires

Santos Plateau

FIC – ANTARCTIC RIDGE

EAST PACIFIC RISE

114

Argentine Rise

7

Mornington Abyssal Plain

Cape Horn

30°

Southeast Pacific Basin

5210

Drake Passage

Falkland Islands

Falkland Plateau

6681

Argentine Basin

Antarctic Circle

8

120°

90°

60°

45°

9

C A

0   1000   2000   3000 KILOMETRES

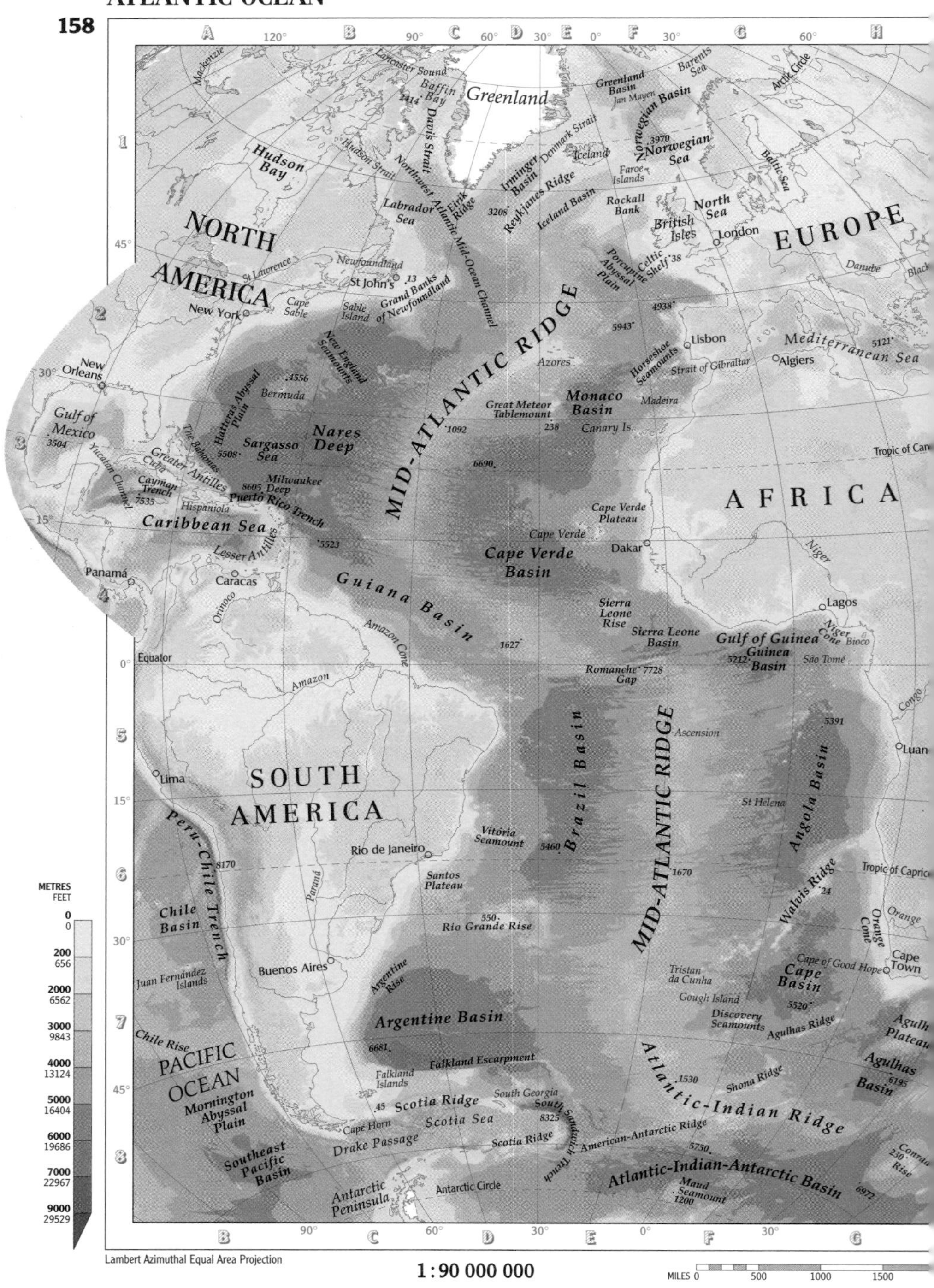

METRES / FEET

METRES	FEET
0	0
200	656
2000	6562
3000	9843
4000	13124
5000	16404
6000	19686
7000	22967
9000	29529

Lambert Azimuthal Equal Area Projection

1 : 90 000 000

MILES 0   500   1000   1500

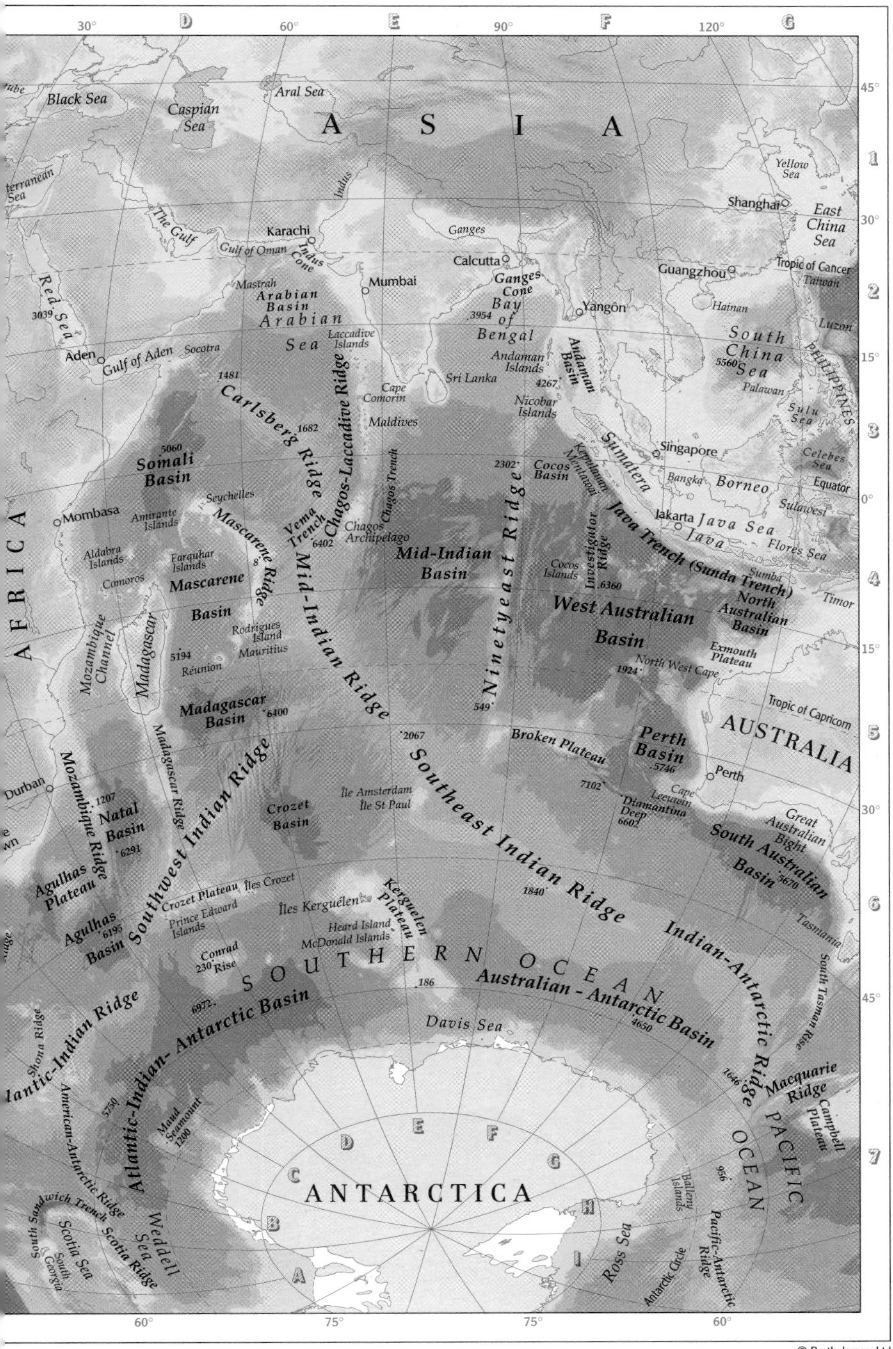

© Bartholomew Ltd

1 : 90 000 000

1000   2000   3000 KILOMETRES

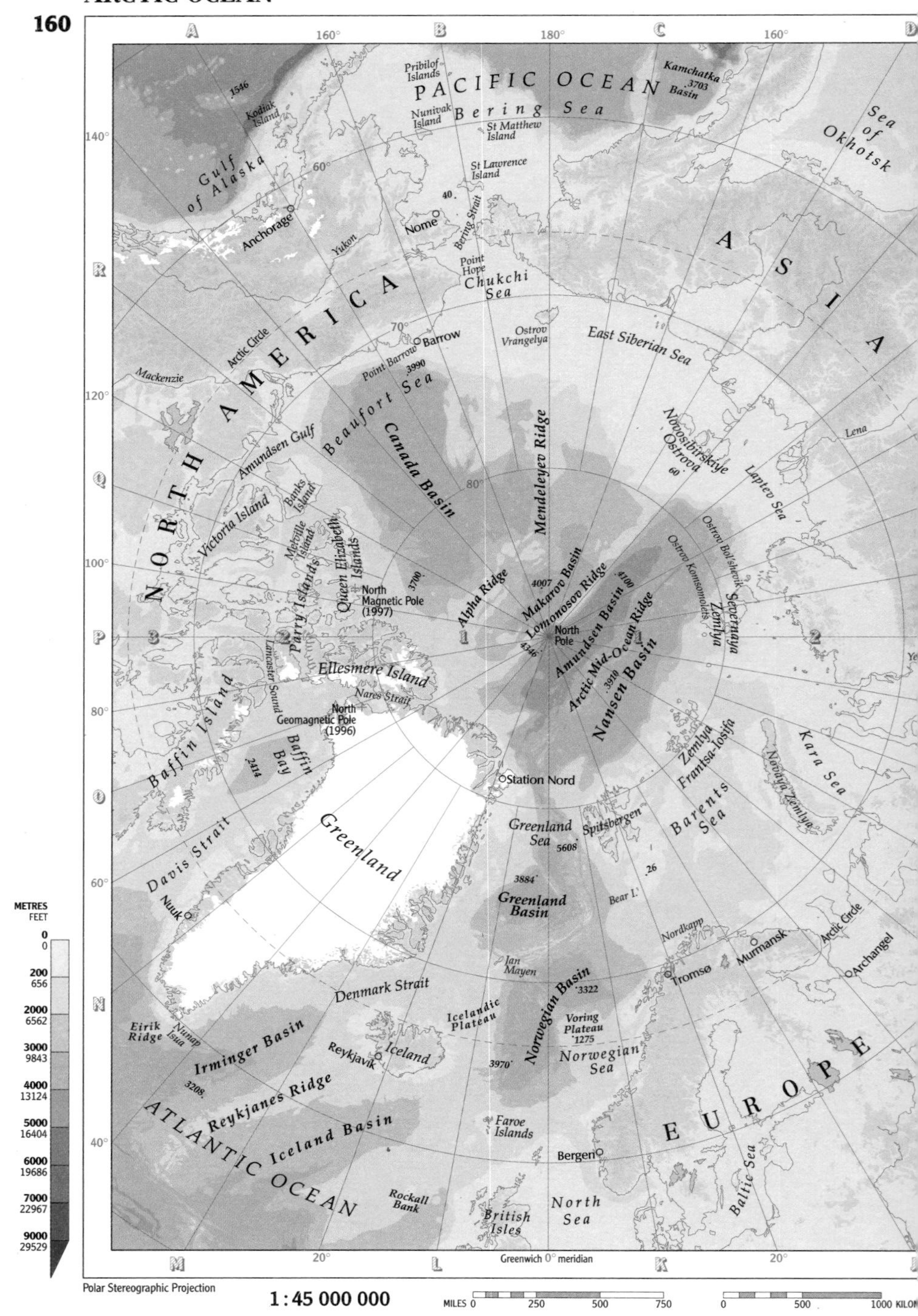

ARCTIC OCEAN

PACIFIC OCEAN

Pribilof Islands
Kamchatka
Basin 3703
Nunivak Island
St Matthew Island
Bering Sea
Sea of Okhotsk
Kodiak Island 1546
Gulf of Alaska
St Lawrence Island
Anchorage
Bering Strait
Nome
40
Point Hope
Yukon
Chukchi Sea
Arctic Circle
ASIA
Mackenzie
Barrow
Point Barrow
70°
Ostrov Vrangelya
East Siberian Sea
Amundsen Gulf
Beaufort Sea
3990
Canada Basin
80°
Mendeleyev Ridge
Novosibirskiye Ostrova
60
Lapter Sea
Lena
Banks Island
Victoria Island
3700
Ostrov Bol'shevik
Ostrov Komsomolets
NORTH AMERICA
Melville Island
Parry Islands
Queen Elizabeth Islands
North Magnetic Pole (1997)
Makarov Basin
4007
Lomonosov Ridge
Amundsen Basin
4100
Severnaya Zemlya
Alpha Ridge
North Pole
4346
Arctic Mid-Ocean Ridge
3910
Nansen Basin
Ellesmere Island
Nares Strait
Zemlya Frantsa-Iosifa
Novaya Zemlya
Kara Sea
North Geomagnetic Pole (1996)
Lancaster Sound
Baffin Island
Baffin Bay
2414
Station Nord
Barents Sea
Davis Strait
Greenland
Greenland Sea
5608
Spitsbergen
Nuuk
3884
Bear I.
Greenland Basin
26
Nordkapp
Murmansk
Arctic Circle
Archangel
Jan Mayen
Tromsø
Denmark Strait
Icelandic Plateau
Norwegian Basin
3322
Voring Plateau
1275
Norwegian Sea
Bergen
Eirik Ridge
Nanup Isua
Reykjavik
Iceland
3970
EUROPE
Irminger Basin
3208
Reykjanes Ridge
ATLANTIC Iceland Basin
Faroe Islands
Bergen
Baltic Sea
OCEAN
Rockall Bank
British Isles
North Sea
Polar Stereographic Projection

1 : 45 000 000

METRES / FEET
0 / 0
200 / 656
2000 / 6562
3000 / 9843
4000 / 13124
5000 / 16404
6000 / 19686
7000 / 22967
9000 / 29529

MILES 0   250   500   750
0   500   1000 KILOM

INTRODUCTION TO THE INDEX

he index includes all names shown on the maps in the
las of the World. Names are referenced by page
mber and by a grid reference. The grid reference
rrelates to the alphanumeric values which appear
thin each map frame. Each entry also includes the
untry or geographical area in which the feature is
cated. Entries relating to names appearing on insets
e indicated by a small box symbol: □, followed by a
id reference if the inset has its own alphanumeric
lues.

ame forms are as they appear on the maps, with
dditional alternative names or name forms included as
oss-references which refer the user to the entry for
e map form of the name. Names beginning with Mc
Mac are alphabetized exactly as they appear. The
rms Saint, Sainte, etc, are abbreviated to St, Ste, etc,
t alphabetized as if in the full form.

Names of physical features beginning with generic
geographical terms are permuted – the descriptive term
is placed after the main part of the name. For example,
Lake Superior is indexed as Superior, Lake; Mount
Everest as Everest, Mount. This policy is applied to all
languages.

Entries, other than those for towns and cities, include a
descriptor indicating the type of geographical feature.
Descriptors are not included where the type of feature is
implicit in the name itself.

Administrative divisions are included to differentiate
entries of the same name and feature type within the
one country. In such cases, duplicate names are
alphabetized in order of administrative division.
Additional qualifiers are also included for names within
selected geographical areas.

NDEX ABBREVIATIONS

min. div.	administrative division	g.	gulf	Port.	Portugal
t. comm.	autonomous community	Ger.	Germany	prov.	province
gh.	Afghanistan	Guat.	Guatemala	pt	point
g.	Algeria	hd	headland	r.	river
g.	Argentina	Hond.	Honduras	r. mouth	river mouth
str.	Australia	i.	island	reg.	region
t. reg.	autonomous region	imp. l.	impermanent lake	resr	reservoir
t. rep.	autonomous republic	Indon.	Indonesia	rf	reef
er.	Azerbaijan	is.	islands	Rus. Fed.	Russian Federation
	bay	isth.	isthmus	S.	South
.O.T.	British Indian Ocean	Kazakh.	Kazakhstan	salt l.	salt lake
	Territory	Kyrg.	Kyrgyzstan	sea chan.	sea channel
ngl.	Bangladesh	l.	lake	special admin. reg.	special administrative
l.	Bolivia	lag.	lagoon		region
s.-Herz.	Bosnia Herzegovina	Lith.	Lithuania	str.	strait
lg.	Bulgaria	Lux.	Luxembourg	Switz.	Switzerland
	cape	Madag.	Madagascar	Tajik.	Tajikistan
n.	Canada	Maur.	Mauritania	Tanz.	Tanzania
A.R.	Central African Republic	Mex.	Mexico	terr.	territory
l.	Colombia	Moz.	Mozambique	Thai.	Thailand
ech Rep.	Czech Republic	mt.	mountain	Trin. and Tob.	Trinidad and Tobago
m. Rep.	Democratic	mts	mountains	Turkm.	Turkmenistan
ongo	Republic of Congo	mun.	municipality	U.A.E.	United Arab Emirates
pr.	depression	N.	North	U.K.	United Kingdom
s.	desert	Neth.	Netherlands	Ukr.	Ukraine
m. Rep.	Dominican Republic	Neth. Antilles	Netherland Antilles	union terr.	union territory
	east	Nic.	Nicaragua	Uru.	Uruguay
c.	escarpment	N.Z.	New Zealand	U.S.A.	United States of America
t.	estuary	Pak.	Pakistan	Uzbek.	Uzbekistan
h.	Ethiopia	Para.	Paraguay	val.	valley
uat. Guinea	Equatorial Guinea	pen.	peninsula	Venez.	Venezuela
n.	Finland	Phil.	Philippines	vol.	volcano
r.	forest	plat.	plateau	vol. crater	volcanic crater
Guiana	French Guiana	P.N.G.	Papua New Guinea	W.	west
Polynesia	French Polynesia	Pol.	Poland	Yugo.	Yugoslavia

A

100 C2 **Aachen** Ger.
102 C2 **Aalen** Ger.
100 B2 **Aalst** Belgium
93 I3 **Äänekoski** Fin.
105 D2 **Aarau** Switz.
100 B2 **Aarschot** Belgium
70 A2 **Aba** China
119 D2 **Aba** Dem. Rep. Congo
115 C4 **Aba** Nigeria
81 C2 **Ābādān** Iran
81 D2 **Ābādeh** Iran
81 D3 **Ābādeh Ţashk** Iran
114 B1 **Abadla** Alg.
155 C1 **Abaeté** Brazil
Abagnar Qi China *see* **Xilinhot**
135 E3 **Abajo Peak** U.S.A.
115 C4 **Abakaliki** Nigeria
83 H3 **Abakan** Rus. Fed.
150 B4 **Abancay** Peru
81 D2 **Abarqū** Iran
66 D2 **Abashiri** Japan
66 D2 **Abashiri-wan** *b.* Japan
59 D3 **Abau** P.N.G.
Abaya, Lake Eth. *see* **Ābaya Hāyk'**
117 B4 **Ābaya Hāyk'** *l.* Eth.
Ābay Wenz *r.* Eth. *see* **Blue Nile**
83 H3 **Abaza** Rus. Fed.
108 A2 **Abbasanta** *Sardinia* Italy
104 C1 **Abbeville** France
143 C2 **Abbeville** *AL* U.S.A.
142 B3 **Abbeville** *LA* U.S.A.
97 B2 **Abbeyfeale** Rep. of Ireland
74 B1 **Abbottabad** Pak.
55 R2 **Abbott Ice Shelf** Antarctica
115 E3 **Abéché** Chad
114 B4 **Abengourou** Côte d'Ivoire
93 E4 **Åbenrå** Denmark
114 C4 **Abeokuta** Nigeria
99 A3 **Aberaeron** U.K.
96 C2 **Aberchirder** U.K.
Abercorn Zambia *see* **Mbala**
99 B4 **Aberdare** U.K.
99 A3 **Aberdaron** U.K.
53 D2 **Aberdeen** Austr.
122 B3 **Aberdeen** S. Africa
96 C2 **Aberdeen** U.K.
141 D3 **Aberdeen** *MD* U.S.A.
137 D1 **Aberdeen** *SD* U.S.A.
134 B1 **Aberdeen** *WA* U.S.A.
129 E1 **Aberdeen Lake** Can.
96 C2 **Aberfeldy** U.K.
96 B2 **Aberfoyle** U.K.
99 B4 **Abergavenny** U.K.
Abergwaun U.K. *see* **Fishguard**
Aberhonddu U.K. *see* **Brecon**
139 C2 **Abernathy** U.S.A.
134 B2 **Abert, Lake** U.S.A.
Abertawe U.K. *see* **Swansea**
Aberteifi U.K. *see* **Cardigan**
99 B4 **Abertillery** U.K.
99 A3 **Aberystwyth** U.K.
86 F2 **Abez'** Rus. Fed.
78 B3 **Abhā** Saudi Arabia
81 C2 **Abhar** Iran
Abiad, Bahr el *r.* Sudan/Uganda *see* **White Nile**
114 B4 **Abidjan** Côte d'Ivoire
137 D3 **Abilene** *KS* U.S.A.
139 D2 **Abilene** *TX* U.S.A.
99 C4 **Abingdon** U.K.
140 C3 **Abingdon** U.S.A.
91 D3 **Abinsk** Rus. Fed.
130 B3 **Abitibi, Lake** Can.
Åbo Fin. *see* **Turku**
74 B1 **Abohar** India
114 B4 **Aboisso** Côte d'Ivoire
114 C4 **Abomey** Benin
60 A1 **Abongabong, Gunung** *mt.* Indon.
118 B2 **Abong Mbang** Cameroon
64 A3 **Aborlan** Phil.
115 D3 **Abou Déia** Chad
106 B2 **Abrantes** Port.
152 B2 **Abra Pampa** Arg.
138 A3 **Abreojos, Punta** *pt* Mex.
116 B2 **'Abri** Sudan
136 A2 **Absaroka Range** *mts* U.S.A.
81 C1 **Abşeron Yarımadası** *pen.* Azer.
78 B3 **Abū 'Arīsh** Saudi Arabia
116 A2 **Abu Ballûs** *hill* Egypt
79 C2 **Abu Dhabi** U.A.E.
116 B3 **Abu Hamed** Sudan
116 B3 **Abu Haraz** Sudan
115 C4 **Abuja** Nigeria
81 C2 **Abū Kamāl** Syria
118 C2 **Abumombazi** Dem. Rep. Congo
152 B1 **Abunã** *r.* Bol.
150 C3 **Abunã** Brazil
74 B2 **Abu Road** India
78 B2 **Abū Şādi, Jabal** *hill* Saudi Arabia
116 B2 **Abu Simbel** Egypt
116 A3 **Abu Zabad** Sudan
Abū Ẓabī U.A.E. *see* **Abu Dhabi**
117 A4 **Abyei** Sudan
145 B2 **Acambaro** Mex.
120 B2 **Acampamento de Caça do Mucusso** Angola
106 B1 **A Cañiza** Spain
144 B2 **Acaponeta** Mex.
145 C3 **Acapulco** Mex.
151 E3 **Acará** Brazil
154 A3 **Acaray, Represa de** *resr* Para.
150 C2 **Acarigua** Venez.
110 B1 **Acâş** Romania
145 C3 **Acatlan** Mex.
145 C3 **Acayucán** Mex.
114 B4 **Accra** Ghana
98 B3 **Accrington** U.K.
74 B2 **Achalpur** India
97 A2 **Achill Island** Rep. of Ireland
101 D1 **Achim** Ger.
96 B2 **Achnasheen** U.K.
91 D2 **Achuyevo** Rus. Fed.
111 C3 **Acıpayam** Turkey
109 C3 **Acireale** *Sicily* Italy
147 C2 **Acklins Island** Bahamas
153 A3 **Aconcagua, Cerro** *mt.* Arg.
106 B1 **A Coruña** Spain
108 A2 **Acqui Terme** Italy
103 D2 **Ács** Hungary
49 N6 **Actéon, Groupe** *is* Fr. Polynesia
145 C2 **Actopán** Mex.
139 D2 **Ada** U.S.A.
Adabazar Turkey *see* **Sakarya**
79 C2 **Adam** Oman
111 B3 **Adamas** Greece
135 B3 **Adams Peak** U.S.A.
'Adan Yemen *see* **Aden**
80 B2 **Adana** Turkey
Adapazari Turkey *see* **Sakarya**
97 B2 **Adare** Rep. of Ireland
55 M2 **Adare, Cape** Antarctica
108 A1 **Adda** *r.* Italy
78 B2 **Ad Dafīnah** Saudi Arabia
78 B2 **Ad Dahnā'** *des.* Saudi Arabia
79 B2 **Ad Dahnā'** *des.* Saudi Arabia
114 A2 **Ad Dakhla** Western Sahara
79 C2 **Ad Dammām** Saudi Arabia
78 A2 **Ad Dār al Ḩamrā'** Saudi Arabia
78 B3 **Ad Darb** Saudi Arabia
78 B2 **Ad Dawādimī** Saudi Arabia
Ad Dawḩah Qatar *see* **Doha**
78 B2 **Ad Dilam** Saudi Arabia
78 B2 **Ad Dir'īyah** Saudi Arabia
117 B4 **Addis Ababa** Eth.
81 C2 **Ad Dīwānīyah** Iraq
143 D2 **Adel** U.S.A.
52 A2 **Adelaide** Austr.
55 A3 **Adelaide Island** Antarctica
50 C1 **Adelaide River** Austr.
101 D2 **Adelebsen** Ger.
55 K2 **Adélie Land** Antarctica
78 B3 **Aden** Yemen
116 C3 **Aden, Gulf of** Somalia/Yemen
100 C2 **Adenau** Ger.
115 C3 **Aderbissinat** Niger
79 C2 **Adh Dhayd** U.A.E.
59 C3 **Adi** *i.* Indon.
116 B3 **Ādī Ārk'ay** Eth.
108 B1 **Adige** *r.* Italy
116 B3 **Ādīgrat** Eth.
78 A3 **Adi Keyih** Eritrea
74 B3 **Adilabad** India
115 D2 **Adīrī** Libya
141 E2 **Adirondack Mountains** U.S.A.
Ādīs Ābeba Eth. *see* **Addis Ababa**
117 B4 **Ādīs Alem** Eth.
80 B2 **Adıyaman** Turkey
110 C1 **Adjud** Romania
50 B1 **Admiralty Gulf** Austr.
128 A2 **Admiralty Island** U.S.A.
59 D3 **Admiralty Islands** P.N.G.
73 B3 **Adoni** India
104 B3 **Adour** *r.* France
106 C2 **Adra** Spain
114 B2 **Adrar** Alg.
140 C2 **Adrian** *MI* U.S.A.
139 C1 **Adrian** *TX* U.S.A.
108 B2 **Adriatic Sea** Europe
Adua Eth. *see* **Ādwa**
116 B3 **Ādwa** Eth.
83 K2 **Adycha** *r.* Rus. Fed.
91 D3 **Adygeysk** Rus. Fed.
114 B4 **Adzopé** Côte d'Ivoire
111 B3 **Aegean Sea** Greece/Turkey
101 D1 **Aerzen** Ger.
106 B1 **A Estrada** Spain
116 B3 **Afabet** Eritrea
Affreville Alg. *see* **Khemis Miliana**
76 C3 **Afghanistan** *country* Asia
78 B2 **'Afīf** Saudi Arabia
136 A2 **Afton** U.S.A.
80 B2 **Afyon** Turkey
115 C3 **Agadez** Niger
114 B1 **Agadir** Morocco
77 D2 **Agadyr'** Kazakh.
113 I7 **Agalega Islands** Mauritius
Agana Guam *see* **Hagåtña**
74 B2 **Agar** India
119 D2 **Āgaro** Eth.
75 D2 **Agartala** India
81 C2 **Ağdam** Azer.
105 C3 **Agde** France
Agedabia Libya *see* **Ajdābiyā**
104 C3 **Agen** France
122 A2 **Aggeneys** S. Africa
111 C3 **Agia Vervara** Greece
111 B3 **Agios Dimitrios** Greece
111 C3 **Agios Efstratios** *i.* Greece
111 C3 **Agios Kirykos** Greece
111 C3 **Agios Nikolaos** Greece
78 A3 **Agirwat Hills** Sudan
123 C2 **Agisanang** S. Africa
110 B1 **Agnita** Romania
74 B2 **Agra** India
81 C2 **Ağrı** Turkey
Ağrı Dağı *mt.* Turkey *see* **Ararat, Mount**
108 B3 **Agrigento** *Sicily* Italy
111 B3 **Agrinio** Greece
109 B2 **Agropoli** Italy
87 E3 **Agryz** Rus. Fed.
144 B2 **Agua Brava, Laguna** *lag.* Mex.
154 B2 **Água Clara** Brazil
145 C3 **Aguada** Mex.
146 B4 **Aguadulce** Panama
144 B2 **Aguanaval** *r.* Mex.
144 B1 **Agua Prieta** Mex.
144 B2 **Aguascalientes** Mex.
155 D1 **Águas Formosas** Brazil
154 C2 **Agudos** Brazil
106 B1 **Águeda** Port.
114 C3 **Aguelhok** Mali
106 C1 **Aguilar de Campóo** Spain
107 C2 **Águilas** Spain
144 B3 **Aguililla** Mex.
122 B3 **Agulhas, Cape** S. Africa
158 F7 **Agulhas Basin** *sea feature* Southern Ocean
155 D2 **Agulhas Negras** *mt.* Brazil
158 F7 **Agulhas Plateau** *sea feature* Southern Ocean
158 F7 **Agulhas Ridge** *sea feature* S. Atlantic Ocean
111 C2 **Ağva** Turkey
81 C2 **Ahar** Iran
100 C1 **Ahaus** Ger.
81 C2 **Ahlat** Turkey
100 C2 **Ahlen** Ger.
74 B2 **Ahmadabad** India
74 B3 **Ahmadnagar** India
74 B2 **Ahmadpur East** Pak.
74 B1 **Ahmadpur Sial** Pak.
117 C4 **Ahmar Mountains** Eth.
Ahmedabad India *see* **Ahmadabad**
Ahmednagar India *see* **Ahmadnagar**
144 B2 **Ahome** Mex.
81 D3 **Ahram** Iran
101 E1 **Ahrensburg** Ger.
104 C2 **Ahun** France
93 F4 **Åhus** Sweden
81 C2 **Ahvāz** Iran
Ahvenanmaa *is* Fin. *see* **Åland**
122 A2 **Ai-Ais** Namibia
80 B2 **Aigialousa** Cyprus
111 B3 **Aigio** Greece
Aihui China *see* **Heihe**
Aijal India *see* **Aizawl**
143 D2 **Aiken** U.S.A.
155 D1 **Aimorés** Brazil
155 D1 **Aimorés, Serra dos** *hill* Brazil
105 D2 **Ain** *r.* France
107 E2 **Aïn Azel** Alg.
115 C1 **Aïn Beïda** Alg.
114 B2 **'Aïn Ben Tili** Maur.
107 D2 **Aïn Defla** Alg.
114 B1 **Aïn Sefra** Alg.
136 D2 **Ainsworth** U.S.A.
Aintab Turkey *see* **Gaziantep**
107 D2 **Aïn Taya** Alg.
107 D2 **Aïn Tédélès** Alg.
107 C2 **Aïn Temouchent** Alg.
60 A1 **Airbangis** Indon.
128 C2 **Airdrie** Can.
96 C3 **Airdrie** U.K.
104 B3 **Aire-sur-l'Adour** Franc
101 E3 **Aisch** *r.* Ger.
128 A1 **Aishihik Lake** Can.
100 A3 **Aisne** *r.* France
59 D3 **Aitape** P.N.G.
137 E1 **Aitkin** U.S.A.
110 B1 **Aiud** Romania
105 D3 **Aix-en-Provence** Franc
Aix-la-Chapelle Ger. *se* **Aachen**
105 D2 **Aix-les-Bains** France
75 D2 **Aizawl** India
88 C2 **Aizkraukle** Latvia
88 B2 **Aizpute** Latvia
67 C3 **Aizu-wakamatsu** Japa
105 D3 **Ajaccio** *Corsica* France
Ajayameru India *see* **Aj**
115 E1 **Ajdābiyā** Libya
79 C2 **'Ajman** U.A.E.
74 B2 **Ajmer** India
Ajmer-Merwara India *s* **Ajmer**
138 A2 **Ajo** U.S.A.
119 D2 **Āk'ak'ī Beseka** Eth.
Akamagaseki Japan *se* **Shimonoseki**
54 B2 **Akaroa** N.Z.
87 E3 **Akbulak** Rus. Fed.
80 B2 **Akçakale** Turkey
114 A3 **Akchâr** *reg.* Maur.
111 C3 **Akdağ** *mt.* Turkey
80 B2 **Akdağmadeni** Turkey
88 A2 **Åkersberga** Sweden
118 C2 **Aketi** Dem. Rep. Congo
81 C1 **Akhalk'alak'i** Georgia
81 C1 **Akhalts'ikhe** Georgia
79 C2 **Akhḑar, Jabal** *mts* Oma
111 C3 **Akhisar** Turkey
87 D4 **Akhtubinsk** Rus. Fed.
118 B3 **Akiéni** Gabon
130 B2 **Akimiski Island** Can.
66 D3 **Akita** Japan
114 A3 **Akjoujt** Maur.
Akkerman Ukr. *see* **Bilhorod-Dnistrovs'kyy**
77 D1 **Akkol'** Kazakh.
Ak-Mechet Kazakh. *see* **Kyzylorda**
88 B2 **Akmenrags** *pt* Latvia
Akmola Kazakh. *see* **Astana**
Akmolinsk Kazakh. *see* **Astana**
67 B4 **Akō** Japan
117 B4 **Akobo** Sudan
74 B2 **Akola** India
118 B2 **Akonolinga** Cameroon
78 A3 **Akordat** Eritrea
131 D1 **Akpatok Island** Can.
77 D2 **Akqi** China
92 □A3 **Akranes** Iceland
111 B2 **Akrathos, Akra** *pt* Gree
136 C2 **Akron** *CO* U.S.A.
140 C2 **Akron** *OH* U.S.A.
75 B1 **Aksai Chin** *terr.* Asia
80 B2 **Aksaray** Turkey
86 F2 **Aksarka** Rus. Fed.

B1 **Aksay** Kazakh.
D2 **Aksay** Rus. Fed.
B2 **Akşehir** Turkey
C2 **Akshiganak** Kazakh.
E2 **Aksu** China
B3 **Āksum** Eth.
B2 **Aktau** Kazakh.
D2 **Aktogay** Kazakh.
C3 **Aktsyabrski** Belarus
B1 **Aktyubinsk** Kazakh.
B4 **Akune** Japan
C4 **Akure** Nigeria
□B2 **Akureyri** Iceland
Akyab Myanmar *see* **Sittwe**
D2 **Akyazı** Turkey
C2 **Akzhaykyn, Ozero** *salt l.* Kazakh.
C2 **Alabama** *r.* U.S.A.
C2 **Alabama** *state* U.S.A.
C2 **Alabaster** U.S.A.
C3 **Alaçatı** Turkey
D2 **Alacrán, Arrecife** *rf* Mex.
C1 **Alagir** Rus. Fed.
F4 **Alagoinhas** Brazil
C1 **Alagón** Spain
B2 **Al Aḥmadī** Kuwait
E2 **Alakol', Ozero** *salt l.* Kazakh.
J2 **Alakurtti** Rus. Fed.
B3 **Al 'Alayyah** Saudi Arabia
C2 **Al 'Amādīyah** Iraq
C2 **Al 'Amārah** Iraq
C3 **Alamo** U.S.A.
B2 **Alamogordo** U.S.A.
A2 **Alamos** Mex.
B2 **Alamos** Mex.
B2 **Alamos** *r.* Mex.
B3 **Alamosa** U.S.A.
G3 **Åland** *is* Fin.
Åland Islands Fin. *see* Åland
B2 **Alanya** Turkey
Alappuzha India *see* Alleppey
B3 **Al 'Aqabah** Jordan
B2 **Al 'Aqīq** Saudi Arabia
C2 **Alarcón, Embalse de** *resr* Spain
B2 **Al Arṭāwīyah** Saudi Arabia
C2 **Alas** Indon.
C3 **Alaşehir** Turkey
A2 **Alaska** *state* U.S.A.
D4 **Alaska, Gulf of** U.S.A.
B3 **Alaska Peninsula** U.S.A.
C2 **Alaska Range** *mts* U.S.A.
C2 **Älät** Azer.
D3 **Alatyr'** Rus. Fed.
B3 **Alausí** Ecuador
H3 **Alavus** Fin.
B2 **Alawoona** Austr.
C2 **Al 'Ayn** U.A.E.
A2 **Alba** Italy
C2 **Albacete** Spain
A2 **Al Badā'i'** Saudi Arabia
B2 **Al Badī'** Saudi Arabia
B1 **Alba Iulia** Romania
C2 **Albania** *country* Europe
A3 **Albany** Austr.
B2 **Albany** *r.* Can.
D2 **Albany** *GA* U.S.A.
E2 **Albany** *NY* U.S.A.
B2 **Albany** *OR* U.S.A.
E1 **Al Bardī** Libya
Al Başrah Iraq *see* **Basra**
D1 **Albatross Bay** Austr.
E1 **Al Bayḍā'** Libya
B3 **Al Bayḍā'** Yemen
D1 **Albemarle** U.S.A.
E1 **Albemarle Sound** *sea chan.* U.S.A.
A2 **Albenga** Italy
C2 **Alberga** *watercourse* Austr.
D2 **Albert, Lake** Dem. Rep. Congo/Uganda
C2 **Alberta** *prov.* Can.
B2 **Albert Kanaal** *canal* Belgium
E2 **Albert Lea** U.S.A.
B4 **Albert Nile** *r.* Sudan/Uganda
C2 **Alberton** S. Africa
Albertville Dem. Rep. Congo *see* **Kalémié**
D2 **Albertville** France
C3 **Albi** France
D2 **Albina** Suriname
A2 **Al Bi'r** Saudi Arabia
B3 **Al Birk** Saudi Arabia
B2 **Al Biyāḍh** *reg.* Saudi Arabia
93 E4 **Ålborg** Denmark
81 C2 **Alborz, Reshteh-ye** *mts* Iran
107 C2 **Albox** Spain
106 B2 **Albufeira** Port.
138 B1 **Albuquerque** U.S.A.
79 C2 **Al Buraymī** Oman
53 C3 **Albury** Austr.
106 B2 **Alcácer do Sal** Port.
106 C1 **Alcalá de Henares** Spain
106 C2 **Alcalá la Real** Spain
108 B3 **Alcamo** *Sicily* Italy
107 C1 **Alcañiz** Spain
106 B2 **Alcántara** Spain
107 C2 **Alcantarilla** Spain
106 C2 **Alcaraz** Spain
106 C2 **Alcaraz, Sierra de** *mts* Spain
106 C2 **Alcaudete** Spain
106 C2 **Alcázar de San Juan** Spain
Alcazarquivir Morocco *see* Ksar el Kebir
91 D2 **Alchevs'k** Ukr.
155 E1 **Alcobaça** Brazil
107 C1 **Alcora** Spain
107 C2 **Alcoy** Spain
107 D2 **Alcúdia** Spain
113 H6 **Aldabra Islands** Seychelles
138 B3 **Aldama** Mex.
145 C2 **Aldama** Mex.
83 J3 **Aldan** Rus. Fed.
83 J2 **Aldan** *r.* Rus. Fed.
99 D3 **Aldeburgh** U.K.
95 C4 **Alderney** *i.* Channel Is
99 C4 **Aldershot** U.K.
114 A3 **Aleg** Maur.
155 D2 **Alegre** Brazil
152 C2 **Alegrete** Brazil
89 D1 **Alekhovshchina** Rus. Fed.
89 E2 **Aleksandrov** Rus. Fed.
Aleksandrovsk Ukr. *see* Zaporizhzhya
83 K3 **Aleksandrovsk-Sakhalinskiy** Rus. Fed.
Alekseyevka Kazakh. *see* Akkol'
91 D1 **Alekseyevka** Rus. Fed.
91 D1 **Alekseyevka** Rus. Fed.
89 E3 **Aleksin** Rus. Fed.
109 D2 **Aleksinac** Yugo.
118 B3 **Alèmbé** Gabon
155 D2 **Além Paraíba** Brazil
93 F3 **Ålen** Norway
104 C2 **Alençon** France
80 B2 **Aleppo** Syria
150 B4 **Alerta** Peru
128 B2 **Alert Bay** Can.
105 C3 **Alès** France
110 B1 **Aleşd** Romania
Aleshki Ukr. *see* Tsyurupyns'k
108 A2 **Alessandria** Italy
Alessio Albania *see* **Lezhë**
93 E3 **Ålesund** Norway
156 D2 **Aleutian Basin** *sea feature* Bering Sea
124 A4 **Aleutian Islands** U.S.A.
83 L3 **Alevina, Mys** *c.* Rus. Fed.
128 A2 **Alexander Archipelago** *is* U.S.A.
122 A2 **Alexander Bay** S. Africa
142 C2 **Alexander City** U.S.A.
55 A2 **Alexander Island** Antarctica
53 C3 **Alexandra** Austr.
54 A3 **Alexandra** N.Z.
153 E5 **Alexandra, Cape** S. Georgia
Alexandra Land *i.* Rus. Fed. *see* Zemlya Aleksandry
111 B2 **Alexandreia** Greece
116 A1 **Alexandria** Egypt
110 C2 **Alexandria** Romania
123 C3 **Alexandria** S. Africa
96 B3 **Alexandria** U.K.
142 B2 **Alexandria** *LA* U.S.A.
137 D1 **Alexandria** *MN* U.S.A.
141 D3 **Alexandria** *VA* U.S.A.
52 A3 **Alexandrina, Lake** Austr.
111 C2 **Alexandroupoli** Greece
131 E2 **Alexis** *r.* Can.
128 B2 **Alexis Creek** Can.
77 E1 **Aleysk** Rus. Fed.
107 C1 **Alfaro** Spain
81 C3 **Al Fāw** Iraq
101 D2 **Alfeld (Leine)** Ger.
155 C2 **Alfenas** Brazil
96 C2 **Alford** U.K.
Al Fujayrah U.A.E. *see* Fujairah
Al Furāt *r.* Iraq/Syria *see* Euphrates
93 E4 **Ålgård** Norway
106 B2 **Algarve** *reg.* Port.
106 B2 **Algeciras** Spain
107 C2 **Algemesí** Spain
78 A3 **Algena** Eritrea
Alger Alg. *see* **Algiers**
114 C1 **Algeria** *country* Africa
79 C3 **Al Ghayḍah** Yemen
108 A2 **Alghero** *Sardinia* Italy
79 B2 **Al Ghwaybiyah** Saudi Arabia
115 C1 **Algiers** Alg.
123 C3 **Algoa Bay** S. Africa
137 E2 **Algona** U.S.A.
Algueirao Moz. *see* Hacufera
81 C2 **Al Ḥadīthah** Iraq
79 C2 **Al Ḥajar al Gharbī** *mts* Oman
115 D2 **Al Ḥamādah al Ḥamrā'** *plat.* Libya
107 C2 **Alhama de Murcia** Spain
78 B2 **Al Ḥanākīyah** Saudi Arabia
81 C2 **Al Ḥasakah** Syria
78 B2 **Al Ḥawīyah** Saudi Arabia
81 C2 **Al Ḥayy** Iraq
78 B3 **Al Ḥazm al-Jawf** Yemen
79 C3 **Al Ḥibāk** *des.* Saudi Arabia
81 C2 **Al Ḥillah** Iraq
78 B2 **Al Ḥillah** Saudi Arabia
79 B2 **Al Ḥinnāh** Saudi Arabia
78 B3 **Al Ḥudaydah** Yemen
79 B2 **Al Hufūf** Saudi Arabia
115 D2 **Al Ḥulayq al Kabīr** *hills* Libya
79 C2 **'Alīābād** Iran
111 C3 **Aliağa** Turkey
111 B2 **Aliakmonas** *r.* Greece
81 C2 **Äli Bayramlı** Azer.
107 C2 **Alicante** Spain
139 D3 **Alice** U.S.A.
109 C3 **Alice, Punta** *pt* Italy
51 C2 **Alice Springs** Austr.
77 D3 **Alichur** Tajik.
74 B2 **Aligarh** India
81 C2 **Alīgūdarz** Iran
69 E1 **Alihe** China
118 B3 **Alima** *r.* Congo
118 C2 **Alindao** C.A.R.
111 C3 **Aliova** *r.* Turkey
74 B2 **Alīrājpur** India
117 C3 **Ali Sabieh** Djibouti
78 A1 **Al 'Īsāwīyah** Saudi Arabia
123 C3 **Aliwal North** S. Africa
115 E2 **Al Jaghbūb** Libya
78 B2 **Al Jahrah** Kuwait
79 C2 **Al Jamalīyah** Qatar
115 E2 **Al Jawf** Libya
78 A2 **Al Jawf** Saudi Arabia
115 D1 **Al Jawsh** Libya
106 B2 **Aljezur** Port.
79 B2 **Al Jubayl** Saudi Arabia
78 B2 **Al Jubaylah** Saudi Arabia
115 D2 **Al Jufra Oasis** Libya
78 B2 **Al Junaynah** Saudi Arabia
106 B2 **Aljustrel** Port.
78 B2 **Al Kahfah** Saudi Arabia
79 C2 **Al Kāmil** Oman
80 B2 **Al Karak** Jordan
81 C2 **Al Kāẓimīyah** Iraq
79 C2 **Al Khābūrah** Oman
78 B2 **Al Khamāsīn** Saudi Arabia
79 C2 **Al Khaşab** Oman
78 B3 **Al Khawkhah** Yemen
79 C2 **Al Khawr** Qatar
115 E2 **Al Khufrah** Libya
115 D1 **Al Khums** Libya
79 B2 **Al Khunn** Saudi Arabia
79 C2 **Al Kidan** *well* Saudi Arabia
79 C2 **Al Kir'ānah** Qatar
100 B1 **Alkmaar** Neth.
81 C2 **Al Kūt** Iraq
Al Kuwayt Kuwait *see* Kuwait
80 B2 **Al Lādhiqīyah** Syria
75 C2 **Allahabad** India
83 K2 **Allakh-Yun'** Rus. Fed.
62 A2 **Allanmyo** Myanmar
78 A2 **'Allâqi, Wâdi el** *watercourse* Egypt
141 D2 **Allegheny** *r.* U.S.A.
141 C3 **Allegheny Mountains** U.S.A.
97 B1 **Allen, Lough** *l.* Rep. of Ireland
145 B2 **Allende** Mex.
145 B2 **Allende** Mex.
141 D2 **Allentown** U.S.A.
73 B4 **Alleppey** India
101 D1 **Aller** *r.* Ger.
136 C2 **Alliance** *NE* U.S.A.
140 C2 **Alliance** *OH* U.S.A.
78 B2 **Al Līth** Saudi Arabia
96 C2 **Alloa** U.K.
131 C3 **Alma** Can.
Alma-Ata Kazakh. *see* Almaty
106 B2 **Almada** Port.
106 C2 **Almadén** Spain
Al Madīnah Saudi Arabia *see* **Medina**
80 B2 **Al Mafraq** Jordan
114 B2 **Al Mahbas** Western Sahara
78 B3 **Al Maḥwīt** Yemen
78 B2 **Al Majma'ah** Saudi Arabia
77 C2 **Almalyk** Uzbek.
Al Manāmah Bahrain *see* Manama
135 B2 **Almanor, Lake** U.S.A.
107 C2 **Almansa** Spain
79 C2 **Al Mariyyah** U.A.E.
115 E1 **Al Marj** Libya
77 D2 **Almaty** Kazakh.
81 C2 **Al Mawşil** Iraq
81 C2 **Al Mayādīn** Syria
106 C1 **Almazán** Spain
151 D3 **Almeirim** Brazil
100 C1 **Almelo** Neth.
155 D1 **Almenara** Brazil
106 B1 **Almendra, Embalse de** *resr* Spain
106 B2 **Almendralejo** Spain
106 C2 **Almería** Spain
106 C2 **Almería, Golfo de** *b.* Spain
87 E3 **Al'met'yevsk** Rus. Fed.
78 B2 **Al Mindak** Saudi Arabia
79 B2 **Al Mish'āb** Saudi Arabia
106 B2 **Almodôvar** Port.
106 B2 **Almonte** Spain
75 B2 **Almora** India
79 B2 **Al Mubarrez** Saudi Arabia
79 C2 **Al Muḍaibī** Oman
80 B3 **Al Mudawwarah** Jordan
79 B3 **Al Mukallā** Yemen
78 B3 **Al Mukhā** Yemen
106 C2 **Almuñécar** Spain
81 C2 **Al Muqdādīyah** Iraq
78 A2 **Al Musayjīd** Saudi Arabia
78 A2 **Al Muwayliḥ** Saudi Arabia
111 B3 **Almyros** Greece
96 B2 **Alness** U.K.
98 C2 **Alnwick** U.K.
62 A1 **Along** India
111 B3 **Alonnisos** *i.* Greece
59 C3 **Alor** *i.* Indon.
59 C3 **Alor, Kepulauan** *is* Indon.
60 B1 **Alor Setar** Malaysia
Alor Star Malaysia *see* Alor Setar
Alost Belgium *see* **Aalst**
59 E3 **Alotau** P.N.G.
86 C2 **Alozero** Rus. Fed.
140 C1 **Alpena** U.S.A.
160 Q1 **Alpha Ridge** *sea feature* Arctic Ocean
100 B1 **Alphen aan den Rijn** Neth.
138 B2 **Alpine** *AZ* U.S.A.
139 C2 **Alpine** *TX* U.S.A.
84 E4 **Alps** *mts* Europe
79 B3 **Al Qa'āmīyāt** *reg.* Saudi Arabia
115 D1 **Al Qaddāḥīyah** Libya
78 B2 **Al Qā'īyah** Saudi Arabia
81 C2 **Al Qāmishlī** Syria
80 B2 **Al Qaryatayn** Syria
79 B2 **Al Qaşab** Saudi Arabia
79 B3 **Al Qaṭn** Yemen
115 D2 **Al Qaṭrūn** Libya
80 B2 **Al Qunayṭirah** Syria
78 B3 **Al Qunfidhah** Saudi Arabia
78 B2 **Al Quwārah** Saudi Arabia
78 B2 **Al Quwayīyah** Saudi Arabia
101 D2 **Alsfeld** Ger.
98 B2 **Alston** U.K.
92 H2 **Alta** Norway
92 H2 **Altaelva** *r.* Norway
68 B1 **Altai Mountains** Asia
143 D2 **Altamaha** *r.* U.S.A.
151 D3 **Altamira** Brazil
109 C2 **Altamura** Italy
144 A1 **Altar, Desierto de** *des.* Mex.
77 E2 **Altay** China
68 C1 **Altay** Mongolia

105 D2 **Altdorf** Switz.
107 C2 **Altea** Spain
92 H1 **Alteidet** Norway
101 F2 **Altenburg** Ger.
100 C2 **Altenkirchen (Westerwald)** Ger.
101 F1 **Altentreptow** Ger.
111 C3 **Altınoluk** Turkey
111 D3 **Altıntaş** Turkey
152 B1 **Altiplano** *plain* Bol.
96 B1 **Altnaharra** U.K.
154 B1 **Alto Araguaia** Brazil
107 C1 **Alto del Moncayo** *mt.* Spain
154 B1 **Alto Garças** Brazil
121 C2 **Alto Ligonha** Moz.
121 C2 **Alto Molócuè** Moz.
99 C4 **Alton** U.K.
137 E3 **Alton** U.S.A.
129 E3 **Altona** Can.
141 D2 **Altoona** U.S.A.
154 B1 **Alto Sucuriú** Brazil
102 C2 **Altötting** Ger.
68 C2 **Altun Shan** *mt.* China
68 B2 **Altun Shan** *mts* China
134 B2 **Alturas** U.S.A.
139 D2 **Altus** U.S.A.
88 C2 **Alūksne** Latvia
78 A2 **Al 'Ulā** Saudi Arabia
115 D1 **Al 'Uqaylah** Libya
91 C3 **Alushta** Ukr.
115 E2 **Al 'Uwaynāt** Libya
139 D1 **Alva** U.S.A.
145 C3 **Alvarado** Mex.
93 F3 **Älvdalen** Sweden
93 F3 **Älvdalen** *val.* Sweden
92 H2 **Älvsbyn** Sweden
78 A2 **Al Wajh** Saudi Arabia
79 C2 **Al Wakrah** Qatar
74 B2 **Alwar** India
81 C2 **Al Widyān** *plat.* Iraq/Saudi Arabia
Alxa Youqi China *see* **Ehen Hudag**
Alxa Zuoqi China *see* **Bayan Hot**
51 C1 **Alyangula** Austr.
88 B3 **Alytus** Lith.
136 C1 **Alzada** U.S.A.
101 D3 **Alzey** Ger.
50 C2 **Amadeus, Lake** *salt flat* Austr.
127 H2 **Amadjuak Lake** Can.
106 B2 **Amadora** Port.
78 B2 **Amā'ir** Saudi Arabia
67 B4 **Amakusa-Shimo-shima** *i.* Japan
93 F4 **Åmål** Sweden
111 B3 **Amaliada** Greece
59 D3 **Amamapare** Indon.
154 A2 **Amambaí** Brazil
154 B2 **Amambaí** *r.* Brazil
154 A2 **Amambaí, Serra de** *hills* Brazil/Para.
69 E3 **Amami-Ō-shima** *i.* Japan
69 E3 **Amami-shotō** *is* Japan
77 C1 **Amangel'dy** Kazakh.
109 C3 **Amantea** Italy
123 D3 **Amanzimtoti** S. Africa
151 D2 **Amapá** Brazil
106 B2 **Amareleja** Port.
88 B2 **Ämari** Estonia
139 C1 **Amarillo** U.S.A.
108 B2 **Amaro, Monte** *mt.* Italy
80 B1 **Amasya** Turkey
150 D2 **Amazon** *r.* S. America
151 E2 **Amazon, Mouths of the** Brazil
Amazonas *r.* S. America *see* **Amazon**
157 I5 **Amazon Cone** *sea feature* S. Atlantic Ocean
74 B1 **Ambala** India
121 □D3 **Ambalavao** Madag.
121 □D2 **Ambanja** Madag.
104 B3 **Ambarès-et-Lagarve** France
150 B3 **Ambato** Ecuador
121 □D2 **Ambato Boeny** Madag.
121 □D3 **Ambato Finandrahana** Madag.
121 □D2 **Ambatolampy** Madag.
121 □D2 **Ambatondrazaka** Madag.
101 E3 **Amberg** Ger.
146 B3 **Ambergris Cay** *i.* Belize
75 C2 **Ambikapur** India
121 □D2 **Ambilobe** Madag.
98 C2 **Amble** U.K.
98 B2 **Ambleside** U.K.
121 □D3 **Amboasary** Madag.
121 □D2 **Ambodifotatra** Madag.
121 □D2 **Ambohidratrimo** Madag.
121 □D3 **Ambohimahasoa** Madag.
Amboina Indon. *see* **Ambon**
59 C3 **Ambon** Indon.
59 C3 **Ambon** *i.* Indon.
121 □D3 **Ambositra** Madag.
121 □D3 **Ambovombe** Madag.
135 C4 **Amboy** U.S.A.
Ambre, Cap d' *c.* Madag. *see* **Bobaomby, Tanjona**
120 A1 **Ambriz** Angola
Ambrizete Angola *see* **N'zeto**
86 F2 **Amderma** Rus. Fed.
75 D1 **Amdo** China
145 B2 **Amealco** Mex.
144 B2 **Ameca** Mex.
100 B1 **Ameland** *i.* Neth.
154 C2 **Americana** Brazil
55 D4 **American-Antarctic Ridge** *sea feature* S. Atlantic Ocean
134 D2 **American Falls** U.S.A.
134 D2 **American Falls Reservoir** U.S.A.
135 D2 **American Fork** U.S.A.
49 J5 **American Samoa** *terr.* S. Pacific Ocean
143 D2 **Americus** U.S.A.
100 B1 **Amersfoort** Neth.
55 H2 **Amery Ice Shelf** Antarctica
137 E2 **Ames** U.S.A.
111 B3 **Amfissa** Greece
83 J2 **Amga** Rus. Fed.
66 C1 **Amgu** Rus. Fed.
115 C2 **Amguid** Alg.
83 K3 **Amgun'** *r.* Rus. Fed.
131 D3 **Amherst** Can.
104 C2 **Amiens** France
79 C3 **Amilḥayt, Wādī al** *r.* Oman
73 B3 **Amindivi Islands** India
122 A1 **Aminuis** Namibia
74 A2 **Amir Chah** Pak.
129 D2 **Amisk Lake** Can.
139 C3 **Amistad Reservoir** Mex./U.S.A.
98 A3 **Amlwch** U.K.
80 B2 **'Ammān** Jordan
127 J2 **Ammassalik** Greenland
78 B3 **Am Nābiyah** Yemen
81 D2 **Amol** Iran
111 C3 **Amorgos** *i.* Greece
142 C2 **Amory** U.S.A.
130 C3 **Amos** Can.
Amoy China *see* **Xiamen**
121 □D3 **Ampanihy** Madag.
155 C2 **Amparo** Brazil
121 □D2 **Ampasimanolotra** Madag.
107 D1 **Amposta** Spain
78 B3 **Amrān** Yemen
Amraoti India *see* **Amravati**
74 B2 **Amravati** India
74 B2 **Amreli** India
74 B1 **Amritsar** India
100 B1 **Amstelveen** Neth.
100 B1 **Amsterdam** Neth.
123 D2 **Amsterdam** S. Africa
156 A8 **Amsterdam, Île** *i.* Indian Ocean
103 C2 **Amstetten** Austria
115 E3 **Am Timan** Chad
76 B2 **Amudar'ya** *r.* Asia
126 F1 **Amund Ringnes Island** Can.
55 J3 **Amundsen, Mount** Antarctica
160 H1 **Amundsen Basin** *sea feature* Arctic Ocean
126 D2 **Amundsen Gulf** Can.
55 P2 **Amundsen Ridge** *sea feature* Southern Ocean
55 P2 **Amundsen Sea** Antarctica
61 C2 **Amuntai** Indon.
Amur *r.* China/Rus. Fed. *see* **Heilong Jiang**
78 A3 **'Amur, Wadi** *watercourse* Sudan
61 D2 **Anabanua** Indon.
83 I2 **Anabar** *r.* Rus. Fed.
83 I2 **Anabarskiy Zaliv** *b.* Rus. Fed.
150 C2 **Anaco** Venez.
134 D1 **Anaconda** U.S.A.
134 B1 **Anacortes** U.S.A.
139 D1 **Anadarko** U.S.A.
80 B1 **Anadolu Dağları** *mts* Turkey
83 M2 **Anadyr'** Rus. Fed.
83 M2 **Anadyr'** *r.* Rus. Fed.
81 C2 **'Ānah** Iraq
145 B2 **Anáhuac** Mex.
73 B3 **Anai Mudi Peak** India
121 □D2 **Analalava** Madag.
121 □D3 **Analavelona** *mts* Madag.
60 B1 **Anambas, Kepulauan** *is* Indon.
137 E2 **Anamosa** U.S.A.
80 B2 **Anamur** Turkey
67 B4 **Anan** Japan
73 B3 **Anantapur** India
74 B1 **Anantnag** Jammu and Kashmir
90 B2 **Anan'yiv** Ukr.
91 D3 **Anapa** Rus. Fed.
154 C1 **Anápolis** Brazil
81 D2 **Anār** Iran
152 B2 **Añatuya** Arg.
65 B2 **Anbyon** N. Korea
104 B2 **Ancenis** France
126 C2 **Anchorage** U.S.A.
108 B2 **Ancona** Italy
153 A4 **Ancud** Chile
Anda China *see* **Daqing**
93 E3 **Åndalsnes** Norway
106 C2 **Andalucía** *aut. comm.* Spain
Andalusia *aut. comm.* Spain *see* **Andalucía**
142 C2 **Andalusia** U.S.A.
159 F3 **Andaman Basin** *sea feature* Indian Ocean
73 D3 **Andaman Islands** India
63 A2 **Andaman Sea** Indian Ocean
121 □D2 **Andapa** Madag.
100 B2 **Andelst** Neth.
92 G2 **Andenes** Norway
100 B2 **Andenne** Belgium
100 B2 **Anderlecht** Belgium
105 D2 **Andermatt** Switz.
126 D2 **Anderson** *r.* Can.
126 C2 **Anderson** *AK* U.S.A.
140 B2 **Anderson** *IN* U.S.A.
143 D2 **Anderson** *SC* U.S.A.
148 C3 **Andes** *mts* S. America
121 □D2 **Andilamena** Madag.
121 □D2 **Andilanatoby** Madag.
77 D2 **Andizhan** Uzbek.
74 A1 **Andkhvoy** Afgh.
121 □D2 **Andoany** Madag.
Andong China *see* **Dandong**
65 B2 **Andong** S. Korea
104 C3 **Andorra** *country* Europe
104 C3 **Andorra la Vella** Andorra
99 C4 **Andover** U.K.
154 B2 **Andradina** Brazil
89 D2 **Andreapol'** Rus. Fed.
155 D2 **Andrelândia** Brazil
139 C2 **Andrews** U.S.A.
109 C2 **Andria** Italy
121 □D3 **Androka** Madag.
Andropov Rus. Fed. *see* **Rybinsk**
146 C2 **Andros** *i.* Bahamas
111 B3 **Andros** Greece
111 B3 **Andros** *i.* Greece
143 E4 **Andros Town** Bahamas
73 B3 **Āndrott** *i.* India
90 B1 **Andrushivka** Ukr.
92 G2 **Andselv** Norway
106 C2 **Andújar** Spain
120 A2 **Andulo** Angola
114 C3 **Anéfis** Mali
147 D3 **Anegada Passage** Virgin Is (U.K.)
114 C4 **Aného** Togo
107 D1 **Aneto** *mt.* Spain
115 D3 **Aney** Niger
83 H3 **Angara** *r.* Rus. Fed.
68 C1 **Angarsk** Rus. Fed.
93 G3 **Ånge** Sweden
Angel, Salto del *waterfall* Venez. *see* **Angel Falls**
144 A2 **Ángel de la Guarda, Isla** *i.* Mex.
64 B2 **Angeles** Phil.
150 C2 **Angel Falls** Venez.
93 F4 **Ängelholm** Sweden
92 G3 **Ångermanälven** *r.* Sweden
104 B2 **Angers** France
129 E1 **Angikuni Lake** Can.
52 B3 **Anglesea** Austr.
98 A3 **Anglesey** *i.* U.K.
121 C2 **Angoche** Moz.
79 C2 **Angohrān** Iran
120 A2 **Angola** *country* Africa
140 C2 **Angola** U.S.A.
158 F6 **Angola Basin** *sea featur* S. Atlantic Ocean
128 A2 **Angoon** U.S.A.
104 C2 **Angoulême** France
155 D2 **Angra dos Reis** Brazil
77 D2 **Angren** Uzbek.
147 D3 **Anguilla** *terr.* West Indie
93 F4 **Anholt** *i.* Denmark
71 B3 **Anhua** China
70 A2 **Anhui** *prov.* China
154 B1 **Anhumas** Brazil
Anhwei *prov.* China *see* **Anhui**
154 C1 **Anicuns** Brazil
66 D1 **Aniva, Mys** *c.* Rus. Fed.
66 D1 **Aniva, Zaliv** *b.* Rus. Fed
88 C1 **Anjalankoski** Fin.
104 B2 **Anjou** *reg.* France
65 B2 **Anjŭ** N. Korea
70 A2 **Ankang** China
80 B2 **Ankara** Turkey
121 □D3 **Ankazoabo** Madag.
121 □D2 **Ankazobe** Madag.
137 E2 **Ankeny** U.S.A.
102 C1 **Anklam** Ger.
121 □D2 **Ankofa** *mt.* Madag.
70 B2 **Anlu** China
55 G3 **Ann, Cape** Antarctica
141 E2 **Ann, Cape** U.S.A.
89 F3 **Anna** Rus. Fed.
115 C1 **Annaba** Alg.
101 F2 **Annaberg-Buchholtz** G
80 B2 **An Nabk** Syria
78 B2 **An Nafūd** *des.* Saudi Arabia
150 D2 **Annai** Guyana
81 C2 **An Najaf** Iraq
63 B2 **Annam Highlands** *mts* Laos/Vietnam
96 C3 **Annan** U.K.
141 D3 **Annapolis** U.S.A.
75 C2 **Annapurna I** *mt.* Jammu and Kashmir/Ne
140 C2 **Ann Arbor** U.S.A.
150 D2 **Anna Regina** Guyana
An Nás Rep. of Ireland s **Naas**
81 C2 **An Nāṣirīyah** Iraq
115 D1 **An Nawfalīyah** Libya
105 D2 **Annecy** France
78 B3 **An Nimāş** Saudi Arabia
71 A3 **Anning** China
142 C2 **Anniston** U.S.A.
105 C2 **Annonay** France
79 B2 **An Nu'ayrīyah** Saudi Arabia
121 □D2 **Anorontany, Tanjona** *h* Madag.
111 C3 **Ano Viannos** Greece
71 B3 **Anpu** China
70 B2 **Anqing** China
101 E3 **Ansbach** Ger.
70 C1 **Anshan** China
71 A3 **Anshun** China
78 A1 **An Sirhān, Wādī** *watercourse* Saudi Arabi
139 D2 **Anson** U.S.A.
114 C3 **Ansongo** Mali
96 C2 **Anstruther** U.K.
150 B4 **Antabamba** Peru
80 B2 **Antakya** Turkey
121 □E2 **Antalaha** Madag.
80 B2 **Antalya** Turkey
80 B2 **Antalya Körfezi** *g.* Turk
121 □D2 **Antananarivo** Madag.
55 A2 **Antarctic Peninsula** Antarctica
96 B2 **An Teallach** *mt.* U.K.
106 C2 **Antequera** Spain
138 B2 **Anthony** U.S.A.
114 B2 **Anti Atlas** *mts* Morocco
105 D3 **Antibes** France
131 D3 **Anticosti, Île d'** *i.* Can.
Anticosti Island Can. *se* **Anticosti, Île d'**
131 D3 **Antigonish** Can.
147 D3 **Antigua** *i.* Antigua
147 D3 **Antigua and Barbuda** *country* West Indies
145 C2 **Antiguo-Morelos** Mex.
111 B3 **Antikythira** *i.* Greece
Antioch Turkey *see* **Antakya**
49 I8 **Antipodes Islands** N.Z.
An t-Ob U.K. *see* **Leverburgh**
152 A2 **Antofagasta** Chile
154 C3 **Antonina** Brazil
António Enes Moz. *see* **Angoche**
97 C1 **Antrim** U.K.

7 C1 **Antrim Hills** U.K.
1 □D2 **Antsalova** Madag.
Antseranana Madag. *see* Antsirañana
1 □D2 **Antsirabe** Madag.
1 □D2 **Antsirañana** Madag.
1 □D2 **Antsohihy** Madag.
Antwerp Belgium *see* Antwerpen
0 B2 **Antwerpen** Belgium
An Uaimh Rep. of Ireland *see* **Navan**
5 C2 **Anugul** India
4 B2 **Anupgarh** India
3 C4 **Anuradhapura** Sri Lanka
Anvers Belgium *see* Antwerpen
3 C2 **Anxi** China
4 C3 **Anxious Bay** Austr.
0 B2 **Anyang** China
5 B2 **Anyang** S. Korea
8 B2 **Anzio** Italy
7 C4 **Aoga-shima** *i.* Japan
5 D2 **Aomori** Japan
Aoraki *mt.* N.Z. *see* **Cook, Mount**
8 A1 **Aosta** Italy
4 B2 **Aoukâr** *reg.* Mali/Maur.
4 C2 **Aoulef** Alg.
5 D2 **Aozou** Chad
3 D3 **Apalachee Bay** U.S.A.
0 C3 **Apaporis** *r.* Col.
4 B2 **Aparecida do Tabuado** Brazil
4 B2 **Aparri** Phil.
5 C2 **Apatity** Rus. Fed.
4 B3 **Apatzingán** Mex.
0 B1 **Apeldoorn** Neth.
0 C1 **Apen** Ger.
Apennines *mts* Italy *see* Appennino
9 J5 **Apia** Samoa
4 C2 **Apiaí** Brazil
4 B3 **Apo, Mount** *vol.* Phil.
1 E2 **Apolda** Ger.
2 B3 **Apollo Bay** Austr.
3 D3 **Apopka** U.S.A.
3 D3 **Apopka, Lake** U.S.A.
4 B1 **Aporé** Brazil
4 B1 **Aporé** *r.* Brazil
0 A1 **Apostle Islands** U.S.A.
0 B2 **Apostolos Andreas, Cape** Cyprus
1 C2 **Apostolove** Ukr.
3 F3 **Appalachian Mountains** U.S.A.
8 A2 **Appennino** *mts* Italy
3 D2 **Appin** Austr.
0 C1 **Appingedam** Neth.
3 B2 **Appleby-in-Westmorland** U.K.
0 B2 **Appleton** U.S.A.
8 B2 **Aprilia** Italy
2 A1 **Aprunyi** India
1 D3 **Apsheronsk** Rus. Fed.
Apsheronskaya Rus. Fed. *see* **Apsheronsk**
4 B2 **Apucarana** Brazil
4 B2 **Apucarana, Serra da** *hills* Brazil
4 A3 **Apurahuan** Phil.
7 D4 **Apure** *r.* Venez.
8 A2 **Aqaba, Gulf of** Asia
1 D2 **'Aqdā** Iran
5 C1 **Aqqikkol Hu** *salt l.* China
4 A1 **Aquidauana** *r.* Brazil
4 B3 **Aquitaine** *reg.* France
5 C2 **Ara** India
7 A4 **Arab, Bahr el** *watercourse* Sudan
6 B4 **Arabian Sea** Indian Ocean
1 F4 **Aracaju** Brazil
4 A2 **Aracanguy, Montes de** *hills* Para.
1 F3 **Aracati** Brazil
4 B2 **Araçatuba** Brazil
5 D1 **Aracruz** Brazil
5 D1 **Araçuaí** Brazil
0 B1 **Arad** Romania
5 E3 **Arada** Chad
9 C2 **'Arādah** U.A.E.
6 C6 **Arafura Sea** Austr./Indon.
4 B1 **Aragarças** Brazil
7 C1 **Aragón** *aut. comm.* Spain
7 C1 **Aragón** *r.* Spain
1 E3 **Araguaia** *r.* Brazil
4 B1 **Araguaiana** Brazil
1 E3 **Araguaína** Brazil
4 C1 **Araguari** Brazil
7 C3 **Arai** Japan
5 C2 **Arak** Alg.
81 C2 **Arāk** Iran
62 A1 **Arakan Yoma** *mts* Myanmar
81 C1 **Araks** *r.* Armenia/Turkey
76 C2 **Aral Sea** *salt l.* Kazakh./Uzbek.
76 C2 **Aral'sk** Kazakh.
Aral'skoye More *salt l.* Kazakh./Uzbek. *see* Aral Sea
106 C1 **Aranda de Duero** Spain
109 D2 **Aranđelovac** Yugo.
97 B1 **Aran Island** Rep. of Ireland
97 B2 **Aran Islands** Rep. of Ireland
106 C1 **Aranjuez** Spain
122 A1 **Aranos** Namibia
139 D3 **Aransas Pass** U.S.A.
67 B4 **Arao** Japan
114 B3 **Araouane** Mali
151 F3 **Arapiraca** Brazil
154 B2 **Arapongas** Brazil
154 C3 **Araquari** Brazil
78 B1 **'Ar'ar** Saudi Arabia
154 C2 **Araraquara** Brazil
151 D3 **Araras** Brazil
154 C2 **Araras** Brazil
154 B1 **Araras, Serra das** *hills* Brazil
154 B3 **Araras, Serra das** *mts* Brazil
81 C2 **Ararat** Armenia
52 B3 **Ararat** Austr.
81 C2 **Ararat, Mount** Turkey
155 D2 **Araruama, Lago de** *lag.* Brazil
155 E1 **Arataca** Brazil
Aratürük China *see* **Yiwu**
150 B2 **Arauca** Col.
154 C1 **Araxá** Brazil
81 C2 **Arbīl** Iraq
129 E2 **Arborg** Can.
96 C2 **Arbroath** U.K.
74 A2 **Arbu Lut, Dasht-e** *des.* Afgh.
104 B3 **Arcachon** France
143 D3 **Arcadia** U.S.A.
134 B2 **Arcata** U.S.A.
145 B3 **Arcelia** Mex.
86 D2 **Archangel** Rus. Fed.
51 D1 **Archer** *r.* Austr.
134 D2 **Arco** U.S.A.
106 B2 **Arcos de la Frontera** Spain
127 G2 **Arctic Bay** Can.
Arctic Institute Islands Rus. Fed. *see* **Arkticheskogo Instituta, Ostrova**
160 J1 **Arctic Mid-Ocean Ridge** *sea feature* Arctic Ocean
160 **Arctic Ocean**
126 D2 **Arctic Red** *r.* Can.
81 C2 **Ardabīl** Iran
81 C1 **Ardahan** Turkey
93 E3 **Årdalstangen** Norway
97 C2 **Ardee** Rep. of Ireland
100 B3 **Ardennes** *plat.* Belgium
135 B3 **Arden Town** U.S.A.
81 D2 **Ardestān** Iran
97 D1 **Ardglass** U.K.
53 C2 **Ardlethan** Austr.
139 D2 **Ardmore** U.S.A.
96 A2 **Ardnamurchan, Point of** U.K.
52 A2 **Ardrossan** Austr.
96 B3 **Ardrossan** U.K.
96 B2 **Ardvasar** U.K.
135 B3 **Arena, Point** U.S.A.
93 E4 **Arendal** Norway
100 B2 **Arendonk** Belgium
101 E1 **Arendsee (Altmark)** Ger.
150 B4 **Arequipa** Peru
151 D3 **Arere** Brazil
106 C1 **Arévalo** Spain
108 B2 **Arezzo** Italy
108 B2 **Argenta** Italy
104 B2 **Argentan** France
153 C2 **Argentina** *country* S. America
158 D7 **Argentine Basin** *sea feature* S. Atlantic Ocean
157 I8 **Argentine Rise** *sea feature* S. Atlantic Ocean
153 A5 **Argentino, Lago** *l.* Arg.
104 C2 **Argenton-sur-Creuse** France
110 C2 **Argeș** *r.* Romania
74 A1 **Arghandab** *r.* Afgh.
111 B3 **Argolikos Kolpos** *b.* Greece
111 B3 **Argos** Greece
111 B3 **Argostoli** Greece
107 C1 **Arguís** Spain
69 E1 **Argun'** *r.* China/Rus. Fed.
131 D3 **Argyle** Can.
50 B1 **Argyle, Lake** Austr.
Argyrokastron Albania *see* Gjirokastër
Ar Horqin Qi China *see* Tianshan
93 F4 **Århus** Denmark
122 A2 **Ariamsvlei** Namibia
152 A1 **Arica** Chile
96 A2 **Arinagour** U.K.
155 C1 **Arinos** Brazil
150 D4 **Aripuanã** Brazil
150 C3 **Aripuanã** *r.* Brazil
150 C3 **Ariquemes** Brazil
154 B1 **Ariranhá** *r.* Brazil
96 B2 **Arisaig** U.K.
96 B2 **Arisaig, Sound of** *sea chan.* U.K.
138 A2 **Arizona** *state* U.S.A.
144 A1 **Arizpe** Mex.
78 B2 **'Arjah** Saudi Arabia
61 C2 **Arjasa** Indon.
92 G2 **Arjeplog** Sweden
142 B2 **Arkadelphia** U.S.A.
77 C1 **Arkalyk** Kazakh.
142 B2 **Arkansas** *r.* U.S.A.
142 B1 **Arkansas** *state* U.S.A.
137 D3 **Arkansas City** U.S.A.
Arkhangel'sk Rus. Fed. *see* **Archangel**
97 C2 **Arklow** Rep. of Ireland
102 C1 **Arkona, Kap** *c.* Ger.
82 G1 **Arkticheskogo Instituta, Ostrova** *is* Rus. Fed.
105 C3 **Arles** France
139 D2 **Arlington** U.S.A.
140 B2 **Arlington Heights** U.S.A.
115 C3 **Arlit** Niger
100 B3 **Arlon** Belgium
97 C1 **Armagh** U.K.
116 B2 **Armant** Egypt
87 D4 **Armavir** Rus. Fed.
81 C1 **Armenia** *country* Asia
150 B2 **Armenia** Col.
Armenopolis Romania *see* Gherla
144 B3 **Armeria** Mex.
53 D2 **Armidale** Austr.
134 D1 **Armington** U.S.A.
130 B2 **Armstrong** Can.
91 C2 **Armyans'k** Ukr.
Armyanskaya S.S.R. *country* Asia *see* **Armenia**
80 B2 **Arnaoutis, Cape** Cyprus
130 D2 **Arnaud** *r.* Can.
Arnauti, Cape Cyprus *see* Arnaoutis, Cape
100 B2 **Arnhem** Neth.
51 C1 **Arnhem, Cape** Austr.
51 C1 **Arnhem Bay** Austr.
51 C1 **Arnhem Land** *reg.* Austr.
108 B2 **Arno** *r.* Italy
52 A2 **Arno Bay** Austr.
130 C3 **Arnprior** Can.
101 D2 **Arnsberg** Ger.
101 E2 **Arnstadt** Ger.
122 A2 **Aroab** Namibia
154 B2 **Aroeira** Brazil
101 D2 **Arolsen** Ger.
78 A3 **Aroma** Sudan
108 A1 **Arona** Italy
144 B2 **Aros** *r.* Mex.
Arquipélago dos Açores *aut. reg.* N. Atlantic Ocean *see* **Azores**
Arrah India *see* **Ara**
81 C2 **Ar Ramādī** Iraq
96 B3 **Arran** *i.* U.K.
80 B2 **Ar Raqqah** Syria
105 C1 **Arras** France
78 B2 **Ar-Rass** Saudi Arabia
79 C2 **Ar Rayyān** Qatar
150 C2 **Arrecifal** Col.
145 C3 **Arriagá** Mex.
79 C2 **Ar Rimāl** *reg.* Saudi Arabia
Ar Riyāḍ Saudi Arabia *see* Riyadh
54 A2 **Arrowtown** N.Z.
135 B3 **Arroyo Grande** U.S.A.
145 C2 **Arroyo Seco** Mex.
79 C2 **Ar Rustāq** Oman
81 C2 **Ar Ruṭbah** Iraq
78 B2 **Ar Ruwayḍah** Saudi Arabia
81 D3 **Arsenajān** Iran
66 B2 **Arsen'yev** Rus. Fed.
111 B3 **Arta** Greece
144 B3 **Arteaga** Mex.
66 B2 **Artem** Rus. Fed.
91 D2 **Artemivs'k** Ukr.
104 C2 **Artenay** France
138 C2 **Artesia** U.S.A.
51 E2 **Arthur Point** Austr.
54 B2 **Arthur's Pass** N.Z.
152 C3 **Artigas** Uru.
129 D1 **Artillery Lake** Can.
123 C1 **Artisia** Botswana
104 C1 **Artois** *reg.* France
90 B2 **Artsyz** Ukr.
Artur de Paiva Angola *see* Kuvango
77 D3 **Artux** China
81 C1 **Artvin** Turkey
59 C3 **Aru, Kepulauan** *is* Indon.
119 D2 **Arua** Uganda
147 D3 **Aruba** *terr.* West Indies
75 C2 **Arun** *r.* Nepal
119 D3 **Arusha** Tanz.
136 B3 **Arvada** U.S.A.
68 C1 **Arvayheer** Mongolia
129 E1 **Arviat** Can.
92 G2 **Arvidsjaur** Sweden
93 F4 **Arvika** Sweden
108 A2 **Arzachena** *Sardinia* Italy
87 D3 **Arzamas** Rus. Fed.
107 C2 **Arzew** Alg.
100 C2 **Arzfeld** Ger.
Arzila Morocco *see* **Asilah**
101 F2 **Aš** Czech Rep.
115 C4 **Asaba** Nigeria
66 D2 **Asahi-dake** *vol.* Japan
66 D2 **Asahikawa** Japan
78 B3 **Āsalē** *l.* Eth.
75 C2 **Asansol** India
117 C3 **Āsayita** Eth.
130 C3 **Asbestos** Can.
122 B2 **Asbestos Mountains** S. Africa
119 E2 **Āsbe Teferi** Eth.
109 C2 **Ascea** Italy
152 B1 **Ascensión** Bol.
113 B6 **Ascension** *i.* S. Atlantic Ocean
101 D3 **Aschaffenburg** Ger.
100 C2 **Ascheberg** Ger.
101 E2 **Aschersleben** Ger.
108 B2 **Ascoli Piceno** Italy
119 D2 **Āsela** Eth.
92 G3 **Åsele** Sweden
111 B2 **Asenovgrad** Bulg.
78 B2 **Asharat** Saudi Arabia
50 A2 **Ashburton** *watercourse* Austr.
54 B2 **Ashburton** N.Z.
142 B2 **Ashdown** U.S.A.
143 D1 **Asheville** U.S.A.
53 D1 **Ashford** Austr.
97 C2 **Ashford** Rep. of Ireland
99 D4 **Ashford** U.K.
76 B3 **Ashgabat** Turkm.
66 D2 **Ashibetsu** Japan
98 C2 **Ashington** U.K.
67 B4 **Ashizuri-misaki** *pt* Japan
Ashkhabad Turkm. *see* Ashgabat
136 D3 **Ashland** *KS* U.S.A.
140 C3 **Ashland** *KY* U.S.A.
140 C2 **Ashland** *OH* U.S.A.
134 B2 **Ashland** *OR* U.S.A.
140 A1 **Ashland** *WI* U.S.A.
53 C1 **Ashley** Austr.
88 C3 **Ashmyany** Belarus
66 D2 **Ashoro** Japan
81 C2 **Ash Shabakah** Iraq
78 B3 **Ash Sharawrah** Saudi Arabia
Ash Shāriqah U.A.E. *see* Sharjah
81 C2 **Ash Sharqāṭ** Iraq
81 C2 **Ash Shaṭrah** Iraq
78 B3 **Ash Shaykh 'Uthman** Yemen
79 B3 **Ash Shiḥr** Yemen
79 C2 **Ash Shināṣ** Oman
78 B2 **Ash Shu'āybah** Saudi Arabia
78 B2 **Ash Shu'bah** Saudi Arabia
78 B2 **Ash Shubaykīyah** Saudi Arabia
78 B2 **Ash Shumlūl** Saudi Arabia
78 B3 **Ash Shuqayq** Saudi Arabia
115 D2 **Ash Shuwayrif** Libya
140 C2 **Ashtabula** U.S.A.
131 D2 **Ashuanipi Lake** Can.
75 B3 **Asifabad** India
106 B2 **Asilah** Morocco

108 A2 **Asinara, Golfo dell'** *b.* *Sardinia* Italy
108 A2 **Asinara, Isola** *i. Sardinia* Italy
82 G3 **Asino** Rus. Fed.
88 C3 **Asipovichy** Belarus
78 B2 **'Asīr** *reg.* Saudi Arabia
93 F4 **Asker** Norway
93 F4 **Askim** Norway
68 C1 **Askiz** Rus. Fed.
116 B3 **Asmara** Eritrea
93 F4 **Åsnen** *l.* Sweden
116 B2 **Asoteriba, Jebel** *mt.* Sudan
103 D2 **Aspang-Markt** Austria
136 B3 **Aspen** U.S.A.
139 C2 **Aspermont** U.S.A.
54 A2 **Aspiring, Mount** N.Z.
116 C3 **Assab** Eritrea
78 B3 **Aş Şahīf** Yemen
78 B2 **As Salamiyah** Saudi Arabia
75 D2 **Assam** *state* India
81 C2 **As Samāwah** Iraq
79 C2 **Aş Şanām** *reg.* Saudi Arabia
115 E2 **As Sarīr** *reg.* Libya
108 A3 **Assemini** *Sardinia* Italy
100 C1 **Assen** Neth.
100 B2 **Assesse** Belgium
115 D1 **As Sidrah** Libya
129 D3 **Assiniboia** Can.
128 C2 **Assiniboine, Mount** Can.
154 B2 **Assis** Brazil
78 B2 **Aş Şubayhīyah** Kuwait
81 C2 **As Sulaymānīyah** Iraq
78 B2 **As Sulaymī** Saudi Arabia
78 B2 **As Sulayyil** Saudi Arabia
78 B2 **As Sūq** Saudi Arabia
80 B2 **As Suwaydā'** Syria
79 C2 **As Suwayq** Oman
111 B3 **Astakos** Greece
77 D1 **Astana** Kazakh.
81 C2 **Astara** Iran
100 B2 **Asten** Neth.
Asterabad Iran *see* **Gorgān**
108 A2 **Asti** Italy
74 B1 **Astor** Jammu and Kashmir
106 B1 **Astorga** Spain
134 B1 **Astoria** U.S.A.
Astrabad Iran *see* **Gorgān**
87 D4 **Astrakhan'** Rus. Fed.
Astrakhan' Bazar Azer. *see* **Cälilabad**
88 C3 **Astravyets** Belarus
Astrida Rwanda *see* **Butare**
106 B1 **Asturias** *aut. comm.* Spain
111 C3 **Astypalaia** *i.* Greece
152 C2 **Asunción** Para.
116 B2 **Aswân** Egypt
116 B2 **Asyût** Egypt
152 B2 **Atacama, Desierto de** *des.* Chile
152 B2 **Atacama, Salar de** *salt flat* Chile
114 C4 **Atakpamé** Togo
111 B3 **Atalanti** Greece
150 B4 **Atalaya** Peru
155 D1 **Ataléia** Brazil
78 B3 **'Ataq** Yemen
114 A2 **Atâr** Maur.
135 B3 **Atascadero** U.S.A.
77 D2 **Atasu** Kazakh.
116 B3 **Atbara** Sudan
116 B3 **Atbara** *r.* Sudan
77 C1 **Atbasar** Kazakh.
142 B3 **Atchafalaya Bay** U.S.A.
137 D3 **Atchison** U.S.A.
Ateransk Kazakh. *see* **Atyrau**
108 B2 **Aterno** *r.* Italy
108 B2 **Atessa** Italy
100 A2 **Ath** Belgium
128 C2 **Athabasca** Can.
129 C2 **Athabasca** *r.* Can.
129 D2 **Athabasca, Lake** Can.
97 C2 **Athboy** Rep. of Ireland
97 B2 **Athenry** Rep. of Ireland
111 B3 **Athens** Greece
142 C2 **Athens** *AL* U.S.A.
143 D2 **Athens** *GA* U.S.A.
140 C3 **Athens** *OH* U.S.A.
143 D1 **Athens** *TN* U.S.A.
139 D2 **Athens** *TX* U.S.A.
51 D1 **Atherton** Austr.
Athina Greece *see* **Athens**
97 C2 **Athlone** Rep. of Ireland
111 B2 **Athos** *mt.* Greece
97 C2 **Athy** Rep. of Ireland
115 D3 **Ati** Chad
130 A3 **Atikokan** Can.
87 D3 **Atkarsk** Rus. Fed.
143 D2 **Atlanta** U.S.A.
137 D2 **Atlantic** U.S.A.
143 D2 **Atlantic Beach** U.S.A.
141 E3 **Atlantic City** U.S.A.
55 D3 **Atlantic-Indian-Antarctic Basin** *sea feature* S. Atlantic Ocean
158 E8 **Atlantic-Indian Ridge** *sea feature* Southern Ocean
158 **Atlantic Ocean**
122 A3 **Atlantis** S. Africa
114 B1 **Atlas Mountains** Africa
114 C1 **Atlas Saharien** *mts* Alg.
128 A2 **Atlin** Can.
128 A2 **Atlin Lake** Can.
142 C2 **Atmore** U.S.A.
152 B2 **Atocha** Bol.
139 D2 **Atoka** U.S.A.
75 C2 **Atrai** *r.* India
80 B2 **Aţ Ţafīlah** Jordan
78 B2 **Aţ Ţā'if** Saudi Arabia
63 B2 **Attapu** Laos
111 C3 **Attavyros** *mt.* Greece
130 B2 **Attawapiskat** Can.
130 B2 **Attawapiskat** *r.* Can.
130 B2 **Attawapiskat Lake** Can.
100 C2 **Attendorn** Ger.
100 A3 **Attichy** France
78 B3 **At Turbah** Yemen
135 B3 **Atwater** U.S.A.
76 B2 **Atyrau** Kazakh.
105 D3 **Aubagne** France
105 C3 **Aubenas** France
126 D2 **Aubry Lake** Can.
142 C2 **Auburn** *AL* U.S.A.
135 B3 **Auburn** *CA* U.S.A.
140 B2 **Auburn** *IN* U.S.A.
141 E2 **Auburn** *ME* U.S.A.
137 D2 **Auburn** *NE* U.S.A.
141 D2 **Auburn** *NY* U.S.A.
104 C2 **Aubusson** France
104 C3 **Auch** France
54 B1 **Auckland** N.Z.
48 H9 **Auckland Islands** N.Z.
117 C4 **Audo Range** *mts* Eth.
101 F2 **Aue** Ger.
101 F2 **Auerbach** Ger.
102 C2 **Augsburg** Ger.
50 A3 **Augusta** Austr.
109 C3 **Augusta** *Sicily* Italy
143 D2 **Augusta** *GA* U.S.A.
137 D3 **Augusta** *KS* U.S.A.
141 F2 **Augusta** *ME* U.S.A.
155 D1 **Augusto de Lima** Brazil
103 E1 **Augustów** Pol.
50 A2 **Augustus, Mount** Austr.
100 A2 **Aulnoye-Aymeries** France
Aumale Alg. *see* **Sour el Ghozlane**
122 B2 **Auob** *watercourse* Namibia/S. Africa
131 D2 **Aupaluk** Can.
74 B3 **Aurangābād** India
104 B2 **Auray** France
100 C1 **Aurich** Ger.
154 B1 **Aurilândia** Brazil
104 C3 **Aurillac** France
136 C3 **Aurora** *CO* U.S.A.
140 B2 **Aurora** *IL* U.S.A.
137 E3 **Aurora** *MO* U.S.A.
137 D2 **Aurora** *NE* U.S.A.
122 A2 **Aus** Namibia
140 C2 **Au Sable** *r.* U.S.A.
137 E2 **Austin** *MN* U.S.A.
135 C3 **Austin** *NV* U.S.A.
139 D2 **Austin** *TX* U.S.A.
49 L6 **Australes, Îles** *is* Fr. Polynesia
50 B2 **Australia** *country* Oceania
55 K4 **Australian-Antarctic Basin** *sea feature* Southern Ocean
53 C3 **Australian Capital Territory** *admin. div.* Austr.
102 C2 **Austria** *country* Europe
150 D3 **Autazes** Brazil
144 B3 **Autlán** Mex.
105 C2 **Autun** France
104 C3 **Auvergne** *reg.* France
105 C2 **Auvergne, Monts d'** *mts* France
105 C2 **Auxerre** France
105 D2 **Auxonne** France
105 C2 **Avallon** France
131 E3 **Avalon Peninsula** Can.
154 C2 **Avaré** Brazil
91 D2 **Avdiyivka** Ukr.
106 B1 **Aveiro** Port.
109 B2 **Avellino** Italy
108 B2 **Aversa** Italy
100 A2 **Avesnes-sur-Helpe** France
93 G3 **Avesta** Sweden
104 C3 **Aveyron** *r.* France
108 B2 **Avezzano** Italy
96 C2 **Aviemore** U.K.
109 C2 **Avigliano** Italy
105 C3 **Avignon** France
106 C1 **Ávila** Spain
106 B1 **Avilés** Spain
52 B3 **Avoca** Austr.
141 D2 **Avoca** U.S.A.
109 C3 **Avola** *Sicily* Italy
99 C4 **Avon** *r. England* U.K.
99 B3 **Avon** *r. England* U.K.
99 B4 **Avon** *r. England* U.K.
138 A2 **Avondale** U.S.A.
104 B2 **Avranches** France
54 B1 **Awanui** N.Z.
119 D2 **Āwasa** Eth.
117 C4 **Āwash** Eth.
117 C3 **Āwash** *r.* Eth.
115 D2 **Awbārī** Libya
117 C4 **Aw Dheegle** Somalia
96 B2 **Awe, Loch** *l.* U.K.
117 A4 **Aweil** Sudan
115 C4 **Awka** Nigeria
114 A2 **Awserd** Western Sahara
126 F1 **Axel Heiberg Island** Can.
114 B4 **Axim** Ghana
150 B4 **Ayacucho** Peru
77 E2 **Ayagoz** Kazakh.
Ayaguz Kazakh. *see* **Ayagoz**
77 C2 **Ayakkuduk** Uzbek.
68 B2 **Ayakkum Hu** *salt l.* China
106 B2 **Ayamonte** Spain
83 K3 **Ayan** Rus. Fed.
150 B4 **Ayaviri** Peru
74 A1 **Āybak** Afgh.
76 A2 **Aybas** Kazakh.
91 D2 **Aydar** *r.* Ukr.
77 C2 **Aydarkul', Ozero** *l.* Uzbek.
111 C3 **Aydın** Turkey
77 C2 **Ayeat, Gora** *hill* Kazakh.
Ayers Rock *hill* Austr. *see* **Uluru**
83 I2 **Aykhal** Rus. Fed.
99 C4 **Aylesbury** U.K.
106 C1 **Ayllón** Spain
129 D1 **Aylmer Lake** Can.
117 B4 **Ayod** Sudan
83 M2 **Ayon, Ostrov** *i.* Rus. Fed.
114 B3 **'Ayoûn el 'Atroûs** Maur.
51 D1 **Ayr** Austr.
96 B3 **Ayr** U.K.
98 A2 **Ayre, Point of** Isle of Man
76 C2 **Ayteke Bi** Kazakh.
110 C2 **Aytos** Bulg.
145 C3 **Ayutla** Mex.
63 B2 **Ayutthaya** Thai.
111 C3 **Ayvacık** Turkey
111 C3 **Ayvalık** Turkey
91 C3 **Ayya, Mys** *pt* Ukr.
114 B3 **Azaouâd** *reg.* Mali
114 C3 **Azaouagh, Vallée de** *watercourse* Mali/Niger
115 D3 **Azare** Nigeria
Azbine *mts* Niger *see* **L'Aïr, Massif de**
81 C1 **Azerbaijan** *country* Asia
Azerbaydzhanskaya S.S.R. *country* Asia *see* **Azerbaijan**
150 B3 **Azogues** Ecuador
86 D2 **Azopol'ye** Rus. Fed.
112 A2 **Azores** *aut. reg.* N. Atlantic Ocean
91 D2 **Azov** Rus. Fed.
91 D2 **Azov, Sea of** Rus. Fed./Ukr.
Azraq, Bahr el *r.* Sudan *see* **Blue Nile**
106 B2 **Azuaga** Spain
146 B4 **Azuero, Península de** *pen.* Panama
153 C3 **Azul** Arg.
108 A3 **Azzaba** Alg.
Az Zahrān Saudi Arabia *see* **Dhahran**
80 B2 **Az Zarqā'** Jordan
115 D1 **Az Zāwiyah** Libya
78 B3 **Az Zaydīyah** Yemen
114 C2 **Azzel Matti, Sebkha** *salt pan* Alg.
78 B2 **Az Zilfī** Saudi Arabia
78 B3 **Az Zuqur** *i.* Yemen
78 B3 **Az Zuqur** *i.* Yemen

B

117 C4 **Baardheere** Somalia
77 C3 **Bābā, Kūh-e** *mts* Afgh.
111 C3 **Baba Burnu** *pt* Turkey
110 C2 **Babadag** Romania
111 C2 **Babaeski** Turkey
116 C3 **Bāb al Mandab** *str.* Africa/Asia
61 C2 **Babana** Indon.
119 C1 **Babanusa** Sudan
59 C3 **Babar** *i.* Indon.
119 D3 **Babati** Tanz.
89 E2 **Babayevo** Rus. Fed.
59 C2 **Babeldaob** *i.* Palau
128 B2 **Babine** *r.* Can.
128 B2 **Babine Lake** Can.
59 C3 **Babo** Indon.
81 D2 **Bābol** Iran
122 A3 **Baboon Point** S. Africa
88 C3 **Babruysk** Belarus
Babu China *see* **Hexian**
64 B2 **Babuyan** *i.* Phil.
64 B2 **Babuyan Channel** Phil.
64 B2 **Babuyan Islands** Phil.
151 E3 **Bacabal** Brazil
145 D3 **Bacalar** Mex.
59 C3 **Bacan** *i.* Indon.
110 C1 **Bacău** Romania
52 B3 **Bacchus Marsh** Austr.
77 D3 **Bachu** China
129 E1 **Back** *r.* Can.
109 C1 **Bačka Palanka** Yugo.
109 C1 **Bačka Topola** Yugo.
52 A3 **Backstairs Passage** Au
62 B1 **Bac Lac** Vietnam
63 B3 **Bac Liêu** Vietnam
62 B1 **Băc Ninh** Vietnam
138 B3 **Bacobampo** Mex.
64 B2 **Bacolod** Phil.
130 C2 **Bacqueville, Lac** *l.* Can
Bada China *see* **Xilin**
70 A1 **Badain Jaran Shamo** *d* China
106 B2 **Badajoz** Spain
Badaojiang China *see* **Baishan**
75 D2 **Badarpur** India
101 E2 **Bad Berka** Ger.
101 D2 **Bad Berleburg** Ger.
101 E1 **Bad Bevensen** Ger.
101 D3 **Bad Dürkheim** Ger.
100 C2 **Bad Ems** Ger.
103 D2 **Baden** Austria
102 B2 **Baden-Baden** Ger.
101 E2 **Bad Harzburg** Ger.
101 D2 **Bad Hersfeld** Ger.
102 C2 **Bad Hofgastein** Austria
101 D2 **Bad Homburg vor der Höhe** Ger.
101 D1 **Bad Iburg** Ger.
74 A2 **Badin** Pak.
Bādiyat ash Shām *des.* Asia *see* **Syrian Desert**
101 E2 **Bad Kissingen** Ger.
100 C3 **Bad Kreuznach** Ger.
136 C1 **Badlands** *reg. ND* U.S.A.
136 C2 **Badlands** *reg. SD* U.S.A.
101 E2 **Bad Lauterberg im Har**
Ger.
101 D2 **Bad Lippspringe** Ger.
101 D3 **Bad Mergentheim** Ger.
101 D2 **Bad Nauheim** Ger.
100 C2 **Bad Neuenahr-Ahrweil** Ger.
101 E2 **Bad Neustadt an der Saale** Ger.
101 E1 **Bad Oldesloe** Ger.
101 D2 **Bad Pyrmont** Ger.
78 A2 **Badr Ḥunayn** Saudi Arab
101 D1 **Bad Salzuflen** Ger.
101 E2 **Bad Salzungen** Ger.
102 C1 **Bad Schwartau** Ger.
101 E1 **Bad Segeberg** Ger.
73 C4 **Badulla** Sri Lanka
101 D1 **Bad Zwischenahn** Ger.
106 C2 **Baeza** Spain
114 A3 **Bafatá** Guinea-Bissau
127 H2 **Baffin Bay** *sea* Can./Greenland
127 H2 **Baffin Island** Can.
118 B2 **Bafia** Cameroon
114 A3 **Bafing** *r.* Guinea/Mali
114 A3 **Bafoulabé** Mali
118 B2 **Bafoussam** Cameroon
81 D2 **Bāfq** Iran
80 B1 **Bafra** Turkey
79 C2 **Bāft** Iran
119 C2 **Bafwasende** Dem. Rep. Congo

9 D3 **Bagamoyo** Tanz.
Bagan Datoh Malaysia *see* Bagan Datuk
0 B1 **Bagan Datuk** Malaysia
4 B3 **Baganga** Phil.
0 B2 **Bagani** Namibia
0 B1 **Bagansiapiapi** Indon.
8 B3 **Bagata** Dem. Rep. Congo
4 E2 **Bagayevskiy** Rus. Fed.
8 A2 **Bagdad** U.S.A.
2 C3 **Bagé** Brazil
1 C2 **Baghdād** Iraq
9 C1 **Bāghīn** Iran
7 C3 **Baghlān** Afgh.
4 C3 **Bagnères-de-Luchon** France
5 C3 **Bagnols-sur-Cèze** France
Bago Myanmar *see* **Pegu**
3 B3 **Bagrationovsk** Rus. Fed.
Bagrax China *see* **Bohu**
4 B2 **Baguio** Phil.
5 C3 **Bagzane, Monts** *mts* Niger
5 C2 **Baharampur** India
6 A2 **Bahariya Oasis** Egypt
0 B1 **Bahau** Malaysia
4 B2 **Bahawalnagar** Pak.
4 B2 **Bahawalpur** Pak.
Bahia Brazil *see* **Salvador**
3 B3 **Bahía Blanca** Arg.
4 A2 **Bahía Kino** Mex.
2 C2 **Bahía Negra** Para.
4 A2 **Bahía Tortugas** Mex.
7 B3 **Bahir Dar** Eth.
9 C2 **Bahlā** Oman
5 C2 **Bahraich** India
9 C2 **Bahrain** *country* Asia
9 D2 **Bāhū Kālāt** Iran
9 D3 **Bahushewsk** Belarus
0 C2 **Baia** Romania
0 A2 **Baía dos Tigres** Angola
0 B1 **Baia Mare** Romania
8 B2 **Baïbokoum** Chad
9 E1 **Baicheng** China
Baidoa Somalia *see* Baydhabo
Baie-aux-Feuilles Can. *see* **Tasiujaq**
1 D3 **Baie-Comeau** Can.
Baie-du-Poste Can. *see* **Mistissini**
1 C3 **Baie-St-Paul** Can.
1 E3 **Baie Verte** Can.
2 A1 **Baihanchang** China
5 B1 **Baihe** China
9 D1 **Baikal, Lake** Rus. Fed.
Baile Átha Cliath Rep. of Ireland *see* **Dublin**
0 B2 **Băilești** Romania
3 C2 **Baima** China
5 C2 **Bainang** China
3 D2 **Bainbridge** U.S.A.
5 D1 **Baingoin** China
3 I3 **Bairiki** Kiribati
Bairin Youqi China *see* **Daban**
3 C3 **Bairnsdale** Austr.
5 B1 **Baishan** *Jilin* China
5 B1 **Baishan** *Jilin* China
0 A2 **Baixo-Longa** Angola
0 A2 **Baiyin** China
6 B3 **Baiyuda Desert** Sudan
3 D2 **Baja** Hungary
4 A1 **Baja California** *pen.* Mex.
4 D2 **Bajawa** Indon.
3 B3 **Bājil** Yemen
5 D3 **Bajoga** Nigeria
9 D2 **Bajram Curri** Albania
4 A3 **Bakel** Senegal
5 C3 **Baker** *CA* U.S.A.
2 B2 **Baker** *LA* U.S.A.
6 C1 **Baker** *MT* U.S.A.
4 C2 **Baker** *OR* U.S.A.
4 B1 **Baker, Mount** *vol.* U.S.A.
9 E1 **Baker Foreland** *hd* Can.
9 J3 **Baker Island** *terr.* N. Pacific Ocean
9 E1 **Baker Lake** Can.
9 E1 **Baker Lake** *l.* Can.
5 C3 **Bakersfield** U.S.A.
Bakharden Turkm. *see* **Bakherden**
4 C3 **Bakhchysaray** Ukr.
6 B3 **Bakherden** Turkm.
4 C1 **Bakhmach** Ukr.
Bakhmut Ukr. *see* **Artemivs'k**
Bākhtarān Iran *see* **Kermānshāh**
Bakı Azer. *see* **Baku**
4 C2 **Bakırköy** Turkey
92 □C2 **Bakkaflói** *b.* Iceland
118 C2 **Bakouma** C.A.R.
81 C1 **Baku** Azer.
99 B3 **Bala** U.K.
64 A3 **Balabac** Phil.
64 A3 **Balabac** *i.* Phil.
61 C1 **Balabac Strait** Malaysia/Phil.
75 C2 **Balaghat** India
60 C2 **Balaiberkuak** Indon.
52 A2 **Balaklava** Austr.
91 C3 **Balaklava** Ukr.
91 D2 **Balakliya** Ukr.
87 D3 **Balakovo** Rus. Fed.
76 C3 **Bālā Morghāb** Afgh.
145 C3 **Balancán** Mex.
111 C3 **Balan Dağı** *hill* Turkey
64 B2 **Balanga** Phil.
75 C2 **Balāngīr** India
87 D3 **Balashov** Rus. Fed.
103 D2 **Balaton** *l.* Hungary
Balaton, Lake Hungary *see* **Balaton**
103 D2 **Balatonboglár** Hungary
150 D3 **Balbina, Represa de** *resr* Brazil
97 C2 **Balbriggan** Rep. of Ireland
52 A2 **Balcanoona** Austr.
110 C2 **Balchik** Bulg.
54 A3 **Balclutha** N.Z.
139 C3 **Balcones Escarpment** U.S.A.
129 E2 **Baldock Lake** Can.
140 D2 **Baldwin** U.S.A.
129 D2 **Baldy Mountain** *hill* Can.
138 B2 **Baldy Peak** U.S.A.
Baleares, Islas *is* Spain *see* **Balearic Islands**
107 D2 **Balearic Islands** *is* Spain
155 E1 **Baleia, Ponta da** *pt* Brazil
75 C2 **Bāleshwar** India
50 B2 **Balgo** Austr.
79 B3 **Bālḥaf** Yemen
61 C2 **Bali** *i.* Indon.
60 A1 **Balige** Indon.
75 C2 **Baliguda** India
111 C3 **Balıkesir** Turkey
61 C2 **Balikpapan** Indon.
64 A3 **Balimbing** Phil.
59 D3 **Balimo** P.N.G.
102 B2 **Balingen** Ger.
64 B2 **Balintang Channel** Phil.
61 C2 **Bali Sea** Indon.
78 B3 **Baljurshī** Saudi Arabia
110 B2 **Balkan Mountains** Bulg./Yugo.
77 C1 **Balkashino** Kazakh.
77 D2 **Balkhash** Kazakh.
Balkhash, Lake Kazakh. *see* **Balkhash, Ozero**
77 D2 **Balkhash, Ozero** *l.* Kazakh.
Balla Balla Zimbabwe *see* **Mbalabala**
96 B2 **Ballachulish** U.K.
50 B3 **Balladonia** Austr.
97 B2 **Ballaghaderreen** Rep. of Ireland
92 G2 **Ballangen** Norway
96 B3 **Ballantrae** U.K.
52 B3 **Ballarat** Austr.
50 B2 **Ballard, Lake** *salt flat* Austr.
96 C2 **Ballater** U.K.
114 B3 **Ballé** Mali
55 M3 **Balleny Islands** Antarctica
53 D1 **Ballina** Austr.
97 B1 **Ballina** Rep. of Ireland
97 B2 **Ballinasloe** Rep. of Ireland
97 B3 **Ballineen** Rep. of Ireland
139 D2 **Ballinger** U.S.A.
97 B2 **Ballinrobe** Rep. of Ireland
97 B1 **Ballycastle** Rep. of Ireland
97 C1 **Ballycastle** U.K.
97 D1 **Ballyclare** U.K.
97 B2 **Ballyhaunis** Rep. of Ireland
97 C1 **Ballymena** U.K.
97 C1 **Ballymoney** U.K.
97 D1 **Ballynahinch** U.K.
97 B1 **Ballyshannon** Rep. of Ireland
95 B2 **Ballyvoy** U.K.
52 B3 **Balmoral** Austr.
139 C2 **Balmorhea** U.S.A.
120 A2 **Balombo** Angola
51 D2 **Balonne** *r.* Austr.
74 B2 **Balotra** India
77 D2 **Balpyk Bi** Kazakh.
75 C2 **Balrampur** India
52 B2 **Balranald** Austr.
110 B2 **Balș** Romania
151 E3 **Balsas** Brazil
145 C3 **Balsas** Mex.
145 B3 **Balsas** *r.* Mex.
90 B2 **Balta** Ukr.
90 B2 **Bălți** Moldova
93 G4 **Baltic Sea** *g.* Europe
80 B2 **Balṭîm** Egypt
97 B3 **Baltimore** Rep. of Ireland
123 C1 **Baltimore** S. Africa
141 D3 **Baltimore** U.S.A.
97 C2 **Baltinglass** Rep. of Ireland
88 A3 **Baltiysk** Rus. Fed.
75 D2 **Balu** India
52 A2 **Balumbah** Austr.
88 C2 **Balvi** Latvia
77 D2 **Balykchy** Kyrg.
87 E4 **Balykshi** Kazakh.
79 C2 **Bam** Iran
71 A3 **Bama** China
51 D1 **Bamaga** Austr.
130 A2 **Bamaji Lake** Can.
114 B3 **Bamako** Mali
118 C2 **Bambari** C.A.R.
101 E3 **Bamberg** Ger.
119 C2 **Bambili** Dem. Rep. Congo
118 B2 **Bambio** C.A.R.
119 C2 **Bambouti** C.A.R.
155 C2 **Bambuí** Brazil
98 C2 **Bamburgh** U.K.
118 B2 **Bamenda** Cameroon
77 C3 **Bāmīān** Afgh.
118 C2 **Bamingui** C.A.R.
79 D2 **Bampūr** Iran
79 C2 **Bampūr** *watercourse* Iran
48 H4 **Banaba** *i.* Kiribati
152 B1 **Bañados del Izozog** *swamp* Bol.
119 C2 **Banalia** Dem. Rep. Congo
71 A3 **Banan** China
151 D4 **Bananal, Ilha do** *i.* Brazil
74 B2 **Banas** *r.* India
111 C3 **Banaz** Turkey
62 B2 **Ban Ban** Laos
97 C1 **Banbridge** U.K.
99 C3 **Banbury** U.K.
96 C2 **Banchory** U.K.
130 C3 **Bancroft** Can.
Bancroft Zambia *see* Chililabombwe
119 C2 **Banda** Dem. Rep. Congo
75 C2 **Banda** India
59 C3 **Banda, Kepulauan** *is* Indon.
60 A1 **Banda Aceh** Indon.
Bandar India *see* Machilipatnam
Bandar Abbas Iran *see* Bandar-e 'Abbās
75 D2 **Bandarban** Bangl.
79 C2 **Bandar-e 'Abbās** Iran
81 C2 **Bandar-e Anzalī** Iran
79 C2 **Bandar-e Chārak** Iran
81 C2 **Bandar-e Emām Khomeynī** Iran
79 C2 **Bandar-e Lengeh** Iran
79 C2 **Bandar-e Maqām** Iran
Bandar-e Pahlavī Iran *see* Bandar-e Anzalī
Bandar-e Shāhpūr Iran *see* Bandar-e Emām Khomeynī
Bandar Lampung Indon. *see* Tanjungkarang-Telukbetung
61 C1 **Bandar Seri Begawan** Brunei
59 C3 **Banda Sea** Indon.
155 D2 **Bandeiras, Pico de** *mt.* Brazil
123 C1 **Bandelierkop** S. Africa
144 B2 **Banderas, Bahía de** *b.* Mex.
114 B3 **Bandiagara** Mali
111 C2 **Bandırma** Turkey
Bandjarmasin Indon. *see* Banjarmasin
97 B3 **Bandon** Rep. of Ireland
97 B3 **Bandon** *r.* Rep. of Ireland
118 B3 **Bandundu** Dem. Rep. Congo
60 B2 **Bandung** Indon.
128 C2 **Banff** Can.
96 C2 **Banff** U.K.
114 B3 **Banfora** Burkina
64 B3 **Banga** Phil.
73 B3 **Bangalore** India
118 C2 **Bangassou** C.A.R.
61 D2 **Banggai** Indon.
61 D2 **Banggai, Kepulauan** *is* Indon.
59 C3 **Banggai, Kepulauan** *is* Indon.
61 C1 **Banggi** *i. Sabah* Malaysia
115 E1 **Banghāzī** Libya
60 B2 **Bangka** *i.* Indon.
60 B2 **Bangka, Selat** *sea chan.* Indon.
61 C2 **Bangkalan** Indon.
60 B1 **Bangkinang** Indon.
60 B2 **Bangko** Indon.
63 B2 **Bangkok** Thai.
75 C2 **Bangladesh** *country* Asia
97 D1 **Bangor** *Northern Ireland* U.K.
98 A3 **Bangor** *Wales* U.K.
141 F2 **Bangor** U.S.A.
63 A2 **Bang Saphan Yai** Thai.
64 B2 **Bangued** Phil.
118 B2 **Bangui** C.A.R.
64 B2 **Bangui** Phil.
121 B2 **Bangweulu, Lake** Zambia
62 B1 **Ban Houayxay** Laos
118 C2 **Bani** C.A.R.
115 D1 **Banī Walīd** Libya
80 B2 **Bāniyās** Syria
109 C2 **Banja Luka** Bos.-Herz.
61 C2 **Banjarmasin** Indon.
114 A3 **Banjul** Gambia
63 A3 **Ban Khok Kloi** Thai.
128 A2 **Banks Island** *B.C.* Can.
126 D2 **Banks Island** *N.W.T.* Can.
48 H5 **Banks Islands** Vanuatu
129 E1 **Banks Lake** Can.
54 B2 **Banks Peninsula** N.Z.
51 D4 **Banks Strait** Austr.
75 C2 **Bankura** India
62 A1 **Banmauk** Myanmar
62 B2 **Ban Mouang** Laos
97 C1 **Bann** *r.* U.K.
62 B2 **Ban Napè** Laos
63 A3 **Ban Na San** Thai.
146 C2 **Bannerman Town** Bahamas
Banningville Dem. Rep. Congo *see* Bandundu
71 A4 **Ban Nong Kung** Thai.
74 B1 **Bannu** Pak.
103 D2 **Banská Bystrica** Slovakia
111 B2 **Bansko** Bulg.
74 B2 **Banswara** India
62 B2 **Ban Taviang** Laos
63 A3 **Ban Tha Kham** Thai.
62 A2 **Ban Tha Song Yang** Thai.
63 B2 **Ban Tôp** Laos
97 B3 **Bantry** Rep. of Ireland
97 B3 **Bantry Bay** Rep. of Ireland
60 A1 **Banyak, Pulau-pulau** *is* Indon.
118 B2 **Banyo** Cameroon
107 D1 **Banyoles** Spain
61 C2 **Banyuwangi** Indon.
Banzyville Dem. Rep. Congo *see* **Mobayi-Mbongo**
Bao'an China *see* **Shenzhen**
70 B1 **Baochang** China
70 B2 **Baoding** China
70 A2 **Baoji** China
63 B2 **Bao Lôc** Vietnam
66 B1 **Baoqing** China
118 B2 **Baoro** C.A.R.
62 A1 **Baoshan** China
70 B1 **Baotou** China
74 B2 **Bap** India
81 C2 **Ba'qūbah** Iraq
90 B2 **Bar** Ukr.
109 C2 **Bar** Yugo.
116 B3 **Bara** Sudan
117 C4 **Baraawe** Somalia
147 C2 **Baracoa** Cuba
53 C2 **Baradine** Austr.
147 C3 **Barahona** Dom. Rep.
116 B3 **Baraka** *watercourse* Eritrea/Sudan
106 C1 **Barakaldo** Spain
61 C1 **Baram** *r. Sarawak* Malaysia
150 D2 **Baramanni** Guyana
89 D3 **Baran'** Belarus
74 B2 **Baran** India
88 C3 **Baranavichy** Belarus
90 B1 **Baranivka** Ukr.
128 A2 **Baranof Island** U.S.A.
Baranowicze Belarus *see* Baranavichy
59 C3 **Barat Daya, Kepulauan** *is* Indon.
155 D2 **Barbacena** Brazil
147 E3 **Barbados** *country* West Indies

107 D1 **Barbastro** Spain
106 B2 **Barbate de Franco** Spain
123 D2 **Barberton** S. Africa
104 B2 **Barbezieux-St-Hilaire** France
51 D2 **Barcaldine** Austr.
107 D1 **Barcelona** Spain
150 C1 **Barcelona** Venez.
105 D3 **Barcelonnette** France
150 C3 **Barcelos** Brazil
114 B4 **Barclayville** Liberia
51 D2 **Barcoo** *watercourse* Austr.
Barcoo Creek *watercourse* Austr. *see* **Cooper Creek**
103 D2 **Barcs** Hungary
92 □B3 **Bárðarbunga** *mt.* Iceland
75 C2 **Barddhamān** India
103 E2 **Bardejov** Slovakia
Bardera Somalia *see* Baardheere
79 C2 **Bardsīr** Iran
75 B2 **Bareilly** India
82 D1 **Barents Sea** Arctic Ocean
78 A3 **Barentu** Eritrea
108 B2 **Barga** Italy
75 C2 **Barh** India
52 B3 **Barham** Austr.
141 F2 **Bar Harbor** U.S.A.
109 C2 **Bari** Italy
107 E2 **Barika** Alg.
74 B1 **Barikot** Afgh.
150 B2 **Barinas** Venez.
75 C2 **Baripada** India
75 D2 **Barisal** Bangl.
60 B2 **Barisan, Pegunungan** *mts* Indon.
61 C2 **Barito** *r.* Indon.
79 C2 **Barkā** Oman
88 C2 **Barkava** Latvia
74 A2 **Barkhan** Pak.
51 C1 **Barkly Tableland** *reg.* Austr.
122 B2 **Barkly West** S. Africa
68 C2 **Barkol** China
110 C1 **Bârlad** Romania
105 D2 **Bar-le-Duc** France
50 A2 **Barlee, Lake** *salt flat* Austr.
109 C2 **Barletta** Italy
53 C2 **Barmedman** Austr.
Barmen-Elberfeld Ger. *see* **Wuppertal**
74 B2 **Barmer** India
52 B2 **Barmera** Austr.
99 A3 **Barmouth** U.K.
101 D1 **Barmstedt** Ger.
98 C2 **Barnard Castle** U.K.
53 B2 **Barnato** Austr.
82 G3 **Barnaul** Rus. Fed.
127 H2 **Barnes Icecap** Can.
100 B1 **Barneveld** Neth.
98 C3 **Barnsley** U.K.
99 A4 **Barnstaple** U.K.
Barnstaple Bay U.K. *see* **Bideford Bay**
143 D2 **Barnwell** U.S.A.
Baroda India *see* **Vadodara**
150 C1 **Barquisimeto** Venez.
96 A2 **Barra** *i.* U.K.
53 D2 **Barraba** Austr.
151 D4 **Barra do Bugres** Brazil
151 E3 **Barra do Corda** Brazil
154 B1 **Barra do Garças** Brazil
150 D3 **Barra do São Manuel** Brazil
Barraigh *i.* U.K. *see* **Barra**
150 B4 **Barranca** Peru
150 B3 **Barranca** Peru
152 C2 **Barranqueras** Arg.
150 B1 **Barranquilla** Col.
105 D3 **Barre des Ecrins** *mt.* France
151 E4 **Barreiras** Brazil
63 A2 **Barren Island** India
154 C2 **Barretos** Brazil
128 C2 **Barrhead** Can.
130 C3 **Barrie** Can.
128 B2 **Barrière** Can.
52 B2 **Barrier Range** *hills* Austr.
53 D2 **Barrington, Mount** Austr.
129 D2 **Barrington Lake** Can.
53 C1 **Barringun** Austr.
97 C2 **Barrow** *r.* Rep. of Ireland
126 B2 **Barrow** U.S.A.
126 B2 **Barrow, Point** U.S.A.
51 C2 **Barrow Creek** Austr.
98 B2 **Barrow-in-Furness** U.K.
50 A2 **Barrow Island** Austr.
126 F2 **Barrow Strait** Can.
99 B4 **Barry** U.K.
122 B3 **Barrydale** S. Africa
130 C3 **Barrys Bay** Can.
74 B2 **Barsalpur** India
101 D1 **Barsinghausen** Ger.
135 C4 **Barstow** U.S.A.
105 C2 **Bar-sur-Aube** France
102 C1 **Barth** Ger.
80 B1 **Bartın** Turkey
51 D1 **Bartle Frere, Mount** Austr.
139 D1 **Bartlesville** U.S.A.
137 D2 **Bartlett** *NE* U.S.A.
142 C1 **Bartlett** *TN* U.S.A.
98 C3 **Barton-upon-Humber** U.K.
103 E1 **Bartoszyce** Pol.
61 C2 **Barung** *i.* Indon.
69 D1 **Baruun Urt** Mongolia
91 D2 **Barvinkove** Ukr.
53 C2 **Barwon** *r.* Austr.
88 C3 **Barysaw** Belarus
118 B2 **Basankusu** Dem. Rep. Congo
110 C2 **Basarabi** Romania
104 B3 **Basauri** Spain
64 B1 **Basco** Phil.
105 D2 **Basel** Switz.
71 C3 **Bashi Channel** Taiwan
91 C2 **Bashtanka** Ukr.
64 B3 **Basilan** *i.* Phil.
99 D4 **Basildon** U.K.
99 C4 **Basingstoke** U.K.
81 C2 **Başkale** Turkey
130 C3 **Baskatong, Réservoir** *resr* Can.
Basle Switz. *see* **Basel**
118 C2 **Basoko** Dem. Rep. Congo
81 C2 **Basra** Iraq
128 C2 **Bassano** Can.
114 C4 **Bassar** Togo
63 A2 **Bassein** Myanmar
147 D3 **Basse-Terre** Guadeloupe
147 D3 **Basseterre** St Kitts and Nevis
114 B3 **Bassikounou** Maur.
114 C4 **Bassila** Benin
51 D3 **Bass Strait** Austr.
79 C2 **Bastak** Iran
101 E2 **Bastheim** Ger.
75 C2 **Basti** India
105 D3 **Bastia** *Corsica* France
100 B2 **Bastogne** Belgium
142 B2 **Bastrop** U.S.A.
Basuo China *see* **Dongfang**
Basutoland *country* Africa *see* **Lesotho**
118 A2 **Bata** Equat. Guinea
146 B2 **Batabanó, Golfo de** *b.* Cuba
83 J2 **Batagay** Rus. Fed.
154 B2 **Bataguaçu** Brazil
74 B1 **Batala** India
106 B2 **Batalha** Port.
64 B1 **Batan** *i.* Phil.
118 B2 **Batangafo** C.A.R.
64 B2 **Batangas** Phil.
60 B2 **Batanghari** *r.* Indon.
64 B1 **Batan Islands** Phil.
154 C2 **Batatais** Brazil
141 D2 **Batavia** U.S.A.
91 D2 **Bataysk** Rus. Fed.
130 B3 **Batchawana Mountain** *hill* Can.
50 C1 **Batchelor** Austr.
63 B2 **Bătdâmbâng** Cambodia
118 B3 **Batéké, Plateaux** Congo
53 D3 **Batemans Bay** Austr.
142 B1 **Batesville** *AR* U.S.A.
142 C2 **Batesville** *MS* U.S.A.
89 D2 **Batetskiy** Rus. Fed.
99 B4 **Bath** U.K.
96 C3 **Bathgate** U.K.
74 B1 **Bathinda** India
53 C2 **Bathurst** Austr.
131 D3 **Bathurst** Can.
Bathurst Gambia *see* Banjul
126 E2 **Bathurst Inlet** Can.
126 E2 **Bathurst Inlet** *inlet* Can.
50 C1 **Bathurst Island** Austr.
126 F1 **Bathurst Island** Can.
78 B1 **Bāṭin, Wādī al** *watercourse* Asia
53 C3 **Batlow** Austr.
81 C2 **Batman** Turkey
115 C1 **Batna** Alg.
142 B2 **Baton Rouge** U.S.A.
144 B2 **Batopilas** Mex.
118 B2 **Batouri** Cameroon
154 B1 **Batovi** Brazil
Batrā' *tourist site* Jordan *see* **Petra**
92 I1 **Båtsfjord** Norway
73 C4 **Batticaloa** Sri Lanka
109 B2 **Battipaglia** Italy
128 D2 **Battle** *r.* Can.
140 B2 **Battle Creek** U.S.A.
135 C2 **Battle Mountain** U.S.A.
74 B1 **Battura Glacier** Jammu and Kashmir
117 B4 **Batu** *mt.* Eth.
60 A2 **Batu, Pulau-pulau** *is* Indon.
61 D2 **Batudaka** *i.* Indon.
64 B3 **Batulaki** Phil.
Batum Georgia *see* Bat'umi
81 C1 **Bat'umi** Georgia
60 B1 **Batu Pahat** Malaysia
61 D2 **Baubau** Indon.
115 C3 **Bauchi** Nigeria
137 E1 **Baudette** U.S.A.
Baudouinville Dem. Rep. Congo *see* **Moba**
104 B2 **Baugé** France
105 D2 **Baume-les-Dames** France
154 C2 **Bauru** Brazil
154 B1 **Baús** Brazil
88 B2 **Bauska** Latvia
102 C1 **Bautzen** Ger.
144 B2 **Bavispe** *r.* Mex.
87 E3 **Bavly** Rus. Fed.
62 A1 **Bawdwin** Myanmar
61 C2 **Bawean** *i.* Indon.
116 A2 **Bawiti** Egypt
114 B3 **Bawku** Ghana
Baxian China *see* **Banan**
146 C2 **Bayamo** Cuba
Bayan Gol China *see* **Dengkou**
68 C1 **Bayanhongor** Mongolia
70 A2 **Bayan Hot** China
70 A1 **Bayan Obo Kuangqu** China
136 C2 **Bayard** *NE* U.S.A.
138 B2 **Bayard** *NM* U.S.A.
64 B3 **Bayawan** Phil.
81 C1 **Bayburt** Turkey
140 C2 **Bay City** *MI* U.S.A.
139 D3 **Bay City** *TX* U.S.A.
86 F2 **Baydaratskaya Guba** Rus. Fed.
117 C4 **Baydhabo** Somalia
104 B2 **Bayeux** France
136 B3 **Bayfield** U.S.A.
78 B3 **Bayḥan al Qiṣab** Yemen
Bay Islands *is* Hond. *see* **La Bahía, Islas de**
81 C2 **Bayjī** Iraq
Baykal, Ozero *l.* Rus. Fed. *see* **Baikal, Lake**
Baykal Range *mts* Rus. Fed. *see* **Baykal'skiy Khrebet**
83 I3 **Baykal'skiy Khrebet** *mts* Rus. Fed.
76 C2 **Baykonur** Kazakh.
87 E3 **Baymak** Rus. Fed.
64 B2 **Bayombong** Phil.
104 B3 **Bayonne** France
76 C3 **Bayramaly** Turkm.
111 C3 **Bayramiç** Turkey
101 E3 **Bayreuth** Ger.
78 B3 **Bayt al Faqīh** Yemen
139 D3 **Baytown** U.S.A.
106 C2 **Baza** Spain
106 C2 **Baza, Sierra de** *mts* Spain
76 A2 **Bazardyuzi, Gora** *mt.* Azer./Rus. Fed.
104 B3 **Bazas** France
74 A2 **Bazdar** Pak.
70 A2 **Bazhong** China
79 D2 **Bazmān** Iran
79 D2 **Bazmān, Kūh-e** *mt.* Iran
Bé, Nossi *i.* Madag. *see* Nosy Bé
136 C1 **Beach** U.S.A.
52 B3 **Beachport** Austr.
99 D4 **Beachy Head** *hd* U.K.
123 C3 **Beacon Bay** S. Africa
50 B1 **Beagle Gulf** Austr.
121 □D2 **Bealanana** Madag.
121 □D3 **Beampingaratra** *mts* Madag.
134 D2 **Bear** *r.* U.S.A.
130 B3 **Beardmore** Can.
53 C1 **Beardmore Reservoir** Austr.
82 C2 **Bear Island** Arctic Ocean
134 E1 **Bear Paw Mountain** U.S.A.
147 C3 **Beata, Cabo** *c.* Dom. R
147 C3 **Beata, Isla** *i.* Dom. Rep
137 D2 **Beatrice** U.S.A.
135 C3 **Beatty** U.S.A.
53 D1 **Beaudesert** Austr.
52 B3 **Beaufort** Austr.
61 C1 **Beaufort** *Sabah* Malays
143 D2 **Beaufort** U.S.A.
126 D2 **Beaufort Sea** Can./U.S
122 B3 **Beaufort West** S. Afric
96 B2 **Beauly** U.K.
96 B2 **Beauly** *r.* U.K.
100 B2 **Beaumont** Belgium
54 A3 **Beaumont** N.Z.
139 E2 **Beaumont** U.S.A.
105 C2 **Beaune** France
100 B2 **Beauraing** Belgium
129 E2 **Beauséjour** Can.
104 C2 **Beauvais** France
129 D2 **Beauval** Can.
129 D2 **Beaver** *r.* Can.
135 D3 **Beaver** U.S.A.
128 A1 **Beaver Creek** Can.
140 B2 **Beaver Dam** U.S.A.
129 E2 **Beaver Hill Lake** Can.
140 B1 **Beaver Island** U.S.A.
128 C2 **Beaverlodge** Can.
74 B2 **Beawar** India
154 C2 **Bebedouro** Brazil
101 D2 **Bebra** Ger.
99 D3 **Beccles** U.K.
109 D1 **Bečej** Yugo.
106 B1 **Becerreá** Spain
114 B1 **Béchar** Alg.
Bechuanaland *country* Africa *see* **Botswana**
140 C3 **Beckley** U.S.A.
117 B4 **Bedelē** Eth.
99 C3 **Bedford** U.K.
140 B3 **Bedford** U.S.A.
98 C2 **Bedlington** U.K.
100 C1 **Bedum** Neth.
53 C3 **Beechworth** Austr.
53 D2 **Beecroft Peninsula** Au
101 F1 **Beelitz** Ger.
53 D1 **Beenleigh** Austr.
Beersheba Israel *see* Be'ér Sheva'
80 B2 **Be'ér Sheva'** Israel
139 D3 **Beeville** U.S.A.
121 □D2 **Befandriana Avaratra** Madag.
53 C3 **Bega** Austr.
107 D1 **Begur, Cap de** *c.* Spain
81 D2 **Behbehān** Iran
81 D2 **Behshahr** Iran
69 E1 **Bei'an** China
71 A3 **Beihai** China
70 B2 **Beijing** China
100 C1 **Beilen** Neth.
118 B2 **Béinamar** Chad
96 B3 **Beinn an Oir** *hill* U.K.
96 A2 **Beinn Mhòr** *hill* U.K.
Beinn na Faoghlia *i.* U. *see* **Benbecula**
121 C2 **Beira** Moz.
80 B2 **Beirut** Lebanon
123 C1 **Beitbridge** Zimbabwe
106 B2 **Beja** Port.
115 C1 **Bejaïa** Alg.
106 B1 **Béjar** Spain
74 A2 **Beji** *r.* Pak.
76 B2 **Bekdash** Turkm.
103 E2 **Békés** Hungary
103 E2 **Békéscsaba** Hungary
121 □D3 **Bekily** Madag.
66 D2 **Bekkai** Japan
114 B4 **Bekwai** Ghana
75 C2 **Bela** India
74 A2 **Bela** Pak.
123 C1 **Bela-Bela** S. Africa
118 B2 **Bélabo** Cameroon
109 D2 **Bela Crkva** Yugo.
61 C1 **Belaga** *Sarawak* Malays
60 C2 **Belangiran** Indon.
88 C3 **Belarus** *country* Europe
121 C3 **Bela Vista** Moz.
60 A1 **Belawan** Indon.
83 M2 **Belaya** *r.* Rus. Fed.
Belchatow Pol. *see* Bełchatów
103 D1 **Bełchatów** Pol.
130 C2 **Belcher Islands** Can.
87 E3 **Belebey** Rus. Fed.
117 C4 **Beledweyne** Somalia
118 B2 **Bélèl** Cameroon
151 E3 **Belém** Brazil
138 B2 **Belen** U.S.A.
110 C2 **Belene** Bulg.

9 E3 **Belev** Rus. Fed.
7 D1 **Belfast** U.K.
1 F2 **Belfast** U.S.A.
6 C1 **Belfield** U.S.A.
5 D2 **Belfort** France
3 B3 **Belgaum** India
Belgian Congo *country* Africa *see* **Congo, Democratic Republic of**
0 B2 **Belgium** *country* Europe
4 D1 **Belgorod** Rus. Fed.
4 D1 **Belgrade** U.S.A.
9 D2 **Belgrade** Yugo.
5 D4 **Beli** Nigeria
9 C1 **Beli Manastir** Croatia
0 B2 **Belinyu** Indon.
0 B2 **Belitung** *i.* Indon.
8 B3 **Belize** Angola
6 B3 **Belize** Belize
6 B3 **Belize** *country* Central America
3 K1 **Bel'kovskiy, Ostrov** *i.* Rus. Fed.
8 B2 **Bella Bella** Can.
4 C2 **Bellac** France
8 B2 **Bella Coola** Can.
3 B3 **Bellary** India
3 C1 **Bellata** Austr.
0 C2 **Bellefontaine** U.S.A.
6 C2 **Belle Fourche** U.S.A.
6 C2 **Belle Fourche** *r.* U.S.A.
3 D3 **Belle Glade** U.S.A.
4 B2 **Belle-Île** *i.* France
1 E2 **Belle Isle** *i.* Can.
1 E2 **Belle Isle, Strait of** Can.
0 C3 **Belleville** Can.
0 B3 **Belleville** *IL* U.S.A.
7 D3 **Belleville** *KS* U.S.A.
4 D2 **Bellevue** *ID* U.S.A.
4 B1 **Bellevue** *WA* U.S.A.
Bellin Can. *see* **Kangirsuk**
3 D2 **Bellingen** Austr.
4 B1 **Bellingham** U.S.A.
5 R2 **Bellingshausen Sea** Antarctica
5 D2 **Bellinzona** Switz.
8 B1 **Belluno** Italy
2 A3 **Bellville** S. Africa
3 D2 **Belmont** Austr.
5 E1 **Belmonte** Brazil
6 B3 **Belmopan** Belize
7 B1 **Belmullet** Rep. of Ireland
9 E1 **Belogorsk** Rus. Fed.
1 □D3 **Beloha** Madag.
5 D1 **Belo Horizonte** Brazil
0 B2 **Beloit** U.S.A.
5 C2 **Belomorsk** Rus. Fed.
9 E3 **Beloomut** Rus. Fed.
4 D3 **Belorechensk** Rus. Fed.
Belorechenskaya Rus. Fed. *see* **Belorechensk**
7 E3 **Beloretsk** Rus. Fed.
Belorussia *country* Europe *see* **Belarus**
Belorusskaya S.S.R. *country* Europe *see* **Belarus**
Belostok Pol. *see* **Białystok**
1 □D2 **Belo Tsiribihina** Madag.
5 F2 **Beloyarskiy** Rus. Fed.
9 E1 **Beloye, Ozero** *l.* Rus. Fed.
Beloye More *sea* Rus. Fed. *see* **White Sea**
9 E1 **Belozersk** Rus. Fed.
2 A2 **Beltana** Austr.
9 D2 **Belton** U.S.A.
Bel'ts' Moldova *see* **Bălţi**
Bel'tsy Moldova *see* **Bălţi**
7 C1 **Belturbet** Rep. of Ireland
7 E2 **Belukha, Gora** *mt.* Kazakh./Rus. Fed.
5 D2 **Belush'ye** Rus. Fed.
0 B2 **Belvidere** U.S.A.
4 D2 **Belyando** *r.* Austr.
9 D2 **Belyy** Rus. Fed.
2 F2 **Belyy, Ostrov** *i.* Rus. Fed.
4 F1 **Belzig** Ger.
7 E1 **Bemidji** U.S.A.
8 C3 **Bena Dibele** Dem. Rep. Congo
3 C3 **Benalla** Austr.
Benares India *see* **Varanasi**
5 D1 **Ben Arous** Tunisia
8 C3 **Bena-Sungu** Dem. Rep. Congo
6 B1 **Benavente** Spain
6 A2 **Benbecula** *i.* U.K.
134 B2 **Bend** U.S.A.
123 C3 **Bendearg** *mt.* S. Africa
Bender Moldova *see* **Tighina**
Bendery Moldova *see* **Tighina**
52 B3 **Bendigo** Austr.
121 C2 **Bene** Moz.
102 C2 **Benešov** Czech Rep.
109 B2 **Benevento** Italy
73 C3 **Bengal, Bay of** *sea* Indian Ocean
70 B2 **Bengbu** China
Benghazi Libya *see* **Banghāzī**
60 B1 **Bengkalis** Indon.
60 B1 **Bengkayang** Indon.
60 B2 **Bengkulu** Indon.
120 A2 **Benguela** Angola
80 B2 **Benha** Egypt
96 B1 **Ben Hope** *hill* U.K.
152 B1 **Beni** *r.* Bol.
119 C2 **Beni** Dem. Rep. Congo
114 B1 **Beni-Abbès** Alg.
107 C2 **Benidorm** Spain
80 B3 **Benī Mazār** Egypt
114 B1 **Beni Mellal** Morocco
114 C4 **Benin** *country* Africa
114 C4 **Benin, Bight of** *g.* Africa
115 C4 **Benin City** Nigeria
107 C2 **Beni-Saf** Alg.
116 B2 **Beni Suef** Egypt
153 C3 **Benito Juárez** Arg.
150 C3 **Benjamim Constant** Brazil
144 A1 **Benjamín Hill** Mex.
59 C3 **Benjina** Indon.
136 C2 **Benkelman** U.S.A.
96 B2 **Ben Lawers** *mt.* U.K.
96 B2 **Ben Lomond** *hill* U.K.
96 C2 **Ben Macdui** *mt.* U.K.
96 A2 **Ben More** *hill* U.K.
96 B2 **Ben More** *mt.* U.K.
54 B2 **Benmore, Lake** N.Z.
96 B1 **Ben More Assynt** *hill* U.K.
128 A2 **Bennett** Can.
83 K1 **Bennetta, Ostrov** *i.* Rus. Fed.
Bennett Island Rus. Fed. *see* **Bennetta, Ostrov**
96 B2 **Ben Nevis** *mt.* U.K.
141 E2 **Bennington** U.S.A.
123 C2 **Benoni** S. Africa
115 D4 **Bénoy** Chad
101 D3 **Bensheim** Ger.
114 B1 **Ben Slimane** Morocco
138 A2 **Benson** U.S.A.
61 D2 **Benteng** Indon.
117 A4 **Bentiu** Sudan
140 B2 **Benton Harbor** U.S.A.
142 B1 **Bentonville** U.S.A.
63 B2 **Bên Tre** Vietnam
115 C4 **Benue** *r.* Nigeria
97 B1 **Benwee Head** *hd* Rep. of Ireland
96 B2 **Ben Wyvis** *mt.* U.K.
70 C1 **Benxi** China
Beograd Yugo. *see* **Belgrade**
75 C2 **Beohari** India
114 B4 **Béoumi** Côte d'Ivoire
67 B4 **Beppu** Japan
109 C2 **Berane** Yugo.
109 C2 **Berat** Albania
59 C3 **Berau, Teluk** *b.* Indon.
116 B3 **Berber** Sudan
117 C3 **Berbera** Somalia
118 B2 **Berbérati** C.A.R.
104 C1 **Berck** France
91 D2 **Berdyans'k** Ukr.
90 B2 **Berdychiv** Ukr.
90 A2 **Berehove** Ukr.
59 D3 **Bereina** P.N.G.
116 B2 **Berenice** Egypt
129 E2 **Berens River** Can.
137 D2 **Beresford** U.S.A.
91 D2 **Berezanskaya** Rus. Fed.
90 A2 **Berezhany** Ukr.
90 C2 **Berezivka** Ukr.
90 B1 **Berezne** Ukr.
86 D2 **Bereznik** Rus. Fed.
86 E3 **Berezniki** Rus. Fed.
Berezov Rus. Fed. *see* **Berezovo**
86 F2 **Berezovo** Rus. Fed.
107 D1 **Berga** Spain
111 C3 **Bergama** Turkey
108 A1 **Bergamo** Italy
102 C1 **Bergen** Ger.
101 D1 **Bergen** Ger.
100 B1 **Bergen** Neth.
93 E3 **Bergen** Norway
100 B2 **Bergen op Zoom** Neth.
104 C3 **Bergerac** France
100 C2 **Bergheim (Erft)** Ger.
100 C2 **Bergisch Gladbach** Ger.
122 A1 **Bergland** Namibia
93 G3 **Bergsjö** Sweden
92 H2 **Bergsviken** Sweden
Berhampur India *see* **Baharampur**
83 M3 **Beringa, Ostrov** *i.* Rus. Fed.
100 B2 **Beringen** Belgium
124 A4 **Bering Sea** N. Pacific Ocean
124 B3 **Bering Strait** Rus. Fed./U.S.A.
100 C1 **Berkel** *r.* Neth.
135 B3 **Berkeley** U.S.A.
100 B1 **Berkhout** Neth.
55 B2 **Berkner Island** Antarctica
110 B2 **Berkovitsa** Bulg.
92 I1 **Berlevåg** Norway
101 F1 **Berlin** Ger.
141 E2 **Berlin** U.S.A.
101 E2 **Berlingerode** Ger.
53 D3 **Bermagui** Austr.
144 B2 **Bermejillo** Mex.
152 B2 **Bermejo** Bol.
125 L6 **Bermuda** *terr.* N. Atlantic Ocean
105 D2 **Bern** Switz.
101 E2 **Bernburg (Saale)** Ger.
127 G2 **Bernier Bay** Can.
50 A2 **Bernier Island** Austr.
100 C3 **Bernkastel-Kues** Ger.
121 □D3 **Beroroha** Madag.
52 B2 **Berri** Austr.
115 C1 **Berriane** Alg.
53 C3 **Berrigan** Austr.
107 D2 **Berrouaghia** Alg.
53 D2 **Berry** Austr.
146 C2 **Berry Islands** Bahamas
122 A2 **Berseba** Namibia
101 C1 **Bersenbrück** Ger.
90 B2 **Bershad'** Ukr.
131 D2 **Berté, Lac** *l.* Can.
118 B2 **Bertoua** Cameroon
150 C3 **Beruri** Brazil
98 B2 **Berwick-upon-Tweed** U.K.
91 C2 **Beryslav** Ukr.
121 □D2 **Besalampy** Madag.
105 D2 **Besançon** France
81 D3 **Beshneh** Iran
129 D2 **Besnard Lake** Can.
142 C2 **Bessemer** U.S.A.
76 B2 **Besshoky, Gora** *hill* Kazakh.
100 B2 **Best** Neth.
121 □D2 **Betafo** Madag.
106 B1 **Betanzos** Spain
118 B2 **Bétaré Oya** Cameroon
122 A2 **Bethanie** Namibia
100 B3 **Bétheny** France
141 D3 **Bethesda** U.S.A.
123 C2 **Bethlehem** S. Africa
141 D2 **Bethlehem** U.S.A.
123 C3 **Bethulie** S. Africa
105 C1 **Béthune** France
121 □D3 **Betioky** Madag.
51 D2 **Betoota** Austr.
77 D2 **Betpak-Dala** *plain* Kazakh.
121 □D3 **Betroka** Madag.
131 D3 **Betsiamites** Can.
121 □D2 **Betsiboka** *r.* Madag.
137 E2 **Bettendorf** U.S.A.
75 C2 **Bettiah** India
74 B2 **Betul** India
74 B2 **Betwa** *r.* India
99 B3 **Betws-y-coed** U.K.
100 C2 **Betzdorf** Ger.
136 C1 **Beulah** U.S.A.
98 C3 **Beverley** U.K.
101 D2 **Beverungen** Ger.
100 B1 **Beverwijk** Neth.
99 D4 **Bexhill** U.K.
111 C2 **Beykoz** Turkey
114 B4 **Beyla** Guinea
76 B2 **Beyneu** Kazakh.
80 B1 **Beypazarı** Turkey
Beyrouth Lebanon *see* **Beirut**
80 B2 **Beyşehir** Turkey
80 B2 **Beyşehir Gölü** *l.* Turkey
91 D2 **Beysug** *r.* Rus. Fed.
91 D2 **Beysugskiy Liman** *lag.* Rus. Fed.
88 C2 **Bezhanitsy** Rus. Fed.
89 E2 **Bezhetsk** Rus. Fed.
105 C3 **Béziers** France
75 C2 **Bhadgaon** Nepal
75 C2 **Bhadrakh** India
73 B3 **Bhadravati** India
75 C2 **Bhagalpur** India
74 A2 **Bhairi Hol** *mt.* Pak.
74 B1 **Bhakkar** Pak.
Bhaktapur Nepal *see* **Bhadgaon**
62 A1 **Bhamo** Myanmar
75 C3 **Bhanjanagar** India
74 B2 **Bharatpur** India
74 B2 **Bharuch** India
74 B2 **Bhavnagar** India
75 C3 **Bhawanipatna** India
123 D2 **Bhekuzulu** S. Africa
74 B1 **Bhera** Pak.
74 B2 **Bhilwara** India
73 B3 **Bhima** *r.* India
74 B2 **Bhind** India
74 B2 **Bhiwani** India
123 C3 **Bhongweni** S. Africa
74 B2 **Bhopal** India
75 C2 **Bhubaneshwar** India
Bhubaneswar India *see* **Bhubaneshwar**
74 A2 **Bhuj** India
62 A2 **Bhumiphol Dam** Thai.
74 B2 **Bhusawal** India
75 D2 **Bhutan** *country* Asia
62 B2 **Bia, Phou** *mt.* Laos
Biafra, Bight of *g.* Africa *see* **Benin, Bight of**
59 D3 **Biak** Indon.
59 D3 **Biak** *i.* Indon.
103 E1 **Biała Podlaska** Pol.
103 D1 **Białogard** Pol.
103 E1 **Białystok** Pol.
109 C3 **Bianco** Italy
74 B2 **Biaora** India
104 B3 **Biarritz** France
105 D2 **Biasca** Switz.
66 D2 **Bibai** Japan
120 A2 **Bibala** Angola
53 C3 **Bibbenluke** Austr.
102 B2 **Biberach an der Riß** Ger.
155 D2 **Bicas** Brazil
73 B3 **Bid** India
115 C4 **Bida** Nigeria
73 B3 **Bidar** India
141 E2 **Biddeford** U.S.A.
96 B2 **Bidean nam Bian** *mt.* U.K.
99 A4 **Bideford** U.K.
99 A4 **Bideford Bay** U.K.
Bié Angola *see* **Kuito**
101 D2 **Biedenkopf** Ger.
105 D2 **Biel** Switz.
101 D1 **Bielefeld** Ger.
108 A1 **Biella** Italy
103 D2 **Bielsko-Biała** Pol.
63 B2 **Biên Hoa** Vietnam
130 C2 **Bienville, Lac** *l.* Can.
120 A2 **Bié Plateau** Angola
100 B3 **Bièvre** Belgium
118 B3 **Bifoun** Gabon
111 C2 **Biga** Turkey
134 D1 **Big Belt Mountains** U.S.A.
123 D2 **Big Bend** Swaziland
129 D2 **Biggar** Can.
96 C3 **Biggar** U.K.
99 C3 **Biggleswade** U.K.
134 D1 **Big Hole** *r.* U.S.A.
134 E1 **Bighorn** U.S.A.
136 B1 **Bighorn** *r.* U.S.A.
136 B2 **Bighorn Mountains** U.S.A.
139 C2 **Big Lake** U.S.A.
140 B2 **Big Rapids** U.S.A.
129 D2 **Big River** Can.
129 E2 **Big Sand Lake** Can.
137 D2 **Big Sioux** *r.* U.S.A.
139 C2 **Big Spring** U.S.A.
134 E1 **Big Timber** U.S.A.
130 B2 **Big Trout Lake** Can.
130 A2 **Big Trout Lake** *l.* Can.
109 C2 **Bihać** Bos.-Herz.
75 C2 **Bihar** *state* India
75 C2 **Bihar Sharif** India
110 B1 **Bihor, Vârful** *mt.* Romania
114 A3 **Bijagós, Arquipélago dos** *is* Guinea-Bissau
73 B3 **Bijapur** India
81 C2 **Bījār** Iran
109 C2 **Bijeljina** Bos.-Herz.
109 C2 **Bijelo Polje** Yugo.
71 A3 **Bijie** China
74 B2 **Bikaner** India
66 B1 **Bikin** Rus. Fed.
66 B1 **Bikin** *r.* Rus. Fed.
118 B3 **Bikoro** Dem. Rep. Congo
79 C2 **Bilād Banī Bū 'Alī** Oman
75 C2 **Bilaspur** India
81 C2 **Biläsuvar** Azer.
90 C2 **Bila Tserkva** Ukr.

63 A2 **Bilauktaung Range** *mts* Myanmar/Thai.
106 C1 **Bilbao** Spain
109 C2 **Bileća** Bos.-Herz.
111 C2 **Bilecik** Turkey
103 E1 **Biłgoraj** Pol.
119 D3 **Bilharamulo** Tanz.
90 C2 **Bilhorod-Dnistrovs'kyy** Ukr.
119 C2 **Bili** Dem. Rep. Congo
83 M2 **Bilibino** Rus. Fed.
109 D2 **Bilisht** Albania
104 B3 **Billère** France
134 E1 **Billings** U.S.A.
99 B4 **Bill of Portland** *hd* U.K.
138 A1 **Bill Williams Mountain** U.S.A.
115 D3 **Bilma** Niger
51 E2 **Biloela** Austr.
91 C2 **Bilohirs'k** Ukr.
90 B1 **Bilohir"ya** Ukr.
91 C1 **Bilopillya** Ukr.
91 D2 **Bilovods'k** Ukr.
142 C2 **Biloxi** U.S.A.
51 C2 **Bilpa Morea Claypan** *salt flat* Austr.
101 E2 **Bilshausen** Ger.
115 E3 **Biltine** Chad
90 C2 **Bilyayivka** Ukr.
114 C4 **Bimbila** Ghana
143 E3 **Bimini Islands** Bahamas
74 B2 **Bina-Etawa** India
59 C3 **Binaija, Gunung** *mt.* Indon.
53 C1 **Bindle** Austr.
118 B3 **Bindu** Dem. Rep. Congo
121 C2 **Bindura** Zimbabwe
107 D1 **Binefar** Spain
120 B2 **Binga** Zimbabwe
53 D1 **Bingara** Austr.
100 C3 **Bingen am Rhein** Ger.
114 B4 **Bingerville** Côte d'Ivoire
141 F1 **Bingham** U.S.A.
141 D2 **Binghamton** U.S.A.
115 D2 **Bin Ghanīmah, Jabal** *hills* Libya
81 C2 **Bingöl** Turkey
62 A1 **Bingzhongluo** China
60 A1 **Binjai** Indon.
53 C2 **Binnaway** Austr.
60 B1 **Bintan** *i.* Indon.
60 B2 **Bintuhan** Indon.
61 C1 **Bintulu** *Sarawak* Malaysia
115 C3 **Bin-Yauri** Nigeria
70 B2 **Binzhou** China
118 A2 **Bioco** *i.* Equat. Guinea
109 C2 **Biograd na Moru** Croatia
155 C1 **Biquinhas** Brazil
115 D2 **Birāk** Libya
118 C1 **Birao** C.A.R.
75 C2 **Biratnagar** Nepal
52 B3 **Birchip** Austr.
128 C2 **Birch Mountains** Can.
100 B1 **Birdaard** Neth.
51 C2 **Birdsville** Austr.
80 B2 **Birecik** Turkey
Birendranagar Nepal *see* Surkhet
60 A1 **Bireun** Indon.
75 C2 **Birganj** Nepal
117 B3 **Birhan** *mt.* Eth.
154 B2 **Birigüi** Brazil
118 C2 **Birini** C.A.R.
76 B3 **Bīrjand** Iran
98 B3 **Birkenhead** U.K.
99 C3 **Birmingham** U.K.
142 C2 **Birmingham** U.S.A.
114 A2 **Bîr Mogreïn** Maur.
115 C3 **Birnin-Kebbi** Nigeria
115 C3 **Birnin Konni** Niger
69 E1 **Birobidzhan** Rus. Fed.
97 C2 **Birr** Rep. of Ireland
96 C1 **Birsay** U.K.
78 A2 **Bîr Shalatein** Egypt
88 B2 **Biržai** Lith.
75 B2 **Bisalpur** India
138 B2 **Bisbee** U.S.A.
104 A2 **Biscay, Bay of** *sea* France/Spain
143 D3 **Biscayne Bay** U.S.A.
102 C2 **Bischofshofen** Austria
77 D2 **Bishkek** Kyrg.
123 C3 **Bisho** S. Africa
135 C3 **Bishop** U.S.A.
98 C2 **Bishop Auckland** U.K.
69 E1 **Bishui** China
150 C2 **Bisinaca** Col.
115 C1 **Biskra** Alg.
64 B3 **Bislig** Phil.
136 C1 **Bismarck** U.S.A.
59 D3 **Bismarck Archipelago** *is* P.N.G.
59 D3 **Bismarck Sea** P.N.G.
107 D2 **Bissa, Djebel** *mt.* Alg.
114 A3 **Bissau** Guinea-Bissau
129 E2 **Bissett** Can.
128 C2 **Bistcho Lake** Can.
110 B1 **Bistrița** Romania
110 C1 **Bistrița** *r.* Romania
100 C3 **Bitburg** Ger.
105 D2 **Bitche** France
115 D3 **Bitkine** Chad
81 C2 **Bitlis** Turkey
111 B2 **Bitola** Macedonia
Bitolj Macedonia *see* Bitola
109 C2 **Bitonto** Italy
101 F2 **Bitterfeld** Ger.
122 A3 **Bitterfontein** S. Africa
134 D1 **Bitterroot** *r.* U.S.A.
134 C1 **Bitterroot Range** *mts* U.S.A.
89 E3 **Bityug** *r.* Rus. Fed.
115 D3 **Biu** Nigeria
67 C3 **Biwa-ko** *l.* Japan
77 E1 **Biysk** Rus. Fed.
Bizerta Tunisia *see* **Bizerte**
115 C1 **Bizerte** Tunisia
92 □A2 **Bjargtangar** *hd* Iceland
92 G3 **Bjästa** Sweden
109 C1 **Bjelovar** Croatia
92 G2 **Bjerkvik** Norway
Björneborg Fin. *see* **Pori**
Bjørnøya *i.* Arctic Ocean *see* **Bear Island**
114 B3 **Bla** Mali
137 E3 **Black** *r.* U.S.A.
51 D2 **Blackall** Austr.
98 B3 **Blackburn** U.K.
134 D2 **Blackfoot** U.S.A.
Black Forest *mts* Ger. *see* Schwarzwald
136 C2 **Black Hills** U.S.A.
96 B2 **Black Isle** *pen.* U.K.
129 D2 **Black Lake** Can.
129 D2 **Black Lake** *l.* Can.
99 B4 **Black Mountains** *hills* U.K.
138 A1 **Black Mountains** U.S.A.
98 B3 **Blackpool** U.K.
138 B2 **Black Range** *mts* U.S.A.
Black River *r.* Vietnam *see* **Đa, Sông**
140 A2 **Black River Falls** U.S.A.
134 C2 **Black Rock Desert** U.S.A.
140 C3 **Blacksburg** U.S.A.
80 B1 **Black Sea** Asia/Europe
131 D3 **Blacks Harbour** Can.
97 A1 **Blacksod Bay** Rep. of Ireland
97 C2 **Blackstairs Mountains** *hills* Rep. of Ireland
114 B4 **Black Volta** *r.* Africa
51 D2 **Blackwater** Austr.
97 C2 **Blackwater** *r.* Rep. of Ireland
128 B1 **Blackwater Lake** Can.
50 A3 **Blackwood** *r.* Austr.
87 D4 **Blagodarnyy** Rus. Fed.
111 B2 **Blagoevgrad** Bulg.
69 E1 **Blagoveshchensk** Rus. Fed.
129 D2 **Blaine Lake** Can.
137 D2 **Blair** U.S.A.
96 C2 **Blair Atholl** U.K.
96 C2 **Blairgowrie** U.K.
143 D2 **Blakely** U.S.A.
153 B3 **Blanca, Bahía** *b.* Arg.
52 A1 **Blanche, Lake** *salt flat* Austr.
152 B1 **Blanco** *r.* Bol.
134 B2 **Blanco, Cape** U.S.A.
131 E2 **Blanc-Sablon** Can.
92 □A2 **Blanda** *r.* Iceland
99 B4 **Blandford Forum** U.K.
135 E3 **Blanding** U.S.A.
107 D1 **Blanes** Spain
60 A1 **Blangkejeren** Indon.
100 A2 **Blankenberge** Belgium
100 C2 **Blankenheim** Ger.
100 C2 **Blankenrath** Ger.
147 D3 **Blanquilla, Isla** *i.* Venez.
103 D2 **Blansko** Czech Rep.
121 C2 **Blantyre** Malawi
97 B3 **Blarney** Rep. of Ireland
98 C2 **Blaydon** U.K.
53 C2 **Blayney** Austr.
54 B2 **Blenheim** N.Z.
115 C1 **Blida** Alg.
130 B3 **Blind River** Can.
123 C2 **Bloemfontein** S. Africa
123 C2 **Bloemhof** S. Africa
123 C2 **Bloemhof Dam** S. Africa
104 C2 **Blois** France
92 □A2 **Blönduós** Iceland
97 B1 **Bloody Foreland** *pt* Rep. of Ireland
138 B1 **Bloomfield** U.S.A.
140 B2 **Bloomington** *IL* U.S.A.
140 B3 **Bloomington** *IN* U.S.A.
102 B2 **Bludenz** Austria
137 E2 **Blue Earth** U.S.A.
140 C3 **Bluefield** U.S.A.
146 B3 **Bluefields** Nic.
53 C2 **Blue Mountains** Austr.
134 C1 **Blue Mountains** U.S.A.
116 B3 **Blue Nile** *r.* Eth./Sudan
126 E2 **Bluenose Lake** Can.
140 C3 **Blue Ridge** *mts* U.S.A.
128 C2 **Blue River** Can.
97 B1 **Blue Stack Mountains** *hills* Rep. of Ireland
54 A3 **Bluff** N.Z.
135 E3 **Bluff** U.S.A.
154 C3 **Blumenau** Brazil
52 A2 **Blyth** Austr.
98 C2 **Blyth** U.K.
135 D4 **Blythe** U.S.A.
142 C1 **Blytheville** U.S.A.
114 A4 **Bo** Sierra Leone
64 B2 **Boac** Phil.
146 B3 **Boaco** Nic.
151 E3 **Boa Esperança, Açude** *resr* Brazil
134 C1 **Boardman** U.S.A.
123 C1 **Boatlaname** Botswana
151 F3 **Boa Viagem** Brazil
150 C2 **Boa Vista** Brazil
53 C2 **Bobadah** Austr.
71 B3 **Bobai** China
121 □D2 **Bobaomby, Tanjona** *c.* Madag.
114 B3 **Bobo-Dioulasso** Burkina
121 B3 **Bobonong** Botswana
Bobriki Rus. Fed. *see* Novomoskovsk
89 F3 **Bobrov** Rus. Fed.
91 C1 **Bobrovytsya** Ukr.
91 C2 **Bobrynets'** Ukr.
121 □D3 **Boby** *mt.* Madag.
150 C3 **Boca do Acre** Brazil
155 D1 **Bocaiúva** Brazil
154 A2 **Bocajá** Brazil
118 B2 **Bocaranga** C.A.R.
143 D3 **Boca Raton** U.S.A.
146 B4 **Bocas del Toro** Panama
103 E2 **Bochnia** Pol.
100 B2 **Bocholt** Belgium
100 C2 **Bocholt** Ger.
100 C2 **Bochum** Ger.
123 C1 **Bochum** S. Africa
101 E1 **Bockenem** Ger.
110 B1 **Bocșa** Romania
118 B2 **Boda** C.A.R.
83 I3 **Bodaybo** Rus. Fed.
96 D2 **Boddam** U.K.
115 D3 **Bodélé** *reg.* Chad
92 H2 **Boden** Sweden
Bodensee *l.* Ger./Switz. *see* **Constance, Lake**
99 A4 **Bodmin** U.K.
99 A4 **Bodmin Moor** *moorland* U.K.
92 F2 **Bodø** Norway
111 C3 **Bodrum** Turkey
118 C3 **Boende** Dem. Rep. Congo
63 A2 **Bogale** Myanmar
142 C2 **Bogalusa** U.S.A.
114 B3 **Bogandé** Burkina
118 B2 **Bogangolo** C.A.R.
80 B2 **Boğazlıyan** Turkey
68 B2 **Bogda Shan** *mts* China
53 D1 **Boggabilla** Austr.
53 D2 **Boggabri** Austr.
97 B2 **Boggeragh Mountains** *hills* Rep. of Ireland
Boghari Alg. *see* Ksar el Boukhari
59 D3 **Bogia** P.N.G.
100 B3 **Bogny-sur-Meuse** France
97 C2 **Bog of Allen** *reg.* Rep. of Ireland
53 C3 **Bogong, Mount** Austr.
60 B2 **Bogor** Indon.
89 E3 **Bogoroditsk** Rus. Fed.
150 B2 **Bogotá** Col.
83 G3 **Bogotol** Rus. Fed.
Bogoyavlenskoye Rus. Fed. *see* Pervomayskiy
83 H3 **Boguchany** Rus. Fed.
91 E2 **Boguchar** Rus. Fed.
114 A3 **Bogué** Maur.
70 B2 **Bo Hai** *g.* China
100 A3 **Bohain-en-Vermandois** France
70 B2 **Bohai Wan** *b.* China
Bohemian Forest *mts* *see* **Böhmer Wald**
123 C2 **Bohlokong** S. Africa
101 F3 **Böhmer Wald** *mts* Ger.
91 D1 **Bohodukhiv** Ukr.
64 B3 **Bohol** *i.* Phil.
64 B3 **Bohol Sea** Phil.
77 E2 **Bohu** China
155 C2 **Boi, Ponta do** *pt* Brazil
123 C2 **Boikhutso** S. Africa
154 B3 **Boi Preto, Serra de** *hil* Brazil
154 B1 **Bois** *r.* Brazil
126 D2 **Bois, Lac des** *l.* Can.
134 C2 **Boise** U.S.A.
139 C1 **Boise City** U.S.A.
129 D3 **Boissevain** Can.
123 C2 **Boitumelong** S. Africa
154 C2 **Boituva** Brazil
101 E1 **Boizenburg** Ger.
76 B3 **Bojnūrd** Iran
75 C2 **Bokaro** India
118 B3 **Bokatola** Dem. Rep. Congo
114 A3 **Boké** Guinea
118 C3 **Bokele** Dem. Rep. Cong
93 E4 **Boknafjorden** *sea chan* Norway
115 D3 **Bokoro** Chad
63 A2 **Bokpyin** Myanmar
89 D2 **Boksitogorsk** Rus. Fed.
122 B2 **Bokspits** S. Africa
118 C3 **Bokungu** Dem. Rep. Congo
115 D3 **Bol** Chad
114 A3 **Bolama** Guinea-Bissau
104 C2 **Bolbec** France
77 E2 **Bole** China
118 B3 **Boleko** Dem. Rep. Cong
114 B3 **Bolgatanga** Ghana
90 B2 **Bolhrad** Ukr.
66 B1 **Boli** China
118 B3 **Bolia** Dem. Rep. Congo
92 H3 **Boliden** Sweden
110 C2 **Bolintin-Vale** Romania
137 E3 **Bolivar** *MO* U.S.A.
142 C1 **Bolivar** *TN* U.S.A.
150 B2 **Bolívar, Pico** *mt.* Venez.
152 B1 **Bolivia** *country* S. Amer
89 E3 **Bolkhov** Rus. Fed.
105 C3 **Bollène** France
93 G3 **Bollnäs** Sweden
53 C1 **Bollon** Austr.
101 E2 **Bollstedt** Ger.
93 F4 **Bolmen** *l.* Sweden
118 B3 **Bolobo** Dem. Rep. Cong
108 B2 **Bologna** Italy
89 D2 **Bologovo** Rus. Fed.
89 D2 **Bologoye** Rus. Fed.
123 C2 **Bolokanang** S. Africa
118 B2 **Bolomba** Dem. Rep. Congo
63 B2 **Bolovens, Phouphieng** *plat.* Laos
108 B2 **Bolsena, Lago di** *l.* Italy
83 H1 **Bol'shevik, Ostrov** *i.* Rus. Fed.
86 E2 **Bol'shezemel'skaya Tundra** *lowland* Rus. Fe
83 L2 **Bol'shoy Aluy** *r.* Rus. Fe
66 B2 **Bol'shoy Kamen'** Rus. Fed.
Bol'shoy Kavkaz *mts* Asia/Europe *see* **Caucas**
83 K2 **Bol'shoy Lyakhovskiy, Ostrov** *i.* Rus. Fed.
Bol'shoy Tokmak Kyrg. *see* **Tokmak**
Bol'shoy Tokmak Ukr. *s* **Tokmak**
100 B1 **Bolsward** Neth.
98 B3 **Bolton** U.K.
80 B1 **Bolu** Turkey
59 E3 **Bolubolu** P.N.G.
92 □A2 **Bolungarvík** Iceland
108 B1 **Bolzano** Italy
118 B3 **Boma** Dem. Rep. Congo
53 D2 **Bomaderry** Austr.
53 C3 **Bombala** Austr.
Bombay India *see* **Mum**
155 C1 **Bom Despacho** Brazil
75 D2 **Bomdila** India
154 B1 **Bom Jardim de Goiás** Brazil
151 E4 **Bom Jesus da Lapa** Br
155 D2 **Bom Jesus do Itabapoana** Brazil

5 D1 **Bon, Cap** *c.* Tunisia
7 D3 **Bonaire** *i.* Neth. Antilles
4 C1 **Bonaparte, Mount** U.S.A.
0 B1 **Bonaparte Archipelago** *is* Austr.
1 E3 **Bonavista** Can.
1 E3 **Bonavista Bay** Can.
8 C2 **Bondo** Dem. Rep. Congo
4 B4 **Bondoukou** Côte d'Ivoire
Bône Alg. *see* **Annaba**
1 D2 **Bonerate, Kepulauan** *is* Indon.
5 C1 **Bonfinópolis de Minas** Brazil
7 B4 **Bonga** Eth.
5 D2 **Bongaigaon** India
8 C2 **Bongandanga** Dem. Rep. Congo
2 B2 **Bongani** S. Africa
8 C2 **Bongo, Massif des** *mts* C.A.R.
1 □D2 **Bongolava** *mts* Madag.
5 D3 **Bongor** Chad
4 B4 **Bongouanou** Côte d'Ivoire
3 B2 **Bông Sơn** Vietnam
9 D2 **Bonham** U.S.A.
5 D3 **Bonifacio** *Corsica* France
8 A2 **Bonifacio, Strait of** France/Italy
Bonin Islands Japan *see* Ogasawara-shotō
0 C2 **Bonn** Ger.
4 C1 **Bonners Ferry** U.S.A.
5 D2 **Bonneville** France
0 A3 **Bonnie Rock** Austr.
9 C2 **Bonnyville** Can.
8 A2 **Bonorva** *Sardinia* Italy
3 D1 **Bonshaw** Austr.
1 C1 **Bontang** Indon.
4 A4 **Bonthe** Sierra Leone
4 B2 **Bontoc** Phil.
1 C2 **Bontosunggu** Indon.
3 C3 **Bontrug** S. Africa
3 C1 **Boolba** Austr.
2 B2 **Booligal** Austr.
3 C1 **Boomi** Austr.
3 D1 **Boonah** Austr.
7 E2 **Boone** U.S.A.
2 C2 **Booneville** U.S.A.
7 E3 **Boonville** U.S.A.
2 B2 **Booroorban** Austr.
3 C2 **Boorowa** Austr.
7 C3 **Boosaaso** Somalia
6 G2 **Boothia, Gulf of** Can.
6 F2 **Boothia Peninsula** Can.
8 B3 **Booué** Gabon
0 C2 **Boppard** Ger.
7 B4 **Bor** Sudan
0 B2 **Bor** Turkey
9 D2 **Bor** Yugo.
3 F4 **Borås** Sweden
1 D3 **Borāzjān** Iran
0 D3 **Borba** Brazil
4 B3 **Bordeaux** France
6 E1 **Borden Island** Can.
7 G2 **Borden Peninsula** Can.
2 B3 **Bordertown** Austr.
7 D2 **Bordj Bou Arréridj** Alg.
7 D2 **Bordj Bounaama** Alg.
4 B2 **Bordj Flye Ste-Marie** Alg.
5 C1 **Bordj Messaouda** Alg.
4 C2 **Bordj Mokhtar** Alg.
Bordj Omar Driss Alg. *see* Bordj Omer Driss
5 C2 **Bordj Omer Driss** Alg.
4 B1 **Borðoy** *i.* Faroe Is
4 B1 **Borðoy** *i.* Faroe Is
Borgå Fin. *see* **Porvoo**
2 □A3 **Borgarnes** Iceland
9 C1 **Borger** U.S.A.
3 G4 **Borgholm** Sweden
0 B2 **Borgloon** Belgium
8 A1 **Borgosesia** Italy
7 D3 **Borisoglebsk** Rus. Fed.
9 E2 **Borisoglebskiy** Rus. Fed.
1 D1 **Borisovka** Rus. Fed.
9 C2 **Bo River Post** Sudan
0 C2 **Borken** Ger.
2 G2 **Borkenes** Norway
0 C1 **Borkum** Ger.
0 C1 **Borkum** *i.* Ger.
3 G3 **Borlänge** Sweden
1 F2 **Borna** Ger.
0 C1 **Borne** Neth.
1 C1 **Borneo** *i.* Asia
3 F4 **Bornholm** *i.* Denmark
1 C3 **Bornova** Turkey
0 B1 **Borodyanka** Ukr.
7 E2 **Borohoro Shan** *mts* China
4 B3 **Boron** Mali
9 D2 **Borovichi** Rus. Fed.
89 E2 **Borovsk** Rus. Fed.
76 C1 **Borovskoy** Kazakh.
51 C1 **Borroloola** Austr.
110 B1 **Borşa** Romania
90 B2 **Borshchiv** Ukr.
69 D1 **Borshchovochnyy Khrebet** *mts* Rus. Fed.
101 E1 **Börßum** Ger.
Bortala China *see* **Bole**
81 C2 **Borūjerd** Iran
90 A2 **Boryslav** Ukr.
90 C1 **Boryspil'** Ukr.
91 C1 **Borzna** Ukr.
69 D1 **Borzya** Rus. Fed.
109 C1 **Bosanska Dubica** Bos.-Herz.
109 C1 **Bosanska Gradiška** Bos.-Herz.
109 C2 **Bosanska Krupa** Bos.-Herz.
109 C1 **Bosanski Novi** Bos.-Herz.
109 C2 **Bosansko Grahovo** Bos.-Herz.
71 A3 **Bose** China
123 C2 **Boshof** S. Africa
109 C2 **Bosnia-Herzegovina** *country* Europe
118 B2 **Bosobolo** Dem. Rep. Congo
111 C2 **Bosporus** *str.* Turkey
138 B2 **Bosque** U.S.A.
118 B2 **Bossangoa** C.A.R.
118 B2 **Bossembélé** C.A.R.
142 B2 **Bossier City** U.S.A.
122 A2 **Bossiesvlei** Namibia
68 B2 **Bosten Hu** *l.* China
99 C3 **Boston** U.K.
141 E2 **Boston** U.S.A.
142 B1 **Boston Mountains** U.S.A.
53 D2 **Botany Bay** Austr.
120 B3 **Boteti** *r.* Botswana
110 B2 **Botev** *mt.* Bulg.
80 A1 **Botevgrad** Bulg.
92 G3 **Bothnia, Gulf of** Fin./Sweden
110 C1 **Botoşani** Romania
70 B2 **Botou** China
123 C2 **Botshabelo** S. Africa
120 B3 **Botswana** *country* Africa
109 C3 **Botte Donato, Monte** *mt.* Italy
136 C1 **Bottineau** U.S.A.
100 C2 **Bottrop** Ger.
154 C2 **Botucatu** Brazil
114 B4 **Bouaké** Côte d'Ivoire
118 B2 **Bouar** C.A.R.
114 B1 **Bouârfa** Morocco
131 D3 **Bouctouche** Can.
107 E2 **Bougaa** Alg.
48 G4 **Bougainville Island** P.N.G.
Bougie Alg. *see* **Bejaïa**
114 B3 **Bougouni** Mali
100 B3 **Bouillon** Belgium
107 D2 **Bouira** Alg.
114 A2 **Boujdour** Western Sahara
50 B3 **Boulder** Austr.
136 B2 **Boulder** *CO* U.S.A.
134 D1 **Boulder** *MT* U.S.A.
135 D3 **Boulder City** U.S.A.
Boulhaut Morocco *see* Ben Slimane
51 C2 **Boulia** Austr.
104 C2 **Boulogne-Billancourt** France
104 C1 **Boulogne-sur-Mer** France
118 C2 **Boulouba** C.A.R.
118 B3 **Boumango** Gabon
118 B2 **Boumba** *r.* Cameroon
107 D2 **Boumerdes** Alg.
114 B4 **Bouna** Côte d'Ivoire
114 B4 **Boundiali** Côte d'Ivoire
134 D2 **Bountiful** U.S.A.
49 I8 **Bounty Islands** N.Z.
114 B3 **Bourem** Mali
104 C2 **Bourganeuf** France
105 D2 **Bourg-en-Bresse** France
104 C2 **Bourges** France
105 C2 **Bourgogne** *reg.* France
105 D2 **Bourgoin-Jallieu** France
53 C2 **Bourke** Austr.
99 C3 **Bourne** U.K.
99 C4 **Bournemouth** U.K.
118 C1 **Bourtoutou** Chad
115 C1 **Bou Saâda** Alg.
115 D3 **Bousso** Chad
100 A2 **Boussu** Belgium
114 A3 **Boutilimit** Maur.
128 C3 **Bow** *r.* Can.
Bowa China *see* **Muli**
51 D2 **Bowen** Austr.
53 C3 **Bowen, Mount** Austr.
129 C3 **Bow Island** Can.
140 B3 **Bowling Green** *KY* U.S.A.
137 E3 **Bowling Green** *MO* U.S.A.
140 C2 **Bowling Green** *OH* U.S.A.
136 C1 **Bowman** U.S.A.
53 D2 **Bowral** Austr.
101 D3 **Boxberg** Ger.
100 B2 **Boxtel** Neth.
80 B1 **Boyabat** Turkey
71 B3 **Boyang** China
97 B2 **Boyle** Rep. of Ireland
97 C2 **Boyne** *r.* Rep. of Ireland
136 B2 **Boysen Reservoir** U.S.A.
152 B2 **Boyuibe** Bol.
111 C3 **Bozburun** Turkey
111 C3 **Bozcaada** *i.* Turkey
111 C3 **Bozdağ** *mt.* Turkey
111 C3 **Boz Dağları** *mts* Turkey
111 C3 **Bozdoğan** Turkey
134 D1 **Bozeman** U.S.A.
118 B2 **Bozoum** C.A.R.
111 D3 **Bozüyük** Turkey
109 C2 **Brač** *i.* Croatia
130 C3 **Bracebridge** Can.
131 D3 **Brachet, Lac au** *l.* Can.
93 G3 **Bräcke** Sweden
99 C4 **Bracknell** U.K.
109 C2 **Bradano** *r.* Italy
143 D3 **Bradenton** U.S.A.
98 C3 **Bradford** U.K.
141 D2 **Bradford** U.S.A.
139 D2 **Brady** U.S.A.
96 C2 **Braemar** U.K.
106 B1 **Braga** Port.
151 E3 **Bragança** Brazil
106 B1 **Bragança** Port.
155 C2 **Bragança Paulista** Brazil
89 D3 **Brahin** Belarus
75 D2 **Brahmanbaria** Bangl.
75 C3 **Brahmapur** India
62 A1 **Brahmaputra** *r.* China/India
53 C3 **Braidwood** Austr.
110 C1 **Brăila** Romania
137 E1 **Brainerd** U.S.A.
99 D4 **Braintree** U.K.
100 B2 **Braives** Belgium
101 D1 **Brake (Unterweser)** Ger.
122 A1 **Brakwater** Namibia
98 B2 **Brampton** U.K.
101 D1 **Bramsche** Ger.
150 C3 **Branco** *r.* Brazil
101 F1 **Brandenburg** Ger.
129 E3 **Brandon** Can.
142 C2 **Brandon** U.S.A.
97 A2 **Brandon Mountain** *hill* Rep. of Ireland
122 B3 **Brandvlei** S. Africa
103 D1 **Braniewo** Pol.
130 B3 **Brantford** Can.
53 D2 **Branxton** Austr.
131 D3 **Bras d'Or Lake** Can.
155 D1 **Brasil, Planalto do** *plat.* Brazil
154 C1 **Brasilândia** Brazil
154 C1 **Brasília** Brazil
155 D1 **Brasília de Minas** Brazil
88 C2 **Braslaw** Belarus
110 C1 **Braşov** Romania
103 D2 **Bratislava** Slovakia
83 H3 **Bratsk** Rus. Fed.
102 C2 **Braunau am Inn** Austria
101 E1 **Braunschweig** Ger.
92 □A2 **Brautarholt** Iceland
Bravo del Norte, Río *r.* Mex./U.S.A. *see* Rio Grande
135 C4 **Brawley** U.S.A.
97 C2 **Bray** Rep. of Ireland
150 D2 **Brazil** *country* S. America
158 E6 **Brazil Basin** *sea feature* S. Atlantic Ocean
139 D3 **Brazos** *r.* U.S.A.
118 B3 **Brazzaville** Congo
109 C2 **Brčko** Bos.-Herz.
96 C2 **Brechin** U.K.
100 B2 **Brecht** Belgium
139 D2 **Breckenridge** U.S.A.
103 D2 **Břeclav** Czech Rep.
99 B4 **Brecon** U.K.
99 B4 **Brecon Beacons** *reg.* U.K.
100 B2 **Breda** Neth.
122 B3 **Bredasdorp** S. Africa
102 B2 **Bregenz** Austria
92 H1 **Breivikbotn** Norway
92 E3 **Brekstad** Norway
101 D1 **Bremen** Ger.
101 D1 **Bremerhaven** Ger.
Bremersdorp Swaziland *see* **Manzini**
134 B1 **Bremerton** U.S.A.
101 D1 **Bremervörde** Ger.
139 D2 **Brenham** U.S.A.
108 B1 **Brennero** Italy
102 C2 **Brenner Pass** Austria/Italy
99 D4 **Brentwood** U.K.
108 B1 **Brescia** Italy
100 A2 **Breskens** Neth.
108 B1 **Bressanone** Italy
96 □ **Bressay** *i.* U.K.
104 B2 **Bressuire** France
88 B3 **Brest** Belarus
104 B2 **Brest** France
Brest-Litovsk Belarus *see* Brest
104 B2 **Bretagne** *reg.* France
142 C3 **Breton Sound** *b.* U.S.A.
151 D3 **Breves** Brazil
53 C1 **Brewarrina** Austr.
134 C1 **Brewster** U.S.A.
89 E2 **Breytovo** Rus. Fed.
Brezhnev Rus. Fed. *see* **Naberezhnyye Chelny**
109 C1 **Brezovo Polje** *hill* Croatia
118 C2 **Bria** C.A.R.
105 D3 **Briançon** France
90 B2 **Briceni** Moldova
Brichany Moldova *see* Briceni
99 B4 **Bridgend** U.K.
141 E2 **Bridgeport** *CT* U.S.A.
136 C2 **Bridgeport** *NE* U.S.A.
147 E3 **Bridgetown** Barbados
131 D3 **Bridgewater** Can.
99 B3 **Bridgnorth** U.K.
99 B4 **Bridgwater** U.K.
99 B4 **Bridgwater Bay** U.K.
98 C2 **Bridlington** U.K.
98 C2 **Bridlington Bay** U.K.
99 B4 **Bridport** U.K.
105 D2 **Brig** Switz.
134 D2 **Brigham City** U.S.A.
53 C3 **Bright** Austr.
54 B3 **Brighton** N.Z.
99 C4 **Brighton** U.K.
136 C3 **Brighton** *CO* U.S.A.
140 C2 **Brighton** *MI* U.S.A.
105 D3 **Brignoles** France
114 A3 **Brikama** Gambia
101 D2 **Brilon** Ger.
109 C2 **Brindisi** Italy
97 B1 **Brinlack** Rep. of Ireland
53 D1 **Brisbane** Austr.
99 B4 **Bristol** U.K.
141 E2 **Bristol** *CT* U.S.A.
143 D1 **Bristol** *TN* U.S.A.
99 A4 **Bristol Channel** *est.* U.K.
128 B2 **British Columbia** *prov.* Can.
British Guiana *country* S. America *see* **Guyana**
British Honduras *country* Central America *see* **Belize**
56 C6 **British Indian Ocean Territory** *terr.* Indian Ocean
British Solomon Islands *country* S. Pacific Ocean *see* **Solomon Islands**
123 C2 **Brits** S. Africa
122 B3 **Britstown** S. Africa
Brittany *reg.* France *see* Bretagne
104 C2 **Brive-la-Gaillarde** France
106 C1 **Briviesca** Spain
99 B4 **Brixham** U.K.
103 D2 **Brno** Czech Rep.
Broach India *see* **Bharuch**
143 D2 **Broad** *r.* U.S.A.
130 C2 **Broadback** *r.* Can.
96 A1 **Broad Bay** U.K.
53 C3 **Broadford** Austr.
96 B2 **Broadford** U.K.
96 C3 **Broad Law** *hill* U.K.
136 B1 **Broadus** U.S.A.
129 D2 **Brochet** Can.
129 D2 **Brochet, Lac** *l.* Can.
101 E1 **Bröckel** Ger.
101 E2 **Brocken** *mt.* Ger.
126 E1 **Brock Island** Can.
130 C3 **Brockville** Can.
127 G2 **Brodeur Peninsula** Can.
96 B3 **Brodick** U.K.
103 D1 **Brodnica** Pol.
90 B1 **Brody** Ukr.
139 D1 **Broken Arrow** U.S.A.
137 D2 **Broken Bow** U.S.A.
52 B2 **Broken Hill** Austr.
Broken Hill Zambia *see* **Kabwe**
159 F6 **Broken Plateau** *sea feature* Indian Ocean
151 D2 **Brokopondo** Suriname

99 B3 **Bromsgrove** U.K.
93 E4 **Brønderslev** Denmark
123 C2 **Bronkhorstspruit** S. Africa
92 F2 **Brønnøysund** Norway
64 A3 **Brooke's Point** Phil.
142 B2 **Brookhaven** U.S.A.
134 B2 **Brookings** *OR* U.S.A.
137 D2 **Brookings** *SD* U.S.A.
128 C2 **Brooks** Can.
126 C2 **Brooks Range** *mts* U.S.A.
143 D3 **Brooksville** U.S.A.
141 D2 **Brookville** U.S.A.
96 B2 **Broom, Loch** *inlet* U.K.
50 B1 **Broome** Austr.
134 B2 **Brothers** U.S.A.
Broughton Island Can. *see* **Qikiqtarjuaq**
90 C1 **Brovary** Ukr.
139 C2 **Brownfield** U.S.A.
128 C3 **Browning** U.S.A.
142 C1 **Brownsville** *TN* U.S.A.
139 D3 **Brownsville** *TX* U.S.A.
139 D2 **Brownwood** U.S.A.
92 □A2 **Brú** Iceland
104 C1 **Bruay-la-Bussière** France
140 B1 **Bruce Crossing** U.S.A.
130 B3 **Bruce Peninsula** Can.
103 D2 **Bruck an der Mur** Austria
100 A2 **Bruges** Belgium
Brugge Belgium *see* Bruges
62 A1 **Bruint** India
128 C2 **Brûlé** Can.
151 E4 **Brumado** Brazil
93 F3 **Brumunddal** Norway
61 C1 **Brunei** *country* Asia
Brunei Brunei *see* Bandar Seri Begawan
102 C2 **Brunico** Italy
Brünn Czech Rep. *see* Brno
101 D1 **Brunsbüttel** Ger.
143 D2 **Brunswick** *GA* U.S.A.
141 F2 **Brunswick** *ME* U.S.A.
53 D1 **Brunswick Head** Austr.
123 D2 **Bruntville** S. Africa
136 C2 **Brush** U.S.A.
100 B2 **Brussels** Belgium
Bruxelles Belgium *see* Brussels
139 D2 **Bryan** U.S.A.
89 D3 **Bryansk** Rus. Fed.
91 D2 **Bryn'kovskaya** Rus. Fed.
91 D2 **Bryukhovetskaya** Rus. Fed.
103 D1 **Brzeg** Pol.
Brześć nad Bugiem Belarus *see* **Brest**
114 A3 **Buba** Guinea-Bissau
111 C3 **Buca** Turkey
80 B2 **Bucak** Turkey
150 B2 **Bucaramanga** Col.
90 B2 **Buchach** Ukr.
53 C3 **Buchan** Austr.
114 A4 **Buchanan** Liberia
110 C2 **Bucharest** Romania
101 D1 **Bucholz in der Nordheide** Ger.
110 C1 **Bucin, Pasul** *pass* Romania
101 D1 **Bückeburg** Ger.
138 A2 **Buckeye** U.S.A.
96 C2 **Buckhaven** U.K.
96 C2 **Buckie** U.K.
99 C3 **Buckingham** U.K.
51 C1 **Buckingham Bay** Austr.
51 D2 **Buckland Tableland** *reg.* Austr.
52 A2 **Buckleboo** Austr.
141 F2 **Bucksport** U.S.A.
103 D2 **Bučovice** Czech Rep.
București Romania *see* Bucharest
89 D3 **Buda-Kashalyova** Belarus
103 D2 **Budapest** Hungary
75 B2 **Budaun** India
108 A2 **Buddusò** *Sardinia* Italy
99 A4 **Bude** U.K.
87 D4 **Budennovsk** Rus. Fed.
Budennoye Rus. Fed. *see* **Krasnogvardeyskoye**
89 D2 **Budogoshch'** Rus. Fed.
108 A2 **Budoni** *Sardinia* Italy
Budweis Czech Rep. *see* **České Budějovice**
118 A2 **Buea** Cameroon
135 B4 **Buellton** U.S.A.
150 B2 **Buenaventura** Col.
144 B2 **Buenaventura** Mex.
Buena Vista *i.* N. Mariana Is *see* **Tinian**
106 C1 **Buendia, Embalse de** *resr* Spain
155 D1 **Buenópolis** Brazil
153 C3 **Buenos Aires** Arg.
153 A4 **Buenos Aires, Lago** *l.* Arg./Chile
141 D2 **Buffalo** *NY* U.S.A.
136 C1 **Buffalo** *SD* U.S.A.
139 D2 **Buffalo** *TX* U.S.A.
136 B2 **Buffalo** *WY* U.S.A.
129 D2 **Buffalo Narrows** Can.
121 C3 **Buffalo Range** Zimbabwe
122 A2 **Buffels** *watercourse* S. Africa
123 C1 **Buffels Drift** S. Africa
110 C2 **Buftea** Romania
103 E1 **Bug** *r.* Pol.
61 C2 **Bugel, Tanjung** *pt* Indon.
109 C2 **Bugojno** Bos.-Herz.
86 D2 **Bugrino** Rus. Fed.
64 A3 **Bugsuk** *i.* Phil.
87 E3 **Bugul'ma** Rus. Fed.
87 E3 **Buguruslan** Rus. Fed.
121 C2 **Buhera** Zimbabwe
110 C1 **Buhuşi** Romania
99 B3 **Builth Wells** U.K.
69 D1 **Buir Nur** *l.* Mongolia
120 A3 **Buitepos** Namibia
109 D2 **Bujanovac** Yugo.
119 C3 **Bujumbura** Burundi
69 D1 **Bukachacha** Rus. Fed.
120 B2 **Bukalo** Namibia
119 C3 **Bukavu** Dem. Rep. Congo
76 C3 **Bukhara** Uzbek.
60 B2 **Bukittinggi** Indon.
119 D3 **Bukoba** Tanz.
103 D1 **Bukowiec** *hill* Pol.
59 C3 **Bula** Indon.
53 D2 **Bulahdelal** Austr.
121 B3 **Bulawayo** Zimbabwe
111 C3 **Buldan** Turkey
123 D2 **Bulembu** Swaziland
68 C1 **Bulgan** Mongolia
110 C2 **Bulgaria** *country* Europe
54 B2 **Buller** *r.* N.Z.
138 A1 **Bullhead City** U.S.A.
52 B1 **Bulloo** *watercourse* Austr.
52 B1 **Bulloo Downs** Austr.
122 A1 **Büllsport** Namibia
61 D2 **Bulukumba** Indon.
118 B3 **Bulungu** Dem. Rep. Congo
118 B3 **Bumba** Dem. Rep. Congo
118 C2 **Bumba** Dem. Rep. Congo
62 A1 **Bumhkang** Myanmar
118 B3 **Buna** Dem. Rep. Congo
97 B1 **Bunbeg** Rep. of Ireland
50 A3 **Bunbury** Austr.
97 C2 **Bunclody** Rep. of Ireland
97 C1 **Buncrana** Rep. of Ireland
119 D3 **Bunda** Tanz.
51 E2 **Bundaberg** Austr.
53 C1 **Bundaleer** Austr.
53 D2 **Bundarra** Austr.
74 B2 **Bundi** India
97 B1 **Bundoran** Rep. of Ireland
75 C2 **Bundu** India
53 C3 **Bungendore** Austr.
119 D2 **Bungoma** Kenya
67 B4 **Bungo-suidō** *sea chan.* Japan
119 D2 **Bunia** Dem. Rep. Congo
118 C3 **Bunianga** Dem. Rep. Congo
63 B2 **Buôn Mê Thuôt** Vietnam
119 D3 **Bura** Kenya
117 C3 **Buraan** Somalia
75 C1 **Burang** China
117 C4 **Burao** Somalia
78 B2 **Buraydah** Saudi Arabia
101 D2 **Burbach** Ger.
111 D3 **Burdur** Turkey
Burdwan India *see* Barddhamān
117 B3 **Burē** Eth.
99 D3 **Bure** *r.* U.K.
69 E1 **Bureinskiy Khrebet** *mts* Rus. Fed.
101 D2 **Büren** Ger.
Bureya Range *mts* Rus. Fed. *see* Bureinskiy Khrebet
110 C2 **Burgas** Bulg.
101 E1 **Burg bei Magdeburg** Ger.
101 E1 **Burgdorf** Ger.
101 E1 **Burgdorf** Ger.
131 E3 **Burgeo** Can.
123 C3 **Burgersdorp** S. Africa
123 D1 **Burgersfort** S. Africa
100 A2 **Burgh-Haamstede** Neth.
101 F3 **Burglengenfeld** Ger.
145 C2 **Burgos** Mex.
106 C1 **Burgos** Spain
Burgundy *reg.* France *see* Bourgogne
111 C3 **Burhaniye** Turkey
74 B2 **Burhanpur** India
75 C2 **Burhar-Dhanpuri** India
101 D1 **Burhave (Butjadingen)** Ger.
154 C2 **Buri** Brazil
60 B2 **Buriai** Indon.
64 B2 **Burias** *i.* Phil.
131 E3 **Burin** Can.
63 B2 **Buriram** Thai.
154 C1 **Buriti Alegre** Brazil
151 E3 **Buriti Bravo** Brazil
155 C1 **Buritis** Brazil
107 C2 **Burjassot** Spain
139 D2 **Burkburnett** U.S.A.
51 C1 **Burketown** Austr.
114 B3 **Burkina** *country* Africa
134 D2 **Burley** U.S.A.
136 C3 **Burlington** *CO* U.S.A.
137 E2 **Burlington** *IA* U.S.A.
143 E1 **Burlington** *NC* U.S.A.
141 E2 **Burlington** *VT* U.S.A.
134 B2 **Burney** U.S.A.
51 D4 **Burnie** Austr.
98 B3 **Burnley** U.K.
134 C2 **Burns** U.S.A.
134 C2 **Burns Junction** U.S.A.
128 B2 **Burns Lake** Can.
137 E2 **Burnsville** U.S.A.
101 F1 **Burow** Ger.
77 E2 **Burqin** China
52 A2 **Burra** Austr.
109 D2 **Burrel** Albania
97 B2 **Burren** *reg.* Rep. of Ireland
53 C2 **Burrendong Reservoir** Austr.
53 C2 **Burren Junction** Austr.
107 C2 **Burriana** Spain
53 C2 **Burrinjuck Reservoir** Austr.
144 B2 **Burro, Serranías del** *mts* Mex.
111 C2 **Bursa** Turkey
116 B2 **Bûr Safâga** Egypt
Bûr Sa'îd Egypt *see* Port Said
Bûr Sudan Sudan *see* Port Sudan
130 C2 **Burton, Lac** *l.* Can.
97 B1 **Burtonport** Rep. of Ireland
99 C3 **Burton upon Trent** U.K.
52 B2 **Burtundy** Austr.
59 C3 **Buru** *i.* Indon.
119 D3 **Burundi** *country* Africa
119 C3 **Bururi** Burundi
96 C1 **Burwick** U.K.
98 B3 **Bury** U.K.
91 C1 **Buryn'** Ukr.
76 B2 **Burynshyk** Kazakh.
99 D3 **Bury St Edmunds** U.K.
118 C3 **Busanga** Dem. Rep. Congo
81 D3 **Būshehr** Iran
119 D3 **Bushenyi** Uganda
Bushire Iran *see* **Būshehr**
118 C2 **Businga** Dem. Rep. Congo
50 A3 **Busselton** Austr.
139 C3 **Bustamante** Mex.
108 A1 **Busto Arsizio** Italy
64 A2 **Busuanga** Phil.
118 C2 **Buta** Dem. Rep. Congo
119 C3 **Butare** Rwanda
96 B3 **Bute** *i.* U.K.
119 C2 **Butembo** Dem. Rep. Congo
123 C2 **Butha Buthe** Lesotho
141 D2 **Butler** U.S.A.
61 D2 **Buton** *i.* Indon.
134 D1 **Butte** U.S.A.
60 B1 **Butterworth** Malaysia
96 A1 **Butt of Lewis** *hd* U.K.
129 E2 **Button Bay** Can.
131 D1 **Button Islands** Can.
64 B3 **Butuan** Phil.
89 F3 **Buturlinovka** Rus. Fed.
75 C2 **Butwal** Nepal
101 D2 **Butzbach** Ger.
117 C4 **Buulobarde** Somalia
117 C5 **Buur Gaabo** Somalia
117 C4 **Buurhabaka** Somalia
78 A2 **Buwātah** Saudi Arabia
101 D1 **Buxtehude** Ger.
98 C3 **Buxton** U.K.
89 F2 **Buy** Rus. Fed.
87 D4 **Buynaksk** Rus. Fed.
111 C3 **Büyükmenderes** *r.* Turkey
65 A1 **Buyun Shan** *mt.* China
74 B1 **Buzai Gumbad** Afgh.
110 C1 **Buzău** Romania
110 C1 **Buzău** *r.* Romania
121 C2 **Búzi** Moz.
87 E3 **Buzuluk** Rus. Fed.
88 C3 **Byahoml'** Belarus
110 C2 **Byala** Bulg.
110 C2 **Byala** Bulg.
88 C3 **Byalynichy** Belarus
88 D3 **Byarezina** *r.* Belarus
88 B3 **Byaroza** Belarus
88 C3 **Byarozawka** Belarus
103 D1 **Bydgoszcz** Pol.
Byelorussia *country* Europe *see* **Belarus**
88 C3 **Byerazino** Belarus
88 C2 **Byeshankovichy** Belaru
89 D3 **Bykhaw** Belarus
127 G2 **Bylot Island** Can.
53 C2 **Byrock** Austr.
53 D1 **Byron Bay** Austr.
83 J2 **Bytantay** *r.* Rus. Fed.
103 D1 **Bytom** Pol.
103 D1 **Bytów** Pol.

C

120 A2 **Caála** Angola
154 B2 **Caarapó** Brazil
155 C1 **Caatinga** Brazil
106 B1 **Cabañaquinta** Spain
64 B2 **Cabanatuan** Phil.
117 C3 **Cabdul Qaadir** Somalia
154 A1 **Cabeceira Rio Manso** Brazil
154 C1 **Cabeceiras** Brazil
106 B2 **Cabeza del Buey** Spair
152 B1 **Cabezas** Bol.
150 B1 **Cabimas** Venez.
120 A1 **Cabinda** Angola
118 B3 **Cabinda** *prov.* Angola
151 F3 **Cabo** Brazil
155 D2 **Cabo Frio** Brazil
155 D2 **Cabo Frio, Ilha do** *i.* Br
130 C3 **Cabonga, Réservoir** *resr* Can.
53 D1 **Caboolture** Austr.
150 B3 **Cabo Pantoja** Peru
Cabora Bassa, Lake *re* Moz. *see* Cahora Bassa, Lago de
144 A1 **Caborca** Mex.
131 D3 **Cabot Strait** Can.
106 C2 **Cabra** Spain
155 D1 **Cabral, Serra do** *mts* Brazil
107 D2 **Cabrera** *i.* Spain
129 D2 **Cabri** Can.
107 C2 **Cabriel** *r.* Spain
154 B3 **Caçador** Brazil
109 D2 **Čačak** Yugo.
108 A2 **Caccia, Capo** *c. Sardini* Italy
106 B2 **Cacém** Port.
151 D4 **Cáceres** Brazil
106 B2 **Cáceres** Spain
128 B2 **Cache Creek** Can.
114 A3 **Cacheu** Guinea-Bissau
151 D3 **Cachimbo, Serra do** *hi* Brazil
154 B1 **Cachoeira Alta** Brazil
155 D2 **Cachoeiro de Itapemir** Brazil
114 A3 **Cacine** Guinea-Bissau
120 A2 **Cacolo** Angola
120 A2 **Caconda** Angola
154 B1 **Caçu** Brazil
103 D2 **Čadca** Slovakia
101 D1 **Cadenberge** Ger.
145 B2 **Cadereyta** Mex.
140 B2 **Cadillac** U.S.A.
64 B2 **Cadiz** Phil.
106 B2 **Cádiz** Spain
106 B2 **Cádiz, Golfo de** *g.* Spai
128 C2 **Cadotte Lake** Can.
104 B2 **Caen** France
Caerdydd U.K. *see* **Card**
Caerfyrddin U.K. *see* Carmarthen
Caergybi U.K. *see* Holyhead
98 A3 **Caernarfon** U.K.
99 A3 **Caernarfon Bay** U.K.
Caernarvon U.K. *see* Caernarfon
152 B2 **Cafayate** Arg.
154 C2 **Cafelândia** Brazil
64 B3 **Cagayan de Oro** Phil.
108 B2 **Cagli** Italy
108 A3 **Cagliari** *Sardinia* Italy

8 A3 Cagliari, Golfo di b. Sardinia Italy
0 A2 Cahama Angola
7 B3 Caha Mountains hills Rep. of Ireland
7 A3 Cahermore Rep. of Ireland
7 A3 Cahersiveen Rep. of Ireland
7 C2 Cahir Rep. of Ireland
1 C2 Cahora Bassa, Lago de resr Moz.
7 C2 Cahore Point Rep. of Ireland
4 C3 Cahors France
0 B2 Cahul Moldova
1 C2 Caia Moz.
1 D4 Caiabis, Serra dos hills Brazil
0 B2 Caianda Angola
4 B1 Caiapó, Serra do mts Brazil
4 B1 Caiapônia Brazil
7 C2 Caicos Islands Turks and Caicos Is
6 C2 Cairngorm Mountains U.K.
6 B3 Cairnryan U.K.
1 D1 Cairns Austr.
6 B1 Cairo Egypt
Caisleán an Bharraigh Rep. of Ireland see Castlebar
6 C3 Caistor U.K.
0 A2 Caiundo Angola
0 B3 Cajamarca Peru
9 C1 Čakovec Croatia
3 C3 Cala S. Africa
5 C4 Calabar Nigeria
0 C2 Calabozo Venez.
0 B2 Calafat Romania
3 A5 Calafate Arg.
7 C1 Calahorra Spain
0 A2 Calai Angola
4 C1 Calais France
1 F1 Calais U.S.A.
2 B2 Calama Chile
4 A2 Calamian Group is Phil.
7 C1 Calamocha Spain
0 A1 Calandula Angola
0 A1 Calang Indon.
5 E1 Calanscio Sand Sea des. Libya
4 B2 Calapan Phil.
0 C2 Călărași Romania
7 C1 Calatayud Spain
4 B2 Calayan i. Phil.
4 B2 Calbayog Phil.
1 F3 Calcanhar, Ponta do pt Brazil
1 D2 Calçoene Brazil
5 C2 Calcutta India
6 B2 Caldas da Rainha Port.
4 C1 Caldas Novas Brazil
2 A2 Caldera Chile
1 D2 Caldervale Austr.
4 C2 Caldwell U.S.A.
3 C3 Caledon r. Lesotho/S. Africa
2 A3 Caledon S. Africa
3 B4 Caleta Olivia Arg.
8 A2 Calf of Man i. Isle of Man
8 C2 Calgary Can.
0 B2 Cali Col.
3 B3 Calicut India
5 D3 Caliente U.S.A.
5 B2 California state U.S.A.
4 A1 California, Golfo de g. Mex.
5 B3 California Aqueduct canal U.S.A.
1 C2 Călilabad Azer.
2 B3 Calitzdorp S. Africa
5 C2 Calkiní Mex.
2 B1 Callabonna, Lake salt flat Austr.
5 C3 Callaghan, Mount U.S.A.
7 C2 Callan Rep. of Ireland
6 B2 Callander U.K.
0 B4 Callao Peru
9 A4 Callington U.K.
8 B3 Caltagirone Sicily Italy
8 B3 Caltanissetta Sicily Italy
0 A1 Calulo Angola
0 B2 Calunda Angola
0 A2 Caluquembe Angola
7 D3 Caluula Somalia
5 D3 Calvi Corsica France
7 D2 Calvià Spain
4 B2 Calvillo Mex.
2 A3 Calvinia S. Africa
9 C2 Calvo, Monte mt. Italy
120 A1 Camabatela Angola
151 F4 Camaçari Brazil
144 B2 Camacho Mex.
120 A2 Camacupa Angola
146 C2 Camagüey Cuba
146 C2 Camagüey, Archipiélago de is Cuba
150 B4 Camana Peru
120 B2 Camanongue Angola
154 B1 Camapuã Brazil
145 C2 Camargo Mex.
63 B3 Ca Mau Vietnam
Cambay India see Khambhat
63 B2 Cambodia country Asia
99 A4 Camborne U.K.
105 C1 Cambrai France
99 B3 Cambrian Mountains hills U.K.
140 C2 Cambridge Can.
54 C1 Cambridge N.Z.
99 D3 Cambridge U.K.
141 E2 Cambridge MA U.S.A.
141 D3 Cambridge MD U.S.A.
137 E1 Cambridge MN U.S.A.
140 C2 Cambridge OH U.S.A.
126 E2 Cambridge Bay Can.
131 D2 Cambrien, Lac l. Can.
120 B1 Cambulo Angola
53 D2 Camden Austr.
142 B2 Camden AR U.S.A.
141 F2 Camden ME U.S.A.
141 D3 Camden NJ U.S.A.
137 E3 Camdenton U.S.A.
137 E3 Cameron U.S.A.
118 B2 Cameroon country Africa
118 A2 Cameroun, Mont vol. Cameroon
151 E3 Cametá Brazil
64 B3 Camiguin i. Phil.
64 B2 Camiguin i. Phil.
152 B2 Camiri Bol.
151 E3 Camocim Brazil
51 C1 Camooweal Austr.
63 A3 Camorta i. India
153 A4 Campana, Isla i. Chile
155 D1 Campanário Brazil
155 C2 Campanha Brazil
122 B2 Campbell S. Africa
54 B2 Campbell, Cape N.Z.
48 H9 Campbell Island N.Z.
156 D9 Campbell Plateau sea feature S. Pacific Ocean
128 B2 Campbell River Can.
140 B3 Campbellsville U.S.A.
131 D3 Campbellton Can.
53 D2 Campbelltown Austr.
96 B3 Campbeltown U.K.
145 C3 Campeche Mex.
145 C3 Campeche, Bahía de g. Mex.
52 B3 Camperdown Austr.
110 C1 Câmpina Romania
151 F3 Campina Grande Brazil
154 C2 Campinas Brazil
154 C1 Campina Verde Brazil
108 B2 Campobasso Italy
155 C2 Campo Belo Brazil
154 C1 Campo Florido Brazil
152 B2 Campo Gallo Arg.
154 B2 Campo Grande Brazil
154 C3 Campo Largo Brazil
151 E3 Campo Maior Brazil
106 B2 Campo Maior Port.
109 C2 Campomarino Italy
154 B2 Campo Mourão Brazil
155 D2 Campos Brazil
155 C1 Campos Altos Brazil
155 C2 Campos do Jordão Brazil
110 C1 Câmpulung Romania
138 A2 Camp Verde U.S.A.
63 B2 Cam Ranh Vietnam
63 B2 Cam Ranh, Vinh b. Vietnam
Cam Ranh Bay Vietnam see Cam Ranh, Vinh
128 C2 Camrose Can.
129 D2 Camsell Portage Can.
111 C2 Çan Turkey
126 G3 Canada country N. America
160 A2 Canada Basin sea feature Arctic Ocean
139 C1 Canadian U.S.A.
139 D1 Canadian r. U.S.A.
111 C2 Çanakkale Turkey
144 A1 Cananea Mex.
154 C2 Cananéia Brazil
114 A2 Canary Islands terr. N. Atlantic Ocean
155 C1 Canastra, Serra da mts Brazil
154 B1 Canastra, Serra da mts Brazil
144 B2 Canatlán Mex.
143 D3 Canaveral, Cape U.S.A.
155 E1 Canavieiras Brazil
53 C2 Canbelego Austr.
53 C3 Canberra Austr.
145 D2 Cancún Mex.
111 C3 Çandarlı Turkey
155 C2 Candeias Brazil
145 C3 Candelaria Mex.
154 B2 Cândido de Abreu Brazil
129 D2 Candle Lake Can.
137 D1 Cando U.S.A.
120 A2 Cangamba Angola
106 B1 Cangas Spain
106 B1 Cangas del Narcea Spain
120 B2 Cangombe Angola
152 C3 Canguçu Brazil
70 B2 Cangzhou China
131 D2 Caniapiscau Can.
131 D2 Caniapiscau r. Can.
131 C2 Caniapiscau, Lac l. Can.
Caniçado Moz. see Guija
108 B3 Canicattì Sicily Italy
151 F3 Canindé Brazil
144 B2 Cañitas de Felipe Pescador Mex.
80 B1 Çankırı Turkey
128 C2 Canmore Can.
96 A2 Canna i. U.K.
73 B3 Cannanore India
105 D3 Cannes France
99 B3 Cannock U.K.
53 C3 Cann River Austr.
152 C2 Canoas Brazil
129 D2 Canoe Lake Can.
154 B3 Canoinhas Brazil
136 B3 Canon City U.S.A.
52 B2 Canopus Austr.
129 D2 Canora Can.
53 C2 Canowindra Austr.
131 D3 Canso Can.
Cantabrian Mountains Spain see Cantábrica, Cordillera
106 B1 Cantabrian Sea Spain
106 C1 Cantábrica, Cordillera mts Spain
Cantábrico, Mar sea Spain see Cantabrian Sea
99 D4 Canterbury U.K.
54 B2 Canterbury Bight b. N.Z.
54 B2 Canterbury Plains N.Z.
63 B2 Cân Thơ Vietnam
151 E3 Canto do Buriti Brazil
Canton China see Guangzhou
137 E2 Canton MO U.S.A.
142 C2 Canton MS U.S.A.
141 D2 Canton NY U.S.A.
140 C2 Canton OH U.S.A.
139 C1 Canyon U.S.A.
134 D1 Canyon Ferry Lake U.S.A.
134 B2 Canyonville U.S.A.
62 B1 Cao Bằng Vietnam
109 C2 Capaccio Italy
154 C2 Capão Bonito Brazil
155 D2 Caparaó, Serra do mts Brazil
141 E1 Cap-de-la-Madeleine Can.
51 D4 Cape Barren Island Austr.
158 F7 Cape Basin sea feature S. Atlantic Ocean
52 A3 Cape Borda Austr.
131 D3 Cape Breton Island Can.
143 D3 Cape Canaveral U.S.A.
141 D3 Cape Charles U.S.A.
114 B4 Cape Coast Ghana
141 E2 Cape Cod Bay U.S.A.
143 D3 Cape Coral U.S.A.
127 G2 Cape Dorset Can.
143 E2 Cape Fear r. U.S.A.
137 F3 Cape Girardeau U.S.A.
155 D1 Capelinha Brazil
100 B2 Capelle aan de IJssel Neth.
Capelongo Angola see Kuvango
141 E3 Cape May Point U.S.A.
120 A1 Capenda-Camulemba Angola
122 A3 Cape Town S. Africa
158 E3 Cape Verde country N. Atlantic Ocean
158 D4 Cape Verde Basin sea feature N. Atlantic Ocean
51 D1 Cape York Peninsula Austr.
147 C3 Cap-Haïtien Haiti
151 E3 Capim r. Brazil
154 A2 Capitán Bado Para.
154 B2 Capivara, Represa resr Brazil
109 C2 Čapljina Bos.-Herz.
109 B3 Capo d'Orlando Sicily Italy
108 A2 Capraia, Isola di i. Italy
108 A2 Caprara, Punta pt Sardinia Italy
108 B2 Capri, Isola di i. Italy
51 E2 Capricorn Channel Austr.
120 B2 Caprivi Strip reg. Namibia
139 C2 Cap Rock Escarpment U.S.A.
139 C1 Capulin U.S.A.
150 C3 Caquetá r. Col.
110 B2 Caracal Romania
150 C2 Caracarai Brazil
150 C1 Caracas Venez.
151 E3 Caracol Brazil
155 C2 Caraguatatuba Brazil
153 A3 Carahue Chile
155 D1 Caraí Brazil
151 D3 Carajás, Serra dos hills Brazil
155 D2 Carandaí Brazil
155 D2 Carangola Brazil
110 B1 Caransebeș Romania
131 D3 Caraquet Can.
146 B3 Caratasca, Laguna lag. Hond.
155 D1 Caratinga Brazil
150 C3 Carauari Brazil
107 C2 Caravaca de la Cruz Spain
155 E1 Caravelas Brazil
129 E3 Carberry Can.
144 A2 Carbó Mex.
108 A3 Carbonara, Capo c. Sardinia Italy
136 B3 Carbondale CO U.S.A.
140 B3 Carbondale IL U.S.A.
141 D2 Carbondale PA U.S.A.
131 E3 Carbonear Can.
155 D1 Carbonita Brazil
107 C2 Carcaixent Spain
104 C3 Carcassonne France
128 A1 Carcross Can.
146 B2 Cárdenas Cuba
145 C3 Cárdenas Mex.
99 B4 Cardiff U.K.
99 A3 Cardigan U.K.
99 A3 Cardigan Bay U.K.
154 C2 Cardoso Brazil
128 C3 Cardston Can.
110 B1 Carei Romania
104 B2 Carentan France
50 B2 Carey, Lake salt flat Austr.
155 D2 Cariacica Brazil
146 B3 Caribbean Sea N. Atlantic Ocean
128 B2 Cariboo Mountains Can.
141 F1 Caribou U.S.A.
130 B2 Caribou Lake Can.
128 C2 Caribou Mountains Can.
144 B2 Carichic Mex.
100 B3 Carignan France
53 C2 Carinda Austr.
107 C1 Cariñena Spain
130 C3 Carleton Place Can.
123 C2 Carletonville S. Africa
135 C2 Carlin U.S.A.
97 C1 Carlingford Lough inlet Rep. of Ireland/U.K.
140 B3 Carlinville U.S.A.
98 B2 Carlisle U.K.
141 D2 Carlisle U.S.A.
155 D1 Carlos Chagas Brazil
97 C2 Carlow Rep. of Ireland
96 A1 Carloway U.K.
135 C4 Carlsbad CA U.S.A.
138 C2 Carlsbad NM U.S.A.
129 D3 Carlyle Can.
128 A1 Carmacks Can.
129 E3 Carman Can.
99 A4 Carmarthen U.K.
99 A4 Carmarthen Bay U.K.
104 C3 Carmaux France
145 C3 Carmelita Guat.
144 A2 Carmen, Isla i. Mex.
155 C1 Carmo do Paranaíba Brazil
Carmona Angola see Uíge
106 B2 Carmona Spain
104 B2 Carnac France
50 A2 Carnarvon Austr.
122 B3 Carnarvon S. Africa

97 C1 **Carndonagh** Rep. of Ireland
129 D3 **Carnduff** Can.
50 B2 **Carnegie, Lake** *salt flat* Austr.
96 B2 **Carn Eighe** *mt.* U.K.
55 P2 **Carney Island** Antarctica
73 D4 **Car Nicobar** *i.* India
118 B2 **Carnot** C.A.R.
52 A2 **Carnot, Cape** Austr.
96 C2 **Carnoustie** U.K.
97 C2 **Carnsore Point** Rep. of Ireland
151 E3 **Carolina** Brazil
49 L4 **Caroline Island** Kiribati
59 D2 **Caroline Islands** N. Pacific Ocean
122 A2 **Carolusberg** S. Africa
103 D2 **Carpathian Mountains** Europe
110 B1 **Carpații Meridionali** *mts* Romania
51 C1 **Carpentaria, Gulf of** Austr.
105 D3 **Carpentras** France
108 B2 **Carpi** Italy
143 D3 **Carrabelle** U.S.A.
97 B3 **Carrantuohill** *mt.* Rep. of Ireland
108 B2 **Carrara** Italy
97 D1 **Carrickfergus** U.K.
97 C2 **Carrickmacross** Rep. of Ireland
97 B2 **Carrick-on-Shannon** Rep. of Ireland
97 C2 **Carrick-on-Suir** Rep. of Ireland
137 D1 **Carrington** U.S.A.
139 D3 **Carrizo Springs** U.S.A.
138 B2 **Carrizozo** U.S.A.
137 E2 **Carroll** U.S.A.
143 C2 **Carrollton** U.S.A.
129 D2 **Carrot River** Can.
135 C3 **Carson City** U.S.A.
135 C3 **Carson Sink** *l.* U.S.A.
Carstensz-top *mt.* Indon. *see* **Jaya, Puncak**
150 B1 **Cartagena** Col.
107 C2 **Cartagena** Spain
146 B4 **Cartago** Costa Rica
54 C2 **Carterton** N.Z.
137 E3 **Carthage** *MO* U.S.A.
139 E2 **Carthage** *TX* U.S.A.
131 E2 **Cartwright** Can.
151 F3 **Caruarú** Brazil
150 C1 **Carúpano** Venez.
52 B1 **Caryapundy Swamp** Austr.
114 B1 **Casablanca** Morocco
154 C2 **Casa Branca** Brazil
144 B1 **Casa de Janos** Mex.
138 A2 **Casa Grande** U.S.A.
108 A1 **Casale Monferrato** Italy
109 C2 **Casarano** Italy
144 B1 **Casas Grandes** Mex.
134 C2 **Cascade** U.S.A.
134 B2 **Cascade Range** *mts* Can./U.S.A.
106 B2 **Cascais** Port.
151 F3 **Cascavel** Brazil
154 B2 **Cascavel** Brazil
141 F2 **Casco Bay** U.S.A.
108 B2 **Caserta** Italy
117 D3 **Caseyr, Raas** *c.* Somalia
97 C2 **Cashel** Rep. of Ireland
153 B3 **Casilda** Arg.
53 D1 **Casino** Austr.
Casnewydd U.K. *see* **Newport**
107 C1 **Caspe** Spain
136 B2 **Casper** U.S.A.
Caspian Lowland Kazakh./Rus. Fed. *see* **Prikaspiyskaya Nizmennost'**
81 C1 **Caspian Sea** Asia/Europe
Cassaigne Alg. *see* **Sidi Ali**
154 C2 **Cássia** Brazil
128 B2 **Cassiar** Can.
128 A2 **Cassiar Mountains** Can.
154 B1 **Cassilândia** Brazil
120 A2 **Cassinga** Angola
108 B2 **Cassino** Italy
96 B2 **Cassley** *r.* U.K.
151 E3 **Castanhal** Brazil
152 B3 **Castaño** *r.* Arg.
144 B2 **Castaños** Mex.
104 C3 **Casteljaloux** France
105 D3 **Castellane** France
107 C2 **Castelló de la Plana** Spain
155 D2 **Castelo** Brazil
106 B2 **Castelo Branco** Port.
104 C3 **Castelsarrasin** France
108 B3 **Castelvetrano** *Sicily* Italy
52 B3 **Casterton** Austr.
108 B2 **Castiglione della Pescaia** Italy
106 C2 **Castilla - La Mancha** *aut. comm.* Spain
106 C1 **Castilla y León** *aut. comm.* Spain
97 B2 **Castlebar** Rep. of Ireland
96 A2 **Castlebay** U.K.
97 C1 **Castleblayney** Rep. of Ireland
97 C1 **Castlederg** U.K.
96 C3 **Castle Douglas** U.K.
128 C3 **Castlegar** Can.
97 B2 **Castleisland** Rep. of Ireland
52 B3 **Castlemaine** Austr.
97 C2 **Castlepollard** Rep. of Ireland
97 B2 **Castlerea** Rep. of Ireland
53 C2 **Castlereagh** *r.* Austr.
136 C3 **Castle Rock** U.S.A.
128 C2 **Castor** Can.
104 C3 **Castres** France
100 B1 **Castricum** Neth.
147 D3 **Castries** St Lucia
154 C2 **Castro** Brazil
153 A4 **Castro** Chile
106 B2 **Castro Verde** Port.
109 C3 **Castrovillari** Italy
150 A3 **Catacaos** Peru
155 D2 **Cataguases** Brazil
154 C1 **Catalão** Brazil
Catalonia *aut. comm.* Spain *see* **Cataluña**
107 D1 **Cataluña** *aut. comm.* Spain
152 B2 **Catamarca** Arg.
64 B2 **Catanduanes** *i.* Phil.
154 C2 **Catanduva** Brazil
154 B3 **Catanduvas** Brazil
109 C3 **Catania** *Sicily* Italy
109 C3 **Catanzaro** Italy
64 B2 **Catarman** Phil.
107 C2 **Catarroja** Spain
64 B2 **Catbalogan** Phil.
145 C3 **Catemaco** Mex.
120 A1 **Catete** Angola
147 C2 **Cat Island** Bahamas
130 A2 **Cat Lake** Can.
145 D2 **Catoche, Cabo** *c.* Mex.
141 E2 **Catskill Mountains** U.S.A.
123 D2 **Catuane** Moz.
64 B3 **Cauayan** Phil.
131 D2 **Caubvick, Mount** Can.
150 B2 **Cauca** *r.* Col.
151 F3 **Caucaia** Brazil
81 C1 **Caucasus** *mts* Asia/Europe
100 A2 **Caudry** France
109 C3 **Caulonia** Italy
120 A1 **Caungula** Angola
150 C2 **Caura** *r.* Venez.
131 D3 **Causapscal** Can.
90 B2 **Căușeni** Moldova
105 D3 **Cavaillon** France
151 E4 **Cavalcante** Brazil
114 B4 **Cavally** *r.* Côte d'Ivoire
97 C2 **Cavan** Rep. of Ireland
154 B3 **Cavernoso, Serra do** *mts* Brazil
151 D2 **Caviana, Ilha** *i.* Brazil
Cawnpore India *see* **Kanpur**
151 E3 **Caxias** Brazil
152 C2 **Caxias do Sul** Brazil
120 A1 **Caxito** Angola
151 D2 **Cayenne** Fr. Guiana
146 B3 **Cayman Islands** *terr.* West Indies
158 C3 **Cayman Trench** *sea feature* Caribbean Sea
117 C4 **Caynabo** Somalia
120 B2 **Cazombo** Angola
Ceará Brazil *see* **Fortaleza**
Ceatharlach Rep. of Ireland *see* **Carlow**
144 B2 **Ceballos** Mex.
64 B2 **Cebu** Phil.
64 B2 **Cebu** *i.* Phil.
108 B2 **Cecina** Italy
137 F2 **Cedar** *r.* U.S.A.
135 D3 **Cedar City** U.S.A.
137 E2 **Cedar Falls** U.S.A.
129 D2 **Cedar Lake** Can.
137 E2 **Cedar Rapids** U.S.A.
144 A2 **Cedros, Isla** *i.* Mex.
51 C3 **Ceduna** Austr.
117 C4 **Ceeldheere** Somalia
117 C3 **Ceerigaabo** Somalia
108 B3 **Cefalù** *Sicily* Italy
145 B2 **Celaya** Mex.
Celebes *i.* Indon. *see* Sulawesi
156 C5 **Celebes Sea** Indon./Phil.
145 C2 **Celestún** Mex.
101 E1 **Celle** Ger.
95 B3 **Celtic Sea** Rep. of Ireland/U.K.
59 D3 **Cenderawasih, Teluk** *b.* Indon.
142 C2 **Center Point** U.S.A.
150 B2 **Central, Cordillera** *mts* Col.
150 B4 **Central, Cordillera** *mts* Peru
64 B2 **Central, Cordillera** *mts* Phil.
Central African Empire *country* Africa *see* Central African Republic
118 C2 **Central African Republic** *country* Africa
74 A2 **Central Brahui Range** *mts* Pak.
137 D2 **Central City** U.S.A.
140 B3 **Centralia** *IL* U.S.A.
134 B1 **Centralia** *WA* U.S.A.
74 A2 **Central Makran Range** *mts* Pak.
156 D5 **Central Pacific Basin** *sea feature* Pacific Ocean
134 B2 **Central Point** U.S.A.
Central Provinces *state* India *see* **Madhya Pradesh**
59 D3 **Central Range** *mts* P.N.G.
Central Russian Upland *hills* Rus. Fed. *see* **Sredne-Russkaya Vozvyshennost'**
Central Siberian Plateau Rus. Fed. *see* **Sredne-Sibirskoye Ploskogor'ye**
142 C2 **Century** U.S.A.
Ceos *i.* Greece *see* **Kea**
111 B3 **Cephalonia** *i.* Greece
Ceram *i.* Indon. *see* Seram
Ceram Sea Indon. *see* Seram Sea
101 F3 **Čerchov** *mt.* Czech Rep.
152 B2 **Ceres** Arg.
154 C1 **Ceres** Brazil
122 A3 **Ceres** S. Africa
105 C3 **Céret** France
106 C1 **Cerezo de Abajo** Spain
109 C2 **Cerignola** Italy
Cerigo *i.* Greece *see* **Kythira**
110 C2 **Cernavodă** Romania
145 C2 **Cerralvo** Mex.
144 B2 **Cerralvo, Isla** *i.* Mex.
145 B2 **Cerritos** Mex.
154 C2 **Cerro Azul** Brazil
145 C2 **Cerro Azul** Mex.
150 B4 **Cerro de Pasco** Peru
105 D3 **Cervione** *Corsica* France
106 B1 **Cervo** Spain
108 B2 **Cesena** Italy
108 B2 **Cesenatico** Italy
88 C2 **Cēsis** Latvia
102 C2 **České Budějovice** Czech Rep.
101 F3 **Český Les** *mts* Czech Rep./Ger.
111 C3 **Çeşme** Turkey
53 D2 **Cessnock** Austr.
104 B2 **Cesson-Sévigné** France
104 B3 **Cestas** France
109 C2 **Cetinje** Yugo.
109 C3 **Cetraro** Italy
106 B2 **Ceuta** N. Africa
105 C3 **Cévennes** *mts* France
Ceylon *country* Asia *see* Sri Lanka
79 D2 **Chābahār** Iran
75 C1 **Chabyêr Caka** *salt l.* China
150 B3 **Chachapoyas** Peru
89 D3 **Chachersk** Belarus
63 B2 **Chachoengsao** Thai.
152 C2 **Chaco Boreal** *reg.* Para.
138 B1 **Chaco Mesa** *plat.* U.S.A.
115 D3 **Chad** *country* Africa
115 D3 **Chad, Lake** Africa
68 C1 **Chadaasan** Mongolia
68 C1 **Chadan** Rus. Fed.
123 C1 **Chadibe** Botswana
153 B3 **Chadileo** *r.* Arg.
136 C2 **Chadron** U.S.A.
Chadyr-Lunga Moldova *see* **Ciadâr-Lunga**
77 D2 **Chaek** Kyrg.
65 B2 **Chaeryŏng** N. Korea
74 A2 **Chagai** Pak.
77 C3 **Chaghcharān** Afgh.
89 E2 **Chagoda** Rus. Fed.
56 I10 **Chagos Archipelago** *is* B.I.O.T.
159 E4 **Chagos-Laccadive Ridg** *sea feature* Indian Ocean
159 E4 **Chagos Trench** *sea feature* Indian Ocean
76 B2 **Chagyl** Turkm.
75 C2 **Chāībāsa** India
63 B2 **Chainat** Thai.
63 A3 **Chaiya** Thai.
63 B2 **Chaiyaphum** Thai.
152 C3 **Chajarí** Arg.
119 D3 **Chake Chake** Tanz.
131 D2 **Chakonipau, Lake** Can.
150 B4 **Chala** Peru
74 A1 **Chalap Dalan** *mts* Afgh.
121 C2 **Chaláua** Moz.
131 D3 **Chaleur Bay** *inlet* Can.
74 B2 **Chalisgaon** India
111 C3 **Chalki** *i.* Greece
111 B3 **Chalkida** Greece
139 C3 **Chalk Mountains** U.S.A.
104 B2 **Challans** France
134 D2 **Challis** U.S.A.
105 C2 **Châlons-en-Champagne** France
Châlons-sur-Marne France *see* **Châlons-en-Champagne**
105 C2 **Chalon-sur-Saône** France
101 F3 **Cham** Ger.
138 B1 **Chama** U.S.A.
121 C2 **Chama** Zambia
74 A1 **Chaman** Pak.
74 B1 **Chamba** India
74 B2 **Chambal** *r.* India
137 D2 **Chamberlain** U.S.A.
138 B1 **Chambers** U.S.A.
141 D3 **Chambersburg** U.S.A.
105 D2 **Chambéry** France
121 C2 **Chambeshi** Zambia
121 B2 **Chambeshi** *r.* Zambia
Chamdo China *see* **Qamd**
119 D2 **Ch'amo Hāyk'** *l.* Eth.
105 D2 **Chamonix-Mont-Blanc** France
140 B2 **Champaign** U.S.A.
141 E2 **Champlain, Lake** Can./U.S.A.
145 C3 **Champotón** Mex.
Chanak Turkey *see* Çanakkale
152 A2 **Chañaral** Chile
Chanda India *see* Chandrapur
126 C2 **Chandalar** *r.* U.S.A.
142 C3 **Chandeleur Islands** U.S.A.
74 B1 **Chandigarh** India
131 D3 **Chandler** Can.
138 A2 **Chandler** U.S.A.
75 D2 **Chandpur** Bangl.
75 B3 **Chandrapur** India
63 B2 **Chang, Ko** *i.* Thai.
Chang'an China *see* Rong'an
121 C3 **Changane** *r.* Moz.
121 C2 **Changara** Moz.
65 B1 **Changbai** China
Changbai Shan *mt.* China/N. Korea *see* Paekdu-san
65 B1 **Changbai Shan** *mts* China/N. Korea
Changchow China *see* Zhangzhou
Changchow China *see* Changzhou
69 E2 **Changchun** China
71 B3 **Changde** China
65 B2 **Ch'angdo** N. Korea
70 B2 **Changge** China
65 A2 **Changhai** China
71 C3 **Changhua** Taiwan
65 B3 **Changhŭng** S. Korea
Chang Jiang *r.* China *see* Yangtze
Changjiang Kou *r. mouth* China *see* Yangtze, Mouth of the
65 B1 **Changjin** N. Korea
65 B1 **Changjin-gang** *r.* N. Korea

Changkiang China see Zhanjiang
Changning China see Xunwu
Ch'ang-pai Shan mts China/N. Korea see Changbai Shan
1 B3 Changsha China
0 C2 Changshu China
5 B2 Changsŏng S. Korea
Changteh China see Changde
1 B3 Changting Fujian China
6 A2 Changting Heilong. China
5 A1 Changtu China
6 B4 Changuinola Panama
5 B2 Ch'angwŏn S. Korea
5 B2 Changyŏn N. Korea
0 B2 Changyuan China
0 B2 Changzhi China
0 B2 Changzhou China
1 B3 Chania Greece
5 C4 Channel Islands Europe
5 C4 Channel Islands U.S.A.
1 E3 Channel-Port-aux-Basques Can.
6 B1 Chantada Spain
3 B2 Chanthaburi Thai.
4 C2 Chantilly France
7 D3 Chanute U.S.A.
2 G3 Chany, Ozero salt l. Rus. Fed.
0 B2 Chaohu China
1 B3 Chaoyang Guangdong China
Chaoyang China see Huinan
0 C1 Chaoyang Liaoning China
1 B3 Chaozhou China
4 B2 Chapala, Laguna de l. Mex.
6 B1 Chapayevo Kazakh.
7 D3 Chapayevsk Rus. Fed.
2 C2 Chapecó Brazil
3 E1 Chapel Hill U.S.A.
0 B3 Chapleau Can.
9 E3 Chaplygin Rus. Fed.
1 C2 Chaplynka Ukr.
Chapra India see Chhapra
5 B2 Charcas Mex.
9 B4 Chard U.K.
6 C3 Chardzhev Turkm.
Chardzhou Turkm. see Chardzhev
4 B2 Charente r. France
8 B1 Chari r. Cameroon/Chad
7 C3 Chārīkār Afgh.
6 E2 Charkayuvom Rus. Fed.
Charkhlik China see Ruoqiang
0 B2 Charleroi Belgium
1 D3 Charles, Cape U.S.A.
1 E1 Charlesbourg Can.
7 E2 Charles City U.S.A.
0 B3 Charleston IL U.S.A.
7 F3 Charleston MO U.S.A.
3 E2 Charleston SC U.S.A.
0 C3 Charleston WV U.S.A.
5 C3 Charleston Peak U.S.A.
1 D2 Charleville Austr.
5 C2 Charleville-Mézières France
0 B1 Charlevoix U.S.A.
3 D1 Charlotte U.S.A.
3 D3 Charlotte Harbor b. U.S.A.
1 D3 Charlottesville U.S.A.
1 D3 Charlottetown Can.
2 B3 Charlton Austr.
0 C2 Charlton Island Can.
1 D2 Charters Towers Austr.
4 C2 Chartres France
8 C2 Chase Can.
8 C3 Chashniki Belarus
4 A3 Chaslands Mistake c. N.Z.
5 B1 Chasŏng N. Korea
4 B2 Chassiron, Pointe de pt France
4 B2 Châteaubriant France
4 C2 Château-du-Loir France
4 C2 Châteaudun France
4 B2 Château-Gontier France
4 B2 Châteaulin France
5 D3 Châteauneuf-les-Martigues France
4 C2 Châteauneuf-sur-Loire France
4 C2 Châteauroux France
5 C2 Château-Thierry France
8 C2 Chateh Can.
0 B2 Châtelet Belgium
104 C2 Châtellerault France
131 D3 Chatham N.B. Can.
140 C2 Chatham Ont. Can.
99 D4 Chatham U.K.
49 J8 Chatham Islands N.Z.
105 C2 Châtillon-sur-Seine France
143 D2 Chattahoochee r. U.S.A.
143 C1 Chattanooga U.S.A.
63 B2 Châu Đôc Vietnam
62 A1 Chauk Myanmar
105 D2 Chaumont France
105 C2 Chauny France
Chau Phu Vietnam see Châu Đôc
151 E3 Chaves Brazil
106 B1 Chaves Port.
130 C2 Chavigny, Lac l. Can.
89 D3 Chavusy Belarus
89 E2 Chayevo Rus. Fed.
86 E3 Chaykovskiy Rus. Fed.
142 C2 Cheaha Mountain hill U.S.A.
102 C1 Cheb Czech Rep.
87 D3 Cheboksary Rus. Fed.
140 C1 Cheboygan U.S.A.
65 B2 Chech'ŏn S. Korea
142 A1 Checotah U.S.A.
62 A2 Cheduba Island Myanmar
Chefoo China see Yantai
126 B2 Chefornak U.S.A.
114 B2 Chegga Maur.
121 C2 Chegutu Zimbabwe
134 B1 Chehalis U.S.A.
65 B3 Cheju S. Korea
65 B3 Cheju-do i. S. Korea
65 B3 Cheju-haehyŏp sea chan. S. Korea
89 E2 Chekhov Rus. Fed.
Chekiang prov. China see Zhejiang
134 B1 Chelan, Lake U.S.A.
81 D2 Cheleken Turkm.
107 D2 Chélif, Oued r. Alg.
76 B2 Chelkar Kazakh.
103 E1 Chełm Pol.
99 D4 Chelmer r. U.K.
103 D1 Chełmno Pol.
99 D4 Chelmsford U.K.
99 B4 Cheltenham U.K.
87 F3 Chelyabinsk Rus. Fed.
83 H1 Chelyuskin Rus. Fed.
101 F2 Chemnitz Ger.
Chemulpo S. Korea see Inch'ŏn
134 B2 Chemult U.S.A.
74 B2 Chenab r. India/Pak.
114 B2 Chenachane Alg.
134 C1 Cheney U.S.A.
Chengchow China see Zhengzhou
70 B1 Chengde China
70 A2 Chengdu China
Chengjiang China see Taihe
71 B4 Chengmai China
Chengshou China see Yingshan
Chengtu China see Chengdu
70 A2 Chengxian China
Chengxiang China see Wuxi
Chengxiang China see Mianning
Chengyang China see Juxian
73 C3 Chennai India
Chenstokhov Pol. see Częstochowa
71 B3 Chenzhou China
99 B4 Chepstow U.K.
143 E2 Cheraw U.S.A.
104 B2 Cherbourg France
Cherchen China see Qiemo
89 E3 Cheremisinovo Rus. Fed.
68 C1 Cheremkhovo Rus. Fed.
89 E2 Cherepovets Rus. Fed.
91 C2 Cherkasy Ukr.
87 D4 Cherkessk Rus. Fed.
89 E3 Chern' Rus. Fed.
91 C1 Chernihiv Ukr.
91 D2 Cherninivka Ukr.
90 B2 Chernivtsi Ukr.
68 C1 Chernogorsk Rus. Fed.
90 B1 Chernyakhiv Ukr.
88 B3 Chernyakhovsk Rus. Fed.
89 E3 Chernyanka Rus. Fed.
69 D1 Chernyshevsk Rus. Fed.
83 I2 Chernyshevskiy Rus. Fed.
Chernyy Rynok Rus. Fed. see Kochubey
137 D2 Cherokee U.S.A.
83 L2 Cherskiy Rus. Fed.
83 K2 Cherskogo, Khrebet mts Rus. Fed.
91 E2 Chertkovo Rus. Fed.
Chervonoarmeyskoye Ukr. see Vil'nyans'k
Chervonoarmiys'k Ukr. see Krasnoarmiys'k
Chervonoarmiys'k Ukr. see Radyvyliv
90 A1 Chervonohrad Ukr.
88 C3 Chervyen' Belarus
89 D3 Cherykaw Belarus
141 D3 Chesapeake Bay U.S.A.
86 D2 Cheshskaya Guba b. Rus. Fed.
98 B3 Chester U.K.
140 B3 Chester IL U.S.A.
143 D2 Chester SC U.S.A.
141 D3 Chester VA U.S.A.
98 C3 Chesterfield U.K.
137 E3 Chesterfield U.S.A.
129 E1 Chesterfield Inlet Can.
129 E1 Chesterfield Inlet inlet Can.
141 F1 Chesuncook Lake U.S.A.
108 A3 Chetaïbi Alg.
131 D3 Chéticamp Can.
145 D3 Chetumal Mex.
128 B2 Chetwynd Can.
98 B2 Cheviot Hills U.K.
119 D2 Che'w Bahir salt l. Eth.
136 C2 Cheyenne U.S.A.
136 C2 Cheyenne r. U.S.A.
136 C3 Cheyenne Wells U.S.A.
75 C2 Chhapra India
75 B2 Chhatarpur India
74 B2 Chhindwara India
75 C2 Chhukha Bhutan
71 C3 Chiai Taiwan
62 A2 Chiang Dao Thai.
120 A2 Chiange Angola
62 A2 Chiang Mai Thai.
62 A2 Chiang Rai Thai.
145 C3 Chiapa Mex.
108 A1 Chiavenno Italy
69 F2 Chiba Japan
Chibizovka Rus. Fed. see Zherdevka
121 C3 Chiboma Moz.
130 C3 Chibougamau Can.
123 D1 Chibuto Moz.
75 D1 Chibuzhang Hu l. China
140 B2 Chicago U.S.A.
128 A2 Chichagof Island U.S.A.
99 C4 Chichester U.K.
50 A2 Chichester Range mts Austr.
139 D1 Chickasha U.S.A.
106 B2 Chiclana de la Frontera Spain
150 B3 Chiclayo Peru
153 B4 Chico r. Arg.
153 B4 Chico r. Arg.
135 B3 Chico U.S.A.
141 E2 Chicopee U.S.A.
64 B2 Chico Sapocoy, Mount Phil.
131 C3 Chicoutimi Can.
131 D1 Chidley, Cape Can.
63 A3 Chieo Lan Reservoir Thai.
108 B2 Chieti Italy
70 B1 Chifeng China
155 D1 Chifre, Serra do mts Brazil
121 C2 Chifunde Moz.
77 D2 Chiganak Kazakh.
145 C3 Chignahuapán Mex.
121 C3 Chigubo Moz.
62 A1 Chigu Co l. China
144 B2 Chihuahua Mex.
77 C2 Chiili Kazakh.
88 C2 Chikhachevo Rus. Fed.
67 C3 Chikuma-gawa r. Japan
128 B2 Chilanko r. Can.
74 B1 Chilas Jammu and Kashmir
139 C2 Childress U.S.A.
153 A3 Chile country S. America
158 C6 Chile Basin sea feature S. Pacific Ocean
152 B2 Chilecito Arg.
157 G8 Chile Rise sea feature S. Pacific Ocean
77 D2 Chilik Kazakh.
75 C3 Chilika Lake India
121 B2 Chililabombwe Zambia
128 B2 Chilko r. Can.
128 B2 Chilko Lake Can.
153 A3 Chillán Chile
140 B2 Chillicothe IL U.S.A.
137 E3 Chillicothe MO U.S.A.
140 C3 Chillicothe OH U.S.A.
128 B3 Chilliwack Can.
153 A4 Chiloé, Isla de i. Chile
145 C3 Chilpancingo Mex.
53 C3 Chiltern Austr.
99 C4 Chiltern Hills U.K.
120 B1 Chiluage Angola
71 C3 Chilung Taiwan
119 D3 Chimala Tanz.
121 C2 Chimanimani Zimbabwe
152 B3 Chimbas Arg.
76 B2 Chimbay Uzbek.
150 B3 Chimborazo mt. Ecuador
150 B3 Chimbote Peru
Chimishliya Moldova see Cimişlia
Chimkent Kazakh. see Shymkent
121 C2 Chimoio Moz.
77 C3 Chimtargha, Qullai mt. Tajik.
68 B2 China country Asia
145 C2 China Mex.
77 C2 Chinaz Uzbek.
150 B4 Chincha Alta Peru
128 C2 Chinchaga r. Can.
145 D3 Chinchorro, Banco sea feature Mex.
121 C2 Chinde Moz.
65 B3 Chindo S. Korea
65 B3 Chin-do i. S. Korea
68 C2 Chindu China
62 A1 Chindwin r. Myanmar
Chinese Turkestan aut. reg. China see Xinjiang Uygur Zizhiqu
65 B2 Chinghwa N. Korea
121 B2 Chingola Zambia
120 A2 Chinguar Angola
65 B2 Chinhae S. Korea
121 C2 Chinhoyi Zimbabwe
Chini India see Kalpa
Chining China see Jining
74 B1 Chiniot Pak.
144 B2 Chinipas Mex.
65 B2 Chinju S. Korea
118 C2 Chinko r. C.A.R.
138 B1 Chinle U.S.A.
71 B3 Chinmen Taiwan
Chinnamp'o N. Korea see Namp'o
67 C3 Chino Japan
135 C4 Chino U.S.A.
104 C2 Chinon France
134 E1 Chinook U.S.A.
138 A2 Chino Valley U.S.A.
121 C2 Chinsali Zambia
108 B1 Chioggia Italy
111 C3 Chios Greece
111 C3 Chios i. Greece
121 C2 Chipata Zambia
120 A2 Chipindo Angola
Chipinga Zimbabwe see Chipinge
121 C3 Chipinge Zimbabwe
73 B3 Chiplun India
99 B4 Chippenham U.K.
140 A2 Chippewa Falls U.S.A.
99 C4 Chipping Norton U.K.
Chipuriro Zimbabwe see Guruve
145 D3 Chiquimula Guat.
77 C2 Chirchik Uzbek.
121 C3 Chiredzi Zimbabwe
138 B2 Chiricahua Peak U.S.A.
146 B4 Chiriquí, Golfo de b. Panama
65 B2 Chiri-san mt. S. Korea
146 B4 Chirripo mt. Costa Rica
121 B2 Chirundu Zimbabwe
130 C2 Chisasibi Can.
137 E1 Chisholm U.S.A.
Chisimaio Somalia see Kismaayo
90 B2 Chişinău Moldova
87 E3 Chistopol' Rus. Fed.
69 D1 Chita Rus. Fed.
120 A2 Chitado Angola
Chitaldrug India see Chitradurga
121 C2 Chitambo Zambia
120 B1 Chitato Angola
121 C1 Chitipa Malawi
121 C3 Chitobe Moz.
Chitor India see Chittaurgarh
66 D2 Chitose Japan

73 B3 **Chitradurga** India
74 B1 **Chitral** Pak.
146 B4 **Chitré** Panama
75 D2 **Chittagong** Bangl.
74 B2 **Chittaurgarh** India
73 B3 **Chittoor** India
Chittorgarh India *see* Chittaurgarh
121 C2 **Chitungwiza** Zimbabwe
120 B2 **Chiume** Angola
121 C2 **Chivhu** Zimbabwe
Chkalov Rus. Fed. *see* Orenburg
101 F2 **Chodov** Czech Rep.
153 B3 **Choele Choel** Arg.
Chogori Feng *mt.* China/Jammu and Kashmir *see* **K2**
48 G4 **Choiseul** *i.* Solomon Is
144 B2 **Choix** Mex.
102 C1 **Chojna** Pol.
103 D1 **Chojnice** Pol.
117 B3 **Ch'ok'ē Mountains** Eth.
Chokue Moz. *see* **Chókwé**
83 K2 **Chokurdakh** Rus. Fed.
121 C3 **Chókwé** Moz.
104 B2 **Cholet** France
145 C3 **Cholula** Mex.
120 B2 **Choma** Zambia
Chomo China *see* **Yadong**
102 C1 **Chomutov** Czech Rep.
83 I2 **Chona** *r.* Rus. Fed.
65 B2 **Ch'ŏnan** S. Korea
58 A2 **Chon Buri** Thai.
150 A3 **Chone** Ecuador
Chong'an China *see* Wuyishan
65 B1 **Ch'ŏngjin** N. Korea
65 B2 **Chŏngju** N. Korea
65 B2 **Ch'ŏngju** S. Korea
65 B2 **Chŏngp'yŏng** N. Korea
70 A3 **Chongqing** China
70 A2 **Chongqing** *mun.* China
65 B2 **Chŏngŭp** S. Korea
121 B2 **Chongwe** Zambia
71 A3 **Chongzuo** China
65 B2 **Chŏnju** S. Korea
154 B3 **Chopimzinho** Brazil
98 B3 **Chorley** U.K.
91 C2 **Chornobay** Ukr.
90 C1 **Chornobyl'** Ukr.
91 C2 **Chornomors'ke** Ukr.
90 B2 **Chortkiv** Ukr.
65 B2 **Ch'ŏrwŏn** S. Korea
65 B1 **Ch'osan** N. Korea
67 D3 **Chōshi** Japan
153 A3 **Chos Malal** Arg.
103 D1 **Choszczno** Pol.
134 D1 **Choteau** U.S.A.
114 A2 **Choûm** Maur.
69 D1 **Choybalsan** Mongolia
69 D1 **Choyr** Mongolia
54 B2 **Christchurch** N.Z.
99 C4 **Christchurch** U.K.
127 H2 **Christian, Cape** Can.
123 C2 **Christiana** S. Africa
Christianshåb Greenland *see* **Qasigiannguit**
54 A2 **Christina, Mount** N.Z.
58 B3 **Christmas Island** *terr.* Indian Ocean
111 C3 **Chrysi** *i.* Greece
111 B2 **Chrysoupoli** Greece
Chu Kazakh. *see* **Shu**
Chubarovka Ukr. *see* Polohy
153 B4 **Chubut** *r.* Arg.
89 F3 **Chuchkovo** Rus. Fed.
90 B1 **Chudniv** Ukr.
89 D2 **Chudovo** Rus. Fed.
126 C2 **Chugach Mountains** U.S.A.
67 B4 **Chūgoku-sanchi** *mts* Japan
Chuguchak China *see* Tacheng
66 B2 **Chuguyevka** Rus. Fed.
91 D2 **Chuhuyiv** Ukr.
Chukchi Peninsula Rus. Fed. *see* **Chukotskiy Poluostrov**
160 J3 **Chukchi Sea** *sea* Rus. Fed./U.S.A.
89 F2 **Chukhloma** Rus. Fed.
83 N2 **Chukotskiy Poluostrov** *pen.* Rus. Fed.
Chulaktau Kazakh. *see* Karatau
135 C4 **Chula Vista** U.S.A.
82 G3 **Chulym** Rus. Fed.
152 B2 **Chumbicha** Arg.
83 K3 **Chumikan** Rus. Fed.
63 A2 **Chumphon** Thai.
65 B2 **Ch'unch'ŏn** S. Korea
Chungking China *see* Chongqing
Ch'ungmu S. Korea *see* T'ongyŏng
71 C3 **Chungyang Shanmo** *mts* Taiwan
83 H2 **Chunya** *r.* Rus. Fed.
119 D3 **Chunya** Tanz.
150 B4 **Chuquibamba** Peru
152 B2 **Chuquicamata** Chile
105 D2 **Chur** Switz.
62 A1 **Churachandpur** India
83 J2 **Churapcha** Rus. Fed.
129 E2 **Churchill** Can.
129 E2 **Churchill** *r. Man.* Can.
131 D2 **Churchill** *r. Nfld.* Can.
129 E2 **Churchill, Cape** Can.
131 D2 **Churchill Falls** Can.
129 D2 **Churchill Lake** Can.
74 B2 **Churu** India
138 B1 **Chuska Mountains** U.S.A.
86 E3 **Chusovoy** Rus. Fed.
131 C3 **Chute-des-Passes** Can.
48 G3 **Chuuk** *is* Micronesia
62 B1 **Chuxiong** China
63 B2 **Chư Yang Sin** *mt.* Vietnam
91 C2 **Chyhyryn** Ukr.
Chymyshliya Moldova *see* Cimişlia
90 B2 **Ciadâr-Lunga** Moldova
Ciadîr-Lunga Moldova *see* Ciadâr-Lunga
60 B2 **Ciamis** Indon.
60 B2 **Cianjur** Indon.
154 B2 **Cianorte** Brazil
138 A2 **Cibuta, Sierra** *mt.* Mex.
80 B1 **Cide** Turkey
103 E1 **Ciechanów** Pol.
146 C2 **Ciego de Avila** Cuba
147 C3 **Ciénaga** Col.
146 B2 **Cienfuegos** Cuba
107 C2 **Cieza** Spain
106 C2 **Cigüela** *r.* Spain
80 B2 **Cihanbeyli** Turkey
144 B3 **Cihuatlán** Mex.
106 C2 **Cijara, Embalse de** *resr* Spain
109 C2 **Çikes, Maja e** *mt.* Albania
60 B2 **Cilacap** Indon.
Cill Airne Rep. of Ireland *see* **Killarney**
Cill Chainnigh Rep. of Ireland *see* Kilkenny
139 C1 **Cimarron** *r.* U.S.A.
90 B2 **Cimişlia** Moldova
108 B2 **Cimone, Monte** *mt.* Italy
Cîmpina Romania *see* Câmpina
Cîmpulung Romania *see* Câmpulung
60 B2 **Cina, Tanjung** *c.* Indon.
140 C3 **Cincinnati** U.S.A.
Cinco de Outubro Angola *see* **Xá-Muteba**
111 C3 **Çine** Turkey
100 B2 **Ciney** Belgium
134 C2 **Cinnabar Mountain** U.S.A.
145 C3 **Cintalapa** Mex.
Ciping China *see* Jinggangshan
153 B3 **Cipolletti** Arg.
126 C2 **Circle** *AK* U.S.A.
136 B1 **Circle** *MT* U.S.A.
60 B2 **Cirebon** Indon.
99 C4 **Cirencester** U.K.
108 A1 **Ciriè** Italy
109 C3 **Cirò Marina** Italy
110 B1 **Cisnădie** Romania
109 C2 **Čitluk** Bos.-Herz.
122 A3 **Citrusdal** S. Africa
135 B3 **Citrus Heights** U.S.A.
110 C1 **Ciucaş, Vârful** *mt.* Romania
145 B2 **Ciudad Acuña** Mex.
145 B3 **Ciudad Altamirano** Mex.
150 C2 **Ciudad Bolívar** Venez.
147 C4 **Ciudad Bolivia** Venez.
144 B2 **Ciudad Camargo** Mex.
145 C3 **Ciudad Cuauhtémoc** Mex.
145 C3 **Ciudad del Carmen** Mex.
154 B3 **Ciudad del Este** Para.
144 B2 **Ciudad Delicias** Mex.
145 C2 **Ciudad de Valles** Mex.
150 C2 **Ciudad Guayana** Venez.
138 B3 **Ciudad Guerrero** Mex.
144 B3 **Ciudad Guzmán** Mex.
145 C3 **Ciudad Hidalgo** Mex.
145 C3 **Ciudad Ixtepec** Mex.
144 B1 **Ciudad Juárez** Mex.
145 C2 **Ciudad Madero** Mex.
145 C2 **Ciudad Mante** Mex.
145 C2 **Ciudad Mier** Mex.
144 B2 **Ciudad Obregón** Mex.
106 C2 **Ciudad Real** Spain
145 C2 **Ciudad Río Bravo** Mex.
106 B1 **Ciudad Rodrigo** Spain
Ciudad Trujillo Dom. Rep. *see* **Santo Domingo**
145 C2 **Ciudad Victoria** Mex.
107 D1 **Ciutadella de Menorca** Spain
108 B1 **Cividale del Friuli** Italy
108 B2 **Civitanova Marche** Italy
108 B2 **Civitavecchia** Italy
104 C2 **Civray** France
111 C3 **Çivril** Turkey
70 C2 **Cixi** China
99 D4 **Clacton-on-Sea** U.K.
128 C2 **Claire, Lake** Can.
105 C2 **Clamecy** France
142 C2 **Clanton** U.S.A.
122 A3 **Clanwilliam** S. Africa
97 C2 **Clara** Rep. of Ireland
52 A2 **Clare** Austr.
140 C2 **Clare** U.S.A.
97 A2 **Clare Island** Rep. of Ireland
141 E2 **Claremont** U.S.A.
97 B2 **Claremorris** Rep. of Ireland
54 B2 **Clarence** N.Z.
55 B3 **Clarence Island** Antarctica
131 E3 **Clarenville** Can.
128 C2 **Claresholm** Can.
137 D2 **Clarinda** U.S.A.
144 A3 **Clarión, Isla** *i.* Mex.
123 C3 **Clarkebury** S. Africa
134 C1 **Clark Fork** *r.* U.S.A.
143 D2 **Clark Hill Reservoir** U.S.A.
140 C3 **Clarksburg** U.S.A.
142 B2 **Clarksdale** U.S.A.
134 C1 **Clarkston** U.S.A.
142 B1 **Clarksville** *AR* U.S.A.
142 C1 **Clarksville** *TN* U.S.A.
154 B1 **Claro** *r.* Brazil
139 C1 **Claude** U.S.A.
139 C1 **Clayton** U.S.A.
97 B3 **Clear, Cape** Rep. of Ireland
126 C3 **Cleare, Cape** U.S.A.
137 E2 **Clear Lake** U.S.A.
135 B3 **Clear Lake** *l.* U.S.A.
128 C2 **Clearwater** Can.
129 C2 **Clearwater** *r.* Can.
143 D3 **Clearwater** U.S.A.
134 C1 **Clearwater** *r.* U.S.A.
139 D2 **Cleburne** U.S.A.
101 E1 **Clenze** Ger.
51 D2 **Clermont** Austr.
105 C2 **Clermont-Ferrand** France
100 C2 **Clervaux** Lux.
52 A2 **Cleve** Austr.
142 B2 **Cleveland** *MS* U.S.A.
140 C2 **Cleveland** *OH* U.S.A.
143 D1 **Cleveland** *TN* U.S.A.
134 D1 **Cleveland, Mount** U.S.A.
154 B3 **Clevelândia** Brazil
97 B2 **Clew Bay** Rep. of Ireland
143 D3 **Clewiston** U.S.A.
97 A2 **Clifden** Rep. of Ireland
53 D1 **Clifton** Austr.
138 B2 **Clifton** U.S.A.
138 B1 **Clines Corners** U.S.A.
128 B2 **Clinton** Can.
137 E2 **Clinton** *IA* U.S.A.
137 E3 **Clinton** *MO* U.S.A.
139 D1 **Clinton** *OK* U.S.A.
125 H8 **Clipperton, Île** *terr.* N. Pacific Ocean
96 A2 **Clisham** *hill* U.K.
98 B3 **Clitheroe** U.K.
97 B3 **Clonakilty** Rep. of Ireland
51 D2 **Cloncurry** Austr.
97 C1 **Clones** Rep. of Ireland
97 C2 **Clonmel** Rep. of Ireland
101 D1 **Cloppenburg** Ger.
137 E1 **Cloquet** U.S.A.
136 B2 **Cloud Peak** U.S.A.
135 C3 **Clovis** *CA* U.S.A.
139 C2 **Clovis** *NM* U.S.A.
Cluain Meala Rep. of Ireland *see* Clonmel
129 D2 **Cluff Lake Mine** Can.
110 B1 **Cluj-Napoca** Romania
51 C2 **Cluny** Austr.
105 D2 **Cluses** France
54 A3 **Clutha** *r.* N.Z.
96 B3 **Clyde** *r.* U.K.
96 B3 **Clyde, Firth of** *est.* U.K.
96 B3 **Clydebank** U.K.
127 H2 **Clyde River** Can.
144 B3 **Coalcomán** Mex.
128 C3 **Coaldale** Can.
135 C3 **Coaldale** U.S.A.
128 B2 **Coal River** Can.
150 C3 **Coari** Brazil
150 C3 **Coari** *r.* Brazil
143 C2 **Coastal Plain** U.S.A.
128 B2 **Coast Mountains** Can.
134 B2 **Coast Ranges** *mts* U.S.A
96 B3 **Coatbridge** U.K.
129 F1 **Coats Island** Can.
55 C2 **Coats Land** *reg.* Antarcti
145 C3 **Coatzacoalcos** Mex.
146 A3 **Cobán** Guat.
53 C2 **Cobar** Austr.
97 B3 **Cóbh** Rep. of Ireland
152 B1 **Cobija** Bol.
Coblenz Ger. *see* **Koblen**
130 C3 **Cobourg** Can.
50 C1 **Cobourg Peninsula** Aus
53 C3 **Cobram** Austr.
101 E2 **Coburg** Ger.
152 B1 **Cochabamba** Bol.
100 C2 **Cochem** Ger.
73 B4 **Cochin** India
128 C2 **Cochrane** *Alta* Can.
130 B3 **Cochrane** *Ont.* Can.
153 A4 **Cochrane** Chile
52 A2 **Cockaleechie** Austr.
52 B2 **Cockburn** Austr.
Cockburn Town Turks and Caicos Is *see* Grand Turk
98 B2 **Cockermouth** U.K.
50 B3 **Cocklebiddy** Austr.
122 B3 **Cockscomb** *mt.* S. Africa
146 B3 **Coco** *r.* Hond./Nic.
125 J9 **Coco, Isla de** *i.* N. Pacific Ocean
159 F4 **Cocos Basin** *sea feature* Indian Ocean
58 A3 **Cocos Islands** *terr.* Indian Ocean
144 B2 **Cocula** Mex.
150 B2 **Cocuy, Sierra Nevada d** *mt.* Col.
141 E2 **Cod, Cape** U.S.A.
150 C3 **Codajás** Brazil
108 B2 **Codigoro** Italy
131 D2 **Cod Island** Can.
151 E3 **Codó** Brazil
136 B2 **Cody** U.S.A.
51 D1 **Coen** Austr.
100 C2 **Coesfeld** Ger.
113 I6 **Coëtivy** *i.* Seychelles
134 C1 **Coeur d'Alene** U.S.A.
100 C1 **Coevorden** Neth.
123 C3 **Coffee Bay** S. Africa
137 D3 **Coffeyville** U.S.A.
52 A2 **Coffin Bay** Austr.
53 D2 **Coffs Harbour** Austr.
123 C3 **Cofimvaba** S. Africa
104 B2 **Cognac** France
118 A2 **Cogo** Equat. Guinea
52 B3 **Cohuna** Austr.
146 B4 **Coiba, Isla** *i.* Panama
153 A4 **Coihaique** Chile
73 B3 **Coimbatore** India
106 B1 **Coimbra** Port.
152 B1 **Coipasa, Salar de** *salt fl* Bol.
52 B3 **Colac** Austr.
155 D1 **Colatina** Brazil
136 C3 **Colby** U.S.A.
99 D4 **Colchester** U.K.
129 C2 **Cold Lake** Can.
96 C3 **Coldstream** U.K.
53 C2 **Coleambally** Austr.
139 D2 **Coleman** U.S.A.
52 B3 **Coleraine** Austr.
97 C1 **Coleraine** U.K.
123 C3 **Colesberg** S. Africa
153 A3 **Colico** Chile
144 B3 **Colima** Mex.
144 B3 **Colima, Nevado de** *vol.* Mex.
96 A2 **Coll** *i.* U.K.
53 C1 **Collarenebri** Austr.
139 D2 **College Station** U.S.A.
53 C1 **Collerina** Austr.
50 A3 **Collie** Austr.
50 B1 **Collier Bay** Austr.
140 C2 **Collingwood** Can.
54 B2 **Collingwood** N.Z.

6 F2 Collinson Peninsula Can.
1 F2 Collmberg *hill* Ger.
8 A3 Collo Alg.
7 B1 Collooney Rep. of Ireland
5 D2 Colmar France
3 B3 Colne U.K.
0 C2 Cologne Ger.
Colomb-Béchar Alg. *see* Béchar
4 C2 Colômbia Brazil
0 B2 Colombia *country* S. America
3 B4 Colombo Sri Lanka
4 C3 Colomiers France
2 C3 Colón Arg.
6 C4 Colón Panama
9 D2 Colonia Micronesia
3 B4 Colonia Las Heras Arg.
9 C3 Colonna, Capo *c.* Italy
6 A2 Colonsay *i.* U.K.
3 B3 Colorado *r.* Arg.
8 A2 Colorado *r.* Mex./U.S.A.
9 D3 Colorado *r.* U.S.A.
6 B3 Colorado *state* U.S.A.
5 C4 Colorado Desert U.S.A.
5 E3 Colorado Plateau U.S.A.
6 C3 Colorado Springs U.S.A.
4 B2 Colotlán Mex.
2 B1 Colquiri Bol.
6 B1 Colstrip U.S.A.
0 B3 Columbia *KY* U.S.A.
1 D3 Columbia *MD* U.S.A.
7 E3 Columbia *MO* U.S.A.
3 D2 Columbia *SC* U.S.A.
2 C1 Columbia *TN* U.S.A.
4 B1 Columbia *r.* U.S.A.
8 C2 Columbia, Mount Can.
4 D1 Columbia Falls U.S.A.
8 B2 Columbia Mountains Can.
4 C1 Columbia Plateau U.S.A.
3 D2 Columbus *GA* U.S.A.
0 B3 Columbus *IN* U.S.A.
2 C2 Columbus *MS* U.S.A.
4 E1 Columbus *MT* U.S.A.
7 D2 Columbus *NE* U.S.A.
8 B2 Columbus *NM* U.S.A.
0 C3 Columbus *OH* U.S.A.
9 D3 Columbus *TX* U.S.A.
4 C1 Colville U.S.A.
6 B2 Colville *r.* U.S.A.
6 D2 Colville Lake Can.
6 B3 Colwyn Bay U.K.
8 B2 Comacchio Italy
5 C3 Comalcalco Mex.
0 C1 Comănești Romania
0 C2 Comencho, Lac *l.* Can.
7 C2 Comeragh Mountains *hills* Rep. of Ireland
9 D2 Comfort U.S.A.
5 D2 Comilla Bangl.
8 A2 Comino, Capo *c. Sardinia* Italy
5 C3 Comitán de Domínguez Mex.
5 C2 Commentry France
9 D2 Commerce U.S.A.
7 G2 Committee Bay Can.
8 A1 Como Italy
8 A1 Como, Lago di *l.* Italy
Como, Lake Italy *see* Como, Lago di
3 B4 Comodoro Rivadavia Arg.
5 B2 Comonfort Mex.
1 D2 Comoros *country* Africa
8 B3 Comox Can.
5 C2 Compiègne France
4 B2 Compostela Mex.
0 B2 Comrat Moldova
4 A4 Conakry Guinea
4 B2 Concarneau France
5 E1 Conceição da Barra Brazil
1 E3 Conceição do Araguaia Brazil
5 D1 Conceição do Mato Dentro Brazil
2 B2 Concepción Arg.
3 A3 Concepción Chile
4 B2 Concepción Mex.
6 B4 Concepción Panama
5 B4 Conception, Point U.S.A.
4 C2 Conchas Brazil
8 C1 Conchas Lake U.S.A.
4 B2 Conchos *r.* Mex.
5 C2 Conchos *r.* Mex.
5 B3 Concord *CA* U.S.A.
1 E2 Concord *NH* U.S.A.
2 C3 Concordia Arg.
2 A2 Concordia S. Africa
7 D3 Concordia U.S.A.
3 C2 Condobolin Austr.
104 C3 Condom France
134 B1 Condon U.S.A.
108 B1 Conegliano Italy
51 E1 Conflict Group *is* P.N.G.
104 C2 Confolens France
135 D3 Confusion Range *mts* U.S.A.
98 B3 Congleton U.K.
118 B3 Congo *country* Africa
118 B3 Congo *r.* Congo/Dem. Rep. Congo
118 C3 Congo, Democratic Republic of *country* Africa
118 C3 Congo Basin Dem. Rep. Congo
Congo (Brazzaville) *country* Africa *see* Congo
Congo Free State *country* Africa *see* Congo, Democratic Republic of
Congo (Kinshasa) *country* Africa *see* Congo, Democratic Republic of
129 C2 Conklin Can.
97 B1 Conn, Lough *l.* Rep. of Ireland
97 B2 Connaught *reg.* Rep. of Ireland
141 E2 Connecticut *r.* U.S.A.
141 E2 Connecticut *state* U.S.A.
96 B2 Connel U.K.
97 B2 Connemara *reg.* Rep. of Ireland
134 D1 Conrad U.S.A.
159 D7 Conrad Rise *sea feature* Southern Ocean
139 D2 Conroe U.S.A.
155 D2 Conselheiro Lafaiete Brazil
155 D1 Conselheiro Pena Brazil
100 B3 Consenvoye France
98 C2 Consett U.K.
63 B3 Côn Sơn *i.* Vietnam
Constance Ger. *see* Konstanz
105 D2 Constance, Lake Ger./Switz.
110 C2 Constanța Romania
106 B2 Constantina Spain
115 C1 Constantine Alg.
134 D2 Contact U.S.A.
155 D2 Contagalo Brazil
150 B3 Contamana Peru
153 A5 Contreras, Isla *i.* Chile
126 E2 Contwoyto Lake Can.
142 B1 Conway *AR* U.S.A.
141 E2 Conway *NH* U.S.A.
51 C2 Coober Pedy Austr.
Cooch Behar India *see* Koch Bihār
54 B2 Cook, Mount N.Z.
143 C1 Cookeville U.S.A.
126 B2 Cook Inlet *sea chan.* U.S.A.
49 K5 Cook Islands *terr.* S. Pacific Ocean
131 E2 Cook's Harbour Can.
97 C1 Cookstown U.K.
54 B2 Cook Strait N.Z.
51 D1 Cooktown Austr.
53 C2 Coolabah Austr.
53 C2 Coolamon Austr.
53 D1 Coolangatta Austr.
50 B3 Coolgardie Austr.
53 C3 Cooma Austr.
52 B2 Coombah Austr.
53 C2 Coonabarabran Austr.
52 A3 Coonalpyn Austr.
53 C2 Coonamble Austr.
53 C1 Coongoola Austr.
137 E1 Coon Rapids U.S.A.
52 A1 Cooper Creek *watercourse* Austr.
143 E3 Cooper's Town Bahamas
134 B2 Coos Bay U.S.A.
53 C2 Cootamundra Austr.
97 C1 Cootehill Rep. of Ireland
145 C3 Copainalá Mex.
145 C3 Copala Mex.
93 F4 Copenhagen Denmark
109 C2 Copertino Italy
53 D1 Copeton Reservoir Austr.
152 A2 Copiapó Chile
139 D2 Copperas Cove U.S.A.
140 B1 Copper Harbor U.S.A.
Coppermine Can. *see* Kugluktuk
126 E2 Coppermine *r.* Can.
122 B2 Copperton S. Africa
Coquilhatville Dem. Rep. Congo *see* Mbandaka
152 A2 Coquimbo Chile
152 A2 Coquimbo, Bahía de *b.* Chile
110 B2 Corabia Romania
155 D1 Coração de Jesus Brazil
150 B4 Coracora Peru
53 D1 Coraki Austr.
50 A2 Coral Bay Austr.
127 G2 Coral Harbour Can.
156 D7 Coral Sea S. Pacific Ocean
48 G5 Coral Sea Islands Territory *terr.* Austr.
137 E2 Coralville U.S.A.
52 B3 Corangamite, Lake Austr.
99 C3 Corby U.K.
Corcaigh Rep. of Ireland *see* Cork
135 C3 Corcoran U.S.A.
153 A4 Corcovado, Golfo de *sea chan.* Chile
143 D2 Cordele U.S.A.
64 B2 Cordilleras Range *mts* Phil.
155 D1 Cordisburgo Brazil
152 B3 Córdoba Arg.
145 C3 Córdoba Mex.
106 C2 Córdoba Spain
153 B3 Córdoba, Sierras de *mts* Arg.
126 C2 Cordova U.S.A.
51 D2 Corfield Austr.
111 A3 Corfu *i.* Greece
154 B1 Corguinho Brazil
106 B2 Coria Spain
106 B2 Coria del Río Spain
53 D2 Coricudgy *mt.* Austr.
Corinth Greece *see* Korinthos
142 C2 Corinth U.S.A.
Corinth, Gulf of *sea chan.* Greece *see* Korinthiakos Kolpos
155 D1 Corinto Brazil
97 B3 Cork Rep. of Ireland
111 C2 Çorlu Turkey
154 B2 Cornélio Procópio Brazil
131 E3 Corner Brook Can.
53 C3 Corner Inlet *b.* Austr.
135 B3 Corning *CA* U.S.A.
141 D2 Corning *NY* U.S.A.
Corn Islands *is* Nic. *see* Maíz, Islas del
108 B2 Corno, Monte *mt.* Italy
130 C3 Cornwall Can.
126 F1 Cornwallis Island Can.
150 C1 Coro Venez.
155 D1 Coroaci Brazil
154 C1 Coromandel Brazil
73 C3 Coromandel Coast India
54 C1 Coromandel Peninsula N.Z.
64 B2 Coron Phil.
129 C2 Coronation Can.
126 E2 Coronation Gulf Can.
55 B3 Coronation Island S. Atlantic Ocean
155 D1 Coronel Fabriciano Brazil
152 C2 Coronel Oviedo Para.
154 B1 Coronel Ponce Brazil
153 B3 Coronel Pringles Arg.
154 A2 Coronel Sapucaia Brazil
153 B3 Coronel Suárez Arg.
109 D2 Çorovodë Albania
145 D3 Corozal Belize
139 D3 Corpus Christi U.S.A.
152 B1 Corque Bol.
151 E4 Corrente Brazil
154 B1 Correntes Brazil
151 E4 Correntina Brazil
97 B2 Corrib, Lough *l.* Rep. of Ireland
152 C2 Corrientes Arg.
153 C3 Corrientes, Cabo *c.* Arg.
144 B2 Corrientes, Cabo *c.* Mex.
139 E2 Corrigan U.S.A.
53 C3 Corryong Austr.
Corse *i.* France *see* Corsica
105 D3 Corse, Cap *c. Corsica* France
105 D3 Corsica *i.* France
139 D2 Corsicana U.S.A.
105 D3 Corte *Corsica* France
106 B2 Cortegana Spain
136 B3 Cortez U.S.A.
108 B1 Cortina d'Ampezzo Italy
141 D2 Cortland U.S.A.
108 B2 Cortona Italy
106 B2 Coruche Port.
Çoruh Turkey *see* Artvin
80 B1 Çorum Turkey
151 D4 Corumbá Brazil
154 C1 Corumbá *r.* Brazil
154 C1 Corumbá de Goiás Brazil
Corunna Spain *see* A Coruña
134 B2 Corvallis U.S.A.
99 B3 Corwen U.K.
Cos *i.* Greece *see* Kos
144 B2 Cosalá Mex.
145 C3 Cosamaloapan Mex.
109 C3 Cosenza Italy
105 C2 Cosne-Cours-sur-Loire France
152 B3 Cosquín Arg.
107 C2 Costa Blanca *coastal area* Spain
107 D1 Costa Brava *coastal area* Spain
106 B2 Costa de la Luz *coastal area* Spain
107 C2 Costa del Azahar *coastal area* Spain
106 B2 Costa del Sol *coastal area* Spain
146 B3 Costa de Mosquitos *coastal area* Nic.
107 D1 Costa Dorada *coastal area* Spain
150 C4 Costa Marques Brazil
154 B1 Costa Rica Brazil
146 B3 Costa Rica *country* Central America
144 B2 Costa Rica Mex.
Costermansville Dem. Rep. Congo *see* Bukavu
110 B2 Costești Romania
64 B3 Cotabato Phil.
137 D1 Coteau des Prairies *slope* U.S.A.
136 C1 Coteau du Missouri *slope* U.S.A.
147 C3 Coteaux Haiti
105 D3 Côte d'Azur *coastal area* France
114 B4 Côte d'Ivoire *country* Africa
Côte Française de Somalis *country* Africa *see* Djibouti
105 C2 Côtes de Meuse *ridge* France
150 B3 Cotopaxi, Volcán *vol.* Ecuador
99 B4 Cotswold Hills U.K.
134 B2 Cottage Grove U.S.A.
102 C1 Cottbus Ger.
105 D3 Cottian Alps *mts* France/Italy
52 A3 Couëdic, Cape de Austr.
105 C2 Coulommiers France
137 D2 Council Bluffs U.S.A.
88 B2 Courland Lagoon *b.* Lith./Rus. Fed.
100 A3 Courmelles France
128 B3 Courtenay Can.
104 B2 Coutances France
104 B2 Coutras France
100 B2 Couvin Belgium
99 C3 Coventry U.K.
106 B1 Covilhã Port.
143 D2 Covington *GA* U.S.A.
140 C3 Covington *KY* U.S.A.
140 C3 Covington *VA* U.S.A.
50 B3 Cowan, Lake *salt flat* Austr.
96 C2 Cowdenbeath U.K.
52 A2 Cowell Austr.
53 C3 Cowes Austr.
134 B1 Cowlitz *r.* U.S.A.
53 C2 Cowra Austr.
154 B1 Coxim Brazil
154 B1 Coxim *r.* Brazil
75 D2 Cox's Bazar Bangl.
145 B3 Coyuca de Benítez Mex.
145 D2 Cozumel Mex.
145 D2 Cozumel, Isla de *i.* Mex.
52 A2 Cradock Austr.
123 C3 Cradock S. Africa
136 B2 Craig U.S.A.
102 C2 Crailsheim Ger.
110 B2 Craiova Romania
129 D2 Cranberry Portage Can.
53 C3 Cranbourne Austr.
128 C3 Cranbrook Can.
151 E3 Crateús Brazil
151 F3 Crato Brazil

154 C2 **Cravinhos** Brazil
136 C2 **Crawford** U.S.A.
140 B2 **Crawfordsville** U.S.A.
99 C4 **Crawley** U.K.
134 D1 **Crazy Mountains** U.S.A.
129 D2 **Cree** *r.* Can.
144 B2 **Creel** Mex.
129 D2 **Cree Lake** Can.
129 D2 **Creighton** Can.
104 C2 **Creil** France
100 B1 **Creil** Neth.
108 A1 **Crema** Italy
108 B1 **Cremona** Italy
108 B2 **Cres** *i.* Croatia
134 B2 **Crescent City** U.S.A.
53 D2 **Crescent Head** Austr.
135 E3 **Crescent Junction** U.S.A.
128 C3 **Creston** Can.
137 E2 **Creston** U.S.A.
142 C2 **Crestview** U.S.A.
111 B3 **Crete** *i.* Greece
107 D1 **Creus, Cap de** *c.* Spain
107 C2 **Crevillente** Spain
98 B3 **Crewe** U.K.
96 B2 **Crianlarich** U.K.
152 D2 **Criciúma** Brazil
96 C2 **Crieff** U.K.
108 B1 **Crikvenica** Croatia
91 C2 **Crimea** *pen.* Ukr.
101 F2 **Crimmitschau** Ger.
96 B2 **Crinan** U.K.
118 B2 **Cristal, Monts de** *mts* Equat. Guinea/Gabon
154 C1 **Cristalina** Brazil
110 B1 **Crişul Alb** *r.* Romania
101 E1 **Crivitz** Ger.
Crna Gora *aut. rep.* Yugo. *see* **Montenegro**
109 C1 **Črnomelj** Slovenia
97 B2 **Croagh Patrick** *hill* Rep. of Ireland
109 C1 **Croatia** *country* Europe
61 C1 **Crocker, Banjaran** *mts* Malaysia
139 D2 **Crockett** U.S.A.
59 C3 **Croker Island** Austr.
96 B2 **Cromarty** U.K.
99 D3 **Cromer** U.K.
54 A3 **Cromwell** N.Z.
147 C2 **Crooked Island** Bahamas
137 D1 **Crookston** U.S.A.
53 C2 **Crookwell** Austr.
53 D1 **Croppa Creek** Austr.
136 C1 **Crosby** U.S.A.
143 D3 **Cross City** U.S.A.
142 B2 **Crossett** U.S.A.
98 B2 **Cross Fell** *hill* U.K.
129 E2 **Cross Lake** Can.
143 C1 **Crossville** U.S.A.
109 C3 **Crotone** Italy
134 E1 **Crow Agency** U.S.A.
99 D4 **Crowborough** U.K.
142 B2 **Crowley** U.S.A.
53 D1 **Crows Nest** Austr.
128 C3 **Crowsnest Pass** Can.
159 D7 **Crozet, Îles** *is* Indian Ocean
146 C3 **Cruz, Cabo** *c.* Cuba
152 C2 **Cruz Alta** Brazil
152 B3 **Cruz del Eje** Arg.
155 D2 **Cruzeiro** Brazil
150 B3 **Cruzeiro do Sul** Brazil
52 A2 **Crystal Brook** Austr.
139 D3 **Crystal City** U.S.A.
140 B1 **Crystal Falls** U.S.A.
142 B2 **Crystal Springs** U.S.A.
103 E2 **Csongrád** Hungary
103 D2 **Csorna** Hungary
121 C2 **Cuamba** Moz.
120 B2 **Cuando** *r.* Angola/Zambia
120 A2 **Cuangar** Angola
118 B3 **Cuango** *r.* Angola/Dem. Rep. Congo
120 A1 **Cuanza** *r.* Angola
144 B2 **Cuatro Ciénegas** Mex.
144 B2 **Cuauhtémoc** Mex.
145 C3 **Cuautla** Mex.
146 B2 **Cuba** *country* West Indies
120 A2 **Cubal** Angola
120 B2 **Cubango** *r.* Angola/Namibia
150 B2 **Cúcuta** Col.
73 B3 **Cuddalore** India
73 B3 **Cuddapah** India
50 A2 **Cue** Austr.
106 C1 **Cuéllar** Spain
120 A2 **Cuemba** Angola
150 B3 **Cuenca** Ecuador
107 C1 **Cuenca** Spain
107 C1 **Cuenca, Serranía de** *mts* Spain
145 C3 **Cuernavaca** Mex.
139 D3 **Cuero** U.S.A.
104 C3 **Cugnaux** France
151 D4 **Cuiabá** Brazil
151 D4 **Cuiabá** *r.* Brazil
96 A2 **Cuillin Sound** *sea chan.* U.K.
120 A1 **Cuilo** Angola
120 B2 **Cuito** *r.* Angola
120 A2 **Cuito Cuanavale** Angola
60 B1 **Cukai** Malaysia
64 B2 **Culasi** Phil.
53 C3 **Culcairn** Austr.
100 B2 **Culemborg** Neth.
53 C1 **Culgoa** Austr.
144 B2 **Culiacán** Mex.
64 A2 **Culion** *i.* Phil.
107 C2 **Cullera** Spain
142 C2 **Cullman** U.S.A.
97 C1 **Cullybackey** U.K.
141 D3 **Culpeper** U.S.A.
151 D4 **Culuene** *r.* Brazil
54 B2 **Culverden** N.Z.
150 C1 **Cumaná** Venez.
141 D3 **Cumberland** U.S.A.
140 B3 **Cumberland** *r.* U.S.A.
143 D2 **Cumberland Island** U.S.A.
129 D2 **Cumberland Lake** Can.
127 H2 **Cumberland Peninsula** Can.
142 C1 **Cumberland Plateau** U.S.A.
127 H2 **Cumberland Sound** *sea chan.* Can.
96 C3 **Cumbernauld** U.K.
135 B3 **Cummings** U.S.A.
96 B3 **Cumnock** U.K.
144 B1 **Cumpas** Mex.
145 C3 **Cunduacán** Mex.
120 A2 **Cunene** *r.* Angola/Namibia
108 A2 **Cuneo** Italy
53 C1 **Cunnamulla** Austr.
108 A1 **Cuorgnè** Italy
96 C2 **Cupar** U.K.
110 B2 **Ćuprija** Yugo.
147 D3 **Curaçao** *i.* Neth. Antilles
150 B3 **Curaray** *r.* Ecuador
153 A3 **Curicó** Chile
154 C3 **Curitiba** Brazil
52 A2 **Curnamona** Austr.
135 C3 **Currant** U.S.A.
51 D3 **Currie** Austr.
135 D2 **Currie** U.S.A.
51 E2 **Curtis Island** Austr.
151 D3 **Curuá** *r.* Brazil
60 B2 **Curup** Indon.
151 E3 **Cururupu** Brazil
155 D1 **Curvelo** Brazil
150 B4 **Cusco** Peru
97 C1 **Cushendun** U.K.
139 D1 **Cushing** U.S.A.
136 C2 **Custer** U.S.A.
134 D1 **Cut Bank** U.S.A.
142 B3 **Cut Off** U.S.A.
75 C2 **Cuttack** India
120 A2 **Cuvelai** Angola
101 D1 **Cuxhaven** Ger.
64 B2 **Cuyo Islands** Phil.
Cuzco Peru *see* **Cusco**
99 B4 **Cwmbran** U.K.
119 C3 **Cyangugu** Rwanda
111 B3 **Cyclades** *is* Greece
129 C3 **Cypress Hills** Can.
80 B2 **Cyprus** *country* Asia
80 B2 **Cyprus** *i.* Asia
102 C2 **Czech Republic** *country* Europe
103 D1 **Czersk** Pol.
103 D1 **Częstochowa** Pol.

D

62 B1 **Đa, Sông** *r.* Vietnam
69 D2 **Daban** China
103 D2 **Dabas** Hungary
114 A3 **Dabola** Guinea
103 D1 **Dąbrowa Górnicza** Pol.
110 B2 **Dăbuleni** Romania
Dacca Bangl. *see* **Dhaka**
102 C2 **Dachau** Ger.
70 A2 **Dachuan** China
143 D3 **Dade City** U.S.A.
Dadong China *see* **Donggang**
Dadra India *see* **Achalpur**
74 B2 **Dadra and Nagar Haveli** *union terr.* India
74 A2 **Dadu** Pak.
64 B2 **Daet** Phil.
114 A3 **Dagana** Senegal
119 D2 **Daga Post** Sudan
88 C2 **Dagda** Latvia
64 B2 **Dagupan** Phil.
Dahalach, Isole *is* Eritrea *see* **Dahlak Archipelago**
74 B3 **Dahanu** India
69 D2 **Da Hinggan Ling** *mts* China
116 C3 **Dahlak Archipelago** *is* Eritrea
100 C2 **Dahlem** Ger.
74 B2 **Dāhod** India
Dahomey *country* Africa *see* **Benin**
Dahra Senegal *see* **Dara**
81 C2 **Dahūk** Iraq
60 B2 **Daik** Indon.
106 C2 **Daimiel** Spain
Dairen China *see* **Dalian**
51 C2 **Dajarra** Austr.
70 A2 **Dajing** China
114 A3 **Dakar** Senegal
117 C4 **Daketa Shet'** *watercourse* Eth.
116 A2 **Dakhla Oasis** Egypt
63 A3 **Dakoank** India
88 C3 **Dakol'ka** *r.* Belarus
109 D2 **Đakovica** Yugo.
109 C1 **Đakovo** Croatia
120 B2 **Dala** Angola
70 A1 **Dalain Hob** China
93 G3 **Dalälven** *r.* Sweden
111 C3 **Dalaman** Turkey
111 C3 **Dalaman** *r.* Turkey
68 C2 **Dalandzadgad** Mongolia
64 B2 **Dalanganem Islands** Phil.
48 I3 **Dalap-Uliga-Djarrit** Marshall Is
63 B2 **Đa Lat** Vietnam
Dalatando Angola *see* **N'dalatando**
74 A2 **Dalbandin** Pak.
96 C3 **Dalbeattie** U.K.
53 D1 **Dalby** Austr.
93 E3 **Dale** Norway
143 C1 **Dale Hollow Lake** U.S.A.
53 C3 **Dalgety** Austr.
139 C1 **Dalhart** U.S.A.
131 D3 **Dalhousie** Can.
62 B1 **Dali** China
70 C2 **Dalian** China
96 C3 **Dalkeith** U.K.
139 D2 **Dallas** U.S.A.
128 A2 **Dall Island** U.S.A.
109 C2 **Dalmacija** *reg.* Croatia
96 B2 **Dalmally** U.K.
Dalmatia *reg.* Croatia *see* **Dalmacija**
96 B3 **Dalmellington** U.K.
66 C2 **Dal'negorsk** Rus. Fed.
66 B1 **Dal'nerechensk** Rus. Fed.
Dalny China *see* **Dalian**
114 B4 **Daloa** Côte d'Ivoire
71 A3 **Dalou Shan** *mts* China
51 D2 **Dalrymple, Mount** Austr.
92 □A3 **Dalsmynni** Iceland
75 C2 **Daltenganj** India
143 D2 **Dalton** U.S.A.
Daltonganj India *see* **Daltenganj**
60 B1 **Daludalu** Indon.
71 B3 **Daluo Shan** *mt.* China
92 □B2 **Dalvík** Iceland
96 B2 **Dalwhinnie** U.K.
50 C1 **Daly** *r.* Austr.
51 C1 **Daly Waters** Austr.
74 B2 **Damān** India
74 B2 **Daman and Diu** *union terr.* India
116 B1 **Damanhûr** Egypt
59 C3 **Damar** *i.* Indon.
118 B2 **Damara** C.A.R.
80 B2 **Damascus** Syria
115 D3 **Damaturu** Nigeria
76 B3 **Damāvand, Qolleh-ye** *mt.* Iran
120 A1 **Damba** Angola
118 B1 **Damboa** Nigeria
81 D2 **Damghan** Iran
Damietta Egypt *see* **Dumyât**
Dammam Saudi Arabia *see* **Ad Dammām**
101 D1 **Damme** Ger.
75 B2 **Damoh** India
114 B4 **Damongo** Ghana
50 A2 **Dampier** Austr.
59 C3 **Dampir, Selat** *sea chan.* Indon.
62 A1 **Damroh** India
75 D1 **Damxung** China
114 B4 **Danané** Côte d'Ivoire
63 B2 **Đa Năng** Vietnam
141 E2 **Danbury** U.S.A.
70 C1 **Dandong** China
117 B3 **Dangila** Eth.
146 B3 **Dangriga** Belize
70 B2 **Dangshan** China
89 F2 **Danilov** Rus. Fed.
89 E2 **Danilovskaya Vozvyshennost'** *hills* Rus. Fed.
70 B2 **Danjiangkou** China
79 C2 **Ḍank** Oman
89 E3 **Dankov** Rus. Fed.
146 B3 **Danlí** Hond.
101 E1 **Dannenberg (Elbe)** Ger.
54 C2 **Dannevirke** N.Z.
62 B2 **Dan Sai** Thai.
Dantu China *see* **Zhenjia**
110 A1 **Danube** *r.* Europe
Danube Delta Romania *see* **Dunării, Delta**
62 A2 **Danubyu** Myanmar
140 B2 **Danville** *IL* U.S.A.
140 C3 **Danville** *KY* U.S.A.
141 D3 **Danville** *VA* U.S.A.
Danxian China *see* **Danzhou**
71 A4 **Danzhou** China
Danzig, Gulf of Pol./Rus. Fed. *see* **Gdańsk, Gulf of**
Daojiang China *see* **Daoxian**
115 D2 **Dao Timmi** Niger
Daoud Alg. *see* **Aïn Beïd**
114 B4 **Daoukro** Côte d'Ivoire
71 B3 **Daoxian** China
64 B3 **Dapa** Phil.
114 C3 **Dapaong** Togo
68 C2 **Da Qaidam Zhen** China
69 E1 **Daqing** China
114 A3 **Dara** Senegal
80 B2 **Dar'ā** Syria
81 D3 **Dārāb** Iran
115 D1 **Daraj** Libya
81 D2 **Dārān** Iran
63 B2 **Đa Răng, Sông** *r.* Vietna
109 D2 **Đaravica** *mt.* Yugo.
75 C2 **Darbhanga** India
Dardo China *see* **Kangdi**
119 D3 **Dar es Salaam** Tanz.
74 B1 **Dargai** Pak.
54 B1 **Dargaville** N.Z.
53 C3 **Dargo** Austr.
68 D1 **Darhan** Mongolia
150 B2 **Darién, Golfo del** *g.* Col.
Darjeeling India *see* **Dārjiling**
75 C2 **Dārjiling** India
68 C2 **Darlag** China
52 B2 **Darling** *r.* Austr.
53 C1 **Darling Downs** *hills* Aust
50 A3 **Darling Range** *hills* Aust
98 C2 **Darlington** U.K.
53 C2 **Darlington Point** Austr.
103 D1 **Darłowo** Pol.
101 D3 **Darmstadt** Ger.
115 E1 **Darnah** Libya
52 B2 **Darnick** Austr.
55 H3 **Darnley, Cape** Antarctica
107 C1 **Daroca** Spain
99 D4 **Dartford** U.K.
99 A4 **Dartmoor** *hills* U.K.
131 D3 **Dartmouth** Can.
99 B4 **Dartmouth** U.K.
97 B1 **Darty Mountains** *hills* Rep. of Ireland
59 D3 **Daru** P.N.G.
59 C2 **Daruba** Indon.
50 C1 **Darwin** Austr.
79 C2 **Dārzīn** Iran
65 A1 **Dashiqiao** China
76 B2 **Dashkhovuz** Turkm.
74 A2 **Dasht** *r.* Pak.
61 C1 **Datadian** Indon.
111 C3 **Datça** Turkey
66 D2 **Date** Japan
71 B3 **Datian** China
70 B1 **Datong** China
64 B3 **Datu Piang** Phil.
74 B1 **Daud Khel** Pak.
88 B2 **Daugava** *r.* Latvia
88 C2 **Daugavpils** Latvia
100 C2 **Daun** Ger.
129 D2 **Dauphin** Can.
129 E2 **Dauphin Lake** Can.
73 B3 **Davangere** India
64 B3 **Davao** Phil.
64 B3 **Davao Gulf** Phil.

7 E2 **Davenport** U.S.A.
9 C3 **Daventry** U.K.
3 C2 **Daveyton** S. Africa
6 B4 **David** Panama
9 D2 **Davidson** Can.
6 F3 **Davidson Lake** Can.
5 B3 **Davis** U.S.A.
1 D2 **Davis Inlet** Can.
5 I3 **Davis Sea** *sea* Antarctica
0 P3 **Davis Strait** *str.* Can./Greenland
5 D2 **Davos** Switz.
9 C3 **Davyd-Haradok** Belarus
9 C3 **Dawqah** Oman
3 B3 **Dawqah** Saudi Arabia
6 C2 **Dawson** Can.
3 D2 **Dawson** U.S.A.
8 B2 **Dawson Creek** Can.
8 B2 **Dawsons Landing** Can.
3 C2 **Dawu** China
Dawukou China *see* **Shizuishan**
9 C2 **Dawwah** Oman
4 B3 **Dax** France
Daxian China *see* **Dachuan**
3 C2 **Daxue Shan** *mts* China
2 B3 **Daylesford** Austr.
1 B3 **Dayong** China
1 C2 **Dayr az Zawr** Syria
0 C3 **Dayton** U.S.A.
3 D3 **Daytona Beach** U.S.A.
1 B3 **Dayu** China
2 B3 **De Aar** S. Africa
3 D3 **Deadman Bay** U.S.A.
0 B2 **Dead Sea** *salt l.* Asia
9 D4 **Deal** U.K.
1 B3 **De'an** China
2 B3 **Deán Funes** Arg.
8 B2 **Dease Lake** Can.
6 E2 **Dease Strait** Can.
5 C3 **Death Valley** *depr.* U.S.A.
4 C2 **Deauville** France
1 C1 **Debak** *Sarawak* Malaysia
1 B2 **Debar** Macedonia
3 E1 **Dębica** Pol.
3 E1 **Dęblin** Pol.
4 B3 **Débo, Lac** *l.* Mali
3 E2 **Debrecen** Hungary
7 B3 **Debre Markos** Eth.
9 D2 **Debre Sīna** Eth.
7 B3 **Debre Tabor** Eth.
7 B4 **Debre Zeyit** Eth.
2 C2 **Decatur** *AL* U.S.A.
0 B3 **Decatur** *IL* U.S.A.
3 B3 **Deccan** *plat.* India
3 D1 **Deception Bay** Austr.
1 A3 **Dechang** China
2 C1 **Děčín** Czech Rep.
7 E2 **Decorah** U.S.A.
4 C2 **Dedo de Deus** *mt.* Brazil
3 C2 **Dedovichi** Rus. Fed.
1 C2 **Dedza** Malawi
9 B3 **Dee** *r. England/Wales* U.K.
6 C2 **Dee** *r. Scotland* U.K.
0 C3 **Deep River** Can.
3 D1 **Deepwater** Austr.
1 E3 **Deer Lake** Can.
4 D1 **Deer Lodge** U.S.A.
0 C2 **Defiance** U.S.A.
2 C2 **De Funiak Springs** U.S.A.
3 C2 **Dêgê** China
7 C4 **Degeh Bur** Eth.
1 F1 **Dégelis** Can.
2 C2 **Deggendorf** Ger.
1 E2 **Degtevo** Rus. Fed.
1 D2 **Deh Bīd** Iran
1 C2 **Dehlorān** Iran
4 B1 **Dehra Dun** India
5 C2 **Dehri** India
9 E2 **Dehui** China
0 A2 **Deinze** Belgium
0 B1 **Dej** Romania
0 B2 **De Kalb** U.S.A.
6 B3 **Dekemhare** Eritrea
8 C3 **Dekese** Dem. Rep. Congo
8 B2 **Dékoa** C.A.R.
3 D3 **De Land** U.S.A.
5 C3 **Delano** U.S.A.
5 D3 **Delano Peak** U.S.A.
4 A1 **Delārām** Afgh.
3 C2 **Delareyville** S. Africa
9 D2 **Delaronde Lake** Can.
0 C2 **Delaware** U.S.A.
1 D3 **Delaware** *r.* U.S.A.
1 D3 **Delaware** *state* U.S.A.
1 D3 **Delaware Bay** U.S.A.
3 C3 **Delegate** Austr.
8 C2 **Délembé** C.A.R.
5 D2 **Delémont** Switz.
0 B1 **Delft** Neth.
0 C1 **Delfzijl** Neth.
121 D2 **Delgado, Cabo** *c.* Moz.
68 C2 **Delhi** China
74 B2 **Delhi** India
60 B2 **Deli** *i.* Indon.
128 B1 **Déline** Can.
Delingha China *see* **Delhi**
101 F2 **Delitzsch** Ger.
107 D2 **Dellys** Alg.
135 C4 **Del Mar** U.S.A.
101 D1 **Delmenhorst** Ger.
109 B1 **Delnice** Croatia
136 B3 **Del Norte** U.S.A.
83 L1 **De-Longa, Ostrova** *is* Rus. Fed.
De Long Islands Rus. Fed. *see* **De-Longa, Ostrova**
De Long Strait Rus. Fed. *see* **Longa, Proliv**
129 D3 **Deloraine** Can.
111 B3 **Delphi** *tourist site* Greece
143 D3 **Delray Beach** U.S.A.
139 C3 **Del Rio** U.S.A.
136 B3 **Delta** *CO* U.S.A.
135 D3 **Delta** *UT* U.S.A.
126 C2 **Delta Junction** U.S.A.
109 D3 **Delvinë** Albania
Demavend *mt.* Iran *see* **Damāvand, Qolleh-ye**
118 C3 **Demba** Dem. Rep. Congo
119 D1 **Dembech'a** Eth.
117 B4 **Dembī Dolo** Eth.
Demerara Guyana *see* **Georgetown**
91 C3 **Demerdzhi** *mt.* Ukr.
89 D2 **Demidov** Rus. Fed.
138 B2 **Deming** U.S.A.
111 C3 **Demirci** Turkey
111 C2 **Demirköy** Turkey
102 C1 **Demmin** Ger.
142 C2 **Demopolis** U.S.A.
60 B2 **Dempo, Gunung** *vol.* Indon.
89 D2 **Demyansk** Rus. Fed.
122 B3 **De Naawte** S. Africa
117 C3 **Denakil** *reg.* Eritrea/Eth.
77 C3 **Denau** Uzbek.
98 B3 **Denbigh** U.K.
100 B1 **Den Burg** Neth.
62 B2 **Den Chai** Thai.
60 B2 **Dendang** Indon.
100 B2 **Dendermonde** Belgium
100 B2 **Dendre** *r.* Belgium
Dengjiabu China *see* **Yujiang**
70 A1 **Dengkou** China
Dengxian China *see* **Dengzhou**
70 B2 **Dengzhou** China
Dengzhou China *see* **Penglai**
Den Haag Neth. *see* **The Hague**
50 A2 **Denham** Austr.
100 B1 **Den Helder** Neth.
107 D2 **Denia** Spain
52 B3 **Deniliquin** Austr.
134 C2 **Denio** U.S.A.
137 D2 **Denison** *IA* U.S.A.
139 D2 **Denison** *TX* U.S.A.
111 C3 **Denizli** Turkey
53 D2 **Denman** Austr.
50 A3 **Denmark** Austr.
93 F4 **Denmark** *country* Europe
84 B2 **Denmark Strait** Greenland/Iceland
61 C2 **Denpasar** Indon.
139 D2 **Denton** U.S.A.
50 A3 **D'Entrecasteaux, Point** Austr.
59 E3 **D'Entrecasteaux Islands** P.N.G.
143 D2 **Dentsville** U.S.A.
136 B3 **Denver** U.S.A.
75 C2 **Deogarh** *Orissa* India
74 B2 **Deogarh** *Rajasthan* India
75 C2 **Deoghar** India
140 B2 **De Pere** U.S.A.
83 K2 **Deputatskiy** Rus. Fed.
62 A1 **Dêqên** China
142 B2 **De Queen** U.S.A.
74 A2 **Dera Bugti** Pak.
74 B1 **Dera Ghazi Khan** Pak.
74 B1 **Dera Ismail Khan** Pak.
87 D4 **Derbent** Rus. Fed.
50 B1 **Derby** Austr.
99 C3 **Derby** U.K.
137 D3 **Derby** U.S.A.
97 B2 **Derg, Lough** *l.* Rep. of Ireland
91 D1 **Derhachi** Ukr.
142 B2 **De Ridder** U.S.A.
91 D2 **Derkul** *r.* Rus. Fed./Ukr.
Dêrub China *see* **Rutog**
116 B3 **Derudeb** Sudan
122 B3 **De Rust** S. Africa
109 C2 **Derventa** Bos.-Herz.
98 C3 **Derwent** *r. England* U.K.
98 C3 **Derwent** *r. England* U.K.
98 B2 **Derwent Water** *l.* U.K.
77 C1 **Derzhavinsk** Kazakh.
Derzhavinskiy Kazakh. *see* **Derzhavinsk**
152 B1 **Desaguadero** *r.* Bol.
49 M5 **Désappointement, Îles du** *is* Fr. Polynesia
129 D2 **Deschambault Lake** Can.
134 B1 **Deschutes** *r.* U.S.A.
117 B3 **Desē** Eth.
153 B4 **Deseado** Arg.
153 B4 **Deseado** *r.* Arg.
138 A2 **Desemboque** Mex.
137 E2 **Des Moines** U.S.A.
137 E2 **Des Moines** *r.* U.S.A.
91 C1 **Desna** *r.* Rus. Fed./Ukr.
89 D3 **Desnogorsk** Rus. Fed.
101 F2 **Dessau** Ger.
Dessye Eth. *see* **Desē**
128 A1 **Destruction Bay** Can.
128 C1 **Detah** Can.
120 B2 **Dete** Zimbabwe
101 D2 **Detmold** Ger.
140 C2 **Detroit** U.S.A.
137 D1 **Detroit Lakes** U.S.A.
Dett Zimbabwe *see* **Dete**
100 B2 **Deurne** Neth.
110 B1 **Deva** Romania
100 C1 **Deventer** Neth.
96 C2 **Deveron** *r.* U.K.
103 D2 **Devét Skal** *hill* Czech Rep.
137 D1 **Devil's Lake** U.S.A.
128 A2 **Devil's Paw** *mt.* U.S.A.
99 C4 **Devizes** U.K.
74 B2 **Devli** India
110 C2 **Devnya** Bulg.
128 C2 **Devon** Can.
126 F1 **Devon Island** Can.
51 D4 **Devonport** Austr.
74 B2 **Dewas** India
137 F3 **Dexter** U.S.A.
70 A2 **Deyang** China
59 D3 **Deyong, Tanjung** *pt* Indon.
79 C2 **Deyyer** Iran
81 C2 **Dezfūl** Iran
70 B2 **Dezhou** China
79 C2 **Dhahran** Saudi Arabia
75 D2 **Dhaka** Bangl.
78 B3 **Dhamār** Yemen
75 C2 **Dhamtari** India
75 C2 **Dhanbad** India
74 B2 **Dhandhuka** India
75 C2 **Dhankuta** Nepal
74 B2 **Dhar** India
75 D2 **Dharmanagar** India
73 B3 **Dharmapuri** India
75 C2 **Dharmjaygarh** India
114 B3 **Ḍhar Oualâta** *hills* Maur.
114 B3 **Ḍhar Tîchît** *hills* Maur.
73 B3 **Dhārwād** India
Dharwar India *see* **Dhārwād**
74 B2 **Dhasa** India
75 C2 **Dhaulagiri** *mt.* Nepal
78 B3 **Dhubāb** Yemen
74 B2 **Dhule** India
Dhulia India *see* **Dhule**
117 C4 **Dhuusa Marreeb** Somalia
144 A1 **Diablo, Picacho del** *mt.* Mex.
138 B2 **Diablo Plateau** U.S.A.
121 C2 **Diaca** Moz.
51 C2 **Diamantina** *watercourse* Austr.
155 D1 **Diamantina** Brazil
151 E4 **Diamantina, Chapada** *plat.* Brazil
159 F6 **Diamantina Deep** *sea feature* Indian Ocean
154 B1 **Diamantino** Brazil
151 D4 **Diamantino** Brazil
71 B3 **Dianbai** China
151 E4 **Dianópolis** Brazil
114 B4 **Dianra** Côte d'Ivoire
114 C3 **Diapaga** Burkina
79 C2 **Dibā al Ḥiṣn** U.A.E.
79 C2 **Ḍibab** Oman
118 C3 **Dibaya** Dem. Rep. Congo
122 B2 **Dibeng** S. Africa
72 D2 **Dibrugarh** India
136 C1 **Dickinson** U.S.A.
142 C1 **Dickson** U.S.A.
Dicle *r.* Turkey *see* **Tigris**
105 D3 **Die** France
Diedenhofen France *see* **Thionville**
129 D2 **Diefenbaker, Lake** Can.
Diégo Suarez Madag. *see* **Antsirañana**
114 B3 **Diéma** Mali
101 D2 **Diemel** *r.* Ger.
62 B1 **Điên Biên Phu** Vietnam
62 B2 **Diên Châu** Vietnam
101 D1 **Diepholz** Ger.
104 C2 **Dieppe** France
100 B2 **Diest** Belgium
115 D3 **Diffa** Niger
131 D3 **Digby** Can.
105 D3 **Digne-les-Bains** France
105 C2 **Digoin** France
64 B3 **Digos** Phil.
59 D3 **Digul** *r.* Indon.
105 D2 **Dijon** France
115 D4 **Dik** Chad
117 C3 **Dikhil** Djibouti
111 C3 **Dikili** Turkey
100 A2 **Diksmuide** Belgium
82 G2 **Dikson** Rus. Fed.
115 D3 **Dikwa** Nigeria
117 B4 **Dīla** Eth.
59 C3 **Dili** East Timor
101 D2 **Dillenburg** Ger.
117 A3 **Dilling** Sudan
126 B3 **Dillingham** U.S.A.
134 D1 **Dillon** *MT* U.S.A.
143 E2 **Dillon** *SC* U.S.A.
118 C4 **Dilolo** Dem. Rep. Congo
72 D2 **Dimapur** India
Dimashq Syria *see* **Damascus**
52 B3 **Dimboola** Austr.
110 C2 **Dimitrovgrad** Bulg.
87 D3 **Dimitrovgrad** Rus. Fed.
Dimitrovo Bulg. *see* **Pernik**
64 B2 **Dinagat** *i.* Phil.
75 C2 **Dinajpur** Bangl.
104 B2 **Dinan** France
100 B2 **Dinant** Belgium
111 D3 **Dinar** Turkey
81 D2 **Dīnār, Kūh-e** *mt.* Iran
104 B2 **Dinard** France
Dinbych U.K. *see* **Denbigh**
73 B3 **Dindigul** India
118 B1 **Dindima** Nigeria
123 D1 **Dindiza** Moz.
101 E2 **Dingelstädt** Ger.
97 A2 **Dingle** Rep. of Ireland
97 A2 **Dingle Bay** Rep. of Ireland
71 B3 **Dingnan** China
102 C2 **Dingolfing** Ger.
114 A3 **Dinguiraye** Guinea
96 B2 **Dingwall** U.K.
70 A2 **Dingxi** China
75 C2 **Dinngyê** China
123 C1 **Dinokwe** Botswana
91 D2 **Dinskaya** Rus. Fed.
100 C2 **Dinslaken** Ger.
135 C3 **Dinuba** U.S.A.
114 B3 **Dioïla** Mali
154 B3 **Dionísio Cerqueira** Brazil
114 A3 **Diourbel** Senegal
75 D2 **Diphu** India
64 B3 **Dipolog** Phil.
74 B1 **Dir** Pak.
51 D1 **Direction, Cape** Austr.
117 C4 **Dirē Dawa** Eth.
120 B2 **Dirico** Angola
50 A2 **Dirk Hartog Island** Austr.
53 C1 **Dirranbandi** Austr.
78 B3 **Ḍirs** Saudi Arabia
153 E5 **Disappointment, Cape** S. Georgia
134 B1 **Disappointment, Cape** U.S.A.
50 B2 **Disappointment, Lake** *salt flat* Austr.
52 B3 **Discovery Bay** Austr.
Disko *i.* Greenland *see* **Qeqertarsuaq**
143 E1 **Dismal Swamp** U.S.A.
99 D3 **Diss** U.K.
108 B3 **Dittaino** *r. Sicily* Italy
74 B2 **Diu** India
155 D2 **Divinópolis** Brazil
87 D4 **Divnoye** Rus. Fed.
114 B4 **Divo** Côte d'Ivoire
80 B2 **Divriği** Turkey
74 A2 **Diwana** Pak.
140 B2 **Dixon** U.S.A.
128 A2 **Dixon Entrance** *sea chan.* Can./U.S.A.
81 C2 **Diyarbakır** Turkey
74 A2 **Diz** Pak.
115 D2 **Djado** Niger

115 D2 **Djado, Plateau du** Niger
Djakarta Indon. *see* **Jakarta**
118 B3 **Djambala** Congo
115 C2 **Djanet** Alg.
115 D3 **Djédaa** Chad
115 C1 **Djelfa** Alg.
119 C2 **Djéma** C.A.R.
114 B3 **Djenné** Mali
114 B3 **Djibo** Burkina
117 C3 **Djibouti** *country* Africa
117 C3 **Djibouti** Djibouti
Djidjelli Alg. *see* **Jijel**
118 C2 **Djolu** Dem. Rep. Congo
114 C4 **Djougou** Benin
118 B2 **Djoum** Cameroon
92 □C3 **Djúpivogur** Iceland
89 F3 **Dmitriyevka** Rus. Fed.
89 E3 **Dmitriyev-L'govskiy** Rus. Fed.
Dmitriyevsk Ukr. *see* **Makiyivka**
89 E2 **Dmitrov** Rus. Fed.
Dmytriyevs'k Ukr. *see* **Makiyivka**
Dnepr *r.* Rus. Fed. *see* **Dnieper**
89 D3 **Dnieper** *r.* Europe
Dniester *r.* Ukr. *see* **Dnister**
Dnipro *r.* Ukr. *see* **Dnieper**
91 C2 **Dniprodzerzhyns'k** Ukr.
91 D2 **Dnipropetrovs'k** Ukr.
91 C2 **Dniprorudne** Ukr.
90 B2 **Dnister** *r.* Ukr.
90 C2 **Dnistrov'ky Lyman** *l.* Ukr.
88 C2 **Dno** Rus. Fed.
121 C2 **Doa** Moz.
115 D4 **Doba** Chad
88 B2 **Dobele** Latvia
101 F2 **Döbeln** Ger.
59 C3 **Doberai, Jazirah** *pen.* Indon.
Doberai Peninsula Indon. *see* **Doberai, Jazirah**
59 C3 **Dobo** Indon.
109 C2 **Doboj** Bos.-Herz.
103 E1 **Dobre Miasto** Pol.
110 C2 **Dobrich** Bulg.
89 F3 **Dobrinka** Rus. Fed.
89 E3 **Dobroye** Rus. Fed.
89 D3 **Dobrush** Belarus
86 E3 **Dobryanka** Rus. Fed.
155 E1 **Doce** *r.* Brazil
145 B2 **Doctor Arroyo** Mex.
144 B2 **Doctor Belisario Domínguez** Mex.
Doctor Petru Groza Romania *see* **Ştei**
111 C3 **Dodecanese** *is* Greece
Dodekanisos *is* Greece *see* **Dodecanese**
136 C3 **Dodge City** U.S.A.
119 D3 **Dodoma** Tanz.
100 C1 **Doesburg** Neth.
100 C2 **Doetinchem** Neth.
59 C3 **Dofa** Indon.
75 C1 **Dogai Coring** *salt l.* China
128 B2 **Dog Creek** Can.
67 B3 **Dōgo** *i.* Japan
115 C3 **Dogondoutchi** Niger
81 C2 **Doğubeyazıt** Turkey
79 C2 **Doha** Qatar
62 A2 **Doi Saket** Thai.
81 D2 **Dokali** Iran
100 B1 **Dokkum** Neth.
88 C3 **Dokshytsy** Belarus
91 D2 **Dokuchayevs'k** Ukr.
59 D3 **Dolak, Pulau** *i.* Indon.
138 A1 **Dolan Springs** U.S.A.
130 C3 **Dolbeau** Can.
104 B2 **Dol-de-Bretagne** France
105 D2 **Dole** France
91 D2 **Dolgaya, Kosa** *spit* Rus. Fed.
99 B3 **Dolgellau** U.K.
89 E3 **Dolgorukovo** Rus. Fed.
89 E3 **Dolgoye** Rus. Fed.
69 F1 **Dolinsk** Rus. Fed.
103 D2 **Dolný Kubín** Slovakia
Dolomites *mts* Italy *see* **Dolomiti**
108 B1 **Dolomiti** *mts* Italy
Dolonnur China *see* **Duolun**
117 C4 **Dolo Odo** Eth.
144 A2 **Dolores** Mex.
126 E2 **Dolphin and Union Strait** Can.
90 A2 **Dolyna** Ukr.
102 C2 **Domažlice** Czech Rep.
93 E3 **Dombås** Norway
103 D2 **Dombóvár** Hungary
Dombrovitsa Ukr. *see* **Dubrovytsya**
Dombrowa Pol. *see* **Dąbrowa Górnicza**
128 B2 **Dome Creek** Can.
147 D3 **Dominica** *country* West Indies
147 C3 **Dominican Republic** *country* West Indies
118 C3 **Domiongo** Dem. Rep. Congo
117 C4 **Domo** Eth.
89 E2 **Domodedovo** Rus. Fed.
111 B3 **Domokos** Greece
61 C2 **Dompu** Indon.
138 B3 **Don** Mex.
89 E3 **Don** *r.* Rus. Fed.
96 C2 **Don** *r.* U.K.
97 D1 **Donaghadee** U.K.
52 B3 **Donald** Austr.
Donau *r.* Austria/Ger. *see* **Danube**
102 C2 **Donauwörth** Ger.
106 B2 **Don Benito** Spain
98 C3 **Doncaster** U.K.
120 A1 **Dondo** Angola
121 C2 **Dondo** Moz.
73 C4 **Dondra Head** *hd* Sri Lanka
97 B1 **Donegal** Rep. of Ireland
97 B1 **Donegal Bay** Rep. of Ireland
91 D2 **Donets'k** Ukr.
91 D2 **Donets'kyy Kryazh** *hills* Rus. Fed./Ukr.
118 B2 **Donga** Nigeria
50 A2 **Dongara** Austr.
71 A3 **Dongchuan** China
71 A4 **Dongfang** China
66 B1 **Dongfanghong** China
61 C2 **Donggala** Indon.
65 A2 **Donggang** China
Donggou China *see* **Donggang**
62 B2 **Đông Ha** Vietnam
Dong Hai *sea* N. Pacific Ocean *see* **East China Sea**
62 B2 **Đông Hôi** Vietnam
116 B3 **Dongola** Sudan
118 B2 **Dongou** Congo
63 B2 **Dong Phraya Fai** *mts* Thai.
63 B2 **Dong Phraya Yen** *esc.* Thai.
Dongping China *see* **Anhua**
71 B3 **Dongshan** China
70 B2 **Dongsheng** China
70 C2 **Dongtai** China
71 B3 **Dongting Hu** *l.* China
Dong Ujimqin Qi China *see* **Uliastai**
71 C3 **Dongyang** China
70 B2 **Dongying** China
139 D3 **Donna** U.S.A.
54 B1 **Donnellys Crossing** N.Z.
100 C3 **Donnersberg** *hill* Ger.
107 C1 **Donostia - San Sebastián** Spain
81 D1 **Donyztau, Sor** *dry lake* Kazakh.
51 C1 **Doomadgee** Austr.
140 B2 **Door Peninsula** U.S.A.
117 C4 **Dooxo Nugaaleed** *val.* Somalia
50 B2 **Dora, Lake** *salt flat* Austr.
99 B4 **Dorchester** U.K.
122 A1 **Dordabis** Namibia
104 B2 **Dordogne** *r.* France
100 B2 **Dordrecht** Neth.
123 C3 **Dordrecht** S. Africa
122 A1 **Doreenville** Namibia
129 D2 **Doré Lake** Can.
101 D1 **Dorfmark** Ger.
114 B3 **Dori** Burkina
122 A3 **Doring** *r.* S. Africa
100 C2 **Dormagen** Ger.
96 B2 **Dornoch** U.K.
96 B2 **Dornoch Firth** *est.* U.K.
114 B3 **Doro** Mali
89 D3 **Dorogobuzh** Rus. Fed.
110 C1 **Dorohoi** Romania
68 C1 **Döröö Nuur** *salt l.* Mongolia
92 G3 **Dorotea** Sweden
50 A2 **Dorre Island** Austr.
53 D2 **Dorrigo** Austr.
118 B2 **Dorsale Camerounaise** *slope* Cameroon/Nigeria
100 C2 **Dorsten** Ger.
100 C2 **Dortmund** Ger.
100 C2 **Dortmund-Ems-Kanal** *canal* Ger.
153 B4 **Dos Bahías, Cabo** *c.* Arg.
101 F1 **Dosse** *r.* Ger.
114 C3 **Dosso** Niger
143 C2 **Dothan** U.S.A.
101 D1 **Dötlingen** Ger.
105 C1 **Douai** France
118 A2 **Douala** Cameroon
104 B2 **Douarnenez** France
105 D2 **Doubs** *r.* France/Switz.
54 A3 **Doubtful Sound** N.Z.
114 B3 **Douentza** Mali
98 A2 **Douglas** Isle of Man
122 B2 **Douglas** S. Africa
128 A2 **Douglas** *AK* U.S.A.
138 B2 **Douglas** *AZ* U.S.A.
143 D2 **Douglas** *GA* U.S.A.
136 B2 **Douglas** *WY* U.S.A.
104 C1 **Doullens** France
154 B1 **Dourada, Serra** *hills* Brazil
154 B2 **Dourados** Brazil
154 B2 **Dourados** *r.* Brazil
154 B2 **Dourados, Serra dos** *hills* Brazil
106 B1 **Douro** *r.* Port.
99 D4 **Dover** U.K.
141 D3 **Dover** U.S.A.
95 D3 **Dover, Strait of** France/U.K.
141 F1 **Dover-Foxcroft** U.S.A.
121 C2 **Dowa** Malawi
81 D3 **Dowlatābād** Iran
79 C2 **Dowlatābād** Iran
97 D1 **Downpatrick** U.K.
81 C2 **Dow Rūd** Iran
77 C3 **Dowshī** Afgh.
67 B3 **Dōzen** *is* Japan
130 C3 **Dozois, Réservoir** *resr* Can.
154 B2 **Dracena** Brazil
100 C1 **Drachten** Neth.
110 B2 **Drăgănești-Olt** Romania
110 B2 **Drăgășani** Romania
105 D3 **Draguignan** France
88 C3 **Drahichyn** Belarus
53 D1 **Drake** Austr.
123 C2 **Drakensberg** *mts* Lesotho/S. Africa
123 C2 **Drakensberg** *mts* S. Africa
149 C8 **Drake Passage** S. Atlantic Ocean
111 B2 **Drama** Greece
93 F4 **Drammen** Norway
109 C1 **Drava** *r.* Europe
128 C2 **Drayton Valley** Can.
101 D2 **Dreieich** Ger.
111 B3 **Drepano, Akra** *pt* Greece
102 C1 **Dresden** Ger.
104 C2 **Dreux** France
100 B1 **Driemond** Neth.
98 C2 **Driffield** U.K.
137 D1 **Drift Prairie** *reg.* U.S.A.
109 C2 **Drina** *r.* Bos.-Herz./Yugo.
142 B2 **Driskill Mountain** *hill* U.S.A.
Drissa Belarus *see* **Vyerkhnyadzvinsk**
109 C2 **Drniš** Croatia
110 B2 **Drobeta-Turnu Severin** Romania
90 B2 **Drochia** Moldova
101 D1 **Drochtersen** Ger.
97 C2 **Drogheda** Rep. of Ireland
90 A2 **Drohobych** Ukr.
99 B3 **Droitwich** U.K.
Drokiya Moldova *see* **Drochia**
97 B1 **Dromahair** Rep. of Ireland
97 C1 **Dromore** U.K.
100 B1 **Dronten** Neth.
74 B1 **Drosh** Pak.
53 C3 **Drouin** Austr.
128 C2 **Drumheller** Can.
140 C1 **Drummond Island** U.S.A.
131 C3 **Drummondville** Can.
96 B3 **Drummore** U.K.
96 B2 **Drumnadrochit** U.K.
Druskieniki Lith. *see* **Druskininkai**
88 B3 **Druskininkai** Lith.
88 C2 **Druya** Belarus
91 D2 **Druzhkivka** Ukr.
88 D2 **Druzhnaya Gorka** Rus. Fed.
89 D3 **Drybin** Belarus
130 A3 **Dryden** Can.
50 B1 **Drysdale** *r.* Austr.
147 C3 **Duarte, Pico** *mt.* Dom. Rep.
78 A2 **Ḍubā** Saudi Arabia
79 C2 **Ḍubai** U.A.E.
90 B2 **Dubăsari** Moldova
129 D1 **Dubawnt Lake** Can.
Dubayy U.A.E. *see* **Duba**
78 A2 **Dubbagh, Jabal ad** *mt.* Saudi Arabia
53 C2 **Dubbo** Austr.
Dubesar' Moldova *see* **Dubăsari**
97 C2 **Dublin** Rep. of Ireland
143 D2 **Dublin** U.S.A.
89 E2 **Dubna** Rus. Fed.
90 B1 **Dubno** Ukr.
141 D2 **Du Bois** U.S.A.
Dubossary Moldova *see* **Dubăsari**
114 A4 **Dubréka** Guinea
109 C2 **Dubrovnik** Croatia
90 B1 **Dubrovytsya** Ukr.
89 D3 **Dubrowna** Belarus
137 E2 **Dubuque** U.S.A.
135 D2 **Duchesne** U.S.A.
129 D2 **Duck Bay** Can.
63 B2 **Đức Trong** Vietnam
101 E2 **Duderstadt** Ger.
82 G2 **Dudinka** Rus. Fed.
99 B3 **Dudley** U.K.
106 B1 **Duero** *r.* Spain
48 H4 **Duff Islands** Solomon Is
96 C2 **Dufftown** U.K.
131 C2 **Dufreboy, Lac** *l.* Can.
109 C2 **Dugi Otok** *i.* Croatia
109 C2 **Dugi Rat** Croatia
100 C2 **Duisburg** Ger.
123 D1 **Duiwelskloof** S. Africa
123 C3 **Dukathole** S. Africa
117 B4 **Duk Fadiat** Sudan
79 C2 **Dukhān** Qatar
89 D2 **Dukhovshchina** Rus. Fed.
Dukou China *see* **Panzhihua**
88 C2 **Dūkštas** Lith.
68 C2 **Dulan** China
152 B3 **Dulce** *r.* Arg.
138 B1 **Dulce** U.S.A.
97 C2 **Duleek** Rep. of Ireland
100 C2 **Dülmen** Ger.
110 C2 **Dulovo** Bulg.
137 E1 **Duluth** U.S.A.
64 B3 **Dumaguete** Phil.
60 B1 **Dumai** Indon.
64 B2 **Dumaran** *i.* Phil.
142 B2 **Dumas** *AR* U.S.A.
139 C1 **Dumas** *TX* U.S.A.
96 B3 **Dumbarton** U.K.
103 D2 **Ďumbier** *mt.* Slovakia
96 C3 **Dumfries** U.K.
89 E3 **Duminichi** Rus. Fed.
75 C2 **Dumka** India
55 L3 **Dumont d'Urville Sea** Antarctica
116 B1 **Dumyât** Egypt
Duna *r.* Hungary *see* **Danube**
Dünaburg Latvia *see* **Daugavpils**
103 D2 **Dunakeszi** Hungary
97 C2 **Dunany Point** Rep. of Ireland
Dunărea *r.* Romania *see* **Danube**
110 C1 **Dunării, Delta** Romania
103 D2 **Dunaújváros** Hungary
Dunav *r.* Bulg./Croatia/Yugo. *see* **Danube**
90 B2 **Dunayivtsi** Ukr.
96 C2 **Dunbar** U.K.
96 C1 **Dunbeath** U.K.
128 B3 **Duncan** Can.
139 D2 **Duncan** U.S.A.
96 C1 **Duncansby Head** *hd* U.K.
88 B2 **Dundaga** Latvia
97 C1 **Dundalk** Rep. of Ireland
141 D3 **Dundalk** U.S.A.
97 C2 **Dundalk Bay** Rep. of Ireland
Dundas Greenland *see* **Uummannaq**
Dún Dealgan Rep. of Ireland *see* **Dundalk**
123 D2 **Dundee** S. Africa
96 C2 **Dundee** U.K.
97 D1 **Dundrum Bay** U.K.
54 B3 **Dunedin** N.Z.
53 C2 **Dunedoo** Austr.
96 C2 **Dunfermline** U.K.
97 C1 **Dungannon** U.K.
74 B2 **Dungarpur** India

7 C2 Dungarvan Rep. of Ireland
9 D4 Dungeness *hd* U.K.
7 C1 Dungiven U.K.
3 D2 Dungog Austr.
9 C2 Dungu Dem. Rep. Congo
0 B1 Dungun Malaysia
6 B2 Dungunab Sudan
9 E2 Dunhua China
3 C2 Dunhuang China
6 C2 Dunkeld U.K.
Dunkerque France *see* Dunkirk
4 C1 Dunkirk France
1 D2 Dunkirk U.S.A.
7 C2 Dún Laoghaire Rep. of Ireland
7 B3 Dunmanway Rep. of Ireland
7 D1 Dunmurry U.K.
6 C1 Dunnet Head *hd* U.K.
6 C3 Duns U.K.
4 B2 Dunsmuir U.S.A.
9 C4 Dunstable U.K.
0 B3 Dun-sur-Meuse France
6 A2 Dunvegan U.K.
0 B1 Duolun China
Duperré Alg. *see* Aïn Defla
0 B2 Dupnitsa Bulg.
6 C1 Dupree U.S.A.
Duque de Bragança Angola *see* Calandula
0 B3 Du Quoin U.S.A.
0 B1 Durack *r.* Austr.
5 C3 Durance *r.* France
4 B2 Durango Mex.
6 C1 Durango Spain
6 B3 Durango U.S.A.
9 D2 Durant U.S.A.
3 C3 Durazno Uru.
Durazzo Albania *see* Durrës
3 D2 Durban S. Africa
5 C3 Durban-Corbières France
2 A3 Durbanville S. Africa
0 B2 Durbuy Belgium
0 C2 Düren Ger.
5 C2 Durg India
8 C2 Durham U.K.
3 E1 Durham U.S.A.
0 B1 Duri Indon.
9 C2 Durmitor *mt.* Yugo.
6 B1 Durness U.K.
9 C2 Durrës Albania
7 A3 Dursey Island Rep. of Ireland
1 C3 Dursunbey Turkey
7 C4 Durukhsi Somalia
9 D3 D'Urville, Tanjung *pt* Indon.
4 B2 D'Urville Island N.Z.
1 A3 Dushan China
7 C3 Dushanbe Tajik.
0 C2 Düsseldorf Ger.
Dutch East Indies *country* Asia *see* Indonesia
Dutch Guiana *country* S. America *see* Suriname
Dutch West Indies *terr.* West Indies *see* Netherlands Antilles
Duvno Bos.-Herz. *see* Tomislavgrad
1 A3 Duyun China
0 B1 Düzce Turkey
1 D2 Dvorichna Ukr.
4 A2 Dwarka India
23 C1 Dwarsberg S. Africa
34 C1 Dworshak Reservoir U.S.A.
9 D3 Dyat'kovo Rus. Fed.
6 C2 Dyce U.K.
27 H2 Dyer, Cape Can.
42 C1 Dyersburg U.S.A.
9 B3 Dyfi *r.* U.K.
03 D2 Dyje *r.* Austria/Czech Rep.
03 D1 Dylewska Góra *hill* Pol.
1 D2 Dymytrov Ukr.
23 C3 Dyoki S. Africa
1 D2 Dysart Austr.
22 B3 Dysselsdorp S. Africa
7 E3 Dyurtyuli Rus. Fed.
9 D2 Dzamïn Üüd Mongolia
1 D2 Dzerzhyns'k Ukr.
Dzhaltyr Kazakh. *see* Zhaltyr
Dzhambul Kazakh. *see* Taraz
31 D1 Dzhanga Turkm.
76 B2 Dzhangala Kazakh.
1 C2 Dzhankoy Ukr.
76 A2 Dzhanybek Kazakh.
Dzharkent Kazakh. *see* Zharkent
81 D2 Dzhebel Turkm.
Dzhetygara Kazakh. *see* Zhitikara
Dzhezkazgan Kazakh. *see* Zhezkazgan
77 C2 Dzhizak Uzbek.
91 D3 Dzhubga Rus. Fed.
83 K3 Dzhugdzhur, Khrebet *mts* Rus. Fed.
77 D2 Dzhungarskiy Alatau, Khrebet *mts* China/Kazakh.
76 C2 Dzhusaly Kazakh.
103 E1 Działdowo Pol.
145 D2 Dzilam de Bravo Mex.
69 D1 Dzuunmod Mongolia
88 C3 Dzyarzhynsk Belarus
88 C3 Dzyatlavichy Belarus

E

131 E2 Eagle *r.* Can.
134 C1 Eagle Cap *mt.* U.S.A.
130 A3 Eagle Lake Can.
134 B2 Eagle Lake U.S.A.
139 C3 Eagle Pass U.S.A.
126 C2 Eagle Plain Can.
Eap *i.* Micronesia *see* Yap
130 A2 Ear Falls Can.
135 C3 Earlimart U.S.A.
96 C2 Earn *r.* U.K.
55 J2 East Antarctica *reg.* Antarctica
East Bengal *country* Asia *see* Bangladesh
99 D4 Eastbourne U.K.
59 D2 East Caroline Basin *sea feature* N. Pacific Ocean
69 E2 East China Sea N. Pacific Ocean
54 B1 East Coast Bays N.Z.
99 D3 East Dereham U.K.
129 D3 Eastend Can.
157 G7 Easter Island S. Pacific Ocean
123 C3 Eastern Cape *prov.* S. Africa
116 B2 Eastern Desert Egypt
73 B3 Eastern Ghats *mts* India
Eastern Samoa *terr.* S. Pacific Ocean *see* American Samoa
Eastern Sayan Mountains Rus. Fed. *see* Vostochnyy Sayan
Eastern Transvaal *prov.* S. Africa *see* Mpumalanga
129 E2 Easterville Can.
153 C5 East Falkland *i.* Falkland Is
100 C1 East Frisian Islands Ger.
135 C3 Eastgate U.S.A.
137 D1 East Grand Forks U.S.A.
96 B3 East Kilbride U.K.
140 C2 East Lansing U.S.A.
99 C4 Eastleigh U.K.
96 C3 East Linton U.K.
140 C2 East Liverpool U.S.A.
123 C3 East London S. Africa
130 C2 Eastmain Can.
130 C2 Eastmain *r.* Can.
143 D2 Eastman U.S.A.
157 G8 East Pacific Rise *sea feature* N. Pacific Ocean
East Pakistan *country* Asia *see* Bangladesh
140 A3 East St Louis U.S.A.
83 K2 East Siberian Sea Rus. Fed.
59 C3 East Timor *terr.* Asia
53 C2 East Toorale Austr.
141 D2 East York Can.
140 A2 Eau Claire U.S.A.
59 D2 Eauripik *atoll* Micronesia
145 C2 Ebano Mex.
99 B4 Ebbw Vale U.K.
118 B2 Ebebiyin Equat. Guinea
102 C1 Eberswalde-Finow Ger.
66 D2 Ebetsu Japan
77 E2 Ebinur Hu *salt l.* China
118 C2 Ebola *r.* Dem. Rep. Congo
109 C2 Eboli Italy
118 B2 Ebolowa Cameroon
107 D1 Ebro *r.* Spain
107 C1 Echarri-Aranaz Spain
114 C1 Ech Chélif Alg.
Echeng China *see* Ezhou
144 A2 Echeverria, Pico *mt.* Mex.
129 E2 Echoing *r.* Can.
100 C3 Echternach Lux.
52 B3 Echuca Austr.
106 B2 Écija Spain
102 B1 Eckernförde Ger.
127 G2 Eclipse Sound *sea chan.* Can.
150 B3 Ecuador *country* S. America
116 C3 Ed Eritrea
96 C1 Eday *i.* U.K.
117 A3 Ed Da'ein Sudan
117 B3 Ed Damazin Sudan
116 B3 Ed Damer Sudan
116 B3 Ed Debba Sudan
116 B3 Ed Dueim Sudan
51 D4 Eddystone Point Austr.
100 B1 Ede Neth.
118 B2 Edéa Cameroon
154 C1 Edéia Brazil
53 C3 Eden Austr.
98 B2 Eden *r.* U.K.
139 D2 Eden U.S.A.
123 C2 Edenburg S. Africa
97 C2 Edenderry Rep. of Ireland
52 B3 Edenhope Austr.
143 E1 Edenton U.S.A.
111 B2 Edessa Greece
141 E2 Edgartown U.S.A.
Edge Island Svalbard *see* Edgeøya
82 C1 Edgeøya *i.* Svalbard
143 D3 Edgewater U.S.A.
140 C2 Edinboro U.S.A.
139 D3 Edinburg U.S.A.
96 C3 Edinburgh U.K.
90 B2 Edineţ Moldova
111 C2 Edirne Turkey
Edith Ronne Land *ice feature* Antarctica *see* Ronne Ice Shelf
128 C2 Edmonton Can.
131 D3 Edmundston Can.
111 C3 Edremit Turkey
111 C3 Edremit Körfezi *b.* Turkey
128 C2 Edson Can.
119 C3 Edward, Lake Dem. Rep. Congo/Uganda
Edwardesabad Pak. *see* Bannu
139 D2 Edwards Plateau U.S.A.
55 O2 Edward VII Peninsula Antarctica
96 C2 Edzell U.K.
100 A2 Eeklo Belgium
135 B2 Eel *r.* U.S.A.
100 C1 Eemskanaal *canal* Neth.
100 C1 Eenrum Neth.
140 B3 Effingham U.S.A.
135 C3 Egan Range *mts* U.S.A.
103 E2 Eger Hungary
93 E4 Egersund Norway
100 B2 Eghezée Belgium
92 □C2 Egilsstaðir Iceland
80 B2 Eğirdir Turkey
80 B2 Eğirdir Gölü *l.* Turkey
104 C2 Égletons France
54 B1 Egmont, Mount *vol.* N.Z.
83 M2 Egvekinot Rus. Fed.
116 B2 Egypt *country* Africa
70 A2 Ehen Hudag China
106 C1 Eibar Spain
100 C1 Eibergen Neth.
100 C2 Eifel *hills* Ger.
96 A2 Eigg *i.* U.K.
73 B4 Eight Degree Channel India/Maldives
50 B1 Eighty Mile Beach Austr.
Eilat Israel *see* Elat
101 F2 Eilenburg Ger.
101 D2 Einbeck Ger.
100 B2 Eindhoven Neth.
160 N4 Eirik Ridge *sea feature* N. Atlantic Ocean
150 C3 Eirunepé Brazil
120 B2 Eiseb *watercourse* Namibia
101 E2 Eisenach Ger.
101 E2 Eisenberg Ger.
102 C1 Eisenhüttenstadt Ger.
103 D2 Eisenstadt Austria
101 E2 Eisleben Lutherstadt Ger.
107 D2 Eivissa Spain
Eivissa *i.* Spain *see* Ibiza
107 C1 Ejea de los Caballeros Spain
121 □D3 Ejeda Madag.
Ejin Qi China *see* Dalain Hob
93 H4 Ekenäs Fin.
77 D1 Ekibastuz Kazakh.
92 J2 Ekostrovskaya Imandra, Ozero *l.* Rus. Fed.
93 F4 Eksjö Sweden
122 A2 Eksteenfontein S. Africa
130 B2 Ekwan *r.* Can.
62 A2 Ela Myanmar
El Aaiún Western Sahara *see* Laâyoune
80 A2 El 'Âmirîya Egypt
123 C2 Elandsdoorn S. Africa
El Araïche Morocco *see* Larache
80 B2 El 'Arîsh Egypt
El Asnam Alg. *see* Ech Chélif
111 B3 Elassona Greece
80 B3 Elat Israel
80 B2 Elazığ Turkey
108 B2 Elba, Isola d' *i.* Italy
150 B2 El Banco Col.
109 D2 Elbasan Albania
150 C2 El Baúl Venez.
114 C1 El Bayadh Alg.
101 D1 Elbe *r.* Ger.
136 B3 Elbert, Mount U.S.A.
143 D2 Elberton U.S.A.
104 C2 Elbeuf France
80 B2 Elbistan Turkey
103 D1 Elbląg Pol.
153 A4 El Bolsón Arg.
87 D4 Elbrus *mt.* Rus. Fed.
Elburz Mountains Iran *see* Alborz, Reshteh-ye
150 C2 El Callao Venez.
139 D3 El Campo U.S.A.
135 C4 El Centro U.S.A.
152 B1 El Cerro Bol.
107 C2 Elche Spain
107 C2 Elda Spain
119 D2 Eldama Ravine Kenya
137 E3 Eldon U.S.A.
154 B3 Eldorado Arg.
154 C2 Eldorado Brazil
144 B2 El Dorado Mex.
142 B2 El Dorado *AR* U.S.A.
137 D3 El Dorado *KS* U.S.A.
134 D1 Electric Peak U.S.A.
114 B2 El Eglab *plat.* Alg.
106 C2 El Ejido Spain
89 E2 Elektrostal' Rus. Fed.
150 B3 El Encanto Col.
146 C2 Eleuthera *i.* Bahamas
80 B3 El Faiyûm Egypt
116 A3 El Fasher Sudan
144 B2 El Fuerte Mex.
117 A3 El Fula Sudan
116 A3 El Geneina Sudan
116 B3 El Geteina Sudan
96 C2 Elgin U.K.
140 B2 Elgin U.S.A.
83 K2 El'ginskiy Rus. Fed.
116 B2 El Gîza Egypt
115 C1 El Goléa Alg.
144 A1 El Golfo de Santa Clara Mex.
119 D2 Elgon, Mount Uganda
108 A3 El Hadjar Alg.
80 A2 El Hammâm Egypt
114 A2 El Ḥammâmi *reg.* Maur.
114 B2 El Ḥank *esc.* Mali/Maur.
114 A2 El Hierro *i.* Canary Is
145 C2 El Higo Mex.
114 C2 El Homr Alg.
Elichpur India *see* Achalpur
126 B2 Elim U.S.A.
Élisabethville Dem. Rep. Congo *see* Lubumbashi
El Iskandarîya Egypt *see* Alexandria
87 D4 Elista Rus. Fed.
141 E2 Elizabeth U.S.A.
143 E1 Elizabeth City U.S.A.
140 B3 Elizabethtown U.S.A.
114 B1 El Jadida Morocco
103 E1 Ełk Pol.
108 A3 El Kala Alg.
88 C2 Elkas kalns *hill* Latvia
139 D1 Elk City U.S.A.
114 B1 El Kelaâ des Srarhna Morocco
128 C2 Elkford Can.
116 B2 El Khârga Egypt
140 B2 Elkhart U.S.A.
El Khartûm Sudan *see* Khartoum

110 C2 Elkhovo Bulg.
141 D3 Elkins U.S.A.
128 C3 Elko Can.
134 C2 Elko U.S.A.
129 C2 Elk Point Can.
137 E1 Elk River U.S.A.
126 F1 Ellef Ringnes Island Can.
137 D1 Ellendale U.S.A.
134 B1 Ellensburg U.S.A.
54 B2 Ellesmere, Lake N.Z.
127 G1 Ellesmere Island Can.
98 B3 Ellesmere Port U.K.
126 F2 Ellice r. Can.
Ellice Islands country S. Pacific Ocean see Tuvalu
123 C3 Elliotdale S. Africa
140 C1 Elliot Lake Can.
123 C1 Ellisras S. Africa
96 C2 Ellon U.K.
141 F2 Ellsworth U.S.A.
55 R2 Ellsworth Mountains Antarctica
116 B2 El Maks el Bahari Egypt
111 C3 Elmalı Turkey
80 B2 El Manṣûra Egypt
115 C1 El Meghaïer Alg.
116 B2 El Minya Egypt
141 D2 Elmira U.S.A.
107 C2 El Moral Spain
101 D1 Elmshorn Ger.
117 A3 El Muglad Sudan
150 B2 El Nevado, Cerro mt. Col.
64 A2 El Nido Phil.
116 B3 El Obeid Sudan
144 B2 El Oro Mex.
115 C1 El Oued Alg.
138 A2 Eloy U.S.A.
El Paso U.S.A. see Derby
138 B2 El Paso U.S.A.
145 D3 El Pinalón, Cerro mt. Guat.
144 B1 El Porvenír Mex.
107 D1 El Prat de Llobregat Spain
106 B2 El Puerto de Santa María Spain
El Qâhira Egypt see Cairo
116 A2 El Qasr Egypt
El Quds Israel/West Bank see Jerusalem
139 D1 El Reno U.S.A.
128 A1 Elsa Can.
145 B2 El Salado Mex.
144 B2 El Salto Mex.
146 B3 El Salvador country Central America
152 B2 El Salvador Chile
145 B2 El Salvador Mex.
138 B3 El Sauz Mex.
144 A1 El Socorro Mex.
138 B3 El Sueco Mex.
El Suweis Egypt see Suez
108 A3 El Tarf Alg.
106 B1 El Teleno mt. Spain
145 C2 El Temascal Mex.
150 C2 El Tigre Venez.
147 D4 El Tocuyo Venez.
116 B2 El Tûr Egypt
El Uqṣur Egypt see Luxor
73 C3 Eluru India
88 C2 Elva Estonia
106 B2 Elvas Port.
93 F3 Elverum Norway
119 E2 El Wak Kenya
99 D3 Ely U.K.
137 E1 Ely MN U.S.A.
135 D3 Ely NV U.S.A.
81 D2 Emāmrūd Iran
93 G4 Emån r. Sweden
76 B2 Emba Kazakh.
76 B2 Emba r. Kazakh.
123 C2 Embalenhle S. Africa
118 B2 Embondo Dem. Rep. Congo
154 C1 Emborcação, Represa de resr Brazil
119 D3 Embu Kenya
100 C1 Emden Ger.
51 D2 Emerald Austr.
129 E3 Emerson Can.
111 C3 Emet Turkey
123 D2 eMgwenya S. Africa
123 D2 eMijindini S. Africa
115 D3 Emi Koussi mt. Chad
145 C3 Emiliano Zapata Mex.
110 C2 Emine, Nos pt Bulg.
80 B2 Emirdağ Turkey
88 B2 Emmaste Estonia
100 B1 Emmeloord Neth.
100 C2 Emmelshausen Ger.
100 C1 Emmen Neth.
139 C3 Emory Peak U.S.A.
144 A2 Empalme Mex.
123 D2 Empangeni S. Africa
156 D2 Emperor Trough sea feature N. Pacific Ocean
108 B2 Empoli Italy
111 C3 Emponas Greece
137 D3 Emporia KS U.S.A.
141 D3 Emporia VA U.S.A.
Empty Quarter des. Saudi Arabia see Rub' al Khālī
100 C1 Ems r. Ger.
100 C1 Emsdetten Ger.
88 C2 Emumägi hill Estonia
123 C2 Emzinoni S. Africa
59 D3 Enarotali Indon.
144 B2 Encarnación Mex.
152 C2 Encarnación Para.
155 D1 Encruzilhada Brazil
60 B1 Endau Malaysia
61 D2 Endeh Indon.
55 G2 Enderby Land reg. Antarctica
126 B2 Endicott Mountains U.S.A.
50 A2 Eneabba Austr.
91 C2 Enerhodar Ukr.
111 C2 Enez Turkey
97 C2 Enfield Rep. of Ireland
87 D3 Engel's Rus. Fed.
60 B2 Enggano i. Indon.
99 C3 England admin. div. U.K.
130 C3 Englehart Can.
143 D3 Englewood U.S.A.
130 A2 English r. Can.
English Bazar India see Ingrāj Bāzār
95 C4 English Channel France/U.K.
139 D1 Enid U.S.A.
Enkeldoorn Zimbabwe see Chivhu
100 B1 Enkhuizen Neth.
93 G4 Enköping Sweden
108 B3 Enna Sicily Italy
129 D1 Ennadai Lake Can.
116 A3 En Nahud Sudan
115 E3 Ennedi, Massif mts Chad
53 C1 Enngonia Austr.
97 B2 Ennis Rep. of Ireland
139 D2 Ennis U.S.A.
97 C2 Enniscorthy Rep. of Ireland
97 C2 Enniskerry Rep. of Ireland
97 C1 Enniskillen U.K.
97 B2 Ennistymon Rep. of Ireland
102 C2 Enns Austria
102 C2 Enns r. Austria
92 J3 Eno Fin.
92 H2 Enontekiö Fin.
53 C3 Ensay Austr.
100 C1 Enschede Neth.
144 A1 Ensenada Mex.
70 A2 Enshi China
119 D2 Entebbe Uganda
128 C1 Enterprise Can.
142 C2 Enterprise AL U.S.A.
134 C1 Enterprise OR U.S.A.
152 B2 Entre Ríos Bol.
106 B2 Entroncamento Port.
115 C4 Enugu Nigeria
150 B3 Envira Brazil
118 B2 Epéna Congo
105 C2 Épernay France
135 D3 Ephraim U.S.A.
134 C1 Ephrata U.S.A.
105 D2 Épinal France
99 D4 Epping U.K.
99 C4 Epsom U.K.
118 A2 Equatorial Guinea country Africa
104 B2 Équerdreville-Hainneville France
101 D3 Erbach Ger.
101 F3 Erbendorf Ger.
100 C3 Erbeskopf hill Ger.
81 C2 Erciş Turkey
80 B2 Erciyes Dağı mt. Turkey
103 D2 Érd Hungary
Erdaobaihe China see Baihe
65 B1 Erdao Jiang r. China
111 C2 Erdek Turkey
80 B2 Erdemli Turkey
154 B2 Eré, Campos hills Brazil
55 M2 Erebus, Mount vol. Antarctica
152 C2 Erechim Brazil
69 D1 Ereentsav Mongolia
80 B2 Ereğli Turkey
80 B1 Ereğli Turkey
69 D2 Erenhot China
Erevan Armenia see Yerevan
101 E2 Erfurt Ger.
80 B2 Ergani Turkey
114 B2 'Erg Chech des. Alg./Mali
115 D3 Erg du Djourab des. Chad
115 D3 Erg du Ténéré des. Niger
111 C2 Ergene r. Turkey
114 B2 Erg Iabès des. Alg.
114 B2 Erg Iguidi des. Alg./Maur.
78 A3 Erheib Sudan
96 B2 Ericht, Loch l. U.K.
140 C2 Erie U.S.A.
140 C2 Erie, Lake Can./U.S.A.
66 D2 Erimo-misaki c. Japan
116 B3 Eritrea country Africa
101 E3 Erlangen Ger.
50 C2 Erldunda Austr.
123 C2 Ermelo S. Africa
80 B2 Ermenek Turkey
111 B3 Ermoupoli Greece
73 B4 Ernakulam India
97 B1 Erne r. Rep. of Ireland/U.K.
73 B3 Erode India
100 B2 Erp Neth.
114 B1 Er Rachidia Morocco
116 B3 Er Rahad Sudan
97 B1 Errigal hill Rep. of Ireland
97 A1 Erris Head hd Rep. of Ireland
48 H5 Erromango i. Vanuatu
109 D2 Ersekë Albania
89 F3 Ertil' Rus. Fed.
101 D2 Erwitte Ger.
101 F2 Erzgebirge mts Czech Rep./Ger.
80 B2 Erzincan Turkey
81 C2 Erzurum Turkey
66 D2 Esashi Japan
93 E4 Esbjerg Denmark
135 D3 Escalante U.S.A.
135 D3 Escalante Desert U.S.A.
144 B2 Escalón Mex.
140 B1 Escanaba U.S.A.
145 C3 Escárcega Mex.
107 C1 Escatrón Spain
100 A2 Escaut r. Belgium
101 E1 Eschede Ger.
100 B3 Esch-sur-Alzette Lux.
101 E2 Eschwege Ger.
100 C2 Eschweiler Ger.
135 C4 Escondido U.S.A.
144 B2 Escuinapa Mex.
111 C3 Eşen Turkey
81 D2 Eşfahān Iran
123 D2 Eshowe S. Africa
123 D2 Esikhawini S. Africa
98 B2 Esk r. U.K.
131 D2 Esker Can.
92 □C2 Eskifjörður Iceland
93 G4 Eskilstuna Sweden
Eskimo Point Can. see Arviat
111 D3 Eskişehir Turkey
81 C2 Eslāmābād-e Gharb Iran
111 C3 Esler Dağı mt. Turkey
111 C3 Eşme Turkey
146 C2 Esmeralda Cuba
150 B2 Esmeraldas Ecuador
79 D2 Espakeh Iran
105 C3 Espalion France
130 B3 Espanola Can.
138 B1 Espanola U.S.A.
50 B3 Esperance Austr.
153 A5 Esperanza Arg.
144 B2 Esperanza Mex.
106 B2 Espichel, Cabo c. Port.
154 B3 Espigão, Serra do mts Brazil
139 C3 Espinazo Mex.
155 D1 Espinhaço, Serra do mts Brazil
151 E4 Espinosa Brazil
Espirito Santo Brazil see Vila Velha
48 H5 Espíritu Santo i. Vanuatu
144 A2 Espíritu Santo, Isla i. Mex.
93 H3 Espoo Fin.
153 A4 Esquel Arg.
114 B1 Essaouira Morocco
114 A2 Es Semara Western Sahara
100 C2 Essen Ger.
150 D2 Essequibo r. Guyana
141 E2 Essex Junction U.S.A.
83 L3 Esso Rus. Fed.
106 B1 Estaca de Bares, Pun da pt Spain
81 D3 Eşţahbān Iran
151 F4 Estância Brazil
123 C2 Estcourt S. Africa
107 C1 Estella Spain
106 B2 Estepona Spain
106 C1 Esteras de Medinaceli Spain
129 D2 Esterhazy Can.
152 B2 Esteros Para.
136 B2 Estes Park U.S.A.
129 D3 Estevan Can.
137 E2 Estherville U.S.A.
129 D2 Eston Can.
88 C2 Estonia country Europe
Estonskaya S.S.R. country Europe see Est
106 B1 Estrela, Serra da mts Port.
106 B2 Estremoz Port.
52 A1 Etadunna Austr.
104 C2 Étampes France
104 C1 Étaples France
75 B2 Etawah India
123 D2 eThandakukhanya S. Africa
122 B2 E'Thembini S. Africa
117 B4 Ethiopia country Africa
109 C3 Etna, Monte vol. Sicily Italy
Etna, Mount vol. Italy s Etna, Monte
93 E4 Etne Norway
128 A2 Etolin Island U.S.A.
120 A2 Etosha Pan salt pan Namibia
110 B2 Etropole Bulg.
100 C3 Ettelbruck Lux.
100 B2 Etten-Leur Neth.
99 D4 Eu France
53 C2 Euabalong Austr.
Euboea i. Greece see Evvoia
50 B3 Eucla Austr.
140 C2 Euclid U.S.A.
143 C2 Eufaula U.S.A.
139 D1 Eufaula Lake resr U.S.
134 B2 Eugene U.S.A.
144 A2 Eugenia, Punta pt Mex
53 C1 Eulo Austr.
53 C2 Eumungerie Austr.
139 C2 Eunice U.S.A.
81 C2 Euphrates r. Asia
134 B2 Eureka CA U.S.A.
134 C1 Eureka MT U.S.A.
135 C3 Eureka NV U.S.A.
52 B2 Euriowie Austr.
53 C3 Euroa Austr.
106 B2 Europa Point Gibraltar
142 C2 Eutaw U.S.A.
128 B2 Eutsuk Lake Can.
123 C2 Evander S. Africa
130 C2 Evans, Lac l. Can.
53 D1 Evans Head Austr.
127 G2 Evans Strait Can.
140 B2 Evanston IL U.S.A.
136 A2 Evanston WY U.S.A.
140 B3 Evansville U.S.A.
Eva Perón Arg. see La Plata
123 C2 Evaton S. Africa
79 C2 Evaz Iran
83 L2 Evensk Rus. Fed.
50 C2 Everard Range hills Aus
75 C2 Everest, Mount China/Nepal
134 B1 Everett U.S.A.
100 A2 Evergem Belgium
143 D3 Everglades swamp U.S
142 C2 Evergreen U.S.A.
99 C3 Evesham U.K.
118 B2 Evinayong Equat. Guine
93 E4 Evje Norway
106 B2 Évora Port.
69 F1 Evoron, Ozero l. Rus. F
111 B2 Evosmo Greece
104 C2 Évreux France
111 C2 Evros r. Greece/Turkey
111 B3 Evrotas r. Greece
104 C2 Évry France
80 B2 Evrychou Cyprus
111 B3 Evvoia i. Greece
119 E2 Ewaso Ngiro r. Kenya
152 B1 Exaltación Bol.
99 B4 Exe r. U.K.
99 B4 Exeter U.K.
99 B4 Exmoor hills U.K.
50 A2 Exmouth Austr.
99 B4 Exmouth U.K.

0 A2 **Exmouth Gulf** Austr.
6 B2 **Extremadura** *aut. comm.* Spain
6 C2 **Exuma Cays** *is* Bahamas
1 D2 **Eya** *r.* Rus. Fed.
8 C3 **Eyangu** Dem. Rep. Congo
9 D3 **Eyasi, Lake** *salt l.* Tanz.
5 C3 **Eyemouth** U.K.
2 □B2 **Eyjafjörður** *inlet* Iceland
7 C4 **Eyl** Somalia
2 A1 **Eyre, Lake** *salt flat* Austr.
2 A2 **Eyre Peninsula** Austr.
4 B1 **Eysturoy** *i.* Faroe Is
4 B1 **Eysturoy** *i.* Faroe Is
3 D2 **Ezakheni** S. Africa
3 C2 **Ezenzeleni** S. Africa
0 B2 **Ezhou** China
6 E2 **Ezhva** Rus. Fed.
1 C3 **Ezine** Turkey

F

8 B2 **Fabens** U.S.A.
2 C1 **Fåborg** Denmark
8 B2 **Fabriano** Italy
5 D3 **Fachi** Niger
4 C3 **Fada-Ngourma** Burkina
8 B2 **Faenza** Italy
Faeroes *terr.* N. Atlantic Ocean *see* **Faroe Islands**
9 C3 **Fafanlap** Indon.
0 B1 **Făgăraş** Romania
9 J5 **Fagatogo** American Samoa
3 E3 **Fagernes** Norway
3 G4 **Fagersta** Sweden
3 B5 **Fagnano, Lago** *l.* Arg./Chile
4 B3 **Faguibine, Lac** *l.* Mali
2 □B3 **Fagurhólsmýri** Iceland
6 C2 **Fairbanks** U.S.A.
7 D2 **Fairbury** U.S.A.
5 B3 **Fairfield** *CA* U.S.A.
0 C3 **Fairfield** *OH* U.S.A.
6 □ **Fair Isle** *i.* U.K.
7 E2 **Fairmont** *MN* U.S.A.
0 C3 **Fairmont** *WV* U.S.A.
8 C2 **Fairview** Can.
8 A2 **Fairweather, Mount** Can./U.S.A.
9 D2 **Fais** *i.* Micronesia
4 B1 **Faisalabad** Pak.
6 C1 **Faith** U.S.A.
5 C2 **Faizabad** India
6 E6 **Fakaofo** *atoll* Tokelau
9 D3 **Fakenham** U.K.
9 C3 **Fakfak** Indon.
5 A1 **Faku** China
4 A4 **Falaba** Sierra Leone
7 B1 **Falcarragh** Rep. of Ireland
9 D3 **Falcon Lake** Mex./U.S.A.
Faleshty Moldova *see* **Făleşti**
0 B2 **Făleşti** Moldova
9 D3 **Falfurrias** U.S.A.
8 C2 **Falher** Can.
1 F2 **Falkenberg** Ger.
3 F4 **Falkenberg** Sweden
1 F1 **Falkensee** Ger.
6 C3 **Falkirk** U.K.
8 D8 **Falkland Escarpment** *sea feature* S. Atlantic Ocean
3 C5 **Falkland Islands** *terr.* S. Atlantic Ocean
7 I9 **Falkland Plateau** *sea feature* S. Atlantic Ocean
3 F4 **Falköping** Sweden
1 D1 **Fallingbostel** Ger.
5 C3 **Fallon** U.S.A.
1 E2 **Fall River** U.S.A.
7 D2 **Falls City** U.S.A.
9 A4 **Falmouth** U.K.
2 A3 **False Bay** S. Africa
4 B2 **Falso, Cabo** *c.* Mex.
3 F5 **Falster** *i.* Denmark
0 C1 **Fălticeni** Romania
3 G3 **Falun** Sweden
2 B2 **Famailla** Arg.
1 □D3 **Fandriana** Madag.
Fangcheng China *see* Fangchenggang
1 A3 **Fangchenggang** China
1 C3 **Fangshan** Taiwan
6 A1 **Fangzheng** China
8 B2 **Fano** Italy
2 B1 **Fan Si Pan** *mt.* Vietnam
9 C2 **Faradje** Dem. Rep. Congo
121 □D3 **Farafangana** Madag.
116 A2 **Farafra Oasis** Egypt
76 C3 **Farāh** Afgh.
114 A3 **Faranah** Guinea
79 C3 **Fararah** Oman
78 B3 **Farasān, Jazā'ir** *is* Saudi Arabia
59 D2 **Faraulep** *atoll* Micronesia
Farewell, Cape Greenland *see* **Nunap Isua**
54 B2 **Farewell, Cape** N.Z.
137 D1 **Fargo** U.S.A.
137 E2 **Faribault** U.S.A.
130 C2 **Faribault, Lac** *l.* Can.
74 B2 **Faridabad** India
75 C2 **Faridpur** Bangl.
141 E2 **Farmington** *ME* U.S.A.
138 B1 **Farmington** *NM* U.S.A.
141 D3 **Farmville** U.S.A.
99 C4 **Farnborough** U.K.
128 C2 **Farnham, Mount** Can.
128 A1 **Faro** Can.
106 B2 **Faro** Port.
88 A2 **Fårö** *i.* Sweden
147 C3 **Faro, Punta** *pt* Col.
106 B1 **Faro, Serra do** *mts* Spain
94 B1 **Faroe Islands** *terr.* N. Atlantic Ocean
113 I6 **Farquhar Group** *atoll* Seychelles
81 D3 **Farrāshband** Iran
Farrukhabad India *see* Fatehgarh
79 C3 **Fartak, Ra's** *c.* Yemen
154 B3 **Fartura, Serra da** *mts* Brazil
Farvel, Kap *c.* Greenland *see* **Nunap Isua**
139 C2 **Farwell** U.S.A.
79 C2 **Fāryāb** Iran
79 C2 **Fāryāb** Iran
81 D3 **Fasā** Iran
109 C2 **Fasano** Italy
90 B1 **Fastiv** Ukr.
119 D2 **Fataki** Dem. Rep. Congo
75 B2 **Fatehgarh** India
75 C2 **Fatehpur** India
114 A3 **Fatick** Senegal
131 D3 **Fatima** Can.
123 C2 **Fauresmith** S. Africa
92 G2 **Fauske** Norway
92 □A3 **Faxaflói** *b.* Iceland
92 G3 **Faxälven** *r.* Sweden
115 D3 **Faya** Chad
142 B1 **Fayetteville** *AR* U.S.A.
143 E1 **Fayetteville** *NC* U.S.A.
142 C1 **Fayetteville** *TN* U.S.A.
74 B1 **Fazilka** India
114 A2 **Fdérik** Maur.
143 E2 **Fear, Cape** U.S.A.
54 C2 **Featherston** N.Z.
104 C2 **Fécamp** France
Federated Malay States *country* Asia *see* **Malaysia**
48 G3 **Federated States of Micronesia** *country* N. Pacific Ocean
102 C1 **Fehmarn** *i.* Ger.
101 F1 **Fehrbellin** Ger.
155 D2 **Feia, Lagoa** *lag.* Brazil
150 B3 **Feijó** Brazil
54 C2 **Feilding** N.Z.
151 F4 **Feira de Santana** Brazil
107 D2 **Felanitx** Spain
101 F1 **Feldberg** Ger.
145 D3 **Felipe C. Puerto** Mex.
155 D1 **Felixlândia** Brazil
99 D4 **Felixstowe** U.K.
101 D2 **Felsberg** Ger.
108 B1 **Feltre** Italy
93 F3 **Femunden** *l.* Norway
Fénérive Madag. *see* Fenoarivo Atsinanana
Fengcheng China *see* Fengshan
71 B3 **Fengcheng** *Jiangxi* China
65 A1 **Fengcheng** *Liaoning* China
62 A1 **Fengqing** China
71 A3 **Fengshan** China
Fengshan China *see* Fengqing
70 B2 **Fengxian** *Jiangsu* China
70 A2 **Fengxian** *Shaanxi* China
Fengxiang China *see* Lincang
Fengyi China *see* Zheng'an
71 C3 **Fengyüan** Taiwan
70 B1 **Fengzhen** China
105 D3 **Feno, Capo di** *c. Corsica* France
121 □D2 **Fenoarivo Atsinanana** Madag.
70 B2 **Fenyang** China
91 D2 **Feodosiya** Ukr.
108 A3 **Fer, Cap de** *c.* Alg.
77 D2 **Fergana** Uzbek.
137 D1 **Fergus Falls** U.S.A.
51 E1 **Fergusson Island** P.N.G.
114 B4 **Ferkessédougou** Côte d'Ivoire
108 B2 **Fermo** Italy
131 D2 **Fermont** Can.
106 B1 **Fermoselle** Spain
97 B2 **Fermoy** Rep. of Ireland
143 D2 **Fernandina Beach** U.S.A.
154 B2 **Fernandópolis** Brazil
Fernando Poó *i.* Equat. Guinea *see* **Bioco**
134 B1 **Ferndale** U.S.A.
99 C4 **Ferndown** U.K.
128 C3 **Fernie** Can.
135 C3 **Fernley** U.S.A.
97 C2 **Ferns** Rep. of Ireland
Ferozepore India *see* Firozpur
108 B2 **Ferrara** Italy
154 B2 **Ferreiros** Brazil
108 A2 **Ferro, Capo** *c. Sardinia* Italy
106 B1 **Ferrol** Spain
Ferryville Tunisia *see* **Menzel Bourguiba**
100 B1 **Ferwerd** Neth.
114 B1 **Fès** Morocco
118 B3 **Feshi** Dem. Rep. Congo
137 E3 **Festus** U.S.A.
110 C2 **Feteşti** Romania
97 C2 **Fethard** Rep. of Ireland
111 C3 **Fethiye** Turkey
96 □ **Fetlar** *i.* U.K.
130 C2 **Feuilles, Rivière aux** *r.* Can.
77 D3 **Feyzābād** Afgh.
Fez Morocco *see* **Fès**
121 □D3 **Fianarantsoa** Madag.
115 D4 **Fianga** Chad
117 B4 **Fichē** Eth.
109 C2 **Fier** Albania
96 C2 **Fife Ness** *pt* U.K.
104 C3 **Figeac** France
106 B1 **Figueira da Foz** Port.
107 D1 **Figueres** Spain
114 B1 **Figuig** Morocco
49 I5 **Fiji** *country* S. Pacific Ocean
152 B2 **Filadélfia** Para.
55 B2 **Filchner Ice Shelf** Antarctica
98 C2 **Filey** U.K.
108 B3 **Filicudi, Isola** *i.* Italy
114 C3 **Filingué** Niger
111 B3 **Filippiada** Greece
93 F4 **Filipstad** Sweden
92 E3 **Fillan** Norway
135 D3 **Fillmore** U.S.A.
119 E2 **Filtu** Eth.
55 D2 **Fimbull Ice Shelf** Antarctica
96 C2 **Findhorn** *r.* U.K.
140 C2 **Findlay** U.S.A.
51 D4 **Fingal** Austr.
141 D2 **Finger Lakes** U.S.A.
111 D3 **Finike** Turkey
Finisterre, Cape Spain *see* **Fisterra, Cabo**
93 I3 **Finland** *country* Europe
93 H4 **Finland, Gulf of** Europe
128 B2 **Finlay** *r.* Can.
53 C3 **Finley** Austr.
134 C1 **Finley** U.S.A.
101 E2 **Finne** *ridge* Ger.
92 H2 **Finnmarksvidda** *reg.* Norway
92 G2 **Finnsnes** Norway
93 G4 **Finspång** Sweden
97 C1 **Fintona** U.K.
96 A2 **Fionnphort** U.K.
Fırat *r.* Turkey *see* Euphrates
Firenze Italy *see* **Florence**
105 C2 **Firminy** France
74 B2 **Firozabad** India
74 B1 **Firozpur** India
81 D3 **Fīrūzābād** Iran
122 A2 **Fish** *watercourse* Namibia
122 B3 **Fish** *r.* S. Africa
129 F1 **Fisher Strait** Can.
99 A4 **Fishguard** U.K.
105 C2 **Fismes** France
106 B1 **Fisterra, Cabo** *c.* Spain
141 E2 **Fitchburg** U.S.A.
128 C2 **Fitzgerald** Can.
143 D2 **Fitzgerald** U.S.A.
50 B1 **Fitzroy Crossing** Austr.
Fiume Croatia *see* **Rijeka**
54 A3 **Five Rivers** N.Z.
108 B2 **Fivizzano** Italy
119 C3 **Fizi** Dem. Rep. Congo
93 F3 **Fjallnäs** Sweden
92 G3 **Fjällsjöälven** *r.* Sweden
123 C3 **Flagstaff** S. Africa
138 A1 **Flagstaff** U.S.A.
130 C2 **Flaherty Island** Can.
98 C2 **Flamborough Head** *hd* U.K.
101 F1 **Fläming** *hills* Ger.
136 B2 **Flaming Gorge Reservoir** U.S.A.
134 D1 **Flathead** *r.* U.S.A.
134 D1 **Flathead Lake** U.S.A.
51 D1 **Flattery, Cape** Austr.
134 B1 **Flattery, Cape** U.S.A.
98 B3 **Fleetwood** U.K.
93 E4 **Flekkefjord** Norway
102 B1 **Flensburg** Ger.
104 B2 **Flers** France
100 B2 **Fleurus** Belgium
104 C2 **Fleury-les-Aubrais** France
51 D1 **Flinders** *r.* Austr.
50 A3 **Flinders Bay** Austr.
51 D3 **Flinders Island** Austr.
52 A2 **Flinders Ranges** *mts* Austr.
129 D2 **Flin Flon** Can.
98 B3 **Flint** U.K.
140 C2 **Flint** U.S.A.
49 L5 **Flint Island** Kiribati
101 F2 **Flöha** Ger.
107 D1 **Florac** France
100 C3 **Florange** France
108 B2 **Florence** Italy
142 C2 **Florence** *AL* U.S.A.
138 A2 **Florence** *AZ* U.S.A.
134 B2 **Florence** *OR* U.S.A.
143 E2 **Florence** *SC* U.S.A.
150 B2 **Florencia** Col.
146 B3 **Flores** Guat.
61 D2 **Flores** *i.* Indon.
Floreshty Moldova *see* Floreşti
61 C2 **Flores Sea** Indon.
151 F3 **Floresta** Brazil
90 B2 **Floreşti** Moldova
139 D3 **Floresville** U.S.A.
151 E3 **Floriano** Brazil
152 D2 **Florianópolis** Brazil
153 C3 **Florida** Uru.
143 D2 **Florida** *state* U.S.A.
143 D4 **Florida, Straits of** Bahamas/U.S.A.
143 D4 **Florida Bay** U.S.A.
143 D4 **Florida Keys** *is* U.S.A.
111 B2 **Florina** Greece
93 E3 **Florø** Norway
129 D2 **Foam Lake** Can.
109 C2 **Foča** Bos.-Herz.
110 C1 **Focşani** Romania
71 B3 **Fogang** China
109 C2 **Foggia** Italy
131 E3 **Fogo Island** Can.
104 C3 **Foix** France
89 D3 **Fokino** Rus. Fed.
130 B3 **Foleyet** Can.
108 B2 **Foligno** Italy
99 D4 **Folkestone** U.K.
143 D2 **Folkston** U.S.A.
108 B2 **Follonica** Italy
129 D2 **Fond-du-Lac** Can.
129 D2 **Fond du Lac** *r.* Can.
140 B2 **Fond du Lac** U.S.A.
106 B1 **Fondevila** Spain
108 B2 **Fondi** Italy
146 B3 **Fonseca, Golfo de** *b.* Central America
150 C3 **Fonte Boa** Brazil
104 B2 **Fontenay-le-Comte** France
92 □C2 **Fontur** *pt* Iceland
Foochow China *see* Fuzhou
53 C2 **Forbes** Austr.
75 C2 **Forbesganj** India
101 E3 **Forchheim** Ger.
93 E3 **Førde** Norway
53 C1 **Fords Bridge** Austr.
142 B2 **Fordyce** U.S.A.
142 C2 **Forest** U.S.A.
53 C3 **Forest Hill** Austr.
131 D3 **Forestville** Can.
96 C2 **Forfar** U.K.
134 B1 **Forks** U.S.A.
108 B2 **Forlì** Italy

107 D2 **Formentera** *i.* Spain
107 D2 **Formentor, Cap de** *c.* Spain
155 C2 **Formiga** Brazil
152 C2 **Formosa** Arg.
Formosa Asia *see* **Taiwan**
154 C1 **Formosa** Brazil
Formosa Strait China/Taiwan *see* **Taiwan Strait**
Føroyar *terr.* N. Atlantic Ocean *see* **Faroe Islands**
96 C2 **Forres** U.K.
50 B3 **Forrest** Austr.
142 B1 **Forrest City** U.S.A.
51 D1 **Forsayth** Austr.
93 H3 **Forssa** Fin.
53 D2 **Forster** Austr.
136 B1 **Forsyth** U.S.A.
74 B2 **Fort Abbas** Pak.
130 B2 **Fort Albany** Can.
151 F3 **Fortaleza** Brazil
Fort Archambault Chad *see* **Sarh**
128 C2 **Fort Assiniboine** Can.
96 B2 **Fort Augustus** U.K.
123 C3 **Fort Beaufort** S. Africa
134 D1 **Fort Benton** U.S.A.
Fort Brabant Can. *see* **Tuktoyaktuk**
135 B3 **Fort Bragg** U.S.A.
Fort Carnot Madag. *see* **Ikongo**
Fort Charlet Alg. *see* **Djanet**
Fort Chimo Can. *see* **Kuujjuaq**
129 C2 **Fort Chipewyan** Can.
136 B2 **Fort Collins** U.S.A.
Fort Crampel C.A.R. *see* **Kaga Bandoro**
Fort-Dauphin Madag. *see* **Tôlañaro**
147 D3 **Fort-de-France** Martinique
Fort de Polignac Alg. *see* **Illizi**
137 E2 **Fort Dodge** U.S.A.
141 D2 **Fort Erie** Can.
Fort Flatters Alg. *see* **Bordj Omer Driss**
Fort Foureau Cameroon *see* **Kousséri**
130 A3 **Fort Frances** Can.
Fort Franklin Can. *see* **Délı̨ne**
Fort Gardel Alg. *see* **Zaouatallaz**
Fort George Can. *see* **Chisasibi**
126 D2 **Fort Good Hope** Can.
Fort Gouraud Maur. *see* **Fdérik**
96 C2 **Forth** *r.* U.K.
96 C2 **Forth, Firth of** *est.* U.K.
Fort Hall Kenya *see* **Muranga**
Fort Hertz Myanmar *see* **Putao**
152 C2 **Fortín Madrejón** Para.
Fort Jameson Zambia *see* **Chipata**
Fort Johnston Malawi *see* **Mangochi**
Fort Lamy Chad *see* **Ndjamena**
Fort Laperrine Alg. *see* **Tamanrasset**
143 D3 **Fort Lauderdale** U.S.A.
128 B1 **Fort Liard** Can.
128 C2 **Fort Mackay** Can.
137 E2 **Fort Madison** U.S.A.
Fort Manning Malawi *see* **Mchinji**
128 C2 **Fort McMurray** Can.
126 D2 **Fort McPherson** Can.
136 C2 **Fort Morgan** U.S.A.
143 D3 **Fort Myers** U.S.A.
128 B2 **Fort Nelson** Can.
128 B2 **Fort Nelson** *r.* Can.
Fort Norman Can. *see* **Tulít'a**
142 C2 **Fort Payne** U.S.A.
136 B1 **Fort Peck** U.S.A.
136 B1 **Fort Peck Reservoir** U.S.A.
143 D3 **Fort Pierce** U.S.A.
119 D2 **Fort Portal** Uganda
128 C1 **Fort Providence** Can.
129 D2 **Fort Qu'Appelle** Can.
128 C1 **Fort Resolution** Can.
96 B2 **Fortrose** U.K.
Fort Rosebery Zambia *see* **Mansa**
Fort Rousset Congo *see* **Owando**
Fort Rupert Can. *see* **Waskaganish**
128 B2 **Fort St James** Can.
Fort Sandeman Pak. *see* **Zhob**
128 B2 **Fort St John** Can.
128 C2 **Fort Saskatchewan** Can.
137 E3 **Fort Scott** U.S.A.
130 B2 **Fort Severn** Can.
76 B2 **Fort-Shevchenko** Kazakh.
128 B1 **Fort Simpson** Can.
128 C1 **Fort Smith** Can.
142 B1 **Fort Smith** U.S.A.
139 C2 **Fort Stockton** U.S.A.
138 C2 **Fort Sumner** U.S.A.
Fort Trinquet Maur. *see* **Bîr Mogreïn**
134 B2 **Fortuna** U.S.A.
131 E3 **Fortune Bay** Can.
128 C2 **Fort Vermilion** Can.
Fort Victoria Zimbabwe *see* **Masvingo**
Fort Walton U.S.A. *see* **Fort Walton Beach**
142 C2 **Fort Walton Beach** U.S.A.
136 B2 **Fort Washakie** U.S.A.
140 B2 **Fort Wayne** U.S.A.
96 B2 **Fort William** U.K.
139 D2 **Fort Worth** U.S.A.
126 C2 **Fort Yukon** U.S.A.
71 B3 **Foshan** China
92 F3 **Fosna** *pen.* Norway
93 E3 **Fosnavåg** Norway
92 □B3 **Foss** Iceland
92 □A2 **Fossá** Iceland
108 A2 **Fossano** Italy
137 D1 **Fosston** U.S.A.
53 C3 **Foster** Austr.
118 B3 **Fougamou** Gabon
104 B2 **Fougères** France
96 □ **Foula** *i.* U.K.
99 D4 **Foulness Point** U.K.
118 B2 **Foumban** Cameroon
111 C3 **Fournoi** *i.* Greece
114 A3 **Fouta Djallon** *reg.* Guinea
54 A3 **Foveaux Strait** N.Z.
136 C3 **Fowler** U.S.A.
50 C3 **Fowlers Bay** Austr.
81 C2 **Fowman** Iran
128 C2 **Fox Creek** Can.
127 G2 **Foxe Basin** *g.* Can.
127 G2 **Foxe Channel** Can.
127 G2 **Foxe Peninsula** Can.
54 B2 **Fox Glacier** N.Z.
128 C2 **Fox Lake** Can.
128 A1 **Fox Mountain** Can.
54 C2 **Foxton** N.Z.
129 D2 **Fox Valley** Can.
97 C1 **Foyle** *r.* Rep. of Ireland/U.K.
97 C1 **Foyle, Lough** *b.* Rep. of Ireland/U.K.
97 B2 **Foynes** Rep. of Ireland
154 B3 **Foz de Areia, Represa de** *resr* Brazil
120 A2 **Foz do Cunene** Angola
154 B3 **Foz do Iguaçu** Brazil
107 D1 **Fraga** Spain
100 A2 **Frameries** Belgium
154 C2 **Franca** Brazil
109 C2 **Francavilla Fontana** Italy
104 C2 **France** *country* Europe
118 B3 **Franceville** Gabon
137 D2 **Francis Case, Lake** U.S.A.
155 D1 **Francisco Sá** Brazil
120 B3 **Francistown** Botswana
128 B2 **François Lake** Can.
100 B1 **Franeker** Neth.
101 D2 **Frankenberg (Eder)** Ger.
101 D3 **Frankenthal (Pfalz)** Ger.
101 E2 **Frankenwald** *mts* Ger.
140 C3 **Frankfort** *KY* U.S.A.
140 B2 **Frankfort** *MI* U.S.A.
101 D2 **Frankfurt am Main** Ger.
102 C1 **Frankfurt an der Oder** Ger.
102 C2 **Fränkische Alb** *hills* Ger.
101 E3 **Fränkische Schweiz** *reg.* Ger.
141 E2 **Franklin** *NH* U.S.A.
141 D2 **Franklin** *PA* U.S.A.
142 C1 **Franklin** *TN* U.S.A.
126 D2 **Franklin Bay** Can.
134 C1 **Franklin D. Roosevelt Lake** U.S.A.
128 B1 **Franklin Mountains** Can.
126 F2 **Franklin Strait** Can.
53 C3 **Frankston** Austr.
54 B2 **Franz Josef Glacier** N.Z.
Franz Josef Land *is* Rus. Fed. *see* **Zemlya Frantsa-Iosifa**
108 A3 **Frasca, Capo della** *c.* *Sardinia* Italy
128 B3 **Fraser** *r. B.C.* Can.
131 D2 **Fraser** *r. Nfld.* Can.
122 B3 **Fraserburg** S. Africa
96 C2 **Fraserburgh** U.K.
130 B3 **Fraserdale** Can.
51 E2 **Fraser Island** Austr.
128 B2 **Fraser Lake** Can.
128 B2 **Fraser Plateau** Can.
153 C3 **Fray Bentos** Uru.
93 E4 **Fredericia** Denmark
139 D2 **Frederick** U.S.A.
139 D2 **Fredericksburg** *TX* U.S.A.
141 D3 **Fredericksburg** *VA* U.S.A.
128 A2 **Frederick Sound** *sea chan.* U.S.A.
131 D3 **Fredericton** Can.
Frederikshåb Greenland *see* **Paamiut**
93 F4 **Frederikshavn** Denmark
Fredrikshamn Fin. *see* **Hamina**
93 F4 **Fredrikstad** Norway
140 B2 **Freeport** *IL* U.S.A.
139 D3 **Freeport** *TX* U.S.A.
146 C2 **Freeport City** Bahamas
139 D3 **Freer** U.S.A.
123 C2 **Free State** *prov.* S. Africa
114 A4 **Freetown** Sierra Leone
106 B2 **Fregenal de la Sierra** Spain
104 B2 **Fréhel, Cap** *c.* France
102 B2 **Freiburg im Breisgau** Ger.
102 C2 **Freising** Ger.
102 C2 **Freistadt** Austria
105 D3 **Fréjus** France
50 A3 **Fremantle** Austr.
135 B3 **Fremont** *CA* U.S.A.
137 D2 **Fremont** *NE* U.S.A.
140 C2 **Fremont** *OH* U.S.A.
French Congo *country* Africa *see* **Congo**
151 D2 **French Guiana** *terr.* S. America
French Guinea *country* Africa *see* **Guinea**
134 E1 **Frenchman** *r.* U.S.A.
49 M5 **French Polynesia** *terr.* S. Pacific Ocean
French Somaliland *country* Africa *see* **Djibouti**
French Sudan *country* Africa *see* **Mali**
French Territory of the Afars and Issas *country* Africa *see* **Djibouti**
151 D3 **Fresco** *r.* Brazil
144 B2 **Fresnillo** Mex.
135 C3 **Fresno** U.S.A.
107 D2 **Freu, Cap des** *c.* Spain
105 D2 **Freyming-Merlebach** France
114 A3 **Fria** Guinea
152 B2 **Frias** Arg.
101 D2 **Friedberg (Hessen)** Ger.
102 B2 **Friedrichshafen** Ger.
101 F1 **Friesack** Ger.
100 C1 **Friesoythe** Ger.
139 C2 **Friona** U.S.A.
136 B3 **Frisco** U.S.A.
Frobisher Bay Can. *see* **Iqaluit**
127 H2 **Frobisher Bay** *b.* Can.
101 F2 **Frohburg** Ger.
87 D4 **Frolovo** Rus. Fed.
103 D1 **Frombork** Pol.
99 B4 **Frome** U.K.
52 A2 **Frome, Lake** *salt flat* Austr.
52 A2 **Frome Downs** Austr.
100 C2 **Fröndenberg** Ger.
139 C3 **Frontera** Mex.
145 C3 **Frontera** Mex.
144 B1 **Fronteras** Mex.
141 D3 **Front Royal** U.S.A.
108 B2 **Frosinone** Italy
92 E3 **Frøya** *i.* Norway
Frunze Kyrg. *see* **Bishkek**
154 C2 **Frutal** Brazil
105 D2 **Frutigen** Switz.
103 D2 **Frýdek-Místek** Czech Rep.
71 B3 **Fu'an** China
71 C3 **Fuding** China
106 C1 **Fuenlabrada** Spain
152 C2 **Fuerte Olimpo** Para.
114 A2 **Fuerteventura** *i.* Canar
64 B2 **Fuga** *i.* Phil.
79 C2 **Fujairah** U.A.E.
67 C3 **Fuji** Japan
71 B3 **Fujian** *prov.* China
67 C3 **Fujinomiya** Japan
67 C3 **Fuji-san** *vol.* Japan
Fukien *prov.* China *see* **Fujian**
67 A4 **Fukue** Japan
67 A4 **Fukue-jima** *i.* Japan
67 C3 **Fukui** Japan
67 B4 **Fukuoka** Japan
67 D3 **Fukushima** Japan
101 D2 **Fulda** Ger.
101 D2 **Fulda** *r.* Ger.
70 A3 **Fuling** China
137 E3 **Fulton** U.S.A.
105 C2 **Fumay** France
49 I4 **Funafuti** *atoll* Tuvalu
114 A1 **Funchal** Madeira
155 D1 **Fundão** Brazil
106 B1 **Fundão** Port.
131 D3 **Fundy, Bay of** *g.* Can.
121 C3 **Funhalouro** Moz.
70 B2 **Funing** *Jiangsu* China
71 A3 **Funing** *Yunnan* China
115 C3 **Funtua** Nigeria
79 C2 **Fūrgun, Kūh-e** *mt.* Iran
89 F2 **Furmanov** Rus. Fed.
Furmanovka Kazakh. *se* **Moyynkum**
Furmanovo Kazakh. *see* **Zhalpaktal**
155 C2 **Furnas, Represa** *resr* Brazil
51 D4 **Furneaux Group** *is* Aust
Furong China *see* **Wan'a**
100 C1 **Fürstenau** Ger.
101 E3 **Fürth** Ger.
66 D3 **Furukawa** Japan
127 G2 **Fury and Hecla Strait** Can.
70 C1 **Fushun** China
65 B1 **Fusong** China
79 C2 **Fuwayriţ** Qatar
Fuxian China *see* **Wafangdian**
70 A2 **Fuxian** China
70 C1 **Fuxin** China
70 B2 **Fuyang** China
69 E1 **Fuyu** China
Fuyu China *see* **Songyua**
68 B1 **Fuyun** China
71 B3 **Fuzhou** China
Fuzhou China *see* **Linchuan**
93 F4 **Fyn** *i.* Denmark
96 B3 **Fyne, Loch** *inlet* U.K.
F.Y.R.O.M. *country* Euro *see* **Macedonia**

G

117 C4 **Gaalkacyo** Somalia
120 A2 **Gabela** Angola
Gaberones Botswana *se* **Gaborone**
115 D1 **Gabès** Tunisia
115 D1 **Gabès, Golfe de** *g.* Tuni
118 B3 **Gabon** *country* Africa
123 C1 **Gaborone** Botswana
79 C2 **Gābrīk** Iran
110 C2 **Gabrovo** Bulg.
114 A3 **Gabú** Guinea-Bissau
73 B3 **Gadag** India
101 E1 **Gadebusch** Ger.
142 C2 **Gadsden** U.S.A.
118 B2 **Gadzi** C.A.R.
110 C2 **Găeşti** Romania
108 B2 **Gaeta** Italy
108 B2 **Gaeta, Golfo di** *g.* Italy
143 D1 **Gaffney** U.S.A.
115 C1 **Gafsa** Tunisia
89 E2 **Gagarin** Rus. Fed.
109 C3 **Gagliano del Capo** Italy
114 B4 **Gagnoa** Côte d'Ivoire
131 D2 **Gagnon** Can.
Gago Coutinho Angola *see* **Lumbala N'guimbo**
81 C1 **Gagra** Georgia
122 A2 **Gaiab** *watercourse* Namibia
104 C3 **Gaillac** France
Gaillimh Rep. of Ireland *see* **Galway**

3 D3 Gainesville FL U.S.A.
3 D2 Gainesville GA U.S.A.
9 D2 Gainesville TX U.S.A.
3 C3 Gainsborough U.K.
2 A2 Gairdner, Lake salt flat Austr.
5 B2 Gairloch U.K.
2 B2 Gakarosa mt. S. Africa
9 E3 Galana r. Kenya
3 D2 Galanta Slovakia
Galápagos, Islas is Pacific Ocean see Galapagos Islands
5 I10 Galapagos Islands is Pacific Ocean
7 G6 Galapagos Rise sea feature Pacific Ocean
5 C3 Galashiels U.K.
0 D3 Galați Romania
8 E3 Galdhøpiggen mt. Norway
5 B2 Galeana Mex.
3 C2 Galena Bay Can.
0 A2 Galesburg U.S.A.
2 B2 Galeshewe S. Africa
0 F2 Galich Rus. Fed.
6 B1 Galicia aut. comm. Spain
7 B2 Galilee, Sea of l. Israel
3 A3 Gallabat Sudan
2 C1 Gallatin U.S.A.
3 C4 Galle Sri Lanka
7 G6 Gallego Rise sea feature Pacific Ocean
0 B1 Gallinas, Punta pt Col.
9 C2 Gallipoli Italy
Gallipoli Turkey see Gelibolu
2 H2 Gällivare Sweden
2 A3 Gallup U.S.A.
4 A2 Galtat Zemmour Western Sahara
7 B2 Galtymore hill Rep. of Ireland
9 E3 Galveston U.S.A.
9 E3 Galveston Bay U.S.A.
9 E3 Galveston Island U.S.A.
7 B2 Galway Rep. of Ireland
7 B2 Galway Bay Rep. of Ireland
4 C1 Gamá Brazil
3 D3 Gamalakhe S. Africa
7 B4 Gambēla Eth.
4 A3 Gambia r. Gambia
3 N6 Gambier, Îles is Fr. Polynesia
2 B2 Gambier Islands Austr.
1 E3 Gambo Can.
3 B3 Gamboma Congo
2 H2 Gammelstaden Sweden
8 B1 Ganado U.S.A.
1 D3 Ganāveh Iran
1 D3 Gäncä Azer.
Gand Belgium see Gent
1 C2 Gandadiwata, Bukit mt. Indon.
8 C3 Gandajika Dem. Rep. Congo
6 B1 Gándara Spain
1 E3 Gander Can.
1 E3 Gander r. Can.
1 D1 Ganderkesee Ger.
7 D1 Gandesa Spain
8 B2 Gāndhīdhām India
8 B2 Gandhinagar India
8 B2 Gāndhī Sāgar resr India
7 C2 Gandía Spain
5 C4 Gand-i-Zureh plain Afgh.
Ganga r. Bangl./India see Ganges
3 B4 Gángán Arg.
8 B2 Ganganagar India
2 A1 Gangaw Myanmar
3 C2 Gangca China
5 C1 Gangdisê Shan mts China
5 D2 Ganges r. Bangl./India
5 C2 Ganges France
5 C2 Ganges, Mouths of the Bangl./India
9 E2 Ganges Cone sea feature Indian Ocean
5 C2 Gangtok India
5 C2 Ganjam India
3 B3 Gan Jiang r. China
4 A3 Ganluo China
5 C2 Gannat France
5 B2 Gannett Peak U.S.A.
2 A3 Gansbaai S. Africa
0 A1 Gansu prov. China
5 D4 Ganye Nigeria
1 B3 Ganzhou China
4 B3 Gao Mali

Gaoleshan China see Xianfeng
114 B3 Gaoua Burkina
114 A3 Gaoual Guinea
70 B2 Gaoyou China
70 B2 Gaoyou Hu l. China
105 D3 Gap France
64 B2 Gapan Phil.
107 C2 Gap Carbon hd Alg.
75 C1 Gar China
97 B2 Gara, Lough l. Rep. of Ireland
117 C4 Garacad Somalia
53 C1 Garah Austr.
151 F3 Garanhuns Brazil
123 C2 Ga-Rankuwa S. Africa
118 C1 Garar, Plaine de plain Chad
117 C4 Garbahaarey Somalia
135 B2 Garberville U.S.A.
81 D2 Garbosh, Kūh-e mt. Iran
101 D1 Garbsen Ger.
154 C2 Garça Brazil
154 B2 Garcias Brazil
108 B1 Garda, Lago di l. Italy
108 A3 Garde, Cap de c. Alg.
101 E1 Gardelegen Ger.
136 C3 Garden City U.S.A.
129 E2 Garden Hill Can.
77 C3 Gardez Afgh.
141 F2 Gardiner U.S.A.
Gardner atoll Micronesia see Faraulep
135 C3 Gardnerville U.S.A.
136 B3 Garfield U.S.A.
88 B2 Gargždai Lith.
75 C2 Garhchiroli India
123 C3 Gariep Dam resr S. Africa
122 A3 Garies S. Africa
119 D3 Garissa Kenya
88 B2 Garkalne Latvia
139 D2 Garland U.S.A.
102 C2 Garmisch-Partenkirchen Ger.
153 B3 Garmo, Qullai mt. Tajik.
153 B3 Garnpung Lake imp. l. Austr.
104 B3 Garonne r. France
117 C4 Garoowe Somalia
74 B2 Garoth India
118 B2 Garoua Cameroon
118 B2 Garoua Boulaï Cameroon
Garqêntang China see Sogxian
96 B2 Garry r. U.K.
81 D2 Garrygala Turkm.
126 F2 Garry Lake Can.
119 E3 Garsen Kenya
122 A2 Garub Namibia
60 B2 Garut Indon.
140 B2 Gary U.S.A.
145 B2 Garza García Mex.
68 C2 Garzê China
104 B3 Gascogne reg. France
Gascogne, Golfe de g. France/Spain see Gascony, Gulf of
53 C3 Gascony reg. France see Gascogne
104 B3 Gascony, Gulf of France/Spain
50 A2 Gascoyne r. Austr.
118 B2 Gashaka Nigeria
115 D3 Gashua Nigeria
59 E3 Gasmata P.N.G.
131 D3 Gaspé Can.
131 D3 Gaspé, Péninsule de pen. Can.
143 E1 Gaston, Lake U.S.A.
143 D1 Gastonia U.S.A.
107 C2 Gata, Cabo de c. Spain
88 D2 Gatchina Rus. Fed.
98 C2 Gateshead U.K.
139 D2 Gatesville U.S.A.
141 D1 Gatineau Can.
130 C3 Gatineau r. Can.
Gatooma Zimbabwe see Kadoma
53 D1 Gatton Austr.
129 E2 Gauer Lake Can.
93 E4 Gausta mt. Norway
123 C2 Gauteng prov. S. Africa
79 C2 Gāvbandī Iran
111 B3 Gavdos i. Greece
104 B3 Gave r. France
93 G3 Gävle Sweden
93 G3 Gävlebukten b. Sweden
89 F2 Gavrilov Posad Rus. Fed.
89 E2 Gavrilov-Yam Rus. Fed.
122 A2 Gawachab Namibia
62 A1 Gawai Myanmar

52 A2 Gawler Austr.
52 A2 Gawler Ranges hills Austr.
75 C2 Gaya India
114 C3 Gaya Niger
114 C3 Gayéri Burkina
140 C1 Gaylord U.S.A.
86 E2 Gayny Rus. Fed.
116 B1 Gaza terr. Asia
80 B2 Gaza Gaza
76 C2 Gaz-Achak Turkm.
76 B3 Gazandzhyk Turkm.
80 B2 Gaziantep Turkey
114 B4 Gboko Nigeria
118 A2 Gbarnga Liberia
103 D1 Gdańsk Pol.
88 A3 Gdańsk, Gulf of Pol./Rus. Fed.
88 C2 Gdov Rus. Fed.
103 D1 Gdynia Pol.
116 B3 Gedaref Sudan
101 D2 Gedern Ger.
111 C3 Gediz Turkey
111 C3 Gediz r. Turkey
102 C1 Gedser Denmark
100 B2 Geel Belgium
52 B3 Geelong Austr.
101 E1 Geesthacht Ger.
75 C1 Gê'gyai China
129 D2 Geikie r. Can.
93 E3 Geilo Norway
119 D3 Geita Tanz.
71 A3 Gejiu China
108 B3 Gela Sicily Italy
108 B3 Gela, Golfo di g. Sicily Italy
91 D3 Gelendzhik Rus. Fed.
111 C2 Gelibolu Turkey
100 C2 Gelsenkirchen Ger.
118 B2 Gemena Dem. Rep. Congo
111 C2 Gemlik Turkey
108 B1 Gemona del Friuli Italy
78 A2 Gemsa Egypt
117 C4 Genalē Wenz r. Eth.
153 B3 General Acha Arg.
153 B3 General Alvear Arg.
153 B3 General Belgrano Arg.
144 B2 General Cepeda Mex.
General Freire Angola see Muxaluando
General Machado Angola see Camacupa
153 B3 General Pico Arg.
153 B3 General Roca Arg.
154 B2 General Salgado Brazil
64 B3 General Santos Phil.
141 D2 Genesee r. U.S.A.
140 C2 Geneseo IL U.S.A.
141 D2 Geneseo NY U.S.A.
Geneva Switz. see Genève
141 D2 Geneva U.S.A.
Geneva, Lake France/Switz. see Léman, Lac
105 D2 Genève Switz.
106 B2 Genil r. Spain
100 B2 Genk Belgium
108 A2 Genoa Italy
Genova Italy see Genoa
108 A2 Genova, Golfo di g. Italy
100 A2 Gent Belgium
61 C2 Genteng i. Indon.
101 F1 Genthin Ger.
50 A3 Geographe Bay Austr.
131 D2 George r. Can.
122 B3 George S. Africa
143 D3 George, Lake Austr.
143 D3 George, Lake FL U.S.A.
141 E2 George, Lake NY U.S.A.
146 C2 George Town Bahamas
114 A3 Georgetown Gambia
151 D2 Georgetown Guyana
60 B1 George Town Malaysia
140 C3 Georgetown KY U.S.A.
143 E2 Georgetown SC U.S.A.
139 D2 Georgetown TX U.S.A.
55 L2 George V Land reg. Antarctica
81 C1 Georgia country Asia
143 D2 Georgia state U.S.A.
130 B3 Georgian Bay Can.
51 C2 Georgina watercourse Austr.
Georgiu-Dezh Rus. Fed. see Liski
77 E2 Georgiyevka Kazakh.
87 D4 Georgiyevsk Rus. Fed.
151 E4 Geral de Goiás, Serra hills Brazil
54 B2 Geraldine N.Z.

50 A2 Geraldton Austr.
80 B1 Gerede Turkey
76 C3 Gereshk Afgh.
102 C2 Geretsried Ger.
135 C2 Gerlach U.S.A.
103 E2 Gerlachovský štit mt. Slovakia
141 D3 Germantown U.S.A.
102 C1 Germany country Europe
100 C2 Gerolstein Ger.
101 E3 Gerolzhofen Ger.
53 D2 Gerringong Austr.
101 D2 Gersfeld (Rhön) Ger.
Géryville Alg. see El Bayadh
75 C1 Gêrzê China
106 C1 Getafe Spain
141 D3 Gettysburg PA U.S.A.
136 D1 Gettysburg SD U.S.A.
55 P2 Getz Ice Shelf Antarctica
111 B2 Gevgelija Macedonia
106 C1 Gexto Spain
111 C3 Geyikli Turkey
122 B2 Ghaap Plateau S. Africa
Ghadamis Libya see Ghadāmis
115 C1 Ghadāmis Libya
75 C2 Ghaghara r. India
76 C2 Ghalkarteniz, Solonchak salt marsh Kazakh.
114 B4 Ghana country Africa
120 B3 Ghanzi Botswana
115 C1 Ghardaïa Alg.
78 A2 Ghârib, Gebel mt. Egypt
115 D1 Gharyān Libya
115 D2 Ghāt Libya
75 C2 Ghatal India
75 C2 Ghazipur India
77 C3 Ghazni Afgh.
78 B2 Ghazzālah Saudi Arabia
Ghent Belgium see Gent
Gheorghe Gheorghiu-Dej Romania see Oneşti
110 C1 Gheorgheni Romania
110 B1 Gherla Romania
105 D3 Ghisonaccia Corsica France
74 B2 Ghotāru India
74 A2 Ghotki Pak.
75 C2 Ghuari r. India
76 C3 Ghurian Afgh.
91 E3 Giaginskaya Rus. Fed.
97 C1 Giant's Causeway lava field U.K.
61 C2 Gianyar Indon.
109 C3 Giarre Sicily Italy
108 A1 Giaveno Italy
122 A2 Gibeon Namibia
106 B2 Gibraltar terr. Europe
106 B2 Gibraltar, Strait of Morocco/Spain
142 B2 Gibsland U.S.A.
50 B2 Gibson Desert Austr.
68 C1 Gichgeniyn Nuruu mts Mongolia
117 B4 Gīdolē Eth.
105 C2 Gien France
101 D2 Gießen Ger.
101 E1 Gifhorn Ger.
128 C2 Gift Lake Can.
67 C3 Gifu Japan
96 B3 Gigha i. U.K.
106 B1 Gijón Spain
138 A2 Gila r. U.S.A.
138 A2 Gila Bend U.S.A.
51 D1 Gilbert r. Austr.
48 I4 Gilbert Islands country Pacific Ocean
156 D5 Gilbert Ridge sea feature Pacific Ocean
151 E3 Gilbués Brazil
134 D1 Gildford U.S.A.
116 A2 Gilf Kebir Plateau Egypt
53 C2 Gilgandra Austr.
74 B1 Gilgit Jammu and Kashmir
74 B1 Gilgit r. Jammu and Kashmir
53 C2 Gilgunnia Austr.
129 E2 Gillam Can.
50 B2 Gillen, Lake imp. l. Austr.
136 B2 Gillette U.S.A.
99 D4 Gillingham U.K.
130 C2 Gilmour Island Can.
135 B3 Gilroy U.S.A.
129 E2 Gimli Can.
64 B3 Gingoog Phil.
117 C4 Ginir Eth.
109 C2 Ginosa Italy
109 C2 Gioia del Colle Italy
53 C3 Gippsland reg. Austr.
74 A2 Girdar Dhor r. Pak.
79 D1 Girdi Iran

Giresun

186

80 B1 **Giresun** Turkey
116 B2 **Girga** Egypt
Girgenti Italy see Agrigento
53 C2 **Girilambone** Austr.
Giron Sweden see Kiruna
107 D1 **Girona** Spain
104 B2 **Gironde** est. France
53 C2 **Girral** Austr.
96 B3 **Girvan** U.K.
54 C1 **Gisborne** N.Z.
93 F4 **Gislaved** Sweden
119 C3 **Gitarama** Rwanda
119 C3 **Gitega** Burundi
Giuba r. Somalia see Jubba
108 B2 **Giulianova** Italy
110 C2 **Giurgiu** Romania
110 C1 **Giuvala, Pasul** pass Romania
105 C2 **Givors** France
123 D1 **Giyani** S. Africa
119 D2 **Giyon** Eth.
Giza Egypt see El Gîza
80 B3 **Giza Pyramids** tourist site Egypt
76 C2 **Gizhduvan** Uzbek.
103 E1 **Giżycko** Pol.
109 D2 **Gjirokastër** Albania
126 F2 **Gjoa Haven** Can.
93 F3 **Gjøvik** Norway
131 E3 **Glace Bay** Can.
134 B1 **Glacier Peak** vol. U.S.A.
139 E2 **Gladewater** U.S.A.
51 E2 **Gladstone** Qld Austr.
52 A2 **Gladstone** S.A. Austr.
92 □A2 **Gláma** mts Iceland
109 C2 **Glamoč** Bos.-Herz.
100 C3 **Glan** r. Ger.
97 B2 **Glanaruddery Mountains** hills Rep. of Ireland
96 B3 **Glasgow** U.K.
140 B3 **Glasgow** KY U.S.A.
136 B1 **Glasgow** MT U.S.A.
99 B4 **Glastonbury** U.K.
101 F2 **Glauchau** Ger.
86 E3 **Glazov** Rus. Fed.
89 E3 **Glazunovka** Rus. Fed.
123 D2 **Glencoe** S. Africa
96 B2 **Glen Coe** val. U.K.
138 A2 **Glendale** AZ U.S.A.
140 B2 **Glendale** WI U.S.A.
53 D2 **Glen Davis** Austr.
51 D2 **Glenden** Austr.
136 C1 **Glendive** U.S.A.
52 B3 **Glenelg** r. Austr.
96 B2 **Glenfinnan** U.K.
53 D1 **Glen Innes** Austr.
96 B2 **Glen More** val. U.K.
53 C1 **Glenmorgan** Austr.
126 C2 **Glennallen** U.S.A.
134 C2 **Glenns Ferry** U.S.A.
138 B2 **Glenrock** U.S.A.
96 C2 **Glenrothes** U.K.
141 E2 **Glens Falls** U.S.A.
96 C2 **Glen Shee** val. U.K.
97 B1 **Glenties** Rep. of Ireland
138 B2 **Glenwood** U.S.A.
136 B3 **Glenwood Springs** U.S.A.
101 E1 **Glinde** Ger.
103 D1 **Gliwice** Pol.
138 A2 **Globe** U.S.A.
103 D1 **Głogów** Pol.
92 F2 **Glomfjord** Norway
93 F4 **Glomma** r. Norway
53 D2 **Gloucester** Austr.
99 B4 **Gloucester** U.K.
131 E3 **Glovertown** Can.
101 F1 **Glöwen** Ger.
77 E1 **Glubokoye** Kazakh.
101 D1 **Glückstadt** Ger.
103 C2 **Gmünd** Austria
102 C2 **Gmunden** Austria
101 D1 **Gnarrenburg** Ger.
103 D1 **Gniezno** Pol.
109 D2 **Gnjilane** Yugo.
75 D2 **Goalpara** India
96 B3 **Goat Fell** hill U.K.
117 C4 **Goba** Eth.
122 A1 **Gobabis** Namibia
153 A4 **Gobernador Gregores** Arg.
152 C2 **Gobernador Virasoro** Arg.
68 D2 **Gobi** des. China/Mongolia
67 C4 **Gobō** Japan
100 C2 **Goch** Ger.
122 A1 **Gochas** Namibia
74 B3 **Godavari** r. India
73 C3 **Godavari, Mouths of the** India
75 C2 **Godda** India

117 C4 **Godē** Eth.
130 B3 **Goderich** Can.
Godhavn Greenland see Qeqertarsuaq
74 B2 **Godhra** India
129 E2 **Gods** r. Can.
129 E2 **Gods Lake** Can.
Godthåb Greenland see Nuuk
Godwin-Austen, Mount China/Jammu and Kashmir see K2
Goedgegun Swaziland see Nhlangano
130 C3 **Goéland, Lac au** l. Can.
131 D2 **Goélands, Lac aux** l. Can.
100 A2 **Goes** Neth.
140 B1 **Gogebic Range** hills U.S.A.
88 C1 **Gogland, Ostrov** i. Rus. Fed.
Gogra r. India see Ghaghara
119 C2 **Gogrial** Sudan
154 C1 **Goiandira** Brazil
154 C1 **Goianésia** Brazil
154 C1 **Goiânia** Brazil
154 B1 **Goiás** Brazil
154 C1 **Goiatuba** Brazil
154 B2 **Goio-Erê** Brazil
111 C2 **Gökçeada** i. Turkey
111 C3 **Gökçedağ** Turkey
121 B2 **Gokwe** Zimbabwe
93 E3 **Gol** Norway
62 A1 **Golaghat** India
111 C2 **Gölcük** Turkey
103 E1 **Gołdap** Pol.
101 F1 **Goldberg** Ger.
Gold Coast country Africa see Ghana
53 D1 **Gold Coast** Austr.
114 B4 **Gold Coast** coastal area Ghana
128 C2 **Golden** Can.
54 B2 **Golden Bay** N.Z.
134 B1 **Goldendale** U.S.A.
128 B3 **Golden Hinde** mt. Can.
97 B2 **Golden Vale** lowland Rep. of Ireland
135 C3 **Goldfield** U.S.A.
128 B3 **Gold River** Can.
143 E1 **Goldsboro** U.S.A.
103 C1 **Goleniów** Pol.
135 C4 **Goleta** U.S.A.
Golfe du St-Laurent g. Can. see St Lawrence, Gulf of
111 C3 **Gölhisar** Turkey
Gollel Swaziland see Lavumisa
75 D1 **Golmud** China
81 D2 **Golpāyegān** Iran
96 C2 **Golspie** U.K.
Golyshi Rus. Fed. see Vetluzhskiy
119 C3 **Goma** Dem. Rep. Congo
75 C2 **Gomati** r. India
115 D3 **Gombe** Nigeria
115 D3 **Gombi** Nigeria
Gomel' Belarus see Homyel'
144 B2 **Gómez Palacio** Mex.
81 D2 **Gomīshān** Iran
75 C1 **Gomo** China
147 C3 **Gonaïves** Haiti
81 D2 **Gonbad-e Kavus** Iran
74 B2 **Gondal** India
Gondar Eth. see Gonder
116 B3 **Gonder** Eth.
75 C2 **Gondia** India
111 C2 **Gönen** Turkey
62 A1 **Gonggar** China
70 A3 **Gongga Shan** mt. China
68 C2 **Gonghe** China
115 D4 **Gongola** r. Nigeria
53 C2 **Gongolgon** Austr.
Gongtang China see Damxung
123 C3 **Gonubie** S. Africa
145 C2 **Gonzáles** Mex.
139 D3 **Gonzales** U.S.A.
122 A3 **Good Hope, Cape of** S. Africa
134 D2 **Gooding** U.S.A.
136 C3 **Goodland** U.S.A.
53 C1 **Goodooga** U.S.A.
98 C3 **Goole** U.K.
53 C2 **Goolgowi** Austr.
52 A3 **Goolwa** Austr.
53 D1 **Goondiwindi** Austr.
134 B2 **Goose Lake** U.S.A.

102 B2 **Göppingen** Ger.
75 C2 **Gorakhpur** India
109 C2 **Goražde** Bos.-Herz.
111 C3 **Gördes** Turkey
89 D3 **Gordeyevka** Rus. Fed.
136 C2 **Gordon** U.S.A.
51 D4 **Gordon, Lake** Austr.
115 D4 **Goré** Chad
117 B4 **Gorë** Eth.
54 A3 **Gore** N.Z.
97 C2 **Gorey** Rep. of Ireland
81 D2 **Gorgān** Iran
81 C1 **Gori** Georgia
100 B2 **Gorinchem** Neth.
108 B1 **Gorizia** Italy
Gor'kiy Rus. Fed. see Nizhniy Novgorod
89 F2 **Gor'kovskoye Vodokhranilishche** resr Rus. Fed.
103 E2 **Gorlice** Pol.
103 C1 **Görlitz** Ger.
Gorna Dzhumaya Bulg. see Blagoevgrad
109 D2 **Gornji Milanovac** Yugo.
109 C2 **Gornji Vakuf** Bos.-Herz.
77 E1 **Gorno-Altaysk** Rus. Fed.
86 F2 **Gornopravdinsk** Rus. Fed.
110 C2 **Gornotrakiyska Nizina** lowland Bulg.
66 D1 **Gornozavodsk** Rus. Fed.
77 E1 **Gornyak** Rus. Fed.
59 D3 **Goroka** P.N.G.
52 B3 **Goroke** Austr.
114 B3 **Gorom Gorom** Burkina
121 C2 **Gorongosa** Moz.
61 D1 **Gorontalo** Indon.
89 E3 **Gorshechnoye** Rus. Fed.
97 B2 **Gorumna Island** Rep. of Ireland
91 D3 **Goryachiy Klyuch** Rus. Fed.
103 D1 **Gorzów Wielkopolski** Pol.
59 E3 **Goschen Strait** P.N.G.
53 D2 **Gosford** U.S.A.
74 A2 **Goshanak** Pak.
66 D2 **Goshogawara** Japan
101 E2 **Goslar** Ger.
109 C2 **Gospić** Croatia
99 C4 **Gosport** U.K.
111 B2 **Gostivar** Macedonia
Göteborg Sweden see Gothenburg
101 E2 **Gotha** Ger.
93 F4 **Gothenburg** Sweden
136 C2 **Gothenburg** U.S.A.
93 G4 **Gotland** i. Sweden
111 B2 **Gotse Delchev** Bulg.
93 G4 **Gotska Sandön** i. Sweden
67 B4 **Gōtsu** Japan
101 D2 **Göttingen** Ger.
128 B2 **Gott Peak** Can.
102 C2 **Gottwaldow** Czech Rep. see Zlín
Gotval'd Ukr. see Zmiyiv
100 B1 **Gouda** Neth.
114 A3 **Goudiri** Senegal
115 D3 **Goudoumaria** Niger
158 E7 **Gough Island** S. Atlantic Ocean
130 C3 **Gouin, Réservoir** resr Can.
53 C2 **Goulburn** Austr.
53 B3 **Goulburn** r. N.S.W. Austr.
53 B3 **Goulburn** r. Vic. Austr.
114 B3 **Goundam** Mali
107 D2 **Gouraya** Alg.
114 B3 **Gourcy** Burkina
104 C3 **Gourdon** France
115 D3 **Gouré** Niger
122 B3 **Gourits** r. S. Africa
114 B3 **Gourma-Rharous** Mali
53 C3 **Gourock Range** mts Austr.
155 D1 **Governador Valadares** Brazil
143 E3 **Governor's Harbour** Bahamas
68 C2 **Govĭ Altayn Nuruu** mts Mongolia
75 C2 **Govind Ballash Pant Sāgar** resr India
99 A3 **Gower** pen. U.K.
152 C2 **Goya** Arg.
81 C1 **Göyçay** Azer.
80 B1 **Göynük** Turkey
115 E3 **Goz-Beïda** Chad
75 C1 **Gozha Co** salt l. China
122 B3 **Graaf-Reinet** S. Africa
122 A3 **Graafwater** S. Africa
101 E1 **Grabow** Ger.
109 C2 **Gračac** Croatia

87 E3 **Grachevka** Rus. Fed.
109 C2 **Gradačac** Bos.-Herz.
104 B3 **Gradignan** France
101 F2 **Gräfenhainichen** Ger.
53 D1 **Grafton** Austr.
137 D1 **Grafton** U.S.A.
139 D2 **Graham** U.S.A.
138 B2 **Graham, Mount** U.S.A.
Graham Bell Island Rus. Fed. see Greem-Bell, Ostrov
128 A2 **Graham Island** Can.
55 A3 **Graham Land** reg. Antarctica
123 C3 **Grahamstown** S. Africa
97 C2 **Graiguenamanagh** Rep. of Ireland
151 E3 **Grajaú** Brazil
103 E1 **Grajewo** Pol.
111 B2 **Grámmos** mt. Greece
96 B2 **Grampian Mountains** U...
52 B3 **Grampians** mts Austr.
146 B3 **Granada** Nic.
106 C2 **Granada** Spain
92 C2 **Granard** Rep. of Ireland
141 E1 **Granby** Can.
114 A2 **Gran Canaria** i. Canary
152 B3 **Gran Chaco** reg. Arg./Para.
136 F2 **Grand** r. MO U.S.A.
136 C1 **Grand** r. SD U.S.A.
146 C2 **Grand Bahama** i. Bahamas
131 E3 **Grand Bank** Can.
158 D2 **Grand Banks of Newfoundland** sea feat... N. Atlantic Ocean
Grand Canary i. Canary see Gran Canaria
138 A1 **Grand Canyon** U.S.A.
138 A1 **Grand Canyon** gorge U.S.A.
146 B3 **Grand Cayman** i. Cayman Is
129 C2 **Grand Centre** Can.
134 C1 **Grand Coulee** U.S.A.
152 B1 **Grande** r. Bol.
154 B2 **Grande** r. Brazil
153 B5 **Grande, Bahía** b. Arg.
155 D2 **Grande, Ilha** i. Brazil
150 C2 **Grande, Serra** mt. Braz...
128 C2 **Grande Cache** Can.
121 D2 **Grande Comore** i. Comoros
128 C2 **Grande Prairie** Can.
115 D3 **Grand Erg de Bilma** des. Niger
114 B1 **Grand Erg Occidental** des. Alg.
115 C2 **Grand Erg Oriental** des... Alg.
131 D3 **Grande-Rivière** Can.
130 C2 **Grande Rivière de la Baleine** r. Can.
152 B3 **Grandes, Salinas** salt marsh Arg.
131 D3 **Grand Falls** N.B. Can.
131 E3 **Grand Falls** Nfld. Can.
128 C3 **Grand Forks** Can.
137 D1 **Grand Forks** U.S.A.
140 B2 **Grand Haven** U.S.A.
128 C1 **Grandin, Lac** l. Can.
137 D2 **Grand Island** U.S.A.
142 B3 **Grand Isle** U.S.A.
136 B3 **Grand Junction** U.S.A.
114 B4 **Grand-Lahou** Côte d'Iv...
131 D3 **Grand Lake** N.B. Can.
131 E3 **Grand Lake** Nfld. Can.
137 E1 **Grand Marais** U.S.A.
130 C3 **Grand-Mère** Can.
106 B2 **Grândola** Port.
129 E2 **Grand Rapids** Can.
140 B2 **Grand Rapids** MI U.S.A.
137 E1 **Grand Rapids** MN U.S.A...
136 A2 **Grand Teton** mt. U.S.A.
147 C2 **Grand Turk** Turks and Caicos Is
129 D2 **Grandview** Can.
134 C1 **Grandview** U.S.A.
134 C1 **Grangeville** U.S.A.
128 B2 **Granisle** Can.
137 D2 **Granite Falls** U.S.A.
134 E1 **Granite Peak** MT U.S.A.
135 C3 **Granite Peak** NV U.S.A.
108 B3 **Granitola, Capo** c. Sicil... Italy
93 F4 **Gränna** Sweden
101 F1 **Gransee** Ger.
99 C3 **Grantham** U.K.
96 C2 **Grantown-on-Spey** U.K...
138 B1 **Grants** U.S.A.

B2 **Grants Pass** U.S.A.
B2 **Granville** France
D2 **Granville Lake** Can.
D1 **Grão Mogol** Brazil
D1 **Graskop** S. Africa
D3 **Grasse** France
B3 **Grass Patch** Austr.
D1 **Graus** Spain
F2 **Gravdal** Norway
B2 **Grave, Pointe de** *pt* France
D3 **Gravelbourg** Can.
C3 **Gravenhurst** Can.
D1 **Gravesend** Austr.
D4 **Gravesend** U.K.
D2 **Gray** France
D1 **Gray** U.S.A.
C2 **Grayling** U.S.A.
D4 **Grays** U.K.
D2 **Graz** Austria
C2 **Great Abaco** *i.* Bahamas
B3 **Great Australian Bight** *g.* Austr.
C2 **Great Bahama Bank** *sea feature* Bahamas
C1 **Great Barrier Island** N.Z.
D1 **Great Barrier Reef** Austr.
C3 **Great Basin** U.S.A.
C1 **Great Bear Lake** Can.
Great Belt *sea chan.* Denmark *see* **Store Bælt**
D3 **Great Bend** U.S.A.
A2 **Great Coco Island** Cocos Is
B3 **Great Dividing Range** *mts* Austr.
Great Eastern Erg *des.* Alg. *see* **Grand Erg Oriental**
B2 **Greater Antilles** *is* Caribbean Sea
Greater Khingan Mountains China *see* **Da Hinggan Ling**
D1 **Great Falls** U.S.A.
C3 **Great Fish** *r.* S. Africa
C3 **Great Fish Point** S. Africa
C2 **Great Inagua** *i.* Bahamas
B3 **Great Karoo** *plat.* S. Africa
C3 **Great Kei** *r.* S. Africa
B3 **Great Malvern** U.K.
D4 **Great Nicobar** *i.* India
B3 **Great Ormes Head** *hd* U.K.
D3 **Great Ouse** *r.* U.K.
C2 **Great Plains** U.S.A.
D3 **Great Rift Valley** Africa
D3 **Great Ruaha** *r.* Tanz.
D2 **Great Salt Lake** U.S.A.
D2 **Great Salt Lake Desert** U.S.A.
A2 **Great Sand Sea** *des.* Egypt/Libya
B2 **Great Sandy Desert** Austr.
C1 **Great Slave Lake** Can.
D1 **Great Smoky Mountains** U.S.A.
A4 **Great Torrington** U.K.
B2 **Great Victoria Desert** Austr.
B1 **Great Wall** *tourist site* China
Great Western Erg *des.* Alg. *see* **Grand Erg Occidental**
D3 **Great Yarmouth** U.K.
Grebenkovskiy Ukr. *see* **Hrebinka**
B1 **Gredos, Sierra de** *mts* Spain
B3 **Greece** *country* Europe
C2 **Greeley** U.S.A.
F1 **Greem-Bell, Ostrov** *i.* Rus. Fed.
F1 **Green** *r.* Can.
B3 **Green** *r. KY* U.S.A.
B3 **Green** *r. WY* U.S.A.
B2 **Green Bay** U.S.A.
B1 **Green Bay** *b.* U.S.A.
C3 **Greenbrier** *r.* U.S.A.
B3 **Greencastle** U.S.A.
D1 **Greeneville** U.S.A.
E2 **Greenfield** U.S.A.
D2 **Green Lake** Can.
J2 **Greenland** *terr.* N. America
L2 **Greenland Basin** *sea feature* Arctic Ocean
R2 **Greenland Sea** *sea* Greenland/Svalbard
B3 **Greenock** U.K.
C1 **Greenore** Rep. of Ireland
135 D3 **Green River** *UT* U.S.A.
136 B2 **Green River** *WY* U.S.A.
140 B3 **Greensburg** *IN* U.S.A.
141 D2 **Greensburg** *PA* U.S.A.
143 E2 **Green Swamp** U.S.A.
138 A2 **Green Valley** U.S.A.
114 B4 **Greenville** Liberia
142 C2 **Greenville** *AL* U.S.A.
141 F1 **Greenville** *ME* U.S.A.
142 B2 **Greenville** *MS* U.S.A.
143 E1 **Greenville** *NC* U.S.A.
143 D2 **Greenville** *SC* U.S.A.
139 D2 **Greenville** *TX* U.S.A.
53 D2 **Greenwell Point** Austr.
131 D3 **Greenwood** Can.
142 B2 **Greenwood** *MS* U.S.A.
143 D2 **Greenwood** *SC* U.S.A.
50 B2 **Gregory, Lake** *salt flat* Austr.
51 D1 **Gregory Range** *hills* Austr.
102 C1 **Greifswald** Ger.
101 F2 **Greiz** Ger.
86 C2 **Gremikha** Rus. Fed.
93 F4 **Grenå** Denmark
142 C2 **Grenada** U.S.A.
147 D3 **Grenada** *country* West Indies
104 C3 **Grenade** France
93 F4 **Grenen** *spit* Denmark
53 C2 **Grenfell** Austr.
129 D2 **Grenfell** Can.
105 D2 **Grenoble** France
51 D1 **Grenville, Cape** Austr.
134 B1 **Gresham** U.S.A.
142 B3 **Gretna** *LA* U.S.A.
141 D3 **Gretna** *VA* U.S.A.
100 C1 **Greven** Ger.
111 B2 **Grevena** Greece
100 C2 **Grevenbroich** Ger.
101 E1 **Grevesmühlen** Ger.
136 B2 **Greybull** U.S.A.
128 A1 **Grey Hunter Peak** Can.
131 E2 **Grey Islands** Can.
54 B2 **Greymouth** N.Z.
52 B1 **Grey Range** *hills* Austr.
97 C2 **Greystones** Rep. of Ireland
123 D2 **Greytown** S. Africa
91 E1 **Gribanovskiy** Rus. Fed.
118 B2 **Gribingui** *r.* C.A.R.
101 D3 **Griesheim** Ger.
143 D2 **Griffin** U.S.A.
53 C2 **Griffith** Austr.
88 C3 **Grigiškės** Lith.
118 C2 **Grimari** C.A.R.
101 F2 **Grimma** Ger.
102 C1 **Grimmen** Ger.
98 C3 **Grimsby** U.K.
128 C2 **Grimshaw** Can.
92 □B2 **Grímsstaðir** Iceland
93 E4 **Grimstad** Norway
92 □A3 **Grindavík** Iceland
93 E4 **Grindsted** Denmark
137 E2 **Grinnell** U.S.A.
123 C3 **Griqualand East** *reg.* S. Africa
122 B2 **Griqualand West** *reg.* S. Africa
122 B2 **Griquatown** S. Africa
127 G1 **Grise Fiord** Can.
Grishino Ukr. *see* **Krasnoarmiys'k**
99 D4 **Gris Nez, Cap** *c.* France
96 C1 **Gritley** U.K.
123 C2 **Groblersdal** S. Africa
122 B2 **Groblershoop** S. Africa
66 B2 **Grodekovo** Rus. Fed.
Grodno Belarus *see* **Hrodna**
103 D1 **Grodzisk Wielkopolski** Pol.
92 □A3 **Gröf** Iceland
104 B2 **Groix, Île de** *i.* France
100 C1 **Gronau (Westfalen)** Ger.
92 F3 **Grong** Norway
100 C1 **Groningen** Neth.
122 B3 **Groot Brakrivier** S. Africa
122 B2 **Grootdrink** S. Africa
51 C1 **Groote Eylandt** *i.* Austr.
120 A2 **Grootfontein** Namibia
122 A2 **Groot Karas Berg** *plat.* Namibia
122 B3 **Groot Swartberge** *mts* S. Africa
122 B2 **Grootvloer** *salt pan* S. Africa
123 C3 **Groot Winterberg** *mt.* S. Africa
101 D2 **Großenlüder** Ger.
101 E2 **Großer Beerberg** *hill* Ger.
102 C2 **Großer Rachel** *mt.* Ger.
103 C2 **Grosser Speikkogel** *mt.* Austria
108 B2 **Grosseto** Italy
101 D3 **Groß-Gerau** Ger.
102 C2 **Großglockner** *mt.* Austria
100 C1 **Groß-Hesepe** Ger.
101 E2 **Großlohra** Ger.
122 A1 **Gross Ums** Namibia
136 A2 **Gros Ventre Range** *mts* U.S.A.
131 E2 **Groswater Bay** Can.
130 B3 **Groundhog** *r.* Can.
135 B3 **Grover Beach** U.S.A.
142 B3 **Groves** U.S.A.
141 E2 **Groveton** U.S.A.
87 D4 **Groznyy** Rus. Fed.
109 C1 **Grubišno Polje** Croatia
Grudovo Bulg. *see* **Sredets**
103 D1 **Grudziądz** Pol.
122 A2 **Grünau** Namibia
92 □A3 **Grundarfjörður** Iceland
Gruzinskaya S.S.R. *country* Asia *see* **Georgia**
89 E3 **Gryazi** Rus. Fed.
89 F2 **Gryazovets** Rus. Fed.
103 D1 **Gryfice** Pol.
102 C1 **Gryfino** Pol.
153 E5 **Grytviken** S. Georgia
146 C2 **Guacanayabo, Golfo de** *b.* Cuba
144 B2 **Guadalajara** Mex.
106 C1 **Guadalajara** Spain
48 H4 **Guadalcanal** *i.* Solomon Is
107 C1 **Guadalope** *r.* Spain
106 B2 **Guadalquivir** *r.* Spain
132 B4 **Guadalupe** *i.* Mex.
106 B2 **Guadalupe, Sierra de** *mts* Spain
138 C2 **Guadalupe Peak** U.S.A.
144 B2 **Guadalupe Victoria** Mex.
144 B2 **Guadalupe y Calvo** Mex.
106 C1 **Guadarrama, Sierra de** *mts* Spain
147 D3 **Guadeloupe** *terr.* West Indies
147 D3 **Guadeloupe Passage** Caribbean Sea
106 B2 **Guadiana** *r.* Port./Spain
106 C2 **Guadix** Spain
154 B2 **Guaíra** Brazil
147 C3 **Guajira, Península de la** *pen.* Col.
150 B3 **Gualaceo** Ecuador
59 D2 **Guam** *terr.* N. Pacific Ocean
144 B2 **Guamúchil** Mex.
144 B2 **Guanacevi** Mex.
151 E4 **Guanambi** Brazil
150 C2 **Guanare** Venez.
146 B2 **Guane** Cuba
70 A2 **Guang'an** China
71 B3 **Guangchang** China
71 B3 **Guangdong** *prov.* China
Guanghua China *see* **Laohekou**
71 A3 **Guangxi Zhuangzu Zizhiqu** *aut. reg.* China
70 A2 **Guangyuan** China
71 B3 **Guangzhou** China
155 D1 **Guanhães** Brazil
147 D4 **Guanipa** *r.* Venez.
71 A3 **Guanling** China
65 A1 **Guanshui** China
Guansuo China *see* **Guanling**
147 C2 **Guantánamo** Cuba
155 C2 **Guapé** Brazil
150 C4 **Guaporé** *r.* Bol./Brazil
155 D2 **Guarapari** Brazil
154 B3 **Guarapuava** Brazil
154 C3 **Guaraqueçaba** Brazil
155 C2 **Guaratinguetá** Brazil
154 C3 **Guaratuba** Brazil
106 B1 **Guarda** Port.
Guardafui, Cape Somalia *see* **Caseyr, Raas**
154 C1 **Guarda Mor** Brazil
106 C1 **Guardo** Spain
155 C2 **Guarujá** Brazil
144 B2 **Guasave** Mex.
146 A3 **Guatemala** *country* Central America
146 A3 **Guatemala** Guat.
157 G5 **Guatemala Basin** *sea feature* N. Pacific Ocean
Guatemala City Guat. *see* **Guatemala**
150 C2 **Guaviare** *r.* Col.
155 C2 **Guaxupé** Brazil
150 B3 **Guayaquil** Ecuador
150 A3 **Guayaquil, Golfo de** *g.* Ecuador
152 B1 **Guayaramerín** Bol.
144 A2 **Guaymas** Mex.
117 B3 **Guba** Eth.
86 E1 **Guba Dolgaya** Rus. Fed.
108 B2 **Gubbio** Italy
89 E3 **Gubkin** Rus. Fed.
73 C3 **Gudivada** India
105 D2 **Guebwiller** France
114 A2 **Guelb er Rîchât** *hill* Maur.
115 C1 **Guelma** Alg.
114 A2 **Guelmine** Morocco
130 B3 **Guelph** Can.
145 C2 **Guémez** Mex.
104 B2 **Guérande** France
115 E2 **Guerende** Libya
104 C2 **Guéret** France
95 C4 **Guernsey** *i.* Channel Is
95 C4 **Guernsey** *terr.* Channel Is
144 A2 **Guerrero Negro** Mex.
131 D2 **Guers, Lac** *l.* Can.
158 D4 **Guiana Basin** *sea feature* N. Atlantic Ocean
70 B2 **Guichi** China
118 B2 **Guider** Cameroon
108 B2 **Guidonia-Montecelio** Italy
71 A3 **Guigang** China
100 A3 **Guignicourt** France
123 D1 **Guija** Moz.
99 C4 **Guildford** U.K.
71 B3 **Guilin** China
130 C2 **Guillaume-Delisle, Lac** *l.* Can.
106 B1 **Guimarães** Port.
114 A3 **Guinea** *country* Africa
113 D5 **Guinea, Gulf of** Africa
114 A3 **Guinea-Bissau** *country* Africa
104 B2 **Guingamp** France
104 B2 **Guipavas** France
154 B1 **Guiratinga** Brazil
150 C1 **Güiria** Venez.
151 D2 **Guisanbourg** Fr. Guiana
98 C2 **Guisborough** U.K.
100 A3 **Guise** France
64 B2 **Guiuan** Phil.
71 A3 **Guiyang** China
71 A3 **Guizhou** *prov.* China
104 B3 **Gujan-Mestras** France
74 B2 **Gujarat** *state* India
Gujerat *state* India *see* **Gujarat**
74 B1 **Gujranwala** Pak.
74 B1 **Gujrat** Pak.
91 D2 **Gukovo** Rus. Fed.
76 B2 **Gulabie** Uzbek.
70 A2 **Gulang** China
53 C2 **Gulargambone** Austr.
73 B3 **Gulbarga** India
88 C2 **Gulbene** Latvia
Gulf of California Mex. *see* **California, Golfo de**
Gulf of Chihli China *see* **Bo Hai**
142 C2 **Gulfport** U.S.A.
53 C2 **Gulgong** Austr.
69 E1 **Gulian** China
77 C2 **Gulistan** Uzbek.
Gulja China *see* **Yining**
129 D2 **Gull Lake** Can.
111 C3 **Güllük** Turkey
Gulü China *see* **Xincai**
119 D2 **Gulu** Uganda
120 B2 **Gumare** Botswana
76 B3 **Gumdag** Turkm.
115 C3 **Gumel** Nigeria
75 C2 **Gumla** India
100 C2 **Gummersbach** Ger.
87 C4 **Gümüşhane** Turkey
74 B2 **Guna** India
Gunan China *see* **Qijiang**
53 C3 **Gundagai** Austr.
111 C3 **Güney** Turkey
118 B3 **Gungu** Dem. Rep. Congo
129 E2 **Gunisao** *r.* Can.
53 D2 **Gunnedah** Austr.
136 B3 **Gunnison** *CO* U.S.A.
135 D3 **Gunnison** *UT* U.S.A.
136 B3 **Gunnison** *r.* U.S.A.
73 B3 **Guntakal** India
73 C3 **Guntur** India
51 C1 **Gununa** Austr.
60 A1 **Gunungsitoli** Indon.
60 A1 **Gunungtua** Indon.
102 C2 **Günzburg** Ger.
102 C2 **Gunzenhausen** Ger.
Guoluezhen China *see* **Lingbao**
74 B2 **Gurgaon** India
151 E3 **Gurgueia** *r.* Brazil

150 C2 **Guri, Embalse de** *resr* Venez.
154 C1 **Gurinhatã** Brazil
121 C2 **Guro** Moz.
151 E4 **Gurupi** Brazil
151 E3 **Gurupi** *r.* Brazil
74 B2 **Guru Sikhar** *mt.* India
121 C2 **Guruve** Zimbabwe
Gur'yev Kazakh. *see* **Atyrau**
115 C3 **Gusau** Nigeria
88 B3 **Gusev** Rus. Fed.
65 A2 **Gushan** China
74 A1 **Gushgy** Turkm.
70 B2 **Gushi** China
83 I3 **Gusinoozersk** Rus. Fed.
89 F2 **Gus'-Khrustal'nyy** Rus. Fed.
108 A3 **Guspini** *Sardinia* Italy
128 A2 **Gustavus** U.S.A.
101 F1 **Güstrow** Ger.
101 D2 **Gütersloh** Ger.
139 D1 **Guthrie** U.S.A.
152 B1 **Gutiérrez** Bol.
121 C2 **Gutu** Zimbabwe
75 D2 **Guwahati** India
150 D2 **Guyana** *country* S. America
Guyi China *see* **Sanjiang**
139 C1 **Guymon** U.S.A.
53 D2 **Guyra** Austr.
70 A2 **Guyuan** China
77 C3 **Guzar** Uzbek.
Guzhou China *see* **Rongjiang**
144 B1 **Guzmán** Mex.
144 B1 **Guzmán, Lago de** *l.* Mex.
88 B3 **Gvardeysk** Rus. Fed.
74 A2 **Gwadar** Pak.
Gwador Pak. *see* **Gwadar**
74 B2 **Gwalior** India
121 B3 **Gwanda** Zimbabwe
97 B1 **Gweebarra Bay** Rep. of Ireland
97 B1 **Gweedore** Rep. of Ireland
Gwelo Zimbabwe *see* **Gweru**
121 B2 **Gweru** Zimbabwe
115 D3 **Gwoza** Nigeria
53 D2 **Gwydir** *r.* Austr.
Gya'gya China *see* **Saga**
Gyandzha Azer. *see* **Gäncä**
Gyangkar China *see* **Dinngyê**
Gyangtse China *see* **Gyangzê**
75 C2 **Gyangzê** China
75 C1 **Gyaring Co** *l.* China
68 C2 **Gyaring Hu** *l.* China
86 G1 **Gydanskiy Poluostrov** *pen.* Rus. Fed.
Gyêgu China *see* **Yushu**
Gyixong China *see* **Gonggar**
51 E2 **Gympie** Austr.
62 A2 **Gyobingauk** Myanmar
103 D2 **Gyöngyös** Hungary
103 D2 **Győr** Hungary
136 B3 **Gypsum** U.S.A.
129 E2 **Gypsumville** Can.
131 D2 **Gyrfalcon Islands** Can.
111 B3 **Gytheio** Greece
103 E2 **Gyula** Hungary
81 C1 **Gyumri** Armenia
76 B3 **Gyzylarbat** Turkm.
Gzhatsk Rus. Fed. *see* **Gagarin**

H

88 B2 **Haapsalu** Estonia
100 B1 **Haarlem** Neth.
122 B3 **Haarlem** S. Africa
101 C2 **Haarstrang** *ridge* Ger.
54 A2 **Haast** N.Z.
74 A2 **Hab** *r.* Pak.
79 C3 **Ḩabarūt** Oman
78 B3 **Ḩabbān** Yemen
81 C2 **Ḩabbānīyah, Hawr al** *l.* Iraq
70 B1 **Habirag** China
67 C4 **Hachijō-jima** *i.* Japan
66 D2 **Hachinohe** Japan
67 C3 **Hachiōji** Japan
121 C3 **Hacufera** Moz.
79 C2 **Ḩadd, Ra's al** *pt* Oman
96 C3 **Haddington** U.K.
115 D3 **Hadejia** Nigeria
93 E4 **Haderslev** Denmark
78 B2 **Ḩādhah** Saudi Arabia
79 B3 **Ḩaḑramawt** *reg.* Yemen
79 B3 **Ḩaḑramawt, Wādī** *watercourse* Yemen
91 C1 **Hadyach** Ukr.
65 B2 **Haeju** N. Korea
65 B2 **Haeju-man** *b.* N. Korea
65 B3 **Haenam** S. Korea
78 B2 **Ḩafar al Bāţin** Saudi Arabia
74 B1 **Hafizabad** Pak.
75 D2 **Hāflong** India
92 □A3 **Hafnarfjörður** Iceland
78 A3 **Hagar Nish Plateau** Eritrea
59 D2 **Hagåtña** Guam
101 F1 **Hagelberg** *hill* Ger.
100 C2 **Hagen** Ger.
101 E1 **Hagenow** Ger.
128 B2 **Hagensborg** Can.
141 D3 **Hagerstown** U.S.A.
93 F3 **Hagfors** Sweden
134 D1 **Haggin, Mount** U.S.A.
67 B4 **Hagi** Japan
62 B1 **Ha Giang** Vietnam
97 B2 **Hag's Head** *hd* Rep. of Ireland
69 F3 **Hahajima-rettō** *is* Japan
119 D3 **Hai** Tanz.
Haicheng China *see* **Haifeng**
70 C1 **Haicheng** China
62 B1 **Hai Dương** Vietnam
Haifa Israel *see* **Ḩefa**
71 B3 **Haifeng** China
Haikang China *see* **Leizhou**
71 B3 **Haikou** China
78 B2 **Ḩā'il** Saudi Arabia
69 D1 **Hailar** China
Hailong China *see* **Meihekou**
92 H2 **Hailuoto** *i.* Fin.
69 D3 **Hainan** *i.* China
71 A4 **Hainan** *prov.* China
128 A2 **Haines** U.S.A.
128 A1 **Haines Junction** Can.
101 E2 **Hainich** *ridge* Ger.
101 E2 **Hainleite** *ridge* Ger.
62 B1 **Hai Phong** Vietnam
Haiphong Vietnam *see* **Hai Phong**
147 C3 **Haiti** *country* West Indies
116 B3 **Haiya** Sudan
103 E2 **Hajdúböszörmény** Hungary
103 E2 **Hajdúszoboszló** Hungary
67 C3 **Hajiki-zaki** *pt* Japan
78 B3 **Ḩajjah** Yemen
81 D3 **Ḩājjīābād** Iran
103 E1 **Hajnówka** Pol.
62 A1 **Haka** Myanmar
81 C2 **Hakkârı** Turkey
66 D2 **Hakodate** Japan
122 B2 **Hakseen Pan** *salt pan* S. Africa
Ḩalab Syria *see* **Aleppo**
78 B2 **Ḩalabān** Saudi Arabia
81 C2 **Ḩalabja** Iraq
116 B2 **Halaib** Sudan
78 A2 **Halaib Triangle** *terr.* Egypt/Sudan
79 C3 **Ḩalāniyāt, Juzur al** *is* Oman
78 A2 **Ḩālat 'Ammār** Saudi Arabia
68 C1 **Halban** Mongolia
101 E2 **Halberstadt** Ger.
64 B2 **Halcon, Mount** Phil.
93 F4 **Halden** Norway
101 E1 **Haldensleben** Ger.
75 B2 **Haldwani** India
79 C2 **Ḩāleh** Iran
54 A3 **Halfmoon Bay** N.Z.
141 D1 **Haliburton Highlands** *hills* Can.
131 D3 **Halifax** Can.
98 C3 **Halifax** U.K.
141 D3 **Halifax** U.S.A.
65 B3 **Halla-san** *mt.* S. Korea
127 G2 **Hall Beach** Can.
100 B2 **Halle** Belgium
102 C2 **Hallein** Austria
101 E2 **Halle-Neustadt** Ger.
101 E2 **Halle (Saale)** Ger.
48 G3 **Hall Islands** Micronesia
137 D1 **Hallock** U.S.A.
127 H2 **Hall Peninsula** Can.
50 B1 **Halls Creek** Austr.
59 C2 **Halmahera** *i.* Indon.
93 F4 **Halmstad** Sweden
Hälsingborg Sweden *see* **Helsingborg**
100 B2 **Halsteren** Neth.
98 B2 **Haltwhistle** U.K.
67 B4 **Hamada** Japan
81 C2 **Hamadān** Iran
80 B2 **Ḩamāh** Syria
67 C4 **Hamamatsu** Japan
93 F3 **Hamar** Norway
116 B2 **Hamâta, Gebel** *mt.* Egypt
73 C4 **Hambantota** Sri Lanka
101 D1 **Hamburg** Ger.
123 C3 **Hamburg** S. Africa
142 B2 **Hamburg** U.S.A.
78 A2 **Ḩamḑ, Wādī al** *watercourse* Saudi Arabia
78 B3 **Ḩamḑah** Saudi Arabia
141 E2 **Hamden** U.S.A.
93 H3 **Hämeenlinna** Fin.
101 D1 **Hameln** Ger.
50 A2 **Hamersley Range** *mts* Austr.
65 B1 **Hamgyŏng-sanmaek** *mts* N. Korea
65 B2 **Hamhŭng** N. Korea
68 C2 **Hami** China
116 B2 **Hamid** Sudan
52 B3 **Hamilton** Austr.
130 C3 **Hamilton** Can.
Hamilton *r.* Can. *see* **Churchill**
54 C1 **Hamilton** N.Z.
96 B3 **Hamilton** U.K.
142 C2 **Hamilton** *AL* U.S.A.
134 D1 **Hamilton** *MT* U.S.A.
140 C3 **Hamilton** *OH* U.S.A.
115 E1 **Hamīm, Wādī al** *watercourse* Libya
93 I3 **Hamina** Fin.
100 C2 **Hamm** Ger.
114 B2 **Hammada du Drâa** *plat.* Alg.
115 D1 **Hammamet, Golfe de** *g.* Tunisia
81 C2 **Ḩammār, Hawr al** *imp. l.* Iraq
101 D2 **Hammelburg** Ger.
92 G3 **Hammerdal** Sweden
92 H1 **Hammerfest** Norway
142 B2 **Hammond** U.S.A.
141 E3 **Hammonton** U.S.A.
141 D3 **Hampton** U.S.A.
141 E2 **Hampton Bays** U.S.A.
79 C2 **Hāmūn-e Jaz Mūrīān** *salt marsh* Iran
74 A2 **Hamun-i-Lora** *dry lake* Pak.
74 A2 **Hamun-i-Mashkel** *salt flat* Pak.
78 A2 **Ḩanalc** Saudi Arabia
66 D3 **Hanamaki** Japan
101 D2 **Hanau** Ger.
70 B2 **Hancheng** China
140 B1 **Hancock** U.S.A.
70 B2 **Handan** China
119 D3 **Handeni** Tanz.
135 C3 **Hanford** U.S.A.
68 C1 **Hangayn Nuruu** *mts* Mongolia
Hangchow China *see* **Hangzhou**
Hanggin Houqi China *see* **Xamba**
Hangö Fin. *see* **Hanko**
70 B2 **Hangu** China
70 C2 **Hangzhou** China
70 C2 **Hangzhou Wan** *b.* China
79 B2 **Ḩanīdh** Saudi Arabia
Hanjia China *see* **Pengshui**
Hanjiang China *see* **Yangzhou**
93 H4 **Hanko** Fin.
135 D3 **Hanksville** U.S.A.
54 B2 **Hanmer Springs** N.Z.
128 C2 **Hanna** Can.
136 B2 **Hanna** U.S.A.
137 E3 **Hannibal** U.S.A.
101 D1 **Hannover** Ger.
101 D2 **Hannoversch Münden** Ger.
93 F4 **Hanöbukten** *b.* Sweden
Hanoi Vietnam *see* **Ha Nôi**
62 B1 **Ha Nôi** Vietnam
130 B3 **Hanover** Can.
Hanover Ger. *see* **Hannover**
122 B3 **Hanover** S. Africa
141 E2 **Hanover** *NH* U.S.A.
141 D3 **Hanover** *PA* U.S.A.
92 G2 **Hansnes** Norway
93 E4 **Hanstholm** Denmark
88 C3 **Hantsavichy** Belarus
75 C2 **Hanumana** India
74 B2 **Hanumangarh** India
70 A2 **Hanzhong** China
49 M5 **Hao** *atoll* Fr. Polynesia
75 C2 **Hāora** India
92 H2 **Haparanda** Sweden
100 B2 **Hapert** Neth.
131 D2 **Happy Valley-Goose B** Can.
78 A2 **Ḩaql** Saudi Arabia
79 B2 **Ḩaraḑh** Saudi Arabia
88 C2 **Haradok** Belarus
78 B3 **Ḩarajā** Saudi Arabia
121 C2 **Harare** Zimbabwe
79 C3 **Ḩarāsīs, Jiddat al** *des* Oman
69 D1 **Har-Ayrag** Mongolia
115 E3 **Haraze-Mangueigne** C
114 A4 **Harbel** Liberia
69 E1 **Harbin** China
140 C2 **Harbor Beach** U.S.A.
131 E3 **Harbour Breton** Can.
74 B2 **Harda Khās** India
61 C1 **Harden, Bukit** *mt.* Indo
100 C1 **Hardenberg** Neth.
100 B1 **Harderwijk** Neth.
122 A3 **Hardeveld** *mts* S. Afric
134 E1 **Hardin** U.S.A.
128 C1 **Hardisty Lake** Can.
93 E3 **Hareid** Norway
100 C1 **Haren (Ems)** Ger.
117 C4 **Härer** Eth.
117 C4 **Hargeysa** Somalia
110 C1 **Harghita-Mădăraş, Vâ** *mt.* Romania
68 C2 **Har Hu** *l.* China
88 B2 **Hari kurk** *sea chan.* Estonia
74 B1 **Haripur** Pak.
74 A1 **Hari Rūd** *r.* Afgh./Iran
110 C1 **Hârlău** Romania
100 B1 **Harlingen** Neth.
139 D3 **Harlingen** U.S.A.
99 D4 **Harlow** U.K.
134 E1 **Harlowton** U.S.A.
134 C2 **Harney Basin** U.S.A.
134 C2 **Harney Lake** U.S.A.
93 G3 **Härnösand** Sweden
69 E1 **Har Nur** China
68 C1 **Har Nuur** *l.* Mongolia
96 □ **Haroldswick** U.K.
114 B4 **Harper** Liberia
101 D1 **Harpstedt** Ger.
130 C2 **Harricanaw** *r.* Can.
53 D2 **Harrington** Austr.
131 E2 **Harrington Harbour** C
96 A2 **Harris** *pen.* U.K.
96 A2 **Harris, Sound of** *sea chan.* U.K.
140 B3 **Harrisburg** *IL* U.S.A.
134 B2 **Harrisburg** *OR* U.S.A.
141 D2 **Harrisburg** *PA* U.S.A.
123 C2 **Harrismith** S. Africa
142 B1 **Harrison** U.S.A.
131 E2 **Harrison, Cape** Can.
126 B2 **Harrison Bay** U.S.A.
141 D3 **Harrisonburg** U.S.A.
128 B3 **Harrison Lake** Can.
137 E3 **Harrisonville** U.S.A.
98 C3 **Harrogate** U.K.
110 C2 **Hârşova** Romania
92 G2 **Harstad** Norway
122 B2 **Hartbees** *watercourse* S. Africa
103 D2 **Hartberg** Austria
141 E2 **Hartford** *CT* U.S.A.
137 D2 **Hartford** *SD* U.S.A.
99 A4 **Hartland Point** U.K.
98 C2 **Hartlepool** U.K.
Hartley Zimbabwe *see* Chegutu
128 B2 **Hartley Bay** Can.
123 B2 **Harts** *r.* S. Africa
143 D2 **Hartwell Reservoir** U.S
68 C1 **Har Us Nuur** *l.* Mongol
136 C1 **Harvey** U.S.A.
99 D4 **Harwich** U.K.
74 B2 **Haryana** *state* India
101 E2 **Harz** *hills* Ger.
101 E2 **Harzgerode** Ger.
78 B2 **Ḩasan, Jabal** *hill* Saudi Arabia
80 B2 **Hasan Dağı** *mts* Turkey
99 C4 **Haslemere** U.K.
73 B3 **Hassan** India
100 B2 **Hasselt** Belgium
101 E2 **Haßfurt** Ger.
115 C2 **Hassi Bel Guebbour** A
115 C1 **Hassi Messaoud** Alg.
93 F4 **Hässleholm** Sweden

B2 **Hastière-Lavaux** Belgium
C3 **Hastings** *Vic.* Austr.
C3 **Hastings** *Vic.* Austr.
C1 **Hastings** N.Z.
D4 **Hastings** U.K.
E2 **Hastings** *MN* U.S.A.
D2 **Hastings** *NE* U.S.A.
Hatay Turkey *see* **Antakya**
B2 **Hatch** U.S.A.
D2 **Hatchet Lake** Can.
B1 **Hațeg** Romania
B2 **Hatfield** Austr.
C1 **Hatgal** Mongolia
B2 **Ha Tĩnh** Vietnam
B2 **Hattah** Austr.
E1 **Hatteras, Cape** U.S.A.
H3 **Hatteras Abyssal Plain** *sea feature* S. Atlantic Ocean
C2 **Hattiesburg** U.S.A.
C2 **Hattingen** Ger.
B3 **Hat Yai** Thai.
C4 **Haud** *reg.* Eth.
E4 **Haugesund** Norway
E4 **Haukeligrend** Norway
I2 **Haukipudas** Fin.
C1 **Hauraki Gulf** N.Z.
A3 **Hauroko, Lake** N.Z.
B1 **Haut Atlas** *mts* Morocco
D3 **Hauterive** Can.
Haute-Volta *country* Africa *see* **Burkina**
B1 **Hauts Plateaux** Alg.
B2 **Havana** Cuba
C4 **Havant** U.K.
E1 **Havel** *r.* Ger.
F1 **Havelberg** Ger.
B2 **Havelock** N.Z.
Havelock Swaziland *see* Bulembu
C1 **Havelock North** N.Z.
A4 **Haverfordwest** U.K.
C2 **Havixbeck** Ger.
D2 **Havlíčkův Brod** Czech Rep.
H1 **Havøysund** Norway
C3 **Havran** Turkey
E1 **Havre** U.S.A.
D3 **Havre Aubert** Can.
D2 **Havre-St-Pierre** Can.
L2 **Hawaii** *i.* U.S.A.
A5 **Hawaiian Islands** *is* N. Pacific Ocean
B2 **Ḥawallī** Kuwait
B3 **Hawarden** U.K.
A2 **Hawea, Lake** N.Z.
B1 **Hawera** N.Z.
B2 **Hawes** U.K.
C3 **Hawick** U.K.
C1 **Hawke Bay** N.Z.
A2 **Hawker** Austr.
B1 **Hawkers Gate** Austr.
A3 **Hawston** S. Africa
C3 **Hawthorne** U.S.A.
B2 **Hay** Austr.
C1 **Hay** *r.* Can.
A1 **Haya** China
C3 **Hayange** France
C2 **Haydarābad** Iran
C1 **Hayden** U.S.A.
E2 **Hayes** *r. Man.* Can.
F2 **Hayes** *r. Nunavut* Can.
C3 **Haymā'** Oman
C2 **Hayrabolu** Turkey
C1 **Hay River** Can.
D3 **Hays** U.S.A.
B3 **Ḥays** Yemen
B2 **Haysyn** Ukr.
B3 **Hayward** U.S.A.
C4 **Haywards Heath** U.K.
A1 **Hazarajat** *reg.* Afgh.
C3 **Hazard** U.S.A.
C2 **Hazārībāg** India
C2 **Hazaribagh Range** *mts* India
C1 **Hazebrouck** France
B2 **Hazelton** Can.
D2 **Hazleton** U.S.A.
B3 **Healdsburg** U.S.A.
C3 **Healesville** Austr.
E7 **Heard Island** Indian Ocean
D2 **Hearne** U.S.A.
B3 **Hearst** Can.
A3 **Hearst Island** Antarctica
B2 **Hebei** *prov.* China
C1 **Hebel** Austr.
B1 **Heber Springs** U.S.A.
B2 **Hebi** China
D2 **Hebron** Can.
A2 **Hecate Strait** Can.
A3 **Hechi** China
100 B2 **Hechtel** Belgium
54 C2 **Hector, Mount** N.Z.
93 F3 **Hede** Sweden
100 C1 **Heerde** Neth.
100 B1 **Heerenveen** Neth.
100 B1 **Heerhugowaard** Neth.
100 B2 **Heerlen** Neth.
80 B2 **Ḥefa** Israel
70 B2 **Hefei** China
70 B3 **Hefeng** China
69 E1 **Hegang** China
119 D1 **Heiban** Sudan
102 B1 **Heide** Ger.
122 A1 **Heide** Namibia
101 D3 **Heidelberg** Ger.
122 B3 **Heidelberg** S. Africa
69 E1 **Heihe** China
102 B2 **Heilbronn** Ger.
69 E1 **Heilong Jiang** *r.* China/Rus. Fed.
93 I3 **Heinola** Fin.
Hejaz *reg.* Saudi Arabia *see* **Hijaz**
92 F3 **Helagsfjället** *mt.* Sweden
70 A2 **Helan Shan** *mts* China
142 B2 **Helena** *AR* U.S.A.
134 D1 **Helena** *MT* U.S.A.
96 B2 **Helensburgh** U.K.
102 B1 **Helgoland** *i.* Ger.
102 B1 **Helgoländer Bucht** *b.* Ger.
Heligoland *i.* Ger. *see* **Helgoland**
Heligoland Bight *b.* Ger. *see* **Helgoländer Bucht**
Helixi China *see* **Ningguo**
92 □A3 **Hella** Iceland
100 B2 **Hellevoetsluis** Neth.
107 C2 **Hellín** Spain
Hell-Ville Madag. *see* **Andoany**
76 C3 **Helmand** *r.* Afgh.
101 E2 **Helmbrechts** Ger.
122 A2 **Helmeringhausen** Namibia
100 B2 **Helmond** Neth.
96 C1 **Helmsdale** U.K.
96 C1 **Helmsdale** *r.* U.K.
98 C2 **Helmsley** U.K.
101 E1 **Helmstedt** Ger.
65 B1 **Helong** China
139 D3 **Helotes** U.S.A.
93 F4 **Helsingborg** Sweden
Helsingfors Fin. *see* **Helsinki**
93 F4 **Helsingør** Denmark
93 H3 **Helsinki** Fin.
99 A4 **Helston** U.K.
97 C2 **Helvick Head** *hd* Rep. of Ireland
99 C4 **Hemel Hempstead** U.K.
101 D1 **Hemmoor** Ger.
92 F2 **Hemnesberget** Norway
70 B2 **Henan** *prov.* China
111 D2 **Hendek** Turkey
140 B3 **Henderson** *KY* U.S.A.
143 E1 **Henderson** *NC* U.S.A.
135 D3 **Henderson** *NV* U.S.A.
139 E2 **Henderson** *TX* U.S.A.
49 O6 **Henderson Island** Pitcairn Is
143 D1 **Hendersonville** U.S.A.
99 C4 **Hendon** U.K.
62 A1 **Hengduan Shan** *mts* China
100 C1 **Hengelo** Neth.
Hengnan China *see* **Hengyang**
71 B3 **Hengshan** China
70 B2 **Hengshui** China
71 A3 **Hengxian** China
71 B3 **Hengyang** China
Hengzhou China *see* **Hengxian**
91 C2 **Heniches'k** Ukr.
141 D3 **Henlopen, Cape** U.S.A.
100 C2 **Hennef (Sieg)** Ger.
130 B2 **Henrietta Maria, Cape** Can.
Henrique de Carvalho Angola *see* **Saurimo**
141 D3 **Henry, Cape** U.S.A.
139 D1 **Henryetta** U.S.A.
127 H2 **Henry Kater, Cape** Can.
101 D1 **Henstedt-Ulzburg** Ger.
120 A3 **Hentiesbaai** Namibia
62 A2 **Henzada** Myanmar
101 D3 **Heppenheim (Bergstraße)** Ger.
71 A3 **Hepu** China
76 C3 **Herāt** Afgh.
129 D2 **Herbert** Can.
54 C2 **Herbertville** N.Z.
101 D2 **Herbstein** Ger.
109 C2 **Herceg-Novi** Yugo.
99 B3 **Hereford** U.K.
139 C2 **Hereford** U.S.A.
101 D1 **Herford** Ger.
100 C2 **Herkenbosch** Neth.
96 □ **Herma Ness** *hd* U.K.
122 A3 **Hermanus** S. Africa
53 C2 **Hermidale** Austr.
134 C1 **Hermiston** U.S.A.
59 D3 **Hermit Islands** P.N.G.
144 A2 **Hermosillo** Mex.
154 B3 **Hernandarias** Para.
100 C2 **Herne** Ger.
93 E4 **Herning** Denmark
104 B2 **Hérouville-St-Clair** France
106 B2 **Herrera del Duque** Spain
141 D2 **Hershey** U.S.A.
99 C4 **Hertford** U.K.
123 C2 **Hertzogville** S. Africa
51 E2 **Hervey Bay** Austr.
101 F2 **Herzberg** Ger.
101 E3 **Herzogenaurach** Ger.
71 A3 **Heshan** China
135 C4 **Hesperia** U.S.A.
128 A1 **Hess** *r.* Can.
101 E1 **Hessen** Ger.
101 D2 **Hessisch Lichtenau** Ger.
136 C1 **Hettinger** U.S.A.
101 E2 **Hettstedt** Ger.
98 B2 **Hexham** U.K.
71 B3 **Hexian** China
98 B2 **Heysham** U.K.
71 B3 **Heyuan** China
52 B3 **Heywood** Austr.
70 B2 **Heze** China
143 D3 **Hialeah** U.S.A.
137 D3 **Hiawatha** U.S.A.
137 E1 **Hibbing** U.S.A.
143 D1 **Hickory** U.S.A.
54 C1 **Hicks Bay** N.Z.
66 D2 **Hidaka-sanmyaku** *mts* Japan
139 D3 **Hidalgo** Mex.
145 C2 **Hidalgo** Mex.
144 B2 **Hidalgo del Parral** Mex.
154 C1 **Hidrolândia** Brazil
67 A4 **Higashi-suidō** *sea chan.* Japan
High Atlas *mts* Morocco *see* **Haut Atlas**
134 B2 **High Desert** U.S.A.
128 C2 **High Level** Can.
143 E1 **High Point** U.S.A.
128 C2 **High Prairie** Can.
128 C2 **High River** Can.
129 D2 **Highrock Lake** Can.
High Tatras *mts* Pol./Slovakia *see* **Tatra Mountains**
99 C4 **High Wycombe** U.K.
88 B2 **Hiiumaa** *i.* Estonia
78 A2 **Hijaz** *reg.* Saudi Arabia
54 C1 **Hikurangi** *mt.* N.Z.
101 E2 **Hildburghausen** Ger.
100 C2 **Hilden** Ger.
101 E2 **Hilders** Ger.
101 D1 **Hildesheim** Ger.
Hillah Iraq *see* **Al Ḥillah**
100 B1 **Hillegom** Neth.
100 C2 **Hillesheim** Ger.
140 C3 **Hillsboro** *OH* U.S.A.
139 D2 **Hillsboro** *TX* U.S.A.
53 C2 **Hillston** Austr.
96 □ **Hillswick** U.K.
49 L2 **Hilo** U.S.A.
143 D2 **Hilton Head Island** U.S.A.
100 B1 **Hilversum** Neth.
74 B1 **Himachal Pradesh** *state* India
68 B2 **Himalaya** *mts* Asia
74 B2 **Himatnagar** India
67 B4 **Himeji** Japan
123 C2 **Himeville** S. Africa
67 C3 **Himi** Japan
80 B2 **Ḥimṣ** Syria
147 C3 **Hinche** Haiti
51 D1 **Hinchinbrook Island** Austr.
52 B3 **Hindmarsh, Lake** *dry lake* Austr.
74 A1 **Hindu Kush** *mts* Afgh./Pak.
73 B3 **Hindupur** India
134 C2 **Hines** U.S.A.
143 D2 **Hinesville** U.S.A.
74 B2 **Hinganghat** India
81 C2 **Hınıs** Turkey
92 G2 **Hinnøya** *i.* Norway
106 B2 **Hinojosa del Duque** Spain
100 C1 **Hinte** Ger.
128 C2 **Hinton** Can.
75 C2 **Hirakud Reservoir** India
Hîrlău Romania *see* **Hârlău**
66 D2 **Hiroo** Japan
66 D2 **Hirosaki** Japan
67 B4 **Hiroshima** Japan
101 E3 **Hirschaid** Ger.
101 E2 **Hirschberg** Ger.
105 C2 **Hirson** France
Hîrșova Romania *see* **Hârșova**
93 E4 **Hirtshals** Denmark
74 B2 **Hisar** India
147 C2 **Hispaniola** *i.* Caribbean Sea
81 C2 **Hīt** Iraq
67 D3 **Hitachi** Japan
67 D3 **Hitachinaka** Japan
92 E3 **Hitra** *i.* Norway
49 N4 **Hiva Oa** *i.* Fr. Polynesia
93 G4 **Hjälmaren** *l.* Sweden
129 D1 **Hjalmar Lake** Can.
93 F4 **Hjørring** Denmark
123 D2 **Hlabisa** S. Africa
92 □B2 **Hlíð** Iceland
91 C2 **Hlobyne** Ukr.
123 C2 **Hlohlowane** S. Africa
123 C2 **Hlotse** Lesotho
91 C1 **Hlukhiv** Ukr.
88 C3 **Hlusk** Belarus
88 C2 **Hlybokaye** Belarus
114 C4 **Ho** Ghana
122 A1 **Hoachanas** Namibia
120 A2 **Hoanib** *watercourse* Namibia
120 A2 **Hoarusib** *watercourse* Namibia
51 D4 **Hobart** Austr.
139 D1 **Hobart** U.S.A.
139 C2 **Hobbs** U.S.A.
93 E4 **Hobro** Denmark
117 C4 **Hobyo** Somalia
63 B2 **Hô Chi Minh** Vietnam
Ho Chi Minh City Vietnam *see* **Hô Chi Minh**
114 B3 **Ḥôḍ** *reg.* Maur.
117 D3 **Ḥodda** *mt.* Somalia
Hodeidah Yemen *see* **Al Ḥudaydah**
103 E2 **Hódmezővásárhely** Hungary
100 B2 **Hoek van Holland** Neth.
65 B2 **Hoeyang** N. Korea
101 E2 **Hof** Ger.
101 E2 **Hofheim in Unterfranken** Ger.
92 □B3 **Höfn** Iceland
92 □A2 **Höfn** Iceland
92 □B3 **Hofsjökull** *ice cap* Iceland
67 B4 **Hōfu** Japan
115 C2 **Hoggar** *plat.* Alg.
93 G4 **Högsby** Sweden
93 E3 **Høgste Breakulen** *mt.* Norway
101 D2 **Hohe Rhön** *mts* Ger.
100 C2 **Hohe Venn** *moorland* Belgium
75 C1 **Hoh Xil Shan** *mts* China
63 B2 **Hôi An** Vietnam
119 D2 **Hoima** Uganda
62 B1 **Hôi Xuân** Vietnam
75 D2 **Hojai** India
54 B2 **Hokitika** N.Z.
66 D2 **Hokkaidō** *i.* Japan
91 C2 **Hola Prystan'** Ukr.
128 B2 **Holberg** Can.
53 C3 **Holbrook** Austr.
138 A2 **Holbrook** U.S.A.
137 D2 **Holdrege** U.S.A.
146 C2 **Holguín** Cuba
92 □B2 **Hóll** Iceland
103 D2 **Hollabrunn** Austria
140 B2 **Holland** U.S.A.
Hollandia Indon. *see* **Jayapura**
135 B3 **Hollister** U.S.A.
103 E2 **Hollóháza** Hungary
93 I3 **Hollola** Fin.
100 B1 **Hollum** Neth.
142 C2 **Holly Springs** U.S.A.
143 D3 **Hollywood** U.S.A.
92 F2 **Holm** Norway
126 E2 **Holman** Can.
92 H3 **Holmsund** Sweden
122 A2 **Holoog** Namibia
93 E4 **Holstebro** Denmark
143 D1 **Holston** *r.* U.S.A.
98 A3 **Holyhead** U.K.
98 C2 **Holy Island** *England* U.K.
98 A3 **Holy Island** *Wales* U.K.

136 C2 **Holyoke** U.S.A.
Holy See Europe *see* **Vatican City**
101 D2 **Holzminden** Ger.
62 A1 **Homalin** Myanmar
101 D2 **Homberg (Efze)** Ger.
114 B3 **Hombori** Mali
100 C3 **Homburg** Ger.
127 H2 **Home Bay** Can.
142 B2 **Homer** U.S.A.
143 D3 **Homestead** U.S.A.
92 F3 **Hommelvik** Norway
143 D3 **Homosassa Springs** U.S.A.
Homs Syria *see* **Ḥimṣ**
89 D3 **Homyel'** Belarus
Honan *prov.* China *see* **Henan**
122 A3 **Hondeklipbaai** S. Africa
145 D3 **Hondo** *r.* Belize/Mex.
138 B2 **Hondo** *NM* U.S.A.
139 D3 **Hondo** *TX* U.S.A.
146 B3 **Honduras** *country* Central America
146 B3 **Honduras, Gulf of** Belize/Hond.
93 F3 **Hønefoss** Norway
135 B2 **Honey Lake** U.S.A.
104 C2 **Honfleur** France
62 B1 **Hông Gai** Vietnam
70 B3 **Honghu** China
71 A3 **Hongjiang** China
69 D3 **Hong Kong** China
71 B3 **Hong Kong** *special admin. reg.* China
Hongqizhen China *see* **Tongshi**
131 D3 **Honguedo, Détroit d'** *sea chan.* Can.
65 B1 **Hongwŏn** N. Korea
70 B2 **Hongze Hu** *l.* China
48 H4 **Honiara** Solomon Is
99 B4 **Honiton** U.K.
66 D3 **Honjō** Japan
92 I1 **Honningsvåg** Norway
49 L1 **Honolulu** U.S.A.
67 B3 **Honshū** *i.* Japan
134 B1 **Hood, Mount** *vol.* U.S.A.
50 A3 **Hood Point** Austr.
134 B1 **Hood River** U.S.A.
100 B2 **Hoogerheide** Neth.
100 C1 **Hoogeveen** Neth.
100 C1 **Hoogezand-Sappemeer** Neth.
100 C2 **Hoog-Keppel** Neth.
Hook of Holland Neth. *see* **Hoek van Holland**
128 A2 **Hoonah** U.S.A.
123 C2 **Hoopstad** S. Africa
100 B1 **Hoorn** Neth.
49 J5 **Hoorn, Îles de** *is* Wallis and Futuna Is
128 B3 **Hope** Can.
142 B2 **Hope** U.S.A.
83 N2 **Hope, Point** U.S.A.
131 D2 **Hopedale** Can.
Hopei *prov.* China *see* **Hebei**
145 D3 **Hopelchén** Mex.
131 D2 **Hope Mountains** Can.
Hopes Advance Bay Can. *see* **Aupaluk**
52 B3 **Hopetoun** Austr.
122 B2 **Hopetown** S. Africa
141 D3 **Hopewell** U.S.A.
130 C2 **Hopewell Islands** Can.
50 B2 **Hopkins, Lake** *salt flat* Austr.
140 B3 **Hopkinsville** U.S.A.
134 B1 **Hoquiam** U.S.A.
81 C1 **Horasan** Turkey
93 F4 **Hörby** Sweden
89 D3 **Horki** Belarus
91 D2 **Horlivka** Ukr.
79 D2 **Hormak** Iran
79 C2 **Hormuz, Strait of** Iran/Oman
103 D2 **Horn** Austria
92 □A2 **Horn** *c.* Iceland
153 B5 **Horn, Cape** Chile
141 D2 **Hornell** U.S.A.
130 B3 **Hornepayne** Can.
Hornos, Cabo de *c.* Chile *see* **Horn, Cape**
53 D2 **Hornsby** Austr.
98 C3 **Hornsea** U.K.
90 B2 **Horodenka** Ukr.
91 C1 **Horodnya** Ukr.
90 B2 **Horodok** Ukr.
90 A2 **Horodok** Ukr.
90 A1 **Horokhiv** Ukr.
Horqin Youyi Qianqi China *see* **Ulanhot**
131 E2 **Horse Islands** Can.
52 B3 **Horsham** Austr.
99 C4 **Horsham** U.K.
93 F4 **Horten** Norway
126 D2 **Horton** *r.* Can.
117 B4 **Hosa'ina** Eth.
74 A2 **Hoshab** Pak.
74 B1 **Hoshiarpur** India
138 B1 **Hosta Butte** *mt.* U.S.A.
75 C1 **Hotan** China
122 B2 **Hotazel** S. Africa
92 G3 **Hoting** Sweden
142 B2 **Hot Springs** *AR* U.S.A.
Hot Springs U.S.A. *see* **Truth or Consequences**
136 C2 **Hot Springs** *SD* U.S.A.
128 C1 **Hottah Lake** Can.
100 B2 **Houffalize** Belgium
140 B1 **Houghton** U.S.A.
141 F1 **Houlton** U.S.A.
70 B2 **Houma** China
142 B3 **Houma** U.S.A.
128 B2 **Houston** Can.
139 D3 **Houston** U.S.A.
50 A2 **Houtman Abrolhos** *is* Austr.
122 B3 **Houwater** S. Africa
68 C1 **Hovd** Mongolia
99 C4 **Hove** U.K.
90 A2 **Hoverla, Hora** *mt.* Ukr.
68 C1 **Hövsgöl Nuur** *l.* Mongolia
68 C2 **Hövüün** Mongolia
116 A3 **Howar, Wadi** *watercourse* Sudan
98 C3 **Howden** U.K.
53 C3 **Howe, Cape** Austr.
123 D2 **Howick** S. Africa
49 J3 **Howland Island** *terr.* N. Pacific Ocean
53 C3 **Howlong** Austr.
Howrah India *see* **Hāora**
142 B1 **Hoxie** U.S.A.
101 D2 **Höxter** Ger.
96 C1 **Hoy** *i.* U.K.
93 E3 **Høyanger** Norway
102 C1 **Hoyerswerda** Ger.
103 D1 **Hradec Králové** Czech Rep.
109 C2 **Hrasnica** Bos.-Herz.
92 □B2 **Hraun** Iceland
91 C1 **Hrebinka** Ukr.
88 B3 **Hrodna** Belarus
62 A1 **Hsi-hseng** Myanmar
71 C3 **Hsinchu** Taiwan
71 C3 **Hsinying** Taiwan
62 A1 **Hsipaw** Myanmar
70 A2 **Huachi** China
150 B4 **Huacho** Peru
70 B1 **Huade** China
65 B1 **Huadian** China
70 B2 **Huaibei** China
70 B2 **Huai He** *r.* China
71 A3 **Huaihua** China
70 B2 **Huainan** China
70 B2 **Huaiyang** China
70 B2 **Huaiyin** China
145 C3 **Huajuápan de León** Mex.
59 C3 **Huaki** Indon.
71 C3 **Hualien** Taiwan
150 B3 **Huallaga** *r.* Peru
120 A2 **Huambo** Angola
150 B4 **Huancavelica** Peru
150 B4 **Huancayo** Peru
Huangcaoba China *see* **Xingyi**
70 B2 **Huangchuan** China
Huang Hai *sea* N. Pacific Ocean *see* **Yellow Sea**
70 B2 **Huang He** *r.* China
71 A4 **Huangliu** China
70 B3 **Huangshan** China
70 B2 **Huangshi** China
70 A2 **Huangtu Gaoyuan** *plat.* China
71 C3 **Huangyan** China
70 A2 **Huangyuan** China
65 B1 **Huanren** China
150 B3 **Huánuco** Peru
152 B1 **Huanuni** Bol.
150 B4 **Huaral** Peru
150 B3 **Huaráz** Peru
150 B4 **Huarmey** Peru
152 A2 **Huasco** Chile
152 A2 **Huasco** *r.* Chile
144 B2 **Huatabampo** Mex.
145 C3 **Huatusco** Mex.
71 A3 **Huayuan** China
70 B2 **Hubei** *prov.* China
73 B3 **Hubli** India
100 C2 **Hückelhoven** Ger.
99 C3 **Hucknall** U.K.
98 C3 **Huddersfield** U.K.
93 G3 **Hudiksvall** Sweden
141 E2 **Hudson** *r.* U.S.A.
129 D2 **Hudson Bay** Can.
127 G3 **Hudson Bay** *sea* Can.
128 B2 **Hudson's Hope** Can.
127 H2 **Hudson Strait** Can.
63 B2 **Huê** Vietnam
146 A3 **Huehuetenango** Guat.
144 B2 **Huehueto, Cerro** *mt.* Mex.
145 C2 **Huejutla** Mex.
106 B2 **Huelva** Spain
107 C2 **Huércal-Overa** Spain
107 C1 **Huesca** Spain
106 C2 **Huéscar** Spain
51 D2 **Hughenden** Austr.
50 B3 **Hughes** Austr.
75 C2 **Hugli** *r. mouth* India
139 D2 **Hugo** U.S.A.
Huhehot China *see* **Huhhot**
70 B1 **Huhhot** China
122 B2 **Huhudi** S. Africa
122 A2 **Huib-Hoch Plateau** Namibia
71 B3 **Huichang** China
Huicheng China *see* **Huilai**
65 B1 **Huich'ŏn** N. Korea
71 B3 **Huilai** China
120 A2 **Huíla Plateau** Angola
71 A3 **Huili** China
70 B2 **Huimin** China
69 E2 **Huinan** China
Huinan China *see* **Nanhui**
93 H3 **Huittinen** Fin.
145 C3 **Huixtla** Mex.
Huiyang China *see* **Huizhou**
71 A3 **Huize** China
71 B3 **Huizhou** China
68 C1 **Hujirt** Mongolia
78 B2 **Hujr** Saudi Arabia
122 B1 **Hukuntsi** Botswana
78 B2 **Ḥulayfah** Saudi Arabia
66 B1 **Hulin** China
130 C3 **Hull** Can.
70 C1 **Huludao** China
Hulun China *see* **Hailar**
69 D1 **Hulun Nur** *l.* China
91 D2 **Hulyaypole** Ukr.
69 E1 **Huma** China
150 C3 **Humaitá** Brazil
122 B3 **Humansdorp** S. Africa
98 C2 **Humber** *est.* U.K.
139 D3 **Humble** U.S.A.
129 D2 **Humboldt** Can.
135 C2 **Humboldt** *NV* U.S.A.
142 C1 **Humboldt** *TN* U.S.A.
135 C2 **Humboldt** *r.* U.S.A.
103 E2 **Humenné** Slovakia
53 C3 **Hume Reservoir** Austr.
138 A1 **Humphreys Peak** U.S.A.
65 A1 **Hun** *r.* China
115 D2 **Hūn** Libya
92 □A2 **Húnaflói** *b.* Iceland
71 B3 **Hunan** *prov.* China
65 C1 **Hunchun** China
110 B1 **Hunedoara** Romania
101 D2 **Hünfeld** Ger.
103 D2 **Hungary** *country* Europe
52 B1 **Hungerford** Austr.
65 B2 **Hŭngnam** N. Korea
Hunjiang China *see* **Baishan**
99 D3 **Hunstanton** U.K.
101 D1 **Hunte** *r.* Ger.
48 I6 **Hunter Island** S. Pacific Ocean
51 D4 **Hunter Islands** Austr.
99 C3 **Huntingdon** U.K.
140 B2 **Huntington** *IN* U.S.A.
140 C3 **Huntington** *WV* U.S.A.
135 C4 **Huntington Beach** U.S.A.
54 C1 **Huntly** N.Z.
96 C2 **Huntly** U.K.
130 C3 **Huntsville** Can.
142 C2 **Huntsville** *AL* U.S.A.
139 D2 **Huntsville** *TX* U.S.A.
Hunyani *r.* Moz./Zimbabwe *see* **Manyame**
59 D3 **Huon Peninsula** P.N.G.
Huoxian China *see* **Huozhou**
70 B2 **Huozhou** China
Hupeh *prov.* China *see* **Hubei**
116 B2 **Hurghada** Egypt
137 D2 **Huron** U.S.A.
140 C2 **Huron, Lake** Can./U.S.A.
135 D3 **Hurricane** U.S.A.
100 C2 **Hürth** Ger.
92 □B2 **Húsavík** Iceland
110 C1 **Huşi** Romania
126 B2 **Huslia** U.S.A.
78 B3 **Ḥusn Āl 'Abr** Yemen
102 B1 **Husum** Ger.
68 C1 **Hutag** Mongolia
60 A1 **Hutanopan** Indon.
137 D3 **Hutchinson** U.S.A.
143 D3 **Hutchinson Island** U.S
70 B2 **Hutuo** *r.* China
100 B2 **Huy** Belgium
70 C2 **Huzhou** China
92 □C3 **Hvalnes** Iceland
92 □B3 **Hvannadalshnúkur** *vol* Iceland
109 C2 **Hvar** Croatia
109 C2 **Hvar** *i.* Croatia
91 C2 **Hvardiys'ke** Ukr.
120 B2 **Hwange** Zimbabwe
Hwang Ho *r.* China *see* **Huang He**
136 C2 **Hyannis** U.S.A.
68 C1 **Hyargas Nuur** *salt l.* Mongolia
50 A3 **Hyden** Austr.
73 B3 **Hyderabad** India
74 A2 **Hyderabad** Pak.
Hydra *i.* Greece *see* **Yd**
105 D3 **Hyères** France
105 D3 **Hyères, Îles d'** *is* Franc
65 B1 **Hyesan** N. Korea
128 B2 **Hyland Post** Can.
67 B3 **Hyōno-sen** *mt.* Japan
99 D4 **Hythe** U.K.
67 B4 **Hyūga** Japan
93 H3 **Hyvinkää** Fin.

I

150 C3 **Iaco** *r.* Brazil
110 C2 **Ialomița** *r.* Romania
110 C1 **Ianca** Romania
110 C1 **Iași** Romania
64 A2 **Iba** Phil.
115 C4 **Ibadan** Nigeria
150 B2 **Ibagué** Col.
154 B2 **Ibaiti** Brazil
150 B2 **Ibarra** Ecuador
78 B3 **Ibb** Yemen
100 C1 **Ibbenbüren** Ger.
115 C4 **Ibi** Nigeria
107 C2 **Ibi** Spain
155 C1 **Ibiá** Brazil
155 D1 **Ibiaí** Brazil
155 D1 **Ibiraçu** Brazil
107 D2 **Ibiza** *i.* Spain
151 E4 **Ibotirama** Brazil
79 C2 **Ibrā'** Oman
79 C2 **Ibrī** Oman
150 B4 **Ica** Peru
Icaria *i.* Greece *see* **Ika**
80 B2 **İçel** Turkey
92 □A3 **Iceland** *country* Europe
160 M4 **Iceland Basin** *sea featu* N. Atlantic Ocean
160 L3 **Icelandic Plateau** *sea feature* N. Atlantic Ocean
66 D3 **Ichinoseki** Japan
91 C1 **Ichnya** Ukr.
65 B2 **Ich'ŏn** N. Korea
151 F3 **Icó** Brazil
155 D2 **Iconha** Brazil
139 E2 **Idabel** U.S.A.
115 C4 **Idah** Nigeria
134 D2 **Idaho** *state* U.S.A.
134 D2 **Idaho Falls** U.S.A.
100 C3 **Idar-Oberstein** Ger.
68 C1 **Ideriyn Gol** *r.* Mongolia
116 B2 **Idfu** Egypt
115 D2 **Idhān Awbārī** *des.* Liby
115 D2 **Idhān Murzūq** *des.* Liby
Idi Amin Dada, Lake Dem. Rep. Congo/Ugan *see* **Edward, Lake**
118 B3 **Idiofa** Dem. Rep. Congo
80 B2 **Idlib** Syria
123 C3 **Idutywa** S. Africa
88 B2 **Iecava** Latvia
154 B2 **Iepê** Brazil
100 A2 **Ieper** Belgium
111 C3 **Ierapetra** Greece
119 D3 **Ifakara** Tanz.
121 □D3 **Ifanadiana** Madag.
115 C4 **Ife** Nigeria
114 C3 **Ifôghas, Adrar des** *hills* Mali

C3 **Ifumo** Dem. Rep. Congo
C1 **Igan** *Sarawak* Malaysia
D2 **Iganga** Uganda
C2 **Igarapava** Brazil
G2 **Igarka** Rus. Fed.
A2 **Igatimí** Para.
B3 **Igatpuri** India
C2 **Iğdır** Turkey
A3 **Iglesias** *Sardinia* Italy
G2 **Igloolik** Can.
Igluligaarjuk Can. *see* **Chesterfield Inlet**
A3 **Ignace** Can.
C2 **Ignalina** Lith.
C2 **İğneada** Turkey
C2 **İğneada Burnu** *pt* Turkey
B3 **Igoumenitsa** Greece
E3 **Igra** Rus. Fed.
F2 **Igrim** Rus. Fed.
B3 **Iguaçu** *r.* Brazil
B3 **Iguaçu Falls** Arg./Brazil
C3 **Iguala** Mex.
D1 **Igualada** Spain
C2 **Iguape** Brazil
B2 **Iguatemi** Brazil
B2 **Iguatemi** *r.* Brazil
F3 **Iguatu** Brazil
A3 **Iguéla** Gabon
D3 **Igunga** Tanz.
□D2 **Iharaña** Madag.
D2 **Ihbulag** Mongolia
□D3 **Ihosy** Madag.
2 **Iijoki** *r.* Fin.
3 **Iisalmi** Fin.
B4 **Iizuka** Japan
C4 **Ijebu-Ode** Nigeria
B1 **IJmuiden** Neth.
B1 **IJssel** *r.* Neth.
B1 **IJsselmeer** *l.* Neth.
C2 **Ijuí** Brazil
Ikaahuk Can. *see* **Sachs Harbour**
C2 **Ikageleng** S. Africa
C2 **Ikageng** S. Africa
C3 **Ikaria** *i.* Greece
C3 **Ikela** Dem. Rep. Congo
B2 **Ikhtiman** Bulg.
A4 **Iki** *i.* Japan
A2 **Ikom** Nigeria
□D3 **Ikongo** Madag.
B2 **Iksan** S. Korea
D3 **Ikungu** Tanz.
C2 **Ilaferh, Oued** *watercourse* Alg.
B2 **Ilagan** Phil.
C2 **Īlām** Iran
C2 **Ilam** Nepal
C1 **Iława** Pol.
C2 **Ilazārān, Kūh-e** *mt.* Iran
D2 **Île-à-la-Crosse** Can.
D2 **Île-à-la-Crosse, Lac** *l.* Can.
C3 **Ilebo** Dem. Rep. Congo
D2 **Ileret** Kenya
D4 **Ilford** U.K.
A4 **Ilfracombe** U.K.
C2 **Ilhabela** Brazil
D2 **Ilha Grande, Baía da** *b.* Brazil
B2 **Ilha Grande, Represa** *resr* Brazil
B2 **Ilha Solteíra, Represa** *resr* Brazil
B1 **Ílhavo** Port.
F4 **Ilhéus** Brazil
Ili Kazakh. *see* **Kapchagay**
B3 **Iliamna Lake** U.S.A.
B3 **Iligan** Phil.
Iliysk Kazakh. *see* **Kapchagay**
C3 **Ilkley** U.K.
A3 **Illapel** Chile
C2 **Illichivs'k** Ukr.
A3 **Illinois** *r.* U.S.A.
B3 **Illinois** *state* U.S.A.
B2 **Illintsi** Ukr.
C2 **Illizi** Alg.
D2 **Il'men', Ozero** *l.* Rus. Fed.
E2 **Ilmenau** Ger.
B4 **Ilo** Peru
B2 **Iloilo** Phil.
J3 **Ilomantsi** Fin.
C4 **Ilorin** Nigeria
D4 **Ilovlya** Rus. Fed.
D1 **Iluka** Austr.
2 **Ilulissat** Greenland
Iman Rus. Fed. *see* **Dal'nerechensk**
B1 **Iman** *r.* Rus. Fed.
A4 **Imari** Japan
93 I3 **Imatra** Fin.
imeni Petra Stuchki Latvia *see* **Aizkraukle**
117 C4 **Īmī** Eth.
65 B2 **Imjin-gang** *r.* N. Korea/S. Korea
143 D3 **Immokalee** U.S.A.
108 B2 **Imola** Italy
151 E3 **Imperatriz** Brazil
108 A2 **Imperia** Italy
136 C2 **Imperial** U.S.A.
118 B2 **Impfondo** Congo
72 D2 **Imphal** India
111 C2 **İmroz** Turkey
67 C3 **Ina** Japan
150 C4 **Inambari** *r.* Peru
115 C2 **In Aménas** Alg.
115 C2 **In Amguel** Alg.
54 B2 **Inangahua Junction** N.Z.
59 C3 **Inanwatan** Indon.
92 I2 **Inari** Fin.
92 I2 **Inarijärvi** *l.* Fin.
67 D3 **Inawashiro-ko** *l.* Japan
80 B1 **İnce Burun** *pt* Turkey
65 B2 **Inch'ŏn** S. Korea
121 C2 **Inchope** Moz.
123 D2 **Incomati** *r.* Moz.
116 B3 **Inda Silasē** Eth.
144 B2 **Indé** Mex.
135 C3 **Independence** *CA* U.S.A.
137 E2 **Independence** *IA* U.S.A.
137 D3 **Independence** *KS* U.S.A.
137 E3 **Independence** *MO* U.S.A.
134 C2 **Independence Mountains** U.S.A.
76 B2 **Inderborskiy** Kazakh.
72 D2 **India** *country* Asia
141 D2 **Indiana** U.S.A.
140 B2 **Indiana** *state* U.S.A.
140 B3 **Indianapolis** U.S.A.
129 D2 **Indian Head** Can.
159 **Indian Ocean**
137 E2 **Indianola** *IA* U.S.A.
142 B2 **Indianola** *MS* U.S.A.
135 D3 **Indian Peak** U.S.A.
135 C3 **Indian Springs** U.S.A.
86 D2 **Indiga** Rus. Fed.
83 K2 **Indigirka** *r.* Rus. Fed.
109 D1 **Inđija** Yugo.
135 C4 **Indio** U.S.A.
58 B3 **Indonesia** *country* Asia
74 B2 **Indore** India
60 B2 **Indramayu, Tanjung** *pt* Indon.
Indrapura, Gunung *vol.* Indon. *see* **Kerinci, Gunung**
75 C3 **Indravati** *r.* India
104 C2 **Indre** *r.* France
74 A2 **Indus** *r.* China/Pak.
74 A2 **Indus, Mouths of the** Pak.
159 E2 **Indus Cone** *sea feature* Indian Ocean
80 B1 **İnebolu** Turkey
111 C2 **İnegöl** Turkey
Infantes Spain *see* **Villanueva de los Infantes**
144 B3 **Infiernillo, Presa** *resr* Mex.
51 D1 **Ingham** Austr.
53 D1 **Inglewood** Austr.
102 C2 **Ingolstadt** Ger.
75 C2 **Ingrāj Bāzār** India
123 D2 **Ingwavuma** S. Africa
120 B2 **Ingwe** Zambia
123 D2 **Inhaca** Moz.
121 C3 **Inhambane** Moz.
121 C2 **Inhaminga** Moz.
151 D2 **Inini** Fr. Guiana
Inis Rep. of Ireland *see* **Ennis**
97 A2 **Inishbofin** *i.* Rep. of Ireland
97 B2 **Inishmore** *i.* Rep. of Ireland
97 C1 **Inishowen** *pen.* Rep. of Ireland
54 B2 **Inland Kaikoura Range** *mts* N.Z.
Inland Sea Japan *see* **Seto-naikai**
102 C2 **Inn** *r.* Europe
127 H1 **Innaanganeq** *c.* Greenland
52 B1 **Innamincka** Austr.
Inner Mongolia *aut. reg.* China *see* **Nei Mongol Zizhiqu**
96 B2 **Inner Sound** *sea chan.* U.K.
51 D1 **Innisfail** Austr.
102 C2 **Innsbruck** Austria
97 C2 **Inny** *r.* Rep. of Ireland
154 B1 **Inocência** Brazil
118 B3 **Inongo** Dem. Rep. Congo
111 D3 **İnönü** Turkey
Inoucdjouac Can. *see* **Inukjuak**
103 D1 **Inowrocław** Pol.
114 C2 **In Salah** Alg.
62 A2 **Insein** Myanmar
110 C2 **Însurăţei** Romania
86 F2 **Inta** Rus. Fed.
105 D2 **Interlaken** Switz.
137 E1 **International Falls** U.S.A.
63 A2 **Interview Island** India
130 C2 **Inukjuak** Can.
126 D2 **Inuvik** Can.
96 B2 **Inveraray** U.K.
96 C2 **Inverbervie** U.K.
54 A3 **Invercargill** N.Z.
53 D1 **Inverell** Austr.
96 B2 **Invergordon** U.K.
128 C2 **Invermere** Can.
131 D3 **Inverness** Can.
96 B2 **Inverness** U.K.
96 C2 **Inverurie** U.K.
159 F4 **Investigator Ridge** *sea feature* Indian Ocean
52 A3 **Investigator Strait** Austr.
77 E1 **Inya** Rus. Fed.
Inyanga Zimbabwe *see* **Nyanga**
119 D3 **Inyonga** Tanz.
87 D3 **Inza** Rus. Fed.
111 B3 **Ioannina** Greece
137 D3 **Iola** U.S.A.
96 A2 **Iona** *i.* U.K.
111 B3 **Ionian Islands** Greece
109 C3 **Ionian Sea** Greece/Italy
Ionioi Nisoi *is* Greece *see* **Ionian Islands**
111 C3 **Ios** *i.* Greece
137 E2 **Iowa** *state* U.S.A.
137 E2 **Iowa City** U.S.A.
154 C1 **Ipameri** Brazil
155 D1 **Ipatinga** Brazil
81 C1 **Ipatovo** Rus. Fed.
123 C2 **Ipelegeng** S. Africa
150 B2 **Ipiales** Col.
151 F4 **Ipiaú** Brazil
154 B3 **Ipiranga** Brazil
150 B3 **Ipixuna** Brazil
60 B1 **Ipoh** Malaysia
154 B1 **Iporá** Brazil
118 C2 **Ippy** C.A.R.
111 C2 **İpsala** Turkey
53 D1 **Ipswich** Austr.
99 D3 **Ipswich** U.K.
127 H2 **Iqaluit** Can.
152 A2 **Iquique** Chile
150 B3 **Iquitos** Peru
Irakleio Greece *see* **Iraklion**
111 C3 **Iraklion** Greece
81 D2 **Iran** *country* Asia
61 C1 **Iran, Pegunungan** *mts* Indon.
79 D2 **Īrānshahr** Iran
144 B2 **Irapuato** Mex.
81 C2 **Iraq** *country* Asia
154 B3 **Irati** Brazil
88 B2 **Irbe Strait** Estonia/Latvia
80 B2 **Irbid** Jordan
86 F3 **Irbit** Rus. Fed.
151 E4 **Irecê** Brazil
97 C2 **Ireland, Republic of** *country* Europe
118 C3 **Irema** Dem. Rep. Congo
76 C2 **Irgiz** Kazakh.
Iri S. Korea *see* **Iksan**
59 D3 **Irian Jaya** *reg.* Indon.
115 E3 **Iriba** Chad
114 B3 **Irîgui** *reg.* Mali/Maur.
119 D3 **Iringa** Tanz.
151 D3 **Iriri** *r.* Brazil
Irish Free State *country* Europe *see* **Ireland, Republic of**
95 B3 **Irish Sea** Rep. of Ireland/U.K.
68 C1 **Irkutsk** Rus. Fed.
160 M4 **Irminger Basin** *sea feature* N. Atlantic Ocean
141 D2 **Irondequoit** U.S.A.
52 A2 **Iron Knob** Austr.
140 B1 **Iron Mountain** U.S.A.
140 C3 **Ironton** U.S.A.
140 A1 **Ironwood** U.S.A.
130 B3 **Iroquois Falls** Can.
64 B2 **Irosin** Phil.
67 C4 **Irō-zaki** *pt* Japan
90 C1 **Irpin'** Ukr.
62 A2 **Irrawaddy** *r.* Myanmar
63 A2 **Irrawaddy, Mouths of the** Myanmar
86 F2 **Irtysh** *r.* Kazakh./Rus. Fed.
107 C1 **Irún** Spain
96 B3 **Irvine** U.K.
139 D2 **Irving** U.S.A.
64 B3 **Isabela** Phil.
146 B3 **Isabelia, Cordillera** *mts* Nic.
92 □A2 **Ísafjarðardjúp** *est.* Iceland
92 □A2 **Ísafjörður** Iceland
67 B4 **Isahaya** Japan
102 C2 **Isar** *r.* Ger.
96 □ **Isbister** U.K.
108 B2 **Ischia, Isola d'** *i.* Italy
67 C4 **Ise** Japan
118 C2 **Isengi** Dem. Rep. Congo
105 C3 **Isère** *r.* France
100 C2 **Iserlohn** Ger.
101 D1 **Isernhagen** Ger.
67 C4 **Ise-wan** *b.* Japan
114 C4 **Iseyin** Nigeria
Isfahan Iran *see* **Eşfahān**
66 D2 **Ishikari-wan** *b.* Japan
77 D1 **Ishim** *r.* Kazakh./Rus. Fed.
82 F3 **Ishim** Rus. Fed.
67 D3 **Ishinomaki** Japan
67 D3 **Ishioka** Japan
67 B4 **Ishizuchi-san** *mt.* Japan
74 B1 **Ishkoshim** Tajik.
140 B1 **Ishpeming** U.S.A.
111 C2 **Işıklar Dağı** *mts* Turkey
111 C3 **Işıklı** Turkey
123 D2 **Isipingo** S. Africa
119 C2 **Isiro** Dem. Rep. Congo
80 B2 **İskenderun** Turkey
82 G3 **Iskitim** Rus. Fed.
110 B2 **Iskŭr** *r.* Bulg.
117 D3 **Iskushuban** Somalia
128 A2 **Iskut** *r.* Can.
74 B1 **Islamabad** Pak.
143 D4 **Islamorada** U.S.A.
52 A2 **Island Lagoon** *salt flat* Austr.
129 E2 **Island Lake** Can.
54 B1 **Islands, Bay of** N.Z.
Islas Canarias *is* N. Atlantic Ocean *see* **Canary Islands**
96 A3 **Islay** *i.* U.K.
98 A2 **Isle of Man** *i.* Irish Sea
Ismail Ukr. *see* **Izmayil**
116 B1 **Ismâ'ilîya** Egypt
116 B2 **Isna** Egypt
121 □D3 **Isoanala** Madag.
121 C2 **Isoka** Zambia
93 H3 **Isokyrö** Fin.
109 C3 **Isola di Capo Rizzuto** Italy
Ispahan Iran *see* **Eşfahān**
80 B2 **Isparta** Turkey
110 C2 **Isperikh** Bulg.
Ispisar Tajik. *see* **Khŭjand**
80 B2 **Israel** *country* Asia
50 B3 **Israelite Bay** Austr.
105 C2 **Issoire** France
Issyk-Kul' Kyrg. *see* **Balykchy**
111 C2 **İstanbul** Turkey
İstanbul Boğazı *str.* Turkey *see* **Bosporus**
103 D2 **Isten dombja** *hill* Hungary
111 B3 **Istiaia** Greece
143 D3 **Istokpoga, Lake** U.S.A.
108 B1 **Istra** *pen.* Croatia
105 C3 **Istres** France
Istria *pen.* Croatia *see* **Istra**
155 D2 **Itabapoana** Brazil
151 E4 **Itaberaba** Brazil
154 C1 **Itaberaí** Brazil
155 D1 **Itabira** Brazil
155 D2 **Itabirito** Brazil
151 F4 **Itabuna** Brazil
150 D3 **Itacoatiara** Brazil
155 D2 **Itaguaí** Brazil
154 B2 **Itaguajé** Brazil
154 C2 **Itaí** Brazil
154 C3 **Itaiópolis** Brazil
154 B3 **Itaipu, Represa de** *resr* Brazil
151 D3 **Itaituba** Brazil
154 C3 **Itajaí** Brazil
155 C2 **Itajubá** Brazil
108 B2 **Italy** *country* Europe
155 E1 **Itamaraju** Brazil
155 D1 **Itamarandiba** Brazil
155 D1 **Itambacuri** Brazil
155 D1 **Itambé, Pico de** *mt.* Brazil
75 D2 **Itanagar** India

154 C2 **Itanhaém** Brazil
155 D1 **Itanhém** Brazil
155 D1 **Itaobím** Brazil
154 C1 **Itapajipe** Brazil
155 E1 **Itapebi** Brazil
155 D2 **Itapemirim** Brazil
155 D2 **Itaperuna** Brazil
155 D1 **Itapetinga** Brazil
154 C2 **Itapetininga** Brazil
154 C2 **Itapeva** Brazil
151 F4 **Itapicuru** *r.* Brazil
151 E3 **Itapicuru Mirim** Brazil
155 C2 **Itapira** Brazil
154 C2 **Itaporanga** Brazil
154 C1 **Itapuranga** Brazil
154 C2 **Itararé** Brazil
74 B2 **Itarsi** India
154 B1 **Itarumã** Brazil
155 D2 **Itaúna** Brazil
155 E1 **Itaúnas** Brazil
64 B1 **Itbayat** *i.* Phil.
141 D2 **Ithaca** U.S.A.
101 D1 **Ith Hils** *ridge* Ger.
118 C2 **Itimbiri** *r.* Dem. Rep. Congo
155 D1 **Itinga** Brazil
154 B1 **Itiquira** Brazil
154 A1 **Itiquira** *r.* Brazil
67 C4 **Itō** Japan
154 C2 **Itu** Brazil
150 B3 **Ituí** *r.* Brazil
154 C1 **Ituiutaba** Brazil
119 C3 **Itula** Dem. Rep. Congo
154 C1 **Itumbiara** Brazil
154 C1 **Itumbiara, Barragem** *resr* Brazil
154 B1 **Iturama** Brazil
101 D1 **Itzehoe** Ger.
83 N2 **Iul'tin** Rus. Fed.
155 D2 **Iúna** Brazil
154 B2 **Ivaí** *r.* Brazil
92 I2 **Ivalo** Fin.
88 C3 **Ivanava** Belarus
109 C1 **Ivanec** Croatia
Ivangrad Yugo. *see* **Berane**
52 B2 **Ivanhoe** Austr.
90 B1 **Ivankiv** Ukr.
90 A2 **Ivano-Frankivs'k** Ukr.
89 F2 **Ivanovo** Rus. Fed.
88 C3 **Ivatsevichy** Belarus
111 C2 **Ivaylovgrad** Bulg.
86 F2 **Ivdel'** Rus. Fed.
110 C1 **Iveşti** Romania
154 B2 **Ivinheima** Brazil
154 B2 **Ivinheima** *r.* Brazil
127 I2 **Ivittuut** Greenland
Iviza *i.* Spain *see* **Ibiza**
89 E3 **Ivnya** Rus. Fed.
Ivory Coast *country* Africa *see* **Côte d'Ivoire**
108 A1 **Ivrea** Italy
111 C3 **İvrindi** Turkey
Ivugivik Can. *see* **Ivujivik**
127 G2 **Ivujivik** Can.
67 D3 **Iwaki** Japan
67 B4 **Iwakuni** Japan
66 D2 **Iwamizawa** Japan
66 D2 **Iwanai** Japan
66 D3 **Iwate-san** *vol.* Japan
88 C3 **Iwye** Belarus
123 D3 **Ixopo** S. Africa
144 B2 **Ixtlán** Mex.
146 B3 **Izabal, Lago de** *l.* Guat.
145 D2 **Izamal** Mex.
81 C1 **Izberbash** Rus. Fed.
86 E3 **Izhevsk** Rus. Fed.
86 E2 **Izhma** Rus. Fed.
Izhma Rus. Fed. *see* Sosnogorsk
89 E3 **Izmalkovo** Rus. Fed.
90 B2 **Izmayil** Ukr.
111 C3 **İzmir** Turkey
İzmit Turkey *see* **Kocaeli**
111 C2 **İznik Gölü** *l.* Turkey
145 C3 **Izúcar de Matamoros** Mex.
67 A4 **Izuhara** Japan
67 B3 **Izumo** Japan
156 C4 **Izu-Ogasawara Trench** *sea feature* N. Pacific Ocean
67 C4 **Izu-shotō** *is* Japan
90 B1 **Izyaslav** Ukr.
91 D2 **Izyum** Ukr.

J

74 A1 **Jabal as Sirāj** Afgh.
106 C2 **Jabalón** *r.* Spain
75 B2 **Jabalpur** India
50 C1 **Jabiru** Austr.
109 C2 **Jablanica** Bos.-Herz.
151 E2 **Jaboatão** Brazil
154 C2 **Jaboticabal** Brazil
107 C1 **Jaca** Spain
145 C2 **Jacala** Mex.
151 D3 **Jacareacanga** Brazil
155 C2 **Jacareí** Brazil
154 B1 **Jaciara** Brazil
155 D1 **Jacinto** Brazil
141 E1 **Jackman** U.S.A.
142 C2 **Jackson** *AL* U.S.A.
140 C2 **Jackson** *MI* U.S.A.
142 B2 **Jackson** *MS* U.S.A.
142 C1 **Jackson** *TN* U.S.A.
136 A2 **Jackson** *WY* U.S.A.
54 A2 **Jackson Head** *hd* N.Z.
142 B2 **Jacksonville** *AR* U.S.A.
143 D2 **Jacksonville** *FL* U.S.A.
140 A3 **Jacksonville** *IL* U.S.A.
143 E2 **Jacksonville** *NC* U.S.A.
139 D2 **Jacksonville** *TX* U.S.A.
147 C3 **Jacmel** Haiti
74 A2 **Jacobabad** Pak.
151 E4 **Jacobina** Brazil
131 D3 **Jacques Cartier, Mont** *mt.* Can.
151 E3 **Jacunda** Brazil
154 C2 **Jacupiranga** Brazil
101 D1 **Jadebusen** *b.* Ger.
Jadotville Dem. Rep. Congo *see* **Likasi**
109 C2 **Jadovnik** *mt.* Bos.-Herz.
150 B3 **Jaén** Peru
106 C2 **Jaén** Spain
Jaffa Israel *see* **Tel Aviv-Yafo**
52 A3 **Jaffa, Cape** Austr.
73 B4 **Jaffna** Sri Lanka
75 C3 **Jagdalpur** India
123 C2 **Jagersfontein** S. Africa
79 C2 **Jaghīn** Iran
152 C3 **Jaguarão** Uru.
154 C2 **Jaguariaíva** Brazil
81 D3 **Jahrom** Iran
74 B2 **Jaipur** India
74 B2 **Jaisalmer** India
74 B2 **Jaitgarh** *hill* India
75 C2 **Jajarkot** Nepal
109 C2 **Jajce** Bos.-Herz.
Jajnagar *state* India *see* **Orissa**
60 B2 **Jakarta** Indon.
128 A1 **Jakes Corner** Can.
92 G2 **Jäkkvik** Sweden
Jakobshavn Greenland *see* **Ilulissat**
92 H3 **Jakobstad** Fin.
77 D3 **Jalālābād** Afgh.
77 D2 **Jalal-Abad** Kyrg.
74 B1 **Jalandhar** India
145 C3 **Jalapa Enríquez** Mex.
154 B2 **Jales** Brazil
74 B2 **Jalgaon** India
115 D4 **Jalingo** Nigeria
74 B3 **Jalna** India
74 B2 **Jalor** India
144 B2 **Jalostotitlán** Mex.
144 B2 **Jalpa** Mex.
75 C2 **Jalpaiguri** India
145 C2 **Jalpan** Mex.
115 E2 **Jālū** Libya
146 C3 **Jamaica** *country* West Indies
146 C3 **Jamaica Channel** Haiti/Jamaica
75 C2 **Jamalpur** Bangl.
60 B2 **Jambi** Indon.
137 D2 **James** *r. ND/SD* U.S.A.
141 D3 **James** *r. VA* U.S.A.
130 B2 **James Bay** Can.
52 A2 **Jamestown** Austr.
Jamestown Can. *see* **Wawa**
123 C3 **Jamestown** S. Africa
137 D1 **Jamestown** *ND* U.S.A.
141 D2 **Jamestown** *NY* U.S.A.
74 B1 **Jammu** Jammu and Kashmir
74 B1 **Jammu and Kashmir** *terr.* Asia
74 B2 **Jamnagar** India
74 B2 **Jampur** Pak.
93 I3 **Jämsä** Fin.
75 C2 **Jamshedpur** India
75 C2 **Jamuna** *r.* Bangl.
75 C2 **Janakpur** Nepal
155 D1 **Janaúba** Brazil
81 D2 **Jandaq** Iran
114 A2 **Jandía** *hill* Canary Is
135 B2 **Janesville** *CA* U.S.A.
140 B2 **Janesville** *WI* U.S.A.
154 A2 **Jango** Brazil
82 A2 **Jan Mayen** *i.* Arctic Ocean
122 B3 **Jansenville** S. Africa
155 D1 **Januária** Brazil
74 B2 **Jaora** India
66 C3 **Japan** *country* Asia
66 B3 **Japan, Sea of** N. Pacific Ocean
150 C3 **Japurá** *r.* Brazil
154 C1 **Jaraguá** Brazil
154 C3 **Jaraguá, Serra** *mts* Brazil
154 C3 **Jaraguá do Sul** Brazil
154 B2 **Jaraguari** Brazil
152 C2 **Jardim** Brazil
69 D1 **Jargalant** Mongolia
103 D1 **Jarocin** Pol.
103 E1 **Jarosław** Pol.
92 F3 **Järpen** Sweden
70 A2 **Jartai** China
150 C4 **Jarú** Brazil
Jarud China *see* **Lubei**
88 C1 **Järvenpää** Fin.
49 K4 **Jarvis Island** *terr.* S. Pacific Ocean
93 G3 **Järvsö** Sweden
79 C2 **Jāsk** Iran
103 E2 **Jasło** Pol.
55 A3 **Jason Peninsula** Antarctica
128 C2 **Jasper** Can.
142 C2 **Jasper** *AL* U.S.A.
140 B3 **Jasper** *IN* U.S.A.
139 E2 **Jasper** *TX* U.S.A.
Jassy Romania *see* **Iaşi**
103 D2 **Jastrzębie-Zdrój** Pol.
103 D2 **Jászberény** Hungary
154 B1 **Jataí** Brazil
74 A2 **Jati** Pak.
154 C2 **Jaú** Brazil
150 C3 **Jaú** *r.* Brazil
145 C2 **Jaumave** Mex.
75 C2 **Jaunpur** India
154 B1 **Jauru** Brazil
61 B2 **Java** *i.* Indon.
107 C1 **Javalambre, Sierra de** *mts* Spain
69 D1 **Javarthushuu** Mongolia
60 C2 **Java Sea** Indon.
156 B6 **Java Trench** *sea feature* Indian Ocean
Jawa *i.* Indon. *see* **Java**
117 C4 **Jawhar** Somalia
103 D1 **Jawor** Pol.
103 D1 **Jaworzno** Pol.
59 D3 **Jaya, Puncak** *mt.* Indon.
59 D3 **Jayapura** Indon.
128 B1 **Jean Marie River** Can.
131 D2 **Jeannin, Lac** *l.* Can.
Jebel, Bahr el *r.* Sudan/Uganda *see* White Nile
116 A3 **Jebel Abyad Plateau** Sudan
96 C3 **Jedburgh** U.K.
78 A2 **Jeddah** Saudi Arabia
108 A3 **Jedeida** Tunisia
101 E1 **Jeetze** *r.* Ger.
137 E2 **Jefferson** U.S.A.
135 C3 **Jefferson, Mount** U.S.A.
137 E3 **Jefferson City** U.S.A.
122 B3 **Jeffrey's Bay** S. Africa
88 C2 **Jēkabpils** Latvia
103 D1 **Jelenia Góra** Pol.
88 B2 **Jelgava** Latvia
60 B1 **Jemaja** *i.* Indon.
61 C2 **Jember** Indon.
101 E2 **Jena** Ger.
77 E2 **Jengish Chokusu** *mt.* China/Kyrg.
80 B2 **Jenīn** West Bank
142 B2 **Jennings** U.S.A.
151 E4 **Jequié** Brazil
155 D1 **Jequitaí** Brazil
155 D1 **Jequitinhonha** Brazil
155 E1 **Jequitinhonha** *r.* Brazil
147 C3 **Jérémie** Haiti
144 B2 **Jerez** Mex.
106 B2 **Jerez de la Frontera** Spain
109 D3 **Jergucat** Albania
115 C1 **Jerid, Chott el** *salt l.* Tunisia
134 D2 **Jerome** U.S.A.
95 C4 **Jersey** *i.* Channel Is
95 C4 **Jersey** *terr.* Channel Is
151 E3 **Jerumenha** Brazil
80 B2 **Jerusalem** Israel/West Bank
53 D3 **Jervis Bay Territory** *admin. div.* Austr.
108 B1 **Jesenice** Slovenia
108 B2 **Jesi** Italy
Jesselton Malaysia *se* Kota Kinabalu
101 F2 **Jessen** Ger.
75 C2 **Jessore** Bangl.
143 D2 **Jesup** U.S.A.
137 D3 **Jesus, Mount** *hill* U.S.
145 C3 **Jesús Carranza** Mex.
100 C1 **Jever** Ger.
74 B2 **Jhalawar** India
74 B1 **Jhang** Pak.
74 B2 **Jhansi** India
75 C2 **Jharsuguda** India
74 B1 **Jhelum** *r.* India/Pak.
74 B1 **Jhelum** Pak.
74 B2 **Jhunjhunūn** India
70 C2 **Jiading** China
69 E1 **Jiamusi** China
71 B3 **Ji'an** *Jiangxi* China
65 B1 **Ji'an** *Jilin* China
Jianchang China *see* Nancheng
62 A1 **Jianchuan** China
Jiandaoyu China *see* Zigui
70 B3 **Jiande** China
Jiangling China *see* Jingzhou
71 B3 **Jiangmen** China
70 B2 **Jiangsu** *prov.* China
71 B3 **Jiangxi** *prov.* China
70 A2 **Jiangyou** China
70 B3 **Jianli** China
71 B3 **Jianyang** *Fujian* China
70 A2 **Jianyang** *Sichuan* Chin
70 B2 **Jiaohe** *Hebei* China
69 E2 **Jiaohe** *Jilin* China
Jiaojiang China *see* Taizhou
70 C2 **Jiaozhou** China
70 B2 **Jiaozuo** China
Jiashan China *see* Mingguang
70 C2 **Jiaxing** China
68 C2 **Jiayuguan** China
Jiddah Saudi Arabia *s* Jeddah
92 G2 **Jiehkkevarri** *mt.* Norw
70 B2 **Jiexiu** China
70 A2 **Jigzhi** China
103 D2 **Jihlava** Czech Rep.
115 C1 **Jijel** Alg.
117 C4 **Jijiga** Eth.
117 C4 **Jilib** Somalia
69 E2 **Jilin** China
65 B1 **Jilin** *prov.* China
65 A1 **Jilin Handa Ling** *mts* China
117 B4 **Jīma** Eth.
110 B1 **Jimbolia** Romania
144 B2 **Jiménez** Mex.
139 C3 **Jiménez** Mex.
145 C2 **Jiménez** Mex.
70 B2 **Jinan** China
70 A2 **Jinchang** China
70 B2 **Jincheng** China
Jinchuan China *see* Jinchang
53 C3 **Jindabyne** Austr.
103 D2 **Jindřichův Hradec** Czech Rep.
Jin'e China *see* Longchang
70 A2 **Jingbian** China
71 B3 **Jingdezhen** China
62 B1 **Jingdong** China
53 C3 **Jingellic** Austr.
71 B3 **Jinggangshan** China
62 B1 **Jinghong** China
70 B2 **Jingmen** China
70 A2 **Jingning** China
70 B2 **Jingsha** China
70 A2 **Jingtai** China
71 A3 **Jingxi** China
Jingxian China *see* Jingzhou
65 B1 **Jingyu** China
70 A2 **Jingyuan** China
70 B2 **Jingzhou** *Hubei* China
71 A3 **Jingzhou** *Hunan* China
71 B3 **Jinhua** China
70 B1 **Jining** *Nei Mongol* Chin
70 B2 **Jining** *Shandong* China
119 D2 **Jinja** Uganda
117 B4 **Jinka** Eth.
146 B3 **Jinotega** Nic.
146 B3 **Jinotepe** Nic.
71 A3 **Jinping** China

Jinsha Jiang *r.* China *see* Yangtze
Jinshi China *see* **Xinning**
B3 **Jinshi** China
Jinxi China *see* **Lianshan**
C1 **Jinzhou** China
C3 **Jiparaná** *r.* Brazil
Jirang China *see* **Burang**
C2 **Jīroft** Iran
C2 **Jirwān** Saudi Arabia
A3 **Jishou** China
B2 **Jiu** *r.* Romania
A2 **Jiuding Shan** *mt.* China
B3 **Jiujiang** China
Jiulian China *see* **Mojiang**
D2 **Jiwani** Pak.
B1 **Jixi** China
B3 **Jīzān** Saudi Arabia
D1 **Joaíma** Brazil
João Belo Moz. *see* Xai-Xai
F3 **João Pessoa** Brazil
C1 **João Pinheiro** Brazil
B2 **Jodhpur** India
I3 **Joensuu** Fin.
C3 **Jōetsu** Japan
C3 **Jofane** Moz.
C2 **Jõgeva** Estonia
Jogjakarta Indon. *see* Yogyakarta
C2 **Johannesburg** S. Africa
C2 **John Day** U.S.A.
B1 **John Day** *r.* U.S.A.
C2 **John d'Or Prairie** Can.
E1 **John H. Kerr Reservoir** U.S.A.
C1 **John o'Groats** U.K.
D1 **Johnson City** U.S.A.
A1 **Johnson's Crossing** Can.
B3 **Johnston, Lake** *salt flat* Austr.
J2 **Johnston Atoll** N. Pacific Ocean
B3 **Johnstone** U.K.
Johnstone Lake Can. *see* Old Wives Lake
D2 **Johnstown** U.S.A.
B1 **Johor Bahru** Malaysia
C2 **Jõhvi** Estonia
C3 **Joinville** Brazil
D2 **Joinville** France
B3 **Joinville Island** Antarctica
G2 **Jokkmokk** Sweden
B2 **Jökulsá á Fjöllum** *r.* Iceland
B2 **Joliet** U.S.A.
C3 **Joliette** Can.
B3 **Jolo** Phil.
B3 **Jolo** *i.* Phil.
C2 **Jombang** Indon.
C2 **Jomsom** Nepal
B2 **Jonava** Lith.
B1 **Jonesboro** *AR* U.S.A.
B2 **Jonesboro** *LA* U.S.A.
F2 **Jonesport** U.S.A.
G1 **Jones Sound** *sea chan.* Can.
F4 **Jönköping** Sweden
C3 **Jonquière** Can.
C3 **Jonuta** Mex.
E3 **Joplin** U.S.A.
B2 **Jordan** *country* Asia
B2 **Jordan** *r.* Asia
E1 **Jordan** U.S.A.
D1 **Jordânia** Brazil
C2 **Jordan Valley** U.S.A.
D2 **Jorhat** India
D1 **Jork** Ger.
E4 **Jørpeland** Norway
C4 **Jos** Nigeria
C3 **José Cardel** Mex.
D2 **Joseph, Lac** *l.* Can.
B1 **Joseph Bonaparte Gulf** Austr.
C4 **Jos Plateau** Nigeria
E3 **Jotunheimen** *mts* Norway
B3 **Joubertina** S. Africa
C2 **Jouberton** S. Africa
C2 **Joué-lès-Tours** France
I3 **Joutseno** Fin.
B1 **Juan de Fuca Strait** Can./U.S.A.
B6 **Juan Fernández Islands** S. Pacific Ocean
Juanshui China *see* Tongcheng
B2 **Juaréz** Mex.
A1 **Juárez, Sierra de** *mts* Mex.
E3 **Juàzeiro** Brazil
F3 **Juàzeiro do Norte** Brazil

117 B4 **Juba** Sudan
117 C5 **Jubba** *r.* Somalia
78 B2 **Jubbah** Saudi Arabia
Jubbulpore India *see* Jabalpur
107 C2 **Júcar** *r.* Spain
154 B1 **Juçara** Brazil
145 C3 **Juchitán** Mex.
155 E1 **Jucuruçu** Brazil
102 C2 **Judenburg** Austria
155 E1 **Juerana** Brazil
101 D2 **Jühnde** Ger.
146 B3 **Juigalpa** Nic.
150 D4 **Juína** Brazil
100 C1 **Juist** *i.* Ger.
155 D2 **Juiz de Fora** Brazil
136 C2 **Julesburg** U.S.A.
150 B4 **Juliaca** Peru
Julianatop *mt.* Indon. *see* Mandala, Puncak
151 D2 **Juliana Top** *mt.* Suriname
Jullundur India *see* Jalandhar
107 C2 **Jumilla** Spain
75 C2 **Jumla** Nepal
Jumna *r.* India *see* **Yamuna**
74 B2 **Junagadh** India
139 D2 **Junction** U.S.A.
137 D3 **Junction City** U.S.A.
154 C2 **Jundiaí** Brazil
128 A2 **Juneau** U.S.A.
53 C2 **Junee** Austr.
105 D2 **Jungfrau** *mt.* Switz.
141 D2 **Juniata** *r.* U.S.A.
153 B3 **Junín** Arg.
92 G3 **Junsele** Sweden
134 C2 **Juntura** U.S.A.
Junxi China *see* **Datian**
Junxian China *see* Danjiangkou
154 B2 **Jupía, Represa** *resr* Brazil
143 D3 **Jupiter** U.S.A.
154 C2 **Juquiá** Brazil
117 A4 **Jur** *r.* Sudan
105 D2 **Jura** *mts* France/Switz.
96 B2 **Jura** *i.* U.K.
96 B3 **Jura, Sound of** *sea chan.* U.K.
88 B2 **Jurbarkas** Lith.
88 B2 **Jūrmala** Latvia
150 C3 **Juruá** *r.* Brazil
150 D3 **Juruena** *r.* Brazil
154 C2 **Jurumirim, Represa de** *resr* Brazil
151 D3 **Juruti** Brazil
150 C3 **Jutaí** *r.* Brazil
101 F2 **Jüterbog** Ger.
154 B2 **Juti** Brazil
145 D3 **Jutiapa** Guat.
Jutland *pen.* Denmark *see* Jylland
70 B2 **Juxian** China
81 D3 **Jūyom** Iran
122 B1 **Jwaneng** Botswana
93 E4 **Jylland** *pen.* Denmark
93 I3 **Jyväskylä** Fin.

K

74 B1 **K2** *mt.* China/Jammu and Kashmir
Kaakhka Turkm. *see* **Kaka**
92 I2 **Kaamanen** Fin.
61 D2 **Kabaena** *i.* Indon.
119 C3 **Kabalo** Dem. Rep. Congo
119 C3 **Kabambare** Dem. Rep. Congo
119 C3 **Kabare** Dem. Rep. Congo
119 C3 **Kabemba** Dem. Rep. Congo
130 B3 **Kabinakagami Lake** Can.
118 C3 **Kabinda** Dem. Rep. Congo
118 B2 **Kabo** C.A.R.
120 B2 **Kabompo** Zambia
119 C3 **Kabongo** Dem. Rep. Congo
77 C3 **Kābul** Afgh.
64 B3 **Kaburuang** *i.* Indon.
121 B2 **Kabwe** Zambia
109 D2 **Kačanik** Yugo.
74 A2 **Kachchh, Gulf of** India
83 I3 **Kachug** Rus. Fed.
81 C1 **Kaçkar Dağı** *mt.* Turkey
111 C2 **Kadıköy** Turkey
52 A2 **Kadina** Austr.
114 B3 **Kadiolo** Mali
Kadiyevka Ukr. *see* Stakhanov
73 B3 **Kadmat** *i.* India

89 F2 **Kadnikov** Rus. Fed.
121 B2 **Kadoma** Zimbabwe
63 A2 **Kadonkani** Myanmar
117 A3 **Kadugli** Sudan
115 C3 **Kaduna** Nigeria
89 E2 **Kaduy** Rus. Fed.
86 E2 **Kadzherom** Rus. Fed.
114 A3 **Kaédi** Maur.
118 B1 **Kaélé** Cameroon
65 B2 **Kaesŏng** N. Korea
118 C3 **Kafakumba** Dem. Rep. Congo
114 A3 **Kaffrine** Senegal
111 B3 **Kafireas, Akra** *pt* Greece
80 B2 **Kafr el Sheikh** Egypt
121 B2 **Kafue** Zambia
120 B2 **Kafue** *r.* Zambia
67 C3 **Kaga** Japan
118 B2 **Kaga Bandoro** C.A.R.
91 E2 **Kagal'nitskaya** Rus. Fed.
Kaganovichi Pervyye Ukr. *see* **Polis'ke**
60 A2 **Kagologolo** Indon.
67 B4 **Kagoshima** Japan
Kagul Moldova *see* **Cahul**
119 D3 **Kahama** Tanz.
90 C2 **Kaharlyk** Ukr.
61 C2 **Kahayan** *r.* Indon.
118 B3 **Kahemba** Dem. Rep. Congo
101 E2 **Kahla** Ger.
79 C2 **Kahnūj** Iran
92 H2 **Kahperusvaarat** *mts* Fin.
80 B2 **Kahramanmaraş** Turkey
79 C2 **Kahūrak** Iran
59 C3 **Kai, Kepulauan** *is* Indon.
115 C4 **Kaiama** Nigeria
54 B2 **Kaiapoi** N.Z.
59 C3 **Kai Besar** *i.* Indon.
70 B2 **Kaifeng** China
Kaihua China *see* Wenshan
122 B2 **Kaiingveld** *reg.* S. Africa
59 C3 **Kai Kecil** *i.* Indon.
54 B2 **Kaikoura** N.Z.
114 A4 **Kailahun** Sierra Leone
Kailas Range *mts* China *see* **Gangdisê Shan**
71 A3 **Kaili** China
59 C3 **Kaimana** Indon.
54 C1 **Kaimanawa Mountains** N.Z.
72 C2 **Kaimur Range** *hills* India
88 B2 **Käina** Estonia
67 C4 **Kainan** Japan
115 C3 **Kainji Reservoir** Nigeria
54 B1 **Kaipara Harbour** N.Z.
74 B2 **Kairana** India
115 D1 **Kairouan** Tunisia
100 C3 **Kaiserslautern** Ger.
55 I2 **Kaiser Wilhelm II Land** *reg.* Antarctica
54 B1 **Kaitaia** N.Z.
54 C1 **Kaitawa** N.Z.
Kaitong China *see* **Tongyu**
59 C3 **Kaiwatu** Indon.
65 A1 **Kaiyuan** *Liaoning* China
71 A3 **Kaiyuan** *Yunnan* China
92 I3 **Kajaani** Fin.
51 D2 **Kajabbi** Austr.
76 B3 **Kaka** Turkm.
122 B2 **Kakamas** S. Africa
119 D2 **Kakamega** Kenya
114 A4 **Kakata** Liberia
91 C2 **Kakhovka** Ukr.
91 C2 **Kakhovs'ke Vodoskhovyshche** *resr* Ukr.
Kakhul Moldova *see* **Cahul**
73 C3 **Kākināda** India
128 C1 **Kakisa** Can.
67 B4 **Kakogawa** Japan
119 C3 **Kakoswa** Dem. Rep. Congo
126 C2 **Kaktovik** U.S.A.
Kalaallit Nunaat *terr.* N. America *see* **Greenland**
59 C3 **Kalabahi** Indon.
120 B2 **Kalabo** Zambia
91 E1 **Kalach** Rus. Fed.
119 D2 **Kalacha Dida** Kenya
87 D4 **Kalach-na-Donu** Rus. Fed.
62 A1 **Kaladan** *r.* India/Myanmar
120 B3 **Kalahari Desert** Africa
92 H3 **Kalajoki** Fin.
123 C1 **Kalamare** Botswana
111 B2 **Kalamaria** Greece
111 B3 **Kalamata** Greece
140 B2 **Kalamazoo** U.S.A.
111 B3 **Kalampaka** Greece
88 B2 **Kalana** Estonia

91 C2 **Kalanchak** Ukr.
61 D2 **Kalao** *i.* Indon.
61 D2 **Kalaotoa** *i.* Indon.
63 B2 **Kalasin** Thai.
79 C2 **Kalāt** Iran
74 A2 **Kalat** Pak.
50 A2 **Kalbarri** Austr.
111 C3 **Kale** Turkey
80 B1 **Kalecik** Turkey
118 C3 **Kalema** Dem. Rep. Congo
119 C3 **Kalémié** Dem. Rep. Congo
62 A1 **Kalemyo** Myanmar
86 C2 **Kalevala** Rus. Fed.
Kalgan China *see* Zhangjiakou
50 B3 **Kalgoorlie** Austr.
109 C2 **Kali** Croatia
110 C2 **Kaliakra, Nos** *pt* Bulg.
60 A2 **Kaliet** Indon.
119 C3 **Kalima** Dem. Rep. Congo
61 C2 **Kalimantan** *reg.* Indon.
Kalinin Rus. Fed. *see* Tver'
88 B3 **Kaliningrad** Rus. Fed.
91 D2 **Kalininskaya** Rus. Fed.
88 C3 **Kalinkavichy** Belarus
134 D1 **Kalispell** U.S.A.
103 D1 **Kalisz** Pol.
91 E2 **Kalitva** *r.* Rus. Fed.
92 H2 **Kalix** Sweden
92 H2 **Kalixälven** *r.* Sweden
111 C3 **Kalkan** Turkey
120 A3 **Kalkfeld** Namibia
100 C2 **Kall** Ger.
92 I3 **Kallavesi** *l.* Fin.
92 F3 **Kallsjön** *l.* Sweden
93 G4 **Kalmar** Sweden
93 G4 **Kalmarsund** *sea chan.* Sweden
73 C4 **Kalmunai** Sri Lanka
119 C3 **Kalole** Dem. Rep. Congo
120 B2 **Kalomo** Zambia
128 B2 **Kalone Peak** Can.
74 B1 **Kalpa** India
73 B3 **Kalpeni** *i.* India
75 B2 **Kalpi** India
126 B2 **Kaltag** U.S.A.
101 D1 **Kaltenkirchen** Ger.
118 B2 **Kaltungo** Nigeria
89 E3 **Kaluga** Rus. Fed.
93 F4 **Kalundborg** Denmark
74 B1 **Kalur Kot** Pak.
90 A2 **Kalush** Ukr.
74 B3 **Kalyan** India
89 E2 **Kalyazin** Rus. Fed.
111 C3 **Kalymnos** Greece
111 C3 **Kalymnos** *i.* Greece
119 C3 **Kama** Dem. Rep. Congo
62 A2 **Kama** Myanmar
86 E3 **Kama** *r.* Rus. Fed.
66 D3 **Kamaishi** Japan
80 B2 **Kaman** Turkey
120 A2 **Kamanjab** Namibia
78 B3 **Kamarān** *i.* Yemen
Kamaran Island Yemen *see* **Kamarān**
74 A2 **Kamarod** Pak.
50 B3 **Kambalda** Austr.
119 C4 **Kambove** Dem. Rep. Congo
160 C4 **Kamchatka Basin** *sea feature* Bering Sea
110 C2 **Kamchiya** *r.* Bulg.
108 B2 **Kamenjak, Rt** *pt* Croatia
76 B1 **Kamenka** Kazakh.
86 D2 **Kamenka** Rus. Fed.
87 D3 **Kamenka** Rus. Fed.
66 C2 **Kamenka** Rus. Fed.
91 D1 **Kamenka** Rus. Fed.
Kamenka-Strumilovskaya Ukr. *see* **Kam"yanka-Buz'ka**
91 E3 **Kamennomostskiy** Rus. Fed.
91 E2 **Kamenolomni** Rus. Fed.
Kamenongue Angola *see* Camanongue
83 M2 **Kamenskoye** Rus. Fed.
Kamenskoye Ukr. *see* **Dniprodzerzhyns'k**
91 E2 **Kamensk-Shakhtinskiy** Rus. Fed.
86 F3 **Kamensk-Ural'skiy** Rus. Fed.
89 F2 **Kameshkovo** Rus. Fed.
75 B1 **Kamet** *mt.* China
122 A3 **Kamiesberge** *mts* S. Africa
122 A3 **Kamieskroon** S. Africa
129 D1 **Kamilukuak Lake** Can.
119 C3 **Kamina** Dem. Rep. Congo
129 E1 **Kaminak Lake** Can.

90 A1 **Kamin'-Kashyrs'kyy** Ukr.
119 C3 **Kamituga** Dem. Rep. Congo
128 B2 **Kamloops** Can.
54 B1 **Kamo** N.Z.
116 B3 **Kamob Sanha** Sudan
118 C3 **Kamonia** Dem. Rep. Congo
119 D2 **Kampala** Uganda
60 B1 **Kampar** *r.* Indon.
60 B1 **Kampar** Malaysia
100 B1 **Kampen** Neth.
119 C3 **Kampene** Dem. Rep. Congo
63 A2 **Kamphaeng Phet** Thai.
63 B2 **Kâmpóng Cham** Cambodia
63 B2 **Kâmpóng Chhnăng** Cambodia
Kâmpóng Saôm Cambodia see **Sihanoukville**
63 B2 **Kâmpóng Spoe** Cambodia
63 B2 **Kâmpôt** Cambodia
Kampuchea *country* Asia see **Cambodia**
129 D2 **Kamsack** Can.
86 E3 **Kamskoye Vodokhranilishche** *resr* Rus. Fed.
117 C4 **Kamsuuma** Somalia
90 B2 **Kam"yanets'-Podil's'kyy** Ukr.
90 A1 **Kam"yanka-Buz'ka** Ukr.
88 B3 **Kamyanyets** Belarus
91 D2 **Kamyshevatskaya** Rus. Fed.
87 D3 **Kamyshin** Rus. Fed.
135 D3 **Kanab** U.S.A.
118 C3 **Kananga** Dem. Rep. Congo
87 D3 **Kanash** Rus. Fed.
140 C3 **Kanawha** *r.* U.S.A.
67 C3 **Kanazawa** Japan
62 A1 **Kanbalu** Myanmar
63 A2 **Kanchanaburi** Thai.
73 B3 **Kanchipuram** India
77 C3 **Kandahār** Afgh.
86 C2 **Kandalaksha** Rus. Fed.
61 C2 **Kandangan** Indon.
74 A2 **Kandhkot** Pak.
114 C3 **Kandi** Benin
74 A2 **Kandiaro** Pak.
74 B2 **Kandla** India
53 C2 **Kandos** Austr.
121 □D2 **Kandreho** Madag.
73 C4 **Kandy** Sri Lanka
76 B2 **Kandyagash** Kazakh.
127 H1 **Kane Bassin** *b.* Greenland
91 D2 **Kanevskaya** Rus. Fed.
122 B1 **Kang** Botswana
127 I2 **Kangaatsiaq** Greenland
114 B3 **Kangaba** Mali
80 B2 **Kangal** Turkey
79 C2 **Kangān** Iran
60 B1 **Kangar** Malaysia
52 A3 **Kangaroo Island** Austr.
93 H3 **Kangasala** Fin.
81 C2 **Kangāvar** Iran
75 C2 **Kangchenjunga** *mt.* India/Nepal
70 A2 **Kangding** China
65 B2 **Kangdong** N. Korea
61 C2 **Kangean, Kepulauan** *is* Indon.
119 D2 **Kangen** *r.* Sudan
127 J2 **Kangeq** *c.* Greenland
127 J2 **Kangerlussuaq** *inlet* Greenland
127 I2 **Kangerlussuaq** *inlet* Greenland
127 I2 **Kangersuatsiaq** Greenland
65 B1 **Kanggye** N. Korea
131 D2 **Kangiqsualujjuaq** Can.
127 H2 **Kangiqsujuaq** Can.
131 C1 **Kangirsuk** Can.
75 C2 **Kangmar** China
65 B2 **Kangnŭng** S. Korea
65 A1 **Kangping** China
72 D2 **Kangto** *mt.* China/India
62 A1 **Kani** Myanmar
118 C3 **Kaniama** Dem. Rep. Congo
61 C1 **Kanibongan** *Sabah* Malaysia
86 D2 **Kanin, Poluostrov** *pen.* Rus. Fed.
86 D2 **Kanin Nos** Rus. Fed.
86 D2 **Kanin Nos, Mys** *c.* Rus. Fed.
91 C2 **Kaniv** Ukr.
52 B3 **Kaniva** Austr.
93 H3 **Kankaanpää** Fin.
140 B2 **Kankakee** U.S.A.
114 B3 **Kankan** Guinea
75 C2 **Kanker** India
Kannur India see **Cannanore**
115 C3 **Kano** Nigeria
122 B3 **Kanonpunt** *pt* S. Africa
67 B4 **Kanoya** Japan
75 C2 **Kanpur** India
136 C3 **Kansas** *r.* U.S.A.
137 D3 **Kansas** *state* U.S.A.
137 E3 **Kansas City** *KS* U.S.A.
137 E3 **Kansas City** *MO* U.S.A.
83 H3 **Kansk** Rus. Fed.
Kansu *prov.* China see **Gansu**
63 B2 **Kantaralak** Thai.
114 C3 **Kantchari** Burkina
91 D2 **Kantemirovka** Rus. Fed.
49 J4 **Kanton** *i.* Kiribati
97 B2 **Kanturk** Rep. of Ireland
123 D2 **KaNyamazane** S. Africa
123 C1 **Kanye** Botswana
71 C3 **Kaohsiung** Taiwan
120 A2 **Kaokoveld** *plat.* Namibia
114 A3 **Kaolack** Senegal
120 B2 **Kaoma** Zambia
118 C3 **Kapanga** Dem. Rep. Congo
88 C3 **Kapatkyevichy** Belarus
77 D2 **Kapchagay** Kazakh.
77 D2 **Kapchagayskoye Vodokhranilishche** *resr* Kazakh.
100 B2 **Kapellen** Belgium
121 B2 **Kapiri Mposhi** Zambia
127 I2 **Kapisillit** Greenland
130 B2 **Kapiskau** *r.* Can.
61 C1 **Kapit** *Sarawak* Malaysia
63 A3 **Kapoe** Thai.
117 B4 **Kapoeta** Sudan
103 D2 **Kaposvár** Hungary
102 B1 **Kappeln** Ger.
65 B1 **Kapsan** N. Korea
Kapsukas Lith. see **Marijampolė**
61 B2 **Kapuas** *r.* Indon.
52 A2 **Kapunda** Austr.
130 B3 **Kapuskasing** Can.
53 D2 **Kaputar** *mt.* Austr.
103 D2 **Kapuvár** Hungary
88 C3 **Kapyl'** Belarus
77 D3 **Kaqung** China
114 C4 **Kara** Togo
111 C3 **Kara Ada** *i.* Turkey
77 D2 **Kara-Balta** Kyrg.
76 C3 **Karabil', Vozvyshennost'** *hills* Turkm.
Kara-Bogaz-Gol Turkm. see **Karabogazkel'**
76 B2 **Kara-Bogaz Gol, Zaliv** *b.* Turkm.
76 B2 **Karabogazkel'** Turkm.
80 B1 **Karabük** Turkey
76 C2 **Karabutak** Kazakh.
111 C2 **Karacabey** Turkey
111 C2 **Karacaköy** Turkey
81 C1 **Karachayevsk** Rus. Fed.
89 D3 **Karachev** Rus. Fed.
74 A2 **Karachi** Pak.
77 D2 **Karaganda** Kazakh.
77 D2 **Karagayly** Kazakh.
83 L3 **Karaginskiy Zaliv** *b.* Rus. Fed.
81 D2 **Karaj** Iran
Kara-Kala Turkm. see **Garrygala**
76 B2 **Karakalpakiya** Kazakh.
64 B3 **Karakelong** *i.* Indon.
Karaklis Armenia see **Vanadzor**
77 D2 **Kara-Köl** Kyrg.
77 D2 **Karakol** Kyrg.
74 B1 **Karakoram** *mts* Asia
72 B1 **Karakoram Range** *mts* Asia
117 B3 **Kara K'orē** Eth.
76 B2 **Karakum, Peski** *des.* Kazakh.
76 C3 **Karakum Desert** Turkm.
Karakumy, Peski *des.* Turkm. see **Karakum Desert**
80 B2 **Karaman** Turkey
77 E2 **Karamay** China
54 B2 **Karamea** N.Z.
54 B2 **Karamea Bight** *b.* N.Z.
80 B2 **Karapınar** Turkey
122 A2 **Karasburg** Namibia
86 F1 **Kara Sea** Rus. Fed.
92 I2 **Karasjok** Norway
Kara Strait Rus. Fed. see **Karskiye Vorota, Proliv**
111 D2 **Karasu** Turkey
Karasubazar Ukr. see **Bilohirs'k**
77 D1 **Karasuk** Rus. Fed.
77 D2 **Karatau** Kazakh.
77 C2 **Karatau, Khrebet** *mts* Kazakh.
86 F2 **Karatayka** Rus. Fed.
67 A4 **Karatsu** Japan
111 B3 **Karavas** Greece
60 B2 **Karawang** Indon.
81 C2 **Karbalā'** Iraq
103 E2 **Karcag** Hungary
Kardeljevo Croatia see **Ploče**
111 B3 **Karditsa** Greece
88 B2 **Kärdla** Estonia
122 B3 **Kareeberge** *mts* S. Africa
75 B2 **Kareli** India
88 C3 **Karelichy** Belarus
92 H2 **Karesuando** Sweden
Karghalik China see **Yecheng**
74 B1 **Kargil** Jammu and Kashmir
Kargilik China see **Yecheng**
86 C2 **Kargopol'** Rus. Fed.
118 B1 **Kari** Nigeria
121 B2 **Kariba** Zimbabwe
121 B2 **Kariba, Lake** *resr* Zambia/Zimbabwe
60 B2 **Karimata, Pulau-pulau** *is* Indon.
60 B2 **Karimata, Selat** *str.* Indon.
73 B3 **Karimnagar** India
61 C2 **Karimunjawa, Pulau-pulau** *is* Indon.
91 C2 **Karkinits'ka Zatoka** *g.* Ukr.
91 D2 **Karlivka** Ukr.
Karl-Marx-Stadt Ger. see **Chemnitz**
109 C1 **Karlovac** Croatia
102 C1 **Karlovy Vary** Czech Rep.
Karlsburg Romania see **Alba Iulia**
93 F4 **Karlshamn** Sweden
93 F4 **Karlskoga** Sweden
93 G4 **Karlskrona** Sweden
102 B2 **Karlsruhe** Ger.
93 F4 **Karlstad** Sweden
101 D3 **Karlstadt** Ger.
89 D3 **Karma** Belarus
93 E4 **Karmøy** *i.* Norway
75 D2 **Karnafuli Reservoir** Bangl.
74 B2 **Karnal** India
110 C2 **Karnobat** Bulg.
74 A2 **Karodi** Pak.
121 B2 **Karoi** Zimbabwe
121 C1 **Karonga** Malawi
116 B3 **Karora** Eritrea
111 C3 **Karpathos** Greece
111 C3 **Karpathos** *i.* Greece
111 B3 **Karpenisi** Greece
Karpilovka Belarus see **Aktsyabrski**
86 D2 **Karpogory** Rus. Fed.
50 A2 **Karratha** Austr.
81 C1 **Kars** Turkey
88 C2 **Kārsava** Latvia
76 B2 **Karshi** Turkm.
77 C3 **Karshi** Uzbek.
111 C3 **Karşıyaka** Turkey
86 E2 **Karskiye Vorota, Proliv** *str.* Rus. Fed.
Karskoye More *sea* Rus. Fed. see **Kara Sea**
101 E1 **Karstädt** Ger.
111 C2 **Kartal** Turkey
87 F3 **Kartaly** Rus. Fed.
81 C2 **Kārūn, Rūd-e** *r.* Iran
73 B3 **Karwar** India
83 I3 **Karymskoye** Rus. Fed.
111 B3 **Karystos** Greece
111 C3 **Kaş** Turkey
130 B2 **Kasabonika Lake** Can.
118 C3 **Kasai, Plateau du** Dem. Rep. Congo
118 C4 **Kasaji** Dem. Rep. Congo
121 C2 **Kasama** Zambia
120 B2 **Kasane** Botswana
118 B3 **Kasangulu** Dem. Rep. Congo
73 B3 **Kasaragod** India
129 D1 **Kasba Lake** Can.
120 B2 **Kasempa** Zambia
119 C4 **Kasenga** Dem. Rep. Congo
119 C3 **Kasese** Dem. Rep. Cong
119 D2 **Kasese** Uganda
Kasevo Rus. Fed. see **Neftekamsk**
81 D2 **Kāshān** Iran
Kashgar China see **Kash**
77 D3 **Kashi** China
67 D3 **Kashima-nada** *b.* Japar
89 E2 **Kashin** Rus. Fed.
89 E3 **Kashira** Rus. Fed.
89 E3 **Kashirskoye** Rus. Fed.
67 C3 **Kashiwazaki** Japan
76 B3 **Kāshmar** Iran
Kashmir *terr.* Asia see **Jammu and Kashmir**
74 A2 **Kashmor** Pak.
119 C3 **Kashyukulu** Dem. Rep. Congo
89 F3 **Kasimov** Rus. Fed.
140 B3 **Kaskaskia** *r.* U.S.A.
93 H3 **Kaskinen** Fin.
119 C3 **Kasongo** Dem. Rep. Congo
118 B3 **Kasongo-Lunda** Dem. Rep. Congo
111 C3 **Kasos** *i.* Greece
Kaspiyskiy Rus. Fed. se **Lagan'**
116 B3 **Kassala** Sudan
101 D2 **Kassel** Ger.
115 C1 **Kasserine** Tunisia
80 B1 **Kastamonu** Turkey
111 B3 **Kastelli** Greece
Kastellorizon *i.* Greece see **Megisti**
111 B2 **Kastoria** Greece
89 D3 **Kastsyukovichy** Belarus
119 D3 **Kasulu** Tanz.
121 C2 **Kasungu** Malawi
141 F1 **Katahdin, Mount** U.S.A.
118 C3 **Katako-Kombe** Dem. Rep. Congo
119 D2 **Katakwi** Uganda
50 A3 **Katanning** Austr.
63 A3 **Katchall** *i.* India
111 B2 **Katerini** Greece
119 D3 **Katesh** Tanz.
128 A2 **Kate's Needle** *mt.* Can./U.S.A.
121 C2 **Katete** Zambia
62 A1 **Katha** Myanmar
80 B3 **Katherîna, Gebel** *mt.* Egypt
50 C1 **Katherine** Austr.
50 C1 **Katherine** *r.* Austr.
74 B2 **Kathiawar** *pen.* India
123 C2 **Kathlehong** S. Africa
75 C2 **Kathmandu** Nepal
122 B2 **Kathu** S. Africa
74 B1 **Kathua** Jammu and Kashmir
114 B3 **Kati** Mali
75 C2 **Katihar** India
54 C1 **Katikati** N.Z.
123 C3 **Kati-Kati** S. Africa
120 B2 **Katima Mulilo** Namibia
114 B4 **Katiola** Côte d'Ivoire
Katmandu Nepal see **Kathmandu**
111 B3 **Kato Achaïa** Greece
119 C3 **Katompi** Dem. Rep. Cor
53 D2 **Katoomba** Austr.
103 D1 **Katowice** Pol.
93 G4 **Katrineholm** Sweden
115 C3 **Katsina** Nigeria
115 C4 **Katsina-Ala** Nigeria
67 D3 **Katsuura** Japan
77 C3 **Kattakurgan** Uzbek.
93 F4 **Kattegat** *str.* Denmark/Sweden
100 B1 **Katwijk aan Zee** Neth.
101 D3 **Katzenbuckel** *hill* Ger.
49 L1 **Kauai** *i.* U.S.A.
93 H3 **Kauhajoki** Fin.
88 B3 **Kaunas** Lith.
115 C3 **Kaura-Namoda** Nigeria
Kaushany Moldova see **Căușeni**
92 H2 **Kautokeino** Norway
109 D2 **Kavadarci** Macedonia
109 C2 **Kavajë** Albania
111 B2 **Kavala** Greece
66 C2 **Kavalerovo** Rus. Fed.
73 C3 **Kavali** India
73 B3 **Kavaratti** *i.* India
110 C2 **Kavarna** Bulg.
59 E3 **Kavieng** P.N.G.
81 D2 **Kavīr, Dasht-e** *des.* Iran

C3 **Kawagoe** Japan
B1 **Kawakawa** N.Z.
B1 **Kawambwa** Zambia
C3 **Kawanishi** Japan
C3 **Kawartha Lakes** Can.
C3 **Kawasaki** Japan
C1 **Kawerau** N.Z.
A2 **Kawkareik** Myanmar
A1 **Kawlin** Myanmar
A2 **Kawmapyin** Myanmar
A2 **Kawthaung** Myanmar
Kaxgar China *see* **Kashi**
D3 **Kaxgar He** *r.* China
B3 **Kaya** Burkina
C3 **Kayacı Dağı** *hill* Turkey
C1 **Kayambi** Zambia
C1 **Kayan** *r.* Indon.
B2 **Kaycee** U.S.A.
Kaydanovo Belarus *see* **Dzyarzhynsk**
A1 **Kayenta** U.S.A.
A3 **Kayes** Mali
D2 **Kaynar** Kazakh.
B2 **Kayseri** Turkey
D2 **Kaysville** U.S.A.
B2 **Kayuagung** Indon.
Kazakhskaya S.S.R. *country* Asia *see* Kazakhstan
D1 **Kazakhskiy Melkosopochnik** *plain* Kazakh.
B2 **Kazakhskiy Zaliv** *b.* Kazakh.
E2 **Kazakhstan** *country* Asia
Kazakhstan Kazakh. *see* **Aksay**
D3 **Kazan'** Rus. Fed.
Kazandzhik Turkm. *see* **Gazandzhyk**
C2 **Kazanlŭk** Bulg.
F3 **Kazan-rettō** *is* Japan
A2 **Kazbek** *mt.* Georgia/Rus. Fed.
D3 **Kāzerūn** Iran
E2 **Kazincbarcika** Hungary
C3 **Kazumba** Dem. Rep. Congo
D2 **Kazuno** Japan
F2 **Kazymskiy Mys** Rus. Fed.
B3 **Kea** *i.* Greece
C1 **Keady** U.K.
D2 **Kearney** U.S.A.
A2 **Kearny** U.S.A.
C1 **Kebili** Tunisia
A3 **Kebkabiya** Sudan
G2 **Kebnekaise** *mt.* Sweden
C4 **K'ebrī Dehar** Eth.
C2 **Kebumen** Indon.
B2 **Kechika** *r.* Can.
D3 **Keçiborlu** Turkey
D2 **Kecskemét** Hungary
B2 **Kėdainiai** Lith.
A3 **Kédougou** Senegal
D1 **Kędzierzyn-Koźle** Pol.
B1 **Keele** *r.* Can.
A1 **Keele Peak** Can.
Keelung Taiwan *see* **Chilung**
E2 **Keene** U.S.A.
A2 **Keetmanshoop** Namibia
E3 **Keewatin** Can.
Kefallonia *i.* Greece *see* **Cephalonia**
C3 **Kefamenanu** Indon.
A3 **Keflavík** Iceland
D2 **Kegen** Kazakh.
C2 **Keg River** Can.
C2 **Kehra** Estonia
A1 **Kehsi Mansam** Myanmar
C3 **Keighley** U.K.
B2 **Keila** Estonia
B2 **Keimoes** S. Africa
I3 **Keitele** *l.* Fin.
B3 **Keith** Austr.
C2 **Keith** U.K.
B1 **Keith Arm** *b.* Can.
B2 **Keizer** U.S.A.
E2 **Kékes** *mt.* Hungary
C4 **K'elafo** Eth.
B1 **Kelang** Malaysia
J2 **Keles-Uayv, Gora** *hill* Rus. Fed.
C2 **Kelheim** Ger.
C3 **Kelifskiy Uzboy** *marsh* Turkm.
B1 **Kelkit** *r.* Turkey
B1 **Keller Lake** Can.
C1 **Kellogg** U.S.A.
I2 **Kelloselkä** Fin.
C2 **Kells** Rep. of Ireland
88 B2 **Kelmė** Lith.
115 D4 **Kelo** Chad
128 C3 **Kelowna** Can.
96 C3 **Kelso** U.K.
134 B1 **Kelso** U.S.A.
60 B1 **Keluang** Malaysia
129 D2 **Kelvington** Can.
86 C2 **Kem'** Rus. Fed.
Ke Macina Mali *see* Massina
128 B2 **Kemano** Can.
118 C2 **Kembé** C.A.R.
111 C3 **Kemer** Turkey
82 G3 **Kemerovo** Rus. Fed.
92 H2 **Kemi** Fin.
92 I2 **Kemijärvi** Fin.
92 I2 **Kemijärvi** *l.* Fin.
92 I2 **Kemijoki** *r.* Fin.
136 A2 **Kemmerer** U.S.A.
92 I3 **Kempele** Fin.
55 G2 **Kemp Land** *reg.* Antarctica
55 A2 **Kemp Peninsula** Antarctica
53 D2 **Kempsey** Austr.
130 C3 **Kempt, Lac** *l.* Can.
102 C2 **Kempten (Allgäu)** Ger.
123 C2 **Kempton Park** S. Africa
61 C2 **Kemujan** *i.* Indon.
126 B2 **Kenai** U.S.A.
129 D2 **Kenaston** Can.
98 B2 **Kendal** U.K.
143 D3 **Kendall** U.S.A.
61 D2 **Kendari** Indon.
60 C2 **Kendawangan** Indon.
115 D3 **Kendégué** Chad
75 C2 **Kendujhargarh** India
114 A4 **Kenema** Sierra Leone
118 B3 **Kenge** Dem. Rep. Congo
62 A1 **Kengtung** Myanmar
122 B2 **Kenhardt** S. Africa
114 B1 **Kénitra** Morocco
97 B3 **Kenmare** Rep. of Ireland
136 C1 **Kenmare** U.S.A.
97 A3 **Kenmare River** *inlet* Rep. of Ireland
100 C3 **Kenn** Ger.
139 C2 **Kenna** U.S.A.
141 F2 **Kennebec** *r.* U.S.A.
Kennedy, Cape U.S.A. *see* **Canaveral, Cape**
142 B3 **Kenner** U.S.A.
99 C4 **Kennet** *r.* U.K.
137 E3 **Kennett** U.S.A.
134 C1 **Kennewick** U.S.A.
130 A3 **Kenora** Can.
140 B2 **Kenosha** U.S.A.
138 C2 **Kent** U.S.A.
77 C2 **Kentau** Kazakh.
140 B3 **Kentucky** *r.* U.S.A.
140 C3 **Kentucky** *state* U.S.A.
140 B3 **Kentucky Lake** U.S.A.
142 B2 **Kentwood** U.S.A.
119 D2 **Kenya** *country* Africa
Kenya, Mount Kenya *see* Kirinyaga
60 B1 **Kenyir, Tasik** *resr* Malaysia
137 E2 **Keokuk** U.S.A.
111 C3 **Kepsut** Turkey
52 B3 **Kerang** Austr.
91 D2 **Kerch** Ukr.
59 D3 **Kerema** P.N.G.
128 C3 **Keremeos** Can.
116 B3 **Keren** Eritrea
81 C2 **Kerend** Iran
159 E7 **Kerguélen, Îles** *is* Indian Ocean
159 E7 **Kerguelen Plateau** *sea feature* Indian Ocean
119 D3 **Kericho** Kenya
54 B1 **Kerikeri** N.Z.
60 B2 **Kerinci, Gunung** *vol.* Indon.
Kerintji *vol.* Indon. *see* **Kerinci, Gunung**
77 C3 **Kerki** Turkm.
100 C2 **Kerkrade** Neth.
111 A3 **Kerkyra** Greece
Kerkyra *i.* Greece *see* **Corfu**
116 B3 **Kerma** Sudan
49 J7 **Kermadec Islands** S. Pacific Ocean
79 C1 **Kermān** Iran
81 C2 **Kermānshāh** Iran
Kermine Uzbek. *see* **Navoi**
139 C2 **Kermit** U.S.A.
135 C3 **Kern** *r.* U.S.A.
114 B4 **Kérouané** Guinea
100 C2 **Kerpen** Ger.
129 D2 **Kerrobert** Can.
139 D2 **Kerrville** U.S.A.
97 B2 **Kerry Head** *hd* Rep. of Ireland
80 B2 **Keryneia** Cyprus
130 B2 **Kesagami Lake** Can.
111 C2 **Keşan** Turkey
66 D3 **Kesennuma** Japan
74 B2 **Keshod** India
100 C2 **Kessel** Neth.
98 B2 **Keswick** U.K.
103 D2 **Keszthely** Hungary
82 G3 **Ket'** *r.* Rus. Fed.
60 C2 **Ketapang** Indon.
128 A2 **Ketchikan** U.S.A.
134 D2 **Ketchum** U.S.A.
114 B4 **Kete Krachi** Ghana
118 B2 **Kétté** Cameroon
99 C3 **Kettering** U.K.
140 C3 **Kettering** U.S.A.
134 C1 **Kettle River Range** *mts* U.S.A.
93 H3 **Keuruu** Fin.
100 C2 **Kevelaer** Ger.
140 B2 **Kewanee** U.S.A.
140 B1 **Keweenaw Bay** U.S.A.
140 B1 **Keweenaw Peninsula** U.S.A.
143 D3 **Key Largo** U.S.A.
99 B4 **Keynsham** U.K.
141 D3 **Keyser** U.S.A.
143 D4 **Key West** U.S.A.
123 C2 **Kgotsong** S. Africa
69 F1 **Khabarovsk** Rus. Fed.
91 D3 **Khadyzhensk** Rus. Fed.
75 D2 **Khagrachari** Bangl.
74 A2 **Khairpur** Pak.
122 B1 **Khakhea** Botswana
76 B3 **Khalilabad** Iran
86 F2 **Khal'mer-Yu** Rus. Fed.
68 C1 **Khamar-Daban, Khrebet** *mts* Rus. Fed.
74 B2 **Khambhat** India
74 B3 **Khambhat, Gulf of** India
74 B2 **Khamgaon** India
79 C2 **Khamīr** Iran
78 B3 **Khamir** Yemen
78 B3 **Khamis Mushayṭ** Saudi Arabia
77 C3 **Khānābād** Afgh.
74 B2 **Khandwa** India
83 K2 **Khandyga** Rus. Fed.
74 B1 **Khanewal** Pak.
Khan Hung Vietnam *see* Soc Trăng
83 J3 **Khani** Rus. Fed.
66 B2 **Khanka, Lake** China/Rus. Fed.
115 C2 **Khannfoussa** *hill* Alg.
74 B2 **Khanpur** Pak.
77 D2 **Khantau** Kazakh.
83 H2 **Khantayskoye, Ozero** *l.* Rus. Fed.
86 F2 **Khanty-Mansiysk** Rus. Fed.
63 A3 **Khao Chum Thong** Thai.
63 A2 **Khao Laem Reservoir** Thai.
74 B1 **Khapalu** Jammu and Kashmir
87 D4 **Kharabali** Rus. Fed.
75 C2 **Kharagpur** India
79 C2 **Khārān** *r.* Iran
Kharga Oasis Egypt *see* **The Great Oasis**
74 B2 **Khargon** India
91 D2 **Kharkiv** Ukr.
Khar'kov Ukr. *see* **Kharkiv**
111 C2 **Kharmanli** Bulg.
89 F2 **Kharovsk** Rus. Fed.
116 B3 **Khartoum** Sudan
87 D4 **Khasav'yurt** Rus. Fed.
79 D2 **Khāsh** Iran
86 F2 **Khashgort** Rus. Fed.
78 A3 **Khashm el Girba** Sudan
78 A3 **Khashm el Girba Dam** Sudan
81 C1 **Khashuri** Georgia
75 D2 **Khāsi Hills** India
111 C2 **Khaskovo** Bulg.
83 H2 **Khatanga** Rus. Fed.
123 C3 **Khayamnandi** S. Africa
77 C2 **Khayatbashi, Gora** *mt.* Uzbek.
78 A2 **Khaybar** Saudi Arabia
122 A3 **Khayelitsha** S. Africa
62 B2 **Khê Bo** Vietnam
107 D2 **Khemis Miliana** Alg.
63 B2 **Khemmarat** Thai.
115 C1 **Khenchela** Alg.
81 D3 **Kherāmeh** Iran
91 C2 **Kherson** Ukr.
83 H2 **Kheta** *r.* Rus. Fed.
69 D1 **Khilok** Rus. Fed.
89 E2 **Khimki** Rus. Fed.
89 E3 **Khlevnoye** Rus. Fed.
63 B2 **Khlung** Thai.
90 B2 **Khmel'nyts'kyy** Ukr.
Khmer Republic *country* Asia *see* **Cambodia**
76 B1 **Khobda** Kazakh.
76 B2 **Khodzheyli** Uzbek.
89 E3 **Khokhol'skiy** Rus. Fed.
74 B2 **Khokhropar** Pak.
74 A1 **Kholm** Afgh.
89 D2 **Kholm** Rus. Fed.
89 D2 **Kholm-Zhirkovskiy** Rus. Fed.
122 A1 **Khomas Highland** *hills* Namibia
89 E3 **Khomutovo** Rus. Fed.
79 C2 **Khonj** Iran
63 B2 **Khon Kaen** Thai.
62 A1 **Khonsa** India
83 K2 **Khonuu** Rus. Fed.
86 E2 **Khoreyver** Rus. Fed.
69 D1 **Khorinsk** Rus. Fed.
120 A3 **Khorixas** Namibia
66 B2 **Khorol** Rus. Fed.
91 C2 **Khorol** Ukr.
81 C2 **Khorramābād** Iran
81 C2 **Khorramshahr** Iran
77 D3 **Khorugh** Tajik.
Khotan China *see* **Hotan**
90 B2 **Khotyn** Ukr.
114 B1 **Khouribga** Morocco
77 C3 **Khowst** Afgh.
88 C3 **Khoyniki** Belarus
62 A1 **Khreum** Myanmar
76 B1 **Khromtau** Kazakh.
Khrushchev Ukr. *see* Svitlovods'k
90 B2 **Khrystynivka** Ukr.
123 B1 **Khudumelapye** Botswana
77 C2 **Khŭjand** Tajik.
63 B2 **Khu Khan** Thai.
78 A2 **Khulays** Saudi Arabia
75 C2 **Khulna** Bangl.
Khūnīnshahr Iran *see* Khorramshahr
81 D2 **Khunsar** Iran
79 B2 **Khurayṣ** Saudi Arabia
74 B1 **Khushab** Pak.
90 A2 **Khust** Ukr.
123 C2 **Khutsong** S. Africa
74 A2 **Khuzdar** Pak.
81 D3 **Khvormūj** Iran
81 C2 **Khvoy** Iran
89 D2 **Khvoynaya** Rus. Fed.
77 D3 **Khyber Pass** Afgh./Pak.
53 D2 **Kiama** Austr.
64 B3 **Kiamba** Phil.
119 C3 **Kiambi** Dem. Rep. Congo
Kiangsi *prov.* China *see* Jiangxi
Kiangsu *prov.* China *see* Jiangsu
119 D3 **Kibaha** Tanz.
119 D3 **Kibaya** Tanz.
119 D3 **Kibiti** Tanz.
119 C3 **Kibombo** Dem. Rep. Congo
119 D3 **Kibondo** Tanz.
119 D2 **Kibre Mengist** Eth.
119 D3 **Kibungo** Rwanda
111 B2 **Kičevo** Macedonia
114 C3 **Kidal** Mali
99 B3 **Kidderminster** U.K.
114 A3 **Kidira** Senegal
74 B1 **Kidmang** Jammu and Kashmir
54 C1 **Kidnappers, Cape** N.Z.
102 C1 **Kiel** Ger.
103 E1 **Kielce** Pol.
98 B2 **Kielder Water** *resr* U.K.
119 C4 **Kienge** Dem. Rep. Congo
90 C1 **Kiev** Ukr.
114 A3 **Kiffa** Maur.
119 D3 **Kigali** Rwanda
119 C3 **Kigoma** Tanz.
88 B2 **Kihnu** *i.* Estonia
92 I2 **Kiiminki** Fin.
67 B4 **Kii-suidō** *sea chan.* Japan
109 D1 **Kikinda** Yugo.
119 C3 **Kikondja** Dem. Rep. Congo
59 D3 **Kikori** P.N.G.
59 D3 **Kikori** *r.* P.N.G.
118 B3 **Kikwit** Dem. Rep. Congo
65 B1 **Kilchu** N. Korea
97 C2 **Kilcock** Rep. of Ireland
97 C2 **Kildare** Rep. of Ireland
118 B3 **Kilembe** Dem. Rep. Congo

139 E2 **Kilgore** U.S.A.
119 D3 **Kilifi** Kenya
119 D3 **Kilimanjaro** *vol.* Tanz.
119 D3 **Kilindoni** Tanz.
80 B2 **Kılıs** Turkey
90 B2 **Kiliya** Ukr.
97 B2 **Kilkee** Rep. of Ireland
97 D1 **Kilkeel** U.K.
97 C2 **Kilkenny** Rep. of Ireland
111 B2 **Kilkis** Greece
97 B1 **Killala** Rep. of Ireland
97 B1 **Killala Bay** Rep. of Ireland
97 B2 **Killaloe** Rep. of Ireland
128 C2 **Killam** Can.
97 B2 **Killarney** Rep. of Ireland
139 D2 **Killeen** U.S.A.
96 B2 **Killin** U.K.
131 D1 **Killiniq** Can.
97 B2 **Killorglin** Rep. of Ireland
97 B1 **Killybegs** Rep. of Ireland
96 B3 **Kilmarnock** U.K.
53 B3 **Kilmore** Austr.
119 D3 **Kilosa** Tanz.
97 B2 **Kilrush** Rep. of Ireland
119 C3 **Kilwa** Dem. Rep. Congo
119 D3 **Kilwa Masoko** Tanz.
119 D3 **Kimambi** Tanz.
52 A2 **Kimba** Austr.
136 C2 **Kimball** U.S.A.
59 E3 **Kimbe** P.N.G.
128 C3 **Kimberley** Can.
122 B2 **Kimberley** S. Africa
50 B1 **Kimberley Plateau** Austr.
65 B1 **Kimch'aek** N. Korea
65 B2 **Kimch'ŏn** S. Korea
65 B2 **Kimhae** S. Korea
127 H2 **Kimmirut** Can.
89 E3 **Kimovsk** Rus. Fed.
118 C3 **Kimpanga** Dem. Rep. Congo
118 B3 **Kimpese** Dem. Rep. Congo
89 E2 **Kimry** Rus. Fed.
61 C1 **Kinabalu, Gunung** *mt.* *Sabah* Malaysia
128 C2 **Kinbasket Lake** Can.
96 C1 **Kinbrace** U.K.
130 B3 **Kincardine** Can.
62 A1 **Kinchang** Myanmar
119 C3 **Kinda** Dem. Rep. Congo
98 C3 **Kinder Scout** *hill* U.K.
129 D2 **Kindersley** Can.
114 A3 **Kindia** Guinea
119 C3 **Kindu** Dem. Rep. Congo
89 F2 **Kineshma** Rus. Fed.
118 B3 **Kingandu** Dem. Rep. Congo
51 E2 **Kingaroy** Austr.
135 B3 **King City** U.S.A.
130 C2 **King George Islands** Can.
88 C2 **Kingisepp** Rus. Fed.
51 D3 **King Island** Austr.
Kingisseppa Estonia *see* Kuressaare
50 B1 **King Leopold Ranges** *hills* Austr.
138 A1 **Kingman** U.S.A.
135 B3 **Kings** *r.* U.S.A.
52 A3 **Kingscote** Austr.
97 C2 **Kingscourt** Rep. of Ireland
99 D3 **King's Lynn** U.K.
50 B1 **King Sound** *b.* Austr.
134 D2 **Kings Peak** U.S.A.
143 D1 **Kingsport** U.S.A.
51 D4 **Kingston** Austr.
130 C3 **Kingston** Can.
146 C3 **Kingston** Jamaica
141 E2 **Kingston** U.S.A.
52 A3 **Kingston South East** Austr.
98 C3 **Kingston upon Hull** U.K.
147 D3 **Kingstown** St Vincent
139 D3 **Kingsville** U.S.A.
99 B4 **Kingswood** U.K.
96 B2 **Kingussie** U.K.
126 F2 **King William Island** Can.
123 C3 **King William's Town** S. Africa
67 D3 **Kinka-san** *i.* Japan
96 B2 **Kinlochleven** U.K.
93 F4 **Kinna** Sweden
97 B3 **Kinsale** Rep. of Ireland
118 B3 **Kinshasa** Dem. Rep. Congo
143 E1 **Kinston** U.S.A.
88 B2 **Kintai** Lith.
114 B4 **Kintampo** Ghana
96 C2 **Kintore** U.K.
96 B3 **Kintyre** *pen.* U.K.
119 D3 **Kiomboi** Tanz.
130 C3 **Kipawa, Lac** *l.* Can.
119 D3 **Kipembawe** Tanz.
119 D3 **Kipengere Range** *mts* Tanz.
129 D2 **Kipling** Can.
Kipling Station Can. *see* Kipling
119 C4 **Kipushi** Dem. Rep. Congo
119 C4 **Kipushia** Dem. Rep. Congo
101 D2 **Kirchhain** Ger.
101 D3 **Kirchheim-Bolanden** Ger.
83 I3 **Kirenga** *r.* Rus. Fed.
83 I3 **Kirensk** Rus. Fed.
89 E3 **Kireyevsk** Rus. Fed.
Kirghizia *country* Asia *see* Kyrgyzstan
77 D2 **Kirghiz Range** *mts* Asia
Kirgizskaya S.S.R. *country* Asia *see* Kyrgyzstan
49 J4 **Kiribati** *country* Pacific Ocean
80 B2 **Kırıkkale** Turkey
89 E2 **Kirillov** Rus. Fed.
Kirin China *see* **Jilin**
Kirin *prov.* China *see* **Jilin**
119 D3 **Kirinyaga** *mt.* Kenya
89 D2 **Kirishi** Rus. Fed.
48 L3 **Kiritimati** *i.* Kiribati
111 C3 **Kırkağaç** Turkey
98 B3 **Kirkby** U.K.
98 B2 **Kirkby Stephen** U.K.
96 C2 **Kirkcaldy** U.K.
96 B3 **Kirkcudbright** U.K.
92 J2 **Kirkenes** Norway
88 B1 **Kirkkonummi** Fin.
130 B3 **Kirkland Lake** Can.
111 C2 **Kırklareli** Turkey
137 E2 **Kirksville** U.S.A.
81 C2 **Kirkūk** Iraq
96 C1 **Kirkwall** U.K.
Kīrov Kazakh. *see* Balpyk Bi
89 D3 **Kirov** Rus. Fed.
86 D3 **Kirov** Rus. Fed.
Kirovabad Azer. *see* **Gäncä**
Kirovakan Armenia *see* Vanadzor
Kirovo Ukr. *see* **Kirovohrad**
86 E3 **Kirovo-Chepetsk** Rus. Fed.
Kirovo-Chepetskiy Rus. Fed. *see* **Kirovo-Chepetsk**
91 C2 **Kirovohrad** Ukr.
86 C2 **Kirovsk** Rus. Fed.
91 D2 **Kirovs'ke** Ukr.
Kirovskiy Kazakh. *see* Balpyk Bi
66 B1 **Kirovskiy** Rus. Fed.
96 C2 **Kirriemuir** U.K.
86 E3 **Kirs** Rus. Fed.
87 D3 **Kirsanov** Rus. Fed.
80 B2 **Kırşehir** Turkey
74 A2 **Kirthar Range** *mts* Pak.
92 H2 **Kiruna** Sweden
67 C3 **Kiryū** Japan
89 E2 **Kirzhach** Rus. Fed.
119 D3 **Kisaki** Tanz.
119 C2 **Kisangani** Dem. Rep. Congo
118 B3 **Kisantu** Dem. Rep. Congo
60 A1 **Kisaran** Indon.
82 G3 **Kiselevsk** Rus. Fed.
75 C2 **Kishanganj** India
Kishinev Moldova *see* Chişinău
67 C4 **Kishiwada** Japan
77 D1 **Kishkenekol'** Kazakh.
75 D2 **Kishorganj** Bangl.
74 B1 **Kishtwar** Jammu and Kashmir
115 C4 **Kisi** Nigeria
119 D3 **Kisii** Kenya
103 D2 **Kiskunfélegyháza** Hungary
103 D2 **Kiskunhalas** Hungary
87 D4 **Kislovodsk** Rus. Fed.
117 C5 **Kismaayo** Somalia
Kismayu Somalia *see* Kismaayo
119 C3 **Kisoro** Uganda
114 A4 **Kissidougou** Guinea
143 D3 **Kissimmee** U.S.A.
143 D3 **Kissimmee, Lake** U.S.A.
129 D2 **Kississing Lake** Can.
Kistna *r.* India *see* **Krishna**
119 D3 **Kisumu** Kenya
103 E2 **Kisvárda** Hungary
Kisykkamys Kazakh. *see* Dzhangala
114 B3 **Kita** Mali
67 D3 **Kitaibaraki** Japan
66 D3 **Kitakami** Japan
66 D3 **Kitakami-gawa** *r.* Japan
67 B4 **Kita-Kyūshū** Japan
119 D2 **Kitale** Kenya
66 D2 **Kitami** Japan
130 B3 **Kitchener** Can.
93 J3 **Kitee** Fin.
119 D2 **Kitgum** Uganda
128 B2 **Kitimat** Can.
118 B3 **Kitona** Dem. Rep. Congo
92 H2 **Kittilä** Fin.
143 E1 **Kitty Hawk** U.S.A.
119 D3 **Kitunda** Tanz.
128 B2 **Kitwanga** Can.
121 B2 **Kitwe** Zambia
102 C2 **Kitzbühel** Austria
101 E3 **Kitzingen** Ger.
59 D3 **Kiunga** P.N.G.
92 I3 **Kiuruvesi** Fin.
92 I2 **Kivalo** *ridge* Fin.
90 B1 **Kivertsi** Ukr.
88 C2 **Kiviõli** Estonia
91 D2 **Kivsharivka** Ukr.
119 C3 **Kivu, Lake** Dem. Rep. Congo/Rwanda
111 C2 **Kıyıköy** Turkey
86 E3 **Kizel** Rus. Fed.
111 C3 **Kızılca Dağ** *mt.* Turkey
80 B1 **Kızılırmak** *r.* Turkey
87 D4 **Kizlyar** Rus. Fed.
Kizyl-Arbat Turkm. *see* Gyzylarbat
92 I1 **Kjøllefjord** Norway
92 G2 **Kjøpsvik** Norway
102 C1 **Kladno** Czech Rep.
102 C2 **Klagenfurt** Austria
88 B2 **Klaipėda** Lith.
94 B1 **Klaksvík** Faroe Is
134 B2 **Klamath** *r.* U.S.A.
134 B2 **Klamath Falls** U.S.A.
134 B2 **Klamath Mountains** U.S.A.
Klang Malaysia *see* **Kelang**
102 C2 **Klatovy** Czech Rep.
122 A3 **Klawer** S. Africa
128 A2 **Klawock** U.S.A.
128 B2 **Kleena Kleene** Can.
122 B2 **Kleinbegin** S. Africa
122 A2 **Klein Karas** Namibia
122 A2 **Kleinsee** S. Africa
123 C2 **Klerksdorp** S. Africa
90 B1 **Klesiv** Ukr.
89 D3 **Kletnya** Rus. Fed.
100 C2 **Kleve** Ger.
88 C3 **Klichaw** Belarus
89 D3 **Klimavichy** Belarus
89 D3 **Klimovo** Rus. Fed.
89 E2 **Klimovsk** Rus. Fed.
89 E2 **Klin** Rus. Fed.
101 F2 **Klingenthal** Ger.
101 F2 **Klínovec** *mt.* Czech Rep.
93 G4 **Klintehamn** Sweden
89 D3 **Klintsy** Rus. Fed.
109 C2 **Ključ** Bos.-Herz.
103 D1 **Kłodzko** Pol.
100 C1 **Kloosterhaar** Neth.
103 D2 **Klosterneuburg** Austria
101 E1 **Klötze (Altmark)** Ger.
128 A1 **Kluane Lake** Can.
Kluang Malaysia *see* Keluang
103 D1 **Kluczbork** Pol.
Klukhori Rus. Fed. *see* Karachayevsk
128 A2 **Klukwan** U.S.A.
74 A2 **Klupro** Pak.
89 F2 **Klyaz'ma** *r.* Rus. Fed.
88 C3 **Klyetsk** Belarus
83 L3 **Klyuchi** Rus. Fed.
98 C2 **Knaresborough** U.K.
93 F3 **Knästen** *hill* Sweden
129 E2 **Knee Lake** Can.
101 E1 **Knesebeck** Ger.
101 E3 **Knetzgau** Ger.
109 C2 **Knin** Croatia
103 C2 **Knittelfeld** Austria
109 D2 **Knjaževac** Yugo.
Knob Lake Can. *see* Schefferville
97 B3 **Knockaboy** *hill* Rep. of Ireland
100 A2 **Knokke-Heist** Belgium
143 D1 **Knoxville** U.S.A.
127 H1 **Knud Rasmussen Land** *reg.* Greenland
122 B3 **Knysna** S. Africa
60 B2 **Koba** Indon.
67 C4 **Kōbe** Japan
København Denmark s[ee] Copenhagen
100 C2 **Koblenz** Ger.
59 C3 **Kobroör** *i.* Indon.
88 B3 **Kobryn** Belarus
111 C2 **Kocaeli** Turkey
111 B2 **Kočani** Macedonia
111 C2 **Kocasu** *r.* Turkey
109 B1 **Kočevje** Slovenia
75 C2 **Koch Bihār** India
89 F3 **Kochetovka** Rus. Fed.
Kochi India *see* **Cochin**
67 B4 **Kōchi** Japan
87 D4 **Kochubey** Rus. Fed.
75 C2 **Kodarma** India
126 B3 **Kodiak** U.S.A.
126 B3 **Kodiak Island** U.S.A.
123 C1 **Kodibeleng** Botswana
117 B4 **Kodok** Sudan
90 B2 **Kodyma** Ukr.
111 C2 **Kodzhaele** *mt.* Bulg./Greece
122 A2 **Koës** Namibia
122 C2 **Koffiefontein** S. Africa
114 B4 **Koforidua** Ghana
67 C3 **Kōfu** Japan
131 D2 **Kogaluk** *r.* Can.
114 B3 **Kogoni** Mali
74 B1 **Kohat** Pak.
72 D2 **Kohima** India
88 C2 **Kohtla-Järve** Estonia
128 A1 **Koidern** Can.
77 D2 **Kokand** Uzbek.
88 B2 **Kökar** Fin.
Kokchetav Kazakh. *see* Kokshetau
122 A2 **Kokerboom** Namibia
88 C3 **Kokhanava** Belarus
89 F2 **Kokhma** Rus. Fed.
92 H3 **Kokkola** Fin.
88 C2 **Koknese** Latvia
140 B2 **Kokomo** U.S.A.
122 B1 **Kokong** Botswana
123 C2 **Kokosi** S. Africa
77 E2 **Kokpekti** Kazakh.
77 C1 **Kokshetau** Kazakh.
131 D2 **Koksoak** *r.* Can.
123 C3 **Kokstad** S. Africa
Koktokay China *see* **Fu**
61 D2 **Kolaka** Indon.
86 C2 **Kola Peninsula** Rus. F
92 H2 **Kolari** Fin.
Kolarovgrad Bulg. *see* Shumen
114 A3 **Kolda** Senegal
93 E4 **Kolding** Denmark
119 C2 **Kole** Dem. Rep. Congo
107 D2 **Koléa** Alg.
86 D2 **Kolguyev, Ostrov** *i.* Rus. Fed.
73 B3 **Kolhapur** India
88 B2 **Kolkasrags** *pt* Latvia
Kolkata India *see* **Calc**
Kollam India *see* **Quilo**
100 C1 **Kollum** Neth.
Köln Ger. *see* **Cologne**
103 D1 **Koło** Pol.
103 D1 **Kołobrzeg** Pol.
114 B3 **Kolokani** Mali
89 E2 **Kolomna** Rus. Fed.
90 B2 **Kolomyya** Ukr.
114 B3 **Kolondiéba** Mali
61 D2 **Kolonedale** Indon.
122 B2 **Kolonkwane** Botswana
82 G3 **Kolpashevo** Rus. Fed.
89 E3 **Kolpny** Rus. Fed.
Kol'skiy Poluostrov *pe* Rus. Fed. *see* Kola Peninsula
78 B3 **Koluli** Eritrea
92 F3 **Kolvereid** Norway
119 C4 **Kolwezi** Dem. Rep. Co
83 L2 **Kolyma** *r.* Rus. Fed.
Kolyma Lowland Rus. Fed. *see* Kolymskaya Nizmenno
Kolyma Range *mts* Rus. Fed. *see* Kolymskiy, Khrebet
83 L2 **Kolymskaya Nizmenno** *lowland* Rus. Fed.
83 M2 **Kolymskiy, Khrebet** *m* Rus. Fed.
122 A2 **Komaggas** S. Africa
67 C3 **Komaki** Japan
83 M3 **Komandorskiye Ostro** *is* Rus. Fed.
103 D2 **Komárno** Slovakia
123 D2 **Komati** *r.* Swaziland
123 D2 **Komatipoort** S. Africa

7 C3 **Komatsu** Japan
20 A2 **Kombat** Namibia
19 C3 **Kombe** Dem. Rep. Congo
Komintern Ukr. *see* **Marhanets'**
0 C2 **Kominternivs'ke** Ukr.
09 C2 **Komiža** Croatia
03 D2 **Komló** Hungary
Kommunarsk Ukr. *see* **Alchevs'k**
16 B2 **Kôm Ombo** Egypt
18 B3 **Komono** Congo
11 C2 **Komotini** Greece
Kompong Som Cambodia *see* **Sihanoukville**
Komrat Moldova *see* **Comrat**
22 B3 **Komsberg** *mts* S. Africa
6 C1 **Komsomolets** Kazakh.
33 H1 **Komsomolets, Ostrov** *i.* Rus. Fed.
39 F2 **Komsomol'sk** Rus. Fed.
91 C2 **Komsomol's'k** Ukr.
33 M2 **Komsomol'skiy** Rus. Fed.
Komsomol'skiy Rus. Fed. *see* **Yugorsk**
37 D4 **Komsomol'skiy** Rus. Fed.
33 K3 **Komsomol'sk-na-Amure** Rus. Fed.
39 E2 **Konakovo** Rus. Fed.
75 C3 **Kondagaon** India
36 F2 **Kondinskoye** Rus. Fed.
Kondinskoye Rus. Fed. *see* **Oktyabr'skoye**
19 D3 **Kondoa** Tanz.
36 C2 **Kondopoga** Rus. Fed.
39 E3 **Kondrovo** Rus. Fed.
27 J2 **Kong Christian IX Land** *reg.* Greenland
27 K2 **Kong Christian X Land** *reg.* Greenland
27 J2 **Kong Frederik VI Kyst** *coastal area* Greenland
35 B2 **Kongju** S. Korea
19 C3 **Kongolo** Dem. Rep. Congo
93 E4 **Kongsberg** Norway
93 F3 **Kongsvinger** Norway
77 D3 **Kongur Shan** *mt.* China
00 C2 **Königswinter** Ger.
03 D1 **Konin** Pol.
09 C2 **Konjic** Bos.-Herz.
22 A2 **Konkiep** *watercourse* Namibia
36 D2 **Konosha** Rus. Fed.
91 C1 **Konotop** Ukr.
03 E1 **Końskie** Pol.
Konstantinograd Ukr. *see* **Krasnohrad**
02 B2 **Konstanz** Ger.
15 C3 **Kontagora** Nigeria
63 B2 **Kon Tum** Vietnam
63 B2 **Kontum, Plateau du** Vietnam
80 B2 **Konya** Turkey
77 D2 **Konyrat** Kazakh.
00 C3 **Konz** Ger.
36 E3 **Konzhakovskiy Kamen', Gora** *mt.* Rus. Fed.
34 C1 **Kooskia** U.S.A.
28 C3 **Kootenay Lake** Can.
53 D2 **Kootingal** Austr.
22 B3 **Kootjieskolk** S. Africa
92 □B2 **Kópasker** Iceland
08 B1 **Koper** Slovenia
93 G4 **Köping** Sweden
23 C1 **Kopong** Botswana
93 G4 **Kopparberg** Sweden
09 C1 **Koprivnica** Croatia
89 F3 **Korablino** Rus. Fed.
73 C3 **Koraput** India
75 C2 **Korba** India
01 D2 **Korbach** Ger.
09 D2 **Korçë** Albania
09 C2 **Korčula** Croatia
09 C2 **Korčula** *i.* Croatia
65 B1 **Korea, North** *country* Asia
65 B2 **Korea, South** *country* Asia
70 C2 **Korea Bay** *g.* China/N. Korea
65 B3 **Korea Strait** Japan/S. Korea
89 D3 **Korenevo** Rus. Fed.
91 D2 **Korenovsk** Rus. Fed.
Korenovskaya Rus. Fed. *see* **Korenovsk**
90 B1 **Korets'** Ukr.
11 C2 **Körfez** Turkey
14 B4 **Korhogo** Côte d'Ivoire
11 B3 **Korinthiakos Kolpos** *sea chan.* Greece
11 B3 **Korinthos** Greece
103 D2 **Kőris-hegy** *hill* Hungary
109 D2 **Koritnik** *mt.* Albania
Koritsa Albania *see* **Korçë**
67 D3 **Kōriyama** Japan
87 F3 **Korkino** Rus. Fed.
111 D3 **Korkuteli** Turkey
77 E2 **Korla** China
103 D2 **Körmend** Hungary
49 I5 **Koro** *i.* Fiji
114 B3 **Koro** Mali
131 D2 **Koroc** *r.* Can.
91 D1 **Korocha** Rus. Fed.
119 D3 **Korogwe** Tanz.
59 C2 **Koror** Palau
103 E2 **Körös** *r.* Romania
90 B1 **Korosten'** Ukr.
90 B1 **Korostyshiv** Ukr.
115 D3 **Koro Toro** Chad
93 H3 **Korpo** Fin.
66 D1 **Korsakov** Rus. Fed.
91 C2 **Korsun'-Shevchenkivs'kyy** Ukr.
103 E1 **Korsze** Pol.
116 B3 **Korti** Sudan
100 A2 **Kortrijk** Belgium
83 L3 **Koryakskaya, Sopka** *vol.* Rus. Fed.
83 M2 **Koryakskiy Khrebet** *mts* Rus. Fed.
86 D2 **Koryazhma** Rus. Fed.
65 B2 **Koryŏng** S. Korea
91 C1 **Koryukivka** Ukr.
111 C3 **Kos** Greece
111 C3 **Kos** Greece
111 C3 **Kos** *i.* Greece
91 D2 **Kosa Biryuchyy Ostriv** *i.* Ukr.
65 B2 **Kosan** N. Korea
103 D1 **Kościan** Pol.
Kosciusko, Mount Austr. *see* **Kosciuszko, Mount**
53 C3 **Kosciuszko, Mount** Austr.
77 E2 **Kosh-Agach** Rus. Fed.
67 A4 **Koshikijima-rettō** *is* Japan
103 E2 **Košice** Slovakia
92 H2 **Koskullskulle** Sweden
65 B2 **Kosŏng** N. Korea
109 D2 **Kosovo** *prov.* Yugo.
109 D2 **Kosovska Mitrovica** Yugo.
48 H3 **Kosrae** *atoll* Micronesia
114 B4 **Kossou, Lac de** *l.* Côte d'Ivoire
76 C1 **Kostanay** Kazakh.
110 B2 **Kostenets** Bulg.
123 C2 **Koster** S. Africa
116 B3 **Kosti** Sudan
92 J3 **Kostomuksha** Rus. Fed.
90 B1 **Kostopil'** Ukr.
89 F2 **Kostroma** Rus. Fed.
89 F2 **Kostroma** *r.* Rus. Fed.
102 C1 **Kostrzyn** Pol.
91 D2 **Kostyantynivka** Ukr.
103 D1 **Koszalin** Pol.
103 D2 **Kőszeg** Hungary
74 B2 **Kota** India
60 B2 **Kotaagung** Indon.
61 C2 **Kotabaru** Indon.
61 C1 **Kota Belud** *Sabah* Malaysia
60 B1 **Kota Bharu** Malaysia
60 B2 **Kotabumi** Indon.
61 C1 **Kota Kinabalu** *Sabah* Malaysia
75 C3 **Kotapārh** India
61 C1 **Kota Samarahan** *Sarawak* Malaysia
86 D3 **Kotel'nich** Rus. Fed.
87 D4 **Kotel'nikovo** Rus. Fed.
83 K1 **Kotel'nyy, Ostrov** *i.* Rus. Fed.
91 C1 **Kotel'va** Ukr.
101 E2 **Köthen (Anhalt)** Ger.
119 D2 **Kotido** Uganda
93 I3 **Kotka** Fin.
86 D2 **Kotlas** Rus. Fed.
126 B2 **Kotlik** U.S.A.
115 C3 **Kotorkoshi** Nigeria
109 C2 **Kotor Varoš** Bos.-Herz.
87 D3 **Kotovo** Rus. Fed.
91 E1 **Kotovsk** Rus. Fed.
90 B2 **Kotovs'k** Ukr.
73 C3 **Kottagudem** India
118 C2 **Kotto** *r.* C.A.R.
83 H2 **Kotuy** *r.* Rus. Fed.
126 B2 **Kotzebue** U.S.A.
126 B2 **Kotzebue Sound** *sea chan.* U.S.A.
114 A3 **Koubia** Guinea
100 A2 **Koudekerke** Neth.
114 B3 **Koudougou** Burkina
122 B3 **Kougaberge** *mts* S. Africa
118 B3 **Koulamoutou** Gabon
114 B3 **Koulikoro** Mali
118 B2 **Koum** Cameroon
118 B2 **Koumra** Chad
114 A3 **Koundâra** Guinea
Kounradskiy Kazakh. *see* Konyrat
151 D2 **Kourou** Fr. Guiana
114 B3 **Kouroussa** Guinea
115 D3 **Kousséri** Cameroon
114 B3 **Koutiala** Mali
93 I3 **Kouvola** Fin.
109 D1 **Kovačica** Yugo.
92 J2 **Kovdor** Rus. Fed.
90 A1 **Kovel'** Ukr.
Kovno Lith. *see* **Kaunas**
89 F2 **Kovrov** Rus. Fed.
51 D1 **Kowanyama** Austr.
54 B2 **Kowhitirangi** N.Z.
71 B3 **Kowloon** China
111 C3 **Köyceğiz** Turkey
86 D2 **Koyda** Rus. Fed.
126 B2 **Koyukuk** *r.* U.S.A.
111 B2 **Kozani** Greece
90 C1 **Kozelets'** Ukr.
89 E3 **Kozel'sk** Rus. Fed.
Kozhikode India *see* Calicut
90 B2 **Kozyatyn** Ukr.
114 C4 **Kpalimé** Togo
63 A2 **Kra, Isthmus of** Thai.
63 A3 **Krabi** Thai.
63 A2 **Kra Buri** Thai.
63 B2 **Krâchéh** Cambodia
93 E4 **Kragerø** Norway
100 B1 **Kraggenburg** Neth.
109 D2 **Kragujevac** Yugo.
60 B2 **Krakatau** *i.* Indon.
103 D1 **Kraków** Pol.
109 D2 **Kraljevo** Yugo.
91 D2 **Kramators'k** Ukr.
93 G3 **Kramfors** Sweden
111 B3 **Kranidi** Greece
102 C2 **Kranj** Slovenia
123 D2 **Kranskop** S. Africa
86 E1 **Krasino** Rus. Fed.
88 C2 **Krāslava** Latvia
101 F2 **Kraslice** Czech Rep.
89 D3 **Krasnapollye** Belarus
89 D3 **Krasnaya Gora** Rus. Fed.
89 F2 **Krasnaya Gorbatka** Rus. Fed.
Krasnoarmeysk Kazakh. *see* **Tayynsha**
87 D3 **Krasnoarmeysk** Rus. Fed.
Krasnoarmeyskaya Rus. Fed. *see* **Poltavskaya**
91 D2 **Krasnoarmiys'k** Ukr.
86 D2 **Krasnoborsk** Rus. Fed.
91 D2 **Krasnodar** Rus. Fed.
91 D2 **Krasnodon** Ukr.
88 C2 **Krasnogorodskoye** Rus. Fed.
91 D1 **Krasnogvardeyskoye** Rus. Fed.
91 D2 **Krasnohrad** Ukr.
91 C2 **Krasnohvardiys'ke** Ukr.
86 E3 **Krasnokamsk** Rus. Fed.
89 D2 **Krasnomayskiy** Rus. Fed.
91 C2 **Krasnoperekops'k** Ukr.
87 D3 **Krasnoslobodsk** Rus. Fed.
86 F3 **Krasnotur'insk** Rus. Fed.
86 E3 **Krasnoufimsk** Rus. Fed.
86 E2 **Krasnovishersk** Rus. Fed.
Krasnovodsk Turkm. *see* Turkmenbashi
83 H3 **Krasnoyarsk** Rus. Fed.
89 E3 **Krasnoye** Rus. Fed.
83 M2 **Krasnoye, Ozero** *l.* Rus. Fed.
89 F2 **Krasnoye-na-Volge** Rus. Fed.
103 E1 **Krasnystaw** Pol.
89 D3 **Krasnyy** Rus. Fed.
Krasnyy Kamyshanik Rus. Fed. *see* Komsomol'skiy
89 E2 **Krasnyy Kholm** Rus. Fed.
91 D2 **Krasnyy Luch** Ukr.
91 E2 **Krasnyy Sulin** Rus. Fed.
90 B2 **Krasyliv** Ukr.
Kraulshavn Greenland *see* Nuussuaq
100 C2 **Krefeld** Ger.
91 C2 **Kremenchuk** Ukr.
91 C2 **Kremenchuts'ka Vodoskhovyshche** *resr* Ukr.
90 B1 **Kremenets'** Ukr.
103 D2 **Křemešník** *hill* Czech Rep.
Kremges Ukr. *see* **Svitlovods'k**
91 D2 **Kreminna** Ukr.
136 B2 **Kremmling** U.S.A.
103 D2 **Krems an der Donau** Austria
89 D2 **Kresttsy** Rus. Fed.
88 B2 **Kretinga** Lith.
100 C2 **Kreuzau** Ger.
101 C2 **Kreuztal** Ger.
118 A2 **Kribi** Cameroon
123 C2 **Kriel** S. Africa
111 B3 **Krikellos** Greece
66 D1 **Kril'on, Mys** *c.* Rus. Fed.
111 B3 **Krios, Akra** *pt* Greece
73 C3 **Krishna** *r.* India
73 C3 **Krishna, Mouths of the** India
75 C2 **Krishnanagar** India
93 E4 **Kristiansand** Norway
93 F4 **Kristianstad** Sweden
92 E3 **Kristiansund** Norway
93 F4 **Kristinehamn** Sweden
Kristinopol' Ukr. *see* Chervonohrad
Kriti *i.* Greece *see* **Crete**
110 B2 **Kriva Palanka** Macedonia
Krivoy Rog Ukr. *see* **Kryvyy Rih**
109 C1 **Križevci** Croatia
108 B1 **Krk** *i.* Croatia
92 F3 **Krokom** Sweden
91 C1 **Krolevets'** Ukr.
89 E3 **Kromy** Rus. Fed.
101 E2 **Kronach** Ger.
63 B2 **Krŏng Kaôh Kŏng** Cambodia
127 J2 **Kronprins Frederik Bjerge** *nunataks* Greenland
123 C2 **Kroonstad** S. Africa
91 E2 **Kropotkin** Rus. Fed.
103 E2 **Krosno** Pol.
103 D1 **Krotoszyn** Pol.
60 B2 **Krui** Indon.
122 B3 **Kruisfontein** S. Africa
109 C2 **Krujë** Albania
111 C2 **Krumovgrad** Bulg.
Krung Thep Thai. *see* Bangkok
88 C3 **Krupki** Belarus
109 D2 **Kruševac** Yugo.
101 E2 **Krušné Hory** *mts* Czech Rep.
128 A2 **Kruzof Island** U.S.A.
89 D3 **Krychaw** Belarus
91 D2 **Krylovskaya** Rus. Fed.
91 D3 **Krymsk** Rus. Fed.
Krymskaya Rus. Fed. *see* Krymsk
Kryms'kyy Pivostriv *pen.* Ukr. *see* **Crimea**
Krystynopol Ukr. *see* Chervonohrad
111 C3 **Krytiko Pelagos** *sea* Greece
91 C2 **Kryvyy Rih** Ukr.
90 B2 **Kryzhopil'** Ukr.
114 B2 **Ksabi** Alg.
107 D2 **Ksar el Boukhari** Alg.
114 B1 **Ksar el Kebir** Morocco
Ksar-es-Souk Morocco *see* **Er Rachidia**
89 E3 **Kshenskiy** Rus. Fed.
78 B2 **Kūʻ, Jabal al** *hill* Saudi Arabia
61 C1 **Kuala Belait** Brunei
Kuala Dungun Malaysia *see* **Dungun**
60 B1 **Kuala Kangsar** Malaysia
60 B1 **Kuala Kerai** Malaysia
60 B1 **Kuala Lipis** Malaysia
60 B1 **Kuala Lumpur** Malaysia
61 C2 **Kualapembuang** Indon.
60 B1 **Kuala Terengganu** Malaysia
60 B2 **Kualatungal** Indon.
61 C1 **Kuamut** *Sabah* Malaysia
65 A1 **Kuandian** China
60 B1 **Kuantan** Malaysia
91 D2 **Kuban'** *r.* Rus. Fed.
89 E2 **Kubenskoye, Ozero** *l.* Rus. Fed.
110 C2 **Kubrat** Bulg.
60 B2 **Kubu** Indon.
61 C1 **Kubuang** Indon.
60 C1 **Kuching** *Sarawak* Malaysia
109 C2 **Kuçovë** Albania
61 C2 **Kudus** Indon.
102 C2 **Kufstein** Austria
91 D2 **Kugey** Rus. Fed.
126 E2 **Kugluktuk** Can.

126 D2 **Kugmallit Bay** Can.
92 I3 **Kuhmo** Fin.
79 C2 **Kūhrān, Kūh-e** *mt.* Iran
122 A1 **Kuis** Namibia
Kuitin China *see* **Kuytun**
120 A2 **Kuito** Angola
128 A2 **Kuiu Island** U.S.A.
92 I2 **Kuivaniemi** Fin.
65 B2 **Kujang** N. Korea
66 D2 **Kuji** Japan
67 B4 **Kujū-san** *vol.* Japan
109 D2 **Kukës** Albania
76 B3 **Kukurtli** Turkm.
111 C3 **Kula** Turkey
75 D2 **Kula Kangri** *mt.* Bhutan
76 B2 **Kulandy** Kazakh.
88 B2 **Kuldīga** Latvia
Kuldja China *see* **Yining**
122 B1 **Kule** Botswana
101 E2 **Kulmbach** Ger.
77 C3 **Kŭlob** Tajik.
76 B2 **Kul'sary** Kazakh.
111 D3 **Kulübe Tepe** *mt.* Turkey
77 D1 **Kulunda** Rus. Fed.
77 D1 **Kulundinskoye, Ozero** *salt l.* Rus. Fed.
127 J2 **Kulusuk** Greenland
67 C3 **Kumagaya** Japan
67 B4 **Kumamoto** Japan
67 C4 **Kumano** Japan
110 B2 **Kumanovo** Macedonia
114 B4 **Kumasi** Ghana
118 A2 **Kumba** Cameroon
Kum-Dag Turkm. *see* Gumdag
78 B2 **Kumdah** Saudi Arabia
87 E3 **Kumertau** Rus. Fed.
65 B2 **Kumi** S. Korea
119 D2 **Kumi** Uganda
111 C3 **Kumkale** Turkey
93 G4 **Kumla** Sweden
115 D3 **Kumo** Nigeria
62 A1 **Kumon Range** *mts* Myanmar
62 B2 **Kumphawapi** Thai.
Kumul China *see* **Hami**
66 D2 **Kunashir, Ostrov** *i.* Rus. Fed.
61 C1 **Kundat** *Sabah* Malaysia
77 D2 **Kungei Alatau** *mts* Kazakh./Kyrg.
76 B2 **Kungrad** Uzbek.
93 F4 **Kungsbacka** Sweden
118 B2 **Kungu** Dem. Rep. Congo
86 E3 **Kungur** Rus. Fed.
62 A1 **Kunhing** Myanmar
62 A1 **Kunlong** Myanmar
75 B1 **Kunlun Shan** *mts* China
71 A3 **Kunming** China
65 B2 **Kunsan** S. Korea
50 B1 **Kununurra** Austr.
101 D3 **Künzelsau** Ger.
92 I3 **Kuopio** Fin.
109 C1 **Kupa** *r.* Croatia/Slovenia
59 C3 **Kupang** Indon.
88 B2 **Kupiškis** Lith.
111 C2 **Küplü** Turkey
128 A2 **Kupreanof Island** U.S.A.
91 D2 **Kup"yans'k** Ukr.
77 E2 **Kuqa** China
81 C2 **Kür** *r.* Azer.
67 B4 **Kurashiki** Japan
75 C2 **Kurasia** India
67 B3 **Kurayoshi** Japan
89 E3 **Kurchatov** Rus. Fed.
77 E2 **Kurchum** Kazakh.
111 C2 **Kŭrdzhali** Bulg.
67 B4 **Kure** Japan
57 T7 **Kure Atoll** U.S.A.
88 B2 **Kuressaare** Estonia
87 F3 **Kurgan** Rus. Fed.
Kuria Muria Islands Oman *see* Ḥalāniyāt, Juzur al
93 H3 **Kurikka** Fin.
156 C2 **Kuril Basin** *sea feature* Sea of Okhotsk
Kuril Islands Rus. Fed. *see* **Kuril'skiye Ostrova**
69 F1 **Kuril'sk** Rus. Fed.
69 F1 **Kuril'skiye Ostrova** *is* Rus. Fed.
156 C3 **Kuril Trench** *sea feature* N. Pacific Ocean
89 E3 **Kurkino** Rus. Fed.
Kurmashkino Kazakh. *see* Kurchum
117 B3 **Kurmuk** Sudan
73 B3 **Kurnool** India
67 D3 **Kuroiso** Japan
101 E2 **Kurort Schmalkalden** Ger.
53 D2 **Kurri Kurri** Austr.
88 B2 **Kuršėnai** Lith.
78 B2 **Kursh, Jabal** *hill* Saudi Arabia
89 E3 **Kursk** Rus. Fed.
109 D2 **Kuršumlija** Yugo.
122 B2 **Kuruman** S. Africa
122 B2 **Kuruman** *watercourse* S. Africa
67 B4 **Kurume** Japan
83 I3 **Kurumkan** Rus. Fed.
73 C4 **Kurunegala** Sri Lanka
81 D1 **Kuryk** Kazakh.
111 C3 **Kuşadası** Turkey
111 C3 **Kuşadası Körfezi** *b.* Turkey
111 C2 **Kuş Gölü** *l.* Turkey
91 D2 **Kushchevskaya** Rus. Fed.
66 D2 **Kushiro** Japan
Kushka Turkm. *see* Gushgy
76 C1 **Kushmurun** Kazakh.
75 C2 **Kushtia** Bangl.
126 B2 **Kuskokwim** *r.* U.S.A.
126 B2 **Kuskokwim Mountains** U.S.A.
66 D2 **Kussharo-ko** *l.* Japan
Kustanay Kazakh. *see* Kostanay
63 B2 **Kut, Ko** *i.* Thai.
111 C3 **Kütahya** Turkey
81 C1 **K'ut'aisi** Georgia
Kutaraja Indon. *see* Banda Aceh
Kutch, Gulf of India *see* Kachchh, Gulf of
109 C1 **Kutjevo** Croatia
103 D1 **Kutno** Pol.
118 B3 **Kutu** Dem. Rep. Congo
116 A3 **Kutum** Sudan
126 E2 **Kuujjua** *r.* Can.
131 D2 **Kuujjuaq** Can.
130 C2 **Kuujjuarapik** Can.
92 I2 **Kuusamo** Fin.
120 A2 **Kuvango** Angola
89 D2 **Kuvshinovo** Rus. Fed.
78 B2 **Kuwait** *country* Asia
78 B2 **Kuwait** Kuwait
82 G3 **Kuybyshev** Rus. Fed.
Kuybyshev Rus. Fed. *see* Samara
91 D2 **Kuybysheve** Ukr.
Kuybyshevka-Vostochnaya Rus. Fed. *see* Belogorsk
87 D3 **Kuybyshevskoye Vodokhranilishche** *resr* Rus. Fed.
77 E2 **Kuytun** China
111 C3 **Kuyucak** Turkey
87 D3 **Kuznetsk** Rus. Fed.
90 B1 **Kuznetsovs'k** Ukr.
86 C2 **Kuzomen'** Rus. Fed.
92 H1 **Kvalsund** Norway
123 D2 **KwaMashu** S. Africa
61 D1 **Kwandang** Indon.
Kwangchow China *see* Guangzhou
65 B2 **Kwangju** S. Korea
Kwangsi Chuang Autonomous Region *aut. reg.* China *see* Guangxi Zhuangzu Zizhiqu
Kwangtung *prov.* China *see* **Guangdong**
65 B1 **Kwanmo-bong** *mt.* N. Korea
123 C3 **Kwanobuhle** S. Africa
123 C3 **KwaNojoli** S. Africa
122 B3 **Kwanonzame** S. Africa
123 C3 **Kwatinidubu** S. Africa
123 C2 **KwaZamokhule** S. Africa
122 B3 **Kwazamukucinga** S. Africa
123 C2 **KwaZanele** S. Africa
123 D2 **Kwazulu-Natal** *prov.* S. Africa
Kweichow *prov.* China *see* **Guizhou**
Kweiyang China *see* Guiyang
121 B2 **Kwekwe** Zimbabwe
118 B3 **Kwenge** *r.* Dem. Rep. Congo
123 C3 **Kwezi-Naledi** S. Africa
103 D1 **Kwidzyn** Pol.
59 D3 **Kwikila** P.N.G.
118 B3 **Kwilu** *r.* Angola/Dem. Rep. Congo
59 C3 **Kwoka** *mt.* Indon.
118 B2 **Kyabé** Chad
53 C3 **Kyabram** Austr.
62 A2 **Kyaikto** Myanmar
63 A2 **Kya-in Seikkyi** Myanmar
68 D1 **Kyakhta** Rus. Fed.
52 A2 **Kyancutta** Austr.
62 A1 **Kyaukpadaung** Myanmar
62 A2 **Kyaukpyu** Myanmar
88 B3 **Kybartai** Lith.
62 A2 **Kyebogyi** Myanmar
54 B3 **Kyeburn** N.Z.
62 A2 **Kyeintali** Myanmar
74 B1 **Kyelang** India
Kyiv Ukr. *see* **Kiev**
Kyklades *is* Greece *see* Cyclades
129 D2 **Kyle** Can.
96 B2 **Kyle of Lochalsh** U.K.
100 C3 **Kyll** *r.* Ger.
111 B3 **Kyllini** *mt.* Greece
111 B3 **Kymi** Greece
52 B3 **Kyneton** Austr.
119 D2 **Kyoga, Lake** Uganda
53 D1 **Kyogle** Austr.
65 B2 **Kyŏnggi-man** *b.* S. Korea
65 B2 **Kyŏngju** S. Korea
67 C4 **Kyōto** Japan
111 B3 **Kyparissia** Greece
111 B3 **Kyparissiakos Kolpos** *b.* Greece
77 C1 **Kypshak, Ozero** *salt l.* Kazakh.
111 B3 **Kyra Panagia** *i.* Greece
Kyrenia Cyprus *see* Keryneia
77 D2 **Kyrgyzstan** *country* Asia
101 F1 **Kyritz** Ger.
93 H3 **Kyrönjoki** *r.* Fin.
86 E2 **Kyrta** Rus. Fed.
86 D2 **Kyssa** Rus. Fed.
83 J2 **Kytalyktakh** Rus. Fed.
111 B3 **Kythira** *i.* Greece
111 B3 **Kythnos** *i.* Greece
128 B2 **Kyuquot** Can.
67 B4 **Kyūshū** *i.* Japan
110 B2 **Kyustendil** Bulg.
62 A2 **Kywebwe** Myanmar
90 C1 **Kyyivs'ke Vodoskhovyshche** *resr* Ukr.
92 H3 **Kyyjärvi** Fin.
68 C1 **Kyzyl** Rus. Fed.
76 C2 **Kyzylkum Desert** Kazakh./Uzbek.
77 C2 **Kyzylorda** Kazakh.
Kzyl-Orda Kazakh. *see* Kyzylorda
Kzyltu Kazakh. *see* Kishkenekol'

L

145 C3 **La Angostura, Presa de** *resr* Mex.
117 C4 **Laascaanood** Somalia
145 D3 **La Ascensión, Bahía de** *b.* Mex.
117 C3 **Laasgoray** Somalia
150 C1 **La Asunción** Venez.
114 A2 **Laâyoune** Western Sahara
87 D4 **Laba** *r.* Rus. Fed.
144 B2 **La Babia** Mex.
146 B3 **La Bahía, Islas de** *is* Hond.
61 D2 **Labala** Indon.
131 D2 **La Baleine, Rivière à** *r.* Can.
152 B2 **La Banda** Arg.
61 C1 **Labang** *Sarawak* Malaysia
104 B2 **La Baule-Escoublac** France
102 C1 **Labe** *r.* Czech Rep.
114 A3 **Labé** Guinea
128 A1 **Laberge, Lake** Can.
128 C2 **La Biche, Lac** *l.* Can.
108 B1 **Labin** Croatia
87 D4 **Labinsk** Rus. Fed.
64 B2 **Labo** Phil.
144 B2 **La Boquilla, Presa de** *resr* Mex.
104 B3 **Labouheyre** France
153 B3 **Laboulaye** Arg.
131 D2 **Labrador** *reg.* Can.
131 D2 **Labrador City** Can.
127 I2 **Labrador Sea** Can./Greenland
150 C3 **Lábrea** Brazil
61 C1 **Labuan** Malaysia
61 C2 **Labuhanbajo** Indon.
60 B1 **Labuhanbilik** Indon.
59 C3 **Labuna** Indon.
63 A2 **Labutta** Myanmar
86 F2 **Labytnangi** Rus. Fed.
109 C2 **Laç** Albania
106 B1 **La Cabrera, Sierra de** *mts* Spain
La Calle Alg. *see* **El Kala**
105 C2 **La Capelle** France
131 D2 **Lac Bermen** *l.* Can.
73 B3 **Laccadive Islands** India
129 E2 **Lac du Bonnet** Can.
146 B3 **La Ceiba** Hond.
52 A3 **Lacepede Bay** Austr.
134 B1 **Lacey** U.S.A.
105 D2 **La Chaux-de-Fonds** Switz.
53 B2 **Lachlan** *r.* Austr.
146 C4 **La Chorrera** Panama
141 E1 **Lachute** Can.
105 D3 **La Ciotat** France
128 C2 **Lac La Biche** Can.
Lac la Martre Can. *see* Wha Ti
141 E1 **Lac-Mégantic** Can.
128 C2 **Lacombe** Can.
145 C3 **La Concordia** Mex.
108 A3 **Laconi** *Sardinia* Italy
141 E2 **Laconia** U.S.A.
104 B2 **La Coubre, Pointe de** *pt* France
128 C2 **La Crete** Can.
140 A2 **La Crosse** U.S.A.
144 B2 **La Cruz** Mex.
144 B2 **La Cuesta** Mex.
155 D1 **Ladainha** Brazil
74 B1 **Ladakh Range** *mts* India
106 C1 **La Demanda, Sierra de** *mts* Spain
122 B3 **Ladismith** S. Africa
79 D2 **Lādīz** Iran
89 D1 **Ladoga, Lake** Rus. Fed.
Ladozhskoye Ozero *l.* Rus. Fed. *see* Ladoga, Lake
143 D2 **Ladson** U.S.A.
123 C3 **Lady Grey** S. Africa
128 B3 **Ladysmith** Can.
123 C2 **Ladysmith** S. Africa
59 D3 **Lae** P.N.G.
62 B2 **Lae** Thai.
139 C3 **La Encantada, Sierra** *mt* Mex.
152 B2 **La Esmeralda** Bol.
93 F4 **Læsø** *i.* Denmark
Lafayette Alg. *see* **Bouga**
143 C2 **La Fayette** U.S.A.
140 B2 **Lafayette** *IN* U.S.A.
142 B2 **Lafayette** *LA* U.S.A.
115 C4 **Lafia** Nigeria
104 B2 **La Flèche** France
143 D1 **La Follette** U.S.A.
130 C2 **Laforge** Can.
79 C2 **Lāft** Iran
108 A3 **La Galite** *i.* Tunisia
87 D4 **Lagan'** Rus. Fed.
151 F4 **Lagarto** Brazil
118 B2 **Lagdo, Lac de** *l.* Cameroon
119 E2 **Lagh Bor** *watercourse* Kenya/Somalia
115 C1 **Laghouat** Alg.
155 D1 **Lagoa Santa** Brazil
114 A2 **La Gomera** *i.* Canary Is
147 C3 **La Gonâve, Île de** *i.* Haiti
114 C4 **Lagos** Nigeria
106 B2 **Lagos** Port.
134 C1 **La Grande** U.S.A.
130 C2 **La Grande 2, Réservoir** *resr* Can.
130 C2 **La Grande 3, Réservoir** *resr* Can.
130 C2 **La Grande 4, Réservoir** *resr* Can.
50 B1 **Lagrange** Austr.
143 C2 **La Grange** U.S.A.
150 C2 **La Gran Sabana** *plat.* Venez.
152 D2 **Laguna** Brazil
150 B3 **Lagunas** Peru
147 C3 **Lagunillas** Venez.
La Habana Cuba *see* Havana
61 C1 **Lahad Datu** *Sabah* Malaysia
104 B2 **La Hague, Cap de** *c.* France
60 B2 **Lahat** Indon.
78 B3 **Laḥij** Yemen
81 C2 **Lāhījān** Iran
100 C2 **Lahnstein** Ger.
74 B1 **Lahore** Pak.

A2 Lahri Pak.
I3 Lahti Fin.
D4 Laï Chad
D1 Laidley Austr.
C2 L'Aigle France
B3 Laingsburg S. Africa
H2 Lainioälven r. Sweden
C3 L'Aïr, Massif de mts Niger
B1 Lairg U.K.
B1 Laives Italy
B2 Laiwu China
C2 Laiyang China
B2 Laiyuan China
B2 Laizhou China
B2 Laizhou Wan b. China
C1 Lajamanu Austr.
B2 Lajes Brazil
B2 La Junta Mex.
C3 La Junta U.S.A.
B2 La Juventud, Isla de i. Cuba
C2 Lake Cargelligo Austr.
C3 Lake Cathie Austr.
B2 Lake Charles U.S.A.
D2 Lake City FL U.S.A.
E2 Lake City SC U.S.A.
B3 Lake Cowichan Can.
   Lake Harbour Can. see Kimmirut
A2 Lake Havasu City U.S.A.
D3 Lake Jackson U.S.A.
A3 Lake King Austr.
A3 Lakeland U.S.A.
C2 Lake Louise Can.
B1 Lake Oswego U.S.A.
A2 Lake Paringa N.Z.
B2 Lake Providence U.S.A.
C3 Lake Pukaki N.Z.
C3 Lakes Entrance Austr.
E2 Lakeview U.S.A.
B4 Lakeville U.S.A.
C3 Lakewood CO U.S.A.
D3 Lakewood NJ U.S.A.
E3 Lake Worth U.S.A.
B1 Lakhpat India
B1 Lakki Pak.
B3 Lakonikos Kolpos b. Greece
B4 Lakota Côte d'Ivoire
H1 Lakselv Norway
A2 La Laguna, Picacho de mt. Mex.
B3 La Libertad Guat.
B1 Lalín Spain
B2 La Línea de la Concepción Spain
B2 Lalitpur India
   Lalitpur Nepal see Patan
D2 La Loche Can.
D2 La Louvière Belgium
A2 La Maddalena Sardinia Italy
D3 La Madeleine, Îles de is Can.
C1 Lamag Sabah Malaysia
   La Manche str. France/U.K. see English Channel
C3 Lamar U.S.A.
C3 Lamard Iran
A3 La Marmora, Punta mt. Sardinia Italy
C1 La Martre, Lac l. Can.
B3 Lamballe France
A3 Lambaréné Gabon
A2 Lambert's Bay S. Africa
A2 Lambeyri Iceland
B1 Lamego Port.
D3 Lameque, Île i. Can.
B4 La Merced Peru
B2 Lameroo Austr.
C2 Lamesa U.S.A.
B3 Lamia Greece
E2 Lamoni U.S.A.
D2 Lampang Thai.
D2 Lampasas U.S.A.
B2 Lampazos Mex.
A3 Lampeter U.K.
D2 Lamphun Thai.
E3 Lamu Kenya
D2 La Nao, Cabo de c. Spain
D2 Lanark U.K.
A2 Lanbi Kyun i. Myanmar
A1 Lancang China
   Lancang Jiang r. China see Mekong
B2 Lancaster CA U.S.A.
C4 Lancaster OH U.S.A.
C3 Lancaster OH U.S.A.
B2 Lancaster PA U.S.A.

143 D2 Lancaster SC U.S.A.
127 G2 Lancaster Sound str. Can.
50 A3 Lancelin Austr.
   Lanchow China see Lanzhou
102 C2 Landeck Austria
136 B2 Lander U.S.A.
99 A4 Land's End pt U.K.
102 C2 Landshut Ger.
93 F4 Landskrona Sweden
143 C2 Lanett U.S.A.
122 B2 Langberg mts S. Africa
137 D1 Langdon U.S.A.
93 F4 Langeland i. Denmark
101 D1 Langen Ger.
100 C1 Langeoog Ger.
100 C1 Langeoog i. Ger.
82 G2 Langepas Rus. Fed.
70 B2 Langfang China
101 D2 Langgöns Ger.
96 C3 Langholm U.K.
92 ☐A3 Langjökull ice cap Iceland
60 A1 Langkawi i. Malaysia
105 C3 Langogne France
104 B3 Langon France
106 B1 Langreo Spain
105 D2 Langres France
60 A1 Langsa Indon.
62 B1 Lang Son Vietnam
105 C3 Languedoc reg. France
101 D1 Langwedel Ger.
129 D2 Lanigan Can.
153 A3 Lanín, Volcán vol. Arg./Chile
81 C2 Länkäran Azer.
104 B2 Lannion France
140 B1 L'Anse U.S.A.
141 E1 L'Anse-St-Jean Can.
140 C2 Lansing U.S.A.
71 B3 Lanxi China
117 B4 Lanya Sudan
114 A2 Lanzarote i. Canary Is
70 A2 Lanzhou China
64 B2 Laoag Phil.
62 B1 Lao Cai Vietnam
70 B2 Laohekou China
   Laojunmiao China see Yumen
65 B1 Laoling China
65 B1 Lao Ling mts China
105 C2 Laon France
62 B2 Laos country Asia
65 B1 Laotougou China
66 A2 Laoye Ling mts China
154 C3 Lapa Brazil
114 A2 La Palma i. Canary Is
146 C4 La Palma Panama
150 C2 La Paragua Venez.
152 B1 La Paz Bol.
145 D3 La Paz Hond.
144 A2 La Paz Mex.
150 C3 La Pedrera Col.
140 C2 Lapeer U.S.A.
66 D1 La Pérouse Strait Japan/Rus. Fed.
145 C2 La Pesca Mex.
144 B2 La Piedad Mex.
153 C3 La Plata Arg.
153 C3 La Plata, Rio de sea chan. Arg./Uru.
92 H3 Lappajärvi l. Fin.
93 I3 Lappeenranta Fin.
92 G2 Lappland reg. Europe
111 C2 Lâpseki Turkey
   Laptevo Rus. Fed. see Yasnogorsk
83 J1 Laptev Sea Rus. Fed.
   Laptevykh, More sea Rus. Fed. see Laptev Sea
93 H3 Lapua Fin.
152 B2 La Quiaca Arg.
108 B2 L'Aquila Italy
135 C4 La Quinta U.S.A.
79 C2 Lār Iran
114 B1 Larache Morocco
136 B2 Laramie U.S.A.
136 B2 Laramie Mountains U.S.A.
154 B3 Laranjeiras do Sul Brazil
61 D2 Larantuka Indon.
59 C3 Larat i. Indon.
107 D2 Larba Alg.
   L'Ardenne, Plateau de Belgium see Ardennes
106 C1 Laredo Spain
139 D3 Laredo U.S.A.
153 A5 La Reina Adelaida, Archipiélago de is Chile
143 D3 Largo U.S.A.
96 B3 Largs U.K.
115 D1 L'Ariana Tunisia

152 B2 La Rioja Arg.
111 B3 Larisa Greece
74 A2 Larkana Pak.
   Larnaca Cyprus see Larnaka
80 B2 Larnaka Cyprus
97 D1 Larne U.K.
100 B2 La Roche-en-Ardenne Belgium
104 B2 La Rochelle France
104 B2 La Roche-sur-Yon France
107 C2 La Roda Spain
147 D3 La Romana Dom. Rep.
129 D2 La Ronge Can.
129 D2 La Ronge, Lac l. Can.
50 C1 Larrimah Austr.
55 A3 Larsen Ice Shelf Antarctica
93 F4 Larvik Norway
136 C3 Las Animas U.S.A.
   Las Anod Somalia see Laascaanood
130 C3 La Sarre Can.
138 B2 Las Cruces U.S.A.
153 A4 La Serena Chile
153 C3 Las Flores Arg.
153 B3 Las Heras Arg.
62 A1 Lashio Myanmar
76 C3 Lashkar Gāh Afgh.
109 C3 La Sila reg. Italy
152 B2 Las Lomitas Arg.
106 B2 Las Marismas marsh Spain
145 D3 Las Minas, Cerro de mt. Hond.
144 B2 Las Nieves Mex.
114 A2 Las Palmas de Gran Canaria Canary Is
108 A2 La Spezia Italy
153 C3 Las Piedras Uru.
150 C4 Las Piedras, Río de r. Peru
153 B4 Las Plumas Arg.
155 D1 Lassance Brazil
129 D2 Last Mountain Lake Can.
152 B2 Las Tórtolas, Cerro mt. Chile
118 B3 Lastoursville Gabon
109 C2 Lastovo i. Croatia
144 A2 Las Tres Vírgenes, Volcán vol. Mex.
146 C2 Las Tunas Cuba
144 B2 Las Varas Mex.
144 B2 Las Varas Mex.
138 B1 Las Vegas NM U.S.A.
135 C3 Las Vegas NV U.S.A.
131 E2 La Tabatière Can.
   Latakia Syria see Al Lādhiqīyah
104 B3 La Teste France
108 B2 Latina Italy
147 D3 La Tortuga, Isla i. Venez.
64 B2 La Trinidad Phil.
89 E2 Latskoye Rus. Fed.
130 C3 La Tuque Can.
88 B2 Latvia country Europe
   Latviyskaya S.S.R. country Europe see Latvia
102 C1 Lauchhammer Ger.
101 E3 Lauf an der Pegnitz Ger.
105 D2 Laufen Switz.
92 ☐A3 Laugarás Iceland
127 H1 Lauge Koch Kyst reg. Greenland
138 C1 Laughlin Peak U.S.A.
51 D4 Launceston Austr.
99 A4 Launceston U.K.
62 A1 Launggyaung Myanmar
153 A4 La Unión Chile
51 D1 Laura Austr.
142 C2 Laurel MS U.S.A.
134 E1 Laurel MT U.S.A.
96 C2 Laurencekirk U.K.
109 C2 Lauria Italy
143 D2 Laurinburg U.S.A.
105 D2 Lausanne Switz.
61 C2 Laut i. Indon.
63 D3 Laut i. Indon.
101 D2 Lautersbach (Hessen) Ger.
61 C2 Laut Kecil, Kepulauan is Indon.
100 C1 Lauwersmeer l. Neth.
141 E1 Laval Can.
104 B2 Laval France
   Lavar Meydān salt marsh Iran
50 B1 Laverton Austr.
154 B3 La Victoria, Sierra de hills Arg.

155 D2 Lavras Brazil
123 D2 Lavumisa Swaziland
61 C1 Lawas Sarawak Malaysia
78 B3 Lawdar Yemen
62 A1 Lawksawk Myanmar
114 B3 Lawra Ghana
140 B3 Lawrence IN U.S.A.
137 D3 Lawrence KS U.S.A.
141 E2 Lawrence MA U.S.A.
142 C1 Lawrenceburg U.S.A.
143 D2 Lawrenceville U.S.A.
139 D2 Lawton U.S.A.
78 A2 Lawz, Jabal al mt. Saudi Arabia
93 F4 Laxå Sweden
122 B2 Laxey S. Africa
78 B2 Laylá Saudi Arabia
109 D2 Lazarevac Yugo.
144 A1 Lázaro Cárdenas Mex.
144 B3 Lázaro Cárdenas Mex.
88 B3 Lazdijai Lith.
66 B2 Lazo Rus. Fed.
83 K2 Lazo Rus. Fed.
136 C2 Lead U.S.A.
129 D2 Leader Can.
136 B3 Leadville U.S.A.
   Leaf Bay Can. see Tasiujaq
129 D2 Leaf Rapids Can.
139 D3 League City U.S.A.
139 D3 Leakey U.S.A.
99 C3 Leamington Spa, Royal U.K.
97 B2 Leane, Lough l. Rep. of Ireland
130 C2 L'Eau Claire, Lac à l. Can.
137 E3 Leavenworth U.S.A.
64 B3 Lebak Phil.
80 B2 Lebanon country Asia
137 D3 Lebanon MO U.S.A.
141 E2 Lebanon NH U.S.A.
134 B2 Lebanon OR U.S.A.
141 D2 Lebanon PA U.S.A.
142 C1 Lebanon TN U.S.A.
89 E3 Lebedyan' Rus. Fed.
91 C1 Lebedyn Ukr.
130 C3 Lebel-sur-Quévillon Can.
104 C1 Le Blanc France
103 D1 Lębork Pol.
123 C1 Lebowakgomo S. Africa
106 B2 Lebrija Spain
153 A3 Lebu Chile
104 C3 Le Bugue France
108 B1 Lecco Italy
102 C2 Lech r. Austria/Ger.
111 B3 Lechaina Greece
71 B3 Lechang China
102 B1 Leck Ger.
142 B2 Lecompte U.S.A.
105 C2 Le Creusot France
104 C3 Lectoure France
106 B1 Ledesma Spain
104 C2 Le Dorat France
128 C2 Leduc Can.
   Lee r. Rep. of Ireland
137 E1 Leech Lake U.S.A.
98 C3 Leeds U.K.
99 B3 Leek U.K.
97 B2 Leenane Rep. of Ireland
100 C1 Leer (Ostfriesland) Ger.
143 D3 Leesburg U.S.A.
142 B2 Leesville U.S.A.
53 C2 Leeton Austr.
122 B3 Leeu-Gamka S. Africa
100 B1 Leeuwarden Neth.
50 A3 Leeuwin, Cape Austr.
147 D3 Leeward Islands Caribbean Sea
111 B3 Lefkada Greece
111 B3 Lefkada i. Greece
   Lefkosia Cyprus see Nicosia
74 B1 Legaspi Phil.
103 D1 Legionowo Pol.
108 B1 Legnago Italy
103 D1 Legnica Pol.
74 B1 Leh Jammu and Kashmir
104 C2 Le Havre France
101 E1 Lehre Ger.
123 C1 Lehututu Botswana
74 B1 Leiah Pak.
102 C2 Leibnitz Austria
99 C3 Leicester U.K.
51 C1 Leichhardt r. Austr.
51 D2 Leichhardt Range mts Austr.
100 B1 Leiden Neth.
100 A2 Leie r. Belgium
52 A2 Leigh Creek Austr.

97 C2 **Leighlinbridge** Rep. of Ireland
99 C4 **Leighton Buzzard** U.K.
93 E3 **Leikanger** Norway
101 D1 **Leine** *r.* Ger.
50 B2 **Leinster** Austr.
97 C2 **Leinster** *reg.* Rep. of Ireland
97 C2 **Leinster, Mount** *hill* Rep. of Ireland
101 F2 **Leipzig** Ger.
92 F2 **Leiranger** Norway
106 B2 **Leiria** Port.
93 E4 **Leirvik** Norway
97 C2 **Leixlip** Rep. of Ireland
71 B3 **Leiyang** China
71 B3 **Leizhou** China
71 A3 **Leizhou Bandao** *pen.* China
118 B3 **Lékana** Congo
122 A2 **Lekkersing** S. Africa
142 B2 **Leland** U.S.A.
Leli China *see* **Tianlin**
100 B1 **Lelystad** Neth.
153 B5 **Le Maire, Estrecho de** *sea chan.* Arg.
105 D2 **Léman, Lac** *l.* France/Switz.
104 C2 **Le Mans** France
137 D2 **Le Mars** U.S.A.
102 B2 **Lemberg** *mt.* Ger.
154 C2 **Leme** Brazil
80 B2 **Lemesos** Cyprus
101 D1 **Lemförde** Ger.
127 H2 **Lemieux Islands** Can.
136 C1 **Lemmon** U.S.A.
135 C3 **Lemoore** U.S.A.
131 D2 **Le Moyne, Lac** *l.* Can.
62 A1 **Lemro** *r.* Myanmar
109 C2 **Le Murge** *hills* Italy
83 J2 **Lena** *r.* Rus. Fed.
100 C1 **Lengerich** Ger.
70 A2 **Lenglong Ling** *mts* China
71 B3 **Lengshuijiang** China
71 B3 **Lengshuitan** China
Leninabad Tajik. *see* **Khŭjand**
Leninakan Armenia *see* **Gyumri**
91 D2 **Lenine** Ukr.
Leningrad Rus. Fed. *see* **St Petersburg**
91 D2 **Leningradskaya** Rus. Fed.
Leninobod Tajik. *see* **Khŭjand**
77 E1 **Leninogorsk** Kazakh.
77 D3 **Lenin Peak** Kyrg./Tajik.
Leninsk Kazakh. *see* **Baykonur**
89 E3 **Leninskiy** Rus. Fed.
53 D1 **Lennox Head** Austr.
143 D1 **Lenoir** U.S.A.
100 A2 **Lens** Belgium
105 C1 **Lens** France
83 I2 **Lensk** Rus. Fed.
103 D2 **Lenti** Hungary
109 C3 **Lentini** *Sicily* Italy
114 B3 **Léo** Burkina
103 D2 **Leoben** Austria
Leodhais, Eilean *i.* U.K. *see* **Lewis, Isle of**
99 B3 **Leominster** U.K.
144 B2 **León** Mex.
146 B3 **León** Nic.
106 B1 **León** Spain
122 A1 **Leonardville** Namibia
108 B3 **Leonforte** *Sicily* Italy
53 C3 **Leongatha** Austr.
50 B2 **Leonora** Austr.
Léopold II, Lac *l.* Dem. Rep. Congo *see* **Mai-Ndombe, Lac**
155 D2 **Leopoldina** Brazil
Léopoldville Dem. Rep. Congo *see* **Kinshasa**
90 B2 **Leova** Moldova
Leovo Moldova *see* **Leova**
123 C1 **Lephepe** Botswana
123 C3 **Lephoi** S. Africa
71 B3 **Leping** China
77 D2 **Lepsy** Kazakh.
105 C2 **Le-Puy-en-Velay** France
123 C1 **Lerala** Botswana
123 C2 **Leratswana** S. Africa
150 B3 **Lérida** Col.
Lérida Spain *see* **Lleida**
106 C1 **Lerma** Spain
111 C3 **Leros** *i.* Greece
130 C2 **Le Roy, Lac** *l.* Can.
93 F4 **Lerum** Sweden
96 □ **Lerwick** U.K.
111 C3 **Lesbos** *i.* Greece
147 C3 **Les Cayes** Haiti
104 C3 **Les Escaldes** Andorra
141 F1 **Les Escoumins** Can.
107 D1 **Le Seu d'Urgell** Spain
70 A3 **Leshan** China
104 B2 **Les Herbiers** France
86 D2 **Leshukonskoye** Rus. Fed.
Leskhimstroy Ukr. *see* **Syeverodonets'k**
109 D2 **Leskovac** Yugo.
104 B2 **Lesneven** France
Lesnoy Rus. Fed. *see* **Umba**
89 E2 **Lesnoye** Rus. Fed.
83 H3 **Lesosibirsk** Rus. Fed.
123 C2 **Lesotho** *country* Africa
66 B1 **Lesozavodsk** Rus. Fed.
104 B2 **Les Sables-d'Olonne** France
147 D3 **Lesser Antilles** *is* Caribbean Sea
Lesser Caucasus *mts* Asia *see* **Malyy Kavkaz**
Lesser Khingan Mountains China *see* **Xiao Hinggan Ling**
128 C2 **Lesser Slave Lake** Can.
105 C3 **Les Vans** France
Lesvos *i.* Greece *see* **Lesbos**
103 D1 **Leszno** Pol.
123 D1 **Letaba** S. Africa
99 C4 **Letchworth** U.K.
128 C3 **Lethbridge** Can.
150 D2 **Lethem** Guyana
59 C3 **Leti, Kepulauan** *is* Indon.
150 C3 **Leticia** Col.
120 B3 **Letlhakane** Botswana
123 C1 **Letlhakeng** Botswana
104 C1 **Le Touquet-Paris-Plage** France
99 D4 **Le Tréport** France
123 D1 **Letsitele** S. Africa
63 A2 **Letsok-aw Kyun** *i.* Myanmar
123 C2 **Letsopa** S. Africa
97 C1 **Letterkenny** Rep. of Ireland
105 C3 **Leucate, Étang de** *l.* France
Leukas Greece *see* **Lefkada**
60 A1 **Leuser, Gunung** *mt.* Indon.
100 B2 **Leuven** Belgium
111 B3 **Levadeia** Greece
92 F3 **Levanger** Norway
139 C2 **Levelland** U.S.A.
50 B1 **Lévêque, Cape** Austr.
96 A2 **Leverburgh** U.K.
100 C2 **Leverkusen** Ger.
103 D2 **Levice** Slovakia
54 C2 **Levin** N.Z.
131 C3 **Lévis** Can.
141 E2 **Levittown** U.S.A.
89 E3 **Lev Tolstoy** Rus. Fed.
99 D4 **Lewes** U.K.
96 A1 **Lewis, Isle of** *i.* U.K.
141 D2 **Lewisburg** *PA* U.S.A.
142 C1 **Lewisburg** *TN* U.S.A.
140 C3 **Lewisburg** *WV* U.S.A.
134 D1 **Lewis Range** *mts* U.S.A.
134 C1 **Lewiston** *ID* U.S.A.
141 E2 **Lewiston** *ME* U.S.A.
134 E1 **Lewistown** U.S.A.
140 C3 **Lexington** *KY* U.S.A.
136 D2 **Lexington** *NE* U.S.A.
139 D1 **Lexington** *OK* U.S.A.
141 D3 **Lexington** *VA* U.S.A.
64 B2 **Leyte** *i.* Phil.
109 C2 **Lezhë** Albania
89 F2 **Lezhnevo** Rus. Fed.
89 E3 **L'gov** Rus. Fed.
75 C2 **Lhagoi Kangri** *mt.* China
Lharigarbo China *see* **Amdo**
75 D2 **Lhasa** China
75 C2 **Lhazê** China
60 A1 **Lhokseumawe** Indon.
62 A1 **Lhünzê** China
67 B3 **Liancourt Rocks** *i.* N. Pacific Ocean
70 B2 **Liangaz Hu** *l.* China
Liangzhou China *see* **Wuwei**
Lianhe China *see* **Qianjiang**
71 B3 **Lianhua** China
71 B3 **Lianjiang** China
Lianran China *see* **Anning**
70 C1 **Lianshan** China
Liantang China *see* **Nanchang**
Lianxian China *see* **Lianzhou**
70 B2 **Lianyungang** China
71 B3 **Lianzhou** China
Lianzhou China *see* **Hepu**
65 A1 **Liao** *r.* China
70 B2 **Liaocheng** China
70 C1 **Liaodong Bandao** *pen.* China
70 C1 **Liaodong Wan** *b.* China
70 C1 **Liaoning** *prov.* China
70 C1 **Liaoyang** China
65 B1 **Liaoyuan** China
128 B1 **Liard** *r.* Can.
134 C1 **Libby** U.S.A.
118 B2 **Libenge** Dem. Rep. Congo
136 C3 **Liberal** U.S.A.
103 D1 **Liberec** Czech Rep.
114 B4 **Liberia** *country* Africa
146 B3 **Liberia** Costa Rica
150 C2 **Libertad** Venez.
137 E3 **Liberty** U.S.A.
100 B3 **Libin** Belgium
64 B2 **Libmanan** Phil.
71 A3 **Libo** China
123 C3 **Libode** S. Africa
119 E2 **Liboi** Kenya
104 B3 **Libourne** France
100 B3 **Libramont** Belgium
138 A3 **Libre, Sierra** *mts* Mex.
118 A2 **Libreville** Gabon
115 D2 **Libya** *country* Africa
115 E2 **Libyan Desert** Egypt/Libya
116 A1 **Libyan Plateau** Egypt
108 B3 **Licata** *Sicily* Italy
Licheng China *see* **Lipu**
99 C3 **Lichfield** U.K.
121 C2 **Lichinga** Moz.
101 E2 **Lichte** Ger.
123 C2 **Lichtenburg** S. Africa
101 E2 **Lichtenfels** Ger.
88 C3 **Lida** Belarus
93 F4 **Lidköping** Sweden
50 C2 **Liebig, Mount** Austr.
105 D2 **Liechtenstein** *country* Europe
100 B2 **Liège** Belgium
92 J3 **Lieksa** Fin.
119 C2 **Lienart** Dem. Rep. Congo
102 C2 **Lienz** Austria
88 B2 **Liepāja** Latvia
100 B2 **Lier** Belgium
102 C2 **Liezen** Austria
97 C2 **Liffey** *r.* Rep. of Ireland
97 C1 **Lifford** Rep. of Ireland
53 C1 **Lightning Ridge** Austr.
121 C2 **Ligonha** *r.* Moz.
105 D3 **Ligurian Sea** France/Italy
119 C4 **Likasi** Dem. Rep. Congo
118 C2 **Likati** Dem. Rep. Congo
128 B2 **Likely** Can.
Likhachevo Ukr. *see* **Pervomays'kyy**
Likhachyovo Ukr. *see* **Pervomays'kyy**
89 E2 **Likhoslavl'** Rus. Fed.
60 B1 **Liku** Indon.
105 D3 **L'Île-Rousse** *Corsica* France
71 B3 **Liling** China
93 F4 **Lilla Edet** Sweden
100 B2 **Lille** Belgium
105 C1 **Lille** France
93 E4 **Lille Bælt** *sea chan.* Denmark
93 F3 **Lillehammer** Norway
93 F4 **Lillestrøm** Norway
128 B2 **Lillooet** Can.
121 C2 **Lilongwe** Malawi
64 B3 **Liloy** Phil.
150 B4 **Lima** Peru
140 C2 **Lima** U.S.A.
155 D2 **Lima Duarte** Brazil
79 C2 **Līmah** Oman
Limassol Cyprus *see* **Lemesos**
97 C1 **Limavady** U.K.
153 B3 **Limay** *r.* Arg.
101 F2 **Limbach-Oberfrohna** Ger.
88 B2 **Limbaži** Latvia
118 A2 **Limbe** Cameroon
101 D2 **Limburg an der Lahn** Ger.
122 B2 **Lime Acres** S. Africa
154 C2 **Limeira** Brazil
97 B2 **Limerick** Rep. of Ireland
93 E4 **Limfjorden** *sea chan.* Denmark
92 I3 **Liminka** Fin.
111 C3 **Limnos** *i.* Greece
104 C2 **Limoges** France
146 B3 **Limón** Costa Rica
136 C3 **Limon** U.S.A.
104 C2 **Limousin, Plateaux du** France
104 C3 **Limoux** France
121 C3 **Limpopo** *r.* S. Africa/Zimbabwe
64 A2 **Linapacan** *i.* Phil.
153 A3 **Linares** Chile
145 C2 **Linares** Mex.
106 C2 **Linares** Spain
108 A3 **Linas, Monte** *mt. Sardir* Italy
62 B1 **Lincang** China
71 B3 **Linchuan** China
98 C3 **Lincoln** U.K.
140 B2 **Lincoln** *IL* U.S.A.
141 F1 **Lincoln** *ME* U.S.A.
137 D2 **Lincoln** *NE* U.S.A.
134 B2 **Lincoln City** U.S.A.
151 D2 **Linden** Guyana
142 C1 **Linden** U.S.A.
119 C2 **Lindi** *r.* Dem. Rep. Cong
119 D3 **Lindi** Tanz.
Lindisfarne *i.* U.K. *see* **Holy Island**
111 C3 **Lindos** Greece
130 C3 **Lindsay** Can.
48 K3 **Line Islands** Kiribati
70 B2 **Linfen** China
64 B2 **Lingayen** Phil.
70 B2 **Lingbao** China
Lingcheng China *see* **Lingshan**
Lingcheng China *see* **Lingshui**
123 C3 **Lingelethu** S. Africa
123 C3 **Lingelihle** S. Africa
100 C1 **Lingen (Ems)** Ger.
60 B2 **Lingga** *i.* Indon.
60 B2 **Lingga, Kepulauan** *is* Indon.
71 A3 **Lingshan** China
71 A4 **Lingshui** China
114 A3 **Linguère** Senegal
155 D1 **Linhares** Brazil
70 A1 **Linhe** China
Linjiang China *see* **Shanghang**
65 B1 **Linjiang** China
93 G4 **Linköping** Sweden
66 B1 **Linkou** China
71 B3 **Linli** China
96 B2 **Linnhe, Loch** *inlet* U.K.
70 B2 **Linqing** China
154 C2 **Lins** Brazil
136 C1 **Linton** U.S.A.
69 D2 **Linxi** China
70 A2 **Linxia** China
70 B2 **Linyi** *Shandong* China
70 B2 **Linyi** *Shandong* China
70 B2 **Linying** China
102 C2 **Linz** Austria
90 A1 **Lioboml'** Ukr.
105 C3 **Lion, Golfe du** *g.* Franc
Lions, Gulf of France *se* Lion, Golfe du
109 B3 **Lipari** Italy
108 B3 **Lipari, Isole** *is* Italy
89 E3 **Lipetsk** Rus. Fed.
110 B1 **Lipova** Romania
101 D2 **Lippstadt** Ger.
53 C3 **Liptrap, Cape** Austr.
71 B3 **Lipu** China
119 D2 **Lira** Uganda
108 B2 **Liri** *r.* Italy
76 C1 **Lisakovsk** Kazakh.
118 C2 **Lisala** Dem. Rep. Congo
Lisboa Port. *see* **Lisbon**
106 B2 **Lisbon** Port.
97 C1 **Lisburn** U.K.
97 B2 **Liscannor Bay** Rep. of Ireland
97 B2 **Lisdoonvarna** Rep. of Ireland
Lishi China *see* **Dingnan**
71 B3 **Lishui** China
104 C2 **Lisieux** France
99 A4 **Liskeard** U.K.
89 E3 **Liski** Rus. Fed.
53 D1 **Lismore** Austr.
97 C2 **Lismore** Rep. of Ireland
97 C1 **Lisnaskea** U.K.
97 B2 **Listowel** Rep. of Ireland
71 A3 **Litang** *Guangxi* China
68 C2 **Litang** *Sichuan* China
140 B3 **Litchfield** *IL* U.S.A.
137 E1 **Litchfield** *MN* U.S.A.

3 D2 **Lithgow** Austr.
1 B3 **Lithino, Akra** *pt* Greece
3 B2 **Lithuania** *country* Europe
1 B2 **Litochoro** Greece
2 C1 **Litoměřice** Czech Rep.
Litovskaya S.S.R. *country* Europe *see* **Lithuania**
6 C2 **Little Abaco** *i.* Bahamas
3 D3 **Little Andaman** *i.* India
3 E3 **Little Bahama Bank** *sea feature* Bahamas
Little Belt *sea chan.* Denmark *see* **Lille Bælt**
6 B3 **Little Cayman** *i.* Cayman Is
3 A1 **Little Colorado** *r.* U.S.A.
) C1 **Little Current** Can.
7 E1 **Little Falls** U.S.A.
9 C2 **Littlefield** U.S.A.
) C4 **Littlehampton** U.K.
2 A2 **Little Karas Berg** *plat.* Namibia
2 B3 **Little Karoo** *plat.* S. Africa
5 A2 **Little Minch** *sea chan.* U.K.
6 C1 **Little Missouri** *r.* U.S.A.
3 D4 **Little Nicobar** *i.* India
2 B2 **Little Rock** U.S.A.
1 E2 **Littleton** U.S.A.
1 C2 **Litunde** Moz.
) B2 **Lityn** Ukr.
Liuchow China *see* **Liuzhou**
) B2 **Liujiachang** China
Liupanshui China *see* **Lupanshui**
1 C2 **Liupo** Moz.
1 A3 **Liuzhou** China
3 C2 **Līvāni** Latvia
3 D2 **Live Oak** U.S.A.
) B1 **Liveringa** Austr.
8 C2 **Livermore, Mount** U.S.A.
3 D2 **Liverpool** Austr.
1 D3 **Liverpool** Can.
8 B3 **Liverpool** U.K.
7 G2 **Liverpool, Cape** Can.
3 C2 **Liverpool Range** *mts* Austr.
6 C3 **Livingston** U.K.
4 D1 **Livingston** *MT* U.S.A.
9 E2 **Livingston** *TX* U.S.A.
9 D2 **Livingston, Lake** U.S.A.
0 B2 **Livingstone** Zambia
5 A3 **Livingston Island** Antarctica
9 C2 **Livno** Bos.-Herz.
9 E3 **Livny** Rus. Fed.
0 C2 **Livonia** U.S.A.
8 B2 **Livorno** Italy
9 D3 **Liwale** Tanz.
0 B2 **Liyang** China
9 A5 **Lizard Point** U.K.
8 B1 **Ljubljana** Slovenia
3 G3 **Ljungan** *r.* Sweden
3 F4 **Ljungby** Sweden
3 G3 **Ljusdal** Sweden
3 G3 **Ljusnan** *r.* Sweden
9 B4 **Llandeilo** U.K.
9 B4 **Llandovery** U.K.
9 B3 **Llandrindod Wells** U.K.
8 B3 **Llandudno** U.K.
9 A4 **Llanelli** U.K.
6 C1 **Llanes** Spain
8 A3 **Llangefni** U.K.
9 B3 **Llangollen** U.K.
9 B3 **Llangurig** U.K.
9 C2 **Llano Estacado** *plain* U.S.A.
0 C2 **Llanos** *reg.* Col./Venez.
7 D1 **Lleida** Spain
9 A3 **Lleyn Peninsula** U.K.
7 C2 **Lliria** Spain
6 C1 **Llodio** Spain
8 B2 **Lloyd George, Mount** Can.
9 D2 **Lloyd Lake** Can.
9 C2 **Lloydminster** Can.
2 B2 **Llullaillaco, Volcán** *vol.* Chile
4 B2 **Loanda** Brazil
3 C2 **Lobatse** Botswana
3 D1 **Łobez** Pol.
0 A2 **Lobito** Angola
1 F1 **Loburg** Ger.
6 B2 **Lochaber** *mts* U.K.
6 B2 **Lochaline** U.K.
Loch Baghasdail U.K. *see* **Lochboisdale**
6 A2 **Lochboisdale** U.K.
4 C2 **Loches** France
6 B2 **Lochgilphead** U.K.
96 B1 **Lochinver** U.K.
96 A2 **Lochmaddy** U.K.
96 C2 **Lochnagar** *mt.* U.K.
Loch nam Madadh U.K. *see* **Lochmaddy**
96 B3 **Lochranza** U.K.
52 A2 **Lock** Austr.
96 C3 **Lockerbie** U.K.
53 C3 **Lockhart** Austr.
139 D3 **Lockhart** U.S.A.
51 D1 **Lockhart River** Austr.
141 D2 **Lock Haven** U.S.A.
141 D2 **Lockport** U.S.A.
63 B2 **Lôc Ninh** Vietnam
105 C3 **Lodève** France
86 C2 **Lodeynoye Pole** Rus. Fed.
74 B2 **Lodhran** Pak.
108 A1 **Lodi** Italy
135 B3 **Lodi** U.S.A.
92 F2 **Løding** Norway
92 G2 **Lødingen** Norway
118 C3 **Lodja** Dem. Rep. Congo
119 D2 **Lodwar** Kenya
103 D1 **Łódź** Pol.
62 B2 **Loei** Thai.
122 A3 **Loeriesfontein** S. Africa
92 F2 **Lofoten** *is* Norway
134 D2 **Logan** U.S.A.
128 A1 **Logan, Mount** Can.
140 B2 **Logansport** U.S.A.
108 B1 **Logatec** Slovenia
115 D3 **Logone** *r.* Africa
106 C1 **Logroño** Spain
93 H3 **Lohja** Fin.
101 D1 **Löhne** Ger.
101 D1 **Lohne (Oldenburg)** Ger.
62 A2 **Loikaw** Myanmar
62 A2 **Loi Lan** *mt.* Myanmar/Thai.
93 H3 **Loimaa** Fin.
104 B2 **Loire** *r.* France
150 B3 **Loja** Ecuador
106 C2 **Loja** Spain
92 I2 **Lokan tekojärvi** *l.* Fin.
100 B2 **Lokeren** Belgium
122 B1 **Lokgwabe** Botswana
91 C1 **Lokhvytsya** Ukr.
119 D2 **Lokichar** Kenya
119 D2 **Lokichokio** Kenya
93 E4 **Løkken** Denmark
89 D2 **Loknya** Rus. Fed.
115 C4 **Lokoja** Nigeria
89 D3 **Lokot'** Rus. Fed.
88 C2 **Loksa** Estonia
127 H2 **Loks Land** *i.* Can.
114 B4 **Lola** Guinea
93 F5 **Lolland** *i.* Denmark
119 D3 **Lollondo** Tanz.
118 C2 **Lolo** Dem. Rep. Congo
122 B2 **Lolwane** S. Africa
110 B2 **Lom** Bulg.
93 E3 **Lom** Norway
119 C2 **Lomami** *r.* Dem. Rep. Congo
153 C3 **Lomas de Zamora** Arg.
50 B1 **Lombardina** Austr.
61 C2 **Lombok** *i.* Indon.
61 C2 **Lombok, Selat** *sea chan.* Indon.
114 C4 **Lomé** Togo
118 C3 **Lomela** *r.* Dem. Rep. Congo
100 B2 **Lommel** Belgium
96 B2 **Lomond, Loch** *l.* U.K.
160 A1 **Lomonosov Ridge** *sea feature* Arctic Ocean
88 C2 **Lomoriosov** Rus. Fed.
61 C2 **Lompobattang, Gunung** *mt.* Indon.
135 B4 **Lompoc** U.S.A.
63 B2 **Lom Sak** Thai.
103 E1 **Łomża** Pol.
130 B3 **London** Can.
99 C4 **London** U.K.
140 C3 **London** U.S.A.
97 C1 **Londonderry** U.K.
50 B1 **Londonderry, Cape** Austr.
154 B2 **Londrina** Brazil
135 C3 **Lone Pine** U.S.A.
83 M2 **Longa, Proliv** *sea chan.* Rus. Fed.
61 C1 **Long Akah** *Sarawak* Malaysia
143 E2 **Long Bay** U.S.A.
135 C4 **Long Beach** U.S.A.
71 A3 **Longchang** China
99 C3 **Long Eaton** U.K.
97 C2 **Longford** Rep. of Ireland
96 C1 **Longhope** U.K.
119 D3 **Longido** Tanz.
61 C2 **Longiram** Indon.
147 C2 **Long Island** Bahamas
130 C2 **Long Island** Can.
59 D3 **Long Island** P.N.G.
141 E2 **Long Island** U.S.A.
130 B3 **Longlac** Can.
130 B3 **Long Lake** Can.
71 A3 **Longli** China
71 A3 **Longming** China
136 B2 **Longmont** U.S.A.
Longping China *see* **Luodian**
140 C2 **Long Point** Can.
71 B3 **Longquan** China
131 E3 **Long Range Mountains** Can.
51 D2 **Longreach** Austr.
Longshan China *see* **Longli**
99 D3 **Long Stratton** U.K.
98 B2 **Longtown** U.K.
105 D2 **Longuyon** France
139 E2 **Longview** *TX* U.S.A.
134 B1 **Longview** *WA* U.S.A.
61 C1 **Longwai** Indon.
70 A2 **Longxi** China
Longxian China *see* **Wengyuan**
71 B3 **Longxi Shan** *mt.* China
63 B2 **Long Xuyên** Vietnam
71 B3 **Longyan** China
82 C1 **Longyearbyen** Svalbard
108 B1 **Lonigo** Italy
100 C1 **Löningen** Ger.
105 D2 **Lons-le-Saunier** France
143 E2 **Lookout, Cape** U.S.A.
119 D3 **Loolmalasin** *vol. crater* Tanz.
50 B3 **Loongana** Austr.
97 B2 **Loop Head** *hd* Rep. of Ireland
Lopasnya Rus. Fed. *see* **Chekhov**
63 B2 **Lop Buri** Thai.
64 B2 **Lopez** Phil.
118 A3 **Lopez, Cap** *c.* Gabon
68 C2 **Lop Nur** *salt l.* China
118 B2 **Lopori** *r.* Dem. Rep. Congo
92 H1 **Lopphavet** *b.* Norway
106 B2 **Lora del Río** Spain
140 C2 **Lorain** U.S.A.
74 A1 **Loralai** Pak.
107 C2 **Lorca** Spain
51 E3 **Lord Howe Island** Austr.
138 B2 **Lordsburg** U.S.A.
155 C2 **Lorena** Brazil
59 D3 **Lorengau** P.N.G.
59 D3 **Lorentz** *r.* Indon.
152 B1 **Loreto** Bol.
144 A2 **Loreto** Mex.
104 B2 **Lorient** France
96 B2 **Lorn, Firth of** *est.* U.K.
52 B3 **Lorne** Austr.
105 D2 **Lorraine** *reg.* France
139 C3 **Los Alamítos, Sierra de** *mt.* Mex.
138 B1 **Los Alamos** U.S.A.
139 D3 **Los Aldamas** Mex.
153 A3 **Los Angeles** Chile
135 C4 **Los Angeles** U.S.A.
135 B3 **Los Banos** U.S.A.
152 B2 **Los Blancos** Arg.
144 B2 **Los Caballos Mesteños, Llano de** *plain* Mex.
153 A4 **Los Chonos, Archipiélago de** *is* Chile
149 C5 **Los Desventurados, Islas de** *is* S. Pacific Ocean
153 B5 **Los Estados, Isla de** *i.* Arg.
89 F3 **Losevo** Rus. Fed.
108 B2 **Lošinj** *i.* Croatia
144 B2 **Los Mochis** Mex.
146 B4 **Los Mosquitos, Golfo de** *b.* Panama
118 B2 **Losombo** Dem. Rep. Congo
106 B2 **Los Pedroches** *plat.* Spain
147 D3 **Los Roques, Islas** *is* Venez.
96 C2 **Lossiemouth** U.K.
150 C1 **Los Teques** Venez.
59 E3 **Losuia** P.N.G.
152 A3 **Los Vilos** Chile
104 C3 **Lot** *r.* France
96 C1 **Loth** U.K.
134 D1 **Lothair** U.S.A.
Lothringen *reg.* France *see* **Lorraine**
119 D2 **Lotikipi Plain** Kenya
118 C3 **Loto** Dem. Rep. Congo
89 E2 **Lotoshino** Rus. Fed.
62 B1 **Louang Namtha** Laos
62 B2 **Louangphrabang** Laos
118 B3 **Loubomo** Congo
104 B2 **Loudéac** France
71 B3 **Loudi** China
118 B3 **Loudima** Congo
114 A3 **Louga** Senegal
99 C3 **Loughborough** U.K.
97 B2 **Loughrea** Rep. of Ireland
105 D2 **Louhans** France
97 B2 **Louisburgh** Rep. of Ireland
51 E1 **Louisiade Archipelago** *is* P.N.G.
142 B2 **Louisiana** *state* U.S.A.
123 C1 **Louis Trichardt** S. Africa
140 B3 **Louisville** *KY* U.S.A.
142 C2 **Louisville** *MS* U.S.A.
86 C2 **Loukhi** Rus. Fed.
118 B3 **Loukoléla** Congo
106 B2 **Loulé** Port.
118 A2 **Loum** Cameroon
130 C2 **Loups-Marins, Lacs des** *lakes* Can.
104 B3 **Lourdes** France
151 D2 **Lourenço** Brazil
Lourenço Marques Moz. *see* **Maputo**
106 B1 **Lousã** Port.
53 C2 **Louth** Austr.
98 C3 **Louth** U.K.
Louvain Belgium *see* **Leuven**
122 A1 **Louwater-Suid** Namibia
89 D2 **Lovat'** *r.* Rus. Fed.
110 B2 **Lovech** Bulg.
136 B2 **Loveland** U.S.A.
136 B2 **Lovell** U.S.A.
135 C2 **Lovelock** U.S.A.
88 C1 **Loviisa** Fin.
139 C2 **Lovington** U.S.A.
86 C2 **Lovozero** Rus. Fed.
119 C3 **Lowa** Dem. Rep. Congo
141 E2 **Lowell** U.S.A.
119 D2 **Lowelli** Sudan
128 C3 **Lower Arrow Lake** Can.
Lower California *pen.* Mex. *see* **Baja California**
54 B2 **Lower Hutt** N.Z.
97 C1 **Lower Lough Erne** *l.* U.K.
128 B2 **Lower Post** Can.
137 E1 **Lower Red Lake** U.S.A.
Lower Tunguska *r.* Rus. Fed. *see* **Nizhnyaya Tunguska**
99 D3 **Lowestoft** U.K.
103 D1 **Łowicz** Pol.
141 D2 **Lowville** U.S.A.
52 B2 **Loxton** Austr.
48 H6 **Loyalty Islands** New Caledonia
Loyang China *see* **Luoyang**
89 D3 **Loyew** Belarus
92 F2 **Løypskardtinden** *mt.* Norway
109 C2 **Loznica** Yugo.
91 D2 **Lozova** Ukr.
120 B2 **Luacano** Angola
70 B2 **Lu'an** China
120 A1 **Luanda** Angola
121 C2 **Luangwa** *r.* Zambia
121 B2 **Luanshya** Zambia
Luao Angola *see* **Luau**
106 B1 **Luarca** Spain
120 B2 **Luau** Angola
103 E1 **Lubaczów** Pol.
103 D1 **Lubań** Pol.
64 A2 **Lubang Islands** Phil.
120 A2 **Lubango** Angola
119 C3 **Lubao** Dem. Rep. Congo
103 E1 **Lubartów** Pol.
101 D1 **Lübbecke** Ger.
102 C1 **Lübben** Ger.
139 C2 **Lubbock** U.S.A.
101 E1 **Lübeck** Ger.
69 E2 **Lubei** China
76 B1 **Lubenka** Kazakh.
119 C3 **Lubero** Dem. Rep. Congo
103 D1 **Lubin** Pol.
103 E1 **Lublin** Pol.
91 C1 **Lubny** Ukr.
61 C1 **Lubok Antu** *Sarawak* Malaysia
101 E1 **Lübow** Ger.
101 E1 **Lübtheen** Ger.
119 C3 **Lubudi** Dem. Rep. Congo
60 B2 **Lubuklinggau** Indon.
119 C4 **Lubumbashi** Dem. Rep. Congo
120 B2 **Lubungu** Zambia
119 C3 **Lubutu** Dem. Rep. Congo
120 A1 **Lucala** Angola
97 C2 **Lucan** Rep. of Ireland

120 B1 **Lucapa** Angola
108 B2 **Lucca** Italy
96 B3 **Luce Bay** U.K.
154 B2 **Lucélia** Brazil
64 B2 **Lucena** Phil.
106 C2 **Lucena** Spain
103 D2 **Lučenec** Slovakia
109 C2 **Lucera** Italy
Lucerne Switz. *see* **Luzern**
66 B1 **Luchegorsk** Rus. Fed.
101 E1 **Lüchow** Ger.
120 A2 **Lucira** Angola
Łuck Ukr. *see* **Luts'k**
101 F1 **Luckenwalde** Ger.
122 B2 **Luckhoff** S. Africa
75 C2 **Lucknow** India
120 A1 **Lucunga** Angola
120 B2 **Lucusse** Angola
Lüda China *see* **Dalian**
100 C2 **Lüdenscheid** Ger.
101 E1 **Lüder** Ger.
120 A3 **Lüderitz** Namibia
119 D4 **Ludewa** Tanz.
74 B1 **Ludhiana** India
140 B2 **Ludington** U.S.A.
99 B3 **Ludlow** U.K.
135 C4 **Ludlow** U.S.A.
110 C2 **Ludogorie** *reg.* Bulg.
93 G3 **Ludvika** Sweden
102 B2 **Ludwigsburg** Ger.
101 F1 **Ludwigsfelde** Ger.
101 D3 **Ludwigshafen am Rhein** Ger.
101 E1 **Ludwigslust** Ger.
88 C2 **Ludza** Latvia
118 C3 **Luebo** Dem. Rep. Congo
120 A2 **Luena** Angola
70 A2 **Lüeyang** China
71 B3 **Lufeng** China
119 C3 **Lufira** *r.* Dem. Rep. Congo
139 E2 **Lufkin** U.S.A.
88 C2 **Luga** Rus. Fed.
88 C2 **Luga** *r.* Rus. Fed.
105 D2 **Lugano** Switz.
121 C2 **Lugenda** *r.* Moz.
106 B1 **Lugo** Spain
110 B1 **Lugoj** Romania
91 D2 **Luhans'k** Ukr.
119 D3 **Luhombero** Tanz.
90 B1 **Luhyny** Ukr.
120 B2 **Luiana** Angola
Luichow Peninsula China *see* **Leizhou Bandao**
118 C3 **Luilaka** *r.* Dem. Rep. Congo
Luimneach Rep. of Ireland *see* **Limerick**
105 D2 **Luino** Italy
92 I2 **Luiro** *r.* Fin.
118 C3 **Luiza** Dem. Rep. Congo
70 B2 **Lujiang** China
Lukapa Angola *see* **Lucapa**
109 C2 **Lukavac** Bos.-Herz.
118 B3 **Lukenie** *r.* Dem. Rep. Congo
138 A2 **Lukeville** U.S.A.
89 E3 **Lukhovitsy** Rus. Fed.
Lukou China *see* **Zhuzhou**
103 E1 **Łuków** Pol.
120 B2 **Lukulu** Zambia
92 H2 **Luleå** Sweden
92 H2 **Luleälven** *r.* Sweden
111 C2 **Lüleburgaz** Turkey
70 B2 **Lüliang Shan** *mts* China
139 D3 **Luling** U.S.A.
Luluabourg Dem. Rep. Congo *see* **Kananga**
61 C2 **Lumajang** Indon.
75 C1 **Lumajangdong Co** *salt l.* China
Lumbala Angola *see* **Lumbala Kaquengue**
Lumbala Angola *see* **Lumbala N'guimbo**
120 B2 **Lumbala Kaquengue** Angola
120 B2 **Lumbala N'guimbo** Angola
142 C2 **Lumberton** *MS* U.S.A.
143 E2 **Lumberton** *NC* U.S.A.
61 C1 **Lumbis** Indon.
106 B1 **Lumbrales** Spain
63 B2 **Lumphăt** Cambodia
129 D2 **Lumsden** Can.
54 A3 **Lumsden** N.Z.
93 F4 **Lund** Sweden
121 C2 **Lundazi** Zambia
99 A4 **Lundy Island** U.K.
101 E1 **Lüneburg** Ger.
101 E1 **Lüneburger Heide** *reg.* Ger.
100 C2 **Lünen** Ger.
105 D2 **Lunéville** France
120 B2 **Lunga** *r.* Zambia
114 A4 **Lungi** Sierra Leone
Lungleh India *see* **Lunglei**
75 D2 **Lunglei** India
97 C2 **Lungnaquilla Mountain** *hill* Rep. of Ireland
120 B2 **Lungwebungu** *r.* Zambia
74 B2 **Luni** *r.* India
88 C3 **Luninyets** Belarus
104 C3 **L'Union** France
114 A4 **Lunsar** Sierra Leone
77 E2 **Luntai** China
71 A3 **Luodian** China
71 B3 **Luoding** China
70 B2 **Luohe** China
70 B2 **Luoyang** China
118 B3 **Luozi** Dem. Rep. Congo
121 B2 **Lupane** Zimbabwe
71 A3 **Lupanshui** China
110 B1 **Lupeni** Romania
121 C2 **Lupilichi** Moz.
101 F2 **Luppa** Ger.
95 B3 **Lurgan** U.K.
Luring China *see* **Gêrzê**
121 D2 **Lúrio** Moz.
121 D2 **Lurio** *r.* Moz.
92 F2 **Lurøy** Norway
121 B2 **Lusaka** Zambia
118 C3 **Lusambo** Dem. Rep. Congo
109 C2 **Lushnjë** Albania
70 C2 **Lushunkou** China
123 C3 **Lusikisiki** S. Africa
136 C2 **Lusk** U.S.A.
Luso Angola *see* **Luena**
76 B3 **Lut, Dasht-e** *des.* Iran
101 F2 **Lutherstadt Wittenberg** Ger.
99 C4 **Luton** U.K.
61 C1 **Lutong** *Sarawak* Malaysia
129 C1 **Łutselk'e** Can.
90 B1 **Luts'k** Ukr.
55 F3 **Lützow-Holm Bay** Antarctica
122 B2 **Lutzputs** S. Africa
122 A3 **Lutzville** S. Africa
117 C4 **Luuq** Somalia
137 D2 **Luverne** U.S.A.
119 C3 **Luvua** *r.* Dem. Rep. Congo
120 B2 **Luvuei** Angola
123 D1 **Luvuvhu** *r.* S. Africa
119 D3 **Luwegu** *r.* Tanz.
119 D2 **Luwero** Uganda
61 D2 **Luwuk** Indon.
100 C3 **Luxembourg** *country* Europe
100 C3 **Luxembourg** Lux.
105 D2 **Luxeuil-les-Bains** France
62 A1 **Luxi** China
123 C3 **Luxolweni** S. Africa
116 B2 **Luxor** Egypt
100 B2 **Luyksgestel** Neth.
86 D2 **Luza** Rus. Fed.
105 D2 **Luzern** Switz.
62 B1 **Luzhai** China
71 A3 **Luzhi** China
71 A3 **Luzhou** China
154 C1 **Luziânia** Brazil
151 E3 **Luzilândia** Brazil
64 B2 **Luzon** *i.* Phil.
64 B1 **Luzon Strait** Phil.
109 C3 **Luzzi** Italy
90 A2 **L'viv** Ukr.
L'vov Ukr. *see* **L'viv**
Lwów Ukr. *see* **L'viv**
88 C3 **Lyakhavichy** Belarus
Lyallpur Pak. *see* **Faisalabad**
89 D2 **Lychkovo** Rus. Fed.
92 G3 **Lycksele** Sweden
55 C2 **Lyddan Island** Antarctica
123 D2 **Lydenburg** S. Africa
88 C3 **Lyel'chytsy** Belarus
88 C3 **Lyepyel'** Belarus
136 A2 **Lyman** U.S.A.
99 B4 **Lyme Bay** U.K.
99 B4 **Lyme Regis** U.K.
141 D3 **Lynchburg** U.S.A.
52 A2 **Lyndhurst** Austr.
129 D2 **Lynn Lake** Can.
134 B1 **Lynnwood** U.S.A.
129 D1 **Lynx Lake** Can.
105 C2 **Lyon** France
Lyons France *see* **Lyon**
89 D2 **Lyozna** Belarus
103 E1 **Łysica** *hill* Pol.
86 E3 **Lys'va** Rus. Fed.
91 D2 **Lysychans'k** Ukr.
87 D3 **Lysyye Gory** Rus. Fed.
98 B3 **Lytham St Anne's** U.K.
88 C3 **Lyuban'** Belarus
90 C2 **Lyubashivka** Ukr.
89 E2 **Lyubertsy** Rus. Fed.
90 B1 **Lyubeshiv** Ukr.
89 F2 **Lyubim** Rus. Fed.
91 D2 **Lyubotyn** Ukr.
89 D2 **Lyubytino** Rus. Fed.
89 D3 **Lyudinovo** Rus. Fed.

M

80 B2 **Ma'an** Jordan
70 B2 **Ma'anshan** China
88 C2 **Maardu** Estonia
78 B3 **Ma'āriḍ, Banī** *des.* Saudi Arabia
80 B2 **Ma'arrat an Nu'mān** Syria
100 B1 **Maarssen** Neth.
100 B2 **Maas** *r.* Neth.
100 B2 **Maaseik** Belgium
64 B2 **Maasin** Phil.
100 B2 **Maastricht** Neth.
121 C3 **Mabalane** Moz.
78 B3 **Ma'bar** Yemen
150 D2 **Mabaruma** Guyana
98 D3 **Mablethorpe** U.K.
123 C2 **Mabopane** S. Africa
121 C3 **Mabote** Moz.
122 B2 **Mabule** Botswana
122 B1 **Mabutsane** Botswana
155 D2 **Macaé** Brazil
121 C2 **Macaloge** Moz.
126 F2 **MacAlpine Lake** Can.
151 D2 **Macapá** Brazil
150 B3 **Macará** Ecuador
155 D1 **Macarani** Brazil
Macassar Indon. *see* **Ujung Pandang**
61 C2 **Macassar Strait** Indon.
121 C2 **Macatanja** Moz.
151 F3 **Macau** Brazil
69 D3 **Macau** China
71 B3 **Macau** *special admin. reg.* China
121 C3 **Maccaretane** Moz.
98 B3 **Macclesfield** U.K.
50 B2 **Macdonald, Lake** *salt flat* Austr.
50 C2 **Macdonnell Ranges** *mts* Austr.
130 A2 **MacDowell Lake** Can.
96 C2 **Macduff** U.K.
106 B1 **Macedo de Cavaleiros** Port.
52 B3 **Macedon** *mt.* Austr.
111 B2 **Macedonia** *country* Europe
151 F3 **Maceió** Brazil
108 B2 **Macerata** Italy
52 A2 **Macfarlane, Lake** *salt flat* Austr.
97 B3 **Macgillycuddy's Reeks** *mts* Rep. of Ireland
74 A2 **Mach** Pak.
155 C2 **Machado** Brazil
121 C3 **Machaila** Moz.
119 D3 **Machakos** Kenya
150 B3 **Machala** Ecuador
121 C3 **Machanga** Moz.
Machaze Moz. *see* **Chitobe**
70 B2 **Macheng** China
140 B2 **Machesney Park** U.S.A.
141 F2 **Machias** U.S.A.
73 C3 **Machilipatnam** India
121 C2 **Machinga** Malawi
150 B1 **Machiques** Venez.
150 B4 **Machupicchu** Peru
99 B3 **Machynlleth** U.K.
123 D2 **Macia** Moz.
Macias Nguema *i.* Equat. Guinea *see* **Bioco**
110 C1 **Măcin** Romania
53 D1 **Macintyre** *r.* Austr.
51 D2 **Mackay** Austr.
50 B2 **Mackay, Lake** *salt flat* Austr.
128 C1 **MacKay Lake** Can.
128 B2 **Mackenzie** Can.
128 A1 **Mackenzie** *r.* Can.
Mackenzie Guyana *see* **Linden**
Mackenzie *atoll* Micronesia *see* **Ulithi**
55 H3 **Mackenzie Bay** Antarctica
126 C2 **Mackenzie Bay** Can.
126 E1 **Mackenzie King Island** Can.
128 A1 **Mackenzie Mountains** Can.
Mackillop, Lake *salt flat* Austr. *see* **Yamma Yamma, Lake**
129 D2 **Macklin** Can.
53 D2 **Macksville** Austr.
53 D1 **Maclean** Austr.
123 C3 **Maclear** S. Africa
50 A2 **MacLeod, Lake** *imp. l.* Austr.
140 A2 **Macomb** U.S.A.
108 A2 **Macomer** *Sardinia* Italy
121 D2 **Macomia** Moz.
105 C2 **Mâcon** France
143 D2 **Macon** *GA* U.S.A.
137 E3 **Macon** *MO* U.S.A.
142 C2 **Macon** *MS* U.S.A.
53 C2 **Macquarie** *r.* Austr.
48 G9 **Macquarie Island** S. Pacific Ocean
53 C2 **Macquarie Marshes** Austr.
53 C2 **Macquarie Mountain** Austr.
156 D9 **Macquarie Ridge** *sea feature* S. Pacific Ocean
55 H2 **Mac. Robertson Land** *reg.* Antarctica
97 B3 **Macroom** Rep. of Ireland
52 A1 **Macumba** *watercourse* Austr.
145 C3 **Macuspana** Mex.
144 B2 **Macuzari, Presa** *resr* Me
123 D2 **Madadeni** S. Africa
121 □D3 **Madagascar** *country* Africa
159 D5 **Madagascar Ridge** *sea feature* Indian Ocean
115 D2 **Madama** Niger
111 B2 **Madan** Bulg.
59 D3 **Madang** P.N.G.
141 D1 **Madawaska** *r.* Can.
62 A1 **Madaya** Myanmar
150 D3 **Madeira** *r.* Brazil
114 A1 **Madeira** *terr.* N. Atlantic Ocean
158 E2 **Madeira** *is* Port.
99 B3 **Madeley** U.K.
144 B2 **Madera** Mex.
135 B3 **Madera** U.S.A.
73 B3 **Madgaon** India
74 B2 **Madhya Pradesh** *state* India
123 C2 **Madibogo** S. Africa
118 B3 **Madingou** Congo
121 □D2 **Madirovalo** Madag.
140 B3 **Madison** *IN* U.S.A.
137 D2 **Madison** *SD* U.S.A.
140 B2 **Madison** *WI* U.S.A.
140 C3 **Madison** *WV* U.S.A.
134 D1 **Madison** *r.* U.S.A.
140 B3 **Madisonville** U.S.A.
61 C2 **Madiun** Indon.
119 D2 **Mado Gashi** Kenya
68 C2 **Madoi** China
88 C2 **Madona** Latvia
78 A2 **Madrakah** Saudi Arabia
79 C3 **Madrakah, Ra's** *c.* Oman
Madras India *see* **Chenna**
134 B2 **Madras** U.S.A.
145 C2 **Madre, Laguna** *lag.* Mex.
139 D3 **Madre, Laguna** *lag.* U.S.
152 B1 **Madre de Dios** *r.* Peru
145 B3 **Madre del Sur, Sierra** *m* Mex.
144 B2 **Madre Occidental, Sierr** *mts* Mex.
145 B2 **Madre Oriental, Sierra** *mts* Mex.
106 C1 **Madrid** Spain
106 C2 **Madridejos** Spain
61 C2 **Madura** *i.* Indon.
61 C2 **Madura, Selat** *sea chan.* Indon.
73 B4 **Madurai** India
121 B2 **Madziwadzido** Zimbabwe
67 C3 **Maebashi** Japan
62 A2 **Mae Hong Son** Thai.
62 A2 **Mae Sariang** Thai.
99 B4 **Maesteg** U.K.
62 A2 **Mae Suai** Thai.
121 □D2 **Maevatanana** Madag.
Mafeking S. Africa *see* **Mafikeng**
123 C2 **Mafeteng** Lesotho
53 C3 **Maffra** Austr.

D3 **Mafia Island** Tanz.
C2 **Mafikeng** S. Africa
D3 **Mafinga** Tanz.
C3 **Mafra** Brazil
L3 **Magadan** Rus. Fed.
Magallanes Chile *see* Punta Arenas
A5 **Magallanes, Estrecho de** *sea chan.* Chile
B2 **Magangue** Col.
B1 **Magazine Mountain** *hill* U.S.A.
A4 **Magburaka** Sierra Leone
E1 **Magdagachi** Rus. Fed.
A1 **Magdalena** Mex.
B2 **Magdalena** U.S.A.
A2 **Magdalena, Bahía** *b.* Mex.
E1 **Magdeburg** Ger.
Magellan, Strait of Chile *see* **Magallanes, Estrecho de**
A1 **Maggiore, Lago** *l.* Italy
Maggiore, Lake Italy *see* **Maggiore, Lago**
B2 **Maghâgha** Egypt
C1 **Magherafelt** U.K.
E3 **Magnitogorsk** Rus. Fed.
B2 **Magnolia** U.S.A.
C2 **Màgoé** Moz.
C3 **Magog** Can.
D2 **Magpie, Lac** *l.* Can.
A3 **Magṭa' Laḥjar** Maur.
D3 **Magu** Tanz.
E3 **Maguarinho, Cabo** *c.* Brazil
D2 **Magude** Moz.
B2 **Măgura, Dealul** *hill* Moldova
A1 **Magwe** Myanmar
C2 **Mahābād** Iran
B2 **Mahajan** India
□D2 **Mahajanga** Madag.
C2 **Mahakam** *r.* Indon.
C1 **Mahalapye** Botswana
□D2 **Mahalevona** Madag.
C2 **Mahanadi** *r.* India
□D2 **Mahanoro** Madag.
B3 **Maharashtra** *state* India
B2 **Maha Sarakham** Thai.
□D2 **Mahavavy** *r.* Madag.
B3 **Mahbubnagar** India
B2 **Mahd adh Dhahab** Saudi Arabia
D2 **Mahdia** Alg.
D2 **Mahdia** Guyana
I6 **Mahé** *i.* Seychelles
C3 **Mahendragiri** *mt.* India
D3 **Mahenge** Tanz.
B3 **Maheno** N.Z.
B2 **Mahesāna** India
B2 **Mahi** *r.* India
C1 **Mahia Peninsula** N.Z.
D3 **Mahilyow** Belarus
D2 **Mahón** Spain
B3 **Mahou** Mali
Mahsana India *see* Mahesāna
B2 **Mahuva** India
C2 **Mahya Dağı** *mt.* Turkey
B1 **Maia** Port.
Maiaia Moz. *see* **Nacala**
C3 **Maicao** Col.
C3 **Maidstone** Can.
D4 **Maidstone** U.K.
D3 **Maiduguri** Nigeria
D3 **Maijdi** Bangl.
C2 **Mailani** India
D2 **Main** *r.* Ger.
B3 **Mai-Ndombe, Lac** *l.* Dem. Rep. Congo
E3 **Main-Donau-Kanal** *canal* Ger.
F1 **Maine** *state* U.S.A.
D3 **Maine, Gulf of** Can./U.S.A.
A1 **Maingkwan** Myanmar
C1 **Mainland** *i. Scotland* U.K.
□ **Mainland** *i. Scotland* U.K.
□D2 **Maintirano** Madag.
D2 **Mainz** Ger.
C1 **Maiquetía** Venez.
B3 **Maitengwe** Botswana
D2 **Maitland** *N.S.W.* Austr.
A2 **Maitland** *S.A.* Austr.
B3 **Maíz, Islas del** *is* Nic.
C3 **Maizuru** Japan
C2 **Maja Jezercë** *mt.* Albania
C2 **Majene** Indon.
D2 **Majī** Eth.
Majorca *i.* Spain *see* Mallorca
Majunga Madag. *see* Mahajanga
123 C2 **Majwemasweu** S. Africa
118 B3 **Makabana** Congo
61 C2 **Makale** Indon.
119 C3 **Makamba** Burundi
77 E2 **Makanchi** Kazakh.
118 B2 **Makanza** Dem. Rep. Congo
90 B1 **Makariv** Ukr.
69 F1 **Makarov** Rus. Fed.
160 B1 **Makarov Basin** *sea feature* Arctic Ocean
109 C2 **Makarska** Croatia
Makassar Indon. *see* **Ujung Pandang**
76 B2 **Makat** Kazakh.
119 D3 **Makatapora** Tanz.
123 D2 **Makatini Flats** *lowland* S. Africa
114 A4 **Makeni** Sierra Leone
120 B3 **Makgadikgadi** *salt pan* Botswana
87 D4 **Makhachkala** Rus. Fed.
76 B2 **Makhambet** Kazakh.
119 D3 **Makindu** Kenya
77 D1 **Makinsk** Kazakh.
91 D2 **Makiyivka** Ukr.
Makkah Saudi Arabia *see* **Mecca**
131 E2 **Makkovik** Can.
103 E2 **Makó** Hungary
118 B2 **Makokou** Gabon
119 D3 **Makongolosi** Tanz.
122 B2 **Makopong** Botswana
119 C2 **Makoro** Dem. Rep. Congo
118 B3 **Makoua** Congo
111 B3 **Makrakomi** Greece
79 D2 **Makran** *reg.* Iran/Pak.
89 E2 **Maksatikha** Rus. Fed.
81 C2 **Mākū** Iran
62 A1 **Makum** India
67 B4 **Makurazaki** Japan
115 C4 **Makurdi** Nigeria
92 G2 **Malå** Sweden
146 B4 **Mala, Punta** *pt* Panama
73 B3 **Malabar Coast** India
118 A2 **Malabo** Equat. Guinea
155 D1 **Malacacheta** Brazil
Malacca Malaysia *see* Melaka
60 A1 **Malacca, Strait of** Indon./Malaysia
134 D2 **Malad City** U.S.A.
88 C3 **Maladzyechna** Belarus
106 C2 **Málaga** Spain
Malagasy Republic *country* Africa *see* Madagascar
121 □D3 **Malaimbandy** Madag.
48 H4 **Malaita** *i.* Solomon Is
117 B4 **Malakal** Sudan
48 H5 **Malakula** *i.* Vanuatu
61 D2 **Malamala** Indon.
61 C2 **Malang** Indon.
Malange Angola *see* Malanje
120 A1 **Malanje** Angola
93 G4 **Mälaren** *l.* Sweden
153 B3 **Malargüe** Arg.
130 C3 **Malartic** Can.
88 B3 **Malaryta** Belarus
80 B2 **Malatya** Turkey
121 C2 **Malawi** *country* Africa
Malawi, Lake Africa *see* **Nyasa, Lake**
89 D2 **Malaya Vishera** Rus. Fed.
64 B3 **Malaybalay** Phil.
81 C2 **Malāyer** Iran
60 B1 **Malaysia** *country* Asia
60 B1 **Malaysia, Semenanjung** *pen.* Malaysia
81 C2 **Malazgirt** Turkey
103 D1 **Malbork** Pol.
101 F1 **Malchin** Ger.
100 A2 **Maldegem** Belgium
48 L4 **Malden Island** Kiribati
56 C5 **Maldives** *country* Indian Ocean
99 D4 **Maldon** U.K.
153 C3 **Maldonado** Uru.
56 I9 **Male** Maldives
111 B3 **Maleas, Akra** *pt* Greece
103 D2 **Malé Karpaty** *hills* Slovakia
119 C3 **Malela** Dem. Rep. Congo
116 A3 **Malha** Sudan
134 C2 **Malheur Lake** U.S.A.
114 B3 **Mali** *country* Africa
114 A3 **Mali** Guinea
59 C3 **Maliana** East Timor
58 C3 **Malili** Indon.
97 C1 **Malin** Rep. of Ireland
119 E3 **Malindi** Kenya
97 C1 **Malin Head** *hd* Rep. of Ireland
97 B1 **Malin More** Rep. of Ireland
111 C2 **Malkara** Turkey
88 C3 **Mal'kavichy** Belarus
110 C2 **Malko Tŭrnovo** Bulg.
53 C3 **Mallacoota** Austr.
53 C3 **Mallacoota Inlet** *b.* Austr.
96 B2 **Mallaig** U.K.
116 B2 **Mallawi** Egypt
129 E1 **Mallery Lake** Can.
107 D2 **Mallorca** *i.* Spain
97 B2 **Mallow** Rep. of Ireland
92 F3 **Malm** Norway
92 H2 **Malmberget** Sweden
100 C2 **Malmédy** Belgium
122 A3 **Malmesbury** S. Africa
93 F4 **Malmö** Sweden
71 A3 **Malong** China
118 C4 **Malonga** Dem. Rep. Congo
86 C2 **Maloshuyka** Rus. Fed.
93 E3 **Måløy** Norway
89 E2 **Maloyaroslavets** Rus. Fed.
89 E2 **Maloye Borisovo** Rus. Fed.
86 D2 **Malozemel'skaya Tundra** *lowland* Rus. Fed.
125 J9 **Malpelo, Isla de** *i.* N. Pacific Ocean
84 F5 **Malta** *country* Europe
88 C2 **Malta** Latvia
134 E1 **Malta** U.S.A.
122 A1 **Maltahöhe** Namibia
98 C2 **Malton** U.K.
59 C3 **Maluku** *is* Indon.
93 F3 **Malung** Sweden
123 C2 **Maluti Mountains** Lesotho
73 B3 **Malvan** India
142 B2 **Malvern** U.S.A.
117 B4 **Malwal** Sudan
90 B1 **Malyn** Ukr.
83 L2 **Malyy Anyuy** *r.* Rus. Fed.
81 C1 **Malyy Kavkaz** *mts* Asia
83 K2 **Malyy Lyakhovskiy, Ostrov** *i.* Rus. Fed.
123 C2 **Mamafubedu** S. Africa
151 F3 **Mamanguape** Brazil
64 B3 **Mambajao** Phil.
119 C2 **Mambasa** Dem. Rep. Congo
118 B2 **Mambéré** *r.* C.A.R.
64 B2 **Mamburao** Phil.
123 C2 **Mamelodi** S. Africa
118 A2 **Mamfé** Cameroon
135 C3 **Mammoth Lakes** U.S.A.
88 A3 **Mamonovo** Rus. Fed.
150 C4 **Mamoré** *r.* Bol./Brazil
114 A3 **Mamou** Guinea
114 B4 **Mampong** Ghana
61 C2 **Mamuju** Indon.
114 B4 **Man** Côte d'Ivoire
150 C3 **Manacapuru** Brazil
107 D2 **Manacor** Spain
59 C2 **Manado** Indon.
146 B3 **Managua** Nic.
121 □D3 **Manakara** Madag.
78 B3 **Manākhah** Yemen
79 C2 **Manama** Bahrain
59 D3 **Manam Island** P.N.G.
121 □D3 **Mananara** *r.* Madag.
121 □D2 **Mananara Avaratra** Madag.
121 □D3 **Mananjary** Madag.
114 A3 **Manantali, Lac de** *l.* Mali
54 A3 **Manapouri, Lake** N.Z.
77 E2 **Manas Hu** *l.* China
75 C2 **Manaslu** *mt.* Nepal
Manastir Macedonia *see* **Bitola**
59 C3 **Manatuto** East Timor
150 C3 **Manaus** Brazil
80 B2 **Manavgat** Turkey
116 A3 **Manawashei** Sudan
98 B3 **Manchester** U.K.
141 E2 **Manchester** *CT* U.S.A.
141 E2 **Manchester** *NH* U.S.A.
142 C1 **Manchester** *TN* U.S.A.
81 D3 **Mand, Rūd-e** *r.* Iran
117 A4 **Manda, Jebel** *mt.* Sudan
121 □D3 **Mandabe** Madag.
93 E4 **Mandal** Norway
59 D3 **Mandala, Puncak** *mt.* Indon.
62 A1 **Mandalay** Myanmar
68 D1 **Mandalgovĭ** Mongolia
136 C1 **Mandan** U.S.A.
118 B1 **Mandara Mountains** Cameroon/Nigeria
108 A3 **Mandas** *Sardinia* Italy
119 E2 **Mandera** Kenya
100 C2 **Manderscheid** Ger.
74 B1 **Mandi** India
114 B3 **Mandiana** Guinea
74 B1 **Mandi Burewala** Pak.
Mandidzuzure Zimbabwe *see* **Chimanimani**
75 C2 **Mandla** India
121 □D2 **Mandritsara** Madag.
74 B2 **Mandsaur** India
50 A3 **Mandurah** Austr.
73 B3 **Mandya** India
108 B1 **Manerbio** Italy
90 B1 **Manevychi** Ukr.
109 C2 **Manfredonia** Italy
109 C2 **Manfredonia, Golfo di** *g.* Italy
114 B3 **Manga** Burkina
118 B3 **Mangai** Dem. Rep. Congo
49 L6 **Mangaia** *i.* Cook Is
54 C1 **Mangakino** N.Z.
110 C2 **Mangalia** Romania
73 B3 **Mangalore** India
123 C2 **Mangaung** S. Africa
60 B2 **Manggar** Indon.
Mangghyshlaq Kazakh. *see* **Mangistau**
76 B2 **Mangistau** Kazakh.
61 C1 **Mangkalihat, Tanjung** *pt* Indon.
68 C2 **Mangnai** China
121 C2 **Mangochi** Malawi
121 □D3 **Mangoky** *r.* Madag.
59 C3 **Mangole** *i.* Indon.
54 B1 **Mangonui** N.Z.
Mangshi China *see* **Luxi**
106 B1 **Mangualde** Port.
154 B3 **Mangueirinha** Brazil
69 E1 **Mangui** China
Mangyshlak Kazakh. *see* Mangistau
137 D3 **Manhattan** U.S.A.
121 C3 **Manhica** Moz.
155 D2 **Manhuaçu** Brazil
121 □D2 **Mania** *r.* Madag.
108 B1 **Maniago** Italy
121 C2 **Maniamba** Moz.
150 C3 **Manicoré** Brazil
131 D3 **Manicouagan** *r.* Can.
131 D2 **Manicougan, Réservoir** *resr* Can.
79 B2 **Manīfah** Saudi Arabia
49 K5 **Manihiki** *atoll* Cook Is
64 B2 **Manila** Phil.
53 D2 **Manilla** Austr.
Manipur India *see* **Imphal**
111 C3 **Manisa** Turkey
107 C2 **Manises** Spain
140 B2 **Manistee** U.S.A.
140 B1 **Manistique** U.S.A.
129 E2 **Manitoba** *prov.* Can.
129 E2 **Manitoba, Lake** Can.
140 B1 **Manitou Islands** U.S.A.
130 B3 **Manitoulin Island** Can.
136 C3 **Manitou Springs** U.S.A.
130 B3 **Manitouwadge** Can.
140 B2 **Manitowoc** U.S.A.
130 C3 **Maniwaki** Can.
150 B2 **Manizales** Col.
121 □D3 **Manja** Madag.
121 C3 **Manjacaze** Moz.
137 E2 **Mankato** U.S.A.
114 B4 **Mankono** Côte d'Ivoire
129 D3 **Mankota** Can.
73 C4 **Mankulam** Sri Lanka
74 B2 **Manmad** India
52 A2 **Mannahill** Austr.
73 B4 **Mannar** Sri Lanka
73 B4 **Mannar, Gulf of** India/Sri Lanka
101 D3 **Mannheim** Ger.
128 C2 **Manning** Can.
52 A2 **Mannum** Austr.
129 C2 **Mannville** Can.
59 C3 **Manokwari** Indon.
119 C3 **Manono** Dem. Rep. Congo
63 A2 **Manoron** Myanmar
105 D3 **Manosque** France
131 C2 **Manouane, Lac** *l.* Can.
65 B1 **Manp'o** N. Korea
107 D1 **Manresa** Spain
121 B2 **Mansa** Zambia
127 G2 **Mansel Island** Can.
92 I2 **Mansel'kya** *ridge* Fin./Rus. Fed.
53 C3 **Mansfield** Austr.
98 C3 **Mansfield** U.K.
142 B1 **Mansfield** *AR* U.S.A.
142 B2 **Mansfield** *LA* U.S.A.
140 C2 **Mansfield** *OH* U.S.A.

141 D2 **Mansfield** *PA* U.S.A.
150 A3 **Manta** Ecuador
64 A3 **Mantalingajan, Mount** Phil.
155 D1 **Mantena** Brazil
143 E1 **Manteo** U.S.A.
104 C2 **Mantes-la-Jolie** France
155 C2 **Mantiqueira, Serra da** *mts* Brazil
108 B1 **Mantova** Italy
88 C1 **Mäntsälä** Fin.
Mantua Italy *see* Mantova
86 D3 **Manturovo** Rus. Fed.
151 D3 **Manuelzinho** Brazil
61 D2 **Manui** *i.* Indon.
54 B1 **Manukau** N.Z.
59 D3 **Manus Island** P.N.G.
142 B2 **Many** U.S.A.
121 C2 **Manyame** *r.* Moz./Zimbabwe
119 D3 **Manyara, Lake** *salt l.* Tanz.
Manyas Gölü *l.* Turkey *see* Kuş Gölü
87 D4 **Manych-Gudilo, Ozero** *l.* Rus. Fed.
138 B1 **Many Farms** U.S.A.
119 D3 **Manyoni** Tanz.
106 C2 **Manzanares** Spain
146 C2 **Manzanillo** Cuba
144 B3 **Manzanillo** Mex.
119 C3 **Manzanza** Dem. Rep. Congo
69 D1 **Manzhouli** China
123 D2 **Manzini** Swaziland
115 D3 **Mao** Chad
Maó Spain *see* Mahón
59 D3 **Maoke, Pegunungan** *mts* Indon.
123 C2 **Maokeng** S. Africa
65 A1 **Maokui Shan** *mt.* China
70 A2 **Maomao Shan** *mt.* China
71 B3 **Maoming** China
121 C3 **Mapai** Moz.
75 C1 **Mapam Yumco** *l.* China
61 D2 **Mapane** Indon.
145 C3 **Mapastepec** Mex.
144 B2 **Mapimí** Mex.
144 B2 **Mapimí, Bolsón de** *des.* Mex.
64 A3 **Mapin** *i.* Phil.
121 C3 **Mapinhane** Moz.
129 D3 **Maple Creek** Can.
156 D4 **Mapmakers Seamounts** *sea feature* N. Pacific Ocean
59 D3 **Maprik** P.N.G.
123 D1 **Mapulanguene** Moz.
121 C3 **Maputo** Moz.
123 D2 **Maputo** *r.* Moz./S. Africa
123 C2 **Maputsoe** Lesotho
114 A2 **Maqteïr** *reg.* Maur.
75 C2 **Maquan He** *r.* China
120 A1 **Maquela do Zombo** Angola
153 B4 **Maquinchao** Arg.
137 E2 **Maquoketa** U.S.A.
123 C1 **Mara** S. Africa
150 B1 **Mara** Venez.
150 C3 **Maraã** Brazil
151 E3 **Maraba** Brazil
151 D2 **Maracá, Ilha de** *i.* Brazil
150 B1 **Maracaibo** Venez.
150 B2 **Maracaibo, Lago de** *l.* Venez.
Maracaibo, Lake Venez. *see* Maracaibo, Lago de
154 A2 **Maracaju** Brazil
154 A2 **Maracaju, Serra de** *hills* Brazil
150 C1 **Maracay** Venez.
115 D2 **Marādah** Libya
115 C3 **Maradi** Niger
81 C2 **Marāgheh** Iran
150 C2 **Marahuaca, Cerro** *mt.* Venez.
151 E3 **Marajó, Baia de** *est.* Brazil
151 D3 **Marajó, Ilha de** *i.* Brazil
79 C2 **Marāki** Iran
119 D2 **Maralal** Kenya
Maralbashi China *see* Bachu
50 C3 **Maralinga** Austr.
Maralwexi China *see* Bachu
138 A2 **Marana** U.S.A.
81 C2 **Marand** Iran
Marandellas Zimbabwe *see* Marondera
150 B3 **Marañón** *r.* Peru
Maraş Turkey *see* Kahramanmaraş

110 C1 **Mărăşeşti** Romania
130 B3 **Marathon** Can.
143 D4 **Marathon** U.S.A.
106 C2 **Marbella** Spain
50 A2 **Marble Bar** Austr.
123 C1 **Marble Hall** S. Africa
123 D3 **Marburg** S. Africa
101 D2 **Marburg an der Lahn** Ger.
103 D2 **Marcali** Hungary
137 E3 **Marceline** U.S.A.
99 D3 **March** U.K.
100 B2 **Marche-en-Famenne** Belgium
106 B2 **Marchena** Spain
152 B3 **Mar Chiquita, Lago** *l.* Arg.
150 B4 **Marcona** Peru
141 E2 **Marcy, Mount** U.S.A.
74 B1 **Mardan** Pak.
153 C3 **Mar del Plata** Arg.
81 C2 **Mardın** Turkey
96 B2 **Maree, Loch** *l.* U.K.
51 D1 **Mareeba** Austr.
108 B3 **Marettimo, Isola** *i. Sicily* Italy
89 D2 **Marevo** Rus. Fed.
138 C2 **Marfa** U.S.A.
Margao India *see* Madgaon
50 A3 **Margaret River** Austr.
150 C1 **Margarita, Isla de** *i.* Venez.
123 D3 **Margate** S. Africa
99 D4 **Margate** U.K.
62 A1 **Margherita** India
Margherita, Lake Eth. *see* Abaya Häyk'
119 C2 **Margherita Peak** Dem. Rep. Congo/Uganda
76 C3 **Margo, Dasht-i** *des.* Afgh.
91 C2 **Marhanets'** Ukr.
62 A1 **Mari** Myanmar
152 B2 **María Elena** Chile
156 C5 **Mariana Trench** *sea feature* N. Pacific Ocean
Mariánica, Cordillera *mts* Spain *see* Morena, Sierra
142 B2 **Marianna** *AR* U.S.A.
143 C2 **Marianna** *FL* U.S.A.
102 C2 **Mariánské Lázně** Czech Rep.
144 B2 **Marías, Islas** *is* Mex.
78 B3 **Ma'rib** Yemen
109 C1 **Maribor** Slovenia
Maricourt Can. *see* Kangiqsujuaq
119 C2 **Maridi** Sudan
117 A4 **Maridi** *watercourse* Sudan
55 P2 **Marie Byrd Land** *reg.* Antarctica
147 D3 **Marie-Galante** *i.* Guadeloupe
93 G3 **Mariehamn** Fin.
122 A1 **Mariental** Namibia
93 F4 **Mariestad** Sweden
143 D2 **Marietta** *GA* U.S.A.
140 C3 **Marietta** *OH* U.S.A.
105 D3 **Marignane** France
83 K3 **Marii, Mys** *pt* Rus. Fed.
88 B3 **Marijampolė** Lith.
154 C2 **Marília** Brazil
106 B1 **Marin** Spain
135 B3 **Marina** U.S.A.
109 C3 **Marina di Gioiosa Ionica** Italy
88 C3 **Mar"ina Horka** Belarus
140 B1 **Marinette** U.S.A.
154 B2 **Maringá** Brazil
106 B2 **Marinha Grande** Port.
140 B2 **Marion** *IN* U.S.A.
140 C2 **Marion** *OH* U.S.A.
143 E2 **Marion** *SC* U.S.A.
140 C3 **Marion** *VA* U.S.A.
143 D2 **Marion, Lake** U.S.A.
52 A3 **Marion Bay** Austr.
152 B2 **Mariscal Estigarribia** Para.
105 D3 **Maritime Alps** *mts* France/Italy
110 C2 **Maritsa** *r.* Bulg.
91 D2 **Mariupol'** Ukr.
117 C4 **Marka** Somalia
68 C3 **Markam** China
123 C1 **Marken** S. Africa
100 B1 **Markermeer** *l.* Neth.
98 C3 **Market Rasen** U.K.
98 C3 **Market Weighton** U.K.
83 I2 **Markha** *r.* Rus. Fed.
141 D2 **Markham** Can.
91 D2 **Markivka** Ukr.
118 B2 **Markounda** C.A.R.

142 B2 **Marksville** U.S.A.
101 D3 **Marktheidenfeld** Ger.
101 F2 **Marktredwitz** Ger.
100 C2 **Marl** Ger.
51 C2 **Marla** Austr.
100 A3 **Marle** France
139 D2 **Marlin** U.S.A.
53 C3 **Marlo** Austr.
104 C3 **Marmande** France
Marmara, Sea of *g.* Turkey *see* Marmara Denizi
111 C2 **Marmara Denizi** *g.* Turkey
111 C3 **Marmaris** Turkey
105 C2 **Marne** *r.* France
105 C2 **Marne-la-Vallée** France
118 B2 **Maro** Chad
121 □D2 **Maroantsetra** Madag.
54 B1 **Marokopa** N.Z.
101 E2 **Maroldsweisach** Ger.
121 □D2 **Maromokotro** *mt.* Madag.
121 C2 **Marondera** Zimbabwe
151 D2 **Maroni** *r.* Fr. Guiana
51 E2 **Maroochydore** Austr.
61 C2 **Maros** Indon.
49 M6 **Marotiri** *is* Fr. Polynesia
118 B1 **Maroua** Cameroon
121 □D2 **Marovoay** Madag.
49 N4 **Marquesas Islands** Fr. Polynesia
143 D4 **Marquesas Keys** *is* U.S.A.
155 D2 **Marquês de Valença** Brazil
140 B1 **Marquette** U.S.A.
116 A3 **Marra, Jebel** *mt.* Sudan
123 D2 **Marracuene** Moz.
114 B1 **Marrakech** Morocco
Marrakesh Morocco *see* Marrakech
116 A3 **Marra Plateau** Sudan
52 A1 **Marree** Austr.
86 F2 **Marresale** Rus. Fed.
121 C2 **Marromeu** Moz.
121 C2 **Marrupa** Moz.
116 B2 **Marsa Alam** Egypt
115 D1 **Marsa al Burayqah** Libya
119 D2 **Marsabit** Kenya
78 A2 **Marsa Delwein** Sudan
108 B3 **Marsala** *Sicily* Italy
116 A1 **Marsa Matrûh** Egypt
101 D2 **Marsberg** Ger.
108 B2 **Marsciano** Italy
52 B2 **Marsden** Austr.
100 B1 **Marsdiep** *sea chan.* Neth.
105 D3 **Marseille** France
Marseilles France *see* Marseille
142 B1 **Marshall** *AR* U.S.A.
137 D2 **Marshall** *MN* U.S.A.
137 E3 **Marshall** *MO* U.S.A.
139 E2 **Marshall** *TX* U.S.A.
48 H2 **Marshall Islands** *country* N. Pacific Ocean
137 E2 **Marshalltown** U.S.A.
140 A2 **Marshfield** U.S.A.
146 C2 **Marsh Harbour** Bahamas
142 B3 **Marsh Island** U.S.A.
93 G4 **Märsta** Sweden
63 A2 **Martaban** Myanmar
63 A2 **Martaban, Gulf of** Myanmar
61 C2 **Martapura** Indon.
60 B2 **Martapura** Indon.
141 E2 **Martha's Vineyard** *i.* U.S.A.
105 D2 **Martigny** Switz.
103 D2 **Martin** Slovakia
136 C2 **Martin** U.S.A.
145 C2 **Martínez** Mex.
143 D2 **Martinez** U.S.A.
155 C1 **Martinho Campos** Brazil
147 D3 **Martinique** *terr.* West Indies
147 D3 **Martinique Passage** Dominica/Martinique
140 C3 **Martinsburg** U.S.A.
140 C3 **Martinsville** U.S.A.
54 C2 **Marton** N.Z.
107 D1 **Martorell** Spain
106 C2 **Martos** Spain
76 B1 **Martuk** Kazakh.
81 D3 **Marv Dasht** Iran
105 C3 **Marvejols** France
76 C3 **Mary** Turkm.
51 E2 **Maryborough** Austr.
122 B2 **Marydale** S. Africa
141 D3 **Maryland** *state* U.S.A.
98 B2 **Maryport** U.K.
75 C2 **Marysville** U.S.A.
137 E2 **Maryville** *MO* U.S.A.
143 D1 **Maryville** *TN* U.S.A.
119 D3 **Masai Steppe** *plain* Tanz.

119 D3 **Masaka** Uganda
61 C2 **Masalembu Besar** *i.* Indon.
61 D2 **Masamba** Indon.
65 B2 **Masan** S. Korea
119 D4 **Masasi** Tanz.
64 B2 **Masbate** Phil.
64 B2 **Masbate** *i.* Phil.
72 D2 **Mascara** Alg.
155 E1 **Mascote** Brazil
123 C2 **Maseru** Lesotho
Mashaba Zimbabwe *see* Mashava
121 C3 **Mashava** Zimbabwe
76 B3 **Mashhad** Iran
123 C3 **Masibambane** S. Afri
79 C3 **Masilah, Wādī al** *watercourse* Yemen
123 C2 **Masilo** S. Africa
118 B3 **Masi-Manimba** Dem. Rep. Congo
119 D2 **Masindi** Uganda
122 B3 **Masinyusane** S. Afric
Masira, Gulf of Oman *see* Maşīrah, Gulf of
79 C2 **Maşīrah** *i.* Oman
79 C3 **Maşīrah, Gulf of** Oma
81 C2 **Masjed Soleymān** Ira
97 B2 **Mask, Lough** *l.* Rep. of Ireland
121 □E2 **Masoala, Tanjona** *c.* Madag.
137 E2 **Mason City** U.S.A.
Masqaţ Oman *see* Muscat
108 B2 **Massa** Italy
141 E2 **Massachusetts** *state* U.S.A.
141 E2 **Massachusetts Bay** U.S.A.
115 D3 **Massaguet** Chad
115 D3 **Massakory** Chad
121 C3 **Massangena** Moz.
120 A1 **Massango** Angola
116 B3 **Massawa** Eritrea
141 E2 **Massena** U.S.A.
115 D3 **Massenya** Chad
128 A2 **Masset** Can.
105 C2 **Massif Central** *mts* France
140 C2 **Massillon** U.S.A.
114 B3 **Massina** Mali
121 C3 **Massinga** Moz.
123 D1 **Massingir** Moz.
78 A2 **Mastābah** Saudi Arab
54 C2 **Masterton** N.Z.
74 B1 **Mastuj** Pak.
74 A2 **Mastung** Pak.
78 A2 **Mastūrah** Saudi Arabi
88 B3 **Masty** Belarus
67 B4 **Masuda** Japan
Masuku Gabon *see* Franceville
121 C3 **Masvingo** Zimbabwe
119 D3 **Maswe** Tanz.
118 B3 **Matadi** Dem. Rep. Cor
146 B3 **Matagalpa** Nic.
130 C3 **Matagami** Can.
130 C3 **Matagami, Lac** *l.* Can.
139 D3 **Matagorda Island** U.S
139 D3 **Matagorda Peninsula** U.S.A.
120 A2 **Matala** Angola
114 A3 **Matam** Senegal
54 C1 **Matamata** N.Z.
144 B2 **Matamoros** Mex.
145 C2 **Matamoros** Mex.
119 D3 **Matandu** *r.* Tanz.
131 D3 **Matane** Can.
146 B2 **Matanzas** Cuba
Matapan, Cape *pt* Gre *see* Tainaro, Akra
73 C4 **Matara** Sri Lanka
61 C2 **Mataram** Indon.
50 C1 **Mataranka** Austr.
107 D1 **Mataró** Spain
123 C3 **Matatiele** S. Africa
54 A3 **Mataura** N.Z.
54 A3 **Mataura** *r.* N.Z.
54 C1 **Matawai** N.Z.
152 B1 **Mategua** Bol.
145 B2 **Matehuala** Mex.
109 C2 **Matera** Italy
108 A3 **Mateur** Tunisia
139 D3 **Mathis** U.S.A.
74 B2 **Mathura** India
64 B2 **Mati** Phil.
145 C3 **Matías Romero** Mex.
98 C3 **Matlock** U.K.
150 D4 **Mato Grosso** Brazil

4 B1 **Mato Grosso, Planalto do** *plat.* Brazil
3 D2 **Matola** Moz.
6 B1 **Matosinhos** Port.
Matou China *see* **Pingguo**
9 C2 **Maṭraḥ** Oman
7 B3 **Matsue** Japan
6 D2 **Matsumae** Japan
7 C3 **Matsumoto** Japan
7 C4 **Matsusaka** Japan
1 C3 **Matsu Tao** *i.* Taiwan
7 B4 **Matsuyama** Japan
0 B2 **Mattagami** *r.* Can.
0 C3 **Mattawa** Can.
5 D2 **Matterhorn** *mt.* Italy/Switz.
4 C2 **Matterhorn** *mt.* U.S.A.
3 D1 **Matthews** U.S.A.
9 C2 **Maṭṭī, Sabkhat** *salt pan* Saudi Arabia
0 B3 **Mattoon** U.S.A.
0 C2 **Maturín** Venez.
D2 **Matveyev Kurgan** Rus. Fed.
3 C2 **Matwabeng** S. Africa
5 C2 **Mau** India
5 C1 **Maubeuge** France
4 C3 **Maubourguet** France
5 E3 **Maud Seamount** *sea feature* S. Atlantic Ocean
9 L1 **Maui** *i.* U.S.A.
3 D2 **Mauldin** U.S.A.
0 C2 **Maumee** *r.* U.S.A.
1 D2 **Maumere** Indon.
0 B2 **Maun** Botswana
3 C1 **Maunatlala** Botswana
2 A1 **Maungdaw** Myanmar
5 B2 **Mau Rampur** India
0 C2 **Maurice, Lake** *salt flat* Austr.
4 A3 **Mauritania** *country* Africa
3 I8 **Mauritius** *country* Indian Ocean
0 B2 **Mavinga** Angola
3 C3 **Mavuya** S. Africa
6 B2 **Māwān, Khashm** *hill* Saudi Arabia
8 B3 **Mawanga** Dem. Rep. Congo
1 B3 **Mawei** China
2 A1 **Mawkmai** Myanmar
2 A1 **Mawlaik** Myanmar
8 B2 **Mawqaq** Saudi Arabia
5 L3 **Mawson Peninsula** Antarctica
8 B3 **Mawza** Yemen
8 A3 **Maxia, Punta** *mt. Sardinia* Italy
1 C3 **Maxixe** Moz.
4 B1 **Maxwell** N.Z.
3 J2 **Maya** *r.* Rus. Fed.
7 C2 **Mayaguana** *i.* Bahamas
7 D3 **Mayagüez** Puerto Rico
1 D2 **Mayamey** Iran
6 B3 **Maybole** U.K.
6 B3 **Maych'ew** Eth.
7 C3 **Maydh** Somalia
0 C2 **Mayen** Ger.
4 B2 **Mayenne** France
4 B2 **Mayenne** *r.* France
8 C2 **Mayerthorpe** Can.
0 B3 **Mayfield** U.S.A.
1 E3 **Maykop** Rus. Fed.
2 A1 **Maymyo** Myanmar
8 A1 **Mayo** Can.
8 B3 **Mayoko** Congo
Mayo Landing Can. *see* **Mayo**
4 B2 **Mayon** *vol.* Phil.
1 D2 **Mayotte** *terr.* Africa
3 J3 **Mayskiy** Rus. Fed.
0 C3 **Maysville** U.S.A.
8 B3 **Mayumba** Gabon
7 D1 **Mayville** U.S.A.
0 B2 **Mazabuka** Zambia
Mazagan Morocco *see* **El Jadida**
1 D3 **Mazagão** Brazil
4 C3 **Mazamet** France
4 B1 **Mazar** China
8 B3 **Mazara del Vallo** *Sicily* Italy
7 C3 **Mazār-e Sharīf** Afgh.
7 C2 **Mazarrón** Spain
7 C2 **Mazarrón, Golfo de** *b.* Spain
4 A2 **Mazatán** Mex.
6 A3 **Mazatenango** Guat.
4 B2 **Mazatlán** Mex.
8 B2 **Mažeikiai** Lith.
8 B2 **Mazirbe** Latvia
121 B3 **Mazunga** Zimbabwe
103 E1 **Mazurskie, Pojezierze** *reg.* Pol.
88 C3 **Mazyr** Belarus
123 D2 **Mbabane** Swaziland
118 B2 **Mbaïki** C.A.R.
118 B2 **Mbakaou, Lac de** *l.* Cameroon
121 C1 **Mbala** Zambia
121 B3 **Mbalabala** Zimbabwe
119 D2 **Mbale** Uganda
118 B2 **Mbalmayo** Cameroon
118 B3 **Mbandaka** Dem. Rep. Congo
118 B2 **Mbandjok** Cameroon
118 A2 **Mbanga** Cameroon
120 A1 **M'banza Congo** Angola
118 B3 **Mbanza-Ngungu** Dem. Rep. Congo
119 D3 **Mbarara** Uganda
118 B2 **Mbé** Cameroon
119 D3 **Mbeya** Tanz.
119 D4 **Mbinga** Tanz.
119 D3 **Mbizi Mountains** Tanz.
119 C2 **Mboki** C.A.R.
118 B2 **Mbomo** Congo
118 B2 **Mbouda** Cameroon
114 A3 **Mbour** Senegal
114 A3 **Mbout** Maur.
118 C3 **Mbuji-Mayi** Dem. Rep. Congo
119 D3 **Mbuyuni** Tanz.
141 F1 **McAdam** Can.
139 D2 **McAlester** U.S.A.
139 D3 **McAllen** U.S.A.
128 B2 **McBride** Can.
134 C2 **McCall** U.S.A.
139 C2 **McCamey** U.S.A.
126 F2 **McClintock Channel** Can.
126 E2 **McClure Strait** Can.
142 B2 **McComb** U.S.A.
136 C2 **McConaughy, Lake** U.S.A.
136 C2 **McCook** U.S.A.
134 C2 **McDermitt** U.S.A.
159 E7 **McDonald Islands** Indian Ocean
134 D1 **McDonald Peak** U.S.A.
135 D3 **McGill** U.S.A.
126 B2 **McGrath** U.S.A.
134 D1 **McGuire, Mount** U.S.A.
121 C2 **Mchinji** Malawi
142 C1 **McKenzie** U.S.A.
51 D2 **McKinlay** Austr.
134 B2 **McKinleyville** U.S.A.
128 C2 **McLennan** Can.
128 B2 **McLeod Lake** Can.
134 B1 **McMinnville** *OR* U.S.A.
142 C1 **McMinnville** *TN* U.S.A.
137 D3 **McPherson** U.S.A.
128 C1 **McTavish Arm** *b.* Can.
123 C3 **Mdantsane** S. Africa
135 D3 **Mead, Lake** *resr* U.S.A.
136 C3 **Meade** U.S.A.
129 D2 **Meadow Lake** Can.
140 C2 **Meadville** U.S.A.
66 D2 **Meaken-dake** *vol.* Japan
106 B1 **Mealhada** Port.
131 E2 **Mealy Mountains** Can.
128 C2 **Meander River** Can.
78 A2 **Mecca** Saudi Arabia
141 D3 **Mechanicsville** U.S.A.
100 B2 **Mechelen** Belgium
100 B2 **Mechelen** Neth.
100 C2 **Mechernich** Ger.
100 C2 **Meckenheim** Ger.
101 E1 **Mecklenburgische Seenplatte** *reg.* Ger.
106 B1 **Meda** Port.
60 A1 **Medan** Indon.
153 B4 **Medanosa, Punta** *pt* Arg.
73 C4 **Medawachchiya** Sri Lanka
107 D2 **Médéa** Alg.
150 B2 **Medellín** Col.
115 D1 **Medenine** Tunisia
134 B2 **Medford** U.S.A.
110 C2 **Medgidia** Romania
110 B1 **Mediaş** Romania
136 B2 **Medicine Bow Mountains** U.S.A.
136 B2 **Medicine Bow Peak** U.S.A.
129 C2 **Medicine Hat** Can.
137 D3 **Medicine Lodge** U.S.A.
155 D1 **Medina** Brazil
78 A2 **Medina** Saudi Arabia
106 C1 **Medinaceli** Spain
106 C1 **Medina del Campo** Spain
106 B1 **Medina de Rioseco** Spain
75 C2 **Medinīpur** India
84 E5 **Mediterranean Sea**
129 C2 **Medley** Can.
87 E3 **Mednogorsk** Rus. Fed.
62 A1 **Mêdog** China
88 B2 **Medvėgalio kalnis** *hill* Lith.
83 L2 **Medvezh'i, Ostrova** *is* Rus. Fed.
86 C2 **Medvezh'yegorsk** Rus. Fed.
50 A2 **Meekatharra** Austr.
136 B2 **Meeker** U.S.A.
74 B2 **Meerut** India
100 A2 **Meetkerke** Belgium
119 D2 **Mēga** Eth.
119 D2 **Mega Escarpment** Eth./Kenya
111 B3 **Megalopoli** Greece
75 D2 **Meghalaya** *state* India
75 C2 **Meghāsani** *mt.* India
111 C3 **Megisti** *i.* Greece
92 I1 **Mehamn** Norway
50 A2 **Meharry, Mount** Austr.
137 E3 **Mehlville** U.S.A.
79 C2 **Mehrān** *watercourse* Iran
74 B1 **Mehtar Lām** Afgh.
119 D3 **Meia Meia** Tanz.
154 C1 **Meia Ponte** *r.* Brazil
118 B2 **Meiganga** Cameroon
65 B1 **Meihekou** China
Meijiang China *see* **Ningdu**
62 A1 **Meiktila** Myanmar
101 E2 **Meiningen** Ger.
102 C1 **Meißen** Ger.
Meixian China *see* **Meizhou**
71 B3 **Meizhou** China
152 B2 **Mejicana** *mt.* Arg.
152 A2 **Mejillones** Chile
118 B2 **Mékambo** Gabon
116 B3 **Mek'elē** Eth.
114 C2 **Mekerrhane, Sebkha** *salt pan* Alg.
114 B1 **Meknès** Morocco
63 B2 **Mekong** *r.* Asia
63 B3 **Mekong, Mouths of the** Vietnam
60 B1 **Melaka** Malaysia
156 D6 **Melanesia** International Feature
156 D5 **Melanesian Basin** *sea feature* Pacific Ocean
53 B3 **Melbourne** Austr.
143 D3 **Melbourne** U.S.A.
108 A2 **Mele, Capo** *c.* Italy
Melekess Rus. Fed. *see* **Dimitrovgrad**
89 F2 **Melenki** Rus. Fed.
131 C2 **Mélèzes, Rivière aux** *r.* Can.
115 D3 **Mélfi** Chad
109 C2 **Melfi** Italy
129 D2 **Melfort** Can.
92 F3 **Melhus** Norway
106 B1 **Melide** Spain
114 B1 **Melilla** N. Africa
129 D3 **Melita** Can.
91 D2 **Melitopol'** Ukr.
119 D2 **Melka Guba** Eth.
101 D1 **Melle** Ger.
93 F4 **Mellerud** Sweden
101 E2 **Mellrichstadt** Ger.
101 D1 **Mellum** *i.* Ger.
123 D2 **Melmoth** S. Africa
152 C3 **Melo** Uru.
115 C1 **Melrhir, Chott** *salt l.* Alg.
96 C3 **Melrose** U.K.
Melsetter Zimbabwe *see* **Chimanimani**
52 B3 **Melton** Austr.
99 C3 **Melton Mowbray** U.K.
105 C2 **Melun** France
129 D2 **Melville** Can.
51 D1 **Melville, Cape** Austr.
131 E2 **Melville, Lake** Can.
50 C1 **Melville Island** Austr.
126 E1 **Melville Island** Can.
127 G2 **Melville Peninsula** Can.
61 C2 **Memboro** Indon.
102 C2 **Memmingen** Ger.
60 B1 **Mempawah** Indon.
80 B3 **Memphis** *tourist site* Egypt
142 B1 **Memphis** *TN* U.S.A.
139 C2 **Memphis** *TX* U.S.A.
91 C1 **Mena** Ukr.
142 B2 **Mena** U.S.A.
121 □D3 **Menabe** *mts* Madag.
114 C3 **Ménaka** Mali
Mènam Khong *r.* Laos/Thai. *see* **Mekong**
105 C3 **Mende** France
117 B4 **Mendebo Mountains** Eth.
116 B3 **Mendefera** Eritrea
160 B1 **Mendeleyev Ridge** *sea feature* Arctic Ocean
145 C2 **Méndez** Mex.
117 B4 **Mendī** Eth.
59 D3 **Mendi** P.N.G.
99 B4 **Mendip Hills** U.K.
140 B2 **Mendota** U.S.A.
153 B3 **Mendoza** Arg.
111 C3 **Menemen** Turkey
100 A2 **Menen** Belgium
70 B2 **Mengcheng** China
60 B2 **Menggala** Indon.
71 A3 **Mengzi** China
131 D2 **Menihek** Can.
52 B2 **Menindee** Austr.
52 B2 **Menindee Lake** Austr.
52 A3 **Meningie** Austr.
104 C2 **Mennecy** France
140 B1 **Menominee** U.S.A.
120 A2 **Menongue** Angola
107 D1 **Menorca** *i.* Spain
61 C1 **Mensalong** Indon.
60 A2 **Mentawai, Kepulauan** *is* Indon.
60 B2 **Mentok** Indon.
61 C1 **Menyapa, Gunung** *mt.* Indon.
108 A3 **Menzel Bourguiba** Tunisia
50 B2 **Menzies** Austr.
144 B2 **Meoqui** Mex.
100 C1 **Meppel** Neth.
100 C1 **Meppen** Ger.
121 C3 **Mepuze** Moz.
123 C2 **Meqheleng** S. Africa
140 B2 **Mequon** U.S.A.
108 B1 **Merano** Italy
59 D3 **Merauke** Indon.
52 B2 **Merbein** Austr.
Merca Somalia *see* **Marka**
107 D2 **Mercadal** Spain
135 B3 **Merced** U.S.A.
152 C2 **Mercedes** Arg.
153 B3 **Mercedes** Arg.
139 D3 **Mercedes** U.S.A.
127 H2 **Mercy, Cape** Can.
139 C1 **Meredith, Lake** U.S.A.
91 D2 **Merefa** Ukr.
116 A3 **Merga Oasis** Sudan
63 A2 **Mergui** Myanmar
63 A2 **Mergui Archipelago** *is* Myanmar
110 C2 **Meriç** *r.* Greece/Turkey
111 C2 **Meriç** Turkey
145 D2 **Mérida** Mex.
106 B2 **Mérida** Spain
150 B2 **Mérida** Venez.
147 C4 **Mérida, Cordillera de** *mts* Venez.
134 C2 **Meridian** *ID* U.S.A.
142 C2 **Meridian** *MS* U.S.A.
139 D2 **Meridian** *TX* U.S.A.
104 B3 **Mérignac** France
93 H3 **Merikarvia** Fin.
53 C3 **Merimbula** Austr.
88 B3 **Merkinė** Lith.
116 B3 **Merowe** Sudan
50 A3 **Merredin** Austr.
96 B3 **Merrick** *hill* U.K.
140 B1 **Merrill** U.S.A.
140 B2 **Merrillville** U.S.A.
136 C2 **Merriman** U.S.A.
128 B2 **Merritt** Can.
53 C2 **Merrygoen** Austr.
116 C3 **Mersa Fatma** Eritrea
100 C3 **Mersch** Lux.
101 E2 **Merseburg (Saale)** Ger.
98 B2 **Mersey** *r.* U.K.
Mersin Turkey *see* **İçel**
60 B1 **Mersing** Malaysia
99 D4 **Mers-les-Bains** France
74 B2 **Merta** India
99 B4 **Merthyr Tydfil** U.K.
119 D2 **Merti Plateau** Kenya
106 B2 **Mértola** Port.
119 D3 **Meru** *vol.* Tanz.
122 B3 **Merweville** S. Africa
80 B1 **Merzifon** Turkey
100 C3 **Merzig** Ger.
138 A2 **Mesa** *AZ* U.S.A.
138 C2 **Mesa** *NM* U.S.A.
137 E1 **Mesabi Range** *hills* U.S.A.
109 C2 **Mesagne** Italy
138 B2 **Mescalero** U.S.A.
139 C2 **Mescalero Ridge** U.S.A.
101 D2 **Meschede** Ger.
89 E3 **Meshchovsk** Rus. Fed.
Meshed Iran *see* **Mashhad**
91 E2 **Meshkovskaya** Rus. Fed.
138 B2 **Mesilla** U.S.A.
111 B2 **Mesimeri** Greece

111 B3 **Mesolongi** Greece
115 C1 **Messaad** Alg.
121 D2 **Messalo** *r.* Moz.
109 C3 **Messina** *Sicily* Italy
123 D1 **Messina** S. Africa
Messina, Strait of Italy *see* **Messina, Stretta di**
109 C3 **Messina, Stretta di** *str.* Italy
111 B3 **Messini** Greece
111 B3 **Messiniakos Kolpos** *b.* Greece
111 B2 **Mesta** *r.* Bulg.
Mesta *r.* Greece *see* **Nestos**
150 C2 **Meta** *r.* Col./Venez.
130 C3 **Métabetchouan** Can.
127 H2 **Meta Incognita Peninsula** Can.
142 B3 **Metairie** U.S.A.
152 B2 **Metán** Arg.
111 B3 **Methoni** Greece
109 C2 **Metković** Croatia
121 C2 **Metoro** Moz.
60 B2 **Metro** Indon.
100 C3 **Mettlach** Ger.
135 C3 **Mettler** U.S.A.
117 B4 **Metu** Eth.
105 D2 **Metz** France
100 B2 **Meuse** *r.* Belgium/France
139 D2 **Mexia** U.S.A.
144 A1 **Mexicali** Mex.
144 A1 **Mexico** *country* Central America
145 C3 **México** Mex.
137 E3 **Mexico** U.S.A.
125 I7 **Mexico, Gulf of** Mex./U.S.A.
Mexico City Mex. *see* **México**
81 D2 **Meybod** Iran
101 F1 **Meyenburg** Ger.
76 C3 **Meymaneh** Afgh.
83 M2 **Meynypil'gyno** Rus. Fed.
86 D2 **Mezen'** Rus. Fed.
86 D2 **Mezen'** *r.* Rus. Fed.
86 E1 **Mezhdusharskiy, Ostrov** *i.* Rus. Fed.
103 E2 **Mezőtúr** Hungary
132 C4 **Mezquital** *r.* Mex.
144 B2 **Mezquitic** Mex.
88 C2 **Mežvidi** Latvia
121 C2 **Mfuwe** Zambia
89 D3 **Mglin** Rus. Fed.
123 D2 **Mhlume** Swaziland
74 B2 **Mhow** India
145 C3 **Miahuatlán** Mex.
106 B2 **Miajadas** Spain
143 D3 **Miami** *FL* U.S.A.
139 E1 **Miami** *OK* U.S.A.
143 D3 **Miami Beach** U.S.A.
81 C2 **Miandowāb** Iran
121 □D2 **Miandrivazo** Madag.
81 C2 **Mīāneh** Iran
71 A3 **Mianning** China
74 B1 **Mianwali** Pak.
Mianyang China *see* **Xiantao**
70 A2 **Mianyang** China
121 □D2 **Miarinarivo** Madag.
87 F3 **Miass** Rus. Fed.
103 D1 **Miastko** Pol.
128 C2 **Mica Creek** Can.
103 E2 **Michalovce** Slovakia
140 B1 **Michigan** *state* U.S.A.
140 B2 **Michigan, Lake** U.S.A.
140 B2 **Michigan City** U.S.A.
140 B1 **Michipicoten Bay** Can.
130 B3 **Michipicoten Island** Can.
130 B3 **Michipicoten River** Can.
Michurin Bulg. *see* **Tsarevo**
89 F3 **Michurinsk** Rus. Fed.
156 D5 **Micronesia** *is* Pacific Ocean
158 E6 **Mid-Atlantic Ridge** *sea feature* Atlantic Ocean
100 A2 **Middelburg** Neth.
123 C3 **Middelburg** S. Africa
123 C2 **Middelburg** S. Africa
100 B2 **Middelharnis** Neth.
134 B2 **Middle Alkali Lake** U.S.A.
73 D3 **Middle Andaman** *i.* India
Middle Congo *country* Africa *see* **Congo**
136 D2 **Middle Loup** *r.* U.S.A.
140 C3 **Middlesboro** U.S.A.
98 C2 **Middlesbrough** U.K.
141 E2 **Middletown** *NY* U.S.A.
140 C3 **Middletown** *OH* U.S.A.
78 B3 **Mīdī** Yemen
130 C3 **Midland** Can.
140 C2 **Midland** *MI* U.S.A.
139 C2 **Midland** *TX* U.S.A.
97 B3 **Midleton** Rep. of Ireland
Midnapore India *see* **Medinīpur**
94 B1 **Miðvágur** Faroe Is
Midway Oman *see* **Thamarīt**
57 T7 **Midway Islands** *terr.* N. Pacific Ocean
109 D2 **Midzhur** *mt.* Bulg./Yugo.
103 E1 **Mielec** Pol.
110 C1 **Miercurea-Ciuc** Romania
106 B1 **Mieres** Spain
101 E1 **Mieste** Ger.
145 C3 **Miguel Alemán, Presa** *resr* Mex.
144 B2 **Miguel Auza** Mex.
144 B2 **Miguel Hidalgo, Presa** *resr* Mex.
63 A2 **Migyaunglaung** Myanmar
67 B4 **Mihara** Japan
89 E3 **Mikhaylov** Rus. Fed.
Mikhaylovgrad Bulg. *see* **Montana**
66 B2 **Mikhaylovka** Rus. Fed.
Mikhaylovka Rus. Fed. *see* **Kimovsk**
87 D3 **Mikhaylovka** Rus. Fed.
77 D1 **Mikhaylovskiy** Rus. Fed.
93 I3 **Mikkeli** Fin.
86 E2 **Mikun'** Rus. Fed.
67 C3 **Mikuni-sanmyaku** *mts* Japan
73 B4 **Miladhunmadulu Atoll** Maldives
108 A1 **Milan** Italy
121 C2 **Milange** Moz.
Milano Italy *see* **Milan**
111 C3 **Milas** Turkey
137 D1 **Milbank** U.S.A.
99 D3 **Mildenhall** U.K.
52 B2 **Mildura** Austr.
71 A3 **Mile** China
136 B1 **Miles City** U.S.A.
141 D3 **Milford** *DE* U.S.A.
135 D3 **Milford** *UT* U.S.A.
99 A4 **Milford Haven** U.K.
54 A2 **Milford Sound** N.Z.
Milḩ, Baḩr al *l.* Iraq *see* **Razāzah, Buḩayrat ar**
107 D2 **Miliana** Alg.
50 C1 **Milikapiti** Austr.
51 C1 **Milingimbi** Austr.
134 E1 **Milk** *r.* U.S.A.
116 B3 **Milk, Wadi el** *watercourse* Sudan
83 L3 **Mil'kovo** Rus. Fed.
128 C3 **Milk River** Can.
105 C3 **Millau** France
143 D2 **Milledgeville** U.S.A.
137 E1 **Mille Lacs** *lakes* U.S.A.
130 A3 **Mille Lacs, Lac des** *l.* Can.
137 D2 **Miller** U.S.A.
91 E2 **Millerovo** Rus. Fed.
52 A2 **Millers Creek** Austr.
96 B3 **Milleur Point** U.K.
52 B3 **Millicent** Austr.
142 C1 **Millington** U.S.A.
141 F1 **Millinocket** U.S.A.
55 J3 **Mill Island** Antarctica
53 D1 **Millmerran** Austr.
98 B2 **Millom** U.K.
136 B2 **Mills** U.S.A.
128 C1 **Mills Lake** Can.
111 B3 **Milos** *i.* Greece
89 E3 **Miloslavskoye** Rus. Fed.
91 E2 **Milove** Ukr.
52 B1 **Milparinka** Austr.
54 A3 **Milton** N.Z.
99 C3 **Milton Keynes** U.K.
140 B2 **Milwaukee** U.S.A.
158 C3 **Milwaukee Deep** *sea feature* Caribbean Sea
104 B3 **Mimizan** France
118 B3 **Mimongo** Gabon
155 D2 **Mimoso do Sul** Brazil
79 C2 **Mīnāb** Iran
61 D1 **Minahasa, Semenanjung** *pen.* Indon.
Minahassa Peninsula Indon. *see* **Minahasa, Semenanjung**
79 C2 **Mina Jebel Ali** U.A.E.
Minaker Can. *see* **Prophet River**
60 B1 **Minas** Indon.
153 C3 **Minas** Uru.
79 B2 **Mīnā' Sa'ūd** Kuwait
155 D1 **Minas Novas** Brazil
145 C3 **Minatitlán** Mex.
62 A1 **Minbu** Myanmar
64 B3 **Mindanao** *i.* Phil.
52 B2 **Mindarie** Austr.
101 D1 **Minden** Ger.
142 B2 **Minden** *LA* U.S.A.
137 D2 **Minden** *NE* U.S.A.
64 B2 **Mindoro** *i.* Phil.
64 A2 **Mindoro Strait** Phil.
118 B3 **Mindouli** Congo
99 B4 **Minehead** U.K.
154 B1 **Mineiros** Brazil
139 D2 **Mineral Wells** U.S.A.
75 C1 **Minfeng** China
119 C4 **Minga** Dem. Rep. Congo
81 C1 **Mingäçevir** Azer.
131 D2 **Mingan** Can.
52 B2 **Mingary** Austr.
70 B2 **Mingguang** China
62 A1 **Mingin** Myanmar
107 C2 **Minglanilla** Spain
119 D4 **Mingoyo** Tanz.
69 E1 **Mingshui** China
96 A2 **Mingulay** *i.* U.K.
71 B3 **Mingxi** China
Mingzhou China *see* **Suide**
70 A2 **Minhe** China
73 B4 **Minicoy** *i.* India
50 A2 **Minilya** Austr.
114 B3 **Mininian** Côte d'Ivoire
131 D2 **Minipi Lake** Can.
130 A2 **Miniss Lake** Can.
52 A2 **Minlaton** Austr.
115 C4 **Minna** Nigeria
137 E2 **Minneapolis** U.S.A.
129 E2 **Minnedosa** Can.
137 E2 **Minnesota** *r.* U.S.A.
137 E1 **Minnesota** *state* U.S.A.
106 B1 **Miño** *r.* Port./Spain
Minorca *i.* Spain *see* **Menorca**
136 C1 **Minot** U.S.A.
88 C3 **Minsk** Belarus
103 E1 **Mińsk Mazowiecki** Pol.
96 D2 **Mintlaw** U.K.
131 D3 **Minto** Can.
130 C2 **Minto, Lac** *l.* Can.
68 C1 **Minusinsk** Rus. Fed.
62 A1 **Minutang** India
70 A2 **Minxian** China
155 D1 **Mirabela** Brazil
155 D1 **Miralta** Brazil
111 C3 **Mirampelou, Kolpos** *b.* Greece
152 C2 **Miranda** Brazil
152 C1 **Miranda** *r.* Brazil
Miranda Moz. *see* **Macaloge**
106 C1 **Miranda de Ebro** Spain
106 B1 **Mirandela** Port.
154 B2 **Mirandópolis** Brazil
154 B2 **Mirante, Serra do** *hills* Brazil
79 C3 **Mirbāţ** Oman
61 C1 **Miri** *Sarawak* Malaysia
153 C3 **Mirim, Lagoa** *l.* Brazil
79 D2 **Mīrjāveh** Iran
89 D3 **Mirnyy** Rus. Fed.
83 I2 **Mirnyy** Rus. Fed.
101 F1 **Mirow** Ger.
74 A2 **Mirpur Khas** Pak.
Mirtoan Sea Greece *see* **Mirtoö Pelagos**
111 B3 **Mirtoö Pelagos** *sea* Greece
65 B2 **Miryang** S. Korea
Mirzachirla Turkm. *see* **Murzechirla**
Mirzachul Uzbek. *see* **Gulistan**
75 C2 **Mirzapur** India
77 E3 **Misalay** China
66 B1 **Mishan** China
51 E1 **Misima Island** P.N.G.
146 B3 **Miskitos, Cayos** *is* Nic.
103 E2 **Miskolc** Hungary
59 C3 **Misoöl** *i.* Indon.
115 D1 **Mişrātah** Libya
130 B2 **Missinaibi** *r.* Can.
130 B3 **Missinaibi Lake** Can.
128 B3 **Mission** Can.
130 B2 **Missisa Lake** Can.
142 C3 **Mississippi** *r.* U.S.A.
142 C2 **Mississippi** *state* U.S.A.
142 C3 **Mississippi Delta** U.S.A.
142 C2 **Mississippi Sound** *sea chan.* U.S.A.
Missolonghi Greece *see* **Mesolongi**
134 D1 **Missoula** U.S.A.
137 E3 **Missouri** *r.* U.S.A.
137 E3 **Missouri** *state* U.S.A.
130 C3 **Mistassibi** *r.* Can.
130 C2 **Mistassini, Lac** *l.* Can.
131 D2 **Mistastin Lake** Can.
103 D2 **Mistelbach** Austria
131 D2 **Mistinibi, Lac** *l.* Can.
130 C2 **Mistissini** Can.
51 D2 **Mitchell** Austr.
51 D1 **Mitchell** *r.* Austr.
136 C2 **Mitchell** *NE* U.S.A.
137 D2 **Mitchell** *SD* U.S.A.
97 B2 **Mitchelstown** Rep. of Ireland
74 A2 **Mithi** Pak.
67 D3 **Mito** Japan
119 D3 **Mitole** Tanz.
53 D2 **Mittagong** Austr.
101 E2 **Mittelhausen** Ger.
101 D1 **Mittellandkanal** *canal* Ger.
101 F3 **Mitterteich** Ger.
Mittimatalik Can. *see* **Pond Inlet**
150 B2 **Mitú** Col.
119 C4 **Mitumba, Chaîne des** *m* Dem. Rep. Congo
119 C3 **Mitumba, Monts** *mts* Dem. Rep. Congo
119 C3 **Mitwaba** Dem. Rep. Congo
118 B2 **Mitzic** Gabon
78 B2 **Miyah, Wādī al** *watercourse* Saudi Arabia
67 C4 **Miyake-jima** *i.* Japan
66 D3 **Miyako** Japan
67 B4 **Miyakonojō** Japan
76 B2 **Miyaly** Kazakh.
Miyang China *see* **Mile**
67 B4 **Miyazaki** Japan
67 C3 **Miyazu** Japan
115 D1 **Mizdah** Libya
97 B3 **Mizen Head** *hd* Rep. of Ireland
90 A2 **Mizhhir"ya** Ukr.
Mizo Hills *state* India *see* **Mizoram**
75 D2 **Mizoram** *state* India
93 G4 **Mjölby** Sweden
93 F3 **Mjøsa** *l.* Norway
119 D3 **Mkomazi** Tanz.
103 C1 **Mladá Boleslav** Czech Rep.
109 D2 **Mladenovac** Yugo.
103 E1 **Mława** Pol.
109 C2 **Mljet** *i.* Croatia
123 C3 **Mlungisi** S. Africa
90 B1 **Mlyniv** Ukr.
123 C2 **Mmabatho** S. Africa
123 C2 **Mmathethe** Botswana
93 E3 **Mo** Norway
135 E3 **Moab** U.S.A.
123 D2 **Moamba** Moz.
54 B2 **Moana** N.Z.
118 B3 **Moanda** Gabon
97 C2 **Moate** Rep. of Ireland
119 C3 **Moba** Dem. Rep. Congo
118 C2 **Mobayi-Mbongo** Dem. Rep. Congo
137 E3 **Moberly** U.S.A.
142 C2 **Mobile** U.S.A.
142 C2 **Mobile Bay** U.S.A.
142 C2 **Mobile Point** U.S.A.
136 C1 **Mobridge** U.S.A.
Mobutu, Lake Dem. Rep. Congo/Uganda *see* **Albert, Lake**
Mobutu Sese Seko, Lak Dem. Rep. Congo/Uganda *see* **Albert, Lake**
121 C2 **Moçambicano, Planalto** *plat.* Moz.
121 D2 **Moçambique** Moz.
Moçâmedes Angola *see* **Namibe**
62 B1 **Môc Châu** Vietnam
Mocha Yemen *see* **Al Mukhā**
123 C1 **Mochudi** Botswana
121 D2 **Mocimboa da Praia** Moz
101 D3 **Möckmühl** Ger.
150 B2 **Mocoa** Col.
154 C2 **Mococa** Brazil
144 B2 **Mocorito** Mex.
144 B1 **Moctezuma** Mex.
145 B2 **Moctezuma** Mex.
144 B2 **Moctezuma** Mex.
121 C2 **Mocuba** Moz.

D2 **Modane** France
B2 **Modder** *r.* S. Africa
B2 **Modena** Italy
B3 **Modesto** U.S.A.
B3 **Modica** *Sicily* Italy
C3 **Moe** Austr.
Moero, Lake Dem. Rep. Congo/Zambia *see* **Mweru, Lake**
C2 **Moers** Ger.
C3 **Moffat** U.K.
Mogadishu Somalia *see* **Muqdisho**
Mogador Morocco *see* **Essaouira**
B1 **Mogadouro, Serra de** *mts* Port.
C1 **Mogalakwena** *r.* S. Africa
A1 **Mogaung** Myanmar
Mogilev Belarus *see* **Mahilyow**
C2 **Mogi-Mirim** Brazil
I3 **Mogocha** Rus. Fed.
C1 **Mogoditshane** Botswana
A1 **Mogok** Myanmar
A2 **Mogollon Plateau** U.S.A.
D2 **Mohács** Hungary
C3 **Mohale's Hoek** Lesotho
D2 **Mohammadia** Alg.
A2 **Mohave Mountains** U.S.A.
E2 **Mohawk** *r.* U.S.A.
A1 **Mohnyin** Myanmar
D3 **Mohoro** Tanz.
B2 **Mohyliv Podil's'kyy** Ukr.
C1 **Moijabana** Botswana
C1 **Moinești** Romania
Mointy Kazakh. *see* **Moyynty**
F2 **Mo i Rana** Norway
C2 **Mõisaküla** Estonia
C3 **Moissac** France
C3 **Mojave** U.S.A.
C3 **Mojave Desert** U.S.A.
B1 **Mojiang** China
C2 **Moji das Cruzes** Brazil
C2 **Moji-Guaçu** *r.* Brazil
C2 **Mojkovac** Yugo.
B1 **Mokau** N.Z.
C2 **Mokhotlong** Lesotho
J2 **Mokhsogollokh** Rus. Fed.
B1 **Mokolo** Cameroon
B3 **Mokp'o** S. Korea
C2 **Mola di Bari** Italy
C2 **Molango** Mex.
Moldavia *country* Europe *see* **Moldova**
Moldavskaya S.S.R. *country* Europe *see* **Moldova**
E3 **Molde** Norway
B2 **Moldova** *country* Europe
B2 **Moldova Nouă** Romania
B1 **Moldoveanu, Vârful** *mt.* Romania
B1 **Moldovei, Podișul** *plat.* Romania
B2 **Moldovei Centrale, Podișul** *plat.* Moldova
C1 **Molepolole** Botswana
C2 **Molėtai** Lith.
C2 **Molfetta** Italy
Molière Alg. *see* **Bordj Bounaama**
C1 **Molina de Aragón** Spain
C2 **Molina de Segura** Spain
D3 **Moliro** Dem. Rep. Congo
B4 **Mollendo** Peru
F4 **Mölnlycke** Sweden
D2 **Molochna** *r.* Ukr.
E2 **Molokovo** Rus. Fed.
C2 **Molong** Austr.
B2 **Molopo** *watercourse* Botswana/S. Africa
Molotov Rus. Fed. *see* **Perm'**
Molotovsk Rus. Fed. *see* **Severodvinsk**
Molotovsk Rus. Fed. *see* **Nolinsk**
B2 **Moloundou** Cameroon
Moluccas *is* Indon. *see* **Maluku**
C3 **Molucca Sea** Indon.
B2 **Momba** Austr.
D3 **Mombasa** Kenya
B1 **Mombuca, Serra da** *hills* Brazil
C2 **Momchilgrad** Bulg.
F4 **Møn** *i.* Denmark
D3 **Monaco** *country* Europe
96 B2 **Monadhliath Mountains** U.K.
97 C1 **Monaghan** Rep. of Ireland
139 C2 **Monahans** U.S.A.
147 D3 **Mona Passage** Dom. Rep./Puerto Rico
120 A1 **Mona Quimbundo** Angola
Monastir Macedonia *see* **Bitola**
89 D3 **Monastyrshchina** Rus. Fed.
90 B2 **Monastyryshche** Ukr.
118 B2 **Monatélé** Cameroon
66 D2 **Monbetsu** Japan
108 A1 **Moncalieri** Italy
86 C2 **Monchegorsk** Rus. Fed.
100 C2 **Mönchengladbach** Ger.
144 B2 **Monclova** Mex.
131 D3 **Moncton** Can.
106 B1 **Mondego** *r.* Port.
118 C2 **Mondjamboli** Dem. Rep. Congo
123 D2 **Mondlo** S. Africa
108 A2 **Mondovì** Italy
106 C1 **Mondragón** Spain
111 B3 **Monemvasia** Greece
66 D1 **Moneron, Ostrov** *i.* Rus. Fed.
141 D1 **Monet** Can.
137 E3 **Monett** U.S.A.
108 B1 **Monfalcone** Italy
106 B1 **Monforte** Spain
119 D2 **Mongbwalu** Dem. Rep. Congo
62 B1 **Mông Cai** Vietnam
62 A1 **Mong Hang** Myanmar
Monghyr India *see* **Munger**
62 B1 **Mong Lin** Myanmar
62 A1 **Mong Nawng** Myanmar
115 D3 **Mongo** Chad
68 C1 **Mongolia** *country* Asia
74 B1 **Mongora** Pak.
62 A1 **Mong Pawk** Myanmar
62 A1 **Mong Ping** Myanmar
120 B2 **Mongu** Zambia
135 C3 **Monitor Range** *mts* U.S.A.
103 E1 **Mońki** Pol.
99 B4 **Monmouth** U.K.
114 C4 **Mono** *r.* Togo
135 C3 **Mono Lake** U.S.A.
109 C2 **Monopoli** Italy
107 C1 **Monreal del Campo** Spain
142 B2 **Monroe** *LA* U.S.A.
140 C2 **Monroe** *MI* U.S.A.
140 B2 **Monroe** *WI* U.S.A.
142 C2 **Monroeville** U.S.A.
114 A4 **Monrovia** Liberia
100 A2 **Mons** Belgium
155 E1 **Monsarás, Ponta de** *pt* Brazil
100 C2 **Montabaur** Ger.
122 B3 **Montagu** S. Africa
109 C3 **Montalto** *mt.* Italy
110 B2 **Montana** Bulg.
134 E1 **Montana** *state* U.S.A.
105 C2 **Montargis** France
104 C3 **Montauban** France
141 E2 **Montauk Point** U.S.A.
123 C2 **Mont-aux-Sources** *mt.* Lesotho
105 C2 **Montbard** France
105 D2 **Montbéliard** France
105 D2 **Mont Blanc** *mt.* France/Italy
105 C2 **Montbrison** France
100 B3 **Montcornet** France
104 B3 **Mont-de-Marsan** France
104 C2 **Montdidier** France
151 D3 **Monte Alegre** Brazil
154 C1 **Monte Alegre de Minas** Brazil
141 E1 **Montebello** Can.
154 B3 **Montecarlo** Arg.
105 D3 **Monte-Carlo** Monaco
154 C1 **Monte Carmelo** Brazil
152 C3 **Monte Caseros** Arg.
123 C1 **Monte Christo** S. Africa
146 C3 **Montego Bay** Jamaica
105 C3 **Montélimar** France
109 C2 **Montella** Italy
145 C2 **Montemorelos** Mex.
104 B2 **Montendre** France
109 C2 **Montenegro** *aut. rep.* Yugo.
121 C2 **Montepuez** Moz.
108 B2 **Montepulciano** Italy
135 B3 **Monterey** U.S.A.
135 B3 **Monterey Bay** U.S.A.
150 B2 **Montería** Col.
152 B1 **Montero** Bol.
145 B2 **Monterrey** Mex.
109 C2 **Montesano sulla Marcellana** Italy
109 C2 **Monte Sant'Angelo** Italy
151 F4 **Monte Santo** Brazil
108 A2 **Monte Santu, Capo di** *c.* *Sardinia* Italy
155 D1 **Montes Claros** Brazil
153 C3 **Montevideo** Uru.
137 D2 **Montevideo** U.S.A.
136 B3 **Monte Vista** U.S.A.
142 C2 **Montgomery** U.S.A.
100 B3 **Monthermé** France
105 D2 **Monthey** Switz.
142 B2 **Monticello** *AR* U.S.A.
143 D2 **Monticello** *FL* U.S.A.
135 E3 **Monticello** *UT* U.S.A.
104 C2 **Montignac** France
100 B2 **Montignies-le-Tilleul** Belgium
106 B2 **Montijo** Port.
106 B2 **Montijo** Spain
106 C2 **Montilla** Spain
154 B1 **Montividiu** Brazil
131 D3 **Mont-Joli** Can.
130 C3 **Mont-Laurier** Can.
104 C2 **Montluçon** France
131 C3 **Montmagny** Can.
104 C2 **Montmorillon** France
51 E2 **Monto** Austr.
134 D2 **Montpelier** *ID* U.S.A.
141 E2 **Montpelier** *VT* U.S.A.
105 C3 **Montpellier** France
130 C3 **Montréal** Can.
Montreal Can. *see* **Montréal**
129 D2 **Montreal Lake** Can.
129 D2 **Montreal Lake** *l.* Can.
99 D4 **Montreuil** France
105 D2 **Montreux** Switz.
96 C2 **Montrose** U.K.
136 B3 **Montrose** U.S.A.
147 D3 **Montserrat** *terr.* West Indies
62 A1 **Monywa** Myanmar
108 A1 **Monza** Italy
107 D1 **Monzón** Spain
123 C1 **Mookane** Botswana
52 A1 **Moolawatana** Austr.
52 B1 **Moomba** Austr.
53 D1 **Moonie** Austr.
53 C1 **Moonie** *r.* Austr.
52 A2 **Moonta** Austr.
50 A3 **Moora** Austr.
50 A2 **Moore, Lake** *salt flat* Austr.
137 D1 **Moorhead** U.S.A.
53 C3 **Mooroopna** Austr.
122 A3 **Moorreesburg** S. Africa
130 B2 **Moose** *r.* Can.
130 B2 **Moose Factory** Can.
141 F1 **Moosehead Lake** U.S.A.
129 D2 **Moose Jaw** Can.
137 E1 **Moose Lake** U.S.A.
129 D2 **Moosomin** Can.
130 B2 **Moosonee** Can.
52 B2 **Mootwingee** Austr.
107 E2 **M'Oukal** Alg.
123 C1 **Mopane** S. Africa
114 B3 **Mopti** Mali
150 B4 **Moquegua** Peru
103 D2 **Mór** Hungary
118 B1 **Mora** Cameroon
93 F3 **Mora** Sweden
137 E1 **Mora** U.S.A.
74 B2 **Moradabad** India
121 □D2 **Morafenobe** Madag.
121 □D2 **Moramanga** Madag.
136 A2 **Moran** U.S.A.
51 D2 **Moranbah** Austr.
103 D2 **Morava** *r.* Europe
96 B2 **Moray Firth** *b.* U.K.
100 C3 **Morbach** Ger.
74 B2 **Morbi** India
93 G4 **Mörbylånga** Sweden
104 B3 **Morcenx** France
69 E1 **Mordaga** China
129 E3 **Morden** Can.
89 F3 **Mordovo** Rus. Fed.
98 B2 **Morecambe** U.K.
98 B2 **Morecambe Bay** U.K.
53 C1 **Moree** Austr.
59 D3 **Morehead** P.N.G.
140 C3 **Morehead** U.S.A.
143 E2 **Morehead City** U.S.A.
145 B3 **Morelia** Mex.
107 C1 **Morella** Spain
74 B2 **Morena** India
106 B2 **Morena, Sierra** *mts* Spain
110 C2 **Moreni** Romania
138 A3 **Moreno** Mex.
128 A2 **Moresby, Mount** Can.
128 A2 **Moresby Island** Can.
53 D1 **Moreton Island** Austr.
52 A2 **Morgan** Austr.
142 B3 **Morgan City** U.S.A.
143 D1 **Morganton** U.S.A.
141 D3 **Morgantown** U.S.A.
105 D2 **Morges** Switz.
68 C2 **Mori** China
66 D2 **Mori** Japan
53 C1 **Moriarty's Range** *hills* Austr.
128 B2 **Morice Lake** Can.
66 D3 **Morioka** Japan
53 D2 **Morisset** Austr.
104 B2 **Morlaix** France
98 C3 **Morley** U.K.
157 G9 **Mornington Abyssal Plain** *sea feature* S. Atlantic Ocean
51 C1 **Mornington Island** Austr.
59 D3 **Morobe** P.N.G.
114 B1 **Morocco** *country* Africa
119 D3 **Morogoro** Tanz.
64 B3 **Moro Gulf** Phil.
122 B2 **Morokweng** S. Africa
121 □D3 **Morombe** Madag.
68 C1 **Mörön** Mongolia
121 □D3 **Morondava** Madag.
106 B2 **Morón de la Frontera** Spain
121 D2 **Moroni** Comoros
59 C2 **Morotai** *i.* Indon.
119 D2 **Moroto** Uganda
98 C2 **Morpeth** U.K.
142 B1 **Morrilton** U.S.A.
154 C1 **Morrinhos** Brazil
54 C1 **Morrinsville** N.Z.
129 E3 **Morris** Can.
137 D1 **Morris** U.S.A.
143 D1 **Morristown** U.S.A.
154 C2 **Morro Agudo** Brazil
155 E1 **Morro d'Anta** Brazil
55 K3 **Morse, Cape** Antarctica
87 D3 **Morshanka** Rus. Fed.
Morshansk Rus. Fed. *see* **Morshanka**
154 B1 **Mortes, Rio das** *r.* Brazil
52 B3 **Mortlake** Austr.
48 G3 **Mortlock Islands** Micronesia
140 B2 **Morton** U.S.A.
53 C2 **Morundah** Austr.
53 D3 **Moruya** Austr.
96 B2 **Morvern** *reg.* U.K.
Morvi India *see* **Morbi**
53 C3 **Morwell** Austr.
101 D3 **Mosbach** Ger.
89 E2 **Moscow** Rus. Fed.
134 C1 **Moscow** U.S.A.
100 C2 **Mosel** *r.* Ger.
122 B2 **Moselebe** *watercourse* Botswana
105 D2 **Moselle** *r.* France
134 C1 **Moses Lake** U.S.A.
92 □A3 **Mosfellsbær** Iceland
54 B3 **Mosgiel** N.Z.
88 C2 **Moshchnyy, Ostrov** *i.* Rus. Fed.
89 D2 **Moshenskoye** Rus. Fed.
119 D3 **Moshi** Tanz.
92 F2 **Mosjøen** Norway
Moskva Rus. Fed. *see* **Moscow**
89 E2 **Moskva** *r.* Rus. Fed.
103 D2 **Mosonmagyaróvár** Hungary
93 F4 **Moss** Norway
Mossâmedes Angola *see* **Namibe**
122 B3 **Mossel Bay** S. Africa
122 B3 **Mossel Bay** *b.* S. Africa
118 B3 **Mossendjo** Congo
52 B2 **Mossgiel** Austr.
51 D1 **Mossman** Austr.
151 F3 **Mossoró** Brazil
53 D2 **Moss Vale** Austr.
102 C1 **Most** Czech Rep.
114 C1 **Mostaganem** Alg.
109 C2 **Mostar** Bos.-Herz.
152 C3 **Mostardas** Brazil
106 C1 **Móstoles** Spain
Mosul Iraq *see* **Al Mawșil**
145 D3 **Motagua** *r.* Guat.
93 G4 **Motala** Sweden
123 C2 **Motetema** S. Africa
96 C3 **Motherwell** U.K.
75 C2 **Motihari** India
107 C2 **Motilla del Palancar** Spain
122 B1 **Motokwe** Botswana
106 C2 **Motril** Spain

110 B2 **Motru** Romania
136 C1 **Mott** U.S.A.
54 B2 **Motueka** N.Z.
145 D2 **Motul** Mex.
49 L5 **Motu One** *atoll* Fr. Polynesia
114 A3 **Moudjéria** Maur.
111 C3 **Moudros** Greece
118 B3 **Mouila** Gabon
52 B3 **Moulamein** Austr.
105 C2 **Moulins** France
63 A2 **Moulmein** Myanmar
143 D2 **Moultrie** U.S.A.
143 E2 **Moultrie, Lake** U.S.A.
140 B3 **Mound City** U.S.A.
115 D4 **Moundou** Chad
140 C3 **Moundsville** U.S.A.
137 E3 **Mountain Grove** U.S.A.
142 B1 **Mountain Home** *AR* U.S.A.
134 C2 **Mountain Home** *ID* U.S.A.
143 D1 **Mount Airy** U.S.A.
123 C3 **Mount Ayliff** S. Africa
52 A3 **Mount Barker** Austr.
53 C3 **Mount Beauty** Austr.
97 B2 **Mount Bellew** Rep. of Ireland
121 C2 **Mount Darwin** Zimbabwe
141 F2 **Mount Desert Island** U.S.A.
123 C3 **Mount Fletcher** S. Africa
123 C3 **Mount Frere** S. Africa
52 B3 **Mount Gambier** Austr.
59 D3 **Mount Hagen** P.N.G.
53 C2 **Mount Hope** Austr.
51 C2 **Mount Isa** Austr.
52 A3 **Mount Lofty Range** *mts* Austr.
50 A2 **Mount Magnet** Austr.
52 B2 **Mount Manara** Austr.
54 C1 **Mount Maunganui** N.Z.
97 C2 **Mountmellick** Rep. of Ireland
137 E2 **Mount Pleasant** *IA* U.S.A.
140 C2 **Mount Pleasant** *MI* U.S.A.
143 E2 **Mount Pleasant** *SC* U.S.A.
139 E2 **Mount Pleasant** *TX* U.S.A.
135 D3 **Mount Pleasant** *UT* U.S.A.
99 A4 **Mount's Bay** U.K.
134 B2 **Mount Shasta** U.S.A.
54 B2 **Mount Somers** N.Z.
140 B3 **Mount Vernon** *IL* U.S.A.
140 C2 **Mount Vernon** *OH* U.S.A.
134 B1 **Mount Vernon** *WA* U.S.A.
51 D2 **Moura** Austr.
106 B2 **Moura** Port.
115 E3 **Mourdi, Dépression du** *depr.* Chad
97 C1 **Mourne Mountains** *hills* U.K.
100 A2 **Mouscron** Belgium
115 D3 **Moussoro** Chad
61 D1 **Moutong** Indon.
115 C2 **Mouydir, Monts du** *plat.* Alg.
100 B3 **Mouzon** France
97 B1 **Moy** *r.* Rep. of Ireland
117 B4 **Moyale** Eth.
Moyen Congo *country* Africa *see* **Congo**
123 C3 **Moyeni** Lesotho
119 D2 **Moyo** Uganda
77 D2 **Moyynkum** Kazakh.
77 D2 **Moyynty** Kazakh.
121 C3 **Mozambique** *country* Africa
113 G8 **Mozambique Channel** Africa
81 C1 **Mozdok** Rus. Fed.
89 E2 **Mozhaysk** Rus. Fed.
119 D3 **Mpanda** Tanz.
121 C2 **Mpika** Zambia
118 B2 **Mpoko** *r.* C.A.R.
121 C1 **Mporokoso** Zambia
123 C2 **Mpumalanga** *prov.* S. Africa
119 D3 **Mpwapwa** Tanz.
115 D1 **M'Saken** Tunisia
119 D3 **Msambweni** Kenya
119 D3 **Msata** Tanz.
88 C2 **Mshinskaya** Rus. Fed.
115 C1 **M'Sila** Alg.
89 D2 **Msta** *r.* Rus. Fed.
89 D2 **Mstinskiy Most** Rus. Fed.
89 D3 **Mstsislaw** Belarus
Mtoko Zimbabwe *see* **Mutoko**
89 E3 **Mtsensk** Rus. Fed.
123 D2 **Mtubatuba** S. Africa
119 E4 **Mtwara** Tanz.
151 E3 **Muana** Brazil
118 B3 **Muanda** Dem. Rep. Congo
62 B1 **Muang Hiam** Laos
62 B2 **Muang Hinboun** Laos
62 B2 **Muang Khammouan** Laos
63 B2 **Muang Không** Laos
63 B2 **Muang Khôngxédôn** Laos
62 B1 **Muang Ngoy** Laos
62 B2 **Muang Pakbeng** Laos
62 B2 **Muang Pakxan** Laos
63 B2 **Muang Phalan** Laos
62 B2 **Muang Phôn-Hông** Laos
62 B1 **Muang Sing** Laos
62 B2 **Muang Vangviang** Laos
62 B2 **Muang Xaignabouri** Laos
60 B1 **Muar** Malaysia
60 B2 **Muarabungo** Indon.
60 B2 **Muaradua** Indon.
61 C2 **Muaralaung** Indon.
60 A2 **Muarasiberut** Indon.
60 B2 **Muaratembesi** Indon.
61 C2 **Muarateweh** Indon.
Muara Tuang Malaysia *see* Kota Samarahan
119 D2 **Mubende** Uganda
115 D3 **Mubi** Nigeria
120 B2 **Muconda** Angola
120 A2 **Mucope** Angola
121 C2 **Mucubela** Moz.
155 E1 **Mucuri** Brazil
155 E1 **Mucuri** *r.* Brazil
66 A2 **Mudanjiang** China
66 A1 **Mudan Jiang** *r.* China
111 C2 **Mudanya** Turkey
136 B2 **Muddy Gap** U.S.A.
101 E1 **Müden (Örtze)** Ger.
53 C2 **Mudgee** Austr.
63 A2 **Mudon** Myanmar
80 B1 **Mudurnu** Turkey
121 C2 **Mueda** Moz.
121 B2 **Mufulira** Zambia
120 B2 **Mufumbwe** Zambia
111 C3 **Muğla** Turkey
116 B2 **Muhammad Qol** Sudan
Muhammarah Iran *see* Khorramshahr
101 F2 **Mühlberg** Ger.
101 E2 **Mühlhausen (Thüringen)** Ger.
88 B2 **Muhu** *i.* Estonia
63 B3 **Mui Ca Mau** *c.* Vietnam
97 C2 **Muine Bheag** Rep. of Ireland
96 B3 **Muirkirk** U.K.
121 C2 **Muite** Moz.
65 B2 **Muju** S. Korea
Mukačevo Ukr. *see* Mukacheve
90 A2 **Mukacheve** Ukr.
61 C1 **Mukah** *Sarawak* Malaysia
Mukalla Yemen *see* Al Mukallā
63 B2 **Mukdahan** Thai.
Mukden China *see* Shenyang
Mukhtuya Rus. Fed. *see* Lensk
50 A3 **Mukinbudin** Austr.
60 B2 **Mukomuko** Indon.
121 C2 **Mulanje, Mount** Malawi
101 F2 **Mulde** *r.* Ger.
119 D3 **Muleba** Tanz.
144 A2 **Mulegé** Mex.
139 C2 **Muleshoe** U.S.A.
106 C2 **Mulhacén** *mt.* Spain
100 C2 **Mülheim an der Ruhr** Ger.
105 D2 **Mulhouse** France
62 B1 **Muli** China
66 B2 **Muling** China
66 B1 **Muling** *r.* China
96 B2 **Mull** *i.* U.K.
53 C2 **Mullaley** Austr.
136 C2 **Mullen** U.S.A.
61 C1 **Muller, Pegunungan** *mts* Indon.
50 A2 **Mullewa** Austr.
97 C2 **Mullingar** Rep. of Ireland
96 B3 **Mull of Galloway** *c.* U.K.
96 B3 **Mull of Kintyre** *hd* U.K.
96 A3 **Mull of Oa** *hd* U.K.
53 D1 **Mullumbimby** Austr.
120 B2 **Mulobezi** Zambia
74 B1 **Multan** Pak.
86 F2 **Mulym'ya** Rus. Fed.
74 B3 **Mumbai** India
120 B2 **Mumbeji** Zambia
120 B2 **Mumbwa** Zambia
61 D2 **Muna** *i.* Indon.
145 D2 **Muna** Mex.
101 E2 **Münchberg** Ger.
München Ger. *see* **Munich**
München-Gladbach Ger. *see* **Mönchengladbach**
140 B2 **Muncie** U.S.A.
50 B3 **Mundrabilla** Austr.
140 B3 **Munfordville** U.S.A.
119 C2 **Mungbere** Dem. Rep. Congo
75 C2 **Munger** India
52 A1 **Mungeranie** Austr.
53 C1 **Mungindi** Austr.
75 C2 **Mungla** Bangl.
102 C2 **Munich** Ger.
155 D2 **Muniz Freire** Brazil
101 E1 **Münster** Ger.
100 C2 **Münster** Ger.
97 B2 **Munster** *reg.* Rep. of Ireland
100 C2 **Münsterland** *reg.* Ger.
62 B1 **Mương Nhie** Vietnam
92 H2 **Muonio** Fin.
92 H2 **Muonioälven** *r.* Fin./Sweden
117 C4 **Muqdisho** Somalia
155 D2 **Muqui** Brazil
103 D2 **Mur** *r.* Austria
67 C3 **Murakami** Japan
119 C3 **Muramvya** Burundi
119 D3 **Muranga** Kenya
86 D3 **Murashi** Rus. Fed.
81 B2 **Murat** *r.* Turkey
111 C2 **Muratlı** Turkey
67 D3 **Murayama** Japan
50 A2 **Murchison** *watercourse* Austr.
107 C2 **Murcia** Spain
107 C2 **Murcia** *aut. comm.* Spain
136 C2 **Murdo** U.S.A.
131 D3 **Murdochville** Can.
111 C2 **Mürefte** Turkey
110 B1 **Mureș** *r.* Romania
104 C3 **Muret** France
142 C1 **Murfreesboro** U.S.A.
77 C3 **Murghab** *r.* Afgh.
77 D3 **Murghob** Tajik.
155 D2 **Muriaé** Brazil
120 B1 **Muriege** Angola
101 F1 **Müritz** *l.* Ger.
92 J2 **Murmansk** Rus. Fed.
86 C2 **Murmanskiy Bereg** *coastal area* Rus. Fed.
87 D3 **Murom** Rus. Fed.
66 D2 **Muroran** Japan
106 B1 **Muros** Spain
67 B4 **Muroto** Japan
67 B4 **Muroto-zaki** *pt* Japan
143 D1 **Murphy** U.S.A.
53 C1 **Murra Murra** Austr.
52 A3 **Murray** *r.* Austr.
128 B2 **Murray** *r.* Can.
140 B3 **Murray** U.S.A.
59 D3 **Murray, Lake** P.N.G.
143 D2 **Murray, Lake** U.S.A.
52 A3 **Murray Bridge** Austr.
122 B3 **Murraysburg** S. Africa
52 B3 **Murrayville** Austr.
52 B2 **Murrumbidgee** *r.* Austr.
53 C2 **Murrumburrah** Austr.
121 C2 **Murrupula** Moz.
53 D2 **Murrurundi** Austr.
109 C1 **Murska Sobota** Slovenia
54 C1 **Murupara** N.Z.
49 N6 **Mururoa** *atoll* Fr. Polynesia
75 C2 **Murwara** India
53 D1 **Murwillumbah** Austr.
76 C3 **Murzechirla** Turkm.
115 D2 **Murzūq** Libya
103 D2 **Mürzzuschlag** Austria
81 C2 **Muş** Turkey
110 B2 **Musala** *mt.* Bulg.
65 B1 **Musan** N. Korea
78 B3 **Musaymir** Yemen
79 C2 **Muscat** Oman
Muscat and Oman *country* Asia *see* **Oman**
137 E2 **Muscatine** U.S.A.
50 C2 **Musgrave Ranges** *mts* Austr.
118 B3 **Mushie** Dem. Rep. Congo
60 B2 **Musi** *r.* Indon.
140 B2 **Muskegon** U.S.A.
140 B2 **Muskegon** *r.* U.S.A.
140 C3 **Muskingum** *r.* U.S.A.
139 D1 **Muskogee** U.S.A.
141 D1 **Muskoka, Lake** Can.
128 B2 **Muskwa** *r.* Can.
74 A1 **Muslimbagh** Pak.
116 B3 **Musmar** Sudan
119 D3 **Musoma** Tanz.
59 D3 **Mussau Island** P.N.G.
96 C3 **Musselburgh** U.K.
117 C4 **Mustahīl** Eth.
88 B2 **Mustjala** Estonia
53 D2 **Muswellbrook** Austr.
116 A2 **Mut** Egypt
121 C2 **Mutare** Zimbabwe
121 C2 **Mutoko** Zimbabwe
66 D2 **Mutsu** Japan
66 D2 **Mutsu-wan** *b.* Japan
121 C2 **Mutuali** Moz.
155 D1 **Mutum** Brazil
92 I2 **Muurola** Fin.
70 A2 **Mu Us Shamo** *des.* Ch
120 A1 **Muxaluando** Angola
86 C2 **Muyezerskiy** Rus. Fed.
119 D3 **Muyinga** Burundi
76 B2 **Muynak** Uzbek.
74 B1 **Muzaffargarh** Pak.
75 C2 **Muzaffarpur** India
123 D1 **Muzamane** Moz.
155 C2 **Muzambinho** Brazil
144 B2 **Múzquiz** Mex.
75 C1 **Muztag** *mt. Xinjiang* Ch
117 A4 **Mvolo** Sudan
119 C3 **Mwanza** Dem. Rep. Co
119 D3 **Mwanza** Tanz.
118 C3 **Mweka** Dem. Rep. Con
121 B2 **Mwenda** Zambia
118 C3 **Mwene-Ditu** Dem. Rep. Congo
121 C3 **Mwenezi** Zimbabwe
121 C3 **Mwenezi** *r.* Zimbabwe
119 C3 **Mweru, Lake** Dem. Rep. Congo/Zamb
121 B1 **Mweru Wantipa, Lake** Zambia
118 C3 **Mwimba** Dem. Rep. Co
120 B2 **Mwinilunga** Zambia
88 C3 **Myadzyel** Belarus
62 A2 **Myanaung** Myanmar
62 A1 **Myanmar** *country* Asia
63 A2 **Myaungmya** Myanmar
62 A1 **Myingyan** Myanmar
62 A1 **Myitkyina** Myanmar
90 A2 **Mykolayiv** Ukr.
91 C2 **Mykolayiv** Ukr.
111 C3 **Mykonos** Greece
111 C3 **Mykonos** *i.* Greece
86 E2 **Myla** Rus. Fed.
75 D2 **Mymensingh** Bangl.
62 A1 **Myohaung** Myanmar
65 B1 **Myŏnggan** N. Korea
88 C2 **Myory** Belarus
92 □B3 **Mýrdalsjökull** *ice cap* Iceland
92 G2 **Myre** Norway
91 C2 **Myrhorod** Ukr.
111 C3 **Myrina** Greece
90 C2 **Myronivka** Ukr.
143 E2 **Myrtle Beach** U.S.A.
53 C3 **Myrtleford** Austr.
134 B2 **Myrtle Point** U.S.A.
89 E2 **Myshkin** Rus. Fed.
Myshkino Rus. Fed. *se* Myshkin
103 C1 **Myślibórz** Pol.
73 B3 **Mysore** India
83 N2 **Mys Shmidta** Rus. Fed.
63 B2 **My Tho** Vietnam
111 C3 **Mytilini** Greece
89 E3 **Mytishchi** Rus. Fed.
123 C3 **Mzamomhle** S. Africa
121 C2 **Mzimba** Malawi
121 C2 **Mzuzu** Malawi

N

101 F3 **Naab** *r.* Ger.
100 B1 **Naarden** Neth.
97 C2 **Naas** Rep. of Ireland
122 A2 **Nababeep** S. Africa
87 E3 **Naberezhnyye Chelny** Rus. Fed.
59 D3 **Nabire** Indon.
80 B2 **Nāblus** West Bank
123 C1 **Naboomspruit** S. Africa
121 D2 **Nacala** Moz.
119 D4 **Nachingwea** Tanz.
103 D1 **Náchod** Czech Rep.
73 D3 **Nachuge** India
139 E2 **Nacogdoches** U.S.A.
144 B1 **Nacozari de García** Me
Nada China *see* **Danzho**
74 B2 **Nadiad** India
90 A2 **Nadvirna** Ukr.
86 C2 **Nadvoitsy** Rus. Fed.
86 G2 **Nadym** Rus. Fed.
93 F4 **Næstved** Denmark
111 B3 **Nafpaktos** Greece
111 B3 **Nafplio** Greece
115 D1 **Nafūsah, Jabal** *hills* Lib
78 B2 **Nafy** Saudi Arabia
64 B2 **Naga** Phil.

B2 **Nagagami** *r.* Can.
C3 **Nagano** Japan
C3 **Nagaoka** Japan
D2 **Nagaon** India
B1 **Nagar** India
B2 **Nagar Parkar** Pak.
A4 **Nagasaki** Japan
B4 **Nagato** Japan
B2 **Nagaur** India
B4 **Nagercoil** India
A2 **Nagha Kalat** Pak.
B2 **Nagina** India
C3 **Nagoya** Japan
B2 **Nagpur** India
D1 **Nagqu** China
E1 **Nags Head** U.S.A.
E1 **Nagurskoye** Rus. Fed.
D2 **Nagyatád** Hungary
D2 **Nagykanizsa** Hungary
B1 **Nahanni Butte** Can.
C2 **Nahāvand** Iran
E1 **Nahrendorf** Ger.
A4 **Nahuel Huapí, Lago** *l.* Arg.
D2 **Nahunta** U.S.A.
D2 **Nain** Can.
D2 **Nā'īn** Iran
C2 **Naiopué** Moz.
C2 **Nairn** U.K.
D3 **Nairobi** Kenya
Naissus Yugo. *see* **Niš**
D3 **Naivasha** Kenya
D2 **Najafābād** Iran
B2 **Najd** *reg.* Saudi Arabia
C1 **Nájera** Spain
C1 **Najin** N. Korea
B3 **Najrān** Saudi Arabia
D2 **Nakasongola** Uganda
C3 **Nakatsugawa** Japan
A3 **Nakfa** Eritrea
B2 **Nakhodka** Rus. Fed.
B2 **Nakhon Nayok** Thai.
B2 **Nakhon Pathom** Thai.
B2 **Nakhon Phanom** Thai.
B2 **Nakhon Ratchasima** Thai.
B2 **Nakhon Sawan** Thai.
A3 **Nakhon Si Thammarat** Thai.
Nakhrachi Rus. Fed. *see* **Kondinskoye**
B2 **Nakina** Can.
B3 **Naknek** U.S.A.
C1 **Nakonde** Zambia
F5 **Nakskov** Denmark
D3 **Nakuru** Kenya
C2 **Nakusp** Can.
D2 **Nalbari** India
D4 **Nal'chik** Rus. Fed.
D1 **Nālūt** Libya
D2 **Namaacha** Moz.
C2 **Namahadi** S. Africa
D2 **Namak, Daryācheh-ye** *salt flat* Iran
B3 **Namak, Kavīr-i-** *salt flat* Iran
C1 **Namakzar-e Shadad** *salt flat* Iran
D2 **Namangan** Uzbek.
D3 **Namanyere** Tanz.
A2 **Namaqualand** *reg.* Namibia
A2 **Namaqualand** *reg.* S. Africa
E2 **Nambour** Austr.
D2 **Nambucca Heads** Austr.
B3 **Năm Căn** Vietnam
B2 **Namch'ŏn** N. Korea
A2 **Nam Chon Reservoir** Thai.
D1 **Nam Co** *salt l.* China
B1 **Nam Định** Vietnam
C2 **Namialo** Moz.
A3 **Namib Desert** Namibia
A2 **Namibe** Angola
A3 **Namibia** *country* Africa
D2 **Namjagbarwa Feng** *mt.* China
C3 **Namlea** Indon.
B2 **Nam Ngum Reservoir** Laos
C2 **Namoi** *r.* Austr.
C2 **Nampa** U.S.A.
B3 **Nampala** Mali
B2 **Namp'o** N. Korea
C2 **Nampula** Moz.
D2 **Namrup** India
A1 **Namsang** Myanmar
F3 **Namsos** Norway
F3 **Namsskogan** Norway
A2 **Nam Tok** Thai.
J2 **Namtsy** Rus. Fed.
A1 **Namtu** Myanmar

121 C2 **Namuno** Moz.
100 B2 **Namur** Belgium
120 B2 **Namwala** Zambia
65 B2 **Namwŏn** S. Korea
62 A1 **Namya Ra** Myanmar
62 B2 **Nan** Thai.
128 B3 **Nanaimo** Can.
71 B3 **Nan'an** China
122 A1 **Nananib Plateau** Namibia
Nan'ao China *see* **Dayu**
67 C3 **Nanao** Japan
71 B3 **Nanchang** *Jiangxi* China
71 B3 **Nanchang** *Jiangxi* China
71 B3 **Nancheng** China
70 A2 **Nanchong** China
63 A3 **Nancowry** *i.* India
105 D2 **Nancy** France
75 C1 **Nanda Devi** *mt.* India
71 A3 **Nandan** China
74 B3 **Nānded** India
Nander India *see* **Nānded**
53 D2 **Nandewar Range** *mts* Austr.
74 B2 **Nandurbar** India
73 B3 **Nandyal** India
71 B3 **Nanfeng** China
62 A1 **Nang** China
118 B2 **Nanga Eboko** Cameroon
61 C2 **Nangahpinoh** Indon.
77 D3 **Nanga Parbat** *mt.* Jammu and Kashmir
61 C2 **Nangatayap** Indon.
63 A2 **Nangin** Myanmar
65 B1 **Nangnim-sanmaek** *mts* N. Korea
70 B2 **Nangong** China
119 D3 **Nangulangwa** Tanz.
70 C2 **Nanhui** China
70 B2 **Nanjing** China
Nanking China *see* **Nanjing**
67 B4 **Nankoku** Japan
120 A2 **Nankova** Angola
70 B2 **Nanle** China
71 B3 **Nan Ling** *mts* China
71 A3 **Nanning** China
127 I2 **Nanortalik** Greenland
71 A3 **Nanpan Jiang** *r.* China
75 C2 **Nanpara** India
71 B3 **Nanping** China
Nanpu China *see* **Pucheng**
69 E3 **Nansei-shotō** *is* Japan
160 I1 **Nansen Basin** *sea feature* Arctic Ocean
126 F1 **Nansen Sound** *sea chan.* Can.
104 B2 **Nantes** France
70 C2 **Nantong** China
141 E2 **Nantucket** U.S.A.
141 F2 **Nantucket Island** U.S.A.
99 B3 **Nantwich** U.K.
49 I4 **Nanumea** *i.* Tuvalu
155 D1 **Nanuque** Brazil
64 B3 **Nanusa, Kepulauan** *is* Indon.
71 B3 **Nanxiong** China
70 B2 **Nanyang** China
119 D3 **Nanyuki** Kenya
70 B2 **Nanzhang** China
Nanzhao China *see* **Zhao'an**
131 C2 **Naococane, Lac** *l.* Can.
74 A2 **Naokot** Pak.
71 B3 **Naozhou Dao** *i.* China
135 B3 **Napa** U.S.A.
126 E2 **Napaktulik Lake** Can.
141 D2 **Napanee** Can.
127 I2 **Napasoq** Greenland
137 F2 **Naperville** U.S.A.
54 C1 **Napier** N.Z.
108 B2 **Naples** Italy
143 D3 **Naples** U.S.A.
150 B3 **Napo** *r.* Ecuador
Napoli Italy *see* **Naples**
Napug China *see* **Gê'gyai**
114 B3 **Nara** Mali
88 C3 **Narach** Belarus
52 B3 **Naracoorte** Austr.
53 C2 **Naradhan** Austr.
145 C2 **Naranjos** Mex.
63 B3 **Narathiwat** Thai.
74 B3 **Narayangaon** India
105 C3 **Narbonne** France
63 A2 **Narcondam Island** India
127 H1 **Nares Strait** Can./Greenland
103 E1 **Narew** *r.* Pol.
122 A1 **Narib** Namibia
87 D4 **Narimanov** Rus. Fed.
67 D3 **Narita** Japan
74 B2 **Narmada** *r.* India
74 B2 **Narnaul** India

108 B2 **Narni** Italy
86 F2 **Narodnaya, Gora** *mt.* Rus. Fed.
90 B1 **Narodychi** Ukr.
89 E2 **Naro-Fominsk** Rus. Fed.
53 D3 **Narooma** Austr.
88 C3 **Narowlya** Belarus
93 H3 **Närpes** Fin.
53 C2 **Narrabri** Austr.
53 C2 **Narrandera** Austr.
53 C2 **Narromine** Austr.
67 B4 **Naruto** Japan
88 C2 **Narva** Estonia
88 C2 **Narva Bay** Estonia/Rus. Fed.
92 G2 **Narvik** Norway
88 C2 **Narvskoye Vodokhranilishche** *resr* Estonia/Rus. Fed.
86 E2 **Nar'yan-Mar** Rus. Fed.
77 D2 **Naryn** Kyrg.
74 B2 **Nashik** India
141 E2 **Nashua** U.S.A.
142 C1 **Nashville** U.S.A.
137 E1 **Nashwauk** U.S.A.
109 C1 **Našice** Croatia
117 B4 **Nasir** Sudan
Nasirabad Bangl. *see* **Mymensingh**
119 C4 **Nasondoye** Dem. Rep. Congo
76 B3 **Naṣrābād** Iran
128 B2 **Nass** *r.* Can.
146 C2 **Nassau** Bahamas
116 B2 **Nasser, Lake** *resr* Egypt
93 F4 **Nässjö** Sweden
130 C2 **Nastapoca** *r.* Can.
130 C2 **Nastapoka Islands** Can.
89 D2 **Nasva** Rus. Fed.
120 B3 **Nata** Botswana
151 F3 **Natal** Brazil
60 A1 **Natal** Indon.
Natal *prov.* S. Africa *see* **Kwazulu-Natal**
159 D6 **Natal Basin** *sea feature* Indian Ocean
139 D3 **Natalia** U.S.A.
131 D2 **Natashquan** Can.
131 D2 **Natashquan** *r.* Can.
142 B2 **Natchez** U.S.A.
142 B2 **Natchitoches** U.S.A.
53 C3 **Nathalia** Austr.
107 D1 **Nati, Punta** *pt* Spain
114 C3 **Natitingou** Benin
151 E4 **Natividade** Brazil
67 D3 **Natori** Japan
119 D3 **Natron, Lake** *salt l.* Tanz.
60 B1 **Natuna, Kepulauan** *is* Indon.
60 B1 **Natuna Besar** *i.* Indon.
122 A1 **Nauchas** Namibia
101 F1 **Nauen** Ger.
64 B2 **Naujan** Phil.
88 B2 **Naujoji Akmenė** Lith.
101 E2 **Naumburg (Saale)** Ger.
48 H34 **Nauru** *country* S. Pacific Ocean
150 B3 **Nauta** Peru
145 C2 **Nautla** Mex.
88 C3 **Navahrudak** Belarus
106 B2 **Navalmoral de la Mata** Spain
106 B2 **Navalvillar de Pela** Spain
97 C2 **Navan** Rep. of Ireland
Navangar India *see* **Jamnagar**
88 C2 **Navapolatsk** Belarus
83 M2 **Navarin, Mys** *c.* Rus. Fed.
153 B5 **Navarino, Isla** *i.* Chile
107 C1 **Navarra** *aut. comm.* Spain
Navarre *aut. comm.* Spain *see* **Navarra**
96 B1 **Naver** *r.* U.K.
89 D3 **Navlya** Rus. Fed.
110 C2 **Năvodari** Romania
77 C2 **Navoi** Uzbek.
144 B2 **Navojoa** Mex.
144 B2 **Navolato** Mex.
74 A2 **Nawabshah** Pak.
75 C2 **Nawada** India
62 A1 **Nawnghkio** Myanmar
62 A1 **Nawngleng** Myanmar
81 C2 **Naxçıvan** Azer.
111 C3 **Naxos** Greece
111 C3 **Naxos** *i.* Greece
144 B2 **Nayar** Mex.
66 D2 **Nayoro** Japan
80 B2 **Nazareth** Israel
144 B2 **Nazas** Mex.
144 B2 **Nazas** *r.* Mex.
150 B4 **Nazca** Peru

157 H7 **Nazca Ridge** *sea feature* S. Pacific Ocean
111 C3 **Nazilli** Turkey
117 B4 **Nazrēt** Eth.
79 C2 **Nazwá** Oman
121 B1 **Nchelenge** Zambia
122 B1 **Ncojane** Botswana
120 A1 **N'dalatando** Angola
118 C2 **Ndélé** C.A.R.
118 B3 **Ndendé** Gabon
115 D3 **Ndjamena** Chad
118 A3 **Ndogo, Lagune** *lag.* Gabon
121 B2 **Ndola** Zambia
97 C1 **Neagh, Lough** *l.* U.K.
50 C2 **Neale, Lake** *salt flat* Austr.
111 B3 **Neapoli** Greece
111 B2 **Nea Roda** Greece
99 B4 **Neath** U.K.
119 D2 **Nebbi** Uganda
53 C1 **Nebine Creek** *r.* Austr.
76 B3 **Nebitdag** Turkm.
150 C2 **Neblina, Pico da** *mt.* Brazil
135 D3 **Nebo, Mount** U.S.A.
89 D2 **Nebolchi** Rus. Fed.
136 C2 **Nebraska** *state* U.S.A.
137 D2 **Nebraska City** U.S.A.
108 B3 **Nebrodi, Monti** *mts Sicily* Italy
139 E3 **Neches** *r.* U.S.A.
156 E4 **Necker Island** U.S.A.
153 C3 **Necochea** Arg.
139 E3 **Nederland** U.S.A.
100 B2 **Neder Rijn** *r.* Neth.
130 C2 **Nedlouc, Lac** *l.* Can.
141 E2 **Needham** U.S.A.
135 D4 **Needles** U.S.A.
Neemuch India *see* **Nimach**
129 E2 **Neepawa** Can.
87 E3 **Neftekamsk** Rus. Fed.
82 F2 **Nefteyugansk** Rus. Fed.
108 A3 **Nefza** Tunisia
120 A1 **Negage** Angola
117 B4 **Negēlē** Eth.
109 D2 **Negotin** Yugo.
111 B2 **Negotino** Macedonia
150 A3 **Negra, Punta** *pt* Peru
155 D1 **Negra, Serra** *mts* Brazil
63 A2 **Negrais, Cape** Myanmar
153 B4 **Negro** *r.* Arg.
150 D3 **Negro** *r.* S. America
152 C3 **Negro** *r.* Uru.
106 B2 **Negro, Cabo** *c.* Morocco
64 B3 **Negros** *i.* Phil.
79 D1 **Nehbandān** Iran
69 E1 **Nehe** China
70 A3 **Neijiang** China
129 D2 **Neilburg** Can.
70 A1 **Nei Mongol Zizhiqu** *aut. reg.* China
150 B2 **Neiva** Col.
129 E2 **Nejanilini Lake** Can.
Nejd *reg.* Saudi Arabia *see* **Najd**
117 B4 **Nek'emtē** Eth.
89 F2 **Nekrasovskoye** Rus. Fed.
89 D2 **Nelidovo** Rus. Fed.
73 B3 **Nellore** India
128 C3 **Nelson** Can.
129 E2 **Nelson** *r.* Can.
54 B2 **Nelson** N.Z.
52 B3 **Nelson, Cape** Austr.
53 D2 **Nelson Bay** Austr.
129 E2 **Nelson House** Can.
134 E1 **Nelson Reservoir** U.S.A.
123 D2 **Nelspruit** S. Africa
114 B3 **Néma** Maur.
88 B2 **Neman** Rus. Fed.
105 C2 **Nemours** France
66 D2 **Nemuro** Japan
90 B2 **Nemyriv** Ukr.
97 B2 **Nenagh** Rep. of Ireland
99 D3 **Nene** *r.* U.K.
69 E1 **Nenjiang** China
137 E3 **Neosho** U.S.A.
75 C2 **Nepal** *country* Asia
75 C2 **Nepalganj** Nepal
141 D1 **Nepean** Can.
135 D3 **Nephi** U.S.A.
97 B1 **Nephin** *hill* Rep. of Ireland
97 B1 **Nephin Beg Range** *hills* Rep. of Ireland
131 D3 **Nepisiguit** *r.* Can.
119 C2 **Nepoko** *r.* Dem. Rep. Congo
141 E2 **Neptune** U.S.A.
108 B2 **Nera** *r.* Italy
104 C3 **Nérac** France
53 D1 **Nerang** Austr.

69 D1 **Nerchinsk** Rus. Fed.
89 F2 **Nerekhta** Rus. Fed.
109 C2 **Neretva** *r.* Bos.-Herz./Croatia
120 B2 **Neriquinha** Angola
88 B3 **Neris** *r.* Lith.
89 E2 **Nerl'** *r.* Rus. Fed.
86 F2 **Nerokhi** Rus. Fed.
154 C1 **Nerópolis** Brazil
83 J3 **Neryungri** Rus. Fed.
92 □C2 **Neskaupstaður** Iceland
96 B2 **Ness, Loch** *l.* U.K.
136 D3 **Ness City** U.S.A.
Nesterov Ukr. *see* **Zhovkva**
111 B2 **Nestos** *r.* Greece
100 B1 **Netherlands** *country* Europe
147 D3 **Netherlands Antilles** *terr.* West Indies
127 H2 **Nettilling Lake** Can.
101 F1 **Neubrandenburg** Ger.
105 D2 **Neuchâtel** Switz.
105 D2 **Neuchâtel, Lac de** *l.* Switz.
100 C2 **Neuerburg** Ger.
100 B3 **Neufchâteau** Belgium
105 D2 **Neufchâteau** France
104 C2 **Neufchâtel-en-Bray** France
101 D2 **Neuhof** Ger.
101 E3 **Neumarkt in der Oberpfalz** Ger.
102 B1 **Neumünster** Ger.
100 C3 **Neunkirchen** Ger.
153 B3 **Neuquén** Arg.
153 B3 **Neuquén** *r.* Arg.
101 F1 **Neuruppin** Ger.
100 C2 **Neuss** Ger.
101 D1 **Neustadt am Rübenberge** Ger.
101 E3 **Neustadt an der Aisch** Ger.
Neustadt an der Hardt Ger. *see* **Neustadt an der Weinstraße**
101 D3 **Neustadt an der Weinstraße** Ger.
101 E1 **Neustadt-Glewe** Ger.
101 F1 **Neustrelitz** Ger.
99 D5 **Neuville-lès-Dieppe** France
100 C2 **Neuwied** Ger.
137 E3 **Nevada** U.S.A.
135 C3 **Nevada** *state* U.S.A.
106 C2 **Nevada, Sierra** *mts* Spain
135 B2 **Nevada, Sierra** *mts* U.S.A.
88 C2 **Nevaišių kalnis** *hill* Lith.
88 C2 **Nevel'** Rus. Fed.
105 C2 **Nevers** France
53 C2 **Nevertire** Austr.
109 C2 **Nevesinje** Bos.-Herz.
87 D4 **Nevinnomyssk** Rus. Fed.
80 B2 **Nevşehir** Turkey
99 C4 **New Addington** U.K.
128 B2 **New Aiyansh** Can.
119 D4 **Newala** Tanz.
140 B3 **New Albany** U.S.A.
151 D2 **New Amsterdam** Guyana
141 E2 **Newark** *NJ* U.S.A.
140 C2 **Newark** *OH* U.S.A.
99 C3 **Newark-on-Trent** U.K.
141 E2 **New Bedford** U.S.A.
143 E1 **New Bern** U.S.A.
140 B1 **Newberry** *MI* U.S.A.
143 D2 **Newberry** *SC* U.S.A.
139 E2 **New Boston** U.S.A.
139 D3 **New Braunfels** U.S.A.
97 C2 **Newbridge** Rep. of Ireland
59 D3 **New Britain** *i.* P.N.G.
131 D3 **New Brunswick** *prov.* Can.
99 C4 **Newbury** U.K.
48 H6 **New Caledonia** *terr.* S. Pacific Ocean
156 D7 **New Caledonia Trough** *sea feature* Tasman Sea
53 D2 **Newcastle** Austr.
131 D3 **Newcastle** Can.
123 C2 **Newcastle** S. Africa
97 D1 **Newcastle** U.K.
140 C2 **New Castle** U.S.A.
136 C2 **Newcastle** U.S.A.
99 B3 **Newcastle-under-Lyme** U.K.
98 C2 **Newcastle upon Tyne** U.K.
51 C1 **Newcastle Waters** Austr.
97 B2 **Newcastle West** Rep. of Ireland
74 B2 **New Delhi** India
128 C3 **New Denver** Can.
53 D2 **New England Range** *mts* Austr.
157 H3 **New England Seamounts** *sea feature* N. Atlantic Ocean
131 E3 **Newfoundland** *i.* Can.
131 E2 **Newfoundland** *prov.* Can.
96 B3 **New Galloway** U.K.
48 G4 **New Georgia Islands** Solomon Is
131 D3 **New Glasgow** Can.
59 D3 **New Guinea** *i.* Indon./P.N.G.
78 A3 **New Halfa** Sudan
141 E2 **New Hampshire** *state* U.S.A.
59 E3 **New Hanover** *i.* P.N.G.
141 E2 **New Haven** U.S.A.
128 B2 **New Hazelton** Can.
New Hebrides *country* S. Pacific Ocean *see* Vanuatu
156 D7 **New Hebrides Trench** *sea feature* S. Pacific Ocean
142 B2 **New Iberia** U.S.A.
59 E3 **New Ireland** *i.* P.N.G.
141 E3 **New Jersey** *state* U.S.A.
130 C3 **New Liskeard** Can.
140 B2 **New London** U.S.A.
50 A2 **Newman** Austr.
54 C2 **Newman** N.Z.
97 B2 **Newmarket** Rep. of Ireland
99 D3 **Newmarket** U.K.
97 B2 **Newmarket-on-Fergus** Rep. of Ireland
138 B2 **New Mexico** *state* U.S.A.
143 D2 **Newnan** U.S.A.
142 B3 **New Orleans** U.S.A.
140 C2 **New Philadelphia** U.S.A.
54 B1 **New Plymouth** N.Z.
99 C4 **Newport** *England* U.K.
99 B4 **Newport** *Wales* U.K.
142 B1 **Newport** *AR* U.S.A.
134 B2 **Newport** *OR* U.S.A.
141 E2 **Newport** *RI* U.S.A.
143 D1 **Newport** *TN* U.S.A.
141 E2 **Newport** *VT* U.S.A.
134 C1 **Newport** *WA* U.S.A.
141 D3 **Newport News** U.S.A.
143 E3 **New Providence** *i.* Bahamas
99 A4 **Newquay** U.K.
142 B2 **New Roads** U.S.A.
97 C2 **New Ross** Rep. of Ireland
97 C1 **Newry** U.K.
New Siberia Islands Rus. Fed. *see* Novosibirskiye Ostrova
52 B2 **New South Wales** *state* Austr.
137 E2 **Newton** *IA* U.S.A.
137 D3 **Newton** *KS* U.S.A.
99 B4 **Newton Abbot** U.K.
98 C2 **Newton Aycliffe** U.K.
96 B3 **Newton Mearns** U.K.
96 B2 **Newtonmore** U.K.
96 B3 **Newton Stewart** U.K.
97 B2 **Newtown** Rep. of Ireland
99 B3 **Newtown** U.K.
136 C1 **New Town** U.S.A.
97 D1 **Newtownabbey** U.K.
97 D1 **Newtownards** U.K.
Newtownbarry Rep. of Ireland *see* Bunclody
97 C1 **Newtownbutler** U.K.
96 C3 **Newtown St Boswells** U.K.
97 C1 **Newtownstewart** U.K.
137 E2 **New Ulm** U.S.A.
141 E2 **New York** U.S.A.
141 D2 **New York** *state* U.S.A.
54 B2 **New Zealand** *country* Oceania
86 D3 **Neya** Rus. Fed.
81 D3 **Neyrīz** Iran
76 B3 **Neyshābūr** Iran
145 C3 **Nezahualcóyotl, Presa** *resr* Mex.
60 B1 **Ngabang** Indon.
118 B3 **Ngabé** Congo
75 C2 **Ngamring** China
119 D2 **Ngangala** Sudan
75 C1 **Ngangla Ringco** *salt l.* China
75 C1 **Nganglong Kangri** *mt.* China
75 C1 **Nganglong Kangri** *mts* China
75 C1 **Ngangzê Co** *salt l.* China
62 A2 **Ngao** Thai.
118 B2 **Ngaoundal** Cameroon
118 B2 **Ngaoundéré** Cameroon
54 C1 **Ngaruawahia** N.Z.
62 A2 **Ngathainggyaung** Myanmar
Ngiva Angola *see* **Ondjiva**
118 B3 **Ngo** Congo
63 B2 **Ngoc Linh** *mt.* Vietnam
115 D4 **Ngol Bembo** Nigeria
68 C2 **Ngoring Hu** *l.* China
115 D3 **Ngourti** Niger
115 D3 **Nguigmi** Niger
59 D2 **Ngulu** *atoll* Micronesia
61 C2 **Ngunut** Indon.
Ngunza Angola *see* **Sumbe**
Ngunza-Kabolu Angola *see* **Sumbe**
115 D3 **Nguru** Nigeria
62 B1 **Nguyên Binh** Vietnam
123 C2 **Ngwathe** S. Africa
123 D2 **Ngwelezana** S. Africa
121 C2 **Nhamalabué** Moz.
120 A2 **N'harea** Angola
63 B2 **Nha Trang** Vietnam
52 B3 **Nhill** Austr.
123 D2 **Nhlangano** Swaziland
51 C1 **Nhulunbuy** Austr.
141 D2 **Niagara Falls** Can.
114 C3 **Niamey** Niger
119 C2 **Niangara** Dem. Rep. Congo
114 B3 **Niangay, Lac** *l.* Mali
119 C2 **Nia-Nia** Dem. Rep. Congo
60 A1 **Nias** *i.* Indon.
88 B2 **Nīca** Latvia
146 B3 **Nicaragua** *country* Central America
146 B3 **Nicaragua, Lago de** *l.* Nic.
Nicaragua, Lake Nic. *see* Nicaragua, Lago de
109 C3 **Nicastro** Italy
105 D3 **Nice** France
73 D4 **Nicobar Islands** India
80 B2 **Nicosia** Cyprus
146 B4 **Nicoya, Golfo de** *b.* Costa Rica
88 B2 **Nida** Lith.
103 E1 **Nidzica** Pol.
102 B1 **Niebüll** Ger.
101 D2 **Niederaula** Ger.
118 B2 **Niefang** Equat. Guinea
101 F1 **Niemegk** Ger.
101 D1 **Nienburg (Weser)** Ger.
103 C1 **Niesky** Ger.
100 B1 **Nieuwegein** Neth.
100 B1 **Nieuwe-Niedorp** Neth.
151 D2 **Nieuw Nickerie** Suriname
122 A3 **Nieuwoudtville** S. Africa
100 A2 **Nieuwpoort** Belgium
80 B2 **Niğde** Turkey
115 D3 **Niger** *country* Africa
115 C4 **Niger** *r.* Africa
115 C4 **Niger, Mouths of the** Nigeria
115 C4 **Nigeria** *country* Africa
130 B3 **Nighthawk Lake** Can.
111 B2 **Nigrita** Greece
67 C3 **Niigata** Japan
67 B4 **Niihama** Japan
67 C4 **Nii-jima** *i.* Japan
67 B4 **Niimi** Japan
67 C3 **Niitsu** Japan
107 C2 **Níjar** Spain
100 B1 **Nijkerk** Neth.
100 B2 **Nijmegen** Neth.
100 C1 **Nijverdal** Neth.
92 J2 **Nikel'** Rus. Fed.
Nikolayev Ukr. *see* Mykolayiv
87 D3 **Nikolayevsk** Rus. Fed.
Nikolayevskiy Rus. Fed. *see* **Nikolayevsk**
86 D3 **Nikol'sk** Rus. Fed.
Nikol'skiy Kazakh. *see* Satpayev
83 M3 **Nikol'skoye** Rus. Fed.
Nikol'skoye Rus. Fed. *see* Sheksna
91 C2 **Nikopol'** Ukr.
80 B1 **Niksar** Turkey
79 D2 **Nīkshahr** Iran
109 C2 **Nikšić** Yugo.
Nīl, Bahr el *r.* Africa *see* Nile
135 C4 **Niland** U.S.A.
116 B1 **Nile** *r.* Africa
140 B2 **Niles** U.S.A.
74 B2 **Nimach** India
105 C3 **Nîmes** France
53 C3 **Nimmitabel** Austr.
117 B4 **Nimule** Sudan
Nimwegen Neth. *see* Nijmegen
53 C1 **Nindigully** Austr.
73 B4 **Nine Degree Channel** India
53 C3 **Ninety Mile Beach** Aus
54 B1 **Ninety Mile Beach** N.Z.
70 C3 **Ningbo** China
71 B3 **Ningde** China
71 B3 **Ningdu** China
70 B2 **Ningguo** China
71 C3 **Ninghai** China
Ninghsia Hui Autonomous Region *aut. reg.* China *see* **Ningx**
72 D2 **Ninging** India
Ningjiang China *see* Songyuan
68 C2 **Ningjing Shan** *mts* Chin
70 A2 **Ningxia** *aut. reg.* China
70 B2 **Ningyang** China
62 B1 **Ninh Binh** Vietnam
63 B2 **Ninh Hoa** Vietnam
66 D2 **Ninohe** Japan
137 D2 **Niobrara** *r.* U.S.A.
62 A1 **Nioko** India
114 B3 **Niono** Mali
114 B3 **Nioro** Mali
104 B2 **Niort** France
129 D2 **Nipawin** Can.
130 B3 **Nipigon** Can.
130 B3 **Nipigon, Lake** Can.
131 D2 **Nipishish Lake** Can.
130 C3 **Nipissing, Lake** Can.
135 C3 **Nipton** U.S.A.
151 E4 **Niquelândia** Brazil
74 B3 **Nirmal** India
109 D2 **Niš** Yugo.
109 D2 **Nišava** *r.* Yugo.
108 B3 **Niscemi** *Sicily* Italy
67 B4 **Nishino-omote** Japan
90 B2 **Nisporeni** Moldova
155 D2 **Niterói** Brazil
96 C3 **Nith** *r.* U.K.
103 D2 **Nitra** Slovakia
49 K5 **Niue** *terr.* S. Pacific Oce
92 H3 **Nivala** Fin.
100 B2 **Nivelles** Belgium
73 B3 **Nizamabad** India
87 E3 **Nizhnekamsk** Rus. Fed.
87 E3 **Nizhnekamskoye Vodokhranilishche** *resr* Rus. Fed.
83 H3 **Nizhneudinsk** Rus. Fed.
82 G2 **Nizhnevartovsk** Rus. Fe
Nizhnevolzhsk Rus. Fed *see* **Narimanov**
83 K2 **Nizhneyansk** Rus. Fed.
Nizhniye Kresty Rus. Fe *see* **Cherskiy**
Nizhniye Ustriki Pol. *see* Ustrzyki Dolne
89 F3 **Nizhniy Kislyay** Rus. Fe
87 D3 **Nizhniy Lomov** Rus. Fed
87 D3 **Nizhniy Novgorod** Rus. Fed.
86 E2 **Nizhniy Odes** Rus. Fed.
86 E3 **Nizhniy Tagil** Rus. Fed.
83 G2 **Nizhnyaya Tunguska** *r.* Rus. Fed.
86 E3 **Nizhnyaya Tura** Rus. Fe
91 C1 **Nizhyn** Ukr.
103 E1 **Nizina** *reg.* Pol.
Njazidja *i.* Comoros *see* Grande Comore
119 D3 **Njinjo** Tanz.
119 D3 **Njombe** Tanz.
118 B2 **Nkambe** Cameroon
119 D4 **Nkhata Bay** Malawi
121 C2 **Nkhotakota** Malawi
118 A3 **Nkomi, Lagune** *lag.* Gabon
119 D3 **Nkondwe** Tanz.
118 A2 **Nkongsamba** Cameroon
123 C3 **Nkululeko** S. Africa
123 C3 **Nkwenkwezi** S. Africa
67 B4 **Nobeoka** Japan
140 B2 **Noblesville** U.S.A.
52 B1 **Noccundra** Austr.
144 A1 **Nogales** Mex.
138 A2 **Nogales** U.S.A.
104 C2 **Nogent-le-Rotrou** France
83 H2 **Noginsk** Rus. Fed.
89 E2 **Noginsk** Rus. Fed.
83 K3 **Nogliki** Rus. Fed.
74 B2 **Nohar** India
100 C3 **Nohfelden** Ger.
104 B2 **Noires, Montagnes** *hills* France

B2	Noirmoutier, Île de i. France	
B2	Noirmoutier-en-l'Île France	
C4	Nojima-zaki c. Japan	
B2	Nokha India	
H3	Nokia Fin.	
A2	Nok Kundi Pak.	
B2	Nola C.A.R.	
D3	Nolinsk Rus. Fed.	
A2	Nome U.S.A.	
C3	Nomonde S. Africa	
D2	Nondweni S. Africa	
	Nonghui China see Guang'an	
B2	Nong Khai Thai.	
D2	Nongstoin India	
A2	Nonning Austr.	
B2	Nonoava Mex.	
B2	Nonsan S. Korea	
B2	Nonthaburi Thai.	
B2	Nonzwakazi S. Africa	
B1	Noordwijk-Binnen Neth.	
C3	Norak Tajik.	
C3	Noranda Can.	
C1	Nordaustlandet i. Svalbard	
C2	Nordegg Can.	
C1	Norden Ger.	
H1	Nordenshel'da, Arkhipelag is Rus. Fed.	
	Nordenskjold Archipelago is Rus. Fed. see Nordenshel'da, Arkhipelag	
C1	Norderney Ger.	
C1	Norderney i. Ger.	
E1	Norderstedt Ger.	
B1	Nordfjordeid Norway	
B1	Nordfriesische Inseln is Ger.	
E2	Nordhausen Ger.	
D1	Nordholz Ger.	
C1	Nordhorn Ger.	
I1	Nordkapp c. Norway	
F3	Nordli Norway	
C2	Nördlingen Ger.	
G3	Nordmaling Sweden	
B1	Norðoyar i. Faroe Is	
B2	Nore r. Rep. of Ireland	
B3	Noreikiškės Lith.	
D2	Norfolk NE U.S.A.	
D3	Norfolk VA U.S.A.	
H6	Norfolk Island terr. S. Pacific Ocean	
E1	Norheimsund Norway	
G2	Noril'sk Rus. Fed.	
D1	Norman U.S.A.	
	Normandes, Îles is Europe see Channel Islands	
D2	Normandia Brazil	
B2	Normandie reg. France Normandy reg. France see Normandie	
D1	Normanton Austr.	
B1	Norman Wells Can.	
G4	Norrköping Sweden	
G4	Norrtälje Sweden	
B3	Norseman Austr.	
G3	Norsjö Sweden	
M2	North, Cape Antarctica	
C2	Northallerton U.K.	
A3	Northam Austr.	
A2	Northampton Austr.	
A3	Northampton U.K.	
D3	North Andaman i. India	
F4	North Australian Basin sea feature Indian Ocean	
D2	North Battleford Can.	
C3	North Bay Can.	
C2	North Belcher Islands Can.	
C2	North Berwick U.K.	
	North Borneo state Malaysia see Sabah	
	North Cape Norway see Nordkapp	
B1	North Cape N.Z.	
A2	North Caribou Lake Can.	
E1	North Carolina state U.S.A.	
B3	North Channel lake channel Can.	
A3	North Channel U.K.	
E2	North Charleston U.S.A.	
B3	North Cowichan Can.	
C1	North Dakota state U.S.A.	
C4	North Downs hills U.K.	
E3	Northeast Pacific Basin sea feature N. Pacific Ocean	

143 E3	Northeast Providence Channel Bahamas	
101 D2	Northeim Ger.	
123 C1	Northern prov. S. Africa	
122 A2	Northern Cape prov. S. Africa	
	Northern Dvina r. Rus. Fed. see Severnaya Dvina	
129 E2	Northern Indian Lake Can.	
97 C1	Northern Ireland prov. U.K.	
59 D1	Northern Mariana Islands terr. N. Pacific Ocean	
	Northern Rhodesia country Africa see Zambia	
50 C1	Northern Territory admin. div. Austr.	
	Northern Transvaal prov. S. Africa see Northern	
96 C2	North Esk r. U.K.	
137 E2	Northfield U.S.A.	
99 D4	North Foreland c. U.K.	
	North Frisian Islands Ger. see Nordfriesische Inseln	
160 O2	North Geomagnetic Pole Greenland	
54 B1	North Island N.Z.	
129 E2	North Knife Lake Can.	
72 D2	North Lakhimpur India	
	North Land is Rus. Fed. see Severnaya Zemlya	
160 Q2	North Magnetic Pole Can.	
136 C2	North Platte U.S.A.	
136 C2	North Platte r. U.S.A.	
96 C1	North Ronaldsay i. U.K.	
129 D2	North Saskatchewan r. Can.	
94 D2	North Sea Europe	
63 A2	North Sentinel Island India	
130 A2	North Spirit Lake Can.	
53 D1	North Stradbroke Island Austr.	
131 D3	North Sydney Can.	
54 B1	North Taranaki Bight b. N.Z.	
130 C2	North Twin Island Can.	
98 B2	North Tyne r. U.K.	
96 A2	North Uist i. U.K.	
131 D3	Northumberland Strait Can.	
99 D3	North Walsham U.K.	
123 C2	North West prov. S. Africa	
158 D1	Northwest Atlantic Mid-Ocean Channnel sea chan. N. Atlantic Ocean	
50 A2	North West Cape Austr.	
156 D3	Northwest Pacific Basin sea feature N. Pacific Ocean	
143 E3	Northwest Providence Channel Bahamas	
131 E2	North West River Can.	
128 B1	Northwest Territories admin. div. Can.	
98 C2	North York Moors moorland U.K.	
140 C3	Norton U.S.A.	
121 C2	Norton Zimbabwe	
	Norton de Matos Angola see Balombo	
126 B2	Norton Sound sea chan. U.S.A.	
55 D2	Norvegia, Cape Antarctica	
140 C2	Norwalk U.S.A.	
93 F3	Norway country Europe	
129 E2	Norway House Can.	
160 L3	Norwegian Basin sea feature N. Atlantic Ocean	
92 E2	Norwegian Sea N. Atlantic Ocean	
99 D3	Norwich U.K.	
141 E2	Norwich CT U.S.A.	
141 D2	Norwich NY U.S.A.	
66 D2	Noshiro Japan	
91 C1	Nosivka Ukr.	
122 B2	Nosop watercourse Africa	
86 E2	Nosovaya Rus. Fed.	
79 C2	Noşratābād Iran	
121 □D2	Nosy Bé i. Madag.	
121 □E2	Nosy Boraha i. Madag.	
103 D1	Noteć r. Pol.	
93 E4	Notodden Norway	
67 C3	Noto-hantō pen. Japan	
131 D3	Notre Dame, Monts mts Can.	

131 E3	Notre Dame Bay Can.	
130 C2	Nottaway r. Can.	
99 C3	Nottingham U.K.	
114 A2	Nouâdhibou Maur.	
114 A3	Nouakchott Maur.	
114 A3	Nouâmghâr Maur.	
63 B2	Nouei Vietnam	
48 H6	Nouméa New Caledonia	
114 B3	Nouna Burkina	
122 B3	Noupoort S. Africa	
	Nouveau-Comptoir Can. see Wemindji	
	Nouvelle Anvers Dem. Rep. Congo see Makanza	
	Nouvelles Hébrides country S. Pacific Ocean see Vanuatu	
103 D1	Nova Chaves Angola see Muconda	
154 B2	Nova Esperança Brazil	
	Nova Freixa Moz. see Cuamba	
155 D2	Nova Friburgo Brazil	
109 C1	Nova Gradiška Croatia	
154 C2	Nova Granada Brazil	
155 D2	Nova Iguaçu Brazil	
91 C2	Nova Kakhovka Ukr.	
155 D1	Nova Lima Brazil	
	Nova Lisboa Angola see Huambo	
154 B2	Nova Londrina Brazil	
91 C2	Nova Odesa Ukr.	
150 C2	Nova Paraíso Brazil	
154 C1	Nova Ponte Brazil	
108 A1	Novara Italy	
151 E3	Nova Remanso Brazil	
131 D3	Nova Scotia prov. Can.	
155 D1	Nova Venécia Brazil	
83 K1	Novaya Sibir', Ostrov i. Rus. Fed.	
86 E1	Novaya Zemlya is Rus. Fed.	
107 C2	Novelda Spain	
103 D2	Nové Zámky Slovakia	
	Novgorod Rus. Fed. see Velikiy Novgorod	
91 C1	Novhorod-Sivers'kyy Ukr.	
110 B2	Novi Iskŭr Bulg.	
66 D1	Novikovo Rus. Fed.	
108 A2	Novi Ligure Italy	
109 D2	Novi Pazar Yugo.	
109 C1	Novi Sad Yugo.	
	Novoalekseyevka Kazakh. see Khobda	
87 D3	Novoanninskiy Rus. Fed.	
150 C3	Novo Aripuanã Brazil	
91 D2	Novoazovs'k Ukr.	
89 D2	Novodugino Rus. Fed.	
86 D2	Novodvinsk Rus. Fed.	
	Novoekonomicheskoye Ukr. see Dymytrov	
152 C2	Novo Hamburgo Brazil	
154 C2	Novo Horizonte Brazil	
90 B1	Novohrad-Volyns'kyy Ukr.	
	Novokazalinsk Kazakh. see Ayteke Bi	
91 E1	Novokhopersk Rus. Fed.	
68 B1	Novokuznetsk Rus. Fed.	
109 C1	Novo Mesto Slovenia	
91 D3	Novomikhaylovskiy Rus. Fed.	
89 E3	Novomoskovsk Rus. Fed.	
91 D2	Novomoskovs'k Ukr.	
91 C2	Novomyrhorod Ukr.	
	Novonikolayevsk Rus. Fed. see Novosibirsk	
91 C2	Novooleksiyivka Ukr.	
91 E2	Novopokrovskaya Rus. Fed.	
91 D2	Novopskov Ukr.	
	Novo Redondo Angola see Sumbe	
91 D2	Novorossiysk Rus. Fed.	
88 C2	Novorzhev Rus. Fed.	
87 E3	Novosergiyevka Rus. Fed.	
91 D2	Novoshakhtinsk Rus. Fed.	
52 A2	Novosibirsk Rus. Fed.	
92 I3	Novosibirskiye Ostrova is Rus. Fed.	
89 E3	Novosil' Rus. Fed.	
89 D2	Novosokol'niki Rus. Fed.	
91 C2	Novotroyits'ke Ukr.	
91 C2	Novoukrayinka Ukr.	
90 A1	Novovolyns'k Ukr.	
89 D3	Novovoronezhskiy Rus. Fed. see Novovoronezh	
89 D3	Novovoronezh	

89 D3	Novozybkov Rus. Fed.	
103 D2	Nový Jičín Czech Rep.	
86 E2	Novyy Bor Rus. Fed.	
91 C2	Novyy Buh Ukr.	
	Novyy Donbass Ukr. see Dymytrov	
	Novyye Petushki Rus. Fed. see Petushki	
	Novyy Margelan Uzbek. see Fergana	
89 E2	Novyy Nekouz Rus. Fed.	
91 D1	Novyy Oskol Rus. Fed.	
86 G2	Novyy Port Rus. Fed.	
86 G2	Novyy Urengoy Rus. Fed.	
69 E1	Novyy Urgal Rus. Fed.	
	Novyy Uzen' Kazakh. see Zhanaozen	
103 D1	Nowogard Pol.	
	Noworadomsk Pol. see Radomsko	
53 D2	Nowra Austr.	
81 D2	Now Shahr Iran	
74 B1	Nowshera Pak.	
103 E2	Nowy Sącz Pol.	
103 E2	Nowy Targ Pol.	
82 G2	Noyabr'sk Rus. Fed.	
105 C2	Noyon France	
121 C2	Nsanje Malawi	
121 B2	Nsombo Zambia	
118 B3	Ntandembele Dem. Rep. Congo	
123 C2	Ntha S. Africa	
118 A2	Ntoum Gabon	
119 D3	Ntungamo Uganda	
	Nuanetsi r. Zimbabwe see Mwenezi	
79 C2	Nu'aym reg. Oman	
116 B2	Nubian Desert Sudan	
150 B4	Nudo Coropuna mt. Peru	
139 D3	Nueces r. U.S.A.	
129 E1	Nueltin Lake Can.	
150 B2	Nueva Loja Ecuador	
153 A4	Nueva Lubecka Arg.	
145 B2	Nueva Rosita Mex.	
144 B1	Nueve Casas Grandes Mex.	
144 B2	Nuevo Ideal Mex.	
145 C2	Nuevo Laredo Mex.	
117 C4	Nugaal watercourse Somalia	
	Nuits-St-Georges France	
62 A1	Nu Jiang r. China	
	Nukha Azer. see Şäki	
49 J6	Nuku'alofa Tonga	
49 M4	Nuku Hiva i. Fr. Polynesia	
48 G4	Nukumanu Islands P.N.G.	
76 B2	Nukus Uzbek.	
50 B2	Nullagine Austr.	
50 C3	Nullarbor Austr.	
50 B3	Nullarbor Plain Austr.	
115 D4	Numan Nigeria	
67 C3	Numazu Japan	
51 C1	Numbulwar Austr.	
93 E3	Numedal val. Norway	
59 C3	Numfoor i. Indon.	
53 C3	Numurkah Austr.	
127 J2	Nunap Isua c. Greenland	
129 E1	Nunavut admin. div. Can.	
99 C3	Nuneaton U.K.	
126 A3	Nunivak Island U.S.A.	
106 B1	Nuñomoral Spain	
78 B2	Nuoro Sardinia Italy	
78 B2	Nuqrah Saudi Arabia	
77 C1	Nura r. Kazakh.	
	Nuremberg Ger. see Nürnberg	
122 A3	Nuriootpa Austr.	
92 I3	Nurmes Fin.	
101 E3	Nürnberg Ger.	
53 C2	Nurri, Mount hill Austr.	
62 A1	Nu Shan mts China	
74 A2	Nushki Pak.	
127 I2	Nuuk Greenland	
127 I2	Nuussuaq Greenland	
127 I2	Nuussuaq pen. Greenland	
80 B3	Nuweiba al Muzeina Egypt	
122 A3	Nuwerus S. Africa	
122 B3	Nuweveldberge mts S. Africa	
86 F2	Nyagan' Rus. Fed.	
75 D1	Nyainqêntanglha Feng mt. China	
75 D2	Nyainqêntanglha Shan mts China	
	Nyakh Rus. Fed. see Nyagan'	
117 A3	Nyala Sudan	
75 C2	Nyalam China	
119 D4	Nyamtumbo Tanz.	

Nyande Zimbabwe *see* Masvingo
86 D2 **Nyandoma** Rus. Fed.
118 B3 **Nyanga** Congo
118 B3 **Nyanga** *r.* Gabon
121 C2 **Nyanga** Zimbabwe
121 C1 **Nyasa, Lake** Africa
Nyasaland *country* Africa *see* **Malawi**
88 C3 **Nyasvizh** Belarus
62 A2 **Nyaunglebin** Myanmar
93 F4 **Nyborg** Denmark
92 I1 **Nyborg** Norway
93 G4 **Nybro** Sweden
Nyenchen Tanglha Range *mts* China *see* **Nyainqêntanglha Shan**
119 D3 **Nyeri** Kenya
75 C1 **Nyima** China
68 C3 **Nyingchi** China
103 E2 **Nyíregyháza** Hungary
93 F5 **Nykøbing** Denmark
93 G4 **Nyköping** Sweden
123 C1 **Nylstroom** S. Africa
53 C2 **Nymagee** Austr.
93 G4 **Nynäshamn** Sweden
53 C2 **Nyngan** Austr.
88 B3 **Nyoman** *r.* Belarus/Lith.
105 D3 **Nyons** France
86 E2 **Nyrob** Rus. Fed.
103 D1 **Nysa** Pol.
134 C2 **Nyssa** U.S.A.
119 C3 **Nyunzu** Dem. Rep. Congo
83 I2 **Nyurba** Rus. Fed.
91 C2 **Nyzhni Sirohozy** Ukr.
91 C2 **Nyzhn'ohirs'kyy** Ukr.
118 B3 **Nzambi** Congo
119 D3 **Nzega** Tanz.
114 B4 **Nzérékoré** Guinea
120 A1 **N'zeto** Angola

O

136 C2 **Oahe, Lake** U.S.A.
49 L1 **Oahu** *i.* U.S.A.
52 B2 **Oakbank** Austr.
142 B2 **Oakdale** U.S.A.
53 D1 **Oakey** Austr.
140 B3 **Oak Grove** U.S.A.
99 C3 **Oakham** U.K.
134 B1 **Oak Harbor** U.S.A.
140 C3 **Oak Hill** U.S.A.
135 B3 **Oakland** *CA* U.S.A.
141 D3 **Oakland** *MD* U.S.A.
140 B2 **Oak Lawn** U.S.A.
136 C3 **Oakley** U.S.A.
50 B2 **Oakover** *r.* Austr.
134 B2 **Oakridge** U.S.A.
143 D1 **Oak Ridge** U.S.A.
54 B3 **Oamaru** N.Z.
64 B2 **Oas** Phil.
145 C3 **Oaxaca** Mex.
86 F2 **Ob'** *r.* Rus. Fed.
Ob, Gulf of *sea chan.* Rus. Fed. *see* **Obskaya Guba**
88 C2 **Obal'** Belarus
118 B2 **Obala** Cameroon
96 B2 **Oban** U.K.
106 B1 **O Barco** Spain
Obbia Somalia *see* **Hobyo**
136 C3 **Oberlin** U.S.A.
53 C2 **Oberon** Austr.
101 F3 **Oberviechtach** Ger.
59 C3 **Obi** *i.* Indon.
151 D3 **Óbidos** Brazil
66 D2 **Obihiro** Japan
69 E1 **Obluch'ye** Rus. Fed.
89 E2 **Obninsk** Rus. Fed.
119 C2 **Obo** C.A.R.
117 C3 **Obock** Djibouti
103 D1 **Oborniki** Pol.
118 B3 **Obouya** Congo
89 E3 **Oboyan'** Rus. Fed.
86 D2 **Obozerskiy** Rus. Fed.
144 B2 **Obregón, Presa** *resr* Mex.
109 D2 **Obrenovac** Yugo.
134 B2 **O'Brien** U.S.A.
87 E3 **Obshchiy Syrt** *hills* Rus. Fed.
86 G2 **Obskaya Guba** *sea chan.* Rus. Fed.
114 B4 **Obuasi** Ghana
90 C1 **Obukhiv** Ukr.
86 D2 **Ob"yachevo** Rus. Fed.
143 D3 **Ocala** U.S.A.
144 B2 **Ocampo** Mex.
106 C2 **Ocaña** Spain
150 B2 **Occidental, Cordillera** *mts* Col.
150 B4 **Occidental, Cordillera** *mts* Peru
141 D3 **Ocean City** *MD* U.S.A.
141 E3 **Ocean City** *NJ* U.S.A.
128 B2 **Ocean Falls** Can.
135 C4 **Oceanside** U.S.A.
91 C2 **Ochakiv** Ukr.
86 E3 **Ocher** Rus. Fed.
101 E3 **Ochsenfurt** Ger.
110 B1 **Ocna Mureș** Romania
90 B2 **Ocnița** Moldova
143 D2 **Oconee** *r.* U.S.A.
145 C3 **Ocosingo** Mex.
143 E1 **Ocracoke Island** U.S.A.
October Revolution Island Rus. Fed. *see* **Oktyabr'skoy Revolyutsii, Ostrov**
116 B2 **Oda, Jebel** *mt.* Sudan
66 D2 **Ōdate** Japan
67 C3 **Odawara** Japan
93 E3 **Odda** Norway
106 B2 **Odemira** Port.
111 C3 **Ödemiș** Turkey
93 F4 **Odense** Denmark
101 D3 **Odenwald** *reg.* Ger.
102 C1 **Oder** *r.* Ger.
102 C1 **Oderbucht** *b.* Ger.
90 C2 **Odesa** Ukr.
139 C2 **Odessa** U.S.A.
114 B4 **Odienné** Côte d'Ivoire
89 E3 **Odoyev** Rus. Fed.
103 D1 **Odra** *r.* Pol.
151 E3 **Oeiras** Brazil
101 D2 **Oelde** Ger.
136 C2 **Oelrichs** U.S.A.
101 F2 **Oelsnitz** Ger.
100 B1 **Oenkerk** Neth.
137 E3 **O'Fallon** U.S.A.
109 C2 **Ofanto** *r.* Italy
101 D2 **Offenbach am Main** Ger.
102 B2 **Offenburg** Ger.
66 C3 **Oga** Japan
117 C4 **Ogadēn** *reg.* Eth.
66 C3 **Oga-hantō** *pen.* Japan
67 C3 **Ōgaki** Japan
136 C2 **Ogallala** U.S.A.
69 F3 **Ogasawara-shotō** *is* Japan
115 C4 **Ogbomoso** Nigeria
134 D2 **Ogden** U.S.A.
141 D2 **Ogdensburg** U.S.A.
126 C2 **Ogilvie** *r.* Can.
126 C2 **Ogilvie Mountains** Can.
143 D2 **Oglethorpe, Mount** U.S.A.
130 B2 **Ogoki** *r.* Can.
130 B2 **Ogoki Reservoir** Can.
88 B2 **Ogre** Latvia
109 C1 **Ogulin** Croatia
81 D2 **Ogurchinskiy, Ostrov** *i.* Turkm.
115 C2 **Ohanet** Alg.
140 B3 **Ohio** *r.* U.S.A.
140 C2 **Ohio** *state* U.S.A.
101 E2 **Ohrdruf** Ger.
101 F2 **Ohře** *r.* Czech Rep.
111 B2 **Ohrid** Macedonia
151 D2 **Oiapoque** Brazil
141 D2 **Oil City** U.S.A.
100 A3 **Oise** *r.* France
67 B4 **Ōita** Japan
144 B2 **Ojinaga** Mex.
152 B2 **Ojos del Salado, Nevado** *mt.* Arg./Chile
89 F2 **Oka** *r.* Rus. Fed.
120 A3 **Okahandja** Namibia
120 A3 **Okakarara** Namibia
128 C3 **Okanagan Falls** Can.
128 C3 **Okanagan Lake** Can.
134 C1 **Okanogan** U.S.A.
134 C1 **Okanogan** *r.* U.S.A.
74 B1 **Okara** Pak.
120 B2 **Okavango** *r.* Botswana/Namibia
120 B2 **Okavango Delta** *swamp* Botswana
67 C3 **Okaya** Japan
67 B4 **Okayama** Japan
67 C4 **Okazaki** Japan
143 D3 **Okeechobee** U.S.A.
143 D3 **Okeechobee, Lake** U.S.A.
143 D2 **Okefenokee Swamp** U.S.A.
99 A4 **Okehampton** U.K.
115 C4 **Okene** Nigeria
101 E1 **Oker** *r.* Ger.
74 A2 **Okha** India
83 K3 **Okha** Rus. Fed.
75 C2 **Okhaldhunga** Nepal
83 K3 **Okhotka** *r.* Rus. Fed.
83 K3 **Okhotsk** Rus. Fed.
83 K3 **Okhotsk, Sea of** Japan/Rus. Fed.
Okhotskoye More *sea* Japan/Rus. Fed. *see* Okhotsk, Sea of
91 C1 **Okhtyrka** Ukr.
69 E3 **Okinawa** *i.* Japan
67 B3 **Oki-shotō** *is* Japan
139 D1 **Oklahoma** *state* U.S.A.
139 D1 **Oklahoma City** U.S.A.
139 D1 **Okmulgee** U.S.A.
Oknitsa Moldova *see* Ocnița
78 A2 **Oko, Wadi** *watercourse* Sudan
118 B3 **Okondja** Gabon
128 C2 **Okotoks** Can.
89 D3 **Okovskiy Les** *for.* Rus. Fed.
118 B3 **Okoyo** Congo
92 H1 **Øksfjord** Norway
62 A2 **Oktwin** Myanmar
Oktyabr' Kazakh. *see* Kandyagash
Oktyabr'sk Kazakh. *see* Kandyagash
86 D2 **Oktyabr'skiy** Rus. Fed.
83 L3 **Oktyabr'skiy** Rus. Fed.
87 E3 **Oktyabr'skiy** Rus. Fed.
86 F2 **Oktyabr'skoye** Rus. Fed.
83 H1 **Oktyabr'skoy Revolyutsii, Ostrov** *i.* Rus. Fed.
89 D2 **Okulovka** Rus. Fed.
66 C2 **Okushiri-tō** *i.* Japan
92 □B2 **Ólafsfjörður** Iceland
92 □A3 **Ólafsvík** Iceland
88 B2 **Olaine** Latvia
93 G4 **Öland** *i.* Sweden
52 B2 **Olary** Austr.
136 B3 **Olathe** *CO* U.S.A.
137 E3 **Olathe** *KS* U.S.A.
153 B3 **Olavarría** Arg.
103 D1 **Oława** Pol.
108 A2 **Olbia** *Sardinia* Italy
126 C2 **Old Crow** Can.
101 D1 **Oldenburg** Ger.
102 C1 **Oldenburg in Holstein** Ger.
100 C1 **Oldenzaal** Neth.
98 B3 **Oldham** U.K.
97 B3 **Old Head of Kinsale** *hd* Rep. of Ireland
96 C2 **Oldmeldrum** U.K.
128 C2 **Olds** Can.
129 D2 **Old Wives Lake** Can.
141 D2 **Olean** U.S.A.
103 E1 **Olecko** Pol.
83 J2 **Olekminsk** Rus. Fed.
91 C2 **Oleksandrivka** Ukr.
Oleksandrivs'k Ukr. *see* **Zaporizhzhya**
91 C2 **Oleksandriya** Ukr.
86 C2 **Olenegorsk** Rus. Fed.
83 I2 **Olenek** Rus. Fed.
83 I2 **Olenek** *r.* Rus. Fed.
89 D2 **Olenino** Rus. Fed.
Olenivs'ki Kar"yery Ukr. *see* **Dokuchayevs'k**
Olenya Rus. Fed. *see* Olenegorsk
Oleshky Ukr. *see* **Tsyurupyns'k**
103 D1 **Olesno** Pol.
90 B1 **Olevs'k** Ukr.
106 B2 **Olhão** Port.
122 A2 **Olifants** *watercourse* Namibia
123 D1 **Olifants** S. Africa
123 D1 **Olifants** *r.* S. Africa
122 A3 **Olifants** *r.* S. Africa
122 B2 **Olifantshoek** S. Africa
154 C2 **Olímpia** Brazil
151 F3 **Olinda** Brazil
123 C1 **Oliphants Drift** S. Africa
107 C2 **Oliva** Spain
155 D2 **Oliveira** Brazil
Olivença Moz. *see* Lupilichi
106 B2 **Olivenza** Spain
142 B2 **Olla** U.S.A.
152 B2 **Ollagüe** Chile
106 C1 **Olmedo** Spain
105 D3 **Olmeto** *Corsica* France
150 B3 **Olmos** Peru
140 B3 **Olney** U.S.A.
103 D2 **Olomouc** Czech Rep.
86 C2 **Olonets** Rus. Fed.
64 B2 **Olongapo** Phil.
104 B3 **Oloron-Ste-Marie** France
107 D1 **Olot** Spain
69 D1 **Olovyannaya** Rus. Fed.
100 C2 **Olpe** Ger.
103 E1 **Olsztyn** Pol.
110 B2 **Olt** *r.* Romania
110 C2 **Oltenița** Romania
139 C2 **Olton** U.S.A.
81 C1 **Oltu** Turkey
Ol'viopol' Ukr. *see* **Pervomays'k**
111 B3 **Olympia** *tourist site* Greece
134 B1 **Olympia** U.S.A.
111 B2 **Olympos** *mt.* Greece
Olympus, Mount Gree *see* **Olympos**
134 B1 **Olympus, Mount** U.S.A
83 M2 **Olyutorskiy** Rus. Fed.
83 M3 **Olyutorskiy, Mys** *c.* Rus. Fed.
66 D2 **Ōma** Japan
97 C1 **Omagh** U.K.
137 D2 **Omaha** U.S.A.
79 C3 **Oman** *country* Asia
79 C2 **Oman, Gulf of** Asia
54 A2 **Omarama** N.Z.
120 A3 **Omaruru** Namibia
120 B2 **Omatako** *watercourse* Namibia
122 B2 **Omaweneno** Botswana
116 B3 **Omdurman** Sudan
53 C3 **Omeo** Austr.
145 C3 **Ometepec** Mex.
78 A3 **Om Hajēr** Eritrea
81 C2 **Omīdīyeh** Iran
128 B2 **Omineca Mountains** C
120 A3 **Omitara** Namibia
67 C3 **Ōmiya** Japan
100 C1 **Ommen** Neth.
83 L2 **Omolon** *r.* Rus. Fed.
100 B3 **Omont** France
82 F3 **Omsk** Rus. Fed.
83 L2 **Omsukchan** Rus. Fed.
110 C1 **Omu, Vârful** *mt.* Roma
67 A4 **Ōmura** Japan
140 A2 **Onalaska** U.S.A.
141 D3 **Onancock** U.S.A.
140 C1 **Onaping Lake** Can.
131 C3 **Onatchiway, Lac** *l.* Car
63 A2 **Onbingwin** Myanmar
120 A2 **Oncócua** Angola
122 B3 **Onderstedorings** S. Af
120 A2 **Ondjiva** Angola
69 D1 **Öndörhaan** Mongolia
122 B1 **One** Botswana
86 C2 **Onega** Rus. Fed.
86 C2 **Onega** *r.* Rus. Fed.
86 C2 **Onega, Lake** Rus. Fed.
128 B2 **One Hundred Mile Ho** Can.
141 D2 **Oneida Lake** U.S.A.
137 D2 **O'Neill** U.S.A.
141 D2 **Oneonta** U.S.A.
110 C1 **Onești** Romania
Onezhskoye Ozero *l.* Rus. Fed. *see* **Onega, L**
122 B2 **Ongers** *watercourse* S. Africa
65 B2 **Ongjin** N. Korea
73 C3 **Ongole** India
121 □D3 **Onilahy** *r.* Madag.
115 C4 **Onitsha** Nigeria
120 A3 **Onjati Mountain** Namil
67 C3 **Ōno** Japan
156 D6 **Onotoa** *atoll* Kiribati
122 A2 **Onseepkans** S. Africa
50 A2 **Onslow** Austr.
143 E2 **Onslow Bay** U.S.A.
130 A2 **Ontario** *prov.* Can.
134 C2 **Ontario** U.S.A.
141 D2 **Ontario, Lake** Can./U.S
107 C2 **Ontinyent** Spain
51 C2 **Oodnadatta** Austr.
Oostende Belgium *see* Ostend
100 B2 **Oosterhout** Neth.
100 A2 **Oosterschelde** *est.* Ne
100 B1 **Oost-Vlieland** Neth.
128 B2 **Ootsa Lake** Can.
128 B2 **Ootsa Lake** *l.* Can.
118 C3 **Opala** Dem. Rep. Cong
130 C2 **Opataca, Lac** *l.* Can.
103 D2 **Opava** Czech Rep.
143 C2 **Opelika** U.S.A.
142 B2 **Opelousas** U.S.A.
117 A4 **Opienge** Dem. Rep. Co
130 C2 **Opinaca, Réservoir** *res* Can.
131 D2 **Opiscotéo, Lac** *l.* Can.
88 C2 **Opochka** Rus. Fed.
144 A2 **Opodepe** Mex.

3 D1 Opole Pol.
B2 Opornyy Kazakh.
5 B1 Oporto Port.
C1 Opotiki N.Z.
E3 Oppdal Norway
C1 Opportunity U.S.A.
B1 Opunake N.Z.
A2 Opuwo Namibia
B1 Oradea Romania
D2 Orahovac Yugo.
B1 Oran Alg.
2 B2 Orán Arg.
B1 Ôrang N. Korea
C2 Orange Austr.
C3 Orange France
2 A2 Orange r. Namibia/S. Africa
E2 Orange U.S.A.
D2 Orangeburg U.S.A.
Orange Free State prov. S. Africa see Free State
D2 Orange Park U.S.A.
C2 Orangeville Can.
D3 Orange Walk Belize
F1 Oranienburg Ger.
A2 Oranjemund Namibia
C3 Oranjestad Aruba
B3 Orapa Botswana
B1 Orăştie Romania
Oraşul Stalin Romania see Braşov
B2 Orbetello Italy
C3 Orbost Austr.
D3 Orchid Island U.S.A.
B3 Orchomenos Greece
B1 Ord, Mount hill Austr.
B1 Ordes Spain
B1 Ordu Turkey
Ordzhonikidze Rus. Fed. see Vladikavkaz
C2 Ordzhonikidze Ukr.
G4 Örebro Sweden
B2 Oregon state U.S.A.
B1 Oregon City U.S.A.
E1 Oregon Inlet U.S.A.
C3 Orekhovo-Zuyevo Rus. Fed.
E3 Orel Rus. Fed.
K3 Orel', Ozero l. Rus. Fed.
D2 Orem U.S.A.
A3 Ören Turkey
F3 Orenburg Rus. Fed.
A3 Orepuki N.Z.
C2 Orestiada Greece
F4 Öresund str. Denmark/Sweden
Oretana, Cordillera mts Spain see Toledo, Montes de
D3 Orford Ness hd U.K.
D2 Orgtrud Rus. Fed.
A1 Orgün Afgh.
C3 Orhaneli Turkey
C2 Orhangazi Turkey
D1 Orhon Gol r. Mongolia
B1 Oriental, Cordillera mts Bol.
B2 Oriental, Cordillera mts Col.
B4 Oriental, Cordillera mts Peru
C2 Orihuela Spain
C1 Orikhiv Ukr.
C2 Orillia Can.
I3 Orimattila Fin.
C2 Orinoco r. Col./Venez.
C2 Orinoco Delta Venez.
C2 Orissa state India
E2 Orissaare Estonia
A3 Oristano Sardinia Italy
I3 Orivesi l. Fin.
D3 Oriximiná Brazil
C3 Orizaba Mex.
C3 Orizaba, Pico de vol. Mex.
C1 Orizona Brazil
E3 Örkanger Norway
F4 Örkelljunga Sweden
E3 Orkla r. Norway
C2 Orkney Islands U.K.
C2 Orlândia Brazil
D3 Orlando U.S.A.
C2 Orléans France
F2 Orléans Can.
E1 Orléans, Île d' i. Can.
Orléansville Alg. see Ech Chélif
A2 Ormara Pak.
B2 Ormoc Phil.
D3 Ormond Beach U.S.A.
B3 Ormskirk U.K.
A2 Orne r. France

92 F2 Ørnes Norway
92 G3 Örnsköldsvik Sweden
114 B3 Orodara Burkina
134 C1 Orofino U.S.A.
141 F2 Orono U.S.A.
Oroqen Zizhiqi China see Alihe
64 B3 Oroquieta Phil.
108 A2 Orosei Sardinia Italy
108 A2 Orosei, Golfo di b. Sardinia Italy
103 E2 Orosháza Hungary
135 B3 Oroville U.S.A.
52 A2 Orroroo Austr.
93 F3 Orsa Sweden
89 D3 Orsha Belarus
87 E3 Orsk Rus. Fed.
110 B2 Orşova Romania
93 E3 Ørsta Norway
106 B1 Ortegal, Cabo c. Spain
104 B3 Orthez France
106 B1 Ortigueira Spain
108 B1 Ortles mt. Italy
108 B2 Ortona Italy
137 D1 Ortonville U.S.A.
83 J2 Orulgan, Khrebet mts Rus. Fed.
81 C2 Orūmīyeh Iran
81 C2 Orūmīyeh, Daryācheh-ye salt l. Iran
152 B1 Oruro Bol.
104 B2 Orvault France
108 B2 Orvieto Italy
93 F3 Os Norway
146 B4 Osa, Península de pen. Costa Rica
137 E3 Osage r. U.S.A.
137 D3 Osage City U.S.A.
67 C4 Ōsaka Japan
77 D1 Osakarovka Kazakh.
101 E1 Oschersleben (Bode) Ger.
108 A2 Oschiri Sardinia Italy
140 C2 Oscoda U.S.A.
89 E3 Osetr r. Rus. Fed.
141 D1 Osgoode Can.
77 D2 Osh Kyrg.
120 A2 Oshakati Namibia
130 C3 Oshawa Can.
120 A2 Oshikango Namibia
66 C2 Ō-shima i. Japan
67 C4 Ō-shima i. Japan
140 B2 Oshkosh U.S.A.
81 C2 Oshnovīyeh Iran
119 C2 Oshogbo Nigeria
109 C1 Osijek Croatia
128 B2 Osilinka r. Can.
108 B2 Osimo Italy
Osipenko Ukr. see Berdyans'k
123 D2 Osizweni S. Africa
137 E2 Oskaloosa U.S.A.
93 G4 Oskarshamn Sweden
89 E3 Oskol r. Rus. Fed.
93 F4 Oslo Norway
93 F4 Oslofjorden sea chan. Norway
80 B1 Osmancık Turkey
111 C2 Osmaneli Turkey
80 B2 Osmaniye Turkey
88 C2 Os'mino Rus. Fed.
101 D1 Osnabrück Ger.
153 A4 Osorno Chile
106 C1 Osorno Spain
128 C3 Osoyoos Can.
100 B2 Oss Neth.
51 D4 Ossa, Mount Austr.
83 L3 Ossora Rus. Fed.
89 D2 Ostashkov Rus. Fed.
101 D1 Oste r. Ger.
100 A2 Ostend Belgium
101 E1 Osterburg (Altmark) Ger.
93 F3 Österdalälven l. Sweden
101 D1 Osterholz-Scharmbeck Ger.
101 E2 Osterode am Harz Ger.
92 F3 Östersund Sweden
Ostfriesische Inseln is Ger. see East Frisian Islands
101 D1 Ostfriesland reg. Ger.
93 G3 Östhammar Sweden
103 D2 Ostrava Czech Rep.
103 D1 Ostróda Pol.
89 E3 Ostrogozhsk Rus. Fed.
90 B1 Ostroh Ukr.
103 E1 Ostrołęka Pol.
101 F2 Ostrov Czech Rep.
88 C2 Ostrov Rus. Fed.
Ostrovets Pol. see Ostrowiec Świętokrzyski
92 H2 Ostrovnoy Rus. Fed.

89 F2 Ostrovskoye Rus. Fed.
103 E1 Ostrowiec Świętokrzyski Pol.
103 E1 Ostrów Mazowiecka Pol.
Ostrowo Pol. see Ostrów Wielkopolski
103 D1 Ostrów Wielkopolski Pol.
109 C2 Ostuni Italy
110 B2 Osům r. Bulg.
67 B4 Ōsumi-kaikyō sea chan. Japan
67 B4 Ōsumi-shotō is Japan
106 B2 Osuna Spain
141 D2 Oswego U.S.A.
99 B3 Oswestry U.K.
67 C3 Ōta Japan
54 B3 Otago Peninsula N.Z.
54 C2 Otaki N.Z.
77 D2 Otar Kazakh.
66 D2 Otaru Japan
120 A2 Otavi Namibia
67 D3 Ōtawara Japan
92 G2 Oteren Norway
134 C1 Othello U.S.A.
120 A3 Otjiwarongo Namibia
109 C2 Otočac Croatia
Otog Qi China see Ulan
117 B3 Otoro, Jebel mt. Sudan
Otpor Rus. Fed. see Zabaykal'sk
93 E4 Otra r. Norway
109 C2 Otranto, Strait of Albania/Italy
67 C3 Ōtsu Japan
93 E3 Otta Norway
130 C3 Ottawa r. Can.
130 C3 Ottawa r. Can.
140 B2 Ottawa IL U.S.A.
137 D3 Ottawa KS U.S.A.
130 B2 Ottawa Islands Can.
98 B2 Otterburn U.K.
130 B2 Otter Rapids Can.
100 B2 Ottignies Belgium
137 E2 Ottumwa U.S.A.
150 B3 Otuzco Peru
52 B3 Otway, Cape Austr.
142 B2 Ouachita r. U.S.A.
142 B2 Ouachita, Lake U.S.A.
142 B2 Ouachita Mountains U.S.A.
115 D3 Ouadda C.A.R.
115 D3 Ouaddaï reg. Chad
114 B3 Ouagadougou Burkina
114 B3 Ouahigouya Burkina
114 B3 Oualâta Maur.
118 C2 Ouanda-Djailé C.A.R.
114 B2 Ouarâne reg. Maur.
115 C1 Ouargla Alg.
100 A2 Ouarzazate Morocco
100 A2 Oudenaarde Belgium
122 B3 Oudtshoorn S. Africa
107 C2 Oued Tlélat Alg.
114 B1 Oued Zem Morocco
104 A2 Ouessant, Île d' i. France
118 B2 Ouésso Congo
97 D2 Oughterard Rep. of Ireland
118 B2 Ouham r. C.A.R./Chad
114 B1 Oujda Morocco
92 H3 Oulainen Fin.
107 D2 Ouled Farès Alg.
92 I2 Oulu Fin.
92 I3 Oulujärvi l. Fin.
108 A1 Oulx Italy
115 E3 Oum-Chalouba Chad
115 D3 Oum-Hadjer Chad
115 E3 Ounianga Kébir Chad
100 B2 Oupeye Belgium
100 C3 Our, Vallée de l' val. Ger./Lux.
106 B1 Ourense Spain
151 D3 Ourinhos Brazil
155 D2 Ouro Preto Brazil
100 B2 Ourthe r. Belgium
98 C3 Ouse r. U.K.
Outaouais, Rivière des r. Can. see Ottawa
131 D3 Outardes r. Can.
131 D2 Outardes Quatre, Réservoir resr Can.
96 A2 Outer Hebrides is U.K.
Outer Mongolia country Asia see Mongolia
120 A3 Outjo Namibia
129 D2 Outlook Can.
92 I3 Outokumpu Fin.
51 E3 Ouyen Austr.
108 A2 Ovace, Punta d' mt. Corsica France
153 A3 Ovalle Chile
106 B1 Ovar Port.
92 H2 Överkalix Sweden

137 E3 Overland Park U.S.A.
135 D3 Overton U.S.A.
92 H2 Övertorneå Sweden
106 B1 Oviedo Spain
143 D3 Oviedo U.S.A.
88 B2 Ovišrags hd Latvia
93 E3 Øvre Årdal Norway
93 F3 Øvre Rendal Norway
90 B1 Ovruch Ukr.
118 B3 Owando Congo
67 C4 Owase Japan
139 D1 Owasso U.S.A.
137 E2 Owatonna U.S.A.
141 D2 Owego U.S.A.
141 D2 Owensboro U.S.A.
135 C3 Owens Lake U.S.A.
130 B3 Owen Sound Can.
51 D1 Owen Stanley Range mts P.N.G.
115 C4 Owerri Nigeria
115 C4 Owo Nigeria
140 C2 Owosso U.S.A.
134 C2 Owyhee U.S.A.
134 C2 Owyhee r. U.S.A.
129 D3 Oxbow Can.
54 B2 Oxford N.Z.
99 C4 Oxford U.K.
142 C2 Oxford U.S.A.
129 E2 Oxford Lake Can.
145 D2 Oxkutzcab Mex.
52 B2 Oxley Austr.
Ox Mountains hills Rep. of Ireland see Slieve Gamph
135 C4 Oxnard U.S.A.
67 C3 Oyama Japan
118 B2 Oyem Gabon
129 C2 Oyen Can.
105 D2 Oyonnax France
64 B3 Ozamiz Phil.
142 C2 Ozark AL U.S.A.
137 E3 Ozark MO U.S.A.
137 E3 Ozark Plateau U.S.A.
137 E3 Ozarks, Lake of the U.S.A.
83 L3 Ozernovskiy Rus. Fed.
89 E3 Ozersk Rus. Fed.
89 E3 Ozery Rus. Fed.
87 D3 Ozinki Rus. Fed.

P

127 I2 Paamiut Greenland
122 A3 Paarl S. Africa
103 D1 Pabianice Pol.
75 C2 Pabna Bangl.
88 C3 Pabradė Lith.
74 A2 Pab Range mts Pak.
150 C2 Pacaraima Mountains mts Brazil
150 B3 Pacasmayo Peru
138 B2 Pacheco Mex.
109 C3 Pachino Sicily Italy
145 C2 Pachuca Mex.
157 E9 Pacific-Antarctic Ridge sea feature
156 Pacific Ocean
61 C2 Pacitan Indon.
52 B2 Packsaddle Austr.
103 D1 Paczków Pol.
60 B2 Padang Indon.
60 A1 Padangpanjang Indon.
60 B2 Padangsidimpuan Indon.
101 D2 Paderborn Ger.
Padova Italy see Padua
139 D3 Padre Island U.S.A.
99 A4 Padstow U.K.
52 B3 Padthaway Austr.
58 B3 Padua Italy
108 B1 Paducah KY U.S.A.
139 C2 Paducah TX U.S.A.
65 B1 Paegam N. Korea
65 B1 Paekdu-san mt. China/N. Korea
65 A2 Paengnyŏng-do i. S. Korea
54 C1 Paeroa N.Z.
80 B2 Pafos Cyprus
109 C2 Pag Croatia
109 C2 Pag i. Croatia
64 B3 Pagadian Phil.
60 B2 Pagai Selatan i. Indon.
60 B2 Pagai Utara i. Indon.
59 D1 Pagan i. N. Mariana Is
61 C2 Pagatan Indon.
138 A1 Page U.S.A.
88 B2 Pagėgiai Lith.

153 E5 **Paget, Mount** S. Georgia
136 B3 **Pagosa Springs** U.S.A.
88 C2 **Paide** Estonia
99 B4 **Paignton** U.K.
93 I3 **Päijänne** *l.* Fin.
75 C2 **Paikü Co** *l.* China
60 B2 **Painan** Indon.
140 C2 **Painesville** U.S.A.
138 A1 **Painted Desert** U.S.A.
Paint Hills Can. *see* **Wemindji**
96 B3 **Paisley** U.K.
92 H2 **Pajala** Sweden
150 A3 **Pajan** Ecuador
150 D2 **Pakaraima Mountains** Guyana
74 A2 **Pakistan** *country* Asia
62 A1 **Pakokku** Myanmar
88 B2 **Pakruojis** Lith.
103 D2 **Paks** Hungary
130 A2 **Pakwash Lake** Can.
63 B2 **Pakxé** Laos
115 D4 **Pala** Chad
60 B2 **Palabuhanratu, Teluk** *b.* Indon.
111 C3 **Palaikastro** Greece
111 B3 **Palaiochora** Greece
Palakkat India *see* **Palghat**
122 B1 **Palamakoloi** Botswana
107 D1 **Palamós** Spain
83 L3 **Palana** Rus. Fed.
64 B2 **Palanan** Phil.
61 C2 **Palangkaraya** Indon.
74 B2 **Palanpur** India
123 C1 **Palapye** Botswana
83 L2 **Palatka** Rus. Fed.
143 D3 **Palatka** U.S.A.
59 C2 **Palau** *country* N. Pacific Ocean
156 C5 **Palau Islands** Palau
63 A2 **Palaw** Myanmar
64 A3 **Palawan** *i.* Phil.
64 A3 **Palawan Passage** *str.* Phil.
88 B2 **Paldiski** Estonia
89 F2 **Palekh** Rus. Fed.
60 B2 **Palembang** Indon.
106 C1 **Palencia** Spain
145 C3 **Palenque** Mex.
108 B3 **Palermo** *Sicily* Italy
139 D2 **Palestine** U.S.A.
62 A1 **Paletwa** Myanmar
73 B3 **Palghat** India
74 B2 **Pali** India
48 G4 **Palikir** Micronesia
109 C2 **Palinuro, Capo** *c.* Italy
111 B3 **Paliouri, Akra** *pt* Greece
100 B3 **Paliseul** Belgium
92 I3 **Paljakka** *hill* Fin.
88 C2 **Palkino** Rus. Fed.
73 B4 **Palk Strait** India/Sri Lanka
Palla Bianca *mt.* Austria/Italy *see* **Weißkugel**
54 C2 **Palliser, Cape** N.Z.
157 F7 **Palliser, Îles** *is* Fr. Polynesia
106 B2 **Palma del Río** Spain
107 D2 **Palma de Mallorca** Spain
154 B3 **Palmas** Brazil
154 B3 **Palmas, Campos de** *hills* Brazil
114 B4 **Palmas, Cape** Liberia
143 D3 **Palm Bay** U.S.A.
135 C4 **Palmdale** U.S.A.
154 C3 **Palmeira** Brazil
151 E3 **Palmeirais** Brazil
126 C2 **Palmer** U.S.A.
55 A2 **Palmer Land** *reg.* Antarctica
49 K5 **Palmerston** *atoll* Cook Is
54 C2 **Palmerston North** N.Z.
109 C3 **Palmi** Italy
145 C2 **Palmillas** Mex.
150 B2 **Palmira** Col.
154 B2 **Palmital** Brazil
135 C4 **Palm Springs** U.S.A.
Palmyra Syria *see* **Tadmur**
49 K3 **Palmyra Atoll** N. Pacific Ocean
135 B3 **Palo Alto** U.S.A.
117 B3 **Paloich** Sudan
145 C3 **Palomares** Mex.
61 D2 **Palopo** Indon.
107 C2 **Palos, Cabo de** *c.* Spain
92 I3 **Paltamo** Fin.
61 C2 **Palu** Indon.
83 M2 **Palyavaam** *r.* Rus. Fed.
150 B3 **Pamar** Col.
121 C3 **Pambarra** Moz.
104 C3 **Pamiers** France
77 D3 **Pamir** *mts* Asia
143 E1 **Pamlico Sound** *sea chan.* U.S.A.
152 B1 **Pampa Grande** Bol.
153 B3 **Pampas** *reg.* Arg.
150 B2 **Pamplona** Col.
107 C1 **Pamplona** Spain
111 D2 **Pamukova** Turkey
60 B2 **Panaitan** *i.* Indon.
73 B3 **Panaji** India
146 B4 **Panama** *country* Central America
146 C4 **Panamá** Panama
146 C4 **Panamá, Golfo de** *g.* Panama
Panama, Gulf of Panama *see* **Panamá, Golfo de**
146 C4 **Panama Canal** *canal* Panama
Panama City Panama *see* **Panamá**
142 C2 **Panama City** U.S.A.
135 C3 **Panamint Range** *mts* U.S.A.
60 B1 **Panarik** Indon.
64 B2 **Panay** *i.* Phil.
109 D2 **Pančevo** Yugo.
64 B2 **Pandan** Phil.
64 B2 **Pandan** Phil.
75 C2 **Pandaria** India
73 B3 **Pandharpur** India
88 B2 **Panevėžys** Lith.
Panfilov Kazakh. *see* **Zharkent**
61 C2 **Pangkalanbuun** Indon.
60 A1 **Pangkalansusu** Indon.
60 B2 **Pangkalpinang** Indon.
61 D2 **Pangkalsiang, Tanjung** *pt* Indon.
127 H2 **Pangnirtung** Can.
86 G2 **Pangody** Rus. Fed.
89 F3 **Panino** Rus. Fed.
74 B2 **Panipat** India
74 A2 **Panjgur** Pak.
Panjim India *see* **Panaji**
118 A2 **Pankshin** Nigeria
65 C1 **Pan Ling** *mts* China
75 C2 **Panna** India
50 A2 **Pannawonica** Austr.
154 B2 **Panorama** Brazil
65 B1 **Panshi** China
145 C2 **Pánuco** Mex.
145 C2 **Pánuco** *r.* Mex.
71 A3 **Panxian** China
62 B1 **Panzhihua** China
109 C3 **Paola** Italy
118 B2 **Paoua** C.A.R.
63 B2 **Paôy Pêt** Cambodia
103 D2 **Pápa** Hungary
54 B1 **Papakura** N.Z.
145 C2 **Papantla** Mex.
96 □ **Papa Stour** *i.* U.K.
54 B1 **Papatoetoe** N.Z.
49 M5 **Papeete** Fr. Polynesia
100 C1 **Papenburg** Ger.
Paphos Cyprus *see* **Pafos**
137 D2 **Papillion** U.S.A.
59 D3 **Papua, Gulf of** P.N.G.
59 D3 **Papua New Guinea** *country* Oceania
62 A2 **Papun** Myanmar
89 F3 **Para** *r.* Rus. Fed.
50 A2 **Paraburdoo** Austr.
154 C1 **Paracatu** Brazil
155 C1 **Paracatu** *r.* Brazil
52 A2 **Parachilna** Austr.
109 D2 **Paraćin** Yugo.
155 D1 **Pará de Minas** Brazil
151 D2 **Paradise** Guyana
135 B3 **Paradise** U.S.A.
142 B1 **Paragould** U.S.A.
151 D3 **Paraguai** *r.* Brazil
147 D3 **Paraguaná, Península de** *pen.* Venez.
152 C2 **Paraguay** *r.* Arg./Para.
152 C2 **Paraguay** *country* S. America
155 D2 **Paraíba do Sul** *r.* Brazil
154 B1 **Paraíso** Brazil
145 C3 **Paraíso** Mex.
114 C4 **Parakou** Benin
52 A2 **Parakylia** Austr.
151 D2 **Paramaribo** Suriname
83 L3 **Paramushir, Ostrov** *i.* Rus. Fed.
152 B3 **Paraná** Arg.
154 A3 **Paraná** *r.* S. America
154 C1 **Paraná, Serra do** *hills* Brazil
154 C3 **Paranaguá** Brazil
154 B1 **Paranaíba** Brazil
154 B2 **Paranaíba** *r.* Brazil
154 B2 **Paranapanema** *r.* Brazil
154 B2 **Paranapiacaba, Serra** *mts* Brazil
154 B2 **Paranavaí** Brazil
90 A2 **Parângul Mare, Vârful** *mt.* Romania
54 B2 **Paraparaumu** N.Z.
155 D2 **Parati** Brazil
52 A2 **Paratoo** Austr.
151 D3 **Parauaquara, Serra** *hill* Brazil
154 B1 **Paraúna** Brazil
105 C2 **Paray-le-Monial** France
74 B2 **Parbati** *r.* India
74 B3 **Parbhani** India
101 E1 **Parchim** Ger.
103 E1 **Parczew** Pol.
155 E1 **Pardo** *r.* Brazil
154 B2 **Pardo** *r.* Brazil
154 C2 **Pardo** *r.* Brazil
103 D1 **Pardubice** Czech Rep.
152 C1 **Parecis, Serra dos** *hills* Brazil
150 C4 **Parecis, Serra dos** *hills* Brazil
130 C3 **Parent** Can.
130 C3 **Parent, Lac** *l.* Can.
61 C2 **Parepare** Indon.
89 D2 **Parfino** Rus. Fed.
111 B3 **Parga** Greece
109 C3 **Parghelia** Italy
147 D3 **Paria, Gulf of** Trin. and Tob./Venez.
150 C2 **Parima, Serra** *mts* Brazil
151 D3 **Parintins** Brazil
104 C2 **Paris** France
142 C1 **Paris** *TN* U.S.A.
139 D2 **Paris** *TX* U.S.A.
93 H3 **Parkano** Fin.
138 A2 **Parker** U.S.A.
140 C3 **Parkersburg** U.S.A.
53 C2 **Parkes** Austr.
140 A1 **Park Falls** U.S.A.
134 B1 **Parkland** U.S.A.
137 D1 **Park Rapids** U.S.A.
106 C1 **Parla** Spain
108 B2 **Parma** Italy
134 C2 **Parma** U.S.A.
151 E3 **Parnaíba** Brazil
151 E3 **Parnaíba** *r.* Brazil
111 B3 **Parnassos** *mt.* Greece
54 B2 **Parnassus** N.Z.
111 B3 **Parnon** *mts* Greece
88 B2 **Pärnu** Estonia
65 B2 **P'aro-ho** *l.* S. Korea
52 B2 **Paroo** *watercourse* Austr.
76 C3 **Paropamisus** *mts* Afgh.
111 C3 **Paros** *i.* Greece
135 D3 **Parowan** U.S.A.
153 A3 **Parral** Chile
53 D2 **Parramatta** Austr.
144 B2 **Parras** Mex.
126 D2 **Parry, Cape** Can.
126 E1 **Parry Islands** Can.
130 B3 **Parry Sound** Can.
137 D3 **Parsons** U.S.A.
108 B3 **Partanna** *Sicily* Italy
101 D2 **Partenstein** Ger.
104 B2 **Parthenay** France
108 B3 **Partinico** *Sicily* Italy
66 B2 **Partizansk** Rus. Fed.
97 B2 **Partry Mountains** *hills* Rep. of Ireland
151 D3 **Paru** *r.* Brazil
131 E3 **Pasadena** Can.
135 C4 **Pasadena** *CA* U.S.A.
139 D3 **Pasadena** *TX* U.S.A.
62 A2 **Pasawng** Myanmar
142 C2 **Pascagoula** U.S.A.
110 C1 **Paşcani** Romania
134 C1 **Pasco** U.S.A.
155 E1 **Pascoal, Monte** *hill* Brazil
Pascua, Isla de *i.* S. Pacific Ocean *see* **Easter Island**
Pas de Calais *str.* France/U.K. *see* **Dover, Strait of**
102 C1 **Pasewalk** Ger.
129 D2 **Pasfield Lake** Can.
89 D1 **Pasha** Rus. Fed.
64 B2 **Pasig** Phil.
60 B1 **Pasir Putih** Malaysia
103 D1 **Pasłęk** Pol.
74 A2 **Pasni** Pak.
153 A4 **Paso Río Mayo** Arg.
135 B3 **Paso Robles** U.S.A.
97 B3 **Passage West** Rep. of Ireland
155 D2 **Passa Tempo** Brazil
102 C2 **Passau** Ger.
152 C2 **Passo Fundo** Brazil
155 C2 **Passos** Brazil
88 C2 **Pastavy** Belarus
150 B3 **Pastaza** *r.* Peru
150 B2 **Pasto** Col.
74 B1 **Pasu** Jammu and Kash
61 C2 **Pasuruan** Indon.
88 B2 **Pasvalys** Lith.
103 D2 **Pásztó** Hungary
153 A5 **Patagonia** *reg.* Arg.
75 C2 **Patan** Nepal
54 B1 **Patea** N.Z.
141 E2 **Paterson** U.S.A.
74 B1 **Pathankot** India
Pathein Myanmar *see* **Bassein**
136 B2 **Pathfinder Reservoir** U.S.A.
61 C2 **Pati** Indon.
74 B1 **Patiala** India
62 A1 **Pātkai Bum** *mts* India/Myanmar
111 C3 **Patmos** *i.* Greece
75 C2 **Patna** India
81 C2 **Patnos** Turkey
154 B3 **Pato Branco** Brazil
152 C3 **Patos, Lagoa dos** *l.* Br
155 C1 **Patos de Minas** Brazil
152 B3 **Patquía** Arg.
111 B3 **Patra** Greece
Patras Greece *see* **Patr**
75 C2 **Patratu** India
154 C1 **Patrocínio** Brazil
63 B3 **Pattani** Thai.
63 B2 **Pattaya** Thai.
128 B2 **Pattullo, Mount** Can.
129 D2 **Patuanak** Can.
146 B3 **Patuca** *r.* Hond.
144 B3 **Pátzcuaro** Mex.
104 B3 **Pau** France
104 B2 **Pauillac** France
150 C3 **Pauini** Brazil
62 A1 **Pauk** Myanmar
126 D2 **Paulatuk** Can.
Paulis Dem. Rep. Cong *see* **Isiro**
151 E3 **Paulistana** Brazil
151 F3 **Paulo Afonso** Brazil
123 D2 **Paulpietersburg** S. Afr
139 D2 **Pauls Valley** U.S.A.
62 A2 **Paungde** Myanmar
155 D1 **Pavão** Brazil
108 A1 **Pavia** Italy
88 B2 **Pāvilosta** Latvia
110 C2 **Pavlikeni** Bulg.
77 D1 **Pavlodar** Kazakh.
91 D2 **Pavlohrad** Ukr.
91 E1 **Pavlovsk** Rus. Fed.
91 D2 **Pavlovskaya** Rus. Fed.
141 E2 **Pawtucket** U.S.A.
111 B3 **Paxoi** *i.* Greece
60 B2 **Payakumbuh** Indon.
134 C2 **Payette** U.S.A.
134 C2 **Payette** *r.* U.S.A.
86 F2 **Pay-Khoy, Khrebet** *hills* Rus. Fed.
Payne Can. *see* **Kangirs**
130 C2 **Payne, Lac** *l.* Can.
152 C3 **Paysandú** Uru.
81 C1 **Pazar** Turkey
110 B2 **Pazardzhik** Bulg.
111 C3 **Pazarköy** Turkey
108 B1 **Pazin** Croatia
63 A2 **Pe** Myanmar
128 C2 **Peace** *r.* Can.
128 C2 **Peace River** Can.
53 C2 **Peak Hill** *N.S.W.* Austr.
50 A2 **Peak Hill** *W.A.* Austr.
135 E3 **Peale, Mount** U.S.A.
142 C2 **Pearl** *r.* U.S.A.
139 D3 **Pearsall** U.S.A.
126 F1 **Peary Channel** Can.
121 C2 **Pebane** Moz.
109 D2 **Peć** Yugo.
155 D1 **Peçanha** Brazil
154 C3 **Peças, Ilha das** *i.* Brazil
92 J2 **Pechenga** Rus. Fed.
86 E2 **Pechora** Rus. Fed.
86 E2 **Pechora** *r.* Rus. Fed.
Pechora Sea Rus. Fed. *see* **Pechorskoye More**
86 E2 **Pechorskoye More** *sea* Rus. Fed.
88 C2 **Pechory** Rus. Fed.
138 B1 **Pecos** *NM* U.S.A.
139 C2 **Pecos** *TX* U.S.A.
139 C3 **Pecos** *r.* U.S.A.
103 D2 **Pécs** Hungary
138 B3 **Pedernales** Mex.
155 D1 **Pedra Azul** Brazil
154 C2 **Pedregulho** Brazil

1 E3 **Pedreiras** Brazil
3 C4 **Pedro, Point** Sri Lanka
1 E3 **Pedro Afonso** Brazil
2 B2 **Pedro de Valdivia** Chile
4 B1 **Pedro Gomes** Brazil
2 C2 **Pedro Juan Caballero** Para.
6 B1 **Pedroso** Port.
5 C3 **Peebles** U.K.
3 E2 **Pee Dee** *r.* U.S.A.
6 D2 **Peel** *r.* Can.
3 A2 **Peel** Isle of Man
8 C2 **Peerless Lake** Can.
4 B2 **Pegasus Bay** N.Z.
1 E3 **Pegnitz** Ger.
2 A2 **Pegu** Myanmar
2 A2 **Pegu Yoma** *mts* Myanmar
3 B3 **Pehuajó** Arg.
1 E1 **Peine** Ger.
3 C2 **Peipus, Lake** Estonia/Rus. Fed.
1 B3 **Peiraias** Greece
4 B2 **Peixe** *r.* Brazil
1 D4 **Peixoto de Azevedo** Brazil
3 C2 **Peka** Lesotho
B2 **Pekalongan** Indon.
B1 **Pekan** Malaysia
B1 **Pekanbaru** Indon.
Peking China *see* **Beijing**
0 B3 **Pelee Island** Can.
D2 **Peleng** *i.* Indon.
3 D2 **Pelhřimov** Czech Rep.
2 I2 **Pelkosenniemi** Fin.
2 A2 **Pella** S. Africa
7 E2 **Pella** U.S.A.
9 D3 **Pelleluhu Islands** P.N.G.
2 H2 **Pello** Fin.
8 A1 **Pelly** *r.* Can.
7 G2 **Pelly Bay** Can.
8 A1 **Pelly Mountains** Can.
2 C3 **Pelotas** Brazil
2 C2 **Pelotas, Rio das** *r.* Brazil
1 F1 **Pemadumcook Lake** U.S.A.
B1 **Pemangkat** Indon.
A1 **Pematangsiantar** Indon.
1 D2 **Pemba** Moz.
0 B2 **Pemba** Zambia
9 D3 **Pemba Island** Tanz.
8 B2 **Pemberton** Can.
7 D1 **Pembina** *r.* Can.
7 D1 **Pembina** *r.* U.S.A.
0 C3 **Pembroke** Can.
9 A4 **Pembroke** U.K.
3 D3 **Pembroke Pines** U.S.A.
6 C1 **Peña Cerredo** *mt.* Spain
6 C1 **Peñalara** *mt.* Spain
5 C2 **Peña Nevada, Cerro** *mt.* Mex.
4 B2 **Penápolis** Brazil
6 B1 **Peñaranda de Bracamonte** Spain
7 C1 **Peñarroya** *mt.* Spain
6 B2 **Peñarroya-Pueblonuevo** Spain
6 B1 **Peñas, Cabo de** *c.* Spain
3 A4 **Penas, Golfo de** *g.* Chile
6 B1 **Peña Ubiña** *mt.* Spain
1 C2 **Pendik** Turkey
4 C1 **Pendleton** U.S.A.
8 B2 **Pendleton Bay** Can.
4 C1 **Pend Oreille Lake** U.S.A.
Penfro U.K. *see* **Pembroke**
4 B3 **Penganga** *r.* India
8 C3 **Penge** Dem. Rep. Congo
3 D1 **Penge** S. Africa
C2 **Penglai** China
1 A3 **Pengshui** China
6 B2 **Peniche** Port.
5 C3 **Penicuik** U.K.
8 B2 **Penne** Italy
2 A3 **Penneshaw** Austr.
8 B2 **Pennines** *hills* U.K.
1 D2 **Pennsylvania** *state* U.S.A.
7 H2 **Penny Icecap** Can.
9 D2 **Peno** Rus. Fed.
1 F2 **Penobscot** *r.* U.S.A.
2 B3 **Penola** Austr.
C3 **Penong** Austr.
7 E6 **Penrhyn Basin** *sea feature* S. Pacific Ocean
3 D2 **Penrith** Austr.
8 B2 **Penrith** U.K.
2 C2 **Pensacola** U.S.A.
5 B1 **Pensacola Mountains** Antarctica
1 C1 **Pensiangan** *Sabah* Malaysia
8 C3 **Penticton** Can.
6 C1 **Pentland Firth** *sea chan.* U.K.
99 B3 **Penygadair** *hill* U.K.
87 D3 **Penza** Rus. Fed.
99 A4 **Penzance** U.K.
83 L2 **Penzhinskaya Guba** *b.* Rus. Fed.
138 A2 **Peoria** *AZ* U.S.A.
140 B2 **Peoria** *IL* U.S.A.
107 C1 **Perales del Alfambra** Spain
111 B3 **Perama** Greece
131 D3 **Percé** Can.
50 B2 **Percival Lakes** *salt flat* Austr.
51 E2 **Percy Isles** Austr.
107 D1 **Perdido, Monte** *mt.* Spain
154 C1 **Perdizes** Brazil
86 F2 **Peregrebnoye** Rus. Fed.
150 B2 **Pereira** Col.
154 B2 **Pereira Barreto** Brazil
Pereira de Eça Angola *see* **Ondjiva**
90 A2 **Peremyshlyany** Ukr.
89 E2 **Pereslavl'-Zalesskiy** Rus. Fed.
91 C1 **Pereyaslav-Khmel'nyts'kyy** Ukr.
153 B3 **Pergamino** Arg.
92 H3 **Perhonjoki** *r.* Fin.
131 C2 **Péribonca, Lac** *l.* Can.
152 B2 **Perico** Arg.
144 B2 **Pericos** Mex.
104 C2 **Périgueux** France
150 B2 **Perija, Sierra de** *mts* Venez.
111 B3 **Peristerio** Greece
153 A4 **Perito Moreno** Arg.
101 E1 **Perleberg** Ger.
86 E3 **Perm'** Rus. Fed.
109 D2 **Përmet** Albania
Pernambuco Brazil *see* **Recife**
52 A2 **Pernatty Lagoon** *salt flat* Austr.
110 B2 **Pernik** Bulg.
Pernov Estonia *see* **Pärnu**
105 C2 **Péronne** France
145 C3 **Perote** Mex.
105 C3 **Perpignan** France
99 A4 **Perranporth** U.K.
Perrégaux Alg. *see* **Mohammadia**
143 D2 **Perry** *FL* U.S.A.
143 D2 **Perry** *GA* U.S.A.
137 E2 **Perry** *IA* U.S.A.
139 D1 **Perry** *OK* U.S.A.
140 C2 **Perrysburg** U.S.A.
139 C1 **Perryton** U.S.A.
137 F3 **Perryville** U.S.A.
Pershnotravnevoye Ukr. *see* **Pershotravens'k**
99 B3 **Pershore** U.K.
91 D2 **Pershotravens'k** Ukr.
Persia *country* Asia *see* **Iran**
50 A3 **Perth** Austr.
96 C2 **Perth** U.K.
159 F5 **Perth Basin** *sea feature* Indian Ocean
86 C2 **Pertominsk** Rus. Fed.
105 D3 **Pertuis** France
108 A2 **Pertusato, Capo** *c.* *Corsica* France
150 B3 **Peru** *country* S. America
140 B2 **Peru** U.S.A.
157 H6 **Peru Basin** *sea feature* S. Pacific Ocean
157 H7 **Peru-Chile Trench** *sea feature* S. Pacific Ocean
108 B2 **Perugia** Italy
154 C2 **Peruíbe** Brazil
100 A2 **Péruwelz** Belgium
90 C2 **Pervomays'k** Ukr.
91 C2 **Pervomays'ke** Ukr.
Pervomayskiy Rus. Fed. *see* **Novodvinsk**
89 F3 **Pervomayskiy** Rus. Fed.
91 D2 **Pervomays'kyy** Ukr.
108 B2 **Pesaro** Italy
108 B2 **Pescara** Italy
108 B2 **Pescara** *r.* Italy
74 B1 **Peshawar** Pak.
109 D2 **Peshkopi** Albania
109 C1 **Pesnica** Slovenia
104 B3 **Pessac** France
89 E2 **Pestovo** Rus. Fed.
142 C2 **Petal** U.S.A.
100 B3 **Pétange** Lux.
147 D3 **Petare** Venez.
144 B3 **Petatlán** Mex.
121 C2 **Petauke** Zambia
130 C3 **Petawawa** Can.
140 B2 **Petenwell Lake** U.S.A.
52 A2 **Peterborough** Austr.
130 C3 **Peterborough** Can.
99 C3 **Peterborough** U.K.
96 D2 **Peterhead** U.K.
55 R3 **Peter I Island** Antarctica
129 E1 **Peter Lake** Can.
50 B2 **Petermann Ranges** *mts* Austr.
129 D2 **Peter Pond Lake** Can.
128 A2 **Petersburg** *AK* U.S.A.
141 D3 **Petersburg** *VA* U.S.A.
101 D1 **Petershagen** Ger.
Peter the Great Bay Rus. Fed. *see* **Petra Velikogo, Zaliv**
Petitjean Morocco *see* **Sidi Kacem**
131 D2 **Petit Lac Manicouagan** *l.* Can.
131 E2 **Petit Mécatina** *r.* Can.
145 D2 **Peto** Mex.
140 C1 **Petoskey** U.S.A.
80 B2 **Petra** *tourist site* Jordan
66 B2 **Petra Velikogo, Zaliv** *b.* Rus. Fed.
111 B2 **Petrich** Bulg.
Petroaleksandrovsk Uzbek. *see* **Turtkul'**
88 C2 **Petrodvorets** Rus. Fed.
Petrokov Pol. *see* **Piotrków Trybunalski**
151 E3 **Petrolina** Brazil
77 C1 **Petropavlovsk** Kazakh.
83 L3 **Petropavlovsk-Kamchatskiy** Rus. Fed.
110 B1 **Petroşani** Romania
Petrovskoye Rus. Fed. *see* **Svetlograd**
89 F3 **Petrovskoye** Rus. Fed.
89 E2 **Petrovskoye** Rus. Fed.
69 D1 **Petrovsk-Zabaykal'skiy** Rus. Fed.
86 C2 **Petrozavodsk** Rus. Fed.
123 C2 **Petrusburg** S. Africa
123 C2 **Petrus Steyn** S. Africa
122 B3 **Petrusville** S. Africa
Petsamo Rus. Fed. *see* **Pechenga**
87 F3 **Petukhovo** Rus. Fed.
89 E2 **Petushki** Rus. Fed.
60 A1 **Peureula** Indon.
83 M2 **Pevek** Rus. Fed.
102 B2 **Pforzheim** Ger.
102 C2 **Pfunds** Austria
101 D3 **Pfungstadt** Ger.
123 C2 **Phahameng** S. Africa
123 C1 **Phahameng** S. Africa
123 D1 **Phalaborwa** S. Africa
74 B2 **Phalodi** India
63 A3 **Phangnga** Thai.
63 B2 **Phan Rang** Vietnam
63 B2 **Phan Thiêt** Vietnam
63 B3 **Phatthalung** Thai.
62 A2 **Phayao** Thai.
129 D2 **Phelps Lake** Can.
143 C2 **Phenix City** U.S.A.
63 A2 **Phet Buri** Thai.
63 B2 **Phetchabun** Thai.
63 B2 **Phichit** Thai.
141 D3 **Philadelphia** U.S.A.
136 C2 **Philip** U.S.A.
Philip Atoll Micronesia *see* **Sorol**
Philippeville Alg. *see* **Skikda**
100 B2 **Philippeville** Belgium
51 C2 **Philippi, Lake** *salt flat* Austr.
100 A2 **Philippine** Neth.
156 C4 **Philippine Basin** *sea feature* N. Pacific Ocean
64 B2 **Philippines** *country* Asia
64 B2 **Philippine Sea** N. Pacific Ocean
126 C2 **Philip Smith Mountains** U.S.A.
122 B3 **Philipstown** S. Africa
53 C3 **Phillip Island** Austr.
137 D3 **Phillipsburg** U.S.A.
63 B2 **Phimun Mangsahan** Thai.
123 C2 **Phiritona** S. Africa
63 B2 **Phitsanulok** Thai.
Phnom Penh Cambodia *see* **Phnum Pénh**
63 B2 **Phnum Pénh** Cambodia
138 A2 **Phoenix** U.S.A.
49 J4 **Phoenix Islands** Kiribati
63 B2 **Phon** Thai.
62 B2 **Phong Nha** Vietnam
62 B1 **Phôngsali** Laos
62 B1 **Phong Thô** Vietnam
62 B2 **Phrae** Thai.
Phu Cuong Vietnam *see* **Thu Dâu Môt**
120 B3 **Phuduhudu** Botswana
63 A3 **Phuket** Thai.
63 B2 **Phumĭ Kâmpóng Trâlach** Cambodia
63 B2 **Phumĭ Sâmraông** Cambodia
63 B2 **Phu Nhơn** Vietnam
63 B2 **Phu Quôc, Đao** *i.* Vietnam
123 C2 **Phuthaditjhaba** S. Africa
Phu Vinh Vietnam *see* **Tra Vinh**
108 A1 **Piacenza** Italy
108 B2 **Pianosa, Isola** *i.* Italy
110 C1 **Piatra Neamţ** Romania
151 E3 **Piauí** *r.* Brazil
108 B1 **Piave** *r.* Italy
117 B4 **Pibor** *r.* Sudan
117 B4 **Pibor Post** Sudan
104 C2 **Picardie** *reg.* France
Picardy *reg.* France *see* **Picardie**
142 C2 **Picayune** U.S.A.
152 B2 **Pichanal** Arg.
144 A2 **Pichilingue** Mex.
98 C2 **Pickering** U.K.
130 A2 **Pickle Lake** Can.
151 E3 **Picos** Brazil
153 B4 **Pico Truncado** Arg.
53 D2 **Picton** Austr.
54 B2 **Picton** N.Z.
73 C4 **Pidurutalagala** *mt.* Sri Lanka
154 C2 **Piedade** Brazil
145 C3 **Piedras Negras** Guat.
145 B2 **Piedras Negras** Mex.
93 I3 **Pieksämäki** Fin.
92 I3 **Pielinen** *l.* Fin.
136 C2 **Pierre** U.S.A.
105 C3 **Pierrelatte** France
123 D2 **Pietermaritzburg** S. Africa
Pietersaari Fin. *see* **Jakobstad**
123 C1 **Pietersburg** S. Africa
123 D2 **Piet Retief** S. Africa
110 B1 **Pietrosa** *mt.* Romania
110 C1 **Pietrosu, Vârful** *mt.* Romania
128 C2 **Pigeon Lake** Can.
137 F1 **Pigeon River** U.S.A.
153 B3 **Pigüé** Arg.
93 I3 **Pihlajavesi** *l.* Fin.
92 I3 **Pihtipudas** Fin.
145 C3 **Pijijiapan** Mex.
89 D2 **Pikalevo** Rus. Fed.
130 A2 **Pikangikum** Can.
136 C3 **Pikes Peak** U.S.A.
122 A3 **Piketberg** S. Africa
140 C3 **Pikeville** U.S.A.
103 D1 **Piła** Pol.
153 C3 **Pilar** Arg.
152 C2 **Pilar** Para.
75 B2 **Pilibhit** India
53 C2 **Pilliga** Austr.
154 C1 **Pilões, Serra dos** *mts* Brazil
150 C4 **Pimenta Bueno** Brazil
88 C3 **Pina** *r.* Belarus
153 C3 **Pinamar** Arg.
80 B2 **Pınarbaşı** Turkey
146 B2 **Pinar del Río** Cuba
64 B2 **Pinatubo, Mount** *vol.* Phil.
103 E1 **Pińczów** Pol.
151 E3 **Pindaré** *r.* Brazil
111 B2 **Pindos** *mts* Greece
Pindus Mountains Greece *see* **Pindos**
142 B2 **Pine Bluff** U.S.A.
136 C2 **Pine Bluffs** U.S.A.
50 C1 **Pine Creek** Austr.
136 B2 **Pinedale** U.S.A.
86 D2 **Pinega** Rus. Fed.
129 D2 **Pinehouse Lake** Can.
111 B3 **Pineios** *r.* Greece
143 D3 **Pine Islands** *FL* U.S.A.
143 D4 **Pine Islands** *FL* U.S.A.
128 C1 **Pine Point** Can.
136 C2 **Pine Ridge** U.S.A.
108 A2 **Pinerolo** Italy
Pines, Isle of *i.* Cuba *see* **La Juventud, Isla de**
123 D2 **Pinetown** S. Africa
142 B2 **Pineville** U.S.A.
70 B2 **Pingdingshan** China
70 B2 **Pingdu** China

62 B1 Pingguo China
71 B3 Pingjiang China
70 A2 Pingliang China
70 B1 Pingquan China
71 C3 P'ingtung Taiwan
Pingxi China *see* Yuping
71 A3 Pingxiang *Guangxi* China
71 B3 Pingxiang *Jiangxi* China
70 B2 Pingyin China
155 C2 Pinhal Brazil
151 E3 Pinheiro Brazil
52 B3 Pinnaroo Austr.
101 D1 Pinneberg Ger.
Pinos, Isla de *i.* Cuba *see* La Juventud, Isla de
145 C3 Pinotepa Nacional Mex.
48 H6 Pins, Île des *i.* New Caledonia
88 C3 Pinsk Belarus
152 B2 Pinto Arg.
135 D3 Pioche U.S.A.
119 C3 Piodi Dem. Rep. Congo
108 B2 Piombino Italy
86 F2 Pionerskiy Rus. Fed.
103 E1 Pionki Pol.
103 D1 Piotrków Trybunalski Pol.
137 D2 Pipestone U.S.A.
131 C3 Pipmuacan, Réservoir *resr* Can.
154 B2 Piquiri *r.* Brazil
154 C1 Piracanjuba Brazil
154 C2 Piracicaba Brazil
155 D1 Piracicaba *r.* Brazil
154 C2 Piraçununga Brazil
Piraeus Greece *see* Peiraias
154 C2 Piraí do Sul Brazil
154 C2 Piraju Brazil
154 C2 Pirajuí Brazil
154 B1 Piranhas Brazil
151 F3 Piranhas *r.* Brazil
155 D1 Pirapora Brazil
154 C1 Pirenópolis Brazil
154 C1 Pires do Rio Brazil
Pirineos *mts* Europe *see* Pyrenees
151 E3 Piripiri Brazil
109 D2 Pirot Yugo.
59 C3 Piru Indon.
108 B2 Pisa Italy
152 A1 Pisagua Chile
150 B4 Pisco Peru
102 C2 Písek Czech Rep.
79 D2 Pīshīn Iran
74 A1 Pishin Pak.
145 D2 Pisté Mex.
109 C2 Pisticci Italy
108 B2 Pistoia Italy
106 C1 Pisuerga *r.* Spain
134 B2 Pit *r.* U.S.A.
114 A3 Pita Guinea
154 B2 Pitanga Brazil
155 D1 Pitangui Brazil
49 O6 Pitcairn Islands *terr.* S. Pacific Ocean
49 O6 Pitcairn Islands *terr.* S. Pacific Ocean
92 H2 Piteå Sweden
92 H2 Piteälven *r.* Sweden
110 B2 Pitești Romania
75 C2 Pithoragarh India
138 A2 Pitiquito Mex.
86 C2 Pitkyaranta Rus. Fed.
96 C2 Pitlochry U.K.
128 B2 Pitt Island Can.
137 E3 Pittsburg U.S.A.
140 D2 Pittsburgh U.S.A.
141 E2 Pittsfield U.S.A.
53 D1 Pittsworth Austr.
155 C2 Piumhí Brazil
150 A3 Piura Peru
90 C2 Pivdennyy Buh *r.* Ukr.
131 E3 Placentia Can.
135 B3 Placerville U.S.A.
146 C2 Placetas Cuba
139 C2 Plains U.S.A.
139 C2 Plainview U.S.A.
60 B2 Plaju Indon.
61 C2 Plampang Indon.
154 C1 Planaltina Brazil
137 D2 Plankinton U.S.A.
139 D2 Plano U.S.A.
154 C2 Planura Brazil
142 B2 Plaquemine U.S.A.
106 B1 Plasencia Spain
109 C1 Plaški Croatia
147 C4 Plato Col.
137 D2 Platte *r.* U.S.A.
140 A2 Platteville U.S.A.
141 E2 Plattsburgh U.S.A.
101 F1 Plau Ger.
101 F2 Plauen Ger.
101 F1 Plauer See *l.* Ger.
89 E3 Plavsk Rus. Fed.
106 B2 Playa de Castilla *coastal area* Spain
63 B2 Plây Cu Vietnam
129 E2 Playgreen Lake Can.
153 B3 Plaza Huincul Arg.
139 D3 Pleasanton U.S.A.
54 B2 Pleasant Point N.Z.
140 B3 Pleasure Ridge Park U.S.A.
104 C2 Pleaux France
130 B2 Pledger Lake Can.
54 C1 Plenty, Bay of *g.* N.Z.
136 C1 Plentywood U.S.A.
86 D2 Plesetsk Rus. Fed.
131 C2 Pletipi, Lac *l.* Can.
100 C2 Plettenberg Ger.
122 B3 Plettenberg Bay S. Africa
110 B2 Pleven Bulg.
Plevna Bulg. *see* Pleven
109 C2 Pljevlja Yugo.
108 A2 Ploaghe *Sardinia* Italy
109 C2 Ploče Croatia
103 D1 Płock Pol.
109 C2 Pločno *mt.* Bos.-Herz.
104 B2 Ploemeur France
Ploești Romania *see* Ploiești
110 C2 Ploiești Romania
89 F2 Ploskoye Rus. Fed.
104 B2 Plouzané France
110 B2 Plovdiv Bulg.
Plozk Pol. *see* Płock
121 B3 Plumtree Zimbabwe
88 B2 Plungė Lith.
144 B2 Plutarco Elías Calles, Presa *resr* Mex.
88 C3 Plyeshchanitsy Belarus
147 D3 Plymouth Montserrat
99 A4 Plymouth U.K.
140 B2 Plymouth U.S.A.
99 B3 Plynlimon *hill* U.K.
88 C2 Plyussa Rus. Fed.
102 C2 Plzeň Czech Rep.
114 B3 Pô Burkina
108 B1 Po *r.* Italy
61 C1 Po, Tanjong *pt* Malaysia
Pobeda Peak China/Kyrg. *see* Jengish Chokusu
Pobedy, Pik *mt.* China/Kyrg. *see* Jengish Chokusu
142 B1 Pocahontas U.S.A.
134 D2 Pocatello U.S.A.
90 B1 Pochayiv Ukr.
89 D3 Pochep Rus. Fed.
89 D3 Pochinok Rus. Fed.
145 C3 Pochutla Mex.
141 D3 Pocomoke City U.S.A.
155 C2 Poços de Caldas Brazil
89 D2 Poddor'ye Rus. Fed.
91 D1 Podgorenskiy Rus. Fed.
109 C2 Podgorica Yugo.
82 G3 Podgornoye Rus. Fed.
83 H2 Podkamennaya Tunguska *r.* Rus. Fed.
89 E2 Podol'sk Rus. Fed.
109 D2 Podujevo Yugo.
122 A2 Pofadder S. Africa
89 D3 Pogar Rus. Fed.
105 E3 Poggibonsi Italy
109 D2 Pogradec Albania
Po Hai *g.* China *see* Bo Hai
65 B2 P'ohang S. Korea
48 G3 Pohnpei *atoll* Micronesia
90 B2 Pohrebyshche Ukr.
110 B2 Poiana Mare Romania
118 C3 Poie Dem. Rep. Congo
118 B3 Pointe-Noire Congo
160 B3 Point Hope U.S.A.
128 C1 Point Lake Can.
140 C3 Point Pleasant U.S.A.
104 C2 Poitiers France
104 C2 Poitou, Plaines et Seuil du *plain* France
74 B2 Pokaran India
53 C1 Pokataroo Austr.
75 C2 Pokhara Nepal
119 C2 Poko Dem. Rep. Congo
83 J2 Pokrovsk Rus. Fed.
91 D2 Pokrovskoye Rus. Fed.
Pola Croatia *see* Pula
138 A1 Polacca U.S.A.
106 B1 Pola de Lena Spain
106 B1 Pola de Siero Spain
103 D1 Poland *country* Europe
55 C1 Polar Plateau Antarctica
80 B2 Polatlı Turkey
88 C2 Polatsk Belarus
77 C3 Pol-e Khomrī Afgh.
61 C2 Polewali Indon.
118 B2 Poli Cameroon
102 C1 Police Pol.
109 C2 Policoro Italy
105 D2 Poligny France
64 B2 Polillo Islands Phil.
80 B2 Polis Cyprus
90 B1 Polis'ke Ukr.
109 C3 Polistena Italy
103 D1 Polkowice Pol.
107 D2 Pollença Spain
109 C3 Pollino, Monte *mt.* Italy
86 F2 Polnovat Rus. Fed.
91 D2 Polohy Ukr.
90 B1 Polonne Ukr.
134 D1 Polson U.S.A.
91 C2 Poltava Ukr.
66 B2 Poltavka Rus. Fed.
91 D2 Poltavskaya Rus. Fed.
88 C2 Põltsamaa Estonia
88 C2 Põlva Estonia
Polyanovgrad Bulg. *see* Karnobat
92 J2 Polyarnyy Rus. Fed.
86 C2 Polyarnyye Zori Rus. Fed.
111 B2 Polygyros Greece
111 B2 Polykastro Greece
156 E6 Polynesia International Feature
106 B2 Pombal Port.
108 B2 Pomezia Italy
92 I2 Pomokaira *reg.* Fin.
110 C2 Pomorie Bulg.
102 C1 Pomorska, Zatoka *b.* Pol.
155 D1 Pompéu Brazil
139 D1 Ponca City U.S.A.
147 D3 Ponce Puerto Rico
73 B3 Pondicherry India
127 G2 Pond Inlet Can.
Ponds Bay Can. *see* Pond Inlet
106 B1 Ponferrada Spain
117 A4 Pongo *watercourse* Sudan
123 D2 Pongola *r.* S. Africa
123 D2 Pongolapoort Dam *l.* S. Africa
128 C2 Ponoka Can.
154 B3 Ponta Grossa Brazil
154 C1 Pontalina Brazil
105 D2 Pont-à-Mousson France
154 A2 Ponta Porã Brazil
105 D2 Pontarlier France
102 B2 Pontcharra France
142 B2 Pontchartrain, Lake U.S.A.
154 B1 Ponte de Pedra Brazil
106 B2 Ponte de Sor Port.
154 B1 Ponte do Rio Verde Brazil
98 C3 Pontefract U.K.
129 D3 Ponteix Can.
155 D2 Ponte Nova Brazil
150 D4 Pontes-e-Lacerda Brazil
106 B1 Pontevedra Spain
Ponthierville Dem. Rep. Congo *see* Ubundu
140 B2 Pontiac *IL* U.S.A.
140 C2 Pontiac *MI* U.S.A.
60 B2 Pontianak Indon.
Pontine Islands *is* Italy *see* Ponziane, Isole
104 B2 Pontivy France
151 D2 Pontoetoe Suriname
104 C2 Pontoise France
129 E2 Ponton Can.
99 B4 Pontypool U.K.
99 B4 Pontypridd U.K.
108 B2 Ponziane, Isole *is* Italy
99 C4 Poole U.K.
Poona India *see* Pune
52 B2 Pooncarie Austr.
152 B1 Poopó, Lago de *l.* Bol.
150 B2 Popayán Col.
83 I2 Popigay *r.* Rus. Fed.
52 B2 Popiltah *N.S.W.* Austr.
52 B2 Popiltah *N.S.W.* Austr.
129 E2 Poplar *r.* Can.
137 E3 Poplar Bluff U.S.A.
118 B3 Popokabaka Dem. Rep. Congo
Popovichskaya Rus. Fed. *see* Kalininskaya
110 C2 Popovo Bulg.
103 E2 Poprad Slovakia
151 E4 Porangatu Brazil
74 A2 Porbandar India
126 C2 Porcupine *r.* Can./U.S.A.
108 B1 Pordenone Italy
108 B1 Poreč Croatia
154 B2 Porecatu Brazil
114 C3 Porga Benin
93 H3 Pori Fin.
54 B2 Porirua N.Z.
88 C2 Porkhov Rus. Fed.
104 B2 Pornic France
83 K3 Poronaysk Rus. Fed.
Porong China *see* Baingoin
111 B3 Poros Greece
92 I1 Porsangen *sea chan.* Norway
93 E4 Porsgrunn Norway
111 D3 Porsuk *r.* Turkey
97 C1 Portadown U.K.
97 D1 Portaferry U.K.
140 B2 Portage U.S.A.
129 E3 Portage la Prairie Car
128 B3 Port Alberni Can.
106 B2 Portalegre Port.
139 C2 Portales U.S.A.
128 A2 Port Alexander U.S.A.
128 B2 Port Alice Can.
142 B2 Port Allen U.S.A.
134 B1 Port Angeles U.S.A.
97 C2 Portarlington Rep. of Ireland
51 D4 Port Arthur Austr.
Port Arthur China *see* Lushunkou
139 E3 Port Arthur U.S.A.
96 A3 Port Askaig U.K.
52 A2 Port Augusta Austr.
147 C3 Port-au-Prince Haiti
131 E2 Port aux Choix Can.
122 B3 Port Beaufort S. Africa
73 D3 Port Blair India
52 B3 Port Campbell Austr.
131 D2 Port-Cartier Can.
54 B3 Port Chalmers N.Z.
143 D3 Port Charlotte U.S.A.
147 C3 Port-de-Paix Haiti
128 A2 Port Edward Can.
155 D1 Porteirinha Brazil
151 D3 Portel Brazil
130 B3 Port Elgin Can.
123 C3 Port Elizabeth S. Afric
96 A3 Port Ellen U.K.
98 A2 Port Erin Isle of Man
122 A3 Porterville S. Africa
135 C3 Porterville U.S.A.
Port Étienne Maur. *see* Nouâdhibou
52 B3 Port Fairy Austr.
54 C1 Port Fitzroy N.Z.
Port Francqui Dem. Rep. Congo *see* Il
118 A3 Port-Gentil Gabon
115 C4 Port Harcourt Nigeria
128 B2 Port Hardy Can.
Port Harrison Can. *see* Inukjuak
131 D3 Port Hawkesbury Can.
99 B4 Porthcawl U.K.
50 A2 Port Hedland Austr.
Port Herald Malawi *see* Nsanje
99 A3 Porthmadog U.K.
131 E2 Port Hope Simpson C
140 C2 Port Huron U.S.A.
106 B2 Portimão Port.
Port Keats Austr. *see* Wadeye
Port Láirge Rep. of Irel *see* Waterford
53 C2 Portland *N.S.W.* Austr.
52 B3 Portland *Vic.* Austr.
141 E2 Portland *ME* U.S.A.
134 B1 Portland *OR* U.S.A.
139 D3 Portland *TX* U.S.A.
99 B4 Portland, Isle of *pen.* U
128 A2 Portland Canal *inlet* C
97 C2 Portlaoise Rep. of Irela
139 D3 Port Lavaca U.S.A.
52 A2 Port Lincoln Austr.
114 A4 Port Loko Sierra Leone
113 I8 Port Louis Mauritius
Port-Lyautrey Morocco *see* Kénitra
52 B3 Port MacDonnell Austr.
53 D2 Port Macquarie Austr.
Portmadoc U.K. *see* Porthmadog
128 B2 Port McNeill Can.
131 D3 Port-Menier Can.
59 D3 Port Moresby P.N.G.
96 A3 Portnahaven U.K.
96 A1 Port Nis U.K.
122 A2 Port Nolloth S. Africa
Port-Nouveau-Québec Can. *see* Kangiqsualujju
Porto Port. *see* Oporto

0 C3 **Porto Acre** Brazil
4 B2 **Porto Alegre** Brazil
2 C3 **Porto Alegre** Brazil
Porto Alexandre Angola *see* **Tombua**
Porto Amélia Moz. *see* Pemba
1 D4 **Porto Artur** Brazil
4 B2 **Porto Camargo** Brazil
1 D4 **Porto dos Gaúchos Óbidos** Brazil
0 D4 **Porto Esperidião** Brazil
8 B2 **Portoferraio** Italy
1 E3 **Porto Franco** Brazil
7 D3 **Port of Spain** Trin. and Tob.
8 B1 **Portogruaro** Italy
8 B2 **Portomaggiore** Italy
4 B2 **Porto Mendes** Brazil
2 C2 **Porto Murtinho** Brazil
1 E4 **Porto Nacional** Brazil
4 C4 **Porto-Novo** Benin
4 B2 **Porto Primavera, Represa** *resr* Brazil
4 B2 **Port Orford** U.S.A.
1 D3 **Porto Santana** Brazil
4 B2 **Porto São José** Brazil
8 A3 **Portoscuso** *Sardinia* Italy
5 E1 **Porto Seguro** Brazil
8 B2 **Porto Tolle** Italy
8 A2 **Porto Torres** *Sardinia* Italy
4 B3 **Porto União** Brazil
5 D3 **Porto-Vecchio** *Corsica* France
0 C3 **Porto Velho** Brazil
0 A3 **Portoviejo** Ecuador
6 B3 **Portpatrick** U.K.
2 B3 **Port Phillip Bay** Austr.
2 A2 **Port Pirie** Austr.
6 A2 **Portree** U.K.
8 B3 **Port Renfrew** Can.
7 C1 **Portrush** U.K.
6 B1 **Port Said** Egypt
3 C3 **Port St Joe** U.S.A.
3 C3 **Port St Johns** S. Africa
3 D3 **Port Saint Lucie City** U.S.A.
3 D3 **Port Shepstone** S. Africa
9 C4 **Portsmouth** U.K.
1 E2 **Portsmouth** *NH* U.S.A.
0 C3 **Portsmouth** *OH* U.S.A.
1 D3 **Portsmouth** *VA* U.S.A.
3 B5 **Port Stephens** Falkland Is
7 C1 **Portstewart** U.K.
6 B3 **Port Sudan** Sudan
2 C3 **Port Sulphur** U.S.A.
9 B4 **Port Talbot** U.K.
4 B1 **Port Townsend** U.S.A.
6 B2 **Portugal** *country* Europe
Portugália Angola *see* **Chitato**
Portuguese Guinea *country* Africa *see* **Guinea-Bissau**
Portuguese Timor *terr.* Asia *see* **East Timor**
Portuguese West Africa *country* Africa *see* **Angola**
7 B2 **Portumna** Rep. of Ireland
5 C3 **Port-Vendres** France
8 H5 **Port Vila** Vanuatu
2 A2 **Port Wakefield** Austr.
0 B1 **Port Warrender** Austr.
3 A5 **Porvenir** Chile
3 I3 **Porvoo** Fin.
5 B2 **Poryŏng** S. Korea
2 C2 **Posadas** Arg.
9 E2 **Poshekhon'ye** Rus. Fed.
Poshekhon'ye-Volodarsk Rus. Fed. *see* Poshekhon'ye
2 I2 **Posio** Fin.
1 D2 **Poso** Indon.
1 E4 **Posse** Brazil
1 E2 **Pößneck** Ger.
9 C2 **Post** U.S.A.
Poste-de-la-Baleine Can. *see* **Kuujjuarapik**
2 B2 **Postmasburg** S. Africa
8 B1 **Postojna** Slovenia
4 C2 **Post Weygand** Alg.
Postysheve Ukr. *see* Krasnoarmiys'k
9 C2 **Posušje** Bos.-Herz.
3 C2 **Potchefstroom** S. Africa
9 E1 **Poteau** U.S.A.
9 C2 **Potenza** Italy
8 B2 **Potenza** *r.* Italy
3 C1 **Potgietersrus** S. Africa
1 E3 **Poti** *r.* Brazil
1 C1 **P'ot'i** Georgia
155 E1 **Potiraguá** Brazil
115 D3 **Potiskum** Nigeria
141 D3 **Potomac, South Branch** *r.* U.S.A.
152 B1 **Potosí** Bol.
64 B2 **Pototan** Phil.
138 C3 **Potrero del Llano** Mex.
101 F1 **Potsdam** Ger.
141 E2 **Potsdam** U.S.A.
141 D2 **Pottstown** U.S.A.
141 D2 **Pottsville** U.S.A.
131 E3 **Pouch Cove** Can.
141 E2 **Poughkeepsie** U.S.A.
98 B3 **Poulton-le-Fylde** U.K.
155 C2 **Pouso Alegre** Brazil
63 B2 **Poŭthĭsăt** Cambodia
103 D2 **Považská Bystrica** Slovakia
109 C2 **Povlen** *mt.* Yugo.
106 B1 **Póvoa de Varzim** Port.
136 B2 **Powell** U.S.A.
135 D3 **Powell, Lake** *resr* U.S.A.
128 B3 **Powell River** Can.
154 B1 **Poxoréu** Brazil
Poyang China *see* **Boyang**
71 B3 **Poyang Hu** *l.* China
109 D2 **Požarevac** Yugo.
145 C2 **Poza Rica** Mex.
109 C1 **Požega** Croatia
109 D2 **Požega** Yugo.
79 D2 **Pozm Tīāb** Iran
103 D1 **Poznań** Pol.
106 C2 **Pozoblanco** Spain
152 C2 **Pozo Colorado** Para.
109 B3 **Pozzallo** *Sicily* Italy
108 B2 **Pozzuoli** Italy
60 B2 **Prabumulih** Indon.
102 C2 **Prachatice** Czech Rep.
63 A2 **Prachuap Khiri Khan** Thai.
103 D1 **Praděd** *mt.* Czech Rep.
104 C3 **Prades** France
155 E1 **Prado** Brazil
102 C1 **Prague** Czech Rep.
Praha Czech Rep. *see* Prague
139 C2 **Prairie Dog Town Fork** *r.* U.S.A.
140 A2 **Prairie du Chien** U.S.A.
60 A1 **Prapat** Indon.
154 C1 **Prata** Brazil
108 B2 **Prato** Italy
137 D3 **Pratt** U.S.A.
142 C2 **Prattville** U.S.A.
61 C2 **Praya** Indon.
63 B2 **Preăh Vihear** Cambodia
89 F2 **Prechistoye** Rus. Fed.
129 D2 **Preeceville** Can.
88 C2 **Preiļi** Latvia
53 C2 **Premer** Austr.
105 C2 **Prémery** France
101 F1 **Premnitz** Ger.
102 C1 **Prenzlau** Ger.
66 B2 **Preobrazheniye** Rus. Fed.
63 A2 **Preparis Island** Cocos Is
63 A2 **Preparis North Channel** Cocos Is
63 A2 **Preparis South Channel** Cocos Is
103 D2 **Přerov** Czech Rep.
138 A2 **Prescott** U.S.A.
138 A2 **Prescott Valley** U.S.A.
109 D2 **Preševo** Yugo.
152 B2 **Presidencia Roque Sáenz Peña** Arg.
151 E3 **Presidente Dutra** Brazil
154 B2 **Presidente Epitácio** Brazil
154 B1 **Presidente Murtinho** Brazil
155 C1 **Presidente Olegário** Brazil
154 B2 **Presidente Prudente** Brazil
138 C3 **Presidio** U.S.A.
103 E2 **Prešov** Slovakia
111 B2 **Prespa, Lake** Europe
141 F1 **Presque Isle** U.S.A.
Pressburg Slovakia *see* Bratislava
101 F2 **Pressel** Ger.
98 B3 **Preston** U.K.
134 D2 **Preston** U.S.A.
96 B3 **Prestwick** U.K.
155 C1 **Preto** *r.* Brazil
123 C2 **Pretoria** S. Africa
Pretoria-Witwatersrand-Vereeniging *prov.* S. Africa *see* **Gauteng**
111 B3 **Preveza** Greece
63 B2 **Prey Vêng** Cambodia
124 A4 **Pribilof Islands** U.S.A.
109 C2 **Priboj** Yugo.
135 D3 **Price** U.S.A.
142 C2 **Prichard** U.S.A.
106 C2 **Priego de Córdoba** Spain
88 B3 **Prienai** Lith.
122 B2 **Prieska** S. Africa
103 D2 **Prievidza** Slovakia
109 C2 **Prijedor** Bos.-Herz.
109 C2 **Prijepolje** Yugo.
76 A2 **Prikaspiyskaya Nizmennost'** *lowland* Kazakh./Rus. Fed.
111 B2 **Prilep** Macedonia
101 F3 **Přimda** Czech Rep.
91 D2 **Primorsko-Akhtarsk** Rus. Fed.
129 D2 **Primrose Lake** Can.
129 D2 **Prince Albert** Can.
122 B3 **Prince Albert** S. Africa
126 E2 **Prince Albert Peninsula** Can.
122 B3 **Prince Albert Road** S. Africa
126 D2 **Prince Alfred, Cape** Can.
122 A3 **Prince Alfred Hamlet** S. Africa
127 G2 **Prince Charles Island** Can.
55 H2 **Prince Charles Mountains** Antarctica
131 D3 **Prince Edward Island** *prov.* Can.
128 B2 **Prince George** Can.
51 D1 **Prince of Wales Island** Austr.
126 F2 **Prince of Wales Island** Can.
128 A2 **Prince of Wales Island** U.S.A.
126 E2 **Prince of Wales Strait** Can.
126 E1 **Prince Patrick Island** Can.
126 F2 **Prince Regent Inlet** *sea chan.* Can.
128 A2 **Prince Rupert** Can.
51 D1 **Princess Charlotte Bay** Austr.
55 H2 **Princess Elizabeth Land** *reg.* Antarctica
128 B2 **Princess Royal Island** Can.
128 B3 **Princeton** Can.
140 B3 **Princeton** *IN* U.S.A.
137 E2 **Princeton** *MO* U.S.A.
134 B2 **Prineville** U.S.A.
86 C2 **Priozersk** Rus. Fed.
Pripet *r.* Belarus *see* Prypyats'
90 A1 **Pripet Marshes** Belarus/Ukr.
109 D2 **Priština** Yugo.
101 F1 **Pritzwalk** Ger.
105 C3 **Privas** France
109 C2 **Privlaka** Croatia
89 F2 **Privolzhsk** Rus. Fed.
109 D2 **Prizren** Yugo.
151 D2 **Professor van Blommestein Meer** *resr* Suriname
146 B3 **Progreso** Hond.
145 D2 **Progreso** Mex.
81 C1 **Prokhladnyy** Rus. Fed.
109 D2 **Prokuplje** Yugo.
Prome Myanmar *see* **Pyè**
154 C2 **Promissão** Brazil
154 C2 **Promissão, Represa** *resr* Brazil
126 D3 **Prophet** *r.* Can.
128 B2 **Prophet River** Can.
51 D2 **Proserpine** Austr.
Proskurov Ukr. *see* **Khmel'nyts'kyy**
103 D2 **Prostějov** Czech Rep.
89 E3 **Protvino** Rus. Fed.
110 C2 **Provadiya** Bulg.
105 D3 **Provence** *reg.* France
141 E2 **Providence** U.S.A.
146 B3 **Providencia, Isla de** *i.* Caribbean Sea
83 N2 **Provideniya** Rus. Fed.
105 C2 **Provins** France
135 D2 **Provo** U.S.A.
129 C2 **Provost** Can.
91 C2 **Prubiynyy, Mys** *pt* Ukr.
154 B3 **Prudentópolis** Brazil
126 C2 **Prudhoe Bay** U.S.A.
100 C2 **Prüm** Ger.
105 D3 **Prunelli-di-Fiumorbo** *Corsica* France
103 D1 **Pruszcz Gdański** Pol.
103 E1 **Pruszków** Pol.
110 C1 **Prut** *r.* Europe
88 B3 **Pruzhany** Belarus
91 D2 **Pryazovs'ke** Ukr.
91 C1 **Pryluky** Ukr.
91 D2 **Prymors'k** Ukr.
91 D2 **Prymors'kyy** Ukr.
139 D1 **Pryor** U.S.A.
90 B1 **Prypyats'** *r.* Belarus/Ukr.
103 E2 **Przemyśl** Pol.
103 E1 **Przeworsk** Pol.
Przheval'sk Kyrg. *see* Karakol
111 C3 **Psara** *i.* Greece
81 C1 **Psebay** Rus. Fed.
91 D3 **Pshekha** *r.* Rus. Fed.
88 C2 **Pskov** Rus. Fed.
88 C2 **Pskov, Lake** Estonia/Rus. Fed.
111 B2 **Ptolemaïda** Greece
109 C1 **Ptuj** Slovenia
150 B3 **Pucallpa** Peru
71 B3 **Pucheng** China
65 B2 **Puch'ŏn** S. Korea
103 D1 **Puck** Pol.
92 I2 **Pudasjärvi** Fin.
86 C2 **Pudozh** Rus. Fed.
Puduchcheri India *see* Pondicherry
145 C3 **Puebla** Mex.
136 C3 **Pueblo** U.S.A.
153 B3 **Puelén** Arg.
153 A3 **Puente Alto** Chile
106 C2 **Puente-Genil** Spain
153 A4 **Puerto Aisén** Chile
152 B1 **Puerto Alegre** Bol.
145 C3 **Puerto Ángel** Mex.
146 B4 **Puerto Armuelles** Panama
150 C2 **Puerto Ayacucho** Venez.
146 B3 **Puerto Barrios** Guat.
146 B3 **Puerto Cabezas** Nic.
153 A4 **Puerto Cisnes** Chile
144 A2 **Puerto Cortés** Mex.
145 C3 **Puerto Escondido** Mex.
152 B1 **Puerto Frey** Bol.
150 C2 **Puerto Inírida** Col.
152 C1 **Puerto Isabel** Bol.
150 B3 **Puerto Leguízamo** Col.
146 B3 **Puerto Lempira** Hond.
144 A2 **Puerto Libertad** Mex.
106 C2 **Puertollano** Spain
153 B4 **Puerto Madryn** Arg.
150 C4 **Puerto Maldonado** Peru
Puerto México Mex. *see* Coatzacoalcos
147 D4 **Puerto Miranda** Venez.
153 A4 **Puerto Montt** Chile
153 A5 **Puerto Natáles** Chile
150 C2 **Puerto Nuevo** Col.
150 C2 **Puerto Páez** Venez.
144 A1 **Puerto Peñasco** Mex.
152 C2 **Puerto Pinasco** Para.
147 C3 **Puerto Plata** Dom. Rep.
150 B3 **Puerto Portillo** Peru
Puerto Presidente Stroessner Para. *see* **Ciudad del Este**
64 A3 **Puerto Princesa** Phil.
154 A3 **Puerto Rico** Arg.
147 D3 **Puerto Rico** *terr.* West Indies
158 C3 **Puerto Rico Trench** *sea feature* Caribbean Sea
153 B5 **Puerto Santa Cruz** Arg.
152 C2 **Puerto Sastre** Para.
144 B2 **Puerto Vallarta** Mex.
87 D3 **Pugachev** Rus. Fed.
74 B2 **Pugal** India
54 B2 **Pukaki, Lake** N.Z.
49 K5 **Pukapuka** *atoll* Cook Is
129 D2 **Pukatawagan** Can.
65 B1 **Pukchin** N. Korea
65 B1 **Pukch'ŏng** N. Korea
109 C2 **Pukë** Albania
54 B1 **Pukekohe** N.Z.
65 B1 **Puksubaek-san** *mt.* N. Korea
Pula China *see* **Nyingchi**
108 B2 **Pula** Croatia
108 A3 **Pula** *Sardinia* Italy
152 B2 **Pulacayo** Bol.
103 E1 **Puławy** Pol.
92 I3 **Pulkkila** Fin.
134 C1 **Pullman** U.S.A.
64 B2 **Pulog, Mount** Phil.
64 B3 **Pulutan** Indon.
150 A3 **Puná, Isla** *i.* Ecuador
152 B2 **Puna de Atacama** *plat.* Arg.
54 B2 **Punakaiki** N.Z.
123 D1 **Punda Maria** S. Africa

Pune

73 B3 Pune India
65 B1 P'ungsan N. Korea
121 C2 Púnguè r. Moz.
119 C3 Punia Dem. Rep. Congo
74 B1 Punjab state India
153 B3 Punta Alta Arg.
153 A5 Punta Arenas Chile
108 A2 Punta Balestrieri mt. Sardinia Italy
146 B3 Punta Gorda Belize
146 B3 Puntarenas Costa Rica
150 B1 Punto Fijo Venez.
92 I3 Puolanka Fin.
70 B3 Puqi China
82 G2 Pur r. Rus. Fed.
75 C3 Puri India
100 B1 Purmerend Neth.
 Purnea India see Pūrnia
75 C2 Pūrnia India
75 C2 Puruliya India
150 C3 Purus r. Peru
61 B2 Purwakarta Indon.
61 C2 Purwodadi Indon.
65 B1 Puryŏng N. Korea
74 B3 Pusad India
65 B2 Pusan S. Korea
89 E3 Pushchino Rus. Fed.
 Pushkino Azer. see Biläsuvar
89 E2 Pushkino Rus. Fed.
88 C2 Pushkinskiye Gory Rus. Fed.
88 C2 Pustoshka Rus. Fed.
62 A1 Putao Myanmar
71 B3 Putian China
 Puting China see De'an
61 C2 Puting, Tanjung pt Indon.
101 F1 Putlitz Ger.
60 B1 Putrajaya Malaysia
122 B2 Putsonderwater S. Africa
102 C1 Puttgarden Ger.
150 B3 Putumayo r. Col.
61 C1 Putusibau Indon.
90 B2 Putyla Ukr.
91 C1 Putyvl' Ukr.
93 I3 Puula l. Fin.
130 C1 Puvurnituq Can.
70 B2 Puyang China
104 C3 Puylaurens France
119 C3 Pweto Dem. Rep. Congo
99 A3 Pwllheli U.K.
92 J2 Pyaozerskiy Rus. Fed.
63 A2 Pyapon Myanmar
83 G2 Pyasina r. Rus. Fed.
87 D4 Pyatigorsk Rus. Fed.
91 C2 P"yatykhatky Ukr.
62 A2 Pyè Myanmar
88 C3 Pyetrykaw Belarus
93 H3 Pyhäjärvi l. Fin.
92 H3 Pyhäjoki r. Fin.
92 I3 Pyhäsalmi Fin.
62 A1 Pyingaing Myanmar
62 A2 Pyinmana Myanmar
65 B2 Pyŏksŏng N. Korea
65 B2 P'yŏnggang N. Korea
65 B2 P'yŏngsong N. Korea
65 B2 P'yŏngt'aek S. Korea
65 B2 P'yŏngyang N. Korea
135 C2 Pyramid Lake U.S.A.
107 D1 Pyrenees mts Europe
 Pyrénées mts Europe see Pyrenees
111 B3 Pyrgetos Greece
111 C3 Pyrgi Greece
111 B3 Pyrgos Greece
91 C1 Pyryatyn Ukr.
103 C1 Pyrzyce Pol.
88 C2 Pytalovo Rus. Fed.
62 A2 Pyu Myanmar
111 B3 Pyxaria mt. Greece

Q

127 H1 Qaanaaq Greenland
 Qabqa China see Gonghe
123 C3 Qacha's Nek Lesotho
69 D2 Qagan Nur China
 Qahremänshahr Iran see Kermänshäh
68 C2 Qaidam Pendi basin China
74 A1 Qaisar, Koh-i- mt. Afgh.
79 C2 Qalamat Abū Shafrah Saudi Arabia
77 C3 Qalāt Afgh.
78 A2 Qal'at al Azlam Saudi Arabia
78 A2 Qal'at al Mu'azzam Saudi Arabia

78 B2 Qal'at Bishah Saudi Arabia
76 C3 Qal 'eh-ye Now Afgh.
129 E1 Qamanirjuaq Lake Can.
 Qamanittuaq Can. see Baker Lake
79 C3 Qamar, Ghubbat al b. Yemen
68 C2 Qamdo China
78 B3 Qam Hadīl Saudi Arabia
127 I2 Qaqortoq Greenland
80 A3 Qara Egypt
 Qarkilik China see Ruoqiang
 Qarqan China see Qiemo
78 B2 Qaryat al Ulyā Saudi Arabia
127 I2 Qasigiannguit Greenland
79 D2 Qasr-e-Qand Iran
81 C2 Qaşr-e Shīrīn Iran
116 A2 Qasr Farafra Egypt
127 I2 Qassimiut Greenland
78 B3 Qa'tabah Yemen
79 C2 Qatar country Asia
116 A2 Qattâra Depression Egypt
76 B3 Qâyen Iran
81 C1 Qazax Azer.
81 C1 Qazimämmäd Azer.
81 C2 Qazvīn Iran
116 B2 Qena Egypt
127 I2 Qeqertarsuaq Greenland
127 I2 Qeqertarsuaq i. Greenland
127 I2 Qeqertarsuatsiaat Greenland
127 I2 Qeqertarsuup Tunua b. Greenland
79 C2 Qeshm Iran
70 A3 Qianjiang Chongqing China
70 B2 Qianjiang Hubei China
69 E1 Qianjin China
65 A1 Qian Shan mts China
71 A3 Qianxi China
70 C2 Qidong China
77 E3 Qiemo China
71 A3 Qijiang China
68 C2 Qijiaojing China
127 H2 Qikiqtarjuaq Can.
74 A2 Qila Ladgasht Pak.
68 B2 Qilian Shan mts China
127 J2 Qillak i. Greenland
70 B3 Qimen China
127 H1 Qimusseriarsuaq b. Greenland
 Qincheng China see Nanfeng
70 C2 Qingdao China
68 C2 Qinghai Hu salt l. China
68 C2 Qinghai Nanshan mts China
 Qingjiang China see Huaiyin
 Qingjiang China see Zhangshu
70 B2 Qingshuihe China
70 A2 Qingtongxia China
70 A2 Qingyang China
71 B3 Qingyuan Guangdong China
 Qingyuan China see Yizhou
65 A1 Qingyuan Liaoning China
68 B2 Qing Zang Gaoyuan plat. China
70 B2 Qingzhou China
70 B2 Qinhuangdao China
 Qinjiang China see Shicheng
70 A2 Qin Ling mts China
 Qinting China see Lianhua
71 B3 Qinyang China
71 A3 Qinzhou China
70 B2 Qionghai China
71 A4 Qionglai Shan mts China
71 A4 Qiongshan China
71 A4 Qiongzhong China
69 E1 Qiqihar China
81 D3 Qīr Iran
 Qishan China see Qimen
79 C3 Qishn Yemen
66 B1 Qitaihe China
70 B2 Qixian Henan China
70 B2 Qixian Shanxi China
 Qogir Feng mt. China/Jammu and Kashmir see K2
81 D2 Qom Iran
81 D2 Qomishēh Iran
 Qomolangma Feng mt. China/Nepal see Everest, Mount

 Qoqek China see Tacheng
80 B2 Qornet es Saouda mt. Lebanon
81 C2 Qorveh Iran
79 C2 Qotbābād Iran
101 C1 Quakenbrück Ger.
53 C2 Quambone Austr.
63 B2 Quang Ngai Vietnam
63 B2 Quang Tri Vietnam
 Quan Long Vietnam see Ca Mau
 Quan Phu Quoc i. Vietnam see Phu Quôc, Đao
71 B3 Quanzhou Fujian China
71 B3 Quanzhou Guangxi China
108 A3 Quartu Sant'Elena Sardinia Italy
138 A2 Quartzsite U.S.A.
81 C1 Quba Azer.
76 B3 Quchan Iran
53 C3 Queanbeyan Austr.
131 C3 Québec Can.
131 C2 Québec prov. Can.
101 E2 Quedlinburg Ger.
 Queen Adelaide Islands Chile see La Reina Adelaida, Archipiélago de
128 A2 Queen Charlotte Can.
128 A2 Queen Charlotte Islands Can.
128 B2 Queen Charlotte Sound sea chan. Can.
128 B2 Queen Charlotte Strait Can.
126 E1 Queen Elizabeth Islands Can.
55 I2 Queen Mary Land reg. Antarctica
126 F2 Queen Maud Gulf Can.
55 E2 Queen Maud Land reg. Antarctica
55 P1 Queen Maud Mountains Antarctica
52 B3 Queenscliff Austr.
52 B1 Queensland state Austr.
51 D4 Queenstown Austr.
54 A3 Queenstown N.Z.
 Queenstown Rep. of Ireland see Cóbh
123 C3 Queenstown S. Africa
121 C2 Quelimane Moz.
153 A4 Quellón Chile
 Quelpart Island S. Korea see Cheju-do
138 B2 Quemado U.S.A.
 Que Que Zimbabwe see Kwekwe
154 B2 Queréncia do Norte Brazil
145 B2 Querétaro Mex.
101 E2 Querfurt Ger.
128 B2 Quesnel Can.
128 B2 Quesnel Lake Can.
74 A1 Quetta Pak.
146 A3 Quezaltenango Guat.
64 A3 Quezon Phil.
64 B2 Quezon City Phil.
120 A2 Quibala Angola
150 B2 Quibdó Col.
104 B2 Quiberon France
120 A2 Quilengues Angola
104 C3 Quillan France
153 C5 Quilmes Arg.
73 B4 Quilon India
51 D2 Quilpie Austr.
153 A3 Quilpué Chile
120 A1 Quimbele Angola
152 B2 Quimili Arg.
104 B2 Quimper France
104 B2 Quimperlé France
135 B3 Quincy CA U.S.A.
143 D2 Quincy FL U.S.A.
137 E3 Quincy IL U.S.A.
141 E2 Quincy MA U.S.A.
63 B2 Qui Nhon Vietnam
107 C1 Quinto Spain
121 D2 Quionga Moz.
120 A2 Quirima Angola
53 D2 Quirindi Austr.
154 B1 Quirinópolis Brazil
131 D3 Quispamsis Can.
120 A2 Quissico Moz.
120 A2 Quitapa Angola
150 B3 Quito Ecuador
151 F3 Quixadá Brazil
71 A3 Qujing China
75 D1 Qumar He r. China
123 C3 Qumrha S. Africa
115 E1 Qunayyin, Sabkhat al salt marsh Libya

129 E1 Quoich r. Can.
52 A2 Quorn Austr.
79 C2 Qurayat Oman
77 C3 Qŭrghonteppa Tajik.
116 B2 Quseir Egypt
 Quxar China see Lhazê
 Quyang China see Jingzhou
71 B3 Quzhou China
 Qyteti Stalin Albania see Kuçovë
 Qyzyltū Kazakh. see Kishkenekol'

R

103 D2 Raab r. Austria
92 H3 Raahe Fin.
100 C1 Raalte Neth.
61 C2 Raas i. Indon.
61 C2 Raba Indon.
114 B1 Rabat Morocco
59 E3 Rabaul P.N.G.
50 C2 Rabbit Flat Austr.
78 A2 Rābigh Saudi Arabia
103 D2 Rabka Pol.
90 B2 Răbniţa Moldova
 Rabyānah, Ramlat des. Libya see Rebiana Sand Sea
131 E3 Race, Cape Can.
142 B3 Raceland U.S.A.
141 E2 Race Point U.S.A.
63 B3 Rach Gia Vietnam
103 D1 Racibórz Pol.
140 B2 Racine U.S.A.
78 B3 Radā' Yemen
110 C1 Rădăuți Romania
140 B3 Radcliff U.S.A.
74 B2 Radhanpur India
130 C2 Radisson Can.
103 E1 Radom Pol.
103 D1 Radomsko Pol.
90 B1 Radomyshl' Ukr.
111 B2 Radoviš Macedonia
88 B2 Radviliškis Lith.
78 A2 Radwá, Jabal mt. Saudi Arabia
90 B1 Radyvyliv Ukr.
75 C2 Rae Bareli India
128 C1 Rae-Edzo Can.
128 C1 Rae Lakes Can.
100 C2 Raeren Belgium
54 C1 Raetihi N.Z.
78 A2 Rāf hill Saudi Arabia
152 B3 Rafaela Arg.
118 C2 Rafaï C.A.R.
78 B2 Rafhā' Saudi Arabia
79 C1 Rafsanjān Iran
119 C2 Raga Sudan
64 B3 Ragang, Mount vol. Phil
109 B3 Ragusa Sicily Italy
61 D2 Raha Indon.
88 D3 Rahachow Belarus
78 A3 Rahad r. Sudan
74 B2 Rahimyar Khan Pak.
73 B3 Raichur India
75 C2 Raigarh India
128 C2 Rainbow Lake Can.
134 B1 Rainier, Mount vol. U.S.A.
130 A3 Rainy Lake Can.
129 E3 Rainy River Can.
75 C2 Raipur India
93 H3 Raisio Fin.
88 C2 Raja Estonia
73 C3 Rajahmundry India
61 C1 Rajang r. Sarawak Malays
74 B2 Rajanpur Pak.
73 B4 Rajapalaiyam India
74 B2 Rajasthan state India
74 B2 Rajasthan Canal canal India
74 B2 Rajgarh India
60 B2 Rajik Indon.
74 B2 Rajkot India
75 C2 Raj Nandgaon India
74 B2 Rajpur India
75 C2 Rajshahi Bangl.
54 C2 Rakaia r. N.Z.
74 B1 Rakaposhi mt. Jammu and Kashmir
90 A2 Rakhiv Ukr.
91 D1 Rakitnoye Rus. Fed.
88 C2 Rakke Estonia
88 C2 Rakvere Estonia
143 E1 Raleigh U.S.A.
48 H3 Ralik Chain is Marshall Is
75 C2 Ramanuj Ganj India

3 C2 **Ramatlabama** S. Africa
4 C2 **Rambouillet** France
9 A4 **Rame Head** *hd* U.K.
7 C1 **Ramelton** Rep. of Ireland
9 E2 **Rameshki** Rus. Fed.
4 B2 **Ramgarh** India
1 C2 **Rāmhormoz** Iran
8 B3 **Ramlat Dahm** *des.* Saudi Arabia/Yemen
0 C1 **Râmnicu Sărat** Romania
0 B1 **Râmnicu Vâlcea** Romania
9 E3 **Ramon'** Rus. Fed.
5 C4 **Ramona** U.S.A.
3 C1 **Ramotswa** Botswana
5 B2 **Rampur** India
2 A2 **Ramree Island** Myanmar
8 A2 **Ramsey** Isle of Man
0 B3 **Ramsey Lake** Can.
9 D4 **Ramsgate** U.K.
1 C2 **Rāmshir** Iran
2 A1 **Ramsing** India
5 C2 **Ranaghat** India
1 C1 **Ranau** *Sabah* Malaysia
3 A3 **Rancagua** Chile
4 B2 **Rancharia** Brazil
5 C2 **Ranchi** India
3 F4 **Randers** Denmark
3 B3 **Rangae** Thai.
5 D2 **Rangapara North** India
4 B2 **Rangiora** N.Z.
9 M5 **Rangiroa** *atoll* Fr. Polynesia
4 C1 **Rangitaiki** *r.* N.Z.
0 B2 **Rangkasbitung** Indon.
Rangoon Myanmar *see* **Yangôn**
5 C2 **Rangpur** Bangl.
29 E1 **Rankin Inlet** Can.
3 C2 **Rankin's Springs** Austr.
Rankovićevo Yugo. *see* **Kraljevo**
6 B2 **Rannoch Moor** *moorland* U.K.
4 B2 **Rann of Kachchh** *marsh* India
3 A3 **Ranong** Thai.
9 C3 **Ransiki** Indon.
1 C2 **Rantaupanjang** Indon.
0 A1 **Rantauprapat** Indon.
1 C2 **Rantepao** Indon.
2 I2 **Ranua** Fin.
3 E4 **Ranum** Denmark
8 B2 **Ranyah, Wādī** *watercourse* Saudi Arabia
49 J6 **Raoul Island** Kermadec Is
49 M6 **Rapa** *i.* Fr. Polynesia
08 A2 **Rapallo** Italy
36 C2 **Rapid City** U.S.A.
38 B2 **Rapla** Estonia
4 A2 **Rapur** India
49 L6 **Rarotonga** *i.* Cook Is
53 B4 **Rasa, Punta** *pt* Arg.
Ras al Khaimah U.A.E. *see* **Ra's al Khaymah**
79 C2 **Ra's al Khaymah** U.A.E.
16 B3 **Ras Dashen** *mt.* Eth.
38 B2 **Raseiniai** Lith.
16 B2 **Râs Ghârib** Egypt
31 C2 **Rasht** Iran
4 A2 **Ras Koh** *mt.* Pak.
10 C1 **Râşnov** Romania
38 C2 **Rasony** Belarus
79 C2 **Ra's Şirāb** Oman
08 B3 **Rass Jebel** Tunisia
37 D3 **Rasskazovo** Rus. Fed.
79 C2 **Ras Tannūrah** Saudi Arabia
01 D1 **Rastede** Ger.
48 I2 **Ratak Chain** *is* Marshall Is
93 F3 **Rätan** Sweden
23 C2 **Ratanda** S. Africa
74 B2 **Ratangarh** India
63 A2 **Rat Buri** Thai.
62 A1 **Rathedaung** Myanmar
01 F1 **Rathenow** Ger.
97 C1 **Rathfriland** U.K.
97 C1 **Rathlin Island** U.K.
97 B2 **Rathluirc** Rep. of Ireland
00 C2 **Ratingen** Ger.
74 B2 **Ratlam** India
73 B3 **Ratnagiri** India
73 C4 **Ratnapura** Sri Lanka
90 A1 **Ratne** Ukr.
38 C1 **Raton** U.S.A.
96 D2 **Rattray Head** *hd* U.K.
93 G3 **Rättvik** Sweden
01 E1 **Ratzeburg** Ger.
78 B2 **Raudhatain** Kuwait
92 □B2 **Raufarhöfn** Iceland
54 C1 **Raukumara Range** *mts* N.Z.
93 H3 **Rauma** Fin.
88 C2 **Rauna** Latvia
61 C2 **Raung, Gunung** *vol.* Indon.
75 C2 **Raurkela** India
66 D2 **Rausu** Japan
90 B2 **Răut** *r.* Moldova
134 D1 **Ravalli** U.S.A.
81 C2 **Ravānsar** Iran
108 B2 **Ravenna** Italy
102 B2 **Ravensburg** Ger.
50 B3 **Ravensthorpe** Austr.
74 B1 **Ravi** *r.* Pak.
74 B1 **Rawalpindi** Pak.
103 D1 **Rawicz** Pol.
50 B3 **Rawlinna** Austr.
136 B2 **Rawlins** U.S.A.
153 B4 **Rawson** Arg.
75 C3 **Rāyagarha** India
69 E1 **Raychikhinsk** Rus. Fed.
78 B3 **Raydah** Yemen
87 E3 **Rayevskiy** Rus. Fed.
134 B1 **Raymond** U.S.A.
53 D2 **Raymond Terrace** Austr.
139 D3 **Raymondville** U.S.A.
129 D2 **Raymore** Can.
145 C2 **Rayón** Mex.
63 B2 **Rayong** Thai.
78 A2 **Rayyis** Saudi Arabia
104 B2 **Raz, Pointe du** *pt* France
81 C2 **Razāzah, Buḩayrat ar** *l.* Iraq
110 C2 **Razgrad** Bulg.
110 C2 **Razim, Lacul** *lag.* Romania
111 B2 **Razlog** Bulg.
Raz"yezd 3km Rus. Fed. *see* **Novyy Urgal**
104 B2 **Ré, Île de** *i.* France
99 C4 **Reading** U.K.
140 C3 **Reading** *OH* U.S.A.
141 D2 **Reading** *PA* U.S.A.
123 C2 **Reagile** S. Africa
115 E2 **Rebiana Sand Sea** *des.* Libya
66 D1 **Rebun-tō** *i.* Japan
50 B3 **Recherche, Archipelago of the** *is* Austr.
89 D3 **Rechytsa** Belarus
151 F3 **Recife** Brazil
123 C3 **Recife, Cape** S. Africa
100 C2 **Recklinghausen** Ger.
152 C2 **Reconquista** Arg.
137 D1 **Red** *r.* Can./U.S.A.
142 B2 **Red** *r.* U.S.A.
100 B3 **Redange** Lux.
143 C1 **Red Bank** U.S.A.
Red Basin China *see* **Sichuan Pendi**
131 E2 **Red Bay** Can.
135 B2 **Red Bluff** U.S.A.
98 C2 **Redcar** U.K.
129 C2 **Redcliff** Can.
121 B2 **Redcliff** Zimbabwe
52 B2 **Red Cliffs** Austr.
128 C2 **Red Deer** Can.
126 E3 **Red Deer** *r.* Can.
129 D2 **Red Deer Lake** Can.
135 B2 **Redding** U.S.A.
99 C3 **Redditch** U.K.
137 D2 **Redfield** U.S.A.
137 D3 **Red Hills** U.S.A.
130 A2 **Red Lake** Can.
130 A2 **Red Lake** *l.* Can.
137 E1 **Red Lakes** U.S.A.
134 E1 **Red Lodge** U.S.A.
134 B2 **Redmond** U.S.A.
137 D2 **Red Oak** U.S.A.
104 B2 **Redon** France
106 B1 **Redondela** Spain
106 B2 **Redondo** Port.
78 A2 **Red Sea** Africa/Asia
128 B1 **Redstone** *r.* Can.
128 C2 **Redwater** Can.
137 E2 **Red Wing** U.S.A.
137 D2 **Redwood Falls** U.S.A.
97 C2 **Ree, Lough** *l.* Rep. of Ireland
134 B2 **Reedsport** U.S.A.
54 B2 **Reefton** N.Z.
139 D3 **Refugio** U.S.A.
102 C2 **Regen** Ger.
155 E1 **Regência** Brazil
102 C2 **Regensburg** Ger.
114 C2 **Reggane** Alg.
109 C3 **Reggio di Calabria** Italy
108 B2 **Reggio nell'Emilia** Italy
110 B1 **Reghin** Romania
129 D2 **Regina** Can.
154 C2 **Registro** Brazil
122 A1 **Rehoboth** Namibia
80 B2 **Rehovot** Israel
101 F2 **Reichenbach** Ger.
143 E1 **Reidsville** U.S.A.
99 C4 **Reigate** U.K.
105 C2 **Reims** France
101 E1 **Reinbek** Ger.
129 D2 **Reindeer** *r.* Can.
129 E2 **Reindeer Island** Can.
129 D2 **Reindeer Lake** Can.
92 F2 **Reine** Norway
106 C1 **Reinosa** Spain
100 C3 **Reinsfeld** Ger.
123 C2 **Reitz** S. Africa
122 B2 **Reivilo** S. Africa
129 D1 **Reliance** Can.
107 D2 **Relizane** Alg.
52 A2 **Remarkable, Mount** *hill* Austr.
79 C2 **Remeshk** Iran
105 D2 **Remiremont** France
100 C2 **Remscheid** Ger.
102 B1 **Rendsburg** Ger.
141 D1 **Renfrew** Can.
60 B2 **Rengat** Indon.
90 B2 **Reni** Ukr.
52 B2 **Renmark** Austr.
48 H5 **Rennell** *i.* Solomon Is
101 D2 **Rennerod** Ger.
104 B2 **Rennes** France
129 D1 **Rennie Lake** Can.
108 B2 **Reno** *r.* Italy
135 C3 **Reno** U.S.A.
70 A3 **Renshou** China
140 B2 **Rensselaer** U.S.A.
75 C2 **Renukut** India
54 B2 **Renwick** N.Z.
61 D2 **Reo** Indon.
136 D3 **Republican** *r.* U.S.A.
127 G2 **Repulse Bay** Can.
150 B3 **Requena** Peru
107 C2 **Requena** Spain
60 B2 **Resag, Gunung** *mt.* Indon.
111 B2 **Resen** Macedonia
154 B2 **Reserva** Brazil
91 C2 **Reshetylivka** Ukr.
152 C2 **Resistencia** Arg.
110 B1 **Reşiţa** Romania
126 F2 **Resolute Bay** Can.
127 H2 **Resolution Island** Can.
155 D1 **Resplendor** Brazil
145 C3 **Retalhuleu** Guat.
98 C3 **Retford** U.K.
105 C2 **Rethel** France
111 B3 **Rethymno** Greece
113 I8 **Réunion** *terr.* Indian Ocean
107 D1 **Reus** Spain
Reut *r.* Moldova *see* **Răut**
102 B2 **Reutlingen** Ger.
86 C2 **Revda** Rus. Fed.
128 C2 **Revelstoke** Can.
144 A3 **Revillagigedo, Islas** *is* Mex.
128 A2 **Revillagigedo Island** U.S.A.
75 C2 **Rewa** India
134 D2 **Rexburg** U.S.A.
135 B3 **Reyes, Point** U.S.A.
160 M4 **Reykjanes Ridge** *sea feature* N. Atlantic Ocean
92 □A3 **Reykjanestá** *pt* Iceland
92 □A3 **Reykjavík** Iceland
145 C2 **Reynosa** Mex.
Reẕā'īyeh Iran *see* **Orūmīyeh**
Reẕā'īyeh, Daryācheh-ye *salt l.* Iran *see* **Orūmīyeh, Daryācheh-ye**
88 C2 **Rēzekne** Latvia
Rheims France *see* **Reims**
Rhein *r.* Ger. *see* **Rhine**
100 C1 **Rheine** Ger.
101 F1 **Rheinsberg** Ger.
Rhin *r.* France *see* **Rhine**
100 C2 **Rhine** *r.* Europe
140 B1 **Rhinelander** U.S.A.
101 F1 **Rhinluch** *marsh* Ger.
101 F1 **Rhinow** Ger.
108 A1 **Rho** Italy
141 E2 **Rhode Island** *state* U.S.A.
111 C3 **Rhodes** Greece
111 C3 **Rhodes** *i.* Greece
Rhodesia *country* Africa *see* **Zimbabwe**
111 B2 **Rhodope Mountains** Bulg./Greece
105 C3 **Rhône** *r.* France/Switz.
Rhum *i.* U.K. *see* **Rum**
Rhuthun U.K. *see* **Ruthin**
98 B3 **Rhyl** U.K.
155 D1 **Riacho dos Machados** Brazil
154 C1 **Rialma** Brazil
154 C1 **Rianópolis** Brazil
60 B1 **Riau, Kepulauan** *is* Indon.
106 B1 **Ribadeo** Spain
106 B1 **Ribadesella** Spain
154 B2 **Ribas do Rio Pardo** Brazil
121 C2 **Ribáuè** Moz.
98 B3 **Ribble** *r.* U.K.
93 E4 **Ribe** Denmark
154 C2 **Ribeira** *r.* Brazil
154 C2 **Ribeirão Preto** Brazil
104 C2 **Ribérac** France
152 B1 **Riberalta** Bol.
Rîbniţa Moldova *see* **Râbniţa**
102 C1 **Ribnitz-Damgarten** Ger.
140 A1 **Rice Lake** U.S.A.
123 D2 **Richards Bay** S. Africa
139 D2 **Richardson** U.S.A.
126 C2 **Richardson Mountains** Can.
135 D3 **Richfield** U.S.A.
134 C1 **Richland** U.S.A.
140 A2 **Richland Center** U.S.A.
53 D2 **Richmond** *N.S.W.* Austr.
51 D2 **Richmond** *Qld* Austr.
134 B1 **Richmond** Can.
54 B2 **Richmond** N.Z.
122 B3 **Richmond** S. Africa
98 C2 **Richmond** U.K.
140 C3 **Richmond** *IN* U.S.A.
140 C3 **Richmond** *KY* U.S.A.
141 D3 **Richmond** *VA* U.S.A.
143 D2 **Richmond Hill** U.S.A.
53 D1 **Richmond Range** *hills* Austr.
130 C3 **Rideau Lakes** Can.
135 C3 **Ridgecrest** U.S.A.
142 B2 **Ridgeland** U.S.A.
102 C1 **Riesa** Ger.
101 D1 **Rieste** Ger.
123 B2 **Riet** *r.* S. Africa
101 D2 **Rietberg** Ger.
122 B2 **Rietfontein** S. Africa
108 B2 **Rieti** Italy
136 B3 **Rifle** U.S.A.
88 B2 **Rīga** Latvia
88 B2 **Riga, Gulf of** Estonia/Latvia
79 C2 **Rīgān** Iran
134 D2 **Rigby** U.S.A.
131 E2 **Rigolet** Can.
93 H3 **Riihimäki** Fin.
55 D2 **Riiser-Larsen Ice Shelf** Antarctica
108 B1 **Rijeka** Croatia
134 C2 **Riley** U.S.A.
105 C2 **Rillieux-la-Pape** France
78 B2 **Rimah, Wādī al** *watercourse* Saudi Arabia
103 E2 **Rimavská Sobota** Slovakia
128 C2 **Rimbey** Can.
108 B2 **Rimini** Italy
Rîmnicu Sărat Romania *see* **Râmnicu Sărat**
Rîmnicu Vîlcea Romania *see* **Râmnicu Vâlcea**
131 D3 **Rimouski** Can.
144 B2 **Rincón de Romos** Mex.
93 F3 **Ringebu** Norway
93 E4 **Ringkøbing** Denmark
92 G2 **Ringvassøy** *i.* Norway
99 C4 **Ringwood** U.K.
101 D1 **Rinteln** Ger.
154 B3 **Rio Azul** Brazil
150 B3 **Riobamba** Ecuador
155 D2 **Rio Bonito** Brazil
150 C4 **Rio Branco** Brazil
154 C3 **Rio Branco do Sul** Brazil
154 B2 **Rio Brilhante** Brazil
155 D2 **Rio Casca** Brazil
154 C2 **Rio Claro** Brazil
153 B3 **Río Colorado** Arg.
153 B3 **Río Cuarto** Arg.
155 D2 **Rio de Janeiro** Brazil
153 B5 **Río Gallegos** Arg.
153 B5 **Río Grande** Arg.
152 C3 **Rio Grande** Brazil
144 B2 **Río Grande** Mex.
139 D3 **Rio Grande** *r.* Mex./U.S.A.
139 D3 **Rio Grande City** U.S.A.
150 B1 **Ríohacha** Col.
150 B3 **Rioja** Peru
145 D2 **Río Lagartos** Mex.
151 F3 **Rio Largo** Brazil
105 C2 **Riom** France
152 B1 **Río Mulatos** Bol.
154 C3 **Rio Negro** Brazil
155 D1 **Rio Pardo de Minas** Brazil

154 C1 **Rio Preto, Serra do** *hills* Brazil
138 B1 **Rio Rancho** U.S.A.
150 B3 **Río Tigre** Ecuador
64 A3 **Rio Tuba** Phil.
154 B1 **Rio Verde** Brazil
145 C2 **Río Verde** Mex.
154 B1 **Rio Verde de Mato Grosso** Brazil
90 C1 **Ripky** Ukr.
99 C3 **Ripley** U.K.
107 D1 **Ripoll** Spain
98 C2 **Ripon** U.K.
66 D1 **Rishiri-tō** *i.* Japan
Rîşnov Romania *see* **Râşnov**
93 E4 **Risør** Norway
122 B2 **Ritchie** S. Africa
73 D3 **Ritchie's Archipelago** *is* India
134 C1 **Ritzville** U.S.A.
152 B2 **Rivadavia** Arg.
108 B1 **Riva del Garda** Italy
146 B3 **Rivas** Nic.
152 C3 **Rivera** Uru.
114 B4 **River Cess** Liberia
129 D2 **Riverhurst** Can.
52 C2 **Riverina** *reg.* Austr.
122 B3 **Riversdale** S. Africa
135 C4 **Riverside** U.S.A.
136 B2 **Riverton** U.S.A.
131 D3 **Riverview** Can.
105 C3 **Rivesaltes** France
131 D3 **Rivière-au-Renard** Can.
131 D3 **Rivière-du-Loup** Can.
141 F1 **Rivière-Ouelle** Can.
90 B1 **Rivne** Ukr.
108 A1 **Rivoli** Italy
120 B2 **Rivungo** Angola
54 B2 **Riwaka** N.Z.
78 B2 **Riyadh** Saudi Arabia
81 C1 **Rize** Turkey
70 B2 **Rizhao** China
105 C2 **Roanne** France
140 D3 **Roanoke** U.S.A.
143 E1 **Roanoke** *r.* U.S.A.
143 E1 **Roanoke Rapids** U.S.A.
135 E3 **Roan Plateau** U.S.A.
146 B3 **Roatán** Hond.
52 A3 **Robe** Austr.
52 B2 **Robe, Mount** *hill* Austr.
101 F1 **Röbel** Ger.
53 D1 **Roberts, Mount** Austr.
92 H3 **Robertsfors** Sweden
122 A3 **Robertson** S. Africa
114 A4 **Robertsport** Liberia
Robert Williams Angola *see* **Caála**
130 C3 **Roberval** Can.
50 A2 **Robinson Range** *hills* Austr.
52 B2 **Robinvale** Austr.
129 D2 **Roblin** Can.
128 C2 **Robson, Mount** Can.
139 D3 **Robstown** U.S.A.
Roçadas Angola *see* **Xangongo**
108 B3 **Rocca Busambra** *mt.* *Sicily* Italy
153 C3 **Rocha** Uru.
98 B3 **Rochdale** U.K.
154 B1 **Rochedo** Brazil
100 B2 **Rochefort** Belgium
104 B2 **Rochefort** France
52 B3 **Rochester** Austr.
137 E2 **Rochester** *MN* U.S.A.
141 E2 **Rochester** *NH* U.S.A.
141 D2 **Rochester** *NY* U.S.A.
94 A2 **Rockall** *i.* N. Atlantic Ocean
160 L4 **Rockall Bank** *sea feature* N. Atlantic Ocean
140 B2 **Rockford** U.S.A.
51 E2 **Rockhampton** Austr.
143 D2 **Rock Hill** U.S.A.
50 A3 **Rockingham** Austr.
140 A2 **Rock Island** U.S.A.
136 B1 **Rock Springs** *MT* U.S.A.
139 C3 **Rocksprings** U.S.A.
136 B2 **Rock Springs** *WY* U.S.A.
143 D1 **Rockwood** U.S.A.
136 C3 **Rocky Ford** U.S.A.
143 E1 **Rocky Mount** U.S.A.
128 C2 **Rocky Mountain House** Can.
124 F4 **Rocky Mountains** U.S.A.
100 B3 **Rocroi** France
102 C1 **Rødbyhavn** Denmark
131 E2 **Roddickton** Can.
104 C3 **Rodez** France
Rodi *i.* Greece *see* **Rhodes**
89 F2 **Rodniki** Rus. Fed.
Rodos Greece *see* **Rhodes**
Rodos *i.* Greece *see* **Rhodes**
Rodosto Turkey *see* **Tekirdağ**
50 A2 **Roebourne** Austr.
50 B1 **Roebuck Bay** Austr.
123 C1 **Roedtan** S. Africa
100 B2 **Roermond** Neth.
100 A2 **Roeselare** Belgium
127 G2 **Roes Welcome Sound** *sea chan.* Can.
128 C2 **Rogers** Can.
142 B1 **Rogers** U.S.A.
140 C3 **Rogers, Mount** U.S.A.
140 C1 **Rogers City** U.S.A.
157 G8 **Roggeveen Basin** *sea feature* S. Pacific Ocean
122 B3 **Roggeveldberge** *esc.* S. Africa
92 G2 **Rognan** Norway
134 B2 **Rogue** *r.* U.S.A.
74 B2 **Rohtak** India
49 M5 **Roi Georges, Îles du** *is* Fr. Polynesia
88 B2 **Roja** Latvia
60 B1 **Rokan** *r.* Indon.
88 C2 **Rokiškis** Lith.
90 B1 **Rokytne** Ukr.
154 B2 **Rolândia** Brazil
137 E3 **Rolla** U.S.A.
139 C2 **Rolling Prairies** *reg.* U.S.A.
51 D2 **Roma** Austr.
59 C3 **Roma** *i.* Indon.
Roma Italy *see* **Rome**
123 C2 **Roma** Lesotho
139 D3 **Roma** U.S.A.
143 E2 **Romain, Cape** U.S.A.
110 C1 **Roman** Romania
158 E5 **Romanche Gap** *sea feature* S. Atlantic Ocean
110 B1 **Romania** *country* Europe
91 C3 **Roman-Kosh** *mt.* Ukr.
69 D1 **Romanovka** Rus. Fed.
105 D2 **Romans-sur-Isère** France
105 D2 **Rombas** France
64 B2 **Romblon** Phil.
108 B2 **Rome** Italy
143 C2 **Rome** *GA* U.S.A.
141 D2 **Rome** *NY* U.S.A.
99 D4 **Romford** U.K.
105 C2 **Romilly-sur-Seine** France
91 C1 **Romny** Ukr.
104 C2 **Romorantin-Lanthenay** France
99 C4 **Romsey** U.K.
134 D1 **Ronan** U.S.A.
96 □ **Ronas Hill** U.K.
151 D4 **Roncador, Serra do** *hills* Brazil
106 B2 **Ronda** Spain
154 B2 **Rondon** Brazil
154 B1 **Rondonópolis** Brazil
74 B1 **Rondu** Jammu and Kashmir
71 A3 **Rong'an** China
Rongcheng China *see* **Rongxian**
Rongcheng China *see* **Jianli**
71 A3 **Rongjiang** China
62 A1 **Rongklang Range** *mts* Myanmar
Rongmei China *see* **Hefeng**
71 B3 **Rongxian** China
93 F4 **Rønne** Denmark
93 G4 **Ronneby** Sweden
55 A2 **Ronne Ice Shelf** Antarctica
101 D1 **Ronnenberg** Ger.
100 A2 **Ronse** Belgium
Rooke Island P.N.G. *see* **Umboi**
100 B1 **Roordahuizum** Neth.
74 B2 **Roorkee** India
100 B2 **Roosendaal** Neth.
135 E2 **Roosevelt** U.S.A.
128 B2 **Roosevelt, Mount** Can.
55 N2 **Roosevelt Island** Antarctica
104 B3 **Roquefort** France
150 C2 **Roraima, Mount** Guyana
93 F3 **Røros** Norway
90 C2 **Ros'** *r.* Ukr.
138 B3 **Rosa, Punta** *pt* Mex.
106 B2 **Rosal de la Frontera** Spain
153 B3 **Rosario** Arg.
144 A1 **Rosario** Mex.
144 B2 **Rosario** Mex.
144 B2 **Rosario** Mex.
147 C3 **Rosario** Venez.
152 B2 **Rosario de la Frontera** Arg.
151 D4 **Rosário Oeste** Brazil
144 A2 **Rosarito** Mex.
144 A1 **Rosarito** Mex.
138 A3 **Rosarito** Mex.
109 C3 **Rosarno** Italy
139 C2 **Roscoe** U.S.A.
104 B2 **Roscoff** France
97 B2 **Roscommon** Rep. of Ireland
97 C2 **Roscrea** Rep. of Ireland
147 D3 **Roseau** Dominica
137 D1 **Roseau** U.S.A.
134 B2 **Roseburg** U.S.A.
96 C2 **Rosehearty** U.K.
139 D3 **Rosenberg** U.S.A.
101 D1 **Rosengarten** Ger.
102 C2 **Rosenheim** Ger.
129 D2 **Rosetown** Can.
122 A2 **Rosh Pinah** Namibia
110 C2 **Roşiori de Vede** Romania
93 F4 **Roskilde** Denmark
89 D3 **Roslavl'** Rus. Fed.
134 B1 **Roslyn** U.S.A.
109 C3 **Rossano** Italy
97 B1 **Rossan Point** Rep. of Ireland
51 E1 **Rossel Island** P.N.G.
55 N1 **Ross Ice Shelf** Antarctica
131 D3 **Rossignol, Lake** Can.
128 C3 **Rossland** Can.
97 C2 **Rosslare** Rep. of Ireland
97 C2 **Rosslare Harbour** Rep. of Ireland
101 F2 **Roßlau** Ger.
101 E2 **Roßleben** Ger.
114 A3 **Rosso** Maur.
105 D3 **Rosso, Capo** *c. Corsica* France
99 B4 **Ross-on-Wye** U.K.
91 D1 **Rossosh'** Rus. Fed.
128 A1 **Ross River** Can.
55 N2 **Ross Sea** Antarctica
92 F2 **Røssvatnet** *l.* Norway
81 D3 **Rostāq** Iran
129 D2 **Rosthern** Can.
102 C1 **Rostock** Ger.
89 E2 **Rostov** Rus. Fed.
91 D2 **Rostov-na-Donu** Rus. Fed.
Rostov-on-Don Rus. Fed. *see* **Rostov-na-Donu**
104 B2 **Rostrenen** France
92 G2 **Røsvik** Norway
92 H2 **Rosvik** Sweden
138 C2 **Roswell** U.S.A.
59 D2 **Rota** *i.* N. Mariana Is
59 C3 **Rote** *i.* Indon.
101 D1 **Rotenburg (Wümme)** Ger.
101 E3 **Roth** Ger.
98 C2 **Rothbury** U.K.
101 E3 **Rothenburg ob der Tauber** Ger.
98 C3 **Rotherham** U.K.
96 C2 **Rothes** U.K.
96 B3 **Rothesay** U.K.
53 C2 **Roto** Austr.
105 D3 **Rotondo, Monte** *mt. Corsica* France
54 C1 **Rotorua** N.Z.
54 C1 **Rotorua, Lake** N.Z.
101 E2 **Rottenbach** Ger.
102 C2 **Rottenmann** Austria
100 B2 **Rotterdam** Neth.
102 B2 **Rottweil** Ger.
49 I5 **Rotuma** *i.* Fiji
105 C1 **Roubaix** France
104 C2 **Rouen** France
Roulers Belgium *see* **Roeselare**
53 D2 **Round Mountain** Austr.
131 E3 **Round Pond** *l.* Can.
139 D2 **Round Rock** U.S.A.
134 E1 **Roundup** U.S.A.
96 C1 **Rousay** *i.* U.K.
130 C3 **Rouyn** Can.
Rouyuanchengzi China *see* **Huachi**
92 I2 **Rovaniemi** Fin.
91 D2 **Roven'ki** Rus. Fed.
91 D2 **Roven'ky** Ukr.
108 B1 **Rovereto** Italy
63 B2 **Rôviĕng Tbong** Cambodia
108 B1 **Rovigo** Italy
108 B1 **Rovinj** Croatia
53 C1 **Rowena** Austr.
Równe Ukr. *see* **Rivne**
64 B3 **Roxas** Phil.
64 B2 **Roxas** Phil.
64 A2 **Roxas** Phil.
64 B2 **Roxas** Phil.
52 A2 **Roxby Downs** Austr.
138 C1 **Roy** *NM* U.S.A.
134 D2 **Roy** *UT* U.S.A.
140 B1 **Royale, Isle** *i.* U.S.A.
104 B2 **Royan** France
99 C3 **Royston** U.K.
90 C2 **Rozdil'na** Ukr.
91 C2 **Rozdol'ne** Ukr.
103 E2 **Rožňava** Slovakia
100 B3 **Rozoy-sur-Serre** France
87 D3 **Rtishchevo** Rus. Fed.
Ruanda *country* Africa *se* **Rwanda**
54 C1 **Ruapehu, Mount** *vol.* N.
54 A3 **Ruapuke Island** N.Z.
89 D2 **Ruba** Belarus
79 B3 **Rub' al Khālī** *des.* Saudi Arabia
119 D3 **Rubeho Mountains** Tanz
91 D2 **Rubizhne** Ukr.
77 E1 **Rubtsovsk** Rus. Fed.
126 B2 **Ruby** U.S.A.
135 C2 **Ruby Mountains** U.S.A.
76 C3 **Rudbar** Afgh.
66 C2 **Rudnaya Pristan'** Rus. Fed.
89 D3 **Rudnya** Rus. Fed.
76 C1 **Rudnyy** Kazakh.
Rudolf, Lake *salt l.* Eth./Kenya *see* **Turkana, Lake**
82 E1 **Rudol'fa, Ostrov** *i.* Rus. Fed.
Rudolph Island Rus. Fec *see* **Rudol'fa, Ostrov**
101 E2 **Rudolstadt** Ger.
116 B3 **Rufa'a** Sudan
119 D3 **Rufiji** *r.* Tanz.
153 B3 **Rufino** Arg.
121 B2 **Rufunsa** Zambia
70 C2 **Rugao** China
99 C3 **Rugby** U.K.
136 C1 **Rugby** U.S.A.
102 C1 **Rügen** *i.* Ger.
119 C3 **Ruhengeri** Rwanda
101 E2 **Ruhla** Ger.
88 B2 **Ruhnu** *i.* Estonia
100 C2 **Ruhr** *r.* Ger.
71 C3 **Rui'an** China
138 B2 **Ruidoso** U.S.A.
144 B2 **Ruiz** Mex.
119 D3 **Rukwa, Lake** Tanz.
96 A2 **Rum** *i.* U.K.
109 C1 **Ruma** Yugo.
78 B2 **Rumāh** Saudi Arabia
117 A4 **Rumbek** Sudan
147 C2 **Rum Cay** *i.* Bahamas
141 E2 **Rumford** U.S.A.
103 D1 **Rumia** Pol.
105 D2 **Rumilly** France
50 C1 **Rum Jungle** Austr.
66 D2 **Rumoi** Japan
121 C2 **Rumphi** Malawi
54 B2 **Runanga** N.Z.
98 B3 **Runcorn** U.K.
120 A2 **Rundu** Namibia
119 C2 **Rungu** Dem. Rep. Congo
119 D3 **Rungwa** Tanz.
68 B2 **Ruoqiang** China
130 C2 **Rupert** *r.* Can.
134 D2 **Rupert** U.S.A.
130 C2 **Rupert Bay** Can.
Rusaddir N. Africa *see* **Melilla**
121 C2 **Rusape** Zimbabwe
110 C2 **Ruse** Bulg.
137 E1 **Rush City** U.S.A.
121 C2 **Rushinga** Zimbabwe
77 D3 **Rushon** Tajik.
136 C2 **Rushville** U.S.A.
53 C3 **Rushworth** Austr.
129 D2 **Russell** Can.
54 B1 **Russell** N.Z.
137 D3 **Russell** U.S.A.
142 C2 **Russellville** *AL* U.S.A.
142 B1 **Russellville** *AR* U.S.A.
140 B3 **Russellville** *KY* U.S.A.
101 D2 **Rüsselsheim** Ger.
82 G3 **Russian Federation** *country* Asia/Europe
81 C1 **Rust'avi** Georgia
123 C2 **Rustenburg** S. Africa
142 B2 **Ruston** U.S.A.
61 D2 **Ruteng** Indon.

98 B3 **Ruthin** U.K.
41 E2 **Rutland** U.S.A.
75 B1 **Rutog** China
19 C3 **Rutshuru**
  Dem. Rep. Congo
19 E4 **Ruvuma** *r.* Moz./Tanz.
79 C2 **Ruweis** U.A.E.
39 E2 **Ruza** Rus. Fed.
77 C1 **Ruzayevka** Kazakh.
37 D3 **Ruzayevka** Rus. Fed.
19 C3 **Rwanda** *country* Africa
39 E3 **Ryazan'** Rus. Fed.
39 F3 **Ryazhsk** Rus. Fed.
36 C2 **Rybachiy, Poluostrov** *pen.*
  Rus. Fed.
  Rybach'ye Kyrg. *see*
  Balykchy
39 E2 **Rybinsk** Rus. Fed.
39 E2 **Rybinskoye**
  Vodokhranilishche *resr*
  Rus. Fed.
03 D1 **Rybnik** Pol.
  Rybnitsa Moldova *see*
  Râbnița
39 E3 **Rybnoye** Rus. Fed.
99 D4 **Rye** U.K.
  Rykovo Ukr. *see*
  Yenakiyeve
39 D3 **Ryl'sk** Rus. Fed.
  Ryojun China *see*
  Lushunkou
67 C2 **Ryōtsu** Japan
  Ryukyu Islands Japan *see*
  Nansei-shotō
39 D3 **Ryzhikovo** Rus. Fed.
03 E1 **Rzeszów** Pol.
91 E1 **Rzhaksa** Rus. Fed.
89 D2 **Rzhev** Rus. Fed.

S

79 C2 **Sa'ādatābād** Iran
01 E2 **Saale** *r.* Ger.
01 E2 **Saalfeld** Ger.
34 B1 **Saanich** Can.
00 C3 **Saar** *r.* Ger.
02 B2 **Saarbrücken** Ger.
88 B2 **Sääre** Estonia
88 B2 **Saaremaa** *i.* Estonia
92 I2 **Saarenkylä** Fin.
93 I3 **Saarijärvi** Fin.
00 C3 **Saarlouis** Ger.
80 B2 **Sab' Ābār** Syria
07 D1 **Sabadell** Spain
67 C3 **Sabae** Japan
61 C1 **Sabah** *state* Malaysia
61 C2 **Sabalana** *i.* Indon.
46 B2 **Sabana, Archipiélago de**
  is Cuba
50 B1 **Sabanalarga** Col.
60 A1 **Sabang** Indon.
55 D1 **Sabará** Brazil
08 B2 **Sabaudia** Italy
22 B3 **Sabelo** S. Africa
19 C2 **Sabena Desert** Kenya
15 D2 **Sabhā** Libya
23 D2 **Sabie** *r.* Moz./S. Africa
23 D2 **Sabie** S. Africa
45 B2 **Sabinas** Mex.
45 B2 **Sabinas Hidalgo** Mex.
39 E3 **Sabine**
31 D3 **Sable, Cape** Can.
43 D3 **Sable, Cape** Can.
31 E3 **Sable Island** Can.
78 B3 **Şabyā** Saudi Arabia
76 B3 **Sabzevār** Iran
07 D2 **Sa Cabaneta** Spain
37 D2 **Sac City** U.S.A.
20 A2 **Sachanga** Angola
30 C2 **Sachigo Lake** Can.
65 B3 **Sach'on** S. Korea
26 D2 **Sachs Harbour** Can.
54 C1 **Sacramento** Brazil
35 B3 **Sacramento** U.S.A.
35 B3 **Sacramento** *r.* U.S.A.
35 B3 **Sacramento Mountains**
  U.S.A.
35 B2 **Sacramento Valley** U.S.A.
10 B1 **Săcueni** Romania
23 C3 **Sada** S. Africa
07 C1 **Sádaba** Spain
83 B3 **Sá da Bandeira** Angola
  see Lubango
78 B3 **Şa'dah** Yemen
63 B3 **Sadao** Thai.
79 B3 **Şādārah** Yemen
63 B3 **Sa Dec** Vietnam
74 B2 **Sadiqabad** Pak.

72 D2 **Sadiya** India
67 C3 **Sadoga-shima** *i.* Japan
107 D2 **Sa Dragonera** *i.* Spain
93 F4 **Säffle** Sweden
138 B2 **Safford** U.S.A.
99 D3 **Saffron Walden** U.K.
114 B1 **Safi** Morocco
155 D1 **Safiras, Serra das** *mts*
  Brazil
86 D2 **Safonovo** Rus. Fed.
89 D2 **Safonovo** Rus. Fed.
78 B2 **Safrā' as Sark** *esc.*
  Saudi Arabia
75 C2 **Saga** China
67 B4 **Saga** Japan
62 A1 **Sagaing** Myanmar
67 C3 **Sagamihara** Japan
74 B2 **Sagar** India
  Sagarmatha *mt.*
  China/Nepal *see*
  Everest, Mount
140 C2 **Saginaw** U.S.A.
140 C2 **Saginaw Bay** U.S.A.
  Saglouc Can. *see* Salluit
106 B2 **Sagres** Port.
146 B2 **Sagua la Grande** Cuba
141 F1 **Saguenay** *r.* Can.
107 C2 **Sagunto** Spain
76 B2 **Sagyndyk, Mys** *pt* Kazakh.
106 B1 **Sahagún** Spain
114 C3 **Sahara** *des.* Africa
  Şaḥara el Gharbīya *des.*
  Egypt *see* Western Desert
  Şaḥara el Sharqīya *des.*
  Egypt *see* Eastern Desert
  Saharan Atlas *mts* Alg.
  see Atlas Saharien
74 B2 **Saharanpur** India
75 C2 **Saharsa** India
74 B1 **Sahiwal** Pak.
144 B2 **Sahuayo** Mex.
78 B2 **Şāḥūq** *reg.* Saudi Arabia
114 C1 **Saïda** Alg.
  Saïda Lebanon *see* Sidon
75 C2 **Saidpur** Bangl.
67 B3 **Saigō** Japan
  Saigon Vietnam *see*
  Hồ Chí Minh
75 D2 **Saiha** India
70 B1 **Saihan Tal** China
67 B4 **Saiki** Japan
93 I3 **Saimaa** *l.* Fin.
144 B2 **Sain Alto** Mex.
96 C3 **St Abb's Head** *hd* U.K.
131 E3 **St Alban's** Can.
99 C4 **St Albans** U.K.
140 C3 **St Albans** U.S.A.
99 B4 **St Alban's Head** *hd* U.K.
  St-André, Cap *pt* Madag.
  see Vilanandro, Tanjona
96 C2 **St Andrews** U.K.
131 E2 **St Anthony** Can.
134 D2 **St Anthony** U.S.A.
52 B3 **St Arnaud** Austr.
131 E2 **St-Augustin** Can.
131 E2 **St-Augustin** *r.* Can.
143 D3 **St Augustine** U.S.A.
99 A4 **St Austell** U.K.
104 C2 **St-Avertin** France
147 D3 **St-Barthélemy** *i.*
  West Indies
98 B2 **St Bees Head** *hd* U.K.
105 D3 **St-Bonnet-en-**
  Champsaur France
99 A4 **St Bride's Bay** U.K.
104 B2 **St-Brieuc** France
130 C3 **St Catharines** Can.
143 D2 **St Catherines Island**
  U.S.A.
99 C4 **St Catherine's Point** U.K.
137 E3 **St Charles** U.S.A.
140 C2 **St Clair, Lake** Can./U.S.A.
105 D2 **St-Claude** France
99 A4 **St Clears** U.K.
137 E1 **St Cloud** U.S.A.
140 A1 **St Croix** *r.* U.S.A.
147 D3 **St Croix Island**
  Virgin Is (U.S.A.)
99 A4 **St David's** U.K.
99 A4 **St David's Head** *hd* U.K.
113 I8 **St-Denis** France
104 C2 **St-Denis** France
  St-Denis-du-Sig Alg. *see*
  Sig
105 D2 **St-Dié** France
105 C2 **St-Dizier** France
130 C3 **Ste-Adèle** Can.
131 D3 **Ste-Anne-des-Monts** Can.
141 E1 **Ste-Foy** Can.
105 D2 **St-Égrève** France
128 A1 **St Elias Mountains** Can.

131 D2 **Ste Marguerite** *r.* Can.
141 E1 **Ste-Marie** Can.
  Ste-Marie, Cap *c.* Madag.
  see Vohimena, Tanjona
  Sainte-Marie, Île *i.*
  Madag. *see* Nosy Boraha
  Ste-Rose-du-Dégelé Can.
  see Dégelis
129 E2 **Ste Rose du Lac** Can.
104 B2 **Saintes** France
105 C2 **St-Étienne** France
104 C2 **St-Étienne-du-Rouvray**
  France
130 C3 **St-Félicien** Can.
97 D1 **Saintfield** U.K.
105 D3 **St-Florent** *Corsica* France
105 C2 **St-Flour** France
136 C3 **St Francis** U.S.A.
104 C3 **St-Gaudens** France
53 C1 **St George** Austr.
135 D3 **St George** U.S.A.
143 D3 **St George Island** U.S.A.
131 C3 **St-Georges** Can.
147 D3 **St George's** Grenada
131 E3 **St George's Bay** Can.
97 C3 **St George's Channel**
  Rep. of Ireland/U.K.
  St Gotthard Pass *pass*
  Switz. *see*
  San Gottardo, Passo del
113 C7 **St Helena** *terr.*
  S. Atlantic Ocean
122 A3 **St Helena Bay** S. Africa
122 A3 **St Helena Bay** S. Africa
98 B3 **St Helens** U.K.
134 B1 **St Helens, Mount** *vol.*
  U.S.A.
95 C4 **St Helier** Channel Is
100 B2 **St-Hubert** Belgium
141 E1 **St-Hyacinthe** Can.
140 C1 **St Ignace** U.S.A.
130 B3 **St Ignace Island** Can.
99 A4 **St Ives** U.K.
  St Jacques, Cap Vietnam
  see Vung Tau
128 A2 **St James, Cape** Can.
130 C3 **St-Jean, Lac** *l.* Can.
104 B2 **St-Jean-d'Angély** France
104 B2 **St-Jean-de-Monts** France
130 C3 **St-Jean-sur-Richelieu**
  Can.
141 E1 **St-Jérôme** Can.
134 C1 **St Joe** *r.* U.S.A.
131 D3 **Saint John** Can.
137 D3 **St John** U.S.A.
141 F1 **St John** *r.* U.S.A.
147 D3 **St John's** Antigua
131 E3 **St John's** Can.
138 B2 **St Johns** U.S.A.
143 D3 **St Johns** *r.* U.S.A.
141 E2 **St Johnsbury** U.S.A.
137 E3 **St Joseph** U.S.A.
130 A2 **St Joseph, Lake** Can.
  St-Joseph-d'Alma Can.
  see Alma
130 B3 **St Joseph Island** Can.
141 E1 **St-Junien** France
104 C2 **St-Junien** France
94 B2 **St Kilda** *i.* U.K.
147 D3 **St Kitts and Nevis**
  country West Indies
151 D2 **St-Laurent-du-Maroni**
  Fr. Guiana
131 E3 **St Lawrence** Can.
131 D3 **St Lawrence** *inlet* Can.
131 D3 **St Lawrence, Gulf of** Can.
126 A2 **St Lawrence Island** U.S.A.
104 B2 **St-Lô** France
114 A3 **St Louis** Senegal
137 E3 **St Louis** U.S.A.
137 E1 **St Louis** *r.* U.S.A.
147 D3 **St Lucia** *country*
  West Indies
147 D3 **St Lucia Channel**
  Martinique/St Lucia
123 D2 **St Lucia Estuary**
  S. Africa
147 D3 **St Maarten** *i.* West Indies
96 ☐ **St Magnus Bay** U.K.
104 B2 **St-Malo** France
104 B2 **St-Malo, Golfe de** *g.*
  France
147 D3 **St Marc** Haiti
  St Mark's S. Africa *see*
  Cofimvaba
147 D3 **St Martin** *i.* West Indies
122 A3 **St Martin, Cape** S. Africa
129 E2 **St Martin, Lake** Can.
141 D2 **St Marys** U.S.A.
124 A3 **St Matthew Island** U.S.A.

59 D3 **St Matthias Group** *is*
  P.N.G.
130 C3 **St Maurice** *r.* Can.
130 C3 **St-Michel-des-Saints**
  Can.
104 B2 **St-Nazaire** France
104 C1 **St-Omer** France
129 C2 **St Paul** Can.
137 E2 **St Paul** U.S.A.
156 A8 **St Paul, Île** *i.* Indian Ocean
137 E2 **St Peter** U.S.A.
95 C4 **St Peter Port** Channel Is
143 D3 **St Petersburg** U.S.A.
131 E3 **St-Pierre**
  St Pierre and Miquelon
141 E1 **St-Pierre, Lac** *l.* Can.
131 E3 **St Pierre and Miquelon**
  terr. N. America
104 B2 **St-Pierre-d'Oléron** France
105 C2 **St-Pourçain-sur-Sioule**
  France
131 D3 **St Quentin** Can.
105 C2 **St-Quentin** France
105 D3 **St-Raphaël** France
122 B3 **St Sebastian Bay** S. Africa
104 B2 **St-Sébastien-sur-Loire**
  France
131 D3 **St Siméon** Can.
129 E2 **St Theresa Point** Can.
130 B3 **St Thomas** Can.
105 D3 **St-Tropez** France
105 D3 **St-Tropez, Cap de** *c.*
  France
  St Vincent, Cape Port. *see*
  São Vicente, Cabo de
52 A3 **St Vincent, Gulf** Austr.
147 D3 **St Vincent and the**
  Grenadines *i.* West Indies
  St Lucia/St Vincent
147 D3 **St Vincent Passage**
129 D2 **St Walburg** Can.
104 C2 **St-Yrieix-la-Perche**
  France
59 D1 **Saipan** *i.* N. Mariana Is
152 B1 **Sajama, Nevado** *mt.* Bol.
122 B2 **Sak** *watercourse* S. Africa
67 C4 **Sakai** Japan
67 B4 **Sakaide** Japan
78 B2 **Sakākah** Saudi Arabia
136 C1 **Sakakawea, Lake** U.S.A.
111 D2 **Sakarya** Turkey
111 D2 **Sakarya** *r.* Turkey
66 C3 **Sakata** Japan
65 B1 **Sakchu** N. Korea
66 D1 **Sakhalin** *i.* Rus. Fed.
123 C2 **Sakhile** S. Africa
81 C1 **Şäki** Azer.
114 C4 **Saki** Nigeria
88 B3 **Šakiai** Lith.
69 E3 **Sakishima-shotō** *is* Japan
62 B2 **Sakon Nakhon** Thai.
74 A2 **Sakrand** Pak.
122 B3 **Sakrivier** S. Africa
67 D3 **Sakura** Japan
91 C2 **Saky** Ukr.
93 G4 **Sala** Sweden
130 C3 **Salaberry-de-Valleyfield**
  Can.
88 B2 **Salacgrīva** Latvia
109 C2 **Sala Consilina** Italy
135 C4 **Salada, Laguna** *salt l.*
  Mex.
152 C2 **Saladas** Arg.
152 B3 **Salado** *r.* Arg.
145 C2 **Salado** *r.* Mex.
114 B4 **Salaga** Ghana
122 B1 **Salajwe** Botswana
79 C2 **Salakh, Jabal** *mt.* Oman
115 D3 **Salal** Chad
78 A3 **Salala** Sudan
79 C3 **Salālah** Oman
145 B2 **Salamanca** Mex.
106 B1 **Salamanca** Spain
141 D2 **Salamanca** U.S.A.
106 B1 **Salas** Spain
59 C3 **Salawati** *i.* Indon.
61 D2 **Salayar** *i.* Indon.
157 G7 **Sala y Gómez, Isla** *i.*
  S. Pacific Ocean
  Salazar Angola *see*
  N'dalatando
104 C2 **Salbris** France
88 C3 **Šalčininkai** Lith.
106 C1 **Saldaña** Spain
122 A3 **Saldanha** S. Africa
88 B2 **Saldus** Latvia
53 C3 **Sale** Austr.
88 F2 **Salekhard** Rus. Fed.
73 B3 **Salem** India
140 B3 **Salem** *IL* U.S.A.
137 E3 **Salem** *MO* U.S.A.

134 B2 **Salem** *OR* U.S.A.
137 D2 **Salem** *SD* U.S.A.
96 B2 **Salen** U.K.
109 B2 **Salerno** Italy
108 B2 **Salerno, Golfo di** *g.* Italy
98 B3 **Salford** U.K.
151 E2 **Salgado** *r.* Brazil
103 D2 **Salgótarján** Hungary
151 F3 **Salgueiro** Brazil
136 B3 **Salida** U.S.A.
111 C3 **Salihli** Turkey
88 C3 **Salihorsk** Belarus
121 C2 **Salima** Malawi
121 C2 **Salimo** Moz.
137 D3 **Salina** *KS* U.S.A.
135 D3 **Salina** *UT* U.S.A.
109 B3 **Salina, Isola** *i.* Italy
145 C3 **Salina Cruz** Mex.
155 D1 **Salinas** Brazil
144 B2 **Salinas** Mex.
135 B3 **Salinas** U.S.A.
135 B3 **Salinas** *r.* U.S.A.
151 E3 **Salinópolis** Brazil
99 C4 **Salisbury** U.K.
141 D3 **Salisbury** *MD* U.S.A.
143 D1 **Salisbury** *NC* U.S.A.
Salisbury Zimbabwe *see* Harare
99 B4 **Salisbury Plain** U.K.
151 E3 **Salitre** *r.* Brazil
92 I2 **Salla** Fin.
139 E1 **Sallisaw** U.S.A.
127 G2 **Salluit** Can.
75 C2 **Sallyana** Nepal
81 C2 **Salmās** Iran
128 C3 **Salmo** Can.
134 D1 **Salmon** U.S.A.
134 C1 **Salmon** *r.* U.S.A.
128 C2 **Salmon Arm** Can.
134 C2 **Salmon River Mountains** U.S.A.
100 C3 **Salmtal** Ger.
118 B2 **Salo** C.A.R.
93 H3 **Salo** Fin.
105 D3 **Salon-de-Provence** France
Salonica Greece *see* Thessaloniki
110 B1 **Salonta** Romania
87 D4 **Sal'sk** Rus. Fed.
122 B3 **Salt** *watercourse* S. Africa
107 D1 **Salt** Spain
138 A2 **Salt** *r.* U.S.A.
152 B2 **Salta** Arg.
99 A4 **Saltash** U.K.
96 B3 **Saltcoats** U.K.
145 B2 **Saltillo** Mex.
134 D2 **Salt Lake City** U.S.A.
154 C2 **Salto** Brazil
152 C3 **Salto** Uru.
155 E1 **Salto da Divisa** Brazil
154 B2 **Salto del Guaíra** Para.
135 C4 **Salton Sea** *salt l.* U.S.A.
154 B3 **Salto Osório, Represa** *resr* Brazil
154 B3 **Salto Santiago, Represa de** *resr* Brazil
143 D2 **Saluda** U.S.A.
76 B3 **Saluq, Kūh-e** *mt.* Iran
108 A2 **Saluzzo** Italy
151 F4 **Salvador** Brazil
79 C2 **Salwah** Saudi Arabia
Salween *r.* China *see* Nu Jiang
62 A2 **Salween** *r.* Myanmar
81 C2 **Salyan** Azer.
140 C3 **Salyersville** U.S.A.
122 A1 **Salzbrunn** Namibia
102 C2 **Salzburg** Austria
101 E1 **Salzgitter** Ger.
101 D2 **Salzkotten** Ger.
101 E1 **Salzwedel** Ger.
144 B1 **Samalayuca** Mex.
66 D2 **Samani** Japan
64 B2 **Samar** *i.* Phil.
87 E3 **Samara** Rus. Fed.
Samarahan Malaysia *see* Sri Aman
59 E3 **Samarai** P.N.G.
61 C2 **Samarinda** Indon.
77 C3 **Samarkand** Uzbek.
81 C2 **Sāmarrā'** Iraq
81 C1 **Şamaxı** Azer.
119 C3 **Samba** Dem. Rep. Congo
61 C1 **Sambaliung** *mts* Indon.
75 C2 **Sambalpur** India
60 C2 **Sambar, Tanjung** *pt* Indon.
60 B1 **Sambas** Indon.
121 E2 **Sambava** Madag.
74 B2 **Sambhar** India
90 A2 **Sambir** Ukr.
61 C2 **Sambo** Indon.
61 C2 **Samboja** Indon.
153 C3 **Samborombón, Bahía** *b.* Arg.
65 B2 **Samch'ŏk** S. Korea
Samch'ŏnp'o S. Korea *see* Sach'on
81 C2 **Samdi Dag** *mt.* Turkey
119 D3 **Same** Tanz.
121 B2 **Samfya** Zambia
78 B2 **Samīrah** Saudi Arabia
65 B1 **Samjiyŏn** N. Korea
Sam Neua Laos *see* Xam Hua
48 J5 **Samoa** *country* S. Pacific Ocean
156 E6 **Samoa Basin** *sea feature* S. Pacific Ocean
Samoa i Sisifo *country* S. Pacific Ocean *see* Samoa
109 C1 **Samobor** Croatia
110 B2 **Samokov** Bulg.
111 C3 **Samos** *i.* Greece
Samothrace *i.* Greece *see* Samothraki
111 C2 **Samothraki** Greece
111 C2 **Samothraki** *i.* Greece
61 C2 **Sampit** Indon.
119 C3 **Sampwe** Dem. Rep. Congo
139 E2 **Sam Rayburn Reservoir** U.S.A.
62 B2 **Sâm Sơn** Vietnam
80 B1 **Samsun** Turkey
81 C1 **Samtredia** Georgia
63 B3 **Samui, Ko** *i.* Thai.
63 B2 **Samut Songkhram** Thai.
114 B3 **San** Mali
78 B3 **Şan'ā'** Yemen
118 A2 **Sanaga** *r.* Cameroon
81 C2 **Sanandaj** Iran
146 B3 **San Andrés, Isla de** *i.* Caribbean Sea
106 B1 **San Andrés del Rabanedo** Spain
138 B2 **San Andres Mountains** U.S.A.
145 C3 **San Andrés Tuxtla** Mex.
139 C2 **San Angelo** U.S.A.
139 D3 **San Antonio** U.S.A.
135 C4 **San Antonio, Mount** U.S.A.
107 D2 **San Antonio Abad** Spain
152 B2 **San Antonio de los Cobres** Arg.
153 B4 **San Antonio Oeste** Arg.
108 B2 **San Benedetto del Tronto** Italy
144 A3 **San Benedicto, Isla** *i.* Mex.
135 C4 **San Bernardino** U.S.A.
135 C4 **San Bernardino Mountains** U.S.A.
138 B3 **San Blas** Mex.
143 C3 **San Blas, Cape** U.S.A.
146 C4 **San Blas, Punta** *pt* Panama
152 B1 **San Borja** Bol.
144 B2 **San Buenaventura** Mex.
64 B2 **San Carlos** Phil.
147 D4 **San Carlos** Venez.
153 A4 **San Carlos de Bariloche** Arg.
147 C4 **San Carlos del Zulia** Venez.
104 C2 **Sancerrois, Collines du** *hills* France
135 C4 **San Clemente** U.S.A.
135 C4 **San Clemente Island** U.S.A.
105 C2 **Sancoins** France
48 H5 **San Cristobal** *i.* Solomon Is
150 B2 **San Cristóbal** Venez.
145 C3 **San Cristóbal de las Casas** Mex.
146 C2 **Sancti Spíritus** Cuba
123 D1 **Sand** *r.* S. Africa
61 C1 **Sandakan** *Sabah* Malaysia
93 E3 **Sandane** Norway
111 B2 **Sandanski** Bulg.
114 A3 **Sandaré** Mali
96 C1 **Sanday** *i.* U.K.
139 C2 **Sanderson** U.S.A.
150 C4 **Sandia** Peru
135 C4 **San Diego** U.S.A.
111 D3 **Sandıklı** Turkey
93 E4 **Sandnes** Norway
92 F2 **Sandnessjøen** Norway
118 C3 **Sandoa** Dem. Rep. Congo
103 E1 **Sandomierz** Pol.
89 E2 **Sandovo** Rus. Fed.
62 A2 **Sandoway** Myanmar
94 B1 **Sandoy** *i.* Faroe Is
94 B1 **Sandoy** *i.* Faroe Is
134 C1 **Sandpoint** U.S.A.
71 B3 **Sandu** China
94 B1 **Sandur** Faroe Is
140 C2 **Sandusky** U.S.A.
122 A3 **Sandveld** *mts* S. Africa
122 A2 **Sandverhaar** Namibia
93 F4 **Sandvika** Norway
93 G3 **Sandviken** Sweden
131 E2 **Sandwich Bay** Can.
135 D2 **Sandy** U.S.A.
129 D2 **Sandy Bay** Can.
51 E2 **Sandy Cape** Austr.
130 A2 **Sandy Lake** Can.
130 A2 **Sandy Lake** *l.* Can.
143 D2 **Sandy Springs** U.S.A.
144 A1 **San Felipe** Mex.
145 B2 **San Felipe** Mex.
150 C1 **San Felipe** Venez.
144 A2 **San Fernando** Mex.
145 C2 **San Fernando** Mex.
64 B2 **San Fernando** Phil.
64 B2 **San Fernando** Phil.
106 B2 **San Fernando** Spain
147 D3 **San Fernando** Trin. and Tob.
150 C2 **San Fernando de Apure** Venez.
143 D3 **Sanford** *FL* U.S.A.
141 E2 **Sanford** *ME* U.S.A.
143 E1 **Sanford** *NC* U.S.A.
152 B3 **San Francisco** Arg.
135 B3 **San Francisco** U.S.A.
107 D2 **San Francisco Javier** Spain
74 B3 **Sangamner** India
83 J2 **Sangar** Rus. Fed.
108 A3 **San Gavino Monreale** *Sardinia* Italy
101 E2 **Sangerhausen** Ger.
61 C1 **Sanggau** Indon.
118 B3 **Sangha** *r.* Congo
109 C3 **San Giovanni in Fiore** Italy
59 C2 **Sangir** *i.* Indon.
59 C2 **Sangir, Kepulauan** *is* Indon.
65 B2 **Sangju** S. Korea
63 A2 **Sangkhla Buri** Thai.
61 C1 **Sangkulirang** Indon.
73 B3 **Sangli** India
118 B2 **Sangmélima** Cameroon
121 C3 **Sango** Zimbabwe
105 D2 **San Gottardo, Passo del** *pass* Switz.
136 B3 **Sangre de Cristo Range** *mts* U.S.A.
75 C2 **Sangsang** China
144 A2 **San Hipólito, Punta** *pt* Mex.
145 D3 **San Ignacio** Belize
152 B1 **San Ignacio** Bol.
144 A2 **San Ignacio** Mex.
130 C2 **Sanikiluaq** Can.
71 A3 **Sanjiang** China
Sanjiang China *see* Jinping
67 C3 **Sanjō** Japan
135 B3 **San Joaquin** *r.* U.S.A.
153 B4 **San Jorge, Golfo de** *g.* Arg.
146 B4 **San José** Costa Rica
64 B2 **San Jose** Phil.
64 B2 **San Jose** Phil.
135 B3 **San Jose** U.S.A.
144 A2 **San José, Isla** *i.* Mex.
144 B2 **San José de Bavicora** Mex.
64 B2 **San Jose de Buenavista** Phil.
144 A2 **San José de Comondú** Mex.
144 B2 **San José del Cabo** Mex.
150 B2 **San José del Guaviare** Col.
152 B3 **San Juan** Arg.
146 B3 **San Juan** *r.* Costa Rica/Nic.
147 C3 **San Juan** Dom. Rep.
147 D3 **San Juan** Puerto Rico
135 D3 **San Juan** *r.* U.S.A.
152 C2 **San Juan Bautista** Para.
107 D2 **San Juan Bautista** Spain
145 C3 **San Juan Bautista Tuxtepec** Mex.
147 D4 **San Juan de los Morros** Venez.
145 C2 **San Juan del Río** Mex.
134 B1 **San Juan Islands** U.S.A.
144 B2 **San Juanito** Mex.
136 B3 **San Juan Mountains** U.S.A.
153 B4 **San Julián** Arg.
75 C2 **Sankh** *r.* India
100 C2 **St Augustin** Ger.
105 D2 **St Gallen** Switz.
105 D2 **St Moritz** Switz.
Sankt-Peterburg Rus. Fed. *see* St Petersburg
89 D2 **St Petersburg** Rus. Fed.
102 C2 **St Veit an der Glan** Austria
100 C3 **St Wendel** Ger.
80 B2 **Şanlıurfa** Turkey
138 B3 **San Lorenzo** Mex.
106 B2 **Sanlúcar de Barrameda** Spain
144 B2 **San Lucas** Mex.
153 B3 **San Luis** Arg.
145 B2 **San Luis de la Paz** Mex.
138 A2 **San Luisito** Mex.
135 B3 **San Luis Obispo** U.S.A.
135 B3 **San Luis Obispo Bay** U.S.A.
145 B2 **San Luis Potosí** Mex.
144 A1 **San Luis Río Colorado** Mex.
139 D3 **San Marcos** U.S.A.
108 B2 **San Marino** *country* Europe
108 B2 **San Marino** San Marino
144 B2 **San Martin de Bolaños** Mex.
153 A4 **San Martín de los Andes** Arg.
135 B3 **San Mateo** U.S.A.
153 B4 **San Matías, Golfo** *g.* Arg.
70 B2 **Sanmenxia** China
146 B3 **San Miguel** El Salvador
152 B2 **San Miguel de Tucumán** Arg.
135 B4 **San Miguel Island** U.S.A.
145 C3 **San Miguel Sola de Vega** Mex.
71 B3 **Sanming** China
153 B3 **San Nicolás de los Arroyos** Arg.
135 C4 **San Nicolas Island** U.S.A.
110 B1 **Sânnicolau Mare** Romania
123 C2 **Sannieshof** S. Africa
114 B4 **Sanniquellie** Liberia
103 E2 **Sanok** Pol.
64 B2 **San Pablo** Phil.
144 B2 **San Pablo Balleza** Mex.
152 B2 **San Pedro** Arg.
152 B1 **San Pedro** Bol.
114 B4 **San-Pédro** Côte d'Ivoire
144 A2 **San Pedro** Mex.
152 C2 **San Pedro** Para.
138 A2 **San Pedro** *watercourse* U.S.A.
106 B2 **San Pedro, Sierra de** *mts* Spain
144 B2 **San Pedro de las Colonias** Mex.
138 A3 **San Pedro el Saucito** Mex.
146 B3 **San Pedro Sula** Hond.
108 A3 **San Pietro, Isola di** *i.* *Sardinia* Italy
96 C3 **Sanquhar** U.K.
144 A1 **San Quintín, Cabo** *c.* Mex.
153 B3 **San Rafael** Arg.
108 A2 **San Remo** Italy
139 D2 **San Saba** U.S.A.
147 C2 **San Salvador** *i.* Bahamas
146 B3 **San Salvador** El Salvador
152 B2 **San Salvador de Jujuy** Arg.
108 B2 **Sansepolcro** Italy
109 C2 **San Severo** Italy
109 C2 **Sanski Most** Bos.-Herz.
152 B1 **Santa Ana** Bol.
146 B3 **Santa Ana** El Salvador
144 A1 **Santa Ana** Mex.
135 C4 **Santa Ana** U.S.A.
152 B1 **Santa Ana de Yacuma** Bol.
144 B2 **Santa Bárbara** Mex.
135 C4 **Santa Barbara** U.S.A.
154 B2 **Santa Bárbara, Serra de** *hills* Brazil
152 B2 **Santa Catalina** Chile
135 C4 **Santa Catalina Island** U.S.A.
150 C3 **Santa Clara** Col.
146 C2 **Santa Clara** Cuba
135 B3 **Santa Clara** U.S.A.

5 C4 **Santa Clarita** U.S.A.
7 D1 **Santa Coloma de Gramenet** Spain
Santa Comba Angola *see* **Waku-Kungo**
9 C3 **Santa Croce, Capo** *c. Sicily* Italy
3 B5 **Santa Cruz** *r.* Arg.
2 B1 **Santa Cruz** Bol.
4 B2 **Santa Cruz** Phil.
5 B3 **Santa Cruz** U.S.A.
5 C3 **Santa Cruz Barillas** Guat.
5 E1 **Santa Cruz Cabrália** Brazil
7 C2 **Santa Cruz de Moya** Spain
4 A2 **Santa Cruz de Tenerife** Canary Is
2 C2 **Santa Cruz do Sul** Brazil
5 C4 **Santa Cruz Island** U.S.A.
8 H5 **Santa Cruz Islands** Solomon Is
6 B1 **Santa Eugenia** Spain
7 D2 **Santa Eulalia del Río** Spain
2 B3 **Santa Fé** Arg.
8 B1 **Santa Fe** U.S.A.
4 B2 **Santa Fé do Sul** Brazil
4 B1 **Santa Helena de Goiás** Brazil
3 B3 **Santa Isabel** Arg.
Santa Isabel Equat. Guinea *see* **Malabo**
8 G4 **Santa Isabel** *i.* Solomon Is
4 B1 **Santa Luisa, Serra de** *hills* Brazil
1 E3 **Santa Luzia** Brazil
4 A2 **Santa Margarita, Isla** *i.* Mex.
2 C2 **Santa Maria** Brazil
4 B1 **Santa María** *r.* Mex.
5 B4 **Santa Maria** U.S.A.
3 D2 **Santa Maria, Cabo de** *c.* Moz.
6 B2 **Santa Maria, Cabo de** *c.* Port.
5 C1 **Santa Maria, Chapadão de** *hills* Brazil
1 E3 **Santa Maria das Barreiras** Brazil
9 C3 **Santa Maria di Leuca, Capo** *c.* Italy
5 D1 **Santa Maria do Suaçuí** Brazil
0 B1 **Santa Marta** Col.
5 C4 **Santa Monica** U.S.A.
1 E4 **Santana** Brazil
0 B1 **Sântana** Romania
6 C1 **Santander** Spain
8 A3 **Sant'Antioco** *Sardinia* Italy
8 A3 **Sant'Antioco, Isola di** *i. Sardinia* Italy
1 D3 **Santarém** Brazil
6 B2 **Santarém** Port.
4 B1 **Santa Rita do Araguaia** Brazil
53 B3 **Santa Rosa** Arg.
52 C2 **Santa Rosa** Brazil
35 B3 **Santa Rosa** *CA* U.S.A.
38 C2 **Santa Rosa** *NM* U.S.A.
46 B3 **Santa Rosa de Copán** Hond.
35 B4 **Santa Rosa Island** *CA* U.S.A.
42 C2 **Santa Rosa Island** *FL* U.S.A.
44 A2 **Santa Rosalía** Mex.
34 C2 **Santa Rosa Range** *mts* U.S.A.
54 B1 **Santa Vitória** Brazil
07 D1 **Sant Carles de la Ràpita** Spain
35 C4 **Santee** U.S.A.
52 C2 **Santiago** Brazil
53 A3 **Santiago** Chile
47 C3 **Santiago** Dom. Rep.
44 B2 **Santiago** Mex.
46 B4 **Santiago** Panama
54 B2 **Santiago** Phil.
06 B1 **Santiago de Compostela** Spain
46 C2 **Santiago de Cuba** Cuba
44 B2 **Santiago Ixcuintla** Mex.
44 B2 **Santiago Papasquiaro** Mex.
06 C1 **Santillana** Spain
07 D1 **Sant Jordi, Golf de** *g.* Spain
55 D2 **Santo Amaro de Campos** Brazil
54 B2 **Santo Anastácio** Brazil
155 C2 **Santo André** Brazil
152 C2 **Santo Angelo** Brazil
154 B2 **Santo Antônio da Platina** Brazil
151 F4 **Santo Antônio de Jesus** Brazil
150 C3 **Santo Antônio do Içá** Brazil
155 C2 **Santo Antônio do Monte** Brazil
147 D3 **Santo Domingo** Dom. Rep.
144 A2 **Santo Domingo** Mex.
138 B1 **Santo Domingo Pueblo** U.S.A.
111 C3 **Santorini** *i.* Greece
155 C2 **Santos** Brazil
155 D2 **Santos Dumont** Brazil
157 I7 **Santos Plateau** *sea feature* S. Atlantic Ocean
152 C2 **Santo Tomé** Arg.
153 A4 **San Valentín, Cerro** *mt.* Chile
146 B3 **San Vicente** El Salvador
144 A1 **San Vicente** Mex.
64 B2 **San Vicente** Phil.
150 B4 **San Vicente de Cañete** Peru
108 B2 **San Vincenzo** Italy
108 B3 **San Vito, Capo** *c. Sicily* Italy
71 A4 **Sanya** China
155 C2 **São Bernardo do Campo** Brazil
152 C2 **São Borja** Brazil
154 C2 **São Carlos** Brazil
155 D1 **São Felipe, Serra de** *hills* Brazil
151 D4 **São Félix** Brazil
151 D3 **São Félix** Brazil
155 D2 **São Fidélis** Brazil
155 D1 **São Francisco** Brazil
151 F4 **São Francisco** *r.* Brazil
154 C3 **São Francisco, Ilha de** *i.* Brazil
154 C3 **São Francisco do Sul** Brazil
152 C3 **São Gabriel** Brazil
155 D2 **São Gonçalo** Brazil
155 C1 **São Gonçalo do Abaeté** Brazil
155 C1 **São Gotardo** Brazil
154 B1 **São Jerônimo, Serra de** *hills* Brazil
155 D2 **São João da Barra** Brazil
155 C2 **São João da Boa Vista** Brazil
106 B1 **São João da Madeira** Port.
155 D1 **São João da Ponte** Brazil
155 D2 **São João del Rei** Brazil
155 D1 **São João do Paraíso** Brazil
155 D1 **São João Evangelista** Brazil
155 D2 **São João Nepomuceno** Brazil
154 C2 **São Joaquim da Barra** Brazil
152 D2 **São José** Brazil
154 C2 **São José do Rio Preto** Brazil
155 C2 **São José dos Campos** Brazil
154 C3 **São José dos Pinhais** Brazil
154 A1 **São Lourenço** Brazil
155 C2 **São Lourenço** Brazil
151 E3 **São Luís** Brazil
154 C2 **São Manuel** Brazil
154 C1 **São Marcos** *r.* Brazil
151 E3 **São Marcos, Baía de** *b.* Brazil
155 E1 **São Mateus** Brazil
154 B3 **São Mateus do Sul** Brazil
105 C2 **Saône** *r.* France
155 C2 **São Paulo** Brazil
155 D2 **São Pedro da Aldeia** Brazil
151 E3 **São Raimundo Nonato** Brazil
155 C1 **São Romão** Brazil
São Salvador Angola *see* **M'banza Congo**
São Salvador do Congo Angola *see* **M'banza Congo**
155 C2 **São Sebastião, Ilha do** *i.* Brazil
154 C2 **São Sebastião do Paraíso** Brazil
154 B1 **São Simão** Brazil
154 B1 **São Simão, Barragem de** *resr* Brazil
59 C2 **Sao-Siu** Indon.
113 D5 **São Tomé** São Tomé and Príncipe
113 D5 **São Tomé** *i.* São Tomé and Príncipe
155 D2 **São Tomé, Cabo de** *c.* Brazil
113 D5 **São Tomé and Príncipe** *country* Africa
155 C2 **São Vicente** Brazil
106 B2 **São Vicente, Cabo de** *c.* Port.
59 C3 **Saparua** Indon.
107 D2 **Sa Pobla** Spain
89 F3 **Sapozhok** Rus. Fed.
66 D2 **Sapporo** Japan
109 C2 **Sapri** Italy
139 D1 **Sapulpa** U.S.A.
81 C2 **Saqqez** Iran
81 C2 **Sarāb** Iran
63 B2 **Sara Buri** Thai.
Saragossa Spain *see* **Zaragoza**
89 F3 **Sarai** Rus. Fed.
109 C2 **Sarajevo** Bos.-Herz.
87 E3 **Saraktash** Rus. Fed.
62 A1 **Saramati** *mt.* India/Myanmar
141 E2 **Saranac Lake** U.S.A.
109 D3 **Sarandë** Albania
64 B3 **Sarangani Islands** Phil.
87 D3 **Saransk** Rus. Fed.
87 E3 **Sarapul** Rus. Fed.
143 D3 **Sarasota** U.S.A.
90 B2 **Sarata** Ukr.
136 B2 **Saratoga** U.S.A.
141 E2 **Saratoga Springs** U.S.A.
61 C1 **Saratok** *Sarawak* Malaysia
87 D3 **Saratov** Rus. Fed.
79 D2 **Saravan** Iran
63 B2 **Saravan** Laos
61 C1 **Sarawak** *state* Malaysia
111 C2 **Saray** Turkey
111 C3 **Sarayköy** Turkey
79 D2 **Sarbāz** Iran
76 B3 **Sarbīsheh** Iran
74 B2 **Sardarshahr** India
Sardegna *i.* Italy *see* **Sardinia**
108 A2 **Sardinia** *i.* Italy
92 G2 **Sarektjåkkå** *mt.* Sweden
77 C3 **Sar-e Pol** Afgh.
158 C3 **Sargasso Sea** *sea* Atlantic Ocean
74 B1 **Sargodha** Pak.
115 D4 **Sarh** Chad
79 D2 **Sarhad** *reg.* Iran
81 D2 **Sārī** Iran
111 C3 **Sarıgöl** Turkey
81 C1 **Sarıkamış** Turkey
61 C1 **Sarikei** *Sarawak* Malaysia
51 D2 **Sarina** Austr.
115 D2 **Sarīr Tibesti** *des.* Libya
65 B2 **Sariwŏn** N. Korea
111 C2 **Sarıyer** Turkey
77 D2 **Sarkand** Kazakh.
111 C2 **Şarköy** Turkey
104 C3 **Sarlat-la-Canéda** France
59 D3 **Sarmi** Indon.
153 B4 **Sarmiento** Arg.
140 C2 **Sarnia** Can.
90 B1 **Sarny** Ukr.
60 B2 **Sarolangun** Indon.
111 B3 **Saronikos Kolpos** *g.* Greece
111 C2 **Saros Körfezi** *b.* Turkey
103 E2 **Sárospatak** Hungary
87 D3 **Sarova** Rus. Fed.
Sarpan *i.* N. Mariana Is *see* **Rota**
105 D2 **Sarrebourg** France
106 B1 **Sarria** Spain
107 C1 **Sarrión** Spain
105 D3 **Sartène** *Corsica* France
Sartu China *see* **Daqing**
111 C3 **Saruhanlı** Turkey
103 D2 **Sárvár** Hungary
81 D3 **Sarvestān** Iran
76 B2 **Sarykamyshkoye Ozero** *salt l.* Turkm./Uzbek.
77 D2 **Saryozek** Kazakh.
77 D2 **Saryshagan** Kazakh.
77 C2 **Sarysu** *watercourse* Kazakh.
77 D3 **Sary-Tash** Kyrg.
75 C2 **Sasaram** India
67 A4 **Sasebo** Japan
129 D2 **Saskatchewan** *prov.* Can.
129 D2 **Saskatchewan** *r.* Can.
129 D2 **Saskatoon** Can.
83 I2 **Saskylakh** Rus. Fed.
123 C2 **Sasolburg** S. Africa
87 D3 **Sasovo** Rus. Fed.
114 B4 **Sassandra** Côte d'Ivoire
108 A2 **Sassari** *Sardinia* Italy
102 C1 **Sassnitz** Ger.
114 A3 **Satadougou** Mali
136 C3 **Satanta** U.S.A.
73 B3 **Satara** India
123 D1 **Satara** S. Africa
87 E3 **Satka** Rus. Fed.
75 C2 **Satna** India
77 C2 **Satpayev** Kazakh.
74 B2 **Satpura Range** *mts* India
63 B2 **Sattahip** Thai.
110 B1 **Satu Mare** Romania
63 B3 **Satun** Thai.
144 B2 **Saucillo** Mex.
93 E4 **Sauda** Norway
92 □B2 **Sauðárkrókur** Iceland
78 B2 **Saudi Arabia** *country* Asia
105 C3 **Saugues** France
137 E1 **Sauk Center** U.S.A.
105 C2 **Saulieu** France
88 B2 **Saulkrasti** Latvia
130 B3 **Sault Ste Marie** Can.
140 C1 **Sault Ste Marie** U.S.A.
77 C1 **Saumalkol'** Kazakh.
59 C3 **Saumlakki** Indon.
104 B2 **Saumur** France
120 B1 **Saurimo** Angola
109 D2 **Sava** *r.* Europe
49 J5 **Savai'i** *i.* Samoa
91 E1 **Savala** *r.* Rus. Fed.
114 C4 **Savalou** Benin
143 D2 **Savannah** *GA* U.S.A.
142 C1 **Savannah** *TN* U.S.A.
143 D2 **Savannah** *r.* U.S.A.
63 B2 **Savannakhét** Laos
130 A2 **Savant Lake** Can.
111 C3 **Savaştepe** Turkey
114 C4 **Savè** Benin
105 D2 **Saverne** France
89 F2 **Savino** Rus. Fed.
86 D2 **Savinskiy** Rus. Fed.
105 D2 **Savoie** *reg.* France
108 A2 **Savona** Italy
93 I3 **Savonlinna** Fin.
Savoy *reg.* France *see* **Savoie**
93 F4 **Sävsjö** Sweden
59 C3 **Savu** *i.* Indon.
92 I2 **Savukoski** Fin.
74 B2 **Sawai Madhopur** India
62 A1 **Sawan** Myanmar
62 A2 **Sawankhalok** Thai.
136 B3 **Sawatch Range** *mts* U.S.A.
121 B2 **Sawmills** Zimbabwe
79 C3 **Şawqirah, Dawḩat** *b.* Oman
Şawqirah Bay Oman *see* **Şawqirah, Dawḩat**
53 D2 **Sawtell** Austr.
137 E1 **Sawtooth Mountains** *hills* U.S.A.
134 C2 **Sawtooth Range** *mts* U.S.A.
61 D2 **Sawu Sea** Indon.
68 C1 **Sayano-Shushenskoye Vodokhranilishche** *resr* Rus. Fed.
76 C3 **Sayat** Turkm.
79 C3 **Sayḩūt** Yemen
93 I3 **Säynätsalo** Fin.
69 D2 **Saynshand** Mongolia
141 D2 **Sayre** U.S.A.
144 B3 **Sayula** Mex.
145 C3 **Sayula** Mex.
128 B2 **Sayward** Can.
Sayyod Turkm. *see* **Sayat**
89 E2 **Sazonovo** Rus. Fed.
114 B2 **Sbaa** Alg.
98 B2 **Scafell Pike** *hill* U.K.
109 C3 **Scalea** Italy
96 □ **Scalloway** U.K.
108 B2 **Scandicci** Italy
96 C1 **Scapa Flow** *inlet* U.K.
96 B2 **Scarba** *i.* U.K.
130 C3 **Scarborough** Can.
147 D3 **Scarborough** Trin. and Tob.
98 C2 **Scarborough** U.K.
64 A2 **Scarborough Shoal** *sea feature* Phil.
96 A2 **Scarinish** U.K.

Scarpanto *i.* Greece *see* Karpathos
100 B2 **Schaerbeek** Belgium
105 D2 **Schaffhausen** Switz.
100 B1 **Schagen** Neth.
102 C2 **Schärding** Austria
100 A2 **Scharendijke** Neth.
101 D1 **Scharhörn** *sea feature* Ger.
101 D1 **Scheeßel** Ger.
131 D2 **Schefferville** Can.
135 D3 **Schell Creek Range** *mts* U.S.A.
141 E2 **Schenectady** U.S.A.
139 D3 **Schertz** U.S.A.
101 E3 **Scheßlitz** Ger.
100 C1 **Schiermonnikoog** *i.* Neth.
100 B2 **Schilde** Belgium
108 B1 **Schio** Italy
101 F2 **Schkeuditz** Ger.
101 E1 **Schladen** Ger.
102 C2 **Schladming** Austria
101 E2 **Schleiz** Ger.
102 B1 **Schleswig** Ger.
101 D2 **Schloß Holte-Stukenbrock** Ger.
101 D2 **Schlüchtern** Ger.
101 E3 **Schlüsselfeld** Ger.
101 D2 **Schmallenberg** Ger.
Schmidt Island Rus. Fed. *see* **Shmidta, Ostrov**
101 F2 **Schmölln** Ger.
101 D1 **Schneverdingen** Ger.
101 E1 **Schönebeck (Elbe)** Ger.
101 E1 **Schöningen** Ger.
100 B2 **Schoonhoven** Neth.
59 D3 **Schouten Islands** P.N.G.
97 B3 **Schull** Rep. of Ireland
101 E3 **Schwabach** Ger.
102 B2 **Schwäbische Alb** *mts* Ger.
101 F3 **Schwandorf** Ger.
61 C2 **Schwaner, Pegunungan** *mts* Indon.
101 E1 **Schwarzenbek** Ger.
101 F2 **Schwarzenberg** Ger.
122 A2 **Schwarzrand** *mts* Namibia
102 B2 **Schwarzwald** *mts* Ger.
102 C2 **Schwaz** Austria
102 C1 **Schwedt an der Oder** Ger.
101 E2 **Schweinfurt** Ger.
101 E1 **Schwerin** Ger.
101 E1 **Schweriner See** *l.* Ger.
105 D2 **Schwyz** Switz.
108 B3 **Sciacca** *Sicily* Italy
95 B4 **Scilly, Isles of** U.K.
140 C3 **Scioto** *r.* U.S.A.
136 B1 **Scobey** U.S.A.
53 D2 **Scone** Austr.
110 B2 **Scornicești** Romania
55 C3 **Scotia Ridge** *sea feature* S. Atlantic Ocean
149 F8 **Scotia Sea** S. Atlantic Ocean
96 C2 **Scotland** *admin. div.* U.K.
128 B2 **Scott, Cape** Can.
123 D3 **Scottburgh** S. Africa
136 C3 **Scott City** U.S.A.
136 C2 **Scottsbluff** U.S.A.
142 C2 **Scottsboro** U.S.A.
96 B1 **Scourie** U.K.
141 D2 **Scranton** U.S.A.
98 C3 **Scunthorpe** U.K.
105 E2 **Scuol** Switz.
Scutari Albania *see* **Shkodër**
99 D4 **Seaford** U.K.
98 C2 **Seaham** U.K.
129 E2 **Seal** *r.* Can.
122 B3 **Seal, Cape** S. Africa
52 B3 **Sea Lake** Austr.
139 D3 **Sealy** U.S.A.
142 B1 **Searcy** U.S.A.
98 B2 **Seascale** U.K.
134 B1 **Seattle** U.S.A.
141 E2 **Sebago Lake** U.S.A.
144 A2 **Sebastián Vizcaíno, Bahía** *b.* Mex.
Sebastopol Ukr. *see* **Sevastopol'**
Sebenico Croatia *see* **Šibenik**
110 B1 **Sebeș** Romania
60 B2 **Sebesi** *i.* Indon.
88 C2 **Sebezh** Rus. Fed.
80 B1 **Şebinkarahisar** Turkey
143 D3 **Sebring** U.S.A.
61 C2 **Sebuku** *i.* Indon.
128 B3 **Sechelt** Can.
150 A3 **Sechura** Peru
73 B3 **Secunderabad** India
137 E3 **Sedalia** U.S.A.
105 C2 **Sedan** France
54 B2 **Seddon** N.Z.
114 A3 **Sédhiou** Senegal
138 A2 **Sedona** U.S.A.
101 E2 **Seeburg** Ger.
101 E1 **Seehausen (Altmark)** Ger.
122 A2 **Seeheim** Namibia
104 C2 **Sées** France
101 E2 **Seesen** Ger.
101 E1 **Seevetal** Ger.
114 A4 **Sefadu** Sierra Leone
123 C1 **Sefare** Botswana
93 F3 **Segalstad** Norway
60 B1 **Segamat** Malaysia
86 C2 **Segezha** Rus. Fed.
114 B3 **Ségou** Mali
106 C1 **Segovia** Spain
86 C2 **Segozerskoye, Ozero** *resr* Rus. Fed.
115 D2 **Séguédine** Niger
114 B4 **Séguéla** Côte d'Ivoire
139 D3 **Seguin** U.S.A.
107 C2 **Segura** *r.* Spain
106 C2 **Segura, Sierra de** *mts* Spain
120 B3 **Sehithwa** Botswana
93 H3 **Seinäjoki** Fin.
104 C2 **Seine** *r.* France
104 B2 **Seine, Baie de** *b.* France
105 C2 **Seine, Val de** *val.* France
103 E1 **Sejny** Pol.
60 B2 **Sekayu** Indon.
114 B4 **Sekondi** Ghana
134 B1 **Selah** U.S.A.
59 C3 **Selaru** *i.* Indon.
61 C2 **Selatan, Tanjung** *pt* Indon.
126 B2 **Selawik** U.S.A.
98 C3 **Selby** U.K.
136 C1 **Selby** U.S.A.
111 C3 **Selçuk** Turkey
120 B3 **Selebi-Phikwe** Botswana
Selebi-Pikwe Botswana *see* **Selebi-Phikwe**
105 D2 **Sélestat** France
Seletyteniz, Oz. *salt l.* Kazakh. *see* **Siletiteniz, Ozero**
92 □A3 **Selfoss** Iceland
114 A3 **Sélibabi** Maur.
138 A1 **Seligman** U.S.A.
116 A2 **Selîma Oasis** Sudan
111 C3 **Selimiye** Turkey
114 B3 **Sélingué, Lac de** *l.* Mali
89 D2 **Selizharovo** Rus. Fed.
93 E4 **Seljord** Norway
129 E2 **Selkirk** Can.
96 C3 **Selkirk** U.K.
128 C2 **Selkirk Mountains** Can.
138 A2 **Sells** U.S.A.
142 C2 **Selma** *AL* U.S.A.
135 C3 **Selma** *CA* U.S.A.
105 D2 **Selongey** France
99 C4 **Selsey Bill** *hd* U.K.
89 D3 **Sel'tso** Rus. Fed.
Selukwe Zimbabwe *see* **Shurugwi**
150 B3 **Selvas** *reg.* Brazil
134 C1 **Selway** *r.* U.S.A.
129 D1 **Selwyn Lake** Can.
128 A1 **Selwyn Mountains** Can.
51 C2 **Selwyn Range** *hills* Austr.
60 B2 **Semangka, Teluk** *b.* Indon.
61 C2 **Semarang** Indon.
60 B1 **Sematan** *Sarawak* Malaysia
118 B2 **Sembé** Congo
81 C2 **Şemdinli** Turkey
91 C1 **Semenivka** Ukr.
87 D3 **Semenov** Rus. Fed.
61 C2 **Semeru, Gunung** *vol.* Indon.
91 E2 **Semikarakorsk** Rus. Fed.
89 E3 **Semiluki** Rus. Fed.
136 B2 **Seminoe Reservoir** U.S.A.
139 C2 **Seminole** U.S.A.
143 D2 **Seminole, Lake** U.S.A.
77 E1 **Semipalatinsk** Kazakh.
61 C1 **Semitau** Indon.
Sem Kolodezey Ukr. *see* **Lenine**
81 D2 **Semnān** Iran
61 C1 **Semporna** *Sabah* Malaysia
105 C2 **Semur-en-Auxois** France
Semyonovskoye Rus. Fed. *see* **Bereznik**
Semyonovskoye Rus. Fed. *see* **Ostrovskoye**
150 C3 **Sena Madureira** Brazil
120 B2 **Senanga** Zambia
67 B4 **Sendai** Japan
67 D3 **Sendai** Japan
143 D2 **Seneca** U.S.A.
114 A3 **Senegal** *country* Africa
114 A3 **Sénégal** *r.* Maur./Senegal
102 C1 **Senftenberg** Ger.
119 D3 **Sengerema** Tanz.
151 E4 **Senhor do Bonfim** Brazil
103 D2 **Senica** Slovakia
108 B2 **Senigallia** Italy
109 B2 **Senj** Croatia
92 G2 **Senja** *i.* Norway
122 B2 **Senlac** S. Africa
105 C2 **Senlis** France
63 B2 **Senmonorom** Cambodia
116 B3 **Sennar** Sudan
130 C3 **Senneterre** Can.
123 C3 **Senqu** *r.* Lesotho
105 C2 **Sens** France
109 D1 **Senta** Yugo.
128 B2 **Sentinel Peak** Can.
75 B2 **Seoni** India
65 B2 **Seoul** S. Korea
155 D2 **Sepetiba, Baía de** *b.* Brazil
59 D3 **Sepik** *r.* P.N.G.
61 C1 **Sepinang** Indon.
131 D2 **Sept-Îles** Can.
87 D4 **Serafimovich** Rus. Fed.
100 B2 **Seraing** Belgium
59 C3 **Seram** *i.* Indon.
59 C3 **Seram Sea** Indon.
60 B2 **Serang** Indon.
60 B1 **Serasan, Selat** *sea chan.* Indon.
109 D2 **Serbia** *aut. rep.* Yugo.
117 C3 **Serdo** Eth.
89 E3 **Serebryanyye Prudy** Rus. Fed.
60 B1 **Seremban** Malaysia
119 D3 **Serengeti Plain** Tanz.
121 C2 **Serenje** Zambia
90 B2 **Seret** *r.* Ukr.
87 D3 **Sergach** Rus. Fed.
86 F2 **Sergino** Rus. Fed.
89 E2 **Sergiyev Posad** Rus. Fed.
Sergo Ukr. *see* **Stakhanov**
61 C1 **Seria** Brunei
61 C1 **Serian** *Sarawak* Malaysia
111 B3 **Serifos** *i.* Greece
80 B2 **Serik** Turkey
59 C3 **Sermata, Kepulauan** *is* Indon.
Sernyy Zavod Turkm. *see* **Kukurtli**
86 F3 **Serov** Rus. Fed.
120 B3 **Serowe** Botswana
106 B2 **Serpa** Port.
Serpa Pinto Angola *see* **Menongue**
89 E3 **Serpukhov** Rus. Fed.
155 D2 **Serra** Brazil
155 C1 **Serra das Araras** Brazil
108 A3 **Serramanna** *Sardinia* Italy
154 B1 **Serranópolis** Brazil
100 A3 **Serre** *r.* France
111 B2 **Serres** Greece
151 F4 **Serrinha** Brazil
155 D1 **Sêrro** Brazil
154 C2 **Sertãozinho** Brazil
59 D3 **Serui** Indon.
120 B3 **Serule** Botswana
61 C2 **Seruyan** *r.* Indon.
68 C2 **Sêrxu** China
120 A2 **Sesfontein** Namibia
108 B2 **Sessa Aurunca** Italy
107 D2 **Ses Salines, Cap de** *c.* Spain
108 A2 **Sestri Levante** Italy
105 C3 **Sète** France
155 D1 **Sete Lagoas** Brazil
92 G2 **Setermoen** Norway
93 E4 **Setesdal** *val.* Norway
115 C1 **Sétif** Alg.
67 B4 **Seto-naikai** *sea* Japan
114 B1 **Settat** Morocco
98 B2 **Settle** U.K.
106 B2 **Setúbal** Port.
106 B2 **Setúbal, Baía de** *b.* Port.
130 A2 **Seul, Lac** *l.* Can.
81 C1 **Sevan** Armenia
76 A2 **Sevan, Lake** Armenia
Sevana Lich *l.* Armenia *see* **Sevan, Lake**
91 C3 **Sevastopol'** Ukr.
Seven Islands Can. *see* **Sept-Îles**
131 D2 **Seven Islands Bay** Can.
99 D4 **Sevenoaks** U.K.
105 C3 **Sévérac-le-Château** France
130 B2 **Severn** *r.* Can.
122 B2 **Severn** S. Africa
99 B4 **Severn** *r.* U.K.
86 D2 **Severnaya Dvina** *r.* Rus. Fed.
83 H1 **Severnaya Zemlya** *is* Rus. Fed.
86 D2 **Severnyy** Rus. Fed.
86 F2 **Severnyy** Rus. Fed.
83 I3 **Severobaykal'sk** Rus. Fe
86 C2 **Severodvinsk** Rus. Fed.
83 L3 **Severo-Kuril'sk** Rus. Fed
92 J2 **Severomorsk** Rus. Fed.
86 C2 **Severoonezhsk** Rus. Fed
83 H2 **Severo-Yeniseyskiy** Rus. Fed.
91 D3 **Severskaya** Rus. Fed.
135 D3 **Sevier** *r.* U.S.A.
135 D3 **Sevier Lake** U.S.A.
Sevilla Spain *see* **Seville**
106 B2 **Seville** Spain
Sevlyush Ukr. *see* **Vynohradiv**
89 D3 **Sevsk** Rus. Fed.
126 C2 **Seward** U.S.A.
126 B2 **Seward Peninsula** U.S.A.
128 A2 **Sewell Inlet** Can.
128 C2 **Sexsmith** Can.
144 B2 **Sextín** *r.* Mex.
86 G1 **Seyakha** Rus. Fed.
113 I6 **Seychelles** *country* Indian Ocean
92 □C2 **Seyðisfjörður** Iceland
Seyhan Turkey *see* **Adana**
80 B2 **Seyhan** *r.* Turkey
91 C1 **Seym** *r.* Rus. Fed./Ukr.
83 L2 **Seymchan** Rus. Fed.
53 C3 **Seymour** Austr.
123 C3 **Seymour** S. Africa
140 B3 **Seymour** *IN* U.S.A.
139 D2 **Seymour** *TX* U.S.A.
105 C2 **Sézanne** France
108 B2 **Sezze** Italy
111 B3 **Sfakia** Greece
110 C1 **Sfântu Gheorghe** Romania
115 D1 **Sfax** Tunisia
Sfîntu Gheorghe Romani *see* **Sfântu Gheorghe**
's-Gravenhage Neth. *see* **The Hague**
96 A2 **Sgurr Alasdair** *hill* U.K.
70 A2 **Shaanxi** *prov.* China
Shabani Zimbabwe *see* **Zvishavane**
91 D2 **Shabel'sk** Rus. Fed.
77 D3 **Shache** China
55 C1 **Shackleton Range** *mts* Antarctica
74 A2 **Shadadkot** Pak.
86 F3 **Shadrinsk** Rus. Fed.
99 B4 **Shaftesbury** U.K.
126 B2 **Shageluk** U.S.A.
Shāhābād Iran *see* **Eslāmābād-e Gharb**
75 C2 **Shahdol** India
77 C3 **Shah Fuladi** *mt.* Afgh.
75 B2 **Shahjahanpur** India
76 B3 **Shāh Kūh** *mt.* Iran
81 D2 **Shahr-e Bābak** Iran
81 D2 **Shahr-e Kord** Iran
Shahrezā Iran *see* **Qomishēh**
Shāhrūd Iran *see* **Emāmrūd**
79 B2 **Shaj'ah, Jabal** *hill* Saudi Arabia
89 E2 **Shakhovskaya** Rus. Fed.
77 C3 **Shakhrisabz** Uzbek.
Shakhterskoye Ukr. *see* **Pershotravens'k**
Shakhty Rus. Fed. *see* **Gusinoozersk**
91 E2 **Shakhty** Rus. Fed.
Shakhtyorskoye Ukr. *see* **Pershotravens'k**
86 D3 **Shakhun'ya** Rus. Fed.
66 D2 **Shakotan-hantō** *pen.* Japan
66 D2 **Shakotan-misaki** *c.* Japan
68 C2 **Shaluli Shan** *mts* China
129 E2 **Shamattawa** Can.
139 C1 **Shamrock** U.S.A.
70 A2 **Shandan** China
70 B2 **Shandong** *prov.* China
70 C2 **Shandong Bandao** *pen.* China
121 B2 **Shangani** Zimbabwe
121 B2 **Shangani** *r.* Zimbabwe
70 B1 **Shangdu** China
70 C2 **Shanghai** China

'0 C2 **Shanghai** *mun.* China
'1 B3 **Shanghang** China
'0 B2 **Shangnan** China
'0 B2 **Shangqiu** China
'1 B3 **Shangrao** China
'0 B2 **Shangshui** China
'7 E2 **Shangyou Shuiku** *resr* China
'0 C2 **Shangyu** China
9 E1 **Shangzhi** China
'0 A2 **Shangzhou** China
4 B1 **Shaniko** U.S.A.
7 B2 **Shannon** *r.* Rep. of Ireland
7 B2 **Shannon, Mouth of the** Rep. of Ireland
2 A1 **Shan Plateau** Myanmar
Shansi *prov.* China *see* Shanxi
'1 B3 **Shantou** China
Shantung *prov.* China *see* Shandong
'0 B2 **Shanxi** *prov.* China
'1 B3 **Shaoguan** China
'1 B3 **Shaowu** China
'0 C2 **Shaoxing** China
'1 B3 **Shaoyang** China
6 C1 **Shapinsay** *i.* U.K.
6 C2 **Shaqrā'** Saudi Arabia
0 B2 **Sharhorod** Ukr.
'9 C2 **Sharjah** U.A.E.
8 C2 **Sharkawshchyna** Belarus
0 A2 **Shark Bay** Austr.
'8 A2 **Sharm el Sheikh** Egypt
0 C2 **Sharon** U.S.A.
6 D3 **Shar'ya** Rus. Fed.
21 B3 **Shashe** *r.* Botswana/Zimbabwe
7 B4 **Shashemenē** Eth.
Shashi China *see* **Jingsha**
4 B2 **Shasta, Mount** *vol.* U.S.A.
4 B2 **Shasta Lake** U.S.A.
5 D2 **Shāṭi', Wādī ash** *watercourse* Libya
Shatilki Belarus *see* Svyetlahorsk
9 E2 **Shatura** Rus. Fed.
29 D3 **Shaunavon** Can.
0 B2 **Shawano** U.S.A.
30 C3 **Shawinigan** Can.
39 D1 **Shawnee** U.S.A.
3 M2 **Shayboveyem** *r.* Rus. Fed.
0 B2 **Shay Gap** Austr.
9 E3 **Shchekino** Rus. Fed.
9 E2 **Shchelkovo** Rus. Fed.
Shcherbakov Rus. Fed. *see* **Rybinsk**
Shcherbinovka Ukr. *see* **Dzerzhyns'k**
9 E3 **Shchigry** Rus. Fed.
1 C1 **Shchors** Ukr.
8 B3 **Shchuchyn** Belarus
1 D1 **Shebekino** Rus. Fed.
'7 C3 **Sheberghān** Afgh.
0 B2 **Sheboygan** U.S.A.
1 D3 **Shebsh** *r.* Rus. Fed.
7 C2 **Sheelin, Lough** *l.* Rep. of Ireland
36 B3 **Sheep Mountain** U.S.A.
9 D4 **Sheerness** U.K.
8 C3 **Sheffield** U.K.
39 C2 **Sheffield** U.S.A.
Sheikh Othman Yemen *see* **Ash Shaykh 'Uthman**
Shekhem West Bank *see* **Nāblus**
39 E2 **Sheksna** Rus. Fed.
39 E2 **Sheksninskoye Vodokhranilishche** *resr* Rus. Fed.
3 M2 **Shelagskiy, Mys** *pt* Rus. Fed.
31 D3 **Shelburne** Can.
0 B2 **Shelby** *MI* U.S.A.
34 D1 **Shelby** *MT* U.S.A.
3 D1 **Shelby** *NC* U.S.A.
0 B3 **Shelbyville** *IN* U.S.A.
2 C1 **Shelbyville** *TN* U.S.A.
3 L2 **Shelikhova, Zaliv** *g.* Rus. Fed.
26 B3 **Shelikof Strait** U.S.A.
29 D2 **Shellbrook** Can.
Shelter Bay Can. *see* Port-Cartier
34 B1 **Shelton** U.S.A.
37 D2 **Shenandoah** U.S.A.
1 D3 **Shenandoah** *r.* U.S.A.
1 D3 **Shenandoah Mountains** U.S.A.
18 A2 **Shendam** Nigeria

Shengli Feng *mt.* China/Kyrg. *see* Jengish Chokusu
86 D2 **Shenkursk** Rus. Fed.
70 B2 **Shenmu** China
Shensi *prov.* China *see* Shaanxi
70 C1 **Shenyang** China
71 B3 **Shenzhen** China
90 B1 **Shepetivka** Ukr.
53 C3 **Shepparton** Austr.
99 D4 **Sheppey, Isle of** *i.* U.K.
131 D3 **Sherbrooke** *N.S.* Can.
130 C3 **Sherbrooke** *Que.* Can.
97 C2 **Shercock** Rep. of Ireland
116 B3 **Shereiq** Sudan
136 B2 **Sheridan** U.S.A.
52 A2 **Sheringa** Austr.
86 F2 **Sherkaly** Rus. Fed.
139 D2 **Sherman** U.S.A.
100 B2 **'s-Hertogenbosch** Neth.
96 □ **Shetland Islands** U.K.
76 B2 **Shetpe** Kazakh.
Shevchenko Kazakh. *see* Aktau
91 D2 **Shevchenkove** Ukr.
137 D1 **Sheyenne** *r.* U.S.A.
79 B3 **Shibām** Yemen
67 C3 **Shibata** Japan
66 D2 **Shibetsu** Japan
Shibotsu-jima *i.* Rus. Fed. *see* **Zelenyy, Ostrov**
71 B3 **Shicheng** China
70 C2 **Shidao** China
96 B2 **Shiel, Loch** *l.* U.K.
Shigatse China *see* **Xigazê**
77 E2 **Shihezi** China
Shihkiachwang China *see* Shijiazhuang
Shijiao China *see* **Fogang**
70 B2 **Shijiazhuang** China
Shijiusuo China *see* Rizhao
74 A2 **Shikarpur** Pak.
67 B4 **Shikoku** *i.* Japan
66 D2 **Shikotsu-ko** *l.* Japan
86 D2 **Shilega** Rus. Fed.
75 C2 **Shiliguri** India
97 C2 **Shillelagh** Rep. of Ireland
75 D2 **Shillong** India
89 F3 **Shilovo** Rus. Fed.
69 E1 **Shimanovsk** Rus. Fed.
117 C3 **Shimbiris** *mt.* Somalia
67 C3 **Shimizu** Japan
74 B1 **Shimla** India
67 C4 **Shimoda** Japan
73 B3 **Shimoga** India
66 D2 **Shimokita-hantō** *pen.* Japan
67 B4 **Shimonoseki** Japan
89 D2 **Shimsk** Rus. Fed.
96 B1 **Shin, Loch** *l.* U.K.
62 A1 **Shingbwiyang** Myanmar
67 C4 **Shingū** Japan
123 D1 **Shingwedzi** S. Africa
123 D1 **Shingwedzi** *r.* S. Africa
66 D3 **Shinjō** Japan
119 D3 **Shinyanga** Tanz.
67 D3 **Shiogama** Japan
67 C4 **Shiono-misaki** *c.* Japan
71 A3 **Shiping** China
98 C3 **Shipley** U.K.
138 B1 **Shiprock** U.S.A.
71 A3 **Shiqian** China
Shiqizhen China *see* Zhongshan
70 A2 **Shiquan** China
78 B2 **Shi'r, Jabal** *hill* Saudi Arabia
67 C3 **Shirane-san** *mt.* Japan
67 C3 **Shirane-san** *vol.* Japan
81 D3 **Shīrāz** Iran
66 D2 **Shiretoko-misaki** *c.* Japan
66 D2 **Shiriya-zaki** *c.* Japan
76 B3 **Shīrvān** Iran
74 B2 **Shiv** India
74 B2 **Shivpuri** India
70 B2 **Shiyan** China
70 A2 **Shizuishan** China
67 C4 **Shizuoka** Japan
89 D3 **Shklow** Belarus
109 C2 **Shkodër** Albania
83 H1 **Shmidta, Ostrov** *i.* Rus. Fed.
67 B4 **Shōbara** Japan
Sholapur India *see* Solāpur
158 F8 **Shona Ridge** *sea feature* S. Atlantic Ocean
76 B2 **Shor Barsa-Kel'mes** *salt marsh* Uzbek.

74 B1 **Shorkot** Pak.
135 C3 **Shoshone** *CA* U.S.A.
134 D2 **Shoshone** *ID* U.S.A.
135 C3 **Shoshone Mountains** U.S.A.
123 C1 **Shoshong** Botswana
91 C1 **Shostka** Ukr.
70 B2 **Shouxian** China
78 A3 **Showak** Sudan
138 A2 **Show Low** U.S.A.
91 C2 **Shpola** Ukr.
142 B2 **Shreveport** U.S.A.
99 B3 **Shrewsbury** U.K.
77 D2 **Shu** Kazakh.
Shuangjiang China *see* Tongdao
62 A1 **Shuangjiang** China
Shuangxi China *see* Shunchang
66 B1 **Shuangyashan** China
87 E4 **Shubarkuduk** Kazakh.
116 B1 **Shubrâ el Kheima** Egypt
89 D2 **Shugozero** Rus. Fed.
Shuidong China *see* Dianbai
120 B2 **Shumba** Zimbabwe
110 C2 **Shumen** Bulg.
87 F3 **Shumikha** Rus. Fed.
88 C2 **Shumilina** Belarus
139 C3 **Shumla** U.S.A.
89 D3 **Shumyachi** Rus. Fed.
71 B3 **Shunchang** China
126 B2 **Shungnak** U.S.A.
78 B3 **Shuqrah** Yemen
77 C3 **Shurchi** Uzbek.
121 C2 **Shurugwi** Zimbabwe
89 F2 **Shushkodom** Rus. Fed.
81 C2 **Shushtar** Iran
128 C2 **Shuswap Lake** Can.
89 F2 **Shuya** Rus. Fed.
89 F2 **Shuyskoye** Rus. Fed.
62 A1 **Shwebo** Myanmar
62 A1 **Shwedwin** Myanmar
62 A2 **Shwegun** Myanmar
62 A2 **Shwegyin** Myanmar
62 A1 **Shweli** *r.* Myanmar
77 C2 **Shymkent** Kazakh.
74 B1 **Shyok** *r.* India
91 C2 **Shyroke** Ukr.
90 C2 **Shyryayeve** Ukr.
59 C3 **Sia** Indon.
74 A2 **Siahan Range** *mts* Pak.
74 B1 **Sialkot** Pak.
Siam *country* Asia *see* Thailand
Sian China *see* **Xi'an**
64 B3 **Siargao** *i.* Phil.
64 B3 **Siasi** Phil.
88 B2 **Šiauliai** Lith.
123 D1 **Sibasa** S. Africa
109 C2 **Šibenik** Croatia
83 G2 **Siberia** *reg.* Rus. Fed.
60 A2 **Siberut** *i.* Indon.
74 A2 **Sibi** Pak.
Sibir' *reg.* Rus. Fed. *see* Siberia
118 B3 **Sibiti** Congo
110 B1 **Sibiu** Romania
60 A1 **Sibolga** Indon.
62 A1 **Sibsagar** India
61 C1 **Sibu** *Sarawak* Malaysia
118 B2 **Sibut** C.A.R.
64 A3 **Sibutu** *i.* Phil.
64 B2 **Sibuyan** *i.* Phil.
64 B2 **Sibuyan Sea** Phil.
128 C2 **Sicamous** Can.
63 A3 **Sichon** Thai.
70 A2 **Sichuan** *prov.* China
70 A3 **Sichuan Pendi** *basin* China
105 D3 **Sicié, Cap** *c.* France
Sicilia *i.* Italy *see* **Sicily**
108 B3 **Sicilian Channel** Italy/Tunisia
108 B3 **Sicily** *i.* Italy
150 B4 **Sicuani** Peru
74 B2 **Siddhapur** India
111 C3 **Sideros, Akra** *pt* Greece
122 B3 **Sidesaviwa** S. Africa
75 C2 **Sidhi** India
107 D2 **Sidi Aïssa** Alg.
107 D2 **Sidi Ali** Alg.
114 B1 **Sidi Bel Abbès** Alg.
114 A2 **Sidi Ifni** Morocco
114 B1 **Sidi Kacem** Morocco
60 A1 **Sidikalang** Indon.
111 B2 **Sidirokastro** Greece
96 C2 **Sidlaw Hills** U.K.
99 B4 **Sidmouth** U.K.
134 B1 **Sidney** Can.
136 C1 **Sidney** *MT* U.S.A.

136 C2 **Sidney** *NE* U.S.A.
140 C2 **Sidney** *OH* U.S.A.
143 D2 **Sidney Lanier, Lake** U.S.A.
61 D1 **Sidoan** Indon.
80 B2 **Sidon** Lebanon
154 B2 **Sidrolândia** Brazil
103 E1 **Siedlce** Pol.
100 C2 **Sieg** *r.* Ger.
101 D2 **Siegen** Ger.
63 B2 **Siěmréab** Cambodia
Siem Reap Cambodia *see* Siěmréab
108 B2 **Siena** Italy
103 D1 **Sieradz** Pol.
138 B2 **Sierra Blanca** U.S.A.
153 B4 **Sierra Grande** Arg.
114 A4 **Sierra Leone** *country* Africa
158 E4 **Sierra Leone Basin** *sea feature* N. Atlantic Ocean
158 E4 **Sierra Leone Rise** *sea feature* N. Atlantic Ocean
144 B2 **Sierra Mojada** Mex.
138 A2 **Sierra Vista** U.S.A.
105 D2 **Sierre** Switz.
116 C3 **Sīfenī** Eth.
111 B3 **Sifnos** *i.* Greece
107 C2 **Sig** Alg.
127 I2 **Sigguup Nunaa** *pen.* Greenland
110 B1 **Sighetu Marmației** Romania
110 B1 **Sighișoara** Romania
60 A1 **Sigli** Indon.
92 □B2 **Siglufjörður** Iceland
102 B2 **Sigmaringen** Ger.
100 B3 **Signy-l'Abbaye** France
106 C1 **Sigüenza** Spain
114 B3 **Siguiri** Guinea
88 B2 **Sigulda** Latvia
63 B2 **Sihanoukville** Cambodia
92 I3 **Siilinjärvi** Fin.
81 C2 **Siirt** Turkey
60 B2 **Sijunjung** Indon.
74 B2 **Sikar** India
74 A1 **Sikaram** *mt.* Afgh.
114 B3 **Sikasso** Mali
111 B2 **Sikea** Greece
137 F3 **Sikeston** U.S.A.
66 B2 **Sikhote-Alin'** *mts* Rus. Fed.
111 C3 **Sikinos** *i.* Greece
103 D2 **Siklós** Hungary
88 B2 **Šilalė** Lith.
144 B2 **Silao** Mex.
101 D1 **Silberberg** *hill* Ger.
75 D2 **Silchar** India
77 D1 **Siletiteniz, Ozero** *salt l.* Kazakh.
75 C2 **Silgarhi** Nepal
80 B2 **Silifke** Turkey
75 C1 **Siling Co** *salt l.* China
110 C2 **Silistra** Bulg.
111 C2 **Silivri** Turkey
93 F3 **Siljan** *l.* Sweden
93 E4 **Silkeborg** Denmark
88 C2 **Sillamäe** Estonia
98 B2 **Silloth** U.K.
142 B1 **Siloam Springs** U.S.A.
123 D2 **Silobela** S. Africa
60 B1 **Siluas** Indon.
88 B2 **Šilutė** Lith.
81 C2 **Silvan** Turkey
154 C1 **Silvânia** Brazil
74 B2 **Silvassa** India
137 E1 **Silver Bay** U.S.A.
138 B2 **Silver City** U.S.A.
136 B3 **Silverton** U.S.A.
62 B1 **Simao** China
130 C3 **Simàrd, Lac** *l.* Can.
111 C3 **Simav** Turkey
111 C3 **Simav Dağları** *mts* Turkey
118 C2 **Simba** Dem. Rep. Congo
140 C2 **Simcoe** Can.
141 D2 **Simcoe, Lake** Can.
78 A3 **Simēn Mountains** Eth.
60 A1 **Simeulue** *i.* Indon.
91 C3 **Simferopol'** Ukr.
75 C2 **Simikot** Nepal
135 C4 **Simi Valley** U.S.A.
Simla India *see* **Shimla**
110 B1 **Şimleu Silvaniei** Romania
100 C3 **Simmern (Hunsrück)** Ger.
92 I2 **Simo** Fin.
129 D2 **Simonhouse** Can.
60 B2 **Simpang** Indon.
51 C2 **Simpson Desert** Austr.
93 F4 **Simrishamn** Sweden

60 A1 **Sinabang** Indon.
116 B2 **Sinai** *pen.* Egypt
105 E3 **Sinalunga** Italy
71 A3 **Sinan** China
65 B2 **Sinanju** N. Korea
62 A1 **Sinbo** Myanmar
62 A1 **Sinbyugyun** Myanmar
150 B2 **Sincelejo** Col.
60 B2 **Sindangbarang** Indon.
111 C3 **Sındırgı** Turkey
86 E2 **Sindor** Rus. Fed.
111 C2 **Sinekçi** Turkey
106 B2 **Sines** Port.
106 B2 **Sines, Cabo de** *c.* Port.
116 B3 **Singa** Sudan
75 C2 **Singahi** India
60 B1 **Singapore** *country* Asia
61 C2 **Singaraja** Indon.
63 B2 **Sing Buri** Thai.
119 D3 **Singida** Tanz.
62 A1 **Singkaling Hkamti** Myanmar
61 D2 **Singkang** Indon.
60 B1 **Singkawang** Indon.
60 B2 **Singkep** *i.* Indon.
60 A1 **Singkil** Indon.
53 D2 **Singleton** Austr.
Sin'gosan N. Korea *see* **Kosan**
62 A1 **Singu** Myanmar
Sining China *see* **Xining**
108 A2 **Siniscola** *Sardinia* Italy
109 C2 **Sinj** Croatia
61 D2 **Sinjai** Indon.
116 B3 **Sinkat** Sudan
Sinkiang *aut. reg.* China *see* **Xinjiang Uygur Zizhiqu**
Sinkiang Uighur Autonomous Region *aut. reg.* China *see* **Xinjiang Uygur Zizhiqu**
151 D2 **Sinnamary** Fr. Guiana
Sînnicolau Mare Romania *see* **Sânnicolau Mare**
Sinoia Zimbabwe *see* **Chinhoyi**
80 B1 **Sinop** Turkey
65 B1 **Sinp'o** N. Korea
61 C1 **Sintang** Indon.
100 B2 **St Anthonis** Neth.
100 A2 **St-Laureins** Belgium
100 B2 **St-Niklaas** Belgium
139 D3 **Sinton** U.S.A.
100 C2 **St-Vith** Belgium
65 A1 **Sinŭiju** N. Korea
64 B3 **Siocon** Phil.
103 D2 **Siófok** Hungary
105 D2 **Sion** Switz.
137 D2 **Sioux Center** U.S.A.
137 D2 **Sioux City** U.S.A.
137 D2 **Sioux Falls** U.S.A.
130 A2 **Sioux Lookout** Can.
65 A1 **Siping** China
129 E2 **Sipiwesk Lake** Can.
55 P2 **Siple, Mount** Antarctica
55 P2 **Siple Island** Antarctica
Sipolilo Zimbabwe *see* **Guruve**
60 A2 **Sipura** *i.* Indon.
64 B3 **Siquijor** Phil.
93 E4 **Sira** *r.* Norway
Siracusa Italy *see* **Syracuse**
51 C1 **Sir Edward Pellew Group** *is* Austr.
110 C1 **Siret** Romania
110 C1 **Siret** *r.* Romania
79 C2 **Sīrīk** Iran
61 C1 **Sirik, Tanjong** *pt* Malaysia
62 B2 **Siri Kit Dam** Thai.
128 B1 **Sir James MacBrien, Mount** Can.
79 C2 **Sīrjān** Iran
81 C2 **Şırnak** Turkey
74 B2 **Sirohi** India
60 A1 **Sirombu** Indon.
74 B2 **Sirsa** India
115 D1 **Sirte** Libya
115 D1 **Sirte, Gulf of** Libya
88 B2 **Širvintos** Lith.
109 C1 **Sisak** Croatia
63 B2 **Sisaket** Thai.
145 C2 **Sisal** Mex.
122 B2 **Sishen** S. Africa
81 C2 **Sisian** Armenia
127 I2 **Sisimiut** Greenland
129 D2 **Sisipuk Lake** Can.
63 B2 **Sisŏphŏn** Cambodia
105 D3 **Sisteron** France
Sitang China *see* **Sinan**
75 C2 **Sitapur** India
111 C3 **Siteia** Greece
123 D2 **Siteki** Swaziland
128 A2 **Sitka** U.S.A.
62 A2 **Sittang** *r.* Myanmar
100 B2 **Sittard** Neth.
62 A1 **Sittaung** Myanmar
62 A1 **Sittwe** Myanmar
61 C2 **Situbondo** Indon.
80 B2 **Sivas** Turkey
111 C3 **Sivaslı** Turkey
80 B2 **Siverek** Turkey
88 D2 **Siverskiy** Rus. Fed.
91 D2 **Sivers'kyy Donets'** *r.* Ukr.
80 B2 **Sivrihisar** Turkey
116 A2 **Siwa** Egypt
75 B1 **Siwalik Range** *mts* India/Nepal
116 A2 **Siwa Oasis** Egypt
105 D3 **Six-Fours-les-Plages** France
70 B2 **Sixian** China
123 C2 **Siyabuswa** S. Africa
Sjælland *i.* Denmark *see* **Zealand**
109 D2 **Sjenica** Yugo.
92 G2 **Sjøvegan** Norway
91 C2 **Skadovs'k** Ukr.
93 F4 **Skagen** Denmark
93 E4 **Skagerrak** *str.* Denmark/Norway
134 B1 **Skagit** *r.* U.S.A.
128 A2 **Skagway** U.S.A.
92 G2 **Skaland** Norway
93 F4 **Skara** Sweden
74 B1 **Skardu** Jammu and Kashmir
103 E1 **Skarżysko-Kamienna** Pol.
103 D2 **Skawina** Pol.
114 A2 **Skaymat** Western Sahara
128 B2 **Skeena** *r.* Can.
128 B2 **Skeena Mountains** Can.
98 D3 **Skegness** U.K.
92 H3 **Skellefteå** Sweden
92 H3 **Skellefteälven** *r.* Sweden
97 C2 **Skerries** Rep. of Ireland
93 F4 **Ski** Norway
111 B3 **Skiathos** *i.* Greece
97 B3 **Skibbereen** Rep. of Ireland
92 □B2 **Skíðadals-jökull** *glacier* Iceland
98 B2 **Skiddaw** *hill* U.K.
93 E4 **Skien** Norway
103 E1 **Skierniewice** Pol.
115 C1 **Skikda** Alg.
52 B3 **Skipton** Austr.
98 B3 **Skipton** U.K.
93 E4 **Skive** Denmark
92 H1 **Skjervøy** Norway
Skobelev Uzbek. *see* **Fergana**
111 B3 **Skopelos** *i.* Greece
89 E3 **Skopin** Rus. Fed.
111 B2 **Skopje** Macedonia
111 C3 **Skoutaros** Greece
93 F4 **Skövde** Sweden
83 J3 **Skovorodino** Rus. Fed.
141 F2 **Skowhegan** U.S.A.
92 H2 **Skröven** Sweden
88 B2 **Skrunda** Latvia
128 A1 **Skukum, Mount** Can.
123 D1 **Skukuza** S. Africa
88 B2 **Skuodas** Lith.
90 B2 **Skvyra** Ukr.
96 A2 **Skye** *i.* U.K.
111 B3 **Skyros** Greece
111 B3 **Skyros** *i.* Greece
93 F4 **Slagelse** Denmark
60 B2 **Slamet, Gunung** *vol.* Indon.
97 C2 **Slaney** *r.* Rep. of Ireland
88 C2 **Slantsy** Rus. Fed.
109 C1 **Slatina** Croatia
110 B2 **Slatina** Romania
139 C2 **Slaton** U.S.A.
129 C1 **Slave** *r.* Can.
114 C4 **Slave Coast** Africa
128 C2 **Slave Lake** Can.
77 D1 **Slavgorod** Rus. Fed.
88 C2 **Slavkovichi** Rus. Fed.
Slavonska Požega Croatia *see* **Požega**
109 C1 **Slavonski Brod** Croatia
90 B1 **Slavuta** Ukr.
90 C1 **Slavutych** Ukr.
66 B2 **Slavyanka** Rus. Fed.
Slavyanskaya Rus. Fed. *see* **Slavyansk-na-Kubani**
91 D2 **Slavyansk-na-Kubani** Rus. Fed.
89 D3 **Slawharad** Belarus
103 D1 **Sławno** Pol.
99 C3 **Sleaford** U.K.
97 A2 **Slea Head** *hd* Rep. of Ireland
130 C2 **Sleeper Islands** Can.
97 D1 **Slieve Donard** *hill* U.K.
97 B1 **Slieve Gamph** *hills* Rep. of Ireland
96 A2 **Sligachan** U.K.
Sligeach Rep. of Ireland *see* **Sligo**
97 B1 **Sligo** Rep. of Ireland
97 B1 **Sligo Bay** Rep. of Ireland
93 G4 **Slite** Sweden
110 C2 **Sliven** Bulg.
Sloboda Rus. Fed. *see* **Ezhva**
110 C2 **Slobozia** Romania
128 C3 **Slocan** Can.
88 C3 **Slonim** Belarus
100 B1 **Sloten** Neth.
99 C4 **Slough** U.K.
103 D2 **Slovakia** *country* Europe
108 B1 **Slovenia** *country* Europe
91 D2 **Slov"yans'k** Ukr.
102 C1 **Słubice** Pol.
90 B1 **Sluch** *r.* Ukr.
100 A2 **Sluis** Neth.
103 D1 **Słupsk** Pol.
88 C3 **Slutsk** Belarus
97 A2 **Slyne Head** *hd* Rep. of Ireland
68 C1 **Slyudyanka** Rus. Fed.
131 D2 **Smallwood Reservoir** Can.
88 C3 **Smalyavichy** Belarus
88 C3 **Smarhon'** Belarus
129 D2 **Smeaton** Can.
109 D2 **Smederevo** Yugo.
109 D2 **Smederevska Palanka** Yugo.
91 C2 **Smila** Ukr.
88 C3 **Smilavichy** Belarus
88 C2 **Smiltene** Latvia
137 D3 **Smith Center** U.S.A.
128 B2 **Smithers** Can.
143 E1 **Smithfield** *NC* U.S.A.
134 D2 **Smithfield** *UT* U.S.A.
141 D3 **Smith Mountain Lake** U.S.A.
130 C3 **Smiths Falls** Can.
53 D2 **Smithtown** Austr.
53 D2 **Smoky Cape** Austr.
137 D3 **Smoky Hills** U.S.A.
92 E3 **Smøla** *i.* Norway
89 D3 **Smolensk** Rus. Fed.
89 D3 **Smolensko-Moskovskaya Vozvyshennost'** *hills* Rus. Fed.
111 B2 **Smolyan** Bulg.
66 B2 **Smolyoninovo** Rus. Fed.
130 B3 **Smooth Rock Falls** Can.
Smyrna Turkey *see* **İzmir**
91 D2 **Smyrnove** Ukr.
92 □B3 **Snæfell** *mt.* Iceland
98 A2 **Snaefell** *hill* Isle of Man
128 A1 **Snag** Can.
134 C1 **Snake** *r.* U.S.A.
134 D2 **Snake River Plain** U.S.A.
128 C1 **Snare Lake** Can.
Snare Lakes Can. *see* **Snare Lake**
92 F3 **Snåsvatn** *l.* Norway
100 B1 **Sneek** Neth.
97 B3 **Sneem** Rep. of Ireland
122 B3 **Sneeuberge** *mts* S. Africa
Snegurovka Ukr. *see* **Tetiyiv**
103 D1 **Sněžka** *mt.* Czech Rep.
108 B1 **Snežnik** *mt.* Slovenia
103 E1 **Śniardwy, Jezioro** *l.* Pol.
Sniečkus Lith. *see* **Visaginas**
91 C2 **Snihurivka** Ukr.
93 E3 **Snøhetta** *mt.* Norway
Snovsk Ukr. *see* **Shchors**
129 D1 **Snowbird Lake** Can.
99 A3 **Snowdon** *mt.* U.K.
Snowdrift Can. *see* **Łutselk'e**
129 C1 **Snowdrift** *r.* Can.
138 A2 **Snowflake** U.S.A.
129 D2 **Snow Lake** Can.
134 C1 **Snowshoe Peak** U.S.A.
52 A2 **Snowtown** Austr.
53 C3 **Snowy** *r.* Austr.
53 C3 **Snowy Mountains** Austr.
139 C2 **Snyder** U.S.A.
121 □D2 **Soalala** Madag.
121 □D2 **Soanierana-Ivongo** Madag.
90 B2 **Sob** *r.* Ukr.
65 B2 **Sobaek-sanmaek** *mts* S. Korea
117 B4 **Sobat** *r.* Sudan
100 C3 **Sobernheim** Ger.
89 F2 **Sobinka** Rus. Fed.
151 E4 **Sobradinho, Barragem de** *resr* Brazil
151 E3 **Sobral** Brazil
91 D3 **Sochi** Rus. Fed.
65 B2 **Sŏch'ŏn** S. Korea
49 L5 **Society Islands** Fr. Polynesia
150 B2 **Socorro** Col.
138 B2 **Socorro** *NM* U.S.A.
138 B2 **Socorro** *TX* U.S.A.
144 A3 **Socorro, Isla** *i.* Mex.
56 B4 **Socotra** *i.* Yemen
63 B3 **Soc Trăng** Vietnam
106 C2 **Socuéllamos** Spain
92 I2 **Sodankylä** Fin.
134 D2 **Soda Springs** U.S.A.
93 G3 **Söderhamn** Sweden
93 G4 **Södertälje** Sweden
116 A3 **Sodiri** Sudan
117 B4 **Sodo** Eth.
93 G3 **Södra Kvarken** *str.* Fin./Sweden
123 C1 **Soekmekaar** S. Africa
Soerabaia Indon. *see* **Surabaya**
101 D2 **Soest** Ger.
53 C2 **Sofala** Austr.
110 B2 **Sofia** Bulg.
Sofia Bulg. *see* **Sofia**
121 □D2 **Sofia** *r.* Madag.
Sofiyevka Ukr. *see* **Vil'nyans'k**
93 E3 **Sognefjorden** *inlet* Norwa
111 D2 **Söğüt** Turkey
75 D1 **Sogxian** China
116 B2 **Sohâg** Egypt
Sohar Oman *see* **Şuḩār**
100 B2 **Soignies** Belgium
105 C2 **Soissons** France
90 A1 **Sokal'** Ukr.
65 B2 **Sokch'o** S. Korea
111 C3 **Söke** Turkey
81 C1 **Sokhumi** Georgia
114 C4 **Sokodé** Togo
89 F2 **Sokol** Rus. Fed.
101 F2 **Sokolov** Czech Rep.
115 C3 **Sokoto** Nigeria
115 C3 **Sokoto** *r.* Nigeria
90 B2 **Sokyryany** Ukr.
73 B3 **Solāpur** India
135 B3 **Soledad** U.S.A.
89 F2 **Soligalich** Rus. Fed.
99 C3 **Solihull** U.K.
86 E3 **Solikamsk** Rus. Fed.
87 E3 **Sol'-Iletsk** Rus. Fed.
100 C2 **Solingen** Ger.
122 A1 **Solitaire** Namibia
92 G3 **Sollefteå** Sweden
93 G4 **Sollentuna** Sweden
107 D2 **Sóller** Spain
101 D2 **Solling** *hills* Ger.
89 E2 **Solnechnogorsk** Rus. Fe
60 B2 **Solok** Indon.
48 H4 **Solomon Islands** *country* S. Pacific Ocean
48 G4 **Solomon Sea** P.N.G./Solomon Is
61 D2 **Solor, Kepulauan** *is* Indon
105 D2 **Solothurn** Switz.
81 D2 **Soltānābād** Iran
101 D1 **Soltau** Ger.
89 D2 **Sol'tsy** Rus. Fed.
96 C3 **Solway Firth** *est.* U.K.
120 B2 **Solwezi** Zambia
111 C3 **Soma** Turkey
117 C4 **Somalia** *country* Africa
120 B1 **Sombo** Angola
109 C1 **Sombor** Yugo.
144 B2 **Sombrerete** Mex.
140 C3 **Somerset** U.S.A.
123 C3 **Somerset East** S. Africa
126 F2 **Somerset Island** Can.
122 A3 **Somerset West** S. Africa
110 B1 **Someş** *r.* Romania
101 E2 **Sömmerda** Ger.
146 B3 **Somoto** Nic.
75 C2 **Son** *r.* India
93 E5 **Sønderborg** Denmark
101 E2 **Sondershausen** Ger.
Søndre Strømfjord *inlet* Greenland *see* **Kangerlussuaq**
108 A1 **Sondrio** Italy
63 B2 **Sông Cau** Vietnam
62 B1 **Sông Da, Hô** *resr* Vietnam
119 D4 **Songea** Tanz.

B1 **Sŏnggan** N. Korea
B1 **Songhua Hu** *resr* China
B1 **Songjianghe** China
Sŏngjin N. Korea *see* Kimch'aek
B3 **Songkhla** Thai.
E1 **Songling** China
B2 **Sŏngnam** S. Korea
B2 **Songnim** N. Korea
A1 **Songo** Angola
C2 **Songo** Moz.
Songololo Dem. Rep. Congo *see* **Mbanza-Ngungu**
E1 **Songyuan** China
Sonid Youqi China *see* Saihan Tal
B2 **Sonīpat** India
E2 **Sonkovo** Rus. Fed.
B1 **Sơn La** Vietnam
A2 **Sonmiani** Pak.
A2 **Sonmiani Bay** Pak.
E2 **Sonneberg** Ger.
A2 **Sonora** *r.* Mex.
B3 **Sonora** *CA* U.S.A.
C2 **Sonora** *TX* U.S.A.
A2 **Sonoyta** Mex.
B3 **Sonsonate** El Salvador
Soochow China *see* Suzhou
A4 **Sopo** *watercourse* Sudan
D2 **Sopron** Hungary
B1 **Sopur** Jammu and Kashmir
B2 **Sora** Italy
C3 **Sorel** Can.
D4 **Sorell** Austr.
C1 **Soria** Spain
B2 **Sor Mertvyy Kultuk** *dry lake* Kazakh.
B2 **Soroca** Moldova
C2 **Sorocaba** Brazil
E3 **Sorochinsk** Rus. Fed.
Soroki Moldova *see* Soroca
D2 **Sorol** *atoll* Micronesia
C3 **Sorong** Indon.
D2 **Soroti** Uganda
H1 **Sørøya** *i.* Norway
B2 **Sorrento** Italy
G2 **Sorsele** Sweden
B2 **Sorsogon** Phil.
C2 **Sortavala** Rus. Fed.
G2 **Sortland** Norway
B2 **Sŏsan** S. Korea
C2 **Soshanguve** S. Africa
E3 **Sosna** *r.* Rus. Fed.
B3 **Sosneado** *mt.* Arg.
E2 **Sosnogorsk** Rus. Fed.
D2 **Sosnovka** Rus. Fed.
C2 **Sosnovyy Bor** Rus. Fed.
D1 **Sosnowiec** Pol.
C1 **Sosnytsya** Ukr.
F3 **Sos'va** Rus. Fed.
D2 **Sosyka** *r.* Rus. Fed.
C2 **Soto la Marina** Mex.
B2 **Souanké** Congo
B3 **Souda** Greece
C3 **Souillac** France
Sŏul S. Korea *see* **Seoul**
B2 **Soulac-sur-Mer** France
B3 **Soulom** France
B2 **Soûr** Lebanon
D2 **Sour el Ghozlane** Alg.
D3 **Souris** *Man.* Can.
D3 **Souris** *P.E.I.* Can.
E3 **Souris** *r.* Can.
F3 **Sousa** Brazil
D1 **Sousse** Tunisia
B3 **Soustons** France
B3 **South Africa, Republic of** *country* Africa
C4 **Southampton** U.K.
F1 **Southampton, Cape** Can.
F1 **Southampton Island** Can.
D3 **South Andaman** *i.* India
A1 **South Australia** *state* Austr.
B2 **Southaven** U.S.A.
B2 **South Baldy** *mt.* U.S.A.
B3 **South Baymouth** Can.
B2 **South Bend** U.S.A.
D2 **South Carolina** *state* U.S.A.
B2 **South China Sea** N. Pacific Ocean
South Coast Town Austr. *see* **Gold Coast**
C2 **South Dakota** *state* U.S.A.
C4 **South Downs** *hills* U.K.
E6 **Southeast Indian Ridge** *sea feature* Indian Ocean
55 O2 **Southeast Pacific Basin** *sea feature* S. Pacific Ocean
129 D2 **Southend** Can.
99 D4 **Southend-on-Sea** U.K.
54 B2 **Southern Alps** *mts* N.Z.
50 A3 **Southern Cross** Austr.
129 E2 **Southern Indian Lake** Can.
159 D7 **Southern Ocean**
143 E1 **Southern Pines** U.S.A.
Southern Rhodesia *country* Africa *see* Zimbabwe
96 B3 **Southern Uplands** *hills* U.K.
55 J2 **South Geomagnetic Pole** Antarctica
149 G8 **South Georgia** *terr.* S. Atlantic Ocean
149 G8 **South Georgia and South Sandwich Islands** *terr.* S. Atlantic Ocean
140 B2 **South Haven** U.S.A.
129 E1 **South Henik Lake** Can.
119 D2 **South Horr** Kenya
54 B2 **South Island** N.Z.
135 B3 **South Lake Tahoe** U.S.A.
55 K3 **South Magnetic Pole** Antarctica
128 B1 **South Nahanni** *r.* Can.
149 F9 **South Orkney Islands** S. Atlantic Ocean
136 C2 **South Platte** *r.* U.S.A.
98 B3 **Southport** U.K.
143 E2 **Southport** U.S.A.
130 C3 **South River** Can.
96 C1 **South Ronaldsay** *i.* U.K.
123 D3 **South Sand Bluff** *pt* S. Africa
149 H8 **South Sandwich Islands** S. Atlantic Ocean
55 C4 **South Sandwich Trench** *sea feature* S. Atlantic Ocean
129 D2 **South Saskatchewan** *r.* Can.
129 E2 **South Seal** *r.* Can.
149 E9 **South Shetland Islands** Antarctica
98 C2 **South Shields** U.K.
54 B1 **South Taranaki Bight** *b.* N.Z.
156 C8 **South Tasman Rise** *sea feature* Southern Ocean
130 C2 **South Twin Island** Can.
96 A2 **South Uist** *i.* U.K.
South-West Africa *country* Africa *see* **Namibia**
Southwest Peru Ridge *sea feature* S. Pacific Ocean *see* Nazca Ridge
53 D2 **South West Rocks** Austr.
99 D3 **Southwold** U.K.
109 C3 **Soverato** Italy
88 B2 **Sovetsk** Rus. Fed.
86 F2 **Sovetskiy** Rus. Fed.
91 C2 **Sovyets'kyy** Ukr.
123 C2 **Soweto** S. Africa
66 D1 **Sōya-misaki** *c.* Japan
65 B2 **Soyang-ho** *l.* S. Korea
104 C2 **Soyaux** France
90 C1 **Sozh** *r.* Europe
110 C2 **Sozopol** Bulg.
100 B2 **Spa** Belgium
106 C1 **Spain** *country* Europe
Spalato Croatia *see* **Split**
99 C3 **Spalding** U.K.
135 D2 **Spanish Fork** U.S.A.
Spanish Guinea *country* Africa *see* Equatorial Guinea
97 B2 **Spanish Point** Rep. of Ireland
Spanish Sahara *terr.* Africa *see* **Western Sahara**
146 C3 **Spanish Town** Jamaica
108 B3 **Sparagio, Monte** *mt. Sicily* Italy
135 C3 **Sparks** U.S.A.
140 A2 **Sparta** U.S.A.
143 D2 **Spartanburg** U.S.A.
111 B3 **Sparti** Greece
109 C3 **Spartivento, Capo** *c.* Italy
89 D3 **Spas-Demensk** Rus. Fed.
89 F2 **Spas-Klepiki** Rus. Fed.
66 B2 **Spassk-Dal'niy** Rus. Fed.
89 F3 **Spassk-Ryazanskiy** Rus. Fed.
111 B3 **Spatha, Akra** *pt* Greece
96 B2 **Spean Bridge** U.K.
136 C2 **Spearfish** U.S.A.
139 C1 **Spearman** U.S.A.
Spence Bay Can. *see* Taloyoak
137 D2 **Spencer** *IA* U.S.A.
134 D2 **Spencer** *ID* U.S.A.
52 A2 **Spencer Gulf** *est.* Austr.
98 C2 **Spennymoor** U.K.
54 B2 **Spenser Mountains** N.Z.
101 D3 **Spessart** *reg.* Ger.
96 C2 **Spey** *r.* U.K.
101 D3 **Speyer** Ger.
100 C1 **Spiekeroog** *i.* Ger.
100 B2 **Spijkenisse** Neth.
100 B3 **Spincourt** France
128 C2 **Spirit River** Can.
103 E2 **Spišská Nová Ves** Slovakia
82 C1 **Spitsbergen** *i.* Svalbard
102 C2 **Spittal an der Drau** Austria
93 E3 **Spjelkavik** Norway
109 C2 **Split** Croatia
129 E2 **Split Lake** Can.
129 E2 **Split Lake** *l.* Can.
134 C1 **Spokane** U.S.A.
140 A1 **Spooner** U.S.A.
102 C1 **Spree** *r.* Ger.
122 A2 **Springbok** S. Africa
131 E3 **Springdale** Can.
142 B1 **Springdale** U.S.A.
101 D1 **Springe** Ger.
138 C1 **Springer** U.S.A.
138 B2 **Springerville** U.S.A.
136 C3 **Springfield** *CO* U.S.A.
140 B3 **Springfield** *IL* U.S.A.
141 E2 **Springfield** *MA* U.S.A.
137 E3 **Springfield** *MO* U.S.A.
140 C3 **Springfield** *OH* U.S.A.
134 B2 **Springfield** *OR* U.S.A.
142 C1 **Springfield** *TN* U.S.A.
123 C3 **Springfontein** S. Africa
131 D3 **Springhill** Can.
143 D3 **Spring Hill** U.S.A.
54 B2 **Springs Junction** N.Z.
51 D2 **Springsure** Austr.
135 D2 **Springville** U.S.A.
98 D3 **Spurn Head** *hd* U.K.
128 B3 **Squamish** Can.
109 C3 **Squillace, Golfo di** *g.* Italy
Srbija *aut. rep.* Yugo. *see* Serbia
110 C2 **Sredets** Bulg.
83 L3 **Sredinnyy Khrebet** *mts* Rus. Fed.
83 L2 **Srednekolymsk** Rus. Fed.
89 E3 **Sredne-Russkaya Vozvyshennost'** *hills* Rus. Fed.
83 I2 **Sredne-Sibirskoye Ploskogor'ye** *plat.* Rus. Fed.
110 B2 **Srednogorie** Bulg.
69 D1 **Sretensk** Rus. Fed.
61 C1 **Sri Aman** *Sarawak* Malaysia
73 B4 **Sri Jayewardenepura Kotte** Sri Lanka
73 C3 **Srikakulam** India
73 C4 **Sri Lanka** *country* Asia
74 B1 **Srinagar** Jammu and Kashmir
73 B3 **Srivardhan** India
101 D1 **Stade** Ger.
101 E1 **Stadensen** Ger.
100 C1 **Stadskanaal** Neth.
101 D2 **Stadtallendorf** Ger.
101 D1 **Stadthagen** Ger.
101 E2 **Staffelstein** Ger.
99 B3 **Stafford** U.K.
99 C4 **Staines** U.K.
91 D2 **Stakhanov** Ukr.
Stakhanovo Rus. Fed. *see* Zhukovskiy
Stalin Bulg. *see* **Varna**
Stalinabad Tajik. *see* Dushanbe
Stalingrad Rus. Fed. *see* Volgograd
Staliniri Georgia *see* Ts'khinvali
Stalino Ukr. *see* **Donets'k**
Stalinogorsk Rus. Fed. *see* Novomoskovsk
Stalinogród Pol. *see* Katowice
Stalinsk Rus. Fed. *see* Novokuznetsk
103 E1 **Stalowa Wola** Pol.
140 B1 **Stambaugh** U.S.A.
99 C3 **Stamford** U.K.
141 E2 **Stamford** *CT* U.S.A.
139 D2 **Stamford** *TX* U.S.A.
Stampalia *i.* Greece *see* Astypalaia
122 A1 **Stampriet** Namibia
92 F2 **Stamsund** Norway
123 C2 **Standerton** S. Africa
140 C2 **Standish** U.S.A.
123 D2 **Stanger** S. Africa
Stanislav Ukr. *see* **Ivano-Frankivs'k**
Stanke Dimitrov Bulg. *see* Dupnitsa
153 C5 **Stanley** Falkland Is
136 C1 **Stanley** U.S.A.
Stanleyville Dem. Rep. Congo *see* Kisangani
Stann Creek Belize *see* Dangriga
111 B3 **Stanos** Greece
83 I3 **Stanovoye Nagor'ye** *mts* Rus. Fed.
83 J3 **Stanovoy Khrebet** *mts* Rus. Fed.
53 D1 **Stanthorpe** Austr.
137 E1 **Staples** U.S.A.
103 E1 **Starachowice** Pol.
Stara Planina *mts* Bulg./Yugo. *see* Balkan Mountains
89 D2 **Staraya Russa** Rus. Fed.
89 D2 **Staraya Toropa** Rus. Fed.
110 C2 **Stara Zagora** Bulg.
49 L4 **Starbuck Island** Kiribati
103 D1 **Stargard Szczeciński** Pol.
89 D2 **Staritsa** Rus. Fed.
143 D3 **Starke** U.S.A.
142 C2 **Starkville** U.S.A.
102 C2 **Starnberg** Ger.
91 D2 **Starobil's'k** Ukr.
89 D3 **Starodub** Rus. Fed.
103 D1 **Starogard Gdański** Pol.
90 B2 **Starokostyantyniv** Ukr.
91 D2 **Starominskaya** Rus. Fed.
91 D2 **Staroshcherbinovskaya** Rus. Fed.
91 D2 **Starotitarovskaya** Rus. Fed.
89 F3 **Staroyur'yevo** Rus. Fed.
89 E3 **Starozhilovo** Rus. Fed.
99 B4 **Start Point** U.K.
88 C3 **Staryya Darohi** Belarus
86 G2 **Staryy Nadym** Rus. Fed.
89 E3 **Staryy Oskol** Rus. Fed.
101 E2 **Staßfurt** Ger.
103 E1 **Staszów** Pol.
141 D2 **State College** U.S.A.
143 D2 **Statesboro** U.S.A.
143 D1 **Statesville** U.S.A.
160 L1 **Station Nord** Greenland
141 D3 **Staunton** U.S.A.
93 E4 **Stavanger** Norway
87 D4 **Stavropol'** Rus. Fed.
Stavropol'-na-Volge Rus. Fed. *see* **Tol'yatti**
87 D4 **Stavropol'skaya Vozvyshennost'** *hills* Rus. Fed.
52 B3 **Stawell** Austr.
123 C2 **Steadville** S. Africa
136 B2 **Steamboat Springs** U.S.A.
101 E2 **Stedten** Ger.
128 C2 **Steen River** Can.
134 C2 **Steens Mountain** U.S.A.
100 C1 **Steenwijk** Neth.
126 E2 **Stefansson Island** Can.
Stegi Swaziland *see* **Siteki**
110 B1 **Ştei** Romania
101 E3 **Steigerwald** *mts* Ger.
100 B2 **Stein** Neth.
129 E3 **Steinbach** Can.
100 C1 **Steinfurt** Ger.
120 A3 **Steinhausen** Namibia
92 F3 **Steinkjer** Norway
122 A2 **Steinkopf** S. Africa
122 B2 **Stella** S. Africa
122 A3 **Stellenbosch** S. Africa
105 D3 **Stello, Monte** *mt. Corsica* France
105 D2 **Stenay** France
101 E1 **Stendal** Ger.
Steornabhagh U.K. *see* Stornoway
Stepanakert Azer. *see* Xankändi
52 B2 **Stephens Creek** Austr.
129 E2 **Stephens Lake** Can.

131 E3 Stephenville Can.
139 D2 Stephenville U.S.A.
Stepnoy Rus. Fed. see Elista
122 B3 Sterling S. Africa
136 C2 Sterling *CO* U.S.A.
140 B2 Sterling *IL* U.S.A.
136 C1 Sterling *ND* U.S.A.
140 C2 Sterling Heights U.S.A.
87 E3 Sterlitamak Rus. Fed.
101 E1 Sternberg Ger.
128 C2 Stettler Can.
140 C2 Steubenville U.S.A.
99 C4 Stevenage U.K.
129 E2 Stevenson Lake Can.
140 B2 Stevens Point U.S.A.
126 C2 Stevens Village U.S.A.
134 D1 Stevensville U.S.A.
128 B2 Stewart Can.
128 A1 Stewart *r.* Can.
54 A3 Stewart Island N.Z.
127 G2 Stewart Lake Can.
123 C3 Steynsburg S. Africa
102 C2 Steyr Austria
122 B3 Steytlerville S. Africa
128 A2 Stikine *r.* Can.
128 A2 Stikine Plateau Can.
122 B3 Stilbaai S. Africa
137 E1 Stillwater *MN* U.S.A.
139 D1 Stillwater *OK* U.S.A.
135 C2 Stillwater Range *mts* U.S.A.
109 D2 Štip Macedonia
96 C2 Stirling U.K.
52 A2 Stirling North Austr.
92 F3 Stjørdalshalsen Norway
103 D2 Stockerau Austria
93 G4 Stockholm Sweden
98 B3 Stockport U.K.
135 B3 Stockton U.S.A.
98 C2 Stockton-on-Tees U.K.
139 C2 Stockton Plateau U.S.A.
63 B2 Stœng Trêng Cambodia
96 B1 Stoer, Point of U.K.
99 B3 Stoke-on-Trent U.K.
98 C2 Stokesley U.K.
92 F2 Stokmarknes Norway
109 D2 Stol *mt.* Yugo.
109 C2 Stolac Bos.-Herz.
100 C2 Stolberg (Rheinland) Ger.
82 E2 Stolbovoy Rus. Fed.
88 C3 Stolin Belarus
101 F2 Stollberg Ger.
101 D1 Stolzenau Ger.
96 C2 Stonehaven U.K.
99 C4 Stonehenge *tourist site* U.K.
129 E2 Stonewall Can.
129 D2 Stony Rapids Can.
92 G2 Storavan *l.* Sweden
93 F4 Store Bælt *sea chan.* Denmark
92 F3 Støren Norway
92 I1 Storfjordbotn Norway
92 F2 Storforshei Norway
126 E2 Storkerson Peninsula Can.
137 D2 Storm Lake U.S.A.
93 E3 Stornosa *mt.* Norway
96 A1 Stornoway U.K.
86 E2 Storozhevsk Rus. Fed.
90 B2 Storozhynets' Ukr.
92 F3 Storsjön *l.* Sweden
92 H2 Storslett Norway
92 G2 Storuman Sweden
92 G2 Storuman *l.* Sweden
99 C4 Stour *r. England* U.K.
99 C3 Stour *r. England* U.K.
99 D4 Stour *r. England* U.K.
130 A2 Stout Lake Can.
88 C3 Stowbtsy Belarus
99 D3 Stowmarket U.K.
97 C1 Strabane U.K.
102 C2 Strakonice Czech Rep.
102 C1 Stralsund Ger.
122 A3 Strand S. Africa
93 E3 Stranda Norway
97 D1 Strangford Lough *inlet* U.K.
96 B3 Stranraer U.K.
105 D2 Strasbourg France
130 B3 Stratford Can.
54 B1 Stratford N.Z.
139 C1 Stratford U.S.A.
99 C3 Stratford-upon-Avon U.K.
128 C2 Strathmore Can.
96 C2 Strathspey *val.* U.K.
102 C2 Straubing Ger.
134 C2 Strawberry Mountain U.S.A.
51 C3 Streaky Bay Austr.

140 B2 Streator U.S.A.
99 B4 Street U.K.
110 B2 Strehaia Romania
94 B1 Streymoy *i.* Faroe Is
82 G2 Strezhevoy Rus. Fed.
101 F3 Stříbro Czech Rep.
111 B2 Strimonas *r.* Greece
153 B4 Stroeder Arg.
101 D1 Ströhen Ger.
109 C3 Stromboli, Isola *i.* Italy
96 B2 Stromeferry U.K.
96 C1 Stromness U.K.
92 G3 Strömsund Sweden
96 C1 Stronsay *i.* U.K.
53 D2 Stroud Austr.
99 B4 Stroud U.K.
100 C1 Strücklingen (Saterland) Ger.
111 B2 Struga Macedonia
88 C2 Strugi-Krasnyye Rus. Fed.
122 B3 Struis Bay S. Africa
111 B2 Struma *r.* Bulg.
99 A3 Strumble Head *hd* U.K.
111 B2 Strumica Macedonia
122 B2 Strydenburg S. Africa
93 E3 Stryn Norway
90 A2 Stryy Ukr.
90 A2 Stryy *r.* Ukr.
128 B2 Stuart Lake Can.
53 C2 Stuart Town Austr.
Stuchka Latvia see Aizkraukle
Stučka Latvia see Aizkraukle
130 A2 Stull Lake Can.
89 E3 Stupino Rus. Fed.
55 M3 Sturge Island Antarctica
140 B2 Sturgeon Bay U.S.A.
130 C3 Sturgeon Falls Can.
130 A3 Sturgeon Lake Can.
140 B2 Sturgis *MI* U.S.A.
136 C2 Sturgis *SD* U.S.A.
52 B1 Sturt, Mount *hill* Austr.
50 B1 Sturt Creek *watercourse* Austr.
50 C1 Sturt Plain Austr.
52 B1 Sturt Stony Desert Austr.
123 C3 Stutterheim S. Africa
102 B2 Stuttgart Ger.
142 B2 Stuttgart U.S.A.
92 □A2 Stykkishólmur Iceland
90 B1 Styr *r.* Belarus/Ukr.
155 D1 Suaçui Grande *r.* Brazil
116 B3 Suakin Sudan
71 C3 Suao Taiwan
78 A3 Suara, Mount Eritrea
60 B1 Subi Besar *i.* Indon.
109 C1 Subotica Yugo.
110 C1 Suceava Romania
Suchan Rus. Fed. see Partizansk
97 B2 Suck *r.* Rep. of Ireland
152 B1 Sucre Bol.
154 B2 Sucuriú *r.* Brazil
Suczawa Romania see Suceava
89 E2 Suda Rus. Fed.
91 C2 Sudak Ukr.
116 A3 Sudan *country* Africa
130 B3 Sudbury Can.
99 D3 Sudbury U.K.
117 A4 Sudd *swamp* Sudan
89 F2 Sudislavl' Rus. Fed.
89 F2 Sudogda Rus. Fed.
94 B1 Suðuroy *i.* Faroe Is
89 E3 Sudzha Rus. Fed.
107 C2 Sueca Spain
116 B2 Suez Egypt
116 B2 Suez, Gulf of Egypt
80 B2 Suez Canal *canal* Egypt
141 D3 Suffolk U.S.A.
142 A3 Sugar Land U.S.A.
141 E1 Sugarloaf Mountain U.S.A.
53 D2 Sugarloaf Point Austr.
70 A2 Suhait China
79 C2 Şuḩār Oman
68 D1 Sühbaatar Mongolia
101 E2 Suhl Ger.
109 C1 Suhopolje Croatia
70 B2 Suide China
66 B2 Suifenhe China
69 E1 Suihua China
70 A2 Suining China
70 B2 Suiping China
97 C2 Suir *r.* Rep. of Ireland
Suixian China see Suizhou
70 B2 Suizhou China
74 B2 Sujangarh India
74 B1 Sujanpur India

74 A2 Sujawal Pak.
60 B2 Sukabumi Indon.
60 B2 Sukadana Indon.
67 D3 Sukagawa Japan
Sukarnapura Indon. see Jayapura
Sukarno, Puntjak *mt.* Indon. see Jaya, Puncak
89 E3 Sukhinichi Rus. Fed.
89 F2 Sukhona *r.* Rus. Fed.
62 A2 Sukhothai Thai.
74 A2 Sukkur Pak.
89 E2 Sukromny Rus. Fed.
59 C3 Sula, Kepulauan *is* Indon.
74 A1 Sulaiman Ranges *mts* Pak.
61 D2 Sulawesi *i.* Indon.
101 D1 Sulingen Ger.
150 A3 Sullana Peru
140 B3 Sullivan *IN* U.S.A.
137 E3 Sullivan *MO* U.S.A.
142 B2 Sulphur U.S.A.
139 D2 Sulphur Springs U.S.A.
140 C1 Sultan Can.
Sultanabad Iran see Arāk
64 B3 Sulu Archipelago *is* Phil.
64 A3 Sulu Sea N. Pacific Ocean
101 E3 Sulzbach-Rosenberg Ger.
79 C2 Sumāil Oman
60 A1 Sumatera *i.* Indon.
Sumatra *i.* Indon. see Sumatera
61 D2 Sumba *i.* Indon.
61 C2 Sumba, Selat *sea chan.* Indon.
61 C2 Sumbawa *i.* Indon.
61 C2 Sumbawabesar Indon.
119 D3 Sumbawanga Tanz.
120 A2 Sumbe Angola
96 □ Sumburgh U.K.
96 □ Sumburgh Head *hd* U.K.
119 C2 Sumeih Sudan
61 C2 Sumenep Indon.
67 D4 Sumisu-jima *i.* Japan
131 D3 Summerside Can.
140 C3 Summersville U.S.A.
143 D2 Summerville U.S.A.
137 D1 Summit U.S.A.
128 B2 Summit Lake Can.
103 D2 Šumperk Czech Rep.
81 C1 Sumqayıt Azer.
143 D2 Sumter U.S.A.
91 C1 Sumy Ukr.
75 C2 Sunamganj Bangl.
65 B2 Sunan N. Korea
79 C2 Sunaynah Oman
52 B3 Sunbury Austr.
141 D2 Sunbury U.S.A.
65 B2 Sunch'ŏn N. Korea
65 B3 Sunch'ŏn S. Korea
123 C2 Sun City S. Africa
93 H3 Sund Fin.
60 B2 Sunda, Selat *str.* Indon.
136 C2 Sundance U.S.A.
75 C2 Sundarbans *reg.* Bangl./India
74 B1 Sundarnagar India
Sunda Strait Indon. see Sunda, Selat
Sunda Trench *sea feature* Indian Ocean see Java Trench
98 C2 Sunderland U.K.
128 C2 Sundre Can.
93 G3 Sundsvall Sweden
123 D2 Sundumbili S. Africa
60 B2 Sungailiat Indon.
60 B2 Sungaipenuh Indon.
61 C1 Sungei Petani Malaysia
80 B1 Sungurlu Turkey
75 C2 Sun Kosi *r.* Nepal
93 E3 Sunndalsøra Norway
134 C1 Sunnyside U.S.A.
135 B3 Sunnyvale U.S.A.
143 D3 Sunrise U.S.A.
83 I2 Suntar Rus. Fed.
74 A2 Suntsar Pak.
114 B4 Sunyani Ghana
92 I3 Suomussalmi Fin.
67 B4 Suō-nada *b.* Japan
86 C2 Suoyarvi Rus. Fed.
138 A2 Superior *AZ* U.S.A.
137 D2 Superior *MT* U.S.A.
140 A1 Superior *WI* U.S.A.
140 B1 Superior, Lake Can./U.S.A.
63 B2 Suphan Buri Thai.
81 C2 Süphan Dağı *mt.* Turkey
89 D3 Suponevo Rus. Fed.
81 C2 Sūq ash Shuyūkh Iraq
70 B2 Suqian China

78 A2 Süq Suwayq Saudi Arab
Suquţrā *i.* Yemen see Socotra
79 C2 Şūr Oman
74 A2 Šurab Pak.
61 B2 Surabaya Indon.
61 C2 Surakarta Indon.
74 B2 Surat India
74 B2 Suratgarh India
63 A3 Surat Thani Thai.
89 D3 Surazh Rus. Fed.
109 D2 Surdulica Yugo.
100 C3 Sûre *r.* Lux.
74 B2 Surendranagar India
82 F2 Surgut Rus. Fed.
64 B3 Surigao Phil.
63 B2 Surin Thai.
151 D2 Suriname *country* S. America
75 C2 Surkhet Nepal
Surt Libya see Sirte
Surt, Khalīj *g.* Libya see Sirte, Gulf of
60 B2 Surulangun Indon.
81 C2 Süsangerd Iran
89 F2 Susanino Rus. Fed.
135 B2 Susanville U.S.A.
80 B1 Şuşehri Turkey
141 D3 Susquehanna *r.* U.S.A.
131 D3 Sussex Can.
101 D1 Süstedt Ger.
100 C1 Sustrum Ger.
83 K2 Susuman Rus. Fed.
111 C3 Susurluk Turkey
74 B1 Sutak Jammu and Kash.
53 D2 Sutherland Austr.
122 B3 Sutherland S. Africa
136 C2 Sutherland U.S.A.
134 B2 Sutherlin U.S.A.
74 B2 Sutlej *r.* India/Pak.
140 C3 Sutton U.S.A.
99 C3 Sutton Coldfield U.K.
98 C3 Sutton in Ashfield U.K.
66 D2 Suttsu Japan
49 I5 Suva Fiji
Suvalki Pol. see Suwałki
89 E3 Suvorov Rus. Fed.
90 B2 Suvorove Ukr.
103 E1 Suwałki Pol.
143 D3 Suwanee Sound *b.* U.S.A.
63 B2 Suwannaphum Thai.
143 D3 Suwannee *r.* U.S.A.
Suweis, Qanâ el *canal* Egypt see Suez Canal
65 B2 Suwŏn S. Korea
79 C2 Sūzā Iran
89 F2 Suzdal' Rus. Fed.
89 F2 Suzemka Rus. Fed.
70 C2 Suzhou *Anhui* China
70 C2 Suzhou *Jiangsu* China
67 C3 Suzu Japan
67 C3 Suzu-misaki *pt* Japan
82 B1 Svalbard *terr.* Arctic Ocean
90 A2 Svalyava Ukr.
92 H2 Svappavaara Sweden
91 D2 Svatove Ukr.
63 B2 Svay Riêng Cambodia
93 F3 Sveg Sweden
88 C2 Švenčionys Lith.
93 F4 Svendborg Denmark
Sverdlovsk Rus. Fed. see Yekaterinburg
111 B2 Sveti Nikole Macedonia
66 C1 Svetlaya Rus. Fed.
88 B3 Svetlogorsk Rus. Fed.
87 D4 Svetlograd Rus. Fed.
88 B3 Svetlyy Rus. Fed.
93 I3 Svetogorsk Rus. Fed.
111 B2 Svidník Slovakia
110 B2 Svilengrad Bulg.
110 B2 Svinecea Mare, Vârful *mt.* Romania
110 C2 Svishtov Bulg.
88 B3 Svislach Belarus
103 D2 Svitavy Czech Rep.
91 C2 Svitlovods'k Ukr.
69 E1 Svobodnyy Rus. Fed.
92 F2 Svolvær Norway
88 C3 Svyetlahorsk Belarus
143 D2 Swainsboro U.S.A.
120 A3 Swakopmund Namibia
52 B3 Swan Hill Austr.
128 C2 Swan Hills Can.
129 D2 Swan Lake Can.
97 C1 Swanlinbar Rep. of Ireland
129 D2 Swan River Can.
53 D2 Swansea Austr.
99 B4 Swansea U.K.

22 B3 **Swartkolkvloer** *salt pan* S. Africa
23 C2 **Swartruggens** S. Africa
Swatow China *see* Shantou
23 D2 **Swaziland** *country* Africa
3 G3 **Sweden** *country* Europe
39 C2 **Sweetwater** U.S.A.
36 B2 **Sweetwater** *r.* U.S.A.
22 B3 **Swellendam** S. Africa
3 D1 **Świdnica** Pol.
3 D1 **Świdwin** Pol.
3 D1 **Świebodzin** Pol.
3 D1 **Świecie** Pol.
29 D2 **Swift Current** Can.
7 C1 **Swilly, Lough** *inlet* Rep. of Ireland
9 C4 **Swindon** U.K.
2 C1 **Świnoujście** Pol.
5 D2 **Switzerland** *country* Europe
7 C2 **Swords** Rep. of Ireland
8 C3 **Syanno** Belarus
9 D1 **Syas'troy** Rus. Fed.
9 D2 **Sychevka** Rus. Fed.
3 D2 **Sydney** Austr.
1 D3 **Sydney** Can.
1 D3 **Sydney Mines** Can.
1 D2 **Syeverodonets'k** Ukr.
6 E2 **Syktyvkar** Rus. Fed.
2 C2 **Sylacauga** U.S.A.
5 D2 **Sylhet** Bangl.
2 B1 **Sylt** *i.* Ger.
0 C2 **Sylvania** U.S.A.
1 C1 **Sylvester, Lake** *salt flat* Austr.
1 C3 **Symi** *i.* Greece
1 D2 **Synel'nykove** Ukr.
0 C2 **Synyukha** *r.* Ukr.
9 C3 **Syracuse** *Sicily* Italy
6 C3 **Syracuse** *KS* U.S.A.
1 D2 **Syracuse** *NY* U.S.A.
7 C2 **Syrdar'ya** *r.* Asia
0 B2 **Syria** *country* Asia
3 A2 **Syriam** Myanmar
0 B2 **Syrian Desert** Asia
1 B3 **Syros** *i.* Greece
1 D2 **Syvash, Zatoka** *lag.* Ukr.
1 C2 **Syvas'ke** Ukr.
7 D3 **Syzran'** Rus. Fed.
2 C1 **Szczecin** Pol.
3 D1 **Szczecinek** Pol.
3 E1 **Szczytno** Pol.
Szechwan *prov.* China *see* Sichuan
3 E2 **Szeged** Hungary
3 D2 **Székesfehérvár** Hungary
3 D2 **Szekszárd** Hungary
3 E2 **Szentes** Hungary
3 D2 **Szentgotthárd** Hungary
3 E2 **Szerencs** Hungary
3 D2 **Szigetvár** Hungary
3 E2 **Szolnok** Hungary
3 D2 **Szombathely** Hungary
Sztálinváros Hungary *see* **Dunaújváros**

T

7 C4 **Taagga Duudka** *reg.* Somalia
4 B2 **Tabaco** Phil.
8 B2 **Tābah** Saudi Arabia
8 A3 **Tabarka** Tunisia
6 B3 **Ţabas** Iran
9 C1 **Tabāsin** Iran
1 D3 **Tābask, Kūh-e** *mt.* Iran
0 C3 **Tabatinga** Brazil
4 C2 **Tabatinga** Brazil
4 B2 **Tabelbala** Alg.
28 C3 **Taber** Can.
4 B2 **Tablas** *i.* Phil.
2 C2 **Tábor** Czech Rep.
9 D3 **Tabora** Tanz.
4 B4 **Tabou** Côte d'Ivoire
1 C2 **Tabrīz** Iran
8 L3 **Tabuaeran** *i.* Kiribati
8 A2 **Tabūk** Saudi Arabia
3 G4 **Täby** Sweden
7 E2 **Tacheng** China
2 C2 **Tachov** Czech Rep.
4 B2 **Tacloban** Phil.
0 B4 **Tacna** Peru
4 B1 **Tacoma** U.S.A.
2 C3 **Tacuarembó** Uru.
8 B3 **Tacupeto** Mex.
4 C2 **Tademaït, Plateau du** Alg.
Tadjikistan *country* Asia *see* **Tajikistan**
117 C3 **Tadjoura** Djibouti
80 B2 **Tadmur** Syria
129 E2 **Tadoule Lake** Can.
Tadzhikskaya S.S.R. *country* Asia *see* **Tajikistan**
65 B2 **T'aebaek-sanmaek** *mts* N. Korea/S. Korea
Taech'ŏn S. Korea *see* Poryŏng
65 B2 **Taegu** S. Korea
65 B2 **Taejŏn** S. Korea
65 B3 **Taejŏng** S. Korea
65 B2 **T'aepaek** S. Korea
107 C1 **Tafalla** Spain
152 B2 **Tafi Viejo** Arg.
79 D2 **Taftān, Kūh-e** *mt.* Iran
91 D2 **Taganrog** Rus. Fed.
91 D2 **Taganrog, Gulf of** Rus. Fed./Ukr.
62 A1 **Tagaung** Myanmar
64 B2 **Tagaytay City** Phil.
64 B3 **Tagbilaran** Phil.
64 B2 **Tagudin** Phil.
51 E1 **Tagula Island** P.N.G.
64 B3 **Tagum** Phil.
106 B2 **Tagus** *r.* Port./Spain
60 B1 **Tahan, Gunung** *mt.* Malaysia
115 C2 **Tahat, Mont** *mt.* Alg.
69 E1 **Tahe** China
49 M5 **Tahiti** *i.* Fr. Polynesia
139 E1 **Tahlequah** U.S.A.
135 B3 **Tahoe, Lake** U.S.A.
135 B3 **Tahoe City** U.S.A.
126 E2 **Tahoe Lake** Can.
115 C3 **Tahoua** Niger
79 C2 **Tahrūd** Iran
128 B3 **Tahsis** Can.
116 B2 **Tahta** Egypt
64 B3 **Tahuna** Indon.
70 B2 **Tai'an** China
70 A2 **Taibai Shan** *mt.* China
Taibus Qi China *see* Baochang
71 C3 **T'aichung** Taiwan
70 B2 **Taihang Shan** *mts* China
54 C1 **Taihape** N.Z.
71 B3 **Taihe** China
70 C2 **Tai Hu** *l.* China
52 A3 **Tailem Bend** Austr.
71 C3 **T'ainan** Taiwan
111 B3 **Tainaro, Akra** *pt* Greece
155 D1 **Taiobeiras** Brazil
71 C3 **T'aipei** Taiwan
Taiping China *see* Chongzuo
60 B1 **Taiping** Malaysia
Tairbeart U.K. *see* **Tarbert**
71 B3 **Taishan** China
70 B2 **Tai Shan** *hills* China
153 A4 **Taitao, Península de** *pen.* Chile
71 C3 **T'aitung** Taiwan
92 I2 **Taivalkoski** Fin.
92 H2 **Taivaskero** *hill* Fin.
71 C3 **Taiwan** Asia
Taiwan Shan *mts* Taiwan *see* **Chungyang Shanmo**
71 B3 **Taiwan Strait** China/Taiwan
70 B2 **Taiyuan** China
70 B2 **Taizhou** *Jiangsu* China
71 C3 **Taizhou** *Zhejiang* China
78 B3 **Ta'izz** Yemen
145 C3 **Tajamulco, Volcán de** *vol.* Guat.
77 D3 **Tajikistan** *country* Asia
74 B2 **Taj Mahal** *tourist site* India
Tajo *r.* Spain *see* **Tagus**
63 A2 **Tak** Thai.
54 B2 **Takaka** N.Z.
115 C2 **Takalous, Oued** *watercourse* Alg.
67 B4 **Takamatsu** Japan
67 C3 **Takaoka** Japan
54 B1 **Takapuna** N.Z.
67 C3 **Takasaki** Japan
122 B1 **Takatokwane** Botswana
122 B1 **Takatshwaane** Botswana
67 C3 **Takayama** Japan
67 C3 **Takefu** Japan
60 A1 **Takengon** Indon.
63 B2 **Takêv** Cambodia
Takhiatash Uzbek. *see* **Gulabie**
63 B2 **Ta Khmau** Cambodia
74 B1 **Takht-i-Sulaiman** *mt.* Pak.
66 D2 **Takikawa** Japan
128 B2 **Takla Lake** Can.
128 B2 **Takla Landing** Can.
Takla Makan *des.* China *see* **Taklimakan Shamo**
Taklimakan Desert China *see* **Taklimakan Shamo**
77 E3 **Taklimakan Shamo** *des.* China
128 A2 **Taku** *r.* Can./U.S.A.
63 A3 **Takua Pa** Thai.
115 C4 **Takum** Nigeria
88 C3 **Talachyn** Belarus
74 B1 **Talagang** Pak.
146 B4 **Talamanca, Cordillera de** *mts* Costa Rica
150 A3 **Talara** Peru
74 A2 **Talar-i-Band** *mts* Pak.
59 C2 **Talaud, Kepulauan** *is* Indon.
106 C2 **Talavera de la Reina** Spain
153 A3 **Talca** Chile
153 A3 **Talcahuano** Chile
89 E2 **Taldom** Rus. Fed.
77 D2 **Taldykorgan** Kazakh.
Taldy-Kurgan Kazakh. *see* Taldykorgan
59 C3 **Taliabu** *i.* Indon.
64 B2 **Talisay** Phil.
61 C2 **Taliwang** Indon.
81 C2 **Tall 'Afar** Iraq
143 D2 **Tallahassee** U.S.A.
53 C3 **Tallangatta** Austr.
88 B2 **Tallinn** Estonia
142 B2 **Tallulah** U.S.A.
104 B2 **Talmont-St-Hilaire** France
90 C2 **Tal'ne** Ukr.
117 B3 **Talodi** Sudan
74 A1 **Tāloqān** Afgh.
91 E1 **Talovaya** Rus. Fed.
126 F2 **Taloyoak** Can.
88 B2 **Talsi** Latvia
152 A2 **Taltal** Chile
129 C1 **Taltson** *r.* Can.
60 A1 **Talu** Indon.
53 C1 **Talwood** Austr.
114 B4 **Tamale** Ghana
115 C2 **Tamanrasset** Alg.
99 A4 **Tamar** *r.* U.K.
Tamatave Madag. *see* Toamasina
144 B2 **Tamazula** Mex.
145 C2 **Tamazunchale** Mex.
114 A3 **Tambacounda** Senegal
60 B1 **Tambelan, Kepulauan** *is* Indon.
86 G1 **Tambey** Rus. Fed.
61 C1 **Tambisan** *Sabah* Malaysia
61 C2 **Tambora, Gunung** *vol.* Indon.
91 E1 **Tambov** Rus. Fed.
119 C2 **Tambura** Sudan
62 A1 **Tamenglong** India
145 C2 **Tamiahua, Laguna de** *lag.* Mex.
Tammerfors Fin. *see* Tampere
143 D3 **Tampa** U.S.A.
143 D3 **Tampa Bay** U.S.A.
93 H3 **Tampere** Fin.
145 C2 **Tampico** Mex.
69 D1 **Tamsagbulag** Mongolia
102 C2 **Tamsweg** Austria
53 D2 **Tamworth** Austr.
99 C3 **Tamworth** U.K.
119 E3 **Tana** *r.* Kenya
Tana, Lake Eth. *see* T'ana Hāyk'
67 C4 **Tanabe** Japan
92 I1 **Tana Bru** Norway
117 B3 **T'ana Hāyk'** *l.* Eth.
60 A2 **Tanahbala** *i.* Indon.
61 C2 **Tanahgrogot** Indon.
61 D2 **Tanahjampea** *i.* Indon.
60 A2 **Tanahmasa** *i.* Indon.
50 C1 **Tanami Desert** Austr.
63 B2 **Tân An** Vietnam
126 B2 **Tanana** U.S.A.
Tananarive Madag. *see* Antananarivo
108 A1 **Tanaro** *r.* Italy
65 B1 **Tanch'ŏn** N. Korea
64 B3 **Tandag** Phil.
110 C2 **Ţăndărei** Romania
153 C3 **Tandil** Arg.
74 A2 **Tando Adam** Pak.
74 A2 **Tando Muhammmad Khan** Pak.
52 B2 **Tandou Lake** *imp. l.* Austr.
67 B4 **Tanega-shima** *i.* Japan
114 B2 **Tanezrouft** *reg.* Alg./Mali
119 D3 **Tanga** Tanz.
75 C2 **Tangail** Bangl.
Tanganyika *country* Africa *see* **Tanzania**
119 C3 **Tanganyika, Lake** Africa
55 F3 **Tange Promontory** *hd* Antarctica
Tanger Morocco *see* Tangier
101 E1 **Tangermünde** Ger.
75 D1 **Tanggula Shan** *mt.* China
75 C1 **Tanggula Shan** *mts* China
114 B1 **Tangier** Morocco
75 C1 **Tangra Yumco** *salt l.* China
70 B2 **Tangshan** China
68 C2 **Taniantaweng Shan** *mts* China
59 C3 **Tanimbar, Kepulauan** *is* Indon.
64 B3 **Tanjay** Phil.
61 C2 **Tanjung** Indon.
60 A1 **Tanjungbalai** Indon.
60 B2 **Tanjungkarang-Telukbetung** Indon.
60 B2 **Tanjungpandan** Indon.
60 B1 **Tanjungpinang** Indon.
61 C1 **Tanjungredeb** Indon.
61 C1 **Tanjungselor** Indon.
74 B1 **Tank** Pak.
48 H5 **Tanna** *i.* Vanuatu
115 C3 **Tanout** Niger
75 C2 **Tansen** Nepal
116 B1 **Tanta** Egypt
114 A2 **Tan-Tan** Morocco
145 C2 **Tantoyuca** Mex.
119 D3 **Tanzania** *country* Africa
Tao'an China *see* **Taonan**
Taocheng China *see* Yongchun
Taolanaro Madag. *see* Tôlañaro
69 E1 **Taonan** China
109 C3 **Taormina** *Sicily* Italy
138 B1 **Taos** U.S.A.
114 B2 **Taoudenni** Mali
114 B1 **Taounate** Morocco
114 B1 **Taourirt** Morocco
88 C2 **Tapa** Estonia
145 C3 **Tapachula** Mex.
151 D3 **Tapajós** *r.* Brazil
60 A1 **Tapaktuan** Indon.
145 C3 **Tapanatepec** Mex.
150 C3 **Tapauá** Brazil
152 C2 **Tapera** Brazil
114 B4 **Tapeta** Liberia
74 B2 **Tāpi** *r.* India
141 D3 **Tappahannock** U.S.A.
54 B2 **Tapuaenuku** *mt.* N.Z.
150 C3 **Tapurucuara** Brazil
154 B1 **Taquaral, Serra do** *hills* Brazil
154 B1 **Taquarí** Brazil
154 A1 **Taquarí** *r.* Brazil
154 B1 **Taquari, Serra do** *hills* Brazil
154 C2 **Taquaritinga** Brazil
53 D1 **Tara** Austr.
115 D4 **Taraba** *r.* Nigeria
Ţarābulus Libya *see* **Tripoli**
54 C1 **Taradale** N.Z.
61 C1 **Tarakan** Indon.
111 D2 **Taraklı** Turkey
88 A3 **Taran, Mys** *pt* Rus. Fed.
Taranaki, Mount *vol.* N.Z. *see* **Egmont, Mount**
106 C1 **Tarancón** Spain
109 C2 **Taranto** Italy
109 C2 **Taranto, Golfo di** *g.* Italy
150 B3 **Tarapoto** Peru
90 C2 **Tarashcha** Ukr.
91 E2 **Tarasovskiy** Rus. Fed.
150 B3 **Tarauacá** Brazil
150 C3 **Tarauacá** *r.* Brazil
48 I3 **Tarawa** *atoll* Kiribati
54 C1 **Tarawera** N.Z.
77 D2 **Taraz** Kazakh.
107 C1 **Tarazona** Spain
77 E2 **Tarbagatay, Khrebet** *mts* Kazakh.
96 C2 **Tarbat Ness** *pt* U.K.
97 B2 **Tarbert** Rep. of Ireland
96 A2 **Tarbert** *Scotland* U.K.
96 B3 **Tarbert** *Scotland* U.K.
104 C3 **Tarbes** France
96 B2 **Tarbet** U.K.
143 E1 **Tarboro** U.S.A.
51 C3 **Tarcoola** Austr.
53 D2 **Taree** Austr.
110 C2 **Târgovişte** Romania
110 C1 **Târgu Frumos** Romania
110 B1 **Târgu Jiu** Romania
110 B1 **Târgu Lăpuş** Romania
110 B1 **Târgu Mureş** Romania

110 C1 **Târgu Neamț** Romania
110 C1 **Târgu Ocna** Romania
79 C2 **Tarif** U.A.E.
152 B2 **Tarija** Bol.
79 B3 **Tarīm** Yemen
Tarim Basin China *see* Tarim Pendi
119 D3 **Tarime** Tanz.
77 E2 **Tarim He** *r.* China
77 E3 **Tarim Pendi** *basin* China
77 C3 **Tarīn Kowt** Afgh.
59 D3 **Taritatu** *r.* Indon.
123 C3 **Tarkastad** S. Africa
82 G2 **Tarko-Sale** Rus. Fed.
114 B4 **Tarkwa** Ghana
64 B2 **Tarlac** Phil.
105 C3 **Tarn** *r.* France
92 G2 **Tärnaby** Sweden
77 C3 **Tarnak** *r.* Afgh.
110 B1 **Târnăveni** Romania
103 E1 **Tarnobrzeg** Pol.
Tarnopol Ukr. *see* **Ternopil'**
103 E1 **Tarnów** Pol.
51 D2 **Taroom** Austr.
114 B1 **Taroudannt** Morocco
143 D3 **Tarpon Springs** U.S.A.
108 B2 **Tarquinia** Italy
107 D1 **Tarragona** Spain
107 D1 **Tàrrega** Spain
80 B2 **Tarsus** Turkey
152 B2 **Tartagal** Arg.
104 B3 **Tartas** France
88 C2 **Tartu** Estonia
80 B2 **Ţarţūs** Syria
155 D1 **Tarumirim** Brazil
89 E3 **Tarusa** Rus. Fed.
90 B2 **Tarutyne** Ukr.
108 B1 **Tarvisio** Italy
Tashauz Turkm. *see* **Dashkhovuz**
Tashi Chho Bhutan *see* **Thimphu**
81 D3 **Tashk, Daryācheh-ye** *l.* Iran
77 C2 **Tashkent** Uzbek.
130 C2 **Tasiat, Lac** *l.* Can.
131 D2 **Tasiujaq** Can.
77 E2 **Taskesken** Kazakh.
54 B2 **Tasman Bay** N.Z.
51 D4 **Tasmania** *state* Austr.
54 B2 **Tasman Mountains** N.Z.
156 D8 **Tasman Sea** S. Pacific Ocean
130 C2 **Tassialujjuaq, Lac** *l.* Can.
115 C2 **Tassili du Hoggar** *plat.* Alg.
115 C2 **Tassili n'Ajjer** *plat.* Alg.
61 D2 **Tataba** Indon.
103 D2 **Tatabánya** Hungary
90 B2 **Tatarbunary** Ukr.
83 K3 **Tatarskiy Proliv** *str.* Rus. Fed.
Tatar Strait Rus. Fed. *see* **Tatarskiy Proliv**
67 C4 **Tateyama** Japan
128 C1 **Tathlina Lake** Can.
78 B3 **Tathlīth** Saudi Arabia
78 B2 **Tathlīth, Wādī** *watercourse* Saudi Arabia
53 C3 **Tathra** Austr.
62 A1 **Tatkon** Myanmar
128 B2 **Tatla Lake** Can.
103 D2 **Tatra Mountains** Pol./Slovakia
Tatry *mts* Pol./Slovakia *see* **Tatra Mountains**
74 A2 **Tatta** Pak.
154 C2 **Tatuí** Brazil
139 C2 **Tatum** U.S.A.
81 C2 **Tatvan** Turkey
151 E3 **Taua** Brazil
155 C2 **Taubaté** Brazil
101 D3 **Tauberbischofsheim** Ger.
54 C1 **Taumarunui** N.Z.
122 B2 **Taung** S. Africa
62 A1 **Taunggyi** Myanmar
62 A2 **Taungup** Myanmar
74 B1 **Taunsa** Pak.
99 B4 **Taunton** U.K.
101 C2 **Taunus** *hills* Ger.
54 C1 **Taupo** N.Z.
54 C1 **Taupo, Lake** N.Z.
88 B2 **Tauragė** Lith.
54 C1 **Tauranga** N.Z.
141 E1 **Taureau, Réservoir** *resr* Can.
Taurus Mountains Turkey *see* **Toros Dağları**
111 C3 **Tavas** Turkey
86 F3 **Tavda** Rus. Fed.
106 B2 **Tavira** Port.
99 A4 **Tavistock** U.K.
63 A2 **Tavoy** Myanmar
111 C3 **Tavşanlı** Turkey
99 A4 **Taw** *r.* U.K.
140 C2 **Tawas City** U.S.A.
61 C1 **Tawau** *Sabah* Malaysia
64 A3 **Tawitawi** *i.* Phil.
71 C3 **Tawu** Taiwan
145 C3 **Taxco** Mex.
77 D3 **Taxkorgan** China
96 C2 **Tay** *r.* U.K.
96 C2 **Tay, Firth of** *est.* U.K.
96 B2 **Tay, Loch** *l.* U.K.
128 B2 **Taylor** Can.
140 C2 **Taylor** *MI* U.S.A.
139 D2 **Taylor** *TX* U.S.A.
140 B3 **Taylorville** U.S.A.
78 A2 **Taymā'** Saudi Arabia
83 H2 **Taymura** *r.* Rus. Fed.
83 H2 **Taymyr, Ozero** *l.* Rus. Fed.
83 G2 **Taymyr, Poluostrov** *pen.* Rus. Fed.
Taymyr Peninsula Rus. Fed. *see* **Taymyr, Poluostrov**
63 B2 **Tây Ninh** Vietnam
96 C2 **Tayport** U.K.
64 A2 **Taytay** Phil.
76 C3 **Tayyebād** Iran
77 C1 **Tayynsha** Kazakh.
82 G2 **Taz** *r.* Rus. Fed.
114 B1 **Taza** Morocco
129 D2 **Tazin Lake** Can.
86 G2 **Tazovskaya Guba** *sea chan.* Rus. Fed.
81 C1 **T'bilisi** Georgia
91 E2 **Tbilisskaya** Rus. Fed.
118 B3 **Tchibanga** Gabon
115 C3 **Tchin-Tabaradene** Niger
118 B2 **Tcholliré** Cameroon
103 D1 **Tczew** Pol.
144 B2 **Teacapán** Mex.
54 A3 **Te Anau** N.Z.
54 A3 **Te Anau, Lake** N.Z.
145 C3 **Teapa** Mex.
54 C1 **Te Awamutu** N.Z.
115 C1 **Tébessa** Alg.
60 B2 **Tebingtinggi** Indon.
60 A1 **Tebingtinggi** Indon.
144 A1 **Tecate** Mex.
114 B4 **Techiman** Ghana
144 B3 **Tecomán** Mex.
144 B2 **Tecoripa** Mex.
145 B3 **Técpan** Mex.
144 B2 **Tecuala** Mex.
110 C1 **Tecuci** Romania
76 C3 **Tedzhen** Turkm.
76 C3 **Tedzhen** *r.* Turkm.
68 C1 **Teeli** Rus. Fed.
98 C2 **Tees** *r.* U.K.
111 C3 **Tefenni** Turkey
60 B2 **Tegal** Indon.
146 B3 **Tegucigalpa** Hond.
115 C3 **Teguidda-n-Tessoumt** Niger
129 E1 **Tehek Lake** Can.
Teheran Iran *see* **Tehrān**
114 B4 **Téhini** Côte d'Ivoire
81 D2 **Tehrān** Iran
145 C3 **Tehuacán** Mex.
145 C3 **Tehuantepec, Golfo de** *g.* Mex.
Tehuantepec, Gulf of Mex. *see* **Tehuantepec, Golfo de**
145 C3 **Tehuantepec, Istmo de** *isth.* Mex.
114 A2 **Teide, Pico del** *vol.* Canary Is
99 A3 **Teifi** *r.* U.K.
119 D3 **Teita Hills** Kenya
Teixeira de Sousa Angola *see* **Luau**
Tejo *r.* Port. *see* **Tagus**
145 B3 **Tejupilco** Mex.
54 B2 **Tekapo, Lake** N.Z.
145 D2 **Tekax** Mex.
116 B3 **Tekezē Wenz** *r.* Eritrea/Eth.
111 C2 **Tekirdağ** Turkey
54 C1 **Te Kuiti** N.Z.
75 C2 **Tel** *r.* India
81 C1 **T'elavi** Georgia
80 B2 **Tel Aviv-Yafo** Israel
145 D2 **Telchac Puerto** Mex.
128 A2 **Telegraph Creek** Can.
154 B2 **Telêmaco Borba** Brazil
61 C1 **Telen** *r.* Indon.
50 B2 **Telfer Mining Centre** Austr.
99 B3 **Telford** U.K.
128 B2 **Telkwa** Can.
60 A2 **Telo** Indon.
86 E2 **Tel'pos-Iz, Gora** *mt.* Rus. Fed.
88 B2 **Telšiai** Lith.
60 B1 **Teluk Anson** Malaysia
60 B2 **Telukbatang** Indon.
60 A1 **Telukdalam** Indon.
114 C4 **Tema** Ghana
130 C3 **Temagami Lake** Can.
60 C2 **Temanggung** Indon.
123 C2 **Temba** S. Africa
83 H2 **Tembenchi** *r.* Rus. Fed.
60 B2 **Tembilahan** Indon.
123 C2 **Tembisa** S. Africa
120 A1 **Tembo Aluma** Angola
Tembué Moz. *see* **Chifunde**
99 B3 **Teme** *r.* U.K.
135 C4 **Temecula** U.S.A.
63 B3 **Temengor, Tasik** *resr* Malaysia
60 B1 **Temerloh** Malaysia
77 D1 **Temirtau** Kazakh.
141 D1 **Témiscamingue, Lac** *l.* Can.
53 C2 **Temora** Austr.
138 A2 **Tempe** U.S.A.
139 D2 **Temple** U.S.A.
97 C2 **Templemore** Rep. of Ireland
102 C1 **Templin** Ger.
145 C2 **Tempoal** Mex.
120 A2 **Tempué** Angola
91 D2 **Temryuk** Rus. Fed.
91 D2 **Temryukskiy Zaliv** *b.* Rus. Fed.
153 A3 **Temuco** Chile
54 B2 **Temuka** N.Z.
145 C2 **Tenabo** Mex.
139 E2 **Tenaha** U.S.A.
73 C3 **Tenali** India
63 A2 **Tenasserim** Myanmar
99 A4 **Tenby** U.K.
117 C3 **Tendaho** Eth.
105 D3 **Tende** France
105 D3 **Tende, Col de** *pass* France/Italy
73 D4 **Ten Degree Channel** India
114 A3 **Te-n-Dghâmcha, Sebkhet** *salt marsh* Maur.
67 D3 **Tendō** Japan
114 B3 **Ténenkou** Mali
115 C2 **Ténéré** *reg.* Niger
115 D2 **Ténéré du Tafassâsset** *des.* Niger
114 A2 **Tenerife** *i.* Canary Is
107 D2 **Ténès** Alg.
61 C2 **Tengah, Kepulauan** *is* Indon.
Tengcheng China *see* Tengxian
62 A1 **Tengchong** China
61 C2 **Tenggarong** Indon.
70 A2 **Tengger Shamo** *des.* China
77 C1 **Tengiz, Ozero** *salt l.* Kazakh.
71 B3 **Tengxian** China
119 C4 **Tenke** Dem. Rep. Congo
114 B3 **Tenkodogo** Burkina
51 C1 **Tennant Creek** Austr.
142 C1 **Tennessee** *r.* U.S.A.
142 C1 **Tennessee** *state* U.S.A.
61 C1 **Tenom** *Sabah* Malaysia
145 C3 **Tenosique** Mex.
61 D2 **Tenteno** Indon.
53 D1 **Tenterfield** Austr.
143 D3 **Ten Thousand Islands** U.S.A.
154 B2 **Teodoro Sampaio** Brazil
155 D1 **Teófilo Otôni** Brazil
145 C3 **Teopisca** Mex.
59 C3 **Tepa** Indon.
144 B2 **Tepache** Mex.
54 B1 **Te Paki** N.Z.
144 B3 **Tepalcatepec** Mex.
144 B2 **Tepatitlán** Mex.
144 B2 **Tepehuanes** Mex.
109 D2 **Tepelenë** Albania
144 B2 **Tepic** Mex.
102 C1 **Teplice** Czech Rep.
89 E3 **Teploye** Rus. Fed.
90 B2 **Teplyk** Ukr.
54 C1 **Te Puke** N.Z.
144 B2 **Tequila** Mex.
49 K3 **Teraina** *i.* Kiribati
108 B2 **Teramo** Italy
52 B3 **Terang** Austr.
89 E3 **Terbuny** Rus. Fed.
90 B2 **Terebovlya** Ukr.
87 D4 **Terek** *r.* Rus. Fed.
154 B2 **Terenos** Brazil
151 E3 **Teresina** Brazil
155 D2 **Teresópolis** Brazil
63 A3 **Teressa Island** India
100 A3 **Tergnier** France
80 B1 **Terme** Turkey
77 C3 **Termez** Uzbek.
108 B3 **Termini Imerese** *Sicily* Italy
145 C3 **Términos, Laguna de** *la* Mex.
109 B2 **Termoli** Italy
59 C2 **Ternate** Indon.
100 A2 **Terneuzen** Neth.
66 C1 **Terney** Rus. Fed.
108 B2 **Terni** Italy
90 B2 **Ternopil'** Ukr.
52 A2 **Terowie** Austr.
69 F1 **Terpeniya, Mys** *c.* Rus. Fed.
69 F1 **Terpeniya, Zaliv** *g.* Rus. Fed.
128 B2 **Terrace** Can.
130 B3 **Terrace Bay** Can.
122 B2 **Terra Firma** S. Africa
142 B3 **Terrebonne Bay** U.S.A.
140 B3 **Terre Haute** U.S.A.
131 E3 **Terrenceville** Can.
100 B1 **Terschelling** *i.* Neth.
108 A3 **Tertenia** *Sardinia* Italy
107 C1 **Teruel** Spain
92 H2 **Tervola** Fin.
109 C2 **Tešanj** Bos.-Herz.
116 B3 **Teseney** Eritrea
66 D2 **Teshio** Japan
66 D2 **Teshio-gawa** *r.* Japan
128 A1 **Teslin** Can.
128 A1 **Teslin Lake** Can.
154 B1 **Tesouro** Brazil
115 C3 **Tessaoua** Niger
99 C4 **Test** *r.* U.K.
121 C2 **Tete** Moz.
90 C1 **Teteriv** *r.* Ukr.
101 F1 **Teterow** Ger.
90 B2 **Tetiyiv** Ukr.
114 B1 **Tétouan** Morocco
110 B2 **Tetovo** Macedonia
Tetyukhe Rus. Fed. *see* Dal'negorsk
Teuchezhsk Rus. Fed. *se* Adygeysk
152 B2 **Teuco** *r.* Arg.
144 B2 **Teul de González Orteg** Mex.
101 D1 **Teutoburger Wald** *hills* Ger.
108 B2 **Tevere** *r.* Italy
54 A3 **Teviot** N.Z.
96 C3 **Teviot** *r.* U.K.
96 C3 **Teviothead** U.K.
61 C2 **Tewah** Indon.
51 E2 **Tewantin** Austr.
54 C2 **Te Wharau** N.Z.
99 B4 **Tewkesbury** U.K.
139 E2 **Texarkana** U.S.A.
53 D1 **Texas** Austr.
139 D2 **Texas** *state* U.S.A.
139 E3 **Texas City** U.S.A.
145 C3 **Texcoco** Mex.
100 B1 **Texel** *i.* Neth.
139 D2 **Texoma, Lake** U.S.A.
123 C2 **Teyateyaneng** Lesotho
89 F2 **Teykovo** Rus. Fed.
89 F2 **Teza** *r.* Rus. Fed.
75 D2 **Tezpur** India
72 D2 **Tezu** India
129 E1 **Tha-anne** *r.* Can.
123 C2 **Thabana-Ntlenyana** *mt.* Lesotho
123 C2 **Thaba Nchu** S. Africa
123 C2 **Thaba Putsoa** *mt.* Lesotho
123 C2 **Thaba-Tseka** Lesotho
123 C1 **Thabazimbi** S. Africa
123 C2 **Thabong** S. Africa
63 A2 **Thagyettaw** Myanmar
62 B1 **Thai Binh** Vietnam
63 B2 **Thailand** *country* Asia
63 B2 **Thailand, Gulf of** Asia
62 B1 **Thai Nguyên** Vietnam
74 B1 **Thal** Pak.
63 A3 **Thalang** Thai.
74 B1 **Thal Desert** Pak.
101 E2 **Thale (Harz)** Ger.
63 B3 **Thale Luang** *lag.* Thai.
62 B2 **Tha Li** Thai.
53 C1 **Thallon** Austr.
123 C1 **Thamaga** Botswana
78 B3 **Thamar, Jabal** *mt.* Yeme
79 C3 **Thamarīt** Oman

30 B3 **Thames** *r.* Can.
4 C1 **Thames** N.Z.
9 D4 **Thames** *est.* U.K.
9 D4 **Thames** *r.* U.K.
9 B3 **Thamūd** Yemen
Thana India see **Thāne**
3 A2 **Thanbyuzayat** Myanmar
4 B3 **Thāne** India
2 B2 **Thanh Hoa** Vietnam
3 B3 **Thanjavur** India
4 A2 **Thano Bula Khan** Pak.
2 B1 **Than Uyen** Vietnam
4 A2 **Thar Desert** India/Pak.
2 B1 **Thargomindah** Austr.
2 A2 **Tharrawaddy** Myanmar
1 C2 **Tharthār, Buḥayrat ath** *l.* Iraq
1 B2 **Thasos** Greece
1 B2 **Thasos** *i.* Greece
2 B1 **Thât Khê** Vietnam
2 A2 **Thaton** Myanmar
2 A1 **Thaungdut** Myanmar
3 A2 **Thayetchaung** Myanmar
2 A2 **Thayetmyo** Myanmar
2 A1 **Thazi** Myanmar
6 C2 **The Bahamas** *country* West Indies
8 B2 **The Cheviot** *hill* U.K.
4 B1 **The Dalles** U.S.A.
6 C2 **Thedford** U.S.A.
3 D2 **The Entrance** Austr.
9 C3 **The Fens** *reg.* U.K.
4 A3 **The Gambia** *country* Africa
6 B2 **The Great Oasis** Egypt
9 C2 **The Gulf** Asia
0 B1 **The Hague** Neth.
9 E1 **Thelon** *r.* Can.
1 E2 **Themar** Ger.
3 C2 **Thembalihle** S. Africa
6 A1 **The Minch** *sea chan.* U.K.
7 A1 **The Mullet** *b.* Rep. of Ireland
9 C4 **The Needles** *stack* U.K.
0 C3 **Theodore Roosevelt** *r.* Brazil
9 D2 **The Pas** Can.
1 B2 **Thermaïkos Kolpos** *g.* Greece
6 B2 **Thermopolis** U.S.A.
3 C3 **The Rock** Austr.
The Skaw *spit* Denmark see **Grenen**
9 C4 **The Solent** *str.* U.K.
0 B3 **Thessalon** Can.
1 B2 **Thessaloniki** Greece
9 D3 **Thetford** U.K.
1 C3 **Thetford Mines** Can.
2 A1 **The Triangle** *mts* Myanmar
7 D3 **The Valley** Anguilla
1 D2 **Thévenet, Lac** *l.* Can.
9 D3 **The Wash** *b.* U.K.
9 D4 **The Weald** *reg.* U.K.
9 D2 **The Woodlands** U.S.A.
2 B3 **Thibodaux** U.S.A.
9 E2 **Thicket Portage** Can.
7 D1 **Thief River Falls** U.S.A.
Thiel Neth. see **Tiel**
5 C2 **Thiers** France
4 A3 **Thiès** Senegal
9 D3 **Thika** Kenya
3 B4 **Thiladhunmathee Atoll** Maldives
5 C2 **Thimphu** Bhutan
5 D2 **Thionville** France
1 C3 **Thira** Greece
Thira *i.* Greece see **Santorini**
8 C2 **Thirsk** U.K.
Thiruvananthapuram India see **Trivandrum**
3 E4 **Thisted** Denmark
9 E1 **Thlewiaza** *r.* Can.
2 A2 **Thoen** Thai.
3 D1 **Thohoyandou** S. Africa
1 E1 **Thomasburg** Ger.
7 C2 **Thomastown** Rep. of Ireland
2 C2 **Thomasville** *AL* U.S.A.
3 D2 **Thomasville** *GA* U.S.A.
0 C2 **Thommen** Belgium
9 E2 **Thompson** Can.
8 E3 **Thompson** *r.* U.S.A.
4 C1 **Thompson Falls** U.S.A.
8 B2 **Thompson Sound** Can.
1 D2 **Thomson** *watercourse* Austr.
3 D2 **Thomson** U.S.A.
3 B2 **Thon Buri** Thai.
3 A2 **Thongwa** Myanmar

138 B1 **Thoreau** U.S.A.
96 C3 **Thornhill** U.K.
136 C3 **Thornton** U.S.A.
55 F2 **Thorshavnheiane** *reg.* Antarctica
123 C2 **Thota-ea-Moli** Lesotho
104 B2 **Thouars** France
62 A1 **Thoubal** India
134 D1 **Three Forks** U.S.A.
128 C2 **Three Hills** Can.
63 A2 **Three Pagodas Pass** Myanmar/Thai.
114 B4 **Three Points, Cape** Ghana
140 B2 **Three Rivers** *MI* U.S.A.
139 D3 **Three Rivers** *TX* U.S.A.
Thrissur India see **Trichur**
63 B2 **Thu Dâu Môt** Vietnam
100 B2 **Thuin** Belgium
Thule Greenland see **Qaanaaq**
121 B3 **Thuli** Zimbabwe
102 B2 **Thun** Switz.
130 B3 **Thunder Bay** Can.
130 B3 **Thunder Bay** *b.* Can.
63 A3 **Thung Song** Thai.
101 E2 **Thüringer Becken** *reg.* Ger.
101 E2 **Thüringer Wald** *mts* Ger.
Thuringian Forest *mts* Ger. see **Thüringer Wald**
97 C2 **Thurles** Rep. of Ireland
59 D3 **Thursday Island** Austr.
96 C1 **Thurso** U.K.
96 C1 **Thurso** *r.* U.K.
55 R2 **Thurston Island** Antarctica
101 D1 **Thüster Berg** *hill* Ger.
121 C2 **Thyolo** Malawi
Thysville Dem. Rep. Congo see **Mbanza-Ngungu**
79 C2 **Tiāb** Iran
151 E3 **Tianguá** Brazil
70 B2 **Tianjin** China
70 B2 **Tianjin** *mun.* China
71 A3 **Tianlin** China
70 B2 **Tianmen** China
69 E2 **Tianshan** China
70 A2 **Tianshui** China
70 A2 **Tianzhu** China
107 D2 **Tiaret** Alg.
114 B4 **Tiassalé** Côte d'Ivoire
154 B2 **Tibagi** Brazil
154 B2 **Tibagi** *r.* Brazil
118 B2 **Tibati** Cameroon
Tiber *r.* Italy see **Tevere**
Tiberias, Lake Israel see **Galilee, Sea of**
115 D2 **Tibesti** *mts* Chad
Tibet *aut. reg.* China see **Xizang Zizhiqu**
Tibet, Plateau of China see **Qing Zang Gaoyuan**
52 B1 **Tibooburra** Austr.
144 A2 **Tiburón, Isla** *i.* Mex.
114 B3 **Tîchît** Maur.
114 A2 **Tichla** Western Sahara
105 D2 **Ticino** *r.* Italy/Switz.
141 E2 **Ticonderoga** U.S.A.
145 D2 **Ticul** Mex.
114 A3 **Tidjikja** Maur.
100 B2 **Tiel** Neth.
70 C1 **Tieling** China
75 B1 **Tielongtan** Aksai Chin
100 A2 **Tielt** Belgium
100 B2 **Tienen** Belgium
68 B2 **Tien Shan** *mts* China/Kyrg.
Tientsin China see **Tianjin**
Tientsin *mun.* China see Tianjin
93 G3 **Tierp** Sweden
145 C3 **Tierra Blanca** Mex.
145 C3 **Tierra Colorada** Mex.
153 B5 **Tierra del Fuego, Isla Grande de** *i.* Arg./Chile
106 B1 **Tiétar, Valle de** *val.* Spain
154 C2 **Tietê** Brazil
154 B2 **Tietê** *r.* Brazil
140 C2 **Tiffin** U.S.A.
Tiflis Georgia see **T'bilisi**
143 D2 **Tifton** U.S.A.
90 B2 **Tighina** Moldova
75 C2 **Tigiria** India
118 B2 **Tignère** Cameroon
131 D3 **Tignish** Can.
150 B3 **Tigre** *r.* Ecuador/Peru
81 C2 **Tigris** *r.* Asia
114 A3 **Tiguent** Maur.
114 B2 **Tiguesmat** *hills* Maur.

115 D3 **Tigui** Chad
145 C2 **Tihuatlán** Mex.
144 A1 **Tijuana** Mex.
91 E2 **Tikhoretsk** Rus. Fed.
89 D2 **Tikhvin** Rus. Fed.
89 D2 **Tikhvinskaya Gryada** *ridge* Rus. Fed.
157 F7 **Tiki Basin** *sea feature* S. Pacific Ocean
54 C1 **Tikokino** N.Z.
81 C2 **Tikrīt** Iraq
83 J2 **Tiksi** Rus. Fed.
100 B2 **Tilburg** Neth.
152 B2 **Tilcara** Arg.
52 B1 **Tilcha** Austr.
114 C3 **Tîlemsi, Vallée du** *watercourse* Mali
Tilimsen Alg. see **Tlemcen**
114 C3 **Tillabéri** Niger
134 B1 **Tillamook** U.S.A.
63 A3 **Tillanchong Island** India
111 C3 **Tilos** *i.* Greece
52 B2 **Tilpa** Austr.
86 F2 **Til'tim** Rus. Fed.
89 E3 **Tim** Rus. Fed.
86 D2 **Timanskiy Kryazh** *ridge* Rus. Fed.
54 B2 **Timaru** N.Z.
91 D2 **Timashevsk** Rus. Fed.
Timashevskaya Rus. Fed. see **Timashevsk**
114 B3 **Timbedgha** Maur.
50 C1 **Timber Creek** Austr.
Timbuktu Mali see Tombouctou
115 C3 **Timia** Niger
114 C2 **Timimoun** Alg.
110 B1 **Timiş** *r.* Romania
110 B1 **Timişoara** Romania
130 B3 **Timmins** Can.
89 E2 **Timokhino** Rus. Fed.
151 E3 **Timon** Brazil
59 C3 **Timor** *i.* Indon.
59 C3 **Timor Sea** Austr./Indon.
Timor Timur *terr.* Asia see **East Timor**
93 G3 **Timrå** Sweden
78 B2 **Tīn, Jabal** *hill* Saudi Arabia
114 B2 **Tindouf** Alg.
53 D1 **Tingha** Austr.
75 C2 **Tingri** China
93 F4 **Tingsryd** Sweden
92 E3 **Tingvoll** Norway
Tingzhou China see **Changting**
59 D2 **Tinian** *i.* N. Mariana Is
Tinnelvelly India see **Tirunelveli**
152 B2 **Tinogasta** Arg.
111 C3 **Tinos** Greece
111 C3 **Tinos** *i.* Greece
100 A3 **Tinqueux** France
115 C2 **Tinrhert, Plateau du** Alg.
62 A1 **Tinsukia** India
52 B3 **Tintinara** Austr.
136 C1 **Tioga** U.S.A.
107 D2 **Tipasa** Alg.
97 B2 **Tipperary** Rep. of Ireland
151 E3 **Tiracambu, Serra do** *hills* Brazil
109 C2 **Tirana** Albania
Tiranë Albania see **Tirana**
108 B1 **Tirano** Italy
52 A1 **Tirari Desert** Austr.
90 B2 **Tiraspol** Moldova
122 A2 **Tiraz Mountains** Namibia
111 C3 **Tire** Turkey
96 A2 **Tiree** *i.* U.K.
Tîrgovişte Romania see **Târgovişte**
Tîrgu Frumos Romania see **Târgu Frumos**
Tîrgu Jiu Romania see **Târgu Jiu**
Tîrgu Lăpuş Romania see **Târgu Lăpuş**
Tîrgu Mureş Romania see **Târgu Mureş**
Tîrgu Neamţ Romania see **Târgu Neamţ**
Tîrgu Ocna Romania see **Târgu Ocna**
74 B1 **Tirich Mir** *mt.* Pak.
Tîrnăveni Romania see **Târnăveni**
155 C1 **Tiros** Brazil
118 C2 **Tiroungoulou** C.A.R.
73 B3 **Tiruchchirāppalli** India
73 B4 **Tirunelveli** India
73 B3 **Tirupati** India
73 B3 **Tiruppattur** India

73 B3 **Tiruppur** India
109 D1 **Tisa** *r.* Europe
109 D2 **Tisa** *r.* Yugo.
129 D2 **Tisdale** Can.
107 D2 **Tissemsilt** Alg.
75 C2 **Tista** *r.* India
103 E2 **Tisza** *r.* Hungary
55 L1 **Titan Dome** *ice feature* Antarctica
152 B1 **Titicaca, Lago** *l.* Bol./Peru
Titicaca, Lake Bol./Peru see **Titicaca, Lago**
75 C2 **Titlagarh** India
Titograd Yugo. see **Podgorica**
Titova Mitrovica Yugo. see **Kosovska Mitrovica**
Titovo Užice Yugo. see **Užice**
Titovo Velenje Slovenia see **Velenje**
Titov Veles Macedonia see **Veles**
Titov Vrbas Yugo. see **Vrbas**
110 C2 **Titu** Romania
143 D3 **Titusville** U.S.A.
99 B4 **Tiverton** U.K.
108 B2 **Tivoli** Italy
79 C2 **Ţīwī** Oman
63 A2 **Ti-ywa** Myanmar
145 D2 **Tizimín** Mex.
107 D2 **Tizi Ouzou** Alg.
114 B2 **Tiznit** Morocco
92 G2 **Tjaktjajaure** *l.* Sweden
Tjirebon Indon. see Cirebon
145 C3 **Tlacotalpán** Mex.
144 B2 **Tlahualilo** Mex.
145 C3 **Tlalnepantla** Mex.
145 C3 **Tlapa** Mex.
145 C3 **Tlaxcala** Mex.
145 C3 **Tlaxiaco** Mex.
114 B1 **Tlemcen** Alg.
123 C1 **Tlokweng** Botswana
128 B2 **Toad River** Can.
121 □D2 **Toamasina** Madag.
60 A1 **Toba, Danau** *l.* Indon.
Toba, Lake Indon. see Toba, Danau
74 A1 **Toba and Kakar Ranges** *mts* Pak.
147 D3 **Tobago** *i.* Trin. and Tob.
59 C2 **Tobelo** Indon.
130 B3 **Tobermory** Can.
96 A2 **Tobermory** U.K.
129 D2 **Tobin Lake** Can.
60 B2 **Toboali** Indon.
76 C1 **Tobol** *r.* Kazakh./Rus. Fed.
86 F3 **Tobol'sk** Rus. Fed.
Tobruk Libya see **Tubruq**
151 E3 **Tocantinópolis** Brazil
151 E3 **Tocantins** *r.* Brazil
143 D2 **Toccoa** U.S.A.
108 A1 **Toce** *r.* Italy
152 A2 **Tocopilla** Chile
53 C3 **Tocumwal** Austr.
59 C3 **Todeli** Indon.
108 B2 **Todi** Italy
144 A2 **Todos Santos** Mex.
128 B3 **Tofino** Can.
96 □ **Toft** U.K.
61 D2 **Togian** *i.* Indon.
61 D2 **Togian, Kepulauan** *is* Indon.
Togliatti Rus. Fed. see Tol'yatti
114 C4 **Togo** *country* Africa
74 B2 **Tohana** India
143 D3 **Tohopekaliga, Lake** U.S.A.
126 C2 **Tok** U.S.A.
116 B3 **Tokar** Sudan
69 E3 **Tokara-rettō** *is* Japan
91 E1 **Tokarevka** Rus. Fed.
80 B1 **Tokat** Turkey
49 J4 **Tokelau** *terr.* S. Pacific Ocean
77 D2 **Tokmak** Kyrg.
91 D2 **Tokmak** Ukr.
54 C1 **Tokoroa** N.Z.
68 B2 **Toksun** China
67 B4 **Tokushima** Japan
67 C3 **Tōkyō** Japan
121 □D3 **Tôlañaro** Madag.
Tolbukhin Bulg. see Dobrich
154 B2 **Toledo** Brazil
106 C2 **Toledo** Spain
140 C2 **Toledo** U.S.A.

106 C2 **Toledo, Montes de** *mts* Spain
142 B2 **Toledo Bend Reservoir** U.S.A.
121 □D3 **Toliara** Madag.
Toling China *see* **Zanda**
61 D1 **Tolitoli** Indon.
108 B1 **Tolmezzo** Italy
108 B1 **Tolmin** Slovenia
103 D2 **Tolna** Hungary
104 B3 **Tolosa** Spain
145 C3 **Toluca** Mex.
87 D3 **Tol'yatti** Rus. Fed.
140 A2 **Tomah** U.S.A.
140 B1 **Tomahawk** U.S.A.
66 D2 **Tomakomai** Japan
61 D2 **Tomali** Indon.
61 C1 **Tomani** *Sabah* Malaysia
106 B2 **Tomar** Port.
103 E1 **Tomaszów Lubelski** Pol.
103 E1 **Tomaszów Mazowiecki** Pol.
144 B3 **Tomatlán** Mex.
154 C2 **Tomazina** Brazil
142 C2 **Tombigbee** *r.* U.S.A.
120 A1 **Tomboco** Angola
155 D2 **Tombos** Brazil
114 B3 **Tombouctou** Mali
138 A2 **Tombstone** U.S.A.
120 A2 **Tombua** Angola
123 C1 **Tom Burke** S. Africa
106 C2 **Tomelloso** Spain
53 C2 **Tomingley** Austr.
61 D2 **Tomini, Teluk** *g.* Indon.
109 C2 **Tomislavgrad** Bos.-Herz.
103 D2 **Tompa** Hungary
50 A2 **Tom Price** Austr.
82 G3 **Tomsk** Rus. Fed.
93 F4 **Tomtabacken** *hill* Sweden
83 K2 **Tomtor** Rus. Fed.
145 C3 **Tonalá** Mex.
150 C3 **Tonantins** Brazil
99 D4 **Tonbridge** U.K.
59 C2 **Tondano** Indon.
49 J5 **Tonga** *country* S. Pacific Ocean
123 D2 **Tongaat** S. Africa
49 J6 **Tongatapu Group** *is* Tonga
71 B3 **Tongcheng** China
70 A2 **Tongchuan** China
71 A3 **Tongdao** China
65 B2 **Tongduch'ŏn** S. Korea
100 B2 **Tongeren** Belgium
65 B2 **Tonghae** S. Korea
71 A3 **Tonghai** China
65 B1 **Tonghua** China
65 B2 **Tongjosŏn-man** *b.* N. Korea
62 B1 **Tongking, Gulf of** China/Vietnam
69 E2 **Tongliao** China
70 B2 **Tongling** China
52 B2 **Tongo** Austr.
Tongquan China *see* **Malong**
71 A3 **Tongren** China
Tongshan China *see* **Xuzhou**
71 A4 **Tongshi** China
Tongtian He *r.* China *see* **Yangtze**
96 B1 **Tongue** U.K.
70 B2 **Tongxian** China
65 B3 **T'ongyŏng** S. Korea
69 E2 **Tongyu** China
65 A1 **Tongyuanpu** China
Tongzhou China *see* **Tongxian**
71 A3 **Tongzi** China
119 C2 **Tonj** Sudan
74 B2 **Tonk** India
81 D2 **Tonkābon** Iran
63 B2 **Tônlé Sab** *l.* Cambodia
Tonle Sap *l.* Cambodia *see* **Tônlé Sab**
135 C3 **Tonopah** U.S.A.
93 F4 **Tønsberg** Norway
135 D2 **Tooele** U.S.A.
52 B3 **Tooleybuc** Austr.
53 D1 **Toowoomba** Austr.
137 D3 **Topeka** U.S.A.
144 B2 **Topia** Mex.
144 B2 **Topolobampo** Mex.
86 C2 **Topozero, Ozero** *l.* Rus. Fed.
134 B1 **Toppenish** U.S.A.
111 C3 **Torbalı** Turkey
76 B3 **Torbat-e Heydarīyeh** Iran
76 C3 **Torbat-e Jām** Iran
131 E3 **Torbay** Can.
106 C1 **Tordesillas** Spain
107 C1 **Tordesilos** Spain
92 H2 **Töre** Sweden
107 D1 **Torelló** Spain
100 B1 **Torenberg** *hill* Neth.
Toretam Kazakh. *see* **Baykonur**
101 F2 **Torgau** Ger.
100 A2 **Torhout** Belgium
Torino Italy *see* **Turin**
67 D4 **Tori-shima** *i.* Japan
117 B4 **Torit** Sudan
154 B1 **Torixoreu** Brazil
89 D2 **Torkovichi** Rus. Fed.
106 B1 **Tormes** *r.* Spain
92 H2 **Torneälven** *r.* Sweden
131 D2 **Torngat Mountains** Can.
92 H2 **Tornio** Fin.
106 B1 **Toro** Spain
130 C3 **Toronto** Can.
89 D2 **Toropets** Rus. Fed.
119 D2 **Tororo** Uganda
80 B2 **Toros Dağları** *mts* Turkey
52 B3 **Torquay** Austr.
99 B4 **Torquay** U.K.
135 C4 **Torrance** U.S.A.
106 B2 **Torrão** Port.
106 B1 **Torre** *mt.* Port.
107 D1 **Torreblanca** Spain
106 B1 **Torre de Moncorvo** Port.
106 C1 **Torrelavega** Spain
106 C2 **Torremolinos** Spain
52 A2 **Torrens, Lake** *salt flat* Austr.
107 C2 **Torrent** Spain
144 B2 **Torreón** Mex.
106 B2 **Torres Novas** Port.
156 C6 **Torres Strait** Austr.
106 B2 **Torres Vedras** Port.
107 C2 **Torrevieja** Spain
96 B2 **Torridon** U.K.
96 B2 **Torridon, Loch** *b.* U.K.
106 C2 **Torrijos** Spain
141 E2 **Torrington** *CT* U.S.A.
136 C2 **Torrington** *WY* U.S.A.
107 D1 **Torroella de Montgrí** Spain
94 B1 **Tórshavn** Faroe Is
108 A3 **Tortolì** *Sardinia* Italy
108 A2 **Tortona** Italy
107 D1 **Tortosa** Spain
81 D2 **Torūd** Iran
103 D1 **Toruń** Pol.
97 B1 **Tory Island** Rep. of Ireland
97 B1 **Tory Sound** *sea chan.* Rep. of Ireland
89 D2 **Torzhok** Rus. Fed.
67 B4 **Tosashimizu** Japan
122 B2 **Tosca** S. Africa
108 A2 **Toscano, Arcipelago** *is* Italy
89 D2 **Tosno** Rus. Fed.
68 C1 **Tosontsengel** Mongolia
152 B2 **Tostado** Arg.
101 D1 **Tostedt** Ger.
80 B1 **Tosya** Turkey
86 D3 **Tot'ma** Rus. Fed.
151 D2 **Totness** Suriname
67 B3 **Tottori** Japan
114 B4 **Touba** Côte d'Ivoire
114 B1 **Toubkal, Jbel** *mt.* Morocco
118 B2 **Touboro** Cameroon
114 B3 **Tougan** Burkina
115 C1 **Touggourt** Alg.
105 D2 **Toul** France
71 C3 **Touliu** Taiwan
105 D3 **Toulon** France
104 C3 **Toulouse** France
62 A2 **Toungoo** Myanmar
Tourane Vietnam *see* **Đa Năng**
104 B2 **Tourlaville** France
100 A2 **Tournai** Belgium
115 D2 **Tourndo, Oued** *watercourse* Alg./Niger
105 C2 **Tournus** France
151 F3 **Touros** Brazil
104 C2 **Tours** France
115 D2 **Toussidé, Pic** *mt.* Chad
122 B3 **Touwsrivier** S. Africa
150 B2 **Tovar** Venez.
66 D2 **Towada** Japan
134 D1 **Townsend** U.S.A.
51 D1 **Townsville** Austr.
61 D2 **Towori, Teluk** *b.* Indon.
77 E2 **Toxkan He** *r.* China
66 D2 **Tōya-ko** *l.* Japan
67 C3 **Toyama** Japan
67 C4 **Toyohashi** Japan
67 C3 **Toyota** Japan
115 C1 **Tozeur** Tunisia
81 C1 **Tqvarch'eli** Georgia
80 B2 **Trâblous** Lebanon
80 B1 **Trabzon** Turkey
106 B2 **Trafalgar, Cabo** *c.* Spain
128 C3 **Trail** Can.
88 B3 **Trakai** Lith.
97 B2 **Tralee** Rep. of Ireland
Trá Li Rep. of Ireland *see* **Tralee**
97 C2 **Tramore** Rep. of Ireland
93 F4 **Tranås** Sweden
63 A3 **Trang** Thai.
59 C3 **Trangan** *i.* Indon.
55 L2 **Transantarctic Mountains** Antarctica
Transylvanian Alps *mts* Romania *see* **Carpații Meridionali**
108 B3 **Trapani** *Sicily* Italy
53 C3 **Traralgon** Austr.
75 D2 **Trashigang** Bhutan
63 B2 **Trat** Thai.
102 C2 **Traunstein** Ger.
54 B2 **Travers, Mount** N.Z.
140 B2 **Traverse City** U.S.A.
63 B3 **Tra Vinh** Vietnam
103 D2 **Třebíč** Czech Rep.
109 C2 **Trebinje** Bos.-Herz.
103 E2 **Trebišov** Slovakia
Trebizond Turkey *see* **Trabzon**
109 C1 **Trebnje** Slovenia
Trefynwy U.K. *see* **Monmouth**
153 C3 **Treinta-y-Tres** Uru.
153 B4 **Trelew** Arg.
93 F4 **Trelleborg** Sweden
130 C3 **Tremblant, Mont** *hill* Can.
109 C2 **Tremiti, Isole** *is* Italy
134 D2 **Tremonton** U.S.A.
107 D1 **Tremp** Spain
103 D2 **Trenčín** Slovakia
153 B3 **Trenque Lauquén** Arg.
Trent Italy *see* **Trento**
98 C3 **Trent** *r.* U.K.
108 B1 **Trento** Italy
141 D2 **Trenton** Can.
137 E2 **Trenton** *MO* U.S.A.
141 E2 **Trenton** *NJ* U.S.A.
131 E3 **Trepassey** Can.
153 B3 **Tres Arroyos** Arg.
155 C2 **Três Corações** Brazil
154 B2 **Três Irmãos, Represa** *resr* Brazil
154 B2 **Três Lagoas** Brazil
153 A4 **Tres Lagos** Arg.
155 C1 **Três Marias, Represa** *resr* Brazil
155 C2 **Três Pontas** Brazil
153 B4 **Tres Puntas, Cabo** *c.* Arg.
155 D2 **Três Rios** Brazil
101 F1 **Treuenbrietzen** Ger.
Treves Ger. *see* **Trier**
108 A1 **Treviglio** Italy
108 B1 **Treviso** Italy
99 A4 **Trevose Head** *hd* U.K.
109 C3 **Tricase** Italy
Trichinopoly India *see* **Tiruchchirāppalli**
73 B3 **Trichur** India
53 C2 **Trida** Austr.
100 C3 **Trier** Ger.
108 B1 **Trieste** Italy
108 B1 **Triglav** *mt.* Slovenia
111 B3 **Trikala** Greece
59 D3 **Trikora, Puncak** *mt.* Indon.
97 C2 **Trim** Rep. of Ireland
73 C4 **Trincomalee** Sri Lanka
154 C1 **Trindade** Brazil
152 B1 **Trinidad** Bol.
147 D3 **Trinidad** *i.* Trin. and Tob.
136 C3 **Trinidad** U.S.A.
147 D3 **Trinidad and Tobago** *country* West Indies
139 E3 **Trinity** *r.* U.S.A.
131 E3 **Trinity Bay** Can.
111 B3 **Tripoli** Greece
Tripoli Lebanon *see* **Trâblous**
115 D1 **Tripoli** Libya
75 D2 **Tripura** *state* India
113 B9 **Tristan da Cunha** *i.* S. Atlantic Ocean
73 B4 **Trivandrum** India
108 B2 **Trivento** Italy
103 D2 **Trnava** Slovakia
59 E3 **Trobriand Islands** P.N.G.
92 F2 **Trofors** Norway
109 C2 **Trogir** Croatia
109 C2 **Troia** Italy
100 C2 **Troisdorf** Ger.
106 C2 **Trois Fourches, Cap de** *c.* Morocco
130 C3 **Trois-Rivières** Can.
87 F3 **Troitsk** Rus. Fed.
86 E2 **Troitsko-Pechorsk** Rus. Fed.
151 D3 **Trombetas** *r.* Brazil
Tromelin Island Micronesia *see* **Fais**
123 C3 **Trompsburg** S. Africa
92 G2 **Tromsø** Norway
92 F3 **Trondheim** Norway
75 D2 **Trongsa** Bhutan
96 B3 **Troon** U.K.
89 E3 **Trosna** Rus. Fed.
97 C1 **Trostan** *hill* U.K.
128 C2 **Trout Lake** *Alta* Can.
128 B1 **Trout Lake** *l. N.W.T.* Can
130 A2 **Trout Lake** *l. Ont.* Can.
99 B4 **Trowbridge** U.K.
142 C2 **Troy** *AL* U.S.A.
141 E2 **Troy** *NY* U.S.A.
105 C2 **Troyes** France
135 C3 **Troy Peak** U.S.A.
109 D2 **Trstenik** Yugo.
89 D3 **Trubchevsk** Rus. Fed.
Truc Giang Vietnam *see* **Bên Tre**
106 B1 **Truchas** Spain
Trucial Coast *country* A *see* **United Arab Emirate**
79 C2 **Trucial Coast** U.A.E.
Trucial States *country* Asia *see* **United Arab Emirates**
146 B3 **Trujillo** Hond.
150 B3 **Trujillo** Peru
106 B2 **Trujillo** Spain
147 C4 **Trujillo** Venez.
Trujillo, Monte *mt.* Dom. Rep. *see* **Duarte, Pico**
142 B1 **Trumann** U.S.A.
131 D3 **Truro** Can.
99 A4 **Truro** U.K.
61 C1 **Trus Madi, Gunung** *mt.* Malaysia
138 B2 **Truth or Consequences** U.S.A.
103 D1 **Trutnov** Czech Rep.
93 F3 **Trysil** Norway
103 D1 **Trzebiatów** Pol.
103 D1 **Trzebnica** Pol.
68 B1 **Tsagaannuur** Mongolia
Tsaidam Basin China *se* **Qaidam Pendi**
121 □D2 **Tsaratanana, Massif du** *mts* Madag.
110 C2 **Tsarevo** Bulg.
122 A2 **Tsaukaib** Namibia
Tselinograd Kazakh. *see* **Astana**
Tsementnyy Rus. Fed. *s* **Fokino**
122 A2 **Tses** Namibia
122 B1 **Tsetseng** Botswana
68 C1 **Tsetserleg** Mongolia
Tsetserleg Mongolia *see* **Halban**
122 B2 **Tshabong** Botswana
122 B1 **Tshane** Botswana
91 D2 **Tshchikskoye Vodokhranilishche** *resr* Rus. Fed.
118 B3 **Tshela** Dem. Rep. Congo
118 C3 **Tshikapa** Dem. Rep. Congo
118 C3 **Tshikapa** *r.* Dem. Rep. Congo
123 C2 **Tshing** S. Africa
123 D1 **Tshipise** S. Africa
118 C3 **Tshitanzu** Dem. Rep. Congo
120 B3 **Tshootsha** Botswana
118 C3 **Tshuapa** *r.* Dem. Rep. Congo
87 D4 **Tsimlyanskoye Vodokhranilishche** *resr* Rus. Fed.
Tsinan China *see* **Jinan**
Tsingtao China *see* **Qingdao**
Tsining China *see* **Jining**
121 □D2 **Tsiroanomandidy** Madag.
Tsitsihar China *see* **Qiqih**
76 A2 **Ts'khinvali** Georgia
123 C3 **Tsomo** S. Africa
67 C4 **Tsu** Japan
67 D3 **Tsuchiura** Japan

6 D2 **Tsugarū-kaikyō** *str.* Japan
Tsugaru Strait Japan *see* Tsugarū-kaikyō
20 A2 **Tsumeb** Namibia
22 A1 **Tsumis Park** Namibia
20 B2 **Tsumkwe** Namibia
7 C3 **Tsuruga** Japan
6 C3 **Tsuruoka** Japan
7 A4 **Tsushima** *is* Japan
7 B3 **Tsuyama** Japan
23 C2 **Tswelelang** S. Africa
8 C3 **Tsyelyakhany** Belarus
1 C2 **Tsyurupyns'k** Ukr.
Tthenaagoo Can. *see* Nahanni Butte
9 C3 **Tual** Indon.
7 B2 **Tuam** Rep. of Ireland
9 M5 **Tuamotu Archipelago** *is* Fr. Polynesia
4 A3 **Tuapeka Mouth** N.Z.
1 D3 **Tuapse** Rus. Fed.
4 A3 **Tuatapere** N.Z.
38 A1 **Tuba City** U.S.A.
1 C2 **Tuban** Indon.
52 D2 **Tubarão** Brazil
2 B2 **Tübingen** Ger.
5 E1 **Tubruq** Libya
4 A1 **Tubutama** Mex.
2 C1 **Tucavaca** Bol.
28 B1 **Tuchitua** Can.
38 A2 **Tucson** U.S.A.
39 C1 **Tucumcari** U.S.A.
0 C2 **Tucupita** Venez.
1 E3 **Tucuruí** Brazil
1 E3 **Tucuruí, Represa** *resr* Brazil
7 C1 **Tudela** Spain
6 B1 **Tuela** *r.* Port.
2 A1 **Tuensang** India
7 F2 **Tufts Abyssal Plain** *sea feature* N. Pacific Ocean
23 D2 **Tugela** *r.* S. Africa
4 B2 **Tuguegarao** Phil.
6 B1 **Tui** Spain
9 C3 **Tukangbesi, Kepulauan** *is* Indon.
26 D2 **Tuktoyaktuk** Can.
8 B2 **Tukums** Latvia
9 D3 **Tukuyu** Tanz.
5 C2 **Tula** Mex.
9 E3 **Tula** Rus. Fed.
Tulach Mhór Rep. of Ireland *see* Tullamore
5 C2 **Tulancingo** Mex.
5 C3 **Tulare** U.S.A.
8 B2 **Tularosa** U.S.A.
0 C1 **Tulcea** Romania
0 B2 **Tul'chyn** Ukr.
Tuléar Madag. *see* **Toliara**
29 E1 **Tulemalu Lake** Can.
39 C2 **Tulia** U.S.A.
28 B1 **Tulít'a** Can.
2 C1 **Tullahoma** U.S.A.
3 C2 **Tullamore** Austr.
7 C2 **Tullamore** Rep. of Ireland
4 C2 **Tulle** France
7 C2 **Tullow** Rep. of Ireland
1 D1 **Tully** Austr.
39 D1 **Tulsa** U.S.A.
26 B2 **Tuluksak** U.S.A.
3 H3 **Tulun** Rus. Fed.
0 B2 **Tumaco** Col.
23 C2 **Tumahole** S. Africa
3 G4 **Tumba** Sweden
8 B3 **Tumba, Lac** *l.* Dem. Rep. Congo
1 C2 **Tumbangtiti** Indon.
3 C3 **Tumbarumba** Austr.
0 A3 **Tumbes** Peru
28 B2 **Tumbler Ridge** Can.
2 A2 **Tumby Bay** Austr.
5 B1 **Tumen** China
0 C2 **Tumereng** Guyana
4 A3 **Tumindao** *i.* Phil.
4 A2 **Tump** Pak.
1 D2 **Tumucumaque, Serra** *hills* Brazil
3 C3 **Tumut** Austr.
9 D4 **Tunbridge Wells, Royal** U.K.
0 B2 **Tunceli** Turkey
3 D2 **Tuncurry** Austr.
8 A1 **Tundun-Wada** Nigeria
9 D4 **Tunduru** Tanz.
0 C2 **Tundzha** *r.* Bulg.
28 B1 **Tungsten** Can.
5 D1 **Tunis** Tunisia
8 B3 **Tunis, Golfe de** *g.* Tunisia
5 C1 **Tunisia** *country* Africa
150 B2 **Tunja** Col.
92 F3 **Tunnsjøen** *l.* Norway
Tunxi China *see* Huangshan
75 D1 **Tuotuoheyan** China
154 B2 **Tupã** Brazil
154 C1 **Tupaciguara** Brazil
142 C2 **Tupelo** U.S.A.
152 B2 **Tupiza** Bol.
83 H2 **Tura** Rus. Fed.
86 F3 **Tura** *r.* Rus. Fed.
78 B2 **Turabah** Saudi Arabia
83 J3 **Turana, Khrebet** *mts* Rus. Fed.
54 C1 **Turangi** N.Z.
76 B2 **Turan Lowland** Asia
77 D2 **Tura-Ryskulova** Kazakh.
78 A1 **Turayf** Saudi Arabia
88 B2 **Turba** Estonia
74 A2 **Turbat** Pak.
150 B2 **Turbo** Col.
110 B1 **Turda** Romania
Turfan China *see* **Turpan**
76 C2 **Turgay** Kazakh.
76 C1 **Turgayskaya Stolovaya Strana** *reg.* Kazakh.
110 C2 **Tŭrgovishte** Bulg.
111 C3 **Turgutlu** Turkey
80 B1 **Turhal** Turkey
107 C2 **Turia** *r.* Spain
108 A1 **Turin** Italy
86 F3 **Turinsk** Rus. Fed.
90 A1 **Turiya** *r.* Ukr.
90 A1 **Turiys'k** Ukr.
90 A2 **Turka** Ukr.
119 D2 **Turkana, Lake** *salt l.* Eth./Kenya
77 C2 **Turkestan** Kazakh.
103 E2 **Túrkeve** Hungary
80 B2 **Turkey** *country* Asia/Europe
50 B1 **Turkey Creek** Austr.
76 B2 **Turkmenbashi** Turkm.
76 B2 **Turkmenistan** *country* Asia
Turkmeniya *country* Asia *see* Turkmenistan
Turkmenskaya S.S.R. *country* Asia *see* Turkmenistan
147 C2 **Turks and Caicos Islands** *terr.* West Indies
147 C2 **Turks Islands** Turks and Caicos Is
93 H3 **Turku** Fin.
119 D2 **Turkwel** *watercourse* Kenya
135 B3 **Turlock** U.S.A.
155 D1 **Turmalina** Brazil
54 C2 **Turnagain, Cape** N.Z.
146 B3 **Turneffe Islands** Belize
100 B2 **Turnhout** Belgium
129 D2 **Turnor Lake** Can.
Tŭrnovo Bulg. *see* Veliko Tŭrnovo
110 B2 **Turnu Măgurele** Romania
68 B2 **Turpan** China
96 C2 **Turriff** U.K.
76 C2 **Turtkul'** Uzbek.
64 A3 **Turtle Islands** Phil.
77 D2 **Turugart Pass** China/Kyrg.
82 G2 **Turukhansk** Rus. Fed.
142 C2 **Tuscaloosa** U.S.A.
142 C2 **Tuskegee** U.S.A.
81 C2 **Tutak** Turkey
89 E2 **Tutayev** Rus. Fed.
73 B4 **Tuticorin** India
121 C1 **Tutubu** Tanz.
49 J5 **Tutuila** *i.* American Samoa
120 B3 **Tutume** Botswana
93 H3 **Tuusula** Fin.
49 I4 **Tuvalu** *country* S. Pacific Ocean
78 B2 **Tuwayq, Jabal** *hills* Saudi Arabia
78 B2 **Tuwayq, Jabal** *mts* Saudi Arabia
78 A2 **Tuwwal** Saudi Arabia
144 B2 **Tuxpan** Mex.
145 C2 **Tuxpan** Mex.
145 C3 **Tuxtla Gutiérrez** Mex.
62 B1 **Tuyên Quang** Vietnam
63 B2 **Tuy Hoa** Vietnam
Tuz, Lake *salt l.* Turkey *see* Tuz Gölü
80 B2 **Tuz Gölü** *salt l.* Turkey
81 C2 **Tuz Khurmātū** Iraq
109 C2 **Tuzla** Bos.-Herz.
91 E2 **Tuzlov** *r.* Rus. Fed.
89 E2 **Tver'** Rus. Fed.
98 B2 **Tweed** *r.* U.K.
53 D1 **Tweed Heads** Austr.
122 A2 **Twee Rivier** Namibia
135 C4 **Twentynine Palms** U.S.A.
131 E3 **Twillingate** Can.
134 D2 **Twin Falls** U.S.A.
137 E1 **Two Harbors** U.S.A.
128 C2 **Two Hills** Can.
Tyddewi U.K. *see* St David's
139 D2 **Tyler** U.S.A.
83 J3 **Tynda** Rus. Fed.
Tyndinskiy Rus. Fed. *see* Tynda
96 B2 **Tyndrum** U.K.
98 C2 **Tyne** *r. England* U.K.
95 C2 **Tyne** *r. Scotland* U.K.
93 F3 **Tynset** Norway
Tyre Lebanon *see* **Soûr**
69 E1 **Tyrma** Rus. Fed.
111 B3 **Tyrnavos** Greece
52 B3 **Tyrrell, Lake** *dry lake* Austr.
108 B2 **Tyrrhenian Sea** France/Italy
76 B2 **Tyub-Karagan, Mys** *pt* Kazakh.
87 E3 **Tyul'gan** Rus. Fed.
86 F3 **Tyumen'** Rus. Fed.
83 J2 **Tyung** *r.* Rus. Fed.
Tyuratam Kazakh. *see* Baykonur
99 A4 **Tywi** *r.* U.K.
123 D1 **Tzaneen** S. Africa

U

Uaco Congo Angola *see* Waku-Kungo
120 B2 **Uamanda** Angola
150 C3 **Uarini** Brazil
150 C3 **Uaupés** Brazil
155 D2 **Ubá** Brazil
155 D1 **Ubaí** Brazil
151 F4 **Ubaitaba** Brazil
81 D1 **Ubal Karabaur** *hills* Uzbek.
118 B3 **Ubangi** *r.* C.A.R./Dem. Rep. Congo
Ubangi-Shari *country* Africa *see* Central African Republic
67 B4 **Ube** Japan
106 C2 **Úbeda** Spain
154 C1 **Uberaba** Brazil
154 C1 **Uberlândia** Brazil
123 D2 **Ubombo** S. Africa
63 B2 **Ubon Ratchathani** Thai.
119 C3 **Ubundu** Dem. Rep. Congo
150 B3 **Ucayali** *r.* Peru
100 B2 **Uccle** Belgium
74 B2 **Uch** Pak.
77 E2 **Ucharal** Kazakh.
66 D2 **Uchiura-wan** *b.* Japan
76 C2 **Uchkuduk** Uzbek.
83 J3 **Uchur** *r.* Rus. Fed.
99 D4 **Uckfield** U.K.
128 B3 **Ucluelet** Can.
83 I2 **Udachnyy** Rus. Fed.
74 B2 **Udaipur** India
91 C1 **Uday** *r.* Ukr.
93 F4 **Uddevalla** Sweden
92 G2 **Uddjaure** *l.* Sweden
100 B2 **Uden** Neth.
74 B1 **Udhampur** Jammu and Kashmir
108 B1 **Udine** Italy
89 E2 **Udomlya** Rus. Fed.
62 B2 **Udon Thani** Thai.
73 B3 **Udupi** India
83 K3 **Udyl', Ozero** *l.* Rus. Fed.
67 C3 **Ueda** Japan
61 D2 **Uekuli** Indon.
118 C2 **Uele** *r.* Dem. Rep. Congo
83 N2 **Uelen** Rus. Fed.
101 E1 **Uelzen** Ger.
119 C2 **Uere** *r.* Dem. Rep. Congo
87 E3 **Ufa** Rus. Fed.
119 D3 **Ugalla** *r.* Tanz.
119 D2 **Uganda** *country* Africa
69 F1 **Uglegorsk** Rus. Fed.
89 E2 **Uglich** Rus. Fed.
89 D2 **Uglovka** Rus. Fed.
66 B2 **Uglovoye** Rus. Fed.
89 D3 **Ugra** Rus. Fed.
103 D2 **Uherské Hradiště** Czech Rep.
Uibhist a' Deas *i.* U.K. *see* South Uist
Uibhist a' Tuath *i.* U.K. *see* North Uist
101 E2 **Uichteritz** Ger.
96 A2 **Uig** U.K.
120 A1 **Uíge** Angola
65 B2 **Ŭijŏngbu** S. Korea
65 A1 **Ŭiju** N. Korea
135 D2 **Uinta Mountains** U.S.A.
120 A3 **Uis Mine** Namibia
65 B2 **Ŭisŏng** S. Korea
123 C3 **Uitenhage** S. Africa
100 C1 **Uithuizen** Neth.
131 D2 **Uivak, Cape** Can.
Ujiyamada Japan *see* **Ise**
74 B2 **Ujjain** India
61 C2 **Ujung Pandang** Indon.
89 F3 **Ukholovo** Rus. Fed.
62 A1 **Ukhrul** India
Ukhta Rus. Fed. *see* Kalevala
86 E2 **Ukhta** Rus. Fed.
135 B3 **Ukiah** U.S.A.
127 I2 **Ukkusissat** Greenland
88 B2 **Ukmergė** Lith.
90 C2 **Ukraine** *country* Europe
Ukrainskaya S.S.R. *country* Europe *see* Ukraine
69 D1 **Ulaanbaatar** Mongolia
68 C1 **Ulaangom** Mongolia
59 E3 **Ulamona** P.N.G.
70 A2 **Ulan** China
Ulan Bator Mongolia *see* Ulaanbaatar
Ulanhad China *see* Chifeng
69 E1 **Ulanhot** China
87 D4 **Ulan-Khol** Rus. Fed.
69 D1 **Ulan-Ude** Rus. Fed.
75 D1 **Ulan Ul Hu** *l.* China
65 B2 **Ulchin** S. Korea
Uleåborg Fin. *see* **Oulu**
88 C2 **Ülenurme** Estonia
74 B3 **Ulhasnagar** India
69 D1 **Uliastai** China
68 C1 **Uliastay** Mongolia
59 D2 **Ulithi** *atoll* Micronesia
53 D3 **Ulladulla** Austr.
96 B2 **Ullapool** U.K.
98 B2 **Ullswater** *l.* U.K.
65 C2 **Ullŭng-do** *i.* S. Korea
102 B2 **Ulm** Ger.
65 B2 **Ulsan** S. Korea
96 □ **Ulsta** U.K.
97 C1 **Ulster** *reg.* Rep. of Ireland/U.K.
52 B3 **Ultima** Austr.
145 D3 **Ulúa** *r.* Hond.
111 C3 **Ulubey** Turkey
111 D3 **Uluborlu** Turkey
111 C2 **Uludağ** *mt.* Turkey
123 D2 **Ulundi** S. Africa
77 E2 **Ulungur Hu** *l.* China
Uluqsaqtuuq Can. *see* Holman
50 C2 **Uluru** *hill* Austr.
98 B2 **Ulverston** U.K.
90 C2 **Ul'yanovka** Ukr.
87 D3 **Ul'yanovsk** Rus. Fed.
136 C3 **Ulysses** U.S.A.
90 C2 **Uman'** Ukr.
86 C2 **Umba** Rus. Fed.
59 D3 **Umboi** *i.* P.N.G.
59 D3 **Umbukul** P.N.G.
92 H3 **Umeå** Sweden
92 H3 **Umeälven** *r.* Sweden
123 D2 **Umhlanga** S. Africa
127 J2 **Umiiviip Kangertiva** *inlet* Greenland
126 E2 **Umingmaktok** Can.
123 D2 **Umlazi** S. Africa
78 A2 **Umm al Birak** Saudi Arabia
79 C2 **Umm as Samīm** *salt flat* Oman
116 A3 **Umm Keddada** Sudan
78 A2 **Umm Lajj** Saudi Arabia
78 A2 **Umm Mukhbār, Jabal** *hill* Saudi Arabia
116 B3 **Umm Ruwaba** Sudan
115 E1 **Umm Sa'ad** Libya
134 B2 **Umpqua** *r.* U.S.A.
120 A2 **Umpulo** Angola
Umtali Zimbabwe *see* Mutare
123 C3 **Umtata** S. Africa
123 D3 **Umtentweni** S. Africa
154 B2 **Umuarama** Brazil
123 C3 **Umzimkulu** S. Africa
109 C1 **Una** *r.* Bos.-Herz./Croatia
155 E1 **Una** Brazil

154 C1 **Unaí** Brazil
126 B2 **Unalakleet** U.S.A.
78 B2 **'Unayzah** Saudi Arabia
136 B3 **Uncompahgre Peak** U.S.A.
52 B3 **Underbool** Austr.
136 C1 **Underwood** U.S.A.
89 D3 **Unecha** Rus. Fed.
53 C2 **Ungarie** Austr.
52 A2 **Ungarra** Austr.
127 H2 **Ungava, Péninsule d'** *pen.* Can.
131 D2 **Ungava Bay** Can.
Ungeny Moldova *see* **Ungheni**
65 C1 **Unggi** N. Korea
90 B2 **Ungheni** Moldova
Unguja *i.* Tanz. *see* **Zanzibar Island**
119 E3 **Ungwana Bay** Kenya
154 B3 **União da Vitória** Brazil
150 C3 **Unini** *r.* Brazil
134 C1 **Union** U.S.A.
142 C1 **Union City** U.S.A.
122 B3 **Uniondale** S. Africa
141 D3 **Uniontown** U.S.A.
79 C2 **United Arab Emirates** *country* Asia
United Arab Republic *country* Africa *see* **Egypt**
95 C3 **United Kingdom** *country* Europe
United Provinces *state* India *see* **Uttar Pradesh**
133 B3 **United States of America** *country* N. America
129 D2 **Unity** Can.
100 C2 **Unna** Ger.
96 □ **Unst** *i.* U.K.
101 E2 **Unstrut** *r.* Ger.
89 E3 **Upa** *r.* Rus. Fed.
119 C3 **Upemba, Lac** *l.* Dem. Rep. Congo
122 B2 **Upington** S. Africa
74 B2 **Upleta** India
49 J5 **Upolu** *i.* Samoa
134 B2 **Upper Alkali Lake** U.S.A.
128 C2 **Upper Arrow Lake** Can.
54 C2 **Upper Hutt** N.Z.
134 B2 **Upper Klamath Lake** U.S.A.
128 B1 **Upper Liard** Can.
97 C1 **Upper Lough Erne** *l.* U.K.
137 E1 **Upper Red Lake** U.S.A.
Upper Tunguska *r.* Rus. Fed. *see* **Angara**
Upper Volta *country* Africa *see* **Burkina**
93 G4 **Uppsala** Sweden
78 B2 **'Uqlat aş Şuqūr** Saudi Arabia
Urad Qianqi China *see* **Xishanzui**
76 B2 **Ural** *r.* Kazakh./Rus. Fed.
53 D2 **Uralla** Austr.
87 E3 **Ural Mountains** Rus. Fed.
76 B1 **Ural'sk** Kazakh.
Ural'skiy Khrebet *mts* Rus. Fed. *see* **Ural Mountains**
119 D3 **Urambo** Tanz.
53 C3 **Urana** Austr.
129 D2 **Uranium City** Can.
86 F2 **Uray** Rus. Fed.
98 C2 **Ure** *r.* U.K.
86 D3 **Uren'** Rus. Fed.
82 G2 **Urengoy** Rus. Fed.
144 A2 **Ures** Mex.
Urfa Turkey *see* **Şanlıurfa**
76 C2 **Urgench** Uzbek.
100 B1 **Urk** Neth.
111 C3 **Urla** Turkey
110 C2 **Urlaţi** Romania
Urmia Iran *see* **Orūmīyeh**
Urmia, Lake *salt l.* Iran *see* **Orūmīyeh, Daryācheh-ye**
109 D2 **Uroševac** Yugo.
144 B2 **Uruáchic** Mex.
151 E4 **Uruaçu** Brazil
144 B3 **Uruapan** Mex.
150 B4 **Urubamba** *r.* Peru
151 D3 **Urucara** Brazil
151 E3 **Uruçuí** Brazil
151 E3 **Uruçuí, Serra do** *hills* Brazil
151 D3 **Urucurituba** Brazil
152 C2 **Uruguaiana** Brazil
153 C3 **Uruguay** *country* S. America
Urumchi China *see* **Ürümqi**
68 B2 **Ürümqi** China
Urundi *country* Africa *see* **Burundi**
53 D2 **Urunga** Austr.
78 B3 **'Urūq al Awārik** *des.* Saudi Arabia
119 D3 **Uruwira** Tanz.
110 C2 **Urziceni** Romania
67 B4 **Usa** Japan
86 E2 **Usa** *r.* Rus. Fed.
111 C3 **Uşak** Turkey
120 A3 **Usakos** Namibia
88 C2 **Ushachy** Belarus
82 G1 **Ushakova, Ostrov** *i.* Rus. Fed.
77 D2 **Ushtobe** Kazakh.
Ush-Tyube Kazakh. *see* **Ushtobe**
153 B5 **Ushuaia** Arg.
86 E2 **Usinsk** Rus. Fed.
99 B4 **Usk** *r.* U.K.
88 C3 **Uskhodni** Belarus
89 E3 **Usman'** Rus. Fed.
86 D2 **Usogorsk** Rus. Fed.
104 C2 **Ussel** France
66 C1 **Ussuri** *r.* China/Rus. Fed.
66 B2 **Ussuriysk** Rus. Fed.
Ust'-Abakanskoye Rus. Fed. *see* **Abakan**
Ust'-Balyk Rus. Fed. *see* **Nefteyugansk**
91 E2 **Ust'-Donetskiy** Rus. Fed.
108 B3 **Ustica, Isola di** *i. Sicily* Italy
83 H3 **Ust'-Ilimsk** Rus. Fed.
86 E2 **Ust'-Ilych** Rus. Fed.
102 C1 **Ústí nad Labem** Czech Rep.
Ustinov Rus. Fed. *see* **Izhevsk**
103 D1 **Ustka** Pol.
83 L3 **Ust'-Kamchatsk** Rus. Fed.
77 E2 **Ust'-Kamenogorsk** Kazakh.
86 F2 **Ust'-Kara** Rus. Fed.
86 E2 **Ust'-Kulom** Rus. Fed.
83 I3 **Ust'-Kut** Rus. Fed.
91 D2 **Ust'-Labinsk** Rus. Fed.
Ust'-Labinskaya Rus. Fed. *see* **Ust'-Labinsk**
88 C2 **Ust'-Luga** Rus. Fed.
86 E2 **Ust'-Nem** Rus. Fed.
83 K2 **Ust'-Nera** Rus. Fed.
83 I2 **Ust'-Olenek** Rus. Fed.
83 K2 **Ust'-Omchug** Rus. Fed.
83 H3 **Ust'-Ordynskiy** Rus. Fed.
103 E2 **Ustrzyki Dolne** Pol.
86 E2 **Ust'-Tsil'ma** Rus. Fed.
86 D2 **Ust'-Ura** Rus. Fed.
76 B2 **Ustyurt Plateau** Kazakh./Uzbek.
89 E2 **Ustyuzhna** Rus. Fed.
146 B3 **Usulután** El Salvador
Usumbura Burundi *see* **Bujumbura**
89 D2 **Usvyaty** Rus. Fed.
135 D3 **Utah** *state* U.S.A.
135 D2 **Utah Lake** U.S.A.
88 C2 **Utena** Lith.
119 D3 **Utete** Tanz.
63 B2 **Uthai Thani** Thai.
74 A2 **Uthal** Pak.
141 D2 **Utica** U.S.A.
107 C2 **Utiel** Spain
128 C2 **Utikuma Lake** Can.
93 G4 **Utlängan** *i.* Sweden
100 B1 **Utrecht** Neth.
123 D2 **Utrecht** S. Africa
106 B2 **Utrera** Spain
92 I2 **Utsjoki** Fin.
67 C3 **Utsunomiya** Japan
87 D4 **Utta** Rus. Fed.
62 B2 **Uttaradit** Thai.
75 B2 **Uttar Pradesh** *state* India
127 H1 **Uummannaq** Greenland
127 I2 **Uummannaq** Greenland
127 I2 **Uummannaq Fjord** *inlet* Greenland
93 H3 **Uusikaupunki** Fin.
120 A2 **Uutapi** Namibia
139 D3 **Uvalde** U.S.A.
119 D3 **Uvinza** Tanz.
123 D3 **Uvongo** S. Africa
68 C1 **Uvs Nuur** *salt l.* Mongolia
67 B4 **Uwajima** Japan
78 A2 **'Uwayriḍ, Ḥarrat al** *lava field* Saudi Arabia
116 A2 **Uweinat, Jebel** *mt.* Sudan
83 H3 **Uyar** Rus. Fed.
115 C4 **Uyo** Nigeria
79 B2 **Uyun** Saudi Arabia
152 B2 **Uyuni, Salar de** *salt flat* Bol.
76 C2 **Uzbekistan** *country* Asia
Uzbekskaya S.S.R. *country* Asia *see* **Uzbekistan**
Uzbek S.S.R. *country* Asia *see* **Uzbekistan**
104 C2 **Uzerche** France
105 C3 **Uzès** France
90 C1 **Uzh** *r.* Ukr.
90 A2 **Uzhhorod** Ukr.
Užhorod Ukr. *see* **Uzhhorod**
109 C2 **Užice** Yugo.
89 E3 **Uzlovaya** Rus. Fed.
111 C3 **Üzümlü** Turkey
111 C2 **Uzunköprü** Turkey

V

123 B2 **Vaal** *r.* S. Africa
92 I3 **Vaala** Fin.
123 C2 **Vaal Dam** S. Africa
123 C1 **Vaalwater** S. Africa
92 H3 **Vaasa** Fin.
103 D2 **Vác** Hungary
152 C2 **Vacaria** Brazil
154 B2 **Vacaria, Serra** *hills* Brazil
135 B3 **Vacaville** U.S.A.
74 B2 **Vadodara** India
92 I1 **Vadsø** Norway
105 D2 **Vaduz** Liechtenstein
94 B1 **Vágar** *i.* Faroe Is
94 B1 **Vágar** *i.* Faroe Is
94 B1 **Vágur** Faroe Is
103 D2 **Váh** *r.* Slovakia
49 I4 **Vaiaku** Tuvalu
88 B2 **Vaida** Estonia
136 B3 **Vail** U.S.A.
77 C3 **Vakhsh** Tajik.
Vakhstroy Tajik. *see* **Vakhsh**
79 C2 **Vakīlābād** Iran
108 B1 **Valdagno** Italy
Valdai Hills Rus. Fed. *see* **Valdayskaya Vozvyshennost'**
89 D2 **Valday** Rus. Fed.
89 D2 **Valdayskaya Vozvyshennost'** *hills* Rus. Fed.
106 B2 **Valdecañas, Embalse de** *resr* Spain
93 G4 **Valdemarsvik** Sweden
105 D2 **Val-de-Meuse** France
106 C2 **Valdepeñas** Spain
153 B4 **Valdés, Península** *pen.* Arg.
126 C2 **Valdez** U.S.A.
153 A3 **Valdivia** Chile
130 C3 **Val-d'Or** Can.
143 D2 **Valdosta** U.S.A.
128 C2 **Valemount** Can.
152 E1 **Valença** Brazil
105 C3 **Valence** France
107 C2 **Valencia** Spain
107 C2 **Valencia** *reg.* Spain
150 C1 **Valencia** Venez.
107 D2 **Valencia, Golfo de** *g.* Spain
106 B1 **Valencia de Don Juan** Spain
97 A3 **Valencia Island** Rep. of Ireland
105 C1 **Valenciennes** France
136 C2 **Valentine** U.S.A.
64 B2 **Valenzuela** Phil.
150 B2 **Valera** Venez.
88 C2 **Valga** Estonia
109 C2 **Valjevo** Yugo.
88 C2 **Valka** Latvia
93 H3 **Valkeakoski** Fin.
100 B2 **Valkenswaard** Neth.
91 D2 **Valky** Ukr.
55 G2 **Valkyrie Dome** *ice feature* Antarctica
145 D2 **Valladolid** Mex.
106 C1 **Valladolid** Spain
107 C2 **Vall de Uxó** Spain
93 E4 **Valle** Norway
145 C2 **Vallecillos** Mex.
150 C2 **Valle de la Pascua** Venez.
150 B1 **Valledupar** Col.
145 C2 **Valle Hermoso** Mex.
135 B3 **Vallejo** U.S.A.
152 A2 **Vallenar** Chile
84 F5 **Valletta** Malta
137 D1 **Valley City** U.S.A.
134 B2 **Valley Falls** U.S.A.
128 C2 **Valleyview** Can.
107 D1 **Valls** Spain
129 D3 **Val Marie** Can.
88 C2 **Valmiera** Latvia
104 B2 **Valognes** France
88 C3 **Valozhyn** Belarus
154 B2 **Valparaíso** Brazil
153 A3 **Valparaíso** Chile
105 C3 **Valréas** France
59 D3 **Vals, Tanjung** *c.* Indon.
74 B2 **Valsād** India
122 B2 **Valspan** S. Africa
91 D1 **Valuyki** Rus. Fed.
106 B2 **Valverde del Camino** Spain
81 C2 **Van** Turkey
Van, Lake *salt l.* Turkey *s* **Van Gölü**
81 C1 **Vanadzor** Armenia
83 H2 **Vanavara** Rus. Fed.
142 B1 **Van Buren** *AR* U.S.A.
141 F1 **Van Buren** *ME* U.S.A.
Van Buren U.S.A. *see* **Kettering**
128 B3 **Vancouver** Can.
134 B1 **Vancouver** U.S.A.
128 B3 **Vancouver Island** Can.
140 B3 **Vandalia** *IL* U.S.A.
140 C3 **Vandalia** *OH* U.S.A.
123 C2 **Vanderbijlpark** S. Africa
128 B2 **Vanderhoof** Can.
122 B3 **Vanderkloof Dam** *resr* S. Africa
50 C1 **Van Diemen Gulf** Austr.
88 C2 **Vändra** Estonia
Väner, Lake Sweden *see* **Vänern**
93 F4 **Vänern** *l.* Sweden
93 F4 **Vänersborg** Sweden
121 □D3 **Vangaindrano** Madag.
81 C2 **Van Gölü** *salt l.* Turkey
138 C2 **Van Horn** U.S.A.
59 D3 **Vanimo** P.N.G.
83 K3 **Vanino** Rus. Fed.
104 B2 **Vannes** France
Vannovka Kazakh. *see* **Tura-Ryskulova**
59 D3 **Van Rees, Pegunungan** *mts* Indon.
122 A3 **Vanrhynsdorp** S. Africa
93 H3 **Vantaa** Fin.
49 I5 **Vanua Levu** *i.* Fiji
48 H5 **Vanuatu** *country* S. Pacific Ocean
140 C2 **Van Wert** U.S.A.
122 B3 **Vanwyksvlei** S. Africa
122 B2 **Van Zylsrus** S. Africa
75 C2 **Varanasi** India
92 I1 **Varangerfjorden** *sea cha* Norway
92 I1 **Varanger Halvøya** *pen.* Norway
88 C2 **Varapayeva** Belarus
109 C1 **Varaždin** Croatia
93 F4 **Varberg** Sweden
111 B3 **Varda** Greece
111 B2 **Vardar** *r.* Macedonia
93 E4 **Varde** Denmark
92 J1 **Vardø** Norway
101 D1 **Varel** Ger.
88 B3 **Varėna** Lith.
141 E1 **Varennes** Can.
108 A1 **Varese** Italy
155 C2 **Varginha** Brazil
93 I3 **Varkaus** Fin.
110 C2 **Varna** Bulg.
93 F4 **Värnamo** Sweden
155 D1 **Várzea da Palma** Brazil
86 C2 **Varzino** Rus. Fed.
Vasa Fin. *see* **Vaasa**
88 C3 **Vasilyevichy** Belarus
88 C2 **Vasknarva** Estonia
110 C1 **Vaslui** Romania
93 G4 **Västerås** Sweden
93 G3 **Västerdalälven** *r.* Swede
88 A2 **Västerhaninge** Sweden
93 G4 **Västervik** Sweden
108 B2 **Vasto** Italy
91 D2 **Vasylivka** Ukr.
90 C1 **Vasyl'kiv** Ukr.
91 D2 **Vasyl'kivka** Ukr.
104 C2 **Vatan** France
111 B3 **Vathia** Greece
108 B2 **Vatican City** Europe
92 □B3 **Vatnajökull** *ice cap* Iceland
110 C1 **Vatra Dornei** Romania
Vätter, Lake Sweden *se* **Vättern**
93 F4 **Vättern** *l.* Sweden

8 B2 **Vaughn** U.S.A.
5 C3 **Vauvert** France
1 □D2 **Vavatenina** Madag.
9 J5 **Vava'u Group** *is* Tonga
8 B3 **Vawkavysk** Belarus
3 F4 **Växjö** Sweden
Vayenga Rus. Fed. *see* **Severomorsk**
6 E1 **Vaygach, Ostrov** *i.* Rus. Fed.
4 C1 **Vazante** Brazil
1 D1 **Vechta** Ger.
0 C2 **Vedea** *r.* Romania
0 C1 **Veendam** Neth.
0 B1 **Veenendaal** Neth.
2 F2 **Vega** *i.* Norway
8 C2 **Vegreville** Can.
6 B2 **Vejer de la Frontera** Spain
3 E4 **Vejle** Denmark
0 B2 **Velbŭzhdki Prokhod** *pass* Macedonia
2 A3 **Velddrif** S. Africa
0 B2 **Veldhoven** Neth.
9 B2 **Velebit** *mts* Croatia
0 C2 **Velen** Ger.
9 C1 **Velenje** Slovenia
9 D2 **Veles** Macedonia
6 C2 **Vélez-Málaga** Spain
5 D1 **Velhas** *r.* Brazil
9 D2 **Velika Plana** Yugo.
8 C2 **Velikaya** *r.* Rus. Fed.
9 D2 **Velikiye Luki** Rus. Fed.
9 D2 **Velikiy Novgorod** Rus. Fed.
6 D2 **Velikiy Ustyug** Rus. Fed.
0 C2 **Veliko Tŭrnovo** Bulg.
8 B2 **Veli Lošinj** Croatia
9 D2 **Velizh** Rus. Fed.
8 B2 **Velletri** Italy
3 B3 **Vellore** India
6 D2 **Vel'sk** Rus. Fed.
1 F1 **Velten** Ger.
1 D1 **Velykyy Burluk** Ukr.
Velykyy Tokmak Ukr. *see* **Tokmak**
9 E4 **Vema Trench** *sea feature* Indian Ocean
8 B2 **Venafro** Italy
4 C2 **Venceslau Bráz** Brazil
4 C2 **Vendôme** France
8 B1 **Veneta, Laguna** *lag.* Italy
9 E3 **Venev** Rus. Fed.
Venezia Italy *see* **Venice**
0 C2 **Venezuela** *country* S. America
0 B1 **Venezuela, Golfo de** *g.* Venez.
8 B1 **Venice** Italy
3 D3 **Venice** U.S.A.
8 B1 **Venice, Gulf of** Europe
0 C2 **Venlo** Neth.
3 E4 **Vennesla** Norway
0 B2 **Venray** Neth.
8 B2 **Venta** *r.* Latvia/Lith.
8 B2 **Venta** Lith.
3 C2 **Ventersburg** S. Africa
3 C3 **Venterstad** S. Africa
8 A2 **Ventimiglia** Italy
9 C4 **Ventnor** U.K.
8 B2 **Ventspils** Latvia
5 C4 **Ventura** U.S.A.
9 C3 **Venustiano Carranza, Presa** *resr* Mex.
7 C2 **Vera** Spain
4 C2 **Vera Cruz** Brazil
5 C3 **Veracruz** Mex.
4 B2 **Veraval** India
8 A1 **Verbania** Italy
8 A1 **Vercelli** Italy
5 D3 **Vercors** *reg.* France
2 F3 **Verdalsøra** Norway
4 B1 **Verde** *r.* Brazil
4 B2 **Verde** *r.* Brazil
4 B2 **Verde** *r.* Mex.
8 A2 **Verde** *r.* U.S.A.
5 D1 **Verde Grande** *r.* Brazil
1 D1 **Verden (Aller)** Ger.
4 B1 **Verdinho, Serra do** *mts* Brazil
5 D3 **Verdon** *r.* France
5 D2 **Verdun** France
3 C2 **Vereeniging** S. Africa
6 B1 **Verín** Spain
1 D3 **Verkhnebakanskiy** Rus. Fed.
9 D3 **Verkhnedneprovskiy** Rus. Fed.
2 J2 **Verkhnetulomskiy** Rus. Fed.
92 J2 **Verkhnetulomskoye Vodokhranilishche** *resr* Rus. Fed.
87 D4 **Verkhniy Baskunchak** Rus. Fed.
91 E1 **Verkhniy Mamon** Rus. Fed.
86 D2 **Verkhnyaya Toyma** Rus. Fed.
89 E3 **Verkhov'ye** Rus. Fed.
90 A2 **Verkhovyna** Ukr.
83 J2 **Verkhoyanskiy Khrebet** *mts* Rus. Fed.
129 C2 **Vermilion** Can.
137 D2 **Vermillion** U.S.A.
130 A3 **Vermillion Bay** Can.
141 E2 **Vermont** *state* U.S.A.
135 E2 **Vernal** U.S.A.
122 B2 **Verneuk Pan** *salt pan* S. Africa
128 C2 **Vernon** Can.
139 D2 **Vernon** U.S.A.
143 D3 **Vero Beach** U.S.A.
111 B2 **Veroia** Greece
108 B1 **Verona** Italy
140 B2 **Verona** U.S.A.
104 C2 **Versailles** France
104 B2 **Vertou** France
123 D2 **Verulam** S. Africa
100 B2 **Verviers** Belgium
105 C2 **Vervins** France
105 D3 **Vescovato** *Corsica* France
87 E3 **Veselaya, Gora** *mt.* Rus. Fed.
91 C2 **Vesele** Ukr.
91 E2 **Veselyy** Rus. Fed.
105 D2 **Vesoul** France
142 C2 **Vestavia Hills** U.S.A.
92 F2 **Vesterålen** *is* Norway
92 F2 **Vestfjorden** *sea chan.* Norway
94 B1 **Vestmanna** Faroe Is
92 □A3 **Vestmannaeyjar** Iceland
92 □A3 **Vestmannaeyjar** *is* Iceland
93 E3 **Vestnes** Norway
108 B2 **Vesuvio** *vol.* Italy
Vesuvius *vol.* Italy *see* **Vesuvio**
89 E2 **Ves'yegonsk** Rus. Fed.
103 D2 **Veszprém** Hungary
93 G4 **Vetlanda** Sweden
86 D3 **Vetluga** Rus. Fed.
86 D3 **Vetluzhskiy** Rus. Fed.
100 A2 **Veurne** Belgium
119 D2 **Veveno** *r.* Sudan
105 D2 **Vevey** Switz.
91 D1 **Veydelevka** Rus. Fed.
80 B1 **Vezirköprü** Turkey
Vialar Alg. *see* **Tissemsilt**
152 C3 **Viamao** Brazil
151 E3 **Viana** Brazil
106 B1 **Viana do Castelo** Port.
Viangchan Laos *see* **Vientiane**
62 B1 **Viangphoukha** Laos
154 C1 **Vianópolis** Brazil
108 B2 **Viareggio** Italy
93 E4 **Viborg** Denmark
Viborg Rus. Fed. *see* **Vyborg**
109 C3 **Vibo Valentia** Italy
107 D1 **Vic** Spain
144 A1 **Vicente Guerrero** Mex.
108 B1 **Vicenza** Italy
89 F2 **Vichuga** Rus. Fed.
105 C2 **Vichy** France
142 B2 **Vicksburg** U.S.A.
155 D2 **Viçosa** Brazil
52 A3 **Victor Harbor** Austr.
50 C1 **Victoria** *r.* Austr.
52 B3 **Victoria** *state* Austr.
Victoria Cameroon *see* **Limbe**
128 B3 **Victoria** Can.
153 A3 **Victoria** Chile
Victoria Malaysia *see* **Labuan**
113 I6 **Victoria** Seychelles
139 D3 **Victoria** U.S.A.
119 D3 **Victoria, Lake** Africa
52 B2 **Victoria, Lake** Austr.
62 A1 **Victoria, Mount** Myanmar
59 D3 **Victoria, Mount** P.N.G.
120 B2 **Victoria Falls** *waterfall* Zambia/Zimbabwe
120 B2 **Victoria Falls** Zimbabwe
126 E2 **Victoria Island** Can.
55 M2 **Victoria Land** *coastal area* Antarctica
145 D3 **Victoria Peak** Belize
50 C1 **Victoria River Downs** Austr.
141 E1 **Victoriaville** Can.
122 B3 **Victoria West** S. Africa
135 C4 **Victorville** U.S.A.
143 D2 **Vidalia** U.S.A.
110 C2 **Videle** Romania
92 □A2 **Víðidalsá** Iceland
110 B2 **Vidin** Bulg.
74 B2 **Vidisha** India
142 B2 **Vidor** U.S.A.
153 B4 **Viedma** Arg.
153 A4 **Viedma, Lago** *l.* Arg.
102 C2 **Viehberg** *mt.* Austria
107 D1 **Vielha** Spain
100 B2 **Vielsalm** Belgium
101 E2 **Vienenburg** Ger.
103 D2 **Vienna** Austria
140 C3 **Vienna** U.S.A.
105 C2 **Vienne** France
104 C2 **Vienne** *r.* France
62 B2 **Vientiane** Laos
100 C2 **Viersen** Ger.
104 C2 **Vierzon** France
144 B2 **Viesca** Mex.
109 C2 **Vieste** Italy
62 B2 **Vietnam** *country* Asia
62 B1 **Viêt Tri** Vietnam
64 B2 **Vigan** Phil.
108 A1 **Vigevano** Italy
106 B1 **Vigo** Spain
Viipuri Rus. Fed. *see* **Vyborg**
73 C3 **Vijayawada** India
92 □B3 **Vík** Iceland
111 B2 **Vikhren** *mt.* Bulg.
128 C2 **Viking** Can.
92 F3 **Vikna** *i.* Norway
Vila Alferes Chamusca Moz. *see* **Guija**
Vila Arriaga Angola *see* **Bibala**
Vila Bugaço Angola *see* **Camanongue**
Vila Cabral Moz. *see* **Lichinga**
Vila da Ponte Angola *see* **Kuvango**
Vila de Aljustrel Angola *see* **Cangamba**
Vila de Almoster Angola *see* **Chiange**
Vila de João Belo Moz. *see* **Xai-Xai**
Vila de Trego Morais Moz. *see* **Chókwé**
Vila Fontes Moz. *see* **Caia**
106 B2 **Vila Franca de Xira** Port.
106 B1 **Vilagarcía de Arousa** Spain
123 D1 **Vila Gomes da Costa** Moz.
106 B1 **Vilalba** Spain
Vila Luísa Moz. *see* **Marracuene**
Vila Marechal Carmona Angola *see* **Uíge**
Vila Miranda Moz. *see* **Macaloge**
121 □D2 **Vilanandro, Tanjona** *pt* Madag.
88 C2 **Viļāni** Latvia
106 B1 **Vila Nova de Gaia** Port.
107 D1 **Vilanova i la Geltrú** Spain
Vila Paiva de Andrada Moz. *see* **Gorongosa**
Vila Pery Moz. *see* **Chimoio**
106 B1 **Vila Real** Port.
106 B1 **Vilar Formoso** Port.
Vila Salazar Angola *see* **N'dalatando**
Vila Salazar Zimbabwe *see* **Sango**
Vila Teixeira de Sousa Angola *see* **Luau**
155 D2 **Vila Velha** Brazil
150 B4 **Vilcabamba, Cordillera** *mts* Peru
92 G3 **Vilhelmina** Sweden
150 C4 **Vilhena** Brazil
88 C2 **Viljandi** Estonia
123 C2 **Viljoenskroon** S. Africa
88 B3 **Vilkaviškis** Lith.
83 H1 **Vil'kitskogo, Proliv** *str.* Rus. Fed.
144 B1 **Villa Ahumada** Mex.
106 B1 **Villablino** Spain
102 C2 **Villach** Austria
Villa Cisneros Western Sahara *see* **Ad Dakhla**
144 A2 **Villa Constitución** Mex.
144 B2 **Villa de Cos** Mex.
152 B3 **Villa Dolores** Arg.
145 C3 **Villa Flores** Mex.
153 C3 **Villa Gesell** Arg.
145 C2 **Villagrán** Mex.
145 C3 **Villahermosa** Mex.
144 A2 **Villa Insurgentes** Mex.
107 C2 **Villajoyosa** Spain
152 B3 **Villa María** Arg.
152 B2 **Villa Montes** Bol.
144 B2 **Villanueva** Mex.
106 B2 **Villanueva de la Serena** Spain
106 C2 **Villanueva de los Infantes** Spain
152 C2 **Villa Ocampo** Arg.
138 B3 **Villa Ocampo** Mex.
108 A3 **Villaputzu** *Sardinia* Italy
152 C2 **Villarrica** Para.
106 C2 **Villarrobledo** Spain
Villasalazar Zimbabwe *see* **Sango**
152 B2 **Villa Unión** Arg.
144 B2 **Villa Unión** Mex.
144 B2 **Villa Unión** Mex.
150 B2 **Villavicencio** Col.
152 B2 **Villazon** Bol.
104 C3 **Villefranche-de-Rouergue** France
105 C2 **Villefranche-sur-Saône** France
107 C2 **Villena** Spain
100 A2 **Villeneuve-d'Ascq** France
104 C3 **Villeneuve-sur-Lot** France
142 B2 **Ville Platte** U.S.A.
100 A3 **Villers-Cotterêts** France
105 C2 **Villeurbanne** France
123 C2 **Villiers** S. Africa
102 B2 **Villingen** Ger.
137 E2 **Villisca** U.S.A.
88 C3 **Vilnius** Lith.
91 C2 **Vil'nohirs'k** Ukr.
91 D2 **Vil'nyans'k** Ukr.
100 B2 **Vilvoorde** Belgium
88 C3 **Vilyeyka** Belarus
83 J2 **Vilyuy** *r.* Rus. Fed.
93 G4 **Vimmerby** Sweden
153 A3 **Viña del Mar** Chile
107 D1 **Vinaròs** Spain
140 B3 **Vincennes** U.S.A.
55 J3 **Vincennes Bay** Antarctica
141 D3 **Vineland** U.S.A.
62 B2 **Vinh** Vietnam
63 B2 **Vinh Long** Vietnam
139 D1 **Vinita** U.S.A.
90 B2 **Vinnytsya** Ukr.
55 R2 **Vinson Massif** *mt.* Antarctica
93 E3 **Vinstra** Norway
108 B1 **Vipiteno** Italy
64 B2 **Virac** Phil.
74 B2 **Viramgam** India
80 B2 **Viranşehir** Turkey
129 D3 **Virden** Can.
104 B2 **Vire** France
120 A2 **Virei** Angola
155 D1 **Virgem da Lapa** Brazil
138 A1 **Virgin** *r.* U.S.A.
123 C2 **Virginia** S. Africa
137 E1 **Virginia** U.S.A.
141 D3 **Virginia** *state* U.S.A.
141 D3 **Virginia Beach** U.S.A.
135 C3 **Virginia City** U.S.A.
147 D3 **Virgin Islands (U.K.)** *terr.* West Indies
147 D3 **Virgin Islands (U.S.A.)** *terr.* West Indies
63 B2 **Virôchey** Cambodia
109 C1 **Virovitica** Croatia
100 B3 **Virton** Belgium
88 B2 **Virtsu** Estonia
73 B4 **Virudunagar** India
109 C2 **Vis** *i.* Croatia
88 C2 **Visaginas** Lith.
135 C3 **Visalia** U.S.A.
74 B2 **Visavadar** India
64 B2 **Visayan Sea** Phil.
93 G4 **Visby** Sweden
126 E2 **Viscount Melville Sound** *sea chan.* Can.
151 E3 **Viseu** Brazil
106 B1 **Viseu** Port.
110 B1 **Vişeu de Sus** Romania
73 C3 **Vishakhapatnam** India
88 C2 **Višķi** Latvia
109 C2 **Visoko** Bos.-Herz.
Vistula *r.* Pol. *see* **Wisła**

Vitebsk Belarus see Vitsyebsk
108 B2 Viterbo Italy
49 I5 Viti Levu i. Fiji
83 I3 Vitim r. Rus. Fed.
155 D2 Vitória Brazil
151 E4 Vitória da Conquista Brazil
106 C1 Vitoria-Gasteiz Spain
104 B2 Vitré France
105 C2 Vitry-le-François France
89 D2 Vitsyebsk Belarus
105 D2 Vittel France
108 B3 Vittoria Sicily Italy
108 B1 Vittorio Veneto Italy
106 B1 Viveiro Spain
136 C2 Vivian U.S.A.
Vizagapatam India see Vishakhapatnam
138 A3 Vizcaíno, Desierto de des. Mex.
144 A2 Vizcaíno, Sierra mts Mex.
111 C2 Vize Turkey
73 C3 Vizianagaram India
100 B2 Vlaardingen Neth.
87 D4 Vladikavkaz Rus. Fed.
89 F2 Vladimir Rus. Fed.
66 B2 Vladivostok Rus. Fed.
109 D2 Vlasotince Yugo.
100 B1 Vlieland i. Neth.
100 A2 Vlissingen Neth.
109 C2 Vlorë Albania
102 C1 Vltava r. Czech Rep.
102 C2 Vöcklabruck Austria
109 C2 Vodice Croatia
Vogelkop Peninsula Indon. see Doberai, Jazirah
101 D2 Vogelsberg hills Ger.
Vohémar Madag. see Iharaña
Vohibinany Madag. see Ampasimanolotra
Vohimarina Madag. see Iharaña
121 □D3 Vohimena, Tanjona c. Madag.
121 □D3 Vohipeno Madag.
119 D3 Voi Kenya
105 D2 Voiron France
131 D2 Voisey Bay Can.
109 C1 Vojvodina prov. Yugo.
92 J3 Voknavolok Rus. Fed.
Volcano Bay Japan see Uchiura-wan
Volcano Islands Japan see Kazan-rettō
Volchansk Ukr. see Vovchans'k
89 E2 Volga Rus. Fed.
89 F2 Volga r. Rus. Fed.
87 D4 Volgodonsk Rus. Fed.
87 D4 Volgograd Rus. Fed.
87 D4 Volgogradskoye Vodokhranilishche resr Rus. Fed.
89 D2 Volkhov Rus. Fed.
89 D1 Volkhov r. Rus. Fed.
101 E2 Volkstedt Ger.
91 D2 Volnovakha Ukr.
90 B2 Volochys'k Ukr.
91 D2 Volodars'ke Ukr.
Volodarskoye Kazakh. see Saumalkol'
90 B1 Volodars'k-Volyns'kyy Ukr.
90 B1 Volodymyrets' Ukr.
90 A1 Volodymyr-Volyns'kyy Ukr.
89 E2 Vologda Rus. Fed.
89 E2 Volokolamsk Rus. Fed.
91 D1 Volokonovka Rus. Fed.
111 B3 Volos Greece
88 C2 Volosovo Rus. Fed.
89 D2 Volot Rus. Fed.
89 E3 Volovo Rus. Fed.
87 D3 Vol'sk Rus. Fed.
114 C4 Volta r. Ghana
114 C4 Volta, Lake resr Ghana
155 D2 Volta Redonda Brazil
110 C2 Voluntari Romania
87 D4 Volzhskiy Rus. Fed.
92 □C2 Vopnafjörður Iceland
88 C3 Voranava Belarus
160 K3 Voring Plateau sea feature N. Atlantic Ocean
86 F2 Vorkuta Rus. Fed.
88 B2 Vormsi i. Estonia
83 G2 Vorogovo Rus. Fed.
89 E3 Voronezh Rus. Fed.
89 E3 Voronezh r. Rus. Fed.
91 E1 Vorontsovka Rus. Fed.
Voroshilov Rus. Fed. see Ussuriysk
Voroshilovgrad Ukr. see Luhans'k
Voroshilovsk Rus. Fed. see Stavropol'
Voroshilovsk Ukr. see Alchevs'k
91 C2 Vorskla r. Rus. Fed.
88 C2 Võrtsjärv l. Estonia
88 C2 Võru Estonia
122 B3 Vosburg S. Africa
105 D2 Vosges mts France
89 E2 Voskresensk Rus. Fed.
93 E3 Voss Norway
86 C2 Vostochnaya Litsa Rus. Fed.
Vostochno-Sibirskoye More sea Rus. Fed. see East Siberian Sea
83 H3 Vostochnyy Sayan mts Rus. Fed.
66 C1 Vostok Rus. Fed.
49 L5 Vostok Island Kiribati
86 E3 Votkinsk Rus. Fed.
86 E3 Votkinskoye Vodokhranilishche resr Rus. Fed.
154 C2 Votuporanga Brazil
105 C2 Vouziers France
91 D1 Vovchans'k Ukr.
92 J2 Voynitsa Rus. Fed.
86 E2 Voyvozh Rus. Fed.
91 C2 Voznesens'k Ukr.
76 B2 Vozrozhdeniya, Ostrov i. Uzbek.
93 E4 Vrådal Norway
90 C2 Vradiyivka Ukr.
66 B2 Vrangel' Rus. Fed.
83 N2 Vrangelya, Ostrov i. Rus. Fed.
109 D2 Vranje Yugo.
110 C2 Vratnik pass Bulg.
110 B2 Vratsa Bulg.
109 C1 Vrbas r. Bos.-Herz.
109 C1 Vrbas Yugo.
122 A3 Vredenburg S. Africa
122 A3 Vredendal S. Africa
100 B3 Vresse Belgium
100 C1 Vriezenveen Neth.
109 D1 Vršac Yugo.
122 B2 Vryburg S. Africa
123 D2 Vryheid S. Africa
89 D1 Vsevolozhsk Rus. Fed.
109 D2 Vučitrn Yugo.
109 C1 Vukovar Croatia
86 E2 Vuktyl' Rus. Fed.
123 C2 Vukuzakhe S. Africa
90 B2 Vulcănești Moldova
109 B3 Vulcano, Isola i. Italy
Vulkaneshty Moldova see Vulcănești
63 B2 Vung Tau Vietnam
92 H2 Vuollerim Sweden
92 I2 Vuotso Fin.
74 B2 Vyara India
Vyarkhowye Belarus see Ruba
Vyatka Rus. Fed. see Kirov
89 D2 Vyaz'ma Rus. Fed.
88 C1 Vyborg Rus. Fed.
88 C1 Vyborgskiy Zaliv b. Rus. Fed.
86 D2 Vychegda r. Rus. Fed.
88 C2 Vyerkhnyadzvinsk Belarus
89 D3 Vyetka Belarus
89 D3 Vygonichi Rus. Fed.
86 C2 Vygozero, Ozero l. Rus. Fed.
87 D3 Vyksa Rus. Fed.
90 B2 Vylkove Ukr.
90 A2 Vynohradiv Ukr.
89 D2 Vypolzovo Rus. Fed.
89 D2 Vyritsa Rus. Fed.
91 D2 Vyselki Rus. Fed.
90 C1 Vyshhorod Ukr.
89 D2 Vyshnevolotskaya Gryada ridge Rus. Fed.
89 D2 Vyshniy-Volochek Rus. Fed.
103 D2 Vyškov Czech Rep.
89 E2 Vysokovsk Rus. Fed.
86 C2 Vytegra Rus. Fed.

W

114 B3 Wa Ghana
100 B2 Waal r. Neth.
100 B2 Waalwijk Neth.
119 D2 Waat Sudan
128 C2 Wabasca r. Can.
128 C2 Wabasca-Desmarais Can.
140 B3 Wabash r. U.S.A.
117 C4 Wabē Gestro r. Eth.
117 C4 Wabē Shebelē Wenz r. Eth.
129 E2 Wabowden Can.
103 D1 Wąbrzeźno Pol.
143 D3 Waccasassa Bay U.S.A.
101 D2 Wächtersbach Ger.
139 D2 Waco U.S.A.
74 A2 Wad Pak.
115 D2 Waddān Libya
100 B1 Waddeneilanden is Neth.
Wadden Islands Neth. see Waddeneilanden
100 B1 Waddenzee sea chan. Neth.
128 B2 Waddington, Mount Can.
100 B1 Waddinxveen Neth.
129 D2 Wadena Can.
137 D1 Wadena U.S.A.
50 B1 Wadeye Austr.
Wadhwan India see Surendranagar
116 B2 Wadi Halfa Sudan
116 B3 Wad Medani Sudan
122 B3 Waenhuiskrans S. Africa
70 C2 Wafangdian China
100 B2 Wageningen Neth.
127 G2 Wager Bay Can.
53 C3 Wagga Wagga Austr.
137 D2 Wagner U.S.A.
74 B1 Wah Pak.
137 D2 Wahoo U.S.A.
137 D1 Wahpeton U.S.A.
54 B2 Waiau r. N.Z.
59 C3 Waigeo i. Indon.
61 C2 Waikabubak Indon.
54 C1 Waikaremoana, Lake N.Z.
52 A2 Waikerie Austr.
54 B2 Waimate N.Z.
75 B3 Wainganga r. India
61 D2 Waingapu Indon.
129 C2 Wainwright Can.
126 B2 Wainwright U.S.A.
54 C1 Waiouru N.Z.
54 B2 Waipara N.Z.
54 C1 Waipawa N.Z.
54 B2 Wairau r. N.Z.
54 C1 Wairoa N.Z.
54 B2 Waitaki r. N.Z.
54 B1 Waitara N.Z.
54 B1 Waiuku N.Z.
67 C3 Wajima Japan
119 E2 Wajir Kenya
67 C3 Wakasa-wan b. Japan
54 A3 Wakatipu, Lake N.Z.
129 D2 Wakaw Can.
67 C4 Wakayama Japan
48 H2 Wake Atoll terr. N. Pacific Ocean
136 D3 WaKeeney U.S.A.
54 B2 Wakefield N.Z.
98 C3 Wakefield U.K.
Wakeham Can. see Kangiqsujuaq
66 D1 Wakkanai Japan
123 D2 Wakkerstroom S. Africa
120 A2 Waku-Kungo Angola
103 D1 Wałbrzych Pol.
53 D2 Walcha Austr.
100 C1 Walchum Ger.
103 D1 Wałcz Pol.
99 B3 Wales admin. div. U.K.
53 C2 Walgett Austr.
119 C3 Walikale Dem. Rep. Congo
135 C3 Walker Lake U.S.A.
134 C1 Wallace ID U.S.A.
143 E2 Wallace NC U.S.A.
52 A2 Wallaroo Austr.
98 B3 Wallasey U.K.
134 C1 Walla Walla U.S.A.
101 D3 Walldürn Ger.
122 A3 Wallekraal S. Africa
53 C2 Wallendbeen Austr.
49 J5 Wallis, Îles is Wallis and Futuna Is
49 J5 Wallis and Futuna Islands terr. S. Pacific Ocean
96 □ Walls U.K.
98 B2 Walney, Isle of i. U.K.
99 C3 Walsall U.K.
136 C3 Walsenburg U.S.A.
101 D1 Walsrode Ger.
143 D2 Walterboro U.S.A.
120 A3 Walvis Bay Namibia
158 F6 Walvis Ridge sea feature S. Atlantic Ocean
119 C2 Wamba Dem. Rep. Cong
52 B1 Wanaaring Austr.
54 A2 Wanaka N.Z.
54 A2 Wanaka, Lake N.Z.
71 B3 Wan'an China
130 B3 Wanapitei Lake Can.
154 B3 Wanda Arg.
66 B1 Wanda Shan mts China
62 A1 Wanding China
Wandingzhen China see Wanding
54 C1 Wanganui N.Z.
54 B1 Wanganui r. N.Z.
53 C3 Wangaratta Austr.
65 B1 Wangqing China
62 A1 Wan Hsa-la Myanmar
Wankie Zimbabwe see Hwange
71 B4 Wanning China
100 B2 Wanroij Neth.
99 C4 Wantage U.K.
70 A2 Wanxian China
70 A2 Wanyuan China
117 A4 Warab Sudan
73 B3 Warangal India
101 D2 Warburg Ger.
50 B2 Warburton Austr.
52 A1 Warburton watercourse Austr.
74 B2 Wardha India
96 C1 Ward Hill U.K.
128 B2 Ware Can.
101 F1 Waren Ger.
101 C2 Warendorf Ger.
53 D1 Warialda Austr.
122 A2 Warmbad Namibia
135 C3 Warm Springs U.S.A.
134 C2 Warner Lakes U.S.A.
134 B2 Warner Mountains U.S.
143 D2 Warner Robins U.S.A.
152 B1 Warnes Bol.
52 B3 Warracknabeal Austr.
53 C3 Warrandyte Austr.
53 C2 Warrego r. Austr.
53 C2 Warren Austr.
142 B2 Warren AR U.S.A.
140 C2 Warren OH U.S.A.
141 D2 Warren PA U.S.A.
97 C1 Warrenpoint U.K.
137 E3 Warrensburg U.S.A.
122 B2 Warrenton S. Africa
115 C4 Warri Nigeria
98 B3 Warrington U.K.
52 B3 Warrnambool Austr.
103 E1 Warsaw Pol.
140 B2 Warsaw U.S.A.
Warszawa Pol. see Warsaw
103 C1 Warta r. Pol.
53 D1 Warwick Austr.
99 C3 Warwick U.K.
141 E2 Warwick U.S.A.
134 D3 Wasatch Range mts U.S.A.
135 C3 Wasco U.S.A.
136 C1 Washburn U.S.A.
137 E2 Washington IA U.S.A.
140 B2 Washington IL U.S.A.
140 B3 Washington IN U.S.A.
137 E3 Washington MO U.S.A.
143 E1 Washington NC U.S.A.
140 C2 Washington PA U.S.A.
135 D3 Washington UT U.S.A.
134 B1 Washington state U.S.A.
141 D3 Washington D.C. U.S.A.
141 E2 Washington, Mount U.S.A.
140 C3 Washington Court Hou U.S.A.
74 A2 Washuk Pak.
130 C2 Waskaganish Can.
129 E2 Waskaiowaka Lake Car
122 A2 Wasser Namibia
101 D2 Wasserkuppe hill Ger.
130 C3 Waswanipi, Lac l. Can.
61 D2 Watampone Indon.
Watenstadt-Salzgitter Ger. see Salzgitter
141 E2 Waterbury U.S.A.
129 D2 Waterbury Lake Can.
97 C2 Waterford Rep. of Irelan
97 C2 Waterford Harbour Rep. of Ireland
100 B2 Waterloo Belgium
137 E2 Waterloo U.S.A.
99 C4 Waterlooville U.K.
123 C1 Waterpoort S. Africa
141 D2 Watertown NY U.S.A.
137 D2 Watertown SD U.S.A.
140 B2 Watertown WI U.S.A.
97 A3 Waterville Rep. of Irelan

4 F2 Waterville U.S.A.
9 C4 Watford U.K.
6 C1 Watford City U.S.A.
9 D2 Wathaman r. Can.
      Watling Island Bahamas see San Salvador
9 D1 Watonga U.S.A.
9 D2 Watrous Can.
9 C2 Watsa Dem. Rep. Congo
0 B2 Watseka U.S.A.
8 C3 Watsi Kengo Dem. Rep. Congo
8 B1 Watson Lake Can.
5 B3 Watsonville U.S.A.
9 C3 Watubela, Kepulauan is Indon.
9 D3 Wau P.N.G.
7 A4 Wau Sudan
3 D2 Wauchope Austr.
0 B2 Waukegan U.S.A.
0 B2 Waukesha U.S.A.
9 D2 Waurika U.S.A.
0 B3 Wausau U.S.A.
9 D3 Waveney r. U.K.
7 E2 Waverly U.S.A.
0 B3 Wawa Can.
3 D2 Waycross U.S.A.
7 D2 Wayne U.S.A.
3 D2 Waynesboro GA U.S.A.
1 D3 Waynesboro VA U.S.A.
7 E3 Waynesville MO U.S.A.
3 D1 Waynesville NC U.S.A.
4 B1 Wazirabad Pak.
0 A1 We, Pulau i. Indon.
9 C2 Wear r. U.K.
9 D1 Weatherford OK U.S.A.
9 D2 Weatherford TX U.S.A.
4 B2 Weaverville U.S.A.
0 B3 Webb U.S.A.
0 B2 Webequie Can.
7 C4 Webi Shabeelle r. Somalia
7 D1 Webster U.S.A.
7 E2 Webster City U.S.A.
5 C3 Weddell Abyssal Plain sea feature Southern Ocean
5 B3 Weddell Sea Antarctica
3 D2 Weenen S. Africa
0 B2 Weert Neth.
3 C2 Weethalle Austr.
3 C2 Wee Waa Austr.
0 C2 Wegberg Ger.
3 E1 Węgorzewo Pol.
3 E1 Węgrów Pol.
0 B2 Wei r. China
0 B1 Weichang China
1 F3 Weiden in der Oberpfalz Ger.
      Weidongmen China see Qianjin
0 B2 Weifang China
0 C3 Weihai China
3 C1 Weilmoringle Austr.
1 E2 Weimar Ger.
9 D3 Weimar U.S.A.
0 A2 Weinan China
1 A3 Weining China
1 D1 Weipa Austr.
3 C1 Weir r. Austr.
0 C2 Weirton U.S.A.
2 B1 Weishan China
1 E2 Weiße Elster r. Ger.
1 E2 Weißenfels Ger.
2 C2 Weißkugel mt. Austria/Italy
1 A3 Weixin China
      Weizhou China see Wenchuan
3 D1 Wejherowo Pol.
0 C3 Welch U.S.A.
7 B3 Weldiya Eth.
2 C2 Welkom S. Africa
9 C3 Welland r. U.K.
1 C1 Wellesley Islands Austr.
9 C3 Wellingborough U.K.
2 B2 Wellington N.Z.
2 A3 Wellington S. Africa
6 D2 Wellington CO U.S.A.
7 D3 Wellington KS U.S.A.
5 D3 Wellington UT U.S.A.
3 A4 Wellington, Isla i. Chile
3 C2 Wellington, Lake Austr.
8 B2 Wells Can.
9 B4 Wells U.K.
4 D2 Wells U.S.A.
0 B2 Wells, Lake salt flat Austr.
4 B1 Wellsford N.Z.
9 D3 Wells-next-the-Sea U.K.
8 A2 Wellton U.S.A.
2 C2 Wels Austria
9 B3 Welshpool U.K.

      Welwitschia Namibia see Khorixas
130 C2 Wembesi S. Africa
130 C2 Wemindji Can.
134 B1 Wenatchee U.S.A.
71 B4 Wenchang China
114 B4 Wenchi Ghana
      Wenchow China see Wenzhou
70 A2 Wenchuan China
70 C2 Wendeng China
101 E1 Wendisch Evern Ger.
117 B4 Wendo Eth.
135 D2 Wendover U.S.A.
71 B3 Wengyuan China
      Wenhua China see Weishan
      Wenlan China see Mengzi
      Wenlin China see Renshou
71 C3 Wenling China
      Wenquan China see Yingshan
71 A3 Wenshan China
52 B2 Wentworth Austr.
71 C3 Wenzhou China
123 C2 Wepener S. Africa
122 B2 Werda Botswana
101 F2 Werdau Ger.
101 F1 Werder Ger.
101 F3 Wernberg-Köblitz Ger.
101 E2 Wernigerode Ger.
101 D2 Werra r. Ger.
52 B2 Werrimull Austr.
53 D2 Werris Creek Austr.
101 D3 Wertheim Ger.
100 C2 Wesel Ger.
101 E1 Wesendorf Ger.
101 D1 Weser r. Ger.
101 D1 Weser sea chan. Ger.
51 C1 Wessel, Cape Austr.
51 C1 Wessel Islands Austr.
123 C2 Wesselton S. Africa
55 P2 West Antarctica reg. Antarctica
156 B7 West Australian Basin sea feature Indian Ocean
80 B2 West Bank terr. Asia
140 B2 West Bend U.S.A.
75 C2 West Bengal state India
99 C3 West Bromwich U.K.
141 E2 Westbrook U.S.A.
137 E2 West Des Moines U.S.A.
100 C2 Westerburg Ger.
100 C1 Westerholt Ger.
141 E2 Westerly U.S.A.
50 B2 Western Australia state Austr.
122 B3 Western Cape prov. S. Africa
116 A2 Western Desert Egypt
      Western Dvina r. Europe see Zapadnaya Dvina
73 B3 Western Ghats mts India
114 A2 Western Sahara terr. Africa
      Western Samoa country S. Pacific Ocean see Samoa
      Western Sayan Mountains mts Rus. Fed. see Zapadnyy Sayan
122 B3 Westerschelde est. Neth.
100 A2 Westerstede Ger.
101 C2 Westerwald hills Ger.
153 B5 West Falkland i. Falkland Is
140 B3 West Frankfort U.S.A.
      West Frisian Islands Neth. see Waddeneilanden
96 C2 Westhill U.K.
55 I3 West Ice Shelf Antarctica
147 D2 West Indies N. America
100 A2 Westkapelle Belgium
96 A1 West Loch Roag b. U.K.
128 C2 Westlock Can.
100 B2 Westmalle Belgium
      Westman Islands Iceland see Vestmannaeyjar
53 C1 Westmar Austr.
156 C4 West Mariana Basin sea feature N. Pacific Ocean
140 B3 West Memphis U.S.A.
140 C3 Weston U.S.A.
99 B4 Weston-super-Mare U.K.
143 D3 West Palm Beach U.S.A.
137 E3 West Plains U.S.A.
54 B2 West Point U.S.A.
97 B2 Westport Rep. of Ireland
100 B1 Westport N.Z.
129 D2 Westray Can.

96 C1 Westray i. U.K.
      West Siberian Plain Rus. Fed. see Zapadno-Sibirskaya Ravnina
100 B1 West-Terschelling Neth.
136 A2 West Thumb U.S.A.
97 B1 West Town Rep. of Ireland
135 D2 West Valley City U.S.A.
140 C3 West Virginia state U.S.A.
53 C2 West Wyalong Austr.
134 D2 West Yellowstone U.S.A.
59 C3 Wetar i. Indon.
128 C2 Wetaskiwin Can.
119 D3 Wete Tanz.
101 D2 Wetzlar Ger.
59 D3 Wewak P.N.G.
97 C2 Wexford Rep. of Ireland
97 C2 Wexford Harbour b. Rep. of Ireland
129 D2 Weyakwin Can.
129 D3 Weyburn Can.
101 D1 Weyhe Ger.
99 B4 Weymouth U.K.
54 C1 Whakatane N.Z.
129 E1 Whale Cove Can.
96 □ Whalsay i. U.K.
54 B1 Whangamomona N.Z.
54 B1 Whangaparaoa N.Z.
54 B1 Whangarei N.Z.
98 C3 Wharfe r. U.K.
139 D3 Wharton U.S.A.
128 C1 Wha Ti Can.
136 B2 Wheatland U.S.A.
140 B2 Wheaton U.S.A.
142 C2 Wheeler Lake resr U.S.A.
138 B1 Wheeler Peak NM U.S.A.
135 D3 Wheeler Peak NV U.S.A.
140 C2 Wheeling U.S.A.
98 B2 Whernside hill U.K.
54 C1 Whistler Can.
98 C2 Whitby U.K.
128 A1 White r. Can./U.S.A.
142 B2 White r. AR U.S.A.
140 B3 White r. IN U.S.A.
50 B2 White, Lake salt flat Austr.
54 B2 White Bay Can.
136 C1 White Butte mt. U.S.A.
52 B2 White Cliffs Austr.
128 C2 Whitecourt Can.
134 D1 Whitefish U.S.A.
98 B2 Whitehaven U.K.
98 C2 Whitehead U.K.
128 A1 Whitehorse Can.
141 E2 White Lake U.S.A.
51 D4 Whitemark Austr.
135 C3 White Mountain Peak U.S.A.
116 B3 White Nile r. Sudan/Uganda
      White Russia country Europe see Belarus
86 C2 White Sea Rus. Fed.
134 D1 White Sulphur Springs U.S.A.
143 E2 Whiteville U.S.A.
114 B3 White Volta watercourse Burkina/Ghana
136 B3 Whitewater Baldy mt. U.S.A.
130 B2 Whitewater Lake Can.
130 B2 Whitewood Can.
96 B3 Whithorn U.K.
54 C1 Whitianga N.Z.
135 C3 Whitney, Mount U.S.A.
99 D4 Whitstable U.K.
51 D2 Whitsunday Island Austr.
52 B3 Whittlesea Austr.
52 A2 Whyalla Austr.
62 A2 Wiang Pa Pao Thai.
62 A1 Wiang Phran Thai.
100 A2 Wichelen Belgium
137 D3 Wichita U.S.A.
139 D2 Wichita Falls U.S.A.
139 D2 Wichita Mountains U.S.A.
96 C1 Wick U.K.
138 A2 Wickenburg U.S.A.
97 C2 Wicklow Rep. of Ireland
97 D2 Wicklow Head hd Rep. of Ireland
97 C2 Wicklow Mountains Rep. of Ireland
99 C3 Widnes U.K.
101 D2 Wiehengebirge hills Ger.
100 C2 Wiehl Ger.
103 D1 Wieluń Pol.
      Wien Austria see Vienna
103 D2 Wiener Neustadt Austria
100 B1 Wieringerwerf Neth.
101 D2 Wiesbaden Ger.
100 C1 Wiesmoor Ger.

103 D1 Wieżyca hill Pol.
98 B3 Wigan U.K.
99 C3 Wight, Isle of i. U.K.
96 B3 Wigtown U.K.
100 B2 Wijchen Neth.
130 B3 Wikwemikong Can.
52 B2 Wilcannia Austr.
      Wilczek Land i. Rus. Fed. see Zemlya Vil'cheka
123 C3 Wild Coast S. Africa
101 D1 Wildeshausen Ger.
136 C2 Wild Horse Hill mt. U.S.A.
123 C2 Wilge r. S. Africa
48 F4 Wilhelm, Mount P.N.G.
101 D1 Wilhelmshaven Ger.
141 D2 Wilkes-Barre U.S.A.
55 K3 Wilkes Land reg. Antarctica
129 D2 Wilkie Can.
134 B1 Willamette r. U.S.A.
134 B1 Willapa Bay U.S.A.
138 B2 Willcox U.S.A.
100 B2 Willebroek Belgium
147 D3 Willemstad Neth. Antilles
52 B3 William, Mount Austr.
52 A1 William Creek Austr.
138 A1 Williams U.S.A.
140 C3 Williamsburg KY U.S.A.
141 D3 Williamsburg VA U.S.A.
128 B2 Williams Lake Can.
140 C3 Williamson U.S.A.
141 D2 Williamsport U.S.A.
143 E1 Williamston U.S.A.
122 B3 Williston S. Africa
136 C1 Williston U.S.A.
128 B2 Williston Lake Can.
135 B3 Willits U.S.A.
137 D1 Willmar U.S.A.
122 B3 Willowmore S. Africa
135 B3 Willows U.S.A.
123 C3 Willowvale S. Africa
50 B2 Wills, Lake salt flat Austr.
52 A3 Willunga Austr.
52 A2 Wilmington Austr.
141 D3 Wilmington DE U.S.A.
143 E2 Wilmington NC U.S.A.
140 C3 Wilmington OH U.S.A.
143 D2 Wilmington Island U.S.A.
      Wilno Lith. see Vilnius
101 D2 Wilnsdorf Ger.
101 D1 Wilseder Berg hill Ger.
143 E1 Wilson U.S.A.
53 C3 Wilson's Promontory pen. Austr.
100 B3 Wiltz Lux.
50 B2 Wiluna Austr.
99 B4 Wimereux France
123 C2 Winburg S. Africa
99 C4 Winchester U.K.
140 C3 Winchester KY U.S.A.
141 D3 Winchester VA U.S.A.
98 B2 Windermere l. U.K.
122 A1 Windhoek Namibia
137 D2 Windom U.S.A.
51 D2 Windorah Austr.
136 B2 Wind River Range mts U.S.A.
53 D2 Windsor Austr.
130 B3 Windsor Can.
147 D3 Windward Islands Caribbean Sea
147 C3 Windward Passage Cuba/Haiti
137 D3 Winfield U.S.A.
100 A2 Wingene Belgium
53 D2 Wingham Austr.
130 B2 Winisk Can.
130 B2 Winisk r. Can.
130 B2 Winisk Lake Can.
62 A2 Winkana Myanmar
129 E3 Winkler Can.
114 B4 Winneba Ghana
140 B2 Winnebago, Lake U.S.A.
134 C2 Winnemucca U.S.A.
136 C2 Winner U.S.A.
142 B2 Winnfield U.S.A.
137 E1 Winnibigoshish, Lake U.S.A.
129 E3 Winnipeg Can.
129 E3 Winnipeg r. Can.
129 E2 Winnipeg, Lake Can.
129 D2 Winnipegosis, Lake Can.
141 E2 Winnipesaukee, Lake U.S.A.
142 B2 Winnsboro U.S.A.
137 E2 Winona MN U.S.A.
142 C2 Winona MS U.S.A.
100 C1 Winschoten Neth.
101 D1 Winsen (Aller) Ger.
101 E1 Winsen (Luhe) Ger.

138 A1 **Winslow** U.S.A.
143 D1 **Winston-Salem** U.S.A.
101 D2 **Winterberg** Ger.
143 D3 **Winter Haven** U.S.A.
100 C2 **Winterswijk** Neth.
105 D2 **Winterthur** Switz.
51 D2 **Winton** Austr.
54 A3 **Winton** N.Z.
52 A2 **Wirrabara** Austr.
52 A2 **Wirraminna** Austr.
99 D3 **Wisbech** U.K.
140 A2 **Wisconsin** *r.* U.S.A.
140 B2 **Wisconsin** *state* U.S.A.
140 B2 **Wisconsin Rapids** U.S.A.
103 D1 **Wisła** *r.* Pol.
101 E1 **Wismar** Ger.
123 C2 **Witbank** S. Africa
122 A2 **Witbooisvlei** Namibia
98 D3 **Witham** *r.* U.K.
98 D3 **Withernsea** U.K.
100 B1 **Witmarsum** Neth.
99 C4 **Witney** U.K.
123 D2 **Witrivier** S. Africa
123 C3 **Witteberg** *mts* S. Africa
101 E1 **Wittenberge** Ger.
101 E1 **Wittenburg** Ger.
50 A2 **Wittenoom** Austr.
101 E1 **Wittingen** Ger.
100 C3 **Wittlich** Ger.
100 C1 **Wittmund** Ger.
101 F1 **Wittstock** Ger.
122 A1 **Witvlei** Namibia
101 D2 **Witzenhausen** Ger.
103 D1 **Władysławowo** Pol.
103 D1 **Włocławek** Pol.
53 C3 **Wodonga** Austr.
59 C3 **Wokam** *i.* Indon.
62 A1 **Wokha** India
99 C4 **Woking** U.K.
101 F2 **Wolfen** Ger.
101 E1 **Wolfenbüttel** Ger.
101 D2 **Wolfhagen** Ger.
136 B1 **Wolf Point** U.S.A.
101 E1 **Wolfsburg** Ger.
100 C3 **Wolfstein** Ger.
131 D3 **Wolfville** Can.
102 C1 **Wolgast** Ger.
102 C1 **Wolin** Pol.
129 D2 **Wollaston Lake** Can.
129 D2 **Wollaston Lake** *l.* Can.
126 E2 **Wollaston Peninsula** Can.
53 D2 **Wollongong** Austr.
101 E2 **Wolmirsleben** Ger.
101 E1 **Wolmirstedt** Ger.
100 C1 **Wolvega** Neth.
99 B3 **Wolverhampton** U.K.
65 B2 **Wŏnju** S. Korea
128 B2 **Wonowon** Can.
65 B2 **Wŏnsan** N. Korea
53 C3 **Wonthaggi** Austr.
52 A2 **Woocalla** Austr.
51 C1 **Woodah, Isle** *i.* Austr.
99 D3 **Woodbridge** U.K.
134 B1 **Woodburn** U.S.A.
136 B3 **Woodland Park** U.S.A.
140 A3 **Wood River** U.S.A.
50 C2 **Woodroffe, Mount** Austr.
51 C1 **Woods, Lake** *salt flat* Austr.
129 E3 **Woods, Lake of the** Can./U.S.A.
53 C3 **Woods Point** Austr.
131 D3 **Woodstock** *N.B.* Can.
140 C2 **Woodstock** *Ont.* Can.
54 C2 **Woodville** N.Z.
139 D1 **Woodward** U.S.A.
98 B2 **Wooler** U.K.
53 D2 **Woolgoolga** Austr.
52 A2 **Woomera** Austr.
140 C2 **Wooster** U.S.A.
122 A3 **Worcester** S. Africa
99 B3 **Worcester** U.K.
141 E2 **Worcester** U.S.A.
102 C2 **Wörgl** Austria
98 B2 **Workington** U.K.
98 C3 **Worksop** U.K.
136 B2 **Worland** U.S.A.
101 D3 **Worms** Ger.
99 A4 **Worms Head** *hd* U.K.
122 A1 **Wortel** Namibia
99 C4 **Worthing** U.K.
137 D2 **Worthington** U.S.A.
61 D2 **Wotu** Indon.
61 D2 **Wowoni** *i.* Indon.
Wrangel Island Rus. Fed. *see* **Vrangelya, Ostrov**
128 A2 **Wrangell** U.S.A.
96 B1 **Wrath, Cape** U.K.
136 C2 **Wray** U.S.A.
122 A2 **Wreck Point** S. Africa
Wrecsam U.K. *see* Wrexham
99 B3 **Wrexham** U.K.
136 B2 **Wright** U.S.A.
63 A2 **Wrightmyo** India
138 A2 **Wrightson, Mount** U.S.A.
128 B1 **Wrigley** Can.
103 D1 **Wrocław** Pol.
103 D1 **Września** Pol.
70 B2 **Wu'an** China
Wuchow China *see* Wuzhou
70 A2 **Wudu** China
70 A2 **Wuhai** China
70 B2 **Wuhan** China
70 B2 **Wuhu** China
71 A3 **Wu Jiang** *r.* China
Wujin China *see* Changzhou
115 C4 **Wukari** Nigeria
62 B1 **Wuliang Shan** *mts* China
59 C3 **Wuliaru** *i.* Indon.
118 B2 **Wum** Cameroon
71 A3 **Wumeng Shan** *mts* China
101 D1 **Wümme** *r.* Ger.
130 B2 **Wunnummin Lake** Can.
101 F2 **Wunsiedel** Ger.
101 D1 **Wunstorf** Ger.
62 A1 **Wuntho** Myanmar
100 C2 **Wuppertal** Ger.
122 A3 **Wuppertal** S. Africa
101 E2 **Wurzbach** Ger.
101 D3 **Würzburg** Ger.
101 F2 **Wurzen** Ger.
101 D2 **Wüstegarten** *hill* Ger.
59 D3 **Wuvulu Island** P.N.G.
70 A2 **Wuwei** China
70 A2 **Wuxi** *Chongqing* China
70 C2 **Wuxi** *Jiangsu* China
Wuxing China *see* Huzhou
71 A3 **Wuxuan** China
Wuyang China *see* Zhenyuan
69 E1 **Wuyiling** China
71 B3 **Wuyishan** China
71 B3 **Wuyi Shan** *mts* China
70 A1 **Wuyuan** China
70 A2 **Wuzhong** China
71 B3 **Wuzhou** China
51 D2 **Wyandra** Austr.
53 C2 **Wyangala Reservoir** Austr.
52 B3 **Wycheproof** Austr.
99 B4 **Wye** *r.* U.K.
50 B1 **Wyndham** Austr.
52 B3 **Wyndham-Werribee** Austr.
142 B1 **Wynne** U.S.A.
129 D2 **Wynyard** Can.
140 B2 **Wyoming** U.S.A.
136 B2 **Wyoming** *state* U.S.A.
53 D2 **Wyong** Austr.
103 E1 **Wyszków** Pol.
140 C3 **Wytheville** U.S.A.

X

117 D3 **Xaafuun** Somalia
121 C3 **Xai-Xai** Moz.
70 A1 **Xamba** China
62 B1 **Xam Hua** Laos
120 A1 **Xá-Muteba** Angola
120 A2 **Xangongo** Angola
81 C2 **Xankändi** Azer.
111 B2 **Xanthi** Greece
154 B3 **Xanxerê** Brazil
150 C4 **Xapuri** Brazil
107 C2 **Xátiva** Spain
120 B3 **Xhumo** Botswana
Xiaguan China *see* **Dali**
71 B3 **Xiamen** China
70 A2 **Xi'an** China
70 A3 **Xianfeng** China
62 A1 **Xiangcheng** China
70 B2 **Xiangfan** China
Xianghuang Qi China *see* Xin Bulag
Xiangjiang China *see* Huichang
71 B3 **Xiang Jiang** *r.* China
62 B2 **Xiangkhoang** Laos
71 B3 **Xiangtan** China
Xiangyang China *see* Xiangfan
71 B3 **Xiangyin** China
70 B3 **Xianning** China
70 B2 **Xiantao** China
70 A2 **Xianyang** China
70 B2 **Xiaogan** China
69 E1 **Xiao Hinggan Ling** *mts* China
70 C2 **Xiaoshan** China
70 B2 **Xiaowutai Shan** *mt.* China
Xiayingpan China *see* Luzhi
Xibu China *see* **Dongshan**
71 A3 **Xichang** China
145 C2 **Xicohténcatl** Mex.
70 A2 **Xifeng** *Gansu* China
71 A3 **Xifeng** *Guizhou* China
Xifengzhen China *see* Xifeng
75 C2 **Xigazê** China
71 A3 **Xilin** China
69 D2 **Xilinhot** China
68 C2 **Ximiao** China
70 B3 **Xin'anjiang Shuiku** *resr* China
70 B1 **Xin Bulag** China
70 B2 **Xincai** China
Xincun China *see* Dongchuan
Xindi China *see* **Honghu**
71 B3 **Xing'an** China
Xingba China *see* **Lhünzê**
68 C2 **Xinghai** China
70 B2 **Xinghua** China
71 B3 **Xingning** China
70 A2 **Xingping** China
70 B2 **Xingtai** China
151 D3 **Xingu** *r.* Brazil
151 D3 **Xinguara** Brazil
71 A3 **Xingyi** China
71 B3 **Xinhua** China
70 A2 **Xining** China
75 C1 **Xinjiang Uygur Zizhiqu** *aut. reg.* China
Xinjing China *see* **Jingxi**
65 A1 **Xinmin** China
71 B3 **Xinning** China
71 A3 **Xinping** China
Xinshiba China *see* Ganluo
70 B2 **Xintai** China
Xinxian China *see* **Xinzhou**
70 B2 **Xinxiang** China
70 B2 **Xinyang** China
71 A4 **Xinying** China
71 B3 **Xinyu** China
77 E2 **Xinyuan** China
70 B2 **Xinzhou** *Shanxi* China
106 B1 **Xinzo de Limia** Spain
Xiongshan China *see* Zhenghe
Xiongzhou China *see* Nanxiong
70 A2 **Xiqing Shan** *mts* China
151 E4 **Xique Xique** Brazil
70 A1 **Xishanzui** China
71 A3 **Xiushan** China
Xiushan China *see* Tonghai
71 B3 **Xiushui** China
71 B3 **Xiuying** China
70 B2 **Xixia** China
75 C1 **Xizang Zizhiqu** *aut. reg.* China
63 B2 **Xom Dưc Hanh** Vietnam
Xuancheng China *see* Xuanzhou
70 B1 **Xuanhua** China
71 A3 **Xuanwei** China
70 B2 **Xuanzhou** China
70 B2 **Xuchang** China
Xucheng China *see* **Xuwen**
117 C4 **Xuddur** Somalia
Xuefeng China *see* **Mingxi**
Xujiang China *see* Guangchang
71 B3 **Xun Jiang** *r.* China
71 B3 **Xunwu** China
71 B3 **Xuwen** China
71 A3 **Xuyong** China
70 B2 **Xuzhou** China
111 B3 **Xylokastro** Greece

Y

70 A2 **Ya'an** China
117 B4 **Yabēlo** Eth.
69 D1 **Yablonovyy Khrebet** *mts* Rus. Fed.
143 D1 **Yadkin** *r.* U.S.A.
75 C2 **Yadong** China
55 A4 **Yaghan Basin** *sea feature* S. Atlantic Ocean
89 E2 **Yagnitsa** Rus. Fed.
83 K2 **Yagodnoye** Rus. Fed.
118 B1 **Yagoua** Cameroon
128 C3 **Yahk** Can.
91 C1 **Yahotyn** Ukr.
144 B2 **Yahualica** Mex.
80 B2 **Yahyalı** Turkey
67 C4 **Yaizu** Japan
134 B1 **Yakima** U.S.A.
134 C1 **Yakima** *r.* U.S.A.
74 A2 **Yakmach** Pak.
114 B3 **Yako** Burkina
66 D2 **Yakumo** Japan
67 B4 **Yaku-shima** *i.* Japan
126 C3 **Yakutat** U.S.A.
128 A2 **Yakutat Bay** U.S.A.
83 J2 **Yakutsk** Rus. Fed.
91 D2 **Yakymivka** Ukr.
63 B3 **Yala** Thai.
118 C2 **Yalinga** C.A.R.
53 C3 **Yallourn** Austr.
111 C2 **Yalova** Turkey
90 B2 **Yalpuh, Ozero** *l.* Ukr.
91 C3 **Yalta** Ukr.
65 A1 **Yalu Jiang** *r.* China/N. Korea
86 F3 **Yalutorovsk** Rus. Fed.
67 D3 **Yamagata** Japan
67 B4 **Yamaguchi** Japan
86 F1 **Yamal, Poluostrov** *pen.* Rus. Fed.
Yamal Peninsula Rus. Fed. *see* Yamal, Poluostrov
Yamankhalinka Kazakh. *see* **Makhambet**
53 D1 **Yamba** Austr.
150 B2 **Yambi, Mesa de** *hills* Co
117 A4 **Yambio** Sudan
110 C2 **Yambol** Bulg.
86 G2 **Yamburg** Rus. Fed.
62 A1 **Yamethin** Myanmar
88 C2 **Yamm** Rus. Fed.
51 D2 **Yamma Yamma, Lake** *salt flat* Austr.
114 B4 **Yamoussoukro** Côte d'Ivoire
91 C1 **Yampil'** Ukr.
90 B2 **Yampil'** Ukr.
75 C2 **Yamuna** *r.* India
62 A1 **Yamzho Yumco** *l.* China
83 K2 **Yana** *r.* Rus. Fed.
70 A2 **Yan'an** China
150 B4 **Yanaoca** Peru
78 A2 **Yanbu' al Baḥr** Saudi Arabia
70 C2 **Yancheng** China
50 A3 **Yanchep** Austr.
114 B3 **Yanfolila** Mali
118 C2 **Yangambi** Dem. Rep. Congo
70 B2 **Yangcheng** China
71 B3 **Yangchun** China
65 B2 **Yangdok** N. Korea
71 B3 **Yangjiang** China
63 A2 **Yangôn** Myanmar
70 B2 **Yangquan** China
71 B3 **Yangshuo** China
62 B1 **Yangtouyan** China
70 C23 **Yangtze** *r.* China
70 C2 **Yangtze, Mouth of the** China
Yangtze Kiang *r.* China s Yangtze
70 A2 **Yangxian** China
70 B2 **Yangzhou** China
65 B1 **Yanji** China
137 D2 **Yankton** U.S.A.
83 K2 **Yano-Indigirskaya Nizmennost'** *lowland* Rus. Fed.
70 B1 **Yanqing** China
71 A3 **Yanshan** China
83 K2 **Yanskiy Zaliv** *g.* Rus. Fe
53 C1 **Yantabulla** Austr.
70 C2 **Yantai** China
118 B2 **Yaoundé** Cameroon
59 D2 **Yap** *i.* Micronesia
59 D3 **Yapen** *i.* Indon.
59 D3 **Yapen, Selat** *sea chan.* Indon.
144 A2 **Yaqui** *r.* Mex.
51 D2 **Yaraka** Austr.
86 D3 **Yaransk** Rus. Fed.
48 H4 **Yaren** Nauru
78 B3 **Yarīm** Yemen
Yarkand China *see* **Shach**
Yarkant China *see* **Shach**
77 D3 **Yarkant He** *r.* China
Yarlung Zangbo *r.* China *see* **Brahmaputra**
131 D3 **Yarmouth** Can.
138 A2 **Yarnell** U.S.A.